THE PROPHETIC
FAITH OF OUR FATHERS
VOLUME II

HARRY ANDERSON. ARTIST

THE DRAGON'S PURSUIT OF THE SYMBOLIC WOMAN

Symbolic Portrayal of the Persecution of the Church in Centuries Past, With Portrayal, Below, of Literal Flight of Persecuted Christians to Mountain Fastnesses, Pursued by Soldiers of the Inquisition (See Chapter 4, pages 103 ff.)

The
PROPHETIC FAITH
OF OUR FATHERS

*The Historical Development
of Prophetic Interpretation*

by

LE ROY EDWIN FROOM

VOLUME II
Pre-Reformation and Reformation
Restoration, and Second Departure

REVIEW AND HERALD
WASHINGTON, D.C.

To ALL Students of Bible Prophecy, That the Last Act in the Prophetic Drama of the Ages May Be Seen in Inseparable Relation to the Scenes Witnessed and Recognized by Our Spiritual Forefathers in Centuries Past, This Volume Is Sincerely Dedicated.

Contents

Introduction to Volume II 9

1. Revival of Interpretation in Italy and Bohemia 17
2. Wyclif Expands Exposition of Little Horn 44
3. Lollard Positions Molded by Prophetic Interpretation 66
4. Collective Extermination of Antichrist Opposers 102
5. Cusa Applies Prophetic Time Measurement to 2300 Days 124
6. Death for Applying "Babylon" to Papacy 142
7. Columbus Impelled by Prophecies to Open New World 159
8. Jewish Expositors Stress Rome and Year-Day Principle 184
9. Persecution Accentuates Medieval Jewish Exposition 203
10. Climax of Jewish Interpretation in Centuries Sixteen
      and Seventeen 220
11. The Reformation Born of a Twofold Discovery 241
12. Luther Sets Pattern for Reformation Interpretation 266
13. Luther's Co-Reformers Stress Prophetic Interpretation 283
14. Gradual Clarification of Hazy Points Continues 307
15. Swiss Reformers Parallel German Interpretations 333
16. English Martyrs Nerved for Stake by Prophecies 350
17. Emphasis Centered on Papacy as Prophesied Antichrist 373
18. Anglican Leaders Continue the Prophetic Emphasis 395
19. Calvin Clear Only Regarding Antichrist 426
20. Knox and Napier Notable Scottish Expositors 443
21. Rome's Counterattacks on Protestant Interpretation 464
22. Jesuits Introduce Futurist Counterinterpretation 484
23. Seventeenth Century Begins With Battle 506
24. King James I Turns Prophetic Expositor 533
25. Similar Expositions in Various Protestant Groups 559
26. Approaching End of Papal Period Predated 580
27. German Expositors Parallel British Positions 598
28. French Huguenots Hold Prophetic Banner High 623
29. Eighteenth Century Marked by Contrasting Developments ... 640
30. Advances in Exposition; Lisbon Earthquake Noted 670
31. Pietism's Advances Counterbalanced by Rationalism's Inroads .. 696
32. Predictions of French Revolution and Papal Overthrow 723
33. French Revolution Leads to Papal Wound 731
34. The Deadly Wound Ends the 1260 Years 749

35. END OF PERIOD RECOGNIZED AND PROCLAIMED _____ 765
36. SUMMING UP THE EVIDENCE OF VOLUME II _____ 783
    ACKNOWLEDGMENTS _____ 797
    APPENDICES _____ 801
    BIBLIOGRAPHY _____ 809
    INDEX _____ 847

Illustrations and Charts

The Dragon's Pursuit of the Symbolic Woman 2
Dante's Portrayal of Papal Apostasy Based on Prophecy 26
Cathedral Tapestry Attests Interest in Prophecy 38
Wyclif Sending Forth His Itinerant Evangelical Preachers 50
Vital Scenes in Wyclif's Life 56
Sons and Daughters of the Church Decry Corruption 70
Prophetic Vista of the Future 84
Charts Visualizing Progressive Development of Prophetic
    Interpretation 96, 97
Huss on trial for Life for Identifying Antichrist 108
Huss Faithful Unto Death for Prophetic Faith 120
Cusa Applies Year-Day Principle to 2300 Days 134
Savonarola Martyred for Identifying Antichrist 148
Major Expositions of the Leading Pre-Reformation Writers
    (Chart) 156, 157
Columbus Pressing His Case Before Ferdinand and Isabella 164
Columbus Considers Himself the "Messenger" of God 172
Lateran Church in Rome, Scene of Epochal Councils 182
Chronological Table of Jewish Interpreters 194
Maimonides and Abravanel 214
Jewish Expositor Outlines the Four Kingdoms 234
Luther Presses the Charges of Prophecy at Wittenberg 242
Tetzel Indulgence Brings Forth Theses and Bull 250
Historic Scenes in Luther's Early Life 260
Graphic German Reformation Illustrations of the Prophecies ... 276
Reformation Exposition Carved in Stone at Nürnberg 292
Three Stalwart Reformers Who Expounded Prophecy 303
Timing and Relationship of Seventy Weeks Studied 310
Illustrated Expositions Make Their Appearance 346
Smithfield Martyrs Die for Prophetic Faith 359
Powerful Figures in Reformation Conflict in Britain 388
Principal Interpretations of the Seventy Weeks (Table) 430
Reformation Scenes in Switzerland, Scotland, and France 444
Distinguished Expositors in Three Generations 456
Council of Trent—Rome's Answer to the Reformation 472
Papal Medal Commemorates St. Bartholomew's Massacre 480

Jesuit Counterinterpretations Parry Reformation Exposition 494
Antichrist Shifted Either Forward or Backward (Diagram) 508
First Protestant Works Adopt Preterist Counterinterpretation 524
Reformation Era: Leading Positions of Principal Expositors of
      Daniel (Chart) 528, 529
Reformation Era: Leading Positions of Principal Expositors on
      Revelation (Chart) 530, 531
King James I, of Britain, Expounds the Prophecies 538
Medals Memorialize Papal Claims and Assumptions 556
Cressener Forecasts Blow to Strike Papacy About 1800 590
Coming French Revolution Predicted Throughout Century Prior 644
French Expositors Parallel British and Other Continentals 648
Daniel Whitby Launches His Post-Millennial Theory 650
Whitby Places Millennium Prior to Second Advent 652
University Professors Conspicuous Expositors of Prophecy 664
Lisbon Earthquake (1755) Recognized as Harbinger 674
Wesley Among the Prophetic Expounders of His Day 690
Petri and Wood Begin 2300 Years With 70 Weeks 714
The Bursting Storm of the French Revolution 736
French Ultimatum Restricts Papal Authority in 1798 754
End of 1260 Years in 1798 Attested by Many 768
Post-Reformation Era: Leading Positions of Principal Expositors
      of Daniel (Chart) 784, 785
Post-Reformation Era: Leading Positions of Principal Expositors
      of Revelation (Chart) 786, 787

Introduction to Volume II

VOLUME I in the four-volume set of *The Prophetic Faith of Our Fathers* closes with the fascinating story of the dissentient Waldensian witnesses in the field of prophetic exposition, quite apart from the many writers noted within the dominant church of the Middle Ages. In order to complete the testimony of these Waldensian witnesses, the recital was followed through to the time of the mergence of their witness with that of the sixteenth-century Protestant Reformers. At that junction the torch of evangelical faith, long borne aloft by these and other weary defenders of the apostolic faith, was picked up and carried forward by the fresh stalwarts of the Reformation.

We here return to the fourteenth century to pick up the line of prophetic exposition witness within the Roman church just where we left off, starting with Dante and Petrarch, at the beginning of the Renaissance in Italy. Like the early gray light of dawn, as the curtain of night is lifted slowly, before the sun touches the landscape with roseate hue, so the Renaissance followed the somber spiritual night of the Middle Ages, softened only by the starlight afforded through occasional scholars of note, ere the effulgent glow of the Protestant Reformation was seen.

I. Significance of the Renaissance

The Renaissance, or Revival of Learning, was that intellectual movement, chiefly of the fourteenth and fifteenth centuries, with its revival of letters and art, which marked the transition from medieval to modern history. It included a rediscovery of the past, but it also ushered in a new concept of philosophy and religion, and marked a rebirth of the arts and sciences. It produced a new concept of man's duty and destiny and recipro-

9

cal relations. It emerged from the encompassing decay of church and empire, and resulted in the fuller development of modern nationalities and languages. It liberated the minds of men, bringing to an end the domination of Scholasticism and Feudalism, and challenging the control of the church over secular matters.

The concept of universal monarchy and indivisible Christendom, incorporated in the Holy Roman Empire and the secularized Roman church, had lost its grip, and was gradually supplanted by new theories of church and state. The empire was in its dotage. The visionary restoration of this Western Empire, which had imposed itself upon the imagination of Europe for six long centuries, hampering Italy and impeding the consolidation of Germany, diminished as a political force while the Roman world disintegrated. It was a period of gradual transition and fusion, of preparation and zealous endeavor. It provoked inquiry. It awakened free thought. It encouraged curiosity and criticism. It shattered the narrow mental barriers of the past, and prepared the best minds in Europe for "speculative audacities" from which most medieval schoolmen would have recoiled. Men became intrigued with ancient pagan literature, and this intellectual activity was often accompanied by moral laxity.

Many close the Middle Ages with Dante (d. 1321), the fascinating character with whom we begin this volume, and begin the Renaissance with Petrarch (d. 1374), treated next, who lifted letters to the rank heretofore occupied by logic and philosophy. A remarkable interest in Greek and Latin marked the period, and Humanism came to the forefront as the vital element in the Renaissance. Humanism was, of course, that specific literary movement at the close of the Middle Ages centering in the revival of the classical learning of Greek and Roman antiquity. It was a revolt against authoritarianism. As its name implies, it made man the center of interest, and stressed the humanities, or culture, rather than the divine side. It was secular, not religious. Humanism found its ideals in the golden age of Greece and Rome; the Reformation, in the primitive age of Christianity.

One section of Humanism sought to engraft this classical learning on the tree of Christianity; the other endeavored not only to revive the literature but to inculcate the pagan spirit of the ancient heathen cults as well.

After the fall of Constantinople, in 1453, the scattering of more Greek scholars throughout Europe gave impetus to the revival of scholarship already in progress. The invention of movable type and of printing, new methods of papermaking, the passage of the Cape of Good Hope, the discovery of America, the exploration of the Indian Ocean, the consolidation of the Spanish nationality, the invention of the marine compass and of gunpowder, the substitution of the Copernican system for the Ptolemaic system in astronomy, the struggle for religious freedom as a result of the papal breakdown following the Babylonian captivity and the Great Schism, and the abolition of feudal customs, as well as the further development of the great universities—all helped to make up the picture and to change the face of Europe.

Each country had its own characteristic form and time of the Renaissance. In contrast to Italy, the later Humanistic emphasis in Germany and the Low Countries was soon superseded by the Reformation, and Biblical language studies were earnestly cultivated under the lead of such noted scholars as Erasmus, Melanchthon, Reuchlin, and Von Hutten. Over in England, Wyclif and Chaucer were the forerunners of the Renaissance and the Reformation there. But the main streams of both these movements reached England contemporaneously, and the brilliant Elizabethan literature resulted.

In France the Renaissance is commonly dated from the invasion of Naples by Charles VIII, in 1495, which led to intellectual contact between the two peoples, this in turn ushering in the period of great French literature. Spain, with her wars of imperial aggrandizement, her voyages of discovery, her expulsion of the Jews, her Catholic despotism, along with the Inquisition and the Society of Jesus, headed the reaction against reform, and was largely without a revival of learning.

But they all had their common starting point in reaction against the long dominant medieval ideas that had become obsolete, and in the development of the energizing forces noted. Individualism came of age. The culminating point of the Renaissance was reached. The Rubicon had been crossed. The Reformation soon took hold of Northern Europe, and the Counter Reformation impended. Such is the setting for the early part of Volume·II. It is the background against which the moving figures of the period are to be viewed, the encompassing framework within which the exposition of prophecy is to be understood. The Reformation will follow along naturally, as well as succeeding periods up to the French Revolution, which marks the terminal point of Volume II.

II. Special Scope of This Second Volume

Contemporary recognition of each major event and epoch of history that has fulfilled prophecy is one of the remarkable characteristics of the centuries. Always there have been men—not one or two, but a group, widely scattered over different lands and speaking various languages—who have sensed the prophetic significance of their own times, and have left the record of their understanding for all mankind.

Thrice during the Christian Era have interest and emphasis in prophetic interpretation been ascendant: first in the early centuries; then in the Reformation and post-Reformation periods; and finally in the nineteenth-century Advent Awakening. Volume I covers the early emphasis—the recognition of imperial Rome as the predicted fourth world power of prophecy; next, the contemporary recognition of its prophesied breakup; and lastly, the growing perception in the Middle Ages of the identity of the Antichrist, prophesied under various terms and symbols by Daniel, Paul, and John. This was traced both within and without the dominant church of the period.

Here in Volume II, picking up the line of testimony with the Renaissance, we continue our quest. The preaching of this growing conviction concerning Antichrist, based on the great outline prophecies of Daniel and the Apocalypse, and their prophetic time periods,[1] had a tremendous effect upon the whole nations. It was tied inseparably into the great Protestant Reformation. The violent Catholic reaction to this Antichrist thesis, and the opposing systems of interpretation marking the Counter Reformation, form the next segment in the narrative.

These two antagonistic and opposite schools of prophetic interpretation reach their climax in the seventeenth century. They begin to wane, however, in the eighteenth century, when the Whitbyan postmillennial theory enters the picture. The dramatic events of the French Revolution at the close of the century again sharply revive the serious study of prophecy—now gripping the New World as well as the Old. At this point the dramatic close of the great 1260-year prophetic time period, pertaining to Antichrist's dominance, was heralded by a fresh cluster of scholarly men in various lands on both sides of the Atlantic.

Such, in brief, is the scope of this volume in the series. Volume II therefore compasses the *second* great period of the predominance of prophetic study and exposition, the *third* appearing in the early decades of the nineteenth century, which is the field reserved for Volumes III and IV.

III. Purpose and Method of Procedure

During the centuries of the Christian Era certain canons of sound prophetic exposition have become established, to which Jews, Catholics, and Protestants have each made major contribution. These, in turn, have become the heritage of all mankind, bequeathed to those of us who live in this epoch of revived prophetic study and exposition. Stalwart characters within the Roman church and independent witnesses outside that church were united on certain important positions, which became com-

---

[1] By the term *outline prophecies*, prophetic outlines like Daniel 2 and 7 are meant, which carry us across the centuries through Babylonia, Medo-Persia, Grecia, and Rome, and Rome's divisions, on to the end; or, like the seven churches, the seven seals, and the seven trumpets of the Revelation, which similarly traverse the centuries of the Christian Era. By the term *time prophecies*, is indicated the prophetic time periods of Daniel and the Revelation, such as the 70 weeks, the 1260 days, the 1290, 1335, and 2300 days of Daniel, and similar periods recorded in the Apocalypse.

mon ground. And not only Christians but Jews, up to the seventeenth century, provide a constant succession of important
supporting evidence—an independent but paralleling line, with
a number of basic principles likewise in common.

It is this threefold body of witnesses—Catholic, Jewish, and
Protestant, scattered throughout Germany, Switzerland, Scandinavia, Britain, The Netherlands, France, and even Spain and
Italy, as well as the faraway colonies of New England—and
their concurrence of testimony, that constitutes the crowning
evidence of manifestly sound principles of prophetic exposition.
Coins and medals also, minted through the centuries, present a
unique line of confirmation quite apart from manuscripts, books,
and tractates. Woodcuts and sculptures similarly bear important
testimony.

The high caliber of the men who have devoted themselves
to the study of prophecy is impressive. The leading lights of
the centuries—the spiritual and intellectual peers of their respective generations—were frequently the investigators and
expositors of prophecy. Names known to all in other fields are
found to have been the leading expounders of the inspired predictions and the heralds of their historical fulfillment. Clerics,
statesmen, recluses, poets, scientists, historians, teachers, kings,
and explorers, spread throughout the various nations, are included in the vast sweep.

Like a giant panorama, we see them pass in review before
us. We hear their voices and note their emphasis as they swell in
a resounding chorus. The massed evidence of the various epochs
makes its due impress. And we shall converse with the outstanding figures who pioneered each advance or enunciated new
and important principles. Thus the cumulative force of accred-
ited principles of interpretation will be seen in balanced perspective.

Tabulation, or charting, of the leading expositors and their
basic positions on the prophecies will summarize each major
epoch covered—as the pre-Reformation, Reformation, and post-
Reformation eras. Thus a balanced, over-all picture of each

great epoch under investigation can be had at a glance, and the combined evidence of all witnesses upon a given point will likewise be immediately available. This is not only desirable but imperative for accurate understanding, and for greatest helpfulness to the investigator.

The original sources are used, except in a few instances; authorities merely supplement and give the setting. All quotations are reproduced *verbatim et literatim*, with the precise spelling, punctuation, and capitalization originally employed— strange as they may at times appear. Every effort has been employed to make the footnote credits exact and complete. The index is built upon a threefold breakdown—names, subjects, and prophetic terms employed. The illustrations have been gleaned largely from the archives of Europe, and comprise authentic reproductions of title pages, key extracts, woodcuts, illustrations, and sculptures, as well as original paintings and portraits. Comprehensive historical charts complete this feature.

Painstaking effort has been made to ensure accuracy of citation and fidelity to context. The full facts and their setting have been the undeviating object of this quest. This has been followed by careful analysis and tabulation of the findings. Conscientious evaluation has marked each step of the search. No pains or expense has been spared to present a faithful picture. Competent scholars have given the benefit of helpful suggestion and criticism, and specialists in various historical periods have been consulted. Acknowledgment for these aids is made at the close. Every effort has been put forth to present a dependable record of man's attempt to interpret the divine plan of the ages as revealed through Bible prophecy.

IV. Response of History to the Call of Prophecy

Scattered over Europe are skillfully contrived pantomime-figure clocks that illustrate impressively what we mean by *the response of history to the call of prophecy*. As the clock strikes certain hours, a door opens, and a procession of figures files past in realistic action around the clock dial—ringing bells, blowing trumpets, bowing, gesticulating, or otherwise heralding the coming of the hour. Similarly, in the field of prophetic interpretation, as the key hours on the clock of divine prophecy have struck among the nations, always with the coming of the hour have the heralding figures appeared, announcing to mankind the fulfillment taking place before its eyes.

This phenomenon has been repeated so often and with such regularity, as the attendant circumstance to each major fulfillment, that it becomes a virtual law of prophecy that each fulfillment of a major epoch or event of prophecy will invariably be recognized and proclaimed by a chorus of intelligent voices at the time of fulfillment. This will become increasingly apparent in the centuries traversed by this investigation.

LeRoy Edwin Froom.

September 25, 1947.

CHAPTER ONE

Revival of Interpretation
in Italy and Bohemia

I. Thinkers Disillusioned by Break in Papal Continuity

The medieval church reached its height in the thirteenth century. Probably at no time did it play so dominant a part in the lives of men. Having disposed of the Holy Roman Empire, its rival in the race for leadership, the Papacy seemed secure. But the fourteenth century had scarcely begun when the Papacy found its authority sharply challenged. First came the Babylonian Captivity (1309-1377) at Avignon. At last this ended, and the Papacy returned to Rome under Gregory XI.[1] This was no sooner effected than the Roman group insisted on an Italian pope, Urban VI. This election, however, proved unsatisfactory to some, and so, reinforced by their French colleagues, the cardinals met again and elected another pope, the French-speaking Clement VII. Thus the embarrassment of the Babylonian Captivity was continued for many years in the scandal of the Great Schism.[2]

1. RENAISSANCE PRODUCES FUNDAMENTAL CHANGE OF MIND. —The older writers placed the Middle Ages from 500 to 1500, between the ancient and modern ages. Historians are not agreed on the time of ending the Middle Ages. However, the transi-

---

[1] Warren O. Ault, *Europe in the Middle Ages*, pp. 607-610.
[2] *Ibid.*, pp. 610, 611; see also Joseph R. Strayer and Dana Carleton Munro, *The Middle Ages, 395-1500*, pp. 420-430.

tional epoch is commonly designated the Age of the Renaissance —meaning the reflaming of the old culture, or the intellectual awakening. The medieval mind began to undergo a fundamental change. The authority of the church, supplemented by the writings of a few ancients like Aristotle, had been dominant in Scholasticism. But scholars began to assert that not all knowledge had been discovered, and that some things long unquestioned were not true. Many universities were founded, being developed out of monastic and cathedral schools. Thus the University of Paris came into being sometime between 1150 and 1170, Oxford about 1168, Cambridge about 1209, and Prague in 1348.

The Romance languages developed out of the medieval Latin. In Italy, Spain, and Gaul the Latin was modified as these peoples developed languages of their own. Though the scholars continued to use Latin, Greek had almost disappeared in Western Europe. One of the most influential factors in producing the change was the revival of classical Greek and Roman literature. It was a rediscovery, its promoters taking the name of Humanists. And the first phase of the Renaissance began in Italy, finding its finest expression in Dante and Petrarch.[3]

This intellectual movement, with its revival of letters, therefore marked the transition from medieval to modern history. It was accomplished by the overthrow of Scholasticism, and deliverance from the dominating power of the church in secular matters, which freedom in turn gave rise to the new nationalism. In England, Wyclif's Bible was one of the forerunners of a new day; in Germany and the Low Countries the study of the original Biblical languages paved the way for the Reformation. During the Renaissance came the invention of printing, the expansion of exploration and commerce, the development of navigation and science, the discovery of America, and the foundations of modern astronomy, laid by Copernicus and Galileo.

---

[3] Frederic Austin Ogg, *A Source Book of Mediaeval History*, pp. 444, 445.

2. AVIGNON USHERS IN NEW EPOCH OF PAPAL DECADENCE.
—The Papacy's "dark century," as it is sometimes called, extending from about 1347 to perhaps 1450, included the period of the
Great Schism (1378-1417), with the rival claims of the French
and Italians to the possession of the Papacy. The transfer of
the Papacy to Avignon, the Babylonian Captivity, and the Great
Schism marked the beginning of a new epoch in the church—
a period of definite decadence and loss. Reaction from disap-
pointed hopes and dire predictions of pious churchmen helped
to bring on the revolt of men like Wyclif and Huss, and stimulated the vagaries of the mystics.[4]

The whole theory and system of an infallible election
of the pope collapsed with the Great Schism, as Rome and Avignon fought for the tiara, each hurling spiritual thunderbolts
at the other.[5] Unity was destroyed. Only one pope could be the
true vicar of Christ. The other must be an impostor, as each
anathematized the other.[6] Or perchance both were right.

The conflict of the Papacy with the Hohenstaufen emperors had greatly weakened both powers. It had made it possible
for France to dominate the Papacy, but it had also materially
weakened the empire. The solidarity of Europe was breaking.
The structure which empire and Papacy had built, and upon
which they rested, was giving way. A new nationalism took its
place, and now these new states began to challenge the very
basis of papal power. It gave opportunity for thinkers to attack
the corruptions of the church. It alienated the support of the
states of Europe. It fomented discussion of the principles upon
which the Papacy rested. It aroused public opinion and produced a cry for reform from one end of Europe to the other.[7]

The emperors could not be content at the sight of a Papacy
in the hands of the French and dominated by the monarchy of
France. The friends of the empire were necessarily the enemies

[4] Alfred Owen Legge, *The Growth of the Temporal Power of the Papacy*, pp. 78, 79.
[5] Alexander Clarence Flick, *The Decline of the Medieval Church*, vol. 1, pp. 263-265.
[6] Johann K. L. Gieseler, *A Text-Book of Church History*, vol. 3, p. 82; Johann J. Ignatz
von Döllinger ("Janus"), *The Pope and the Council*, pp. 292 ff; Heinrich Geffcken, *Church and State*, vol. 1, p. 263.
[7] Flick, *op. cit.*, vol. 1, pp. 211-245.

of France and of the Gallicized Papacy. Whether in Italy or in Germany, the protagonists of the imperial political positions were antipapal, and any material upon which they could lay hands, usable against the Papacy, became ammunition hurled at the hierarchy. And antipapal churchmen in the imperial fold found in Scripture much that they could use in attacking the popes seated at Avignon.

3. INCREASING CHORUS DECLARES PAPACY IS ANTICHRIST.— It was a period of confusion, marked by increasing denunciations of the Papacy and predictions concerning the appearance and identification of Antichrist.[8] The Spiritual Franciscans were especially active, both extremists and moderates. But there were irreconcilable differences among these protesters before the Reformation. Nevertheless, men's convictions grew stronger as the predicted marks of Antichrist broke out like plague spots upon the body of "the Man of Sin," as the Catholic Church was frequently called. And the papal church system was compelled to fashion itself anew amid these repeated protests and hostile actions. Foxe lists an imposing array of learned men between 1331 and 1360, including Dante and Petrarch, who contended against the usurpations of the pope.[9] Of these lesser ones, we cite only three, preliminary to major characters.

MICHAEL OF CESENA, general of the Grey Friars, declared the pope "to be Antichrist, and the church of Rome to be the whore of Babylon, drunk with the blood of saints." [10] Michael had numerous followers, not a few of whom were slain. JOHANNES DE RUPESCISSA (sometimes called Jean Roquetaillardes), a Minorite friar under Clement VI, in 1345, preached openly that the Church of Rome was the whore of Babylon, and that the pope, with his cardinals, was "very Antichrist." Foxe's conjecture is that this friar and an unnamed priest were imprisoned and burned at Avignon. Foxe looked upon this violence as

---

[8] *Ibid.*, pp. 191, 192.
[9] John Foxe, *Acts and Monuments*, vol. 1, pp. 443-448, 453. (Unless another edition is specified, the 1684 edition of Foxe's *Acts* is used hereafter.)
[10] Foxe, *Acts*, vol. 1, p. 445; see also M. Creighton, *A History of the Papacy*, vol. 1, p. 35. The custom of employing rather strong expressions, common throughout the Renaissance and Reformation periods, is dealt with in chapter 11, pp. 246-248.

evidence that the devil had been loosed after his thousand-year binding,[11] and regarded these martyrs as voices of resistance to Antichrist, as they longed for his fall and ruin. In the fourteenth century the controversy takes on a broader character and touches more on fundamental principles.

II. Dante's Portrayal of Prophesied Papal Apostasy

DANTE ALIGHIERI (1265-1321), Italian poet and one of the great writers of all time, was born in Florence. While Dante was still a boy, his father died, and his mother placed him with the philosopher Latini, who gave him a liberal education at Bologna, Padua, and Naples. Dante became proficient in theology, as well as in languages, painting, and music. At eighteen he was already winning wide recognition with his sonnets. In childhood he had developed a deep but unreciprocated affection for Beatrice, who married a nobleman. She died in 1290 at the age of twenty-four. Filled with sorrow, Dante took refuge in intensive study. (Portrait of Dante appears on p. 70.)

Florence was the predominant power in central Italy at the time, and head of the Guelphic League. Dante was born just before the liberation of the city. His family belonged to the Guelphs, and he took a strong stand against all lawlessness and external interference with Florentine affairs. He entered public life in 1295, was elected one of the six priors in 1300, and participated in the civil war between the irreconcilable Guelphs and Ghibellines. In 1301 Charles of Valois, brother of King Philip of France, entered Florence with 1,200 horsemen. Joined by others, he burst open the prisons and drove the priors out of their palace. Dante, one of the first victims, was banished from Florence, and the rest of his life was spent in political exile.[12]

Dante stood on the threshold of a new era. He reproved the "Supreme Pastor of the West." [13] What artists endeavored to portray in the pseudo-Joachim *Pope Book*, Dante put into verse,

---

11 Foxe, *Acts*, vol. 1, pp. 445, 446, 451.
12 Edmund G. Gardner, *The Story of Florence*, pp. 36-39; see also Ault, *op. cit.*, p. 534.
13 Flick, *op. cit.*, vol. 1, p. 211.

not sparing the popes. In fact, Döllinger declares him to have
been a Joachimite.[14]

1. DIVINE COMEDY THE DIRGE OF DEPARTING AGE.—No
writer was more conscious of the shame and failure of Rome.
His *Divine Comedy* was like the dirge of the departing Middle
Ages.[15] In canto after canto he poured out his indignation in
classical expression, consigning popes to the hottest hell for their
misdeeds. But his purpose was to correct, not to destroy; to
reform, not demolish. He did not go so far as the Spirituals. To
him the Roman Catholic Church was still the bride of Christ,
but the veil was rent, the orange flowers faded. The spotless
maiden had been sold unto the world. Dante simply pleaded
for the restoration of vanished ideals and the reconstruction of
the ruins.[16] He is "both claimed and condemned, as a disturber
of the church's faith." [17] But before seeking the prophetic significance of *The Divine Comedy*, note Dante's remarkable
conception of the relation of church and state in the light of
his time. Said he:

> " 'Rome, that turn'd it unto good,
> Was wont to boast two suns, whose several beams
> Cast light on either way, the world's and God's.
> One since hath quench'd the other; and the sword
> Is grafted on the crook; and, so conjoin'd,
> Each must perforce decline to worse, unawed
> By fear of other.
>
> .   .   .   .   .
>
> " 'The Church of Rome,
> Mixing two Governments that ill assort,
> Hath miss'd her footing, fallen into the mire,
> And there herself the burden much defiled.' " [18]

Dante developed his *Divine Comedy* into a theodicy, representing the divine philosophy of the world's story. It was a
terrific indictment of his times. According to Döllinger, *The*

[14] Döllinger, *Prophecies and the Prophetic Spirit in the Christian Era*, p. 130.
[15] Richard Chenevix Trench, *Lectures on Medieval Church History*, p. 280; for a comprehensive analysis of Dante's *Divine Comedy*, see Henry Osborn Taylor, *The Mediaeval Mind*,
vol. 2 pp. 568-589.
[16] Herbert B. Workman, *The Dawn of the Reformation*, vol. 1, pp. 13-15.
[17] Richard William Church, *Essays and Reviews*, p. 78.
[18] Dante Alighieri, *The Divine Comedy*, "Purgatory," Canto XVI.

Divine Comedy was "the boldest, most unsparing, most incisive, denunciatory song that has ever been composed." [19]

2. POWERS OF STATE NOT DERIVED FROM CHURCH.— Dante's *De Monarchia* is a fundamental discussion of the relation of temporal and spiritual powers in which he insists that they are of equal rank, and that the empire derives its authority directly from God, and existed before the Christian church. Maintaining the necessity of civil power for the preservation of justice, freedom, and unity, Dante attributes the authority of the Holy Roman Empire to Aeneas and Caesar, holding that it was God's will for the Romans to rule. The question he raises is, Does that power come directly from God, or through some vicar, the successor of Peter?

This he answers negatively by denying spiritual supremacy, and positively by arguments for temporal superiority. In the conflict between the Papacy and imperial power the imperialists made effective use of his arguments. The treatise was admired by one group and abhorred by the other. Burned as heretical, in the sixteenth century it was placed by Roman authorities on the Index as a prohibited book. [20]

In strong, bold strokes Dante disposes of the papal contention, reducing the arguments to syllogisms that he overthrows. "I proceed to refute the above assumption that the two luminaries of the world typify its two ruling powers." [21] First, man was not in existence when they were created; second, they began to minister to man while he was still in the state of innocency, without need of such governmental direction as was later necessary. Therefore the assumption fails. Then, turning to the argument of Peter and the keys, and again putting it in the form of a syllogism which he disproves, he says:

"Therefore I conclude that although the successor of Peter has authority to bind and loose in accordance with the requirements of the pre-

---

[19] Döllinger, *Studies in European History*, pp. 85, 86.
[20] Ogg, *op. cit.*, p. 453; see also *The De Monarchia of Dante Alighieri*, translated by A. Henry.
[21] Dante Alighieri, *De Monarchia*, book 3, chap. 4, sec. 8, translated by Henry; see also Workman, *Dawn of the Reformation*, vol. 1, p. 76.

rogative granted to Peter, it does not follow, as they claim, that he [the Pope] has authority to bind and loose the decrees or statutes of Empire, unless they prove that this also belongs to the office of the keys. But we shall demonstrate farther on that the contrary is true." [22]

After a discussion of the attitude of the early Christians, he declares, "We have stated and rejected the errors on which those chiefly rely who declare that the authority of the Roman Prince is dependent on the Roman Pontiff." [23] And after an extended argument Dante presents this conclusion: "It is established, then, that the authority of temporal Monarchy descends without mediation from the fountain of universal authority." [24]

III. "Divine Comedy" a Prophetic Portrayal of Corruption

Taking the Apocalypse and its interpretation by Joachim for a formula, the exiled poet wrote *The Divine Comedy* in the vernacular. In the poem, the church, bereaved of her first husband, remained over a thousand years without a single suitor. In harmony with the current conception of his day, Dante filled paradise (holiness and happiness), purgatory (penitence and hope), and hell (sin and misery), with the spirits of the departed, painting his picture with vivid colors. Toward the end of the poem, Dante refers to the apostle John as seeing all the grievous times through which the church was destined to pass.

> "The seer
> That, ere he died, saw all the grievous times
> Of the fair bride, who with the lance and nails
> Was won." [25]

1. JOACHIM DEPICTED IN PARADISE AND SHEPHERDS AS WOLVES.—Dante places Joachim in Paradise, as he writes:

> " 'And at my side there shines
> Calabria's abbot, Joachim, endow'd
> With soul prophetic.' " [26]

---

[22] Dante Alighieri, *De Monarchia*, book 3, chap. 8, sec. 5.
[23] *Ibid.*, chap. 13, sec. 1.
[24] *Ibid.*, chap. 16, sec. 8.
[25] Dante Alighieri, *Divine Comedy*, "Paradise," Canto 32.
[26] *Ibid.*, Canto 12.

Then is portrayed the transformation of shepherds into wolves, the departure of the teachers from the gospel, and the substitution of decretals, and with more thought on the Vatican than on Nazareth.[27]

Four lines must suffice:

> "In shepherd's clothing, greedy wolves below
> Range wide o'er all the pastures. Arm of God!
> Why longer sleep'st thou? Cahorsines and Gascons
> Prepare to quaff our blood." [28]

Dante thus assigns one of the most conspicuous places in Paradise to Joachim of Floris, one of whose writings had been solemnly condemned by Innocent III at the fourth Lateran Council, and refuted by Thomas Aquinas. On the other hand, three popes had patronized Joachim during his lifetime, and his more potentially dangerous writings were never condemned.[29] The explanation of this paradox is to be found in the comparative freedom of thought and expression in the thirteenth century in Italy. Dante caused little scandal by consigning one of the canonized popes, Celestine V, to the lower regions. The simple fact is that "the rigid framework and the inexorable discipline of the modern Roman Church are mainly the work of the Counter-Reformation." [30] The thirteenth century tolerated a wide diversity of belief and teaching.[31]

2. THE WOMAN OF REVELATION 17 AND HER LOVERS.—In "Paradise," Dante's language is quite symbolical, but in "Purgatory," Canto 16, the veil is removed. The Roman 'church, intermingling the two powers, has trafficked with kings. Sullied with their vices, she has sunk into the mire. This Dante covertly describes from Revelation 17. The car, symbolizing the church, upon which paganism swoops down as "the bird of Jove," hav-

---

[27] *Ibid.*, Canto 9.   [28] *Ibid.*, Canto 27.
[29] Covered in **Volume I** of *The Prophetic Faith of Our Fathers.*
[30] G. G. Coulton, *From St. Francis to Dante*, p. 150.
[31] It was really Gerard of Borgo San Donnino, professor of theology at the University of Paris, who wrote an *Introduction to the Eternal Gospel*, that created a sensation. He predicted that the Abomination of Desolation would be a simoniacal pope shortly to come. This was brought in 1255 before a papal commission, and his work condemned and suppressed. Yet, in all the storm, Joachim's own prophecies were not condemned, and the whole affair was hushed up as quietly as possible. (*Ibid.*, pp. 152, 153.)

DORE. ARTIST

DANTE'S PORTRAYAL OF PAPAL APOSTASY BASED ON PROPHECY

Dante's *Divine Comedy*, Later Illustrated by Doré, Filled Paradise, Purgatory, and Hell With Spirits of the Departed. He Pictured Papal Corruption Through the Symbolism of Revelation 17 —a Harlot and Her Lover, Borne by the Symbolic Beast (Lower Right)

ing attached itself to imperial powers in the days of Constantine, is tied to a tree. Islam drags a part away. Then a change takes place, as heads and horns appear at the four corners of the car. Such a monster, with seven heads and ten horns, has never before been seen. Above the car sits a shameless woman, and at her side there stands a giant with whom she exchanges kisses. Then the giant scourges her and drags her away to the forest. Thus is pictured what happened under Boniface VIII, who had usurped God's place, and who united with the giant (Philip) and was dragged into the forest (France).[32] And when renewal of her connection with the German emperor was sought, Philip scourged her. Hear it:

> "Like monster, sight hath never seen.
> O'er it methought there sat, secure as rock
> On mountain's lofty top, a shameless whore,
> Whose ken roved loosely round her. At her side,
> As 't were that none might bear her off, I saw
> A giant stand; and ever and anon
> They mingled kisses. But, her lustful eyes
> Chancing on me to wander, that fell minion
> Scourged her from head to foot all o'er; then full
> Of jealousy, and fierce with rage, unloosed
> The monster, and dragg'd on, so far across
> The forest, that from me its shades alone
> Shielded the harlot and the new-form'd brute." [33]

3. THE SEVEN-HEADED, TEN-HORNED MONSTER.—As Dante proceeds through "Inferno," the symbols become more graphic. The beast—symbol of Rome—fastens "to many an animal in wedlock vile," until a greyhound arises as an avenger, supported by love, wisdom, and virtue, and chases the lewd wolf through every town until the monster is destroyed.[34] Then reality takes the place of symbol in the recital. Greedy priests, popes, and cardinals fill hell, so that Cerberus, the hell hound, expresses his delight in fierce barking on account of the rich prey furnished

---

[32] "He [Boniface] who usurps on earth, (my [God's] place, . . . which in the presence of the Son of God is void.)" ("Paradiso," XXVII.) In "Inferno," Canto 27, Dante calls Boniface "the Prince of the new Pharisees."
[33] Dante Alighieri, *Divine Comedy*, "Purgatory," Canto 32.
[34] *Ibid.*, "Inferno," Canto 1.

to hell by the Papacy.[35] Boniface VIII arrives, and the spirit of Nicholas III languishes in the flames.[36]

The Dominicans had chosen the greyhound as a symbol of their order. The chariot refers to the church. In popes like Nicholas the apocalyptic prophecy of the Babylonian woman seemed to be fulfilled. She sits on the beast with seven heads and ten horns, with the cup of abominations in her hand. Dante felt himself impelled to proclaim that there was no longer before God any true pope or any true church. The chair was vacant; the vessel was broken.[37]

Reverence for the keys of Peter restrains Dante from using still stronger language concerning papal corruption and avarice that had overcast the world with mourning. The alleged Donation of Constantine to Sylvester had given birth to all this. As the climax of his poetical interpretation of the Apocalypse, especially Revelation 17, Dante portrays the papal apostasy as worse than heathen idolatry.

> " 'If reverence of the keys restrain'd me not,
> Which thou in happier time didst hold, I yet
> Severer speech might use. Your avarice
> O'ercasts the world with mourning, under foot
> Treading the good, and raising bad men up.
> Of shepherds like to you, the Evangelist
> Was ware, when her, who sits upon the waves,
> With kings in filthy whoredom he beheld;
> She who with seven heads tower'd at her birth,
> And from ten horns her proof of glory drew,
> Long as her spouse in virtue took delight.
> Of gold and silver ye have made your god,
> Differing wherein from the idolater,
> But that he worships one, a hundred ye?
> Ah, Constantine! to how much ill gave birth,
> Not thy conversion, but that plenteous dower,
> Which the first wealthy Father gain'd from thee.' "[38]

Such was the remarkable testimony of the poet of Florence.

---

[35] *Ibid.*, Canto 7.   [36] *Ibid.*, Canto 19.
[37] Döllinger, *Studies,* pp. 97-114.
[38] Dante Alighieri, *Divine Comedy,* "Inferno," Canto 19.

IV. Petrarch Declares Papacy Fulfills Prophetic Terms

Appearing shortly after Dante, FRANCESCO PETRARCH (1304-1374), poet laureate at Rome in his day, is one of the celebrated names in Italian literature. His father was a notary, and destined his son for the law, sending him to study at Montpellier and Bologna. But contact with Latin classics ended his interest in law. Literary interests remained dominant. After his father's death he studied for holy orders, serving as prior, canon, and archdeacon. Through Petrarch the spirit of the Renaissance found its initial expression in Italy, culminating finally in a revolt against Scholasticism, and the fables and superstitions that flourished under its protection. (See portrait on page 70.)

He despised scholastic and mystical learning, and went back further—to the well of antiquity. This led to his attack on astrology and his scorn of the false science of his time. Many treatises in poetic and prose form resulted. In the latter part of his career the cities of Italy vied with one another in showering honor upon him. The Roman senate and the University of Paris invited him to receive the poet's crown, which he accepted from the former, in 1341, in a colorful celebration.[39]

Petrarch formed one of a deputation from Rome, in 1342, which besought Clement VI to return to the Eternal City. Thus he had an opportunity to learn of the unsavory things of Avignon that he reveals in his *Letters*. He contrasts the humility and poverty of the early church with the splendor and power of the church of his time. Petrarch stresses this in his sonnet beginning *Fiamma dal ciel su le tue treccie piova*, in which he inveighs against the court of Rome. Here it is in quaint old English:

> "Vengeaunce must fall on thee, thow filthie whore
> Of Babilon, thow breaker of Christ's fold,
> That from achorns, and from the water colde,
> Art riche become with making many poore.
> Thow treason's neste that in thie harte dost holde
> Of cankard malice, and of myschief more
> Than pen can wryte, or may with tongue be tolde,

[39] David S. Schaff, *The Middle Ages* (Philip Schaff, *History of the Christian Church*, vol. 5), part 2, pp. 573-576; Pierre de Nolhac, *Petrarch and the Ancient World*, pp. 5-12, 15, 29.

> Slave to delights that chastitie hath solde;
> For wyne and ease which settith all thie store
> Uppon whoredome and none other lore,
> In thye pallais of strompetts yonge and olde
> Theare walks Plentie, and Belzebub thye Lorde;
> Guydes thee and them, and doth thye raigne upholde:
> It is but late, as wryting will recorde,
> That poore thow weart withouten lande or goolde;
> Yet how hathe golde and pryde, by one accorde,
> In wickednesse so spreadd thie lyf abrode,
> That it dothe stincke before the face of God." [40]

BABYLON CALLED SHAMELESS.—In wild and untaught notes, the Spirituals had sung of the doom of Rome. But now the strain is taken up by a master, and Europe listens. In eloquent words Petrarch portrayed the same picture of papal corruption as given by Dante. The depravity of the papal court especially attracted the notice of Petrarch, and though the court had taken up residence in Avignon—which Petrarch execrated [41]—he pursued it thither, citing the evangelist John's description in Revelation 17.

"Thou Babylon, seated on the wild banks of the Rhone, shall I call thee famous or infamous, O harlot, who hast committed harlotry with the kings of the earth? Truly thou art the same that the holy Evangelist saw in spirit, the same, I say, and not another, sitting upon many waters. Either literally, being surrounded by three rivers, or, in the profusion of this world's goods, among which thou sittest wanton and secure, unmindful of eternal riches; or, in the sense laid down by him that beheld thee, that the waters on which you the harlot sit are peoples and nations and languages. Recognize thine own features. A woman clothed in purple and scarlet, decked with gold and precious stones and pearls, having a golden cup in her hand, full of abomination in the impurity of her fornication—Dost thou not know thyself, O Eabylon? Unless perhaps what is written upon her forehead is wrong, Babylon the great, you indeed are Babylon the little." [42]

He frequently speaks of western Babylon—that is, Avignon on the Rhone—in a number of the letters in his *Book of Letters Without Title.*[43]

From Petrarch's own observations of the Curia, and the sad

---

[40] Francesco Petrarch, Sonnet CV, translated by Wyatt (?), in *The Sonnets, Triumphs, and Other Poems of Petrarch*, pp. 135, 136.
[41] Flick, *op. cit.*, vol. 1, pp. 211-213.
[42] Translated from Petrarch, *Epistolarum Sine Titulo, Liber*, letter headed *Babylonem Gallicam Describit*, in *Opera*, vol. 2, p. 807.
[43] *Ibid.*, pp. 793-809.

havoc open simony had made upon the church, he drew a fright-
ful description of the perishing, abominable, Gallic Babylon,
and the Apocalyptical woman, "drunk with the blood of the
saints." [44]

This is the word of the second of Italy's great poets.

While Wyclif was protesting papal abuses in England, in
Bohemia Milicz of Kremsier, Conrad of Waldhausen, and
Matthias of Janow, canon of the Cathedral of Prague, similarly
called for reformation, and appealed to the Bible as the source of
Christian faith and practice. [45]

V. Milicz—Bohemian Herald of Already Existent Antichrist

Prophetic light likewise penetrated Bohemia in the fourteenth century, where the Greek church had helped to establish
Christianity in the ninth century. Bohemia was not, however,
brought under papal rule until the fifteenth. In fact, owing to
its Greek origin, the Bohemian church barely tolerated the
Roman constitution and ritual. [46] We now note the first of two
notable prophetic expositors in this region.

JOHN MILICZ (variants: Militz, Miliz, or Milic) of Kremsier
(d. 1374), eminent precursor of the Bohemian reformation, was
born of poor parents in Moravia. Little is known of his early
years, nor are we sure where he received his higher education;
some suggest, besides Prague, even Paris or Italy. The first time
he enters the arena of history is when he became a priest in 1350.
He soon attracted the attention of the emperor Charles IV, king
of Bohemia, who made him his secretary. Then he became
canon and archdeacon of the Cathedral of Prague, and therefore
occupied a conspicuous ecclesiastical position. But his fervent
desire to help his fellow men led him, in 1363, to resign his
handsome income and high position, with its prospects of even
greater promotion. [47]

---

[44] *Ibid.*, p. 807.
[45] John Cunningham Geikie, *The English Reformation*, p. 50.
[46] Johann Heinrich Kurtz, *Church History*, vol. 2, p. 206.
[47] Bernhard Czerwenka, *Geschichte der Evangelischen Kirche in Böhmen*, vol. 1, p. 45;
E. H. Gillett, "Milicz," in M'Clintock and Strong, *Cyclopaedia of Biblical, Theological, and
Ecclesiastical Literature*, vol. 6, p. 256.

Withdrawing to Bischof-Teinitz, he served as a humble minister, his life tinged with ascetic severity and poverty; but he soon returned to Prague. He was a powerful preacher, his preaching being characterized by fiery enthusiasm and soaring eloquence. He often spoke four or five times a day—once in Latin to the students of the University of Prague, and the other times in the vernacular German and Bohemian tongues.[48] Rieger says that Catholic and Protestant writers agree that Milicz favored the fundamental Waldensian truths.[49] He inveighed against the use of an unknown tongue in worship. He reproved sin, and multitudes thronged his meetings. He was noted not only for his moral earnestness but for the spiritual force of his character. He had views concerning Antichrist, which probably connect him with the Spiritual Franciscans.[50]

1. ANTICHRIST'S COMING THE BURDEN OF HIS DISCOURSES.—Milicz stressed the necessity of true conversion, attacked the mendicant system, and delved into the prophecies of the Apocalypse. In fact, his preaching was largely from the Apocalypse, the discourse of Jesus in Matthew 24, and the epistles of Paul. He saw the way preparing for divine judgments on the corrupt church, and foresaw a reformation by which the church would be prepared for the second advent of Christ.[51] He seemed to see Antichrist embodied in the variety of errors and abuses that existed in the church, and his earnest words held the throngs. Erelong, the coming of Antichrist became the burden of his pulpit discourses, as he exposed the iniquities that seemed to herald it. Priests, bishops, magistrates, and even the emperor were not spared.[52] His mind became fired by the prophecies of Antichrist. Says Schaff:

"Milicz's mind became fired with the prophecies of antichrist and the last days, and he dwelt frequently, as later did Huss, on 'the abomination of

[48] Augustus Neander, *General History of the Christian Religion and Church*, vol. 5, pp. 175, 176; Gillett, "Milicz," in M'Clintock and Strong, *op. cit.*, vol. 6, p. 256.
[49] Georg Cunrad Rieger, *Die Alte und Neue Böhmische Brüder* (1734), vol. 1, p. 67.
[50] Reginald Lane Poole, *Wycliffe and Movements for Reform*, p. 121.
[51] Neander, *op. cit.*, vol. 5, p. 178.
[52] Gillett, "Milicz," in M'Clintock and Strong, *op. cit.*, vol. 5, p. 256.

desolation which was spoken of through Daniel the prophet standing in the holy place,' Matt. 24:15." [53]

Such positive preaching soon brought Milicz into prison. But the pope freed him. Milicz is quoted as saying that he was—

"moved contrary to his own will by the Holy Spirit to search the Scriptures concerning the time when Antichrist would appear. While doing so, he found that this Antichrist had already appeared and is dominating the church of Christ. The Church by the negligence of her priests has become miserable and desolate. She has an abundance of worldly goods, but is lacking completely of spiritual values: The idols destroyed Jerusalem and made the temple desolate, but the abomination is covered by hypocrisy. Many deny Christ, because they keep silent and dare not to confess Christ and His truth before those who keep back the truth by their unrighteousness. There is no truth in the pope, cardinals, bishops, prelates, priests, and monks, nor do they teach the way of truth." [54]

2. APPLIES YEAR-DAY PRINCIPLE TO 1335 DAYS.—Many in Bohemia who longed for a deeper understanding of spiritual truths leaned toward the views of the Joachimites. Milicz likewise applied himself with great zeal to the study of time prophecy, and accepted the year-day principle as had Joachim. Combining Daniel 12:12 with Matthew 24:15, he believed the 1335 year-days would end about 1363-1367—taking the crucifixion of Christ as the beginning—and that the already existent Antichrist would be fully revealed at that time. [55]

It is to be observed that, like Joachim, Milicz adopted a true symbolic time principle. But, lacking knowledge as to what it signified and when it should be applied, he naturally erred in its chronological placement. In the initial application the tendency has always been to have these great prophetic time periods end in one's own day. In fact, that seems to be the way in which they have usually been introduced. Fuller knowledge would correct their chronological setting. So Milicz, dating those days from the cross, ended them in his own time.

---

[53] David S. Schaff, *John Huss*, p. 30.
[54] Translated from Rieger, *op. cit.*, vol. 1, pp. 68, 69. Rieger cites this from unnamed Catholic writers.
[55] David S. Schaff, *John Huss*, pp. 30, 31.

3. Posts "Antichrist" Placard on St. Peter's at Rome.—
Milicz' studies, based on the Apocalypse, did not create the desired effects among his fellow countrymen, so he felt himself
called to go directly to Pope Urban V at Rome. He desired to
place his scheme of prophetic interpretation directly before the
pope, and to urge the calling of a general council for the reformation of the church. In 1367, acting on the report that the pope
was about to return from Avignon to Rome, Milicz resolved to
confer with him in the chief city of Christendom, there to utter
his admonitions.[56] He hoped a plan of reformation could be devised by the bishops.

Rieger states that Milicz asked the Lord to free him from these
convictions if they were not from God. "But finding no rest, he
undertook a pilgrimage to Rome, meeting a number of cardinals in their own homes to whom he fearlessly proclaimed that
the Antichrist has already appeared." [57] Milicz took with him a
few companions, and awaited the pope's arrival. But the pope
was delayed. So Milicz gave himself to prayer, fasting, and the
reading of the Scriptures for a full month, preparing for the work
he felt called to do. Gillett and Neander describe the astonishing episode of posting an "Antichrist" placard on the doors of
the original St. Peter's, at Rome:

"Still the pope did not arrive. Milicz could no longer restrain himself.
He posted on the doors of St. Peter's that on a certain day he would appear
and address the multitude. It is said, moreover, that he added, 'The Antichrist is come; he has his seat in the church.' " [58]

"Milicz could no longer keep silent. He caused a notification to be
posted up at the entrance of St. Peter's church, that on a certain day he
would there make his public appearance and address the assembled multitude; that he would announce the coming of Antichrist and exhort the
people to pray for the pope and the emperor, that they might be enabled so
to order the affairs of the church, in things spiritual and temporal, that the
faithful might securely serve their Creator." [59]

---

[56] Workman, *Dawn of the Reformation*, vol. 2, p. 104.
[57] Rieger, *op. cit.*, vol. 1, p. 69. See footnote 54.
[58] E. H. Gillett, *The Life and Times of John Huss*, vol. 1, p. 23; see also Gieseler, *op. cit.*,
vol. 3, pp. 184, 185.
[59] Neander, *op. cit.*, vol. 5, p. 180.

4. PREACHES TO ASSEMBLED CLERGY IN ST. PETER'S.—The terse expression, "The Antichrist is come," epitomized the thought that had long occupied his mind, and he zealously warned both clergy and people to withdraw from iniquity. It was almost as dramatic an act as Luther's later posting of his Theses on the church door at Wittenberg, and was a century and a half earlier. This could not pass. The Inquisitor, spurred by reports of Milicz' course in Bohemia, ordered his arrest and imprisonment. He was turned over to the Franciscans to be kept in close confinement. From his prison he was summoned to address an assembly of the Roman clergy, but his full release did not occur until the pope's arrival in Rome in 1368.[60] Neander describes the remarkable sermon, preached in St. Peter's itself:

"After having been long detained in close confinement [in Rome], he was asked, what it had been his intention to preach. He requested his examiners to give him the Bible, which had been taken from him at the time of his arrest, with paper, pen, and ink, and he would put his discourse in writing. This was granted, and his fetters were removed. Before a large assembly of prelates and learned men, in the church of St. Peter, he delivered a discourse in Latin, which produced a great impression. He was then conducted back to his prison, but treated with less severity." [61]

5. WRITES TRACT ON ANTICHRIST FROM PRISON CELL.— While in his cell at Rome, Milicz composed his remarkable tract De Antichristo (On the Antichrist), which has been preserved by his disciple Matthias of Janow in the latter's writings, and which later influenced Huss,[62] according to Neander.

"Antichrist, he supposes, is not still to come, but has come already. He says in his tract on the Antichrist: Where Christ speaks of the 'abomination' in the temple, he invites us to look round and observe how, through the negligence of her pastors, the church lies desolate; just as, by the negligence of its pastors, the synagogue lay desolate." [63]

This treatise Milicz took back with him to Prague, upon his release from prison by Cardinal Albano, after the return of Urban V.

---

60 Gillett, "Milicz," in M'Clintock and Strong, op. cit., vol. 6, p. 256.
61 Neander, op. cit., vol. 5, p. 181.
62 Neander, op. cit., vol. 5, pp. 178, 181.
63 Ibid., p. 178.

6. ESTABLISHES PREACHERS' TRAINING SCHOOL IN PRAGUE.—
Back in Prague, he was distressed because his influence was limited to his own personal preaching. He often said, "Would that
all were prophets." After the death of Konrad of Waldhausen,[64]
in 1369, a large field of activity opened up before him. So he
set up a school for preachers,[65] multiplying books through copying. These exerted a wide influence, disseminating his doctrines
through Bohemia, Poland, and Silesia. In fact, Raynaud complains that he "weaned away many people from the Catholic
faith in Poland, Bohemia, Moravia, Silesia, and neighboring
countries." [66]

"He founded an association composed of two or three hundred young
men, all of whom resided under the same roof with himself, were trained
under his influence, and by his society. He copied the books which they
were to study, and gave them devotional books to copy themselves, for the
sake of multiplying them." [67]

Prague was stirred by this powerful preaching of the gospel.
Milicz' labors also transformed more than two hundred fallen
women in "Little Venice," an evil district of Prague. For these
women who abandoned their life of shame Milicz established a
chapel dedicated to Mary Magdalene. More than that, the emperor helped him rebuild a large institution for the care of these
reclaimed souls.[68]

7. DIES AT AVIGNON UNDER PAPAL CENSURE.—However,
Milicz was not to escape the wrath of his enemies. Charges against
him were lodged before Pope Gregory XI—that he disparaged

---

[64] KONRAD (OR CONRAD) OF WALDHAUSEN (d. 1369) of Austria, received his education in
an Augustinian convent, becoming a priest in 1345. In 1360, he was called by Emperor Charles
IV to minister at Leitmeritz, and in 1362 to Prague, where he became canon of the cathedral.
Konrad preached chiefly in the German tongue, and with such marked success that the churches
could not accommodate the enormous crowds, so the pulpit was placed outside the church in the
public square. Even the Jews crowded in to hear him. (Czerwenka, op. cit., vol. 1, pp. 43, 44).
He fearlessly lifted his voice against the moral and religious degradation of his time, especially
against the monks. He was regarded as a master preacher, and his sermons were used as models
by other preachers, and extracts circulated for general convenience. In 1364, the Dominicans and
Franciscans combined against Konrad, and exhibited 29 Articles of Accusation, but could not
substantiate the charges when called before the archbishop; therefore Konrad was able to continue without serious interference until his death. (James C. Robertson, History of the Christian
Church, vol. 7, pp. 302, 303.)
[65] Workman, Dawn of the Reformation, vol. 2, p. 105; Neander, op. cit., vol. 5, p. 181.
[66] Rieger, op. cit., vol. 1, p. 68.
[67] Neander, op. cit., vol. 5, p. 181.
[68] Czerwenka, op. cit., vol. 1, pp. 46, 47.

the clergy, from the pope down.[69] In 1372, Gregory XI dispatched bulls to the archbishop of Prague and bishops of Luturmysl, Breslau, Ollmütz, and Krakau, and to Charles IV, based on twelve serious accusations. He commanded them to excommunicate Milicz for asserting that Antichrist was already come.[70] One article specifically asserted that "Antichrist was come." [71] He expressed surprise that they should have so long waited until such heretical, schismatic doctrines had spread through so wide a circle.[72]

Milicz went fearlessly to Avignon for examination in 1374, appearing in person before the pope, under the protection of his friend Cardinal Albano. On May 21 he was permitted to preach before the cardinals,[73] and his accusers were compelled to withdraw their charges. However, he died before judgment was passed on his case,[74] to the sorrow and grief of many.

VI. Janow Makes Complete Break With Rome Over Antichrist

MATTHIAS OF JANOW (d. 1394), the Wyclif of the Bohemian church, was born at Prague of noble parentage. Conspicuously talented and well educated, he was called the "Parisian master" because he continued his studies at the University of Paris, from which he received his doctor's degree after nine years. In 1381 he became canon in the Cathedral of Prague. Janow was a devoted disciple of Milicz, whose writings filled him with "enthusiastic admiration," powerfully influencing his life.

Janow paved the way for the Hussite movement by his writings, just as Milicz had done by his preaching. In these writings the prophetic concepts of Milicz were further developed by Janow, with their influence extending on to Huss.

BIBLICAL AND PROPHETICAL BASIS OF TEACHINGS.—According to his own testimony Janow was converted from his evil hab-

---

[69] Robertson, op. cit., vol. 7, pp. 303-305.
[70] Joseph Milner, The History of the Church of Christ, vol. 2, cent. 14, chap. 1, p. 108; Czerwenka, op. cit., vol. 1, p. 48.
[71] Gieseler, op. cit., vol. 3, pp. 184, 185, note 6.
[72] Neander, op. cit., vol. 5, pp. 182, 183.
[73] Flick, op. cit., vol. 1, p. 362.
[74] Czerwenka, op. cit., vol. 1, p. 48; Gieseler, op. cit., vol. 3, pp. 184, 185.

CATHEDRAL TAPESTRY ATTESTS INTEREST IN PROPHECY

Fourteenth Century Angers Cathedral Tapestry, in France, Portrays the Transfer of Power from the Dragon of Revelation 12 to the Seven-headed Beast From the Sea, of Revelation 13

its through the reading of the Scriptures.[75] In 1388 he wrote a treatise on the Lord's supper, which stirred up severe persecution. He fought for the restoration of the wine at communion, and condemned the worship of images, saints, and relics. He attributed the deplorable conditions of the church to neglect of the study of the Word and the fact that the traditions of men were exalted above the Word of God. He firmly opposed righteousness by works, teaching that justification and sanctification come only through faith by the grace of God and the merits of the blood of Christ.[76] Thus clear rays of divine light penetrated the surrounding darkness.

Janow vigorously opposed the encroachments of the Papacy,

---

[75] Czerwenka, *op. cit.*, vol. 1, p. 48.
[76] *Ibid.*, pp. 50, 51; Flick, *op. cit.*, vol. 1, p. 362.

denouncing the iniquities of the clergy and charging that the church had changed from a spiritual power to a secular force. Under the Western Schism, Janow's ideas of reform ripened into opposition to Rome, which he came to regard as the apostate Antichrist, instead of Christ's vicar.[77] He declared Antichrist had come long ago, and was even then claiming dominion over the church. This he considered imperative to expose, believing "a secularized hierarchy was Antichrist embodied."[78] Janow based these contentions on 2 Thessalonians 2, on Daniel, and on Revelation 13 and 17, and believed Antichrist was to be destroyed at the second advent. His views naturally aroused the ire of the church authorities. He was arraigned before the synod of Prague in 1389, where his views were condemned. But his reformatory ideas paved the way for Huss,[79] and later for Luther.

Janow went further in practical reform than either Konrad or Milicz. He was indeed the Wyclif of the Bohemian church. His efforts toward reformation of the corrupt Latin system were intended to remove entirely the yoke of that system. Though not suffering punishment as a heretic, he was not long permitted to sow seeds that would undermine some of the foundation principles of the papal hierarchy. Suspended from his ministry, he was obliged to leave Prague for a time, though he continued to teach.[80] He especially emphasized that the Scriptures give grand prophetic vistas of the future.

VII. Epitome of Janow's Teachings on Antichrist

1. CALLS FALSE SPOUSE OF CHRIST THE ANTICHRIST.—His chief work was *De Regulis Veteris et Novi Testamenti* (Concerning the Rules of the Old and the New Testament). It contains a number of separate treatises in which Milicz' tract *De Antichristo,* which really should be called *Anatomia Membrorum Antichristi* (Anatomy of the Members of Antichrist), is

---

[77] Robertson, *op. cit.,* vol. 7, pp. 305-307.
[78] Gillett, *Life and Times of John Huss,* vol. 1, p. 31.
[79] There were others—like Thomas of Stitney, John of Stekno, and Matthew of Cracow—who spread the teachings over different lands—Bohemia, Moravia, Austria, Hungary, Thuringia. (Flick, *op. cit.,* vol. 1, p. 362.)
[80] Flick, *op. cit.,* vol. 1, p. 362; Robertson, *op. cit.,* vol. 7, pp. 306, 307.

included. But it is difficult today to establish exactly which portion of this work is to be ascribed to Milicz and which to Janow. The following quotations, therefore, are given under the authorship of Janow.[81]

"I confess, before God and his Christ, that so alluring was this harlot Antichrist, that she so well feigned herself the true spouse of Jesus Christ, or rather, Satan by his arts so tricked her out, that from my early years I was long in doubt what I should choose, or what keep. . . . I confess that between these two courses I hung wavering in doubt; and unless our Lord Jesus be our keeper, none will escape the honeyed face and smile of this harlot—the tricks of Satan and the snares of Antichrist." [82]

2. ANTICHRIST'S REIGN IN CHURCH PRESENT ACTUALITY.— In explicit terms Janow identifies Antichrist as the apostate tyrant who has already come, arrogating to himself dominion over the church. This exposure became his avowed object:

"The Antichrist has already come. He is neither Jew, pagan, Saracen, nor worldly tyrant, but the 'man who opposes Christian truth and the Christian life by way of deception;—he is, and will be, the most wicked Christian, falsely styling himself by that name, assuming the highest station in the church, and possessing the highest consideration, arrogating dominion over all ecclesiastics and laymen;' one who, by the working of Satan, assumes to himself power and wealth and honor, and makes the church, with its goods and sacraments, subservient to his own carnal ends." [83]

3. A FUTURE ANTICHRIST IS THE DEVIL'S TRICK.—Janow explicitly declares the idea of an Antichrist yet to come is a cunning trick of the archenemy, "when, in truth, he is now present and so has been for a long time," and as a result directly contravenes Catholic teaching.

" 'Lest—says he—the abomination of desolation,' (Matt. 24:15,) [']should be plainly manifest to men, he has invented the fiction of another abomination still to come, that the church, plunged still deeper in error, may pay homage to the fearful abomination which is present, while she pictures to herself another which is still in the future. It is a common, everyday fact, that Antichrists go forth in·endless numbers, and still they are looking forward for some other and future Antichrist.' " [84]

---

[81] Workman, *Dawn of the Reformation*, vol. 2, pp. 355, 356; Neander, *op. cit.*, vol. 5, p. 178; Gillett, *Life and Times of John Huss*, vol. 1, p. 33.
[82] Gillett, *Life and Times of John Huss*, vol. 1, pp. 29, 30.
[83] *Ibid.*, pp. 30, 31.
[84] Neander, *op. cit.*, vol. 5, p. 196.

4. INGENIOUS DESCRIPTION IN "ANATOMY OF THE BEAST."—
This ingenious production, glowing with the fire of indignation
against Antichrist, is thus described by Gillett:

"The names of Antichrist are presented in alphabetical order—'Abomination of Desolation,' 'Babylon,' 'Bear of the Wood,' etc. The various
members of his mystical body are then described,—the head, hair, brow,
eyes, nose, neck, breast, loins, etc. Most important are the three false principles which are formed from the tail of Antichrist. The first is, that as soon
as one is elected pope of Rome, he becomes head of the whole militant
church, and supreme vicar of Christ on earth. This is pronounced a bare
lie. The second is, that what the pope determines in matters of faith is to be
received as of equal authority with the gospel. This is likewise pronounced
false; for we must believe him, who has so often erred in matters of faith,
only when he is supported by the scriptures. The third,—that the laws of
the pope are to be obeyed before the gospel,—is declared blasphemous;
for it is blasphemy to believe the pope or any one else, or to accept his laws,
in preference to Christ." [85]

"The various passages of scripture, both in the Old and New Testaments, in which the great apostasy of the church is foretold, or in which the
iniquity of Antichrist is exhibited, are successively considered. Ezekiel's
vision; Gog and Magog; he that sitteth in the temple of God; the locusts
of Revelation; the beast with the seven heads and the ten horns; the woman
seated upon the beast, with her cup of abomination in her hand, and her
forehead branded 'Babylon the great, the mother of harlots,'—are brought
to view, and shown to be exact descriptions of the prevailing apostasy.
Even now, Janow declares that the pious are persecuted. They are re-
proached as Beghards and Turpins, Picards and wretches. . . .
"But Antichrist is to be destroyed. Christ will destroy him by the
breath of his mouth and the brightness of His coming." [86]

5. SECOND ADVENT ENDS CONFLICT OF CHRIST AND ANTI-
CHRIST.—Janow applies 2 Thessalonians 2 to the moral falling
away in the church. He believed that there was to be a gradual
evolution of the two kingdoms of Christ and Antichrist, side by
side. Two movements had already begun—the preaching of the
gospel, and the decline of Antichrist—and both will find their
consummation at the second coming of Christ.

"While Satan, then, was thus gradually to introduce the mysteries of
his Antichrist into the church, keeping his toils concealed; so, on the other
hand, the Lord Christ, gradually manifesting himself in his beloved dis-

---

[85] Gillett, *Life and Times of John Huss*, vol. 1, p. 34.
[86] *Ibid.*, pp. 35, 36.

ciples, was at length, before the final judgment, to reveal himself in a great multitude of preachers. The spiritual revelation of Christ, through his genuine organs, the spiritual annihilation of Antichrist by the same, and a new illumination of the church, were to prepare it for the last personal appearance of Christ, and precede that event." [87]

6. REVIVAL OF PRIMITIVE CHRISTIANITY PREDICTED.—Declaring that before "the end of the world" the "church of Christ shall be reformed" by a great company of preachers of Jesus Christ, Janow rejects the thought that Elias was to appear literally, and believes that this reappearance of Elias is to be "understood only in the spiritual sense."

"Speaking of the signs of these times, he [Janow] says: 'As John the Baptist pointed away to Christ, so these signs point away impressively with their fingers to Antichrist, already coming; they point to him now and will point to him still more; they have revealed him, and will reveal him, till the Lord shall destroy him with the breath of his mouth; and he will consume him by the brightness of his new revelation, until Satan is finally crushed under his feet. The friends of Christ, however, will destroy him, will rob him of his trade, the company of the preachers of Jesus Christ, united and bound together by the love and wisdom which come from God.' All holy Scripture—he says—predicts, that before the end of the world the church of Christ shall be reformed, renovated, and more widely extended; that she shall be restored to her pristine dignity, and that still, in her old age, her fruitfulness shall increase." [88]

7. APOSTLES OF ANTICHRIST PERSECUTE FOLLOWERS OF CHRIST.—As Matthias of Janow was the nucleus of the reform movement in Bohemia, he naturally was the center of papal antagonism. He himself, in various passages, mentions the existence of this antagonism.

" 'They—says he—who are apostles and preachers of Antichrist, oppress the apostles, the wise men and prophets of Christ, persecuting them in various ways, and boldly asserting, that these ministers of Christ are heretics, hypocrites, and Antichrists. And since many and mighty members of Antichrist go forth in a countless variety of ways, they persecute the members of Christ who are few and weak, compelling them to go from one city to another by driving them from the synagogues, (excluding them from the fellowship of the church). Whenever one of the society of such Christians ventures to be somewhat more free of speech, and to live more worthily

---

[87] Neander, *op. cit.*, vol. 5, p. 199.
[88] *Ibid.*, p. 200.

of Christ than is common, he is directly called a béghard, or by some other heretical name, or merely set down as a hypocrite or fool. If he do but in a small degree imitate his crucified master, and confess his truth, he will experience at once a fierce persecution from some side of the thick body of Antichrist.' " [89]

8. Approaching Redemption and Antichrist's Destruction.—With the return of the prophecies to a vital place in the understanding of the conflict between Christ and Antichrist, the second advent hope flamed anew.

" 'All that now remains for us—he says—is to desire and pray for reform by the destruction of Antichrist himself, and to lift up our heads, for our redemption draweth nigh.' " [90]

---

[89] *Ibid.*, pp. 232, 233.
[90] *Ibid.*, p. 234.

CHAPTER TWO

Wyclif Expands Exposition
of Little Horn

I. The Founding of the Universities

The university came into being in the medieval age. The thirst for knowledge, with students wandering over Europe in search of capable teachers, formed the setting and created the demand.[1] Bologna, at the crossroads of northern Italy, became a university center for the study of law about 1100; two centuries later, faculties for the arts, medicine, and theology were added.[2]

The University of Paris came into being about 1200, likewise with faculties for the arts, theology, law, and medicine. Paris in turn became the model for the universities of Northern Europe—Oxford, about 1200; Cambridge, a little later; Prague, in Bohemia, in 1347; and Heidelberg, the first German university, in 1386.[3] By 1300 there were some fourteen universities scattered through Italy, Spain, France, and England.[4]

The need for social control and cheap lodging created the college, the University of Paris founding the first college in 1209. Others followed. At first these were merely dormitories, where students could live inexpensively under supervision. Later, masters were assigned to live with the students and to help them prepare for their examinations.[5]

---

[1] Strayer and Munro, *op. cit.*, pp. 260, 345.
[2] Ault, *op. cit.*, pp. 493, 500, 501. On universities, see also H. O. Taylor, *op. cit.*, vol. 2, pp. 410 ff.
[3] Ault, *op. cit.*, pp. 502, 503.
[4] Strayer and Munro, *op. cit.*, p. 344.
[5] Ault, *op. cit.*, pp. 504, 505.

The Catholic Church did not create the first universities, but it quickly realized that they were ideal for regulating the conduct of students, as well as controlling the content of books and the doctrine of teachers. Thus the universities became the instruments through which the church controlled education and research. The popes aided the foundation of new universities. They gave high offices to university professors, and assisted poor students in their efforts to obtain an education. Thus they secured almost complete orthodoxy among schoolmen. The scholars who taught in the universities succeeded in reconciling the new knowledge with the doctrines of the church. The faculties watched zealously for signs of heresy in books and lectures.[6] Thus the universities came to play an increasingly important role in the coming conflict.

II. The Fourteenth Century Conciliar Movement

The Conciliar movement of the fourteenth century aimed at transforming the Papacy from an absolute monarchy into a limited monarchy, setting up a representative council in the church, vested with legislative powers. The Conciliar movement found its chief support in the universities of Europe, especially in that of Paris, formerly the stronghold of papal orthodoxy.[7] As the schism dragged on, the Conciliar idea found increasing advocates, two of the leaders being Peter d'Ailly and John Gerson.[8] Only a general council, it was argued, could heal the schism, stamp out heresy, and reform the church. England was spotted with "heretics," and Bohemia almost ready to break away.

The cardinals summoned a general council, independent of both popes, to meet at Pisa in 1409. Representatives from England, France, Germany, Poland, and Sicily were present. They deposed both popes and elected a Greek, of Italian training, who took the name Alexander V.[9] But neither of the de-

---

[6] Strayer and Munro, *op. cit.*, pp. 260, 261, 344.
[7] Ault, *op. cit.*, p. 617; also Strayer and Munro, *op. cit.*, pp. 431 ff.
[8] Ault, *op. cit.*, p. 618.
[9] *Ibid.*

posed pontiffs recognized the legality of Pisa and excommunicated the adherents of Alexander.[10] Since the advocates of the
Conciliar idea failed in their full objectives at Pisa, the Council
of Constance was called in 1414. There the election was unanimous, as Martin V became the new pope; the council then addressed itself to uprooting heresy and to crushing the two
Bohemians, Huss and Jerome of Prague. Later councils launched
four crusades against the heretics without success.[11] But the
Conciliar movement had failed, and the papal restoration had
not been effected.[12]

From 1309 to 1377 the papal court was in residence at
Avignon, France. A majority of the cardinals were always
French, and the popes of the period were Frenchmen. There
was strong feeling in England that the Papacy was under
French control, and antipapal hostility developed. Parliament
passed a statute forbidding the pope to fill English clerical
posts,[13] and those who carried an appeal out of England to the
papal court at Rome, without the king's consent, were guilty of
treason.[14] The climax of anticlericalism came, however, in the
career and teachings of John of Wyclif, the Oxford scholar.[15]

III. Morning Star Appears Before Reformation Dawn

The English universities, which had been established about
two centuries prior to Wyclif's day, were largely for sacred
learning—theology being the chief study, and the students
largely novitiates of the monastic orders. The Magna Charta,
secured at Runnymede in 1215, was denounced by the pope.
But this event was an important landmark in the great struggle
between the papal and the secular power in Britain. Kings and
the parliament had long withstood the oppressive yoke of the
hierarchy. John of Salisbury, Robert Grosseteste (or Great-

---

[10] Strayer and Munro, *op. cit.*, p. 432.
[11] Ault, *op. cit.*, pp. 618-621.
[12] Strayer and Munro, *op. cit.*, p. 441.
[13] Statute of Provisors, 1351, quoted in Ault, *op. cit.*, p. 593.
[14] Statute of Praemunire, 1353, quoted in Ault, *op. cit.*, pp. 593, 594.
[15] Ault, *op. cit.*, p. 594; also Strayer and Munro, *op. cit.*, p. 429.

head), Bishop of Lincoln,[16] Roger Bacon, and others had raised their voices against the corruptions of the church. Light was breaking in increasingly upon the dark Middle Ages. By Wyclif's day papal prestige was at a low ebb, unable to command either respect or obedience.

Wyclif was born while the Papacy was in its Babylonian Captivity in Avignon. During the early years of his priesthood he witnessed the enormous loss of prestige suffered by the Papacy. Antipapal elements in the English court sheltered Wyclif for a long time from what would otherwise have been consequences serious to himself, because of his antipapal utterances. The period was a time of controversy and of cross fire of political, religious, and scientific opinion such as Europe had not seen since the collapse of classical culture in the sixth and seventh centuries.

1. ATTACKS OF OXFORD PROFESSOR DRAW PAPAL FIRE.— JOHN WYCLIF (Wiclif, Wycliffe, or Wickliffe) of Lutterworth (c. 1324-1384), "the Morning Star of the Reformation," was born in Yorkshire about the time of Dante's death. Educated at Oxford, and proficient in canon and civil law, he there distinguished himself as a teacher. He was first aroused about his own soul, when still in his twenties, by a fearful pestilence from Asia and the Continent, which swept over England, slaying an appalling number. Wyclif became a spiritual as well as an intellectual giant. He received the degree of D.D., or Doctor of Theology, when it was quite infrequent and stood for conspicuous scholastic achievement. In 1360 he had become master of Balliol College and lecturer on the Scriptures. When he began his public opposition to the ignorant mendicant friars,[17] the issue was over the mendicants versus the gospel.

Wyclif became rector, successively, of Fillingham (1361), Ludgershall (1368), and Lutterworth (1374). In about 1365 he was made chaplain to the king, thus entering into close

---

[16] Matthew Paris, *English History*, vol. 3, pp. 35-39; Charles Maitland, *The Apostles' School of Prophetic Interpretation*, pp. 332, 333.
[17] Arthur Robert Pennington, *Epochs of the Papacy*, p. 196.

relations with the government. In 1374 he was sent as a member of a royal commission to Bruges, Netherlands, to discuss differences with the papal nuncios of Gregory XI, over appointments to ecclesiastical offices. After his return he spoke openly of the papal "Antichrist." [18] He saw clearly the evils of the church and warned against her errors and abominations. He laid the ax at the root of indulgences, crusades, transubstantiation, pilgrimages, and relics. Wyclif strove for two main principles: first, to free the church from its connection with temporal affairs; and second, to effect a doctrinal reform through substituting the "law of the gospel" for the tradition of the church. [19]

In 1377 Wyclif denied the priestly power of absolution, and began to issue popular tracts. In this year his theological views were first called into question. He was summoned to London by Bishop Courtenay, to give account of his teachings. Riots resulted, but nothing came of it. The hierarchy became alarmed. Gregory XI issued five bulls, on May 22, 1377, condemning Wyclif's positions and citing him to answer charges of insubordination and heresy, roundly condemning eighteen propositions from his writings, reproving Oxford for not taking action against Wyclif, and authorizing his imprisonment. [20]

2. GREAT SCHISM DROVE WYCLIF FROM PAPACY.—Wyclif paid little attention to the bulls. A new citation followed, and a second hearing was held at Lambeth in 1378, with a formidable list of charges. But Wyclif was protected by the Princess of Wales. From 1378 to 1382 he continued to write and teach at Oxford, elaborating his views and gaining supporters. In 1378, just as the papal net was closing in about Wyclif, death suddenly stiffened the hand that had woven it. Gregory XI died, and two popes were elected to succeed him—Clement VII at Avignon, and Urban VI at Rome. This schism in the Roman church pre-

---

[18] Kurtz, *op. cit.*, vol. 2, p. 204; Robert Vaughan, *The Life and Opinions of John de Wycliffe*, vol. 1, pp. 337, 338.
[19] Poole, *Wycliffe and Movements for Reform*, p. 113.
[20] Poole, "Wycliffe," *Encyclopaedia Britannica* (1945 ed.), vol. 23, pp. 822, 823; for English translation of bull of Gregory XI against John Wyclif, see Guy Carleton Lee, *Source-Book of English History*, pp. 211, 212; *Translations and Reprints From the Original Sources of European History*, vol. 2, no. 5, "England in the Time of Wycliffe," sec. 3, "Wycliffe and the Lollards," pp. 9 ff.

vented further action for the time, giving Wyclif a breathing spell. Papal authority was crippled, and was unable to enforce its demands.

It was the Great Schism that drove Wyclif from allegiance to the Papacy. This year—1378—was the turning point in his life. His spiritual senses were shocked, his theories overturned. The spectacle of two popes—each claiming to be sole head of the church, each labeling the other Antichrist, and each seeking the destruction of the other—horrified him. The whole institution appeared to be from the evil one. From earlier support, he changed to antagonism. Then, as he came to see its prophetic significance, he threw off his allegiance. No longer holding one pope to be true and the other false, Wyclif ranked both alike false—"two halves of Antichrist, making up the perfect Man of Sin between them." [21] From 1378 onward he concentrated on the reform of doctrine.[22] It was no longer a matter of whether the Papacy enjoined this or that, but the status of the Papacy itself. Meantime, while the popes were hurling anathemas at each other, Wyclif pursued his sublime work of translating the Bible—each verse a ray of light piercing the surrounding darkness.

Then came the issue over transubstantiation, which by 1381 Wyclif assailed as anti-Scriptural in his lectures at Oxford. Since the doctrine promulgated by Wyclif on this point occurs frequently in the course of his sermons, it is probable that it had been introduced from the pulpit prior to its admission into his teaching in the classroom.[23] At approximately the same time he published twelve short theses at Oxford, denying transubstantiation, and challenging all of contrary mind to debate the matter.[24] Summoned to appear before a group of judges at Oxford, two of whom were doctors of laws, and ten doctors of theology, Wyclif stood alone.

---

[21] Trench, *op. cit.*, p. 312.
[22] Pennington, *op. cit.*, p. 207.
[23] Gotthard Lechler, *John Wycliffe and His English Precursors*, pp. 367, 368; Vaughan, *Life and Opinions of . . . Wycliffe*, vol. 2, p. 59.
[24] John Lewis, *The History of the Life and Sufferings of the Reverend and Learned John Wicliffe*, chap. 6; Lechler, *op. cit.*, pp. 367-369.

WYCLIF SENDING FORTH HIS ITINERANT EVANGELICAL PREACHERS

From His Parish at Lutterworth, Wyclif Sent His Russet-robed Itinerant Preachers Throughout All England to Spread the Evangelical Truth, Including the Prophetic Portrayal of the Papacy. Possessing Only the Pages of Wyclif's Bible, Tracts, and Sermons, They Went Out Two by Two Until Thousands Became Persuaded. From England, Wyclif's Teachings Spread to the Continent, and Were the Means of Enlightening Huss

This convocation, sitting with the chancellor of the university, condemned his theses, and prohibited their being taught in the university. Some forty years had passed since Oxford had become the home of the Reformer. Now he was gray with toil and age. Many who had stood with Wyclif when he assailed flagrant ecclesiastical abuses, shrank from following him in doctrinal controversy. Like Elijah, he now stood virtually alone among his countrymen, witnessing uncompromisingly to the truths of Scripture, and refusing to repudiate the mandates of conscience.

This refusal led to an organized attempt to suppress him. A synod convoked by Archbishop Courtenay in London in 1382, at which Wyclif was not present, condemned as heretical many of Wyclif's positions,[25] and threatened heavy penalties upon any who should so teach or listen to them.[26] Banished from Oxford, Wyclif went back to Lutterworth, where he wrote ceaselessly against papal claims and formalism, in full expectation of imprisonment and martyrdom. Tracts poured forth—*De Potestate Papae* (On the Power of the Pope) (*c.* 1379), *De Veritate Sacrae Scripturae* (On the Truth of Sacred Scripture), and so forth.

He attacked the clergy for their wealth and self-seeking, their subservience to the pope as vendors of indulgences, the doctrine of transubstantiation, and the efficacy of confession to priests. Finding a ready response, he soon came to have a substantial following known as the Lollards.[27] As early as 1378 he organized a body of itinerant preachers, who spread his doctrine throughout the land.[28] Clad in long russet robes of undressed wool, staff in hand, their only possession a few pages of Wyclif's Bible, tracts, or sermons, they went out two by two. (Illustrated on page 50.) Half of England was favorable to

[25] Flick, *op. cit.*, vol. 1, p. 350; Joannes Dominicus Mansi, *Sacrorum Conciliorum Nova, et Amplissima Collectio*, vol. 26, cols. 695-706.
[26] Lechler, *op. cit.*, pp. 379-385; J. A. Wylie, *The History of Protestantism*, vol. 1, p. 116.
[27] This name was early given to the English followers of Wyclif. Derived from the Dutch or German *lollen*, signifying to sing with a low voice, it originated on the Continent, especially the Low Countries, and from the middle of the eleventh century was applied to persons distinguished for their piety, generally remarkable for devotional singing. (See Workman, *Dawn of the Reformation*, vol. 1, p. 303, Appendix.)
[28] Pennington, *op. cit.*, p. 209.

Lollardism, which included many knights and nobles.[29] Among his adherents were Walter Brute (Britte), William Thorpe, Lord Cobham (Sir John Oldcastle), and John Purvey. The doctrine likewise spread to the Continent and, carried to Prague, was the means of enlightening Huss.

3. APPEAL TO SCRIPTURE THREATENS PAPAL AUTHORITY.— Wyclif now completed the most abiding work of his life—the translation of the Bible into English.[30] He was possessed with a great longing to bring the Word of Life to the people. "The Scripture only is true," became his golden maxim. These Scriptures, he believed, should be accessible to all. Heretofore portions had been put into the vernacular, mainly the Psalter, for the unlettered clerics.[31] Wyclif's was the first English version of the whole of Sacred Scripture designed for everyone.[32] Groups assembled everywhere to read Wyclif's translation, which was finished about 1382. As it was based on the Vulgate, there was an outcry from opponents that a translation was imperfect; and was not the Vulgate sufficient?—forgetting that the Vulgate itself was a translation.

IV. Exposes Antichrist as False Church of Prophecy

The usurpations of the Papacy—its "spoliation" of the churches, its haughty pride, the worldly character of its government, and its claims to hierarchal domination over the world—were attacked by Wyclif as bearing the stamp of Antichrist—a name he applied to the pope and the Papacy in numberless passages in his later years.[33] In chapter 2 of *De Papa* he asserts that "the pope is antichrist here in earth," and in chapter 7 that the cardinals "are hinges to the fiend's [devil's] house." [34] Wyclif contrasts the true church with "the 'Church of the malignants' "—the members of the holy church with the disciples of

---

29 Trench, *op. cit.*, p. 316.
30 Lechler, *op. cit.*, pp. 216, 217.
31 Trench, *op. cit.*, p. 309.
32 There are various editions of Wyclif's Bible extant. One commonly accessible edition of his New Testament is in *The English Hexapla;* see also Margaret T. Hills, *A Ready Reference History of the English Bible*, Pamphlet no. 1, pp. 3, 4.
33 Lechler, *op. cit.*, pp. 317, 318, 366.
34 *The English Works of Wyclif Hitherto Unprinted*, pp. 458 ff.

Antichrist.[35] He maintains "there are two flocks in the militant church, the flock of Christ and manifold flocks of Antichrist." [36]

Like those of Dante, Wyclif's views on church and state fitted perfectly into the rising nationalism of the time. He denounced the temporal claims of the Papacy in *De Dominio Divino* (Concerning Divine Lordship), declaring the pope ought to have no authority over states and governments. It became a cardinal feature of his teaching, a position he never yielded.

ANTICHRIST IDENTIFIED ON BASIS OF BIBLE PROPHECY.— Wyclif regarded the pope, in bloodstained garments at the high altar of the central church of Christendom, as the Man of Sin, the Little Horn, and the true Antichrist of prophecy. His treatises are replete with such references.[37] In his translation of the "secounde epistle to Tessalonycense" (1380) and of the "Apocalips," he beheld the real character of the Man of Sin and the woman of Revelation 17. His *Speculum de Antichristo* (Mirror of Antichrist) unveils the deceits of Antichrist and his "clerks" (clergy), who object to the preaching of Christ's gospel.[38] To subject Christendom to the bishop of Rome is to subject her to the power of Antichrist.[39] In his tract *Of Good-Preaching Priests,* Wyclif again inveighs against the "heresy and hypocrisy of Antichrist," and calls his prelates "the clerks [clergy] of Antichrist." [40] Writing further on the "fiction" of the "keys of Antichrist," he admonishes his readers to "sever from the church such frauds of Antichrist," and to learn to "detect the devices of Antichrist." [41]

In *How the Office of Curates Is Ordained of God,* which is in manuscript in the Library of Corpus Christi College, Cambridge, Wyclif's point XXIV is explicit:

---

[35] Wyclif, *Sermons,* in *Select English Works of John Wyclif,* vol. 1, p. 50; cited in Lechler, *op. cit.,* p. 293.
[36] Lechler, *op. cit.,* p. 293.
[37] Workman, *Dawn of the Reformation,* vol. 1, pp. 173-175.
[38] *English Works,* pp. 108 ff.
[39] Vaughan, *John de Wycliffe, D.D., a Monograph,* p. 432.
[40] *Tracts and Treatises of John de Wycliffe,* p. 29.
[41] *Ibid.,* p. 198.

"The four and twentieth is, that they put the holy law of God under the feet of antichrist and his clerks, and the truth of the gospel is condemned for error and ignorance by worldly clerks, who presume by their pride to be doomsmen of subtle and high mysteries, proving articles of holy writ, and blindly condemn truths of Christ's gospel, for they are against their worldly life and fleshly lusts, and condemn for heretics true men who teach holy writ, truly and freely, against their sins." [42]

Wyclif applies the name Antichrist to all the popes collectively, and to individuals such as Clement VII, frequently referring to the pope as fulfilling the Pauline prophecy of 2 Thessalonians 2, concerning "the 'Man of Sin.' " The cardinals who opposed Urban VI, before electing a rival pope, had issued a manifesto against Urban, declaring that he ought to be called Antichrist rather than pope. Small wonder that Wyclif called both popes (Urban VI and Clement VII) Antichrist, as well as popedom at large. [43]

V. Wyclif's Remarkable Expositions of Daniel's Prophecies

As might be expected, Wyclif reached his conclusions relative to the Papacy on the basis of the prophecies of Daniel, Paul, and John, just as did the Waldenses of the valleys, Eberhard of Salzburg, [44] and Milicz and Matthias of Janow in Bohemia. By these inspired symbols he was guided and nerved for conflict in the battle and break with Rome. His expositions, however, are not commonly known, as they are in Latin, with no complete English translation thus far available.

1. FOUR PROPHETIC EMPIRES OF DANIEL 2 ENUMERATED.— Naming Assyria (Babylon), Medo-Persia, Grecia, and Rome as the four world powers of prophecy, Wyclif brings in the Medo-Persian ram, the Grecian goat and Alexander as the notable horn of Daniel 8, to establish the identity and sequence of the second and third empires.

"The second prophecy is that . . . in the second chapter of Daniel relating to the dream of Nebuchadnezzar, to whom appeared the image consisting of four parts, signifying four monarchies, so that the head of gold

---

42 *Writings of . . . John Wickliff*, p. 132.
43 Lechler, *op. cit.*, p. 319.
44 Treated in Volume I of *Prophetic Faith*.

represents the kingdom of the Assyrians, as Daniel explains in the same place, the second kingdom represented by the breast and arms of silver, was the kingdom of the Persians and the Medes, and the third kingdom, represented by the belly and thighs of brass, was the kingdom of the Greeks. For in the eighth chapter of Daniel we read, how he saw a ram, brandishing his horns toward the west, toward the north, and toward the south, and how all beasts were unable to resist him, or to be freed from his hands. And afterward Gabriel explains this as related to the king of the Persians and Medes, and the vision in which he saw the he-goat with one notable horn conquering the ram; Gabriel explains as relating to the king of the Greeks, which he had proved after the occurrence of the event, as is shown in the eighth chapter of Daniel and the first of the Maccabees concerning Alexander the Great. Moreover the fourth part of the image, represented by the feet of iron, is explained concerning the kingdom of the Romans, which by civil law and by wars overthrew the four horns coming forth from Alexander." [45]

2. Papal Antichrist Is Little Horn of Daniel 7.—Striking at the popular Catholic fallacy of a future Antichrist, Wyclif, in England, applies the lawless, persecuting Little Horn to the papal Antichrist, as did Eberhard in Austria, and the ten horns to "the whole of our temporal rulers." Here is Wyclif's clear depiction:

"Why is it necessary in unbelief to look for another Antichrist? Hence in the seventh chapter of Daniel Antichrist is forcefully described by a horn arising in the time of the fourth kingdom. For it grew from [among] our powerful ones, more horrible, more cruel, and more greedy, because by reckoning the pagans and our Christians by name, a lesser [greater?] struggle for the temporals is not recorded in any preceding time. Therefore the ten horns are the whole of our temporal rulers, and the horn has arisen from the ten horns, having eyes and a mouth speaking great things against the Lofty One, and wearing out the saints of the Most High, and thinking that he is able to change times and laws." [46]

After quoting Daniel 7:8, 25, concerning this Little Horn "having eyes and a mouth speaking great things against the Lofty One," Wyclif expressly states: "For so our clergy foresee the lord pope, as it is said of the eighth blaspheming little head." [47]

And after quoting Zechariah 3:8, 9, Wyclif applies to Christ

---

[45] Translated from Wyclif's *De Veritate Sacrae Scripturae*, vol. 3, pp. 262, 263.
[46] *Ibid.*, pp. 267, 268. Some texts read *maior;* see footnote.
[47] *Ibid.*, p. 268.

VITAL SCENES IN WYCLIF'S LIFE WITNESS

Interior of Wyclif's Lutterworth Church, With Pulpit at Left, From Which He Thundered Forth
His Message of Saving Truth and His Exposure of the Errors of the Papacy and Its Identity as
Antichrist (Upper); Exterior of Famous Lutterworth Church (Left); Wyclif Battled the Friars
Until His Deathbed, Refusing to Capitulate (Center Right); Little Brook Called the Swift into
Whose Waters Wyclif's Bones Were Cast After Being Burned Near By (Lower)

the very words that for centuries had been usurped by the pope
—*"Servus servorum"* (servant of servants).

"It seems to me that this scripture cannot be more soundly or more
fittingly understood than concerning our Jesus, who was servant of servants,
coming forth from high heaven." [48]

3. APPLIES YEAR-DAY PRINCIPLE TO PROPHETIC TIME.—
After discussing the relationship of the lunar and solar years,
concerning which there is "varied exposition," Wyclif clearly
sets forth the year-day principle (a prophetic day equals a year)
for prophetic time, citing the experience of Laban and Jacob
in Genesis 29.[49]

4. LITTLE HORN'S THREE AND HALF TIMES COVERS CEN-
TURIES.—Concerning the "period" that has been "assigned" to
Antichrist for his "despotic rule, according to the prophetic
sense," Wyclif apparently expounds the first "time" of Daniel
7:25 as covering some three centuries, evidently from Constantine's endowment to Mohammed, the two "times" as the
period from Mohammed forward to the period when the clergy
exercise their powers of excommunication, and the "dividing
of time" as the last segment. That Wyclif understood these
"times" to be precise prophetic years is doubtful. But here are
his words.

"By a *time* Daniel understands the whole period in which the church
apostatizes, from the time of its first endowment even to the time in which
Mahomet prevailed; and by *times* he understands the diversity of times
from this time up to the time when the secular rulers compute harmoniously
their gifts which they bestow upon the poor; and by *half a time* he understands the residue of time during which the clergy by the deceit of their
excommunication and the thunderbolt of their censures against those who
do good to them, foolishly kick back by taking away the remedy of their
sin." [50] (Italics not in the original.)

The remarkable advance in this application lies in the fact
that it is applied to the period assigned to the papal Little Horn,
and that it contravenes the popular fallacy of three and a half
literal years at the end of the age, just as truly as it controverts

[48] *Ibid.*, p. 265.
[49] *Ibid.*, pp. 270, 271.
[50] *Ibid.*, p. 268.

the concept of a yet future Antichrist. It is a truly Protestant interpretation, as clear as could be expected for the time. It is an indirect application of the year-day principle, reaching back across the centuries and tied to the historical Papacy.

5. SEVENTIETH WEEK OF DANIEL 9 A "WEEK OF YEARS."— After declaring that it was "our Jesus" that was promised to the patriarchs, Wyclif discusses Daniel 9 and teaches that Christ was crucified three and a half years after the beheading of John the Baptist, in the seventieth "week of years."

"Moreover in the last week of years our Jesus confirmed those things which He promised the ancient fathers, and in the second half of that week, namely, three and a half years from the beheading of John the Baptist, when Christ preached and suffered, the victim and sacrifice ceased gradually in the temple and a little after the death of Christ more completely." [51]

6. ABOMINATION OF DESOLATION REMOVES CONTINUAL SACRIFICE.—Citing Christ's admonition to understand the "abomination of desolation," as applied to the defiling of the sanctuary in Daniel 11, and the taking away of the "continual sacrifice," Wyclif applies the "abomination of desolation" set up in the holy place to the doctrine of transubstantiation,[52] which he calls "this heresy about the host." [53]

7. LIVING IN "LAST AGE OF THE CHURCH."—Wyclif wrote a library of learned and powerful disquisitions. The earliest work attributed by some to him is a small treatise entitled *The Last Age of the Chirche*, written in 1356. It constitutes an indictment of the sins of the church and her priests—the church that had been cursed with persecutions, heresies, and simony. There is only one more trouble to follow: the devil at work in broad daylight, *i.e.*, the Antichrist, with the end of the age impending. It should be noted that Joachim of Floris, Pierre Jean Olivi (Peter John Olivi, or Oliva), and Bernard of Clairvaux, as well as Bede, are frequently cited.[54]

---

[51] *Ibid.*, p. 272.
[52] *Wycliffe's Wyckett*, reprinted in *Tracts and Treatises*, pp. 274, 282, 284.
[53] Wyclif, *Trialogus*, book 4, chap. 6, translated in *Tracts and Treatises*, p. 149.
[54] Wyclif, *The Last Age of the Chirche*, pp. xxiv, xxv, lii, liii; Lechler, *op. cit.*, pp. 63, 64. These characters, except Bede, are all discussed in Volume I of *Prophetic Faith*.

The calculation of the end is significant, being influenced by the 1260- and 1335-year prophecies. Though Wyclif was persuaded no one could foretell the day of judgment, he was certain the time was nigh at hand. It is said that the occasion of the writing was the terrible earthquakes and fearful pestilences decimating Europe. These were taken as indicating that the great designs of God were hastening toward their close. Believing that the final visitations were soon to take place, he styles the time "the last age of the Chirche."

VI. Wyclifism Condemned as Heresy at Oxford and Constance

In 1382 the church council at London formally condemned Wyclif's doctrines, but he himself remained at large and unmolested. The Reformer, however, was growing old, and now occupied himself in writing tracts and two of his most important works, one of which was the *Trialogus*. Pope Urban cited him to answer for his opinions before him at Rome, but the summons came too late. Wyclif had already, in 1382 or 1383, suffered a paralytic stroke. On the 28th of December, 1384, he had a final stroke, and died on New Year's Eve.[55]

Back in 1383 Oxford had expelled all Lollards from her walls.[56] To many the doctrine seemed suppressed by the time of Wyclif's death.[57] When Wyclif was summoned to Rome by Urban VI to be tried for heresy in 1384, he boldly declared: "No man should follow the pope, nor no saint that now is in heaven, but in as much as he [the pope] follows Christ." And Wyclif tactfully adds, "I suppose of our pope that he will not be Antichrist, and reverse Christ in this working, to the contrary of Christ's will." [58]

The Lollards continued to stress the disparity of papal

---

[55] Flick, *op. cit.*, vol. 1, p. 350; Mansi, *op. cit.*, vol. 26, cols. 695-706.
[56] A Wyclifite, or Lollard, came to indicate one who opposed the hierarchical order and temporal endowments of the church, as well as certain doctrines, chief of which was transubstantiation, and who maintained that public preaching is imperative. (Poole, *Wycliffe and Movements for Reform*, p. 113.)
[57] Workman, *John Wyclif*, vol. 2, p. 330.
[58] Ogg, *op. cit.*, pp. 476, 477; Old English text found in *Select English Works of John Wyclif*, vol. 3, pp. 504-506; see also Lee, *op cit.*, pp. 212-214.

dogmas and practices with New Testament teachings. In 1395 they affixed to the door of St. Paul's and of Westminster Abbey, in London, a placard attacking the Roman clergy. Laws of extreme severity against them were passed through Convocation and Parliament (1399-1400), and for the first time in England "heresy" was punishable with death by fire. Nor did these laws remain a dead letter. Wyclif's followers were arrested. Some recanted. Of those who stood fast, some were imprisoned for life, and others died for their faith.[59]

1. COUNCIL OF OXFORD REPUDIATES WYCLIFISM IN 1408.—
In 1406 a document was issued in the name of the chancellor of Oxford University, and sealed with the university seal, declaring in favor of Wyclif.[60] However, the Council of Oxford (1408)—against the Lollards—forbade reading from any book composed by John Wyclif, or written in his time or since, unless it had first been examined and unanimously approved by a group representing the universities of Oxford or Cambridge (Canon 6). It declared translation of the text of Holy Scripture a dangerous thing, because of the difficulty of preserving the original meaning, and forbade reading Wyclif's translation under pain of excommunication, with the same penalty for making or reading any other unauthorized translation. Finally, it declared the University of Oxford to be "infected with new unprofitable doctrines, and blemished with the new damnable brand of Lollardy." (Canon 11.) [61]

In 1412 the Catholic leaders of the university transmitted to the governing body 267 propositions taken from thirteen treatises by Wyclif, which were declared erroneous and heretical. By 1414—thirty years after Wyclif's death—Oxford had repudiated Wyclifism. It was on Bohemia, however, that Wyclif's real legacy devolved. There his doctrines were planted and nour-

---

[59] Trench, op. cit., p. 317; Kurtz, op. cit., vol. 2, p. 206; see also Albert Henry Newman, A Manual of Church History, vol. 1, p. 592. The death penalty for heresy, which had been authorized for nearly two centuries on the Continent, was officially used as a threat in England in 1389. (Poole, Wycliffe and Movements for Reform, pp. 115, 116.)
[60] Lechler, op. cit., p. 456.
[61] Edward H. Landon, A Manual of Councils of the Holy Catholic Church, vol. 2, pp. 13-15; Mansi, op. cit., vol. 26, cols. 1037-1041.

ished, and grew to power. The recently established University of Prague had adopted the plan of traveling scholarships to assist Bohemian students at Paris or Oxford. Bohemian students continued to flock to England after the death of Anne of Bohemia, the queen of Richard II, in 1394, and Wyclif's writings were transcribed by them. Thus the Lollard teachings were transmitted to Bohemia, where they were earnestly read. They brought fresh vitality to the Reform movement, but by 1403 Wyclif's teachings were solemnly condemned by the University of Prague.[62]

2. COUNCIL OF CONSTANCE ORDERS WYCLIF'S BONES EXHUMED.—In 1414 the Council of Constance opened. In addition to ending the Great Schism, one of its chief objects was "to take cognisance of the heresies of Huss and Wickliff." Forty-five articles, or propositions, were extracted from Wyclif's writings. In 1415 these, together with all his books, were condemned, including Article 37, which declared that "the Church of Rome is the synagogue of Satan." Wyclif's bones were ordered exhumed and cast forth from consecrated ground—if they could be separated from the bones of the faithful.[63] This sentence was not executed, however, until 1428—thirteen years later—when Pope Martin V sent renewed orders to Fleming, bishop of Lincoln,[64] once a favorer of Wyclif's doctrines. The moldering remains were taken from the grave where they had reposed for more than forty years, and burned. The ashes were then cast into an adjoining rivulet called the Swift. Thomas Fuller well observes:

"Thus this brook hath conveyed his ashes into Avon, Avon into Severn, Severn into the narrow seas, they into the main ocean. And thus the ashes of Wyclif are the emblem of his doctrine, which now is dispersed all the world over."[65]

---

[62] Poole, *Wycliffe and Movements for Reform*, pp. 119, 120, 124.
[63] H. J. Schroeder, *Disciplinary Decrees of the General Councils*, p. 449; Mansi, *op. cit.*, vol. 27, cols. 632-636; Foxe, *Acts*, vol. 1, p. 529.
[64] Lechler, *op. cit.*, pp. 466, 467.
[65] Workman, *John Wyclif*, vol. 2, p. 320; also put into verse by William Wordsworth in *Ecclesiastical Sonnets*, Part 2, Sonnet 17, "Wicliffe," in *The Poetical Works of William Wordsworth*, edited by E. de Selincourt [vol. 3], pp. 369, 370.

3. IDENTIFICATION OF ANTICHRIST "PRESENT TRUTH" FOR MIDDLE AGES.—It is obvious that recognition of the historical Papacy as the Antichrist, prophesied by Daniel, Paul, and John, *and seen as a then-present reality,* was the emphasis designed of God as the Middle Ages drew toward their close. The outline prophecies in general, and the papal Little Horn section in particular, along with the anticipation of God's coming kingdom, were again in the forefront, though the other two of the five factors governing the advent hope [66]—the literal resurrection and the true concept of the millennium—were still misconceived. But an increasing number of earnest students knew approximately where they were in the Antichrist period of the grand prophetic outline, as they waited and longed for the closing events at the end of the age, and the return of the Lord Jesus. They had recognized the Little Horn phase when it had come to pass.

Wyclif had threatened the very citadel of papal dogmatism by appealing to the Bible and its prophecies as the primary authority. Asserting every man's right to examine the Bible for himself, he had contended for the literal sense. Verily, Wyclif was a brilliant light shining in the darkness of the late Middle Ages. He stands out like an illuminated mountain peak amid the enshrouding darkness—one of God's true noblemen of the ages.

VII. The Plowman's Prayer and the Lantern of Light

1. PLOWMAN'S APPEAL FOR SHORTENING ANTICHRIST'S DAYS. —An illuminating example of the protesting literature of the time is the anonymous *Prayer and Complaint of the Ploughman,* written about 1360.[67] Foxe recorded it, "neither changing any thing of the matter, neither altering many words of the Phrase thereof." [68] It was likewise "faithfully set forth by William Tindal," according to Foxe. Raising complaint against muddied

---

[66] Treated in Volume I of *Prophetic Faith.*
[67] This work is not to be confused with *The Vision of Piers Plowman,* by William Langland, which treatise is also critical of the clergy and hostile to the Papacy. (Ault, *op. cit.,* p. 594; Thomas Martin Lindsay, "Lollards," *Encyclopaedia Britannica,* vol. 14, p. 341.)
[68] Foxe, *Acts,* vol. 1, p. 453.

water for God's sheep, auricular confession, penance, simony, image worship, withholding knowledge, violating God's law, and being wolves in sheep's clothing, the author continues in quaint old English, reaching this climax concerning the Antichrist:

> " 'For *Peter* knowledged that thou were Christ and God, and kept the Hests [precepts] of thy Law: but these han forsaken the Hests of thy Law, and hath ymaken a Law contrary to thine Hests of thy Law. And so he maketh himself a false Christ, and a false God in Earth. And I trow thou gave him no Power to undo thy Law. And so in taking this Power upon him, maketh him a false Christ and *Antichrist.*' " [69]

This "Antichrist" is immediately identified as he "that in his words maketh himself Christs Vicar in Earth," who makes men worship him as a god:

> " 'Therefore he is *Antichrist* that maketh men worshipen him as a god on Earth, as the proud King *Nabugodonosor* did sometime, that was King of *Babylon.* And therefore we lewde men that knowen not God but thee Jesus Christ, believen in thee that art our God, and our King, and our Christ, and thy Laws; and forsaken *Antichrist* and *Nabugodonosor* that is a false god, and a false Christ, and his Laws ben contrary to thy preaching.' " [70]

The treatise closes with this appeal to God to shorten the prophesied days of the prophesied Antichrist, according to His promise.

> " 'And Lord, geve our King and his Lords heart to defenden thy true Shepherds and thy Sheep from out of the Wolves mouths, and grace to know thee that art the true Christ, the Son of thy heavenly Father, from the *Antichrist;* that is, the Son of Pride. And Lord, geve us thy poor Sheep patience and strength to suffer for thy Law, the cruelness of the mischievous Wolves. And Lord, as thou hast promised, shorten these days. Lord we axen this now, for more need was there never.' " [71]

2. "THE LANTERN OF LIGHT" LOOKS TOWARD COMING DELIVERANCE.—Another searching Lollard treatise, *The Lantern of Light,* written about 1400, had three chapters devoted to strictures on Antichrist.[72] The "open conclusion," based on the

---

[69] *Ibid.,* p. 463.
[70] *Ibid.,* p. 463; cf. pp. 455, 456.
[71] *Ibid.,* p. 463.
[72] Chapters 3-5.

prophecies of Daniel, Paul, and John, looked for the destruction
of Antichrist at the advent.

> "In the court of Rome is the head of antichrist, and in prelates is the
> body of antichrist, but in those clouted sects, as monks, canons, and friars,
> is the venomous tail of antichrist.
> "How this antichrist shall be destroyed, God himself teacheth by the
> prophet Daniel, and saith, This antichrist shall be destroyed without hands,
> that is, without power of man. For Paul saith, 2 Thess. ii., Christ shall slay
> antichrist with the spirit of his mouth, that is, with the holy word of his
> law. And the lord shall destroy him with the shining of his coming, that is,
> with the turning of men's hearts by his grace, to his law, a little before the
> doom." [73]

Chapter 5 concludes with an appeal to look for the appearance of Enoch and Elijah, not in person, "but in spirit and in
power," to make men's hearts "ready before Christ's doom." [74]
Chapters 12 and 13 concern the "Fiend's contrivances" and the
"Fiend's church." Since this work was written just as the burning
alive of the Lollards had begun, these persecuted folk had "recourse to Scripture," and sensed their oneness with the martyrs
of former centuries. A moving appeal in chapter 13 states:

> "The fiend's church in these days praise above the clouds Christ and
> his holy saints, with words and with signs; but they pursue to death the
> lovers of his law! . . . Oh, these shall have a dreadful day when they are
> arraigned at the bar of judgment, when Christ shall rear up his cross, the
> banner of his sufferings!" [75]

This section closes with the impending judgment. Citing
Zephaniah 1, *The Lantern of Light* says:

> "The great day of the Lord is nigh, and cometh fast, and wonders
> approach quickly; it shall not long tarry. In that day, he that is strong and
> mighty shall be troubled; for the voice of the Lord is bitter to the
> damned." [76]

Next is envisioned salvation for the persecuted, with everlasting burning for the persecutors. Then follows this appeal,
calling for separation:

---

[73] *The Lantern of Light,* in *Writings and Examinations of Brute, Thorpe, Cobham, Hilton . . . with The Lantern of Light,* p. 148.
[74] *Ibid.,* p. 150.
[75] *Ibid.,* p. 186.
[76] *Ibid.*

"Strive in this life to leave the fiend's church, and to bring yourself, both body and soul, into the church of Jesus Christ, while grace and mercy may be granted." [77]

So the growing chorus of voices rose in volume and clarity.

---

[77] *Ibid.*, p. 187.

CHAPTER THREE

Lollard Positions Molded
by Prophetic Interpretation

I. Influential Catholics Point the Finger at Rome

In the centuries just preceding the Reformation an ever-increasing number of pious persons began openly to express the conviction that the dire prophecies concerning Antichrist were even then in the process of fulfillment. They felt that the "falling away" had already taken place. They declared that Antichrist was already seated in the churchly temple of God, clothed in scarlet and purple. Numerous individuals of influence spoke mysterious things about seven-hilled Rome, and solemnly pointed the finger at the Roman church as the predicted Man of Sin, which had now become a historical reality.[1] With the Papacy growing in disfavor, the clergy under attack, and heresy rampant, there appeared an outbreak of mysticism. Scholasticism had sought to save theology by buttressing it with argument, whereas mysticism sought to save men by bringing them into direct relationship to God. These mystics included Bridget, or Birgitta, of Sweden (1303-1373) and Catherine of Siena (1347-1380).[2]

Some were sound, scholarly thinkers; others were erratic and visionary. Some were outside the church, but most were still within the Catholic fold, conscious of her corrupted char-

---

[1] Döllinger, *Prophecies*, pp. 53-55.
[2] Ault, *op. cit.*, p. 625.

acter and striving earnestly to effect reforms. There was marked unrest among the heretical sects—Beghards, Beguines, Fraticelli, and so forth—whereas the Spirituals busied themselves preaching and writing against the pope and his court as Antichrist and the Babylonian Harlot.[3] As papal oppression grew, many braced themselves against it. Despairing of reform, they sought religious security outside her pale.[4] The Hildebrandine idea of the church had been questioned, disputed, declined, and condemned, and was never again to dominate the world as before.[5]

1. NICHOLAS DE LYRA, ADMITS YEAR-DAY.—NICHOLAS OF LYRA, or Lyranus (d. 1340), born in Normandy, was a Hebrew and Greek scholar and exegetical writer of high repute, belonging to the Franciscans. Of the five methods of exposition— verbal, subjective, allegoric, cabalistic, and literal—Nicholas chose the literal, endeavoring to find the actual meaning of the writer.[6] Stimulated by the Jewish writers Rashi (d. 1105) and Maimonides (d. 1204), he still held to the seven rules of Ticonius.[7] But Lyra complained that the Catholic expositions had buried the true sense under a superabundance of mystical interpretation. And he, between 1320 and 1340, filled five vast folio volumes without doing much better.[8]

De Lyra could see little in the Apocalypse but Saracens, Byzantines, and Turks, the false prophet being Mohammed.[9] He expected Antichrist to appear at the end of the world, in accordance with the usual medieval understanding. He made the seals, trumpets, and vials consecutive. However, he did expound Daniel's forty-five days (1290 days plus 45 equals 1335) to be forty-five years.[10] Satan was considered bound by the founding of the orders of St. Francis and St. Dominic. De Lyra still thought the first resurrection to be a change from sin to grace, and the

[3] Flick, *op. cit.*, vol. 1, pp. 190-192, 241, 242.
[4] Gieseler, *op. cit.*, vol. 3, p. 182.
[5] Trench, *op. cit.*, p. 303.
[6] Frederic W. Farrar, *History of Interpretation*, pp. 274, 275.
[7] *Ibid.*, pp. 275, 276. Ticonius is discussed in Volume I of *Prophetic Faith*.
[8] *Ibid.*, p. 278, n. 1.
[9] Charles Maitland, *op. cit.*, pp. 349, 430.
[10] E. B. Elliott, *Horae Apocalypticae* (5th ed.), vol. 4, pp. 429, 430.

1,000 years but an indefinite period from Christ's birth to the end.[11]

2. Bridget of Sweden Denounces Corruptions.—The most unsparing denunciations of the corruption of the church at Avignon came from two women honored by the church— Bridget of Sweden and Catherine of Siena. It is anomalous that certain of their writings which so searchingly discuss the prevalent corruption were highly prized by the leaders of the church, but they did nothing to remedy the condition. They contained the gravest charges against the popes, the Roman Curia, and the degeneracy of the clergy. Yet Bridget of Sweden, like Joachim of Floris, was honored by the church.[12]

Bridget, Birgitta, or Brigitta (1303-1373), was the daughter of Birger Persson, lord of Finstad, connected with the reigning house of Sweden. She was married to Ulf Gudmarsson, a Swedish nobleman of royal blood, to whom she bore eight children. Her wedded days were filled with happiness, and her life was one of service to others. In 1343 Gudmarsson became a monk, and died the following year. Mystical voices began to be heard by this Swedish princess, whose messages are recorded in her *Revelations*. She believed herself to be a channel between God and mankind, and denounced the immoral lives of priests and monks. She claimed to have visions, and at times lost consciousness in her trances. She returned to the court to preach repentance. Then she founded the Order of the Holy Saviour, composed of both women and men, with respective convents.

Looking southward to Avignon and Rome, she wrote a letter of rebuke to Pope Clement, urging him to break the fetters of Babylonian Captivity. Failure to accomplish this led to her journey to Rome. The desolation of Rome struck deeply into Bridget's soul and inspired pages of eloquence reminiscent of Petrarch. The rest of her life was lived in Italy. But she saw little hope. For the most part she remained in Rome, laboring

---

[11] Farrar, *op. cit.*, p. 276.
[12] Döllinger, *Prophecies*, p. 143. (Joachim is fully treated in Volume I of *Prophetic Faith*.)

for the souls of men. Her revelations rebuked the excesses and sins of the populace, and stirred up fierce hatred against her, some even threatening to burn her alive.[13] She proclaimed a mighty overthrow of the seat of the Papacy.[14] Decrying the "horrible simony" and the theft of the Lord's sheep, she declared the priests had become the slaves of the devil rather than the servants of God.[15] In one of her visions she bewails the lamentable state of the church in the following words:

"Now I wail over you, you head of my church, who sits on my throne, the one I have given to Peter and his successors, to sit on it in threefold dignity with threefold authority, first: that they should have power to bind souls and to loose them from sin; second, that they open heaven to the penitent; third, to close heaven to the cursed and despisers of my commandments. But you, who should release the souls and present them to me, you are in reality a murderer of souls. I have ordained Peter as a shepherd and guardian of all my sheep, but you destroy and tear them up. You are worse than Lucifer, he was jealous and did only desire to kill me in order to rule in my place, but you are so much worse, because you not only kill me in thrusting me aside by your wicked works, but you kill souls by your bad example. I bought the souls with my blood and committed them to your charge as to my faithful friend, but you surrender them again to the enemy from whom I ransomed them. You are more unjust than Pilate, who condemned nobody to death except me, but you do not only judge me as if I be a powerless and worthless individual but you condemn also innocent souls and free the guilty ones. You are more cruel than Judas, who sold only me, but you do not sell me alone but the souls of my elect for the sake of vile profit and a hollow name. You are more abominable than the Jews; they crucified only my body, but you crucify and punish the souls of mine elect to whom your wickedness and transgression is more bitter than any sword." [16]

3. CATHERINE DECLARES OPPOSING CARDINALS SERVANTS OF ANTICHRIST.—CATHERINE BENINCASA OF SIENA (1347-1389) was a contemporary of Francesco Petrarch, poet laureate of Rome. Matters had changed but little since Dante had written his famous lament in the sixth canto of the *Purgatory*. During the time of the absence of the popes at Avignon, immorality had

---

[13] John Wordsworth, *The National Church of Sweden*, pp. 123-137; Edmund G. Gardner, *Saint Catherine of Siena*, pp. 44-46; Döllinger, *Prophecies*, pp. 54, 55.
[14] Döllinger, *Prophecies*, pp. 54, 55; Karl Hase, *A History of the Christian Church*, pp. 344, 345.
[15] Flick, *op. cit.*, vol. 1, pp. 182, 183.
[16] Translated from the German version, *Leben und Offenbarung en der heiligen Brigitta* (Life and Revelations of Saint Brigitta), pp. 239, 240.

Sons and Daughters of the Church Decry Corruption

Dante and Petrarch, Poets of Italy, Pour Forth Their Indignation Against Church's Depravity, and Europe Listens (Upper); Bridget of Sweden and Catherine of Siena, Honored by the Church, Similarly Denounce the Prevalent Corruption (Lower). (For These Four Characters See Pages 21, 29, 68, and 69.)

grown among the priests, and moral corruption was rampant in the convents and monasteries. Many secular priests openly kept concubines. As the great pestilence of 1348 swept over Italy, scourging everywhere with violence, it seemed like a punishment for the flagrant sins of men. Florence and Siena endured its worst horrors. Catherine's people were of the ruling class at Siena, her father being a dyer. About 1363 Catherine began a life of incredible austerity and of mystical visions. Raw herbs, bread, and water were her diet, and she slept on a bare board. She entered upon a three-year retreat of silence within the enclosure of her cell. It was probably in 1366 that she began to go forth on her missions.[17]

Catherine announced that a great and thorough reformation of the church would come to pass.[18] The bride, now deformed and clothed with foul rags, would then shine forth with bright jewels, crowned with a diadem of virtue. Catherine declared that the appointment of evil shepherds was responsible for the rebellion in the church.[19] She looked upon the opposing cardinals as fallen angels, who place themselves in the service of Antichrist. To Urban VI she wrote, "I have learned that those devils in human form have made an election. They have not chosen a Vicar of Christ, but an Anti-Christ." And to the opposing cardinals she declared, "You, who were angels upon earth, have turned to the work of devils. You would . . . seduce us into obedience to Anti-Christ." [20]

Let us note briefly five others who represent the times.

4. ARNOLD OF VILLANOVA ANTICIPATES THE END.—The celebrated Spanish or French physician and alchemist ARNOLD OF VILLANOVA,[21] or Arnaldus of Bachuone (c. 1235-1313), lecturer at the University of Paris and a zealous Joachimite in certain points, maintained that the church of the West was

---

[17] Gardner, *Saint Catherine of Siena.* This excellent work, based on the sources, contains an extensive bibliography.
[18] Döllinger, *Prophecies,* pp. 67, 68.
[19] Flick, *op. cit.,* vol. 1, pp. 180, 181.
[20] Ludwig Pastor, *The History of the Popes,* vol. 1, pp. 129, 130.
[21] More fully discussed in Volume I of *Prophetic Faith.*

already irretrievably destroyed, and that Antichrist was about to appear and the world to come to its end.[22] His treatise on the coming of Antichrist places that event at the setting up of the abomination of desolation, at the end of the 1290 years, about 1378.[23]

Villanova does not identify the Antichrist, but points out his forerunners as he lashes out at the Paris theologians who have tried to silence him:

"For who of the faithful is ignorant, since the Chaldeans and barbarians are not ignorant, [of the fact] that the Roman pontiff is Christ on earth? . . . How, therefore, without the greatest ruin of the Catholics, can those despise his authority who have been chosen for the protection of the Lord's vineyard? Can it be argued from this that the persecution of Antichrist already hastens exceedingly, since he is to be armed with a whole phalanx of his iniquity against the apostolic see as against the chief and personal see of Jesus Christ, and he is to speak great things against the chief pontiff as against the God of gods in the church militant. Are not such despisers of the apostolic see the exact forerunners of Antichrist?" [24]

The fifteen propositions condemned by the theologians of Paris in 1309 included the following: The papal bulls, decrees, and canonical constitutions are simply the works of men; the monks corrupted the doctrine of Christ; the founding of churches, works, and perpetual masses cannot save one who does not have charity; works of mercy are more pleasing to God than solemn sacrifice.[25]

5. CLEMANGIS OF PARIS PREDICTS RUIN OF ROME.—The learned CLEMANGIS (c. 1360-1440), rector of the University of Paris, wrote a tractate "On the Corrupt State of the Church." In this he laments the corruptions of the church:

"I speak of the temporal power, the glory, and the delicacies, with which the Church has become drunk even to nausea and forgetfulness of herself. Concerning these things it is commanded to the avenging angels, in the condemnation of the harlot, 'How much she hath glorified herself, and lived deliciously, so much torment and sorrow give her.' For, to omit events at a distance, such as the secession of the Greeks, brought about by

---

[22] Döllinger, *Prophecies*, pp. 134, 135.
[23] Arnold of Villanova, *Tractatus de Tempore Adventus Antichristi* (Treatise on the Time of the Coming of Antichrist), in Heinrich Finke, *Aus den Tagen Bonifaz VIII.*, pp. 132, 133.
[24] *Ibid.*, p. 157; see also Carl Mirbt, *Quellen zur Geschichte des Papsttums*, p. 211.
[25] Emmanuel Lalande (under the pseudonym Marc Haven), *La vie et les oeuvres de maitre Arnaud de Villeneuve*, pp. 36, 37.

our own pride and avarice; the now contracted limits of the Catholic religion, once extended over almost the whole breadth of the world; to pass over these, and some other wounds lately inflicted on the Church, there is at least the ruin which we now see befalling the city of Rome, the seat and head of the Church. Does not this ruin declare that the desolation of the Church, as well as of her whole government, is at hand, even as the dispersion of the synagogue and of the Jews followed close upon the destruction of Jerusalem?

"For how can she long endure and flourish, wandering homeless and unstable about the world, her standing destroyed, her head lost, and she herself forced to migrate from place to place, as a pilgrim and a guest in the world? From this she ought to gather certainly that her destruction is at hand; for, quitting the city of Romulus on account of her own hateful corruptions, she has fled to Avignon, where, in proportion to her greater liberty, she has more openly and shamelessly displayed her ways of simony and gain. Her foreign and perverse manners, the forerunners of calamity, she has brought into our Gaul, till that time upright and frugal. . . .

"Gaul herself, impoverished by her, has begun to pay back her injuries, so as to fulfil the prediction of the prophet, 'Thou shalt be ashamed of Egypt as thou wast ashamed of Assyria.' Also this: 'O daughter of Babylon, wasted with misery, happy shall he be that rewardeth thee as thou hast rewarded us.' " [26]

6. VINCENT FERRER ANNOUNCES ANTICHRIST IMMINENT.—The Spanish Dominican preacher of Valencia, VINCENT FERRER (1350-1419), felt called to announce that the public appearance of Antichrist was about to take place.[27]

It is interesting to note that Ferrer used his fiery eloquence to convert the Spanish Jews. In 1411 he traveled over Castile from synagogue to synagogue with a scroll of the law in one hand and a crucifix in the other, exhorting them to embrace Christianity. In view of the facts that his preaching had occasioned mass violence against the Jews in Valencia, and that mobs continued to accompany him, it is not surprising that he won converts. At any rate, thousands were won over by his persuasion to a quasi-voluntary acceptance of nominal Christianity. While some were sincere, and others indifferent enough to be satisfied with halfhearted Christianity, most of them remained secret Jews at heart.[28]

---

[26] Cited in Charles Maitland, op. cit., pp. 347-349.
[27] Döllinger, Prophecies, pp. 67, 144; Charles Maitland, op. cit., p. 352.
[28] Cecil Roth, A History of the Marranos, pp. 17-19.

7. JACOBUS DE PARADISO DISCOURSES ON DEPRAVITY.—
JACOBUS DE PARADISO (1381-1465), the Carthusian doctor at
Erfurt (*c.* 1457), likewise contended that the church would continue in utter depravity until the appearance of Antichrist, then
believed near.[29]

"To me," says Jacobus, "it seems scarcely possible that
the Church in general can be reformed, unless the court of
Rome be reformed first. And how difficult that is, present events
show: for no people or nation of believers make such resistance
to the reformation of any church as the Italians." [30]

8. JACOPONE DA TODI CONNECTS ANTICHRIST WITH PETER'S
CHAIR.—The satires of the celebrated Minorite poet JACOPONE
DA TODI (fl. thirteenth century) commented on the appearance
of a "new Lucifer" in the papal chair, and the idea that the chair
of St. Peter would for a long time be the spoil of the predicted
Antichrist. This idea was confirmed when in 1310, Clement V
subjected his predecessor Boniface VIII to a public prosecution
and a process of inquiry lasting more than a year.[31]

Let us turn next to four remarkable characters in Britain—
Brute, Cobham, Wimbledon, and Purvey.

II. Brute Makes Defense on Basis of Bible Prophecies

WALTER BRUTE (or Britte), fourteenth-century British or
Welsh layman and Lollard scholar, perhaps the most conspicuous prophetic expositor among Wyclif's followers, was a gradu-
ate of Oxford.[32] His stand against the Papacy was occasioned by
the conflict between the rival popes, Urban VI and Clement VII,
and the condemnation of his companion Swinderby.[33] In 1391
a process was served against Brute by John, bishop of Hereford.
Among "sundry other" items of accusation, Article VI stated:

---

[29] Döllinger, *Prophecies*, pp. 69, 70.
[30] Charles Maitland, *op. cit.*, p. 356.
[31] Döllinger, *Prophecies*, pp. 129, 130.
[32] Elliott, *op. cit.*, vol. 4, pp. 431-436; Workman, *Dawn of the Reformation*, vol. 1, p.
235; Lechler, *op. cit.*, pp. 448, 449; Foxe, *Acts*, vol. 1, p. 542.
[33] WILLIAM SWINDERBY, a priest and Lollard, accused of heresy in 1389, also maintained
that "the pope is this Antichrist," and "his law contrary to Christ his law." (Foxe, *Acts*, vol. 1,

"*Item,* The said *Walter* hath oftentimes said, and commonly avouched, that the Pope is Antichrist, and a seducer of the people, and utterly against the Law and life of Christ." [34]

In thus speaking Brute was declared to have blasphemed the high priest of Christendom. A student of the prophetic Word, Brute declared that the pope answered to Paul's prophesied Man of Sin, the chief of the false christs prophesied by Christ, with Rome as the Beast, Babylon, and Harlot of the Apocalypse. He contended that the time for the unmasking of the mystery had come.

Little has been recorded of the life of this learned Welshman. But the account of his pleadings before the bishop of Hereford in 1391-92 shows how fully the basic doctrines of Wyclif—the supremacy of Scripture, Christ's sole headship of the church, and the figurative character of the Lord's supper— had taken root. Brute's interpretation of the prophecies however, went beyond Wyclif.[35] More than those of any others of the time, his writings show the determining place the prophecies had in governing relationships to the church, and in the battle with Rome, under such serious circumstances as ecclesiastical trial for heresy.

When he was brought to trial Brute was denounced as a "child of Belial." He made answer by a brief "exhibit" or defense, which was declared by the bishop of Hereford to be "too short and obscure." So Brute, familiar with Wyclif's Bible, set forth the Biblical and prophetic grounds, submitting an extended defense on "divers Scrouls of paper," which fill sev-

---

p. 540.) Originally a hermit, Swinderby came to Leicester preaching against the corruptions of the age. After becoming a recluse again for a while, he resumed his preaching, this time directing his discourses against the errors and vices of the Papacy. He captivated the people, but was soon excommunicated and forbidden to preach in any church or churchyard. So he made a pulpit of two millstones in the high street of Leicester. There he preached "in contempt of the bishop," and throngs of people heard him. He was cited to appear before the bishop at Lincoln, where he was convicted of heresy and errors. The duke of Lancaster interposed, and he was allowed to escape. He then settled in Coventry and preached with greater power than ever. Swinderby returned to Herefordshire, where proceedings were instituted against him in 1391. These are recorded in the registers of the bishop of Hereford. He was accused of conducting worship in a private house, as the Lollards were then forced to do, which at that time was considered a crime worthy of death. He was excommunicated, and addressed a letter to Parliament urging an examination of the errors and abuses prevalent. He was considered of sufficient importance to be denounced by name through royal proclamation. (*Writings and Examinations of Brute,* pp. 5, 6.)

[34] "Proceedings in the Trial of Walter Brut for Heresy, Etc.," original Latin in *Registrum Johannis Trefnant, Episcopi Herefordensis,* p. 279; translated in Foxe, *Acts,* vol. 1, p. 543.

[35] Lechler, *op. cit.,* p. 449.

enty-three printed pages.[36] This Foxe gives from original sources. After he had presented the written exhibit, Brute was cited to appear October 3, 1393, in the cathedral church of Hereford before numerous prelates, abbots, monks, and doctors for oral examination. The hearing continued three days. He made a hazy statement of submission to the gospel and to the church without specifically recanting any of his points of doctrine. From his writings the papal doctors drew up thirty-seven articles and sent them to the University of Cambridge to be confuted. There is no record of what finally became of Brute.[37]

Before the detailed expositions of Brute are considered, it will be well to have a brief preview of the leading positions he set forth. Then part will fit into part.

PANORAMIC SURVEY OF LEADING PROPHETIC POSITIONS.— Brute lays stress on the fact that the gospel came direct to Britain from the East,[38] not by way of Rome. He contends that the "woman" of Revelation 12, or the church, had fled to Britain in the early centuries, where for the 1260 prophetic days or literal years (elsewhere expressed as forty-two months, or three and a half times), the true faith had been maintained.[39]

Concerning Antichrist, Brute dwells on the futility of the long-received papal ideas of Antichrist, which he had formerly shared—such as the view that Antichrist is to be an individual born in Babylon of the tribe of Dan, and ultimately to seduce Christendom for three and a half literal years. Vain, too, was the thought of 1290 days as the number of literal days Antichrist should be worshiped in God's temple—with the forty-five additional days, totaling 1335, for the repentance of those who have worshiped Antichrist. Similarly futile was the idea of the beast with seven heads and ten horns signifying a yet future Antichrist.

The sixty-two weeks, Brute contends, were weeks of years; and so were the 1290 days, which he dates from Hadrian's plac-

---

[36] *Registrum*, pp. 285-358; translated in Foxe, *Acts*, vol. 1, pp. 545-570; see also Workman, *Dawn of the Reformation*, vol. 1, pp. 235, 236.
[37] *Registrum*, pp. 359-365; Foxe, *Acts*, vol. 1, pp. 570, 571.
[38] *Registrum*, pp. 294, 295; Foxe, *op. cit.*, vol. 1, p. 548.
[39] *Registrum*, p. 294; Foxe, *Acts*, vol. 1, p. 548.

ing an idol, or "abomination," in the holy place—a desolation which in Brute's time had continued for nearly 1290 years, and which he thought was to continue to the full revealing or exposure of Antichrist. He adopts the year-day principle for all prophetic time periods. The first beast of Revelation 13, Brute interprets as pagan Roman emperors, for the woman of Revelation 17—seated thereon—was Rome, the city of the seven hills. Its power was to be for 1260 years, just as the ten days of Diocletian's persecution were ten years, and the five months, or 150 days, of the locusts of Revelation 9 were 150 years.

The bishop of Rome is then identified as the chief of the false christs, as he claims to be both high priest and king, using force as his law against both infidel and Christian. He is also the chief of the false prophets. The pope's law—giving judicial sentence of death and exciting crusading wars against heretics, and changing times as well as laws—was contrary to Christ's doctrine. Then Brute argues against the doctrine of the keys, auricular confession, transubstantiation, a sacrificing priesthood, and the practice of selling prayers and pardons. He stresses justification by faith, quoting in advance Luther's favorite text.[40] The second beast of Revelation 13 he expounds as being the popes with their assumed kingly and priestly powers. They allow none in the church to sell spiritual merchandise unless he have the mark of the beast. The number of the name of the beast, Brute declares to be *"Dux Cleri"* (Captain of the Clergy), "and that name is six hundred and sixty-six." He concluded with a warning and appeal.[41]

III. Tabulation of Individual Points of Interpretation

Though the phrasing is antique, complicated, and ofttimes wearisome, a grasp of his prophetic exposition necessitates acquaintance with Brute's own words. His testimony is so important that his witness is given with considerable completeness.

---

[40] *Registrum*, pp. 304, 336; Foxe, *Acts*, vol. 1, pp. 552, 563; see also Workman, *Dawn of the Reformation*, vol. 1, p. 279.
[41] *Registrum*, p. 356; Foxe, *Acts*, vol. 1, p. 570.

1. Papal Abomination of Desolation in God's Temple.

—In his first, or shorter, exhibit Brute avers that the bishop of Rome, declaring "I am a God," sitting in the "Seat of God" and taking away from Him the continual sacrifice, is the "abomination of desolation" foretold by Daniel—a phrase frequently employed by the Lollards.

"If the high Bishop of *Rome* calling himself the Servant of the Servants of God, and the chief Vicar of Christ in this World, do make and maintain many laws contrary to the Gospel of Jesus Christ; then is he of those that have come in Christs name, saying, I am Christ, and have seduced many a one, by the Testimony of our Saviour in *Matth.* Chap. 24. And the Idol of desolation sitting in the Temple of God and taking away from him the continual sacrifice for a time, times, and half a time, which Idol must be revealed to the Christian people by the Testimony of *Daniel.* Whereof Christ speaketh in the Gospel; When ye shall see the abomination of desolation that was told of by *Daniel* the Prophet, standing in the holy place; let him that readeth understand." [42]

2. Man of Sin, Beasts of Apocalypse, and Chief Antichrist.

—The composite testimony of Paul and John is next declared fulfilled in the "chief *Antichrist* upon the Earth," who is to be destroyed by the brightness of Christ's coming.

"And sitting in the Temple of God, doth advance himself above all things that is called God, or whatsoever is worshipped, by the Testimony of *Paul* to the *Thess.* 2 Epistle, Chap. 2. *And in the defection or falling away shall the man of Sin be revealed, whom the Lord Jesus shall slay with the breath of his mouth.* . . . He is also besides, *The Beast ascending up out of the earth, having two horns like unto a Lamb, but he speaketh like a Dragon,* and as *the cruel Beast ascending up out of the Sea, whose Power shall continue 42 months.* He worketh the things that he hath given to the Image of the Beast. And he compelled Small and Great, Rich and Poor, Free-men and Bond-slaves, to worship the beast, and to take his mark in their Forehead or their Hands, *Apoc.* Chap. 13. And thus by the testimony of all these places is he the chief *Antichrist* upon the Earth, and must be slain with the Sword of Gods Word, and cast with the *Dragon,* the cruel Beast and the false Prophet that hath seduced the Earth, into the lake of fire and brimstone to be tormented world without end." [43]

3. Babylon on Waters Parallels Woman in Wilderness.

—Brute likewise denominates Rome as "Babylon" and the

---

[42] *Registrum*, p. 287; Foxe, *Acts*, vol. 1, p. 545.
[43] *Registrum*, p. 288; Foxe, *Acts*, vol. 1, pp. 545, 546.

"harlot," whose spiritual unfaithfulness merits her destruction destined for the end of the 1260 years (the forty-two months, or three and a half times during which the "woman" is in the wilderness).

"If the City of *Rome* do allow his Traditions, and do disallow Christs holy Commandments, and Christs Doctrine, that it may confirm his Traditions; then is she *Babylon the Great,* or the *Daughter of Babylon,* and the *Great Whore sitting upon many waters,* with whom the Kings of the Earth have committed Fornication, and the Inhabitants of the earth are become drunken with the Wine of her Harlotry lying open to Bawdry. With whose spiritual Whoredom, Enchantments, Witchcrafts, and Simon Magus Merchandises, the whole round world is infected and seduced; saying in her heart, *I sit as a Queen, and* Widow I am not, neither shall I see Sorrow and mourning. Yet is she ignorant that within a little while shall come the day of her destruction and ruine by the Testimony of the Apoc. Chap. 17. Because that from the time of the continual Sacrifice was taken away, and the abomination of Desolation placed, there be passed 1290 days, by the Testimony of *Daniel* [chap. xii.], and the Chronicles added do agree to the same. And the holy City also hath been trodden under foot of the Heathen, for forty two months, and the Woman was nourished up in the Wilderness (unto which she fled for fear of the face of the Serpent) during 1260. days, or else for a time, times, and half a time, which is all one. All these things be manifest by the Testimony of the *Apocalyps,* and the Chronicles thereto agreeing." [44]

As he closes his unique initial exhibit, Brute appeals to Christ to take from him "all manner of mark of Antichrist."

4. SECRETS OF PROPHETS REVEALED TO LAY PERSONS.—In his second, or "more ample Tractation," demanded by the bishop, Brute amplifies the foregoing statements and adds many others. Referring to the prophetic symbols and time prophecies of Daniel, that had formerly been cited, Brute declares significantly that He who hides the "secrets of the Scriptures" from the wise, "revealeth the same to Sinners, and Lay-persons, and simple souls, that he may have the honour and glory in all things." [45]

5. DISCLOSING OF ANTICHRIST PRECEDES SECOND ADVENT.— Then Brute refers to signs that "betoken the second coming of

---

[44] *Registrum,* p. 288; Foxe, *Acts,* vol. 1, p. 546.
[45] *Registrum,* pp. 291, 292; Foxe, *Acts,* vol. 1, p. 547.

Christ to reform his Church, and to call men again, by the disclosing of *Antichrist,* to the perfection of the Gospel, from their Heathenish Rites, and ways of the *Gentiles.* By whom the holy City was trampled under foot, for 42 months." [46]

6. TIME NOW FOR DISCLOSURE OF ANTICHRIST.—After allusion to Isaiah and Paul (2 Thessalonians) on the advent, Brute calls the "abomination of desolation standing in the holy place" the "greatest sign of all." [47] Connecting this with the 1290 year-days from the destruction of Jerusalem, Brute contends that it is time in his day for the exposure of Antichrist.

"Now if any man will behold the *Chronicles,* he shall find, that after the destruction of *Jerusalem* was accomplished, and after the strong hand of the holy people was fully dispersed, and after the placing of the abomination; that is to say, the Idol of Desolation of *Jerusalem,* within the Holy place, where the Temple of God was before, there had passed 1290 days, taking a day for a year, as commonly it is taken in the Prophets. And the times of the Heathen people are fulfilled, after whose Rites and Customs God suffered the holy City to be trampled under foot for forty and two months. For although the Christian Church, which is the holy City, continued in the Faith from the Ascension of Christ, even till this time: yet hath it not observed and kept the perfection of the Faith all this whole season." [48]

7. CALL OF GENTILES TO TRUE FOLD INVOLVES ANTICHRIST. Interpreting the Christian church as the holy city—a carry-over from Augustinianism—the time of the error of the Gentiles is believed fulfilled, and now must come their recall by the Word, that there may be one fold of the Jews and Gentiles under one Shepherd. Thus Antichrist will be "moved."

"For although the Christian Church, which is the holy City, continued in the Faith from the Ascension of Christ, even till this time: yet hath it not observed and kept the perfection of the Faith all this whole season. For soon after the departure of the Apostles, the Faith was kept with the Observation of the Rites of the *Gentiles,* and not of the Rites of *Moses* Law, nor of the Law of the Gospel of Jesus Christ. Wherefore seeing that this time of the Error of the *Gentiles* is fulfilled: it is likely that Christ shall call the *Gentiles* from the Rites of their gentility to the perfection of the

[46] *Ibid.*
[47] *Registrum,* p. 292; Foxe, *Acts,* vol. 1, p. 547.
[48] *Registrum,* p. 293; Foxe, *Acts,* vol. 1, p. 548.

Gospel, as he called the *Jews* from the Law of *Moses* to the same perfection in his first coming: that there may be one Sheepfold of the *Jews* and *Gentiles,* under one Shepherd. Seeing therefore, that *Antichrist* is known, which hath seduced the Nations, then shall the Elect, after that they have forsaken the errors of their gentility, come through the light of Gods Word to the perfection of the Gospel, and that same Seducer shall be slain with the Sword of Gods word. So that by these things it doth partly appear unto me, why at this time rather than at any other time this matter of *Antichrist* is moved." [49]

8. CHURCH IN BRITISH WILDERNESS 1260 YEARS.—Contending that Britain is the "wilderness" offering the "woman" refuge from the dragon's wrath, Brute said, "These sayings may be applied unto this Kingdom rather than to other Kingdoms."

"Unto this place [Britain] fled the Woman; that is to say, the Church (which by Faith did spiritually bring forth Christ into the world) whereas she was fed with the heavenly Bread, the Flesh and Blood of Jesus Christ, for one thousand, two hundred and sixty days, seeing that for so many days, taking a day for a year, the *Britains* continued in the Faith of Christ: which thing cannot be found so of any Christian Kingdom, but of this Desert: and well it is said, That she flew to this place. For from the East came the Faith into Britain, not by walking in journey, nor yet by sailing; for then should it have come by *Rome, Italy, Almaine, France,* which cannot be found: and therefore she flew over those places, and rested not in them, even as a Bird, flying over a place resteth not in the same: but rested in this Wilderness for a time, times, and half a time; that is, one thousand two hundred and sixty years, from the first coming of the Faith into *Britain* until this present." [50]

9. OVERTHROWS ERRONEOUS CONCEPTS OF IMAGINED ANTICHRIST.—Brute next contends against the erroneous tales of an "imagined *Antichrist*"—"born in *Babylon* of the Tribe of *Dan,*" and performing miraculous deeds for three and a half years—and other current misunderstandings. He confutes the arguments one by one. These errors he overthrows by turning to the "Prophecies in Daniel, and in the Apocalyps." [51]

10. BRUTE APPLIES YEAR-DAY PRINCIPLE TO 70 WEEKS AND 1260 AND 1290 DAYS.—Declaring it plain that the seventy weeks had already been fulfilled, and Jerusalem destroyed,[52] Brute says,

---

[49] *Ibid.*
[50] *Registrum,* p. 294; Foxe, *Acts,* vol. 1, p. 548.
[51] *Registrum,* pp. 296-298; Foxe, *Acts,* vol. 1, p. 549
[52] *Registrum,* p. 298; Foxe, *Acts,* vol. 1, p. 549.

"Daniel speaking of 62 weeks, doth not speak of the weeks of days but of years." Then he places the 1290 years to the revealing of Antichrist—"taking a day always for a year, as commonly it is taken in the Prophets." [53] Likewise he interprets the meaning of the five months: "Taking a month for thirty days, and a day for a year. And to Ezekiel were days given for years." Brute then draws the conclusion:

"Wherefore it is an unfit thing to assign the 42 months, being appointed to the power of the Beast, unto three years and a half, for the Reign of that fantastical and imagined *Antichrist*." [54]

11. ANTICHRIST'S IDENTITY ALREADY PERCEIVED BY SOME.— The identification of Antichrist being due, and already discerned by some, Brute believed it should be proclaimed from the housetops.

"Let us go forward to declare whether *Antichrist* be already come, and yet is he hid from many, and must be opened and disclosed within a little while according to the truth of the holy Scripture, for the Salvation of the Faithful.

"And because that in the first conclusion of mine answer I have conditionally put it, who is that Antichrist lying privy in the hid Scriptures of the Prophets: I will pass on the Declaration of that conclusion, bringing to light those things which lay hid in darkness, because nothing is hid which shall not be disclosed, and nothing covered which shall not be known. And therefore the thing which was said in the darkness, let us say in the light; and the thing that we have heard in the ear, let us preach upon the house tops. I therefore, as I have before said, so say, that if the high Bishop of *Rome,* calling himself the Servant of God, and the chief Vicar of Christ in this world, do make and justifie many Laws contrary to the Gospel of Jesus Christ: then is he the chief of many, which coming in the name of Christ have said I am Christ, who have seduced many. Which is the first part of the first conclusion, and is manifest." [55]

12. POPES ARE ANTICHRIST BECAUSE THEY ARE PRIEST-KINGS.—"Seeing then that the Bishops of *Rome* do say that they are the High Priests; they say also therein that they are Kings, because they say that they have the Scriptural Sword pertaining to their Priesthood, and the corporal Sword which agreeth for a Kings State. So is it plain, that really and in very deed, they say, *That they are Christs, albeit that expresly they be not called Christs.* Now that they come in the name of Christ it is manifest, because

---

[53] *Registrum*, p. 299; Foxe, *Acts*, vol. 1, p. 550.
[54] *Registrum*, p. 300; Foxe, *Acts*, vol. 1, p. 550.
[55] *Ibid.*

they say that they are his principal Vicars in this World, ordained of Christ specially for the Government of the Christian Church. Therefore, seeing they say, that really and in very deed they are Christs, and the chief friends of Christ: If they make and justifie many Laws contrary to the Gospel of Jesus Christ, then it is plain that they themselves in earth are the principal *Antichrists,* because there is no worse plague and pestilence, than a familiar enemy. And if in secret they be against Christ, and yet in open appearance they say that they are his friends, they are so much the more meet to seduce and deceive the Christian people." [56]

13. FOUR EMPIRES AND STONE KINGDOM NAMED.—"He [Daniel] applieth therefore four Kingdoms unto the four parts of the image, namely, the Kingdom of the *Babylonians* unto the head of gold; the Kingdom of the *Medes* and *Persians,* unto the breast and arms of silver; the Kingdom of the *Grecians* unto the belly and thighs of brass, but the fourth Kingdom which is of the *Romans,* he applieth unto the feet and legs of iron. And *Daniel* addeth, *in the days of their Kingdoms shall God raise up a Kingdom which shall never be destroyed, and his Kingdom shall not be delivered unto another, but it shall break and destroy those Kingdoms; and it shall stand for ever, according as thou sawest, that the stone was cut out of the mountain without hands, and brake in pieces the clay, and iron, brass, silver and gold.* Seeing therefore it is certain, that this stone signifieth Christ, whose Kingdom is for ever; it is also a thing most assured, that he ought to reign every where, and to break in pieces the other Kingdoms of the world." [57]

14. APOCALYPTIC BABYLON IDENTIFIED AS ROME.—"This *Babylon,* this great City, is the City of *Rome,* as it appeareth by the process of the Apostle. Because the Angel which shewed unto Saint *John* the destruction of the mighty Harlot sitting upon many Waters, with whom the Kings of the Earth have committed fornication, and all they which dwell upon the Earth, are made drunk with the Wine of her Whoredom, said unto him; And the woman which thou sawest, is the great City which hath Dominion above Kings, etc. [Apoc. 18.] And indeed in the days of Saint *John,* the whole World was subject to the temporal Empire of the City of *Rome,* and afterwards it was subject to the spiritual Empire or Dominion of the same. But touching the temporal Government of the City of *Rome,* it is fallen already: and so that other also, for the multitude of her spiritual Fornication, shall fall." [58]

15. IRON LEGS SAME AS DREADFUL ROMAN BEAST.—"Hereupon by the Image of *Nabuchadonozor,* the Empire of the *Romans* is likened to Iron, which beateth together, and hath the Mastery of all Metals. And in the vision of *Daniel,* wherein he saw the four Winds of Heaven to fight in the main Sea; and four very great Beasts coming out of the Sea; the Kingdom of the *Romans* is likened to the fourth terrible and marvellous Beast, the which had great iron Teeth; eating and destroying, and treading the rest

[56] *Registrum,* pp. 300, 301; Foxe, *Acts,* vol. 1, p. 550.
[57] *Registrum,* p. 320; Foxe, *Acts,* vol. 1, p. 557.
[58] *Registrum,* p. 353; Foxe, *Acts,* vol. 1, p. 569.

HARRY ANDERSON. ARTIST

PROPHETIC VISTA OF THE FUTURE

Daniel the Prophet Expounds the Great Metallic Colossus to King Nebuchadnezzar as Symbolic of the Succession of World Powers From Babylon on to Modern Days

under his Feet: And this Beast had Ten Horns, and as *Daniel* saith, he shall speak words against the most high, and shall tear with his Teeth the Saints of the most high: and he shall think that he may be able to change times and laws, and they shall be delivered into his power, until a time, times, and half a time. In the *Apocalyps*, Saint *John saw a Beast coming out of the Sea, having seven Heads and ten Horns, and power was given to him to make Months* 42. So long time endured the Empire of the *Romans;* that is to say, from the beginning of *Julius Cesar,* which was the first Emperor of the *Romans,* unto the end of *Fredericus,* which was the last Emperor of the *Romans."* [59]

After identifying the legs of iron with the fourth dreadful beast of Daniel 7, and this in turn with the first beast of Revelation 13, Brute applies the forty-two months from Julius Caesar to the Emperor Frederick.

16. FEET OF CLAY LINKED WITH BEAST FROM EARTH.—The "feet of the Image," part clay and part iron, betokening the broken "Empire of Rome," which "yet endureth," is linked by Brute to the beast from the earth. (Revelation 13.)

"This |two-horned| Beast as seemeth me, doth betoken the Clay and Earthen part of the feet of the Image, because he came out of the Earth. For that by terrene help he is made the High and chief Priest of the *Romans* in the Church of Christ, and so from below he ascended, on high. But Christ from Heaven descended, because that he which was God, and Author of every Creature, became man; and he that was Lord of Lords, was made in the shape of a Servant. And although that in the Heavens the company of Angels Minister unto him, he himself Ministred or served in Earth, that he might teach us Humility, by which a man ascendeth into Heaven, even as by pride a man goeth down into the bottomless Pit. This Beast hath two Horns most like a Lamb, because that he challengeth to himself both the Priestly and Kingly power above all other here in earth. The Lamb, that is, Christ, is a King for ever upon the Kingly Seat of *David,* and he is a Priest for ever after the Order of *Melchisedech;* but his Kingdom is not of this World: but the Kingdom of this Beast is of this World, because those that be under him fight for him." [60]

17. BISHOP OF ROME SITS IN TEMPLE OF GOD IMPRINTING HIS MARK.— "Also the Bishop of *Rome* doth make man to worship him as God, because that the special Sacrifice that God doth require of us, is to be obedient unto him in keeping of his Commandments. But now the Popes Commandments be commanded to be kept, and be kept in very Deed; but the Commandments of Christ are contemned and rejected. Thus sitteth the Bishop of

---

[59] *Registrum*, pp. 353, 354; Foxe, *Acts*, vol. 1, p. 569.
[60] *Registrum*, p. 354; Foxe, *Acts*, vol. 1, p. 569.

Rome in the Temple of God, shewing himself as God, and extolleth himself above all that which is called God, or worshipped as God. But in his
fall he shall be revealed, because that every Kingdom divided in it self shall
be made desolate. He teaching a truth is the Head of the Church; but the
Prophet teaching a lie is the Tail of the Dragon. He seducing the World
shall be acknowledged to be the verity of the Doctrine of Christ; but after
he is known, he shall be rejected and nought esteemed. He giveth to small
and great, rich and poor, free and bond, Marks in their right Hands, and
in their Foreheads; that no man should buy or sell, but those that shall have
the marks of the name of the Beast, or that look to have of him some recom-
pense, small, mean, or great, or else the number of his name, which number
is 300. The Pope saith, that in the Administration of every Sacrament he
doth Imprint a certain Character or Mark into the soul of him that re-
ceiveth it. In Baptism he saith that he doth Imprint, into the soul of him
that is Baptized, a Mark that cannot be wiped out, and so likewise in other
Sacraments." [61]

18. ANTICHRIST THE MYSTICALLY NUMBERED BEAST.—Brute
states that "some" had set forth *Dux Cleri* (Captain of the
Clergy) as the solution of 666. This was an attempt to find the
pope a name that yields the prophetic number rather than an
attempt to look for a period of years.

"The number of his name, according to the opinion of some men, is,
Dux Cleri, the Captain of the Clergy, because by that name he is named,
and maketh his name known, and that name is *666.*"

"This is my opinion of the Beast ascending out of the Earth, and shall
be, until such time as I shall be of the same Beast better instructed. And
although that this Beast doth signifie the *Roman* Bishops; yet the other
cruel Beast ascending out of the Sea, doth signifie the *Roman* emperors.
And although that the *Dragon* being a cruel Beast, and the false Prophet
giving the mark, must be thrown into the lake of fire and brimstone to be
tormented for ever; I would have no man to judge, but I leave such things
altogether to the final Judgment of Christ to be determined. . . . But I have
partly declared how that the Popes Law is contrary to Christs Law, and
how that he saith, *That he is the chief Vicar of Christ in Earth;* and in his
deeds is contrary to Christ, and doth forsake both his Doctrine and Life.
I cannot see who else may be so well *Antichrist,* and a Seducer of the people.
For there is not a greater Pestilence than a familiar enemy." [62]

Brute's appeal was to this effect:

"My counsel is, let the buyer beware of those marks; because that after
the fall of *Babylon, If any man hath worshipped the Beast and her Image,*

[61] *Registrum,* pp. 355, 356; Foxe, *Acts,* vol. 1, p. 569.
[62] *Registrum,* pp. 356, 357; Foxe, *Acts,* vol. 1, p. 570.

and hath received the mark upon his Forehead, and upon his Hand, he shall drink of the wine of Gods wrath." [63]

And the closing paragraphs of Brute's defense begin, "Thus reverend Father have I made mine Answer to the matter whereof I am accused." [64] Such is the story of Brute, the Briton—a full century and a quarter before the Lutheran Reformation.

IV. Oldcastle Martyred for Maintaining Pope Is Antichrist

SIR JOHN OLDCASTLE (*c.* 1360-1417), famous Christian knight of Herefordshire, also called Lord Cobham,[65] became a prominent follower of Wyclif. Distinguished for military ability and summoned to sit among the barons of England, Sir John was an excellent scholar and a favorite of king and people. He opposed papal abuses and maintained a great number of itinerant Lollard preachers in various parts of the country.[66] He thus disregarded the legislation against the Lollards, who now numbered many thousands. (The term *Lollard,* however, came to be rather indiscriminately used by the papal church to stigmatize those who dissented, without special classification of the grounds and points of dissent.) [67]

1. POPE THE ANTICHRIST; ABOMINATION IN HOLY PLACE.— A number of Lollards had been burned for their faith, with many prosecutions for heresy.[68] In 1413 Archbishop Arundel of Canterbury—under whom the full force of the persecution was let loose—called a synod to repress the Lollards, and particularly to withstand Sir John, maintainer of their preachers. A court of "twelve Inquisitors of Heresies" was appointed, which found Oxford overrun with heretics, the opinions of Wyclif having made their way among the junior students. By stipends Lord Cobham had encouraged scholars from Oxford to propa-

[63] *Registrum,* p. 356; Foxe, *Acts,* vol. 1, p. 570.
[64] *Registrum,* p. 358; Foxe, *Acts,* vol. 1, p. 570.
[65] So called from his marriage to the heiress of the Cobham estate. (David S. Schaff, *The Middle Ages,* part 2, p. 354.)
[66] Foxe, *Acts,* vol. 1, pp. 635, 636; Milner, *op. cit.,* vol. 2, cent. 15, chap. 1, p. 147.
[67] David S. Schaff, *The Middle Ages,* part 2, p. 350; George Waddington, *A History of the Church,* p. 502.
[68] David S. Schaff, *The Middle Ages,* part 2, p. 353.

gate his opinions, and he was considered the chief offender. The archbishop approached the king, who sent for Cobham and sought to reclaim him to the faith, admonishing him to submit to the pope as an obedient child. Cobham then made the famous answer:

> "You most worthy Prince, . . . I am always prompt and willing to obey, forsomuch as I know you a Christian King, and the appointed Minister of God, bearing the Sword to the punishment of evil Doers, and for safeguard of them that be virtuous. Unto you (next my eternal God) owe I my whole Obedience, and submit thereunto (as I have done ever) all that I have, either of Fortune or Nature, ready at all times to fulfil whatsoever ye shall in the Lord command me. But as touching the Pope and his Spirituality, I owe them neither suit nor service, forsomuch as I know him by the Scriptures to be the great Antichrist, the Son of Perdition, the open Adversary of God, and the Abomination standing in the holy place." [69]

The king was irritated and would no longer talk with him. Cobham was then cited by Arundel, and accused of heresy. But he disregarded the various summons. A copy of Wyclif's writings, belonging to Cobham, was burned by the enraged archbishop, who excommunicated Cobham for "contumacy" and "disobedience," and demanded aid of the civil power to apprehend him.[70] Perceiving that the "fury of *Antichrist*" was "kindled against him," Lord Cobham took paper and pen, and put into writing his confession of faith. In this he said:

> "If any Prelates of Church require more, or else any other kind of obedience, than this to be used; he contemneth Christ, exalting himself above God, and so becometh an open Antichrist." [71]

This he took to the king, desiring him to read it. But the king refused to receive it, and in the issue had him arrested and imprisoned in the Tower of London.

2. PROPHECIES CITED DURING EXAMINATIONS.—In the course of subsequent examinations and admonitions to accept the pope as Christ's vicar on earth, one of the papal doctors asked Lord Cobham, "What do ye saye of the Pope?"

---

[69] Foxe, *Acts*, vol. 1, p. 636.
[70] Milner, *op. cit.*, vol. 2, cent. 15, chap. 1, pp. 148, 149; Foxe, *Acts*, vol. 1, p. 636.
[71] Foxe, *Acts*, vol. 1, p. 637.

"The Lorde *Cobham* answered: As I sayd before, he and yow togyther maketh whole the great Antichrist. Of whom he is the great Head, yow Bysshoppes, Prestes, Prelates, and Monkes are the Bodye, and the beggynge Fryers are the Tayle, for they cover the Fylthynesse of yow both, with theyr subtyle Sophistrye. Never will I in Conscience obeye anye of yow all, tyll I se yow with *Peter* folowe *Christ* in Conversacyon." [72]

The prophetic basis of his belief appears in one of Cobham's impressive answers to the archbishop.

"Both *Christ* and his Apostles were accused of Sedycyon makynge, yet were they most peceable Menne. Both *Daniel* and *Christ* prophecyed, that soche a troublouse Tyme shulde come, as hath not bene yet sens the Worldes begynnyng. And this Prophecye is partlye fulfylled in youre Dayes and Doynges. For manye have ye slayne alredye, and more will ye slee here after, yf God fulfyll not his Promes. *Christ* sayth also, yf those Dayes of yours were not shortened, scarslye shuld anye fleshe be saved. Therefore loke for yt justlye, for God will shorten youre Dayes." [73]

It is interesting, incidentally, to observe that appended to this chronicle are several paragraphs from "Prophecyes of Joachim Abbas," translated into English, two brief sections of which follow:

"In the latter Dayes shall apere a Lawe of Lyberte. The Gospell of the Kyngedome of *Christ* shall be taught, and the Churche shall be purged as Wheate is from Chaffe and Tares. . . .

"The Churche of *Rome* is the fleshlye Synagoge of Sathan.

"The Churche of *Rome* shall be destroyed in the thyrde State, as the Synagoge of the *Jewes* was destroyed in the seconde State, And a spirituall Churche shall from thens forth succede, to the Ende of the Worlde." [74]

3. ROME THE "VERY NEST OF ANTICHRIST."—In his second examination Cobham boldly declared:

"My belief is (as I said afore) that all the Scriptures of the sacred Bible are true. All this is grounded upon them I believe throughly. For I know it is Gods pleasure that I should so do. But in your lordly Laws and idle determinations have I no belief. For ye be no part of Christs holy Church, as your open deeds do shew: But ye are very Antichrists, obstinately set against His holy Law and Will. . . .

"And let all Men consider well this, That Christ was meek, and merciful; the Pope is proud, and a tyrant; Christ was poor and forgave, the Pope

---

[72] *A Brefe Chronycle Concernynge the Examynacyon and Death of the Blessed Martyr of Christ, Sir Johan Oldecastell, the Lorde Cobham,* collected by Johan Bale, p. 68.
[73] *Ibid.,* p. 64.
[74] *Ibid.,* pp. 111, 112. (See Volume I of this present work.)

is rich and a malitious Man-slayer, as his daily acts do prove him. *Rome* is the very nest of Antichrist, and out of that nest come all the Disciples of him. Of whom, Prelates, Priests, and Monks, are the body, these pil'd Friers are the tail, which covereth his most filthy part." [75]

4. SENTENCED TO DEATH FOR NAMING ANTICHRIST.—In his letter to the bishop of London, Archbishop Arundel admitted that Sir John was sentenced for naming Antichrist. This is the archbishop's declaration:

"As touching the Power and Authority of the Keys, the Archbishops, Bishops, and other Prelates, he said, That the Pope is very Antichrist, that is the head; that the Archbishops, Bishops, and other Prelates be his members, and that the Friers be his tail. The which Pope, Archbishops, and Bishops, a man ought not to obey, but so far forth as they be followers of Christ and of *Peter,* in their life, manners, and conversation, and that he is the successor of *Peter,* which is best and purest in life and manners. Furthermore, the said Sir *John,* spreading his hands, with a loud voice said thus to those which stood about him: These Men, which judge and would condemn me, will seduce you all and themselves, and will lead you unto Hell; therefore take heed of them. When he had spoken those words, we again, as oftentimes before, with lamentable countenance, spake unto the said Sir *John,* exhorting him with as gentle words as we might, that he would return to the unity of the Church, to believe and hold that which the Church of *Rome* doth believe and hold. Who expressly answered, That he would not believe or hold otherwise than he had before declared. Wherefore, we perceiving, as it appeared by him, that we could not prevail, at the last with bitterness of heart we proceeded to the pronouncing of a definitive Sentence in this matter." [76]

Arundel's court then condemned Cobham and pronounced him to be "a pernicious and detestable heretic," and delivered him over to the secular arm "to do him to death," [77] with abettors excommunicated.[78] The king, Henry V, granted a respite of forty days in the hope that he would recant. But Cobham escaped from the tower, and remained at large for four years. In 1414 he was falsely charged with being a party to an uprising of twenty thousand Lollards against the king, and declared an outlaw.[79] Nearly twoscore Lollards were killed and others taken

---

[75] Foxe, *Acts*, vol. 1, pp. 640, 641.
[76] Foxe, *Acts*, vol. 1, p. 646.
[77] Workman, *Dawn of the Reformation*, vol. 1, p. 265; David S. Schaff, *The Middle Ages,* part 2, p. 354; Foxe, *Acts*, vol. 1, p. 731.
[78] Mansi, *op. cit.*, vol. 27, cols. 511, 512.
[79] Workman, *Dawn of the Reformation*, vol. 1, pp. 265, 266; Foxe, *Acts*, vol. 1, p. 371; David S. Schaff, *The Middle Ages,* part 2, p. 354.

prisoner—some hanged, others burned. Three years later Cobham was apprehended and sentenced to be hanged as a traitor and burned as a heretic. So in 1417 he was dragged to St. Giles, suspended in chains, and was slowly burned to death, praising God.[80] (Portrait of Cobham appears on page 456.)

Others shared his fate. But the Lollards maintained their faith, prizing the prophetic declaration that the papal Antichrist should continue but 1260 year-days. According to Workman, the growth of Lollardism lasted through a century and a half of oppression, until it merged itself in the Reformation.[81]

V. Wimbledon's Sermon on Matthew 24 and Seven Seals

R. WIMBLEDON, another Lollard preacher, delivered a notable sermon at "Pauls-Cross," in London in 1389, that created considerable stir. Also recorded by Foxe, it shows how the prophecies formed a part of leading Lollard sermons, as well as of writings and defenses. Joachim, twelfth-century projector of the year-day principle, is cited as well,[82] as was common with the Lollards. Wimbledon discusses Matthew 24, and the surrounding Roman armies constituting a token of the approaching destruction of Jerusalem in the first century. So the rising of nation against nation, and famines and pestilences, were among the signs of the coming end of the age.

1. 1290 YEAR-DAYS FOR ABOMINATION OF DESOLATION.— The chief token noted was the "abomination of desolation" standing in the holy place. This was declared to come in the days of Antichrist, who was to appear about 1290 years from the time of Titus and Vespasian. The end of this period was anticipated to be within a few years—on the basis that "a day must be taken for a yeare, both by authority of holy Writ in the same place and in other, and also by reason." [83]

---

[80] Oldcastle was one of the great soldiers of his day. Arundel hated him because he was a pupil of Wyclif, a receiver of the new light, and a protector of the Lollards. He read the Bible on his knees, and was the strong friend of free inquiry. (Geikie, *op. cit.*, pp. 57, 59, 60; see also Foxe, *Acts*, vol. 1, pp. 731, 732; Workman, *Dawn of the Reformation*, vol. 1, pp. 266, 267.)
[81] Workman, *John Wyclif*, vol. 2, p. 330.
[82] Foxe, *Acts*, vol. 1, p. 628.   [83] *Ibid.*

2. Seven Seals, Antichrist's Manifestation, and Second Advent.—Turning then to the "seven seales," Wimbledon declares that these comprehend the state of the church from the time of Christ to the end of the world—from the first advent to "the time of Antichrist and his foregoers." [84] An epitome must suffice. The white horse of the first seal "betokeneth the Preachers of Christes Resurrection and his Ascension." The second seal shows the state of the church in the time of the early martyrs from Nero to Constantine, who endowed the church, and includes the persecution of Diocletian. The third denotes the church in the time of the heresies.

The fourth seal denotes the state of the church "in the time of ypocritis." This is the last state that shall be, in the church before the clear unveiling and appearing of the great Antichrist. "The opening of the fifth seale telleth the state of the Church that then God shall follow, and desire that lovers of Goddis law shulleth have after the end of this world to be delivered of this woe." The opening of the sixth seal reveals the state of the church in the time of Antichrist—the devil's ministers stopping the "foure Gospels to be Preached," and so hindering the calling upon men for "amendment." In the seventh seal Jesus Christ shall slay the persecuting "Fiend" with the breath of His mouth.[85] Limited and foreshortened in scope, this view nevertheless reveals the dominating place of prophecy.

VI. Purvey—Projector of First Protestant Commentary

John Purvey (c. 1354-1428), faithful friend and colaborer of Wyclif, was a student at Oxford when Wyclif's influence was at its height. Later serving as his secretary, and evidently curate at Lutterworth, Purvey became the leader of the Lollards after Wyclif's death. He was called "The Library of the Lollards, and Wyclif's glosser." In fact, to Purvey as much as to Wyclif we owe the excellence of the famous English Bible of 1388. We are indebted to his scholarship in translation, revision, and improve-

---

[84] *Ibid.*
[85] *Ibid.*

ment. He smoothed out much of the stiffness and awkwardness of Wyclif's original, many passages of which had been over-literal.[86] He also furnished the glosses for the margin and a prologue of much value. Manuscript copies were multiplied rapidly and circulated widely.

1. BIBLE TRANSLATION AND ANTICHRIST ATTACK BRINGS CONFLICT.—Purvey's denunciation of the errors of the Roman church, and his endeavor to make the English Bible available to the people, drew upon him the severest penalties within the power of the hierarchy to inflict. He had been preaching at Bristol, but in 1387 was forbidden by the bishop of Worcester. His writings were declared erroneous and heretical, and were among those that the bishops of Worcester, Salisbury, and Hereford were authorized to seize in 1388 and 1389. In 1390 Purvey was thrown into prison, and occupied his time with writing a commentary on the Apocalypse, based on Wyclif's former lectures.[87]

In 1395 Purvey assisted the Wyclif party in Parliament by drawing up an indictment of ecclesiastical corruptions—thirty-seven articles from the writings of Wyclif—under the title *Remonstrances Against Romish Corruptions in the Church*. In 1401 he was brought to trial before the Convocation. Stress is laid by his enemies upon the fact that, after being grievously tortured and punished in the Saltwood prison, he recanted certain phrases at Paul's Cross, London, under Arundel, archbishop of Canterbury. He was then made vicar of West Hythe, in Kent.

But it is believed that Purvey subsequently repented of his recantation.[88] Moreover, the articles he had recanted were of a less vital character and did not deal with Antichrist. Resigning the vicarage of West Hythe in 1403, he returned to the simple teaching of the Bible, continuing to decry the errors of the

---

[86] Trench, *op. cit.*, p. 310; Workman, *Dawn of the Reformation*, vol. 1, pp. 199, 200.
[87] Workman, *Dawn of the Reformation*, vol. 1, p. 236.
[88] Trench, *op. cit.*, p. 317; Lechler, *op. cit.*, p. 453.

church—for which he was once more imprisoned, in 1421, under Archbishop Chicheley.[89] This latter time he put forth articles which agreed that the pope—Innocent III—was the "head of Antichrist," [90] the pope is the "great abomination," [91] and the Church of Rome "the great and cursed strumpet, of whom St. *John* writeth in Revel. 17." [92]

2. DIGEST OF PURVEY'S COMMENTARY ON REVELATION.—A copy of Purvey's commentary on the Apocalypse (1390), based on Wyclif's sermons, found its way to Livonia (later part of Latvia), and thence one hundred years later to Luther. It made such an impression upon the Reformer that he had it reprinted at Wittenberg in 1528, describing it as "a Commentary on the Apocalypse Written 100 Years Ago." It comprised 196 leaves. This first Protestant commentary aims in every way possible to expose and protest against papal apostasy, and to testify to the truth of the pure gospel doctrine. Purvey was convinced that they were "already living in the times of Antichrist," that the pope was the prophesied Antichrist, and that all the predicted warnings of prophecy must be given.

3. LUTHER'S DISCLAIMER OF PRIORITY.—This unique reprint of Purvey's *Commentarius in Apocalypsin* is prefaced by an impressive statement by Luther, disclaiming any originality or priority in advancing the premise that the Papacy is the prophesied Antichrist of Scripture. Luther's disclaimer is here rendered rather literally so as to preserve its original phrasing:

"This preface, noble reader, you may understand was written by us for this reason—that we might make known to the world that we are not the first who interpret the Papacy as the kingdom of Antichrist. For many years prior to us, so many and so great men (whose number is large, and their memory eternal) have attempted this so clearly and openly, and that with great spirit and force, that [those] who were driven by the fury of the papal tyranny into the farthest boundaries of the earth, and suffering the most atrocious tortures, nevertheless bravely and faithfully persisted in the confession of the truth. Although we in this age are far more learned and

---

[89] Foxe, *Acts*, vol. 1, pp. 618, 619; M'Clintock and Strong, *op. cit.*, vol. 8, p. 815, art. "Purvey."
[90] Foxe, *Acts*, vol. 1, p. 619.   [91] *Ibid.*, p. 621.   [92] *Ibid.*, p. 622.

free than they, yet we ought to be ashamed that they, held in great barbarity and captivity, were so much braver and bolder than we in spirit and fortitude.

"For as this author was, for his age (as I think), among the first who sought learning and holiness most ardently, yet hindered by the defectiveness of the time and the reign of darkness could neither speak these things so purely nor think so clearly as in this our age we speak and think, yet he rightly and truly pronounces the Pope Antichrist (as he is), . . . a witness, indeed, foreordained by God to confirm our doctrine." [93]

4. PURVEY ASSERTS POPE IS ANTICHRIST.—In his exposition Purvey brings Antichrist into the over-all picture of the seven churches.[94] The express declaration that the pope is "Antichrist" appears in this connection, despite the fact that many claim for him "as great sanctity and authority as if he were Christ when He was on earth." [95] Purvey asserts without reservation that Antichrist "already reigns." [96]

[93] Luther, preface, in John Purvey, *Commentarius in Apocalypsin*, sig. A₂v.
[94] Purvey, *Commentarius*, fols. 2v-28v.
[95] *Ibid.*, fol. 29v; see also fols. 60r and 64r.
[96] *Ibid.*, fol. 30v.

CHARTS VISUALIZING PROGRESSIVE DEVELOPMENT OF PROPHETIC INTERPRETATION

On the Pages Immediately Following, the Complete Upper Chart Pictures in Miniature the Entire Field Covered by the Four Volumes of the *Prophetic Faith* Set. Marked Off by Centuries, From Fourth Century B.C. to Nineteenth Century A.D., the Full Story Is Visualized, Showing Sequences and Relationships

The Lower Chart Is an Enlargement of the Central Section of the Upper Full-Length Chart. The Range Covered in Volume II Is From A.D. 1300 to 1800—or From the Renaissance on Through the Reformation, Counter Reformation, and Post-Reformation Eras, Ending With the French Revolution. Divided by Vertical Century Lines, the Upper Horizontal Band Represents the Jewish Interpreters; the Second Band Indicates the Pre-Reformation Witnesses, Principally in Britain and Bohemia, Expanding Into the Great Protestant Reformation Spread of Prophetic Exposition, Then the Narrowing Post-Reformation Group, With the Whitbyan Post-Millennial Tangent, and Finally the French Revolution Climax. The Broad Third Band Indicates the Widespread Catholic Expositors of Prophecy, from Dante and Petrarch on Through Cusa and Savonarola, Then the Significant Fifth Lateran and Trent Councils. Next Comes the Catholic Counter Reformation, and the Clever Counter Interpretations of Jesuits Ribera and Alcazar, Which Parried and Split the Widespread Protestant Witness on Antichrist and Launched the Popular Futurist and Preterist Views, Later Accepted by Liberal and Conservative Protestants. The Climax of Volume II Is in the French Revolution, and Contemporary Recognition of the Close of the Great 1260-Year Time Period

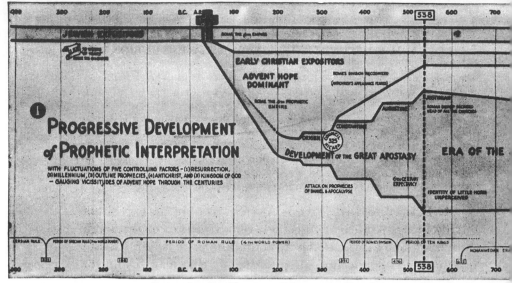

Comprehensive Charting of Progressive Development of Prophetic Interp

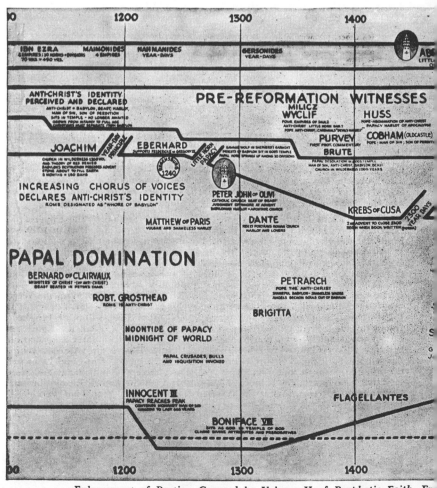

Enlargement of Portion Covered by Volume II of *Prophetic Faith*, Fr

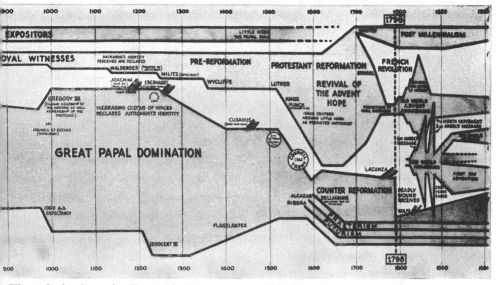

 Through the Centuries, From 4th Century B.C. to 19th Century A.D.

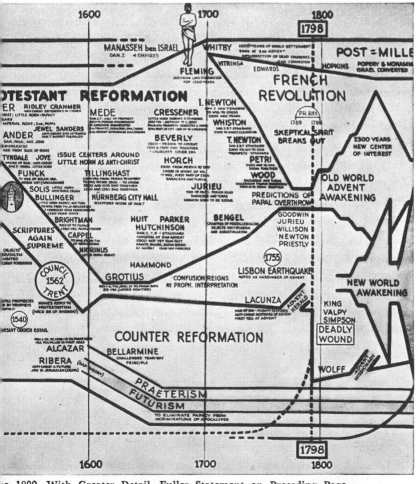

 to 1800, With Greater Detail. Fuller Statement on Preceding Page

5. ANTICHRIST DESTROYED UNDER SEVENTH SEAL.—In commenting on the seven seals, Purvey sees the history of the church repeated through the ages—the apostolic, the pure, the heretics, and the hypocrites,[97] followed by the sword of persecution against those holding the evangelical doctrine, killing them in body or mind.[98] Purvey thought that after the seventh seal, or state of the church, and the accompanying destruction of Antichrist, there would be a period of peace and quiet for the church.[99]

6. TRUMPETS EXPOSE DEPARTURES OF ANTICHRIST.—The seven trumpets, covering the same ages, are similarly asserted to involve the destruction of Antichrist and his helpers. The trumpeters are the preachers against Antichrist. The first is identified as he who first called the pope Antichrist. Others cry out against heresy, and the allegorization and abandonment of the literal interpretation of prophecy, for Antichrist destroys both law and gospel.[100] Under the sixth trumpet Antichrist is openly exposed.[101] The hosts of Antichrist are declared to be the prelates of the church.[102] And the Little Book of Revelation 10 is the knowledge of the present fulfillment of this prophecy, bitter because of persecution over the divulgence of this prophecy.[103]

7. THE WOMAN RECOGNIZED AS THE CHURCH.—The woman of Revelation 12, Purvey recognizes as Christ's church, and the 1260 days as the time of Antichrist's persecution, though he does not attempt to give the length or to suggest the dating.[104]

8. BEAST'S IDENTIFICATION, MARK, AND NUMBER.—The first beast of Revelation 13 symbolizes Antichrist, Purvey continues, the seven heads comprising its princes and prelates, and the ten horns the methods of attacking "the law of the gospel, which leads men to the perfect observance of the decalogue." [105] This beast, he solemnly avers, receives his power from Satan, not God.[106] The second beast embraces those engaged in preaching,

---

[97] *Ibid.*, fols. 51v-58v.   [98] *Ibid.*, fol. 59r, v.   [99] *Ibid.*, fol. 75v.
[100] *Ibid.*, fols. 76r-88r.   [101] *Ibid.*, fol. 88r.   [102] *Ibid.*, fol. 90v.   [103] *Ibid.*, fols. 97v, 98r.
[104] *Ibid.*, fols. 108v, 111v.   [105] *Ibid.*, fol. 116v.   [106] *Ibid.*, fol. 119r,v.

disputing, teaching, and carrying on the business of Antichrist—the pseudo-apostles of Antichrist, including the friars, who kill with the civil sword.[107] These deceive men into receiving the mark in the right hand—works conformed to the Antichrist—or in the forehead—public profession—both alike bringing conformity to Antichrist.[108] The number 666 Purvey attaches to the pope, who, instead of being inerrant, is just a sinner like all others of earth.[109]

9. 144,000 FAITHFUL TO EVANGELICAL FAITH.—The 144,000 are those faithful in the evangelical doctrine, and the new song is that of the evangelical doctrine.[110] They live up to their baptismal vows.[111]

10. FIRST ANGEL EXPOSES ANTICHRIST.—The first angel of Revelation 14 is set forth as a preacher of the evangelical doctrine against Antichrist, proclaimed in the church even in Purvey's own time, and Satan's church is defined as the synagogue of Satan.[112] The dominant position, or rule, of the Beast's preachers in the church is set forth as a definite sign of the nearness of the last judgment.[113]

11. BABYLON'S FALL SPIRITUAL AND TEMPORAL.—The second angel is similarly an evangelical preacher, with Babylon identified as Rome; and "fallen, fallen," repeated, embraces both spiritual and temporal power. "Babylon," Purvey explains, means manifold confusion—simony, avarice, and greed continually.[114]

12. THIRD ANGELIC MESSENGER AGAINST ANTICHRIST.—The third angel's message is directed specifically against the Antichrist-beast, with the image as those who imitate him and receive his mark.[115] The seven angels, with the vials, illuminated with the seven spiritual graces, are thought likewise to be preachers against Antichrist.[116] The vials contain damnation for the followers, high and low, of Antichrist.[117]

---

[107] *Ibid.*, fols. 121v-123v.   [108] *Ibid.*, fol. 123v.; also fol. 128v.   [109] *Ibid.*, fol. 124r.
[110] *Ibid.*, fols. 124v-125v.   [111] *Ibid.*, fol. 126v.   [112] *Ibid.*, fol. 127r.   [113] *Ibid.*, fol. 127v.
[114] *Ibid.*, fol. 128r.   [115] *Ibid.*, fol. 128v.   [116] *Ibid.*, fols. 133v-136v.
[117] *Ibid.*, fol. 137r.

13. SERIOUSLY CONFUSED ON TIME FEATURE.—On the time
feature Purvey is seriously confused. He counts the 1,000 years
of Revelation 20 from the crucifixion to the Antichrist, and
states that about 357 years have passed since their expiration,
thus placing the composition of this work in 1390, although his
figures are not consistent, even after the correction on the last
page. In this view of the thousand years, as dating from the first
advent, he still follows Augustine. In fact, the distortions of the
millennium were the last of the great perversions to be corrected
by the Reformed movement. The three and a half times of Antichrist are, to Purvey, only 350 years—apparently from 1033 to
1383—since which time the pope has been universally demonstrated as the great Antichrist. Purvey, with other Lollards,
believed that they were in the forty-five years (presumably the
difference between the 1290 and 1335) given to the elect for
repentance. Gog and Magog are the persecutors of the preachers
of evangelical doctrine.[118]

Such is the well-defined and clearly expressed concept of
Purvey in 1390, later reprinted under the Reformation.

VII. Relentless Suppression of the Lollards

The story of the Lollards is a moving one. Wyclif's "poor
priests," clad in russet robes of undressed wool, without sandals,
purse, or scrip, went forth from place to place with pages of
Wyclif's Bible, tracts, and sermons. Their number increased,
and they became a power in the land. The effort to suppress
Lollardy was relentless. As early as 1387 commissioners were
appointed in many parts of the kingdom to search out and seize
the books and tracts of Wyclif and his followers, and send them
to the council. All persons were forbidden to defend, maintain,
or teach, openly or privately, the opinions set forth in these
books, or to keep, copy, buy, or sell them, under pain of imprisonment and forfeiture of all their property. Many were
apprehended, compelled to abjure, or to suffer imprisonment

---

[118] *Ibid.*, fols. 170r,v; 195v.

and even death for defiance. The bishops' registers disclose intense activities along this line.

The contest that had developed between the English Government and the papal court was continued. The clergy were alarmed. The Lollards were threatened, and the pope urged their uprooting. Arundel had succeeded to the archbishopric in 1396. At a council in London eighteen conclusions from Wyclif's *Trialogus* were condemned. The university was directed to remove all Lollards, and Wyclif's "errors" were censured to the number of three hundred. Then Henry IV, in 1399, forbade preaching, teaching, or holding anything contrary to the Catholic faith, and demanded that all heretical books be delivered up within forty days—and those who refused to comply were to be burned alive.

Under this provision William Sawtree was burned alive at Smithfield in 1401 and the Lollards were persecuted with unceasing severity. In 1408 constitutions were made by Arundel again prohibiting the perusal of Wyclif's writings. In 1411 forty-five articles attributed to Wyclif were condemned in London. And in 1415 Henry V and the primate Chicheley proceeded against the Lollards with even greater severity. All officers had to take an oath to destroy Lollardy. Lord Cobham was one of the first victims, as noted. In 1416 Inquisitors were appointed in every parish to search out persons suspected of heresy. Then the Council of Constance sat, and forty-five conclusions from Wyclif's writings were condemned as false, heretical, and erroneous. His bones were ordered to be dug up and cast upon a dunghill. This sentence was not executed, however, until 1428 when Pope Martin V sent renewed orders to Fleming, bishop of Lincoln.[119] Such were the tribulations of Lollardy.

---

[119] *Writings and Examinations of Brute*, etc., pp. 7-13.

CHAPTER FOUR

Collective Extermination
of Antichrist Opposers

I. Warring Against the Saints by Council Action

Among all the movements of the Middle Ages that opposed the corruptions of the Roman church and its claim to universal dominion over the consciences and possessions of men, no other body of Christians was subjected to such fearful and continued persecution as were the Waldenses, who are fully treated in Volume I of *Prophetic Faith*.

1. POWER TO RESIST DRAWN FROM THE PROPHECIES.—In vain did the Papacy try time and time again to break the line that connected the Vaudois with the faith of the early church. Rome could not endure their testimony that they must obey God rather than the church; that Rome is Babylon, and the Papacy is Antichrist. So, lighting her fires and drawing her sword, she waged violent war against them. But their power to resist was strengthened by the prophecies of Daniel, Paul, and John, whose inspired visions pierced the centuries, marked out the conflicts and martyrdoms of the true church, and declared her final triumph. Those prophetic texts became their stay and comfort. They were looked upon as windows letting eternal light into their dungeons, far and near, in the days of gross darkness.

Nobly did they keep their evangelical trust. Black clouds gathered, and furious tempests broke. But they watched their lamps while practically all the rest of Christendom stumbled through the night. Among them the mass was not sung. In their midst no image was set up. Excluded from participation in civil rights and natural privileges, they often could not buy or sell. Their goods were confiscated, their houses burned, their lands seized. At last crusades were launched against them, accompanied by ruthless massacres. And what the crusades could not accomplish was left to the Inquisition to accomplish, the horrors of which exceeded the crusades. The Waldenses endured a succession of invasions of their valleys, which had their rise in Rome. The war against them, now authorized by the edicts of councils, which branded them and their Bible translations as heretical, was followed by dreadful collective action. (See symbolic portrayal in Frontispiece.)

2. FIRES KEPT ALIVE DESPITE EFFORTS TO QUENCH.—During the Middle Ages the presence of the Waldenses, under their different names and in various countries of Europe, was brought to light by the fires of the Inquisition. So persistent and effective were these efforts that sometimes assembly for worship had to be abandoned. But the sparks were kept alive in the valleys of the Cottian Alps, whither these exiles for their faith had fled for refuge—the valley fortresses offering resistance to the increasing assaults. As the crusades were launched against them, they at first were slaughtered without resistance. But later they took up arms in their own defense rather than to be helpless spectators to the death and torture of their dear ones.

Rome's efforts to stamp out the fire only scattered the embers over a wider area. But while the bodies of her victims were burned, their words lived on. And a little later the embers blazed forth again in the tremendous fires of the Reformation. The launching of persecution forced dispersion and secrecy, and was the means used of God to spread their doctrine. The Waldenses began traveling in disguise as pilgrims, penitents, or tradesmen, and distributed the Scriptures secretly, making disciples everywhere. Thus the evangel was carried through Europe, winning adherents. In this way the ground was broken up and prepared for the great harvest reaped by the Reformation of the sixteenth century. Thus many Protestant churches are largely the daughters of the old Waldensian church.

3. COLLECTIVE ACTION SUPERSEDES INDIVIDUAL ACTION.—
It was at the Third Lateran Council (1179) that the Papacy aroused itself collectively to extirpate heresy and dissent.[1] Previously, individual members of the system, acting alone or in small groups, had opposed the evangelical truth by force and cruelty. But in the twelfth, thirteenth, fourteenth, and fifteenth centuries Romanism, then in the plenitude of its power, gathered itself together for a determined, united, persistent effort to crush all that opposed its supremacy, and to clear Christendom of "heresy."[2] Thus began in earnest the warfare against the evangelicals, which came to be seen as the deadly onslaught foretold both by Daniel and John, wearing out "the saints of the Most High," and prevailing against them.

Persecution by Catholic council action now became the rule of procedure, for which collective papal responsibility is inescapable. The extirpation of heretics was the professed object of many of the bulls of the general councils of the West in this period, and of the canons of those councils. Death was decreed, and provision made for accomplishing it. In order that the church might not seem to stain herself with blood, the secular princes must serve as executioners.

Joint measures were taken by secular authority, at the instigation of Rome, for the destruction of the heretics. The Fourth Lateran Council (1215) enacted a canon for the extirpation of heresy, urged its enforcement with vigor, and subordinated secular authority to the spiritual powers for that purpose.[3] When resistance was encountered, the interdict was employed. If kings would not clear their dominions of heresy, their subjects were to be absolved from all allegiance to them. Thus crusades against the Waldenses and Albigenses were proclaimed, and

---

[1] Schroeder, *op. cit.*, pp. 214, 234, 235; Mansi, *op. cit.*, vol. 22, cols. 231-233.
[2] Official actions of the councils, authorizing such persecutions, are listed in Volume I of the present work.
[3] Canon 3; see Schroeder, *op. cit.*, pp. 242-244; Landon, *op. cit.*, vol. 1, p. 330; Mansi, *op. cit.*, vol. 22, cols. 986-990.

plenary absolution promised to such as should perish in the holy war.[4]

4. CRUSADES AND INQUISITION THE CHOSEN INSTRUMENTS.—

Innocent III was the first to organize overwhelming war against heresy—the dreadful work of extermination being denominated "sacred," and securing the same privileges and rewards as crusades against the Turks. Opposers were reduced to the silence of the sepulcher. As the fifteenth century drew toward its close, a furious crusade seemed about to accomplish its object. The prophetic "beast" had all but conquered and killed the "witnesses," as the bull of Innocent VIII (1487)[5] called for the "extirpation of the Waldenses," to "rise up in Arms against them, . . . to tread them under foot, as venomous Adders," until they were "exterminated and destroyed."[6]

But the tribunal of the Inquisition, founded early in the thirteenth century, was the primary papal agency for crushing the alleged errors of the Waldenses, and for carrying forward its covert inquest after heresy, with the secular arm as the servile instrument of the orders of the church.[7] The Dominican monks were made primarily responsible for carrying out this process, and bishops gave themselves to the work of ferreting out the heretics. However, despite the vigorous efforts of the popes to destroy the Waldensian "heresy," and despite all that the Inquisition could do, it continued to increase.[8] It obviously had a mission to perform in this Middle Age period.

II. Multiple Background of Bohemian Reforms

During the latter half of the fourteenth century the kingdom of Bohemia occupied a place among the nations of Europe, somewhat comparable to her geographical position in the heart

---

[4] J. C. L. Simonde de Sismondi, *History of the Crusades Against the Albigenses, in the Thirteenth Century*, pp. 20-24.

[5] Samuel Morland, *The History of the Evangelical Churches of the Valleys of Piemont*, pp. 196-214. Here an English translation of the bull appears paralleling the Latin original.

[6] *Ibid.*, pp. 200, 201.

[7] Döllinger, *The Pope and the Council*, pp. 240, 241.

[8] Full information is found in such standard authors as Lea, Llorente, Limborch, Ranke, Sismondi, and Rule, as well as in histories of the Waldenses like Morland, Perrin, Leger, Allix, Monastier. See also Volume I of *Prophetic Faith*.

of the continent. Her population was, in the main, Slavic, and her capital was a residence of the German emperor. Her university at Prague, though but recently founded, was one of the largest and most flourishing—indeed, almost the only one—in that section of Europe.[9] Her churches, cloisters, and palaces kindled admiration and surprise in the stranger, and through her connection with the German Empire, her influence was widely felt.[10] Here a reformation, based on the prophecies, began more than a century before Luther, which, to human view, was quenched in blood—not, however, without leaving behind it most important results. From these persecuted Bohemians later sprang the Moravian missionaries as spiritual descendants.

1. GREEK FAITH GRADUALLY YIELDED FOR ROMAN RITES.— Like Moravia, Bohemia had probably received the Christian faith from the West in the time of Charlemagne. However, because of the unfamiliarity of the Western missionaries with the Slavic tongue, Christianity was completely established by teachers from Greece, and the Eastern ritual was practiced in the national church in Bohemia until in 1079 Gregory VII forbade the use of the mother tongue in public worship.[11] Although the extent of Greek influence is a matter of dispute among historians, such usages as preaching in the vernacular, marriage of the clergy, and communion in both kinds died very slowly.[12] This should be kept in mind, as it was the seed from which the later Reformers, such as Huss, sprang.

During the period following the bull of Gregory VII, when the Papacy became more and more predominant in Bohemia, a new spiritual element was introduced by the Waldenses,[13] who fled from their homelands and found a foothold here, and spread themselves in small colonies all over the Slavic countries, keeping the evangelical message alive until the time of Huss.[14]

---

[9] David S. Schaff, *The Middle Ages,* part 2, pp. 358, 359.
[10] Gillett, *Life and Times of John Huss,* vol. 1, p. 1.
[11] Valerian Krasinski, *Sketch of the Religious History of the Slavonic Nations,* p. 25; Wylie, *op. cit.,* vol. 1, p. 131.
[12] Trench, *op. cit.,* pp. 321, 322; Robertson, *op. cit.,* vol. 4, pp. 85-87; vol. 6, p. 420; vol. 7, pp. 302, 482.
[13] Flick, *op. cit.,* vol. 1, p. 360.
[14] Wylie, *op. cit.,* vol. 1, p. 131.

2. WALDENSIANISM AND WYCLIFISM MAKE THEIR CON-
TRIBUTION.—Rieger says that the Reformer Chytraeus, during a
trip through Bohemia in 1569, was told by the Bohemian Brethren that they were called Waldensians and Picards,[15] their spiritual ancestry being traced first through the Greeks, then the
Waldensians, then the Wyclifites—and of course, Huss. The
Wyclifite movement, at the time of Wyclif, was purely English
in scope. But it was soon destined to acquire European significance. Some sparks of fire were blown halfway across Europe to
remote Bohemia, and there quickened latent embers of reform
into active flame.[16]

Thus it was that the sacred fire passed from Oxford to
Prague, as Huss was influenced by the works of Wyclif. But in
its inception the Bohemian movement was independent, and
eminently a national one, as no Wyclifite writings had, as yet,
made any impress on Bohemia. And, as has been noted, Huss
had several spiritual forerunners—Milicz of Kremsier, Konrad
of Waldhausen, Thomas of Stitny, John of Stekno, and
Matthias of Janow.[17] Many of the Bohemians espoused the teachings of Huss, including his views on the antipapal prophecies.
But, as Comenius expressed it, many sealed their testimony with
their own blood as the Antichrist sought to exterminate them.[18]
The story is a dreadful one. But from their ashes sprang the
later Moravian missionaries.[19]

III. Stormy Career of Huss as Reform Leader

John Huss, or Hus (1369-1415), or John of Husinec (Hussi-
necz), as he is called in the earliest authentic documents, was the
central figure of the Hussite movement. The name Huss meant
"goose" in the Bohemian, and the significance of this term was
more than once impressively applied by the Reformer.[20] Born

---

[15] Rieger, op. cit., vol. 1, pp. 634, 635.
[16] Trench, op. cit., p. 321.
[17] Johann Loserth, Wiclif and Hus, chap. 2; see also chap. 5.
[18] Johann Amos Comenius, The Bequest of the Unity of the Brethren, p. 32.
[19] David S. Schaff, John Huss, p. 334.
[20] At the place of his execution Huss is reported to have said, "This day ye are burning
a goose; but from my ashes will arise a swan, which ye will not be able to roast"—an expression
Luther quoted. (See Döllinger, Prophecies, pp. 14, 15.)

BROZIK, ARTIST

HUSS ON TRIAL FOR LIFE FOR IDENTIFYING ANTICHRIST

John Huss, Professor at University of Prague, and Famous Bohemian Reformer and Defender of Wyclif's Writings, His Safe-Conduct to Council of Constance Violated, He Was Condemned, Degraded, and Turned Over to the Secular Arm to Perish at the Stake

in southern Bohemia, of humble Czech parents, Huss pursued the divinity and liberal arts courses. His higher studies were taken at the University of Prague, where his achievements attracted the attention of his teachers. Working his way by singing and manual labor, Huss rose rapidly to distinction. In 1393, at the age of twenty-four, he received his B.A., in 1394 his Bachelor's degree in theology, and in 1396 his M.A. In 1398 Huss began to lecture at the university. He was ordained a priest in 1400, and was made dean of the faculty of philosophy in 1401. In 1402, at the age of thirty-three, he was chosen rector of the university for one semester, and in 1403 was appointed Synodal preacher.[21]

1. CONNECTING LINKS BETWEEN PRAGUE AND OXFORD.— There were certain connecting links between the universities of Prague and Oxford, which institutions often exchanged students. Of course, the universal use of the Latin language in all books and at all educational institutions in medieval Europe made such migration possible and even natural. In 1383 Richard II of England married Princess Anne of Bohemia, who favored the Lollard doctrines. She habitually read the New Testament, and carried with her to England a book of the Gospels in the Latin, Bohemian, and German languages.[22] This established considerable contact between the two countries. Special scholarships were provided for Czech students at Oxford, where they came under the direct influence of Wyclifism, taking back with them copies of Wyclif's writings.[23] Thus it was that Jerome of Prague, a Bohemian knight who had studied at Oxford, returned about 1402, bringing with him the major writings of Wyclif.[24] The *Dialogus* and *Trialogus*, Jerome copied personally.[25] While in Paris and Vienna, Jerome maintained Wyclif's positions from

[21] Workman, *Dawn of the Reformation*, vol. 2, pp. 117-119; Flick, *op. cit.*, vol. 1, pp. 363-365; Poole, *Wycliffe and Movements for Reform*, pp. 151, 152.
[22] Neander, *op. cit.*, vol. 5, p. 241, citing Palacky.
[23] Workman, *Dawn of the Reformation*, vol. 2, pp. 121, 122; Flick, *op. cit.*, vol. 1, pp. 363, 364.
[24] Flick, *op. cit.*, vol. 2, p. 93.
[25] Loserth, *op. cit.*, pp. 74, 75; Workman, *Dawn of the Reformation*, vol. 2, pp. 122, 123.

Scripture in disputes with scholars. It was these treatises by Wyclif that opened the eyes of Huss.[26]

But there was yet another feature. About this time the rule of the faculty of philosophy at Prague was that lecturers made use of the books of well-known masters of Oxford and Paris. In this way Huss first became acquainted with Wyclif's philosophical writings, and later with his theological works. Such were the links that bound pre-Reformation Bohemia and Britain.

2. BETHLEHEM CHAPEL APPOINTMENT TURNING POINT OF LIFE.—Huss was held in high esteem in university circles, but he entered a new epoch in his lifework when, in 1402, he was appointed preacher of Bethlehem Chapel in Prague.[27] This chapel had been founded in 1391 by a citizen of Prague, with the stipulation that the preaching of the Word was to be in "the tongue of the people." [28] This was one of the direct results of Milicz' preaching.[29] The plan afforded a means of appealing favorably to the popular mind. In preparing his sermons, Huss studied not only the Scriptures but the writings of Wyclif with increasing delight. He became a zealous advocate of Wyclif's writings,[30] their truths penetrating his mind and heart through and through.

Crowds flocked to hear him, as he sought to feed hungry souls with the bread of life and to rebuke prevailing corruptions—with results that made Rome tremble. Queen Sophia was one of his hearers, and in 1403 he was chosen to be her confessor.[31] Familiarity with Wyclif's positions led Huss to place the Bible above the authority of both pope and council —anticipating the clear Protestant platform. Huss demanded reforms similar to those urged by Wyclif. As a result the echo of Wyclif's voice was heard in Bohemia, especially as Huss

---

[26] *Encyclopaedia Britannica*, vol. 13, p. 3, art. "Jerome of Prague"; Workman, *Dawn of the Reformation*, vol. 2, pp. 122-124.
[27] Lechler, *op. cit.*, p. 461.
[28] Workman, *Dawn of the Reformation*, vol. 2, p. 120; David S. Schaff, *The Middle Ages*, part 2, p. 361.
[29] Creighton, *op. cit.*, vol. 1, p. 314.
[30] Trench, *op. cit.*, p. 324; Loserth, *op. cit.*, p. 86.
[31] Flick, *op. cit.*, vol. 1, pp. 363-365.

translated Wyclif's *Trialogus* into Czech for the benefit of the laity.[32] These were the circumstances that led Huss into conflict with the university, which in 1403 condemned forty-five propositions from Wyclif's writings.[33]

3. SUPPRESSION OF WYCLIF'S TEACHINGS BRINGS CRISIS.—
The Reformation in Bohemia really began in 1403, when forty-five propositions from Wyclif's writings were condemned as heretical, at a meeting of the authorities of the University of Prague, and their propagation in lecture or sermon form forbidden.[34] Despite the condemnation Huss persisted in defending and using Wyclif's teachings [35]—and continued to be the preferred speaker at the synods as well. It was this issue that caused the controversy among the clergy.[36] It was complained that Huss had calumniated the clergy in his sermons. Hence, in 1408 he was deposed as synodal preacher, and the university decreed that no discussions should be held on Wyclif's doctrines.[37]

Two parties resulted, one favoring reform and the other opposing. In 1409 national rivalries over control of the university were complicated by the Germans and Bohemians taking opposite sides on the question of the rival popes. As a result of the strong movement of Bohemia for the Bohemians, the Germans were outvoted, and some two thousand of the students then in attendance withdrew from the university.[38] The new University of Leipzig was founded as a result of this secession. Huss, then at the peak of his influence, was again chosen rector when the University of Prague was reorganized. However, the clergy of Prague laid charges of heresy concerning Huss before Archbishop Zbynek (Zybnic). Zbynek in turn appealed to Pope Alexander V, who issued a bull demanding

[32] Lechler, *op. cit.*, p. 461; *Encyclopaedia Britannica*, vol. 11, p. 942, art. "Huss."
[33] Robertson, *op. cit.*, vol. 7, pp. 313, 314; Neander, *op. cit.*, vol. 5, p. 246.
[34] David S. Schaff, *The Middle Ages*, part 2, pp. 361, 362; Kurtz, *op. cit.*, vol. 2, p. 207.
[35] Lechler, *op. cit.*, p. 461.
[36] Loserth, *op. cit.*, pp. 77, 78.
[37] Flick, *op. cit.*, vol. 1, p. 365; Loserth, *op. cit.*, p. 104.
[38] Lechler, *op. cit.*, p. 462; Creighton, *op. cit.*, vol. 1, p. 318, note; Flick, *op. cit.*, vol. 1, p. 363.

that heresy be rooted out of the diocese, calling for the withdrawal of Wyclif's books from the sight of the faithful and
prohibiting all preaching except as authorized in appointed
places.[39]

The university protested against the bull, and Huss and
others appealed to the new pope, John XXIII.[40] Nevertheless
two hundred choice manuscript copies of Wyclif's writings
were publicly burned, together with some works of Milicz
and others, amid the tolling of the church bells.[41] Two days
after the burning, the sentence of excommunication was
launched against Huss and all who might persist in refusing
to deliver up Wyclif's writings. The excitement among all
classes was intense. The act inflamed the soul of Huss, who
vigorously defended Wyclif, denounced the religious war, attacked the indulgence, and uncovered the "putrid sores" of
the church. Defying the papal order, he continued to preach
both in the Bethlehem Chapel and in the university.[42] So John
XXIII pressed the proceedings against Huss, citing him to
appear at Rome. This he failed to do. It was this defiance that
had led to his excommunication, and the placing of Prague,
and any place that should harbor him, under interdict.[43]

4. HUSS TAKES STAND AGAINST ANTICHRIST OF PROPHECY.
—In 1412 Pope John XXIII, by papal bull, proclaimed a crusade against Ladislaus, king of Naples, with full indulgence
as a reward. This led Huss into open opposition to the hierarchy. In a public disputation he maintained that the pope
had no right to grant such indulgences.[44] His most stanch supporter was Jerome, the enthusiastic adherent of Wyclif's doctrines. The discourses of Huss and Jerome were heard with
enthusiasm by the students. A few days later a crowd of sym-
pathizers burned the bulls relating to the crusades after they
had been paraded through the streets on the breast of an

39 Loserth, *op. cit.*, pp. 114, 115.   40 Flick, *op. cit.*, vol. 1, p. 366.
41 Neander, *op. cit.*, vol. 5, p. 261; Robertson, *op. cit.*, vol. 7, pp. 319, 320.
42 David S. Schaff, *The Middle Ages*, part 2, p. 363.
43 Flick, *op. cit.*, vol. 1, p. 367; Trench, *op. cit.*, pp. 326, 327.
44 Flick, *op. cit.*, vol. 1, pp. 367, 368.

alleged public prostitute, representing the prophesied "Harlot of the Apocalypse." [45]

The Curia was infuriated and thundered its curses. The theological faculty of the university renewed its condemnation of Wyclif's propositions, and added six more from Huss. It was at this point that Huss took his public stand on Antichrist, declaring Antichrist was exercising his predicted powers of deception, and that prophecy was obscured, the gift of healing removed, and true doctrine silent.[46] Says Gillett:

"Early in 1412 it was manifest that the spirit of Huss was fully aroused. At one of the regular disputations of the university, Huss maintained that the great Antichrist, which according to the word of God was to come at the end of the world, was even now in possession of the highest dignity of Christendom, and exercised transcendent authority over all Christian people, clerical and lay, and that he is in fact no other than the pope of Rome. Hence Christians are not to obey him, but, as the chief enemy and grand opponent of Christ, they are rather to resist him. Huss subsequently published his argument." [47]

Huss was excommunicated and anathematized. Every place in which he might be was to be interdicted. At the request of King Wenceslaus, of Bohemia, in 1412 Huss withdrew from the tumults of Prague, under the protection of the nobles, after setting forth an appeal to Christ as Judge of all.[48] It was during this exile that he wrote *De Ecclesia* (Concerning the Church), largely based on the doctrines of Wyclif, touching upon the clergy of the two churches—that of Christ and of Antichrist.[49] His *De Sex Erroribus* (Concerning Six Errors) exposed the errors of the Papacy on creation and the Creator, faith, forgiveness of sins, obedience, excommunication, and simony.[50] He set himself against the primacy of Peter, and broke with the church.[51] His views spread far and near through these controversial and doctrinal treatises. Huss de-

[45] Kurtz, *op. cit.*, vol. 2, pp. 298, 209; Robertson, *op. cit.*, vol. 7, p. 324; Loserth, *op. cit.*, p. 142.
[46] Neander, *op. cit.*, vol. 5, p. 266.
[47] Gillett, *Life and Times of John Huss*, vol. 1, p. 205.
[48] Robertson, *op. cit.*, vol. 7, p. 327; Kurtz, *op. cit.*, vol. 2, p. 209.
[49] Neander, *op. cit.*, vol. 5, pp. 299, 300; Flick, *op. cit.*, vol. 1, p. 369.
[50] Loserth, *op. cit.*, pp. 156, 157, 247.
[51] David S. Schaff, *The Middle Ages*, part 2, pp. 369, 370.

clared that it was because he preached Christ and the gospel, and exposed Antichrist, that he was placed under ban.

IV. Faithful Unto Death for Prophetic Faith

1. HUSS SUMMONED TO CONSTANCE; SAFE-CONDUCT VIOLATED.—The Council of Constance (1414-1418), one of Christendom's most brilliant councils, was summoned by Sigismund, king of Hungary and emperor of the Holy Roman Empire, to end the Great Schism of the West—there were now three popes, John XXIII, Benedict XIII, and Gregory XII—to repress heresy, and to reform the church in its head and members.[52] Huss had been cited, in 1413, to appear before the council, to make answer to certain charges. Having been granted a safe-conduct and given assurance of a fair hearing by the emperor, he was nevertheless arrested in direct violation of the imperial safe-conduct, shortly after his arrival at Constance, was charged with heresy, and committed to prison, where he was ill for two months. The council persuaded the emperor that, as a heretic, Huss was beyond civil protection.[53] The trial lasted for months,[54] during which Huss was harassed by private interrogations.

The same commission appointed to handle Huss was likewise to deal with the writings of Wyclif.[55] Wyclif was declared by them, "to have been, while he lived, a notorious heretic," and the forty-five Wyclif articles that had been issued in 1403 and 1408, by the University of Prague, were condemned. His writings were ordered to be burned, and his remains to be disinterred and removed from consecrated ground.[56] In all, 305 heretical Wyclif propositions were condemned by the council.[57] This condemnation of Wyclif practically sealed the fate of Huss.[58]

---

[52] Schroeder, op. cit., p. 443.
[53] David S. Schaff, The Middle Ages, part 2, pp. 371-374; David S. Schaff, John Huss, p. 186.
[54] Workman, Dawn of the Reformation, vol. 2, p. 303.
[55] Loserth, op. cit., p. 172.
[56] Schroeder, op. cit., p. 449; original in Mansi, op. cit., vol. 27, cols. 632-636.
[57] Schroeder, op. cit., p. 449.
[58] Workman, Dawn of the Reformation, vol. 2, p. 307; Loserth, op. cit., pp. 172, 173.

2. HUSS CONDEMNED AS HERETIC; ORDERED DEGRADED.—
Asked if he acknowledged the books charged to him, Huss defended some, disowned others falsely attributed to him, and adhered steadfastly to his opinions.[59] He declared that if any proposition could be shown contrary to God's Word, he would retract.
The basic issue was the supremacy of the Word. But none could
persuade him, and his fate was sealed. He was brought before
the council for sentence and doom. It was a tumultuous hearing,
with hostile cries of "Recant." Then a list of thirty-nine articles
preached and taught by Huss were condemned as heretical, sedi-
tious, deceitful, and offensive. His books were ordered burned.[60]
After the recital of his heresies Huss was condemned to be degraded and turned over to the secular arm, to perish at the
stake.[61]

The ignominious ceremonies known as the degradation and
deconsecration then took place. Huss was placed on a platform
and clad by seven bishops in full ecclesiastical vestments; then
the vestments were one by one stripped from him.[62] The chalice
and paten were put into his hand, and then taken away. His
tonsure was effaced. They put a high conical paper cap on his
head, painted with devils "clawing his soul with their nails," and
bearing the word "heresiarch" (a leader in heresy). This done,
and his soul having been delivered over to the devil, his body
was surrendered to the secular arm.[63]

3. BURNED AT STAKE FOR PROPHETIC FAITH.—Accompanied
by a guard of a thousand armed men and a vast crowd of spectators, Huss was led out of the council precincts. As he passed
through the churchyard, Huss saw a bonfire of his books in the
public square. Reaching the execution ground, called the
"Devil's Place," Huss knelt and prayed. His hands were tied behind him, and he was bound to the stake, facing the west. A

[59] Schroeder, *op. cit.*, p. 449.
[60] Wilhelm Möller, *History of the Christian Church in the Middle Ages*, p. 509.
[61] Schroeder, *op. cit.*, p. 449; Landon, *op. cit.*, vol. 1, p. 180.
[62] Workman, *Dawn of the Reformation*, vol. 2, p. 330; Count Franz Lützow, *The Life & Times of Master John Hus*, p. 282.
[63] Creighton, *op. cit.*, vol. 1, p. 354; Trench, *op. cit.*, pp. 329, 330.

rusty chain was wound round his neck. Straw and wood were piled around him, and rosin sprinkled upon them. The offer of life was renewed if he would recant, but he refused. Then the lighted fagots were applied. Huss began to sing, but the wind swept the flames into his face and silenced his words. Only his lips moved—until they too were stilled in death for his stand against the Antichrist of Bible prophecy. Then his persecutors stirred his bones with a stick, split open his skull, and flung it back into the flames, with the unconsumed portions of his garments. Thus his body was reduced to ashes, which were gathered up and cast into the Rhine.[64]

V. Huss Discussed Antichrist's Identity and Prophesied Doom

Huss was not so much an originator as an incorporator. His Latin writings contained many extracts and phrasings from Wyclif, some being copied almost verbatim.[65] Loserth devotes pages to showing their close parallel on the church, the Antichrist, and the doctrine of the Papacy—placing the two texts in parallel columns.[66] In fact, Huss gave up his life for these very doctrines, so fully did he believe and teach them. Therefore, to know Wyclif's position on the Antichrist of prophecy is to understand Huss, though Huss was no mere copyist.[67]

The writings of Huss constantly refer to Antichrist as the enemy of the church—not as a Jew, pagan, or Turk, but as a false confessor of the name of Christ. Antichrist's location must be within the Roman Empire, subtly finding its way into the church. The pope, with his cardinals and priests, comprises the Mystery of Iniquity and the Spiritual Babylon. And finally Huss avers him to be the vicar of Satan[68] and the great Antichrist.[69] This he stresses in many tracts.

---

[64] Workman, *Dawn of the Reformation*, vol. 2, pp. 330-332; David S. Schaff, *The Middle Ages*, part 2, pp. 382, 383.
[65] Workman, *Dawn of the Reformation*, vol. 2, pp. 176, 177; Loserth, *op. cit.*, pp. xvi, xvii, xviii.
[66] Loserth, *op. cit.*, pp. 182 ff.
[67] David S. Schaff, *The Middle Ages*, part 2, p. 370.
[68] Rieger, *op. cit.*, vol. 2, pp. 54-64.
[69] See, for example, *De Antichristo*, in *Ioannis Hus, et Hieronymi Pragensis Confessorum Christi Historia et Monumenta*.

1. Antichrist's Persecutions Anticipated and Fore-warned.—Huss fully sensed the persecuting anger of Antichrist that was stirred up against him, and dwelt upon the coming kingdom of God and the last judgment. For example:

"And the more circumspect ye ought to be, for that Antichrist labour-eth the more to trouble you. The last judgment is near at hand: death shall swallow up many, but to the elect children of God the Kingdom of God draweth near. . . . Know ye, welbeloved, that Antichrist being stirred up against you, deviseth divers persecutions." [70]

2. Prophetic Symbols Applied to Papal Antichrist.— The intimate letters of Huss, written during his exile (1412-1414), set forth with undisguised conviction and clarity his understanding of Antichrist—embracing the pope and his entire retinue as the prophesied "abomination" and "beast." And Paul's depiction in 2 Thessalonians 2 is clearly implied by the "beast" who was "sitting in a place of honour" and receiving worship as if he were God.

"I beseech you in Christ Jesus, with all your fellow-members of the University, to be prepared for a battle; for the reconnoitres of Antichrist have already begun, and the fight will soon follow. The Goose also must needs flap his wings against the wings of Behemoth, and against his tail, which always conceals the abomination of the beast Antichrist. . . . *The Lord shall destroy the head and the tail*—that is, the Pope and his prophets, masters, doctors, priests, who under the false pretext of sanctity conceal the abomination of the beast. Pray, what greater abomination can there be than a harlot who should parade herself and offer herself publicly? Yes, there is the still greater abomination of the beast sitting in a place of honour and offering himself for worship to all comers, as though he were God: ready to sell whatever a man may wish to buy in matters spiritual. Yea, he sells what he doth not possess. Woe be to me, then, if I shall not preach, weep, and write against such an abomination!" [71]

3. Papacy Is Predicted Abomination of Desolation.— Letter XXIX (1413) warns that men should beware of the "chief Antichrist," whom Huss denominated a thief, robber, wolf, and

---

[70] Foxe, *Acts*, vol. 1, p. 712. Other letters appear in Foxe, but a more complete group, with greater accuracy of translation, is found in Workman and Pope, cited in the next footnote.
[71] *The Letters of John Hus*, edited by Herbert B. Workman and R. Martin Pope, Letter XXVI, pp. 118, 119. The thought of the head and the tail, or the anatomy of Antichrist, seems to have been a favorite one with the Bohemian reformers.

hypocrite. He admonishes all to heed the prophecy of Christ concerning false christs, "popes bearing Christ's name," and adds:

"Blessed is he that considers *the abomination of desolation which was spoken of by Daniel the prophet, standing in the holy place. He that readeth let him understand,* saith Christ, the Head of the Church. For what greater abomination can there be in the holy place—that is, the holy office—than that in the place—that is, the sanctity—where the holiest, most gracious, gentlest, humblest, poorest, most untiring, most patient, most chaste of all men hath sat, there is now sitting one [John XXIII]; in name the holiest, but in reality the worst, the most cruel, the most vengeful, the proudest, the richest in this world's wealth, the most indolent, the most impatient, and the most unclean? Is it not an abomination of desolation in a place apart? Truly is Christ set forth by the false prophets to be in a desert place, which is left forlorn of all the virtues. Christ the Lord prophesied and forewarned His own: When you shall see the abomination in the holy place: he that readeth, let him understand. And afterwards: If they shall say to you, behold Christ (sic) is in the desert, believe it not: go ye not out." [72]

4. CONCERN FOR SHORTENING OF ANTICHRIST'S TRIBULATION.—His letters before his martyrdom revealed the burden Huss bore concerning the Antichrist, and the promised shortening of his days of tribulation for the church. Thus on June 24, 1415, writing "To the Faithful Bohemians," Huss says:

"Remember what the merciful Saviour said to us by way of warning in Matt. xxiv., that before the Judgment Day *shall be great tribulation, such as hath not been from the beginning of the world until now, neither shall be, insomuch as to deceive (if possible) even the elect: but for the sake of the elect those days shall be shortened.* Holding these things in your memory, beloved, press bravely on; for I trust God that the school of Antichrist shall tremble before you and suffer you to enjoy quietness, and that the Council of Constance shall not come to Bohemia." [73]

Antichrist, as comprised of the "Pope and his associates," fulfilling Daniel's prophecy, is then portrayed, together with his concern that God will raise up other witnesses after his own testimony is closed shortly.

"Surely *now* the wickedness, iniquity, and baseness of Antichrist has been revealed in the Pope and his associates in the Council: *now* the faithful servants of God can understand the meaning of the Saviour's words,

---

[72] *Ibid.,* pp. 129, 130; see parallel statements from Wyclif, in Loserth, *op. cit.,* p. 257.
[73] *Ibid.,* Letter LXXIV, p. 255.

*When ye shall see the abomination of desolation which was spoken of by
Daniel the prophet, . . . he that readeth, let him understand.* Verily 'a great
abomination' is pride, avarice, and simony: 'in a place apart'—that is,
dignity which lacks modesty, love, and other virtues; and this is what
we clearly mark in those who win office and dignity. Would that I were
allowed to point out their wickedness, in order that the faithful servants
of God might beware of them! Gladly would I do so; but I am trusting
that God will raise up others after me, braver men than there are to-day,
who shall better reveal the wickedness of Antichrist and lay down their
lives for the truth of the Lord Jesus Christ, who will grant eternal joy
both to you and to me. Amen. I write this letter in prison, on the day of
St. John Baptist, as I lie bound in chains, remembering that St. John also
was beheaded in prison for the sake of God's truth." [74]

5. Denounces Spiritual Unfaithfulness of the Church.
—On June 29, 1415, Huss wrote his farewell letter to Baron
John of Chlum. His conception of Antichrist was unchanged,
and his burden the same. Expecting and longing for martyrdom,
he recites the sufferings of the worthies of old for Christ.[75] In this
connection and setting he makes his final declaration:

"The iniquity of the *great harlot*—that is, of the blaspheming congregation, of which we read in the Apocalypse—is and shall be made bare, with
which harlot *the kings of the earth commit fornication.* In the same place,
likewise, it is written that they commit fornication spiritually, that they
depart from Christ and His truth and consent to the falsehood of Antichrist,
whether by being seduced or terrified, or by being led to hope in the confederacy for the winning of the world's honour." [76]

VI. Hussites Continue Struggle Against Antichrist of Prophecy

The burning of Huss by flagrant breach of imperial promise, followed by that of Jerome, aroused violent protest. Open
insurrection flamed forth. Four hundred and fifty-two Bohemian
and Moravian nobles signed and sent to the Council of Constance an indignant protest, and entered into a solemn six-year
compact to maintain and defend the doctrines of Huss by all
means.[77] In 1417 the University of Prague declared for commu-

---

[74] *Ibid.,* p. 258.
[75] *Ibid.,* Letter LXXX, pp. 270, 271.
[76] *Ibid.;* see also Foxe, *Acts,* vol. 1, p. 712, col. 2.
[77] David S. Schaff, *The Middle Ages,* part 2, pp. 391 ff; Lützow, *op. cit.,* pp. 337-339.

BROZIK, ARTIST

HUSS FAITHFUL UNTO DEATH FOR PROPHETIC FAITH

Huss Is Burned at Stake for Stand Against Prophesied Antichrist (Upper); Hussites Compact to
Continue the Struggle, Celebrating Communion in Both Kinds (Lower)

nion under both kinds. Meetings were called on the hilltop, or "tabor," to celebrate the Lord's supper in both kinds, these tabor gatherings becoming great religious celebrations of the Czechs.[78] In consequence the participants were called Taborites.

1. "TABOR" BECOMES REFUGE FROM ANTICHRIST.—Upon the conclusion of the Council of Constance, Martin V issued a bull, in 1418, ordering the punishment of all, of both sexes, holding the heresy of Wyclif, Huss, and Jerome.[79] All the churches in Prague, except two, were ordered turned over to the Catholics. A crusade, involving 150,000 soldiers, was launched against Bohemian heretics.

John of Selau preached on the Apocalypse, emphasizing the second coming of Christ, and led a procession back from his church, past the town hall, where the magistrate tried to stop it. Through some incident a tremendous turmoil occurred during which the town hall was stormed, several of the city councilors being thrown out of the window and killed. This enraged the king, and the army was ordered out to oppose the Hussites. Thousands gathered in self-defense. The resolute John Ziska ("ziska = the one-eyed")[80] led the Hussite armies in opposition to the papal crusaders, building for the "faithful" a stronghold on a steep mountain, called the city of Tabor—sixty miles from Prague—to which they could "flee from Antichrist." Many were convinced that Prague had become a new Babylon, from which they were to escape.[81] (For medal of Paul II, see page 556.)

2. TABORITES REJECT ERRORS OF PAPAL "BEAST."—Bohemia became the gathering place for a large number of Waldenses who here found excellent soil for their opposition to Catholic tradition. In fact, the Taborites, Waldenses, and Wyclifites were very similar. The Taborites, or more anti-Catholic faction of the Hussites, asserted the sole and absolute authority of Scripture, and repudiated the writings of the fathers of

---

[78] Czerwenka, *op. cit.*, vol. 1, p. 122.
[79] David S. Schaff, *The Middle Ages*, part 2, p. 392.
[80] Flick, *op. cit.*, vol. 2, p. 157.
[81] Czerwenka, *op. cit.*, vol. 1, pp. 123, 136.

the church.[82] In 1420 a statement of faith by a group under the leadership of Martin Hauska was issued, which rejected all ceremonies associated with the mass, purgatory, intercession of saints, shrines, images, and transubstantiation.[83] Two parties developed—the Hussites, who did not go beyond the position of Huss, and simply demanded the cup (*calix*); and the Taborites, who assumed positions of uncompromising hostility toward papal claims.

3. COMPROMISE POSITION REACHED AT COUNCIL OF BASEL.—In 1431 the Hussites were invited to the Council of Basel (1431-1449), in an effort to restore unity to the church, and were given assurances of protection and of freedom of speech.[84] Seven nobles and eight priests, representing the Hussites, rode through Germany bearing a banner reading, "Truth Conquers All!" On their arrival in Basel on January 4, 1433, the Bohemians were assigned to four public taverns. Very lengthy discussions at the council now began. Wyclif and Huss were even praised on the floor of the council.[85] Nicholas of Cusa—to be noted soon—asked whether they would join the council if granted communion in both kinds.

Finally, a compromise, based on the Four Articles of the Prague, which included provision for communion under both kinds for laymen,[86] was reached with the reactionary Calixtines (from *calix*, cup). The main article granted the use of the cup to the laity, where it was asked, but on condition that the doctrine be inculcated that the whole Christ is contained in each of the elements. Compacts were ratified by the Bohemian Diet in 1436. Consequently the Hussite movement was outmaneuvered by the Council of Basel, but the Taborites were not satisfied. Slaughter broke out between the Utraquists (who approached closer to the Catholics) and the Taborites in Prague, and open war followed for a time.[87] The Taborites were defeated in the battle

[82] Lützow, *op. cit.*, p. 358; Albert Henry Newman, *op. cit.*, vol. 1, p. 617.
[83] Czerwenka, *op. cit.*, vol. 1, pp. 131 ff.
[84] Flick, *op. cit.*, vol. 2, pp. 161, 162.
[85] *Ibid.*, p. 163; David S. Schaff, *The Middle Ages*, part 2, p. 395.
[86] Flick, *op. cit.*, vol. 2, pp. 166-171; Mansi, *op. cit.*, vol. 31, cols. 273-278.
[87] David S. Schaff, *The Middle Ages*, part 2, pp. 395, 396.

at Lipan, in 1434. Their power was gone, and in 1452 they lost Mount Tabor.

The *Unitas Fratrum* (commonly called the Bohemian Brethren), the third body that finally emerged from the Hussite movement, formed a separate church (*c.* 1467), and had their chosen leader ordained by the Waldensian bishop Stephen.[88] The Brethren absorbed the Taborites and received many Waldenses. Bishop Lukás (Lucas) of Prague (d. 1528)[89] became their leading spirit. Visiting the Waldenses in their valleys, he is said to have republished their noted *Treatise on Antichrist*. Peter Chelcicky (d. 1460) rejected any union of church and state as the system of Antichrist.[90] He wrote *Sit Very* (The Net of Faith).

---

[88] *Ibid.*, pp. 397, 398.
[89] *Ibid.*, p. 398; Philip Schaff, *The Creeds of Christendom,* vol. 1, pp. 566, 568, 569.
[90] David S. Schaff, *The Middle Ages*, part 2, p. 398, citing Goll (*Untersuchungen,* pp. 107, 112).

CHAPTER FIVE

Cusa Applies Prophetic Time Measurement to 2300 Days

I. Climaxes Application of the Year-Day Principle

As traced in Volume I, the time prophecies of Daniel and the Apocalypse were recognized as slowly but inexorably fulfilling. This was gradually perceived as the predicted events were progressively identified. Many centuries were required for full development, and consequently for clear recognition. Moses and Ezekiel had long before given the inspired key to all prophetic time measurement; namely, that the prophetic time unit is always *a day for a year*,[1] just as on a map one inch may stand for one hundred miles. In the application of this basic principle the fulfillment of the prophesied seventy weeks of years—which were to extend from the time of Persia to the Messiah—was first seen to be exactly accomplished in the baptism and death of Christ in connection with the seventieth week. These sublime transactions sealed forever for the Christian church the "year-day" principle already recognized by the Jews.

Joachim of Floris, in the twelfth century, had seen the 1260-day period to be so many year-days. This great advance was slowly accepted. Meanwhile, the anonymous *De Semine* (1205) interpreted the 2300 days as twenty-three hundred years, approximating the year-day principle. Then in 1292 Villanova, in addition to using this prophetic time unit in the 1290- and 1335-

---

[1] Numbers 14:34; Ezekiel 4:6.

day periods, seems to have been the first Christian writer to apply this established canon of measurement to the longest of the great time prophecies of Daniel—a prophetic period embracing all others—the 2300 days of Daniel 8:14.[2] This was destined to be of utmost interest and importance in later centuries. Finally in 1440 Cusa gave a more definite B.C. and A.D. dating to the period, and through his greater prominence he established the principle in the minds of the prophetic expositors who followed him. To Cusa, then, we now turn our attention, first to note the caliber and type of the man who gave currency to this new step in the application of time prophecy, and then to observe his precise statements.

II. Cusa—Scholar, Philosopher, Churchman, and Reformer

NICHOLAS OF CUSA (Nicholas Cusanus, de Cusa, von Cusa, or Nicholas Krebs of Cusa) (1400?-1464)—theologian, mathematician, scientist, and scholar—often credited by later writers with establishing the year-day principle as applied to the 2300 days—derived his name from the place of his birth, Cusa, or Cues (Kues), near Treves, or Trier. His father was a boatman named Krebs (Krypffs). Not wishing to follow his father's vocation, he left home and found employment with the count of Manderscheid, who sent him first to school at Deventer, and then to the University of Padua.[3] He studied law, as well as Greek, Hebrew, philosophy, mathematics, and astronomy, and in later years, Arabic. At the age of twenty-three Cusa became a Doctor of Laws. But he turned from law to theology, which he studied at Cologne, likewise becoming a Doctor of Theology. After holding several ecclesiastical benefices, he was present as archdeacon of Liége at the Council of Basel.

1. CHAMPIONS AUTHORITY OF COUNCILS OVER THAT OF POPE.—In 1432 the Council of Basel (convoked in 1431, and

---

[2] Joachim and Villanova are discussed in Volume I. For earlier Jewish use of 2300 days as years, see p. 240.
[3] M'Clintock and Strong, *op. cit.*, vol. 2, p. 611, art. "Cusa"; and similar biographical sketches.

continuing intermittently until 1449) became a constitutional battle over the absolutism of the pope versus conciliar supremacy. Cusa, taking the antipapal side along with the Bohemian Hussites, was among the most distinguished champions of the authority of the general council over that of the pope, although he later changed his views.[4] The battle was fought with pen as well as by debate, Cusa there issuing his famous *De Concordantia Catholica* (Concerning Catholic Harmony), dedicated to the council in 1433.[5] In this—one of the ablest works of its kind —he contended that Peter had no more authority than the other apostles, that all bishops are equal, and that ecclesiastical authority is not confined to the Roman See. The Basel council renewed the decrees of Constance concerning the superior authority of the councils—which, of course, threatened the very foundations of the Papacy.

Cusa, having been won over to the adherents of the pope, was entrusted with a number of important missions by the church, being sent to Constantinople to bring about a union of the Eastern and Western churches, for the reunion of Christendom took precedence over all other church objectives.[6] The Greek emperor John VIII (Palaeologus, 1425-1448) and his leading prelates were prevailed upon to attend the Council of Florence (1439), which was a continuation of the Council of Ferrara (1438), to which place the Council of Basel had been transferred.[7]

2. Presses Reform of Ecclesiastical Abuses.—Cusa came back to Germany as papal delegate to the diets between 1441 and 1446. In 1447 he arranged the concordat of Vienna, and in recognition of his services was created a cardinal.[8] About 1450

---

[4] R. Schmid, art. "Cusa," *The New Schaff-Herzog Encyclopedia of Religious Knowledge*, vol. 3, p. 327; Johann von Mosheim, *Institutes of Ecclesiastical History*, vol. 3, p. 41; David S. Schaff, *The Middle Ages*, part 2, pp. 170, 224, 225.

[5] David S. Schaff, *The Middle Ages*, part 2, pp. 170, 224, 225; Neander, *op. cit.*, vol. 5, p. 130. Cusa's works were published in Latin at Paris in 1514. A more complete edition is the *Opera* of Basel, 1565. Cusa's most important works were put into French and German, only a few into English.

[6] David S. Schaff, *The Middle Ages*, part 2, pp. 175, 224.

[7] M'Clintock and Strong, *op. cit.*, vol. 2, p. 611, art. "Cusa"; Schroeder, *op. cit.*, pp. 467-470.

[8] *Encyclopaedia Britannica*, vol. 6, p. 901, art. "Cusanus"; David S. Schaff, *The Middle Ages*, part 2, p. 225.

he was made bishop of Brixen, in the Tyrol, and traveled throughout the larger part of Germany, insisting on reforms of ecclesiastical abuses.[9] In 1451, pursuant to the purpose of effecting reforms, he prohibited all "bleeding Hosts." [10] He preached in the vernacular, and in Magdeburg secured the condemnation of the sale of indulgences for money. At Salzburg he effected reforms in the convents, and established a thirty-three-bed hospital at Cues,[11] to which he bequeathed his manuscript library and his scientific instruments.[12]

He protested against the despotism and covetousness of the church, predicting that it would sink still deeper, to the point of extinction, before rising triumphantly again.[13] Cusa was one of the first to break with Scholasticism, and revealed the influence of the ideas on faith that he received during his early schooling at Deventer.[14]

Though remaining a son of the church, Cusa definitely influenced Faber Stapulensis, who was himself a French forerunner of Luther on justification by faith.[15]

3. DENOUNCES SCHOLASTICISM; EXPOSES FORGED CONSTANTINE "DONATION."—Cusa, whom Döllinger denominates the most profound thinker of his time, denounced perverted Scholasticism in *De Docta Ignorantia* (On Learned Ignorance). He held that man's wisdom lies in recognizing his ignorance, and

---

[9] David S. Schaff, *The Middle Ages,* part 2, p. 225; R. Schmid, *op. cit., The New Schaff-Herzog,* vol. 3, p. 327; M'Clintock and Strong, *op. cit.,* vol. 2, pp. 611, 612, art. "Cusa"; John Fletcher Hurst, *History of the Christian Church,* vol. 2, p. 95.
[10] Gieseler, *op. cit.,* vol. 3, pp. 383, 384; Robertson, *op. cit.,* vol. 8, p. 375.
[11] David S. Schaff, *The Middle Ages,* part 2, p. 226.
[12] R. Schmid, *op. cit., The New Schaff-Herzog,* vol. 3, p. 327; J. G. Hagen, "Nicholas of Cusa," *The Catholic Encyclopedia,* vol. 11, p. 61.
[13] Döllinger, *Prophecies,* pp. 74, 75, citing Cusa's *De Concordantia Catholica.*
[14] The Brethren of the Common Life (or Common Lot), who flourished in the fourteenth and fifteenth centuries in the Netherlands and northwest Germany, were practical mystics akin in some ways to the later pietists. They were associated in voluntary groups without monastic vows or garb, although they renounced worldly goods and remained single, and supported themselves in common by their toil. They also preached in the vernacular, explained the Scriptures to small groups in private homes, copied manuscripts (and later employed printing), translated portions of the Bible and devotional books, and engaged in teaching. They broke away from Scholasticism and combined the crafts and Bible study with a general education given chiefly in the mother tongue. Their schools laid the foundation for the modern literature of those regions, and prepared the ground for the Reformation to come. The school at Deventer, one of the famous grammar schools in the history of education, trained Thomas à Kempis, Nicholas of Cusa, Wessel Gansfort, and Erasmus, who learned his Greek there. (See David S. Schaff, *The Middle Ages,* part 2, pp. 278-284; C. Ullman, *Reformers Before the Reformation,* vol. 2, pp. 57-184.)
[15] David S. Schaff, *The Middle Ages,* part 2, p. 225.

that escape from skepticism lies in sensing the reality of God.[16] Of liberal views and wide mental horizon, he facilitated the transition from Middle Age scholastic theology to the Renaissance. He was interested in the Jews, and sought to lead them to a recognition of the Trinity.

Cusa's *De Concordantia Catholica,* presented to the Basel assembly, was recognized as one of the ablest works of the Middle Ages. In it he favored the subservience of the pope to the council,[17] and insisted on reformation of the church. He and two other men (Reginald Pecock and Lorenzo Valla),[18] in the middle of the fifteenth century, proved on historical grounds that the Donation of Constantine was a forgery.[19] He made little use, however, of the discovery.

Christopher B. Coleman says:

"Nicholas Cusanus some seven years earlier [1433] in his De concordantia catholica covered part of the same ground even better than Valla did, and anticipated some of his arguments. But Valla's treatise is more exhaustive, is in more finished and effective literary form, and in effect established for the world generally the proof of the falsity of the Donation." [20]

4. Anticipated Features of Copernican Theory by a Century.—In the field of science Cusa presented to the Council of Basel in his *Reparatio Kalendarii* (Restoration of the Calendar), published 1436, a proposed correction of the Julian calendar similar in method to the one later adopted by Gregory XIII.[21] Moreover, Cusa anticipated Copernicus in part by nearly a hundred years in holding that the earth is not the center of the

[16] *Ibid.*
[17] M'Clintock and Strong, *op. cit.,* vol. 2, p. 611, art. "Cusa."
[18] Lorenzo Valla (d. 1457) was the initiator of historical criticism. In 1440, while in the employ of the king of Naples, who was then at odds with the pope, Lorenzo demonstrated the spurious character of the celebrated Donation of Constantine. Later, Nicholas V, a great scholar, summoned Valla to Rome as secretary to the papal court. Valla continued his exposure of historical frauds, correcting mistranslations, and stamping as worthless certain popular documents. (Ault, *op. cit.,* p. 680.) Pecock and Valla were regarded as heretical in various aspects of their writings, and barely escaped the stake—one through abjuration, and the other through the intercession of the king. (Robertson, *op. cit.,* vol. 8, pp. 138, 351, 352.)
[19] Döllinger, *Fables Respecting the Popes of the Middle Ages,* p. 174; David S. Schaff, *The Middle Ages,* part 2, p. 226.
[20] Christopher B. Coleman, *The Treatise of Lorenzo Valla on the Donation of Constantine,* Introduction, p. 3.
[21] *Encyclopaedia Britannica,* vol. 6, p. 901, art. "Cusanus."

universe, but is in motion, and that the heavenly bodies do not have strictly spherical form or circular orbits.[22] He was likewise conspicuous as a mathematician, stressing arithmetical and geometrical complements, the "quadrature of the circle," and so forth.[23] Schaff calls him the "most universal scholar of Germany." [24]

These were the intellectual attainments and the achievements of this scholar of the fifteenth century, who was influential in establishing the application of the year-day principle to the 2300 days.[25]

III. Setting and Circumstances of Application to 2300 Days

Cusa's works fill a large volume. The title page of the standard Latin edition (1565) of the *Opera* is in the usual eulogistic strain of the times. But it is of interest, as it discloses the publisher's evaluation. Translated, it reads:

"*The Works of Doctor Nicolas of Cusa, Cardinal, Doctor of Each Law, a Man Unequalled in Every Philosophy.*

"In which the very many mysteries of Theology, Unapproachable apart from the Spirit of God, already veiled and neglected for so many Centuries, are unveiled. Moreover there is no topic of ordinary Theology which is not handled.

"LIKEWISE

"Many Difficulties in Philosophy, especially in Mathematics, which, as being beyond the capacity of the human mind, absolutely no one has dared to approach before this author, are explained and demonstrated."

---

[22] *Ibid.;* David S. Schaff, *The Middle Ages,* part 2, p. 226; Hurst, *op. cit.,* vol. 2, p. 96; *The New International Encyclopaedia,* vol. 6, p. 379, art. "Cusa"; Hagen, *op. cit., The Catholic Encyclopedia,* vol. 11, p. 62.
[23] Mosheim, *op. cit.,* vol. 3, p. 41.
[24] David S. Schaff, *The Middle Ages,* part 2, p. 225.
[25] Indebtedness is here expressed to Dr. Raymond Klibansky, formerly of Heidelberg University and later lecturer on philosophy at the University of London, later of Oxford, authority on Cusa, writer of the article "Niccolo da Cusa," in *Enciclopedia Italiana,* co-editor with Ernst Hoffmann of Cusa's *Opera Omnia* (1932-), and cataloger and reconstructor of his library. From Dr. Klibansky, photostat copies were obtained of certain original Cusa manuscripts, in his own signed handwriting (Codex Cusanus 220), and a portion of an important sermon preached in 1440—"Paulus apostolus ad Galathas scribens." Also, secured from the same source, is a page from Cusa's theory of planetary motion, antedating the position of Copernicus, and illustrated by a diagram—similarly in Cusa's handwriting. Perhaps most significant of all is a page from an old manuscript containing Villanova's *Introductio in librum de semine scripturarum* (Codex Cusanus 42, fol. 194-201). Obviously Cusa had acquaintance with Joachimism, and more specifically, with this commentary on pseudo-Joachim which pioneered in applying the year-day prophetic time measure to the 2300 days.

But the *Coniectura Domini Nicolai de Cusa, de Novissimis Diebus* [26] (Conjecture Concerning the Last Days), though only a few pages in length, has aroused exceptional interest.

1. GLIMPSES OF FUTURE REVEALED THROUGH PROPHECY.—An epitome of the opening paragraphs must suffice. Cusa first declares that the whole world depends upon the will of Almighty God; that the present belongs to us, but the future is known only to Him; that it is not for us to define what belongs only to God; and that we are not to seek a knowledge of the future simply from curiosity. Nearly all, he says, who up to now have written on the calculation of times have been deceived by some erroneous conjecture. Nevertheless, it is our privilege to know something of the future. Yet he does not think it reprehensible to investigate the Scriptures with a spirit of meekness, to conjecture the future and thereby be strengthened and encouraged in our pilgrimage. It is our duty to seek the truth, although it is not possible to know the whole truth, for it is veiled in enigmatic figures.

2. JUBILEES OF CHURCH LIKE YEARS OF CHRIST'S LIFE.—As Christ is the source of knowledge concerning the future, it is therefore necessary to go back to Christ and His life—the church being the mystical body of Christ, which He left as His seed, and also His bride. After His work upon earth Christ ascended to heaven, and the church must ultimately follow Him there. As Eve was Adam's bride, so the church is Christ's bride, and must finally be united with Him in heaven, perfected by her wanderings through the earth. Cusa then presents the conjecture that out of the earthly life of Christ truth is to be read concerning the future of the church. Christ was Lord of the Sabbath, in whom we may find the key of the jubilee years—the Sabbath in which time will find its rest. Wrote Cusa:

"All time is unrolled in periods of seven, as seven days, seven years, seven times seven years, which are forty-nine. Hence the fiftieth year is

---

[26] Originally written in 1452, it appears in the Latin editions of Cusa's works of 1514 and 1565, also in separate French translations of 1562, 1597, and 1700, and the German editions of 1745 and 1862. The original autograph copy is in the Cusa Library.

after a wearisome revolution of time, a sabbathkeeping in which all slavery ceases and returns to liberty." [27]

As fifty years of the church comprise a jubilee, so one year of our Lord's life may represent a jubilee period. Because Christ is the Sun of Righteousness, and the church is the follower of Him, so one "solar revolution" or year, so to speak, in the life of our Lord, may correspond to "one revolution in the journeying of the church." Thus "more than fifty jubilees lead to the resurrection of the church." Such was Cusa's "Conjecture" as he calls it. In 1452, when he wrote it, he states that there were already twenty-nine jubilees in the past. (So, on the basis of this speculation, the end would come about 2502.)

3. LAST-TIME ELIJAH PREACHERS PARALLEL JOHN THE BAPTIST.—Cusa suggests that as John the Baptist prepared the way for Christ's first advent, so likewise men in the last days, arising in the spirit of Elijah, would prepare the way for the last things. Cusa's words are impressive:

"Moreover there was then John the Baptist baptizing in the wilderness and washing by his teaching the filthiness of sinners, that he might prepare for the Lord a perfect people. For in the same spirit of Elijah, in which he [John] himself bore testimony to the light of truth, namely to Christ, we believe that next there ought to rise up disciples of the same spirit, and in them themselves Elijah will manifest himself in their teaching, who with his finger points out to the world Christ and the truth of life and righteousness. And they will wash the body of Christ, namely, the church, so that the spirit of God may descend upon it just as visibly as it descended above Christ in the form of dove-like simplicity." [28]

4. PERSECUTION BY ANTICHRIST FOLLOWS WORLD-WIDE EVANGEL.—Cusa then speaks of the persecution of the church, incited by the spirit of Antichrist, almost destroying the church, and separating the church from the world. He adds:

"Also the spirit of the firmness of Elijah will endure persecution among the foremost preachers themselves, as in the case of John, because the allurement of the harlot of this world, which was the cause of the death of John, will not suffer them to live. But the number of the faithful will

---

[27] Translated from *Coniectura*, in *Opera*, p. 933.   [28] *Ibid.*

be steadily increased, and will be successively enlarged by the light of the doctrine until the fortieth jubilee. And there will be made in the very signs and prodigies explanations of the life of Christ, handed down in the Gospels. And there will not be a dwelling in the world without the knowledge of Christ and of the faith. After this the satanic spirit of Antichrist will stir up persecution against the body of Christ which is the church, and there will be a final tribulation, than which there has never been another greater, which is explanatory of the story of the passion of Christ. And the church itself will seem to be extinguished, because of the holy apostles, the sowers of the word of God, will forsake them and flee. Neither will there remain a successor of Peter or of any apostle; all will undergo temptation." [29]

But the church will rise again, and "the infidel Antichrists, seeing that the church has prevailed and that they are conquered, will submit to Christ as the victor, and all nations will return to him, so that the inheritance of Christ in the whole world will be one fold of one Shepherd." Then comes this curiously interesting expression that is worth pondering:

"And Peter will weep bitterly, because he fled, and so the rest of the apostles, namely, the bishops and priests of the church, and place for repentance will be given them. And the glorious church turns by a glorious resurrection from the oppression of Antichrist, a show to all doubters, so that all who have been in doubt concerning the truth of the life which is in Christ, the bridegroom of the church, become witnesses of the glorious resurrection." [30]

5. AFTER JUDGMENT, BRIDE TO REIGN IN ETERNAL GLORY.— Finally will come "eternal peace," with the church-bride in glory reigning with Christ. But that hour is not yet. So Cusa continues:

"But not yet is the end at hand, in order that the bride may be restored from every wrinkle and spot, worthy of the Bridegroom, who is the Lamb without spot. And then He will come to judge the living and the dead, and the world by fire. And He will receive His bride in glory, to reign eternally with himself. Anyone will be able from the delineations of the evangelists to explain these conclusions more particularly, and hence it is enough now concerning this." [31]

6. SECOND ADVENT IN 34TH JUBILEE, POSSIBLY BY 1734.— On the basis of this analogy of the history of the church with the

---

[29] Ibid.   [30] Ibid.   [31] Ibid., p. 934.

symbolic years of Christ's life—and with the final events of Christ's life likewise paralleled in the life of the church—Cusa applies his theory of the thirty-fourth jubilee as perhaps falling between 1700 and 1734. He stresses, however, that no one knows the exactness of the time:

"As the Christian considers this alone, apart from rash judgment, what is involved in those things which Christ did, and which were done concerning Christ, after the twenty-ninth year, even to the day of his resurrection from death, one year of the Lord, by extending into a jubilee, anyone will be able in a very similar way to forsee what will happen in the church; so that thus in the thirty-fourth jubilee from the resurrection of Christ, Antichrist having been cast down, by the justice of God he will look for the victorious and glorious resurrection of the church. And this will be after the year 1700 of our Lord's birth, and before the year 1734. Moreover after that time will be the ascension of the church, Christ the bridegroom coming to judgment, but when He will come no one will know. For that advent will be unknown beforehand to all, as to the exactness of the time; just as his [first] advent into the world was unknown to all as to the exactness of its time. Then the saints who know, that He will come and will not tarry, will pray that the Desire of all nations may come." [32]

Then, all enemies having been put under the Lord's footstool, and with all the earth as His possession, the faithful will say, "Come, Lord," knowing that "the day of redemption draws near, which will come without a sign as a thief in the night; just as the flood came, so Christ discloses what the future will be." [33]

7. GRIEVOUS OPPRESSION OF CHURCH PREDICTED BY DANIEL. —After asserting the presence of Christ with the church "even to the consummation of the ages," Cusa then turns to the bearing of Daniel's prophecy, noted by Christ in these words:

"He [Christ] predicted that before its [the Church's] glorious resurrection there would come in the last days an oppression of the church than which there has been none greater, as in the last days of his flesh it was done with him. And so he turned our attention to two things, namely to the similitude of the flood, and to the saying of Daniel the prophet." [34]

8. 2300 YEARS FROM DANIEL'S VISION TO END BY 1750.— Extending his conjectures based on speculative jubilee periods

---

[32] *Ibid.*   [33] *Ibid.*   [34] *Ibid.*

CUSA APPLIES YEAR-DAY PRINCIPLE TO 2300 DAYS

Pages From Cusa's Manuscript Copy of a Pseudo-Joachim Book (Upper Left and Right); Cusa Manuscript With Signature at Upper Right (Lower Left); Likeness of Cusa Made Within Year of Death (Insert); Title Page of Printed Collection of Cusa's Writings (Lower Right); Remarkable Treatise Containing His Calculations on the 2300 Year-Days (Insert)

paralleling the thirty-four years of Christ's life, and citing Philo on the flood of water coming in the thirty-fourth jubilee after the first Adam, Cusa conjectures the end of sin about 34 jubilees after Christ, and 2300 years from Daniel:

"So we conjecture that in the 34th jubilee after the second Adam will come the consuming of sin through the fire of the Holy Spirit. In the same way it was opened up to Daniel in what way the last curse would be after the sanctuary shall be cleansed and the vision fulfilled; and this after 2300 days from the hour of the going forth of the word. Whence in the third year of king Belshazzar this revelation was made to him, in the first year of Cyrus the king who, according to Jerome, Africanus, and Josephus, lived about 559 years before Christ, then it is established that the resurrection of the church according to the predicted number by resolving a day into a year, according to the unfolding made to the prophet Ezekiel, [will be] 1700 after Christ and before 1750; which agrees with what had been set forth." [35]

Cusa dated it from the time when he understood the prophecy to have been given—in the last year of Babylon or the first year of Persia—which he believed to be about 559 B.C. Cusa looked for the "sanctuary," which he understood to be the church, to be cleansed from error 2300 years after this time. Moreover, it is desirable to note that this view advanced by Cusa was consistently held by him over a period of years. There is no available evidence to indicate precisely when he reached that conclusion. It is first recorded in a sermon preached in 1440—a full decade before Cusa became a cardinal in 1450. It was put into formal or permanent form in 1452 in his *Coniectura,* appearing afterward in his *Opera.* And there is no record or suggestion of any repudiation or change of view in the twelve years remaining before his death in 1464, at the age of sixty-three. So the interpretation introduced was deliberate, consistent, and mature. Here is a sentence from that 1440 sermon, showing the year-day application and the beginning date, 559 B.C.:

"In like manner, he exactly agrees with Daniel, who held that the 2300 days—a day for a year—from the going forth of the word, are future, and [that] was 559 years before Christ." [36]

---

[35] *Ibid.*

[36] Translated from "Paulus Apostolus ad Galathas Scribens," Predigt 3, fol. 10v., secured through Dr. Klibansky, from Cusa's manuscript library.

9. Says Dating Derived Independently.—Cusa closes his treatise by referring to the recognized periods from Adam to the Flood, from the Flood to Moses, Moses to Christ, and Christ to the end—the last beginning with the resurrection of Christ, and frequently called the "end of the ages." Cusa adds that there are different chronologies (Hebrew and Septuagint) and different interpretations of Daniel, over which "many have wearied themselves"—each having his opinion, and none agreeing with the other in the exposition of the prophetic "times." But concerning the uniqueness of the exposition he has here propounded on the 2300 days, Cusa adds: "I have carefully followed the writings of these persons, and I have found nothing in them concerning the consideration advanced." [37] The "writings of these persons" that he read must have included the prior exposition advanced by Arnold of Villanova.

10. Little Application of the Beast Symbols Recorded. —So far as we know, Cusa did not apply the beast symbols of Daniel and John to the Papacy, and his only prophetic symbol reference of which we have record concerns the first beast of Revelation 13—which comes up out of the sea—with his number 666. With others, Cusa thought this might apply to Mohammed and his work, as it came into prominence about A.D. 666.[38] Cusa lived to see the conquests of the Turks and the fall of Constantinople in 1453, happenings which doubtless revived this old Catholic position in his mind.

The fall of Constantinople, which caused a large number of Greek scholars to take refuge in Italy, together with the newly discovered art of printing, helped to stimulate the revival of letters and art called the Renaissance. During the same time,

---

[37] *Coniectura*, in *Opera*, p. 935. Cusa here announces that his conclusions on the chronology of the various ages of the world, and on the interpretations of Daniel, are his own, but he does not specifically claim originality for his application of the year-day principle to the 2300 days. It is entirely possible that he arrived at this idea independently, although he was familiar with the literature of medieval theology, and he begins the period from the third year of Belshazzar, like Villanova, and like him cites Ezekiel on the principle of a day for a year. He might have been influenced by Villanova's *Introductio*. (See note 25.) Yet his year-day scheme could have been an independent extension of Joachim's use of it in the 1260 days. Although he was not profoundly influenced by Joachim, it is reasonable to suppose that he was acquainted with his exposition of the 1260 days. (Raymond Klibansky, letter to the author, Oct. 17, 1938.)
[38] *Excitationum*, in *Opera*, p. 560; David S. Schaff, *The Middle Ages*, part 2, pp. 225, 226.

however, the papal chair sank to new depths of iniquity. And Cusa, after sensing the failure of all reform councils, and fathoming the despotism and covetousness of the Papacy as the cause of the corruption, foresaw its still deeper degradation.[39]

But although Cusa refuted a number of errors in the Catholic Church and longed sincerely for a reform, he was one of the most prominent cardinals of his time and became, near the end of his life, the vicar general of the papal states.

Yet in the wide scope of his universal spirit he longed and worked for a union of all religions, in order that religious wars and persecution might cease. He expressed these thoughts in his *De Pace seu Concordantia Fidei* (On Peace or the Harmony of Faith): "Thou, O Lord and King of the universe, Thou art sought under different forms in different religions. Thou art called by different names, because in Thy real being Thou art unknown and incomprehensible."[40]

IV. Printing Press Spells Doom of Papal Control

1. PRINTING PRESS BRINGS REVIVAL OF ANCIENT LITERATURE. —Under the Renaissance, dormant intellectual forces awakened from their long slumber. Universities, raised up in the twelfth and thirteenth centuries—at Oxford, Cambridge, Paris, Montpellier, Bologna, Padua, Salamanca, and Prague—were thronged with students. Mankind entered a new era of study and investigation. Many libraries were founded. And, marching hand in hand with this revival of learning, came the invention of printing.[41]

Printing brought a revival of ancient literature, secular and sacred. Preceding and following the fall of Constantinople, Greek scholars, with their manuscript books and learning, fled westward, seeking refuge from the Turkish woe. Not only did dead languages become the object of revived study, but the Scriptures in the originals began to be consulted again. The diffused

---

[39] See his expression of this, already quoted on page 132. See also Döllinger, *Prophecies*, pp. 74, 75, citing *De Concordantia Catholica*.
[40] Translated from F. A. von Scharpff, *Der Cardinal und Bischof Nicolaus von Cusa als Reformator in Kirche, Reich und Philosophie*, p. 245.
[41] Trench, *op. cit.*, p. 434.

light that resulted could no longer be hidden under a bushel. Therefore the printing press became one of the most powerful instruments not only in popularizing the Renaissance but in merging it into the coming Reformation. It contributed materially to the regeneration of Christendom.

2. Prohibitive Costs of Manuscript Books Restricted Circulation.—The coming of the printing press in the fifteenth century, with its amazing power of multiplication—and consequently reduced costs—wrought a miracle in Europe. It flooded the Continent with thousands of important but hitherto rare and virtually inaccessible books. This relative scarcity of books and their consequent inaccessibility, arose from the cost of transcribing and materials—for example, of parchment as against modern book paper. Labor, however, was a heavy factor. It is difficult today to realize the vast toil involved in laboriously copying an entire volume by hand.

Think, for instance, of the sheer labor of reproducing the entire Bible in this way—a year's task for an industrious scribe. That is one reason why complete copies of the Bible were not common before the days of printing, but only portions of books. These rare volumes were lettered with great care, and illuminated and embellished with incredible industry, until they were treasures of costly beauty. Private individuals seldom possessed such books because of the prohibitive cost, these being reserved for churches, monasteries, and universities.

Another cost factor was the necessity of individual verification. Now, when one copy of an edition has been scrutinized in the modern multiplication of printed books, the entire edition has been seen in facsimile. But in ages past, every manuscript copy had its own individuality, and the correctness of one manuscript was no pledge of the accuracy of other copies. The individual correctness could only be established by minute and laborious comparison—likewise a wearisome, time-consuming, and costly process. The value was therefore determined by the reliability of the scribe. No wonder a complete Bible would sometimes cost "two hundred sheep, five quarters

[30 sacks] of wheat, and the same quantity of rye and millet." [42]

That is not alone why the common folk seldom possessed such books, but was the chief reason for the chaining of books— not simply Bibles—in the Middle Ages. The very costliness, and the danger of mutilation or loss, often made access difficult and involved. When books were borrowed, a heavy pledge deposit was required—a thousand pounds, for example, for some from the Bodleian Library, Oxford. [43] And books could not always be obtained even on such terms.

3. DOOMS PAPAL CONTROL OVER MEN'S MINDS.—The pitiless light of learning, which printing multiplied and popularized a thousandfold, was turned upon the abuses and corruptions of the church. Among other things, it brought men into intimate acquaintance with early church history and writers. It revealed those centuries that were without the papal edifice of later times, as well as exposing the changes and perversions that had then been introduced. And now it provided an adequate vehicle for that swelling chorus of remonstrance against ecclesiastical abuses, affording facility of communication. It was easy now to expose forgeries like the false decretals. All this caused discontent with the medieval church, for it made the Bible an open book, explained the past, diffused contemporary knowledge, and enabled public opinion to form and be expressed. [44]

Thus the invention of printing doomed the exclusive control of the Papacy over the minds of men. The rough-appearing book or tract, with ill-cut type and crude illustration, was none the less potent in awakening the minds of men. No longer could priests and scholars monopolize knowledge. The intellectual awakening passed from the scholar downward to the common man, until the whole intellectual life of Europe was revolutionized. [45]

4. VERNACULAR BIBLES HIGH IN RISING TIDE OF BOOKS.— Many German cities became centers of the new industry, with

---

[42] S. R. Maitland, *The Dark Ages*, p. 61.   [43] *Ibid.*, p. 68.
[44] Flick, *op. cit.*, vol. 2, pp. 480, 481.   [45] *Ibid.*, p. 219.

thousands of artisans in the printing field. From Mainz, the noble art was carried to other countries. By 1500 there were printing establishments in 220 places;[46] cloisters and universities, such as the Sorbonne, had their own, and friars changed from scribes to printers. Wood cuts were used to interest the masses.[47] It is estimated that 8,000,000 volumes had been printed and circulated by 1500.

Significantly enough, the first printed book of any size was the Bible, in 1456, followed by the earliest dated book—the famous Mainz Psalter—and the first dated Bible in 1462.[48] In fact, the press was definitely enlisted for the production of vernacular translations of the Scriptures, many of these finding their way into the hands of those suspected of unorthodoxy.[49]

Various editions of the Bible began to come forth—in German (1466), Italian (1471), Dutch (1477), French (1487), and Bohemian (1488). The Jews produced a complete edition of the Old Testament at Soncino in 1488. The *Complutensian Polyglot* was produced in 1514—containing the Old Testament in Hebrew, with the Chaldee paraphrase of the Pentateuch, the Septuagint Old Testament, the Greek New Testament, and the Latin Vulgate.[50] By 1500 there were ninety-eight full editions of the Latin Vulgate,[51] and by 1535 the Waldenses had availed themselves of the press for the production of the French Bible.

5. Censorship Control Sought Over New Invention.—It did not take the Papacy long to scent the potential trouble that printing had introduced. Censorship and an Index of Prohibited Books helped to counteract its perils, but much escaped, or defied, the most vigilant control. This began when Sixtus IV, as early as 1479, empowered the University of Cologne to proceed with censures against printers, purchasers, and readers of heretical books. In 1486 the archbishop of Mainz—where the Gutenberg Bible was produced—endeavored to establish a

46 *The Encyclopedia Americana*, vol. 22, pp. 588, 589, art. "Printing."
47 Flick, *op. cit.*, vol. 2, pp. 252, 253.   48 *Ibid.*, pp. 479, 480.
49 Robertson, *op. cit.*, vol. 8, p. 388.   50 *Ibid.*, pp. 386, 387.
51 Flick, *op. cit.*, vol. 2, p. 479.

crude censorship against translations of the Bible into the vernacular. And Alexander VI took a more comprehensive step in 1501, when he declared that no book should be printed without preliminary examination and license, and existing books be inspected. In 1502 censorship was established in Spain.[52]

By the time of the Fifth Lateran Council (1512-1517), a decree by Pope Leo X was adopted (in session 10) calling for a board of censors for all books, the board consisting of the bishop of each diocese, and the local Inquisitor.[53] In order to check the dissemination of heretical ideas, no printing was lawful without previous censorship and sanction by the pope's Inquisitor of the district and the bishop, or the pope.[54] Thus the battle lines were drawn for the impending Reformation conflict, as Rome sought to extend her repressive control over this new instrument of enlightenment and exposure that was destined to be so potent in the hands of the Reformers.

---

[52] *Ibid.*, pp. 480, 481; Robertson, *op. cit.*, vol. 8, pp. 388, 389.
[53] George Haven Putnam, *The Censorship of the Church of Rome*, vol. 1, pp. 108, 109; Flick, *op. cit.*, vol. 2, p. 481.
[54] David S. Schaff, *The Middle Ages*, part 2, p. 487; Schroeder, *op. cit.*, pp. 484, 504, 505; Mansi, *op. cit.*, vol. 32, cols. 912, 913.

CHAPTER SIX

Death for Applying "Babylon"

to Papacy

Many religious leaders in the latter part of the fifteenth century were moved to protest the papal evils, and some even paid the supreme penalty for their temerity. Most conspicuous among those thus to die was Savonarola.

I. Savonarola Burned for Interpretation of Apocalypse

GIROLAMO SAVONAROLA (1452-1498), most imposing preacher of the century, and moral and religious reformer, was regarded by Luther as a precursor of the Reformation.[1] Born of the nobility at Ferrara, Italy, he was reared in honor and wealth, receiving every educational advantage. His parents desired him to study medicine, but a deepening sense of the corruption of church and state led him to leave home secretly for Bologna, where he became a Dominican monk in 1475. Lecturing for a brief time on physics and philosophy, he turned to the study of Holy Scripture in the Hebrew and Greek. Fifteen years of usual monastic life and laborious study followed. His first attempts to preach proved a failure, but he persevered until he became the greatest spiritual force in Italy since Joachim of Floris, nearly three centuries prior.

1. EXPOUNDS APOCALYPSE TO IMMENSE AUDIENCES.—While still in his novitiate, Savonarola wrote burning poems against

---

[1] Philip Schaff (revised by David S. Schaff), "Savonarola," *The New Schaff-Herzog*, vol. 10, p. 217.

the corruptions of the church, and pointed to the impending judgments of God. In 1481 he moved to Florence, which was wracked with political factions, and soon became professor, or "reader," of Holy Scripture at the Convent of San Marco (St. Mark's).[2] By 1483 he began to preach on prophecy, and in 1486 launched into the soul-stirring scenes of the Apocalypse. In this year he preached a bold sermon that shook men's souls by his portrayal of the wrath to come, and moved them to tears by the tender pathos of his pleadings to seek God's mercy. He aspired to reform the church, and was a fearless preacher of righteousness. He contended that a revival *must* come without further delay, otherwise one would be led to believe that God had irrevocably rejected the Bride, as He rejected the Synagogue of old, a conclusion that was untenable for a Catholic.[3] From 1490 onward, throngs came to hear him. In 1491 he was chosen prior of the Convent of St. Mark. As the head of its theological school he effected important reforms.

Savonarola preached first at St. Mark's church, connected with the convent, and then in the Duomo, or Cathedral (Santa Maria del Fiore). Immense audiences came to hear him expound the book of Revelation[4]—throngs numbering into the thousands waited for hours to hear the Word. Few of these sermons have been preserved, however. His preaching was likened to "flashes of lightning and reverberations of thunder." It was pictorial, eruptive, and startling, as he laid the ax at the root of sin. He won the hearts of his auditors, who often wept aloud with him. His messages were addressed to the clergy, as well as the laity—though so many of the latter attended there was scarcely room for the monks.[5] He declared:

"See, how in these days prelates and preachers are chained to the earth by love of earthly things; the cure of souls is no longer their concern; they are content with the receipt of revenue; the preachers preach for the

---

[2] Herbert Lucas, *Fra Girolamo Savonarola*, p. 12.
[3] Döllinger, *Prophecies*, p. 162.
[4] David S. Schaff, *The Middle Ages*, part 2, pp. 686, 687.
[5] *Ibid.*; Pasquale Villari, *Life and Times of Girolamo Savonarola*, pp. 90, 91; see also Georg Rapp, Introduction to *Die erwecklichen Schriften des Märtyrers Hieronymus Savonarola* (The Devotional Works of the Martyr Girolamo Savonarola), p. xvii.

pleasure of princes, to be praised and magnified by them. . . . And they have done even worse than this, inasmuch as they have not only destroyed the Church of God, but built up another after their own fashion. This is the new Church, no longer built of living rock, namely, of Christians steadfast in the living faith and in the mould of charity; but built of sticks, namely, of Christians dry as tinder for the fires of hell. . . . Go thou to Rome and throughout Christendom; in the mansions of the great prelates and great lords, there is no concern save for poetry and the oratorical art. Go thither and see, thou shalt find them all with books of the humanities in their hands, and telling one another that they can guide men's souls by means of Virgil, Horace, and Cicero. . . . In the primitive Church the chalices were of wood, the prelates of gold; in these days the Church hath chalices of gold and prelates of wood." [6]

Savonarola preached reformation and repentance ere the tempest of divine vengeance, already impending over Italy, should descend and overwhelm it,[7] and multitudes renounced the follies of the world. He was the unofficial leader of Florence, inspiring the populace to form a republic and establish an extreme form of theocracy. People read the Bible and Savonarola. Ill-gotten gains were returned, hymns took the place of ribald songs. Women cast aside their jewels and finery. He won the young people especially to his reforms. A club, or band, was formed to collect pernicious books and voluptuous articles of luxury, which they solicited from the populace and burned publicly in 1497.[8]

2. TOOK SCRIPTURES AS SOLE GUIDE AND AUTHORITY.—The wisdom of Greece was preached from the pulpits of Rome, whereas Savonarola based his preaching on the Bible. Although he used rather extreme allegorical interpretations, he made the exposition of Scripture his main theme.[9] He insisted on "taking the Scriptures as my sole guide," [10] committing great portions to memory. "People of Florence," he admonished, "give yourselves to Bible study." He often invited men to challenge him if they

---

[6] Villari, op. cit., pp. 182-184, citing Sermon XXIII.
[7] George Waddington, A History of the Church, p. 715.
[8] Villari, op. cit., p. 343; Rapp, op. cit., p. xviii.
[9] Lucas, op. cit., p. 28.
[10] David S. Schaff, The Middle Ages, part 2, p. 689; Rapp, op. cit., p. xiv; Villari, op. cit., p. 117.

found him preaching anything contrary thereto.[11] In fact, the only book he read during the last eight years of his life was the Bible, which gave him the blessed assurance of being justified and accepted by grace,[12] a truth he desired to proclaim to his fellow men—not merits of our own; only those inwrought by the Holy Spirit. And the love manifested on the cross was the basis upon which Savonarola built his message. Lorenzo de Medici tried to silence him with gifts in the convent's offering box, but to no avail.[13]

3. PROCLAIMED DIRE WOES TO COME.—In 1492 he began his "prophetic testimony," as he predicted what his soul longed for—an approaching theocracy under the Lord Jesus, in place of a corrupt ecclesiastical government. It was more or less generally believed that he had the gift of prophecy.[14] His vision of the sword called forth his declaration, "Behold the sword of the Lord will descend quickly and suddenly upon the earth." [15] Savonarola saw what appeared to be a black cross in the midst of Rome, with its head touching heaven and its arms stretched forth over the earth. This scene was accompanied by destruction. After this he saw another cross, similar to the first, but of gold, lifted up over Jerusalem, so resplendent that it illuminated the world. Likewise in 1492, after the election of Roderigo Borgia to the Papacy as Alexander VI, Savonarola said he saw a hand in heaven with a sword, and a succession of dire declarations of doom were written in the heavens.[16]

The French army of Charles VIII entered Italy in 1494, sacking and massacring. Savonarola, who had foretold the invasion, induced Charles to be lenient with Florence. The city banished the Medicis, and reorganized under Savonarola's influence, as a theocracy.[17] In February, 1496, preaching in the Duomo from Amos and Zechariah, he denounced the shameless

[11] Foxe, Acts, vol. 1, p. 830.   [12] Rapp, op. cit., p. xiv.   [13] Villari, op. cit., p. 130.
[14] Döllinger, Prophecies, pp. 159-161; Villari, op. cit., p. 154, citing Savonarola's Compendium Revelationum.
[15] Philip Schaff, "Savonarola," The New Schaff-Herzog, vol. 10, p. 214.
[16] Gardner, Story of Florence, pp. 113-115.
[17] David S. Schaff, The Middle Ages, part 2, pp. 695-697.

corruption of Pope Alexander and his court, which had made
Rome the sink of Christendom. Here in the presence of his
vastest audience he uttered his most terrible declaration: Catastrophe was to come upon Rome; she was to be banded with
steel, put to the sword, and consumed with fire. Italy was to be
ravaged with pestilence and famine. Let men fly from corrupted
Rome, the Babylon of confusion, he urged, and come to repentance. The echoes reverberated throughout Europe. In May a
new course of sermons on Ruth and Micah was no less severe.
Fear of excommunication did not deter Savonarola's denunciations. If the pope gave commands contrary to Christian charity,
he was not an instrument of the Lord but a broken tool.

4. ANATHEMATIZED AND CONDEMNED AFTER REJECTING
PAPAL AUTHORITY.—In the latter part of his career Savonarola
was pitted against Pope Alexander VI, whose intrigue, bribery,
extortion, simony, immorality, and judicial murder wrote probably the blackest page in the papal record; and who determined
to silence Savonarola by diplomacy, bribery, or force. The offer
of a cardinal's red hat in return for a change in the content of
his preaching was indignantly spurned, as Savonarola declared,
"I want no hat, nor mitre, great or small: I wish for nothing
more than that which has been given to thy saints—death;—
a red hat, a hat of blood." [18] This gave him proof of Rome's
unholy traffic in holy things.

In July, 1495, he received a papal summons to Rome, which
he courteously declined on the grounds of ill-health and dangers
en route. In October he was forbidden to preach in public or
private. He ceased preaching to avoid arousing scandal in the
church, although he knew the reasons were political and personal. In February he re-entered the pulpit, possibly following
the offer of the hat, and more vigorously denounced the corruptions of the Papacy. So, refusing to submit to papal authority, he
was excommunicated in May, 1497.[19] But Savonarola publicly

---

    18 Villari, op. cit., pp. 400, 401.
    19 David S. Schaff, The Middle Ages, part 2, pp. 697-701; Villari, op. cit., pp. 376, 389,
400-402, 540-544.

declared that Alexander's unjust sentence, which he regarded as invalid, was not binding upon him. He held his peace until the end of the year. On Christmas Day, and on into 1498, Savonarola thundered again from the pulpit of the Duomo and from the Piazza of San Marco. There were hints of a future general council, held to be superior to the pope. The pope threatened an interdict, which would ruin Florence. Savonarola must be forbidden to preach. Yet he preached to greater crowds than ever, and became more intense in his arraignments of the Papacy.[20]

His enemies took counsel against him; he was cited before the city council and declared guilty of heresy. A conspiracy was framed against him, his enemies charging that the reason for his coming forward in Florence as a reformer was to make himself the *Papa Angelicus*. His popular support cooled, reaction set in, and he clearly foresaw his fate. In March, 1498, he declared:

"Rome will not quench this fire, and if this were quenched, God would kindle another, and it is already kindled everywhere, only they do not know it."[21]

5. DEGRADED, HANGED, AND BURNED.—At last the government of Florence forbade Savonarola to preach. His last sermon was delivered on March 18. It was a tense, moving appeal—a solemn warning to Rome. Then, in the silence of his cell, Savonarola prepared his last move. He would appeal to the princes of Christendom to summon a general council to depose the simoniacal usurper, who was no true pope. But the letters were never sent. A preliminary message to each court was forwarded. The dispatch to France was intercepted, and sent to Cardinal Ascanio Sforza in Rome. Soon after, the famous ordeal by fire was demanded by the Franciscans to prove the truth of his doctrines. When this failed to be carried out, the populace turned against him and raged in the streets. The convent was attacked; he surrendered to his enemies, and was imprisoned with two companions in the dark inquisitional prison. The

[20] *Ibid.*, pp. 702, 703; Villari, *op. cit.*, pp. 599, 613-615.
[21] Döllinger, *Prophecies*, pp. 149, 163.

SAVONAROLA MARTYRED FOR IDENTIFYING ANTICHRIST

Interior of St. Mark's Church at Florence, Where Savonarola Was Preacher (Upper Left); Savonarola's Cell in St. Mark's Convent, With His Desk, Chair, and Books, Where He Wrote His Indictments of Papal Corruption (Upper Right); Exterior of Florence Cathedral, Where He Also Preached Occasionally (Center Left); Well-known Profile of Savonarola by Fra Bartolommeo (Center Right); Historic Painting of the Burning of Savonarola at Florence (Lower)

tribunal was composed of his bitterest foes, and he was tortured to secure confession.[22] Savonarola declared under torture that he had preached, not for ecclesiastical preferments, but to bring about a general council for the purifying of the clergy.[23] He was sentenced to be hanged and then burned as a heretic. In a cell he spent his last weeks setting forth his positions through a commentary on the Psalms.[24]

According to Foxe, fourteen articles were gathered out of Savonarola's writings, the first nine of which, in summary, were as follows: (1) Free justification by faith in Christ; (2) communion in both kinds; (3) papal pardons and indulgences of no effect; (4) preaching against the wicked lives of cardinals; (5) denial of pope's supremacy; (6) keys not given to Peter but to universal church; (7) pope is Antichrist; (8) pope's excommunication invalid; and (9) auricular confession not necessary. These were read to Savonarola and his companions, and their recantation demanded. But they steadfastly maintained their position.[25] Such, according to Foxe, was the platform on which Savonarola stood.

The sentence was executed on May 23 in the square in front of the old palace. Savonarola was stripped of his robes, and stood barefoot and with hands bound, as the bishop of Vasona pronounced deposition from the priesthood upon him. The death sentence was declared upon Savonarola and two companions, Domenico and Silvestro, as the bishop made the pronouncement: "I separate thee from the Church militant and the Church triumphant." "Not from the church triumphant," replied Savonarola, "that is not thine to do." [26]

With his two companions preceding him, Savonarola was first hanged on the gallows, and then burned. As the smoke was whisked away, through the flames could be seen the erect figure of Savonarola, who had been placed in the center, between his

[22] David S. Schaff, The Middle Ages, part 2, pp. 703-709; Villari, op. cit., pp. 638-778.
[23] Francesco Guicciardini, The History of Italy, vol. 2, p. 202.
[24] David S. Schaff, The Middle Ages, part 2, p. 710; Villari, op. cit., pp. 734-736.
[25] Foxe, Acts, vol. 1, pp. 830, 831.
[26] David S. Schaff, The Middle Ages, part 2, p. 711; Villari, op. cit., p. 756.

two disciples. A shower of stones fell on the half-consumed bodies.[27] Savonarola had delivered his message, and he died as a witness to truth. His ashes were cast into the near-by river Arno.[28]

Only a few years later Raphael painted the portrait of this "flaming religious luminary," [29] now strangely among the revered doctors of the church. And the bronze plaque, placed in the square at Florence in 1901, reads, "By Unrighteous Sentence." Savonarola's martyrdom convinced Luther that it was useless to hope for the reform of Rome.[30]

II. Fragmentary Glimpses Reveal Positions on Prophecies

Savonarola's views on prophecy were set forth in his sermons, and in his *Compendium Revelationum*[31] (Manual of Revelations), in 1495, and *Dialogo della verità profetica* (Dialogue Concerning Prophetic Truth), in 1497,[32] the latter, together with fifteen of his sermons, being placed on the Index.[33] It is to be remembered that Savonarola's burden was not primarily doctrinal reform. These were still the hazy hours of dawn, before the full noontide implications were yet clearly perceived. Nevertheless, it was Savonarola's interpretation of the Apocalypse that started him on the road to incurring the displeasure of Rome.

1. Four Horsemen—From Apostolic to Contemporary Times.—Savonarola's sermon on *The Renewal of the Church*, given in the Cathedral of Florence, January 13, 1495, declared

---

27 Villari, *op. cit.*, pp. 758-760.
28 What emotions sweep over the soul as one stands in the very church and cathedral where Savonarola thundered against ecclesiastical apostasy, and came into open conflict with Rome! These old buildings stand virtually unchanged, as in his day. In the Duomo, or Cathedral, the old pulpit, formerly attached to the second pillar, has been removed, though the marks are still there. By the side of St. Mark's is the convent of which Savonarola had charge. The rows of cells, each with a tiny, solitary window, are all alike—and Savonarola's with them. His old desk and chair, some of his books, and one of his handwritten manuscripts are all there, and also his old vestments. The original mold of the plaque that appears in the public square where he was burned, is now in the convent, together with the paintings of Savonarola and the execution scene.
29 See David S. Schaff, *The Middle Ages*, vol. 5, part 2, p. 712.
30 Villari, *op. cit.*, p. 771.
31 Only two copies of this manuscript are in existence. It was first printed in Florence (1495), then later Venice (1537) and Paris (1674).
32 Villari, *op. cit.*, p. 315.
33 *Ibid.*, p. 769; Lucas, *op. cit.*, p. 51.

that this renewal must come soon, when God would punish humanity for the iniquities of the age. In support of this, he cites Joachim of Floris, a fact which is both interesting and significant. Savonarola then turns to different symbolical pictures and shows their spiritual meaning. It is only a glimpse, but it shows his general concept.

"The third symbolic picture of which I spoke is that of Revelation 6:2. There the four horsemen are spoken of, the white, the red, the black and the pale. The white horse symbolized the time of the apostles; the red one the time of the martyrs, the second period of the church; the black horse the period of the heretics; the pale horse is the time of the lukewarmness, which is now. Therefore I told you that the renewal of the Church has to take place very soon, or God will surrender his vineyard, that is Rome and the Church, to others to cultivate it, because not a spark of love is left in Rome, but only the devil. So much about symbols." [34]

2. TIMES OF VISITATION MADE KNOWN TO PROPHETS.—Savonarola's acquaintance with certain of the prophetic time periods such as Daniel's seventy weeks, is intimated.

"T[empter]—But did not our Lord say: 'It is not for you to know the times and the moments'?
"S[avonarola]—If you will look more closely at the text you will see that this is not said of all 'times and moments,' but of those times and moments 'which the Father has kept within His own power'; as, for instance, the day of Judgment. But as for other times and moments, that of the deluge was made known to Noe, to Jeremiah the seventy years of captivity, to Daniel the seventy weeks, etc." [35]

3. DANIEL PREDICTS PERSECUTION; MATTHEW WORLD-WIDE PREACHING.—One of Savonarola's widely circulated sermons recognizes Antichrist to be portrayed in the book of Daniel. And the fulfillment of the great commission is checkmated by apostasy in the clergy. Thus:

"Daniel the Prophet hath said that Antichrist shall come to persecute the Christians; . . . Therefore it is necessary to convert the Turks. And how shall they be converted unless the Church be renewed? St. Matthew hath told us that the Gospel shall be preached throughout the world; but

[34] Translated from Hieronymus Savonarola, *Auswahl aus seinen Schriften und Predigten* (German version by Joseph Schnitzer), p. 118.
[35] *Compendium Revelationum*, English translation in Lucas, *op. cit.*, p. 57.

who now is fitted to preach it? Where are good pastors and preachers to be found?" [36]

4. Degenerate Roman Church Denominated Babylon.
—To Savonarola, *Babylon* and *Rome* were synonymous terms. Here is an example:

"The Roman church is full of simony and vileness. . . . I visualized a black cross over Babylon—Rome with the inscription: Wrath of the Lord. And it rained upon her swords and knives, lances and weapons of all kinds, as well as hailstones and brimstones in a terrible thunderstorm in deepest gloom. And I saw another cross of gold which reached from the sky over Jerusalem to the earth with the inscription: Mercy of God. And here was full sunshine. And on the strength of vision I declare again, that the Church must reform herself, and that very soon because God is angry." [37]

This, of course, stirred the papal wrath.

Relationship to Rome is indicated in a Lenten sermon, preached in the midst of his conflict with the pope.

" 'Fly from Rome, for Babylon signifies confusion, and Rome hath confused all the Scriptures, confused all vices together, confused everything. Fly, then, from Rome, and come to repentance.' " [38]

Then, after asserting reformation of the church must come, he cries:

"Be of good cheer, ye righteous. Prepare your hearts for the visitation by reading, meditation and prayer, and you will be saved from the second death. And you godless servants continue to wallow in the mire! Your body may be filled with intoxicating liquor." [39]

Probably the most fearful denunciation recorded was likewise made at the Lenten season, in 1497:

" 'Come here thou ribald Church. The Lord saith: I gave thee beautiful vestments, but thou hast made idols of them. Thou hast dedicated the sacred vessels to vainglory, the sacraments to simony; thou hast become a shameless harlot in thy lusts; thou art lower than a beast, thou art a monster of abomination. . . . And what doeth the harlot? She sitteth on the throne of Solomon, and soliciteth all the world: he that hath gold is made welcome

---

36 Villari, *op. cit.*, p. 333, citing *Predica della Rinnovazione*, Sermon III.
37 Savonarola, *Auswahl*, pp. 120, 121.
38 Villari, *op. cit.*, p. 413, citing Lenten Sermon (1496), for Wednesday after fifth Sunday.
39 Savonarola, *Auswahl*, p. 122.

and may do as he will. . . . O prostitute Church, . . . thou hast multiplied thy fornications in Italy, in France, in Spain, and all other parts. Behold, I will put forth My hand, saith the Lord. I will smite thee, thou infamous wretch.' " [40]

5. VICEGERENT OF DARKNESS IN THE TEMPLE.—The coldness and desolation of the church and the intrusion of the vicegerent of darkness are vividly portrayed. Rapp gives a vivid picture of Savonarola's time thus:

"In the pompous house of night they murmured their prayers and rattled their sermons, but the stream of life did not gush forth. It had turned to ice in this frosty atmosphere. And out of this cloud of incense stepped one and declared: I am the vicar of God on earth. And the nations worshipped him; he could not err, even if he did not speak the truth. He alone could save souls, even if he brought misery. But the people who dwelt in darkness and the shadow of death should see the great light again, the light which brightens the day. And the faithful watchmen on the walls of Zion proclaimed: 'The night is far spent and the day is approaching. Let us cast off the works of darkness and put on the armor of light.'

"Truth stands firm and like the earth turns around the sun, so men turn toward truth. Jesus has given to truth a brightness like the brightness of the morning. He roused new life in the hearts of men. And never will He cease again. He shines like the noonday-sun and like the midsummer-sun in the far north in the hours of the deepest night.

"But the warm glow of heavenly love grew dim; by the coldness of the hearts, an icy winter settled down and night was all around. The walls of the city of God, of the Church of Jesus, loomed high in the utter darkness. They lighted the somber halls with many candles to forget the night. They raised clouds of incense and inhaled its fragrance in order not to be reminded of their withered hearts. Yet the vicar of darkness, who called himself the vicar of Christ, had these watchmen arrested. They had proclaimed what he disliked, and the glare of the stakes which took their lives shone forth against the coming dawn. The time was fulfilled, and these flames kindled a fire from the throne of justice, which men will never quench. Self-centered human power destroys, but the divine power of love can only create." [41]

III. Endless Chain of Individuals Calls for Reformation

As noted, Savonarola was not alone in dying for his faith. Many, about the same time, were aroused by the papal evils,

---

[40] Villari, *op. cit.*, pp. 517, 518, citing Lenten Sermon XXII (1497), afterward suppressed by the Congregation of the Index.
[41] Translated from Rapp, *op. cit.*, pp. vii, viii.

and a number met a similar fate. Only barest mention can be made of a few of these protestors. The Carmelite THOMAS CON-ECTE, of Flanders, was burned in 1432, and the Dominican ANDREW, archbishop and cardinal, died in prison in 1484 for rebuking Sixtus IV.[42] JOHN OF WESEL, a vice-rector of the University of Erfurt, ended his life in prison in 1482 for assailing papal errors and showing the way back to the Bible.[43]

The Franciscan JOHANNES HILTEN, of Thuringia, languished in close confinement in prison from 1477 until his death, about 1500, because of rebuking certain well-known abuses. In prison, about 1485, he wrote a commentary on Daniel and the Apocalypse, parts of which soon came to the attention of the Reformers.[44] Hilten, citing Bridget of Sweden, said that the popes had perverted the vicarship of Christ; he saw the sword of punishment in the Turks. Like Joachim, he looked for a reformation of the church.[45] Melanchthon refers to him in his *Apology* as the one who looked for someone to arise about 1516, whom the church would be unable to resist.[46]

A popular feeling arose in Germany in the fifteenth century that a great crisis for the Papacy impended. Many former declarations of this character were assembled, and formed a sort of treasury of predictions of coming doom. A favorite collection was that attributed to a mythical John Lichtenberger, which contained such names as Reinhard, Bridget of Sweden, and the

---

[42] Gieseler, *op. cit.*, vol. 3, pp. 453, 454.

[43] John Wesel is not to be confused with the better-known Wessel (sometimes called John Wessel or Wessel Gansfort) of Groningen, who was connected with the Brethren of the Common Life. The latter escaped arraignment by the Inquisition, but his writings were not published until after the Reformation began. He died in 1489. It was of Wessel that Luther said, "If I had read Wessel earlier, my enemies might have said that Luther drew everything from Wessel, so well do our two minds agree." (For both Wesel and Wessel see David S. Schaff, *The Middle Ages*, part 2, pp. 681-684; Ullman, *op. cit.*, vol. 1, pp. 161-374, vol. 2, pp. 261-615; Gieseler, *op. cit.*, vol. 3, pp. 461-464, 467-471; Robertson, *op. cit.*, vol. 8, pp. 356-359; Flick, *op. cit.*, vol. 2, pp. 476, 478.)

[44] Friedrich von Bezold, "Geschichte der deutschen Reformation," p. 146, in Wilhelm Oncken, *Allgemeine Geschichte in Einzeldarstellungen;* Gieseler, *op. cit.*, vol. 3, p. 471.

[45] Melchior Adam, *Vitae Germanorum Theologorum* ("Lives of German Theologians"), pp. 3-5.

[46] Philipp Melanchthon, *Apologia Confessionis Augustanae*, in his *Opera (Corpus Reformatorum)*, vol. 27, cols. 627, 628. A footnote in Melanchthon, col. 627, says: "Ioannes Hilten,] this name (fol Pr 4a lin. 3.4.) Luther underscored in a red color, and wrote this in the margin: 'I think this man was still living or recently dead when I received the first schooling in Eisenach. For I remember mention made of him by friend Heinrich Schalden with compassion, as if of one bound in prison. Yet I was then fourteen or fifteen years old.' "

Sibyl. Aytinger, Grünbeck, and Hagen fall into this category.[47] From 1450 to 1517 there were frequent declarations of the retribution about to burst over Rome, the popes, and the clergy, together with cravings for reformation. As Christendom, unaware, yet in a sense expectant, came close to the great epoch of the Reformation and the division of the church, the more threatening became these individual voices from the laity and even the clergy, and the more sharp their sting, directed at the Papacy.

VINCENT FERRER (1357-1419), Spanish Dominican preacher of Valencia, declared that the public manifestation of Antichrist (an individual, he believed) was near, and urged that mankind prepare for the great contest.[48] JACOBUS DE PARADISO, Carthusian and Doctor of Divinity at Erfurt (1457), declared that the church would continue in utter depravity until the appearance of Antichrist, which must now be very near.[49] That the church was in a lamentable condition, all agreed. But one faction said it would be renovated, and the other declared it would go to ruin. Machiavelli (1469-1527), Florentine political writer and humanist, boldly said: "One of two things must come upon the Roman Church, either utter ruin or a very heavy chastisement." [50]

Bishop BERTHOLD OF CHIEMSEE, in 1519, in his *The Burden of the Church* (like the "burden" of Isaiah)—influenced by Joachim, Ferrer, Catherine of Siena, Bridget of Sweden, and Hildegard—draws a dark picture of degradation and gloomy anticipation. So also does the Swiss poet PAMPHILUS GENGENBACH, who quotes Joachim, Bridget of Sweden, Reinhard, and others in the

[47] Döllinger, *Prophecies*, pp. 164-168. W. Grünbeck in his illustrated *Ein spiegel der natürlichen, himlischen, und prophetischen sehungen.* . . . (Mirror of Natural, Celestial, and Prophetical Vision, 1508), published at Nürnberg in German and Latin, pictured on the title page the celestial signs of Christ's advent, the persecution of the saints, and a scattering of priestly paraphernalia. His woodcuts represent the church as a ship in the storm, peasants as ministering priests at the altar, and monks and priests plowing in the field. This is reproduced in Bezold, *op. cit.*, p. 147.
[48] Döllinger, *Prophecies*, p. 67; David Schaff, *The Middle Ages*, part 2, pp. 229-231; Flick, *op. cit.*, vol. 1, p. 264.
[49] Döllinger, *Prophecies*, pp. 69, 70.
[50] *Ibid.*, p. 159, citing *Discorsi Sopra Livio* (Discourse Upon Livy), I, 12, in *Opere* (1843 ed.), p. 273.

No.	Name	Page	Date	Dan. 2		Dan. 7				Dan. 8			Dan. 9	Dan. 12
				Metallic Man	Stone	4 Beasts	10 Horns	Little Horn	3½ Times	Ram	He-Goat	2300 Days	70 Wks.	1290 Days
1	Dante Alighieri	24	c. 1310											
2	Nicholas de Lyra	67	c. 1330										Years	
3	Michael of Cesena	20	c. 1331											
4	Johannes de Rupescissa	20	c. 1345											
5	Francisco Petrarch	29	c. 1350											
6	John Milicz	32	c. 1367											C
7	John Wyclif	52	c. 1379	B-P-G-R		B-P-G-R	Temporal Rulers	Popes	Many Centuries	Per.	Grecia			
8	Matthias of Janow	40	c. 1388											
9	R. Wimbledon	92	c. 1389										Yrs. from Titus	Y
10	John Purvey	94	c. 1390										Years	Years
11	Walter Brute	76	c. 1393	B-P-G-R	Christ	B-P-G-R		Rome	3½ Cent. 1260 Yrs.				Years	Years
12	John Huss	115	c. 1412											
13	Nicholas of Cusa	130	c. 1452									559 B.C.-A.D.1750		
14	Girolamo Savonarola	143	c. 1497										Years	

Positions on the key prophecies held by Europe's leading expositors, between 1300 and 1500, are here disclosed at a glance. The writers are tabulated in chronological order. Reference to the actual text is easily had by turning to the page noted. Certain constantly recurring terms—*Antichrist, Abomination of Desolation, Beast, Babylon,* and *Harlot*—appear in their respective columns, and the interpretation given. The various outline prophecies and time periods of Daniel appear in sequence; then the same follows for Revelation. The preponderance of any given exposition can easily be deduced by scanning the vertical columns. On the other hand, the over-all position of any given expositor can quickly be had by following through this allocated line horizontally. This provides a simplified index and visualized tabulation of his essential teachings.

The abbreviations are simple: "B-P-G-R" means *Babylonia, Persia, Greece,* and *Rome;* "P-G." = *Persia, Greece;* "Ch." = *church;* "Pagan R." = *Pagan Rome,* etc.

This table discloses the fact that the identification of Antichrist, under his various names (Little Horn, Man of Sin, Abomination of Desolation, Beast, Babylon, and Harlot), was uppermost in the minds of men at the time. The four world powers, with Rome followed by the great papal apostasy, was the predominant emphasis of the hour. The year-day principle was likewise by now being slowly perceived and applied to most prophetic time periods—including, for its first time, the 2300 year-days. But the Augus-

form of questions and answers, climaxing with the appearance of Antichrist, and suggesting the reformation of the church.[51]

A seemingly endless succession of calls for reformation came during this period—a living protest in the very bosom of the church. Peasants—such as HANS WERNER, of Villingen, able to repeat almost the entire Bible from memory, and to refer readily to nearly any Scripture text—disputed from the Bible with the priests. The belief that the iniquities of the last days were upon them was increasingly common. Such ideas were rampant throughout the Continent.[52]

---

[51] Döllinger, *Prophecies,* pp. 56, 168-170; Bezold, *op. cit.,* pp. 146, 147.
[52] Bezold, *op. cit.,* p. 113.

Matt. 24:15 Abom. of Desola.	2 Thess. 2 Man of Sin	Rev. 2, 3 7 Churches	Rev. 6, 7 7 Seals	Rev. 8, 9 7 Trumpets	Rev. 12 Dragon	Woman	42 Months 1260 Days 3½ Times	1st Beast	Rev. 13 2d Beast	666	Beast	Rev. 17 Babylon	Harlot	Rev. 20 Millennium
							42 M. 3½ T.				Rome		Roman Ch.	Augustinian
												Ch. of Rome	Ch. of Rome Papal Court	
Papacy	Papacy												Papacy Hierarchy	
Papacy Fallen Church Papacy	Papacy Present Ch.		Eras of Ch.	Apostasy			Yrs. Implied	Papacy				Popes	Papacy Hierarchy	
Bp. of Rome Papacy	Papacy Papacy	10 days-Yrs.	Eras of Ch.	Eras of Ch. 150 Yrs.	True Ch.	True Ch.	Long Period Caesar to Fred. II	Papacy Rom. Emp. Papacy	Hierarchy Pontificate	Pope Dux Cleri		Papacy Papacy Papacy	Papacy Papacy Papacy	Augustinian
	Papacy		Eras of Ch.		Apos. Ch.			Mohammed		Moham.		Papacy	Papacy	

tinian theory of the millennium was still predominant throughout Christendom.

(Similar tabular chart-summaries will appear at the close of each major epoch, as we progress. This will place all the essential information at our finger tips.)

CONCLUSIONS: These two deductions are surely to be made: (1) It was, significantly enough in Britain, far away from Rome—where the Venerable Bede (673-735) was about the only one who attempted any sound exposition of prophecy during the Dark Ages (covered in Volume I)—that the fullest and clearest exposition now appears, under Wyclif, Wimbledon, Purvey, and Brute, all dissentient voices, in conflict with Rome. All others, in these two centuries, saw principally one thing—the contemporary existence and identity of the predicted Antichrist. To this they emphatically testified.

And by now (2) along with the seventy weeks interpreted as years (handed down from the Jews in the third century B.C.), the 1260, 1290, 1335, and 2300 days from Daniel (enunciated as years by Joachim and his successors in the twelfth and thirteenth centuries) we see the ten days, the five months or 150 years, and the 1260 years from the Apocalypse all expounded. The major advance, however, is the fact that now for the first time Cusa gives a specific dating for the 2300 years.

For sequence and over-all relationship, note again the comprehensive chart on pages 96, 97.

IV. Summarization of Pre-Reformation Witnesses

Ere we leave the pre-Reformation section, and turn to the Reformation epoch—though tarrying first to review the thirty paralleling Jewish writers on prophecy spread across the centuries of the Christian Era—let us summarize in convenient tabular form the leading views of the principal fourteenth- and fifteenth-century expositors, in order to bring their voluminous and scattered teachings into compact form. This is achieved by means of the accompanying chart.

Prophetic exposition, be it remembered, was just beginning to grip the minds of godly men again, after a virtual eclipse of interest and exposition for over five long centuries. In fact, be-

157

tween the fifth and eleventh centuries, understanding of the prophetic writings almost passed from among men. Only an occasional gleam was to be seen by the searcher, like the flickering light of some lone star in the night, before the gray light of dawn broke over the earth during the Renaissance, and the prophecies once more became the object of study and elucidation.

CHAPTER SEVEN

Columbus Impelled by Prophecies to Open New World

When we examine the witnesses of the centuries we see that most prophetic expositors are clerics, though some were laymen. Most of these were scholars, but a few were untutored. Some were historians, others scientists, and still others were poets or writers. Not a few were loyal sons of the church; others were outside the pale of those acknowledging the Papacy's claims to spiritual supremacy. Now we come to the great century of discovery, and turn, strange as it may seem, to none other than the renowned discoverer, Christopher Columbus. Here is an example of how a profound conviction of the intent of prophecy —even though faulty—and a consciousness of helping to fulfill these prophecies, dominated the life of the "admiral of the oceans," as he was called.

But before sketching his life and tracing his teachings in this field, we must first glance back over the centuries to get the background of the agelong controversy over the rotundity of the earth, and the conflict over Columbus' conviction that he could reach the Indies by a westward course. Then the relationship to our quest will become evident.

I. Battle of the Centuries Over Globular Earth Theory

Among the ancient Greeks, PYTHAGORAS (fl. 532 B.C.) first declared the great physical truth concerning the earth—that it is spherical in form. Later HERACLIDES (born c. 388 B.C.)

taught the daily rotation of the earth on its own axis and the revolution of Venus and Mercury around the sun. ARISTARCHUS OF SAMOS (fl. 280 B.C.) projected the next great truth—that the earth revolves around the sun. HIPPARCHUS OF NICEA (fl. 146-126 B.C.), father of geometrical astronomy, rejected this theory for the old idea of the earth as the center of the universe. So did PTOLEMY (Claudius Ptolemaeus, c. A.D. 150), of Alexandria, who systematized the theories of Hipparchus, in his famous *Mathematike Syntaxis* (Mathematical Composition), better known under the Arabic title *Almagest*[1] (The Greatest), formed by prefixing the Arabic article *al* to the Greek superlative *megiste,* "greatest." Although a few believed that some of the planets circle the sun, the prejudices of the time doomed the teaching of the heliocentric theory, which lay largely dormant until the time of Copernicus.

1. DARK AGE ECLIPSE OF EARLIER GLOBAL THEORY.—Some of the church fathers were hostile to the heathen Greek concepts of the universe, which included the globular form of the earth and the "sphere" system of planetary motion. The list includes LACTANTIUS (c. 260-c. 325), EUSEBIUS OF CAESAREA (c. 260-c. 340), JEROME (c. 340-420), CHRYSOSTOM (347-407), and AUGUSTINE (354-430). In patristic geography the earth was considered a flat surface, bordered by the waters of the sea, on the yielding support of which rests the crystalline dome of the sky. This concept was for the most part supported by Scripture expressions wrested from their proper meaning.[2] Then COSMAS of Alexandria, surnamed Indicopleustes, after returning from a voyage to India (A.D. 535), put the finishing touch to the rejection of the round-earth theory in his *Christian Topography*— which became the standard authority for hundreds of years— by demanding of its advocates how in the day of judgment, men

---

[1] George Sarton, *Introduction to the History of Science*, vol. 1, pp. 73, 141, 156, 193-195. For a good popular treatment of the development of astronomy see Norton Wagner, *Unveiling the Universe*, pp. 14-35.
[2] John William Draper, *History of the Intellectual Development of Europe*, vol. 2, p. 159; Wagner, *op. cit.*, pp. 20, 21. The prophetic teachings of these writers are discussed in *Prophetic Faith*, Volume I.

on the other side of a globe could see the Lord descending through the air! [3]

For hundreds of years following the dismemberment of the Western Roman Empire, Greek science was rejected, and darkness prevailed concerning the true form of the earth, penetrated only by an occasional gleam. The VENERABLE BEDE (c. 673-735) accepted the theory of the spherical form of the earth.[4] But the twelfth century reintroduced many translations of the ancient Greek writings, and an interest was awakened in mathematics and astronomy, and in the thirteenth century many universities were founded. Under this awakened thought Ptolemy's *Almagest* was restudied, and superior thinkers gradually came to the conclusion that Ptolemy's system was complex and inaccurate. It was becoming evident to thinking minds that the geocentric systems of Hipparchus and Ptolemy were not a correct explanation of our planetary system.

ROGER BACON (c. 1214-1294), English Franciscan, philosopher and scientist, sent writings to the pope in 1268 explaining the importance of a complete and accurate survey of the world. He also indicated the possibility of a westward passage to the Indies.[5] But he assumed that the Indies were nearer Spain than they are. Bacon's position was later made known to Columbus through Pierre d'Ailly's *Imago Mundi* (Picture of the World), as will be seen.

2. SETTLED BY 15TH- AND 16TH-CENTURY ASTRONOMERS AND DISCOVERERS.—In 1444 Cardinal Nicholas of Cusa—as noted in Chapter Five—contended that the earth is not fixed, but moves, rotating upon its axis. And then NICOLAUS COPERNICUS (1473-1543), Polish astronomer and doctor of canon law, after studying Hipparchus and Ptolemy's *Almagest,* about the year 1505 constructed the heliocentric, or sun-centered system, which he explained in his book *The Revolutions of the Heavenly Orbs.*

[3] Draper, *op. cit.,* vol. 2, p. 159; Sarton, *op. cit.,* vol. 1, p. 431.
[4] Sarton, *op. cit.,* vol. 1, p. 510, citing the Venerable Bede, *De natura rerum.* Bede is treated in *Prophetic Faith,* Volume I.
[5] Sarton, *op. cit.,* vol. 2, part 2, pp. 952-958.

With his instruments he proved what others had guessed, but he was reluctant to publish his doctrine because of the attacks it would invite.[6] This work created a revolution in human thought, restoring the ancient Greek glimpse of truth. Then Columbus helped to overcome the prevalent prejudices, and finally Magellan's voyage settled forever the globular form of the earth.

II. Voyages Influenced by Deep Religious Convictions

CHRISTOPHER COLUMBUS, or Cristobal Colón (1451-1506), discoverer, writer on prophecy, and believer in the approaching end of the world, was born at Genoa, Italy. He was the son of a master weaver. Obtaining a good knowledge of arithmetic, drawing, and painting, he early developed a fondness for geography. With strong attachment for the sea and the mysterious regions beyond its horizons, he engaged intermittently in the Syrian trade, and voyaged probably to Ireland and the northern seas.

Columbus was a skilled chartmaker, and when not at sea employed his time making maps and charts for sale. In Portugal, probably in 1478, he married the daughter of a distinguished navigator. Fortunately, Columbus became the possessor of his deceased father-in-law's journals, charts, and memoranda.[7] In Lisbon he read Ptolemy and the Greek philosophers and geographers, and studied Marco Polo and particularly the *Imago Mundi* of Pierre d'Ailly.[8] Through these works he came to believe that the sea is navigable everywhere, that the earth is

[6] Dorothy Stimson, *The Gradual Acceptance of the Copernican Theory of the Universe,* pp. 27-28; Wagner, *op. cit.,* pp. 26, 27.

[7] R. H. Major, editor's introduction to *Select Letters of Christopher Columbus,* pp. xlii, xliii; Samuel Eliot Morison, *Admiral of the Ocean Sea,* vol. 1, pp. 49-51.

[8] PIERRE D'AILLY (Petrus d'Alliaco, 1350-1420), French churchman and schoolman, studied at the College of Navarre of the University of Paris, and became master of the college in 1384, and the same year was made chancellor of Notre Dame. He was created a cardinal in 1411. But he insisted on the superiority of the council over the pope at the Council of Constance (1414-1418), where he took a leading part, presiding over the third session. He held that the church is founded on the living Christ, not on erring Peter; on the Bible not on canon law. Like Cusa, he proposed a tangible reform of the calendar, later carried out. In 1410 he wrote a geographical work, *Imago Mundi,* which showed a possibility of reaching the Indies by sailing west. D'Ailly's views seem to have exercised a greater influence upon Columbus than those of any other writer. D'Ailly also wrote on the chronology of the world, and the concordance of astronomy with history. On the margins of books which belonged to Columbus are found many notes taken from d'Ailly's works.

round, and from the Scriptures concluded that there must be other inhabited lands, since God's command at the Flood was to replenish the earth.[9] He came to believe that he had a lofty mission to perform—a task to which he held with singular firmness.[10]

1. PROJECT A MATTER OF CONVICTION, NOT OPINION.— The shortest route to India had hitherto been the land route along the Euphrates and the Persian Gulf, now largely cut off by the Moslems, who were at war with European Christendom. Columbus had entered into correspondence with Toscanelli, the Florentine astronomer, who likewise held that the Indies could be reached by sailing west, and who sent him a map, or chart, constructed largely on the travels of Marco Polo (*c.* 1254-1324). During his years of entreaty Columbus was ridiculed and disparaged. But he was unmoved, for with him it was not a mere matter of opinion or simply of belief; he felt a profound conviction—*India could be reached by sailing west*. Moreover, he believed himself to be the destined messenger of the Most High. It is plain, from his letter describing his fourth voyage, that he was convinced that he was under the personal guidance and direct protection of God, and felt that he had a divine call to this task of discovery.[11] This conviction came from his study of the prophecies, as will be developed.

Columbus could not sail without substantial aid, and this it seemed impossible to secure. There were years of vexatious delay. He is said to have first gone to some wealthy men at Genoa, but without success. Then he approached King John II, of Portugal, who sent a secret maritime mission to learn the truth of Columbus' claims. But the timid pilots soon returned.[12] In disgust Columbus went to Spain in 1485 to lay his case before Ferdi-

---

[9] Draper, *op. cit.*, vol. 2, p. 160.
[10] Washington Irving, *The Life and Voyages of Christopher Columbus*, vol. 1, p. 24; Henry Harrisse, *Notes on Columbus*, pp. 156 ff. Author identified in Library of Congress catalog.
[11] Columbus, *The Voyages of Christopher Columbus, Being the Journals of His . . . Voyages*, etc., pp. 299, 306; see also Cecil Jane, editor's introduction, *ibid.*, pp. 27, 32, 40, 41; Irving, *op. cit.*, vol. 1, p. 24.
[12] Major, *op. cit.*, in Columbus, *Select Letters*, pp. xlvii, xlviii.

BROZIK, ARTIST

COLUMBUS PRESSING HIS CASE BEFORE FERDINAND AND ISABELLA

Columbus Asked Royal Support at the Spanish Court for His Great Venture. In a Later Letter He Gave Credit to Prophecy for His Achievements,

nand and Isabella, there to plead for his great idea. But the learned would not listen, and others were too busy with war.

2. PREJUDICED COURT RAISES QUESTION OF HERESY.—
Finally the Spanish court referred the project to a council of ecclesiastics, which met first at Cordova and then in one of the colleges of the University of Salamanca. But here Columbus found himself in a theological predicament; the most serious feature was the irreligious implications. Any heresy would, of course, expose its propounder to the newly established Spanish Inquisition. He was able to escape through the support of one learned man who appreciated the eloquent and lucid reasonings of the adventurer, and through whose influence the commission delayed its report.[13] Columbus' ideas were refuted from the Pentateuch, the Psalms, the prophets, the Gospels, the Epistles, and the writings of the church fathers. Moreover, it was argued that if he sailed down under, "the rotundity of the earth would present a kind of mountain up which it was impossible for him to sail, even with the fairest wind," so that he could never get back—such an argument was made in the adverse report four years later.[14] General public opinion considered the project dangerous if not ridiculous; ignorant people thought that Columbus' vessels would fall off the edge of a flat earth, and educated men, who knew that the earth was not flat, believed that all sorts of dangers lurked in the unknown ocean.

All who had heard the project spoken of treated it with contempt, save two friars.[15] After the wearisome delays of evasion, rehearings, and rejections, he was about to start for France. However, after nearly seven years of waiting, the queen was at last prevailed upon. Columbus received his commission, which made him admiral and viceroy of all he should discover for Spain. The courageousness of such a venture, when the distances and the hazards of the voyage were unknown, is, of course, apparent. The popes had given Portugal a monopoly on the sea

---

[13] *Ibid.*, pp. l, li; Morison, *op. cit.*, vol. 1, pp. 116, 117.
[14] Draper, *op. cit.*, vol. 2, p. 161; Morison, *op. cit.*, vol. 1, pp. 131, 132.
[15] Columbus, *Select Letters*, pp. 105, 106.

route to India by way of Good Hope.[16] Spain and Portugal, rival
sea powers, had found it impossible to traffic with the Far East
without violating the papal mandate—until this westward route
was proposed, and against which there was no papal edict.

3. Four Voyages Follow Years of Waiting.—At last, on
Friday, August 3, 1492, the weary struggles and heartsickness of
eighteen years of preparation were over, and at daybreak three
caravels sailed from Palos, Spain, with a sea chart said to have
been constructed by Toscanelli, and Marco Polo's narratives.[17]
Columbus carried with him d'Ailly's *Imago Mundi,* from which
most of his knowledge of Greek and Roman writers on the fea-
sibility of reaching India by a western route was gained—d'Ailly
in turn quoting from Roger Bacon.[18] Columbus' personal copy,
incidentally, has many notations in the margin in his own handwriting.[19] (See reproduction on page 172).

Finally, after weeks of courageous sailing and suspense,
Columbus came in sight of land. On October 12 he touched at
San Salvador, in the Bahamas, and before returning to Spain
discovered Cuba and Haiti. Owing to Ptolemy's understatement
of the earth's circumference,[20] the New World discoverer believed he had reached the islands off the east coast of Asia, the
region of the fabled India, and so gave the name Indians to the
aborigines. The *Santa Maria* was wrecked on the Haitian coast,
so Columbus reached home on the *Niña,* from his first voyage, in
March of 1493. The second expedition, with seventeen ships,
was undertaken in September of that same year. On this voyage
numerous other islands were discovered, including Puerto Rico
and Jamaica, and Columbus returned to Spain in 1494.

The third voyage, begun in 1498, resulted in the discovery
of South America, the significance of which did not at first

---

[16] Edgar Prestage, "Portugal," *The Catholic Encyclopedia*, vol. 12, p. 302.
[17] Alexander von Humboldt, *Cosmos,* vol. 2, pp. 251, 261; but see Harrisse, *op. cit.*, p. 85.
[18] Humboldt, *op. cit.*, vol. 2, pp. xvi, 247; Harrisse, *op. cit.*, pp. 83, 84.
[19] Preserved in the Biblioteca Capitular y Colombina at Seville, Spain; see Justin Winsor,
"Columbus and His Discoveries," chap. 1 in *Narrative and Critical History of America,* vol. 2,
p. 31; John Boyd Thacher, *Christopher Columbus,* vol. 1, p. 480; Harrisse, *op. cit.*, p. 84; Jane,
op. cit., in *Voyages of Christopher Columbus,* p. 35; Major, *op. cit.*, in Columbus, *Select Letters,*
p. xliii.
[20] Sarton, *op. cit.*, vol. 1, p. 273.

impress Columbus, because of his eagerness to revisit the colony at Hispaniola. But he found it necessary to quell revolt and opposition at Santo Domingo, the new capital of the settlement, and at home court favor had turned against him. Although he was confident of rich revenues within three years, a new governor and judge of Hispaniola was appointed, and Columbus was returned to Spain in chains in October, 1500.[21] But when the "admiral of the ocean fleet" arrived home in irons, a wave of popular indignation soon freed him.

After disappointing experiences Columbus sought to circumnavigate the globe, and on the 11th of May, 1502, sailed on his fourth great voyage.[22] After Columbus had touched at Santo Domingo, he reached Honduras and Panama in an attempt to find a passage westward. After a vain attempt to plant a colony, he returned to Jamaica, where his worm-eaten and storm-beaten ships gave out, and he and his men endured terrible privations and illness. At length, in June, 1504, ships were sent to take them home, and after a tempestuous voyage Columbus reached Spain in November, 1504. Soon after this Isabella died, and as a result Columbus' fortunes were materially affected. Thacher contends that he knew the character of his discovery— that he had disclosed another continent, which he called Novus Orbis or Mundus Novus.[23]

4. Chosen to Proclaim God's Name in New World.— Columbus was a voluminous writer, and kept a minute diary of his voyages. These writings reflect a deep religious spirit.[24] There is frequent citation of Scripture concerning Biblical characters and episodes.[25] Columbus found land "with the aid of the Lord." He took possession of San Salvador, the first land of the Western Hemisphere that he sighted, in these words:

[21] Major, *op. cit.*, in Columbus, *Select Letters,* p. lxi.
[22] Many of Columbus' official accounts of his voyages, with the appointments as admiral, viceroy, and governor of whatever lands he should discover, together with the papal bull of 1493, appear in *Christopher Columbus—His Own Book of Privileges,* edited by Benjamin Franklin Stevens; see examples also in *The Authentic Letters of Columbus,* edited by William Eleroy Curtis.
[23] Thacher, *op. cit.,* vol. 2, p. 568.
[24] Columbus, *Authentic Letters,* pp. 101, 105.
[25] Columbus, *Select Letters,* pp. 148, 158, 170, 184, 196, 197.

"O Lord, Eternal and Almighty God, by thy sacred word thou hast created the heavens, the earth and the sea; blessed and glorified be thy name, and praised be thy Majesty, who hath designed to use thy humble servant to make thy sacred name known and proclaimed in this other part of the world." [26]

In his letter of July 7, 1503, about the fourth voyage, he states concerning the material wealth and other favorable aspects of the newly discovered dominion, "All this makes for the security of the Christians and the assurance of their dominion, and gives great hope for the honour and increase of the Christian religion." [27] The story is told that even before his voyages, while he lay ill near Belem, Portugal, an unknown voice whispered to him in a dream, "God will cause thy name to be wonderfully resounded through the earth, and will give thee the keys of the gates of the ocean, which are closed with strong chains!" [28] And Columbus' will begins with the words:

"In the name of the Most Holy Trinity, who inspired me with the idea and afterward made it perfectly clear to me, that I could navigate and go to the Indies from Spain, by traversing the ocean westwardly." [29]

5. POPE DIVIDES GLOBE BETWEEN SPAIN AND PORTUGAL.— The Spanish and Portuguese discoveries offered a wide field for papal extension. However, soon after Christopher Columbus discovered the New World, a hot dispute arose between Spain and Portugal. The pope was called upon to mediate between them, for he was still considered the international arbiter, and the Holy See the highest tribunal. Pope Calixtus III had granted Portugal exclusive rights of trading and founding colonies on the west coast of Africa between Cape Bojador and Guinea. But no sooner had Columbus—whose project had been rejected by Portugal—returned from his famous voyage, than King Emanuel, of Portugal, set up claim to the newly discovered lands on the ground of the former grant. [30] (Medal of Calixtus on page 556.)

---

[26] Harrisse, *op. cit.*, pp. 139, 140.
[27] *Voyages of Christopher Columbus*, p. 303; Columbus, *Select Letters*, p. 201.
[28] Draper, *op. cit.*, vol. 2, p. 160.
[29] Columbus, *Authentic Letters*, p. 193.
[30] Pastor, *op. cit.*, vol. 6, pp. 158 160.

Ferdinand and Isabella at once dispatched an embassy to Alexander VI for the purpose of ensuring their rights to the new territories, on the principle that Martin V had given to the king of Portugal possession of all lands he might discover between Cape Bojador and the East Indies, with plenary indulgence for the souls who perished in the conquest. The pontifical action was based essentially on the principle that pagans and infidels have no lawful rights in their lands and goods, and that the children of God may rightfully take them over.[31]

In two bulls, of May 4 and 5, 1493, Alexander VI presumed to divide the Western world between Portugal and Spain by a line one hundred leagues west of the Azores, north and south. The possession of the lands discovered, and to be discovered, was assigned to the two countries to be held in perpetuity. Again, the principle was that all countries are subject to papal disposal. This was by the authority of the omnipotent God conceded to the pope in St. Peter, and by reason of the vicarship of Jesus Christ, which he administered on earth. Thus half the globe was divided between Spain and Portugal.[32]

As Peter's successor, the pope claimed the right to give away the Western continent, a gift that involved an unending right of tenure. This prerogative of assigning to these two nations the lands in the West was in accordance with the so-called gift or donation of Constantine to Pope Sylvester. Alexander's donation included, "by the authority of Almighty God, whatever there is toward India, but saves the existing rights of any Christian princes." It forbade, under pain of excommunication, anyone to trade in that direction, threatening the indignation of Almighty God. It directed barbarous nations to be subdued, and no pains to be spared in reducing the Indians to Christianity. Thus the obstacles of patristic geography were removed, but the ideas of ethnology that had come down from the fathers led to an appalling tragedy. The terms of the bull of May 4 were

---

[31] Draper, *op. cit.*, vol. 2, p. 164.
[32] David S. Schaff, *The Middle Ages*, part 2, pp. 462, 463; Humboldt, *op. cit.*, vol. 2, p. 280; Pastor, *op. cit.*, vol. 6, pp. 160, 161.

set aside a year later, and the line shifted.[33] One cannot but ponder the thought that had Columbus landed on the continent of North America, a Spanish Catholic rather than an English Protestant population might have resulted.

III. Columbus Both Fulfiller and Expositor of Prophecy

1. EXPLORATORY ENTERPRISE HELPS FULFILL PROPHECIES.— Columbus expressly declares that the discovery of the New World was not prompted by speculation, mathematics, or mere navigation, but by the compulsive conviction that all the divinely inspired prophecies of Scripture must be fulfilled before the approaching end of the world, including the proclamation of the gospel to the ends of the earth. No trial or disappointment could turn him from his purpose.[34]

In a letter written about the end of 1500, while returning from the Indies in chains, Columbus said:

"I offered myself with such earnest devotion to the service of these princes, and I have served them with a fidelity hitherto unequalled and unheard of. God made me the messenger of the new heaven and the new earth, of which He spoke in the Apocalypse by St. John, after having spoken of it by the mouth of Isaiah; and He showed me the spot where to find it. All proved incredulous; except the Queen my mistress, to whom the Lord gave the spirit of intelligence and the necessary courage, and made her the heiress of all, as a dear and well beloved daughter. I want to take possession of it in her royal name. . . . Seven years [had] passed away in deliberations, and nine have been spent in accomplishing things truly memorable, and worthy to be preserved in the history of man. I have now reached that point, that there is no man so vile but thinks it is his right to insult me." [35]

2. BOOK ON PROPHECIES DISCLOSES IMPELLING MOTIVES.— In September, 1501, Columbus began the preparation of his

---

[33] David S. Schaff, *The Middle Ages*, part 2, p. 463; Robertson, *op. cit.*, vol. 8, p. 334; Draper, *op. cit.*, vol. 2, pp. 165, 166. The appalling atrocities that followed later are sometimes called the great American tragedy. Whole populations were treated as if they did not belong to the human race. Their goods were taken, and their persons seized, on the basis of the text, "The heathen for thine inheritance, and the uttermost parts of the earth for thy possession." Ps. 2:8. Unspeakable ruin followed, as literally millions were remorselessly cut off. From Mexico to Peru a civilization was crushed out. (See William H. Prescott, *History of the Conquest of Mexico*.)

[34] Irving, *op. cit.*, p. 24.

[35] Letter to a former nurse of Prince John, in Columbus, *Select Letters*, p. 148.

Libro de las Profecías (Book of the Prophecies) which he further illuminated by citations from the Carthusian friar Gaspar Gorricio. The heading in Lollis' edition shows that he ended it in March, 1502.[36] It comprises some seventy pages. It was evidently written in the convent of Las Cuevas, when he was for a time wearing the gray frock and knotted cord of the Franciscans.[37] It is penned partly in his own hand and partly in that of his brother Bartholomew and of his son Ferdinand. He continually invokes the Bible and the prophets, claiming to owe all he knew and all he had accomplished to the leading of God. He also quotes ecclesiastical writers, Christian and Jewish.

Columbus affirms the world must have an end, and a second advent of Christ, and that the Lord gave an account of the signs preceding it, which are mentioned in the Gospels. He also cites Joachim of Floris, who seems to have indicated that Spain was to have a part in all of this.[38] He touches likewise on the coming of Antichrist, basing his statement on Paul, in 2 Thessalonians, and on Daniel.[39]

3. LED BY LORD WITH LIGHT FROM HOLY SPIRIT.—Columbus' *Libro de las Profecías* contains a letter to the king and queen, a remarkable report, which reads almost like a theological treatise. After rehearsing his careful study, his extensive travels wherever man had gone, his knowledge of the planetary sciences, mathematics, and geography, acquired after many years of study, and his consultations with the learned, as well as his dexterity in making maps and hemispheres, Columbus writes:

"At this time I both read and studied all kinds of literature: cosmography, histories, chronicles, and philosophy and other arts, to which our Lord opened my mind unmistakably to the fact that it was possible to navigate from here to the Indies, and He evoked in me the will for the execution of it; and with this fire I came to Your Highnesses. All those who heard of my plan disregarded it mockingly and with laughter. All the

---

[36] This work is printed complete in *Scritti di Cristoforo Colombo,* ed. by Cesare de Lollis, vol. 2; see also Harrisse, *op. cit.,* p. 156.
[37] Harrisse, *op. cit.,* p. 156; Thacher, *op. cit.,* vol. 2, pp. 566, 567.
[38] Columbus, *Libro de las Profecías,* in *Scritti,* vol. 2, pp. 81, 83.
[39] *Ibid.,* pp. 108, 125.

COLUMBUS CONSIDERS HIMSELF THE "MESSENGER" OF GOD

First Page of Royal Commission Making Columbus Admiral of the Ocean (Left); Sailing West to Reach the East, Columbus Was Moved by the Conviction That He Was Helping to Fulfill Prophecy (Center); Page From Cardinal d'Ailly's *Imago Mundi*, Which Influenced Columbus, Whose Handwritten Notes Appear in Margin With d'Ailly's Picture as Inset (Right)

sciences of which I spoke were of no profit to me nor the authorities in them; only in Your Highnesses remained my faith, and my stay. Who would doubt that this light did not come from the Holy Spirit, anyway as far as I am concerned, which comforted with rays of marvelous clarity and with its Holy and Sacred Scriptures, . . . encouraged me that I should go on, and continually without a moment's pause, they urged me with great haste." [40]

4. RECOVERY OF JERUSALEM BEFORE THE END.—In this letter Columbus presses the providential guidance of his Western discoveries as a miracle intended to encourage the undertaking of the restoration of Jerusalem to the church.

"In this voyage of the Indies, our Lord wished to perform a very evident miracle to comfort me and others in this other one of the holy House [Jerusalem], . . . the restitution of the holy House to the holy Church. I have already said that in order to execute the enterprise of the Indies neither reason, nor mathematics, nor maps profited me; what Isaiah said was fully realized, and this is that which I wish to write here in order to bring to the mind of Your Highnesses, and in order that you rejoice of the other, which I shall tell you about Jerusalem through the same authorities, about whose enterprise, if there is any faith, hold victory for more than certain." [41]

5. IMMINENCE OF END BASIS OF APPEAL TO MONARCHS.— Columbus, following Augustine, said that the world would last seven thousand years. He adopted the creation date of King Alfonso (about 5,344 years before Christ). Therefore he believed that there were only about 150 years remaining until the great consummation. Believing that the ends of the earth were to be brought together and all nations united under the banners of Christ, and convinced of his own selection as the instrument of Providence, he sought to persuade Ferdinand and Isabella to make possible a new voyage, the fourth. The new continent he had discovered must be explored, and if possible, a new passageway found to China and India. [42]

6. 150-YEAR EXPECTATION BASED ON 7,000-YEAR CONCEPT. —According to the astronomical calculations of King Alfonso X,

---

[40] Translated from Columbus, *Libro de las Profecías*, in *Scritti*, vol. 2, pp. 79, 80.
[41] *Ibid.*, pp. 80, 82.
[42] *Ibid.*, p. 107; Thacher, *op. cit.*, vol. 2, pp. 566, 567.

the Wise, Columbus deduced that from Adam to Christ are
5,343 years, and adding 1,501 years since His birth, one has a
total of about 6,844 years since creation. There lacked, therefore,
according to this reckoning, only 155 years for the completion
of 7,000. Columbus consequently concludes that, according to
these authorities, the world must then come to an end. Here are
his own words, addressed to the king and queen, who were thus
made fully aware of Columbus' views:

"From the creation of the world, or from Adam up to the coming of
our Lord Jesus Christ, are 5,343 years and 318 days, according to the reckoning of the king Don Alfonso, which is considered the most accurate. Peter
d'Ailly, in 'Elucidation of the Concordance of Astronomy with Theological
and Historical Truth,' in chapter 10, adds 1,501 [years] incomplete to make
altogether 6,845 incomplete.

"According to this reckoning, there are lacking but 155 years for the
completion of 7,000, in which it says above through the above-mentioned
authorities, that the world is to come to an end. Our Redeemer said that
before the consummation of this world all that was written by the prophets
is to be accomplished. . . . Cardinal Peter d'Ailly writes much concerning
the end of the Mohammedan sect, and of the coming of the Antichrist in
a treatise, which he wrote 'About the Concordance of Astronomical Truth
and Historical Narration,' in which he relates the saying of many astronomers about the ten revolutions of Saturn, and especially at the end of the
said book in the last nine chapters." [43]

7. OPENING OF WORLD TO GOSPEL TO FULFILL PROPHECY.—
Columbus cites the prophecies of the Old Testament, particularly the Psalms, Isaiah, and Jeremiah. He believed that the
whole Gentile world must have the knowledge of the Lord, and
many nations gather to Mount Zion, and Jerusalem come under
the sway of the Redeemer.[44] He expressly believed the discovery
of these lands, and the opening of these pagan countries to the
teachings of the gospel, in which he had a part, was a direct
fulfillment of prophecy.

"Our Redeemer said that before the consummation of this world all
that was written by the prophets is to be accomplished. . . .

[43] Translated from Columbus, *Libro de las Profecías*, in *Scritti*, vol. 2, pp. 81, 83; see
Humboldt's paraphrase of this translated in Harrisse, *op. cit.*, pp. 158, 159.
[44] Thacher, *op. cit.*, vol. 2, pp. 567, 568; see Columbus, letter to the king and queen,
describing his third voyage, in *Select Letters*, p. 106.

"The greatest part of the prophecies and [of] the Holy Scriptures is already finished. . . .

"I said above that much remained for the completion of the prophecies, and I say that there are great things in the world, and I say that the sign is that Our Lord is hastening them; the preaching of this gospel in so many lands, in recent times, tells it to me." [45]

There seemed to Columbus to remain only the recovery of Jerusalem and Mount Zion for the completion of prophecy and the end of the world. In his report to the king and queen, on his third voyage, Columbus expressed his conviction that the project was more than merely a human venture.[46] It was this faith that made Columbus a discoverer. Near the end of a letter to Raphael Sanchez, describing his first voyage, he says: "Let Christ rejoice upon Earth as He rejoices in Heaven, as He foresees that so many souls of so many people heretofore lost are to be saved." [47]

IV. Fifth Lateran Council Boasts Opposers Silenced

There yet remains one incident of great importance to be noted ere we turn to the Reformation. It forms, in fact, the dramatic setting of the great protest that developed soon after under the lead of Luther. It took place in connection with the Fifth Lateran Council, held at Rome (1512-1517), with its twelve sessions, under the pontificates of Julius II (1503-1513) and Leo X (1513-1521). Julius had promised to call a general council, but had failed to do so. So certain dissatisfied French prelates called the second council of Pisa (1511).[48]

To frustrate this assembly, the pope called the Fifth Lateran Council for 1512. This council, whose delegates—ranging from 100 to 150 in number—were mostly Italians, was convened for the reformation of the church, the extirpation of here-

---

[45] Columbus, *Libro de las Profecias*, in *Scritti*, vol. 2, pp. 81-83.
[46] Jane, *op. cit.*, in *Voyages of Christopher Columbus*, p. 28.
[47] *First Letter of Christopher Columbus to the Noble Lord Raphael Sanchez*, dated Lisbon, March 14, 1493.
[48] Schroeder, *op. cit.*, pp. 480-482; Richard Grier, *An Epitome of the General Councils of the Church*, pp. 255-257; see also Edward Maslin Hulme, *The Renaissance, The Protestant Revolution, and the Catholic Reformation*, pp. 157, 317.

sies, the opposition of the Turks, and the healing of schisms in order to preserve the unity of the church.[49] These the Council of Basel had failed to accomplish.

In the opening speech of the Lateran Council, Aegidius of Viterbo sounded the note of reform, but little came of it. The principal achievement of the council, late in the proceedings, was the abolition of the Pragmatic Sanction of Bourges. Through this deal with the king of France, the measure of independence that the French clergy had enjoyed for some time was surrendered, though most of the powers were reconferred on the French king. Thus Rome appeared superficially to have overcome the setbacks of Avignon and the Great Schism. The decrees of the three councils of Pisa, Constance, and Basel, which had sought to place some limits on the absolutism of the popes, had been secretly evaded, set at nought, or solemnly reversed, and the participants at Pisa were now duly excommunicated.[50] The scandal of pope and antipope anathematizing each other ceased.

The sects that had threatened the very existence of the Papacy were now but shadows of their former strength. The flame kindled by the funeral pyre of Huss appeared fairly burned out. The sword and scaffold of crusade and Inquisition seemed more than a match for the "Manichaean" sects. The Waldenses alone, "as a visible body," seemed to have survived in their Alpine retreats. The powerful protests of the later individual leaders in reform had been silenced and had left no successors. Yet beneath the apparently tranquil surface there was widespread bitterness and resentment, which the ecclesiastical rulers largely ignored. The church's peak of power had been left behind, and "weakness, wearing the treacherous semblance of strength," prevented any genuine reform from within. The popes, while claiming to be lords of Christendom, spent much of their time immediately before the Lutheran revolt in build-

---

[49] Schroeder, *op. cit.*, pp. 480, 481; for the bull of convocation by Julius II, see Mansi, *op. cit.*, vol. 32, cols. 687, 688.
[50] Trench, *op. cit.*, p. 427; Schroeder, *op. cit.*, pp. 456, 480.

ing up the temporal states of the pope in Italy, heedless of the storm of discontent that was gathering in Northern Europe.[51]

1. CATHOLIC CHRISTENDOM HAILED AS NEW JERUSALEM.—— This council was marked by oratorical emphasis on the triumph of papal power, and of the submergence of heretics. Catholicism's basic concept of the church was stressed. The Catholic Church was described as the Holy City of Jerusalem—the beatific subject of Isaiah's, David's, and John's depictions. It had come down from God, and was governed by the Vicar of Christ.[52] This thought resounded throughout the sermon of Thomas de Vio (Cardinal Cajetan), in the second session, with Revelation 21:1 ff. as his text.[53] The same thought was stressed by different orators of the fourth, sixth, seventh, ninth, and tenth sessions.[54]

When ultimate reform and renovation should be accomplished, and the world brought into the true faith, the golden age would be revived, the inheritance restored, and the promise fulfilled that the church should rule from sea to sea. Thus the descent of the New Jerusalem would be accomplished, and the establishment of the Lord's house in the top of the mountains in the last days be fulfilled, when all nations should flow into it—the mountain of the Lord's house meaning "the plenitude of the power of his Christ in the Apostolic See." [55]

2. POPE ACCLAIMED ANOTHER GOD ON EARTH.—Particular note should be taken of the orations of the appointed preachers, which ascribe to the pope, as Vice-Christ, the dignity, titles, and relations to the church of Jesus Christ Himself, and present him as the hope and savior of the church, to bring to pass the final oneness and universality of Christ's kingdom. The following example of the adulation of the pope is abridged from an address by the Venetian prelate Christopher Marcellus during

---

[51] Trench, *op. cit.*, pp. 429-436.
[52] Pastor, *op. cit.*, vol. 6, pp. 410, 411.
[53] Mansi, *op. cit.*, vol. 32, col. 720; Elliott, *op. cit.*, vol. 2, p. 80.
[54] Mansi, *op. cit.*, cols. 761, 804, 888, 919, 920.
[55] Speech of archbishop of Patras in 10th session, *ibid.*, col. 920; Elliott, *op. cit.*, vol. 2, pp. 81, 82.

the fourth session, over which Julius II was presiding in person. He represents the church as a suppliant bowed at the feet of Pope Julius.

"I have compassed sea and land, and found none but thee to care for my preservation and dignity. Unhappy, degraded by wicked hands from my original high elevation, and with my heavenly beauty defiled by earthly pollutions, I come to thee as my true Lord and Husband; beseeching thee to look to it that thy bride be renewed in her beauty. And see too that the flock committed to thee be nourished with the best and spiritual aliment; the fold united in one which is now divided; and the sickness healed which has afflicted the whole world." [56]

Such extravagant language was doubtless a reflection of Julius' popularity because of his military and political victories in Italy. It contains, however, a note of warning that all is not well within the church, and an appeal to the pope to bestir himself further in her behalf. The climax is reached in the following well-known sentence: "For thou art our shepherd, thou our physician, thou our ruler, thou our husbandman, thou, finally, another God on earth." [57]

Likewise in the sixth session, under Leo X, the bishop of Modrusium pictures the Holy Roman Church as the "bride of Christ." [58] Then come these words:

"Is this Jerusalem, that city of perfect beauty, . . . the daughter of Zion, the spouse of Christ? . . . But, weep not, daughter of Zion; for the Lion of the tribe of Judah, the root of David, hath come. Behold, God hath raised up a Saviour for thee who shall save thee from the hands of thy desolators. O most blessed Leo, we hope that thou wilt come as a savior." [59]

3. TELLTALE MARKS SEEN IN LEO X'S CEREMONIES.—In the course of the council, Julius II died in 1513, and Leo X began his reign. The tidings of Leo's election were followed by his ornate coronation at St. Peter's. Still grander was the ceremonial of his taking possession of the church of his bishopric—the

---

[56] Abridged translation, Elliott, *op. cit.*, vol. 2, pp. 79, 80; Pastor, *op. cit.*, vol. 6, p. 429.
[57] Mansi, *op. cit.*, vol. 32, col. 761.
[58] Translated from Mansi, *op. cit.*, vol. 32, col. 803.
[59] *Ibid.*

"Holy Lateran Church, the mother and head of all the churches
of the city [Rome] and of the world." [60] Besides the hierarchy,
there appeared the princes, ambassadors, and ecclesiastical
deputies assembled at the Lateran Council. Following the procession of troops and bodyguard officials from the different
parts of Christendom, came the pope riding a white horse and
wearing the tiara. As he traversed the streets strewn with tapestry
and flowers, he was sheltered by a canopy. The multitude fell
to their knees acclaiming, *"Viva Papa Leone!"* (Long live Pope
Leo!)[61] This very scene was powerfully used by the coming Protestants as revealing the earmarks of Antichrist.

Various paintings adorned the scene. One showed kings
kneeling before the pope; another represented the pope as in
Christ's place as vicegerent in the golden age, and another represented the pope as standing on land and sea, holding the keys
of heaven and hell.[62] Thus Leo X, the antagonist-to-be of Luther,
ascended his pontifical throne in the midst of the council proceedings. It was probably this revelation of papal character, and
the acceptance of the deification and ascription of titles and
offices of Christ as the pope's due, that brought most forcibly
to Luther's mind the contrast between the simplicity and
humility of Christ and the pretensions of His professed vicar.
(For reproduction of Leo's medal, see page 556.)

4. Bohemian Hussites Cited to Appear and Plead.—In
the sixth session—after Julius' death and the assumption of
office by Leo—it was made clear that the terms of the Bull of
Convocation had been directed at specific heretics and opposers.
The English Lollards and Piedmontese Waldenses had been
practically silenced. It was the remnants of the Bohemian Hussites—which included many Waldenses and Wyclifites—that
irritated. No time was lost in proceeding against them. Already,
in the interval between the seventh and eighth sessions, held

---

[60] The words are carved in stone in the entry: *Sacros. Lateran. Eccles. Omnium Urbis et
Orbis Ecclesiarum Mater et Caput.* St. John Lateran ranks higher than any other Catholic church
in the world. (See reproduction on p. 182.)
[61] Elliott, *op. cit.*, vol. 2, pp. 51 ff.
[62] A vivid description of these paintings appears in Elliott, *op. cit.*, vol. 2, pp. 55-59.

in June and December, 1513, respectively, Leo had dispatched to Bohemia, Cardinal Archbishop Thomas of Strigonium, in Hungary, giving him full powers to discuss the differences between Rome and the Bohemian schismatics and heretics, in the hope of an agreement.[63] Concessions regarding giving the cup to the laity had been made some eighty years before at Basel.[64]

The cardinal's mission, with its object, was placed before the council in a papal bull in the eighth session (Dec. 16, 1513), together with a citation to the Bohemians and an offer of a safe-conduct, to appear and plead either before the cardinal legate in Hungary, or before the next session of the Lateran Council in Rome, which finally convened May 5, 1514.[65]

5. NOT A VOICE PROTESTS; OPPOSITION APPEARS SILENCED. —Thus the little remnant was put to the test of braving the danger of facing the lordly legate and the possibility of death, or pleading their cause before the great council, as did Huss at Constance. The time for opening the ninth session arrived, and the council assembled. But there was no report from the cardinal legate giving intimation either of pleading or of opposition. No deputies arrived at the session from Bohemia to plead before it. By this time not a lip seemed prepared to move in behalf of the ancient "heresies." [66]

The heretics appeared confused and silenced. Throughout the length and breadth of Christendom the entire pre-Reformation witness seemed crushed and silenced by means of sword, rack, and stake. Rome's authority seemed better established and the pillars of her strength more visible than ever. Antonius Puccius ascended the pulpit and addressed the assembled members of the Lateran Council in a memorable oration of triumph, in which he uttered a startling declaration—an exclamation that Elliott contends was never uttered before, and has not been

---

[63] Elliott, *op. cit.*, vol. 2, pp. 447, 448; Mansi, *op. cit.*, vol. 32, col. 845.
[64] Elliott, *op. cit.*, vol. 2, p. 448, and pp. 567, 568, Appendix VII.
[65] Mansi, *op. cit.*, vol. 32, cols. 843-845; Landon, *op. cit.*, vol. 1, p. 335; Elliott, *op. cit.*, vol. 2, p. 449.
[66] Elliott, *op. cit.*, vol. 2, pp. 449, 450.

pronounced since:[67] *"Jam nemo reclamat, nullus obsistit!"* (Now no one cries out, not one objects.)[68]

And then came the exultant words, "Now all Christendom (*universum illius [Ecclesiae] corpus*) sees that it is subjected to one head, that is, to thee." [69] It seemed that all Christendom acquiesced. Truly the Papacy seemed to be able to say, "I sit a queen, . . . and shall see no sorrow."

6. EPOCH OF PAPAL TRIUMPH INTERRUPTED BY LUTHER.—Never did the court of Rome sound more confident. The council broke up with the name of Rome and the Roman ecclesiastical *civitas,* referring to the Roman church, on its lips as the New and Holy Jerusalem. Yet only a few months later (Oct. 31, 1517) Luther posted his theses at Wittenberg.[70] Just when Roman ecclesiasticism boasted of triumph and anticipated the fulfillment of Christ's promised reign with His saints, as the appointed heir to all the kingdoms of earth, Luther suddenly interrupted the scene. Such was the dramatic setting as Luther issued his Ninety-five Theses. Before long he was denouncing Rome as, not the New Jerusalem from heaven, but the precise opposite—the great Babylon from the abyss. He even called it Sodom and Egypt—the murderous Jerusalem, by whose decrees and acts the Lord was crucified.[71]

V. Council Action Against Identifying of Antichrist

1. DISCUSSION OF "TIMES" OF ANTICHRIST OR JUDGMENT PROHIBITED.—During the eleventh session, on December 19, 1516, the public exposition of Antichrist or the time of the mooted judgment, and the hidden "times and moments" of God, was definitely prohibited.

"Nor shall they presume to announce or predict in their sermons any fixed time of future evils, the coming of Antichrist, or the day of the last

---

[67] *Ibid.*, p. 450.
[68] Oration of Antonius Puccius, in ninth session, in Mansi, *op. cit.*, vol. 32, col. 892.
[69] *Ibid.*
[70] Elliott, *op. cit.*, vol. 2, p. 444; Pennington, *op. cit.*, pp. 276, 277.
[71] Letter to Staupitz, February, 1519, in *Dr. Martin Luthers Sämmtliche Schriften* (Walch ed.), vol. 15, col. 2443; Elliott, *op. cit.*, vol. 2, pp. 444, 445.

Lateran Church in Rome, Scene of Epochal Councils

Exterior View of St. John's Lateran Church, Rome, and Interior View of This Scene of the Famous Fifth Council, Which Sought to Halt Preaching on Antichrist and to Extirpate Heresy. In the Portico, Carved Into a Large Block of Marble, Is the Pretentious Inscription, "Holy Lateran Church Mother and Head of All the Churches of the City and the World" (Insert)

judgment, since the truth says: 'It is not for you to know the times and moments which the Father hath put in His own power.' (Acts 1:7)." [72]

2. ALL UNCENSORED PRINTING OF BOOKS PROHIBITED.—

With printing now in vogue, the tenth session (in 1515) had prohibited all printing of books without previous papal censorship. Here is the action:

"No one shall presume to print or cause to be printed, in Rome or in any other city or diocese, any book or any other writing whatsoever unless it has first been carefully examined and its publication approved by our vicar and the master of the Sacred Palace, in other cities and dioceses by the bishops or by competent persons appointed by them and by the inquisitor of the city or diocese in which the books are to be printed. This approval must be given over the personal signatures of the censors, free of charge and without delay, under penalty of excommunication." [73]

3. ALL CHRISTIANS SUBJECT TO ROMAN PONTIFF.—Leo's

bull, *Pastor aeternus,* renewed and confirmed the famous bull *Unam Sanctam,* of Boniface VIII, in which all faithful Christians were required to be subject to the Roman pontiff.[74]

Such was Rome's own interpretation of prophecy concerning herself. It was the precise opposite of the identification given by her historic opposers. They denominated her as Babylon, the fallen church of Revelation 17, instead of the new Jerusalem bride of Revelation 21. It was the clash of fundamentally opposite concepts. The basic issue lay in opposite interpretations of the prophetic symbols, and therefore of variant understanding of the character of the two opposing churches. Portentous events were in the offing. But before broaching these, let us pause to introduce another pertinent line of evidence.

---

[72] From the bull of Leo X, *Supernae majestatis praesidio,* in Schroeder, *op. cit.,* p. 505; original in Mansi, *op. cit.,* vol. 32, col. 946.

[73] From the bull *Inter sollicitudines* see Schroeder, *op. cit.,* p. 504; Mansi, *op. cit.,* vol. 32, col. 913; Putnam, *op. cit.,* vol. 1, pp. 108, 109.

[74] Eleventh session, in Mansi, *op. cit.,* vol. 32, cols. 969, 970; Elliott, *op. cit.,* vol. 2, p. 85.

Jewish Expositors Stress
Rome and Year-Day Principle

The historical survey of prophetic interpretation, in Volume I, began with Jewish exposition prior to the Christian Era. But from the time of Josephus onward, the tracing has almost entirely concerned Christian exposition of prophecy. This course was followed, first, because of the relative paucity of Jewish interpretation in the early centuries. And it seemed best, instead of scattering such interpretations through other chapters, to assemble them at this point. This was likewise desirable because the Jewish viewpoint, background, and relationship to the Messianic hope are basically different. Under these circumstances, although the Jews had their hearts set simply on the long-delayed coming of the Messiah, prophecy would have quite a different connotation for the Jews from that anticipated by the Christians.

I. Factors Influencing Jewish Interpretation of Prophecy

In order to grasp the significance of Jewish exposition, it will be necessary first to survey the situation in Jewry in the early centuries regarding the Scriptures, the influence of Greek philosophy, and the relationship between the Jews and the Christians. It will also be imperative to define and understand certain terms that will constantly be employed or encountered— the *Talmud*, with its *Mishnah* and *Gemara*, the *Halachah*, the *Haggadah*, the *Targum*, the *Midrash*, and others. To these we

184

now turn for the setting. Then we shall survey thirty remarkable Jewish interpreters of prophecy, spanning the Christian Era, and later summarized and charted on page 194. These men, and the principles they hold and the applications they make, have a material bearing on our quest.

1. Disastrous Effects of Alexandrian Allegorical School.—Prior to the Christian Era, two widely divergent schools of religious thought developed among the Jews. One embraced Palestine and Babylonia, zealously interpreting the sacred books according to the methods of the Talmud and its related writings. The other school—and a virile one—centered in Alexandria, bent on absorbing the very lifeblood of Greek philosophy.[1] This latter school sought to blend and harmonize the traditions of Hebraism with Greek philosophy, softening and explaining away the differences by allegorical treatment. This reached its peak in Philo (B.C.E. 20-53 C.E.).[2] His burden was to show that, by applying the allegorical system of interpretation to the Scriptures, their simple and obvious meaning really embodied everything that was wise and exalted in Greek philosophy.

It was a struggle between Literalism and Allegorism, as Philo regarded the literal to be a concession to the weak and ignorant. To him, Scripture was "not so much a text for criticism as a pretext for theory." Instead of elucidating the literal sense, he transformed it into a philosophic symbol.[3] A complete perversion of Scripture resulted, as he developed out of Moses a vivid semblance to Greek philosophy. The works of Philo, it should be added, contain no direct reference to the prophecies —no Messiah, no restoration of the Jewish state, no interpretation of prophecy. Living through the lifetime of Jesus, he does not even mention His name.

It was this allegorizing feature of Philo's work, however,

---

[1] Farrar, op. cit., pp. 111, 127.
[2] The terms c.e. (Common Era, or Christian Era) and b.c.e. (before the Common Era, or before the Christian Era), instead of a.d. and b.c., will be employed here in accordance with Jewish practice.
[3] Farrar, op. cit., p. 139.

that was laid hold of with avidity by one large group in the early Christian church—particularly by Origen of Alexandria— and with the same disastrous effects. Some resisted these excesses of fanciful allegory; nevertheless, a deep and abiding impress was left. The influence upon Irenaeus, Tertullian, Origen, Cyprian, Lactantius, Jerome, and Augustine was profound.[4] The unity of language brought about by the conquests of the Greeks and the political unity effected through the coming of the Roman Empire only accentuated this form of interpretation.[5] The Jerusalem Jews sought in vain to stem the advance of Hellenistic influence as Alexandria became the focal point of penetrating influence.

2. JEWISH-CHRISTIAN CONTROVERSIES OF EARLY CENTURIES. —The early centuries of the Christian Era were filled with bitter controversy between the Jews and the Christians. Both groups anticipated a millennium, but the church fathers connected it with the second advent of Christ. The church fathers sought to Christianize the Old Testament, and the rabbis opposed it. Because of this, the Jews came to dislike the Septuagint, for the Christians used it in their Messianic controversies with them.[6] During the first five centuries, belief in a coming millennium was widespread, and prophecy was constantly employed by Christians to prove the Messianic character of Jesus, along with emphasis upon His second advent.[7]

As noted, with the church fathers it was the *second* advent of Christ that was stressed, whereas with the Jews it was just the advent of the Messiah that was anticipated. The Christian interpretation of Messianic prophecies led to opposition on the part of some Jews, who denied that the prophecies were decipherable, and others—such as the elder Hillel (Hillel I),[8] whose lifespan extended briefly into the first century, and the Tanna Rabbi

---

[4] Louis Israel Newman, *Jewish Influence on Christian Reform Movements*, pp. 6, 7, 28, 102; Farrar, *op. cit.*, p. 156, n. 2. These men are all discussed in *Prophetic Faith*, Volume I.
[5] Louis I. Newman, *op. cit.*, pp. 16, 17.
[6] Farrar, *op. cit.*, p. 118.
[7] See *Prophetic Faith*, Volume I.
[8] Abba Hillel Silver, *A History of Messianic Speculation in Israel*, pp. 196-198.

Nathan in the second—even denied the Messianic character of any prophecy. This conflict persisted into the Middle Ages. But the majority sought the prophecies of Daniel with pathetic eagerness, to ascertain the time of the Messiah's coming.

3. PROGRESSION OF EVENTS ACCENTUATES MESSIANIC HOPE. —Many events accentuated the Messianic hope through the centuries—the early struggle with Rome (66-70 C.E.), the destruction of the temple (70 C.E.), the Bar Kochba uprising (132-135), the fall of the Roman Empire (476), the rise of Islam (7th century), the Crusades (1096 onward), the coming of the Tartars, the religious wars of the sixteenth and seventeenth centuries,[9] as well as the Inquisition and the Protestant Reformation. Each in its time intensified the Messianic hope and stimulated time speculations. The promise of the Messiah was the one hope of Israel in its often desperate circumstances. It was only natural that the Jews should have turned to the prophecies of Daniel.

The golden age of Jewish prophetic interpretation is usually placed between 900 and 1500 C.E., beginning with Saadia Gaon,[10] and continuing to Don Isaac Abravanel—and spreading over Babylonia, Palestine, Egypt, Spain, France, Germany, and Italy.[11] Some of these writers were addicted to allegory and Gematria; others stood stiffly against tradition. Some followed the fanciful Midrash, and some sought out the obvious sense, or the literal meaning, of each individual prophecy. But with all these differences there was remarkable unity on certain principles of prophetic interpretation.

4. EXPOSITION CENTERS ON FOUR POWERS AND YEAR-DAY PRINCIPLE.—Two primary phases in Jewish prophetic interpretation will be noted: (1) The recognition of the symbols of Rome as the fourth of the four world powers of prophecy; and (2) the application of the year-day principle to the time prophecies

---

[9] *Ibid.*, p. 4.
[10] Farrar, *op. cit.*, p. 461.
[11] *Gaon* was the title of honor given to the Jewish heads of the two Babylonian academies at Sura and Pumbeditha. The first Gaon of Sura entered upon his office in 591 C.E.; the first Gaon of Pumbeditha assumed his duties about the year 598; and the last Gaon died in 1038.

of Daniel. Some stress only one or the other, but nearly half of the thirty expositors blend the time and symbol aspects,[12] as will be noted on the accompanying chronological table (on page 194), summarizing name, date, place, and interpretation. First, the standard ancient writings of the Jews will be noted, and then their leading scholars through the centuries.

II. Talmud, Targum, and Midrash on the Four Kingdoms

1. TALMUD FIRST SUPPLEMENTS, THEN SUPERSEDES, WRITTEN LAW.—The Talmud is that body of Jewish civil and religious law comprising the combined collections of the Mishnah, or amplifications of the text, and the Gemara, or commentary, especially of legendary homiletics. There are really two Talmuds, named from the regions in which they originated. The Palestinian, or Jerusalem, Talmud (*Talmud Yerushalmi*) contains the discussions of the Palestinian scholars, or Amoraim, from the second to about the middle of the fifth century C.E. The Babylonian Talmud (*Talmud Babli*) embodies the teachings of the Babylonian scholars, also known as Amoraim, from about 190 C.E. down to the end of the fifth century—the Babylonian Talmud being much larger, and practically superseding the former as an authority.

This oral law was first exalted as a necessary supplement to the written law; then it was virtually substituted in its place.[13] The Babylonian Talmud, which fills 2,947 folios, is composed of legal disputes, stories, sermons, legends, Scripture comments, moral truths, observations, legal enactments, history, and rationalism.[14] It is a veritable encyclopedia of things Jewish, a vast compendium of Hebrew science and theology. Drawn from the promiscuous notebooks of students, as taken down from lectures

---

[12] Heavy draft is made upon two Jewish scholars who have made extensive and authoritative research into Jewish writers on Messianic expectation through the centuries of the Christian Era, as based upon the prophetic symbols and time periods of Daniel—Abba Hillel Silver, in his *A History of Messianic Speculations in Israel, From the First Through the Seventeenth Centuries;* and Joseph Sarachek, in *The Doctrine of the Messiah in Mediaeval Jewish Literature.* Showing the futility and unsoundness of such time setting, they nevertheless disclose the basis of their calculations as applications of the year-day principle, and their common understanding of the prophetic course of empire.
[13] Farrar, *op. cit.*, p. 62.
[14] *Ibid.*, p. 92.

by noted rabbis in the schools, it has been called a "monument of human industry, human wisdom, and human folly." [15]

It is still regarded as a sacred book by orthodox Jews. But one must search diligently for the gems hidden in the midst of the conglomerate mass of more than 2,500,000 words—the "sea of the Talmud"—the flotsam and jetsam of a thousand years. Thus it came to overshadow and supersede the Living Oracles (Sacred Scriptures), and turned its followers from the River of Life to broken cisterns. It is often so arbitrary or futile as to give radically false concepts of the sacred books. [16]

2. ORAL TRADITIONS MULTIPLY LAW A THOUSANDFOLD.— The *Halachah*, or *Halaka* (pl. *Halachoth*), meaning "rule," "law," or "decision," comprises the accepted decisions of the rabbis of the Talmud on disputed questions—a general term for Jewish oral or traditional law, which supplements and runs parallel to the written law (Scriptures), embracing minute precepts not found in the written law. Although written by men, it was supposed to be of inspired origin, and to serve as an adjunct to the fundamental code, the theory being that the oral law was handed down through a long line of the highest authorities.

These additions multiplied the bulk of the law a thousandfold, as all Scripture was considered capable of infinite expansion. Like ever-widening, yet ever fainter circles on the broken surface of a lake, the ripples of indefinitely expanding legalism spread long after all traces of the first waves had died away. They embraced foolish questions and conflicts between schools of thought—such as the disagreements between the schools of Hillel and Shammai, and whether an egg laid on the Sabbath or holiday might be eaten. Tradition was thrust between men and the Book. There was an almost limitless development of rules to meet every conceivable case. It was Scholasticism, or Dialecticism, applied to ritual. [17]

The *Haggadah* (pl., *Haggadoth*), meaning "narrative," was

---

[15] Henry Hart Milman, *History of the Jews*, vol. 3, p. 13.
[16] Farrar, *op. cit.*, pp. 93, 94.
[17] *Ibid.*, pp. 85-88.

a free interpretation or application. It embraced the illustrative
sayings—stories, legends, fables, aphorisms, proverbs, allegories,
and folklore [18]—as distinguished from the *Halachah,* and was
often in conflict therewith. It developed beginning with the
days of Johanan ben Zakkai (1st century), when the Jews needed
consolation after the destruction of the Temple and their dispersion. These together make up the Talmud.

3. TALMUD MAKES ROME FOURTH IN PROPHETIC SERIES.—
The Talmud of this early period—which was completed by the
fifth century—commonly speaks of the four empires of prophecy, beginning with Babylonia and ending with Rome [19]—which
latter name was usually concealed under the term *Edom.* Thus,
after the Persian bear and the Grecian leopard, the fourth, designated as Edom, is explicitly explained to be "the kingdom
of Rome the wicked." [20] Guttmann further discusses the Jewish
use of the symbol of the wild boar, employed by the Romans
themselves as the symbol of their nation. He then concludes:

"The result was that it was as though it was said specifically with reference to the Romans." [21]

Guttmann then turns from the common designation
"Edom," as "the fourth kingdom, the kingdom of Edom or
Rome," to the Middle Age suspicion of the dominant Christian
church in thinking that the Midrash and Talmud extended the
application to ecclesiastical Rome. His statement is illuminating: [22]

"One more word about the view which began to be spread abroad in
the Christian church of the Middle Ages, i.e. that the designation 'Edom'
which is found in the Midrash and Talmud, and similarly 'the fourth king-

---

[18] *Ibid.,* p. 91.
[19] Sarachek, *The Doctrine of the Messiah,* p. 11.
[20] Translated from Michael Guttmann, *Mafteah Hatalmud (Clavis Talmudis),* vol. 3b,
pp. 55, 62-65.
[21] *Ibid.,* p. 65.
[22] Indebtedness is here expressed to Doctors Louis Ginzberg and Louis Finkelstein of the
Jewish Theological Seminary of America, in New York City, for invaluable service in locating
citations in the Hebrew writings here used, to Dr. Joshua Bloch, chief of the Jewish division of
the New York Public Library, and his associates, for making photostatic copies possible, and to
Rabbi Abraham Shinedling, of the *Universal Jewish Encyclopedia* editorial staff, for the accurate
translations from the old, unvocalized Hebrew.

dom, the kingdom of Edom or Rome,' refers to Christianity. The censorship, too, acted in accordance with this view, and burned many literary treasures, and in many places where it did not decree destruction, it at least deleted the source texts by placing instead of 'Edom,' 'Rome,' 'the fourth kingdom,' or 'the wicked kingdom' other names which confused the subject matter. . . . The jealous ones of the [Christian] church suspected the Talmud for something which is not contained in it. In vain they thought that they would find their name on the ancient pages of the Law of Israel. And their error rolled upon them from two different reasons: from the first side, they thought (from Jerome on) that they were the inheritors of the dominion of the fourth kingdom, and thus necessarily it had as inescapable result that in their eyes all the ancient remainder of Judaism who mentioned the name of this kingdom were referring to them." [23]

4. TALMUD ON WORLD'S END AT 6,000 YEARS.—Many rabbis believed, on the basis of creation week, that the world would last six thousand years and be in chaos the seventh thousand years.[24] The Babylonian Talmud records the discussion of Rab Hanan and Rab Joseph, and concludes with these words:

" 'The Holy One, blessed be He, will renew his world only after seven thousand years.' R. Abba the son of Raba said: The statement was after five thousand years. It has been taught; R. Nathan said: This verse pierces and descends to the very abyss: *For the vision is yet for an appointed time, but at the end it shall speak, and not lie: though he tarry, wait for him; because it will surely come, it will not tarry.* Not as our Masters, who interpreted the verse, *until a time and times and the dividing of time.*" [25]

5. THE TARGUMIM TEACH THE FOUR WORLD POWERS.—The *Targum* (pl. *Targumim*) comprises the vernacular paraphrases of portions of the Old Testament into the Aramaic of Judea—together with oral tradition reaching back to the pre-Christian Roman period, used in the synagogues of Palestine and Babylonia. When Hebrew ceased to be spoken generally, it became necessary to explain the meaning of what was read from the Hebrew Scriptures. Only a minor part of the floating mass of oral *Targumim* produced has survived in written form, chiefly— (1) the Babylonian *Targum Onkelos* on the Penta-

---

[23] *Ibid.*, p. 76.
[24] Silver, *op. cit.*, p. 16, citing Sanhedrin, 97a.
[25] *The Babylonian Talmud, English Translation*, Tractate Sanhedrin, 97b, p. 658.

teuch, (2) the Jerusalem *Pseudo-Jonathan Targum* on the Pentateuch, and (3) the Babylonian *Targum Jonathan ben Uzziel* on the prophets. No Targum has been found for Daniel. In the *Targumim* a few passages bear on the four empires. For example, in the Jerusalem *Targum* of Pseudo-Jonathan:

"Behold, the kingdom of Babylon shall not endure, and shall not exercise rulership over Israel; the kings of Media shall be killed, and the mighty men of the worshipers of the stars and constellations shall not prosper. The Romans shall be destroyed, and they shall not gather rakings from Jerusalem [i.e., they shall not profit from the destruction of Jerusalem.— Translator's note.] [26]

"And I lifted up my eyes, and I saw, and behold, four kings. And I said to the angel who was speaking with me: What are these? And he said unto me: These are the kingdoms which scattered the men of Judah and Israel and the inhabitants of Jerusalem. . . . These are the kingdoms which scattered the men of Judah and did not permit them to walk upright, and these came to terrify them, to break the kingdom of the nations which lifted up weapons against the land of the house of Judah to exile it." [27]

6. MIDRASH DECLARATIONS ON FOUR WORLD POWERS.—The *Midrash* (pl., *Midrashim*), meaning "interpretation," "explanation," with the practical sense of "deeper exegesis," is a body of Scriptural exposition produced over many centuries following the Exile, embracing two leading principles: (1) That nothing in Scripture is indifferent or accidental, and (2) that all Scripture is capable of infinite interpretations. [28] This explains the strange textual basis selected to set forth the four world powers. The comment on Genesis 15:9, recording a discussion between Rabbis Eleazar and Johanan, is an example:

" 'Take Me a heifer of three years old.' This is *Babylon,* which caused three kings to stand, [i.e. which raised up three kings.—Translator's note.] Nebuchadnezzar, Evil-Merodach, and Belshazzar. And a she-goat of three years old. This is *Media,* which raised up three kings, Cyrus, Darius, and Artaxerxes [in Hebrew, *Ahashverosh.*—Trans.] And a ram of three years old. This is *Greece.* Rabbi Eleazar and Rabbi Johanan had a dispute. Rabbi

---

[26] Translated from *Targum Jonathan,* on Hab. 3:17, in *Mikraoth Gedoloth im Lamed Beth Perushim* (The Great Scriptures, with the Thirty-two Commentaries) Part 10, Ezekiel and the 12 Minor Prophets, p. 281; see also Charles Maitland, *op. cit.,* p. 83.
[27] Translated from *Targum Jonathan,* on Zech. 2:1-4 (A.V., Zech. 1:18, 19), p. 326; see also Charles Maitland, *op. cit.,* p. 83.
[28] Farrar, *op. cit.,* pp. 442, 443.

Eleazar said: The children of Greece subdued all the winds, but they did not subdue the east wind. Rabbi Johanan said to him: But it is written (Daniel 8), I saw the ram pushing westward, and northward, and southward; and no beasts could stand before him, neither was there any that could deliver out of his hand; but he did according to his will, and magnified himself. This is the opinion of Rabbi Eleazar, who did not say the east. And a turtle-dove, and a young pigeon. This is Edom." [29]

Similarly in Genesis 15:12, Babylonia, Media, Greece, and Edom are thrice named by Rabbi Simon in connection with various symbols, and the fourth power is declared to be the "fourth beast, fearful and dreadful and exceedingly strong"— the comment closing with the expression, *"the four kingdoms."* [30]

And finally, the *Midrash* on Leviticus 13:5 twice presents by name the same four powers—but under the strange symbols of the camel, rock-badger, hare, and swine—citing Rabbi Akiba [31] and his associates. Thus the four empires of prophecy permeate the Midrash.

III. Expositors From Josephus (1st cent.) to Eliezer (9th cent.)

The survey of prophetic interpretation, in Volume I, began with the key expositions of the Jews before Christ, which in turn were carried over into the Christian Era. We now trace the Jewish expositors of the Christian, or Common, Era.

1. JOSEPHUS CONCEALS VIEWS ON "BEASTS" AND "TIMES".— [I] [32] FLAVIUS JOSEPHUS (*c.* 37-*c.* 100 C.E.), although primarily a historian, indicates that he had a definite interpretation of both the "beasts" and "times" of Daniel. But these he deliberately withheld, in large part, from his readers [33]—evidently from fear of difficulty with the Roman state, which he indicated was the fourth prophetic power. But the available interpretations of Jo-

---

[29] Translated from *Sefer Midrash Rabboth al Hatorah U Chammash Migloth* (The Book of the Midrash Rabboth on the Torah and the Five Scrolls), part 1, chap. 44, comment on Gen. 15:9.

[30] *Ibid.*, comment on Gen. 15:12.

[31] *Ibid.*, chap. 13, comment on Lev. 13:5.

[32] Figure in brackets indicates serial number of the expositor appearing on the Chronological Table of Jewish Interpreters, for facility in locating the different writers. See p. 194.

[33] Flavius Josephus, *Antiquities of the Jews*, book 10, chap. 10, sec. 4; Silver, *op. cit.*, pp. 21, 22.

CHRONOLOGICAL TABLE OF JEWISH INTERPRETERS OF FOUR EMPIRES AND YEAR-DAY PRINCIPLE

	Date	Name	Place	Interpretation
1.	37-c.100	FLAVIUS JOSEPHUS	Palestine-Rome	Four empires = Babylon, Medo-Persia, Greece, Rome.
2.	1st cent.	JOHANAN ben ZAKKAI	Palestine	Fourth empire = Rome.
3.	c.50-132	AKIBA ben JOSEPH	Palestine	Four empires and year-day.
4.	8th-9th cents.	BENJAMIN ben MOSES NAHAWENDI†	Persia	1290 and 2300 = year-days.
5.	8th or 9th cent.	PIRKE de RABBI ELIEZER	Palestine, Syria, or Asia Minor	Four empires and Messianic stone.
6.	882-942	* SAADIA ben JOSEPH (al-FAYYUMI)	Gaon of Sura, Babylonia	Four empires; 490, 1290, 1335, 2300 (÷ 2 = 1150) = year-days.
7.	10th cent.	SOLOMON ben JEROHAM †	Jerusalem	1290 and 1835 = year-days.
8.	10th cent.	SAHL ben MAZLIAH HAKOHEN †	Palestine	1290, 2300 = year-days.
9.	10th cent.	JEPHET ibn ALI (HALEVI) †	Palestine	Four empires: Iron and clay = Romans and Arabs; Stone = Messiah; Little Horn = Mohammedanism; 2300 evening-mornings (÷ 2) = 1150 year-days; 70 weeks = 490 years.
10.	1040-1105	* RASHI (SOLOMON ben ISAAC)	France	Four empires; 3½ times, 70 weeks, 1290, 1835, 2300 = year-days.
11.	1065-1136	ABRAHAM bar HIYYA HANASI	Spain	1290, 1335, 2300 = year-days.
12.	1092-1167	* ABRAHAM ibn EZRA † (?)	Spain	Four kingdoms; 70 weeks = 490 years.
13.	11th cent.	TOBIAH ben ELIEZER	Bulgaria-Pales.	1335 = year-days.
14.	13th cent.	ISAAC ben JUDAH HALEVI	France	1290, 1335 = year-days.
15.	c.1310-1380	HAYYIM GALIPAPA	Spain	All fulfillments historically past.
16.	1135-1204	MAIMONIDES (MOSES ben MAIMON)	Spain & Egypt	Rome = fourth monarchy.
17.	ca.1195-1270	NAHMANIDES (MOSES ben NAHMAN)	Spain	70 weeks, 1290, 1335, 2300 = year-days.
18.	c.1260-1340	BAHYA ben ASHER	Spain	1290, 1335, 2300 (÷ 2) = year-days.
19.	1288-1344	* GERSONIDES (LEVI ben GERSHON)	France	Four Kingdoms; 1290, 1335 = year-days.
20.	1310-1385	MENAHEM ben AARON ben ZERAH	Spain	1290, 1335 = year-days.
21.	1361-1444	SIMON ben ZEMAH DURAN	Spain & Algeria	1290, 2300 = year-days.
22.	1437-1508	* DON ISAAC ben JUDAH ABRAVANEL	Portugal & Spain	Four empires; Little Horn = Papacy; 1290, 1335, 70 weeks, 2300 = year-days.
23.	15th-16th cent.	ABRAHAM SABA	Spain	Four kingdoms.
24.	c.1460-1530	ABRAHAM HALEVI ben ELIEZER	Spain & Palestine	1290, 1335, 2300 = year-days.
25.	1494-1539	* JOSEPH ben DAVID ibn YAHYA	Italy	Four empires; 2300 = year-days.
26.	c.1512-1585	NAPHTALI HERZ ben JACOB ELHANAN	Turkey & Poland	1335 = year-days.
27.	c.1527-1585	MORDECAI ben JUDAH DATO	Italy	Four empires; 1335 = year-days.
28.	c.1550	DANIEL ben PERAHIAH		1335 = year-days.
29.	16th cent.	NAPHTALI HERZ ben JACOB ELHANAN	Germany	1335 = year-days.
30.	1604-1657	MANASSEH ben ISRAEL	Holland	Four kingdoms; illustrated by Rembrandt.

* Names with asterisk (*) held both year-day principle and Rome as fourth of four prophetic world powers.
† Indicates Karaites.
NOTE.—The serial number, in first column, appears in brackets before each name in accompanying sketches.

sephus—whose life paralleled the ministry of the apostles—are presented in Volume I of *Prophetic Faith* and are therefore omitted here.

2. JOHANAN DECLARES ROME THE FOURTH KINGDOM.— [2] JOHANAN BEN ZAKKAI (1st cent. C.E.), of Palestine—sometimes called the "Upright Pillar"—was one of the greatest of the pupils of Hillel. The first president of the academy at Jabneh (near Joppa, only six miles from Jerusalem), he opposed rebellion against the Roman power, which Johanan recognized to be the fourth world power of the prophesied series of four. The *Babylonian Talmud* gives his interpretation of Daniel 7:23 thus:

"Because it is written (Daniel 7:23), 'It shall devour the whole earth, and shall tread it down, and break it in pieces.' Rabbi Johanan said, This is guilt-laden Rome, whose influence has gone out over all the world." [34]

3. AKIBA RECOGNIZES YEAR-DAY PRINCIPLE AND FOUR EMPIRES.—[3] AKIBA (AQIBA) BEN JOSEPH (c. 50-132), of Palestine, one of the most distinguished Jews of his time, was often called the father of rabbinical Judaism.[35] He systematized Rabbinism, and created a scheme of multiple interpretation that was perfected by Rabbi Judah Hanasi, who committed the oral law to written form in the Mishnah.[36] Akiba recognized both the year-day principle and the four empires, and anticipated the world's end in 6093 A.M. (*anno mundi*, "year of the world," from creation).[37]

This famous associate of the false messiah Bar Kochba, in the 132 to 135 C.E. revolt against Hadrian and the Romans, based his action on Messianic time expectation, and this in turn on the prophetic-time basis[38]—his faith in the expectation never wavering. He was taken prisoner and put to death by the Romans about 132 C.E.

---

[34] Translated from *Der babylonische Talmud* (tractate "Abodah Zarah"), fol. 2a-2b, p. 796; see also Giulio Bartolocci, *Bibliotheca Magna Rabbinica*, vol. 3, p. 610.

[35] Louis Ginzberg, "Akiba ben Joseph," *The Jewish Encyclopedia*, vol. 1, p. 304.

[36] Farrar, *op. cit.*, pp. 79, 80.

[37] Silver, *op. cit.*, pp. 14, 60.

[38] Sarachek, *Doctrine*, pp. 12, 17; Elliott, *op. cit.*, vol. 3, pp. 284, 285; cf. Silver, *op. cit.*, pp. 14, 20, 48.

Later the breakup of the Roman Empire in the fifth century and the imminence of the long-anticipated collapse led to a new hope of the appearance of the Messiah in Palestinian quarters.[39] But the Messiah's failure to appear dampened the ardor of interpretation for some time. As the Mohammedan period advanced, however, Messianic expectancy began to appear again in various anonymous writings.[40]

4. NAHAWENDI APPLIES YEAR-DAY PRINCIPLE TO 1290 AND 2300 PERIODS.—[4] BENJAMIN BEN MOSES NAHAWENDI (8th-9th centuries), the Karaite [41]—with all that the name connotes— dated the 2300 year-days from the destruction of Shiloh (942 B.C.E.), and *from the time of the removal of the continual* [sacrifice] *('olath hatamid)"*—and likewise with the 1290 year-days, from the destruction of the second temple (70 C.E.)— thereby arriving at 1358 C.E. as the Messianic year.[42]

IV. Scriptarian Karaites Reject Rabbinical Traditions

Early in the eighth century a strong protest arose among the Jews in the region of Babylonia, over the throttling grip of traditionalism. This crystallized into the sect called the Karaites (or Caraites),[43] so called because they insisted upon following the wording of the Scripture text. They were also called Scriptarians and literalists, likewise "People of the Holy Writ," and "Followers of the Bible." The Karaites have been referred to as the "Protestants of Judaism." [44] Rejecting the Talmud, the oral law, and the traditions of the Rabbinites, they acknowledged only the authority of Scripture, and were determined to abide by the literal sense.[45] The impact of Islam upon Jewry undoubtedly had a stimulating influence.[46]

[39] Silver, *op. cit.*, pp. 29, 30.   [40] *Ibid.*, pp. 36-49.
[41] Heinrich Graetz, *History of the Jews*, vol. 3, p. 151; Silver, *op. cit.*, p. 55. A sketch of Karaism appears as section IV of this chapter.
[42] Silver, *op. cit.*, pp. 55 (citing Simhah Pinsker, *Likkute Kadmoniyoth*, p. 82), 208.
[43] The name is derived from the Arabic *Alkurra* (cf. Hebrew *Mikra*, from *Kara*, "to read," i.e., the Scriptures).
[44] Albiruni, *The Chronology of Ancient Nations*, pp. 68, 69.
[45] Farrar, *op. cit.*, pp. 83, 449, note 5.
[46] Philip Birnbaum, editor's introduction in Jephet ibn Ali, *The Arabic Commentary of Yefet ben Ali on the Book of Hosea*, p. xv.

1. Anan's Revolt Expands to Embrace a Third of Jewry.—Anan ben David (c. 760), the founder of Karaism,[47] having attacked the oral law, and being excluded from the exilarchate of the Jewish community in Babylonia, went to Jerusalem to develop his own system undisturbed. His followers were at first called Ananites. Gathering strength and popularity, Karaism clashed seriously with the parent faith, shook off the yoke of traditionalism, proclaimed the right of private judgment, and maintained that the original Scripture is a full and sufficient guide. Anan gave up the system of rabbinical calendation, and made the intercalation of a leap month dependent upon the ripened barley,[48] according to Moses. By the ninth century, with its center in Jerusalem, it carried forward a strong missionary propaganda in other countries.[49] Its period of ascendancy, especially in Palestine and Egypt, was from the ninth to the twelfth centuries, with the flood tide in the tenth and eleventh.

By the time of the Middle Ages, Karaism had become a powerful factor in Jewry, possessing many able scholars. In fact, it comprised about forty per cent of Jewry,[50] and effectively laid hold of printing, when it came into vogue. Caleb Afendopolo, a fifteenth-century Karaite leader, summarized the points wherein the Karaites differed from the Talmudists, or Rabbinites, thus: (1) In rejecting the oral law; (2) in rejecting traditional exegesis, while maintaining the "perspicuity" of Scripture; and (3) in denying all right to add to or diminish from the law.[51] They claimed, furthermore, the right of constant progress without justifiable charge of unfaithfulness to their earlier leaders.

2. Reject Rabbinical Calendar; Reinstate Mosaic Reckoning.—A fundamental part of Anan's reform was the

[47] Jacob Mann, *Texts and Studies in Jewish History and Literature*, vol. 2, p. v.; Sarachek, *Doctrine*, p. 30.
[48] Albiruni, *op. cit.*, p. 69. This will be fully discussed in Volume IV of *Prophetic Faith*.
[49] Mann, *op. cit.*, vol. 2, pp. 4, 7.
[50] Zvi Cahn, *The Rise of the Karaite Sect*, p. 12.
[51] Farrar, *op. cit.*, p. 449.

abandonment of the fixed rabbinical calendar as contrary to the
Mosaic regulations, together with reinstatement of the original
form of luni-solar calendation. With the Karaites, the new year
could fall on any day of the week, the Passover and the Day of
Atonement frequently differing from those of the Rabbinites.
This rabbinical revision or change of Jewish time (the Karaites
called it a definite perversion) began under Hillel II, back in the
fourth century,[52] which departure resulted in a fixed, artificial
calendar tied to the vernal equinox, and thus the Rabbinites
disregarded the Mosaic regulations and threw the appointed
Jewish feasts usually one moon (month) too early. In the tenth
century the conflict became intense, as the Palestinian school
sought to break down the authority of the Babylonian school as
regards the calendar. The leaders in this controversy were Ben
Meir, head of the Karaite school in Palestine, and Saadia Gaon,
head of the Babylonian rabbinical school.[53]

3. BEN MEIR SEEKS TO WREST CALENDAR CONTROL FROM
BABYLONIA.—AARON BEN MEIR (9th-10th centuries) had denied
the authority of the Babylonian academies to fix the festivals,
and had won the confidence of many. He disputed the Babylonian method of calculation, but he "never ventured to propose a
return to the method of lunar observation," as did "the Karaites,
who had reverted in all respects to the ancient practice of determining the time of the new moon by observation, and the intercalation of the thirteenth month when required by the state
of the crops." [54] He sought, in fact, to transfer the authority from
rabbinical Babylonia back to Palestine, and to wrest the control
of calendar calculation from the Rabbinites. Saadia ben Joseph,
then in Babylonia, had far earlier defended the rabbinical calendation. His opinion came to be accepted, ending in a setback
for Ben Meir, who was excommunicated by the exilarch David
ben Zakkai and the academies of Babylonia, with notification

. [52] Samuel Poznanski, "Calendar (Jewish)," James Hastings, editor, *Encyclopaedia, of Religion and Ethics*, vol. 3, p. 118. See also *Prophetic Faith*, Volume IV.
[53] Poznanski, "The Anti-Karaite Writings of Saadiah Gaon," in *Jewish Quarterly Review*, January, 1898, vol. 10, pp. 238, 239.
[54] Poznanski, "Calendar (Jewish)" in Hastings, *Encyclopaedia*, vol. 3, p. 119.

sent out over the world. Saadia was rewarded by being made Gaon of the Sura academy, notwithstanding the contrary advice of Nahawendi.[55]

The controversy continued, but in the end the Karaite protest lost its momentum, and the Babylonian system of regulation of the Jewish festival year became authority, before which the Holy Land had to bow. This setting and circumstance will assume major importance when we come later to study the prophetic exposition of 1843 and 1844.[56]

V. "Golden Age" of Interpretation Opens With Saadia

1. ELIEZER—MESSIANIC KINGDOM FOLLOWS FOURTH EMPIRE.—[5] The *Pirke de Rabbi Eliezer* (The Chapters of Rabbi Eliezer), an eight- or ninth-century Midrash (exposition —written after the rise of Mohammedanism, but incorporating much old material),[57] refers to "the four kingdoms, their dominion and their downfall." [58] The second power was declared to be Medo-Persia, signified by the ram of Daniel 8, the third being Greece, symbolized by the he-goat, and the fourth beast (Dan. 7:19) Edom [59]—which name is used for Rome, as the translator's footnote indicates: " 'Edom' is the usual term for the Roman Empire. MS.[Moses] Gaster adds: 'This is the fourth Kingdom.' " [60]

Previously, the four kingdoms had been sketchily set forth from Daniel 2—with the monarchs Nebuchadnezzar, Cyrus, and Alexander named. The stone kingdom is declared to be that of "King Messiah, who, in the future, will rule from one end of the world to the other"—citing Daniel 2:35, concerning the stone, which became a great mountain and "filled *the whole earth*." [61]

[55] I. Broydé, "Ben Meir," *The Jewish Encyclopedia*, vol. 2, p. 677.
[56] This will be covered in Volume IV of *Prophetic Faith*.
[57] Silver, *op. cit.*, pp. 37-39; *The Universal Jewish Encyclopedia*, vol. 8, p. 541, art. "Pirke de Rabbi Eliezer."
[58] *Pirke de Rabbi Eliezer*, translated by Gerald Friedlander, p. 198.
[59] *Ibid.*, pp. 198, 199.
[60] *Ibid.*
[61] *Ibid.*, pp. 82, 83.

2. SAADIA INTERPRETS BOTH SYMBOLS AND TIME PROPHECIES.

—[6] SAADIA BEN JOSEPH [al-Fayyumi] (882-942), Gaon of Sura, famous academy of Babylonia, is called the pioneer of "scientific Jewish exegesis." Opening the "Golden Age" of prophetic interpretation, he built primarily on the literal sense, and rejected the naturalistic explanation of miracles.[62] He was a bitter opponent of the Karaites, especially of Solomon ben Jeroham. He believed in the authority and integrity of the Scriptures, but defended rabbinical Judaism, contending that there are two other sources beside the Scriptures—"understanding and tradition." He relied on Scripture, however, in order to fight Karaism with its own weapons.[63] He translated the Old Testament into Arabic.

Saadia was perhaps the first among the Gaonim to formulate a comprehensive view upon the Messianic predictions, presented in his commentary on the book of Daniel, the *Sefer Hagalui*,[64] and the eighth chapter of his *Kitab al-Amanat kal-I'tikadat*. He contends that both the 1290 days of Daniel 12 and the 1335 days —beginning forty-five days earlier—are to be reckoned as years,[65] but he did not fix a beginning for the periods. Similarly with the 2300—only these he divided by two, obtaining 1150. In the field of prophetic exegesis, Saadia says that the stone of Daniel 2 is the Messianic power. He writes thus of the kingdoms symbolized in Daniel 2:

"And after thee [Babylon] shall arise another kingdom lower than thee, just as silver is inferior to gold, and this is the kingdom of Media. Lower means weaker. . . . Another, a third kingdom. Like brass. This is the kingdom of Greece, whose hardness is like brass and whose rulership is over the whole land of Israel. And the fourth kingdom, strong like iron. This is Gog." [66]

The first three beasts of Daniel 7 are denominated by Saadia as Babylonia, Persia, and Greece.[67] The fourth beast he inter-

---

[62] Farrar, *op. cit.*, p. 461, note 1.
[63] Sarachek, *Doctrine*, p. 30.
[64] See Poznanski, *Miscellen über Saadja III. Die Berechnung des Erlösungsjahres bei Saadja*, p. 2.
[65] Silver, *op. cit.*, p. 50; Sarachek, *Doctrine*, pp. 40, 41; Elliott, *op. cit.*, vol. 3, pp. 285, 286.
[66] Translated from Saadia, comment on Dan. 2:39, in *Sefer Kehilloth Mosheh* (The Book of the Communities of Moses, or The Rabbinic Bible), part 4; Sarachek, *Doctrine*, pp. 37, 38.
[67] Saadia, Comment on Dan. 7, in *Mikraoth Gedoloth*, pp. 134, 135.

preted as "Gog and Magog," which will crush the land of Israel. And among the ten horns, or kings, arises a cruel king who will destroy the Temple, enticing to harlotry in the holy of holies for three and a half "times," which time, he declares, no one understands except God. It is for Israel to wait and hope for God's mercy on His people and city.[68] The ram and the he-goat are Medo-Persia and Greece, and the four horns Alexander's generals.[69] As to the seventy weeks of years, Saadia is explicit:

"Seventy weeks are decreed upon thy people. We shall count and know how many years they are. Ten times seven, amounting to seventy; behold, these seventy weeks are 490 years. Subtract from them the seventy years of the Babylonian exile, from the time when Nebuchadnezzar destroyed the Temple until the second year of Darius, and there remain 420 years, which is the length of time that the second Temple existed, as if to say: Seventy weeks he decreed upon thy people and upon thy city Jerusalem thy holy city, which is going to be rebuilt. Behold thou hast learned: Including the Babylonian exile and including the existence of the second Temple, is a period of seventy weeks, which mean 490 years, seventy for the destruction and 420 for the building, . . . in order to rebuild Jerusalem, hitherto there are seven weeks; seven weeks are forty-nine years since God announced to them the tidings to rebuild Jerusalem." [70]

3. YEROHAM CALCULATES MESSIANIC YEAR WITH YEAR-DAYS.

—[7] SOLOMON BEN JEROHAM (Yeroham) (10th century), Karaite contemporary and opponent of Saadia, in his explanation of Daniel, arrived at the date of 968 C.E. He based the 70 weeks on the third year of Cyrus as the starting point, and reckoned the duration of the second temple as sixty-two and a half year-weeks, with the destruction by the Romans in the midst of the last week.[71] Study and discussion of the prophecies appear about equally divided among the opposing Karaites and Rabbinites as to calculation.

4. HAKOHEN HOLDS 2300 AND 1290 AS YEAR-DAYS.—[8]

SAHL BEN MAZLIAH HAKOHEN (10th century) of Jerusalem, like-

---

[68] *Sefer Kehilloth Mosheh*, part 4.
[69] *Mikraoth Gedoloth*, p. 145.
[70] *Ibid.*; see also Sarachek, *Doctrine*, pp. 36, 37.
[71] Silver, *op. cit.*, pp. 50-52; Poznanski, *Miscellen über Saadja III. Die Berechnung des Erlösungsjahres bei Saadja*, pp. 5-7. About a century later Albiruni, an Arabic astronomer and chronologer, says that the Jews count 1335 years from the time of Alexander the Great, and so terminate them about 968 C.E., looking then for the redemption of Israel. (Albiruni, *op. cit.*, p. 18.)

wise a Karaite, and one of Saadia's bitterest opponents, held views similar to those of Jephet Ibn Ali Halevi relative to the time periods of the 2300 and 1290 year-days, and wrote a commentary on Daniel. He reproved the Rabbinites and believed that the rejection of rabbinism would hasten the Messiah's coming.[72] He was also deeply interested in the calendrical issue.[73]

---

[72] Silver, *op. cit.*, p. 54.
[73] Schulim Ochser, "Sahl ben Mazliah Ha-Kohen," *The Jewish Encyclopedia*, vol. 10, p. 636.

CHAPTER NINE

Persecution Accentuates
Medieval Jewish Exposition

I. A Thousand Years of Jewish Oppression

Before tracing further the Middle Ages expositors in Jewry, let us pause to envision the oppression visited upon the Jews throughout the centuries we are traversing. The fate of the Jews during the Christian Era is perhaps the most moving and sorrowful drama in all history.[1] It forms the background through which they looked and longed for the promised Messiah, and gives the actual setting in which their great scholars interpreted the prophecies of Daniel. They became the most widely dispersed of all nations. But the Talmud, like a band of iron, held them together and separated Jew from Gentile. On the whole, they were protected rather than oppressed by the emperors of pagan Rome. However, when Christianity became the religion of the Roman Empire, the synods began to forbid eating with Jews. The earlier tolerance passed, and with few exceptions Christian writings introduced a hostile tone. In 439 Theodosius II excluded the Jews from public office; and this statute was embodied in the Justinian Code that continued in force for centuries in the East as well as in the West.

By the end of the sixth century attempts at compulsory conversion of the Jews were made by the Franks, with the support of the bishops. Coercive laws were passed punishing those

---

[1] Döllinger, *Studies,* p. 211. This section is based upon chapter 9, "The Jews in Europe," by this learned professor of ecclesiastical history in the University of Munich.

who relapsed. Jews were forbidden to marry Christians or to sit in judgment upon them. It was unlawful to call a Jewish physician. And by the close of the eleventh century the religious wars, or Crusades, began to compel heathen and unbeliever to embrace the Christian faith and to plunder and root out those who resisted. This aggravated the misery of the Jews, as this coercive program was applied to them as well. When the Crusaders set out to war against the distant Mohammedans, they often first murdered the Jews at home and plundered their homes. Finally the Papacy, which at first ignored the Jews, assumed a hostile attitude under Pope Stephen VI (885-891), declaring that the Jews, as enemies of God, were being punished for the death of Christ.[2]

There was little protection from the popes. Innocent III declared that the Jewish nation was destined to perpetual slavery because of its sins, and this pronouncement was continually cited. The Jews were compelled to wear a distinctive badge, or garment, and there was frequent mob violence. Merciless legislation was sponsored by Eugene IV. And where popes failed, councils made up for any omissions in oppression. The Talmud was frequently ordered burned because of its alleged anti-Christian passages. And Thomas Aquinas pronounced the whole race condemned to perpetual slavery, with dispossession lawful. Monarchs, like Frederick II and Charles IV, followed up the principle of perpetual slavery, and the Jews were often regarded as chattels. Massacres were frequent, as in 1290. And the great Black Plague of 1348, which depopulated much of Europe, was often falsely attributed to the Jews.[3]

Because they lent money at excessive interest, the Jews were charged with usury. The entire principle of interest was condemned by popes and councils, such as Clement V at the Council of Vienna in 1311. The Jews were ostracized from trades and handicrafts, and often debarred from the medical profession, except in territories controlled by the Mohammed-

---

[2] *Ibid.*, pp. 215-218.   [3] *Ibid.*, pp. 219-223.

ans.[4] In England they were from time to time subject to bloody oppression, and bishops demanded their banishment. This was finally accomplished in 1290 by Edward I. The maltreatment extended into France, and in 1394 Charles VI decreed their expulsion from his kingdom.[5]

In Spain their lot was more tolerable at first. In fact, some rose to power and influence in the twelfth and thirteenth centuries. But priests fanned the flames of persecution. Two hundred thousand Jews saved themselves by receiving Christian baptism, though thousands relapsed into Judaism. And in 1492 a royal edict commanded all Jews to quit the country, leaving their goods.[6] Statistics vary, but between 170,000 and 400,000 withdrew into exile. Thousands perished from pestilence, starvation, and shipwreck. In Portugal their plight was even worse, especially in 1496 under King Manuel, who decreed their expulsion from the land. They could remain only by turning Christian. Jewish children under fourteen were seized and baptized under compulsion. Conditions were better in Italy. Some 30,000 Jews were "converted" under the fiery eloquence of the preaching friar, Vincent Ferrer. But it should be remembered that the supposed conversions took place in conjunction with a reign of terrorism. And when a Jew became a Christian he forfeited intercourse with the Jews without gaining the favor of the Christians. In Rome it was commonly said that a baptized Jew almost invariably relapsed into "apostasy" (Judaism).[7]

The worst of all came with the spiritual tribunals of the Inquisition, under which, upon the merest suspicion, the new convert was seized, tortured, and condemned to fine or imprisonment for secret Judaism. This induced many to enter the Christian church and live a life of hypocrisy. It is scarcely possible to imagine a more painful, frustrated existence than that of the Jew in the Middle Ages—nearly a thousand years of oppression and massacre, banishment and recall.[8] Such is the

---

[4] *Ibid.*, pp. 224-226.   [5] *Ibid.*, pp. 229-231.   [6] *Ibid.*, pp. 231, 232.
[7] *Ibid.*, pp. 56, 232-235.   [8] *Ibid.*, pp. 235-238.

tragic background of their writings on prophecy, as they strove to obtain equal rights of citizenship and protection.

II. Jephet ibn Ali Represents Iron and Clay as Romans-Arabs

[9] JEPHET IBN ALI HALEVI (Yefeth ben Ali Halevi, or Japheth ben Eli) (10th century), of Palestine, was the most able of all Karaite scholars. Commentator and expounder,[9] he was distinguished by the term Teacher of the Exile. Born in Iraq, he spent considerable time in Jerusalem. He wrote a comprehensive Arabic commentary on the entire Jewish Bible, and his writings were translated from Arabic into Hebrew in the eleventh century. Stressing the importance of grammar and lexicography in exposition, he engaged in lengthy discussions with Saadia,[10] charging him with lack of exegetical and grammatical knowledge.

Jephet claimed full freedom for the exegete, often differing from his fellow Karaites, Anan and Nahawendi. He frequently cited the Talmud, Midrash, and Targum,[11] but was opposed to the philosophical and allegorical treatment. He exemplified the difference between the Karaites and Rabbinites, and charged the Rabbinites with changing the divine laws. He also engaged in controversy over the Jewish calendar, and the right beginning of the lunar month for the governing of the Mosaic festivals. Here are Jephet's own significant words: "They have introduced the calculation of the calendar, and changed the divine festivals from their due seasons." [12]

Jephet notes the prophetic calculations made by many rabbis, who had counted the 1335 year-days from the third year of Cyrus, and remarks that, as the terminal date of that calculation is past, it stands discredited.[13] He also states that the 2300 year-days are, by many Karaites, held to be dated from the

---

[9] Graetz, *op. cit.*, vol. 3, pp. 205, 206.
[10] Birnbaum, *op. cit.* in Jephet ibn Ali, *Arabic Commentary . . . on the Book of Hosea*, pp. xxxvi, xxxvii.
[11] *Ibid.*, p. x.
[12] *Ibid.*, pp. xxvii, xxviii. This will be carefully studied in *Prophetic Faith*, Volume IV.
[13] Silver, *op. cit.*, p. 52 (citing Pinsker, p. 81).

Exodus, which took place—according to Karaite chronology—in 1332 B.C.E., and would therefore have ended in 968 C.E.[14]

1. TEN HORNS ROMAN, BUT LITTLE HORN MOHAMMEDANISM.—In expounding the four kingdoms of Daniel 2, the fourth kingdom—following Babylonia, Persia, and Greece—is expressly declared to be "the kingdom of Rome, before the king dom of Arabia arose." Of the divided feet and toes, he holds, "The *iron* represents the Romans, and the *clay* the Arabs." [15] The "stone" cut out of the mountain Jephet expounds as the kingdom of the Messiah, which will never pass away.[16] Coming to the four beasts of Daniel 7, with the earth interpreted as the "sea," Jephet similarly declares the fourth beast to be "Rome, the fourth kingdom," exercising dominion over all mankind; the ten horns are the "ten thrones, belonging to Rome." [17]

It is but natural that Jephet, living in Palestine when Islam controlled the homeland of the Jews, should apply the Little Horn to Mohammedanism, with its changing of appointed times and the law—"holy-days, sabbaths, and feasts." He stresses the fact that they had merely been changed, not abolished. The three and a half times, he says, may be the length of Islam's reign, or the time of its rule over Israel.[18]

2. SYSTEMATIC EXPOSITION OF DANIEL 8 TO 12.—Jephet identifies the Persian ram and the Grecian goat of Daniel 8 with the notable horn replaced by four horns, as Alexander and the four divisions into which his empire was split. He again applies the great horn of Daniel 8—that casts truth to the ground—to the Mohammedan perversion of the words of the law and the prophets, with Mohammedanism's ultimate final destruction.[19] The 2300 evening-mornings of Daniel 8:14 are interpreted as 1150 whole days—a day standing for "a year" in fulfillment.[20]

---

[14] *Ibid.*, p. 54.
[15] Jephet ibn Ali, *A Commentary on the Book of Daniel*, translated by D. S. Margoliouth, pp. 12, 13.
[16] *Ibid.*, p. 14.
[17] *Ibid.*, pp. 33, 37.
[18] *Ibid.*, p. 38.
[19] *Ibid.*, pp. 33, 41, 42.
[20] *Ibid.*, pp. 43, 80.

But no attempt is made to locate the period. Continuing with the time prophecy of the seventy weeks, Jephet says:

"Of these *seventy weeks, seven* passed in the kingdom of the Chaldees (47 years); 57 years the Persians reigned, 180 the Greeks, 206 the Romans; these are the special periods of the seventy weeks. These include the reigns of all four beasts; only the angel does not describe at length what happened to any of them save the history of the Second Temple during the time of Rome. These seventy weeks are *weeks of sabbatical years,* making 490 years; below they are divided into periods." [21]

The 434 years, Jephet calculates, reach to the coming of "Titus the sinner"; the abomination is the "army of the Romans." [22] And the exposition continues in Daniel 11, covering Persia, Greece, and Rome. The running to and fro and seeking knowledge, cited in Daniel 12:4, is a searching of God's Word— "Knowledge shall increase; knowledge of two things: (a) the commandments; (b) the end." [23]

3. ACKNOWLEDGES YEAR-DAY PRINCIPLE BUT QUESTIONS PLACEMENT.—On the larger time periods—the 1290, 1335, and 2300—Jephet is distressed by the futile attempts to pierce the "times" and "seasons," and the unjustified and disappointing calculations that had frequently been made by both Rabbinites and Karaites. He prays God to bring the great consummation "near in our day and yours; not to deny us or you abundant knowledge of His book, revelation of His secrets, and attachment to His faith." [24] Though protesting the rather general practice of calculating the periods extending to the Messiah, he bears witness to the general recognition of the year-day principle. Here is Jephet's rebuke:

"The scholars who preceded Joseph ibn Bakhtawi explained the 2300, 1290, and 1335 as *years;* the Rabbanites, too, spoke of the *end,* and fancied that from the third year of Cyrus to the *end* would be 1335 years; the term is passed some years since, so that their opinion has been disproved, and that of their followers; similarly El-Fayyumi [Saadia] explained it years, and has been proved false; he had however some marvellous inventions with reference to the *time and times.* He was answered by Salmon ben

---

21 *Ibid.,* p. 49.   22 *Ibid.,* pp. 50, 51.   23 *Ibid.,* p. 77.
24 *Ibid.,* p. 86; see also Silver, *op. cit.,* pp. 207, 208.

Jerucham; whom we need not in our turn answer, since his term is past and the end not arrived. Certain of the Karaites, too, made the 2300 years date from the Exodus from Egypt; that term too is past years ago, and their prophecy not come true. Salmon ben Jerucham, in his Commentary on Ps. lxxiv. 9, denied that it was possible to ascertain the *end;* but on Ps. cii. 14 he offered a date which is passed and falsified. He agreed with many others in interpreting the 2300 and 1290 as days, but differed about the interpretation of the *time of the removal of the continual,* which, he thought, meant the *destruction of the Second Temple.* Benjamin Nahawendi agreed with him in the latter point, but differed from him about the days being days and not years. Benjamin took a separate view in believing that they were years. Salmon ben Jerucham referred the 1290 to the three and a half spoken of in chap. x. 27 ('for the half of the week he shall cause the sacrifice and the oblation to cease').

"Each of the commentators has taken a different line, and all have gone wrong in making the days years. Benjamin Nahawendi, indeed, made the 2300 date from the destruction of Shiloh, and *from the time of the removal of the continual* from the destruction of the Second Temple; this leaves still some 400 years; but this is a delusion." [25]

He speaks of one commentator who attempts to apply the three and a half times to the three periods of 2300, 1290, and 1335, but shows its improbability. He closes his commentary by asking God to "pardon any slips or errors." Then "the Almighty Himself has said that *the words are shut up and sealed till the time of the end.* At that time it shall be revealed by the hand of the wise; *the wise shall understand.* God Almighty, in His mercy and lovingkindness, bring near their realisation." [26]

III. Similar Expositions From Rashi to Maimonides

1. RASHI—EXPECTS MESSIANIC KINGDOM TO FOLLOW ROME. —[10] RASHI (SOLOMON BEN ISAAC) (1040-1105), the most celebrated rabbi of the French schools, is often called "The Exegete," his Midrashic and legal commentary on the law (in the Talmud) being considered standard among the Jews,[27] though it came under the ban of the Inquisition. His was the first Jewish book to be printed (1470).[28] He witnessed the beginning of the

---

[25] *Ibid.*
[26] *Ibid.*, p. 87.
[27] Farrar, *op. cit.*, pp. 462, 83; see also Louis I. Newman, *op. cit.*, p. 325.
[28] Farrar, *op. cit.*, p. 462.

period of the Crusades, terrible tragedies coming upon the Jewish communities in northwestern Europe in their wake.

In the field of prophetic interpretation he believes the four monarchies of Daniel 2 and 7 to be Babylonia, Medo-Persia, Greece, and Rome, followed by the Messianic state.[29] He has Daniel 8:14 begin with the Egyptian captivity, and 12:11, 12 terminate in 1352 C.E., as the Messianic year [30]—1290 years after the cessation of the burnt offering in 62 C.E., shortly before the destruction.[31] He interprets the seventy weeks as 490 years.[32]

On Daniel 2, Rashi makes the usual Jewish application to the four kingdoms by name,[33] followed by Rome's weakness and division. It is while these kingdoms are still in existence, he contends, that the eternal Messianic kingdom—the fifth—will be set up, and it will consume all others.[34] In Daniel 7 the same four kingdoms are portrayed, the ten horns being ten Roman kingdoms, with Titus as the little horn.[35] Rashi makes the three and a half times, however, the same as the "1335 years," reckoned from the cessation of the perpetual sacrifice,[36] when the abomination of desolation is removed.

Rashi has recourse to Gematria,[37] however, and adds 574 to the 2300, making 2874, when the sanctuary shall be "victorious" [38]—dating it from the time when Israel went down into Egypt until the "continual offering" was removed, shortly before the destruction of Jerusalem. This arbitrary date Rashi

[29] Sarachek, *Doctrine*, pp. 55, 56.
[30] *Ibid.*, p. 59, noting Sanhedrin 97b; Silver, *op. cit.*, p. 66.
[31] Silver, *op. cit.*, p. 66.
[32] Sarachek, *Doctrine*, pp. 56, 57.
[33] Rashi. comment on Daniel 2, in *Sefer Kehilloth Mosheh*, part 4.
[34] Rashi, comment on Daniel 2, in *Nebiim Ukethubim im Perush Rashi Uperush Mikrae Kodesh Cha-Rav Meir Loeb Malbim.* (The Prophets and Hagiographa With Rashi's Commentary) and the Commentary "Mikrae Kodesh" Which is by Rabbi Meir Loeb Malbim, vol. 10, pp. 9, 10.
[35] *Ibid.*, comment on Dan. 7:24; see also *Mikraoth Gedoloth*, comment on Dan. 7:4.
[36] *Ibid.*, comment on Dan. 7:25; see also *Sefer Kehilloth Mosheh*, comment on Dan. 8.
[37] In Gematria men sought to find numerical equivalents through the mystical value of names, and of the letters by which they were expressed. This led to innumerable fancies, as every name was regarded as a number, and therefore a cognate to any other name which yielded the same number. Then there were also the sizes and shapes of letters, and computations, and interchange of letters in a cabalistic alphabet. (Farrar, *op. cit.*, pp. 97-107.) This often led to letter worship and traditionalism, to exaltation of ceremonialism, and to the ignoring of the literal intent. Bibliolatry slowly but surely undermined the Bible, and the Scriptures came to be buried under masses of legendary distortion. Exegesis became an art of leading astray, as the mystic Cabala was devoid of any sound foundation. Thus the Word was set at nought by human inventions.
[38] *Mikraoth Gedoloth*, comments on Dan. 8:14, and 12:11.

admits is without "specific proof." [39] He apparently believes that the forty-five years beyond the 1290 will yield the 1335, when the Messiah will reveal Himself; but his statement is couched very vaguely. The seventy weeks are sabbatical weeks of years, and are therefore 490 years—the Babylonian Exile seventy years, and the Second Temple 420 years.[40] Despite it all, the year-day principle was acknowledged and applied.

2. BAR HIYYA SEEKS DATE OF END FROM TIME PROPHECIES. —[11] ABRAHAM BAR HIYYA HANASI (c. 1065-1136), Spanish astronomer, mathematician, and philosopher, was surveyor for the state, writer of a textbook on geometry, and interested in calendation. His is the first eschatological work—*Megillath Hamegalleh* (The Scroll of the Revealer)— of a European rabbi, and it later influenced Nahmanides and Abravanel; his is also the most extensive attempt at Messianic calculation thus far essayed, digesting all the literature up to his day. He sought to determine the apocalyptic end.[41] His calculations were derived from the date of creation, as he believed that the world would last 6,000 years, with the seventh as the millennial sabbath.[42]

Bar Hiyya makes the 2300, the 1290, and the 1335 terminate at different dates—with the 2300 from the erection of the First Temple (2928 B.C.E.), which would end these periods in 1468 C.E., with the sanctuary "victorious"; the 1290 he dates from the destruction of the Second Temple, which he placed in 68 C.E., therefore bringing 1358 C.E. as the Messianic year; the 1335 lasts forty-five years longer, for the wars of Gog and Magog.[43] He also invoked astrology—the conjunctions of the planets.[44]

3. IBN EZRA—TITUS LITTLE HORN ON ROMAN FOURTH BEAST.—[12] ABRAHAM IBN EZRA (1092-1167), noted exegete with Karaite leanings, was famous for his scientific discoveries. Born in Spain, he traveled in Northern Africa, Babylonia, Persia,

---

[39] *Ibid.*, comment on Dan. 8:14.
[40] *Ibid.*
[41] Sarachek, *Doctrine*, pp. 313, 314; Silver, *op. cit.*, pp. 69, 70.
[42] Silver, *op. cit.*, p. 79; Sarachek, *Doctrine*, pp. 316, 321.
[43] Sarachek, *Doctrine*, p. 323; Silver, *op. cit.*, p. 72.
[44] Silver, *op. cit.*, pp. 72-74, 257.

India, France, and England. He was interested in philosophy, medicine, mathematics, philology, and theology. His commentaries on the Old Testament developed the literal sense, distrusting allegory. The writings of Jephet ibn Ali Halevi, the Karaite, exerted a marked influence upon him, and he quoted from Jephet more frequently than from any other.[45] Declaring that the book of Daniel contains Messianic prophecies, he deplored astrological attempts to nullify them.

Ibn Ezra distinguished between the five methods of Jewish Biblical exegesis, and chose the last. These were: (1) Verbal—expounding each separate word; (2) subjective—paying no attention to tradition; (3) allegorical—reading mysteries into the sacred text; (4) cabalistic—developing secrets out of letters, numbers, and syllables; and (5) literal—confined to the actual meaning of the writers.[46] Like many others, he stressed the four empires of Daniel 2 and 7, with the eternal kingdom of the Messiah to follow.[47]

The seventy weeks Ibn Ezra holds to be seventy septinates, or 490 years,[48] and cites Saadia in support of the year-day principle.[49] But he is not clear regarding the 2300, 1290, and 1335 numbers.[50] Believing them to be literal days, he says that they may, however, represent that number of years.[51]

In Daniel 2, after enumerating the first three powers as Babylonia, Medo-Persia, and Greece, Ibn Ezra avowedly follows Saadia Gaon in bringing Ishmael into the fourth empire, as the clay, mingled with the Roman iron.[52] In Daniel 7 the Persian element is predominant in the second kingdom, and the three ribs are the three provinces. The four heads of the leopard are the four divisions of Alexander's kingdom. The ten horns of the fourth, or Roman, beast are "ten kings which arose in Rome

[45] Birnbaum, *op. cit.*, in Jephet ibn Ali, *Arabic Commentary . . . on the Book of Hosea*, pp. xi, xliii.
[46] Farrar, *op. cit.*, pp. 274, 275.
[47] Sarachek, *Doctrine*, p. 119; Silver, *op. cit.*, pp. 212, 213.
[48] Sarachek, *Doctrine*, p. 120.
[49] Ibn Ezra, comment on Dan. 9:24, in *Mikraoth Gedoloth*.
[50] Sarachek, *Doctrine*, pp. 119, 120.
[51] Silver, *op. cit.*, p. 213.
[52] Abraham ibn Ezra, comment on Dan. 2, in *Sefer Kehilloth Mosheh*.

before Vespasian, who destroyed the Temple." [53] The Little Horn is "the last king." [54] The words of presumption in the mouth of the Little Horn were spoken by Titus.[55] "The explanation of these 70 weeks is very difficult," Ibn Ezra declares.[56]

So he contents himself with simply repeating the exposition of Saadia Gaon—that they are weeks of years, and the sixty-two weeks are the years of the Second Temple. Ibn Ezra's curious explanation of the seventieth week, and its midst, follows:

"It is well known that Titus made a covenant with Israel seven years, and for three years and a half the continual offering was abolished in the Second Temple before the destruction of the Temple, and thus it is written in the book of Joseph ben Gorion . . . and it is written in the fourth prophecy, And they shall profane the sanctuary, the fortress, this is the day on which Jerusalem was captured in the days of Titus, and they had removed the continual offering before this, and set up there the abomination of desolation, and thus it is written: And from the time when the continual offering was removed, and the abomination of desolation was set up, 1,290 days." [57]

"According to their number, will be the days which Israel will be in great trouble before the coming of the redeemer, and behold it has been made clear according to the explanation that when the king of the north will go out and take Egypt after three and a half years, the redeemer will come to Israel, but we do not know until now when this will be." [58]

4. TOBIAH BEN ELIEZER—MESSIANIC EPOCH AT END OF 1335. —[13] TOBIAH BEN ELIEZER (11th century), of Bulgaria, in his Midrashic commentary, *Lekah Tob,* looked for the ending of the 1335 year-days of Daniel 12:12 to bring the Messianic epoch, but did not know their terminus.[59]

5. JUDAH HALEVI SETS 1358 FOR END OF PERIODS.—[14] ISAAC BEN JUDAH HALEVI (13th century), of Sens, France, in revolt against contemporary philosophy, held that the 1290 and 1335 represent year-days. Beginning with the destruction of

[53] Ibn Ezra, comment on Dan. 7:5-8, in *Mikraoth Gedoloth.*
[54] Ibn Ezra, comment on Dan. 7:5-8, in *Sefer Kehilloth Mosheh.*
[55] Ibn Ezra, comment on Dan. 7:8, in *Mikraoth Gedoloth.*
[56] Ibn Ezra, comment on Dan. 9:24, *ibid.*
[57] Translated from Ibn Ezra's comment on Dan. 9:24, *ibid.*
[58] Ibn Ezra, comment on Dan. 12:11, *ibid.*
[59] Silver, *op. cit.,* pp. 59, 136.

Maimonides, Notable
Twelfth-Century Jew-
ish Scholar, Who Held
Little Horn of Daniel
7 Was Rule of Rome
(Left)

Abravanel, Illustrious
Fifteenth - Century
Spanish Minister of Fi-
nance, Who Declared
Little Horn to Be Rule
of Pope (Right)

Jerusalem, they would probably end in 1358 and 1403, respectively.[60]

6. GALIPAPA THROWS ALL FULFILLMENTS BACK INTO PAST.
—[15] HAYYIM GALIPAPA (c. 1310-1380), Spanish rabbi who
fought against the severities of the Talmudists, sought to throw
all fulfillments back into the past; he applied the Little Horn of
Daniel 7 to Antiochus Epiphanes.[61] In this he is unique among
all Jewish expositors—a Jewish preterist in verity!—and ante-
dates the Catholic preterist Alcazar by three centuries.

7. RATIONALISTIC MAIMONIDES HAZY ON PROPHECY.—[16]
MAIMONIDES, or MOSES BEN MAIMON, sometimes called RaMBaM
(1135-1204), illustrious Jewish scholar, philosopher, physician,
and astronomer, was born in Cordova, Spain. After the Mohammedan invasion he wandered, with his family, throughout Spain,
Palestine, and Northern Africa, settling at Cairo in 1165. Forced
conversions were common, and Maimonides' family had conformed outwardly to Mohammedanism. So Maimonides became
court physician to the reigning sultan. Called the "Light of the
West," he was the leading Jewish scholar and philosopher of
the Middle Ages, and may be regarded as the founder of Jewish
rationalism.[62] Maimonides made a profound and permanent impression upon Judaism, and established the right of free investi-

---

[60] Silver, op. cit., p. 86.
[61] Silver, op. cit., pp. 215, 216; Sarachek, Doctrine, pp. 218, 219.
[62] Milman, History of the Jews, vol. 3, p. 160; Silver, op cit., pp. 74, 80; Farrar, op. cit.,
p. 83.

gation as against the principle of absolute rabbinical authority.

He was author of numerous works, *The Guide to the Perplexed* being his leading production. In this he sought to harmonize Biblical and rabbinical teaching with philosophy, particularly Aristotelianism. However, he held that matter is not eternal, but created, and that immortality is acquired, not inherent. He believed that prophecy was possible, and discussed its nature. He applied the Little Horn of Daniel 7 to the presumption of Jesus, regarding Jesus as a false prophet, like Mohammed.[63]

He was particularly determined that no one should attempt to fix the time of the Messiah's advent from Bible texts, and he placed man's highest aspiration in the future world rather than in a restored state.[64] He believed that Messiah would come upon the termination of Rome's allotted period of prosperity; he defended Saadia on the coming of Messiah, and although reluctant about time setting, looked to the year 1216.[65] He did not hold to the cabalistic 7,000-year theory.[66]

Maimonides is remembered also for his work in Jewish calendar science, particularly on the visibility of the new moon, which he based on Chaldean astronomy. His system of determining the visibility of the new moon in Jerusalem, and his plan of intercalation, appearing in his tractate, have a bearing on some of the later interpreters who dealt with the crucifixion date, as will be discussed in Volume IV of *Prophetic Faith*.

IV. Nahmanides Employs Time Prophecy in Debate With Dominican

[17] NAHMANIDES, or Moses ben Nahman, or RaMBaN (1195-1270), of Spain, was a practicing physician. In marked contrast to Maimonides, he was a conservative, with unbounded respect for Moses and the prophets. He fought against the rationalizing of the Scriptures and the rejection of miracles. He

---

[63] Sarachek, *Doctrine*, p. 137.
[64] Silver, *op. cit.*, p. 214; Sarachek, *Doctrine*, p. 303.
[65] Sarachek, *Doctrine*, pp. 140-145; Silver, *op. cit.*, pp. 74, 75, 214.
[66] Sarachek, *Doctrine*, p. 160.

also rejected the exegesis of Ibn Ezra, and many Karaites attended his lectures. But Nahmanides revived the mystical Cabalism.[67]

In his *Sefer Hagulah* (Book of Redemption), Nahmanides seeks to harmonize the various time periods and dates so as to deduce the Messianic year, setting 1358 c.e. for the Messiah's coming.[68] Nahmanides believes that the six days of creation represent six millennia,[69] at the end of which the Messiah would appear. The seventh would be the millennial Sabbath. The seventy weeks are 490 years, from the close of the first commonwealth to the end of the second, and involving the devastation of Europe. As regards the 1290, 1335, and 2300 periods, when the sanctuary shall be victorious, dated from King David's rule, Nahmanides says, "Days stand for years." [70] He likewise had recourse to Gematria.

1. DRAMATIC DEBATE WITH PABLO CHRISTIANI BEFORE SPANISH KING.—In September, 1263, the Dominican Fra Pablo Christiani (a former Jew) challenged the Jews to a series of public disputations before King James of Aragon, on the differences between Jews and Christians. The three main points were: Had the Messiah appeared? Was He human or divine? And who possesses the true faith? The king ordered Nahmanides to engage him at Barcelona, granting the former full freedom of speech. Four days were consumed in this spectacular dispute, which centered on the Messianic question.[71] Nahmanides explained the 1290 days as 1290 years, referring to Leviticus 25:29

---

[67] Cabala, Cabbala, or Quabbala—a mystical system of philosophy that arose among the Jews at the beginning of the Christian Era, signifying a secret system of theology, metaphysics, and magic. In the thirteenth century the *Zohar* was the great Spanish textbook of medieval Cabala, stressing the approaching millennium on the 6,000-year theory. One of the branches of cabalistic lore consisted in finding the hidden sense of the whole *Masorah* (the traditional Bible text) down to verses, words, letters, and even vowel points and accents, which they thought had been delivered to Moses on Sinai. The numbers of letters, the collations of letters, and the transpositions, or substitutions, were supposed to have a supernatural significance.
[68] Silver, *op. cit.*, pp. 83, 84.
[69] Sarachek, *Doctrine*, p. 166 (citing *Torath Adonai*, p. 32).
[70] *Ibid.*, pp. 172-176.
[71] Sarachek, *Doctrine*, pp. 176, 177, 182; Elliott, *op. cit.*, vol. 3, p. 286, n.; Rabbi Chone, *Nachmanides*. For sources see "Acta Disputationis R. Mosis Nachmanidis cum Fratre Paulo Christiani, et Fratre Raymundo Martini," in *Tela Ignea Satanae*, edited by Johann Christopher Wagenseil (1681); Nahmanides' own report in *Nachmanidis Disputatio*, edited by M. Steinschneider (1860); the Dominican report in Raymund Martini, *Pugio Fidei* (1687); *Ozar Wikuhim*, edited by J. D. Eisenstein (1928).

and Genesis 24:55 to illustrate the year-day principle. Pablo contended that the 490 years reached to the "Most Holy" and the "anointed prince." Nahmanides responded that Jesus was born seventy years before the nation fell. In the course of the debate he said:

"It is now 1195 years since the destruction, or 95 years less than the Messianic figure [1335] of Daniel. We believe that the Messiah will come that year." [72]

Nahmanides was adjudged the winner, the king giving him three hundred gold dinars and royal protection on his homeward journey.[73] But in 1264, by order of a papal bull, all copies of the Talmud in Aragon were confiscated and certain anti-Christian passages stricken out. Nahmanides' published account was condemned to be burned and he was banished from the country, thus suffering under the Catholic government of Spain, which had compelled his participation in the disputation, and which resulted in his exile. Nahmanides looked for a resurgence of Mohammedan power as a preliminary to redemptive deliverance.[74]

It is noteworthy not only that Nahmanides employed the 1290-year time prophecy in his public debate before the king, but that Pablo—a Jewish renegade, and therefore somewhat acquainted with prophecy—projects the 490 years to prove Christ to have been the promised Messiah. But Nahmanides wins the point from him, because Pablo, now a Catholic, was not sufficiently informed rightly to place the period of the seven hebdomads in answer to Nahmanides' rebuttal—Jew and Catholic alike acknowledging the year-day principle. Truly, prophecy has had the spotlight in many a dramatic setting, and not a few times before kings—even in the thirteenth century!

2. OTHER RABBIS OF MIDDLE AGES APPLY YEAR-DAY PRINCIPLE.—Only the barest mention can be made of five other less

---

[72] Silver, *op. cit.*, p. 84, citing Steinschneider, p. 15.
[73] Sarachek, *Doctrine*, p. 177. This prize would have been $1,200, probably worth about $12,000 in present purchasing power, according to information from the American Numismatic Society.
[74] Silver, *op. cit.*, p. 85; see also Louis I. Newman, *op. cit.*, p. 320.

prominent thirteenth- and fourteenth-century expositors of the year-day principle. These were:

[18] BAHYA BEN ASHER (c. 1260-1340), of Spain, who held that the 1290 and 1335, and the 2300 divided by 2 (or 1150 years), were all year-days.[75]

[19] GERSONIDES, OR LEVI BEN GERSHON (RaLBaG) (1288-1344), French philosopher, stated that the last portion of Daniel had clear reference to Rome, with the 1290 years reaching from the destruction to the redemption, which he placed at 1358 C.E.[76] The four beasts of Daniel 7 were explicitly declared to parallel the four kingdoms of Daniel 2—Babylonia, with the swiftness of a lion; Medo-Persia, with the rapacity of a bear; Greece, with its four divisions; and the fourth dreadful, long-enduring beast as "the kingdom of Rome."[77]

[20] MENAHEM BEN AARON BEN ZERAH (1310-1385), of Spain, held the 1290 and 1335 days as years.[78]

[21] SIMON BEN ZEMAH DURAN, or RaSHBaZ (1361-1444), rabbi and physician of Algiers, who had fled thither from Mallorca, because of persecutions of the Jews, in 1394 became chief rabbi of Algiers. He wrote numerous commentaries on the Bible and Talmud, his commentary on Job, *Oheb Mishpat*, giving 1850 C.E. as the Messianic year. Citing Ezekiel 4:4 as evidence that prophetic days stood for literal years, he alluded, among other discussions, to the 2300 days of Daniel 8:14, which he interpreted as so many years. Taking the final destruction of the kingdom of Israel, about 450 B.C.E., as the starting point, he looked for the redemption to take place 2300 years later, or in the year 1850 C.E. Duran similarly applied the 1290 year-days of Daniel 12:11 to the conquest of Jerusalem by the Mohammedans. The end of Mohammedan rule could therefore be looked for 1290 years after the rise of Mohammed (1290 + 622 = 1912 C.E.), and the beginning of the end sixty years earlier, in 1850 C.E.[79]

---

[75] Silver, *op. cit.*, pp. 95-97.   [76] *Ibid.*, p. 94.
[77] Gersonides, comment on Daniel 7, *Sefer Kehilloth Mosheh*, part 4.
[78] Silver, *op. cit.*, p. 103.
[79] *The Universal Jewish Encyclopedia*, vol. 3, p. 612, art. "Duran, Simon ben Zemah"; Silver, *op. cit.*, pp. 107, 108.

V. 16th-Century Expositors Apply Year-Day Principle

[23] ABRAHAM SABA (15th-16th centuries), of Spain, longed for redemption but opposed calculation of the Messianic year. He constantly referred to the four kingdoms and believed that the redemption would take place "hard upon the fall of Rome." [80]

[24] ABRAHAM HALEVI BEN ELIEZER (c. 1460-1530), Spanish exile and Cabalist, in his treatise on Daniel (*The Loosener of Knots*), tries to prove the Messianic year to be 1530 C.E., in close relation to the fall of Constantinople in 1453 C.E. He placed the beginning of the 1290 year-days not from the destruction but from 4000 A.M., which would bring 1462 C.E. But he, too, applied Gematria, and thus adjusted all terminal points. [81]

[25] JOSEPH BEN DAVID IBN YAHYA IV (1494-1539), of Italy, in his commentary on Daniel, advanced the Messianic year to 1931 C.E. in order to discourage early anticipations and to spare disillusionment. He terminated the 2300 years in 5691 A.M. or 1931 C.E. [82]

[26] ELIEZER ASHKENAZI BEN ELIJAH HAROFE (1512-1585), of Turkey and Poland, terminated the 1335 years in 1594. [83]

[27] MORDECAI BEN JUDAH DATO (1527-1585), of Italy, stressed the 1335 year-days from 4000 A.M., when, according to Talmudic tradition, the 2,000 years of the Messianic epoch were to begin. [84] Dato followed the *Pirke* on the four empires. He looked to 1575 as the year of expectation.

[28] DANIEL BEN PERAHIAH (16th century), reckoning on the basis of 1335 year-days, thought that they would terminate in 1575. [85]

[29] NAPHTALI HERZ BEN JACOB ELHANAN (2nd half of the 16th century), of Germany, likewise ended the 1335 years in 1575. [86]

---

[80] Silver, *op. cit.*, pp. 221, 222.   [81] *Ibid.*, pp. 130-132.   [82] *Ibid.*, pp. 142, 143.
[83] *Ibid.*, p. 139.   [84] *Ibid.*, pp. 135, 136 (citing Sanhedrin, 97 a,b).
[85] *Ibid.*, p. 137.   [86] *Ibid.*, p. 138.

CHAPTER TEN

Climax of Jewish Interpretation
in Centuries Sixteen and Seventeen

I. Marranos Infiltrate the Christian Faith

The story of the Marranos is one of the most amazing chapters in all history, perhaps unparalleled in sheer dramatic pathos and appeal. The Marrano was a Christianized Jew who professed Christianity chiefly to escape persecution. The record of these "new Christians," or crypto-Jews, is an inseparable part of the history of Spain and Portugal, particularly from Inquisition times onward, although it was a development that touched nearly every country of Western Europe in the seventeenth and eighteenth centuries. It provides the explanatory background of countless persons of highest eminence, and receives lurid illumination from the flares of the auto-da-fé.[1]

Under the "Great Expulsion" of 1290, Jews to the number of sixteen thousand had been banished from England under Edward I (1273-1307). Similar expulsions from Spain had taken place under Ferdinand and Isabella, resulting in Jewish colonies all over the Levant. Some Jews, refusing to leave Spain and Portugal, professed Christianity and developed this group, called the Marranos, "to outwit the Jesuits with their own weapons."[2] These Marranos penetrated deeply into the ranks of the nations —particularly in Rome, Amsterdam, and London.

---

[1] Cecil Roth, *A History of the Marranos*, pp. xi, xii.
[2] Lucien Wolf, "Introduction. The Return of the Jews to England," *Menasseh ben Israel's Mission to Oliver Cromwell*, p. xii.

The roots of Marranism go back to the early centuries of the Christian Era. They are tied into the Jewish teaching that a man should save his life, if necessary, by any means except murder, incest, or idolatry.[3] Christianity became increasingly dominant in Western Europe from the fourth century onward. And the phenomenon of crypto-Judaism was the common accompaniment of forcible conversion—their following of the practices of Judaism in secret fidelity. With the coming of the Mohammedan Arabs there was considerable toleration of Jews in Spain, but later intolerance sprang up, and most of the Jews sought refuge in Christian kingdoms.[4] A minority outwardly embraced the forms of the dominant faith—paying lip service—but in their homes they remained faithful to Judaism.

In Spain, beginning with the reconquest under Alfonso X of Castile (1065-1109), after certain preliminary difficulties, the life and culture of the Jews prospered under the Christian rule, but later their position deteriorated. The tide of hostility rose against the Jews. Mobs broke loose in 1391, and the Juderia (ghetto) was piteously sacked. Expulsion of the Jews became common throughout Europe—from England, as noted in 1290, from France in 1394, and several from Germany. So, large bodies of Jews accepted baptism en masse in order to escape death. Numbers of them, as noted, were won by Fra Vincent Ferrer's impassioned appeals—some thirty-five thousand in Spain and Portugal in the fifteenth century.[5] But they continued to observe the Sabbath, their special feast days, and their characteristic food regulations. Many held high positions of state.[6] Some even became bishops, as Solomon Levi became Pablo de Santa Maria, bishop of Burgos.[7]

In the fifteenth century the Inquisition was established and the autos-da-fé were continued.[8] In 1482 Thomas de Torquemada sped the burning of heretics. The general "conversion" spread into Portugal. These secret Jews retained their knowledge

[3] Roth, *History of the Marranos*, p. 1.   [4] *Ibid.*, pp. 8, 9.
[5] *Ibid.*, pp. 17, 18.   [6] *Ibid.*, p. 23.
[7] *Ibid.*, pp. 19, 24.   [8] *Ibid.*, pp. 44, 45.

of the Hebrew language. They believed salvation was through
the law of Moses, not through Christ. The New Testament was
neglected. Circumcision was, of course, an impossibility, for it
meant death if discovered. The Jewish calendar gave difficulty,
with its adjustment of intercalary months. So the Day of Atonement was celebrated arbitrarily on the tenth day after the new
moon of September, and the Passover was celebrated in the
period of the first full moon of March.[9]

Columbus sailed on his first voyage in 1492, in the same
month that the expulsion of the Jews from Spain occurred;
several Marranos were, in fact, in the personnel of his expedition and were quick to realize the possibilities of the New
World.[10] The Marranos spread throughout Mexico, but felt the
weight of the Spanish Inquisition from 1574 onward.[11] The
settlement of the Marranos in the Low Countries began in
1512; by 1537 colonies were in Antwerp, and by 1593 Amsterdam was known as the Dutch Jerusalem.[12]

Resettlement in England began later, many Marranos taking refuge in London. Their return was largely the result of
the appeal of Manasseh ben Israel, in the time of the Protectorate under Oliver Cromwell. The Jews had been banished from
England in 1290, and none could live there officially or
lawfully.[13] Nevertheless, many re-entered after the Spanish expulsion of 1492, until under Bloody Mary they had to leave the
country. Under Elizabeth a large colony returned, but from
the time of the defeat of the Spanish Armada in 1588 the Marrano colony declined.[14] The Reformation in England had turned
the eyes of many toward England, and the increased Old Testament tendencies of Puritanism, incorporated into the Common-
wealth, revived the hope of a revocation of their banishment.[15]
The question of readmission was brought to a climax by the
famous mission of Manasseh ben Israel to Oliver Cromwell

9 *Ibid.*, p. 82.   10 *Ibid.*, pp. 271-273.
11 *Ibid.*, pp. 274-276.   12 *Ibid.*, p. 236.
13 *Ibid.*, p. 252.   14 *Ibid.*, pp. 254, 255, 257.
15 Wolf, *op. cit.*, in *Menasseh ben Israel's Mission*, pp. xiv-xv.

(which will be noted in section III), with its appeal based partly on Daniel 12:7 (that the final redemption would begin when the scattering of the Jews was complete).[16] In this negotiation Manuel Martinez, a Marrano, represented the Jewish case before Manasseh came to England,[17] and the indispensability to foreign trade of the Marranos in London was an important consideration in the final result—a recognition of the legality of the residence of Jews in England—which was not formal assent to resettlement of the Jews, but rather an unofficial tolerance and avoidance of the issue, which left them unmolested.[18] After the Restoration the Jews continued to win favor, and during the next hundred years there was considerable expansion.[19] It is interesting to note that the distinguished Disraeli family were Jewish refugees of this category.[20]

II. Abravanel Expounds Little Horn as Papal Antichrist

[22] Don Isaac ben Judah Abravanel (Abrabanel, Abarbanel) (1437-1508), last and most illustrious of a long line of notable Jewish statesmen in the Spanish Golden Age, was a Biblical scholar as well as a statesman. Born in Lisbon of wealthy parentage and possessing extraordinary mental powers, he became master of the learning of his time, and particularly of the Holy Scriptures. Abravanel lived in the age of discovery and social and religious ferment. He was the contemporary of Savonarola, Torquemada, Columbus, Leonardo da Vinci, Copernicus, Machiavelli, Erasmus, and Luther. He lived in the transition age, at the end of the Middle Ages, when the world's horizon was growing wider. The Inquisition against the Marranos was under way, and the Jews were expelled from Spain. Columbus discovered the new world, and the simmering revolt against the church broke forth in the Reformation.[21]

---

[16] *Ibid.*, p. xvi.
[17] Roth, *History of the Marranos*, p. 263.
[18] Wolf, *op. cit.*, in *Menasseh ben Israel's Mission*, pp. xxx, lxvi-lxviii; Roth, *History of the Marranos*, pp. 264, 265.
[19] Roth, *History of the Marranos*, pp. 266, 267.
[20] *Ibid.*, p. 318.
[21] Graetz, *op. cit.*, vol. 4, pp. 337, 342; Sarachek, *Don Isaac Abravanel*, pp. 13-15.

Three kings (of Spain, Portugal and Naples) recognized Abravanel's financial ability, and used his services. Notwithstanding, he was at times a homeless wanderer, fleeing from country to country, falling from honor to disgrace, and from wealth to poverty. His father and grandfather had been financiers in Lisbon and Seville, respectively. He attended a Lisbon college where he studied both the Bible and Talmud. He was proficient in Latin, Spanish, Portuguese, and Italian, and his father's position gave him wealth and prestige. Abravanel's earlier life was perhaps the most eventful and picturesque of that of any Jew of his age. He was the friend of scholars, physicians, church dignitaries, and officials. (Portrait appears on page 214.)

A financial genius, Abravanel became counselor to Alfonso V of Portugal, upon whose death he was banished by the son, John II, and sought refuge in Toledo, Spain. Later he was advanced to the post of minister of finance to Ferdinand and Isabella, which position he filled for eight years (1484-1492)[22]—the crucial period in Columbus' life.

It is most probable that Abravanel met Columbus, who was in Portugal seeking financial support for his mission while the former was fiscal minister, and he later sought help from Queen Isabella during the eight years, from 1484 onward, in which Ferdinand used Abravanel as collector of the royal revenues.[23]

The massacre against the Jews in 1491 had begun a reign of terror that climaxed in the expulsion in 1492. They were forced to wear an identifying badge. Persecution of the Marranos had grown to full proportions under Torquemada. Many of these Jews had been financiers, judges, and legislators—living outwardly as Christians but inwardly as Jews. Then in 1492 the Spanish expulsion came. Through his official position, and by offering his own wealth, Abravanel tried vainly to persuade Ferdinand to revoke the expulsion edict of March 30, 1492.

---

[22] Graetz, *op. cit.*, vol. 4, pp. 340-343; Sarachek, *Don Isaac Abravanel*, pp. 16-27, 40.
[23] Sarachek, *Don Isaac Abravanel*, p. 29.

Failing in this, and with his property confiscated, he had to flee.[24]

It was the breakup of Jewish life in Spain, as three hundred thousand fled in all directions. Abravanel went first to the kingdom of Naples, where he became treasurer to the king, but the French invasion of that kingdom sent him to Sicily for refuge. Later he went to the island of Corfu, then returned to Naples for eight years.[25]

The harrowing experiences of his people sent Abravanel for refuge and hope to the searching of prophecy. Thus led to the study of the coming deliverance of the Jews by the Messiah, he wrote three books on the subject.[26] In 1503, at the age of sixty-six, he came finally to Venice. Here in his commentaries, which were delivered as lectures, he blazed a new trail in Scripture study. Although acquainted with the history of interpretation, he made use of earlier commentators.[27] He rose to the defense of Literalism, taking issue with the naturalizing and rationalizing trend of the times, and strove to revive the "forlorn hope in a Messiah." [28]

In his exposition of Daniel's prophecy he taught that the 1335 years ended in 1503 c.e., and expected the Messiah on the basis of Daniel 8:14 and 12:4, as well as on the basis of the time, times, and a half, of Daniel 7:25, reckoning a time as 410 years (the duration of the first temple).[29]

Sarachek assures us that "Abravanel is the only writer in Jewish theology who alludes to the Antichrist." [30] In the succession of prophetic empires, he sees "the successive sway of the world empires, Babylonia, Persia, Greece and Rome, and the permanent messianic state." [31] And Abravanel was perhaps the first Jewish exegete to envision the prophecies of Daniel as a whole.[32] This did not come through tradition.[33] He was unin-

[24] *Ibid.*, pp. 33, 34, 42-44.
[26] *Ibid.*, pp. 51, 52.
[28] *Ibid.*, pp. 82, 83, 163.
[30] *Ibid.*, p. 186.
[32] Isaac Landman, "Abravanel, Isaac," *The Universal Jewish Encyclopedia*, vol. 1, pp. 53, 54.
[33] Silver, *op. cit.*, p. 117.

[25] *Ibid.*, pp. 48-50.
[27] *Ibid.*, pp. 52, 65-69.
[29] *Ibid.*, pp. 175, 176.
[31] *Ibid.*, p. 183.

8

fluenced by the rationalism of Maimonides, and rejected Cabal-ism.[34] He shook off the fetters of Aristotelianism, restored neg-lected grammatical methods, and made free use of the writings of Christians,[35] who similarly used his writings.

In 1496, during his exile in the kingdom of Naples, in the very land of the Papacy, Abravanel wrote a remarkable exposi-tion of Daniel, titled *Wells* [or Sources] *of Salvation*. Stressing the year-day principle for most of the prophetic time periods, and listing Babylonia, Medo-Persia, Greece, and Rome as the four empires, Abravanel declared the Little Horn to be the first pope of Rome. He is the first Jewish writer of whom we have record so to do.[36] In fact, he is about the only Jewish writer in this period who alludes to Antichrist,[37] although he himself re-jected Jesus as the promised Messiah.[38] Of the *Wells of Salvation*, which is a running commentary on the entire book of Daniel, Silver says, of its completeness and scope, that Abravanel's works are "the most complete and thoroughgoing of their kind in the whole field of Jewish adventist literature." "The content of the book focuses itself in the vision of the Four Kingdoms"— with the fourth as Rome, following Greece, Persia, and Baby-lonia.[39]

1. CHRISTIANS INCLUDED UNDER ROME'S RULE.—Well 2, of Abravanel's commentary, shows that the four kingdoms are the uniform subject of chapters 2, 7, 8, and 11, with the fifth king-dom, that of the Messiah, as the "common feature." Laying a foundation for later conclusions, Abravanel makes this signifi-cant observation on the "Romans":

"And the Romans and the Christians, although they have different names, are one people, and they have one language, i. e. the Latin language. But since Rome was the capital city with ministers in the provinces, not only in matters of rulership and dominion and kingdom but also it became the head in the conduct of their religion and their faith, for there seats were set for the judgment of the pope, and from there he pastures the

---
[34] Sarachek, *Doctrine*, pp. 231-233.   [35] Farrar, *op. cit.*, p. 464.
[36] Sarachek, *Doctrine*, pp. 247, 257.   [37] *Ibid.*, p. 263.
[38] *Ibid.*, p. 230.   [39] Silver, *op. cit.*, pp. 116, 118.

whole people of Edom [Rome], therefore the Christians were called under the category of the Romans." [40]

Then Abravanel observes that Rome became Christianized under Constantine and compelled the nations to accept the religion of Jesus.

2. IRON AND CLAY ARE CHRISTIANITY AND MOHAMMEDANISM.—Well 6 is devoted to Daniel 2, with the nonmingling divisions of iron and clay as Christianity and Mohammedanism, for "some of them accepted the religion of Jesus the Christian, and some of them accepted the religion of Mohammed the Ishmaelite." It is within this latter state of division that the Messianic kingdom is to be set up. The Christians, Abravanel states, explain it as that of "Jesus their God and his house of prayer, which they call ecclesia." The fourth kingdom, he adds, centers in Italy.[41]

3. STONE KINGDOM NOT THE CHRISTIAN CHURCH.—Arguing against the Christian church as being the stone kingdom, for it was established centuries before Rome's division, Abravanel says:

"The kingdom of Rome, which is the fourth kingdom, and the fifth kingdom, which to their [the Christian] knowledge and according to their view, was in the religion of Jesus, are one thing just as even today the emperors do, and they are called Roman emperors and Roman empire, but they themselves are Christian, and therefore the fourth kingdom is still in existence, and the fifth kingdom has not yet come." [42]

4. ACCURATE PORTRAYAL OF FOUR SYMBOLIC BEASTS.—Well 8 deals with Daniel 7 with remarkable accuracy. Abravanel gives the intent of the four symbolic beasts, with details explained, such as the wings of the lion, and the three ribs of the bear, the four heads of the leopard, and the Little Horn on the fourth or Roman beast as the papacy, and the accounting of the fourth beast at the judgment day, followed by the coming of the Messiah.[43]

---

[40] Isaac Abravanel, *Sefer Mayene Hayeshuah (Wells of Salvation)*, Well 2, Palm Tree 3.
[41] *Ibid.*, Well 6, Palm Tree 1.
[42] *Ibid.*, Palm Tree 2.   [43] Silver, *op. cit.*, pp. 119, 120.

5. LITTLE HORN THE RULE OF THE POPE.—Well 8 also deals
with the Little Horn of Daniel 7. Citing Rashi, Nahmanides,
and Maimonides as evidence for Rome as the fourth beast, Abravanel comes to the ten horn-kingdoms springing from Rome,
and the Little Horn. Some Christian commentators, he says,
make them the ten kingdoms. Others, Jews and Christians, had
different views. Then comes this remarkable statement penned
in 1496, repeated in varying forms and places, in which he
differed from Gersonides:

"Gersonides thought that the little horn was that emperor who compelled the world to embrace the religion of Jesus, and I do not know why
he calls him small horn, for was he not Constantine the greatest of the
great among the emperors. And furthermore, why does he mention him
after the ten emperors, when between him and them there came other
emperors, for he was the 39th emperor, and therefore I have come to the
inner conclusion that the little horn was the rule of the pope, who began
in Rome after the destruction of Jerusalem through a disciple of Jesus;
because the pope in his beginning was small and tiny, not mighty, they
called it the little horn. And since its beginning was in Rome. . . ." [44]

Of the plucking up of the three horns, Abravanel narrates
how Constantine gave Sylvester the rulership of Rome and Italy
while he went to the East and established Constantinople, and
compelled the kingdoms under his rule to accept Christianity.
Then Abravanel adds the following, and concludes with the
statement, "This is without doubt the true interpretation of
this verse."

"And Rome specifically became Christian, adhering to the faith of
Jesus unto this day. If so, then it was the little horn which was getting great
and spreading in the land and before which there were uprooted three
kinds of government which had been in Rome, for it no longer had the
rule of the kings or the rule of the old men and the councillors, nor the
rule of the emperors, but only the rule of the leaders and the popes, and
these are the three horns which were uprooted from before the little
horn." [45]

Of the "eyes of a man," and the shrewdness of the rule of
the pope, his rule and government and law are "different from

---

[44] Abravanel, *op. cit.*, Well 8, Palm Tree 5.
[45] *Ibid.*

those of the rest of the nations." And of the mouth speaking great things, after repeating more than once that the Little Horn is the "rule of the pope," Abravanel asserts that its strength was in its mouth. Thus:

"He confesses and puts under the ban and forbids sins and releases and makes atonement for guilt, and it has become one of the principles of their faith that things are done just as he says, and that everything which he. speaks on earth shall be established in heaven, and this is what is meant when it says: 'And a mouth speaking great things.' " [46]

In addition to the feature of the papal persecution, Abravanel describes the pope's attempts to change the law.

"He will plan to change the seasons and the religion, i. e. that the sect of the adherents of the religion of Jesus will plan to change the festivals of the law and to destroy the commandments of the law and to make a new law in the land, different from the law (religion) of Moses." [47]

He proceeds with a discussion of the views of Protestants, that the Little Horn is the "anti-Christ," who was "opposed to Jesus their Messiah," and adds:

"And three of the former horns were uprooted from before him—they are the three kingdoms of Africa, Egypt and Antiochia [Syria] which he will conquer first, and behold eyes like the eyes of men, this means that the anti-Christ will do many wonders and they will believe that he is God, and this is not so, for he is only human. And a mouth speaking great things— that he will entice [deceive] the children of men through the words of his mouth. I looked until thrones were cast—this speaks of the words of the coming of Jesus on the day of judgment to judge the world and to destroy the anti-Christ." [48]

After commenting on the fact that the Christians got the Antichrist idea from their chief apostle in the Revelation, and from Daniel 7, Abravanel says that a "time," in the three and a half times, means a year.[49] But he declares that this "is used with reference to a long time," perhaps the 1335-year period.

6. 2300 YEARS ARE DURATION OF EXILE UNDER ROME.— Wells 9 and 10 deal with the 2300 days, which Abravanel shows could not mean literal days but indicate years, leading to the

[46] Ibid.
[48] Ibid., Palm Tree 6.

[47] Ibid.
[49] Ibid., Palm Tree 5; Well 11, Palm Tree 6.

remote future or "far-off days," at the "time of the end," and not referring to the seventy years of the captivity. They will extend into, or past, the kingdom of Rome, and not end with Greece. It did not refer to Antiochus, but had reference to Rome, at the end of the exile.[50] This was explained in Daniel's second vision, where the previous destruction of Medo-Persia and Greece was involved.

"And indeed in the second vision he [Daniel] saw the destruction of Persia and Media through the hand of the Greeks, and also in the latter period of things, the removal of the continual offering and the holy, and the host trampling under foot, and the number of the two thousand, and three hundred, and he saw in his wisdom that that number of years was required. And therefore he said that he had not understood anything of the vision, for if it was that that exile in which they were then were to last all that time, then the prophet's promise of the seventy years, of Jeremiah, would not be right. And therefore he thought to himself: Perhaps because of the wickedness of the people the exile has been extended all those 2300 years. And therefore he was compelled to pray to God to turn back His anger and wrath." [51]

So Daniel came to understand that—

"thereafter there would come another exile through the hand of the Romans, which would be long and difficult, evil and very bitter, and would last until the conclusion of the 2300 years of the vision." [52]

Adverting to the Little Horn of Daniel 7, Abravanel quotes Ben Gorion on the "arrogant king" as "concerning the pope and the might of his rule," and makes this important declaration concerning the stone:

"A stone will arise, not by human agency, which will smite the image which hints to the kingdom of Rome, as I have explained above, and it will destroy them, whether the iron, which is the children of Edom, the Christians, or the clay, which is the Ishmaelites, and all of them will be brought to an end at that time." [53]

7. SEVENTY WEEKS EQUAL 490 YEARS.—Well 10 expounds the seventy weeks as 490 years, as between the destruction of the First and Second Temples—the forty-nine years from the destruction of the First Temple to Cyrus' permission to rebuild,

---

[50] *Ibid.*, Well 9, Palm Trees 7, 8.   [51] *Ibid.*, Well 10, Palm Tree 1.
[52] *Ibid.*   [53] *Ibid.*, Well 9, Palm Tree 8.

the 434 years from Darius to the second destruction, and the seven years to the period during which Vespasian offered peace to Jerusalem.[54]

8. KINGS OF NORTH AND SOUTH INVOLVE CHRISTIANS AND TURKS.—Well 11 sketches Daniel 11—Persia, Greece, and finally Rome. (Daniel 11:31.) Abravanel has difficulty in interpreting the kings of the north and south, believing that somehow the Turks and Christians are involved, as is the conquest of Constantinople in 1453, and that disregard of the desire of women "refers to the celibacy of pope and priest." [55] Then the Messiah will appear, and the resurrection occur. Abravanel then gives the "Christian" interpretation (of those opposing the Papacy in 1496):

"On the explanation of the rest of the portions of the vision, according to the wise men of the Christians. The angel said to Daniel: And the king will do according to his will, and he will exalt himself, etc., and these verses, unto the end of the book, the Christians interpreted them as referring to the Antichrist, who would come after the world, in their view, as I have mentioned. And they said that he is called a king because of his exaltedness and his rule over many kingdoms, and he would set himself up as a god in the midst of the nations." [56]

Abravanel's familiarity with the historic controversies and counterinterpretations in the Christian church is incidentally disclosed by his reference to Porphyry and his rejection of the Christian view, and his application of the Little Horn to Antiochus.[57]

9. TIME PERIODS ON YEAR-DAY PRINCIPLE.—Well 11 deals with the time periods—the 1290, 1335, and 2300 days and the 70 weeks or 490 years. But by Gematria, Abravanel frequently adds 100 to the year-day reckoning (the numerical value of the word "days"), thus making the 1290 days equal 1290 plus 100, or 1390 years; and similarly the 1335 days mean 1435 years; he ties the 1390 years to the 1453 date, which he believes to be the be-

[54] *Ibid.*, Well 10, Palm Trees 1 and 6; Silver, *op. cit.*, pp. 121, 122; Sarachek, *Doctrine,* p. 258.
[55] Silver, *op. cit.*, pp. 122, 123.
[56] Abravanel, *op. cit.*, Well 11, Palm Tree 6.   [57] *Ibid.*

ginning of the end.[58] In supplemental books—*The Salvation of His Anointed* and *Proclaiming Salvation*—he scrutinizes minutely every reference to the Messiah and ultimate redemption.[59]

With many other Jewish writers he believed that the world would endure six or seven thousand years, and upon its dissolution would be reborn.[60]

III. Manasseh's Exposition of Daniel 2; Illustrated by Rembrandt

[30] MANASSEH (MENASSEH) BEN ISRAEL (1604-1657), theologian, prolific writer, and statesman, was rabbi of the Jewish congregation at Amsterdam. For more than a century his ancestors had lived in Portugal as professing Christians. Manoel of Portugal reluctantly banished all Jews from his realm, except the Christianized Jews. In 1497, at the time of their Passover, Jewish children between four and fourteen were seized, and were to be baptized and brought up as Christians.[61]

The Marranos grew. Their success was phenomenal, until they virtually controlled the economic life of the country. They excelled as scholars, poets, explorers, jurists, professors, and physicians. But their Christianity was largely a mask. In the privacy of their own homes they practiced Judaism characteristically—observing the Sabbath, the Passover, and the Day of Atonement. In 1531 a papal bull established the Portuguese Inquisition, and in 1540 the first auto-da-fé [62] took place in Lisbon. This fundamentally altered the position of the Marranos.

At the close of the sixteenth century Holland cast off the Spanish Catholic yoke. The new toleration attracted many, including the father of Manasseh ben Israel, himself a Marrano. The parents had gone first from Lisbon to the Madeira Islands, so that Manasseh was born there in 1604, and was baptized Manoel Dias Soeiro. Thence the family moved to La Rochelle, France, and finally to Amsterdam, where they threw off the hitherto compulsory Christian mask and were henceforth known

---

[58] Silver, *op. cit.*, pp. 123, 124.
[60] Sarachek, *Doctrine*, p. 306.
[61] Cecil Roth, *A Life of Menasseh ben Israel*, pp. 1-3.

[59] *Ibid.*, pp. 125-130.

[62] *Ibid.*, pp. 6-8.

under Jewish names. Manoel Dias Soeiro, now called Manasseh ben Israel, grew up to become a teacher and rabbi.[63] His linguistic knowledge was phenomenal; he had facility in ten languages. A prodigious reader, he was familiar not only with Jewish writers but with the church fathers, and the Greek and Latin classics; moreover, there is some indication that he practiced medicine.[64] Manasseh attracted notice at a time when public attention was directed toward Biblical prophecy.[65] He functioned as a printer from 1626 to 1652, establishing the first Hebrew press at Amsterdam. This press turned out more than sixty works, including three Hebrew Bibles.[66]

Manasseh wrote in Spanish, often discussing seeming conflicts in the Old Testament. Four hundred of his sermons were printed in Portuguese.

Since mysticism was in the ascendancy at the time, and there was considerable stress, among Christian expositors, on the imminent second advent, linked with the expectation of the speedy conversion of the Jews, many of the English religious leaders were interested in Jewish welfare and were friends of Manasseh ben Israel.[67] Among the Jews also there was widespread hope at this time.

In 1648 the Thirty Years' War closed—a year that was regarded by many a Jew as the Messianic, or miracle, year. Manasseh was profoundly interested in Messianic problems. It was his conviction that the hour of redemption was at hand, waiting only for the complete dispersion of Israel throughout the world.[68]

It was this that led him to petition Cromwell for the readmission of the Jews to England. On friendly terms with not a few noted men, Manasseh undertook to procure abolition of the legal exclusion of the Jews from England, petitioning Oliver Cromwell to this end. He went to London to negotiate with Cromwell, who appointed a commission to hear the petition in December, 1655. As a result the Jewish question became a na-

[63] *Ibid.*, pp. 9-15, 32, 33. [64] *Ibid.*, pp. 40-42.
[65] *Ibid.*, pp. 181, 190, 195. [66] *Ibid.*, pp. 74-77.
[67] Joseph Jacobs, "Manasseh ben Israel," *The Jewish Encyclopedia*, vol. 8, pp. 282-284.
[68] Silver, *op. cit.*, pp. 181, 186, 188.

JEWISH EXPOSITOR OUTLINES THE FOUR KINGDOMS

Title Page of Manasseh ben Israel's Discussions of the Prophecies of Daniel Identifying the Four Kingdoms (Upper Left) ; Rembrandt's Portrait of Rabbi ben Israel of Amsterdam (Upper Right); Prophetic Statue of Daniel 2 and Beasts of Daniel 7, Illustrated by Rembrandt, Signed and Dated (Lower Left and Center); and Reconstruction of Rembrandt's Drawing (Lower Right)

tional issue for some time. Manasseh returned to Holland and shortly afterward died a heartbroken man because the petition was not formally granted, yet the result was that the way was paved for the unopposed infiltration of Jews back into England.[69]

Manasseh ben Israel was opposed to Messianic calculation, but he believed that the Messiah's appearance was nigh at hand.[70] This he averred on the basis of the Old Testament prophecies, even in his "Humble Addresses" to Cromwell.[71]

This conviction is pre-eminently set forth in his book *Piedra Gloriosa o de la Estatua de Nebuchadnesar* (The Glorious Stone; or, On the Image of Nebuchadnezzar), for which Rembrandt made four etchings.[72] The fuller understanding of the prophecies, Manasseh believed, was a sign of the Messianic times and a fulfillment of Daniel 12:4: "Then shall knowledge be increased." [73] The four beasts of Daniel 7, he declared, are the four monarchies of the statue of Daniel 2. The two legs, he believed, were Romanism and Mohammedanism, the ten toes, the ten subdivisions, and the stone the Messianic kingdom, filling the world.[74] He also believed that the Indians in the Americas were possibly the ten lost tribes.[75] His book received the attention of many Protestant theologians, who were likewise convinced of the speedy coming of the Messiah—only they looked for the *second* advent.

1. *The Hope of Israel* CITES BIBLE PROPHECY.—*The Hope of Israel* is permeated with prophetic exposition. Declaring that

---

[69] Silver, *op. cit.*, pp. 151, 188; Milman, *History of the Jews*, vol. 3, pp. 363, 364; Roth, *Life of Menasseh*, pp. 225-273.
[70] Silver, *op. cit.*, p. 188.
[71] This pamphlet, *To His Highnesse The Lord Protector of the Common-Wealth of England, Scotland, and Ireland. The Humble Addresses of Menasseh Ben Israel*, is found in *Menasseh ben Israel's Mission*, pp. 73-103.
[72] The original illustrations for Manasseh ben Israel's 259-page book were made by Rembrandt and are in the British Museum. They are reproduced in "Rembrandt's Etchings for the 'Piedra Gloriosa,' " *The Jewish Chronicle* (London), July 13, 1906, p. 39. In Rembrandt's hand, "Babel" (Babylon) appears on the head, "Media" and "Persia" on the two arms, "Grecia" across the waist, and "Rome" and "Mohammedans" on the legs. The stone of the Messianic kingdom is smashing the feet of the image. The etching is signed "Rembrandt, 1654." The illustrations of the 1655 edition are patterned after Rembrandt, but are the work of another artist.
[73] Manasseh ben Israel, *The Hope of Israel*, sec. 36, p. 42, in *Menasseh ben Israel's Mission*, p. 52.
[74] Manasseh ben Israel, *Piedra Gloriosa*, pp. 209, 256.
[75] Silver, *op. cit.*, p. 191; Roth, *Life of Menasseh*, pp. 176-186.

the prophets speak of the approaching end of the age, which
Manasseh believes will bring the close of the long captivity, he
speaks pathetically of the injuries suffered by his people, especially under the Inquisition, and the long delay in the coming
of the Messiah. Then he says:

"At this day it is said, that ALTHOUGH THE MESSIAH WERE
LAME, HE MIGHT HAVE COME BY THIS TIME. Though we cannot
exactly shew the time of our redemption, yet we judge it to be near. For,
"1. We see many prophesies fulfilled, and others also which are subservient to a preparation for the same redemption; and it appears by this,
that during that long and sore captivity, many calamities are fore-told us
under the four Monarchies." [76]

Again stressing the "shortness of time," and fervently hop-
ing that the "scattering of the holy people" is about over,[77]
Manasseh says of Daniel 12:4:

"To these, let us adde that, which the same Prophet speakes, in ch. 12.
ver. 4. *That knowledge shall be increased;* for then the prophecies shall
better be understood, the meaning of which we can scarce attaine to, till
they be fulfilled. So after the *Otteman* race began to flourish, we understood
the prophesie of the two leggs of the Image of *Nebuchadnezzar,* which is to
be overthrowne by the fifth Monarchy, which shall be in the World." [78]

It is to be particularly noted that Oliver Cromwell thus had
the prophecies brought to his attention through two radically
different avenues—the persecutions of the Jews and the sufferings of the Waldenses. Just about this time the fearful massacre
of the Waldenses greatly stirred Cromwell, who in 1655 appointed Sir Samuel Morland to investigate this bloody slaughter
and intercede for these oppressed people. Morland's published
report to Cromwell stresses the same prophetic views as those
held by the Waldenses.[79]

2. Four Kingdoms Followed by God's "Fifth Monarchy."—Early in 5415 A.M. (1655 C.E.) Manasseh published his
treatise on the Glorious Stone which smites the image of Nebu-

[76] Manasseh ben Israel, *The Hope of Israel,* sec. 29, p. 36, in *Menasseh ben Israel's Mission,* p. 46.
[77] *Ibid.,* sec. 35, p. 42, in *Menasseh ben Israel's Mission,* p. 52.
[78] *Ibid.,* sec. 36.
[79] See *Prophetic Faith,* Volume I, on the Waldenses.

chadnezzar. In the dedicatory letter he states that this prophecy of Daniel 2 is the "most easily understood" and explained of all Daniel's prophecies, manifesting the foreknowledge of God without any ambiguity, with the four world powers followed by the "fifth monarchy." [80] Naming the temporal monarchies as "the Babylonians, the Persians, the Greeks, and the Romans," he speaks of the "Messiah (who is the stone) [who] will destroy with temporal and earthly power all the other monarchies," whose dominion will be "eternal according to this infallible interpretation of Daniel." [81] In this exposition the Midrash and the Targum are cited, together with individual interpreters such as Rabbi Simeon ben Levi, Abravanel, Eliezer, and others. [82]

3. Two Legs of Statue Represent Rome and Turkey.—The "universal history" of the world, as presented "under the figures of animals," as the same four powers of Daniel 7, is next brought in from supporting witness, citing the *Targum Onkelos,* [83] Saadia, and Meir Hakohen. Then, continuing with the statue of Daniel, Manasseh declares: "Turkey and Rome are the two legs of the Statue, which comprise this last monarchy." [84]

4. Usual Exposition of Four Beasts, Ram, and He-Goat.—Turning to Daniel 7, and the four beasts from the "sea," which is declared to be the "world," Manasseh quotes from Augustine's *Civitas Dei.* Proceeding with the exposition, he interprets the lion as Babylonia, citing Abravanel, then follows with the Persian bear and the Greek leopard, this time citing Aristotle. The notable horn of the he-goat is Alexander the Great, and the four divisions are Alexander's "four captains," as supported by citations from Simon the Just, and Josephus' record of the meeting of the Jewish high priest and Alexander. [85]

5. Believes Lawless Little Horn to Be Mohammedanism.—Declaring the fourth beast to be Rome, later divided into "many parts," Manasseh again cites Abravanel. [86] But as regards

[80] Translated from Manasseh ben Israel, *Piedra Gloriosa,* pp. 4, 5.
[81] *Ibid.,* pp. 26, 27, 108. [82] *Ibid.,* pp. 27, 28, 46, 47, 49.
[83] *Ibid.,* p. 46. [84] *Ibid.,* pp. 50, 51.
[85] *Ibid.,* pp. 190-196, 203-208. [86] *Ibid.,* pp. 209-211.

the Little Horn that was against the saints, "changing the Sabbaths and festivals," he differs from Abravanel's application to the pope, "for the Pope is not a king," and he presents this conclusion:

> "For these reasons I rather agree with those who suppose it to be Mahomet, or Mohammed as others call him, who being at first a small horn, and having been born in Arabia, formerly subject to the Romans, in humble circumstances, in the days of the emperors Eraclius and Honorius, attained such strength that in a short space of time he and his descendants became lords of three-quarters of the world." [87]

6. PARALLELS DIVISIONS OF STATUE WITH HORNS OF BEAST. —Of the establishment of the fifth monarchy Manasseh says:

> "When the fourth monarchy ends, declares Daniel, as he saw the fifth given to the Messiah the King, descendant of the House of David, therefore he (the Messiah) must succeed immediately to the empire of the world." [88]

Manasseh then parallels the climax of Daniel 2 and 7 in these words:

> "I. 'These great beasts, which are four, are four kings.' It is described by all its circumstances, and its type was the image of Nebuchadnezzar. II. That the fourth monarchy should be divided into two nations, of diverse laws, whose division would bring about the little horn Mahomet, and that they are the two legs of the statue. III. That this Roman empire would be divided into ten kingdoms, which are the ten horns which arise from this beast, and the ten toes of the feet of the statue. IV. That when these kingdoms come to their end and are destroyed, the monarchy of Israel will follow, which constitutes the people of the saints and the stone that becomes a great mountain that fills the whole earth." [89]

IV. Sound Prophetic Principles but Fallacious Application

The pathetic eagerness with which the leading Jewish scholars of the centuries sought to "read the riddle of redemption," and from the prophecies to discover the hour of the Messiah's promised advent, must be apparent. Yet this candid survey presents a dismal procession of hopeless, disappointing futility, and fallacious application. Speculation on the time of the Messiah's coming overshadowed all else.

---

[87] *Ibid.*, pp. 222, 223.   [88] *Ibid.*, p. 252.   [89] *Ibid.*, p. 256.

1. REJECTION OF TWO FACTORS PREVENTS RIGHT TIME PLACEMENT.—Although the Jews clearly perceived the sound year-day principle of time prophecy,[90] they rejected the basic factor of the death of the prophesied Messiah in the fourth decade of the Christian Era as the key. The seventy weeks of years were never once rightly located by them during the seventeen centuries surveyed. And, since they failed to connect the seventy weeks with the 2300 year-days, from which they were cut off, neither the true beginning nor the correct ending of the 2300 years was ever obtained in all the Jewish attempts to calculate their chronological placement.

The second error was this: Failing to grasp the papal fulfillment of the prophesied Little Horn of the fourth, or Roman, beast in the generally and correctly understood series of prophetic world powers—Babylonia, Medo-Persia, Greece, and Rome—they likewise failed to locate correctly the true time boundaries of any one of the 1260, 1290, or 1335 year-day periods that are related to the key 1260 and the 2300-year periods.

Passionately longing for the Messiah, they fervidly sought some beginning date that would bring the terminus near to their own day—not to mention the Sabbatical seventh-thousand-years element frequently brought in to determine the end, nor the attempts of some to lengthen or adjust the literality of the stated time periods presented by the prophet Daniel through employing the vagaries of Gematria or Cabala. Such has been the pathetic story of the futility and error of Jewish application of time prophecy. But these twin keys—the seventieth week as fulfilled in the death of Jesus the Messiah, and then tied to the 2300-year prophecy of the cleansing of the sanctuary, and the 1260 years of papal ecclesiastical supremacy—were the clues that enabled Christian expositors, living in these same centuries, to come first to be increasingly accurate, and then finally to sound and irrefutably true conclusions.

---

[90] Down to the Protestant Reformation, there is scarcely a Jewish expositor on Daniel who protests the year-day principle (Elliott, *op. cit.*, vol. 3, p. 286), and nearly all support and apply it.

2. Constitute Separate Confirmatory Line of Witness.
—Nevertheless, it was the Jews who, hundreds of years before
the cross, first applied the year-day principle to the seventy
weeks. And it was the Jews who first perceived the fourth empire, in the prophetic series, to be Rome.[91] These were their two
great contributions. Such was part of the "every way" advantage
of the Jew. (Rom. 3:1, 2.) What a tragedy that with these absolutely sound principles—that were simply carried over into the
Christian church, there to find such successful lodgment—they
failed to keep in the lead!

As disclosed by the Chronological Table on page 194, at
least ten Jewish expositors, between Nahawendi in the eighth
century and Tobiah ben Eliezer in the eleventh, applied the
year-day principle to the longer time periods before Abbot
Joachim, of Floris, in 1190, first applied it to the 1260 days. And
some seven Jewish scholars—between the same Nahawendi
in the eighth century and Nahmanides in the thirteenth—
applied the year-day principle to the 2300 days before Villanova
in 1297, and probably two more before Cusa in 1440.
Truly this is a remarkable record, constituting a separate but
strongly confirmatory line of competent witnesses to the fundamental year-day principle of Biblical time prophecy, of the same
race and language as those of the prophet Daniel himself, whom
they studied.

Furthermore, while Catholic Archbishop Eberhard II, of
Salzburg, first applied the Little Horn of Daniel 7 to the historical Papacy, the Jewish Don Isaac Abravanel, counselor successively to the kings of Portugal and Spain, similarly applied the
Little Horn to the Papacy in 1496—before the Protestant applications began early in the next century. Yet this was the climactic
point of the prophecy of Daniel 7. But here again there was
independent harmony of witness before the voices of Protestant
Reformation expositors were added. Such is the panorama of
Jewish interpretation in the Christian Era.

---

[91] See *Prophetic Faith*, Volume I.

CHAPTER ELEVEN

The Reformation
Born of a Twofold Discovery

I. The Secret of the Reformers' Unprecedented Defiance

Like a glorious sunrise after a dismal night, the sixteenth-century Reformation era ushered in an epoch of increasing light, hope, liberty, truth, and progress. Europe began to awake from her long slumber of superstition. The light of the gospel penetrated into many nations, and the teachings of the early church reappeared under the Reformers. The seed of civil and religious liberty was sown, and the printing press and the revival of learning accelerated the movement. Columbus had struck out across the western seas and opened a new world to view, considering himself, under the profound conviction of God's guiding, to be an instrument of fulfilling prophecy. Rome, on her seven hills, was shaken, and lost a good portion of her dominions. Protestant nations came into being. A new era began—a turning point in the history of mankind.

1. HALF OF EUROPE SUNDERED FROM ROMAN COMMUNION. —This Protestant movement, initiated by Luther, split western Christendom into two halves—finally severing Norway, Denmark, Sweden, Germany, Switzerland, Holland, England, and Scotland from the communion of Rome, and seriously affecting other countries like France and Austria. Yet during the period of the Counter Reformation much Protestant territory was lost again, and Rome riveted her fetters more strongly than ever upon her own adherents.

LUTHER PRESSES THE CHARGES OF PROPHECY AT WITTENBERG

Inseparably Tied to His Preaching of Christ, Was Luther's Exposure of the Identity of Antichrist as the Great Roman Apostasy. Upon Great Con-

The Reformation was not the tardy formation of the true church, but rather its *re-formation*. It has been aptly said that Pentecost formed it, the Papacy deformed it, and now Protestantism re-formed it. The church had become frightfully deformed, and needed to be thoroughly re-formed. It had departed from the faith, and desperately needed to be brought back. A restoration of apostolic Christianity was imperative. The Papacy had subverted both the truth of God and the liberties of man. Christ had been eclipsed, and the provisions of salvation grossly perverted. The papal priest had been substituted for the Saviour of sinners, and the mystery of iniquity for the mystery of godliness. God raised up the Reformation to do a work of protest, exposure, condemnation, and deliverance. It took courageous men to face the most powerful ecclesiastical organization that had ever been developed. And such a deliverance came into being under the lead of Luther.

2. REFORMATION RESTS ON A TWOFOLD TESTIMONY.— Luther's break with Rome was a spectacle equaling, if not surpassing, in moral sublimity any other scene unfolded in the Christian Era. Evangelicals of the Waldensian type—and remnants of the Bohemians, Taborites, Spirituals, and Lollards—rejoiced in the bold stand. Melanchthon, Carlstadt, Amsdorf, Jonas, Cellarius, and others took similar steps. Many who secretly had held similar views became avowed evangelicals. Again it was evident that nothing in this old world is more powerful than a prophetic truth whose time has come. It has impelling force and power within it. Thus it was with the Reformation, which was really born of a twofold discovery—first, the rediscovery of Christ and His salvation; and second, the discovery of the identity of Antichrist and his subversions.

This fact is of epochal importance. Luther discovered "Christ and His salvation" before 1517. And before 1520 he had discovered the identity of "Antichrist and his damnation." The entire Reformation rested on this twofold testimony. The reformers were unanimous in its acceptance. And it was this interpretation of prophecy that lent emphasis to their reformatory action. It led them to protest against Rome with extraordinary strength and undaunted courage. It nerved them to resist to the utmost the claims of the apostate church. It sustained them at the martyrs' stake. Verily, this was the rallying point and the battle cry that made the Reformation unconquerable.

Thus it was that the Reformation, founded on the recovered Bible and extended by Bible preaching, emancipated the minds of men from bondage. It gave impetus to the arts and sciences, to enterprise and culture, and to freedom and liberty. It was hailed as a glad deliverance by all who came under its influence. But the aroused wrath of the Papacy soon brought long and cruel persecutions.

3. ENTIRE REFORMATION ENFOLDED WITHIN BIBLE.—The principles of the Reformation were all contained within the complete Latin Bible that Luther discovered in the university library of Erfurt. Staupitz later gave him a copy for his own, and from his refuge in the Wartburg, Luther gave to the world his priceless German translation. He felt that only the Bible, which had liberated him, could liberate the people. Thus it came to be printed and scattered like the leaves of autumn. In vain did Rome kindle her fires and burn copies of the Book. This only increased the demand. Finding it impossible to suppress Luther's translation, papal theologians were constrained, erelong, to print a rival translation of their own. By simple reference to Scripture, Protestantism's newly recovered doctrines had been justified.

Translation of the Bible into the vernacular was necessary, because it was available only in an obsolete language, for Latin was read only by the educated few—a situation which was not so much the case with the Greek and Armenian churches. In fact, the Catholic ritual was so much identified with the Latin that the abandonment of this language and the use of the vernacular became the symbol of the return to the primitive gospel. It was like taking away the veil that covered an age-old treasure. So the Reformation became pre-eminently the Age of the Book. The Scriptures were again made supreme in the Reformer ranks, with traditionism crowded into the background, and the Bible translated into various tongues of Europe.

4. SEPARATION FROM ROME IMPELLED BY PROPHECIES.— Along with this restoration of the Bible came the inevitable revival in prophetic interpretation. Literally hundreds of volumes or tractates were written in the contest of Protestant and Catholic pens regarding the charge that the Papacy was the predicted Antichrist, with its allotted time fast expiring. It was the profound conviction springing from the great outline prophecies, and the inescapable conclusion that the Papacy was the predicted Antichrist, that impelled separation and gave courage to battle the great apostasy.

The prophecies concerning the Antichrist soon became the center of controversy, as the Reformers pointed the incriminating finger of prophecy, saying, Thou art the Man of Sin! Rome was declared to be the Babylon of the Apocalypse, and the papal pontiffs, in their succession, the predicted Man of Sin. Separation from the Church of Rome and its pontifical head therefore came to be regarded as a sacred, bounden duty. Christians were urged to obey the command, "Come out of her, My people." To them, this separation was separation not from Christ and His church but from Antichrist. This was the basic principle upon which the Reformers prosecuted their work from the beginning. It was this that animated and made them invincible. This helps to explain their courage in the face of the uniform papal oppressions, triumphs, and subjugations of the past.

Thus the voices of the Waldenses, Wyclifites, and Hussites, which had almost died away in Christendom, protesting against the Papacy as the Beast and Rome as the Apocalyptic Babylon, were revived in unparalleled power after the temporary suspension. Vain was the authoritative prohibition by the Fifth Lateran Council, in 1516, against writing or preaching on the subject of Antichrist. In Germany, Switzerland, England, France, Denmark, and Sweden, the concept of the Papacy as Antichrist was increasingly received as a self-evident and fundamental truth by the founders of the various Protestant churches, and was therefore a prophetic warrant and sufficient justification for the epochal act of separation.

II. Forthright Language of the Reformation Times

The reader will doubtless be troubled by some of the forthright language employed by the robust figures of the Reformation, which we must occasionally quote hereafter. Not only is this true of the language of the Continental writers, but it is especially noticeable in the extracts from the British Reformers, where the phrasing is not softened by the euphemisms of the translations. To us today their words often sound uncouth and coarse, if not indeed vulgar and sometimes almost obscene. We would not employ them in our generation, but they were an integral part of the temper and terminology of the times. These expressions came not from men of the lower strata of life but from conspicuous leaders in religious, intellectual, and civic circles—noted clergymen, bishops, archbishops, university professors of theology and other subjects, lawyers, and even kings. They included the most upright and godly men of their day.

Moreover, many of the terms used were but variations of the strong symbols and terms constantly employed by Holy Writ in characterizing the great spiritual apostasy, first in the Jewish church, but more especially in the Christian church, and its unlawful union with the world—the commingling of the holy and the vile in the realm of spiritual, doctrinal, and prophetic truth. In Revelation 12 and 17 the church is likened to a "woman"—a pure woman, clothed in spotless white, representing a pure church; a fallen woman clad in suggestive scarlet, symbolizing a fallen church. This unchaste, figurative woman was guilty of spiritual "adultery" with her lovers—the worldly secular states —and hence she was denominated a "harlot," or "whore." These terms were frequently employed with this clearly understood intent. "Beast" was another favorite term, which was simply the symbolic, cartoon-type representation employed for this same politico-religious organization, designated in Revelation 13.

It is to be noted particularly that these terms, which were applied to the dominant church at large, were not epithets directed toward individuals, nor to indicate personal immorality, but were used to describe what they deemed the gross departures and pollutions of the church they once loved and espoused. They believed that she had fallen into the mire, and had sadly soiled herself. They averred she was guilty of spiritual adultery and pollution, as the Bible graphically phrased it, and of trafficking with the world. So they cried out vehemently against it. They were determined to reform her, or to disavow and leave her fold. They were face to face with spiritual despotism and departure, and fought it with a forthrightness of logic and language foreign to our twentieth-century diplomacy and suavity.

To know precisely what these defenders of spiritual truth and purity taught and wrote, it will be necessary, in pursuance of our uniform procedure, to occasionally cite their actual words—and to overlook their seeming crudities. These high-minded men were neither vile nor obscene in thought, life, or intent. But they were desperately in earnest. Their opponents used even stronger language, and the purely Humanistic literature of the day was "not only dirty but wantonly licentious." The Reformers were at close grips with a relentless foe, and they fought without quarter—often yielding life itself at the stake for principle. The issues that confronted them were a grave reality. Heinrich Böhmer, discussing the strong language and strange customs of the sixteenth century, gives us this informative word that sheds light on the actualities of the era:

"Observe the well-known Humanistic historian Sleidan, describing those obscene pictures by Cranach which satirize the Papacy so calmly and cheerfully, as though he were dealing merely with one of the innocent satires on professors in the Fliegende Blaetter. It would seem after all that in order to appreciate this tone we must again take to heart the word about the spirit of the times. If we do that, if we transport ourselves three hundred and fifty years into the past, we will soon clearly see that the tone at Luther's table and in his writings is not at all at variance with polite manners in German, or in French, English, and even Italian society of the day. . . .

"The Humanist Scheurl upon entering the office of Rector at the university ventured an address before the ladies of the court to which in our time the coarsest woman would not listen without resentment. . . .

"The famous preacher Geiler of Kaisersberg compares the perfect Christian with a well-contrived sausage, . . . he praises Christ as our sumpter mule who bears away our sins in a manure bucket. . . .

"Even the polite tone of the sixteenth century was therefore in our estimation not at all polite. Uncleanly as the people in general were in their habits of eating and drinking—forks and handkerchiefs had not yet come into common use—indulgent as they were toward fleas, lice and other vermin, toward the itch and other filthy diseases, so unclean according to our standards they still were everywhere in their literary usages.

"From a generation so rude and coarse Luther had sprung, to such a generation he spoke, and against it he was continually forced to do battle." [1]

III. Luther Sets the Pattern for the Reformation

MARTIN LUTHER (1483-1546), foremost of all the Reformers and master spirit of the Reformation, was born at Eisleben of humble rustic parentage. After preliminary schooling at Magdeburg and Eisenach, Luther began the study of law in 1501, for the usual four years. This was at the University of Erfurt, then one of the best on German soil, with its charter dated in 1392. While here Luther showed unusual intellectual powers and a scholarship that excited the admiration of the university.

1. LATIN BIBLE LEADS TO SOUL AWAKENING.—It was here, when but twenty years of age, that Luther found a complete Latin Bible—a copy of the Vulgate—on the library shelves.[2] Previously all he had known of the Bible was that which was in the Breviary, and the parts sung during the mass and sermonaries.[3] The discovery amazed him. He studied this unfamiliar Book with intense eagerness, and it awakened within him a desire to know God. Shocked by a dangerous illness and the sudden death of a friend, Luther felt unprepared to meet his God. He longed to propitiate Him, but was convinced of the inadequacy of his past performances. The monastery must be the place, and penance the method, he thought. So, gathering his friends around, he made his farewell and, in 1505, betook

---

[1] Heinrich Böhmer, *Luther in Light of Recent Research,* pp. 194-196.
[2] Philip Schaff, *History,* vol. 6, p. 111.
[3] Waddington, *A History of the Reformation on the Continent,* vol. 1, pp. 36, 37; J. H. Merle d'Aubigné, *History of the Reformation of the Sixteenth Century,* p. 54.

himself to the Augustinian monastery. Day and night he gave himself to prayers, penances, fastings, and self-mortification.

When he entered the monastery, a complete copy of the Latin Bible was placed in his hands for study, as was enjoined by the new code of statutes drawn up by Von Staupitz, vicar-general of the German branch of the Augustinians.[4] Here Luther renewed his studies of the Holy Scripture with great intensity. But at first the awful attributes of divine justice and holiness appeared more terrible than ever.

One day Staupitz,[5] who was a man of deep spiritual aspiration and understanding, noticed the eager young monk with a troubled look and a face emaciated by fasting and long vigils, and drew him into his confidence. Step by step Staupitz directed his attention from meditation upon his sins to the merits of Christ, from the law to the cross. Staupitz made him understand that true repentance does not consist in self-imposed penances and punishments but in a change of heart, and that in Christ's sacrifice the secret of God's eternal will was revealed. Thus Staupitz became his best friend, his wisest counselor, and his spiritual father. In these quiet hours the seed of truth was sown in this eager heart which would bring forth an abundant harvest not long thereafter.[6]

2. BEGINS REFORM CAREER WHILE UNIVERSITY PROFESSOR. — In 1502 Frederick III, elector of Saxony, founded the University of Wittenberg,[7] and Staupitz became the first dean of its theological faculty. This was one of the first European universities to teach all three of the ancient languages—Hebrew, Greek, and Latin. In 1508 Staupitz summoned Luther, who had just received his B.D. degree, to teach. In 1512, on being made Doc-

---

[4] Philip Schaff, *History*, vol. 6, p. 115.

[5] Staupitz in 1515 and 1518 respectively published two deeply spiritual small works: *Imitation of Christ* and *The Love of God*.

[6] Philip Schaff, *History*, vol. 6, pp. 118, 119; D'Aubigné, *op. cit.*, vol. 1, pp. 61-63; Albert Henry Newman, *op. cit.*, vol. 2, pp. 45, 46.

[7] Philip Schaff, *History*, vol. 6, pp. 132-134. The little town of Wittenberg, its walls largely intact, still stands, with the parish church where Luther first preached as a monk, then as a university professor. Even the old pulpit is preserved. Also remaining are the castle church, the door on which Luther nailed his theses having been replaced; the university, the old Augustinian monastery, built about 1502, in which is Luther's study and lecturehall; and the Luther oak (replaced), beneath which Luther burned the pope's bull.

Albertus dei gra Aplice sedis gra. sctaq Magdeburgeñ in Germania Archicancellari, princeps el burgeñ. Stetineñ. pomeranie. Cassuba Sclauoruqz duc tru ordinis mioz de obseruatia. couentz Moguntini. per i geñ. Moguntineñ. ac illaru et Halberstadeñ. ciuitates et d chioniu Brandenburgeñ. tpal dñio mediate vel immediate. Uniuersis et singlis psentes lras inspecturis Salute in di pa decim modern: oibus z singlis virtusqz sexus chzistifi de vibe. iurta ordinatione nfam man poingentib adiutri chzistifideles ipi obtiere possint. iurta lraz Aplicaz desu idoneu possint eligere pfessoze psbyteaz seculare. vel cuiu comissis p eligente delictz z excessib ac petis qbuslibet. qz censuraz eccliasticz. etia ab hoie. ad alicui instatia latz. de spealir reuata. pretqz machiatiois in psona sumi potifice taz i illos aut alios plator. Falsificatiois lraz Aplicaz q cesuraz occasioe aluminu tulfe aplice de ptib infideliu...

Moguntine sedis Archiepus. primas. z sacri Roani imperi sac Administrato: Halberstadeñ ecclaz. Marchio Brandeñ ggrauin Aurenbergeñ. Rugieqz pnceps. Et Swardian frat nu dñm nfm Leone Papa decimu. p prouitias Magdebur necnon terras et loca Illustrissimoru principu dñoru Mar cta. nucij z comissarij. ad infra scripta spealic deputati. btu facim q Scrissim dñs noster Leo diuia pruidentia pa adrepatioe fabrice Basilice principis aplo. sancti Petri ltra plenissimas indulgetias ac alias gras et facultates quas taz cotinentia. misericordie etia in dño indulsit atqz pcessit. ue iaz medicatiu ordis regulare. q eoz pfessioe diligeter audita. p anaz grauib z enormib. etia in dicte sedi reseruatis casibus. q i partiu. etia rone indicti i cursis. z qru absolutio eide sedi est liois Epoz. aut alioz supioz platoz. z liectiois manuii violez iois armoz. et alioz. phibitoz ad ptes infideliu. ac sentetia ieles itra phibitione. delatoz. incursaz. semel i vita. z i moztz at casib tociesqztiens id petierit plenarie absolueret z eis pe plenariaz oium. et z indulgentia z remissione impede z z eu

¶ Amore et studio elucidande veritatis, hec subscripta disputabuntur Wittenburge Presidente R. P. Martino Luther Eremitano Augustiniano Artiu et S. Theologie Magistro. eiusdemqz ibidem lectore Ordinario. Quare petit vt qui non possunt verbis presentes nobiscum disceptare / agant id literis absentes. In Nomine dñi nostri Ihesu Christi, Amen.

1 Dñs et magister noster Ihesus Christus. dicendo penitecia agite zc. omne vitam fidelium. penitentiam esse voluit.
2 Qd verbu de penitecia sacrametali (.i. cofessionis et satisfactionis que sacer dotum ministerio celebzatur) non potest intelligi.
3 No tñ sola intedit interioze: immo interioz nulla est .nisi foris opetur varias carnis mortificationes.
4 Manet itaqz pena donec manet odiu sui (.i. penitecia vera intus) sez vsqz ad introitum regni celozum.
5 Papa no vult nec pot; villas penas remittere. preter eas. qs arbitrio vel suo vel canonum imposuit.
6 Papa no potest remittere vlla culpam. nisi declarando et approbando re missaz a deo. Aut certe remittendo casus reseruatos sibi. quibus cotemptis culpa prozsus remaneret.
7 Nulli prozsus remittit deus culpa. quin simul eu subijciat; humiliatu in omnibus: sacerdoti suo vicario.
8 Canones penitentiales solu viuentibus sunt impositi: nihilqz morituris sm

38 Docedi sunt Christiani. q Papa sicut magis eget: ita magis optat: in ve nijs dandis. p se deuotam ozonem: q promptam pecuniam.
39 Docedi sunt Christiani. q venie Pape sunt vtiles si no in eas cofidant: p tiocenissime: Si timozem dei per eas amittant.
40 Docedi sunt Christiani q si Papa noster exactioes venialiu pdicatoz. mal let Basilica S. Petri i cineres ire. q edificaret: cute carne z ossib oiu suaz.
41 Docedi sunt Christiani. q Papa sicut debet ita vellet: etia vedita (si op si) Basilica S. Petri. de suis pecunijs dare illio; a quou plurimis quida con cionatoes veniarum pecuniam eliciunt.
42 Clana est fiducia salutis literas venuarii etia si Comissarius: immo Pa pa ipe suam animam. p illis impignoraret.
43 Hostes Christi et Papesut ij qui propter venias pdicadas verbu dei in alijs ecclesijs penitus silere iubent.
44 Iniuria fit vbo Dei: duu codе fmode zequale vel longius tps impenditur venijs q illi.
45 Adens Pape necessario est q si venie (qo minimu est) vna capana: vnis po

Bulla contra errores Martini Lutheri z sequacium.

TETZEL INDULGENCE BRINGS FORTH THESES AND BULL

Part of a Tetzel Indulgence, Now in Wittenberg Museum, That Precipitated the Crisis With Luther (Upper); Upper Section of 1517 Printing of Luther's Ninety-five Theses (Center); Church Door to Which Theses Were Nailed—Replaced by Bronze Portals in Which Are Cast the Text of the Theses (Lower Right); Front Page of Bull of Leo X Against Luther's Errors (Lower Left)

tor of Divinity *ad Biblia* (Doctor of Holy Scriptures),[8] and having to vow on his appointment to defend the Bible and its doctrines, Luther started on his career as a reformer. It was the beginning of a new epoch in his life, as in his lectures he now opened the gospel of "Christ our righteousness," as the central thought of all his teaching.

In 1517 Luther held the threefold office of subprior, preacher, and professor.[9] Great numbers came to hear the new doctrines so convincingly propounded. Meanwhile, Luther had written his little-known theses against the schoolmen (*Disputatio contra scholasticam theologicam*), and against the scholastic doctrine of man's ability and strength to attain righteousness, as he attacked superstition and Scholasticism.[10] But it was his theses against indulgences that stirred the world.

3. CRISIS PRECIPITATED BY TETZEL INDULGENCES.—The present St. Peter's, at Rome, was built with the proceeds from the sale of indulgences. Begun in 1506 under Julius II, it was completed in 1626 at a cost of $46,000,000.[11] In the bull *Liquet omnibus* of Julius II (Jan. 11, 1510), which excited Luther's revolt, no mention is made of repentance and confession as a condition for gaining the indulgence, but only of payment. For an extra sum the sinner could choose his own confessor. It thus became an expedient of papal finance.[12] In 1514 Leo X began to organize collections for St. Peter's on a large scale. Three commissions were directed to Germany and neighboring lands. In March, 1515, one was given to Albert, archbishop of Mainz. Half the proceeds were to go to the Holy See. This was not carried into execution until 1517, when the business of preaching the indulgence was put into the hands of the Dominican John Tetzel.[13] Offering his indulgences near Wittenberg, with hitherto unheard of claims, Tetzel set forth the pope as heaven's dispenser of mercy, and the source of light, grace, and salvation.

---

[8] Staupitz urged Luther to obtain these academic degrees, to be used in the defense of Holy Scripture against all errors. (*Ibid.*, pp. 136, 137.)
[9] *Ibid.*, p. 136.   [10] *Ibid.*, p. 145.   [11] *Ibid.*, p. 146.
[12] B. J. Kidd, *Documents Illustrative of the Continental Reformation*, p. 5.
[13] *Ibid.*, pp. 12, 13.

Seeing the corrupting influence of these indulgences among his own parishioners, Luther tried to stem the tide, and refused to absolve those from their sins who produced an indulgence purchased from Tetzel. (Facsimile appears on page 250.) Therefore the immediate spark that ignited the Reformation did not come from the theological chair, nor even from the pulpit, but from a faithful pastor who was roused to protect his flock from spiritual harm.[14] When Tetzel heard that Luther did not respect his indulgences, he began to threaten with the Inquisition, but Luther was the last one to be intimidated by such a threat. His indignation became irrepressible, and according to the academic custom of the time, he wrote Ninety-five Theses against the indulgences, and at high noon, on October 31, 1517, he affixed them to the door of the Castle Church.[15] (Pictured on page 250.) These he offered to maintain against all opponents.

They were also sent, with a covering letter, to Archbishop Albert of Mainz. Underwritten by "Martin Luther, Monk of the Order of St. Augustine," they asserted the pope's utter insufficiency to confer forgiveness or salvation, and set forth Christ's self-sufficiency. They asked those desiring to discuss the propositions to do so in person, or by letter. Their immediate effect was startling, and their boldness stunned the populace. Within a few weeks they were copied, printed, and spread all over Europe.[16] Their voice, echoing throughout Christendom, was felt by friend and foe alike. Their impact produced a mighty shock, giving men a new view of Christ that could not be escaped.

4. FIRST INTIMATIONS THAT PAPACY IS ANTICHRIST.—At first Pope Leo X was disposed to ignore the Wittenberg movement as a contemptible monkish quarrel. But five months afterward, in March, 1518, he found it necessary to appoint a com-

---

[14] Waddington, *History of the Reformation*, vol. 1, pp. 75-78.
[15] The door of the castle church in Wittenberg was the usual place for posting notices of university disputations. (Kidd, *Documents*, pp. 20, 21.) An English translation may be found in Philip Schaff, *History*, volume 6, pages 160-166. A graphic human-interest portrayal of the crucial epochs in Luther's life is given by D'Aubigné.
[16] Philip Schaff, *History*, vol. 6, p. 156.

mission of inquiry under the direction of the learned Dominican Sylvester Mazzolini, also called Prierias (Prieras), who was master of the papal palace and official censor at Rome. Prierias was under the impression that Luther was ignorant and a heretic. In his refutation of the theses he identified the pope with the Church of Rome, and the Church of Rome with the Church Universal, and denounced every departure from it as heresy.[17] Luther published a reply in August, 1518. The effect of this controversy was to widen the breach, and so to lift the issue to a different level. Whereas in the beginning it was a matter of stopping certain abuses inside the church, it now became a matter of the authority of the church versus one's own conscience.

Luther's fate had already been decided in Rome. On August 7, 1518, he was summoned there in order to recant, and on the twenty-third of August Elector Frederick was asked to deliver this "Child of the Devil" to the papal legate. Instead, Frederick arranged a peaceful interview with the papal legate at Augsburg, which took place between October 12 and 14.[18] All these experiences troubled and tormented Luther's heart to its depths, for he considered himself still a faithful son of the church. Doubts about the position of the Papacy became stronger and stronger, and on December 11, 1518, in a letter written to Wenceslaus Link, he promised:

"I will send you these compositions of mine, that you may judge whether I am right in my divination when I assert, that that true Antichrist mentioned by St. Paul reigns in the court of Rome and is, as I think I can prove, a greater pest than the Turks." [19]

Before the final decision another attempt from Rome was made to silence Luther. Karl von Miltitz, a Saxon nobleman, was sent as papal nuncio to try by diplomacy to bring the matter to a satisfactory conclusion. On January 6, 1519, he met Luther at

---

[17] *Ibid.*, p. 171.
[18] *Ibid.*, pp. 172-175.
[19] *Dr. Martin Luthers Sämmtliche Schriften*, edited by Johann Georg Walch, vol. 15, col. 2430; translated in Waddington, *History of the Reformation*, vol. 1, p. 201. Hereafter Luther's *Schriften*, without other specification, will mean this Walch edition.

Altenburg, and partly succeeded. They reached a truce, under which Tetzel was reproved, and Luther promised to ask the pardon of the pope and to warn the people against the sin of separating from the mother church.[20] In his letter to the pope on March 3, 1519, Luther expresses his deepest humility to the Holy Father, but without retracting his conscientious convictions. At the same time, however, in his study of church history, grave doubts arose in his mind about the validity of the decretals on which the papal primacy was based. So, only a few days later (March 13) we have a letter from Luther, written to Spalatin confidentially, in which he states:

"I am sifting the pontifical decretals with a view to my disputation [at Leipsig]; and, to whisper to you the truth, I am not determined whether the Pope be Antichrist himself or only his apostle, so cruelly is Christ (which is the truth) corrupted and crucified by him in his decretals. I am in perfect torture when I consider that the people of Christ are thus mocked, under the pretence of the laws and name of Christ." [21]

IV. Reaches Conclusions on Papal Antichrist

A further step in becoming more firmly established in his convictions of the antichristian powers revealed in the Papacy, was precipitated by the disputation with Dr. Eck, which took place in June and July, 1519, at Leipzig. The topics discussed comprised not only "indulgences, purgatory," etc., but centered finally on the question of the "superiority of the Roman Church by human or divine right." [22] Although the disputation was not very satisfactory in itself, it helped Luther to understand the complexity of questions involved, and to realize the wide divergence between his views and those promulgated by Rome, as well as to realize that the gulf had already become practically unbridgeable. Nothing was left to him but to stand solely upon the divine Scriptures and his faith in God.[23] Dr. Eck considered

---

[20] Philip Schaff, *History*, vol. 6, p. 176.
[21] Luther, *Schriften*, vol. 21a, col. 156; translated in Waddington, *History of the Reformation*, vol. 1, p. 201.
[22] Waddington, *History of the Reformation*, vol. 1, p. 226.
[23] Philip Schaff, *History*, vol. 6, p. 182.

himself triumphant, and went to Rome to pursue with all vigor the excommunication of Luther.

1. GROWING CONVICTIONS RECORDED.—On February 24, 1520, Luther wrote a letter to Spalatin, which reveals his growing conviction about the sinister nature of the Papacy:

"I am practically cornered, and can hardly doubt any more, that the Pope is really the Antichrist, whom the world expects according to a general belief, because everything so exactly corresponds to the way of his life, action, words, and commandments." [24]

This year, 1520, also saw the three great Reformation treatises, which kindled the flame in Germany. The first was *To the Christian Nobility of the German Nation*. He sent it, with a covering letter, to Nicolaus von Amsdorf on June 20, 1520. It is a clarion call in more than one respect. It not only calls for religious reform and the abolition of all clerical abuses, but also for a political away-from-Rome movement. In unmistakable language Luther uncovers all the depraved practices of the Roman court and the anti-Biblical requirements of the canon law. And although he does not attack the hierarchical system of the church as such, he wants to have it separated from all secular commitments. He said, "Now the Pope should be the head and leader of the soldiers of Heaven, and yet he engages more in worldly matters than any king or emperor." [25]

Although Luther does not in this tract identify the pope with Antichrist, he shows clearly how the pope has given full scope for antichristian powers to work in the church, and is therefore directly responsible. The following statements will elucidate this thought. If a fire breaks out—

"is not every citizen bound in this case to rouse and call in the rest? How much more should this be done in the spiritual city of Christ, if a fire of offence breaks out, either at the pope's government or wherever it may! . . .

---

[24] Translated from Luther, *Schriften*, vol. 21a, col. 234. In all translation a faithful, literal rendering, rather than a free, literary translation, is followed.
[25] Luther, *First Principles of the Reformation; or, The Ninety-five Theses and the Three Primary Works of Dr. Martin Luther*, edited by Wace and Buchheim, p. 52 (original in *Schriften*, vol. 10, col. 307).

There is no authority in the Church but for reformation. Therefore if the Pope wished to use his power to prevent the calling of a free council, so as to prevent the reformation of the Church, we should not respect him or his power. . . . It is the power of the Devil and Antichrist that prevents what would serve for the reformation of Christendom." [26]

On the next page Luther quotes 2 Thessalonians 2:9.

Speaking against the office of cardinals, as superfluous and only created to extract money, he says:

"Now that Italy is sucked dry, they come to Germany and begin very quietly; but we shall see that Germany is soon to be brought into the same state as Italy. We have a few cardinals already. What the Romanists mean thereby the drunken Germans are not to see until they have lost everything —bishoprics, convents, benefices, fiefs, even to their last farthing. Antichrist must take the riches of this earth, as it is written. (Dan. xi. 8, 39, 43.)" [27]

"Antichrist, I hope, will not insult God in this open way. There you have the Pope, as you have chosen to have him, and why? Why, because if the Church were to be reformed, many things would have to be destroyed, and possibly Rome among them." [28]

About Rome, he adds:

"There is a buying and selling, a changing, exchanging and bargaining, cheating and lying, robbing and stealing, debauchery and villainy, and all kinds of contempt of God, that Antichrist himself could not rule worse." [29]

"All these excessive, over-presumptuous and most wicked claims of the Pope are the invention of the Devil, with the object of bringing in Antichrist in due course, and to raise the Pope above God." [30]

2. CLEAR CONCLUSIONS REACHED.—When his friends Staupitz, Lang, and Link begged Luther to suppress his dangerous book, *To the German Nobility,* he answered under date of August 18, 1520, that it had already left the press, and made the following statement:

"We here are of the conviction that the papacy is the seat of the true and real Antichrist, against whose deceit and vileness all is permitted for the salvation of souls. Personally I declare that I owe the Pope no other obedience than that to Antichrist." [31]

[26] *Ibid.*, pp. 29, 30 (original in *Schriften,* vol. 10, cols. 280, 281).
[27] *Ibid.*, pp. 32, 33 (*Schriften,* vol. 10, col. 283).
[28] *Ibid.*, p. 38 (*Schriften,* vol. 10, col. 290).
[29] *Ibid.*, p. 41 (*Schriften,* vol. 10, col. 293).
[30] *Ibid.*, p. 51 (*Schriften,* vol. 10, col. 305).
[31] Luther, *Schriften,* vol. 15, col. 1639.

V. Religious Freedom Perceived and Proclaimed

In his second treatise, *On the Babylonian Captivity of the Church,* which was published in October, 1520,[32] Luther discussed the different sacraments of the church, revealing their man-made inferences and therefore their futility, by throwing the full light of gospel truth upon them. Finally he comes to a climax in his classic statement on liberty and freedom of conscience. which blazed the trail for all who fought and now fight for religious freedom to this day:

"I cry aloud on behalf of liberty and conscience, and I proclaim with confidence that no kind of law can with any justice be imposed on Christians, whether by men or by angels, except so far as they themselves will; for we are free from all. If such laws are imposed on us, we ought so to endure them as still to preserve the consciousness of our liberty. We ought to know and stedfastly to protest that a wrong is being done to that liberty, though we may bear and even glory in that wrong; taking care neither to justify the tyrant nor to murmur against the tyranny. 'Who is he that will harm you, if ye be followers of that which is good?' (1 Peter iii.13.) All things work together for good to the elect of God. Since, however, there are but few who understand the glory of baptism and the happiness of Christian liberty, or who can understand them for the tyranny of the Pope —I for my part will set free my own mind and deliver my conscience, by declaring aloud to the Pope and to all papists, that, unless they shall throw aside all their laws and traditions, and restore liberty to the churches of Christ, and cause that liberty to be taught, they are guilty of the death of all the souls which are perishing in this wretched bondage, and that the papacy is in truth nothing else than the kingdom of Babylon and of very Antichrist. For who is the man of sin and the son of perdition, but he who by his teaching and his ordinances increases the sin and perdition of souls in the Church; while he yet sits in the Church as if he were God? All these conditions have now for many ages been fulfilled by the papal tyranny. It has extinguished faith, darkened the sacraments, crushed the gospel; while it has enjoined and multiplied without end its own laws, which are not only wicked and sacrilegious, but also most unlearned and barbarous." [33]

His third treatise, *Concerning Christian Liberty* (literally, The Freedom of the Christian), the most spiritual document of the three, he sent with a dedication directed to Pope Leo, after

---

[32] Philip Schaff, *History*, vol. 6, p. 213.
[33] Luther, *First Principles*, pp. 196, 197 (*Schriften*, vol. 19, cols. 70, 71).

October 13, 1520. In the covering letter, which is most polite and apologetic, we find the following statements:

"Therefore, most holy father Leo, pray, accept my apology, and be assured I never attacked your person . . . although I confess to have spoken against the Roman see, the Court of Rome, which not even thyself nor anybody on earth can deny that it is in a worse and more corrupt condition than Sodom, Gomorrha, and Babylon have ever been. . . . Meanwhile thou sittest, most holy father, like a sheep among wolves, like Daniel in the lion's den, like Ezekiel among scorpions. What canst thou do against such like? And even if there be three or four pious and learned cardinals, what are they amongst so many? . . . I have ever regretted, pious Leo, that thou shouldest now be pope when thou wert worthy of better times. The Roman See is not worthy of thee,—the Evil Spirit should be Pope, who rules more than thou in this Babel. . . . Such a honour should be reserved to Judas Iscariot and his tribe, whom God has cast out. . . . The Roman Court surpasses that of Turkey in wickedness. Once it was a gate of heaven; now it is the very jaw of hell. This is why I have attacked it so mercilessly." [34]

VI. The Final Rupture With Rome

1. ROME'S ENDEAVOR TO SILENCE LUTHER.—In the meantime the papal court was at work. On June 15 the notorious bull *Exsurge Domini* was issued in Rome [35] condemning Luther's theses and ordering him to retract his errors within sixty days or be seized and carried as a prisoner to Rome. (Reproduced on page 250.) It was the last bull addressed to Latin Christendom as an undivided whole, and the first one to be disobeyed by a large part of it. It took three months before the bull was published in Germany, and when Dr. Eck came to Leipzig he was ridiculed and the bull defied and torn to pieces. In Erfurt the bull was even thrown into the river. [36] Instead of crushing Luther, it rallied Germany to his side. [37]

2. POPE'S BULL BURNED AS BULL OF ANTICHRIST.—Finally, on December 10, 1520, responding to a call to gather outside the walls of Wittenberg's Elster Gate, a concourse of several hun-

---

[34] Translated from Luther, *Schriften*, vol. 15, cols. 783-787; see also *First Principles*, pp. 96-98.
[35] Kidd, *Documents*, p. 38.
[36] Philip Schaff, *History*, vol. 6, pp. 228-230.
[35] Kidd, *Documents*, p. 38.

dred assembled to witness the burning of the papal bull.[38] Curiously enough, this was near the place where the clothing of those who had died of contagious diseases was burned. A pile of wood was placed near the base of an oak tree. One of the oldest professors on the university faculty lighted the wood.

As the flames arose, Luther advanced in frock and cowl. Amid bursts of approbation from the doctors, professors, and students, he cast the bull into the fire along with the canon law and the decretals, declaring, "As thou hast vexed the Holy One of the Lord, may the eternal fire vex thee." [39] Thus he sealed the rupture with Rome by burning the bull that demanded his recantation, and proclaimed his determination to wage a ceaseless warfare against the papal Antichrist. Students, marching in procession through the town, collected papal books, and returning, threw them on the pile.[40] The next day Luther warned the students against the Roman Antichrist, realizing full well the seriousness of the struggle ahead.[41]

Whereas Luther had at first trembled at the step, now, after the deed was done, returning home together with Melanchthon and Carlstadt, he felt more cheerful and confident than ever. They regarded the excommunication as emancipation from the bonds of the Papacy. Luther then publicly announced his stand in a treatise in Latin and Greek, "Why the Books of the Pope and His Disciples Were Burned by Dr. Martin Luther." [42] Calling the canon law the "abomination of desolation," and antichristian, Luther planted himself stanchly on the Book of Scripture. In his published statement he wrote:

"I think, that whosoever was the author of this Bull he is very Antichrist. . . . But I tell thee, Antichrist, that Luther, being accustomed to war, will not be terrified with these vain Bulls, and has learned to put a difference between a piece of paper and the omnipotent Word of God." [43]

---

[38] James Mackinnon, *Luther and the Reformation*, vol. 2, p. 220.
[39] Philip Schaff, *History*, vol. 6, p. 248.
[40] *Ibid.*
[41] Pennington, *op. cit.*, p. 287.
[42] Philip Schaff, *History*, vol. 6, p. 249. 12-page *Quare Pape ac Discipulorum Eius Libri a Doctore Martino Luthero Combusti Sint* (unpaged), Wittenberg, 1520.
[43] Foxe, *Acts*, vol. 2, p. 542.

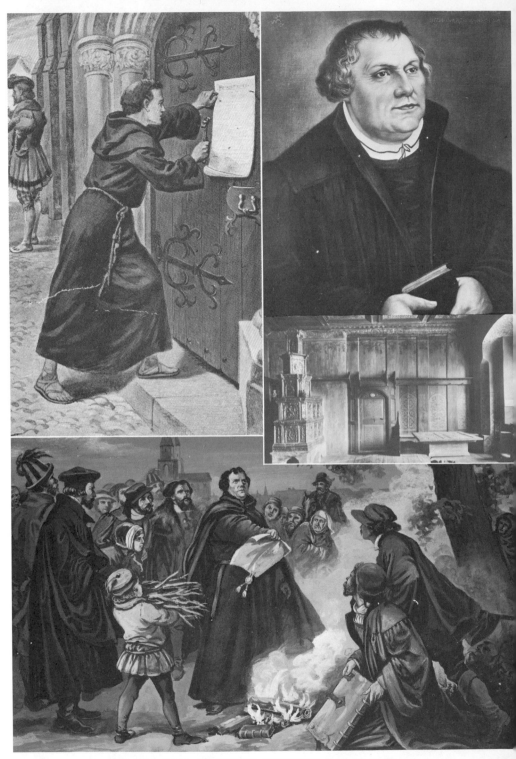

HISTORIC SCENES IN LUTHER'S EARLY LIFE

Nailing the Theses to the Castle Church Door (Upper Left); Luther, the Driving Force of the German Reformation (Upper Right); Luther's Room in the Lutherhaus and the Table at Which He Penned the Ninety-five Theses (Center Right); Burning the Papal Bull as the "Bull of Antichrist" Outside of Wittenberg's East Gate, Under the Famous Luther Oak (Lower)

Such was the remarkable act that launched the Reformation. The issue was Christ versus Antichrist! And it is to be remembered that the subject of Antichrist and the time of the last judgment were then sternly forbidden subjects.[44]

The first bull had anathematized forty-one of Luther's theses. Now the second *(Damnatio et excommunicatio Martini Lutheri . . .),* dated January 4, 1521, placed Luther and his adherents under the actual ban of excommunication.[45] While negotiations were going on, he worked incessantly. Besides several exegetical works, he wrote also an exhaustive reply to the Dominican Catharinus, of Rome, in which he declared that Christ and not Peter was the Rock upon which the church rests, and that the Roman church lacks the seal of the true church. This he proceeded to prove from Daniel and Paul, declaring that Antichrist is not a single person but the whole body of wicked men in the church, and the succession of their rulers. The Papacy was that king in the latter times of the fourth, or Roman, empire, originating out of imperial Rome, which hampering power would first be removed.[46]

3. PROPHECIES USED TO SUPPORT ARGUMENT.—Luther then focused the prophecies of Daniel, Christ, Paul, Peter, Jude, and John upon the Roman Babylon. His main interest was centered on the prophecy of the Little Horn in Daniel 8:9-12, 23-25,[47] and 2 Thessalonians 2 was identified as the antichristian power of the Papacy, or even the pope of Rome himself. Likewise the Little Horn of Daniel 7, coming up among the divisions of Rome, received explicit application.[48] This is Luther's first work to deal largely with prophecy, in which he broadens the foundations of the Reformation and places them on the sure ground of prophetic faith.

---

[44] Fifth Lateran Council, session 11, in Schroeder, *op. cit.,* p. 505; original in Mansi, *op. cit.,* vol. 32, col. 946.

[45] Heinrich, Böhmer, *Luther in Light of Recent Research,* pp. 143, 145; Luther, *Schriften,* vol. 15, cols. 1704, 1705.

[46] Luther, *Schriften,* vol. 18, cols. 1443, 1470, 1471.

[47] *Ibid.,* cols. 1470 ff.

[48] *Ibid.,* cols. 1512, 1513.

4. STAND AT DIET BASED ON DANIEL'S PROPHECIES.—These refutations had just been completed when an imperial herald from Charles V arrived, on April 2, and summoned Luther to the Diet of Worms. With mind convinced of the papal fulfillment of Daniel's prophecies in chapters 8 and 11, he went to give an account of his position and to hold his ground before this great assembly. Such is the fundamental part prophecy played in building the foundations of the great Reformation.

On April 18 Luther testified before the diet that he could not retract.

"Unless I am refuted and convicted by testimonies of the Scriptures or by clear arguments (since I believe neither the Pope nor the councils alone, it being evident that they have often erred and contradicted themselves), I am conquered by the Holy Scriptures quoted by me, and my conscience is bound in the word of God. I can not and will not recant anything, since it is unsafe and dangerous to do anything against the conscience." [49]

Then follow the familiar words, "Here I stand, God help me!" The moral courage involved in thus standing alone before such a brilliant assembly—vindicating long-lost truth against the ancient and almost universal opinion of mankind, fearless of any reproach but his own conscience, and unafraid of any disapproval but that of God—is truly imposing. It is one of the heroics of history. Verily Luther was God's chosen instrument for the time.

5. WARTBURG EXILE RESULTS IN GREATEST GIFT.—As the prophet of old was hid from the wrath of Ahab, so the German Reformer, now under the ban of the empire, was seized by his friends and conveyed to the Wartburg fortress, on the wooded heights south of Eisenach. Here he had safe refuge for a time from the storms that sought to break over him, allowing his beard and his hair to grow long, and donning the costume of a knight. Hidden from his persecutors in the lonely castle, Luther translated the Bible into the vernacular. Though Luther was a

---

[49] Philip Schaff, *History*, vol. 6, pp. 303 ff.

prolific writer, and published about 350 treatises,[50] this German Bible, translated during his exile, was Luther's greatest gift— seventeen editions and fifty reprints being issued subsequently in twelve years. Lufft, of Wittenberg, alone printed 100,000 copies of it within forty years.[51]

VII. Reformation Artists Illuminate the Prophecies

1. Artist Pictures Antichrist in Impressive Series.—The printing press gave wings to the Reformation, and pamphlets and tracts were effectively illustrated by woodcuts. The early *Passional Christi und Antichristi* (1521) is a classic example. Illustrated by the noted Reformation artist Lucas Cranach, Senior, but with captions framed by Luther from the New Testament, and accompanied by appropriate texts, it brought the discussion of Antichrist to every lip.

Bluntly but cleverly and rather violently, as was the custom in those days, it presented a series of graphic contrasts. It showed how Christ fled from an earthly crown, whereas Antichrist ever seeks earthly dominion. Christ wore a crown of thorns; Antichrist wears a triple crown of gold. Christ washed the disciples' feet; Antichrist requires all to kiss his foot. Christ paid taxes; the pope is exempt from taxes. Christ lived in humble poverty; Antichrist fares sumptuously. Christ was bowed to earth with the cross; the pope is carried about in state. Christ rode into Jerusalem on a humble ass; Antichrist rides a beautiful, caparisoned steed. Christ sought neither silver nor gold; Antichrist rules cities and empires. Christ's kingdom was not with observation; Antichrist subjects the whole world. Christ drove the money changers out of the temple (see reproduction on page 276), but—

"The Antichrist sits in the temple of God and professes to be God, as Paul has proclaimed, and changes all divine order as Daniel says, and suppresses Holy Writ, sells dispensations, indulgences, pallia, bishoprics, ten-

---

[50] Böhmer, *op. cit.*, p. 210.
[51] Philip Schaff, *History*, vol. 6, p. 350.

ures, takes taxes, dissolves marriages, burdens the conscience with his laws, makes and annuls laws for the sake of money." [52]

The closing contrast in the series portrays Christ returning from heaven to establish His eternal kingdom, while Antichrist is cast into the bottomless pit, where he will be destroyed. And Luther's appendix note, in a later edition, reads in summarized form:

"Christ and the pope are here presented opposite each other. Please note the case of each. It will not be difficult for you to decide whether or not the pope is the Antichrist, who is against our Lord Jesus Christ." [53]

2. PROPHETIC BEAST SYMBOLS VIVIDLY ILLUSTRATED.—The woodcut illustrations of the prophetic symbols in Luther's German translation of the Scriptures are vivid, and set the pattern for a remarkable group of illustrated commentaries to follow in Germany, Switzerland, England, and Scandinavia. Picturing Daniel 7, the four beasts have arisen in their approximately proper geographical locations around the Mediterranean basin —the lion in Babylon, the bear to the south of it, the leopard in Greece, and the fourth in Western Europe and Northern Africa—with the four winds of strife blowing upon the sea of nations from which they have arisen. [54] (Reproduction on page 276.) The beast of Revelation 13 is portrayed by the artist as wearing an identifying triple crown. The dragon of Revelation 12 is pictured as pouring a flood out of his mouth to overwhelm the woman, symbolic of the pure church, clothed with the sun, and the moon under her feet, while the child Jesus has been caught up to God in heaven. In the background the earlier battle in heaven is presented, with Satan being cast out.

In contrast, the purple-clad woman of Revelation 17, with triple crown upon her head and golden goblet in her hand, is riding the dragon beast, with the kings of the earth on their knees doing obeisance. (Reproduced on page 276.) Again, por-

---

[52] Translated from *Passional Christi und Antichristi*, Leipzig reprint, p. 41.
[53] *Ibid.*, p. 47.
[54] This famous illustration of the four beasts of Daniel 7 appears in the various editions, from the first in 1530 onward.

traying the two beasts of Revelation 13, the lamb-horned beast from the earth is pictured as drawing fire down from heaven, with mankind on bended knees, worshiping the seven-headed first beast from the sea. On another plate the angels, with their vials of wrath, pour them out upon the various objects specified, one in front pouring his upon the ornate, cushioned seat of the Beast, with the triple-crowned Beast receiving its full benefit. In the background church spires topple under the impact of a great earthquake. (Reproduced on page 276.) In Revelation 14 the two harvests of the wheat and the grapes are pictured, and in Revelation 20 the dragon is locked up in the abyss.[55] Thus the talents of the artist played a vital part in the literature of the Reformation.

---

[55] *Biblia, das ist, die gantze Heilige Schrifft, Deudsch,* translated by Martin Luther (Wittenberg, 1534), with woodcuts by Hans Lufft. Luther's introductions to each book of the Bible are brought together in *Dr. Martin Luthers Vorreden zur Heiligen Schrift,* edited by Friedrich Held.

CHAPTER TWELVE

Luther Sets Pattern
for Reformation Interpretation

I. Luther's Deep Interest in Prophecy

In a letter to his friend Johannes Lang, dated December 18, 1521, the idea of translating the New Testament appears for the first time: "I want to translate the New Testament into German. . . . I only wish that this one book could be in everybody's mouth and everybody's hand, and before the eyes and ears of everybody, and in everybody's heart." In eleven weeks he completed this huge task. On the sixth of March he took the manuscript from Wartburg to Wittenberg.[1] Since it left the press in September, 1522, it was sometimes called the *Septemberbibel.*[2]

In his refutations of the attacks against him by Rome-inspired writers, he had made use of the prophecies, first against Catharinus as previously mentioned. But now, when translating the Bible, his interest in the prophecies received a new impetus. He began to dig more deeply into their secrets, and after having translated four of the prophets, he was so much impressed by the prophecies of Daniel that he hastened its publication in order that Daniel might do its good work among rulers and people before the mighty and terrible day of the Lord should overtake

---

[1] Friedrich Held, introductory discussion in *Dr. Martin Luthers Vorreden zur Heiligen Schrift,* p. vi.
[2] British and Foreign Bible Society, *Historical Catalogue of Printed Editions of Holy Scripture* (1911), vol. 2, p. 486.

the world.[3] In this sense he wrote to another friend, Nicolaus Hausmann, "We are working on the book of Daniel, which is a great consolation in these last days." [4] The distraught condition of the world, he explained, and the unparalleled tribulation brought by the pope and Mohammed, led him to decide to publish Daniel without waiting:

"These and similar thoughts caused us to publish this prophet Daniel before the others, which have to be published still, that he [Daniel], may see the light of day before the elements shall melt, and he may do his work and console the distressed Christians for whose sake he was written and spared to these last days." [5]

II. Luther's Comprehensive Exposition of Daniel

1. WORLD ATTESTS THE FOUR EMPIRES OF DANIEL 2.—Because of Luther's key position in the Reformation, and because he set the pattern—though his later associates amplified and perfected the comprehensive expositions he enunciated—disproportionate space must be given his interpretation of Daniel.[6] Luther's explanation of Daniel 2 reiterates the standard progression of the four world powers, as already presented by scores of previous voices over the course of centuries. Here is the heart of his exposition:

"The first kingdom is the Assyrian or Babylonian kingdom; the second, the Medo-Persian; the third, the great kingdom of Alexander and the Greeks; and the fourth, the Roman Empire. In this the whole world agrees, and history supports it fully in detail.

"But the prophet has the most to say about the Roman empire, . . . the legs, the feet, and the toes. The Roman empire will be divided. Spain,

---

[3] Luther, *Schriften*, vol. 6, cols. 892, 893.
[4] *Ibid.*, col. 893.
[5] *Ibid.*
[6] The challenge and the arguments of different men—Eck, Emser, Prierias, and Nanni—forced Luther to investigate and to declare himself increasingly as to his faith in the prophetic outline. Sylvester Prierias, a high official at Rome, contended in his *Epitoma* that the Catholic Church was the kingdom of heaven, and the fifth kingdom following the four earthly monarchies of the Assyrians, the Medes and Persians, the Greeks, and the Romans. (Luther's annotated reprint, in *Dr. Martin Luthers Werke*, Weimar edition, vol. 6, p. 330.) To this Luther retorted in a footnote that no one knows this unless from Sylvester, and that the sacred kingdom is as much like a worldly kingdom as Christ is like Belial, since Christ said, "My kingdom is not of this world." Furthermore, he declared in his preface: "If at Rome it is thus believed and taught with the knowledge of the Pontiff and the Cardinals (which I hope is not so), I freely declare that from these writings, the real Antichrist sits in the temple of God, and reigns in Rome, that scarlet-colored Babylon, and that the Roman Curia is the synagogue of Satan." (*Ibid.*, p. 328.)

France, England, and others emerged from it, some of them weak, others strong, and although it will be divided there will still be some strength, as symbolized by the iron in it. . . . This empire shall last until the end; no one will destroy it but Jesus Himself, when His kingdom comes." [7]

2. Kingdom of Saints Follows Rome's Divisions.—In chapter 7 the same four kingdoms are repeated under beast symbols, Luther asserted, giving special emphasis to the fourth, or Roman, with the day of judgment following the coming of Christ in the time of Rome's divisions, after which the saints receive the kingdom.

"This prophecy of Daniel is by all teachers uniformly explained to represent the kingdoms of Assyria and Babylon, Medo-Persia, Greece, the kingdom of Alexander the Great, and the fourth, the Roman empire, which is the largest, the most cruel, and most powerful, and the last on earth. Daniel states clearly that after the fourth beast or empire the judgment will sit, and no other kingdom shall follow but the kingdom of the saints which will last forever." [8]

But before all this happens, the Roman Empire will long have been divided into ten kingdoms, symbolized by the ten horns, which, he said, are Syria, Egypt, Asia (Minor), Greece, Africa (northern), Spain, Gallia, Italy, Germany, and England.[9]

3. His Position on the Little Horn.—Luther is not always consistent. In his treatise against Catharinus (1521) he had considered the Little Horn of Daniel 7 to refer to the Papacy, but he must have changed his opinion between 1521 and 1529, for in his special sermon against the Turk, which left the press on October 28, 1529,[10] he distinctly expounded the Little Horn as the Turk, or Mohammed's kingdom. This sermon contains a full exegesis of Daniel 7, and among others he makes this explicit statement:

"Since we have for certain in the little horn, Mohammed and his empire, we can easily learn from Daniel, what should be thought about the Turk and Mohammed's kingdom." [11]

---

[7] Translated from Luther, *Schriften*, vol. 6, cols. 898-900.
[8] *Ibid.*, vol. 20, col. 2160.   [10] *Ibid.*, vol. 20, cols. 2158 ff.
[9] *Ibid.*, vol. 6, col. 903.   [11] *Ibid.*, col. 2162.

The same explanation appears in his introduction to the prophet Daniel, wherein he states:

> "A little horn shall also come forth from among them and shall pluck out three of the foremost horns of the ten. This is Mohammed or the Turk, who today has Asia, Egypt, and Greece in his claws. This little horn shall fight the saints and shall blaspheme Christ. All this happens before our own eyes, for the Turk has gained a mighty victory over the Christians, and yet he denies Christ and elevates Mohammed above all. We surely have no more to expect but the day of judgment, because the Turk will not destroy more than three of the ten horns." [12]

Luther seems to have adhered to this opinion for a long time, for in one of his Table Talks, on February 17, 1538, he is quoted as having asserted, "Really the Turk is no small or mean enemy, as Dan. 7:21 shows us, because to him is given the power to fight against the saints of the Lord." [13] This did not, of course, alter his conviction that the pope is Antichrist, which Luther proved from the various other symbols.

We shall not be surprised by Luther's point of view concerning the Turk when we take into consideration the political situation of his time. Western Christianity was in deadly danger of being overwhelmed by the onrushing Ottoman Turks; Eastern Christianity had already succumbed. Soliman the Magnificent had conquered the whole of Southeastern Europe and was knocking at the gates of Vienna, with the resources of a vast empire at his disposal. On the contrary, the Christian princes, disunited as usual, apparently had little with which to oppose him. Luther consequently drew comfort and fortitude from this prophecy, in the belief that this power should pluck out only three horns and not more.

4. ANTIOCHUS REGARDED AS SYMBOL OF ANTICHRIST.—On Daniel 8, after identifying the ram as Medo-Persia, and the goat as Greece under Alexander, who defeated Darius, Luther states that the kingdom of Alexander was "split into four parts: Syria, Egypt, Asia, and Greece." [14] The conspicuous horn, according

---

[12] *Ibid.*, vol. 6, col. 903.   [13] *Ibid.*, vol. 22, col. 1599.   [14] *Ibid.*, vol. 6, col. 904.

to Luther, coming out of Syria, seemed to typify Antiochus initially and his conflict with the Jews, whose country lay between Syria and Egypt, and the duration of the conflict was 2300 literal days, or about six years and three months. "That," said Luther, "is why all the teachers of the past saw a *symbol* of the Antichrist in this Antiochus, and surely they found the truth." [15]

5. APPLIES YEAR-DAY PRINCIPLE TO SEVENTY WEEKS.—On the application of the year-day principle to the seventy weeks of Daniel 9, Luther not only is explicit but declares the harmony of all teachers thereon.

> "All teachers are in harmony that these are year-weeks and not day-weeks, that means, a week encompasses seven years and not seven days. This also is taught by experience, for seventy day-weeks would not even span two years, and that would not be a remarkable period for such a wonderful revelation; therefore, these seventy weeks are 490 years." [16]

Luther divides them into their component parts, but begins them with the commandment of the second year of Darius. And he places the death of Christ at the beginning of the seventieth week, during which last week of years the gospel was preached with power.[17] In this unusual exegesis Luther was followed by Osiander and some others.

6. WILLFUL KING OF CHAPTER 11 APPLIED TO POPE.— Luther firmly believed that the willful king of Daniel 11:36— that exalted and magnified himself above every God, and lorded it over emperors—referred to the pope.

> "Here the pope is clearly pictured, who in all his decrees shouts impudently that all the churches and thrones will be judged by him, but he cannot be judged by anyone. And Cap. Solitae: As the sun is superior to the moon, so the pope is superior to the emperor. And wherever authority is, there is power to command, and the others are obliged to obey." [18]

After discussing the distinctive features of the prophecy— disregard of the desire of women through the prohibiting of the marriage of priests, the construction of strong church-fortresses,

---

15 *Ibid.*, cols. 904, 905.   16 *Ibid.*, col. 906.   17 *Ibid.*, cols. 906-909.
18 *Ibid.*, col. 917; also the same in substance in vol. 22, cols. 918, 919.

and the approach of the last conflict when war with the Papacy shall reach its predicted climax—Luther cites Huss' prediction of 1416, that after roasting a goose (*Huss* meaning goose in Bohemian), a swan would arise after a hundred years whom they would not be able to fry. This, Luther averred, began with the controversy over indulgences in 1517. And although the pope received a mighty shock but still remained on his seat, nevertheless at the time of the end the pope will be pushed against. And he will finally be destroyed, coming to his end between the seas—Rome being between the seas of Tyrrhenum and Adriaticum—with none to help him. In support, he cites Daniel 11:41, 2 Thessalonians 2:8, Revelation 18:4, and Daniel 8:25.[19]

Luther's application of the Antichrist to the Papacy is explicit, though at times he rather inconsistently seeks to include both pope and Turk,[20] while in others he explicitly rules out the Turk.

"Here, in Daniel 11:37, we have a description of the Antichrist. He will not regard God, that is religion, nor the love of women, that is the worldly order and the order of the household and family. Under woman is understood the propagation of the human kind. And who despises that, despises all mankind, because all the civil institutions and orders of the world are made ultimately for the sake of the woman, to protect her and her offspring. Now the Antichrist, that is the pope, will not have God nor a legitimate wife and that means that the Antichrist will despise laws and regulations, customs and principles, kings and princes, principalities in heaven and on earth and accept only his own law. Daniel was a mighty prophet, who was loved by Christ and he spoke in no uncertain terms about the Christ and the Antichrist. The latter shall reign between two seas, at Constantinople, but that place is not holy, they [the Turks] also do not forbid marriage, therefore, believe me, the Pope is the Antichrist."[21]

On the relationship between the pope and the Turk, Luther interestingly observes:

"The body of the Antichrist is as well the pope as the Turk, because a living being consists of body and soul. The spirit of the Antichrist is the pope, his flesh is the Turk; the latter fights against the church with material

[19] *Ibid.*, cols. 922-933.
[20] *Ibid.*, vol. 22, col. 844, no. 1 (Cordatus nos. 1354, 1355).
[21] *Ibid.*, cols. 844, 845, no. 2 (Cordatus, nos. 1409, 40, 1676, 1441); also *Table Talk of Martin Luther* (trans. by Hazlitt), no. 430, pp. 193, 194.

weapons whereas the former with spiritual. But both are from the same master, the devil, because the Pope is a liar and the Turk is a murderer. Make a unit of the Antichrist and you will find both in the pope (lying and murdering).

"But as in the beginning the church was victorious over the saintliness of the Jews and the might of the Romans, in like manner, she will today and forever be victorious over the hypocrites, that is over the pope and the power of the Turk and the emperor. Just let us pray for it." [22]

However, in declaring that Daniel "spoke of that Antichrist persecutor as clearly as if he had been an eyewitness thereof," Luther asserts, in the same Table Talk, that the holy mountain between the seas is at Rome, not at Constantinople. Thus:

"'He shall plant the tabernacles of his palace between the seas, in the glorious holy mountain'; that is, at Rome, in Italy. The Turk rules also between two seas, at Constantinople, but that is not the holy mountain. He does not honor or advance the worship of Maosim, nor does he prohibit matrimony. Therefore Daniel points directly at the pope, who does both with great fierceness." [23]

7. BOOK OF DANIEL BEING OPENED BY STUDY.—On Daniel 12:4, concerning the sealing of the book till the last days, when it "shall be opened and greater knowledge proceed from it," Luther says significantly:

"This is the work which we are doing at the present time. And as formerly stated prophecies can only be perfectly understood after they have been fulfilled." [24]

Dealing last of all with prophetic time, Luther again reverts to the three and a half times of Daniel 12:7. When it will end, and the desolation of the abomination come, we cannot know, he said, until we see it fulfilled. Luther is hazy here, but says that if the 1290 and 1335 are years, as with the seventy weeks, then they should have come to an end about seven years before the great papal schism (1378). They will be "understood only by their fulfillment on the day of judgment," which day he believed near.[25] Luther closes his comment on the indispensability of the book of Daniel thus:

[22] Luther, *Schriften*, vol. 22, col. 844.   [23] Luther, *Table Talk*, no. 430, p. 194.
[24] Luther, *Schriften*, vol. 6, cols. 935, 936.   [25] *Ibid.*, cols. 937-939.

"Therefore we bid that all earnest Christians read the book of Daniel, to whom it will be a consolation and a great profit in these last miserable times. . . . 'But when these things begin to come to pass, look up, and lift up your heads, because your redemption is at hand.' For the same reason we find in Daniel that all the dreams and visions, how fearful they might be, end always in joy and gladness with the coming of Christ and His kingdom, yea, for that chief article of faith, the coming of Christ, these visions were given, explained, and recorded." [26]

8. PROFOUND INFLUENCE OF PROPHECIES ON REFORMATION. —Disavowing originality for the positions presented, but declaring their profound influence upon the course of the Reformation, Luther states:

"Nobody can say or pride himself that these teachings have originated in his head, or have been taught deliberately and on purpose. We all stumbled upon them incidentally, or it happened to us as Isaiah expresses it: [65:1] 'I am sought by them that ask not for me. I am found by them that sought me not.' I myself must confess that I am one of the first of those who originally followed an altogether different purpose. I first directed my writings against the misuse of indulgences, not against indulgences themselves. Neither had I thought of opposing the pope, or to harm even a hair of his head. First I had not rightly understood either the pope or Christ Himself. [But our text states] that tidings also come from the north, that means from the pope's own kingdom, because we ourselves had been papists and antichristians, perhaps even more than they." [27]

III. Luther on the Book of Revelation

The book of Revelation, although it was translated by Luther earlier than the book of Daniel, did not at first have his full approval. He could draw no satisfaction from its symbols. He even hesitated to accept the Apocalypse as an authentic book, and mentioned his doubts freely in his first introduction to the book. In 1545, however, he prepared a new preface in which he gave a general synopsis of the book and its content, particularly with reference to chapters 13-20. [28]

1. OUTLINE OF INTRODUCTION TO BOOK OF REVELATION.— Luther understood the seven churches to be the seven churches in Asia Minor in John's time. The sixth, seventh, and eighth

---

[26] *Ibid.*, cols. 942, 943.   [27] *Ibid.*, col. 932.   [28] *Ibid.*, vol. 14, cols. 130-141.

chapters portray, in vivid pictures, the distress and affliction through which the church was to pass. The sixth seal pertained more to physical sufferings through wars, famines, and pestilence, while the seventh and eighth chapters describe the spiritual afflictions of the church. For instance, Luther regards "the great mountain burning with fire, and cast into the sea," pictured in the second trumpet, as referring to Marcion, Mani, and the Manichaeans, those heretical teachers who had led thousands astray. In the ninth and tenth chapters the misery becomes extreme, as physical and spiritual afflictions are combined. The second woe, for instance, refers to Mohammed and the Saracens. The eleventh and twelfth chapters bring consolation through the two faithful witnesses and the woman clothed with the sun.

The thirteenth chapter contains the third woe on the papal imperium and the imperial Papacy. Here the Papacy receives worldly power and rules not only with the book but also with the sword, as the Catholics boastfully proclaim. Two beasts are shown, the one representing the imperial Roman power, the other with the two horns, the Papacy, which had become a worldly power and rules with indescribable cruelty. Really, Luther asserted, we find in this picture the devil's last wrath. There in the East the second woe, Mohammed and his followers, and here in the West, the pope, and as a further addition the Turk, Gog and Magog, as is clearly shown in the twentieth chapter. Thus the Christian is tormented from all sides by false teachings and wars, by pen and by sword.

In the fourteenth chapter Christ stands ready to slay the Antichrist by the Spirit of His mouth and by the angel with the everlasting gospel. Then follows the other angel, who proclaims the downfall of Babylon, the decline of the spiritual Papacy. In the fifteenth and sixteenth chapters the angels with the seven vials appear; the true gospel light increases, and the seat of the Papacy will be attacked from all sides, until utter darkness covers it. Yet it will defend itself and try to urge the kings into battle on its behalf, though even that will not change its doom.

In Revelation 17 the imperial Papacy and the papal imperium are again portrayed from beginning to end. The Papacy is presented as an evildoer, who is to be tried publicly in order that men might understand in what manner this beast shall be judged and condemned. The eighteenth chapter shows the utter destruction and desolation of the Papacy, though they (the Catholics) nevertheless seek to incite the kings to violence and to warfare. But the One astride the white horse wins the battle. (Revelation 19.)

While all these events are in full progress, Gog and Magog, the Turk, whom Satan had bound 1,000 years prior, enters the picture. But soon he also will be hurled into the sea of fire. The exact time of the beginning of the 1,000 years is difficult to determine, but it is not necessary that all the details should be understood. Then follows the last judgment, and finally, in chapter 21, the holy city of God comes down, and Christ will be Lord of lords through all eternity.[29]

2. DATES PAPAL PERIOD FROM GREGORY I.—The 666 is expounded by Luther as years, possibly from the time of Gregory I (590-604):

"In the decrees [of the pope] are many and even very good passages taken from the Fathers and inserted, but the pope brings them into disrepute, as he claims the right to himself alone, and in this manner he stalks and rules in the name of God, and his reign shall last 666 years according to the number of the beast as John says (Rev. 13:18). This distress started soon after Gregory the First, and thereafter the bishop of Constantinople and the one of Rome quarrelled over the primacy till the time of Charlemagne, in which he, the latter, rose and became a lord over all kings." [30]

3. ANTICHRIST'S KINGDOM PORTRAYED UNDER PERSECUTING BEAST.—Papal, not Turkish, tyranny is portrayed in Revelation 13:

"The kingdom of Antichrist is also described in the revelation of John, where it is said: 'And it was given unto him to make war with the saints, and to overcome them.' [Rev. 13:7.] This might seem prophesied of the

---

[29] *Ibid.*, cols. 130-139.   [30] *Ibid.*, vol. 22, col. 859.

GRAPHIC GERMAN REFORMATION ILLUSTRATIONS OF THE PROPHECIES

Illustration of Daniel 7 From Luther Bible of 1530—the Beasts Plotted Geographically on the Mediterranean Basin, and the Four Winds Blowing on the Sea of Nations (Upper Left); Hans Lufft Portrayal, in 1534, of Plague-Angels Pouring Out Their Vials, One on the Seat of the Triple-crowned Beast (Right); Dragon Pouring Out Flood of Persecution to Destroy the Woman—Also From 1534 Luther Bible (Center Left); Scarlet Woman of Revelation 17, Wearing Triple Crown, Riding the Beast and Worshiped by Notables (Center Right); Contrast Between Christ and Antichrist Portrayed in Famous *Passional* Series (Lower)

Turk and not of the pope, but we must, on investigation, understand it of the pope's abominations and tyranny in temporal respects. It is further said in the Apocalypse: 'It shall be for a time, and times, and half a time.' Here is the question: what is a time? If time be understood a year, the passage signifies three years and a half, and hits Antiochus, who for such a period persecuted the people of Israel, but at length died in his own filth and corruption. In like manner will the pope also be destroyed; for he began his kingdom, not through power or the divine authority, but through superstition and a forced interpretation of some passages of Scripture. Popedom is built on a foundation which will bring about its fall." [31]

4. THREE AND A HALF TIMES BEGIN POSSIBLY WITH PHOCAS. —The time feature perplexed Luther. He alludes to the possible beginning in the time of Phocas, the Eastern Roman Emperor (602-610), which is essentially the time of Gregory I. Says Luther, "I cannot well define or comprehend this prophecy: 'a time, times, and half a time.' " (Rev. 13:14.) He concludes, "God knows how it stands, and how He will deliver those that are His." Then he consoles them with the words:

"The pope is the last blaze in the lamp, which will go out, and ere long be extinguished, the last instrument of the devil, . . . but when he [the Devil] is struck with God's Word, then the pope is turned to a poppy and a frothy flower." [32]

5. SPIRITUAL BABYLON IS PROPHESIED ABOMINATION.—Comparing literal and spiritual Babylon, Luther says:

"The second Babylon is similar to the first, and what the mother has done, that is also practiced by the daughter. The first Babylon defended her faith by fire and burnt the ancestors of Christ. See Genesis 11:9. This Babylon in Rome burns the children of Christ. One Babylon is as pious as the other." [33]

Luther also identified Babylon as the "abomination of desolation" spoken of by Christ:

"This is abomination itself, it is a foul odor of which Jesus speaks in Matthew 24:15, 'When ye therefore shall see the abomination of desolation spoken of by Daniel the prophet, stand in the holy place (whoso readeth, let him understand:)' etc., and Saint Paul: (1 [2] Thess. 2:4) 'He sitteth in

---

[31] Luther, *Table Talk*, p. 194.
[32] *Ibid.*, pp. 195, 196.
[33] *Dr. Martin Luthers sämmtliche Werke*, ed. by J. K. Irmischer (Erlangen edition), vol. 24, p. 140.

the temple of God (that means, in the midst of christendom), showing himself that he is God.' " [34]

IV. Views on Time of the Judgment Day

1. BELIEVED END VERY NEAR.—Luther's views on the probable length of time to elapse until the great judgment day varied from time to time. It was in his Table Talks,[35] scattered over years, that these varying expressions occur. He believed the end near, and hoped he might see it in his day. In 1538, in commenting on the prevalent godlessness, Luther said, "I hope that day is not far off and we shall still see it." [36] And on another occasion he added:

"I hope the last day will not tarry over 100 years, because God's Word will be taken away again and a great darkness will come for the scarcity of ministers of the Word." [37]

In 1536, after identifying his own time as that of the fourth state—the white (pale) horse—he had said:

"We have reached the time of the white [pale] horse of the Apocalypse. This world will not last any more, if God wills it, than another hundred years." [38]

"The world cannot stand much longer, perhaps a hundred years at the outside." [39]

Besides these aforementioned statements of Luther about the soon coming of Christ, others are sometimes quoted which indicate that he believed that a longer period—200, 300, or 400 years—had to elapse before the last events would set in.[40] Though

---

[34] *Ibid.*, p. 161.
[35] Luther's Table Talks sprang from a round table with his companions at the evening meal in the Augustinian Monastery, the same custom being continued after Luther's marriage in 1525. In 1531 Conrad Cordatus, of Austria, began jotting down at the moment the remarks made by Luther at the table. (Böhmer, *op. cit.*, pp. 189-192.) Others—about a dozen—followed suit, exchanging their copies. (For the list see Preserved Smith, *Luther's Table Talk*, p. 16.) Each reporter was a source for comparison, until the sayings became united—like springs pouring into a common stream. Lauterbach began to arrange the collections topically, his notebooks being extant, but Aurifaber, who spent only the last two years at Luther's table, was the first who thought of publishing them. First edition was in 1566.
[36] Luther, *Schriften*, vol. 22, col. 1331.
[37] *Ibid.*, col. 16.
[38] *Ibid.*, col. 1334.
[39] Luther, *Table Talk*, chap. "The Resurrection," p. 325.
[40] For example: "I hope the last Day of Judgment is not far, I persuade myself verily it will not be absent full three hundred years longer." (*The Familiar Discourses of Dr. Martin Luther*, Bell's translation, 1818 ed., chap. 1, p. 7.) See Luther, *Schriften*, vol. 22, cols. 1760, 1761, and 1880, 1881, for the 200 and 400 years respectively.

some of these statements are incorporated in translated *Table Talk*, they are largely taken from the diaries of Luther's associates. Consequently, not too much certainty can be attached to them.

2. CALCULATION BASED ON 6,000-YEAR THEORY.—In 1545 Luther wrote that the world was in its sixth and last thousand years, before the eternal Sabbath rest—typified by the six days of creation week—with the Papacy, established by about A.D. 600, dominating in the sixth millennium, along with Mohammedanism. In this period ended the 1290 days (1290 years from the midst of the seventieth week, or about 1327). The end, with the fall of Antichrist, would be shortened because Christ did not stay in the tomb the full three days. The seventieth week, Luther believed, began with the crucifixion, resurrection, and ascension of Christ in the thirty-fourth year of His life, and the fifth millennium began at the end of the seventieth week (in A.D. 41).[41]

V. Various Signs of Second Advent Enumerated

Luther wrote rather comprehensively on the signs of Christ's second advent, sometimes from Luke 21 and sometimes from Matthew 24. In 1532 he published *Ein tröstliche predigt von der zukunfft Christi und den vorhergehenden Zeichen des Jüngsten tags* (A Consoling Sermon Concerning the Appearing of Christ and the Signs of the Last day).

1. CELESTIAL SIGNS OF MATTHEW 24 AS YET FUTURE.— Luther even discussed the celestial signs of the end. But on these he was hazy and rather speculative.

"We find in this gospel [Matthew] two main points, first: the signs which shall precede His coming, and second: these signs are given to console the Christians, the true believers. . . . Now the first sign shall happen in the sky, in the sun, moon and stars; the second among men, they will wither away for fear. . . . Now I do not want to dispute whether these signs in the sun, moon, and stars have happened already, nor do I want to

---

[41] Luther, *Supputatio Annorum Mundi Emendata* (A Corrected Computation of the Years of the World), unpaged.

command the Christians to believe it. But my own belief and sure hope is, that the majority of these signs have happened already and that we have not to expect many more. If we want to believe it, we have seen enough with our own eyes in our own days. How many great darknesses have followed one another in a few years, which have never been experienced before. . . . But those who do not want to believe, would not believe even if the sun would be darkened every day and the stars would fall in bundles.

"And although the astrologers say that they can predict some of the signs, yet these [aforementioned] signs, especially when they appear in such multitude indicate some fearful events, as they [astrologers] do not deny. . . . Therefore let them be afraid and wither for fear, who know nothing else nor ask for anything else than this temporal life. . . . But let us be full of cheer and hope, because our life and our treasure is not here but hidden with Christ in God, and soon Christ will be revealed before the whole universe in His immortal being and His eternal brightness." [42]

2. SOME WILL RECOGNIZE THEM AS THEY COME.—A thirty-page English translation of this work appeared, in 1661, under the title *The Signs of Christ's Coming and the Last Day*. The discussion is quite full. The signs were to be literal. And despite the blindness and scoffing, there—

"undoubtedly must needs be some living in the time of these signs, who shall both know and acknowledge the signs, and shall also, as the Lord doth admonish, lift up their heads, and expect their redemption, though they cannot certainly know that precise day." [43]

The return of the Jews was likewise alluded to.

3. PAPAL ABOMINATION LISTED AS A SIGN.—The Papacy is clearly listed here as a sign. Thus, in the quaint spelling of the time:

"Neither is that which *Matthew* hath foretold, in ch. 24, touching that Horrible Abomination (to wit) Antichrist, a less certain Signs to me then [than] the former, namely that under his Kingdome, there should be and prevail, extream blindness, the most pernicious Errors, and the highest wickednesses. All which things do most wretchedly flourish in the Kingdom of the Pope, and that in the greatest *impudency* and *tyranny* that can be. Which Sign, (I confess) above all the rest, compells me stedfastly to be-

---

[42] Translated from *Ein tröstliche predigt von der zukunfft Christi und den vorgehenden zeichen des Jüngsten tags* (unpaged).
[43] *The Signs of Christ's Coming and of the Last Day*, the substance of a sermon of Martin Luther, p. 3.

lieve, that Christ will not now stay long. For truly these wickednesses are more great and grievous, and these Blasphemies are more horrible, then that Heaven should long indure to behold them; for they do even provoke the Day of the Lord, and insult over his Divine Vengeance; that it cannot be, but it must needs come quickly upon them, as a snare." [44]

4. SIGNS CONSTITUTED HERALDS OF IMPENDING JUDGMENT DAY.—In a similar treatise Luther declared:

"I will not permit any one to rob me of my opinion that the day of the Lord is not far hence. This conviction is forced upon me by the signs and by the admonitions of Christ himself." [45]

After rehearsing the signs Luther approvingly cites Lactantius (A.D. 320) on the sign conditions before the end of the world —godlessness, strife, war, violence. [46]

5. LONGED FOR DELIVERANCE AT SECOND ADVENT.—Luther longed for the Saviour's return, and in a family letter written in 1540, prayed, "Oh, come thou day of judgment." [47]

"Oh, Christ, my Lord, look down upon us and bring upon us thy day of judgment, and destroy the brood of Satan in Rome. There sits the Man, of whom the Apostle Paul wrote (2 Thess. 2:3,4) that he will oppose and exalt himself above all that is called God,—that Man of Sin, that Son of Perdition. What else is papal power but sin and corruption? It leads souls to destruction under thine own name, O Lord! . . . I hope the day of judgment is soon to dawn. Things can and will not become worse than they are at this time. The papal see is practicing iniquity to its heights. He suppresses the Law of God and exalts his commandments above the commandments of God." [48]

6. LOOKED FOR RESURRECTION AT ADVENT.—Luther believed in the literal resurrection of the dead, to take place at the last trump, the soon-coming day of the Lord. But as the world scoffed at the impending destruction in the days of Sodom, so in his own time it scoffed at the soon-coming day of judgment— which cannot be stayed. [49] And then the last trumpet of God will

---

[44] *Ibid.,* p. 6.
[45] Luther, *Schriften,* vol. 11, col. 47.
[46] Cf. Lactantius, *The Divine Institutes,* book 7, chap. 15, in *The Ante-Nicene Fathers,* vol. 7, p. 212.
[47] *Luther im Kreise der Seinen, Familienbriefe und Fabeln* (Luther in His Own Family Circle, Family Letters and Fables), p. 37, no. 17 (July 16, 1540).
[48] *Dr. Martin Luthers sämmtliche Werke* (Erlangen edition), vol. 21, p. 339.
[49] Luther, *Schriften,* vol. 8, cols. 1334, 1335.

be heard; that is the last clap of thunder, which will suddenly destroy heaven and earth and all that is on it. After which we shall be translated, and this corruptible will put on incorruption and this mortal will put on immortality. All the reverberations we have to experience in our days are only a prelude to that last mighty peal.

And then he quotes Jerome: *"Sive comedam, sive bibam, sive aliquid aliud faciam, semper vox illa videtur sonare in auribus meis: Surgite mortui et venite ad judicium."* (If I eat, or if I drink or do anything else, that voice always seems to sound in my ears: Rise, O dead, and come to the judgment.)[50]

---

[50] *Ibid.*, cols. 1330, 1331.

CHAPTER THIRTEEN

Luther's Co-Reformers

Stress Prophetic Interpretation

I. 1500 Tractates Empower 16th-Century Reformation

The whole throbbing story of the German Reformation is enfolded within the fifteen hundred treatises—though this includes numerous duplicates—issued from more than forty centers of Germany between the years 1511 and 1598—treatises for the first time emancipated from Latin as the classical medium of polemics.[1] These treatises are miscalled "tracts," for some contain up to three hundred pages. Some of the academic disputes were printed as broadsides, that they might be posted where they could come under the notice of all at university centers, as with Luther's theses in Wittenberg.

1. SHEER NUMBER AND RANGE IS PHENOMENAL.—This was the first systematic use of the newly created printing press for controversial purposes. Comparatively speaking, the sheer number was phenomenal. And their influence was so great that soon it was recognized that upon the outcome of this battle of words rested the fate of Europe. These treatises verily made history. The battle was incessant and the language forthright. Pent-up forces capitalized upon the situation and sometimes carried matters beyond the control of the Reformation leaders. Political aspects injected themselves, and revolutionary symptoms ap-

---

[1] James L. Lindsay, *Bibliotheca Lindesiana—Catalogue of Collection of 1500 Tracts by Martin Luther and His Contemporaries*, Preface. Lindsay's list is not, of course, complete.

peared. There were occasional outbursts of violence, as well as the Peasants' War.

The Earl of Crawford assembled this great list mentioned, and it is printed in a quarto volume of 280 pages, beginning with Reuchlin, precursor of the German Reformation. Prominent in the early listing was, of course, Luther's Ninety-five Theses, the attack upon them and their defense, the subsequent bull of condemnation, and Luther's defense after burning it, together with the speech before the Diet of Worms. Then, in addition to the discussions, there are the manifestos, credal declarations, and Biblical expositions, including the prophecies of Daniel and the Apocalypse. Almost every sermon or speech was immediately and inexpensively printed.

2. GREATEST WAR EVER WAGED OVER BIBLE TRUTH.—Old commentaries on Daniel and the Apocalypse were reprinted. The one attributed to John Purvey of England, republished by Luther in 1528, carried Luther's comment that he was not the first to apply the antichristian kingdom to the Papacy, for many great men had done so many years before, and that frankly and openly, under the greatest persecution.[2]

Note the number, frequency, and continuity of treatises from Luther's pen alone: 77 in 1520, 37 in 1521, 72 in 1522, 94 in 1523, 44 in 1524, 36 in 1525, and so on—a total of approximately 360, though not a few were duplicates. But there were some four hundred writers, in all, responsible for the fifteen hundred treatises, though some were anonymous. The people were thus kept in touch with every stage of the conflict. This tabulation represents the greatest doctrinal war ever waged among men over Bible truth to that time. And running all through this vast body of polemical literature was the basic conflict over the prophetic identity of the Papacy, and the predicted marks for its identification.

3. ILLUSTRATED WITH POWERFUL CARTOONS AND SATIRES.—

---

[2] Luther, preface, in John Purvey, *Commentarius in Apocalypsin Ante Centum Annos Editus*, sig. A₂v. This preface is also in German in Luther, *Schriften*, vol. 14, col. 178.

These tractates were often effectively illustrated with woodcuts—about one thousand such appearing [3]—many of them designed by the great Reformation artists. They included portraits of the leading characters, illustrations of their teachings, together with powerful cartoons and satires. Such is the setting of the unfolding story of Reformation literature and prophetic interpretation that we now pursue.[4] There is growing clarity with the years.

II. Melanchthon Holds Prophetic Views Similar to Luther

PHILIPP MELANCHTHON (1497-1560), second leader in the German Reformation and the "Protestant Preceptor of Germany," was born at Bretten. His mother was the niece of the celebrated Hebraist Reuchlin (Capnion). Because the father died during the lad's childhood, Reuchlin took charge of Philipp, and as friend and patron gave him the Greek name Melanchthon. Also he presented him with a rare, early Latin Bible,[5] and several Greek and Latin grammars and lexicons. Reuchlin sent him to the Latin school at Pforzheim in 1507, and to the University of Heidelberg in 1509. There he studied philosophy, mathematics, science, law, and medicine, as well as the Greek and Latin classics, which languages he wrote and spoke better than his native German. He was a precocious student, but modest and amiable in character. (His portrait appears on page 303.)

Melanchthon received his B.A. in 1511, and his M.A. in 1514. Erasmus paid extraordinary tribute to his classical learning. Melanchthon began public life at the University of Tübingen as lecturer on ancient literature. In 1518 he published a Greek grammar that lived through many editions. Upon the

---

[3] James L. Lindsay, *op. cit.*, preface, p. viii.
[4] Doubtless the most graphic modern pictorial review extant of the old German Reformation characters, their environs, their institutions, and above all their writings, with the accompanying illustrations and cartoons of the time, has been prepared by Paul Schreckenbach and Franz Neubert—*Martin Luther, Ein Bild seines Lebens und Wirkens.* (Martin Luther, A Picture of His Life and of His Activities), 184 pages crowded with photographs, woodcuts, and information, biographical sketches, and the great historical documents, which are photographically reproduced.
[5] J. W. Richard, *Philip Melanchthon,* p. 21; Philip Schaff in *Saint Augustin, Melanchthon, Neander,* pp. 107-109. Melanchthon is a blending of two Greek words meaning "black earth," the same as the meaning of his family name, Schwarzerd. Melanchthon usually signed his name simply Phillipus.

recommendation of Reuchlin, Elector Frederick the Wise called Melanchthon to a professorship at Wittenberg. Melanchthon declined calls to Ingolstadt and Leipzig, but accepted that of the University of Wittenberg, to become its first professor of Greek, arriving there August 25, 1518, when only twenty-one—nearly a year after the publication of Luther's theses, and two years before burning the pope's bull.

1. CREATOR OF PROTESTANT EDUCATIONAL SYSTEM.—Although he was small of stature and extremely diffident, his learning was nevertheless conceded by all, and his high character was above suspicion. He fostered the revival of Biblical languages, which did much to promote the success of the Reformation.[6] He was the creator of the Protestant educational system of Germany.[7] Shortly after his arrival in Wittenberg, Melanchthon delivered a remarkable oration on reforming the studies of youth, attacking the prevailing Scholasticism and announcing a plan of reform, particularly regarding "sacred studies" and Biblical languages, that set the pattern for the Reformation emphasis.[8]

There were stormy days, however, in the early Reformation. In 1521 many monks left the monastery, fiercely attacking the mass, the adoration of the host, and monasticism. Some priests married, and turbulent students interrupted the mass. Melanchthon celebrated the Lord's supper, in both kinds, with his students, Carlstadt following his example and employing the German language. During Luther's confinement in the Wartburg, Melanchthon carried on as head of the Reformed cause. Fanaticism, led by Storch and Stübner, as well as Münzer from Zwickau, arose to plague them in 1522. Münzer sent forth twelve apostles and set apart seventy-two evangelists. He went to Prague, and Storch came to Wittenberg. Melanchthon scarcely knew how to handle him and his visionary "prophetic" predictions, as Carlstadt, rector of the university, accepted some of his views.

---

[6] Philip Schaff, *Saint Augustin, Melanchthon, Neander*, pp. 109-111.
[7] Richard, *op. cit.*, pp. 133, 134.
[8] Leading portions appear in F. A. Cox, *The Life of Philip Melancthon*, pp. 30-33.

2. POPULAR TEACHER, APPEALING TO SCHOLARS.—In 1519 Melanchthon had received a B.D. degree, but later declined a proferred degree of Doctor, as he did not especially approve of higher degrees.[9] A member of the theological faculty, he taught ethics, logic, and Greek literature. In later life he devoted himself exclusively to sacred learning. He was never ordained,[10] and never ascended the pulpit, but every Sunday in his lecture room he gave a Latin discourse on the Scripture lesson. He was, nevertheless, the theologian of the Lutheran Church. His complete works *(Opera Omnia)* fill the first twenty-eight volumes of the *Corpus Reformatorum*.[11] His greatest work was the composing of the Augsburg Confession, the most important and generally received creed of the Lutheran Church, and foundation of the German Lutheran faith. This he drew up during the Diet of 1530, and revised it in 1540, in order to make it acceptable to the Reformed groups. This latter has often been subscribed to by the German Reformed Churches.[12]

Melanchthon was the most popular teacher in Wittenberg; sometimes as high as fifteen hundred to two thousand [13] of the three thousand students were recorded in attendance. Among his hearers were princes, knights, and barons from all parts of Europe—France, England, Hungary, Poland, Denmark, Bohemia, Italy, and Greece. The strong personal attachment between Luther and Melanchthon was based on mutual esteem. A highly gifted scholar of untiring industry—a man of order and method—he was the complement to Luther, affording the appeal to the scholars; whereas Luther captivated the masses. Both were prolific writers, but neither he nor Luther received any remuneration for their books.[14]

3. COMPROMISING POLICY TONED DOWN HIS WITNESS.—

---

[9] Richard, *op. cit.*, p. 58.
[10] *Ibid.*; Philip Schaff, *Saint Augustin, Melanchthon, Neander*, p. 112.
[11] Comprising the writings of the professors of the University of Wittenberg, and edited by Bretschneider and Bindseil.
[12] Cox, *op. cit.*, pp. 160-178; Philip Schaff, *Saint Augustin, Melanchthon, Neander*, p. 124; for text, see Philip Schaff, *Creeds*, vol. 3, pp. 3-73.
[13] Richard, *op. cit.*, p. 44; Samuel Leigh Sotheby, *Unpublished Documents, Marginal Notes and Memoranda, in the Autograph of Philip Melanchthon and of Martin Luther*, Plate XXXIV.
[14] Philip Schaff, *Saint Augustin, Melanchthon, Neander*, p. 118.

Melanchthon lacked the bold spirit of Luther, but shared most of his sentiments. He leaned, however, toward compromise. Composing the celebrated Confession of Augsburg, in 1530, which was intended to be read publicly to the hostile Roman Catholic emperor Charles V in the presence of princes and ecclesiastical dignitaries, Melanchthon toned it down as far as possible, avoiding statements concerning the Roman Catholic Church that would cause offense. Luther complained of this omission:

"Satan sees clearly . . . that your Apology has passed lightly over the articles of purgatory, the worship of saints, and above all, of the Pope and of Antichrist." [15]

4. ROME IS BABYLON AND POPE MAN OF SIN.—Melanchthon was clear personally, however, in his conviction that Rome is the Babylon of the Apocalypse and the pope the Man of Sin. In his disputation on marriage, based on First Timothy, he says:

"18. Since it is certain that the pontiffs and the monks have forbidden marriage, it is most manifest, and true without any doubt, that the Roman Pontiff, with his whole order and kingdom, is very Antichrist." [16]

"19. Likewise in 2 Thess. II, Paul clearly says that the man of sin will rule in the church exalting himself above the worship of God, etc.

"20. But it is certain that the popes do rule in the church, and under the title of the church in defending idols.

"21. Wherefore I affirm that no heresy hath arisen, nor indeed shall be, with which these descriptions of Paul can more truly and certainly accord and agree than with this pontifical kingdom. . . .

"25. The prophet Daniel also attributes these two things to Antichrist; namely, that he shall place an idol in the temple, and worship [it] with gold and silver; and that he shall not honor women.

"26. That both of them belong to the Roman Pontiff, who does not clearly see? The idols are clearly the impious masses, the worship of saints, and the statues which are exhibited in gold and silver that they may be worshiped." [17]

5. MESSIAH'S KINGDOM CLIMAX OF DANIEL 2.—Melanchthon's Latin commentary on Daniel (1543) urges earnestly at the outset that the reader should be interested not merely in the

---

[15] Merle d'Aubigné, *op. cit.*, book 14, chap. 8, p. 573.
[16] Translated from Melanchthon, *Disputationes*, No. 56, "De Matrimonio," in *Opera* (*Corpus Reformatorum*), vol. 12, col. 535.
[17] *Ibid.*, cols. 535, 536.

historical fulfillment but in entering the eternal kingdom portrayed as the climax of prophecy. Enumerating the four empires of Daniel 2 as the kingdoms of the Assyrians and Chaldeans, of the Medes and Persians, of Alexander and his successors, of the Roman Empire, it sets forth the feet and the toes as the later kingdoms—Frankish, Germanic, Spanish, Saracenic, and Turkish, and the stone as the Messianic kingdom, soon to be set up.

"Finally, it benefits all to know that the time of the world is a short period, that the day of judgment is already upon [us] and is at the doors, just as also God wished to warn this Babylonian king of the shortness of the times of the world, of the judgment to come, of the salvation of the pious, of the eternal punishments of the wicked. . . .

"The stone means Christ, who from the mountain, that is, from the people of Israel, was born. . . . This signifies that the kingdom of Christ will not be political, but spiritual, because it will be administered through the Word." [18]

6. LITTLE HORN OF DANIEL 7 CONSIDERED MOHAMMEDAN-ISM.—The same four kingdoms, Melanchthon holds, are portrayed by the four beasts of Daniel 7. The four heads of the leopard are the four divisions of Alexander's empire, and the ten horns of the fourth, or Roman beast, are the divisions of the Roman Empire—ten may indicate merely a large number, or, if anyone wants to be specific: Italy, Spain, France, Germany, Illyricum, Grecia, Africa, Egypt, Asia, and Syria. But the Little Horn, Melanchthon conceives to be the Mohammedan Saracens and Turks, rising when Rome fell.[19] The question of the time, times, and half a time, Melanchthon maintains, is rather difficult. He interprets this "dark passage" as a long time and says that the Turkish Empire will suddenly come to an end, but after its fall, the blessed day of the Lord will soon arrive.[20]

7. DANIEL 8 APPLIES TO ANTIOCHUS AND THE PAPACY.—The Persian ram is followed by the Grecian goat, Alexander, and this in turn by the four horns—the four divisions of Alexander's

---

[18] Translated from Melanchthon, *In Danielem Prophetam Commentarius*, in *Opera* (*Corpus Reformatorum*), vol. 13, cols. 833, 834 (for the contemporary German version, see *Der Prophet Daniel ausgelegt durch D. Philipp. Melanth.*, translated from Latin by Justus Jonas).
[19] *In Danielem Prophetam*, in *Opera*, vol. 13, cols. 858-860.
[20] *Ibid.*, cols. 864, 865.

empire. Then comes the Little Horn, which Melanchthon applies to Antiochus as a type of the papal Antichrist. According to the common interpretation of his day, he makes the 2300 days literal, in the time of the oppression of the Jews by Antiochus Epiphanes, but the other characteristics he applies not only to Antiochus but to Paul's Antichrist, who, Melanchthon feels, includes both Mohammedanism and the Papacy. The breaking "without hand" is the gospel triumph over the Papacy before the day of judgment.[21]

8. 70 Weeks Are 490 Years—From Longimanus.—He interprets the seventy weeks as 490 literal years, on the year-day principle. He explains two computations, extending from the second year of "Darius Artaxerxes Longimanus" to the baptism of Christ, or from the first year of Cyrus to the birth of Christ. And even if these computations were not absolutely exact, it suffices pious hearts to know that this period of 490 years agrees with the time that elapsed between the return from Babylon and the coming of the Messiah. But he personally prefers another reckoning of sixty-nine weeks to the baptism of Christ, beginning with the second year of Longimanus, with Jesus crucified in the midst of the seventieth week, three and a half years after his baptism.[22]

9. Papal Transgression of Desolation Depicted.—Declaring that "the history of Antiochus is a type and figure of Antichrist," Melanchthon stresses the Mohammedan and papal perversions of the true worship, and says that Daniel 11:45 may refer to the Turk, who has his seat between the two seas, as well as to the seat of the Roman pope, likewise located between two seas—the Adriatic and the Tyrrhenian.[23]

10. The 1290 and 1335 Days.—Melanchthon conceives Daniel's numbers of 1290 and 1335 to be year-days, which he combines as 2625 years, extending to the end. The first he

---

[21] *Ibid.*, cols. 866, 869-872.   [22] *Ibid.*, cols. 881-897.   [23] *Ibid.*, cols. 951, 962-974.

places from Daniel's time (somewhere near 600 B.C.) to the rise
of Mohammedanism, and of the apostasy in the church in the
seventh century after Christ; the second, to the end of the world
at the end of the sixth millennium, allowing for a shortening of
the time.[24]

11. Believes Judgment Less Than 400 Years Distant.—
Declaring that the great day of God will soon come, and adverting to the 6,000-year theory—2,000 without law, 2,000 under
law, and 2,000 under the Messiah—Melanchthon adds: "It is
settled that Christ was born about the close of the fourth millennium, and now 1545 years have passed. Therefore we are not
far from the end." [25]

12. Calculates 666 From Hebrew "Romith."—Sotheby
gives a photographic reproduction of Melanchthon's own hand-
written calculation of the 666, but first citing and tabulating the
numerical equivalent given by Irenaeus to the Greek *Lateinos*,
and then his own calculation of the Hebrew *Romith* (Roman
kingdom), signing his initials "P. M." [26]

III. Nurnberg Embraces the New Protestant Faith

Four hundred years ago the free town[27] of Nürnberg (Nuremberg) was already famous in Europe. Centrally located on the
River Pegnitz, in the midst of the great Franconian plain between the Danube and the Rhine, it was advantageously situated
at the crossroads of nations. Founded in the tenth century, it
was by the sixteenth a center of industry, art, and letters.[28] It

---

[24] *Ibid.*, col. 978.
[25] *Ibid.*; see also Sotheby, *op. cit.*, Plate XXVIII, which reproduces a note in Melanchthon's own hand, in a 1541 copy of Luther's Bible (p. 4): "Written in the year 1557, after the
birth of our Lord Christ, of the Virgin Mary,—year from the creation of the world 5519; from
this number we may be assured that this aged world is not far from its end."
[26] Sotheby, *op. cit.*, Plate XIII.
[27] There were eighty-four free cities in the empire in 1521. Many of these began to recognize the evangelical preachers. These had been drawn from the Augustinian Friars, the Franciscans, the Canons Regular, and the secular clergy. The Reform began to prevail by decision of
the townsmen at Frankfurt am Main and Magdeburg; and at Ulm, Strassburg, Bremen, and
Nürnberg in 1524. The Lutheran hymns first became popular in northern Germany, and then
in the south. (Kidd, *Documents*, pp. 164, 165.)
[28] The oldest specimens of stained glass are said to have come from Nürnberg. The first
paper mill in Germany was established there in 1360. Cannon were cast there about 1350, fine
watches were made there by 1500, and modern brass in 1556. (Cecil Headlam, *The Story of
Nuremberg*, pp. 212-214; Wylie, *op. cit.*, vol. 1, p. 496.)

REFORMATION EXPOSITION CARVED IN STONE AT NURNBERG

Figure of Nebuchadnezzar, Seated by the Winged Lion, Symbol of Babylon, and of Cyrus at Right by Bear, Symbol of Persia, Carved Over Outer Portal of City Hall in Nürnberg (Upper); at Left, Statue of Alexander the Great by Crecian Leopard, and Julius Caesar at right by the Roman Ten-horned Beast (Center); Exterior View of Rathaus, or City Hall, Showing Left and Extreme Right Portals With These Prophetic Symbols, Sculptured by Leonard Kern in 1607 (Lower)

also became a stronghold of liberty. Nürnberg was first governed
by burgraves. But this form was succeeded by a great Council of
Three Hundred, with a smaller administrative council. Nürnberg, it should be added, was mistress of seven surrounding cities
and about 480 villages.

The Reformation took firm hold there, as Andreas Osiander
began to preach the evangelical faith in the Church of St.
Lorenz, which was noted as one of the best examples of German
Gothic art.[29] Albrecht Dürer, famous painter and sculptor, likewise embraced the Reformed faith and became a friend of
Luther.[30] And Hans Sachs, the noted shoemaker-poet, similarly
became a disciple, his succession of spiritual songs becoming a
power in the Reformation.[31] The Rathaus, or Town Hall, was
the scene of the famous diets of the empire. This great structure,
about 290 feet long, is of Italian design, with three magnificent
Doric portals, over which the prophetic beasts of Daniel 7 are
carved.[32] These impressive figures, authorized by the city council,
were sculptured by the well-known artist, Leonhard Kern, in
1617. They portray in enduring stone the understanding and
conviction of the time in the field of prophecy. Under the building are vaulted dungeons and chambers of torture, earlier employed by the "Holy Office" for the prosecution of dissenters and
confessors of the reformed faith.[33]

Gutenberg's revolutionary invention of movable type was
brought to Nürnberg in 1470, the printer Koberger alone publishing over two hundred different works before 1500 on his
twenty-four presses, with agents for his product in the principal
towns of Christendom. By 1500 twenty-five printers had established themselves in Nürnberg. Significantly enough, the first

---

[29] Austin Patterson Evans, *An Episode in the Struggle for Religious Freedom*, pp. 26, 27;
see also Headlam, *op. cit.*, pp. 239, 240.
[30] Arthur G. and Nancy Bell, *Nuremberg*, p. 140. Dürer illustrated the symbols of the
Apocalypse with a series of wood engravings; Headlam, *op. cit.*, p. 75.
[31] Hans Sachs (1494-1576), "darling of Nuremberg" as Wagner called him, left his imprint upon the town. After five years of travel over Germany, Sachs returned to devote himself
to poetry, and became a Meistersinger (master singer). The Meistersingers flourished in the
fourteenth, fifteenth, and sixteenth centuries. Most of them were of noble birth. They cultivated
poetry and art, lived in kings' palaces, and wandered from court to court composing love poems,
which were always sung. (Headlam, *op. cit.*, pp. 215-224.)
[32] H. J. Whitling, *Pictures of Nuremberg*, vol. 1, pp. 108-114.
[33] Headlam, *op. cit.*, pp. 158-167.

work of art to leave Koberger's presses was a magnificent illustrated Bible, in 1483. Theological and other works poured forth, including criticism and satire of popular established abuses.[34]

Nürnberg was one of the first towns to express sympathy with Martin Luther when he nailed his Ninety-five Theses to the castle-church door at Wittenberg, in 1517, against "the crime of false pardons." Luther came to Nürnberg in the course of the next year, on his way to Augsburg to answer for his "heresies" before Cardinal Cajetan. The council was irked by the excommunication of their own Willibald Pirkheimer and Lazarus Spengler (clerk of the council), in the papal bull of 1519 by which Luther was excommunicated, and refused to interfere with the printing of Luther's works. The council also sent Spengler to represent Nürnberg at the Diet of Worms, called by Charles V in 1521.[35]

When an imperial edict forbade representatives of the towns to meet at Spires to discuss religious matters, they met at Rothenberg, and Nürnberg boldly gave reasons why it should not obey the decree. It determined on a new form of worship. The sacrament was now administered in both kinds, and the mass was read in German, with Lutheran omissions. Other towns followed Nürnberg, and imitated her Lutheran services. Dislike for monasteries and nunneries broke out, and satires and cartoons appeared against nuns and monks. After discussion by the council Osiander called upon the council for immediate action. The council gave its vote for the Lutheran cause and cast in its lot with the Reformation.[36]

Nürnberg threw itself heartily into the tide of the Reform movement. In the churches of St. Sebald and St. Lorenz, beautified by great artists, the tapers were extinguished, the images removed, and the clouds of incense disappeared. Interest centered for the moment in the Diet of Spires. Then, in 1525, the council declared the Evangelical party victorious.[37] Evangelical

---

[34] *Ibid.*, pp. 73, 74.
[36] Headlam, *op. cit.*, pp. 76, 77.
[35] *Ibid.*, pp. 74, 75; Evans, *op. cit.*, p. 25.
[37] Evans, *op. cit.*, pp. 27, 28.

pastors were appointed, and the Reformation established. Luther had first visited the town in 1518, and Melanchthon [38] came in 1525 to found a new gymnasium, or classical preparatory school, in which the principles of the Reformation were to be taught.[39]

IV. Osiander Leads Nurnberg to Adopt Reformation Principles

ANDREAS OSIANDER (1498-1552), resolute champion of the Reformation, was born at Gunzenhausen, near Nürnberg, Bavaria, his real name being Hosemann. Educated at Leipzig, Altenburg, and Ingolstadt, he attained great proficiency in the ancient languages, especially Hebrew, which he studied at the University of Ingolstadt. He was also proficient in theology, mathematics, and medicine. Ordained a priest in 1520, he was appointed instructor in Hebrew in the Augustinian Convent in Nürnberg. In 1522 he issued an improved Latin version of the Bible, and as the city council of Nürnberg, according to its rights, had filled the provost's offices of the parish churches of St. Lorenz and St. Sebald with men of the new school of thought, Osiander was called to be preacher at St. Lorenz, and soon became one of the outstanding figures of the Reformation in Nürnberg.[40]

1. OPENLY DISCOURSES ON ANTICHRIST FROM PROPHECIES.—In March, 1524, when the papal delegate came to attend the Nürnberg Diet, the very next day Osiander openly preached on the Roman Antichrist. This mighty apostate power, he said, speaking terrible words against God, was seated in God's temple, imperial Rome making room for him. He contended that, with the removal of Constantine from Rome, the papal Antichrist moved in.

"I proved to my listeners, solely from the Holy Scriptures, who this Antichrist is, simply by lining up all the texts referring to him, and did

---

[38] Johannes Janssen, *Geschichte des deutschen Volkes*, vol. 2, pp. 352-366.
[39] Bell, *op. cit.*, p. 148; Headlam, *op. cit.*, p. 78.
[40] Johann J. Herzog, *Real-Encyklopädie für protestantische Theologie und Kirche* (1854-1868 ed.), vol. 10, p. 720; *Allgemeine deutsche Biographie*, vol. 24, art. "Osiander."

not need to give any additional comments on them. . . . When Constantine moved out of Rome, the Antichrist moved in." [41]

2. ILLUSTRATES AND REPRINTS JOACHIM'S WRITINGS.—Finding two copies probably of Joachim's writings, which the Spirituals had fittingly illustrated about 1278, Osiander had woodcuts made and adapted to Reformation times. It was titled *Ein wunderliche weissagung, von dem Bapstumb, wie es yhm bis an das ende der welt gehen sol, ynn figuren odder gemelde begriffen, gefunden zu Nurmberg ym Cartheuserkloster vnd ist seer alt* (A Strange Prophecy of the Papacy and What Its Fate Will Be Till the End of the World, Illustrated with Symbols and Pictures Found in the Nürnberg Carthusian Convent).[42] Osiander wrote the foreword, and the Nürnberg master poet, Hans Sachs, wrote suitable verse for the woodcuts.[43] One of the numerous pictures represents the strife between the pope and the emperor, showing the Roman eagle being compelled to kiss the pope's feet, and the tiara above the imperial crown. Luther was highly pleased, but the authorities of the free city of Nürnberg realized that a conflict was nearing, and reprimanded Osiander, the printer, and Hans Sachs. Osiander also republished (1527) Hildegard's so-called prophecy regarding the Papacy.[44] Osiander took no position on the authority of such "prophecies," but said the papists will not profit by any warning, be it by the mouth of Daniel, or Jesus, or the apostles, or by their own bishops, monks, or nuns, any more than the Jews profited by the voices of their prophets, of Christ, and the apostles.[45]

From 1522 on, Osiander thundered against Antichrist, and offered, even while the papal legate Campegius was in the city, both elements of the communion to Queen Isabella of Denmark, sister of Charles V. Nor did he forget the common folk of the town, to whom he carried the Reformation truths. Thus Osiander was instrumental in introducing the Reformation into

[41] Wilhelm Möller, *Andreas Osiander*, pp. 13, 14.
[42] Dated 1527. *Allgemeine deutsche Biographie*, vol. 24, art. "Osiander."
[43] Möller, *Andreas Osiander*, pp. 97, 98.
[44] See *Prophetic Faith*, Volume I.
[45] Möller, *Andreas Osiander*, p. 103.

Nürnberg, and in obtaining its adoption by the city. In 1525 he wrote a severe polemic attacking the doctrine of the sacrifice of the mass. He was present at the Marburg Conference (1529), which sought to reconcile the Lutheran and Swiss theologians, as well as at the Augsburg Diet in 1530, and was one of the signers of the Schmalkalden (Smalkald) Articles in 1537. In this year he also published *Harmoniae Evangelicae* (A Harmony of the Gospels)—the first Protestant work of its kind—at the request of Archbishop Cranmer of England, who had married Osiander's niece in 1532.

3. GOES TO KONIGSBERG BECAUSE OF CONTROVERSIES.—His mathematical and astronomical accomplishments were such that he was invited by Copernicus to make corrections of his work *De revolutionibus orbium coelestium,* and unknown to the author, he wrote a preface to it (1543). Osiander labored with marked success in behalf of the Reformation, defending it in public discussions with the Roman Catholic clergy. However, his violent disputes impaired his popularity, and his vehemence caused many enemies, for though able and learned, he was opinionated and quarrelsome. Cranmer had considered inviting him to England, but refrained because of his combative tendencies.

Osiander left Nürnberg in 1549 because of differences over the *Interim* compromise—that what is not expressly enjoined or forbidden by the divine Word may be accepted but not imposed by authority. He then became the head of the theological faculty—though without a degree—of the newly established University of Königsberg in 1549, and in the next year engaged in controversy with Chemnitz over the nature of justification. In this discussion he held that justification is not to be understood as a judicial act but as a mystical indwelling of Christ and His righteousness in the heart of man.[46] In spite of his agreement with Luther in opposing Romanism and Calvinism, his mysticism led him to interpret justification by faith as an infu-

---

[46] Philip Schaff, *History*, vol. 6, p. 570.

sion of the divine nature of Christ rather than an imputation.
This controversy continued beyond the time of his death.[47]

4. "Conjectures" Relate to Time Prophecy and Papacy.—When Melanchthon sent his revised Commentary on
Daniel to his friend Veit at Nürnberg, in 1543, he asked Osiander to furnish something more definite on the prophetic time
periods of Daniel. In response, Osiander published in Latin and
German (in 1544 and 1545 respectively) his *Conjecture de
Ultimis Temporis, ac de Fine Mundi* (Conjectures Concerning
the Last Times and the End of the World). This was translated
into English by George Joye, and published in 1548—three
years after the German edition. It was dedicated by Osiander
to his patron, Prince Albrecht of Prussia, expressing joy that
one of the ten horns (kingdoms) should hate the "Babylonian
whore." And he said, "May God also arouse the other horns
against that mentioned beast, and make a speedy end of it." [48]
Osiander understood Antichrist to be an ecclesiastical system,
not an individual, to continue on until shortly before the end
of the world.

In this work Osiander mentions Cardinal Cusa (1452), by
whom he was influenced and from whom he evidently borrowed
the essence of the idea as well as the title. In the dedication to
Albrecht, Osiander prays that what he has written may arouse
Christendom to the dangers of wicked Babylonian Rome, spoken
of in Daniel and the Apocalypse. He contends that though no
one knows the day or hour of Christ's coming we may know
the age and time,[49] as the husbandman may detect the approach
of summer.

5. Time Expectation Based on 6,000-Year Theory.—In
chapters 1 and 2 Osiander cites and supports the 6,000-year expectation held both by the Jews in the Talmud and by certain

---

[47] Gieseler, *op. cit.*, vol. 4, pp. 469 ff.
[48] Andreas Osiander, *Vermutung von den letzten Zeiten und dem Ende der welt, aus der
heiligen Schrifft gezogen;* see also Möller, *Andreas Osiander,* pp. 260-265.
[49] Osiander, *Vermutung,* preface.

Christian writers. In fact, Osiander built his time expectation upon the analogy of the six days of creation week, and the 6,000 years of toil, to be followed by the eternal rest in the seventh thousand years.[50] Osiander had a curious "angelic year," containing as many common years as our common year has days.[51] He also followed Cusa's concept of the years of Christ's life as being typical of so many jubilee periods of fifty years.

6. PAPACY FOLLOWS IMPERIAL ROME FOR 1260 YEARS.—In chapter 4 Osiander declares that in the prophecies of Daniel 7, Revelation 13 and 17, and 2 Thessalonians 2, Rome is pictured as twice obtaining world power—once as a nation, and then under the rule of the Papacy. The national dominion ceased at the sack of Rome by Alaric about 412 (410). Adding the 1260 years, the destruction of popery would, he thought, come in 1672, the end of the world following soon thereafter.[52]

7. REAL ANTICHRIST OVERLOOKED WHILE AWAITING FICTITIOUS ONE.—The papal contention—of Antichrist's reign being for but three and a half literal years that were yet future—had caused them to look ahead for a fictitious Antichrist, and overlook the real Antichrist at Rome, who had already exerted his influence for centuries.[53] According to Revelation 13, Satan had given the glory of empire to the Papacy, the pope ruling over the secular and spiritual powers by means of a lie—the pretended Donation of Constantine. Therefore, all who believe that the Papacy is of God, in reality worship the devil. In order to preserve its power, it must forbid the preaching of God's Word. The lamblike power of Revelation 13 is a group, which has the appearance of pious Christian teachers, but in reality these teachers are preaching not the Word of God but pagan philosophy from Aristotle, and they induce people to worship the pope. The speaking image refers to canon law, which is every-

---

[50] *Ibid.*, chaps. 1 and 2. "And as there passed from creation to the time of the flood 1656 years, it is permissible to assume that the same number of years will elapse from the birth of Christ till the end of the world. That would give us another 112 years, but if beginning with the death and resurrection of Christ 145 years [ending about 1688]."
[51] *Ibid.*, chaps. 3 and 4.   [52] *Ibid.*, chap. 4.   [53] *Ibid.*

where obeyed. The pope will fight and overcome the saints of the Lord, because all who do not accept this abomination are considered heretics and will be persecuted.[54]

8. THE MARK AND NUMBER OF THE BEAST.—Applying Revelation 13 to the Papacy, he explains the 666 as the number of its name in Hebrew—*Malchuth Romijth* (Roman kingdom).[55] The mark is subservience to the Papacy, with its bans against buying and selling for those not subject to the pope—they are to be banished and deprived of temporal and spiritual help.[56]

9. SEVEN HILLS AND TEN HORNS IDENTIFIED.—The seven heads of Revelation 17 have a twofold meaning: First, literally, they refer to the seven hills on which the city of Rome was built; and second, symbolically they refer to the seven forms of Roman government; and the ten horns are kingdoms that Rome, as the head of all churches, recognizes—"Spain, Portugal, France, England, Scotland, Denmark, Poland, Bohemia, Hungary, and the Holy Roman Empire." [57]

10. THE POPE IS THE EIGHTH HEAD.—The eighth head is the pope, who took the place of the emperors:

"He is in some respects very similar to them, yet in others very different. Those ruled in worldly fashion and fought against the Word of God with the sword, but he rules under the pretext of religion, and with the help of exegesis he falsifies and perverts the teachings of Christ, sullies His holy sacrament by his own supplements and abuses, and confirms the teaching of the devil; the son of perdition [the Pope], with his whole gang, will be hurtled into hell." [58]

His magniloquence consists of calling himself Christ's vicar on earth, comparing himself with the sun in contrast to the emperor as the moon, and his blasphemy in changing and condemning the right use of the sacrament and establishing false teachings and superstitions.[59]

---

[54] Möller, *Andreas Osiander*, pp. 40, 41.
[56] Möller, *Andreas Osiander*, p. 41.
[58] *Ibid.*
[55] Osiander, *Vermutung*, chap. 4.
[57] Osiander, *Vermutung*, chap. 4.
[59] *Ibid.*

11. 1260 YEARS POSSIBLY IN ANGELIC TIME.—The time period is 1260 years, or forty-two months.

"These are angelic years, or prophetic time. Twelve hundred and sixty literal years which are also mentioned in the 12th chapter of Revelation, where it is also mentioned as a time, and times, and half a time." [60]

12. SECOND BEAST SAME AS FALSE PROPHET.—The two-horned beast of Revelation 13 is the same as the false prophet of Revelation 19 who works miracles before the beast—the deceiving powers of the false teachers of the Papacy. The two-horned beast of Revelation 13 is further explained in Revelation 19:20, where it is called the false prophet, that wrought the signs in his sight wherewith he deceived them. Osiander understands thereby the theologians, scholastics, and doctors of canon law who are the real architects of popedom and who have pledged themselves by oath to do everything to uphold the pope, who is the first beast. The pope sits in the temple of God. [61]

13. TEN HORNS WILL DESTROY THE PAPACY.—The ten horns, and not the Turk, will destroy the Papacy. The Roman emperor prevented the development of the Papacy, until the imperial obstacle was removed by his transfer from Rome to Constantinople. [62]

14. PAPACY PICTURED IN MATTHEW 24.—Jesus also prophesied about this deception in Matthew 24. In its first period or "age" it grew stronger and stronger until it forced the emperor into subjection. During its second period, or "age," it forced people into war against the unbelievers to convert them to Christianity by the sword (Crusades), hereby fulfilling Matthew 24:6-8. Then, in the "third age," its rage turned against the heretics, and the resultant dreadful persecution fulfilled Matthew 24:9-13. Weakened in old age, he thought, the Papacy will be broken without human effort, as the Lord consumes it with the spirit of His mouth. [63] Osiander closes his revealing *Conjectures* with these words:

---

[60] *Ibid.*   [61] *Ibid.*   [62] *Ibid.*   [63] Möller, *Andreas Osiander*, p. 43.

"They are truly only conjectures, and in no wise divine revelations in themselves, but, nevertheless, I hold, that if my senses do not betray me, they are not far from the truth." [64]

V. The First French Recruit Revives Future Millennium

FRANCOIS LAMBERT OF AVIGNON (1487-1530), who had a part in reforming the Hessians, was the first French monk to be converted to Protestantism. Formerly a traveling preacher of the Franciscan Order in southern France, and an able orator, he found no peace in ascetic exercises. He was profoundly moved by a French translation of some of Luther's early tracts. Sent to Germany to join brethren of his order, he traveled on muleback, stopping successively at Geneva, Bern, Zürich, Basel, Eisenach, and Wittenberg—ever seeking light. Half converted by Zwingli, in a public disputation in 1522, he was urged to go on to Luther, by whom he was fully persuaded at Wittenberg, in 1523.[65]

During the year 1523 he delivered exegetical lectures at the university, and wrote several tracts defending his new faith. He also translated Reformation tracts into French and Italian. In 1524 Lambert left Wittenberg for Metz and Strassburg, and in 1526 was called by Count Philip to help organize the Protestant church in Hesse.[66] Here he prepared 158 theses for the Synod of Homberg, demanding that whatever is *deformed* should be *reformed* by the Word as the rule of faith and practice, and that the church should consist of true Christians only.

In 1527 Lambert became professor of theology in the newly opened university of Marburg, and lectured on the prophecies and the Apocalypse. But on account of his leanings toward the Zwinglian position on the Lord's supper, he lost the support of his Lutheran co-reformers.[67] In 1528 Lambert wrote a commentary on the Apocalypse—*Exegeseos in sanctum Divi Joannis Apocalypsim*—dedicated to the Landgrave of Hesse. His com-

---

[64] Osiander, *Vermutung*, chap. 4.
[65] Philip Schaff, *Histo ·y*, vol. 6, p. 582.
[66] *Ibid.*, pp. 582 ff.
[67] Buchberger, *Lexikon für Tl eologie und Kirche*, vol. 6, p. 352.

THREE STALWART REFORMERS WHO EXPOUNDED PROPHECY

Philip Melanchthon, Luther's Yokefellow (Left) ; Nicolaus von Amsdorf, of Naumburg (Center), and Heinrich Bullinger of Zurich (Right), Were Ready Writers on the Prophecies and Markedly Influenced Others Through Their Interpretations. See Pages 285, 304, and 339

mentary shows decided traces of Joachim's influence in the explanation of Revelation 20. The pope and the Turk are types of Antichrist. And after the long persecution set forth by the seals, under the last seal will come the 1,000-year pause of Revelation 20.[68]

VI. Amsdorf Prophesied Antichrist Enforcing Marks of Beast

NICOLAUS VON AMSDORF (1483-1565), friend and zealous coworker of Luther, was born in Torgau. Dedicated to the priesthood by his mother, who was related to Von Staupitz, Amsdorf was educated at Leipzig and Wittenberg, and was given a license in theology in 1511. In the same year he started to lecture on theology and philosophy. He accepted Luther's viewpoint before 1517, and became one of his most steadfast and unswerving followers. He accompanied Luther to Leipzig and Worms, knew about his exile in the Wartburg, and when Luther secretly left the Wartburg and came to Wittenberg, he lived in Amsdorf's house. In 1524 Amsdorf became superintendent in Magdeburg

---

[68] Francis Lambert, *Exegeseus*, p. 491.

at the Church of St. Ulrich, and was instrumental in seeing that
the Reformation took deep root in Magdeburg, which later
became a veritable city of refuge to the Lutherans. In 1528 he
established the Reformation in Goslar and in 1539 in Meissen.

Of all the co-workers of Luther none was so near to the heart
of the great Reformer as Amsdorf. Luther said, "My spirit finds
rest in my dear Amsdorf." Luther was attached to him because
of his piety, sincerity, and unwavering spirit. He esteemed him
highly for his keen, penetrating intellect in judicial matters,
and Amsdorf repaid that trust with unlimited devotion and
fidelity. On the other hand, he lacked the affectionate kindness
that Luther possessed to such a high degree. His harsh and ab-
rupt attitude may have contributed to quite an extent to the failure of the different attempts to bring unity into the Protestant
camp. In 1542, when the bishopric of Naumburg became vacant,
the Elector Frederick appointed von Amsdorf to become the
first Protestant bishop in Naumburg. Luther preached the sermon and officiated at the consecration.[69] A few years later, however, during the Schmalkaldic wars, he lost his see and had to
flee to Jena, where he took part in the founding of the University
of Jena (1548). In his strict adherence to Luther's teaching he
was, of course, firmly opposed to Melanchthon's inclination to
compromise, and urged separation from Melanchthon in the
"Adiaphoristic" controversy.[70]

1. FIVE SIGNS OF THE APPROACHING END.—In addition to
writing numerous polemical treatises, Amsdorf was fully convinced that the end was near. So he published *Fünff fürnemliche und gewisse Zeichen, aus göttlicher heiliger Schrifft, so
Kurtz vor dem Jüngsten tag geschehen sollen* (Five Prominent
and Certain Signs From Holy Writ, Which Are to Happen
Shortly Before the Last Day), based on Luke 21 and Matthew
24. Holding the papal apostasy to be Antichrist, he felt that

---

[69] About twenty-five intimate letters from Luther to Amsdorf appear in *Letters of Martin
Luther*, translated by Margaret Currie.
[70] *Allgemeine deutsche Biographie*, art. "Nicolaus von Amsdorf"; Herzog, *Real-Encyklopädie*, art. "Nicolaus von Amsdorf."

the "daily sacrifice" is the preaching of the gospel, the "desolation of abomination" is human tradition, the real Babylonian harlot is the Papacy, and the mark of the beast the enforced worship by papal canons, decretals, and ceremonies. This is significant.

2. PAPAL PROHIBITIONS OF MARRIAGE AND MEATS.—The first sign is based on 2 Thessalonians 2 and 1 Timothy 4, fulfilled in papal prohibition of marriage of priests and of abstinence from meats. But the kingdom that comes not with observation does not consist of meats and drinks. Such papal practice shows the falling away from the true faith.[71] The second sign indicates that he will remain hidden a long time, working in secret, but nevertheless held to be the true head of the church and vicar of Christ. The Turk is not Antichrist.

"He [the Antichrist] will be revealed and come to naught before the last day, so that every man shall comprehend and recognize that the pope is the real, true Antichrist and not the vicar of Christ. . . . Therefore those who consider the pope and his bishops as Christian shepherds and bishops are deeply in error, but even more are those who believe that the Turk is the Antichrist. Because the Turk rules outside of the church and does not sit in the holy place, nor does he seek to bear the name of Christ but is an open antagonist of Christ and His church. This does not need to be revealed, but it is clear and evident because he persecutes Christians openly and not as the pope does, secretly under the form of godliness."[72]

3. JUDGMENT DAY FOLLOWS PAPAL LITTLE HORN.—The third sign is that after the fourth beast of Daniel 7, the day of judgment will follow, because after the Roman Empire declines and changes, there shall come no other empire, but the last day shall follow soon after and make an end to the "game" of this world.[73]

4. ABOMINATION OF TRADITION NULLIFIES DAILY PREACHING.—"The daily sacrifice (that is, the preaching of the gospel) shall cease, and as Daniel says, the abomination of desolation, that is, human tradition, will be put in its place. This sign is being fulfilled right in our time, not only among the papists but even among us. Wherever people command to believe,

---

[71] Nicolaus von Amsdorf, *Fünff fürnemliche und gewisse Zeichen*, sig. A₂r.,v.
[72] *Ibid.*, sig. A₄v.
[73] *Ibid.*, sig. B₂v.

preach, and accept besides the gospel human traditions, as a certain kind of mass [*Narrenmesse*], chrism [*Schmiere*], abstaining from meats and other marks of the Antichrist.

"And those who refuse to accept besides the gospel the mark of the Antichrist are chased away, deprived of their offices, and hypocrites are accepted in their places. Therefore the daily sacrifice, the undefiled preaching of the gospel, cannot continue very long. It will be put aside and made desolate, and faith will be extinguished and exterminated, and then the last day will not tarry much longer." [74]

5. MARK OF BEAST REPRESENTS ENFORCED CEREMONIALS.— The fifth sign is the enforced mark of the beast John predicts for the last days.

"This beast we know is the Roman Empire, which carries and supports the red Babylonian whore, which is the Papacy. The mark of the beast is the canons, the decrees and ceremonies of the Pope, and all ecclesiastical traditions concerning food, drink, and dress, singing, reading, and other childish things which have nothing to do with, nor belong to, the kingdom of God, which is true Christianity." [75]

Declaring one should have nothing to do with the papal innovations, Amsdorf refers to many other signs that show the nearness of Christ's coming, such as the repetition of the carelessness of the days of Noah and Lot. But even were the day of judgment in the far future, the arraignment for every soul comes when he is called out of this life.[76]

---

[74] *Ibid.*, sig. B₂v., B₃r.
[75] *Ibid.*, sig. B₃v., B₄r.
[76] *Ibid.*, sig. D₁r.-D₂r.

CHAPTER FOURTEEN

Gradual Clarification
of Hazy Points Continues

I. Application of Prophecies to Turks Followed by Some

The application of the Little Horn of Daniel 7 and the beast of Revelation 13 to Mohammed or the Turks, on the part of some of the Reformers, goes back in its origin to the time of the early Crusades. Before 1200 Joachim, on a visit to the Holy Land, conceived the fourth beast and its ten horns to be the Saracens, and the Little Horn to be Mohammed, whom he also assigned to the seventh head of the beast of Revelation 13.[1] In 1213 Innocent III, in a letter preliminary to the Fourth Lateran Council of 1215, doubtless countering the applications to the Papacy, made both the beast and the false prophet to be Mohammed, and applied the 666 to him.[2] A century later De Lyra could see little in the Apocalypse but pagans, Byzantines, and Turks, and the false prophet as Mohammed.[3]

In 1480 GIOVANNI NANNI (Nannis, or Annius), of Viterbo, consolidated these positions. He believed that the mystical Babylon of the Turks and Saracens was to be conquered by the Latin church, and made out Mohammed as the man of sin and Antichrist. In 1580 GENEBRARD, says Maitland, first found 666 in the

---

[1] Charles Maitland, *op. cit.*, pp. 430, 431; Joachim on the Apocalypse (see Volume I of *Prophetic Faith*) is cited in Elliott, *op. cit.*, vol. 4, pp. 406, 407, 421.
[2] Mansi, *op. cit.*, vol. 22, col. 957.
[3] De Lyra, *Postilla in Libros Sacros* (Notes on the Sacred Books); see Elliott, *op. cit.*, vol. 4, p. 430; Charles Maitland, *op. cit.*, p. 430.

name Mohammed.[4] Consequently, when the Reformation was launched, although there was unanimity regarding the Papacy as the Antichrist, the Beast, the Babylon, and the Harlot, some seem to have followed the papal interpretation so far as to also include Mohammed or the Turks. Some had the Turk as the Little Horn, the three horns plucked up being, for example, Egypt, Africa, and Greece; others had both an Eastern and a Western Antichrist—the Turk being a sort of lesser partner in the kingdom of Antichrist. But a growing number contended that the reference was to the Papacy alone. This will be increasingly apparent as the Reformation witnesses continue to testify.

II. Funck Places Seventy Weeks Between 457 B.C. and A.D. 34

JOHANN FUNCK (1518-1566), of Nürnberg, studied theology in Wittenberg, where he received his M.A. degree, and then ministered in his home town. He preached in several places and finally was recommended to Duke Albrecht of Prussia. He went to Königsberg in 1547, where the duke was so pleased with this young clergyman that he made him his court preacher in 1549. Funck championed Osiander's cause in the strife over righteousness by faith,[5] and after Osiander's death (1552), together with Aurifaber, took over the leadership of Osiander's party. After Aurifaber's death (1559) he married his widow, who was a daughter of Osiander, and the whole fury of the opponents of Osiander's teaching was hurled against him.[6] However, Funck submitted a confession of faith to the theologians of Leipzig and Wittenberg that was declared orthodox in 1561. Tragically enough, he fell a victim to political agitations, and was decapitated by Polish authorities in 1566.[7]

Funck wrote a *Chronology*, from creation to his own day.[8] He also probably wrote the German commentary of "J. F." on

---

[4] Giovanni Nanni, *Glosa . . . super Apocalypsim* (Notes . . . on the Apocalypse), fols. c₁v-c₃r; Maitland, *op. cit.*, p. 430.

[5] Gieseler, *op. cit.*, vol. 4, p. 478.

[6] Paul Tschackert, "Funck," *The New Schaff-Herzog*, vol. 4, p. 410.

[7] Gieseler, *op. cit.*, vol. 4, p. 479; Buchberger, *Lexikon*, art. "Funck."

[8] First published (1548-52) *Chronologia ab Urbe Condita* (Chronology From the Founding of the City [Rome]) and then enlarged as *Chronologia . . . ab Initio Mundi*, published after his death in 1570.

the Apocalypse, to which Melanchthon wrote the introduction, and in 1564 he produced a vitally important work explaining and diagramming the seventy weeks of Daniel 9.[9] He gave most complete, thorough, and conscientious study to the data, from both prophecy and history, and was probably the first in Reformation times to begin the seventy weeks in 457 B.C., a date which was later favored by many of the theological writers of the early nineteenth century, particularly in Britain and America, the majority of whom began the 70 weeks and the 2300 days in 457 B.C., as will be seen in Volumes III and IV of the present work. Funck here gives his strong reasons for beginning the seventy weeks with the seventh year of Artaxerxes and, by a series of paralleling reckonings, shows that the 490 years therefore end in A.D. 34.

1. ANONYMOUS COMMENTARY SETS DATES AS 261 AND 1521. —A 700-page German commentary on the book of Revelation with a preface by Melanchthon, is attributed to Funck. This stresses that the pope is the Antichrist and the Babylonian woman in scarlet. It puts the 1260 years from Bishop Samosata, in 261, to the Diet of Worms, in 1521. It has the Two Witnesses as the Old and New Testaments, and understands the red dragon of Revelation 12 as the antichrist of all Antichrists, the devil; the beasts of chapter 13 are the Papacy; the Little Horn of Daniel 7 is not the Turk but the "papal empire"; the daily sacrifice is the true worship; the 666 may point to the years of papal rule; the 1290 years are 261 + 1290 = 1550; and the 1335 years run forty-five years beyond, to 1595. The signs of the times are portrayed from Matthew 24, with the advent as the climax.[10]

2. 490 SOLAR YEARS CUT OFF FOR JEWS.—After an extended discussion of the views of Luther, Melanchthon, Calvin, and Bibliander on the seventy weeks, Funck gives his own reckoning of the "exact date" of the period, which he holds is the

---

[9] Johann Funck, *Anleitung zum Verstand der Apocalypse* (A Guide to the Understanding of the Apocalypse); *Ausslegung des anderntheils des Neundten Capitels Danielis* (Exegesis of the Second Part of the Ninth Chapter of Daniel).
[10] Funck, *Apocalypse. Der Offenbarung Künfftiger geschicht Johannis . . . Auslegung* (a second title of the *Anleitung*).

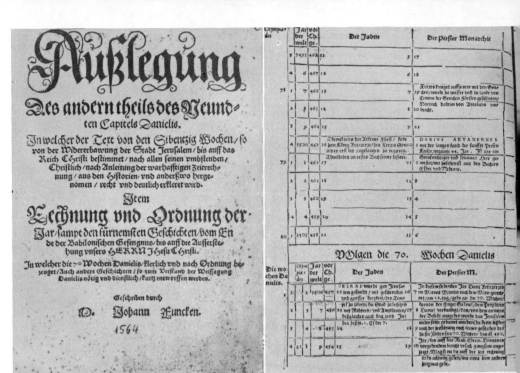

TIMING AND RELATIONSHIP OF SEVENTY WEEKS STUDIED

John Funck, of Germany, in 1564 Begins the 70 Weeks With 457 B.C., and Closes Them in A.D. 34 (Upper); John Tillinghast, Two Centuries Later in England, Asserts the 70 Weeks to Be a Lesser Epoch Within the Larger 2300 Year-Day Period (Lower). See Pages 312 and 570

"correct explanation," connecting it with historical data of Greek and Roman history. The treatise is dedicated to Prince Albrecht, Margrave of Prussia, and was written while Funck was serving as court chaplain, and in fulfillment of a former promise.

These seventy weeks, Funck avers, are weeks of years, and are divided into three parts, totalling the seventy prophetic weeks, or 490 years. Moreover, they are fulfilled in solar, not lunar, time. And the seventy weeks—no more and no less—were "cut off," or "counted off," for the people of Daniel, the Jews. The definite beginning warrants a definite ending, which is connected with the Messiah's death and resurrection. Funck tersely declares, "You must here understand seventy year-weeks; that means seventy times seven years, which is 490 years. Please note this." [11]

3. BEGINS WITH REBUILDING OF CITY, NOT TEMPLE.—Then follows a careful, scholarly analysis of the six prophetically listed events that mark the close of the seventy weeks. Funck then turns to the beginning of the seventy weeks with the going forth of the command to restore and rebuild the city of Jerusalem, from Artaxerxes—not from Cyrus, as Calvin and Luther had reckoned—for Cyrus only restored the *temple*. The difficulties involved in the reckoning of Persian reigns are rehearsed. Funck then contends that the seventy weeks, ending at the crucifixion in A.D. 34, begin with Artaxerxes Longimanus,[12] fifth king of Persia, who began to reign in the fourth year of the seventy-eighth Olympiad, as demonstrated in his other work, the *Chronologia*, and attested by Thucydides, Plutarch, and Xenophon. Funck held that it was impossible to understand and explain prophecy without the aid of world history.

Funck then presents his argument for starting with the seventh year of Artaxerxes. Declaring that the seventy weeks must,

---

[11] Funck, *Ausslegung des anderntheils des Neundten Capitels Danielis*, sig. c₅v.
[12] *Ibid.*, sigs. F₆r,v, and tables. Funck commonly calls him Darius Longimanus, but identifies him as Darius Artaxerxes Longimanus, as in the next quotation. This common identification is attributed to Jewish tradition in an editorial note in Heinrich Bullinger, *Decades* (Parker Society ed.), decade 2, sermon 6, p. 318.

according to the angel, begin with the command to restore and rebuild Jerusalem, Funck succinctly states his thesis in these clear words:

"In the time of Cyrus, only the temple was built, and the religious worship was arranged to some degree. The people themselves, however, were still under the rule of the Persian satraps and judges and there was no freedom, necessary to build a town or a people, but only compulsion, servitude, and slavery. . . .

"However, when Ezra received the order and the authority to install judges and magistrates who knew the law of the Lord and would teach those who were ignorant of it, that really meant freedom. And with it began the building of the town of Jerusalem and of the nation of Judea. . . . Therefore I consider this year, which was the seventh of Darius Artaxerxes Longimanus, the beginning of the seventy weeks of Daniel." [13]

4. VARIOUS MODES OF COMPUTING BEGINNING YEAR.—Funck reaches his final conclusion, and sums up his argument, in these clear words:

"You must begin to figure the 490 years with the other (second) year of the 80th Olympiad, or from the year after Creation 3506, or from B.C. 457, or from the 22nd year of Prince Resa Hesullam in the 16th year of the High Priest Joachim, or in the 7th of the reign of Artaxerxes of the Persians, or 42 years of Alexander Amynte Sone in Macedonia, or from the 294th year of the time of the founding of Rome, or you will find many other dates to which you can link this event." [14]

The "Chronological Tables" presented are most interesting. They represent exhausting toil and scholarly research. In vertical columns, from left to right, appear progressively the years of the Olympiads, the year of the world, the year B.C., the Jewish reckoning, the events of the Persian monarchy, the events of the Macedonian kingdom, the year of the Roman reckoning, and reigns of the Roman rulers. The consecutive years run from top to bottom. In this table the first year of Artaxerxes in the "B.C." column is 463, and therefore the seventh year is 457. Similarly, the seventy weeks are seen, in another table, to end in A.D. 34.

---

[13] Translated from Funck, *Ausslegung*, sig. H₅r.
[14] *Ibid.*, sig. N₆v. For the basis of his B.C. dating see Funck's *Chronologia . . . ab Initia Mundi*, commentaria, book 4, sig. F₅r, also p. 430 of the present volume.

5. SIGNIFICANCE OF CONTRIBUTION NOT SENSED TILL LATER.
—Funck mentions the tremendous toil involved in this investigation, and "the sacrifice of several hundred Gulden, which sum I was obliged to spend for books, and to print and bring to light all this important knowledge for the benefit of Christianity." But he assures us that he would not part with his findings for "much gold." Making no apologies for being "sure" of his convictions, he assures us that he had no intention of placing himself "above others." The real significance and value of Funck's contribution was not, however, sensed at the time. But two centuries later it was destined to have a most important bearing in determining the appointed ending of the 2300-year period, when its relationship to the 70 weeks had been established.

III. Solis—Nurnberg Engraver of Graphic Prophetic Symbols

VIRGIL SOLIS (1514-1562, or 1567), designer and engraver of great ability and versatility, produced an enormous number of woodcuts, etchings, and illuminations—so many that people later have wondered how he could have done it in his short lifetime.[15] In 1531 we find him in Zurich, working with the printer Froschauer, making woodcuts for the Swiss edition of the Bible. From 1540 on we find him in Nürnberg, where he designed coats of arms, illustrated histories,[16] and so forth. But his great contributions were his Bible illustrations (published also in book form).[17] By these pictures he gave to the people a new kind of Bible, and taught them to look at the Scriptures in a new way. In his realistic representation of Biblical scenery, in his enchanting splendor, in his *genre* style, he met the taste of his time. And this Picture Bible, published by Feyerabend in 1560, at Frankfurt am Main, had the most outstanding success. However, it did not meet the approval of Wittenberg, where Solis' pictures were considered innovations, and called outrageous,

---

[15] Michael Bryan, *Dictionary of Painters and Engravers,* vol. 2, art., "Solis, Virgil."
[16] Richard Grafton, *A Chronicle at Large and Meere History* (London, 1569).
[17] Virgil Solis, *Biblische Figuren des Alten und Newen Testaments* (Biblical Illustrations of the Old and New Testaments).

and even vicious, so that Feyerabend discontinued to use them in later editions. Strange to say, they remained favorites among the Catholics, and we find his pictures in all editions of the Dietenberger Bible until far into the seventeenth century, of course with omission of some of the more disconcerting illustrations of Revelation. His monogram, a small *s* superimposed on the right arm of a large *V*, became famous in the world of art and printing.[18]

After picturing Nebuchadnezzar's dream of the metallic statue of a man, symbolizing the kingdoms of man from Babylonia forward, Solis presents the prophetic beast-symbols of Daniel 7. The four beasts, representing the same four successive empires, have arisen from the sea of nations amid the blowing of the four winds, and are placed two in the East—the Babylonian lion and the Persian bear; and two in the West—the Grecian leopard and the Roman beast. Beneath is the legend:

> "Four kingdoms do on earth proclaim,
> Will have power that's much the same.
> The fifth, the Antichrist will build
> Till God pulls down his guile and guilt." [19]

In these illustrations of the book of Revelation we find, among others, Christ walking among the seven candlesticks, with the sword coming forth from His mouth; the four apocalyptic horsemen; the picturing of the seven trumpets; the angel of Revelation 10; the two witnesses of chapter 11; the beast with a triple crown crouching before them, eager to devour them; and the dragon with seven heads casting the flood of water after the woman-church, whose child was caught up to God.

The Beast with seven heads is worshiped by the multitudes, and by prelates and kings alike. The triumphant Lamb is placed on Mount Zion with the redeemed, and the angel is crying, "Babylon is fallen." The Son of man is shown coming in the clouds, sending His angels to harvest the wheat of the earth and to cut the clusters of grapes for the winepress of wrath. The

---

[18] E. von Ubisch, *Virgil Solis und seine Biblischen Illustrationen,* pp. 9, 16 ff., 53, 54, 61.
[19] Solis, *Biblische Figuren,* sig. M_1r.

seven last plagues are being poured out—one of the angels emptying his vial on the seat of the Beast. The woman with the golden cup, seated on the seven-headed Beast, receives homage. The final fall of Babylon is disclosed, the final war is portrayed, with the Beast cast into the bottomless pit. The siege of the Holy City by the hosts of the wicked is presented, and finally the glories of the new earth are pictured. Such was the graphic portrayal of the prophetic symbols that were the constant theme of study and exposition. (Reproduction appears on page 346.)

IV. Flacius—Books Markedly Mold Protestant Interpretation

MATTHIAS FLACIUS (Vlacich) (1520-1575), of Illyria, was one of the great scholars of his time and compiler of the epochal *Magdeburg Centuries,* the first Protestant church history. He studied in Venice, and being fervently inclined toward religion and service for the church, he approached one of his relatives, who was a provincial of the Minorites, requesting that he be accepted into the order. But this man, Lupetinus by name, observing Flacius' great zeal for truth, advised him to go to Germany. He went first to Basel, and was received with paternal love by Grynäus, from there in 1540 to Tübingen, and in the following year to Wittenberg. About 1544 he received a permanent position as professor of Old Testament at the University of Wittenberg.

However, serious trouble soon arose through the acceptance of the Leipzig Interim in 1548, which upheld the Protestant doctrine of justification by faith, yet conceded the so-called "Adiaphora," or things neither forbidden nor enjoined by Scripture, and even reinstituted in the Protestant church such elements as extreme unction, the mass, lights, vestments, vessels, images, the old festivals of Mary, and fast days. Flacius, seeing the pure teaching of Protestantism in danger, but being unable to stop the trend, went to Magdeburg (1549), a city which had not accepted the Interim, and from there he began to fight against the Interim by word and pen, calling the Saxon theologians "Lovers of the Babylonish harlot, secret papists," et cetera.

There in Magdeburg he worked on the *Catalogus Testium Veritatis* (Catalog of Witnesses for the Truth), and began also his comprehensive thirteen-volume *Ecclesiastica Historia* (Church History) better known as the *Magdeburg Centuries,* which became the Protestant arsenal of source material, possessing high permanent value. After a number of years, in 1557, he was called by Duke Johann Friedrich to the professorship of theology at Jena, which became the citadel of the Flacianists, with Wittenberg that of the Philippists. But because of a controversy with the duke about church polity, he was dismissed in 1561. Wandering to Regensburg and to Antwerp (where he was pastor of the Lutheran community), he had continuous breaks with church and civil authorities. He was finally expelled from the city council of Strassburg in 1573, because of his controversy with the clergy, and went to Frankfurt am Main, where he died two years later. He was a passionate defender of Luther, taking issue with the followers of Melanchthon, and published numerous controversial works.[20]

His *Magdeburg Centuries* was a work of "colossal industry," a landmark in church history, although somewhat biased, and was called by the Catholics a *"pestilentissimum opus,"* [21] for it revealed facts they did not desire to have come to light. Yet modern Catholic commentaries, like Buchberger (1932), admit that, although full of hatred against the Catholic Church, it was exemplary in its extensive use of source material, and was superseded later only by the *Annales Ecclesiastici* of Cardinal Caesare Baronius (1538-1607), who had direct approach to the archives of the Vatican.[22]

1. REIGN OF ANTICHRIST TO BE 1260 YEARS.—Flacius' *Catalogus Testium Veritatis,* first issued at Basel in 1556, and citing four hundred witnesses, urges the study and following of the

---

[20] Buchberger, *Lexikon,* art. "Flacius"; Herzog, *Real-Encyklopädia,* arts. "Flacius" and "Interim"; G. Kawerau, "Flacius," and S. Issleib, "Interim," *The New Schaff-Herzog;* Karl R. Hagenbach, *History of the Reformation in Germany and Switzerland Chiefly,* vol. 2, p. 285; Hulme, *op. cit.,* p. 507.
[21] Philip Schaff, *History,* vol. 6, p. 573; Kawerau, "Magdeburg Centuries," *The New Schaff-Herzog,* vol. 7, p. 124.
[22] Buchberger, *Lexikon,* art. "Flacius."

prophecies, which make possible the detection of Antichrist's teachings. The year-day principle is applied to the 1260 days.

In Revelation, John has given the time of his reign—1260 days, which are literal years, for in the Scriptures a day often stands for a year. He also describes the powers which will again, at least in part, establish the declining Empire of Rome. (Revelation 13.) This the Papacy has already accomplished. The place is also mentioned, Babylon, and the papists themselves understand the Babylon of the New Testament to be Rome.

Ambrose, of the fourth century, is also cited as commenting on Antichrist in 2 Thessalonians 2, whose coming would follow upon the passing of the empire.[23]

2. "CENTURIES" IDENTIFIES ANTICHRIST AND LOCATES REIGN. —In the *Magdeburg Centuries,* Flacius defends the Apocalypse, and applies 2 Thessalonians 2 explicitly to the Roman bishop. He endorses the year-day principle, as recognized by Joachim, Cusa, and De Lyra, and contends for the 1260 years of papal spiritual rule from 606 (Phocas and Gregory), in contrast to 666 years of worldly supremacy. In fact, Flacius applied the term *Antichrist* to both the Pope and Mohammed—the one inside the church, and the other outside. The first he dated from 606; the second, a few years later.[24]

3. CHRISTIANS SHOULD SEVER CONNECTIONS WITH ANTI-CHRIST.—In 1570 Flacius also wrote a tractate on the Antichrist, warning all honest Christians to separate from the system of Antichrist—the prophecies forming the basis of separation:

"The sixth and last reason for our separation from the pope and his followers be this: By many writings of our church, by the Divinely Inspired Word, by prophecies concerning the future and by the special characteristics of the papacy, it has been profusely and thoroughly proved that the pope with his prelates and clergy is the real true great Antichrist, that his kingdom is the real Babylon, a never ceasing fountain and a mother of all abominable idolatry." [25]

---

[23] Matthias Flacius, *Catalogus Testium Veritatis* (1597 ed.), book 4, vol. 1, p. 208.
[24] Flacius, and others, *Ecclesiastica Historia* (or the *Magdeburg Centuries*), cent. 1, book 2, chap. 4, cols. 434, 438; cent. 6, chap. 1, col. 16; cent. 7, chap. 1, cols. 21, 22.
[25] Flacius, *Etliche Hochwichtige Ursachen und Gründe, warumb das sich alle Christen von dem Antichrist . . . absondern sollen.*

4. Exercises Molding Influence on Protestant Exposition.—In the same year Flacius published an edition of Erasmus' New Testament with his own *Glossa Compendiaria* (Short
Notes), in which the following prophetic interpretations are
found: 2 Thessalonians 2:3, 4 refers to an apostasy in the church
after the spread of the gospel, or about A.D. 500 to 600, most
particularly to Antichrist's rule in the church—not that of a
single man—extending from apostolic times to the last day; the
Man of Sin is the author of many sins, such as false doctrine,
various idols and abominations, oppression of the saints, the
power of dispensation, impure celibacy, simony, scandals, and
the like.[26] Verse 4 refers, not to Mohammed, but to the assumption by the Roman Antichrist of authority over the Word of
God.[27] The time of Antichrist is the same as the 42 months, 1260
days, and time, times, and a half—possibly from Constantine to
the then present revelation of Antichrist, although certainty
on the time is not necessary—and the Two Witnesses are the
Old and the New Testament.[28]

Irenaeus' third-century allusion to the 666 of Antichrist, as
being *Lateinos,* is presented for the beast of Revelation 13, and
is expressly applied by Flacius to the pope, head of the Latin
church.[29]

Flacius' Latin works were translated into different languages, and many editions were printed, molding Protestant
exposition of prophecy to a marked degree.

V. Conradus—Italian Convert Holds Millennium Yet Future

Alfonsus Conradus (16th century), of Mantua, was one of
the many Italians who were compelled to leave their fatherland
because of religious convictions. Conradus found refuge in
Graubünden, Switzerland, where, in 1560, he wrote a large commentary on the Apocalypse, in which he declared the Roman

---

[26] Flacius, *Glossa Compendiaria . . . in Novum Testamentum,* pp. 1028, 1029.
[27] *Ibid.,* p. 1030.
[28] *Ibid.,* on Rev. 11:2, 3, p. 1352.
[29] *Ibid.,* on Rev. 13:17, 18, pp. 1363, 1364.

Papacy to be the Antichrist.[30] Further biographical details of this energetic opponent of the Roman church are unknown.

1. PROPHESIED ANTICHRIST IS HISTORICAL PAPACY.—Asserting that the seven churches and the seven seals represent the church, and that the trumpets are aspects and periods of the church and its tribulations, Conradus takes the position that it is useless to wait for the coming of Antichrist, for the pope is Antichrist.[31]

The 1260 days of Antichrist are the same as the forty-two months, and the three and a half times, with each day standing for a literal year. This application discloses approximately the duration of the persecution by Antichrist.[32] The first six trumpets signify calamities for the church, Conradus thought, but the seventh will bring victory to the cause of God and defeat for Antichrist.[33]

2. PAPACY IS BEAST, LITTLE HORN, ANTICHRIST, AND BABYLON.—The dragon is Satan, ruler of this world, and the seven heads signify earthly powers.[34] Of the specifications of Revelation 13 and 17, the following is the gist of Conradus' position:

The Beast coming out of the sea is the Antichrist. This same Beast is seen in the seventh chapter of Daniel in the role of the Little Horn. The Beast with the ten horns is the Roman Empire. The Antichrist is the head of the fourth beast. The pope is the Antichrist, the Man of Sin.

The number 666 is the number of the name of the pope.

Babylon the great is Rome. His name is also Egypt, and Sodom.

The seven heads are seven ruling kingdoms.

The woman on the seven hills is the Papacy. The Papacy sits on top of the kingdoms of this world, is supported by them, and controls them. The seven kingdoms are enemies to the people of God.[35]

---

[30] Alfonsus Conradus, *In Apocalypsim D. Ioan. Apostoli Commentarius Alfonsi Conradi,* p. 222.
[31] *Ibid.*
[32] *Ibid.*, p. 240.
[33] *Ibid.*, pp. 251, 252.
[34] *Ibid.*, p. 262.
[35] *Ibid.*, pp. 279, 306, 307, 369, 385-387.

3. SEVEN HEADS ENUMERATED WITH POPE THE SEVENTH.—
The seven heads are Egypt, Israel, Babylonia, Medo-Persia,
Greece, the Rome of the Caesars, and the Rome of the Popes.[36]

4. SATAN'S BINDING BELIEVED FUTURE, NOT PAST.—As to
the one thousand years, and the conflicting views that were current, Conradus is not so clear, but he did not believe that Satan's
one thousand-year binding began in the early centuries, and,
significantly, challenged the standard Catholic view, which had
its origin with Augustine.[37]

VI. Stiefel Sets Day and Hour Despite Luther's Protests

MICHAEL STIEFEL (Styfel, Stiffel, Stifel, Stieffel) (1486-
1567) was born at Esslingen. He became an Augustinian monk,
and was consecrated a priest in 1511. But the spirit of the
Reformation set his heart aflame, and in 1520 he left the cloister
and went to Wittenberg. He later relates that while still a monk,
though not having reached a final decision, he had nevertheless
applied the beast of Revelation 13 to Pope Leo X, and attempted, by a slight manipulation of spelling, to get 666 out of
Leo's name, or from "Mystery." [38] In 1523 Luther appointed him
court preacher to Count Albrecht of Mansfeld, and in 1528 he
became pastor at Lochau. Luther thought very highly of him,
recommending him as a pious, industrious, and well-mannered
man of extensive knowledge. He was also an able mathematician
and is considered by competent critics as one of the outstanding
arithmeticians of his time.

Yet for some time Stiefel had devoted himself to a strange
cabalistic system of transforming letters into so-called trigonal
numbers, seeking to discover the hidden time secrets of the
Bible.[39] Sharing the views of the Reformers on the Papacy as the
Antichrist, he published in 1532, despite Luther's protest,
Ein Rechen Büchlin vom End Christ. Apocalypsis in Apoca-

---

[36] *Ibid.*, pp. 387-389.
[37] *Ibid.*, pp. 451 ff.
[38] Michael Stiefel, *Ein sehr Wunderbarliche wortrechnung* (A Very Wonderful Word Calculation), 1553.
[39] Kawerau, "Stiefel (Styfel), Michael," *The New Schaff-Herzog*, vol. 11, p. 95.

lypsim (A Booklet of Arithmetic About the Antichrist. A Revelation of Revelation).

CONTRIVES EXACT DAY BY CABALISTIC NUMBERS.—Believing he had solved the prophetic times by these curious triangular numbers, he thought that the figure 2300 would designate the beginning of the time of the end, and 1335 that of the blessed time.[40] He claimed to have found the deep meanings of these prophetic numbers, and submitted twenty-two propositions to Luther intended to show that Christ's coming in judgment would occur at 8 A.M., on October 19, 1533.[41] Luther warned Stiefel not to be rash in his conclusions. But Stiefel would not listen, and continued to speak publicly about the exact hour of Christ's advent. According to his explanation, Christ's declaration that only the Father knew the day and the hour did not apply after the resurrection. The word of the calculation spread far and wide.

Three days before the fateful date he gathered the crowds together, exhorted them to be ready, and began to administer the Lord's supper. Peasants from far and near had flocked to Lochau; and as he had given away all his belongings, so they had neglected their work for quite a time, thereby losing their harvest. As the appointed hour passed, and Christ did not come, the resultant disappointment of the people knew no bounds. They took Stiefel, bound him with ropes, and brought him to Wittenberg, where some sued him for damages.[42] This episode brought upon the Reformation cause reproach for which the leaders were in no way responsible. Yet Luther himself did not take it too seriously, merely calling it a mild temptation. He accepted him in his house for further instruction, and in 1535 he was given another chance at Holzdorf.[43]

For fourteen years Stiefel kept himself aloof from prophetic numbers, pursuing purely mathematical studies, and published

---

[40] Stiefel, *Ein sehr Wunderbarliche wortrechnung*, sigs. f₁v, j₃r.
[41] Luther, *Schriften*, vol. 22, cols. 1332, 1333; vol. 21, cols. 1825, 1826.
[42] M'Clintock and Strong, *op. cit.*, vol. 9, p. 1023, art. "Stiefel, Michael."
[43] A detailed "eyewitness" report of the episode at Lochau, made at Luther's request, is given in Weller's letter to Luther dated Nov. 17, 1533. Letter No. 2017, in Luther, *Schriften*, vol. 21b, cols. 1864-1870.

11

his *Arithmetica Integra* in 1543. During the Schmalkaldic Wars, however, his parish was destroyed and he had to flee. He then returned to his cabalistic play with the numbers of Daniel and the Apocalypse, attempting to establish new dates by means of this strange "spiritual arithmetic" that was a plague to his associates. In 1553, in his second treatise, *Ein sehr wunderbarliche Wortrechnung,* Stiefel admitted his error in the 1533 experience, and his refusal to heed Luther's warning." In 1558 he joined the faculty at Jena, where for a decade he continued as a simple teacher of mathematics.

VII. Musculus—World's End Within Few Hundred Years

ANDREAS MUSCULUS (1514-1581), professor of theology at Frankfurt an der Oder, general superintendent of Brandenburg, and spiritual adviser to the elector, was a fervent Lutheran. By his holy but passionate zeal he often got mixed in bitter theological disputes, but on the other hand, he helped the needy wherever he could; poor students especially found in him their great benefactor. The favorite themes of his sermons were the last days, death, resurrection and judgment, and the works of the devil and his destruction. He wrote a number of tracts, among them "About the Last Days," "About the Tyranny of the Devil in the Last Days," and "Consider the End." [45] In these he discussed the coming judgment day and the signs of the approaching end—signs of the second advent, with the attendant resurrection to life or to damnation. These signs include the falling stars, the preaching of the gospel to all the world, and the breaking of the Papacy without hand. Believing the Papacy to be the "Antichrist of the Occident," and the Turk the "Antichrist of the Orient," Musculus wrote:

"But according to the explanation of this picture [Daniel 2] the world has now the last flap in its hands and that will soon slip away from it, as can be proved by the word of Elias, that the world will not stand longer

---

[44] Stiefel, *Ein sehr Wunderbarliche wortrechnung,* foreword.
[45] Herzog, *Real-Encyklopädie,* art. "Musculus"; Kawerau, "Musculus (Meusel), Andreas," *The New Schaff-Herzog,* vol. 8, p. 60.

than 6,000 years. It has continued already for 5556 years and should have some other 500 years to go on, according to Elias' prophecy. But the image being set on feet of mud [clay] is therefore destined to sink down; the days will be shortened. Else, because of the overwhelming iniquity, even the other worlds are in danger. . . . And by many unprecedented signs, our Lord Christ has given us to understand that He has already the knife in His hand to cut the thread and to shorten the days. . . . [Among the signs] when this gospel shall be preached in all the world, then shall the end come. . . . And today we see and hear how the precious word has taken its course straight towards midnight and how it shall reach further and further till it comes to the very last hamlet of this world. . . . [On Matt. 24.9—they shall deliver you up to be afflicted and shall kill you] Whereas this was first fulfilled under the persecution of the emperors . . . now since 800 years the pope of Rome from the beginning of his Antichristian kingdom has started to slay, to kill, and to destroy. Many a learned man, many pious Christians who have comprehended this abomination, protested against it, and refused to worship the Bride of Babylon, were put to death by him and exterminated." [46]

VIII. Selnecker—Stresses Unity of Belief on Prophecies

NIKOLAUS SELNECKER (1530-1592), theologian and hymnist, was born near Nürnberg. Educated at Wittenberg, he studied theology under Melanchthon after completing a law course. In his temperament and attitude he resembled Melanchthon, but in his theological views he inclined toward strict Lutheranism. He became court preacher at Dresden in 1557, but had to resign in 1561 because the controlling power was antagonistic toward Lutheranism. Obtaining a professorship at Jena, the stronghold of ultra-Lutheranism, he was soon discharged because of his mild views. In 1568 he was made a professor at Leipzig and pastor of the Thomaskirche. In 1570 he was charged with heading the Reformation at Brunswick, and helped to found the University of Helmstedt.[47] He was a voluminous though not an original writer, and largely echoed the prophetic teachings of Luther.

1. WORLD OF ONE OPINION ON FOUR EMPIRES.—Selnecker was a firm believer in the return of Christ, on the basis of the prophecies.[48] His volume, *Die Propheten* (The Prophets),

---

[46] Translated from Andreas Musculus, *Vom jüngsten Tage.*
[47] F. W. Dibelius, "Selnecker, Nikolaus," *The New Schaff-Herzog*, vol. 10, p. 346; Herzog, *Real-Encyklopädie*, art. "Selnecker."
[48] Translated from Nikolaus Selnecker, *Die Propheten*, fol. 465 r.

stresses the significant universality of belief in the four world powers of prophecy:

"The first kingdom, Babylon, the second, Medo-Persia, the third, the great kingdom of Alexander the Greek, the fourth, the Romans. In this all the world is of one opinion. . . . The mountain from which the stone was cut off without hands may well signify the whole Jewish nation out of which Jesus came." [49]

2. CONSIDERED LITTLE HORN TO BE TURK.—The four beasts of Daniel 7 symbolized the same, but Selnecker thought the Turk was the Little Horn appearing among the ten horns:

"The fourth has ten horns. These are: Syria, Egypt, Asia, Greece, Africa, Spain, Gallia, Italy, Germania, and Anglia, but the little horn is Mohammed or the Turk who has now conquered Egypt, Asia and Greece. This little horn shall destroy God's people and blaspheme the name of Christ. This all happens in these our days." [50]

3. ALL TEACHERS AGREE SEVENTY WEEKS ARE YEAR-WEEKS.—The seventy weeks of years he dated from the second year of Artaxerxes Longimanus:

"The seventy weeks, as all teachers agree, are year-weeks, and not day-weeks, 490 years. . . . Our opinion is, that the seventy weeks should begin with the second year of Darius [Artaxerxes] Longimanus, as the prophets Haggi and Zechariah plainly state." [51]

4. DANIEL 11 GIVES "PICTURE OF THE POPE".—According to Selnecker, Antichrist is plainly pictured in the latter part of Daniel 11. He states his accord with Luther's belief that it is a "picture of the pope."

"In the eleventh chapter, Daniel gives to his people, the Jews, practically the same prophecy as he did in the eighth chapter. He speaks of the great Alexander and of the two kingdoms, Syria and Egypt, mostly for the sake of Antiochus, who would torment the Jews. But he pictures Antiochus in such a manner, that he describes in him the Antichrist and therewith just hits our last time, the days before the end. For all expounders of Scripture agree that this prophecy on Antiochus points to the Antichrist." [52]

The essential unity of the various writers is impressive, and grows as the list of expositors lengthens.

---

[49] *Ibid.*, fol. 433v.   [50] *Ibid.*, fol. 434v.
[51] *Ibid.*, fol. 435v.   [52] *Ibid.*, fol. 436r.

IX. Nigrinus—Reaches Peak of Reformation Interpretation

GEORG NIGRINUS (1530-1602), Evangelical theologian and satirist, was born in Battenberg, Hesse, Germany. While securing his schooling he supported himself by going from door to door as a minstrel. At seventeen he thought to enter a Catholic monastery at Würzburg, where he could be free from all worries, and study to his heart's content. He was dissuaded from this by an innkeeper on the way, who chided him for thinking of such a thing, being a son of Hesse, the most Protestant country in Germany. He urged him to attend the gymnasium at Schweinfurt, to which he went. But the enforcement of the stipulations of the Leipzig Interim brought his stay in Schweinfurt to an untimely end, and he went to Joachimsthal, where he became acquainted with several well-known expositors of prophecy, including Matthias, Eberhard, and Melanchthon.

Financially unable to attend a university, he became a teacher in Silesia, on the Bohemian frontier. In 1553 he went to Munich and taught in a school for poets. Here he became unfavorably acquainted with the inner aspect of Catholicism and especially with the Jesuits, who sought to harm him because he studied Melanchthon's works in private with his pupils. Considering it wiser to leave Munich, he returned in 1555 to Hesse, studied theology at Marburg, and served as a minister at Homburg ob der Ohm. In a great debate on the Lord's supper his singular ability was brought to the attention of the university, and he won the favor of the landgrave. In 1564 he received the parish of the town of Giessen, one of the most important places in Hesse, where the most fruitful period of his life began.

Nigrinus distinguished himself as a homiletical expositor and a prolific exegete, chiefly on prophecy. He was conspicuous as a controversialist against the Catholic Church. His *Apocalypsis . . . in Sechzig Predigten . . . ausgelegt* (Sixty Sermons on the Apocalypse), of 1573, and his *Daniel . . . ausgelegt in fünfftzig Predigten* (Daniel Explained in Fifty Sermons), of 1574, had been preceded by *Ein wolgegründe Rechnung und Zeitregister*

(A Well-founded Calculation and Time Register), published in 1570, proving the Papacy to be Antichrist. Another treatise was *Von der rechten alten Catholischen Kirche* (Of the True Ancient Catholic Church), published in 1575.

Nigrinus' satires against the church were very popular, especially his burlesque, *Affenspiel F. Johan Nasen Gute Nacht Babst* (Good Night, Pope), of 1571. His most important work appeared in 1582, *Papistische Inquisition und gulden Flüs der Römischen Kirchen* (Papal Inquisition and the Golden Fleece of the Roman Church).[53] Here are his leading positions:

1. TERMINATES SEVENTY WEEKS WITH CROSS IN A.D. 34.—In his chronicle Nigrinus gives special attention to the time of Antichrist, as foretold by the prophecies of Daniel and the Apocalypse. Turning to the time prophecy of Daniel 9, he terminates the seventy weeks of years in A.D. 34, with the death of Christ—three and a half years after His baptism—and reckons backward from that to the beginning of the period in the seventh year of Artaxerxes Longimanus, which he places at 456 B.C.[54]

2. 1260 YEARS PLACED FROM 441 TO 1701.—Nigrinus dated the time and times and half a time, or the 1260 years, from Leo I, in 441, when the idea of papal world power first appeared. That would bring him to 1701 for the end of the Antichrist, which would make the periods end about two hundred years from his day. The end of the three times, or 1080 years, brought him to the year 1521, in which he said that "our blessed Luther proclaimed the holy gospel before the highest authorities of the German nation," and since that time the papacy had lost so much ground that "we have just to pray to the Lord to put some more force to His thunder and to advance the course of His word in order to make the Antichrist tumble" and to complete his ruin. And 50 years of the last "half a time" had passed already.[55]

---

[53] *Allgemeine deutsche Biographie,* art. "Nigrinus, Georg."
[54] Georg Nigrinus, *Ein wolgegründe Rechnung und Zeitregister,* sig. H$_1$v, H$_2$r. Although following Funck, he fell a year short in reaching the starting point, doubtless because of overlooking the fact that chronology has no year zero between 1 B.C. and A.D. 1.
[55] Nigrinus, *Apocalypsis, Die Offenbarunge Sanct Johannis des Apostels,* pp. 282 ff.

On the other hand, believing that the Little Horn in Daniel 7 also refers to the Turk, and that a period of 1260 years had also been given to this Horn, the Turk's end would come in A.D. 1883, starting with the beginning of Islam in A.D. 623, or Mohammed's flight from Mecca to Medina. But he hoped that the Lord would come sooner, and make an end to the abomination of the Turk at the very time He uproots the pope and brings an end to Antichrist.[56] Nigrinus saw in the woman of Revelation 12 the true church persecuted as heretical.[57]

3. MARSHALS PROPHECIES TO MEET JESUIT DISCLAIMERS.— In his *Profound Revelation of Antichrist,* Nigrinus presents a comprehensive thesis against the Jesuits to disprove their claim that the pope is not Antichrist, but that the Antichrist is someone entirely unconnected with the Christian faith. In his reply Nigrinus marshals the collective descriptions of prophecy. He states:

"The Jesuits claim to be sorely offended and have taken my declarations as an insult and blasphemy in branding the papacy as the Antichrist of which Daniel, Paul, Peter, John and even Christ prophesied. But this is as true as it is that Jesus is the Messiah, and I am prepared to show it even by their own definition of the word 'Antichrist.' "[58]

4. ANTICHRIST NOT AN INDIVIDUAL BUT A SYSTEM.—Nigrinus refutes the Jesuit assumption that Antichrist is to be a single individual, by showing that it is a continuing system. This he proves from 2 Thessalonians 2, Daniel 7, and Revelation 13 and 17. That the Beast with seven heads and ten horns is pagan Rome is admitted by the Jesuits. The Beast with two horns, Nigrinus adds, is papal Rome that followed, and took the place of pagan Rome.[59]

5. TO APPEAR IN LATIN CHURCH WITH NUMBER 666.—Referring to the number of the beast, 666, Nigrinus stresses the fact that Antichrist will appear in the Latin church, in the place where the Latins first ruled. But he concludes:

---

[56] Nigrinus, *Wolgegründe Rechnung,* sigs. Q_1r-Q_2r, S_1v-S_2v.
[57] Nigrinus, *Apocalypsis,* p. 325.
[58] Translated from Nigrinus, *Antichrists Gründtliche Offenbarung,* fol. 6v.
[59] *Ibid.,* fols. 14v, 16v, 17v.

"Therefore, even if the name with its secret number would never be known, we have sufficient other signs to be able to recognize the Roman Antichrist, as the Jesuit must admit and has already admitted." [60]

6. RELATIONSHIP OF CONTROVERSY TO SECOND ADVENT.— The relation of this controversy to the second advent is also set forth:

"This Jesuit ridicules the thought of the near coming of Christ and insinuates that the reformers preached it only in order to frighten the people or to bamboozle and trick the common folk as their priests often do. But Luther has never spoken in this manner about the last day, but since the Antichrist has now come to the open, he and the others have concluded that the Day of the Lord cannot be far away." [61]

7. JESUIT CONTENTION OF THREE AND A HALF YEARS RE-FUTED.—Citing Tertullian's recognition of the fact that pagan Rome in his day was holding back the coming of Antichrist, Nigrinus discusses Antichrist's allotted time period, and cites the verdict of the Holy Scriptures.

"This Jesuit further contends that the papacy cannot be antichrist because the papacy has lasted for centuries, but that the antichrist is supposed to reign only 3½ years. . . . But no one doubts today that Daniel spoke of year-days, not literal days. . . . The prophetic time-periods of forty-two months, 1260 days, 1, 2, ½ times are prophetic, and according to Ezekiel 4, a day must be taken for a year. . . . [Antiochus is a type of Antichrist], and as many days as he raged and raved against the Jews, so many *years* shall the spiritual Antiochus or Antichrist rage in the midst of the Christian church." [62]

8. TEN DIVISIONS OF ROME TABULATED.—Finally, in a discussion of Revelation 13, after listing the seven forms of Roman government as the seven heads, Nigrinus tabulates the ten horns thus:

"Italia; Hispania; Gallia; Syria; Egypt; Asia; Grecia; Pannonia; Africa; Anglia. These were all under the power of Rome in the time of John. But practically all were stripped from her at the time we set above, of the beginning of the papacy and the downfall of the first monarchy. The Visigoths and Lombards occupied Italy and ruled over her with force for a long time. The Ostrogoths conquered Spain, and later it was subdued by the Saracens. Syria, Egypt and Asia were conquered by the Mohammedans; they plucked

---

[60] *Ibid.*, fols. 22v, 23r.   [61] *Ibid.*, fol. 26r.   [62] *Ibid.*, fols. 28v, 29r.

up three horns and formed one [kingdom] out of them, which is now the Turkish Empire. Grecia with some surrounding territories remained in the hands of the emperors of Eastern Rome until the Turk overwhelmed them. Pannonia, or Hungary, was occupied by the Huns until the Turk took a share of it. Africa was overrun by the Vandals, Anglia by the Saxons, Gallia by the Franks, Normans, and other German tribes.

"Germany will not be counted because she was not under the sway of the Romans during the time of the first emperors, but was in perpetual warfare with them. The same holds true for Bohemia, Poland, Denmark, and Sweden. These will not be counted, because at that time they were still barbaric nations. They have received their royal titles during the time of the divided empire; . . . that is all history." [63]

Nigrinus' final conclusions are as follows:

"Really this is the time, prophesied by Jesus in Matt. 24, when the gospel will be preached for a witness unto all nations. . . . There is no doubt that the end of the world is much nearer than the pope and his Jesuits believe. . . . And herewith I shall conclude this extract. Even if it is of no avail to the Jesuits and their followers, many pious Christians will by it recognize and accept the truth and be filled with gladness. May the Lord bestow His blessing and His grace upon it." [64]

9. THE ANTICHRIST BOTH POPE AND TURK.—The two powers of iniquity are one. The pope is even the worse of the two, because he has crowded himself into the temple of God. Some say that the pope is the soul, and the Turk the body, of Antichrist. [65]

10. YEAR-DAY PRINCIPLE IN PROPHETIC PERIODS.—Nigrinus reckons the 1290 days and the 1335 days as years, just as he does the 1260 days. These two periods begin together, so that the 1335 days end just 45 days later than the 1290. [66]

X. Chytraeus—Prophetic Fulfillment Soon to End in Judgment

DAVID CHYTRAEUS (1530-1600), last of the "Fathers of the Lutheran church," was born at Ingelfingen, Württemberg. After studying ancient languages at Tübingen, he went to Wittenberg when about fifteen years of age, where he became one of the most beloved pupils of Melanchthon, whom he venerated all

---

[63] *Ibid.*, fol. 59r,v.
[65] Nigrinus, *Ein wolgegründe Rechnung*, sig. S₂r,v.

[64] *Ibid.*, fols. 96v, 97r.
[66] *Ibid.*, sig. S₄r.

through his life, being of a conciliatory nature like his master. A scholar with encyclopedic knowledge, but no preacher, he began to lecture on physics and theology in Wittenberg in 1548.

In 1551 he was called to Rostock, where he was the leading spirit, and had great influence in Mecklenburg, where he became instrumental in founding the University of Rostock. He was also occupied with ecclesiastical regulations, and was opposed to the Flacian adversaries of The Formula of Concord. Being known for his great skill and power in negotiation, he was employed by the emperor Maximilian II to arrange ecclesiastical affairs in Austria on the basis of the modified positions. He was the author of the statutes of the University of Helmstädt, and of numerous works, including expositions of Daniel and the Apocalypse.

1. DAY OF JUDGMENT NOT FAR HENCE.—Chytraeus held that the judgment was "not far hence." This he based on the cumulative evidence of Daniel 2 and 7, Matthew 24 and Mark 13, 2 Thessalonians 2, and Revelation 13. The second advent was tied in as the climax of the prophetic outlines. Here is a comprehensive paragraph:

"The Lord Himself revealed to Daniel how long the four world kingdoms should exist, and how long the little horn should last. This little horn is also described by Paul in 2 Thess. 2 where we are told that this anti-Christian power, the papacy, would be fully revealed just before the judgment should take place. We know today that the four monarchies have long passed off the stage of action, that the two-horned beast which is mentioned in Revelation 13 and which refers to the same power can not last much longer, and so we are forced to conclude that the day of judgment is not far hence. . . . This same thought is given in 2 Thess. 2:1-8 where the Roman antichrist is again mentioned. . . . Most of the other signs have also been fulfilled which our Saviour referred to in Matthew 24." [67]

With these prophecies Chytraeus also connected the six-thousand-year theory, and the thought that the seventh thousand years would usher in the eternal state. But he believed that the allotted time would be shortened. [68]

---

[67] Translated from David Chytraeus, *Auslegung der Offenbarung Johannis* (Explanation of the Revelation of John).
[68] *Ibid.*

2. Rome Substitutes Key of Bottomless Pit.—Chytraeus held that the Word-of-God key, given to the apostles and early bishops, and which unlocks heaven, was thrown away about A.D. 600, and in its place the bishop of Rome accepted the key of the bottomless pit, from which the smoke of false doctrine emerged, darkening and eclipsing the pure gospel. This had already begun when Gregory I (590-604) occupied the papal chair. Soon after, Boniface III received from Phocas his title as universal bishop.[69]

3. Sixth Trumpet Applied to Mohammedanism.—The sixth trumpet describes the rising of Mohammed, king of the locusts, and his followers—appearing about the time that Boniface III received the title of head of the universal church—and penetrating throughout Arabia, Palestine, Syria, Egypt, Northern Africa, Asia Minor, Spain, and Gaul.[70]

4. 1260 Years From 412 to 1672, Or Possibly 1866.— Two possible chronological locations for the papal Little Horn's 1260 years are suggested by others:

"They start to reckon from 412 when the Roman Empire was destroyed by the Goths, and the city of Rome conquered. 412 + 1260 years will bring the day of judgment to 1672. But if one starts to reckon the forty-two months from 606-7 from the time the Roman pope became universal head of the church through Emperor Phocas, he reaches the year 1866." [71]

5. Papacy Symbolized in Daniel 7 and Revelation 13.— Contending that the beast of Revelation 17 is the same as the ten-horned beast of Revelation 13 and Daniel 7, Chytraeus goes on to say:

"This beast rising from the sea, having seven heads or ten horns, is without doubt a symbol of the Roman Empire, which rose from the sea or the world, being constituted of many nations and has seven heads, which, according to the explanation of the angel, signify seven hills or seven kings. For the city of Rome, which had the power over the kings on earth, has seven hills inside her walls." [72]

---

[69] *Ibid.*
[70] *Ibid.*
[71] *Ibid.*
[72] *Ibid.*

6. STILL HOLDS AUGUSTINIAN THEORY OF MILLENNIUM.—
As to the number 666, Chytraeus cites the view mentioned by
Irenaeus as possibly correct, which is based on the Greek word
Lateinos. On Revelation 20 he still follows Augustine, who holds
that the first resurrection is spiritual, and in counting the one
thousand years he follows Bibliander, who begins them in
A.D. 73, when most of the apostles had finished their work of
preaching the gospel. Reckoning from that date, the one thousand years end with Gregory VII, who persecuted with Antichristian tyranny.[73]

---

[73] *Ibid.*

CHAPTER FIFTEEN

Swiss Reformers
Parallel German Interpretations

I. Zwingli and Juda Hold Similar Views on Antichrist

A different path was marked out for the Reformation in Switzerland, where it spread rapidly. The Swiss Republic had gained its liberty at great sacrifice, and the University of Basel soon became the stronghold of the new learning. In 1505-1507 Thomas Wyttenbach (1472-1526) had already fought against certain doctrines of the church. Later Capito preached on Romans in Basel, and in 1514 Erasmus also made Basel his headquarters, but he did not reside there permanently until 1521. Among these Reformers was HULDREICH (ULRICH) ZWINGLI (1484-1531), who received a strong urge to study the Word in the original tongues.

Born at Wildhaus, Zwingli was educated at Berne, the University of Vienna, and at Basel, there studying theology under Wyttenbach. After teaching for three years he was appointed a priest in 1506 in Glarus. His duties as army chaplain with the Swiss guards who fought for the pope brought him to the battlefields of Italy, where he had ample time to observe the variances between professed and practical Christianity. Here he began to preach fearlessly the simple teachings of Jesus. From the very beginning he made it his principle not to cause offense by harmful polemics but to fight error by preaching positive truth.

When he had to leave Glarus in 1516, he was cordially received in the monastery of Einsiedeln, famous for its shrine, to

which people flocked from far and near. Here, too, he preached
the simple gospel. He tried to reach the highest authorities in the
church by word and pen, in order to induce them to begin
reforms. Therefore, when Zwingli raised his voice with all his
power against the seller of indulgences who came to Switzerland
in the autumn of 1518, no reproach fell upon him. In the same
year he was called to become preacher at Zurich, where his sermons caused many to change their evil habits of life.

The main topic of his preaching in 1522 was the supremacy
and sufficiency of the Bible. God alone, the Father of Jesus
Christ, should be our teacher, not doctors and priests, or popes
and councils. Upon the Word alone we have to build our faith.
He prepared sixty-seven theses for a public discussion held on
January 29, 1523. Every one of these theses was built on sure
Scriptural ground. Faith in the gospel of Christ is the only condition to salvation; and Christ, the eternal High Priest, the only
mediator between God and men. The papal party was unable
to furnish Scriptural proof either for the intercession of saints
or for celibacy, the points specially discussed. Thereupon the
magistrate of the city of Zurich resolved that Master Zwingli
should continue to preach and to introduce reforms, and that all
other preachers should proclaim only what they were able to
substantiate from Scripture.[1]

1. ZWINGLI'S ATTITUDE TOWARD THE PAPACY.—Perhaps the
most interesting chapter which throws light upon Zwingli's attitude toward the Papacy, we find in his treatise *Ueber die wahren
Aufrührer* (Against the True Inciters of Sedition). It appeared
on December 28, 1524, and was directed against the machina-
tions of Rome as well as against the riotous behavior of the Anabaptists, who caused Zwingli no end of trouble. He writes:

"Wherever envy and hatred are found, there is also found the rock of
the old Adam. And as Prov. 10. [12] says: Hatred stirreth up strifes, [there-
fore] if they do not know better than to speak scornfully against the Papacy
and to spread its deceit, they are to be rebuked for not working on their
own improvement. Not because they do any injustice to the Papacy, for

---

[1] Herzog, *Real-Encyklopädie*, art. "Zwingli," vol. 18, pp. 701 ff.

I know that in it works the might and power of the Devil, that is, of the Antichrist. Yet I cannot approve their proclaiming of the Word of God solely because of their hatred against the Pope. I desire much more that the love of God would be their motive in resisting Antichrist, and to lessen the burdens of their neighbors." [2]

"If we would live Christlike, everybody would fall away from Popedom, because they would recognize that nothing else than deceitful pomp stands behind it. [In this spirit] everything undertaken toward its fall will succeed. And I request that we break the might of the Papacy not by the power of hate, but by the power of love to God and to our neighbor." [3]

"You are protecting all this disorder, this most wicked profession, this antichristian Papacy, although you see the bright shining light and perceive that all nations rejoice that the wickedness of the harlot, who deceived everybody, has been revealed." [4]

"The Papacy has to be abolished or it conceals itself until it suppresses again the gospel. But by no other means can it be more thoroughly routed than by the word of God (2 Thess. 2), because as soon as the world receives this [the word of God] in the right way, it will turn away from the pope without compulsion." [5]

Zwingli did not base his ideas concerning the Papacy upon the Apocalypse, because he did not regard this book as apostolic and did not use it for prophetic evidence.[6]

LEO JUDA (Jud) (1482-1542) was also first influenced by Wyttenbach at the University of Basel, and became an intimate friend of Zwingli. Zwingli, after being established in Zurich, called this friend to him, and Juda arrived there in 1523. His relationship to Zwingli was somewhat similar to that of Melanchthon to Luther. During the years 1524-1529 he did the main work in translating the Bible into German, which was printed at Froschauer's well-known press. He also translated the Old Testament from Hebrew into Latin.

2. JUDA—ROME FULFILLS REVELATION 13 AND 17.—Leo Juda's quaintly worded *Paraphrase Upon the Revelacion of S. John* interprets the second beast of Revelation 13 as the "kingdome of papacie" taking upon itself "all the power of the . . . romyshe Emperour" in persecuting the saints. Revelation 17 portrays the same power as the scarlet woman of Babylon, to be

[2] Huldreich Zwingli, *Hauptschriften* (Principal Works), vol. 7, p. 135.
[3] *Ibid.*, p. 137.   [4] *Ibid.*, p. 199.
[5] *Ibid.*, p. 205.   [6] Philip Schaff, *History*, vol. 7, p. 90.

"throwen downe" at the judgment, in the conflict between "Christ and antichrist." [7]

3. CONFESSIONS CONDEMN PAPACY AS PREDICTED ANTI-CHRIST.—The genuine Reformation in Switzerland produced the first Helvetic Confession, drawn up at Basel by the Reformed theologians in 1536. Accepted and signed by the Reformed cantons and towns, it was sent to the Lutheran leaders assembled at Schmalkalden, in 1537. In both the Helvetic Confession and the Schmalkaldic Articles the Papacy is condemned as the predicted Antichrist.[8]

It is also to be noted that there was now a marked tendency to defend the Reformation positions (1) by citing reforming Catholics from the Council of Rheims (991) onward; (2) by appealing to the witness of early Christian fathers before the great Roman apostasy became pronounced; and (3) by citing later dissentients—such pre-Reformation witnesses as the Waldenses of Piedmont, the Wyclifites of England, and the Hussites of Bohemia.

II. Oecolampadius—Stone Is God's Kingdom; Little Horn Is Papacy

JOHANN OECOLAMPADIUS (1482-1531), leading figure of the Reformation in Basel, was born at Weinsberg. He studied law in Bologna, and philology, philosophy, and theology in Heidelberg and Tübingen. He was one of the best-trained thinkers of his time, specializing in Greek and Hebrew, and receiving M.A. and D.D. degrees. After 1515 he was several times in Basel, once helping Erasmus in his edition of the New Testament. In 1518 he went to Augsburg and spoke frankly in favor of Luther when the latter was summoned before Cajetan. In 1520 he entered a convent for a short time, but dared to make such unorthodox utterances that they did not enjoy his presence. For instance, "It is not evil to invoke intercessors, but no intercessor can be

---

[7] Leo Juda, *Paraphrase Upon the Revelacion of S. John,* appended to *The Seconde Tome or Volume of the Paraphrase of Erasmus Upon the Newe Testament.*
[8] H. Grattan Guinness, *Romanism and the Reformation,* p. 234.

so merciful as Christ, who is the source of all mercy." In 1522 he became chaplain for Franz von Sickingen. Persuaded by Luther's writings, he attacked Mariolatry, the abuses of the confessional, and transubstantiation. From the end of 1522 we find him in Basel, and he soon became the leading figure of the Reformation there. Like Zwingli, Oecolampadius preached on whole books of the Bible. And he defended the Apocalypse against the depreciations of Luther and Zwingli. He contended that it gives a more extensive description of the Little Horn of Daniel 7. The bulk of his writings have never been collected.[9]

1. Denies Antiochus Is Little Horn of Daniel 7.—In his commentary on the book of Daniel, which he believed contains the divine timetable, Oecolampadius gives the usual interpretation of chapter 2—Babylonia, Persia, Macedonia, and Rome—with the kingdom of God, which is compared to a stone, finally crushing the whole image.[10] The four beasts of Daniel 7 represent the same four powers of prophecy, with the ten horns as ten kingdoms of Europe, including Spain, England, France, Bohemia, and Hungary.[11] On the Little Horn he takes issue with Polychronius' fifth-century view that Antiochus is the power symbolized, holding rather that it is the Antichrist (the same as the two-horned beast of Revelation 13, and Paul's Man of Sin)—the triple-crowned pope and Mohammed, although Antichrist includes whoever, sitting in the place of God, blasphemes His name and persecutes the church.[12]

2. The Seventy Weeks; The Antichrist.—The seventy weeks are reckoned by Oecolampadius from several different points to somewhere near the time of Christ; however, the last week is not considered seven years, but a long period extending to the Jewish wars under the reign of Hadrian.[13] And Daniel 11 climaxes with the career of Antichrist.[14]

---

[9] Philip Schaff, *History*, vol. 7, pp. 107-116.
[10] Johann Oecolampadius, *In Danielem Prophetam*, pp. 22-27.
[11] *Ibid.*, pp. 73-75.
[12] *Ibid.*, pp. 76, 77, 92, 132, 133. On Polychronius, see Volume I of *Prophetic Faith.*
[13] *Ibid.*, pp. 104-109.
[14] *Ibid.*, pp. 132-134.

III. Bibliander—Antichrist Is Papacy; Millennium Yet Future

THEODOR BIBLIANDER (1504-1564), lecturer on the Apocalypse, was born near Constance. Called the "Father of Biblical Exegesis in Switzerland," [15] he studied Hebrew at Zurich, and in 1526 under Oecolampadius at Basel. After teaching high school for two years he became Zwingli's successor as professor of theology and Old Testament literature at Zurich, in 1531. His specialty was linguistics, for he was master of numerous languages. His rendering of the prophets was highly successful, winning the commendation of Bullinger, who attended his lectures. He wrote a Hebrew grammar and also published a Latin translation of the Koran in 1543.[16] Openly attacking the Catholic Church at the Council of Trent, he antagonized the Roman College of the Propaganda, and advocated missions to Jews and Mohammedans. With others he completed the Zurich Bible of Leo Juda. Openly and strenuously opposing Calvinism in its conception of predestination, he was finally dismissed from office in 1560. Many of his manuscripts were never published but are preserved at Zurich.[17]

1. 6,000-YEAR PERIOD FOLLOWED BY MILLENNIUM.—Bibliander's purpose, as expressed on the title page of his *Relatio Fidelis* (1545), was to give a "faithful relation" that "from the only Word and Son of God is to be sought exact knowledge of present and future times, and even of Antichrist himself, as the worst plague of the whole world." He was persuaded that after six thousand years of prevailing wickedness there would come the still future predicted millennium of righteousness, and that it therefore behooves us to study the signs and prophecies to know when it is near.[18] Holding the prophetic time measurement to be a day for a year (Ezekiel 4), he counted the seventy weeks

---

[15] Philip Schaff, *History*, vol. 7, p. 211.
[16] The publication of the Koran aroused such an opposition in certain circles in Basel that the printer was imprisoned, and only by the intervention of Luther and Bullinger was the edition released for the public.
[17] M'Clintock and Strong, *op. cit.*, vol. 1, p. 809, art. "Bibliander"; Emil Egli, "Bibliander," *The New Schaff-Herzog*, vol. 2, p. 169.
[18] Theodor Bibliander, *Ad Omnium Ordinum . . . Principes Viros, Populumque Christianum, Relatio Fidelis*, p. 22 [i.e. 24].

of Daniel 9 from the 32d year of Darius Hystaspes to the birth of Christ (A.D. 1).[19]

2. SEALS AND TRUMPETS ARE SUCCESSIVE AGES.—In the midst of the Turkish inroads he declared that the Papacy was worse than the Turk, and is the Antichrist predicted in 2 Thessalonians 2 and Revelation 17.[20] He held the seals and trumpets to be so many successive periods. According to Revelation 10, the gospel is to be reinstated, whereby Antichrist will be revealed.[21] In 1533 he published appeals to return to the Bible as the only rule of faith and the only means of uniting Protestants.

IV. Bullinger—Little Horn Is Papacy, Not Turk

HEINRICH BULLINGER (1504-1575), of Zurich, one of the greatest prophetic expositors of his time, was the intimate friend of Zwingli, whom he succeeded as chief pastor in 1531. He was the most moderate and blameless among the Reformers, prudent and strong without being harsh, ready to conciliate without being weak. He was born at Bremgarten. His father, Dean Bullinger, was the parish priest who resisted the sale of indulgences in 1518, and in 1529 confessed the Reformation doctrine from his pulpit. In 1516 he sent his son Heinrich to the school of the Brethren of the Common Life,[22] at Emmerich, where, to learn carefulness and sympathy for the poor, he was compelled to support himself as a street singer while obtaining his education. In 1519 he went to Cologne, the seat of opposition to the Reformation, securing his B.A. there in 1520. Turning against scholastic theology, Bullinger began to study Chrysostom, Ambrose, and Augustine. And because they drew their premises from Scripture, he set himself to study the New Testament. Securing a copy of his own, he searched it day and night. Erasmus led him to study the classics.

Deeply impressed by Luther's tractates, especially his *Baby-*

---

[19] *Bibliander, Temporum a Condito Mundo . . . Supputatio,* pp. 102, 120. His dates are A.M. 3489 and 3979, or [B.C. 490] and A.D. 1.
[20] Bibliander, *Relatio Fidelis,* p. 58.
[21] *Ibid.,* p. 138.
[22] Biographical notice in Bullinger, *Decades,* decade 5, pp. vii, viii.

lonian Captivity, Bullinger was persuaded that the Papacy·was hopelessly corrupt, and so abandoned the idea of becoming a priest. Receiving his M.A. degree in 1522, he resolved to teach. He obtained a position in the Cistercian Monastery at Cappel as lecturer on the New Testament, which vocation he held until 1529. But from 1523 on, together with Juda, he began preparing tracts to spread the Reformation in Switzerland, an act which led to considerable Catholic hostility.

1. WIDE FRIENDSHIPS AND IMPORTANT CONTACTS.—In 1527 Bullinger was granted a leave of absence to attend Zwingli's lectures at Zurich and to perfect his Greek and Hebrew, and in 1528 he went with Zwingli to the disputation at Berne. In 1529 he became pastor at Bremgarten, as successor to his father, and two years later was elected successor to Zwingli at Zurich, serving as chief pastor. In 1536, with Leo Juda and others, he drew up the first Helvetic Confession.[23]

An indefatigable writer and preacher, Bullinger rarely preached less than six to eight sermons a week during the first years of his ministry in Zurich, and his more than a hundred works fill ten folio volumes. He harbored the persecuted evangelicals of Italy, France, Germany, and England,[24] such as Hooper, Calvin, and Jewel, and championed the rights of the Huguenots and Waldenses. He carried on extensive correspondence with leading theologians, Reformers, rulers, and statesmen in all parts of Europe, dedicating sermons and books to monarchs, such as Edward VI, king of England.[25] Many of his writings were translated into English, and were widely circulated in other languages, and his sermons were held in such high repute in England that Archbishop Whitgift of Canterbury exhorted the bishops of his province to require every minister not licensed as a preacher to read one sermon from Bullinger's *Decades* each week.[26]

---

[23] Philip Schaff, *Creeds,* vol. 3, pp. 211-231.
[24] Carl Pestalozzi, *Heinrich Bullinger, Leben und ausgewählte Schriften,* p. 295; Philip Schaff, *History,* vol. 7, p. 208.
[25] Bullinger, *Decades,* decade 4, pp. 115-122.
[26] *Ibid.,* decade 5, pp. xv-xxxi.

Significantly enough, Bishop Parkhurst, of Norwich, also wrote to Bullinger in 1561, just after the issuance of the English edition of *Sermons on the Apocalypse.* "I have given directions to all the ministers of the word throughout Suffolk and Norfolk to procure either in Latin or English your sermons on the Apocalypse." [27] And in 1565 Parkhurst wrote, "I am expecting your most learned discourses on Daniel." [28]

2. SERMONS ON ANTICHRIST AROUSE ANTAGONISM.—Bullinger preferred to explain whole books of Scripture, such as the Apocalypse and Daniel, and wrote extensively on the prophecies. He was also active in lifting educational standards by scholarships, and filled professorships with able theologians. He clearly understood the value of the printed word, and many of his sermons were printed. Among them, most enlightening to our study, were his one hundred sermons on the Apocalypse. The Latin edition was published in 1557, a German translation following, and an English edition in 1561, as well as editions in French, Dutch, and Polish. Two large volumes of *Zurich Letters,* comprising the correspondence of several English bishops with the leading Helvetian Reformers, between 1558 and 1602— more than 250 letters in all—form part of the Parker Society reprint of the English Reformation writings. These give an intimate glimpse of the spirit, relationships, and heart burdens of these men, and thus throw light on our quest.

The wonderful Christian attitude which Bullinger exercised is clearly revealed in his answer to Borrhaus, who remarked that he could not follow him in all his explanations of the Apocalypse. Bullinger answered, "I am of the opinion, that I do not see any reason to quarrel with brethren in the faith, or even to sever the ties of friendship, if they differ in the explanation of certain passages, as long as we are united in the doctrines of faith. I have written about the New Testament and the Revelation, but if others write also about it, and offer better and more simple

---

[27] *The Zurich Letters* [1st series], 1558-1579, letter 42, pp. 98, 99.
[28] *Ibid.,* letter 65, p. 144, letter 97, p. 202.

explanations to the church, I shall be very grateful and shall never stick obstinately to my writings." [29]

V. Epitome of Bullinger's Teachings on the Prophecies

Bullinger's *A Hundred Sermons Upon the Apocalips of Jesu Christe* ("Englished" in 1561, but originally written in Latin in 1557) sets forth most clearly and fully his positions. The twenty-four-page preface, addressed "unto all the exiles for the name of Christ in Germany and Swyserland, of Fraunce, England, Italy, and of other Realmes or Nations, and generally to all the faithfull wheresoever they be, abiding and lokyng for the comyng of Christe oure Lorde and Judge," is most revealing.

1. CHRIST AND ANTICHRIST THE CONTINUING THEME.—The high priesthood and the kingship of Christ are continually stressed. The seven churches are "all the churches that shal be in the worlde, untyl the worldes ende," and the seven trumpets portray the grievous conflicts which will befall the church. The Witnesses are those cruelly slain by Antichrist. The beasts of Revelation 13 are the old Roman Empire and the triple-crowned "Papistrie." Out of old Rome's division rises the new Rome, spoken of by Paul and in Daniel 7 and 11. It is also denominated Babylon. The mark of the Beast is his excommunicating power, and the 666 are years, he thought, leading from A.D. 97, the time when the book of Revelation was written, to 763, when the bishop of Rome began to forget his humility. The scarlet woman of Revelation 17 is "the Romish church," and Rome the seat of the Beast.[30]

2. STUDENT OF EARLIER PROPHETIC INTERPRETATIONS.—Bullinger contended that Daniel was understood as far as fulfilled, citing Christ's admonition to understand. But in the Revelation the mystery is made plain. Not only had Bullinger studied it from his youth, but he had searched the writings of

---

[29] Pestalozzi, *op. cit.*, p. 473.
[30] Bullinger, *A Hundred Sermons upon the Apocalips*, preface; see also his *Decades*, decade 4, sermon 7, pp. 273 ff.

other expositors—Bibliander of Zurich, Aretas, Justin, Primasius, Thomas Aquinas, Sebastian Meier, François Lambert, Erasmus, Laurentius Valla. And on the Antichrist he had compassed Irenaeus, Tertullian, Jerome, Arnulf of Orleans (at Rheims, 991), Bernard of Clairvaux, Eberhard of Salzburg (1240), giving a sketch of his great speech identifying the kingdom of the popes as coming up among the divisions of Rome.[31] Then he cites Joachim, Petrarch, Luther, Marsilius of Padua, Savonarola, Pico della Mirandola, and the Waldenses.

This summary, Bullinger continues, was compiled at great labor, and repeats that it is dedicated to the oppressed sufferers for the faith in all lands. Before launching into his sermon-expositions he makes an elaborate defense of the Apocalypse, citing more than twenty witnesses covering the centuries. He stresses that the book can be understood by prayer, and that its dominant theme is the conflict of Christ and Antichrist, and "an absolute and certayne prophecie of thynges to come." [32]

3. Fifth and Sixth Trumpets Are Mohammedans and Turks.—The pope is Antichrist because he usurps the keys of Christ and His kingly and priestly authority.[33] The seat of Satan is, at the time of Pergamos, Rome itself.[34] In Daniel 7, 8, 11, clear indications of Antichrist are given.[35] The fifth and sixth trumpets are the Mohammedans and Saracens, and the Turks and the Tartarians, respectively.[36]

4. Powers of Revelation 13 and Daniel 7 Identical.— After naming the four empires Bullinger declares that the time of the beast is 1260 days, forty-two months, or three and a half times, contending that these are not literal but prophetic time.[37] He reiterates that the Roman beast of Revelation 13 is the same as that of Daniel 7, that the seven heads are named as the seven hills as well as seven kings.[38] Then Bullinger elaborates on the Antichrist's appearing after the fourth empire is taken away,

---

[31] Bullinger, *A Hundred Sermons*, preface.
[33] *Ibid.*, sermon 6, p. 44.
[35] *Ibid.*, sermon 40, p. 265.
[37] *Ibid.*, sermon 47, pp. 314, 315.

[32] *Ibid.*, sermon 1, pp. 3-8, 12.
[34] *Ibid.*, sermon 10, p. 75.
[36] *Ibid.*, sermon 41, pp. 270-273.
[38] *Ibid.*, sermon 55, pp. 370, 371.

and the pope's transition from the simple pastor to the ruling bishop of Rome, about the time of Phocas, reaching the climax of power under Innocent III and Boniface VIII.[39] Arguing as to the number 666, whether a name or years, he concludes that it is years, from 97 to 763.[40]

5. FOLLOWS AUGUSTINE ON THE THOUSAND YEARS.—The angelic message of Revelation 14 symbolizes the preaching of the pure gospel, which is also declared in Matthew 24; and the fall of Babylon is the fall of the Papacy.[41] No attempt is made to list completely the ten horns supporting the Papacy in Revelation 17, but they must include Spain, France, and Hungary.[42] On the thousand years of Revelation 20, however, Bullinger still follows Augustine, and puts them either from 34 to 1034, from 60 to 1060, or from 73 to 1073; and the resurrection he spiritualizes away as the newness of life in the Christian's heart.[43]

6. GLORIOUS SECOND ADVENT TO DESTROY SINNERS.—Bullinger's clear view of the second advent appears often.

"At the second time he shall come gloriously to judgment, to be a judge and revenger that will not be entreated against all unrepentant sinners and wicked doers. And he shall come out of heaven, from the right hand of the Father, in his visible and very human body, to be seen of all flesh, with the incomprehensible power of his Godhead, and being attended on by all the angels." [44]

7. LITTLE HORN IS ROMAN KINGDOM OF POPE.—In his commentary on Daniel he is explicit that the Papacy is the Little Horn of chapter 7, which power begins to blossom forth under Gregory and Boniface:

"By the little horn many understand the kingdom of Mohammed, of the Saracens and of the Turks. . . . But when the apostolic prophecy in Second Thessalonians 2 is more carefully examined, it seems that this prophecy of Daniel and that prophecy of the apostle belong more rightly to the kingdom of the Roman pope, which kingdom has arisen from small beginnings and has increased to an immense size." [45]

---

[39] Ibid., sermon 58, pp. 386-389.   [40] Ibid., sermon 61, pp. 427-434.
[41] Ibid., sermon 63, pp. 445-454.   [42] Ibid., sermon 75, pp. 518, 519.
[43] Ibid., sermon 77, pp. 593, 594; and sermon 78, pp. 605, 606.
[44] Bullinger, Decades, decade 1, sermon 8, p. 152.
[45] Translated from Bullinger, Daniel Sapientissimus Dei Propheta (Daniel the Most Wise Prophet of God), chap. 7, fol. 78v.

8. SEVENTY WEEKS ARE DATED FROM 7TH OF ARTAXERXES.——
The seventy weeks, or 490 years, extending from the seventh
year of Artaxerxes to the death of Christ, are calculated by the
Olympiads:

"The computation of the seventy weeks, that is, of the 490 years, must
begin from the seventh year of Artaxerxes Longimanus and must extend
even to the year of the suffering and death of the Lord, which in one and
the same year was followed by the glorious resurrection, the ascension into
heaven, and the sending of the Holy Spirit upon the apostles, who went
into the whole world, and prepared a kingdom for Christ among all peoples
and nations. Therefore since we have already announced from what terminus the computation of the seventy weeks must be commenced, and
until when it must be extended, namely, from the seventh year of Artaxerxes Longimanus to the suffering and death of the Lord Jesus Christ, the
computation will now be easy and plain, certainly if we progress through
the Olympiads and through the years from the founding of the city. . . .
The seventh year of our Artaxerxes falls in the Eightieth Olympiad, year 2,
and in the year A.U.C. 294. Moreover, the death of the Lord, which I have
also indicated above, falls in the 18th year of Tiberius, that is, in the 4th
year of the 202d Olympiad, and in the year 784 of the founding of the
city." [46]

He gives no B.C. date, although his chronological tables
place the crucifixion in the year of Christ 33. A close inspection
reveals a discrepancy between text and tables which makes it
hard to determine whether he ends the period in 33 or 34, and
consequently whether he begins it in 458 or 457 B.C.[47]

VI. Stimmer Pictures Little Horn Surmounted by Pope's Triple Crown

TOBIAS STIMMER (1539-1584) was born in Schaffhausen,
Switzerland. His father, a teacher, made use of his artistic inclinations to illuminate books in his spare time. We have no
information concerning the education of Tobias or the early de-

[46] *Ibid.*, chap. 9, fol. 105v. He gives Olympiads 80.2 to 202.4, or A.U.C. 294 to 784.
[47] If Bullinger's "years of Christ" are true A.D. dates, as they seem to be, his other datings can be computed. His A.D. 1 is *anno mundi* 3970; he begins the first Olympiad in A.M. 3195,
and puts A.U.C. 1 in A.M. 3219, or 775 and 751 B.C. respectively (compare Funck's 775 B.C., referred to on page 430). His 70 weeks (A.M. 3512-4002) are, then, from 458 B.C. to A.D. 33—in
harmony with his tabulated ending date and his A.U.C. scale—although his Olympiad dates in the
text would actually require 457 B.C. to A.D. 34 if the Olympiad years were accurately placed to
take into account their midsummer beginning point. Bullinger's oversight on this point probably
accounts for the discrepancy, for men of his time relied on tables and had not worked out the
more exact details as in later times.

ILLUSTRATED EXPOSITIONS MAKE THEIR APPEARANCE

Virgil Solis, of Nürnberg, in 1560 Portrays the Four Prophetic World Empires of Daniel 7, Followed by the Fifth, Which "Antichrist Erects" (Upper); and Tobias Stimmer's Depiction, in 1576, of the Same Four Prophetic Beasts, Duly Named, and With the Triple Crown on the Roman Fourth (Lower). See Pages 314 and 347

velopment of his artistic talents. The first time we hear of him is in 1562. From his early style of painting one could probably draw the conclusion that he spent some time in Venice. From 1565 to 1570 he worked in his home town, where he became famous through a great fresco painting. Subsequently he was called to Strassburg to decorate the famous astronomical clock of the cathedral. Here in Strassburg, getting acquainted with the prominent printers of the time, as Fischart, Feyerabend of Frankfurt am Main, and Thomas Gwarin of Basel, he was inspired to attempt wood carving, and reached such perfection in this art that he contributed much to its last golden age.

His most significant contributions were his *New Artistic Illustrations of Scripture History*. These illustrations were so well done that even most brilliant painters in later times, like Rubens, liked to copy them and to learn from them.[48] For our purpose it is important to note how he handled the prophetic subjects. For instance, in Daniel 2 the prophet Daniel is portrayed as expounding to Nebuchadnezzar the meaning of the great image of Daniel 2, which is pictured, with the stone from the mountain prepared to smite the image, and the winds ready to carry away the chaff. Beneath is a descriptive caption concerning the four monarchies soon to be destroyed by the stone.

GRAPHIC CARTOONS OF FOUR POWERS OF DANIEL 7.—However, it is the portrayal of Daniel 7 that is expressive and typical of the Reformation position. The four beasts appear in a row, emerging from the sea of nations. The four winds are blowing upon the sea from angelic mouths. The names Assyria, Persia, Grecia, and Rome appear beneath the respective beasts. And among the ten horns of Rome, the Little Horn has emerged with a man's head upon it surmounted by the triple crown of the pope. The caption reads, "These explain the four world kingdoms." (Facsimile appears on page 346.) So by voice, pen, and graphic cartoon, the prophetic symbols of Daniel and the Apocalypse were presented in an ever-mounting total. And the empha-

---

[48] August Stolberg, *Tobias Stimmer, Sein Leben und seine Werke* (Tobias Stimmer, His Life and His Work), pp. 1-6.

sis was always on the Papacy as the Antichrist of the various prophetic symbols.

VII. Growing Concern Over End-Date of the 1260 Years

The Christian Era was now far advanced. It therefore became a matter of increasing concern with all expositors, in considering the probabilities of the future, to determine if possible the beginning and ending dates of the prophetic periods. This was especially true of the 1260 days, as their ending might well fix the great consummation. BENEDICTUS ARETIUS of Berne (1505-1574), teacher of theology at Marburg, reckons the 1260 years possibly from 312 (Constantine's legalization of Christianity) to 1572.[49] Not only the Swiss but practically all the German and English expositors held to the year-day principle except on the 2300 days. Chytraeus of Germany, for example, set forth two possible dates for the 1260 days—from 412 (Alaric's sack of Rome) to 1672, or from 606 (Phocas' decree) to 1866.[50] Others usually chose a single dating, or were less definite.

The significant feature in it all is that, irrespective of national or geographical variations or theological differences among the Reformed groups, similar views were held on the basic features of the symbolic outline prophecies, and increasingly so on the prophetic time periods. They generally felt that the bulk of the 1260 years was in the past. This was the consensus, but not for another century did their views come to a focus on the dates. For example, note two variant views:

1. BROCARDO PLACES 1260 YEARS BETWEEN 313-1573.— JACOBO BROCARDO (James Brocard) (16th century), Italian Protestant of Venice, was reputed to be of "a visionary turn" because he sought to show that the principal events of his time had been predicted in the Bible. Writing on Bible prophecy, he contended that the 1260 years of papal tyranny extended from 313 to 1573.[51]

---

[49] Benedictus Aretius, *Commentarii in Apocalypsin*, p. 250; Elliott, *op. cit.*, vol. 4, p. 442.
[50] See pp. 329-332.
[51] James Brocard, *The Revelation of St. John Revealed*, fol. 110v.

2. DANEAU MAKES NO ATTEMPT TO LOCATE PERIOD.—LAM-
BERT DANEAU (*c.* 1530-1595), Protestant jurisconsult and theologian, and pastor at Geneva, in his tract on the Antichrist, likewise contends that Antichrist is the pope, not Mohammed, with
Rome as his seat, and that he appears only after the fall of
Rome.[52] He does not locate the 1260 years, but applies 666 to the
time when the Roman bishop reached the peak of his power,
which he places at 666 years after John's prophecy, or, allowing
for differences in computation, in A.D. 666, followed by the thousand years of Revelation 20, from 666 to 1666.[53] Thus he breaks
somewhat with Augustine. He appends the attacks of Bernard of
Cluny, Petrarch, and others on the apostate condition of the
papal church.[54]

---

[52] Lambert Daneau, *Tractatus de Antichristo*, pp. 52, 62-64, 80-82.
[53] *Ibid.*, pp. 87-89, 95-98.
[54] *Ibid.*, appendix following p. 172. (Derived from Flacius, *Catalogus Testium Veritatem.*)

CHAPTER SIXTEEN

English Martyrs
Nerved for Stake by Prophecies

I. English Reform Movement Differs From Continental

1. REFORMED CHURCHES ESTABLISHED IN SEPARATION FROM ROME.—The Protestant Reformation took place in stages during a period of about a century. The commencement is usually reckoned from October 31, 1517, when Luther posted on the Wittenberg church door his theses against indulgences. In Germany its close is dated from the Peace of Augsburg, in 1555, which confirmed Protestantism in its rights and possessions, recognizing complete national and ecclesiastical independence from the pope. In England many place it from the full establishment of the Protestant church under Queen Elizabeth, about 1563.

The Reformation was more than a spiritual formation of the Protestant church. It was more than a spiritual revival, for it brought into being a new ecclesiastical system, establishing the Reformed churches in separation from Rome—national churches, in some cases with secular monarchs at the head. It was a movement of renovation and liberation, spreading in ever-widening circles, from the individual to the group, then to the church, and finally to the nation.

Because of the terrific papal reaction, the struggle to maintain the position gained, occupied a much longer period in Central Europe, extending beyond the Peace of Westphalia in 1648. In France and England it extended till the close of the seventeenth century, when it was settled in favor of Catholicism in France by the Revocation of the Edict of Nantes, and in favor of Protestantism in England by the act which excluded papal monarchs from the throne.

2. Reformation Tide Alternates in Four Successive Reigns.—For a clear picture of the English Reformation it is essential to bear in mind four successive royal reigns, in which the tide of Reformation favor ebbed and flowed alternately. These are:

1. Henry VIII (1509-1547), a Romanist at heart, breaking with Rome over the divorce issue.
2. Protestant Edward VI (1547-1553), son of Henry VIII by Jane Seymour.
3. Catholic "Bloody" Mary (I), or Mary Tudor (1553-1558), daughter of Henry VIII by Catherine of Aragon.
4. Protestant Elizabeth I (1558-1603), daughter of Henry VIII by Anne Boleyn.[1]

It was under Edward VI that Protestantism made its great strides, but the Roman Catholic resurgence under Mary produced that storm period during which the exile of so many Protestant leaders to the Continent took place. Many others— Latimer, Ridley, Hooper, Philpot, Cranmer, et cetera—perished in the fierce fires of Smithfield, and other places. Then, upon Mary's death, the return of the exiles began. The reaction from Mary's persecutions did more to establish the Reformation than the favors of her predecessors.[2] A carefully detailed dating of the events in the lives of the English Reformers will be followed, for only by comparing these years with the ebb and flow of Reformation fortunes under these four monarchs, will the picture assume its true and significant pattern. See medals on page 556.)

3. Two Hundred Perish at Smithfield for Their Faith. —At Smithfield some two hundred persons perished at the stake for religious conviction during a brief four years. In February,

---

[1] Albert Hyma, *Europe From the Renaissance to 1815*, pp. 133-135.
[2] Pennington, *op. cit.*, p. 328.

1555, John Rogers and John Bradford, prebendaries of **St.** Paul's, and John Philpot, archdeacon of Winchester, were led from prison past friends and families to the stake to die rather than to surrender their Protestant faith based on the evangelic and prophetic Scriptures. An impressive memorial tablet marks the place, and the Smithfield Martyrs Memorial Church, not far away, was built in remembrance of sixty-six of the most prominent. The interior walls bear mural scrolls, tabulating the names of these martyrs, the alleged offenses, and the names of the monarchs under whom they suffered. On the outside life-sized figures in stone depict in relief the martyrdoms in progress—portraying John Rogers, Anne Askew, and others. (Illustrations appear on page 359).

Anne Askew, for example, daughter of a Lincolnshire knight, had been in the habit of visiting the cathedral daily, reading there the open Bible in English which, in 1538, Henry VIII had commanded to be placed in all the churches. Anne had been cast out of her home by her Catholic husband because of her deep-rooted religious belief in the Protestant faith. She was finally arrested and put in the Tower of London, and there subjected to the excruciating torture of the rack. On July 16, 1546, suffering from extreme weakness as a result of her tortures, she was carried in a chair to Smithfield, tied with a harsh metal chain to a stake which was surrounded by fagots at the bottom, and under which gunpowder had been placed, and was executed there along with three other Protestants. She was then only about twenty-five years old and the mother of two young children.[3]

On the bench sat the lord chancelor, the duke of Norfolk, the earl of Bedford, and the lord mayor of London to witness the tragedy. The lord bishop of Salisbury was deputed to admonish the victims. After a sermon and prayers, which disturbed the titled spectators, the lord chancelor endeavored to get Anne to recant; but she refused to deny her Lord and Master. So the

---

[3] Geikie, *op. cit.*, pp. 387-391.

order for firing the fagots was given. Scenes such as this helped produce the Protestant reaction in the short reign of Edward VI (1547-1553). But again, in the reign of Bloody Mary, the fires were rekindled (1553-1558) when Bradford and Philpot were burned.

4. Movement Energized and Guided by Prophetic Word. —From the very first, and throughout the Reformation century, the movement was energized and aided by the prophetic Word. Luther never thought of separating from Rome until the pope had given him sufficient reason to recognize in him the predicted Antichrist. The Reformers embodied their prophetic interpretation of Antichrist in their confessions of faith. In this they were united and assured. It determined their reformatory action, and led them to protest against Rome with undaunted courage. It nerved them to resist her claims to the utmost. It made them martyrs, and sustained them at the stake. Moreover, these views were shared by hundreds and thousands.

5. Prophetic Emphasis All Centers About Antichrist.— The fact is conspicuous, and well-nigh universal among English Reformers, that prophetic emphasis now centers on those portions of prophecy dealing with the supremacy and decline of the Papacy as the predicted Antichrist of Daniel, Jesus, Paul, and John—just as in the early centuries it was focused on Rome as the fourth prophetic empire, next upon Rome's division, and then upon the impending Antichrist that had not yet been identified. And now, as in Roman days, a great cluster of witnesses in various countries—Germany, Switzerland, England, France, Scandinavia, and the Low Countries—were giving the same emphasis. It is one of those clear evidences of the trend of the times, and was a fundamental part of the Reformation message.

6. Why Educational and Ecclesiastical Attainments Are Noted.—The educational and ecclesiastical achievements of prophetic interpreters are rather uniformly cited, not to laud scholastic degrees and churchly office, but to show that the leaders in evangelical and prophetic reform were among the most

12

highly trained, capable, and brilliant men that the realm afforded—leaders and molders of thought, keen scholars, and in sheer ability the peers of any of their opposers. The witnesses will appear in chronological sequence, for this will best unfold the developing picture.[4]

II. Tyndale—Centers Emphasis on Pope as Antichrist

WILLIAM TYNDALE *(c.* 1484-1536), Reformer, first translator of the Bible from Greek into English, and martyr, was born near the border of Wales. Educated at Oxford, where he secretly studied the Scriptures, and at Cambridge, he came under the influence of Erasmus' classes in Greek, and above all, of his Greek Testament. Tyndale's conversion through the Scriptures to the doctrines of Wyclif and Luther precipitated numerous disputes with Roman Catholics, in which Tyndale used his Greek Testament effectively. In one of these discussions Tyndale declared that if God would spare his life, ere many years he "would cause a boy that driveth the plow" to know more of the Scripture than did the papal doctor with whom he was disputing.[5]

This stirred the animosity of the Catholics, and the cry of heresy was raised. How to establish the people in truth without the Bible in their mother tongue, Tyndale could not see. This brought to him the sublime conviction that he must translate the New Testament into English. So he began his task. But he soon declared that not only was there "no room in my lord of London's palace to translate the New Testament, but also . . . there was no place to do it in all England." [6] Tyndale tried to preach in London, where he had come intent on translating, but a storm of persecution arose.

---

[4] The documentation for the English Reformers in these chapters will be largely drawn from the Parker Society reprint (over 50 volumes) of the entire printed works of the English Reformers of the sixteenth century, who "flourished in the age of the Roman yoke." The Parker Society set, published by the Cambridge University Press between 1841 and 1855, was stimulated by the Romeward trend of the Oxford Movement. This reprint so alarmed Roman Catholics that it led them to attempt establishment of a counter-society for the republishing of Catholic writings of the period.
[5] "Biographical Notice," William Tyndale, *Works,* vol. 1 *(Doctrinal Treatises* [etc.]), p. xix. 1858; Christopher Wordsworth, *Ecclesiastical Biography,* vol. 2, p. 193.
[6] Tyndale, *Works,* vol. 1, pp. xx, xxii; M'Clintock and Strong, *op. cit.,* vol. 10, p. 607, art. "Tyndale."

Friends urged Tyndale to retire. So he repaired to Germany, never to see his native land again. Arrived in Hamburg, he unpacked his precious Greek Testament and resumed his task. Later he went on to Cologne, where he began to print his New Testament, the Gospels of Matthew and Mark being sent first to England separately. Interrupted by opposers, he took the sheets and completed the task at Worms and Antwerp. Thousands of copies were smuggled into England, where they were vigorously combated by the ecclesiastical authorities.

In 1526 Cardinal Wolsey had ordered Luther's books burned. On the occasion St. Paul's was packed to the doors. During the sermon the great bonfire was kindled outside, and the books burned. But copies of Tyndale's Testament came into England "thick and fast"; the fifth edition issued from Antwerp in 1529, and the sale was rapid on the Continent. The University of Louvain thirsted for his blood, and there were frequent burnings of Tyndale's works in London. But in 1534 there was a new and improved edition of his Testament, which was later incorporated in Coverdale's Bible.

In the same year Tyndale, whose writings had previously been denounced by the English Government, was betrayed by an English acquaintance, Henry Philips, an agent of his enemies in England, and was seized at Antwerp by the authorities of Brussels in the name of the emperor. After about seventeen months of protracted imprisonment and trial for heresy he was strangled and burned at the stake near Brussels in Flanders, on October 6, 1536, praying, "Lord, open the eyes of the King of England." [7]

1. Stresses Literalism; Repudiates Origen's Allegorism. —In his interpretation of the Scriptures, Tyndale stressed the literal sense, declaring that the blindness of past centuries sprang from the allegorizing of Origen.[8] Tyndale believed the first resurrection to be literal, and looked for God's kingdom to be

---

[7] Geikie, *op. cit.*, p. 299.
[8] Tyndale, *The Obedience of a Christian Man*, in *Works*, vol. 1, p. 307.

established by Christ's second coming, for which he longed.[9]

2. CENTERS EMPHASIS ON POPE AS ANTICHRIST.—Tyndale himself did not set a sharp pattern of prophetic interpretation that others followed in England. Luther had done that for all Protestantism, influencing not only Germany but Switzerland, England, Scandinavia, and even France. Like all the English Reformers that followed him—Barnes, Joye, Latimer, Ridley, Hooper, Philpot, Bradford, Cranmer, Becon, Bale, Jewel, Sandys, et cetera—Tyndale held that the Roman church was Babylon, the pope the Man of Sin, or Antichrist, seated in the temple of God, i.e., the church, and to be destroyed at the approaching second advent. In these features there is impressive unity and cumulative force among all English Reformers.

The marginal cross references and wood cuts in Tyndale's illustrated Bible of 1550 were borrowed from Luther's Bible, which provided the standard Protestant prophetic exposition of the Continent. For instance, the standard Luther woodcut illustration of the ten-horned first beast of Revelation 13 is given, and the marginal references definitely connect this beast-symbol with "Apoc. 17" and "Dan. 7." And in Apocalypse 17 the cross references are similarly to "Apoc. 13" and "Dan. 7."

The term *Antichrist* and its strong equivalent terms—the *Man of Sin, Mystery of Iniquity, Babylon,* and *Whore of Babylon,* applied to the Papacy as the prophetic designation—occur constantly throughout Tyndale's writings.[10] One citation will illustrate:

"And [they] have set up that great idol, the whore of Babylon, antichrist of Rome, whom they call pope; and have conspired against all commonwealths, and have made them a several kingdom, wherein it is lawful, unpunished, to work all abomination." [11]

3. APPLIES PROPHESIED NAMES TO PAPACY.—The prophetic basis for such epithets is likewise repeatedly stressed. Paul, in

---

[9] Tyndale, *An Answer to Sir Thomas More's Dialogue,* book 2, chap. 8, in *Works,* vol. 3 (*An Answer to Sir Thomas More's Dialogue* [etc.]), p. 118.
[10] Tyndale, *The Obedience of a Christian Man,* in *Works,* vol. 1, pp. 147, 185, 188, 208, 311; *The Exposition of the First Epistle of Saint John,* in *Works,* vol. 2 (*Expositions and Notes* [etc.]), pp. 179, 183; *An Answer to Sir Thomas More's Dialogue,* in *Works,* vol. 3, p. 102 ("a sure token that the pope is Antichrist").
[11] Tyndale, *The Obedience of a Christian Man,* in *Works,* vol. 1, p. 191.

2 Thessalonians 2, is cited again and again—the apostasy coming and destroying faith, and sitting in the temple of God, demanding the obedience and worship of men.[12] With this was connected the predicted false teachers of 2 Peter 2 and the false prophets foretold in Matthew 24.[13] Of the specifications of Paul, in 1 Timothy 4, Tyndale says:

"The pope's forbidding matrimony, and to eat of meats created of God for man's use, which is devilish doctrine by Paul's prophecy, . . . are tokens good enough that he is the right antichrist, and his doctrine sprung of the devil." [14]

4. DECLARES CHRIST AND ANTICHRIST TO BE CONTRARIES.—In discussing John's declaration concerning Antichrist (1 John 2:18), upon connecting it with Paul's and Peter's prophecies, and declaring "antichrist and Christ are two contraries," Tyndale makes this clear statement of the historical development:

"The apostles were clear-eyed, and espied antichrist at once, and put him to flight, and weeded out his doctrine quickly. But when charity waxed cold, and the preachers began to seek themselves, and to admit glory and honour of riches, then antichrist disguised himself after the fashion of a true apostle, and preached Christ wilily, bringing in now this tradition, and now that, to darken the doctrine of Christ; and set up innumerable ceremonies, and sacraments, and imagery, giving them significations at the first; but at the last, the significations laid apart, preached the work as an holy deed, to justify and to put away sin, and to save the soul, that men should put their trust in works, and in whatsoever was unto his glory and profit; and under the name of Christ ministered Christ out of all together, and became head of the congregation himself.

"The bishop of Rome made a law of his own, to rule his church by, and put Christ's out of the way. All the bishops swear unto the bishop of Rome, and all curates unto the bishops; but all forswear Christ and his doctrine.

"But seeing John took a sign of the last day, that he saw antichrist begin, how nigh ought we to think that it is, which, after eight hundred years reigning in prosperity, see it decay again, and his falsehood to be disclosed, and him to be slain with the spirit of the mouth of Christ." [15]

Then this conclusion is reached:

"Now though the bishop of Rome and his sects give Christ these names, yet in that they rob him of the effect, and take the significations of his

---

[12] Tyndale, *The Obedience of a Christian Man,* in *Works,* vol. 1, pp. 215, 287.
[13] Tyndale, *An Answer to Sir Thomas More's Dialogue,* in *Works,* vol. 3, pp. 102-104.
[14] *Ibid.,* p. 171.
[15] Tyndale, *The Exposition of the First Epistle of St. John,* in *Works,* vol. 2, pp. 179, 180.

names unto themselves, and make of him but an hypocrite, as they themselves be, they be the right antichrists, and deny both the Father and Son." [16]

5. Gives Historical Tracement of Papal Primacy.—In Tyndale's *The Practice of Prelates* (1530), the historical development of the ultimate primacy of the bishop of Rome is given in accurate detail—the earlier great bishoprics; then "those decaying, Constantinople and Rome waxed great, and strove who should be greater." [17] The continued struggle for supremacy is pictured, and "at the last there came an emperor called Phocas," at the time that the ambitious Boniface III was bishop of Rome, and to whom he gave the coveted title of "chiefest of all bishops." [18] Then it was that the pope "exalted his throne above his fellows." Passing the episodes of Pepin and Charlemagne, which further extended the pope's power century by century, Tyndale presents the startling conclusion that "the pope, after he had received the kingdom of the world of the devil, and was become the devil's vicar," had indeed fallen down to worship him, after Lucifer had showed and offered him all the kingdoms of the world. [19]

III. Barnes Burned for Rejection of the Papal Chaff

Robert Barnes (d. 1540), martyr of Smithfield, specializing in the ancient languages, was educated at the universities of Cambridge and Louvain, receiving the D.D. degree from the latter. Then he went back to Cambridge, where he was made prior, and master of the house of the Augustines. Intensively studying Paul's epistles, he became famous as a preacher. The godly and learned flocked to hear him in sermon and disputation. [20] Barnes was one of the early converts to Luther's doctrines, and there were frequent private meetings of friends for study of the new faith.

Barnes' enemies, however, soon accused him of heresy before the vice-chancelor, and the search was made for Luther's

---

[16] *Ibid.*, p. 183.
[17] Tyndale, *The Practice of Prelates*, in *Works*, vol. 2, p. 257.
[18] *Ibid.*, p. 258.   [19] *Ibid.*, p. 274.
[20] Foxe, *Acts*, vol. 2, pp. 435, 436.

SMITHFIELD MARTYRS DIE FOR PROPHETIC FAITH

Robert Barnes, and Companions, Burned at Smithfield Stake for Identifying Antichrist (Upper Left); Oxford Martyrs' Memorial (Upper Right); Tablet Marking Scene of Numerous Smithfield Burnings, Near London (Lower Left); and Smithfield Memorial Martyrs' Church, London (Lower Right) ; Discussion on Pages 352 and 366

books and Lollard writings. Conflict continued for some time. Then Barnes was arrested and taken to London. With him were numerous other suspects. Disputations, threatenings, and imprisonment went on for months, Barnes abjuring certain minor points. Fearing violence, he escaped and fled to Antwerp and then to Germany, where he made contact with Luther. While there he wrote *Acta Romanorum Pontificum* (Acts of the Roman Pontiffs), and his faith was strengthened by conferring with Luther, Melanchthon, Justus Jonas, and others. Bishop Fox found him there and recommended him to Thomas Cromwell. He was later sent as the king's representative to Schmalkalden.

Returning to England, Barnes was once more apprehended, when Roman influence was revived. With Garret and Jerome, likewise Protestant clergymen, he was induced to preach three sermons which were secretly reported and used against him. And with these same men he was taken to the Tower, from which he never emerged until taken out for his execution.

Two days after Thomas Cromwell's death, in 1540,[21] the three were taken to Smithfield. Praying together, they declared their faith and spoke plainly to the people. Then they kissed one another farewell. All were tied to one stake, and suffered without crying out—though condemned without formal trial or due process of law.[22] They prayed on until the fire silenced them. Luther publicized an account of this martyrdom. A graphic picture of the three men appears in *The Workes of Doctour Barnes* (London: Daye, 1572)—the curious crowd, the bundles of branches and lighted fagots, with soldiers and monks in the foreground and royalty peering from the windows of the building in the rear.

1. DECLARES ANTICHRIST REIGNS UNDER NAME OF CHRIST. —Regrettably, not all of Barnes' writings have been preserved. But one sermon—"That all men are bounde to receiue the holy Communion vnder Both Kyndes"—has this statement:

---

[21] Within a short time, hundreds of persons were imprisoned for their faith, including two bishops.

[22] Geikie, *op. cit.*, pp. 354, 355; Mosheim, *op. cit.*, vol. 3, pp. 150, 151n.

"But now seeyng that they will doe the open deedes of Antechrist, they must bee content that I may also geve them his name. And that all the world may openly know, y Antechrist doth raine in the world (yea and that under the name of Christ)." [23]

2. SHOWS SCRIPTURE OUTBALANCES DREGS OF ANTICHRIST.— In this same work a graphic cartoon contrasts the weight of God's Word as against the chaff of papal tradition, and Justice holds the balances. The pope is loading the high end of the balance with bulls, decretals, crosses, and rosaries. A monk tries to even the balance beam with his hands, and the devil himself attaches his weight in vain to the elevated pan. The legend reads:

"How light is chaffe of Popish toyes, if thou desire to trye,
Loe Justice holdes true beame without respect of partiall eye:
One ballance holdes Gods holy word, and on the other parte,
Is layde the dregs of Antichrist, devisde by Popish arte:
Let Friers and Nunnes and baldpate Priestes, with triple crowne of pope,
The Cardinals hatt, and devill him selfe, by force plucke downe the rope:
Bryng bell, booke, candle, crosse, & beades, and mitred Basan bull,
Bryng buls of leade and Popes Decrees, the ballance downe to pull:
Yet shall these tares and filthy dregs, invented by mans brayne,
Through force of Gods most mighty word, be found both light and vayne." [24]

IV. Joye—Systematic Exposition of Daniel's Symbols and Periods

GEORGE JOYE (d. 1553), expositor and associate of Tyndale, was born in Bedfordshire and educated at Peterhouse, Cambridge, receiving his M.A. in 1517. Accused of Reformed heresy in 1527, he was obliged to go to Germany, where he resided for several years. He assisted Tyndale in the translation of his Bible, and then superintended its printing in Antwerp. He was the author of several works, prominent among which was *On the Unity and Schism of the Ancient Church* (1534), and his systematic *Exposition of Daniel* (1545 and 1550). The latter was largely gleaned from Melanchthon's and Oecolampadius' teachings, but printed before either of their expositions was pub-

---

[23] *The Workes of Doctour Barnes*, p. 301, in *The Whole Workes of W. Tyndall, John Frith, and Doct. Barnes* [etc.].
[24] *Ibid.*, closing page.

lished, in 1546 and 1567 respectively. He also translated Andreas Osiander's *Conjectures of the Ende of the Worlde* (1545) in 1548.

1. HOLDS EVERLASTING KINGDOM FOLLOWS DIVISION OF ROME.—Joye's chapter-by-chapter "Exposycion" of Daniel, according to the title page, is "diligentely to be noted of al Emperours & Kinges, in these laste dayes." The prophecy of the four monarchies of Daniel 2 witnesses that "in the ende of the world the everlasting kingdom of ye faithful" shall be established.[25]

The standard listing of the empires is given—with the "Romayn empyre," as the fourth division, dispersed and decayed into "Germanye, Englande, Spayne, France," et cetera, these "shalbe mixt together, but yet shall they not cleave," either by confederations or blood affinities. "They shalbe confedered to make a newe and all one Monarchie, but all in vayne."

2. DECLARES LITTLE HORN IS KINGDOM OF POPE.—In chapter 7 the "iiii great beastes" are the same four kingdoms, and the ten horns the divisions of Rome—"Italy, Spayne, France, Germany," et cetera. Of the "lyttle horne," Joye is explicit:

"This lyttle horne was, & is the Antichristes kingdom of the popes of Rome, with al their unclene clargye." [26]

John, in Revelation 13 and 17 and 1 John 2, and Paul, in 2 Thessalonians 2, are cited as setting forth one and the same power. The Roman Empire had held back the emergence of Antichrist. Expanding on Revelation 13, Joye says, "The x. horned beast ascending out of the sea, is the spiritual Antichryst of Rome" with all his "lawes, rytes, tradicions, decrees and doctryne." Reverting to Daniel 7, Joye expands on the plucking up of the three kingdoms, and on the Papacy's lawless character.[27]

3. PERSIAN RAM, GRECIAN GOAT, AND 70 HEBDOMADS.— Coming to chapter 8, with Babylonia at an end, Joye discusses the Persian "Ram" and the Grecian "Gote," with the notable horn signifying Alexander.[28] Then in chapter 9 he deals with the

---

[25] George Joye, *The Exposycion of Daniel the Prophete*, chap. 2.
[26] *Ibid.*, chap. 7.   [27] *Ibid.*   [28] *Ibid.*, chap. 8.

70 hebdomads and their three divisions as weeks of years. After referring to some as beginning the period with the second year of Darius, he states he inclined to begin them with Cyrus.[29]

4. INCREASED KNOWLEDGE OF PROPHECY AND 1290 YEARS.— Antichrist is also brought into Daniel 11 and 12. On Daniel 12:4 the increase of knowledge is of the prophecies, and comes from reading the book of Daniel—"diligently often studied and labored." And the 1290 days are interpreted as 1290 years, to end in the not distant future.[30]

V. Henry VIII Prohibits English Bibles and Prophetic Expositions

On July 8, 1546, King Henry VIII made a "Proclamation for the Abolishing of English Books," making it unlawful for anyone to "receive, have, take or keep in his or their possession," Tyndale's or Coverdale's English translation of the New Testament, or any book by Tyndale, Wyclif, Joye, Roy, Basil, Turner, Tracy, Frith, Bale, Barnes, or Coverdale bearing upon the prophetic identification of Antichrist, but were to deliver them over for burning.[31]

In the forbidden list, significantly enough, is the record of the "Acts of the Disputation in the council of the Empire at Regensburg," the council where, in 1240, Archbishop Eberhard of Salzburg first applied the Little Horn prophecy to the historical Papacy, coming up among the divisions of the Roman Empire.[32] There was also Joye's translation of the *Exposition of Daniel* by Melanchthon and others, *A Brief Chronicle* concerning the death of Sir John Oldcastle for identifying the Papacy as the Antichrist of prophecy, Bale's treatises on prophecy, and the *Lantern of Light*, the old Lollard tract. There was a total of about ninety prohibited works.[33]

It is therefore apparent that this effort was largely directed

---

[29] *Ibid.*, chap. 9.   [30] *Ibid.*, chap. 12 (1545 ed.).
[31] Given in full in Foxe, *Acts*, vol. 2, pp. 496, 497.
[32] See Volume I of *Prophetic Faith*.
[33] A complete list appears in the Cattley edition of *The Acts and Monuments of John Foxe*, vol. 5, pp. 566-568.

against prophetic interpretation with the disconcerting pressure that it was exerting in the battle between Protestantism and Catholicism.

VI—Ridley Burned for Repudiation of Papal Antichrist

NICHOLAS RIDLEY (c. 1500-1555), famed English martyr, was born in Northumberland. Beginning his higher education in Pembroke College, he went on to the University of Cambridge, then to the Sorbonne in Paris, and to the University of Louvain in Belgium. Impelled ever onward by a thirst for knowledge, he followed a steadily rising university career, becoming a fellow of Cambridge in 1524, then receiving his M.A. in 1526, his B.D. in 1534, and his D.D. in 1540. He was made senior proctor of the university (charged with maintaining discipline) in 1533, master of Pembroke Hall in 1540, and rector of Soham in 1547. But Ridley also gained fame as a preacher who gave great attention to Scripture, especially to the Greek, committing to memory almost all the epistles in Greek. He wrote numerous works.[34]

In 1534, when Ridley was proctor of Cambridge, the question of the pope's supremacy came before the university to be examined by Scripture. The decision was that the bishop of Rome had no authority and jurisdiction derived from God over the kingdom of England, more than any other foreign bishop. This decree against papal supremacy was signed by the vice-chancelor, and by proctors Ridley and Wilkes.[35]

Appointed as domestic chaplain to Cranmer in 1537, Ridley was progressively vicar of Herne in 1538, chaplain to Henry VIII in 1540, canon of Canterbury in 1541, and canon of Westminster in 1545. In 1547, after Henry's death, he became bishop of Rochester, and in 1550 was made bishop of London. About 1545 Ridley renounced the doctrine of transubstantiation, and during the reign of Edward VI (1547-1553) he was very active in pro-

---

[34] A list of Ridley's various works appears in *The Works of Nicholas Ridley, D.D.*, Preface, pp. xii-xvi, and Christopher Wordsworth, *op. cit.*, vol. 3, pp. 12-14.
[35] M'Clintock and Strong, *op. cit.*, vol. 9, p. 25, art. "Ridley, Nicholas."

moting his Reformed views. He was deputed to set forth the doctrines of the Reformation in York, Durham, and other dioceses, and about 1549 to place Protestantism on a firm basis at Cambridge. In 1551, as bishop of London, he assisted Cranmer in composing the Forty-one Articles of Faith. Ridley attempted to convert Princess Mary and offered to preach in her presence, but Mary took offense at his visit and offer.[36]

Upon her accession to the throne Mary I, or Bloody Mary (1553-1558), had Ridley arrested and committed to the Tower of London. In 1554 he was removed, along with Cranmer and Latimer, to Bocardo jail at Oxford for a time. Ridley there took part in an open disputation on the questions dividing Protestants from Roman Catholics. And in 1555 he was ordered to stand trial before the Divinity School of Oxford, where he was declared a heretic.[37]

1. MAKES ISSUE OF SEPARATION FROM ANTICHRIST.— The utter incompatibility of Christ and Antichrist was the theme of one of the recorded conferences between Ridley and Latimer. The unequivocal necessity of separation from Rome was apparent. In their second conference these words from Latimer are recorded:

"Yea, what fellowship hath Christ with Antichrist? Therefore is it not lawful to bear the yoke with papists. 'Come forth from among them, and separate yourselves from them, saith the Lord.' "[38]

2. CHOOSES DEATH RATHER THAN ACCEPT ROME.—Promised life if he would recant, Ridley replied, "So long as the breath is in my body, I will never deny my Lord Christ, and his known truth."[39] During his last examination, in September, 1555, before the queen's commissioners, Ridley said: "'I acknowledge in no point that usurped supremacy of Rome, and

[36] The important conversation between Mary and Ridley appears in Christopher Wordsworth, *op. cit.*, vol. 3, pp. 12-14, and in Ridley, *Works*, Preface, pp. x, xi.
[37] The record of the disputation on the Lord's supper at Oxford, in April, 1555, likewise appears in Foxe, *Acts*, vol. 3, pp. 50 ff, and in Ridley, *Works*, pp. 189-252.
[38] "Conferences . . . Between Nicholas Ridley and Hugh Latimer," in Ridley, *Works*, p. 124.
[39] "The Order and Manner of the Examination of Dr. Ridley," in Ridley, *Works*, p. 295.

therefore contemn and utterly despise all authority coming from him.' " [40]

And in the course of his masterful response Ridley denied the primacy of Peter and the apostolic succession of the Roman bishopric, sustaining his positions from Scripture and history.[41]

Because of his beliefs, Ridley was degraded from his ecclesiastical position the day before he suffered death by fire. On the day of his death, upon reaching the place of execution, he kissed the stake by which he was to suffer for his Master.[42] He attempted to reply to the brief papal sermon, but the bailiffs and the vice-chancelor ran and stopped Ridley's mouth with their hands. As the flames were slow in doing their work, again and again Ridley cried, "Let the fire come unto me; I can not burn." His lower members burned first, the end coming when the fire reached a bag of gunpowder that his brother-in-law had tied about his neck.[43] Those were tremendous times, when one's prophetic faith often meant death. (See Martyrs' Monument, page 359.)

3. IDENTIFIES ANTICHRIST AS "BABYLONICAL BEAST" OF ROME.—In his *Piteous Lamentation*, Ridley gives perhaps the clearest declaration of his prophetic identification of the Papacy. Asserting that Rome "hath bewitched almost the whole world," he says:

"The head, under Satan, of all mischief is Antichrist and his brood; and the same is he which is the Babylonical beast. The beast is he whereupon the whore sitteth. The whore is that city, saith John in plain words, which hath empire over the kings of the earth. This whore hath a golden cup of abominations in her hand, whereof she maketh to drink the kings of the earth, and of the wine of this harlot all nations hath drunk; yea, and kings of the earth have lain by this whore; and merchants of the earth, by virtue of her pleasant merchandise, have been made rich.

"Now what city is there in the whole world, that when John wrote, ruled over the kings of the earth; or what city can be read of in any time, that of the city itself challenged the empire over the kings of the earth, but only the city of Rome, and that since the usurpation of that See hath grown to her full strength? And is it not read, that old and ancient writers under-

---

[40] *Ibid.*, p. 258.   [41] *Ibid.*, pp. 255-291.   [42] *Ibid.*, pp. 294-297.
[43] *Ibid.*, pp. 297, 298. Foxe also gives a complete account of his life and martyrdom. On the burning of Ridley and Latimer, see Guy C. Lee, *op. cit.*, pp. 293-297.

stood Peter's former Epistle to be written at Rome, and it to be called of him in the same Epistle, in plain terms, Babylon! By the abominations thereof, I understand all the whole trade of the Romish religion, under the name and title of Christ, which is contrary to the only rule of all true religion, that is God's word." [44]

4. SAYS MARK OF BEAST INVOLVES ALLEGIANCE TO BEAST.— Declaring that "the abomination that Daniel prophesied of so long before, is now set up in the holy place," Ridley appeals to men to flee out of her. Citing the call of Revelation 18 and 1 Corinthians 6 to come out, he understood this to be to flee out of "the realm." [45] On the mark of the beast he made this observation:

"Wherefore what I suppose is to bear the beast's mark, I will tell thee, and commit the judgment of mine interpretation, as in all other things, to the spiritual man. I suppose he beareth the beast of Babylon's mark in his forehead, which is not ashamed of the beast's ways, but will profess them openly to set forth his master the beast Abaddon. And likewise he beareth his mark in his hand, that will and doth practise the works of the beast with his power and hand." [46]

5. TELLS OF MARKED MEN OF THE BEAST.—In speaking of the beast's "marked" men, Ridley states clearly that this is a spiritual relationship and not a physical mark:

"Thus I suppose these prophecies are spiritually to be understood: and to look for other corporal marks, to be seen in men's foreheads, or in their hands, is nothing else but to look that there should come some brute beast out of Babylon, or some elephant, leopard, lion, or camel, or some other such monstrous beast with ten horns, that should do all the wonderful things spoken in John; and yet of a beast speaketh John; but I understand him so to be called, not for that he shall be any such brute beast, but for that he is and shall be the child of perdition, which for his cruelty and beastly manners is well called a beast." [47]

6. LAST FAREWELL WARNS AGAINST SHARING ANTICHRIST'S FATE.—Ridley's last Farewell (in letter 32) before his martyrdom on October 16, 1555, is a moving message. Bidding good-by to his wife, brothers, sisters, kinsfolk, and countrymen, the Cambridge Cathedral church, and London, and giving a review of his faith and his life, he showed how the Papacy was centuries in develop-

---

[44] Ridley, *A Piteous Lamentation of the Miserable Estate of the Church in England, in the Time of the Late Revolt from the Gospel,* in *Works,* p. 53.
[45] *Ibid.,* pp. 63-65.   [46] *Ibid.,* p. 69.   [47] *Ibid.,* p. 70.

ing, that it had "set up another religion, hath exercised another power, and hath taken upon it to order and rule the church of Christ by other strange laws, canons, and rules." Then he declared in the strong language of the time:

"The see is the seat of Satan; and the bishop of the same, that maintaineth the abominations thereof, is antichrist himself indeed. And for the same causes this see at this day is the same which St. John calleth in his Revelation Babylon, or the whore of Babylon, and spiritually Sodoma and Egyptus, the mother of fornications and of the abominations upon the earth." [48]

"This whore of Babylon and the beast whereupon she doth sit maintaineth at this day with all violence of fire and sword, with spoil and banishment (according to Daniel's prophecy), and finally with all falsehood, deceit, hypocrisy, and all kind of ungodliness—are as clean contrary to God's word as darkness is unto light, or light to darkness, white to black, or black to white, or as Belial unto Christ, or Christ unto antichrist himself." [49]

"The whore of Babylon may well for a time dally with you, and make you so drunk with the wine of her filthy stews and whoredom (as with her dispensations and promises of pardon a poena et culpa), that for drunkenness and blindness ye may think yourselves safe. But be ye assured, . . . the living Lord shall try the matter by the fire, and judge it according to his word. . . . For he that is partner with them in their whoredom and abominations, must also be partner with them of their plagues, and on the latter day shall be thrown with them into the lake burning with brimstone and unquenchable fire. Thus fare ye well, my lords all. I pray God give you understanding of his blessed will and pleasure, and make you to believe and embrace the truth. Amen." [50]

VII. Latimer—Antichrist's End at Close of Prophetic Outline

HUGH LATIMER (c. 1490-1555), one of the most distinguished prelates of the Church of England, was born in Leicestershire. Receiving his B.A. at Cambridge in 1510, and his M.A. in 1514, he entered holy orders. In 1530 he preached before King Henry VIII, and rose in favor at court. He obtained his B.D. in 1534 by a disputation against the teachings of Melanchthon, for Latimer was still bitter against the Reformation. He called himself an "obstinate papist." Won to Protestantism by Thomas Bilney, his antipathy against the Roman church equaled

---

[48] "Letters of Bishop Ridley," letter 32, in *Works*, p. 415.
[49] *Ibid.*, pp. 415, 416.   [50] *Ibid.*, p. 418.

his former fervor for it. His sermons caused great excitement, and his opponents induced the bishop of Ely to prohibit his preaching in the churches of the University of Cambridge. However, Dr. Robert Barnes gave him permission to preach in the church of the Augustine Friars, a church exempt from episcopal jurisdiction.[51]

Many complaints were made against him by Catholics throughout the years of his preaching. In January, 1532, he was cited to appear before the bishop of London on the charge of Protestant heresy, and threatened with excommunication. After being greatly molested, he was freed at the intervention of the king, however, and absolved from the sentence. He had been made a royal chaplain upon recommendation of Cranmer, and in 1535 was appointed bishop of Worcester, where he actively promoted the Reformation. But in 1539 he resigned, refusing the mitre because he would not sign the Six Articles—transubstantiation, communion in one kind, celibacy of the clergy, lawfulness of monastic vows, private masses, and auricular confession.[52]

1. TELLS KING HOW ANTICHRIST MAY BE KNOWN.—After the resignation of his bishopric Latimer was placed "in ward" in the home of Dr. Sampson, the bishop of Chichester. He remained in the custody of the bishop until that prelate was himself imprisoned in the Tower. Latimer was then set at liberty for a while, it is believed, but was finally apprehended and cast into the Tower, where he remained until the death of Henry in 1547. During the reign of Edward VI (1547-1553), Latimer regained his influence at court and identified himself firmly with the Reformation as a zealous and eloquent preacher, sparing no hypocrisy and no tyranny. In a sermon preached before the boy king in a palace garden in 1549, Latimer stated how Antichrist may be known:

"In this we learn to know antichrist, which doth elevate himself in the church, and judgeth at his pleasure before the time. His canonizations,

---

[51] "Memoir of Hugh Latimer," in Latimer, *Works*, vol. 1 (*Sermons*), pp. ii, iii (see also his first sermon on the Lord's prayer on page 334 of the same volume).
[52] *Ibid.*, pp. vii-xi.

and judging of men before the Lord's judgment, be a manifest token of antichrist." [53]

Latimer declined an invitation to resume his former office, however, preferring to live chiefly in the archiepiscopal palace as confidant of Cranmer, with whom he associated in preparing the *Book of Homilies*.[54] Latimer's activities were checked by the accession of Bloody Mary, in 1553. In July of that year he was summoned from Warwickshire to appear before the council in London. He was again arrested and imprisoned in the Tower, in the same room with Cranmer, Ridley, and Bradford.[55] In 1554 they were taken by their enemies to Bocardo, the "common gaol," in Oxford, to defend their position on the mass before the divines of the university. Latimer was examined, basing his arguments solely on Scripture, but refused to dispute. After subjection to a mock trial they were again condemned. In 1555, about to be burned for his faith "at the ditch over against Balliol College," Latimer said to Ridley, who was condemned and burned with him (cut of Martyrs' Memorial on page 359):

" 'Be of good comfort, Master Ridley, and play the man: we shall this day light such a candle, by God's grace, in England, as I trust shall never be put out.' " [56]

2. HOLDS STANDARD VIEW OF FOUR PROPHETIC EMPIRES.— Latimer wrote less on the outline prophecies than his contemporary Reformers. But that he held the same view of the prophesied world outline is seen in his famous third sermon on the Lord's Prayer, of 1552:

"There have been principally four monarchies in the world: the first were the Babylonians, which had great and many nations underneath them: which was God's ordinance and pleasure, for he suffered them so to do. After those came the Persians, which were great rulers and mighty kings; as it appeareth by stories written of learned men at that time. Then came in the Greeks, and took the dominion from the Persians, and ruled themselves for awhile, till they were plucked down. At the last came the Romans,

---

[53] Latimer, third sermon preached before Edward VI, in *Works*, vol. 1, pp. 148, 149.
[54] "A Memoir of Hugh Latimer," in Latimer, *Works*, vol. 1, p. xii.
[55] Latimer, "Protestation" at the Oxford disputation, in *Works*, vol. 2 (*Sermons and Remains*), pp. 258, 259.
[56] "Memoir of Hugh Latimer," in Latimer, *Works*, vol. 1, p. xiii.

with their empire, which shall be the last: and therefore it is a token that the end of the world is not far off." [57]

3. DECLARES PRESENCE OF ANTICHRIST EVIDENCE OF LATTER DAYS.

—Latimer viewed the approaching judgment hour as the "latter day," in relationship to Antichrist's reign. With the appeal, "Therefore, good people, let us make ready towards his coming. And though he cometh not at this time, yet let us make ready," Latimer said:

"I would will and desire you most heartily, for God's sake, to consider that the judgment of God at the latter day shall be right, according unto justice: it will then appear who hath been good or bad. And this is the only comfort of all christian people, that they know that they shall be delivered from all their troubles and vexations. Let us therefore have a desire that this day may come quickly. Let us hasten God forward. Let us cry unto him day and night, *Adveniat regnum tuum;* 'Most merciful Father, thy kingdom come.' St Paul saith, *Non veniet Dominus nisi veniat defectio;* 'The Lord will not come till the swerving from faith cometh:' which thing is already done and past. Antichrist is known throughout all the world. Wherefore the day is not far off. Let us beware, for it will one day fall upon our heads." [58]

4. PUTS ROMAN CHURCH IN DIABOLIC CATEGORY.

—In the "Last Appearance and Examination" we find his testimony before the commissioners, October 1, 1555. Latimer said concerning the church:

" 'I confess there is a catholic church, to the determination of which I will stand; but not the church which you call catholic, which sooner might be termed diabolic. And whereas you join together the Romish and catholic church, stay there, I pray you. For it is one thing to say Romish church, and another thing to say catholic church.' " [59]

In a sermon at Paul's Church, London, on January 18, 1548, Latimer's concept of the Papacy had been plainly told:

"But the devil, by the help of that Italian bishop yonder, his chaplain, hath laboured by all means that he might to frustrate the death of Christ and the merits of his passion. And they have devised for that purpose to make us believe in other vain things by his pardons." [60]

---

[57] Latimer, third sermon on the Lord's prayer, in *Works*, vol. 1, p. 356.
[58] *Ibid.*, p. 364.
[59] Hugh Latimer, *Works*, vol. 2, p. 290.
[60] *Ibid.*, vol. 1, p. 74.

5. BELIEVES END LESS THAN 400 YEARS DISTANT.—As to the approximate time to the end, Latimer only had the six-thousand-year theory, as did many of his contemporaries—some four hundred years till the end, but the time would be shortened for the elect's sake. Latimer continues:

"St Peter saith, *Finis omnium appropinquat;* 'The end of all things draweth very near.' If St Peter said so in his time, how much more shall we say so.' For it is a long time since St Peter spake these words. The world was ordained to endure, as all learned men affirm and prove it with scripture, six thousand years. Now of that number there be passed five thousand (five hundred) and fifty-two; so that there is no more left but four hundred and forty-eight. And furthermore, those days shall be shortened: it shall not be full six thousand years. *Nam abbreviabuntur dies propter electos;* 'The days shall be shortened for the elect's sake.' Therefore all those excellent learned men, which without doubt God hath sent into this world in these latter days to give the world warning, all those men do gather out of scripture that the last day cannot be far off." [61]

[61] *Ibid.,* pp. 364, 365.

CHAPTER SEVENTEEN

Emphasis Centered on Papacy
as Prophesied Antichrist

I. Philpot—Concepts Molded by Predictions of Prophets

JOHN PHILPOT (1516-1555), archdeacon of Winchester and
martyr at Smithfield, was born near Winchester and educated at
New College, Oxford. His love of languages, especially Latin,
Greek, and Hebrew, led him into contact with the writings of
the fathers, and, above all, with Scripture. He studied civil law,
and after leaving Oxford traveled through Italy, where, on
account of his religion, he often faced peril. It was there that the
conviction grew upon him that Romanism was untrue. He returned to England about the time of the accession of Edward
VI, in 1547, when the doors of the prisons holding the Reformers
captive were thrown open, and John Hooper, John Rogers, and
others were freed.

Philpot became archdeacon of Winchester under Edward
VI, but his preaching was "obnoxious" to Stephen Gardiner,
the deprived bishop of Winchester. Upon Mary's accession to
the throne Philpot distinguished himself by his bold stand
for the Protestant cause, taking his position in a convocation of
bishops and dignitaries against changing the established religion
from Protestantism to Catholicism. At the close of this convocation he was haled before the bishop of Winchester (Gardiner),
and was, without any personal citation, illegally deprived of his
archdeaconry and committed to the king's bench prison for
nearly two years. On October 2, 1555, Philpot was removed to

the sessions' house, by Newgate, and, after having been examined before the queen's commissioners, was by them committed to the custody of Bishop Bonner. He was confined in the bishop's coal house, and here met with every insult.

He was examined fifteen or sixteen times. Back in 1554, while still in the king's bench, he had participated in the famous disputations at Oxford, at the close of which Ridley, Latimer, and Cranmer were condemned and excommunicated.

After he had suffered many indignities, still steadfast in purpose, he was condemned as a heretic. When he was brought to the stake at Smithfield in 1555, he kissed the wood, as he said, "Shall I disdain to suffer at this stake, when my Lord and Saviour refused not to suffer a most vile death on the cross for me?" After he was bound to the stake, he repeated psalms and prayed fervently until death ended his sufferings.

1. GREAT APOSTASY ARISES AFTER EMPIRE'S DECAY.—In his fourth examination before four bishops Philpot sets forth Paul's prophecy of the great apostasy in the Christian church after the decay of the empire.

> "*Philpot:*—'St Paul to the Thessalonians prophesieth, that there should come a universal departing from the faith in the latter days, before the coming of Christ; saying, "Christ shall not come, till there come a departing first." '
>
> "*Cole:*—'Yea, I pray you, how take you the departing there in St Paul? It is not meant of faith, but of the departing from the empire: for it is in Greek ἀποστασία [*apostasia*].'
>
> "*Philpot:*—'Marry indeed you, master doctor, put me in good remembrance of the meaning of St Paul in that place; for *apostasia* is properly a departing from the faith, and thereof cometh *apostata,* which properly signifieth one that departeth from his faith: and St Paul in the same place after speaketh of the decay of the empire.' " [1]

2. ALWAYS TWO CHURCHES; ONE IS ANTICHRIST'S.—And in his eleventh examination, before four bishops and other commissioners, Philpot contends that there have always been two churches, and continues:

---

[1] *The Examinations of John Philpot,* in Philpot, *Examinations and Writings,* p. 28.

" 'In the New Testament is mention made of two churches, as it appeareth in the Apocalypse; and also St Paul to the Thessalonians maketh mention that antichrist, with his false generation, shall sit in the temple of God.' " [2]

3. REVELATION 13 AND 18 CITED FOR SEPARATION FROM PAPAL CHURCH.—Writing from prison shortly before his martyrdom, and addressing the Reformed church, Philpot cites the prophecies of Revelation 13 and 18 as the Biblical basis of separation from the Papacy.

"St John in the Apocalypse telleth us plainly, that none of those who are written in the book of life do receive the mark of the beast, which is, of the papistical synagogue, either in their foreheads or else in their hands, that is, apparently or obediently. . . . Finally, in the 18th of the Apocalypse, God biddeth us plainly to depart from this Babylonical synagogue, and not to be partakers of her trespass. St Paul to the Thessalonians commandeth us, in the name of the Lord Jesus Christ, to 'withdraw ourselves from every brother that walketh inordinately, and not according to the institution which he hath received of him.'

"Ponder therefore well, good brethren and sisters, these scriptures, which be written for your erudition and reformation; whereof one iota is not written in vain; which be utterly against all counterfeit collusion to be used of us with the papists in their fantastical religion." [3]

Exhorting his sister to stand for the "truth," Philpot said, "You are at this present in the confines and borders of Babylon, where you are in danger to drink of the whore's cup, unless you be vigilant in prayer." [4]

This cup has "sotted and made drunk the most part of Christendom," he declares in dedicating his translation of a work by the Italian Reformer Curio.[5]

---

[2] Ibid., p. 107.
[3] Philpot, Examinations and Writings, letter 1, p. 222.
[4] Ibid., letter 6, p. 239.
[5] Philpot, A Defence of the True and Old Authority of Christ's Church, in Examinations and Writings, p. 322.

COELIO SECUNDO CURIO (1503-1569) was born and educated in Turin. Influenced by the Bible given him by his father, and by the writings of the Reformers, he became a leading promoter of the Reformation in Italy. In the course of his travels he incurred suspicion and was forced to flee at one time from city to city. Later he went to Switzerland, where he finally became professor of eloquence and the belles-lettres at Basel. This treatise translated by Philpot emphasizes 2 Thessalonians 2—Paul's description of Antichrist sitting in the temple of God, which Paul "seemeth to have taken out of the prophecies of Daniel," and which Curio applies to the pope; he regards the beast and the scarlet woman of Revelation as symbols of the papal church, and counsels the reader to flee to the strong tower of the true church of Christ and His kingdom, which, as the stone cut out without hands, will destroy the "image of kingdoms." (Ibid., pp. 338, 339, 427, 428, 431, 432.)

II. Bradford Burned for Not Acknowledging Antichrist of Rome

JOHN BRADFORD (*c.* 1510-1555), chaplain to Bishop Ridley, and friend of Latimer, popular preacher and ready writer, was born in Manchester. In 1547 he entered the Inner Temple as a student of common law, but turned to divinity through the influence of Thomas Sampson. Soundly converted, he sold his jewelry to help the poor. The following year he went to Cambridge, "to learn by God's law, how to further the building of the Lord's temple." In 1549 the university bestowed upon him, by special grace, the degree of Master of Arts in recognition of eight years of study of the arts, literature, and divinity. In 1550 he was ordained deacon by Bishop Ridley, and received a license to preach. In 1551 he became prebendary of St. Paul's in Kentish Town. A few months later he was appointed chaplain to Edward VI. He faithfully reproved sin, preached Christ crucified, and impugned heresies.[6] Bradford believed in the coming destruction of the earth by fire, and waited for the new heavens and new earth—holding that 1,500 years were past, and it could not be long now.[7] This hope sustained many whose lives were in jeopardy in this troubled time.

Soon after Mary's accession, in 1553, Bradford was arrested and imprisoned. Before the court in which Bishop Gardiner sat as chief, he was tried on a trumped-up charge of raising a tumult, and was condemned as a heretic. He was a fellow prisoner in the Tower with Dr. Edwin Sandys, Cranmer, Ridley, and Latimer. There he wrote many letters, messages, and farewells, both to the lowly and to persons of prominence. In 1555 the three statutes for the punishment of heresy were revived. Bradford's life was spared for a time in the hope that he would recant. But he preferred death to dishonest profession. He pleaded not guilty, challenging any authority on the bishop of Rome's behalf over the kingdom of England.[8] The judges were

---

[6] "Biographical Notice" in *The Writings of John Bradford* [vol. 2] (*Letters, Treatises, Remains*), pp. xiii-xxvi.
[7] John Bradford in *Writings* [vol. 1] (*Sermons, Meditations, Examinations*), pp. 185-187, 393; vol. 2, pp. 71, 249, 339.
[8] *Ibid.*, vol. 2, pp. xxx-xxxvii; vol. 1, pp. 465, 466, 475.

baffled in an attempt to establish incriminating evidence. Nevertheless, sentence was passed.

On June 30, 1555, he was taken, late at night, from the Compter, where he was prisoner, to Newgate, all the prisoners tearfully bidding him farewell. Great crowds were abroad, and as he passed along, the people wept and prayed for him.

When Bradford and his fellow sufferer, John Leaf, a young man, an apprentice, came to the stake in Smithfield to be burned, they lay prostrate in prayer for the space of a minute. But the restive sheriff ordered, "Arise, and make an end; the press of the people is great." At that command they both stood, and Bradford, taking a fagot in his hand, kissed it, and the stake also. Standing by the stake, with both hands uplifted, he cried, "O England, England, repent thee of thy sins, repent thee of thy sins. Beware of idolatry, beware of false antichrists; take heed they do not deceive you." It was just five years from his ordination to his martyrdom.[9]

1. CONDEMNED FOR REPUDIATING POPE AS CHRIST'S VICAR. —Bradford's remarks on prophecy are scattered through his writings as remarks or observations rather than as formal expositions. Thus in a "Letter on the Mass, to Hopkins and Others, at Coventry" (1554), he says in the uncouth language of the day:

"Ah, wretches then that we be, if we will defile either part with the rose-coloured whore of Babylon's filthy mass-abomination! It had been better for us never to have been washed, than so to wallow ourselves in the filthy puddle of popery: it had been better never to have known the truth, than thus to betray it. Surely, surely, let such men fear, that their 'latter end be not worse than the beginning.' "[10]

After he was condemned, looking hourly to be conveyed to the place of burning, Bradford wrote a moving "Farewell to the City of London." He declares he was condemned "for not acknowledging the antichrist of Rome to be Christ's vicar-general and supreme head of his catholic and universal church."[11] Similarly in his "Farewell to the University and Town of Cam-

---

[9] *Ibid.*, pp. xli-xliv.   [10] *Ibid.*, vol. 1, p. 390.   [11] *Ibid.*, pp. 434, 435.

bridge," he inquires, "Dost thou not know Rome to be Baby-lon?" Then he avers:

"Wherefor I now am condemned and shall be burned as an heretic. For, because I will not grant the antichrist of Rome to be Christ's vicar-general and supreme head of his church here and every where upon earth, by God's ordinance." [12]

He appeals to Cambridge, whom he addresses as "dear mother," to "come out of Babylon," "come again to God's truth," contrasting the simple flock of Christ's disciples with Babylon. It is signed, "Ready to the stake, the 11th of February, anno 1555." [13]

2. ANTICHRIST IN CHURCH; NOT TURK, INFIDEL, OR JEW.— In a conference with Archdeacon Harpsfield, Bradford clearly implied that neither the Turk, nor an infidel, nor a Jew is the great deceiver. And denying the apostolic succession of the Roman bishops, Bradford places the apostasy within the church:

" 'If this point fail you, all the church you go about to set forth will fall down. You shall not find in all the scripture this your essential point of succession of bishops,' quoth I. 'In Christ's church antichrist will sit. And Peter telleth us, as it went in the old church afore Christ's coming, so will it be in the new church sithen Christ's coming: that is, as there were false prophets, and such as bare rule were adversaries to the true prophets; so shall there be, sithen Christ's coming, false teachers, even of such as be bishops, and bear rule amongst the people.' " [14]

He pressed this same point with Bishop Heath of York and Bishop Day of Chichester, declaring that "the wicked man which 'sitteth in the temple of God,' that is, in the church," cannot be understood of Mohammed or "any out of the church, but of such as bear rule in the church." [15]

3. BISHOP OF ROME UNDOUBTEDLY GREAT ANTICHRIST.— In "Letter LIII. to Lady Vane," [16] Bradford responds to her desire for facts to arm her in the Reformed faith. He deals with the arguments of Christ's charge to Peter, the primacy of the bishop of Rome, and how that was not achieved till the time of Gregory

---

[12] *Ibid.*, pp. 441, 442.   [13] *Ibid.*, pp. 444, 447.   [14] *Ibid.*, p. 505.
[15] *Ibid.*, p. 523.   [16] *Ibid.*, vol. 2, pp. 142-147.

I and of Phocas. Calling the bishop of Rome a "bitesheep" rather than a bishop, Bradford tells of a large treatise he had begun, entitled "Of Antichrist." To Lady Vane he says:

"This bearer hath told me, that your desire is to have something sent to you concerning the usurped authority of the supremacy of the bishop of Rome, which is undoubtedly that great Antichrist, of whom the apostles do so much admonish us; that you may have as well something the more to stay you on, as also wherewith to answer the adversaries, because you may perchance therein be something apposed. To satisfy this your desire I will briefly go about, and so that I will, by God's grace, fully set forth the same, to enarm you to withstand the assaults of the papists herein, if you mark well and read over again that which I now write." [17]

4. GOD'S PEOPLE TO COME OUT OF ROMISH BABYLON.—In the midst of the conflict over the mass, including persecution to the death, Bradford wrote a vital treatise on *The Hurt of Hearing Mass,* going deeply into the historical development of this rite, which he called the "most detestable device that ever the devil brought out by man." [18] Giving thirty-nine reasons showing that going to mass is sin, Bradford says, intensely in No. 14:

"O deaf ears, that will not hear the blast of the angel's trump, warning us to come from amongst these whorish Babylonians, belly-god massmongers, lest we perish with them! 'Come out from her, my people,' saith God. If thou be one of God's people, thou must come from her: but, if thou be not, tarry still." [19]

5. REIGN OF EMPIRE BEASTS AND ANTICHRIST AT ADVENT.— Bradford tersely sets forth the Antichrist as a usurper in God's kingdom, also showing his accord with the standard Reformation interpretation of the four empire beasts of Daniel 7.

"Paul telleth, that Antichrist shall bear rule in the church until Christ come to judgment: then shall he destroy his kingdom. So that the true church of Christ shall not have worldly dominion and kingdom, but rather be persecuted, and especially towards the end of the world: as Peter telleth, that, as there was before Christ's coming in the church 'false prophets,' and the regiment was with the adversaries, which bare the name of the church, under the which they destroyed the church, so shall it be in the church after Christ's time: 'There will be,' saith he, 'many false teachers,' which will deceive not a few or the fewer part, but many and the greater part, as now the papists have done almost all Christendom. Again he saith, that 'there

---

[17] *Ibid.,* p. 142.   [18] *Ibid.,* p. 312.   [19] *Ibid.,* p. 329.

will come mockers,' which will make a mock of religion; so that the church cannot but be persecuted. Daniel plainly sheweth that the 'beasts,' that is, the empires of the world, shall be cast into the fire when Christ shall come to judgment: so that some wicked empires shall continue until the last day." [20]

III. Hooper—Prophetic Terms Permeate His Writings

JOHN HOOPER, sometimes spelled Hoper, or Houper (*c.* 1495-1555), martyred bishop of Gloucester and Worcester, was born in Somerset. After his education at Oxford he embraced monastic life, entering the Cistercian Order. He was first turned to the Protestant faith by studying the writings of Zwingli and Bullinger's commentaries on St. Paul's epistles, and finally renounced his allegiance to Rome. When the Act of the Six Articles was enforced by Henry VIII, the clerics were stirred against him. He withdrew to the Continent to escape persecution for heresy, residing in Zurich in association with Bullinger. There he studied history and wrote. After the accession of Edward VI, Hooper returned to England, in 1549. He preached to large congregations in London and took an active part in the Reformation proceedings.[21] In parting from Bullinger, Hooper had assured him that he would write, but had added, with a premonition:

"But the last newes of all I shall not be able to write: for there, said hee, (taking M. Bullinger by the hand) where I shall take most paines, there shall you heare of mee to be burned to ashes: and that shall be the last newes which I shall not be able to write unto you, but you shall heare it of me." [22]

Hooper had common ground with Cranmer and Ridley, but felt they did not go far enough, and during the time of this brief variance he was rebuked by them for his impetuosity. But in 1551 Hooper was consecrated bishop of Gloucester after a year's struggle over his objections to an oath by the saints, and to the wearing of some of the priestly vestments, which he felt sprang from Rome. He was also made bishop of Worcester in

---

[20] *Ibid.*, p. 361.
[21] Christopher Wordsworth, *op. cit.*, vol. 2, pp. 357-361.
[22] *Ibid.*, p. 360.

1552, and the two dioceses soon became one. He urged that tables be substituted for altars in the churches, and helped to lay the foundation for the Puritan movement.

On the accession of Mary, in 1553, when the Papacy was restored, Hooper was one of the first to be sent for. He was thrown into Fleet prison for a year and a half. During this time he wrote extensively. False rumors of his recantation were circulated.[23] Deprived of his bishopric, he was treated with severity. "Of the one side of which prison is the sink and filth of all the house," he wrote, "and on the other side the town-ditch; so that the stench of the house hath infected me with sundry diseases. During which time I have been sick."[24] Finally Hooper was degraded, along with John Rogers,[25] and ordered burned at Gloucester. The basis of his death is clear.

"I come not hither as one enforced or compelled to die (for it is well known I might have had my life with worldly gain), but as one willing to offer and give my life for the truth, rather than to consent to the wicked papistical religion of the bishop of Rome, received and set forth by the magistrates in England, to God's high displeasure and dishonour."[26]

A throng of seven thousand gathered, many weeping. While he knelt and prayed, a box said to contain his pardon contingent upon his recantation was placed before him. But he spurned it, saying, "Away with it!"[27] He was bound to the stake with an iron hoop. Piles of reeds were placed about the stake, but the fagots put above the reeds were green and did not burn freely. In the slow agony he cried, "Let me have more fire!" His limbs were burning while his body was almost untouched. Though his tongue was swollen, as long as he retained the power of speech he employed it in prayer. A bag of gunpowder placed between his legs, and one under each arm, did not kill him, and as he prayed he beat his hands upon his breast, falling forward after three quarters of an hour of anguish.[28]

---

[23] *Ibid.,* pp. 386-388.
[24] John Hooper, letter 48, in *Works,* vol. 2 (*Later Writings*), p. 620.
[25] For Mary's orders for the execution of John Hooper (1555) see Guy C. Lee, *op. cit.,* pp. 292, 293.
[26] "Biographical Notice," in Hooper, *Works,* vol. 2 (*Later Writings*), p. xxvi.
[27] *Ibid.,* p. xxviii.
[28] Geikie, *op. cit.,* pp. 455, 456.

1. Papal Antichrist Same as Beast of Apocalypse.—

Hooper complains that the "ungodly bishops of Rome attribute unto themselves to be the heads of Christ's church," and adds, "Thus is true, the see of Rome is not only a tyranny and pestilence of body and soul, but the nest of all abomination." [29] Then comes his identification of the prophesied Antichrist and Beast of the Apocalypse:

"Because God hath given this light unto my countrymen, which be all persuaded, (or else God send them to be persuaded!) that the bishop of Rome nor none other is Christ's vicar upon the earth; it is no need to use any long or copious oration: it is so plain that it needeth no probation; the very properties of antichrist, I mean of Christ's great and principal enemy, is so openly known to all men, that are not blinded with the smoke of Rome, that they know him to be the beast that John describeth in the Apocalypse." [30]

2. The Antichristian Seat of Abomination.—Discussing

the third of the Ten Commandments, Hooper says:

"As the pope, under the title and pretence of God's ministry, hath gotten himself not only a bishopric, but also the whole monarchy, in manner, of all Europe; a richer kingdom than any prince of the world; which never ceased from his beginning to move christian princes to most cruel and bloody war, under the cloak and mantle of God's name. What means and craft hath he found to maintain this whorish and antichrist[ian] seat of abomination; idols, peregrinations, masses, dispensations, absolutions, defensions of all things abominable; tyrannies against virtue, stablishments of his own laws, abrogations of God's laws, emptying of heaven, and filling of hell, blessing of things exterior, oil, bell, bread, water, with other that be not cursed, and cursing of the souls that Christ redeemed with his precious blood; with a thousand more such abominations, under the name and pretence of God and his holy church, the which neither the patriarchs, neither the prophets, Christ, neither his apostles, never knew of, as both the Testaments doth bear record." [31]

3. References to Antichrist Permeate Writings.—In a

confession of faith, which was printed by Christopher Barker (London, 1550), "Printer to the Queene's most excellent Maiestie," Hooper states that the church shall always have enemies,

---

[29] Hooper, *A Declaration of Christ and His Office*, chap. 3, in *Works*, vol. 1 (*Early Writings*), pp. 22, 23.
[30] *Ibid.*, p. 24.
[31] Hooper, *A Declaration of the Ten Commandments*, chap. 6, in *Works*, vol. 1, p. 325.

and be tormented with the "thunderings of Antichrist," Antichrist exercising "great and cruel tyranny upon the faithful children of God." [32] Such expressions as the "kingdom of Antichrist," [33] the "doctrine of Antichrist," and the "mark" of Antichrist [34] are frequent in Hooper's writings. There is also reference to the "synagogue of Antichrist." [35]

4. WOMAN OF BABYLON SITS IN SEVEN-HILLED ROME.—After evil-disposed persons had for eighteen months attempted to secure his condemnation as a heretic by false accusations, Hooper boldly wrote:

"Of that wicked and pestilent see and chair of Rome, which is indeed the very whore of Babylon that St John describeth in the Revelation of Jesus Christ, sitting upon a seven-headed beast, which St John himself interpreteth to be seven hills, and the children in the grammar-school do know that Rome is called *civitas septem montium,* the city of seven hills." [36]

5. INTOXICATED EARTH GIVES POWER TO PAPAL BEAST.— Again and again the prophetic angle is given in this apology. For example:

"Yet, as St John saith, the princes of the earth shall be made so drunken with the cup of the whore of Babylon, that they will deliver their power to the beast: but yet St John saith plainly, although the kings do give to the beast against God's laws their kingdoms, yet be they none of the beast's." [37]

6. COMFORT AND GUIDANCE FROM MATTHEW 24.—Finally, in a letter to his wife, Anne, in 1553, exhorting her to patience, Hooper commends the reading of Matthew 24, concerning the last days, "for such as love the coming of our Saviour Christ to judgment," [38] repeating his admonition in these words:

"Read again the 24th chapter of St Matthew, and mark what difference is between the destruction of Jerusalem, and the destruction of the whole world; and you shall see that then there were left alive many offenders to repent: but at the latter day there shall be absolute judgment and sentence,

---

[32] Hooper, *A Brief and Clear Confession of the Christian Faith,* arts. 52, 56, in *Works,* vol. 2, pp. 42, 44.
[33] *Ibid.,* art. 79, p. 54.
[34] *Ibid.,* art. 83, p. 56.
[35] Hooper, letter 39, in *Works,* vol. 2, p. 603, for example.
[36] Hooper, *An Apology Against the Untrue and Slanderous Reports,* in *Works,* vol. 2, p. 554.
[37] *Ibid.,* p. 559.
[38] Hooper, letter 26, in *Works,* vol. 2, p. 587.

never to be revoked, of eternal life and eternal death upon all men; and yet towards the end of the world we have nothing so much extremity as they had then, but even as we be able to bear." [39]

7. PALE HORSE OF FOURTH SEAL IS PAPAL PERIOD.—In a letter, written while in the Fleet, to "Lovers of the Truth" at beginning of their change of religion, Hooper applied the fourth seal to the period of papal persecution.

"Read ye the sixth chapter of St John's Revelation, and ye shall perceive, among other things, that at the opening of the fourth seal came out a pale horse, and he that sat upon him was called Death, and Hell followed him. This horse is the time wherein hypocrites and dissemblers entered into the church under the pretence of true religion, as monkers, friars, nuns, massing-priests, with such other, that have killed more souls with heresies and superstition than all the tyrants that ever were killed bodies with fire, sword, or banishment, as it appeareth by his name that sitteth upon the horse, who is called Death: for all souls that leave Christ, and trust to these hypocrites, live to the devil in everlasting pain, as is declared by him that followeth the pale horse, which is Hell." [40]

IV. English and Continental Protestantism Compared

A summarizing picture of Protestantism in the latter part of the sixteenth century is desirable at this point, and of Protestantism in England in contrast and comparison with that of the Continent. Lutheranism had spread rapidly in the three Scandinavian countries—Sweden, Denmark, and Norway. In fact, these became more thoroughly Protestant than some parts of Germany. But Lutheranism did not gain the support of the masses of the people in the countries to the west of Germany, where another form of Protestantism became established.[41] In England, still a third type was introduced. And while these three major groups were becoming firmly established, a number of smaller denominations came into being.

On the eve of the Reformation Erasmus' Greek and Latin New Testament came to England. For its time his Greek New Testament was a wonderful work; it relied on the original text, and revealed the fact that the commonly accepted Latin version

---

[39] *Ibid.*, p. 588.   [40] *Ibid.*, letter 27, p. 591.
[41] Hyma, *op. cit.*, pp. 123, 124.

was a secondhand document.[42] Its influence upon opinion was deep and lasting. But the Reformation in England was, perhaps to a greater degree than in any other country on the Continent, brought to pass by the dissemination of the vernacular Scriptures.[43] There was now no overtowering religious leader comparable to Luther or Calvin.

1. ENGLISH PROTESTANTISM TAKES DIFFERENT COURSE.— Protestantism in England was influenced by several factors, among which were the Lollards; the New Learning, with its exposure of ecclesiastical corruption and its promotion of study of the Scriptures; German Protestantism; the banishment of English Protestants, which brought them into close contact with Continental Protestant leaders; Henry's contest with the Papacy, which indirectly favored the religious movement. Thus English Protestantism took a course different from that followed by Lutheranism in Germany and Calvinism in other countries. In the Church of England a compromise between Catholicism and Protestantism was developed whereby the articles of faith were basically evangelical, but the prayer book was Catholic in its tendency. Because of the quarrel which had broken out between Henry VIII and the pope, based on purely selfish motives, a political element was introduced into the Reformation which led to that spirit of compromise between Protestantism and Catholicism noticeable in that church even to our day. Henry VIII made himself head of the national church and separated from Rome, although the majority of the people were still Roman Catholic at heart.[44]

Henry VIII, in 1521, had defended the Catholic faith against Lutheranism. For this the pope called him officially the "Defender of the Faith"—which title he held till his death, and which all later monarchs, both Catholic and Protestant, retained. About 1540 Henry VIII again took his stand, in a booklet,

[42] Wylie, op. cit., vol. 3, p. 358; Geikie, op. cit., p. 91; Mark Pattison, "Erasmus," Encyclopaedia Britannica, vol. 8, p. 679.
[43] Merle d'Aubigne, op. cit., vol. 5, book 18, chap. 1; Albert Henry Newman, op. cit., p. 250.
[44] Albert Henry Newman, op. cit., vol. 2, pp. 250-253; Geikie, op. cit., pp. 235-238, 430, 431.

13

against the Lutheran faith. But having broken with the pope, and having dissolved all the monasteries in England (1535), he gave a certain measure of encouragement to the Protestants in England. After his death, in 1547, Protestantism made substantial progress in England under Edward VI. Though the Reformation was held in check for a few years under Henry's Catholic daughter, Queen Mary (1553-1558), under Queen Elizabeth (1558-1603), England became predominantly Protestant[45]— eighty per cent professing the faith, which approximate percentage continued throughout the seventeenth century.

2. DISSENTING SECTS ENTER THE PICTURE.—Elizabeth was head of the Church of England, or Anglican Church, though, of course, without right to preach, ordain, or dispense the sacrament. Since the Anglican Church retained an organization centered in the bishops (Latin, *episcopus*), the name Episcopal came to be applied. And from the very beginning the Church of England had a prayer book of its own, called the *Book of Common Prayer,* which prescribed the order of worship in the church. Elizabeth also decreed that those who did not attend services should be fined. It was partly because of this Act of Uniformity of the Book of Common Prayer, of 1559, that, near the end of her reign, and later, hundreds of nonconformists, including the Pilgrim Fathers, removed to the Netherlands, where they were given that toleration in the Dutch Republic which they had sought in vain from Elizabeth, and her successor, James I.

By the latter half of the sixteenth century the Anabaptists, or "Again-Baptists" (so named because they thought infant baptism un-Scriptural and inefficacious, and therefore baptized those who had already been christened), had developed the beliefs and church polity that became the heritage of the Baptists of England and the United States. There was a wide variation in the tenets held by the Anabaptists on the Continent, but by 1575 their more extreme elements, which had discredited their

---

45 Hyma, *op. cit.,* pp. 134-137.

cause, had largely disappeared. In the Netherlands a moderate group, the Mennonites, prevailed. Some believe that the English Baptists and Congregationalists, later called Independents, derived from the exiles in Holland the principle of local self-government,[46] which was later so highly prized by the American Congregationalists, such as the Pilgrim Fathers and the Puritans. Among the Independents were also the Quakers, and the Separatists, who drew completely away from the Anglican Church, and such leaders as Roger Williams, who realized in the New World the ideal of separation of church and state. It was later to no small degree through the influence of the dissenting groups that religious toleration, as well as democracy, came to America.

V. Cranmer at the Stake Repudiates Pope as Antichrist

Cranmer, Ridley, Latimer, and Bradford were all burned for their testimony against the prophesied papal Antichrist, just as Cobham, Huss, and Jerome before them. A host of martyrs thus sealed their testimony. Indeed, the Reformation rests on such testimony. To fail to recognize this is to miss the very basis of that work, for the prophetic was inseparably joined to the evangelical, and jointly guided the Reformers in their separation from Rome.

THOMAS CRANMER (1489-1556), archbishop of Canterbury, was born in Nottinghamshire. When he was fourteen he was sent to the University of Cambridge, from which he received his M.A. in 1515. In 1519 he began a systematic study of the Scriptures. The fame of the Lutheran controversy had reached Cambridge, and he set out to find on whose side was truth. Made a reader at Buckingham College, and assiduously studying Greek and Hebrew, he obtained his D.D. in 1523, and was soon chosen public examiner in theology for clerical candidates. Cranmer favored submitting the question of the annulment of Henry's marriage to Catherine of Aragon to the universities for decision, instead of waiting for Rome to decide.

---

[46] *Ibid.*, pp. 138, 139.

POWERFUL FIGURES IN REFORMATION CONFLICT IN BRITAIN

Archbishop William Laud of Canterbury (Left), Who Was Strongly Romanist, Sought Absolutism in Church and State, and Persecuted Dissenters; Archbishop Thomas Cranmer (Right), Whose Activities in the English Reformation Under Edward VI Were Set Back by the Accession of Bloody Mary, and Who, After Imprisonment in the Tower, Went to a Martyr's Death in 1556

About the close of 1529 Cranmer was appointed a member of the embassy to Rome that was to plead the cause of the king's annulment before the pope, but it brought back little definite result. Cranmer was chosen as Henry's sole ambassador to the court of Charles V, in order to win the German divines to the cause of Henry VIII. His mission was unfavorable in its outcome; but Cranmer was summoned by Henry to return to England, to receive the highest ecclesiastical post in the realm, the archbishopric of Canterbury. This elevation was unexpected, as meantime he had married the daughter of Osiander, pastor at Nürnberg, noted German Reformer and expositor of prophecy, previously mentioned.

In 1535 Cranmer formally renounced allegiance to the see of Rome, being followed by other English bishops. The erasure of the pope's name from every prayer book was also directed, and the king of England was announced as head of the English Church. The dissolution of the monasteries was now a project of the king, and a measure for the suppression of the smaller religious houses was passed in 1536. In 1537 a third edition of Coverdale's complete Bible (first finished in 1535) was printed. On the title page of this third edition were the significant words, "Set forth with the Kynges moost gracious licence." In all probability Cranmer had a large share in this transaction. In 1538 Cranmer also endeavored to secure a union between the German Protestants and the Church of England, and doubtless presided at the conferences of visiting German divines with English bishops that year.

1. PENDULUM SWINGS BETWEEN CATHOLICISM AND PROTESTANTISM.—Then disappointments came. The Catholic reaction of 1539 set in, which Cranmer sought to stay. The Act of Six Articles was passed, making it a felony to oppose transubstantiation, communion in one kind, celibacy of the clergy, monastic vows, private masses, and auricular confession. In the year 1544 Cranmer succeeded in mitigating the Act of the Six Articles. However, opposition grew, and the archbishop escaped the Tower only through the friendship of the king. But before Henry VIII died (January, 1547), he had named Cranmer one of the regents of the young Protestant king Edward VI, in whose favor Cranmer steadily advanced. Protestantism became the state religion, and a number of reforms were carried out. The Six Articles and other persecuting statutes were repealed; images were removed from the churches; the first prayer book of Edward was finished; the clergy were allowed to marry; the communion table was substituted for the Roman Catholic altar; the Articles of Religion were published.[47]

Upon the accession of Catholic Mary (1553), England was received back into the bosom of the Papacy.[48] Thousands of

---

[47] "Biographical Notice," in Thomas Cranmer, *Works*, vol. 2 (*Miscellaneous Writings and Letters*), pp. ix, x; Albert Henry Newman, *op. cit.*, vol. 2, p. 263.
[48] A papal medal was struck by Julius III to celebrate the return to England of Roman Catholicism. The obverse side shows the kneeling figure of Queen Mary being welcomed by the pope. Other well-known contemporary figures are looking on. (See p. 556 for reproduction of this medal.)

Protestant leaders went into exile, hundreds were imprisoned, and not a few were burned. Among them was Cranmer, who was arrested, and imprisoned in the Tower in September, 1553. Then in March, 1554, he and his two illustrious fellow prisoners, Ridley and Latimer, were removed to Oxford, where they were subjected to interrogation by Roman prelates.[49] All three— Cranmer, Ridley, and Latimer—were condemned, and excommunicated as heretics. However, they were not executed immediately.

Ridley and Latimer were executed eighteen months later, October 16, 1555, but Cranmer was held for another five months, and subjected to another exhaustive trial. A letter from the pope (Paul IV), dated November 14, 1555, declared him guilty of heresy and commanded his excommunication. On February 14 he was degraded. Finally his courage forsook him, and he was prevailed upon to write or to sign with his own hand a series of recantations.[50]

2. DYING TESTIMONY REJECTS POPE AS ANTICHRIST.—Then Cranmer's firmness returned, and he renounced his recantations. Condemned to death at the stake, he went to the fire with courage and fortitude, and perished in the flames for his faith. Here is his dying testimony, given just before his death. Having made a final exhortation, he finished with these words, written with his own hand:

" 'And now I come to the great thing that so much troubleth my conscience more than any thing that ever I did or said in my whole life, and that is, the setting abroad of a writing contrary to the truth: which now here I renounce and refuse as things written with my hand contrary to the truth which I thought in my heart, and written for fear of death, and to save my life, if it might be; and that is, all such bills and papers which I have written or signed with my hand since my degradation; wherein I have written many things untrue. And forasmuch as my hand offended, writing contrary to my heart, my hand shall first be punished therefore: for, may I come to the fire, it shall be first burned.

---

[49] Cranmer, *Works*, vol. 1 (*Writings and Disputations*), pp. 391-427; see the original account in Foxe, *Acts*, vol. 3, pp. 36 ff.
[50] These appear in Cranmer's *Works*, vol. 2, appendix, pp. 563-566; see also pp. 567-570; also Geikie, *op. cit.*, p. 473.

" 'And as for the pope, I refuse him as Christ's enemy and antichrist, with all his false doctrine.

" 'And as for the sacrament, I believe as I have taught in my book against the bishop of Winchester; the which my book teacheth so true a doctrine of the sacrament, that it shall stand at the last day before the judgment of God, where the papistical doctrine contrary thereto shall be ashamed to shew her face.' " [51]

Upon uttering this, Cranmer was led to the fire. Having put off his outer garments, he stood there in a shirt which hung down to his feet. His thick beard covered his bosom. An iron chain was tied about him, and the fire set to the fagots. As the fire drew close to him he stretched out his right hand, which had signed his recantation, and thrust it into the flame, holding it there immovable, declaring, "This hand hath offended." [52] Finally, he cried out, "Lord Jesus, receive my spirit." In a short time more the flames had left him a blackened corpse. Like Peter, he had wavered in a moment of weakness. But, like Peter also, he fully repented and became adamant for truth.

3. PLACED IN OFFICE TO CALL FLOCK OUT OF BABYLON.— In the Preface to his *A Defense of the True and Catholic Doctrine of the Sacrament* (1550), occurs this solemn declaration of Cranmer's prophetic interpretation of the Papacy as Antichrist and Babylon:

"I know in what office God hath placed me, and to what purpose; that is to say, to set forth his word truly unto his people, to the uttermost of my power, without respect of person, or regard of thing in the world, but of him alone. I know what account I shall make to him hereof at the last day, when every man shall answer for his vocation, and receive for the same good or ill, according as he hath done. I know how antichrist hath obscured the glory of God, and the true knowledge of his word, overcasting the same with mists and clouds of error and ignorance through false glosses and interpretations. It pitieth me to see the simple and hungry flock of Christ led into corrupt pastures, to be carried blindfold they know not whither, and to be fed with poison in the stead of wholesome meats. And moved by the duty, office, and place, whereunto it hath pleased God to call me, I give warning in his name unto all that profess Christ, that they flee far from Babylon, if they will save their souls, and to beware of that great

---

[51] Cranmer, *Works*, vol. 2, appendix, p. 566.
[52] Biographical sketch abridged from Foxe in Cranmer, *Works*, vol. 1, pp. xviii, xix; John Strype, *Memorials of . . . Thomas Cranmer*, vol. 2, p. 558; Geikie, *op. cit.*, p. 474.

harlot, that is to say, the pestiferous see of Rome, that she make you not drunk with her pleasant wine." [53]

4. TRIPLE-CROWNED ANTICHRIST SEATED IN TEMPLE.—In the Preface to his *A Confutation of Unwritten Verities* (1547), Cranmer states:

"After all these sprung up the pope, that triple-crowned monster, and great antichrist, which took upon him authority, not only over the clergy, but also climbed above kings and emperors, deposing them at his pleasure, and settled himself in the temple of God, that is, in the consciences of men, extolling himself above God, dispensing with good laws, and giving men leave to break them, and to regard more his decrees than the everlasting commandments of God." [54]

In chapter 3 of this treatise, on "Canons of the Apostles and Councils Not Kept nor Used," Cranmer cites certain canons, and then states the contrary action of the Papacy.

"But now Antichrist of Rome, contrary to this decree, hath extolled himself above his fellow-bishops, as God's vicar, yea, rather as God himself; and taketh upon him authority over kings and emperors, and sitteth in the temple of God, that is, in the consciences of men, and causeth his decrees to be more regarded than God's laws; yea, and for money he dispenseth with God's laws, and all other, giving men licence to break them." [55]

5. ROME IS APOCALYPTIC BABYLON AND ANTICHRIST.—Applying first the fourth and fifth seals of Revelation, Cranmer shows that the Antichrist of Babylon must reign from seven-hilled Rome.

"And as the true church of Christ can never be long without persecution, in like manner can the false church of Satan and antichrist never cease from persecuting; as it appeareth throughout the histories of the whole bible. Of the tyranny and cruelty of antichrist in persecuting of Christ's true church, prophesied Daniel long before. Speaking of the empire and regiment of Rome: 'The fourth beast,' saith he, 'shall be the fourth kingdom, which shall be greater than all other kingdoms: it shall devour, tread down, and destroy all other lands; he shall speak words against the Highest of all; he shall destroy the saints of the Most Highest, and think that he can change times and laws.' And again, he saith of Antiochus, which was a figure of antichrist: 'There shall arise a king unshamefaced of face; he shall be wise in dark speaking; he shall be mighty and strong, but not in his own strength; he shall destroy above measure, and all that he

---

[53] Cranmer, *Works,* vol. 1, pp. 6, 7.
[54] *Ibid.,* vol. 2, p. 15.   [55] *Ibid.,* p. 39.

goeth about shall prosper in his hand: his heart shall be proud, he shall slay the strong and holy people, and through his craftiness falsehood shall prosper in his hand, and many a one shall be put to death in his wealthiness; he shall stand up against the prince of princes, but he shall be slain without hand.'

"Of the tyranny and prosperous success of antichrist in slaying of the saints of God, and the reward of them that be slain for the witness of God's truth, speaketh also St John, in the sixth chapter of his Apocalypse, under the opening of the four and five seals: and in the seventeenth chapter he lively setteth forth the pope in his own colours, under the person of the whore of Babylon being drunken with the blood of saints; pointing, as it were with his finger, who this whore of Babylon is, and the place where she shall reign, saying: 'The woman which thou sawest is that great city which reigneth over the kings of the earth.' Now what other city reigned at that time, or at any time since, over the christian kings of the earth, but only Rome? Whereof it followeth Rome to be the seat of antichrist, and the pope to be very antichrist himself. I could prove the same by many other scriptures, old writers, and strong reasons." [56]

6. LAST EXAMINATION CONCERNS ARROGATION OF ANTICHRIST.—The full record of Cranmer's "Examination at Oxford Before Brokes," in September, 1555, after the disputations, has been preserved. James Brokes, bishop of Gloucester, was the pope's subdelegate, with other commissioners. Permission being given to speak, Cranmer declared, "I will never consent that the bishop of Rome shall have any jurisdiction within this realm." Citing a dozen reasons for his stand—the last of which was that Antichrist arrogated to himself what was not his own—Cranmer said:

"Christ saith, that antichrist shall be. And who shall he be? Forsooth, he that advanceth himself above all other creatures. Now if there be none already that hath advanced himself after such sort besides the pope, then in the mean time let him be antichrist." [57]

Toward the close of the examination, after charging the pope with being the author of the erroneous teachings of the papal church, and declaring "the author of the same to be very antichrist," Cranmer solemnly asserts:

"Not content herewithal, more insolent than Lucifer, [the Pope] hath occupied not only the highest place in this world above kings and princes,

---

[56] *Ibid.*, pp. 62, 63. [57] *Ibid.*, pp. 213, 214.

but hath further presumed to sit in the seat of Almighty God, which only he reserved to himself, which is the conscience of man; and to keep the possession thereof, he hath promised forgiveness of sins *totiens quotiens.*

"He hath brought in gods of his own framing, and invented a new religion, full of gain and lucre, quite contrary to the doctrine of the holy scripture, only for the maintaining of his kingdom, displacing Christ from his glory, and holding his people in a miserable servitude of blindness, to the loss of a great number of souls, which God at the latter day shall exact at his hand: boasting many times in his canons and decrees, that he can dispense *contra Petrum, contra Paulum, contra vetus et novum Testamentum;* and that he, *plenitudine potestatis, tantum potest quantum Deus:* that is, 'Against Peter, against Paul, against the old and new Testament; and of the fulness of power may do as much as God.' O Lord, who ever heard such blasphemy? If there be any man that can advance himself above him, let him be judged antichrist.

"This enemy of God and of our redemption is so evidently painted out in the scriptures, by such manifest signs and tokens, which all so clearly appear in him, that, except a man will shut up his eyes and heart against the light, he cannot but know him: and therefore, for my part, I will never give my consent to the receiving of him into this church of England, and you, my lord, and the rest that sit here in commission, consider well and examine your own consciences: you have sworn against him; you are learned, and can judge of the truth. I pray God you be not wilfully blind. As for me, I have herein discharged mine own conscience toward the world, and I will write also my mind to her grace [Queen Mary], touching this matter." [58]

A similar declaration, in even stronger language, was made by Cranmer at his degradation.[59]

---

[58] *Ibid.,* pp. 222, 223. The forthright letter written to Queen Mary in that same month, September, 1555, appears on pp. 447-554.
[59] *Ibid.,* pp. 224-228.

CHAPTER EIGHTEEN

Anglican Leaders
Continue the Prophetic Emphasis

I. Bale—Portrays Opposing Churches of Christ and Antichrist

JOHN BALE (1495-1563), bishop of Ossory, Ireland, under Edward VI, and "one of the most distinguished among the minor lights of the English Reformation," was born in Suffolk. His education was begun in a Carmelite convent, and continued at Cambridge, where he turned from the study of civil law to theology. At first Bale was a strenuous opponent of "the new learning," but finally turned Protestant. Embracing the Reformed faith about 1529, he cast aside his monastic habit, and renounced the vows he had taken upon admission to orders, also refusing a degree of Doctor from the faculty. Of his conversion he says, significantly:

" 'I made haste to deface the mark of the wicked antichrist, and entirely threw off his yoke from me, that I might be partaker of the lot and liberty of the sons of God.' " [1]

Bale first received the attention and patronage of Cromwell, then earl of Essex, through his dramatic productions. Upon the latter's death, and because of persecution by the Catholics, Bale fled to Germany in 1540. There he remained until recalled to Ireland upon the accession of Edward VI (1547). He was then made rector of Bishopstoke, and vicar of Swaffham, as well as receiving a D.D. in 1551. He was consecrated as bishop of Ossory

---

[1] John Bale, *Vocacyon of John Bale*, p. 14, cited in "Biographical Notice" in his *Select Works*, p. viii.

in 1553, against his own wishes. A dispute developed, as the Irish ecclesiastics wanted him consecrated according to the "Romish ritual." There were many tumults, for the Reformation was not at all popular in Ireland.

Bale was so hated by the Catholics that upon news of the death of Edward VI, in 1553, and the accession of Mary his very life was in danger. He fled, purposing to go to Holland. But the ship on which he sailed was seized by pirates, and he was sold as a slave. Finally he got to Basel, where he remained until the accession of Elizabeth in 1559. He then returned from his second exile, and was made a prebendary in the Cathedral of Canterbury.

1. CHRONICLED OLDCASTLE'S MARTYRDOM FOR IDENTIFYING ANTICHRIST.—Bale was a prolific writer, producing eighty-five separate productions—some published under assumed names— including sacred drama and a book of hymns. His writings came under the prohibited list of Henry VIII in 1546. He never ceased to expose the perversions, of the Papacy in intense and uncompromising language. Even the closing Scriptural sentence of the preface to his account of the death of Sir John Oldcastle reads: "O Babylon, thy merchants were princes of the earth: and with thine enchantments were all nations deceived. Apocal xviii." [2] The 1729 edition of the treatise also included a section containing some of the writings of Joachim on the Antichrist.

Bale was wholly familiar with such Oldcastle declarations as the following:

" 'As touching the pope and his spirituality, truly I owe them neither suit nor service, forsomuch as I know him by the scriptures to be the great Antichrist, the son of perdition, the open adversary of God, and the abomination standing in the holy place.' " [3]
" 'Rome is the very nest of antichrist.' " [4]

2. HAD AMAZING FAMILIARITY WITH INTERPRETERS OF PROPHECY.—Bale's major contribution to prophetic interpreta-

---

[2] Bale, *A Brief Chronicle Concerning the Examination and Death of the Blessed Martyr of Christ, Sir John Oldcastle, the Lord Cobham,* in *Select Works,* General Preface, p. 14.
[3] *Ibid.,* pp. 17, 18.
[4] *Ibid.,* p. 36.

tion was his extensive *Image of Both Churches,* written while in exile, in 1545, and published in 1550—"image" signifying similitude, symbol, or portrayal of the two conflicting churches of Christ and Antichrist. A verse-by-verse exposition of the Apocalypse, it is more wordy, more vitriolic, and less specific than the German expositors. But one fact was crystal clear: He made the prophesied Antichrist of the various chapters to be the Roman Papacy, from which separation is imperative and specifically called for.

Bale's familiarity with the whole field of prophetic exposition is evidenced by his tabulation of scores of interpreters of the Apocalypse from Justin, Irenaeus, and Hippolytus on through the centuries to the contemporary Luther, Zwingli, Calvin, and Hoffman productions on the Continent. Frequent reference is made to such important past witnesses as Joachim, Wyclif, Savonarola, Valla, and others.[5]

In the margins of the first part of the work appear copious Scripture texts and the names of supporting commentators. For example, Bale cites Oecolampadius and Bibliander, along with Daniel 7 and Revelation 13, where he identifies the pope with the beast that "maketh men to believe he may constitute laws, keep under the gospel, distribute kingdoms, sell promotions and benefices, set up a purgatory, provide satisfactions, make new bodies to Christ, redeem dead men's souls, and remit sin for money." [6] Following through, chapter by chapter and verse by verse, Bale presents first the "text," then the "paraphrase" or exposition—a "compendius elucidation upon the Apocalypse," signing his name "John Bale, an exile also in this life, for the testimony of Jesus." [7]

3. SEVEN CHURCHES COVER ENTIRE CHRISTIAN CHURCH.— The seven churches are expressly declared to be "the whole Christian church in the seven parts," [8] and the Papacy's presence noted within their framework, as "the Romish pope sitting in

[5] Bale, *The Image of Both Churches,* in *Select Works,* pp. 349, 520.
[6] *Ibid.,* p. 262.   [7] *Ibid.,* p. 264.   [8] *Ibid.,* p. 379.

the most pestilent seat of errors," while Mohammed is outside "standing in the way of sinners." [9]

4. SEVEN SEALS EMBRACE APOSTASY IN CHURCH.—The seven seals are likewise "the seven ages of the christian church." [10] Commenting on the pale horse and its rider, death, Bale applies it to the "estate of the christian church" when the bishops "sought for new promotions," seeking the pre-eminence, as when "Boniface the third of that name, bishop of Rome, took upon him to be the head bishop of all the world, and God's only vicar in earth." He alludes to the "church of antichrist, pale as men without health." [11] The souls under the altar, in the fifth seal, are interpreted as referring to the martyred Waldenses and Albigenses. [12]

5. ANTICHRIST OF EUROPE IS HEAD OF PALE HORSE.—Bale's identification of the Antichrist is most explicit. Nothing is left to surmise or imagination. Thus:

"The great antichrist of Europe is the king of faces, the prince of hypocrisy, the man of sin, the father of errors, and the master of lies, the Romish pope. He is the head of the said pale horse, whose body are his patriarchs, cardinals, archbishops, bishops, fat prebends, doctors, priests, abbots, priors, monks, canons, friars, nuns, pardoners, and proctors, with all the sects and shorn swarm of perdition, and with all those that consent with them in the Romish faith, obeying their wicked laws, decrees, bulls, privileges, decretals, rules, traditions, titles, pomps, degrees, blessings, counsels, and constitutions, contrary to God's truth. The wickedness of these hath so darkened the blind world, that scarce was left one sparkle of the verity of the true christian faith. Nowhere can men dwell to greater loss of their souls' health, than under their abominations." [13]

6. SECOND ADVENT IN GLORY AS JUDGE.—Of the second advent Bale declared his faith thus:

"Take heed: for most certain it is, though Christ in his first coming as a merciful Saviour appeared here upon earth poor, simple and ignominious; yet shall he in his latter coming appear in the clouds of heaven with majesty, power and glory, accompanied with the infinite host of angels as a rigorous judge." [14]

---

[9] *Ibid.*, p. 291. Bale in one place speaks of Mohammed as the other member of Antichrist's kingdom. (*Ibid.*, p. 640.) [10] *Ibid.*, p. 380. [11] *Ibid.*, p. 319. [12] *Ibid.*, p. 322. [13] *Ibid.*, pp. 325, 326. [14] *Ibid.*, p. 267.

Bale's vivid description of the wicked crying for the rocks to fall, under the sixth seal, reveals his descriptive style.

"Fall upon us with such stuff as ye have. Cover us with your works more than need. Pray, pray, pray, sing, sing, sing, say, say, say, ring, ring, ring. 'Give us of your oil, for our lamps are out.' Help us with your Latin psalms. Relieve us with your lip-labour, though all be but dung and earth. Comfort us with *Placebo* [the vesper hymn for the dead]. Help us with *Requiem aeternam*. Pour out your trental masses, spew out your commendations. Sing us out of that hot fiery purgatory, before we come there." [15]

7. SEVENTH SEAL AND TRUMPET USHER IN JUDGMENT DAY.
—The trumpets similarly cover "the seven ages of the church." [16] Of the relationship of the seventh seal and seventh trumpet, Bale writes:

"Herein may we conjecture that the seventh seal once opened, and the seventh trumpet blown, the last judgment-day is not far off. Blessed is he that watcheth for the Lord's coming." [17]

8. TEN-HORNED BEAST IS PAPAL ANTICHRIST.—Of the ten-horned beast of Revelation 13, Bale bluntly declares:

"By the monstrous, ugly, and most odious beast rising out of the sea, with seven heads and ten horns, is meant the universal or whole Antichrist, comprehending in him all the wickedness, fury, falsehood, frowardness, deceit, lies, crafts, sleights, subtilties, hypocrisy, tyranny, mischiefs, pride, and all other devilishness, of all his malicious members which have been since the beginning. . . .

"No abomination nor mystery of iniquity, as Paul calleth it, was ever found in these kingdoms, but now reigneth manifold in the detestable papacy or monstrous kingdom of antichrist, as all the world may see." [18]

9. TWO-HORNED BEAST IS PRELATES OF ANTICHRIST'S CHURCH.—The two-horned beast represents "the prelates of antichrist's church . . . rightly described here of the Holy Ghost in this two-horned beast." [19] The various names projected by men to yield the 666 are mentioned.[20] The fall of Babylon, in Revelation 14, is disposed of thus:

"So sure is it that the execrable church of antichrist shall be overthrown, and utterly destroyed, as it were now performed in deed. Nothing

---

[15] *Ibid.*, p. 330.
[18] *Ibid.*, pp. 420, 423.
[16] *Ibid.*, p. 380.
[19] *Ibid.*, p. 438.
[17] *Ibid.*, p. 402.
[20] *Ibid.*, pp. 448, 449

shall be unrooted out, that the heavenly Father hath not planted. Sooner shall heaven and earth perish, than this promise be unfulfilled." [21]

10. SPIRITUAL WICKEDNESS OF FALLEN CHURCH AND NATIONS.—Strong and really offensive language is used of the symbolical woman-church riding the state-beast of Revelation 17:

"With this stinking strumpet have the mighty potentates of the universal earth, the emperors, kings, princes, and other notable governors, committed most shameful whoredom in the spirit by many strange worshippings, agreeing among themselves to her wickedly decreed laws and customs. Too long should we stand here in this place, if we should describe them all severally in their colours at large as they be.

"Through the crafty legerdemain of the priests on the one side, and the cruel constitutions of princes on the other side, the dwellers of the earth or worldly-minded multitude are drunken with the wine of her fornication spiritual, or practised worshippings besides the prescript rules of God's word. . . .

"And I saw (saith St John) in mystery a woman (for a whore at the first blush seemeth only a woman) sitting upon a rose-coloured beast. This beast is the great antichrist that was spoken of afore, or the beastly body of the devil, comprehending in him popes, patriarchs, cardinals, legates, bishops, doctors, abbots, priors, priests, and pardoners, monks, canons, friars, nuns, and so forth; temporal governors also, as emperors, kings, princes, dukes, earls, lords, justices, deputies, judges, lawyers, mayors, bailiffs, constables, and so forth, learning their own duty-offices as to minister rightly, to serve their abominations." [22]

11. GOLDEN CUP OF FALSE RELIGION MINISTERED TO NATIONS.—"Moreover in her hand, which is her exterior ministration, she hath a golden cup full of abominations and filthiness of her execrable whoredom. This cup is the false religion that she daily ministereth, besides the chalice whom her merchants most damnably abuse; and it containeth all doctrine of devils, all beastly errors and lies, all deceitful power, all glittering works of hypocrites, all crafty wisdom of the flesh, and subtle practices of man's wit, besides philosophy, logic, rhetoric, and sophistry; yea, all prodigious kinds of idolatry, fornication, sodomitry, and wickedness. Outwardly it seemeth gold, pretending the glory of God, the holy name of Christ, the sacred scriptures of the Bible, perpetual virginity of life; and all are but counterfeit colours and shadows of hypocrisy in the outward letter and name.

"Full of abominations is the drink of the execrable faith of that Romish religion received of others, and full of filthiness also." [23]

12. BEAST'S SEVENTH HEAD IS PAPISTICAL ROME.—Bale

---

[21] *Ibid.*, pp. 458, 459.   [22] *Ibid.*, pp. 494-496.   [23] *Ibid.*, p. 497.

contends that the Beast's seventh head is the "papistical kingdom of our Romish spirituality." [24] Speaking of the simple Roman bishops' becoming contenders for the primacy (such as Boniface III securing the appointment as head bishop from the emperor Phocas), Bale says:

"When this was once gotten, then rose they up so high that the emperor became their footstool, and all other christian princes their waiting slaves, to tide and run, make and mar, strive and fight, slay and kill, at their commandment and pleasure. Thus became the Romish pope the seventh king that was in John's time yet to come." [25]

13. DATES BEGINNING OF PAPAL POWER WITH PHOCAS.— Speaking of the beginnings of the Roman papal power, Bale says:

"For yet is it not a thousand years since the papacy first began under Phocas, which is but as a day before God; and that day will he shorten by his own promise for his elects' sake, which to remember is their great comfort." [26]

14. TEN HORNS ARE CONTEMPORARY EUROPEAN NATIONS. —The ten horns of the Beast include England, France, Spain, Portugal, et cetera.[27] The closing words of his commentary reveal his heart longing—the second advent:

"Come, most merciful Saviour and Redeemer, and fulfil the godly promises of this book, to the eternal comfort of man. Make haste to the judgment-seat, for a full deliverance of the whole chosen number, that thy servants may be where as thou art in perfect glory and joy." [28]

II. Becon Deals With Antichrist Throughout His Works

THOMAS BECON (c. 1511-1567), facile writer, and author of numerous books on "popery"—sometimes writing under the pen name of Theodore Basille [29] (or Basil)—was born, it is thought, in Norfolk. Educated first at St. John's College, Cambridge, from which he obtained his B.A. in 1530, he later obtained the degree of D.D. also from Cambridge University. He was ordained about the year 1538, and entered the Protestant

---

[24] *Ibid.*, p. 502.   [25] *Ibid.*, p. 503.   [26] *Ibid.*, p. 504.
[27] *Ibid.*, p. 505.   [28] *Ibid.*, p. 635.
[29] *The Century Cyclopedia of Names*, p. 136.

ministry in an era full of danger. Later, charged with heresy because of his opinions and writings, he was brought to Paul's
Cross to recant and to revoke his doctrine. After making some
sort of public submission, he retired to the country.

Upon the accession of Edward VI, Becon had more personal
security and a wider field of usefulness. He was made a rector,
and then one of the six chaplains of Canterbury, under Archbishop Cranmer. He also taught at Oxford "without molesta-
tion," and held other important positions.

However, upon the assumption of the throne by Mary, in
1553, when the Reformed preachers were silenced, deprived of
their parishes, and cast into prison, Becon was one of the first to
be committed to the Tower as a preacher of "sedition." John
Bradford, martyred in 1555, was one of his companions at the
time. Becon was somehow released (some attribute his release to
a mistake as to his name on the part of the state official, Gardiner), and at once repaired to the Continent, going to Strassburg.
While there he wrote constantly. Upon the accession of Elizabeth (1558) he returned to his homeland, and was soon placed in
Canterbury, made rector of Christ's Church, Newgate, and also
given other important positions.

1. Portrays Marks for Identifying Antichrist.—In his
*The Acts of Christ and of Antichrist, Concerning Both Their
Life and Doctrine* (1563)[30]—comprising 226 propositions contrasting the two—Becon paints a very impressive and complete
picture. Presenting the two aspects of teaching and life, it leaves
little to be said, and is completely buttressed by Scripture. An
earlier treatise, *The Displaying of the Popish Mass,* speaks of
"antichrist's brood of Rome" and the "idolatrous priests of
Babylon." [31]

The general preface to his three volumes discloses the whole
tenor of his writing. This rather graphic paragraph must suffice:

"In this third volume, I say, as the time and manners of men justly

---

[30] Thomas Becon, *The Acts of Christ and of Antichrist,* in *Works,* vol. 3 (*Prayers and Other Pieces of Thomas Becon*), pp. 498-539.
[31] Becon, *The Displaying of the Popish Mass,* in *Works,* vol. 3, pp. 259, 261.

required, I have somewhat more sharped my pen in some places against antichrist and his Babylonical brood, than in my books heretofore made and published. In them also I have disclosed a great number of antichrist's jugglings, superstitions, new-found sects [orders], pardons, pilgrimages, ceremonies, and such-like devices. I have also shewed what is to be thought of the bishop of Rome's primacy, which he challengeth over and above all other, yea, and that by the faithful testimonies of certain most faithful writers, both ancient and of this our time. In fine, I have displayed the wicked kingdom of the son of perdition, and set it forth in his lively colours, that all men, if they be not obstinately blind, and willingly set themselves against the manifest truth of God's word, may easily know antichrist, and beware of his wolfish whelps and of their pharisaical leaven." [32]

2. SECOND ADVENT WILL DESTROY ANTICHRIST.—In *A New Catechism* (410 pages), by Becon, in the section on "Prayer," he expresses a desire for the destruction of Antichrist through the second advent, at which time Christ's kingdom will be established. In it the very phrasings of the prophecies concerning Antichrist are used, and with many marginal references to Scripture, such as Daniel 7, 2 Thessalonians 2, and Revelation 17, 18, and 19:

"We desire of our heavenly Father, that antichrist with his kingdom, which hath seduced, and daily doth seduce, an infinite number of miserable and poor wretched souls through his glistering and painted visor of counterfeit, false, and feigned holiness, may shortly be slain and brought unto confusion 'with the breath of the Lord's mouth, and utterly be abolished with the brightness of his coming;' that 'that sinful man, the son of perdition, which is an adversary, and is exalted above all that is called God, or that is worshipped,' may no longer 'sit in the temple of God, boasting himself to be God,' nor be 'drunken' any more 'with the blood of the saints and with the blood of the martyrs of Jesu,' nor yet sell the souls of men, nor utter any more of his false and counterfeit merchandise to the simple ones; that the kingdom may be his alone, which is 'King of kings and Lord of lords.' " [33]

Stronger words are used, consonant with the times, which will not be repeated here. [34]

III. Coverdale—Poem on the Fall of Babylon

Space precludes more than passing reference to certain noted Reformers whose interpretations have not been preserved

[32] Becon, "Preface," in *Works*, vol. 1 (*The Early Works of Thomas Becon*), p. 29.
[33] Becon, *A New Catechism*, in *Works*, vol. 2 (*The Catechism of Thomas Becon . . . With Other Pieces*), p. 152.   [34] *Ibid.*, p. 409.

for us, but who shared the positions of their associates. For instance, there is Coverdale's[35] eighty-eight line poem "Let Go
the Whore of Babylon," the first stanza of which reads:

> "Let go the whore of Babilon,
> Her kyngdome falleth sore;
> Her mechauntes begyne to make theyr mone,
> The Lorde be praysed therfore.
> Theyr ware is naught, it wyll not be bought,
> Great falsheed is founde therin:
> Let go the whore of Babilon,
> The mother of al synne."[36]

IV. Geveren Translated; Eberhard Cited

In 1577 Thomas Rogers, chaplain to Archbishop Bancroft,
made a translation "from the Latin of S. a G." (Sheltco a
Geveren) which was published as a tract with the English title
*Of the Ende of This World, and Second Comming of Christ,
a Comfortable and Necessary Discourse, for These Miserable
and Daungerous Dayes.* After referring to Christ's own prophecy of His second advent, recorded in Matthew 24, Mark 13,
and Luke 21, and the prophecies of His first advent, this unknown author tells of Daniel's prophecy of the course of
empires, calling him "the great historiographer,"[37] with references to Daniel 2, 7, 8, 9, and 11.

1. EVERLASTING KINGDOM TO BE ESTABLISHED THROUGH
ADVENT.—Definite reference is made to the future eternal kingdom to be established by Christ when He shall put all kingdoms
of the world under His feet, and "shall hew them like a stone,
which is cut from the mountain." And similarly with the four
monarchies and the Antichrist of Daniel 7, climaxing with "an

---

[35] MILES COVERDALE (1488-1569), bishop of Exeter, was at Cambridge when Robert Barnes
was prior. It was from Barnes that he imbibed his Reformed views, and he accompanied Barnes
at his trial. Having a Bachelor of Canon Law degree from Cambridge (1531), Coverdale was admitted to the degree of D.D. at Tübingen. In 1563 he obtained the same degree from Cambridge.
After he became known as a writer and preacher, he twice fled to the Continent to escape persecution. He translated the Bible in 1535 (his most notable work). His writings were proscribed
in 1555.
[36] Miles Coverdale, "Let Go the Whore of Babylon," in *Works,* vol. 2 (*Remains of Miles
Coverdale*), p. 586.
[37] *Of the Ende of this World, and Second Coming of Christ,* fol. 3v.

everlasting and perpetual kingdom, which al the Saincts of God after judgment shal possesse world without end." [38]

2. ACQUAINTANCE WITH EBERHARD'S EXPOSITION OF HORN. —A succeeding section deals with the historical aspect. It cites Tertullian, Jerome, and Lactantius on Rome as the "hinderer," restraining the coming of Antichrist; then it recites Archbishop Eberhard's remarkable speech of 1240, identifying the Papacy as the Little Horn emerging in the midst of the ten divisions of Rome and sitting down in the temple of God.[39] The frequent citation of Eberhard's exposition by different men, and in different countries, indicates the general acquaintance of the Reformation writers with the key expositors of the past. This is significant.

V. Jewel—Logical Expositor of Prophecies on Antichrist

JOHN JEWEL (1522-1571), bishop of Salisbury, and one of the great intellectuals of the English Reformation, was born in Devonshire. Graduating from Oxford in 1540 with a B.A., he felt the urge to continued study, which he followed in the fields of Greek, Latin, rhetoric, philosophy, history, and mathematics, while serving as a reader of rhetoric. He was granted a fellowship at Corpus Christi College in 1542, and obtained his M.A. in 1544. An incessant student, his hours were from 4 A.M., until 10 P.M., until excessive study injured his health.

Imbibing a good many of the principles of the Reformation from Peter Martyr,[40] and openly espousing the Protestant faith, he inculcated his beliefs among his students under the reign of Edward VI.[41] Interestingly enough, Jewel was one of the recorders, or notaries, at the famous Oxford Disputations of 1554, when Cranmer, Ridley, and Latimer were under trial.[42] This unquestionably strengthened his faith. Much correspondence over Reformation affairs appears in *Zurich Letters* (1558-

---

[38] *Ibid.*, fol. 4r.   [39] *Ibid.*, fol. 22v, 23r.
[40] Peter Martyr was an Italian, but joined the Reformers at Zurich, and was called to Oxford as professor of divinity.
[41] Christopher Wordsworth, *op. cit.*, vol. 3, p. 334.
[42] Foxe, *Acts*, vol. 3, p. 51.

1559), between Jewel and Bullinger, the Helvetian Reformer, and others.

In 1562 Jewel produced his monumental *Apologia Ecclesiae Anglicanae* [43] (Apology of the Church of England), the product of many years of research. Translated from Latin into English in 1564, and into German, Italian, French, Spanish, and Greek, it was the first methodical statement of the position of the Church of England as against Roman Catholicism. With a wide circulation on the Continent as well, it is said to have done more for the Reformation than any other book of the time. It was, in reality, an answer to the Council of Trent, then sitting.[44] It drew forth a caviling reply by the Romanist, Harding.

In 1565 Jewel was granted a D.D. degree from Oxford. And in 1566 he prepared a heavily documented *Defence* [45] (1567) of his former *Apology* of 1562, against the same Roman opponent Harding. He also had some controversy with the Puritans. Among his last works were discussions with the Romanists about Antichrist.

1. ANTICHRIST'S COMING FORETOLD BY FOUR PROPHETS.— In his masterful commentary on the Thessalonian epistles,[46] in the classical second chapter of the second epistle, Jewel recognizes that whatever he says on Antichrist will be "ill taken of many"; therefore he will only employ the phrasings of Scripture and the fathers. In fact, his language is quite moderate compared to the violent invective generally employed in his day. He avers that many, seeking to avoid Antichrist, are deceived by him. Commenting first on the prophetic prediction of Christ's first coming, which was fulfilled to the letter, Jewel says of Antichrist:

"Now, as the coming of Christ was, such is the coming of antichrist. God hath foretold of his coming. Daniel hath foretold. Christ and his apostles Paul and John have foretold it: the scriptures and old fathers make

43 *The Works of John Jewel, Bishop of Salisbury,* vol. 3, pp. 1-47.
44 Christopher Wordsworth, *op. cit.,* vol. 3, p. 355.
45 Jewel, *A Defence of the Apology of the Church of England,* in *Works,* vol. 3, pp. 113-626; vol. 4, pp. 627-1086.
46 Jewel, *An Exposition Upon the Two Epistles of St. Paul to the Thessalonians,* in *Works,* vol. 2, pp. 813-946.

often mention hereof. There is none, neither old nor young, neither learned nor unlearned, but he hath heard of antichrist. They hate his name, and detest him, before they know him. But here you may mark the wonderful sleight and subtilty of Satan. The world shall look after the coming of antichrist. He shall not fail but come. All men shall carry hatred against him, and reckon him abominable; and yet their eyes shall be blinded and their hearts deceived, so that they shall not know him. They shall hate his name, and embrace his doctrine: he shall cover himself with a cloke of holiness. They shall think they do good service unto Christ, but shall therein do service unto antichrist." [47]

2. PROPHETIC SPECIFICATIONS LISTED FOR IDENTIFICATION.

—After listing the common Catholic misconceptions concerning Antichrist—that he would be a Jew of the tribe of Dan, that he would be born in Babylonia or Syria, or be Mohammed, or overthrow Rome or rebuild Jerusalem, or be Nero, or that he would reign but three and a half years—Jewel sets forth his specifications as depicted by Paul, Daniel, and John:

"These tales have been craftily devised to beguile our eyes, that, whilst we think upon these guesses, and so occupy ourselves in beholding a shadow or probable conjecture of antichrist, he which is antichrist indeed may unawares deceive us.

" 'Except that man of sin be disclosed.' The apostle seemeth to teach us of antichrist as if he should be one man, because he calleth him 'the man of sin.' But we may not so take him. The manner of the scripture is oftentimes, and in divers places it speaketh that of many which seemeth to be spoken but of one. So doth Daniel set forth the kingdom and all the kings of Persia in the name and likeness of a bear, and so describeth the state of other whole kingdoms in such particular names. And so doth the Spirit of God in the Revelation set down under the name of the beast the succession and continuance of many. He meaneth not, therefore, that antichrist shall be any one only man, but one estate or kingdom of men, and a continuance of some one power and tyranny in the church." [48]

3. ANTICHRIST A COVERT ENEMY WITHIN THE CHURCH.—

Although he is Antichrist, he will not be an open enemy, "spitting at" the gospel of God or defying Christ, but be a vicar of Christ. He will come in the name of Christ, yet do things against Christ.

"Under pretence and colour of serving Christ, he shall devour the sheep and people of Christ; he shall deface whatsoever Christ hath taught;

---

[47] *Ibid.*, p. 902.   [48] *Ibid.*, p. 903.

he shall quench that fire which Christ hath kindled; he shall root up those plants which Christ hath planted; he shall undermine that house which Christ hath built.

"He shall be contrary to Christ, his faith contrary to the faith of Christ, and his life contrary to the life of Christ. Is any man desirous to know antichrist? His coming shall be notable, it shall astonne the world. By this mark you may know him: he shall be contrary to Christ. To shew you at large this contrariety, by comparison of things contrary in Christ and antichrist, would ask long time." [49]

4. PROUD AND POMPOUS, TO SIT IN TEMPLE.—Jewel contrasts Christ's one offering with the priests' daily mass, Christ's headship of the church with the pope's usurpation, Christ's disassociation from the kingdoms of this world with papal claims, Christ's payment of tribute with papal exemptions, Christ's humility and the pope's exaltation, carried upon the shoulders of men, and waited upon by kings.[50] Then comes this comprehensive portrayal of Antichrist:

"Now on the other part take view of antichrist. Behold his birth, his place, his chair, his estate, his doctrine, his disciples, and all his life: you shall see nothing but pomp and glory. Gregory calleth him the king of pride. He is proud in life, proud in doctrine, proud in word, and proud in deeds. He is like unto Lucifer, and setteth himself before his brethren, and over nations and kingdoms. He maketh every knee to bow down to him and worship him: he maketh kings to bring him water, to carry his train, to hold his cup, to bear his dish, to lead his bridle, and to hold his stirrup: he claimeth power over heaven and earth: he saith he is lord over all the world, the lord of lords, and the king of kings; that his authority reacheth up into heaven and down into hell; that he can command the angels of God; that he condemneth whom he will condemn; that he maketh saints at his pleasure; that whatsoever he blesseth is blessed; and that it is cursed whatsoever he curseth.

"He selleth merits, the forgiveness of sins, the sacrifice for the quick and the dead. He maketh merchandise of the souls of men. He layeth his filthy hands upon the Lord's anointed. He removeth kings, and deposeth the states and princes of the world. This is antichrist. This is his power. Thus shall he work and make himself manifest. So shall he sit in the temple of God. The people shall wonder at him, and shall have him in reverence: they shall say, 'Who is like unto the beast?' Who is so wise, so mighty, so godly, so virtuous, so holy, so like unto God? So intolerable and monstrous shall be his pride." [51]

---

[49] *Ibid.*, pp. 903, 904.
[50] *Ibid.*, p. 904.
[51] *Ibid.*, p. 905.

5. PROPHESIED "BEAST" IS BISHOP OF ROME.—Declaring, "The people shall receive his [Antichrist's] doctrine, and believe his word. They shall fall down before him and worship him. They shall say, 'Who is like unto the beast?' What creature is so beautiful as he?" Jewel logically observes:

"Here, methinketh, I see the secret motions of your heart. You look that I should name the bishop of Rome, that it is he which hath suffered himself to be called by the name of God." [52]

6. KINGDOM BUILT OUT OF PERVERTED CHURCH INSTITU-TIONS.—Jewel says that Antichrist's "time is appointed." It is a "time of darkness; when shepherd and the guides of the people shall be careless; when the word shall be loathed; when the light shall be put out; when superstition shall reign; when ignorance shall have the upper hand." The Antichrist shall forbid lawful marriage, according to 1 Timothy 4 and Daniel 11, and Jewel comments, "This is the practice of antichrist." He shall build a kingdom out of the perverted Lord's supper, and the keys of the church, and of prayers. Such are the "marks of antichrist." [53]

7. ANTICHRIST SUCCEEDS TO POWER AND TERRITORY OF ROME.—Pagan Rome was the hindering power preventing the development of Antichrist. That passing, then Antichrist shall possess a great part of that empire.

"When the emperor shall fall and decay, then he shall rise up: when the emperor becometh weak, then he shall grow strong. Therefore Paul saith, antichrist shall not come yet; for the emperor letteth him: the emperor shall be removed; and then shall antichrist come.

"But before I proceed to say more of this division of the empire, that we may come to the bottom of this matter, and so see the meaning of this prophecy evidently laid open before us, I will shew more plainly and particularly of antichrist, who he shall be." [54]

8. ANTICHRIST MUST SIT IN SEVEN-HILLED CITY.—Asking *where* Antichrist should appear—and setting aside such "guesses" as Babylonia, Syria, Chaldea—Jewel clinches his prophetic argument thus:

---

[52] *Ibid.*, p. 906.
[53] *Ibid.*, pp. 909-913.
[54] *Ibid.*, p. 914.

"Paul telleth us he shall creep into the empire of Rome. So saith the apostle, and so the fathers. The empire shall be made waste; and then antichrist shall come and invade the church. But the empire was great and wide, it reached over a great part of the world. It did contain England, France, Spain, Germany, Poland, Denmark, Italy, Illyricum, Macedonia, Thracia, Graecia, Asia, Armenia, Egypt, Mauritania, and the rest of Africa. All these were parts of the empire of Rome. In what part, or in what city, or in what church of all these shall he sit? St John saith: 'The seven heads are seven mountains, on which the woman sitteth.' Antichrist shall sit in a city built upon seven hills. Where shall we find such a city in the whole world? Is it Hierusalem, or Athens, or Constantinople, or Antioch? Where we find a city so built, that city is the place of antichrist. There is none but one. The Spirit of God cannot lie. But which is that one? All writers, as well old as new, call that city Rome. Rome is built upon seven hills. They be yet standing. The names of the hills are known to be these, Palatinus, Quirinalis, Aventinus, Coelius, Viminalis, Exquilius, Janicularis. . . . Rome is the city of seven heads: Rome is the city built upon seven hills; therefore the city which John describeth; and therefore it is the tabernacle and stall in which antichrist shall sit." [55]

9. APPEARS AS LITTLE HORN AMONG ROME'S DIVISIONS.— In substantiation Jewel cites Irenaeus, Joachim, Bernard, and John of Paris. The climax and sum of the argument, however, is based on the Little Horn of Daniel 7.

"This whole matter is also expressed in the seventh of Daniel: 'The fourth beast was fearful and terrible and very strong: it had great iron teeth: it devoured and brake in pieces, and stamped the residue under his feet; and it was unlike to the beasts that were before it; for it had ten horns.' 'And, behold, there came up among them another little horn . . . which had eyes like a man, and a mouth speaking presumptuous things.' This beast is the empire of Rome, the greatest empire that ever was. It was divided into ten, or into sundry kingdoms; as I shewed you, and as we see this day. The little horn is antichrist. The empire shall be divided and weakened: then antichrist shall come. 'He shall speak great words against the Most High, and shall consume the saints of the Most High, and think that he may change times and laws; and they shall be given into his hand.' Daniel saith, 'He shall speak great words against the Most High, and shall think he may change times and laws; and they shall be given into his hand.' Wherein he sheweth not only the pride and presumption of antichrist, but that he shall also prevail for a time. Such a one there hath been, and yet is. He blasphemeth God, murdereth the saints, hath changed times and laws, the laws of God and the laws of nature. He is antichrist." [56]

---

[55] *Ibid.*, p. 915.
[56] *Ibid.*, p. 918.

10. Babylon's Fall Preceded by Message of Revelation 14.—There remains only the ruin and fall of Antichrist to be preceded by the message of Revelation 14:6-14, then the overthrow of Babylon portrayed in Revelation 17 and 18.[57]

11. Drafts Upon Testimony of Past Witnesses.—This same teaching runs all the way through Jewel's writings.[58] Particularly is this true of his *Defence of the Apology* (1567), in which draft is made upon such men as Petrarch, Joachim, Arnulf at the Council of Rheims, Dante, and the bishops at Regensberg (Reinspurg).[59] The familiarity of the Reformers with these medieval expositors is noteworthy. This knowledge profoundly strengthened and assured them, tying them into fellowship with the church prior to the great apostasy.

12. Christ's "Abomination" Same as Paul's "Man of Sin."—In this *Defence,* Jewel expands upon Christ's prophesied "abomination of desolation," which is declared to be the same as Paul's Man of Sin, or Antichrist, sitting—or standing—in the church.

"The apostles demanded him [Christ] this question: 'What is the token of thy coming (to judgment), and of the end of the world?' To this question Christ answereth in this wise: 'Take heed that no man deceive you. Many shall come in my name, and shall say, I am Christ, and shall deceive many. Ye shall hear of wars, and talks of wars. But be not ye troubled. All these things must happen: yet this is not the end,' &c. 'Many false prophets shall rise, and shall deceive many. Iniquity shall increase: charity shall wax cold. Whoso continueth unto the end, he shall be saved. And this gospel of the kingdom shall be preached in all the world for a witness unto all nations; and then shall come the end.' The next words that follow are these: 'Therefore, when ye shall see the abomination of desolation, that was spoken of by Daniel,' &c. Thus may ye see, M. Harding, by the very course and tenor of Christ's answer, that, if the judgment be the judgment, if the end be the end, if the world be the world, then must these words needs have relation to the end of the world." [60]

After an involved argument Jewel plainly states, "Then

[57] *Ibid.*, pp. 930-932.
[58] Jewel, *A Reply to M. Harding's Answer* (1565), in *Works*, vol. 1, pp. 81-552, and vol. 2, pp. 553-811; "Sermon on Haggai I. 2-4.," in vol. 2, pp. 986-1004.
[59] Jewel, *A Defence of the Apology*, in *Works*, vol. 4, pp. 628, 714, 715, 744. The entire *Defence* is in vol. 3, pp. 113-626, and vol. 4, pp. 627-1086.
[60] *Ibid.*, vol. 4, pp. 728, 729.

doth St Paul say, 'Antichrist shall sit within the church.' In like
sense Christ saith: 'Antichrist shall sit in the holy place.' By
which words many of the best-learned fathers have expounded
'the church of God.' " [61]

13. SIXTH-CENTURY HEADSHIP OF CHURCHES RECOGNIZED.—
Finally, after dwelling on the historical development of the
Papacy, Jewel lays much stress on Justinian's decision in the
sixth century that the bishop of Rome be head of all the
churches, and his pledge to advance the authority of the Roman
see. He remarks:

> "The emperor's purpose was, as it plainly appeareth by his words, by
> these and all other means to bring the see of Rome into credit. For thus
> he saith: . . . 'We labour to advance the honor and authority of your see." [62]

14. END OF ANTICHRIST ACCOMPLISHED BY SECOND ADVENT.
—As to the end of Antichrist, at the end of the world and the
resurrection, Jewel states:

> "Here may we see the overthrow of Babylon, 'which made all nations
> to drink of the wine of the wrath of her fornication;' how she is destroyed
> with the breath of God's mouth. Here we behold the resurrection of the
> dead; and four and twenty elders sit before God on their seats, and the
> Ancient of days sit upon his throne, and the judgment-seat, and the books
> opened, and all flesh appear before him, and how some are taken into
> everlasting life, and some are sent into everlasting death." [63]

VI. Foxe, the Martyrologist, Writes Commentary on Apocalypse

JOHN FOXE (1516-1587), famed author of *Acts and Monuments*—popularly known as *Foxe's Book of Martyrs*—was born
in Lincolnshire. His childhood had been marked by a love for
reading. In 1533 he entered Oxford as a decided Romanist, and
received his B.A. in 1538, and his M.A. in 1543, being chosen a
fellow of Magdalen College the same year. He also served as a
tutor. Applying himself with great diligence to the study of
theology during his university life, he became a convert to the
principles of the Reformation. This tendency was suspected. He

---

[61] *Ibid.*, p. 729.
[62] *Ibid.*, p. 1032.
[63] Jewel, *Treatise of the Holy Scriptures*, in *Works*, vol. 4, p. 1181.

was charged with heresy, and by a judgment of the college was expelled in 1545—the year, incidentally, that the Council of Trent began.

The religious controversies of the time were vivid realities. In 1543 vernacular Bibles had been prohibited to the lower classes, which prohibition was promptly disregarded. The Romanists and the Reformers were about evenly balanced, and spies and treacherous companions abounded. So, during the reign of Mary, Foxe was driven from the country, remaining abroad from 1554 to 1559. Going first to Strassburg, he occupied himself with writing a Latin history of Christian persecutions, which he began at the suggestion of Lady Jane Grey.[64] It dealt chiefly with Wyclif and Huss, coming down only to A.D. 1500. This was the beginning of his *Book of Martyrs,* and was printed by Wendelin Richelius, at Strassburg, in 1554.

In the same year Foxe moved to Frankfurt, where he found the exiled Protestant refugees divided into two camps—Calvinists and Anglicans. In 1555 he went to Basel, and there sustained himself by correcting proofs for an eminent printer, Johann Herbst, or Oporinus, of that city. Meantime he made steady progress on the remainder of his book. In 1559 he completed the Latin edition, and upon the accession of Elizabeth, returned to his native land. Back in England, Foxe associated with Day, the printer, also a former exile. In 1560 he was ordained by the bishop of London, and made prebendary of Salisbury. But he engaged chiefly in literary work, and consistently maintained his Puritan views.

Meantime his book had been given an enthusiastic reception in England. In 1563 the first English edition of *Acts and Monuments* was produced. Its popularity was immense, for the Marian persecution was still fresh in men's minds, along with that of the Spanish Inquisition. However, it was immediately challenged by the Catholics, but major or willful inaccuracies were never

---

[64] Queen of England for nine days in 1554. She was a great-granddaughter of Henry VII, and briefly succeeded Edward VI, but was imprisoned in the Tower after a nine-day reign, and a few months later was beheaded. (Cf. Richard Davey, *The Nine Days' Queen.*)

proved. Foxe corrected minor inaccuracies in a second revised edition of 1570. This subsequent edition was ordered by the Convocation to be placed in every collegiate church. There were four editions during Foxe's lifetime, and by 1684 it had reached its ninth edition, exerting a powerful influence.

In later full editions more than two hundred pages in volume 1 are devoted to a painstaking examination of the fifteen leading attacks on the book, which still lives on.

1. COMMENTARY ON APOCALYPSE INTERRUPTED BY DEATH.— It is not to be wondered that after producing his monumental *Acts and Monuments* portraying the martyrs, many of whom were notable expositors of the prophecies—and not a few of whom had died for their prophetic faith, identifying the Papacy as the predicted Antichrist—Foxe should himself be an expositor of prophecy. In fact, his exposition of the Apocalypse was interrupted by his death. His four-hundred-page Latin work, *Eicasmi seu Meditationes in Sacram Apocalypsin* (Conjectures on the Apocalypse), was published by his son in 1587.[65]

2. SIXTH TRUMPET TURKS; SEVENTH APPROACHING ADVENT. —Foxe's *Conjectures* was written more than twenty years after his *Acts and Monuments*. In this work there are many outstanding points. Foxe, in speaking of the sixth trumpet, states that it is clearer than light itself that this prophetic trumpet of the sixth angel denotes mostly the Turks and their multitude and arms, and adds that the seventh trumpet, heralding the last judgment and advent, could not be far off.[66] The angel of Revelation 10 symbolizes the restoration of gospel preaching and the certainty of the end.[67]

3. TRUE CHURCH AND CHURCH OF PAPAL ANTICHRIST.—The temple of Revelation 11, with its inner and outer courts, he considered the church with its true and false worshipers, and the measuring is the separation and reformation from previous corruption under Antichrist. And the Antichrist of Scripture is

---

[65] Elliott, *op. cit.*, vol. 2, p. 144, and vol. 4, p. 460.
[66] Foxe, *Eicasmi*, pp. 98-106; Elliott, *op. cit.*, vol. 4, pp. 463, 464.
[67] Foxe, *Eicasmi*, pp. 102, 105.

the pope, not the Turk.[68] On the time periods Foxe cites many expositors, but he himself is not clear either as to the time of beginning or the unit of measurement, whether literal time, or on the year-day principle measured from Constantine, Alaric, or Phocas.[69] The travailing woman is God's true church.[70]

4. TWO BEASTS ARE ROME, PAGAN AND PAPAL.—The first beast of Revelation 13 is pagan Rome, and the second beast is the pope, or Antichrist, who revived the old empire wounded to death.[71] The equivalent of *Romanus* in Hebrew and Greek yields the 666.[72] Foxe had completed his work only through chapter 17 at the time of his death. His view of the thousand years, however, had been given twenty-three years previously in his *Acts and Monuments,* which teachings on prophecy we now note.

5. CHALLENGES PAPISTS TO IDENTIFY BEASTS OF REVELATION 13.—In a series of questions propounded to the Catholics, question 3 begins thus: "My third question I take of the thirteenth Chapter of the Book of Revelation. Which Book as it containeth a Prophetical History of the Church, so likewise it requireth by histories to be opened." [73] After describing the first, or ten-horned beast from the sea, and then the two-horned beast from the earth, Foxe asks:

"Upon this descripcion of these two Beasts riseth my question; wherein I desire all Papists, from the highest to the lowest, either to answer, or to consider with themselves, what the spirit of the Prophesie meaneth by the said two Beasts. Neither is the mystery of this Prophesie so obscure, but being Historical by Histories it may be explained and easily expounded. Writing therefore to the Papists, as men expert in Histories, my question is this, That seeing the Prophesie of these two Beasts must needs prefigure some People or Dominion in the World, of some high estate and power; they will now declare unto us, what people or domination this should be. Which if they will do plainly and truly, according to the marks and properties of the said two Beasts here set forth, they must needs be driven of force inevitable to grant and confess, the same to agree only to the City and Em-

[68] *Ibid.,* pp. 100 [*i.e.* 110] -113 (sig. K₁v-K₃r).
[69] *Ibid.,* pp. 122, 123, 144-148; Elliott, *op. cit.,* vol. 4, p. 464.
[70] Foxe, *Eicasmi,* p. 197; Elliott, *op. cit.,* vol. 4, p. 464.
[71] Foxe, *Eicasmi,* pp. 213-216, 223; Elliott, *op. cit.,* vol. 4, p. 465.
[72] Foxe, *Eicasmi,* pp. 269, 270; Elliott, *op. cit.,* vol. 4, pp. 465, 466.
[73] Foxe, "Four Questions Propounded," in *Acts,* vol. 1, sig. a₆v.

pire of Rome, and to no other; which, by these Reasons following of necessity must needs be concluded." [74]

6. Ten-horned Beast Must Import Rome.—Contending
that the first symbol must be "an Empire or Monarchy of great
force, passing all other Monarchies in the world besides," Foxe
asserts that "this must needs argue the empire of Rome and none
other." [75] Continuing, he avers:

> "In that the Beast had seven heads and ten horns, with ten Diadems
> full of blasphemy upon them; those seven heads being expounded in the
> same book, chap. 17. for seven Hills, notoriously importeth the City of
> Rome, wherein were seven hills contained. The like also may be thought of
> the ten horns, being there expounded for ten Kings (signifying belike the
> ten Provinces and kingdoms of the world, subdued to the Roman Empire)
> with ten Crowns of Blasphemy upon their heads; all which conveniently
> agree to the City of Rome." [76]

7. Second Beast Applied to Bishop of Rome.—The sec-
ond beast is then applied to the bishop of Rome in these words:

> "The description of this second Beast being well viewed, it cannot be
> avoided, but needs must be applied to the Bishop of Rome, and to none
> other; as by History, and order of times is evident to be proved. For who
> else representeth the horns of the *Lamb of God which taketh away the
> sins of the World,* but only he? Who speaketh with the voice of the Dragon
> so proudly as he?" [77]

Foxe's challenge to the Catholics is then repeated, and his
own conviction follows:

> "Now if any Papists whatsoever, in answering to this my question, can
> apply this prophetical mystery of these two Beasts otherwise than thus,
> I would heartily desire him to take so much pains to satisfie this doubt at
> his good pleasure and leisure. In the mean season, let this stand for a
> *Corolarium,* that the Bishop of Rome by this description must be that
> second Beast prophesied to come in the later time of the Church under a
> false pretensed Lamb, to restore again the old Persecutions of Rome, and to
> disturb the whole Church of Christ, as this day too truly it is come to
> pass." [78]

8. Likewise Challenges Catholics as to 2 Thessalo-
nians 2.—Coming to his fourth point, Foxe stresses another

---

[74] *Ibid.*   [75] *Ibid.*   [76] *Ibid.*, sigs. a₆v, b₁r.
[77] *Ibid.*, sig. b₁r.   [78] *Ibid.*

"prophetical place of Scripture, no less evident against the Bishop of Rome," which he takes out of Second Thessalonians:

"As touching my fourth question, although I could urge you with another like prophetical place of Scripture, no less evident against the Bishop of Rome, taken out of the second Epistle of Saint Paul to the Thessalonians, where mention is made of the Son of Perdition, *sitting in the Temple of God, as God, and advancing himself above all that is called God, &c.* Which place ye can by no reasonable evasion avoid." [79]

9. STILL FOLLOWS AUGUSTINE ON THE THOUSAND YEARS.— On the question of the thousand years of Revelation 20, however, Foxe (with many others) still followed the Augustinian theory of the binding of Satan at the first advent, or a little later. He places the "loosing" at "about the thousandth year after the ceasing of Persecution," in the time of Constantine.[80] He refers to the common supposition that the chaining of Satan took place at the birth of Christ, and admits a spiritual binding at the death of Christ "not only for a thousand years, but for ever"; but he applies the prophecy of the thousand years to the restraining of Satan from persecuting the church, namely, the time of Constantine, who ended the three centuries of pagan persecution. He computes it thus: After the forty-two months, counted at seven years each (A.D. 30 + 1294), the thousand years begin with the victory of Constantine over Maxentius, and end in 1324.[81]

VII. Sandys Summarizes Signs and Prophecies of End

EDWIN SANDYS (1519-1588), archbishop of York and primate of England, was born in Lancastershire. He was graduated from St. John's College, Cambridge, when Protestant views were prevalent. He became junior proctor of the university in 1542, and was made master of Catherine Hall in 1547. After receiving his D.D., and becoming prebendary of the Cathedral of Peterborough in 1548 and of Carlisle in 1552, he became vice-chancellor of Cambridge University in 1553, under King Edward VI.

---

[79] *Ibid.*
[80] Foxe, *Acts*, vol. 1, p. 1, and book 1, p. 116; book 2, p. 149.
[81] *Ibid.*, book 1, p. 111; book 5, p. 452.

14

Having embraced Protestantism, Sandys was deprived of office upon the accession of Queen Mary (1553) and, along with John Bradford, was confined in the Tower for twenty-nine weeks. However, he escaped to the Continent in 1554.

Upon the accession of Elizabeth, Sandys returned to England and was successively created bishop of Worcester (1559), bishop of London (1570), and archbishop of York (1576). A man of learning and influence, he was one of nine Protestant leaders appointed by Queen Elizabeth to hold a disputation with an equal number of Romanists before both houses of Parliament. He was also one of a commission appointed to revise the Liturgy, and assisted in the translation of the *Bishops' Bible*.

1. ANTICHRIST DISPENSES SALVATION FOR A PRICE.—Twenty-two of Sandys' impressive sermons have been preserved to us. In the "First Sermon," based on Isaiah 55, "Ho, every one that thirsteth," stressing coming to the waters without money and without price, he contrasts "the contrary"—salvation sold by the papal Antichrist for money:

"He that sitteth in the temple of God, and termeth himself Christ's vicar, doth in like sort offer unto the people bread, water, wine, milk, pardon of sins, grace, mercy, and eternal life; but not freely: he is a merchant, he giveth nothing, and that is nothing which he selleth. For although he make large promises to the buyer, he selleth that which he hath not to deliver. 'Eternal life is the gift of God.' The pope therefore selleth but wind and smoke for fire, shadows for truths: he deceiveth the buyers with false sleights, false measures, false weights. Beware of this merchant, lose not your labour, cast not away your money: it is not meat but poison which he offereth you. His physic cannot heal your diseases; his holy water cannot wash away the spots of a sullied and defiled soul, as he untruly would bear you in hand; his blasphemous masses do not appease, but provoke God's wrath; they cannot benefit the quick, much less the dead, which either need no help, or are past all help; his rotten relics cannot comfort you; his blind, dumb, and worm-eaten idols can do you no good. It is cast away which is spent upon his shameless pardons; they will not prevail—God will not admit them: by his Latin service ye cannot be edified, or made wiser. Yet this trumpery they sell for money, and upon this trash they cause silly men to waste their substance, and to these to commit their souls. Thus you see a manifest difference between Christ and antichrist." [82]

---

[82] Edwin Sandys, *The Sermons of Edwin Sandys*, pp. 11, 12.

2. ROMAN ANTICHRIST DECLARED GUILTY OF TREASON.—
Of similar vein is the phrasing of the eighteenth sermon, "Then There Shall Be Signs":

"Christ is obscured by that great enemy antichrist, 'the man of sin,' who hath set himself in Christ's peculiar place, and will be 'exalted above all that is called God.' To make any other mediator between God and man, saving only Christ Jesus which is not only man, but also God; to seek elsewhere remission of sins, justification, redemption, sanctification, or salvation, that only in this Jesus, and in him crucified, doth darken and make dim both him and his merits. And of this treason the Romish antichristian church, which they term catholic, is found guilty. For the children of this harlot labour by all means to obscure the Son of God, to rob him of the glory of his deserts in our salvation." [83]

3. OUTLINE PROPHECIES AND SIGNS ATTEST IMPENDING JUDG-
ment.—Most remarkable of all is the twentieth sermon, "The End of All Things is At Hand." Discussing how "Christ at His second coming shall finish the course of all this sinful world" and of the impending day of judgment, Sandys succinctly gives the signs and the prophecies by which we may know that it is near. This is his summary:

"Now, as we know not the day and time, so let us be assured that this coming of the Lord is near. He is not slack, as we do count slackness. That it is at hand, it may be probably gathered out of the scriptures in divers places. The signs mentioned by Christ in the gospel, which should be the foreshewers of this terrible day, are almost already all fulfilled. The prophecies of Daniel of the four monarchies, of the little horn, and of the times, weeks, and days, are manifestly come to pass. The defections or fallings away, which are spoken of in holy scriptures, are also in great part accomplished. The provinces, the ten kingdoms, are fallen from the Roman empire, and that wicked one hath wrought the mystery of iniquity." [84]

4. ANTICHRIST'S IDENTITY INDICATED WITH PROPHETIC
FINGER.—Alluding next to the harassments of Mohammedans, and then to the papal falling away from the faith fulfilling the prophecies of Paul and Peter, Sandys admits and defends Protestantism's departure from Catholicism, declaring, "We do utterly abandon this usurped and proud authority: we have happily

---

[83] *Ibid.*, pp. 358, 359.
[84] *Ibid.*, p. 388.

forsaken that synagogue of Satan." Then comes this scorching
denunciation, couched in biting phrases:

"This is our apostasy. We have forsaken him that hath forsaken God,
and whom God hath forsaken: we have left that man of sin, that rose-
coloured harlot with whom the kings of the earth have committed fornication, that triple-crowned beast, that double-sworded tyrant, that thief and
murderer, who hath robbed so many souls of salvation, and sucked so much·
innocent blood of christian martyrs, that adversary unto Christ, that pretensed vicar, who hath displaced the person, not only taking upon him
Christ's room and office, but also boasting himself as if he were a god, and
being content of his parasites so to be called. This wicked man of sin is at
length revealed by the sincere preaching of the gospel. Daniel in his prophecies, Paul in his epistles, and John in his revelations, have most lively
described and pointed him forth even as it were with the finger. Yea,
through his pride and ambition, his usurping authority and worldly rule,
his tyranny and persecuting of Christ in his members, he hath sufficiently
revealed and detected himself, if none had done it for him." [85]

5. END OF ANTICHRIST'S REIGN DRAWS NEAR.—Asserting
that the Lord shall destroy the Papacy with the breath of His
mouth, and then shall be the end, Sandys adds that "the blast
of God's trump hath made him already stagger: he hath caught
such a cramp, that he beginneth now to halt." Iniquity is
abounding and the gospel sounding. Therefore, he concludes,
"The end is near at hand." [86]

VIII. Fulke Identifies Papal Antichrist by Seven Hills of Rome

WILLIAM FULKE (c. 1538-1589), English Puritan, was born
in London and educated at St. Paul's School and St. John's College, Cambridge, which he entered in 1555. After studying law
for six years at Clifford Inn, he returned to Cambridge to study
theology. He was well versed in science and in the Oriental languages. Thus he secured his B.A. in 1558, his M.A. in 1563, and
his B.D. in 1568. He became a lecturer in Hebrew at Cambridge
in 1567. He allied himself with Thomas Cartright (1535-1603),
zealous champion of Puritanism and opponent of Roman
Catholicism. He was also a participant in the vestarian contro-

---

[85] *Ibid.*, p. 389.
[86] *Ibid.*, pp. 389, 390.

versy, to discard surplices in the chapel of St. John's. This led to his expulsion from Cambridge. He became rector of Warley in 1571, and in 1572 went to Paris as chaplain to the earl of Lincoln, England's ambassador to France. He secured his D.D. in 1572.

In 1578 Fulke was made master of Pembroke Hall, Cambridge. The next year, as vice-chancellor of the university, he was deputed to hold a public disputation with Edward Campion in the Tower of London, and in 1582 was one of twenty-five theologians to hold disputations with Roman Catholic priests and Jesuits. His writings were mostly in the field of polemical theology, largely against the papacy. When the Catholics at Rheims published their English version of the New Testament, Fulke reprinted it with added annotations refuting the Catholic notes.[87]

1. CAN SETTLE ANTICHRIST ONLY IN SEE OF ROME.—In an eighteen-chapter controversial treatise, *A Discovery of the Dangerous Rock of the Popish Church* (1580), Fulke reaches the heart of his argument in chapter 17. In the first paragraph he says:

"They [Protestants] can find no place to settle Antichrist in but in the see of Rome, so beautified and dignified by Christ, and all the primitive Church. But seeing Antichrist is appointed to sit in the temple of God, which is a higher place than S. Peter's chair, it is no marvel if Satan have thrust him into that see, which of old time was accounted the top and castle of all religion." [88]

2. GREGORY'S PREDICTION OF ANTICHRIST FULFILLED IN POPE.—Contending that Antichrist is a succession of men, not a single individual, and that the seat of civil empire was removed from Rome "before Antichrist the Pope" was installed, Fulke answers the argument that Antichrist would not come until just before the end of the world, and makes this comprehensive statement:

---

[87] For a discussion of this version see pp. 549-552.
[88] William Fulke, *A Discovery of the Dangerous Rock of the Popish Church,* in **Works,** vol. 2 (Fulke's Answers to Stapleton, Martiall, and Sanders), p. 366.

"Gregory, seeing the ambition of John of Constantinople, affirmed that the time of the revelation of Antichrist was even at hand; and that the same John was the forerunner of Antichrist, and Antichrist should shortly be revealed, and 'an army of Priests' should wait upon him. Now seeing he, whosoever took that which John refused, by Gregory's judgment should be Antichrist; and it is certain that Pope Boniface the third, soon after the death of Gregory and his successors, usurped not only that but more also; it is certain by Gregory's prophecy, that the Pope is Antichrist: who, being within the six hundred years, answereth to M. Sander's fond challenge. And although none within that compass had pointed out the see of Rome, yet the fulfilling of the prophecy in the latter times did sufficiently declare who it should be. And most of the ancient writers name Rome to be the see of Antichrist; although they could not foresee that the bishoprick of that see should degenerate into the tyranny of Antichrist." [89]

3. SEVEN-HILLED CITY STILL SEE OF ROME.—Next, answering the contention that Rome had gone from the "seven hills" to the plain, and that the pope was sitting on the other side of the Tiber, upon Vatican hill, Fulke says that "although the people have removed their habitations from the hills, yet the Pope hath not; for on them be still to this day his churches, monasteries and courts." These he impressively tabulates thus:

"For on the Mount Coelius be the monastery of Saint Gregory, the church of John and Paul, the hospital of our Saviour, the round church, the great minster of Lateran. . . .

"The Mount Aventinus hath three monasteries; of Sabina, Bonifacius, and Alexius.

"The Mount Exquilinus hath the church of Saint Peter himself, surnamed *Ad vincula.*

"The Mount Viminalis hath the church of S. Laurence in Palisperna, [Panisperna,] and S. Potentiana.

"The Mount Tarpeius, or Capitoline, hath an house of Friars Minors called *Ara Coeli:* and there did Boniface the ninth build a fair house of brick for keeping of courts.

"The Mount Palatinus is a place called the Great Palace; and hath an old church of S. Nicholas, and of S. Andrew.

"The Mount Quirinalis is not altogether void of habitation: to which appertaineth the church of S. Maria de Populo.

"The city with seven hills is still the see of Antichrist; described by S. John at such time as those seven hills were most of all inhabited, and garnished with sumptuous buildings." [90]

---

[89] *Ibid.*, p. 371.
[90] *Ibid.*, pp. 372, 373.

4. Having Located the See, the Occupant Is Known.—
Fulke's convincing conclusion follows:

"The see being found, it is easy to find the person by S. Paul's description; and this note especially, that excludeth the heathen tyrants, 'He shall
sit in the temple of God:' which when we see to be fulfilled in the Pope,
although none of the eldest Fathers could see it, because it was performed
after their death, we nothing doubt to say and affirm still, that the Pope
is that 'Man of sin,' and 'Son of perdition,' the adversary that lifteth up
himself 'above all that is called God;' and shall be destroyed 'by the spirit
of the Lord's mouth, and by the glory of His coming.' " [91]

IX. Prophetic Interpretation Woven into Formulas of Church

That the prophecies and their interpretation were woven
right into the catechisms, homilies, and other standard formulas
and instruments of the church, as well as in the writings of individuals, is evident from these extracts from *A Short Catechisme,
or playne instruction, conteynynge the sume of Christian learninge, sett fourth by the kings maiesties authoritie, for all Scholemaisters to teache,* drawn up under Edward VI in 1553, in the
first year of his reign. That the establishment of the kingdom
was yet future, and not the Catholic Church of the Middle Ages,
is clearly stated.

"The end of the world holi scripture calleth the fulfyllynge & par-
formaunce of the kyngdome and mistery of Christ, and the renewing of all
thynges." [92]

1. Catechism States Stone Kingdom Yet Future.—More
important and explicit still is the interpretation of the stone
of Daniel 2, which is held to be yet future. This is the catccheti-
cal response required of the "scholar" to the "maister's" inquiry
as to what way these things were to come to pass:

"For we see not yet all thynges in subiection to Christe: we see not
the stone hewed offron the mountayne wythoute woorke of man, which all
to brosed and brought to nought ye image whiche Daniell, descriveth that
the onlye rocke Christe may obtayn and possesse the dominion of the hole
world, graunted him of his father. Antichrist is not yet slayne. For thys

---

[91] *Ibid.,* p. 373.
[92] *A Short Catechisme,* fol. xxxv r.

cause do we longe for, and praye that it may at length come to passe and be fulfylled, that Christe may reign with his sainctes, accordinge to Gods promises." [93]

Then the master responds, "God graunte hys kyngdome may come: and that spedilye." [94]

2. HOMILIES CALL POPE ANTICHRIST, CHURCH BABYLON.—In 1547 Cranmer and others, including Becon and probably Latimer and Ridley, had prepared the book of homilies, which they called *Certayne Sermons, or Homelies, appoynted by the kynges Maistie, to be declared and redde, by all persones, Vicars, or Curates, every Sondaye in their churches, where they have Cure.* A second book of homilies was published in 1563 by Bishop Jewel and others. These volumes of homilies comprise sermons appointed by Edward VI and Elizabeth, respectively, to be read as part of the divine service, and endorsed in Article 35 in the Thirty-Nine Articles of the Church of England. In one of these homilies we read:

"And concerning the usurped power of the bishop of Rome, which he most wrongfully challengeth, as the successor of Christ and Peter, we may easily perceive how false, feigned, and forged it is, not only in that it hath no sufficient ground in holy Scripture, but also by the fruits and doctrine thereof. For our Saviour Christ and St. Peter teach, most earnestly and agreeably, obedience to kings, as to the chief and supreme rulers in this world next under God; but the bishop of Rome teacheth, that they that are under him are free from all burdens and charges of the commonwealth and obedience towards their prince, most clearly against Christ's doctrine and St. Peter's. He ought therefore rather to be called Antichrist and the successor of the Scribes and Pharisees, than Christ's vicar or St. Peter's successor." [95]

And in *The Second Tome of Homilies,* "of Such Matters as Were Promised and Intituled in the former Part of Homilies Set out by the authority of the Queen's Magesty, and read in every Parish Church agreebly," occur the words:

---

[93] *Ibid.,* fol. lvii v, lviii r.
[94] *Ibid.,* fol. lviii r.
[95] "An Exhortation Concerning Good Order and Obedience To Rulers and Magistrates" (Third Part), in *Certain Sermons or Homilies Appointed To Be Read in Churches in the Time of Queen Elizabeth* (1890 ed.), pp. 119, 120; see also *Wylie,* op. cit., vol. 3, p. 436.

"If they deny it, let them read the eleventh chapter of Daniel the Prophet; who saith of Antichrist, *He shall worship god whom his fathers knew not with golde, silver, and with precious stone, and other things of pleasure."* [96]

The "idolatrious Church" is the unbeautiful but outwardly adorned woman of Revelation 17 and 18, and the decking of images is a token of Antichrist's kingdom.[97]

---

[96] "An Homily Against Peril of Idolatry and Superfluous Decking of Churches" (Third Part), in *Certain Sermons or Homilies*, p. 243.
[97] *Ibid.*, pp. 272, 274.

CHAPTER NINETEEN

Calvin

Clear Only Regarding Antichrist

I. Bird's-eye View of Leading Allocations of 70 Weeks

Before continuing with the line of witnesses on prophetic exposition, particularly in French Switzerland, let us pause long enough to get a bird's-eye view of the leading positions on the chronological placing of the seventy weeks. This will shed light on the frequent expositions and slight variations of this vital time prophecy, held as weeks of years by Jews, Catholics, and Protestants alike. We will first have a glance at the technical or chronological reasons for the slightly divergent datings.

There is general agreement among Christian writers that the beginning point was either from the time of the vision or from some imperial edict connected with the restoration of Jerusalem. Similarly, the ending is placed at or near the time of Christ's death, though a few extend the period to the destruction of Jerusalem. Aside from the prophetic expositors dealt with elsewhere in this volume, notice will here be taken of eight leading writers on the seventy weeks, and a convenient tabular reference list will be given to summarize the leading datings from Luther (1530) to William Hales (1799).

Luther, Melanchthon, Calvin, and Bibliander all interpreted the seventy weeks as weeks of years, beginning them with the edict of Cyrus, the reign of Darius Hystaspes, or the second year of Darius (identified as Artaxerxes Longimanus). Funck produced a more systematic synchronization of the various datings, by which he aligned the canon of Ptolemy with the Olympiad dates, although he placed the first Olympiad a year later in the B.C. scale than the standard dating.[1] Bullinger and Nigrinus followed Funck on the seventy weeks. Then came a series of writers who, while dealing principally with chronology or history, are mentioned in this present volume because they referred to the period of the seventy weeks. They will be considered further in Volume IV, in connection with the nineteenth-century interpretations of the 2300 year-days. Here are the eight not discussed elsewhere in this volume:

1. JOSEPH SCALIGER (1540-1609) was a French Protestant, the most prominent scholar of his time, and the father of modern technical and historical chronology. He devised the chronological system called the Julian Period, based on lunar and solar cycles, which by using a single long scale avoided the difficulty of computing B.C. and A.D. dates in two directions. In the Julian Period dating, J.P. 4713 and J.P. 4714 correspond respectively to 1 B.C. and A.D. 1. Scaliger reckoned the seventy weeks from the second year of Darius Nothus to the destruction of Jerusalem, or from J.P. 4290 to J.P. 4783 (which is 424 B.C.-A.D. 70). He makes the interval 493 years, because he takes the "midst" or "half" of the week, three and a half years, as a separate period in addition to the seventy weeks.[2]

---

[1] Without going into technical chronology, it may be observed that Ptolemy's Egyptian years, numbered by the Nabonassar Era, and the Greek years of the Olympiads, or those of any ancient calendar, cannot be accurately designated by single B.C. dates; for the lunar years of the Olympiads run approximately from midsummer to midsummer, whereas Ptolemy's 365-day years of the Nabonassar Era, beginning on February 26 in 747 B.C. (according to his numerous eclipse data), do not even preserve a uniform overlap with our years, but shift slowly through the seasons for lack of leap-year corrections. Thus Ptolemy's N.E. 1 is really 747/6 B.C., and the first year of the first Olympiad is, as now generally accepted, 776/5 B.C. So, when a chronological table, such as Funck's, prints an Olympic year alongside a corresponding B.C. year, it is necessary to know whether he means that the Olympic year *began* in that B.C. year or *ended* in it. Funck's B.C. numbering runs consistently one year later than the modern standard dating, because, after aligning his canon dating with the Olympiads, he derives his B.C. equivalents from the Olympiads, which he begins (in common with other writers of his time) at 775/4 B.C. instead of 776/5, later generally accepted on the basis of several eclipse dates.

Ptolemy's chronology of the earlier Persian kings is included here for reference. The canon dates each reign from the beginning, not of the Persian, but of the Egyptian calendar year, whose B.C. equivalents are taken from F. K. Ginzel, *Handbuch der mathematischen und technischen Chronologie*, vol. 1, p. 139: Cyrus, Jan. 5, 538; Cambyses, Jan. 3, 529; Darius I (Hystaspes), Jan. 1, 521; Xerxes, Dec. 23, 486; Artaxerxes I (Longimanus), Dec. 17, 465; Darius II (Nothus), Dec. 7, 424; Artaxerxes II (Mnemon), Dec. 2, 405. The first years of these reigns according to the Persian calendar began several months later than the canon years.

[2] Joseph Scaliger, *Opus de Emendatione Temporum* (1629 ed.), pp. 361, 599-608.

2. Denis Petau, better known as Dionysius Petavius (1583-1652), was a noted Jesuit theologian. He also wrote an extended work on chronology (1627), in which he generally followed that of Scaliger, criticized it violently in the polemical fashion of the day, and in many points improved on it. He began the seventy weeks with Nehemiah's return in the twentieth year of Artaxerxes Longimanus (not the twentieth from the death of Xerxes, but from a conjectured coregency beginning ten years earlier), and calculated the period from J.P. 4259, or 455 B.C., with the crucifixion in J.P. 4744, or A.D. 31, in the third year of the seventieth week (which would end the week in A.D. 36).[3] Petavius regards the ceasing of the sacrifices in the midst of the week as the abrogation of the old covenant at the crucifixion, and understands the abomination of desolation as the ruin of the city and temple under the Romans.[4]

3. James Ussher (1581-1656), Anglican archbishop of Armagh, Ireland, published his *Annales* (1650-54), which became the standard for Biblical chronology for nearly two hundred years among both Catholics and Protestants. Ussher, like Petavius, shifts the accession of Artaxerxes, but he puts it nine years earlier, rather than ten. So the seventy weeks, from the twentieth year of Artaxerxes, run from 454 B.C. to A.D. 37, with the cross in A.D. 33.[5] Ussher's dating of the seventy weeks was followed by many later authorities. It appeared in chronological supplements of both Protestant and Catholic Bibles, and was followed by such Catholic writers as Calmet (1672-1757) and

---

[3] Denis Petau, *De Doctrina Temporum* (1757 ed.), book 13 (tables), vol. 2, pp. 316, 374; *Rationarium Temporum* (1733 ed.), part 2, book 3, chap. 10, vol. 2, p. 192. This coregency had no basis except his assumption in order to harmonize Ptolemy's dating of Artaxerxes with a rather uncertain statement of a Greek historian concerning Themistocles, and he uses the earlier beginning only in computing this seventy-week period. (See *Rationarium Temporum*, book 3, chap. 10, vol. 2, pp. 189-192.) The ending date, A.D. 36, as derived from Petavius' A.D. 31 as the third year of the week, is not a slip in addition; the third year of the seventieth week, in which he places the crucifixion, *begins* in A.D. 31, but the last, or 490th year, *ends* in A.D. 36. The apparent difficulty would be avoided by using double dates: If the third year is A.D. 31/2, the seventh is clearly A.D. 35/6. Neither is the equation "455 B.C. + 490 years = A.D. 36" incorrect; for purposes of addition, 455 B.C. is —454, as will be seen in note 11 of this chapter.
[4] Petau, *De Doctrina Temporum*, book 12, chap. 33, vol. 2, p. 265.
[5] James Ussher, *Annales Veteris Testamenti*, p. 195; *The Annals of the World*, pp. 137, 835, 847. He makes the shift for the same reason as Petavius, but he does not conjecture a coregency. He merely subtracts nine years from Xerxes' reign to make the adjustment desired, although the historical records, as well as later archaeological documents, give Xerxes a much longer reign.

Rollin (1661-1741).[6] It is odd that the Protestant Ussher's seventy-week dating should have been more popular among Catholics than that of their own Petavius; perhaps the one year's difference escaped the readers.

4. PHILIPPE LABBE (1607-1667), distinguished Jesuit theologian and writer on history, geography, and philology, was best known for his collaboration with Gabriel Cossart in the compilation of the *Sacrosancta Concilia*. He also wrote an extensive work on chronology (1638). If the posthumous 1670 edition represents his own chronology, he deals with the seventy weeks as follows: On the one hand he gives Artaxerxes a nine-year coregency, like Petavius, yet does not follow his interpretation exactly; on the other hand he, like Ussher, counts the seventy weeks from 454 B.C. to A.D. 37, beginning with the return of Nehemiah, placing the baptism of Jesus at the end of the sixty-nine weeks, and the cross three and a half years later, in the fourth year of the 70th week, A.D. 33.[7]

5. WILLIAM LLOYD (1627-1717), bishop of Worcester, who in 1701 inserted the Ussher chronology (with minor revisions) in the Authorized Version margin, did not follow Ussher on the dating of the seventy weeks. Using the canon dating, he began the period in the twentieth year of Artaxerxes, 445 B.C., but ended it in A.D. 70 by an unusual method. Reckoning 483 years at 360 days each, instead of true solar years, he reached A.D. 32 for the end of the 69th week, with the cross at the next Passover, in 33, followed, after a gap, by the 70th week during the Jewish Wars, from A.D. 63 to the destruction of the temple in A.D. 70.[8]

6. HUMPHREY PRIDEAUX (1648-1724), dean of Norwich and

---

[6] AUGUSTIN CALMET, *Dictionarium . . . Sacrae Scripturae*, vol. 1, "Bibliotheca Sacra," pp. 12, 135, Preface, p. vi, and p. 125, art. "Artaxerxes Longimanus"; British and Foreign Bible Society, *Historical Catalogue of the Printed Editions of Holy Scripture*, vol. 1, p. 248; Douay Bible marginal notes on 2 Esdras 2; Authorized Bible, London, 1701 (and many later editions), chronological "Index," entry under 455 B.C.; CHARLES ROLLIN, *Ancient History*, vol. 2, p. 109. It should be noted that the *marginal* dates for Artaxerxes in the Authorized Version are not Ussher's, but are as revised by Bishop Lloyd. These marginal notes do not mention the seventy weeks, but the dates were used in interpreting that prophecy by many nineteenth-century English and American expositors.

[7] Philippe Labbe, *Concordia Chronologica*, vol. 5, p. 593; see also pp. 81, 83, 85.

[8] This seems to have been followed only by Benjamin Marshall, in whose *Chronological Tables*, table 3 and Appendix, Lloyd's unpublished scheme of the seventy weeks is preserved.

PRINCIPAL INTERPRETATIONS OF SEVENTY WEEKS

Date of Pub.	Expositor	70 Weeks (B.C.-A.D.)	Basis of Chronology	Grouping
1530	Luther	No date	2d yr. of Darius Longimanus to 7th yr. after crucifixion	Dates inexact or incomplete
1543	Melanchthon	No date	2d yr. of Longimanus to 3½ yrs. after crucifixion	
1558	Bibliander	—A.D. 1	32d yr. of Darius Hystaspes to birth of Christ	
1561	Calvin	No date	1st yr. of Cyrus to 3½ yrs. after cross	
1564, 70	Funck	457-34	Olympiads; Ptolemy*	7th year of Artaxerxes to cross; Olympiads from B.C. 775/4*
1570	Nigrinus	456-34	Follows Funck; ignores lack of 0 yr.† in subtracting	
1576	Bullinger	{ 458-33? 457-34?	Follows Funck rather closely; years not exact.	
1583	Scaliger	424-70	Ptolemy; 490 + 3½ yrs. counted back from A.D. 70	Based on A.D. 70
1643	Mede	{ 421-70 417-74	Ptolemy; destruction of temple in end, or preferably midst, of 70th week	
1627	Petavius	455- (36)	Ptolemy; 20th yr. from conjectured coregency of 10 yrs.	20th year of Artaxerxes shifted
1650	Ussher	454- (37)	Abandons Ptolemy here; shifts Artaxerxes' reign 9 yrs. earlier	
1670	Labbe	454-37	Ptolemy; calls shift coregency	
1702	Whiston	445-33+	Ptolemy; 360-day yr.‡; 70th wk. begins A.D. 33	20th yr. of Artaxerxes; 360-day yrs.
(1713)	Lloyd	445-70	Ptolemy; 360-day yrs.; gap (32-63) between 69th wk. and 70th	
1715-18	Prideaux	458-33	Ptolemy; 33 cross by Rabbinical calendar	7th yr. of Artaxerxes to cross
1733	Isaac Newton	457-34	Ptolemy; Olympiads; from supposed accession after Artabanus	
1754	Blair	458-33	Ptolemy; complete tables; same as Prideaux	
1756	Ferguson	—457-33	Ptolemy; astron. reckoning; 0 yr.; therefore 457 = Prideaux's 458	
1768	Petri	454/3?-37?	Ignores secular chron. as uncertain; 453 yrs. before Christ's birth.	Cross + 3½
1787	Wood	420-70	Same as Scaliger, Mede; overlooks absence of 0 yr.	Based on A.D. 70
1799	Hales	420-70	Ptolemy; follows Scaliger, Mede, Wood; overlooks lack of 0 yr.	

* See note 1, p. 427.
† See note 11, p. 431.
‡ See pp. 672, note 6, and 673.

Oriental scholar, follows the canon dating as given by Scaliger and Petavius, but runs the 490 years from 458 B.C. to A.D. 33, or J.P. 4256 to 4746; like many others after him, he begins at the popularly held crucifixion date in A.D. 33 and reckons back to arrive at the starting point, the seventh year of Artaxerxes.[9]

7. JOHN BLAIR (d. 1782), of Edinburgh, published chronological tables (1754) synchronizing the Julian Period, B.C., Roman, Olympiad, and canon dating, which were a standard reference work for two hundred years. He ran the seventy weeks, like Prideaux, from the seventh year of Artaxerxes to the cross (458 B.C. to A.D. 33).[10]

8. JAMES FERGUSON, F.R.S. (1710-1776), Scottish astronomer, published in 1756 an explanation of the seventy weeks, ending the period at the crucifixion. This he placed at A.D. 33 through astronomical calculations similar to those of Roger Bacon in the thirteenth century: By assuming that the Jewish Rabbinical calendar (which actually was revised to its historic form several centuries later) was applicable in the time of Christ, and by calculating for several possible years, the full moon dates on which the Passover, according to that calendar, would have fallen, he arrived at A.D. 33 as the only year in which such a Passover date would fall on Friday. From this year, then (J.P. 4746), he counted back 490 years to reach the starting point of the seventy weeks at J.P. 4256, the seventh year of Artaxerxes Longimanus, which he called 457 "before Christ," according to the astronomical method of numbering (—457, as modern astronomers would write it), but which is the common chronological 458 B.C.[11] His work did much to popularize the 33 cruci-

[9] Humphrey Prideaux, *The Old and New Testament Connected in the History of the Jews* (1719 ed.), part 1, book 5, pp. 113-116; part 2, book 9, pp. 287, 288.
[10] John Blair, *The Chronology and History of the World* (1768 ed.), tables 11, 21.
[11] James Ferguson, *Astronomy Explained Upon Sir Isaac Newton's Principles*, secs. 349-353, 395; also his *Tables and Tracts, Relative to Several Arts and Sciences*, pp. 177-194; and *An Astronomical Lecture, on . . . the True Year of Our Saviour's Crucifixion, . . . and the Prophet Daniel's Seventy Weeks*, pp. 32, 33. That his dates before Christ are astronomical is shown by the presence of the year 0 in his tables. For the difference between the astronomical and chronological dating, due to the fact that chronological tables show 1 B.C. followed immediately by A.D. 1, while astronomers use a 0 year between, see George F. Chambers, *A Handbook of Descriptive and Practical Astronomy*, vol. 2, p. 460.

Astronomical:	—3	—2	—1	0	1	2	3	4
Chronological:	4 B.C.	3 B.C.	2 B.C.	1 B.C.	A.D. 1	A.D. 2	A.D. 3	A.D. 4

fixion date among the prophetic writers of the nineteenth century, as will be seen in Volume IV of the present work.

The accompanying table embraces the foregoing writers on the seventy weeks, together with the leading expositors on this period covered in this present volume. Hales, who closes the series, is treated in Volume III. We now return to the prophetic witness.

II. The Religious Situation on the Continent

Whereas Zwingli's work was mostly confined to the German part of Switzerland, Calvin had planted the Reformation firmly in Geneva, what is now French Switzerland. He is generally considered, next to Luther, the greatest Protestant figure of the sixteenth century. In some ways his influence was more widespread, because it extended into the countries that became great colonizing powers—England and the Dutch Republic. The movement in French Switzerland appeared somewhat later in time, but in essentially the same form.

Calvin was a Frenchman, and although his teaching had a marked influence upon France, the Reformation, however, never became a mass movement there as in northern Germany. The political situation under Francis I was averse to such a development. Spain in the Iberian Peninsula, the kingdom of Naples and Sicily, as well as Austria, were under the firm rule of the emperor Charles V of Hapsburg, a loyal Catholic. Moreover, the Inquisition was holding these countries in its merciless grip so that it was practically impossible for any group of dissenters to organize themselves into a church. Besides, the Latin mentality in general seems to be more in favor of an outward display in matters of religion, which the Roman church, of course, amply provided. In Austria the Reformation had certain success at first. But a Catholic reaction soon started, sponsored mostly by the newly formed order of the Jesuits, and the Reformation was practically rooted out. Through the influence of this order among princes and ruling houses, large sections of southern and western Germany were led back to the Catholic fold.

The Netherlands were well prepared spiritually to receive the seed of the Reformation by the Brethren of the Common Life, who had long established their schools in the Low Countries, and politically by the strong urban communities, which enjoyed a large degree of freedom. Since the country belonged to the crownlands of the Hapsburgs, the Inquisition was established by Charles V in 1522,[12] and a ruthless persecution began, which, however, could not quench the flame of evangelical truth.

In Poland, under the enlightened kings Sigismund I and II, Cracow became the center of Humanistic ideas and Renaissance art. The doctrine of the Reformation influenced Poland's intellectual life, and soon a movement for a Reformed Polish State Church was under way. Protestants of all shades, persecuted elsewhere, streamed into Poland. Not many years later Protestants had won a majority in the diet and elected a Calvinist to be their marshall. But, hopelessly divided in matters of doctrine, they could not consolidate their gains, and political emergencies gave way to a new upsurge of Catholicism.[13] In Ireland, Protestantism was imposed by the English Crown and later became the state religion, but never had any hold on the Irish people generally.

III. Calvin Clear on Antichrist but Uncertain on Other Prophecies

JEAN (JOHN) CALVIN (1509-1564), eminent French Reformer, and generally regarded second only to Luther in Reformation influence, was born at Noyon in northern France, and studied at Paris, Orleans, and Bourges.[14] He first went to the university to prepare himself for the priesthood, but on the request of his father he changed to jurisprudence. While Calvin was at the university, in 1527, his cousin Robert Olivetan induced him

---

[12] George G. Coulton, "Reformation," *Encyclopaedia Britannica*, vol. 19, p. 39.
[13] Robert Nisbet Bain and Roman Dyboski, "Poland: The Reformation to the Partitions," *Ibid.*, vol. 18, pp. 132, 133.
[14] On Calvin consult E. Doumergue, *Jean Calvin*, (7 vols.) ; Eugene Choisy, *Théocratie à Genève au temps de Calvin* (Theocracy at Geneva at the Time of Calvin) (Geneva, 1897) ; and the excellent monograph of Williston Walker, *John Calvin, the Organiser of Reformed Protestantism* (New York, 1906).

to read the Bible, pointing out the conflict between Scripture teachings and the doctrines of the church. Calvin was a serious thinker, and a brilliant student. Moreover, the influence of Wolmar, his instructor in Greek, a professor openly sympathizing with the cause of the Reformation, may have made a deep impression upon his soul, although Calvin himself speaks of his conversion as a sudden act without aid by any human agency. He publicly embraced Protestantism about 1532, beginning to proclaim his new-found faith.

Calvin suddenly found himself the leader of the evangelicals in France. In 1533 a friend of Calvin, Nicolas Cop, became rector of the Sorbonne, and incurred the anger of the faculty by his candid inaugural oration (which was probably prepared by Calvin), and had to flee. Thereupon Calvin left Paris quietly. In 1534 an overzealous Protestant brought on a climax in Paris by publishing an anti-Catholic placard, which caused a violent reaction.[15] Many Protestants were imprisoned, banished, or burned. Between 1533 and 1536 Calvin became a fugitive evangelist for a time, protected by Marguerite of Navarre. Later he went to Strassburg and Basel.

While he was in Basel the first edition of his *Institutio Christianae Religionis* appeared in 1536 [16] and was dedicated to Francis I, king of France. Calvin was only twenty-six years of age when he wrote that remarkable work, which became doubtless the most outstanding systematic presentation of the Protestant faith. Calvin was not satisfied with this first edition, and worked ceaselessly to improve and enlarge his work, until in the eighth edition, which appeared in 1559, it had reached its final form and had grown to five times the size of the original tractate of 1536. In 1536 he also spent some months in Ferrara at the court of the Duchess Renate, and became a spiritual adviser to her until his death. Threatened by the Inquisition, he returned to Switzerland.

---

[15] Philip Schaff, *History*, vol. 7, p. 319.
[16] The first draft was made in 1534-1535, and ten to twelve editions appeared in his lifetime. (Jean Calvin, *Institutes of the Christian Religion*, vol. 1, pp. v, xii ff.)

In the same year Calvin arrived at Geneva, where he was called to be a preacher and teacher of theology. As the apostles of old were circumcised and trained in the Jewish faith, so the Reformers had largely been born, baptized, confirmed, and educated in the Catholic Church. Calvin was no exception. Though prepared for the priesthood, he had never read mass or entered the higher orders, and no bishop had ordained him. He simply responded to the call as pastor and teacher, and was elected at Geneva in 1536 by the presbyters and the council, with the consent of the people.[17]

In 1537, with Farel, Calvin prepared a Confession of Faith. He also introduced stern disciplinary measures of which the city did not approve, and was banished from Geneva in 1538. A few years later the Geneva senate sent Calvin a written invitation to return, which he did in 1541, and sought to make Geneva a model for all Protestant communities. Calvin possessed the iron will, the frankness, and the thorough Bible knowledge necessary to become the second great leader of Protestantism. After a long struggle Geneva became the city of Protestant piety and the training center for missionaries of the evangel.

Calvin insisted on the removal of crosses and other papal emblems from church buildings. And he requested that only psalms and New Testament hymns be sung. He spent the rest of his life in Geneva, where he founded a school, or academy, for training pastors, which later became the university. Until the end of his life he presided over the Little Council, which ruled the city on the theocratic principle. In 1551 he had a controversy with Bolsec on predestination, and in 1553 the burning of Michael Servetus took place. No mercy was shown under the theocracy, since the doctrine of tolerance was not yet recognized. He preached on alternate days, lectured thrice a week, carried on a vast correspondence, and did voluminous writing—his works being published in some fifty volumes.[18]

---

[17] Philip Schaff, *History*, vol. 7, pp. 314, 315.
[18] The first edition of Calvin's complete works was published in 1671.

1. UNSATISFACTORY IN EXPOSITION OF PROPHECIES.—
Though clear in his identification of the Papacy as Antichrist,
Calvin was the least satisfactory of all the Protestant leaders regarding the prophecies in general. He still followed Augustine
in many things—the stone of Daniel 2 as the churchly spiritual
kingdom which will break up all earthly kingdoms, and the
thousand years embracing the various historic troubles that had
afflicted the church militant [19]—but he was averse to giving any
definite explanation to prophetic time periods. The time and
times and half a time should not be considered as years but
might stand for "any period whose termination is in the select
counsel of God." He made the Little Horn refer to Julius Caesar
and the other Caesars, and the forty-two months an indefinite
time.[20] He made the 1290 days to mean anything except 1290,
and he avoided writing on the Apocalypse.[21]

2. IDENTIFICATION OF ANTICHRIST GIVEN EMPEROR.—In
his letter sent to the emperor Charles V on the necessity
of reforming the church, Calvin wrote: "The arrogance of antichrist of which Paul speaks is, that he as God sitteth in the
temple of God, showing himself that he is God." [22]

After declaring that the pope's laws have taken precedence
over God's laws, and alluding to his prohibition of meats and
of marriage as a "doctrine of devils," Calvin avers that the highest impiety is to set man in a higher rank than God. Then he
adds, "If they deny the truth of my statement, I appeal to fact."
The closing portion of the letter reads:

"I deny that See to be Apostolical, wherein nought is seen but a shock-
ing apostasy—I deny him to be the vicar of Christ, who, in furiously persecuting the gospel, demonstrates by his conduct that he is Antichrist—I
deny him to be the successor of Peter, who is doing his utmost to demolish
every edifice that Peter built—and I deny him to be the head of the Church,
who by his tyranny lacerates and dismembers the Church, after dissevering
her from Christ, her true and only Head." [23]

---

[19] Calvin, *Institutes*, vol. 2, p. 25.
[20] Calvin, *Commentaries on the Book of the Prophet Daniel*, vol. 2, pp. 27, 68.
[21] Paul Henry, *The Life and Times of John Calvin*, vol. 1, p. 225, vol. 2, p. 391.
[22] Calvin, *Tracts Relating to the Reformation*, vol. 1, pp. 1 ff; Guinness, *Romanism*, p. 235.
[23] Calvin, *Tracts*, vol. 1, pp. 219, 220; see also Guinness, *Romanism*, p. 236.

3. CITES PAUL AND DANIEL ON ANTICHRIST.—Calvin's identification of the Papacy as the prophesied Antichrist is explicit. In his classic *Institutes* there are at least four sharp applications. Here are two:

"Daniel and Paul had predicted that Antichrist would sit in the temple of God. The head of that cursed and abominable kingdom, in the Western Church, we affirm to be the Pope. When his seat is placed in the temple of God, it suggests, that his kingdom will be such, that he will not abolish the name of Christ or the Church. Hence it appears, that we by no means deny that churches may exist, even under his tyranny; but he has profaned them by sacrilegious impiety, afflicted them by cruel despotism, corrupted and almost terminated their existence by false and pernicious doctrines; like poisonous potions, in such churches, Christ lies half buried, the gospel is suppressed, piety exterminated, and the worship of God almost abolished; in a word, they are altogether in such a state of confusion, that they exhibit a picture of Babylon, rather than of the holy city of God." [24]

"But while the Spirit has expressly predicted, by the mouth of Paul, that there shall come an apostasy, which cannot take place without the pastors being the first to revolt from God, why do we wilfully shut our eyes to our own ruin?" [25]

4. ANTICHRIST LURKS IN THE CHURCH UNDER A MASK.— Explaining that he is only using Bible phraseology when he calls the Roman pontiff "Antichrist," Calvin says:

"Some persons think us too severe and censorious when we call the Roman pontiff Antichrist. But those who are of this opinion do not consider that they bring the same charge of presumption against Paul himself, after whom we speak and whose language we adopt. And lest any one should object, that we improperly pervert to the Roman pontiff those words of Paul, which belong to a different subject, I shall briefly show that they are not capable of any other interpretation than that which applies them to the Papacy. Paul says that Antichrist 'sitteth in the temple of God.' In another place, also, the Holy Spirit, describing his image in the person of Antiochus, declares that his kingdom will consist in 'speaking great words,' or blasphemies, 'against the Most High.' Hence we conclude that it is rather a tyranny over the souls of men, than over their bodies, which is erected in opposition to the spiritual kingdom of Christ. And in the next place, that this tyranny is one which does not abolish the name of Christ or of his Church, but rather abuses the authority of Christ, and conceals itself under the character of the Church, as under a mask. Now, though all the heresies and schisms which have existed from the beginning belong to the kingdom

---

[24] Calvin, *Institutes*, vol. 2, pp. 314, 315. The English translation of 1561, fol. 15v, gives the same thought, only in the quaint but often more vivid phrasing of the time.
[25] *Ibid.*, p. 439.

of Antichrist, yet when Paul predicts an approaching apostasy, he signifies by this description that that seat of abomination shall then be erected when a universal defection shall have seized the church, notwithstanding many members dispersed in different places, persevere in the unity of the faith. But when he adds, that even in his days 'the mystery of iniquity' did 'already work' in secret, what it was afterwards to effect in a more public manner, he gives us to understand that this calamity was neither to be introduced by one man, nor to terminate with one man. Now, when he designates Antichrist by this character,—that he would rob God of His honor in order to assume it to himself,—this is the principal indication which we ought to follow in our inquiries after Antichrist, especially where such pride proceeds to a public desolation of the church. As it is evident therefore that the Roman pontiff has impudently transferred to himself some of the peculiar and exclusive prerogatives of God and Christ, it cannot be doubted that he is the captain and the leader of this impious and abominable kingdom." [26]

A similar statement appears in his work on the Thessalonian epistles, with pagan Rome as the impediment, or historical occasion of delay, and Chrysostom cited as supporting evidence.[27]

5. COMMENTARY ON DANIEL EXCEPTION TO REFORMATION WRITERS.—Calvin's *Commentaries on the Book of the Prophet Daniel,* published in Latin at Geneva, soon after translated into English (1570), is the least satisfactory of all the Reformed expositions, and constitutes an exception. Though it clearly depicts the four world powers of Babylonia, Medo-Persia, Greece, and Rome, it is not clear on the feet and toes of Daniel 2, nor on the ten horns, and the Little Horn of Daniel 7. Of Daniel 2, Calvin does say, "Under one image the whole state of the world is here depicted for us." Again, "The dream was presented to King Nebuchadnezzar, that he might understand all future events to the renovation of the world." [28]

But aside from recognizing the same four empires in Daniel 7, Calvin considers Rome only in its pagan phase, and confines the ten horns and the Little Horn to that era.[29] Calvin is not

---

[26] *Ibid.*, vol. 2, pp. 410, 411 (in 1561 ed., fol. 45v).
[27] Calvin, *Commentaries on the Epistles of Paul the Apostle to the . . . Thessalonians,* pp. 330-333.
[28] Calvin, *Commentaries on the Book of the Prophet Daniel* (1852 ed.), vol. 1, pp. 162-179.
[29] *Ibid.*, vol. 2, pp. 62-68.

too specific on the seventy weeks, and where he is specific he is not chronologically exact. He begins the period with the first decree of Cyrus. The seven weeks, or forty-nine years, extend from Cyrus to the sixth year of Darius. About 480 years elapsed from Darius, Calvin adds, to the death of Christ, who was cut off in the seventieth week. He implies that the crucifixion occurred in the midst of the seventieth week, when the sacrifice and offering end, but does not specifically date the cross.[30]

In many ways Calvin was a Preterist, so far as the book of Daniel was concerned, decades before Alcazar, the Jesuit, popularized Preterism. Nor did Knox's views seem to have induced Calvin to accept the year-day principle. He was, however, very clear and positive on the Papacy as Paul's Man of Sin and the Antichrist of Scripture.

IV. Servetus Persecuted by Calvin, Also Interprets Prophecy

Calvin was a theocrat, persecuting those who differed from his doctrines. His first tract was against the "soul-sleepers" (those who believed in the unconscious sleep of the dead), mostly Anabaptists. In 1537 he had an open discussion with the Anabaptists, and defeated them so thoroughly that they did not dare any longer to show themselves in the city. Torture and the sentence of death were introduced, and several executions and banishments took place between 1542 and 1546. Calvin's most tragic deed was his responsibility for the death of the Spanish physician, MICHAEL SERVETUS (1509-1553), who, although brilliant, had such a haughty and contentious spirit that at the age of twenty he would not take the advice of men like Bucer, Oecolampadius, and Capito, but set out as an independent radical to reform the Reformation. In 1531 he published his antitrinitarian views in his book *Errors of the Trinity*, which appeared blasphemous equally to Catholics and Protestants. The reaction to this book forced him to retire to France, where, under another name, he gained fame as a geographer and a physician, and was

---

[30] *Ibid.*, vol. 2, pp. 212-214, 219-221, 224-227

to all appearances a good Catholic. More than twenty years later he was detected, after publishing his *Christianismi Restitutio* (Restitution of Christianity). This included a revision of his first work, with the addition of an elaborate system of theology, attacking not only the papal Antichrist, but Calvin and Melanchthon in particular. Escaping from imprisonment in Vienne, he went, oddly enough, to Geneva, where Calvin had him apprehended. The French Inquisitors who had tried him at Vienne demanded his extradition, but the Genevan Council preferred to burn its own heretics. So Servetus, with his books, was burned in 1553.[31]

1. ANTICHRIST PORTRAYED BY DANIEL, PAUL, AND JOHN.— Not only was Servetus skilled in the sciences, but he was well versed in Scripture. In his *Christianismi Restitutio*, of 1553, we find many references to the prophetic Word. He viewed church history in the light of Revelation 12—the woman being the true church of the first three centuries, pursued by the dragon, and the pope as the Antichrist predicted by Daniel, Paul, and John, reigning during the 1260 prophetic days or literal years in which the true church was in the wilderness, from 325 to 1585. He placed the beginning of the period with the Council of Nicaea, when the doctrine of the Trinity was triumphant; the union of church and state under Constantine, when the king became a monk; and the establishment of the Papacy under Sylvester, when the bishop became a king. He lists many signs or works of Antichrist from Matthew 24, Daniel 7 and 12, 2 Thessalonians 2, 1 Timothy 4, and Revelation 13 to 18.[32]

2. MILLENNIUM INTRODUCED BY FIRST RESURRECTION.— Servetus believed the first resurrection will take place at the beginning of the millennium, with the general resurrection and final judgment at its close. He called the Roman church the "most beastly of beasts and the most impudent of harlots," but

---

[31] Philip Schaff, *History*, vol. 7, pp. 712-736, 757-786. An "expiatory monument," was erected at Geneva in 1903 by Calvinists, sincerely deploring the burning as an error of their former leaders.
[32] *Ibid.*, pp. 754, 755.

he thought the Protestant churches little better. In fact, he excelled in firing at both Catholics and Protestants the invectives which they customarily hurled at each other. He opposed infant baptism and believed the soul but mortal, with immortality bestowed by the grace of Christ (the doctrine of conditional immortality). Servetus looked for Christ's millennial reign, soon to supersede the papal reign, after which the general judgment would follow, when God would again be all in all—a sort of pantheistic philosophy.[33]

3. Castellio Puts Millennium After Antichrist's Fall. —Calvin tried to justify the execution of Servetus in a booklet,[34] but many disapproved of his arguments, including Castellio of Savoy (1515-1563), professor at Basel, who had been rector of the Genevan Latin School prior to his banishment. Castellio, a language genius, made both a Latin (1551) and a French (1555) translation of the Bible. In the preface to the Latin Bible he declared the thousand years would not begin until after the fall of Antichrist.[35]

V. Vergerius—Venetian Convert Gives Clear Testimony

Petrus Paulus Vergerius, or Pier Paolo Vergerio (1498-1565), first a prominent Catholic lawyer at Venice, and then papal secretary and chaplain, renounced his connection with Rome in 1548, after reading Protestant books.[36] He had formerly been used by the pope in the Augsburg Diet in dealing with the princes and with Luther, but had now become the leading Italian evangelical among the Grisons. In 1553 he accepted a call to Wurttemberg as counselor to Duke Christopher, from which place he undertook several diplomatic missions in behalf of the evangelical cause. He wrote numerous books against the Papacy. Schaff says of him:

---

[33] *Ibid.*, pp. 741-757.
[34] *Ibid.*, p. 790.
[35] Bengel, *Erklärte Offenbarung Johannis*, p. 672; see also Philip Schaff, *History*, vol. 7, pp. 622-628.
[36] Philip Schaff, *History*, vol. 7, pp. 147-155.

"He agreed with Luther that the papacy was an invention of the Devil; that the Pope was the very antichrist seated in the temple of God as predicted by Daniel (11:36) and Paul (2 Thess. 2:3 sq.), and the beast of the Apocalypse; and that he would soon be destroyed by a divine judgment." [37]

So, after surveying the leading allocations of the 70 weeks, and then observing Calvin's none-too-satisfactory excursions into prophecy, as well as noting the positions of Doctor Servetus, the victim of Calvin's antipathy—and with a parting glance at Costellio and Vergerius—we take leave of the Continent, for a time, and turn to Scotland.

---

[37] *Ibid.*, p. 153.

CHAPTER TWENTY

Knox and Napier

Notable Scottish Expositors

I. The Setting of the Reformation in Scotland

England's dominant idea in the Reformation was to free the throne from the pope's supremacy; that of Scotland was the emancipation of conscience from the popish faith. So the chief result of the Reformation in England was a free state, while in Scotland the immediate product was a free church,[1] though these achievements were soon merged.

PRELIMINARY MARTYRDOMS PROFOUNDLY AFFECT KNOX.—In 1525-1527 the Scottish Parliament sought to check the progress of the Reformed faith by stringent laws. All were forbidden to possess or to discuss any of the writings of Luther or his disciples.[2] But stanch Protestants bore their testimony in the face of death at the stake. Patrick Hamilton, studying abroad at the University of Marburg, heard Lambert of Avignon's lectures on the Apocalypse. Inspired by the light of the prophetic Word, he returned to Scotland full of missionary zeal. But after witnessing for a time, he was accused, and died at the stake in 1528.[3]

No threats of burning, however, could deter the Scotch from secret meetings at night, or from bringing forth their Bibles from their secret hiding places and strengthening one another with newly gained light. GEORGE WISHART (*c.* 1513-1546), re-

---

[1] Wylie, *op. cit.*, vol. 3, p. 466.
[2] McCrie, *Life of John Knox*, p. 38.
[3] *Ibid.*, p. 33.

REFORMATION SCENES IN SWITZERLAND, SCOTLAND, AND FRANCE

Famous Reformation Wall in Geneva, With Giant Figures of Farel, Calvin, Beza, and Knox (Upper Left); Knox Thundering His Powerful Message

turning from exile in 1544, when not permitted in churches, preached the gospel with apostolic zeal until he also was burned, in 1546. As a student, Knox learned about the unscriptural character of the Papacy from Wishart, sometimes accompanying him to protect him. But on his last trip Wishart bade him return, saying, "One is sufficient for one sacrifice." [4]

II. Knox Sounds Keynote of Scottish Reformation From Daniel 7

JOHN KNOX (1505-1572), the Reformer of Scotland and founder of the Church of Scotland, was born at the village of Gifford, a suburb of Haddington, sixteen miles east of Edinburgh. After being educated at the school of Haddington, Knox was sent, in 1522, to the University of Glasgow, where he studied under John Major, the most famous teacher of his day in Scotland. After he left college Knox did not come into prominence until about 1546. During this time he took priest's orders. It is supposed that the study of the ancient fathers shook his attachment to the church of Rome as early as 1535, but he did not become an avowed adherent of the Reformed faith until 1545. His religious transition was first from Scholasticism to the fathers, and then to the Scriptures. In 1544, or earlier, he became tutor to several sons of prominent families. At this period Knox met George Wishart, by whom he was greatly influenced. [5]

In 1547, when Knox was forty-two, John Rough, a Protestant preacher, and the occupants of the castle of St. Andrews, then an asylum for the persecuted, observing Knox's manner of teaching, urged him to preach. He was overwhelmed by the unexpected and solemn call, and demurred. But he soon responded, and his first sermon in the parish church of St. Andrews sounded the keynote of the Scottish Reformation—that the Church of Rome is the Antichrist of Scripture prophecy. [6]

1. EXILED TWICE TO CONTINENT THROUGH PERSECUTION.— Others had condemned papal abuses and demanded reforms,

---

[4] *Ibid.*, pp. 40, 41; P. Hume Brown, *John Knox*, vol. 1, pp. 63-68.
[5] McCrie, *op. cit.*, pp. 17, 18, 23, 24, 370; Introductory section in *Works of John Knox*, ed. by David Laing, vol. 1, pp. xiii, xiv; Brown, *op. cit.*, vol. 1, pp. 4-27, 66.
[6] McCrie, *op. cit.*, pp. 46-51; Wylie, *op. cit.*, vol. 3, p. 484; Brown, *op. cit.*, vol. 1, p. 76.

but Knox called insistently for repudiation and separation. A storm of persecution arose, and began to beat against Knox. The castle of St. Andrews was soon besieged by the French, prior to which time Knox preached with power and converted many. In July, 1547, the castle was captured by men from the French fleet, and Knox carried captive to Rouen, France. Following this, he spent nineteen months in slavery in French galleys.[7]

In 1549 Knox was released, and immediately went to England, where the religious changes under Edward VI were well on their way to success. Soon afterward he was sent by the English council to preach at Berwick. According to his own account, Knox must have moved from Berwick to Newcastle early in 1551. At this time he was already one of the important figures in the party of religious reform. In that same year Knox seems to have been made a royal chaplain, and was associated with Cranmer. He assisted in the revision of the *Prayer Book* in 1552, and also of the Articles of Religion. He was offered an English bishopric, but declined it, preferring to hold himself aloof from an office which might compromise him.[8]

Soon after, upon the accession of Mary Tudor, Knox was forced to retire to the Continent, fleeing first to Dieppe early in 1554, and then visiting Calvin at Geneva and Bullinger at Zurich. In the same year he accepted a call to become pastor of the English congregation at Frankfurt am Main, but controversies in connection with vestments, ceremonies, and the use of the *Book of Common Prayer* led to his retirement from that city after less than six months' service. He then returned to Geneva, where he found a more congenial field of labor.[9]

But Knox resolved to visit his native country, and in the latter part of 1555 landed on the east coast of Scotland near Berwick. Most of the winter of 1555 and 1556 he taught in Edinburgh. He was allowed to preach privately for six months in the southern part of Scotland, and he was very happy to find a num-

[7] McCrie, *op. cit.*, pp. 52-56, 60, 399.
[8] *Ibid.*, pp. 60-108, 415, 416; Brown, *op. cit.*, vol. 1, pp. 104-186. In the call to Frankfurt am Main the first name signed is that of "Iohn Bale."
[9] William Lee, "Knox, John," *The New Schaff-Herzog*, vol. 6, p. 363.

ber who had neither "bowed the knee" to established idolatry nor "received the mark of antichrist." [10] Having received a call from the English church at Geneva, Knox left Scotland in July, 1556. Before this time he had married Marjory Bowes. After his farewell services in Scotland, he joined his wife and mother-in-law at Dieppe, whither he had sent them, and together they proceeded to Geneva. From 1556 to 1559, with the exception of some months spent at Dieppe (1557-1558), he was again in Geneva in close association with Calvin—whose influence on Knox was to bear much fruitage in Scotland. At Geneva he studied Hebrew and was employed as pastor of the English congregation. He also helped to make a new translation of the Bible into English, the so-called Geneva Bible. [11]

2. SCOTTISH PROTESTANTISM REARED IN PROPHETIC SETTING. —In July, 1558, Knox wrote a strong appeal to the people of Scotland, entreating them to heed the Bible evidence "that the papal religion is but an abomination before God," and to "flee out of Babylon, that ye perish not with her." [12] The number of Scottish Reformers increased, and their conflict with Rome reached crisis proportions. Returning to Scotland in 1559, Knox became the master spirit of the Scottish Reformation. He preached with such power and persuasion that images, ornaments of the church, shrines, and monasteries were destroyed. CHRISTOPHER GOODMAN (c. 1520-1603), his co-laborer in Geneva, joined Knox in Edinburgh. In the following year Goodman was appointed to St. Andrews, where he lectured on the Apocalypse. Lord Napier and others were encouraged to search the prophecies and to write on them. [13] As a result of the revolt of the Scottish Protestants against the French alliance and the Church of Rome, Protestantism gained the day.

---

[10] Friedrich Brandes, *John Knox, der Reformator Schottlands*, p. 123; McCrie, *op. cit.*, p. 116; Brown, *op. cit.*, vol. 1, p. 191.

[11] McCrie, *op. cit.*, p. 140; Alexander Taylor Innes, "Knox, John," *Encyclopaedia Britannica*, vol. 13, p. 468; Albert Henry Newman, *op. cit.*, vol. 2, p. 241. The Geneva translation, made by English exiles during Queen Mary's reign, was so called because done in that city. The New Testament was published in 1557 and the Old Testament in 1560. (*The English Hexapla*, pp. 130-135.)

[12] Brandes, *op. cit.*, pp. 501, 504.

[13] McCrie, *op. cit.*, pp. 158-179; David Stewart Erskine (earl of Buchan), and Walter Minto, *An Account of the Life, Writings, and Inventions of John Napier*, p. 11.

Even the popular ballads of the time show the temper and understanding of the common people concerning the pope and the papal church. Here is part of a quaint ballad of about 1560:

"The Paip, that Pagane full of pryde,
He hes us blindit lang,
For quhair the blind the blind dois gyde,
Na wounder baith ga wrang;
Lyke Prince and King, he led the Regne [ring],
Of all Iniquitie:
Hay trix, tryme go trix, under the grene [wod tré].

"Bot his abominatioun,
The Lord hes brocht to lycht;
His Popische pryde, and thrinfald Crowne,
Almaist hes loste thair mycht." [14]

The "Lords of the Congregation" entered into a "band" to "renounce the congregation of Satan," set up a provisional reform of their own, and sent for Knox. Here was their bold declaration:

"WE, perceaving how Sathan in his memberis, the Antichristis of our tyme, cruelly doeth rage, seaking to dounethring and to destroy the Evangell of Christ, and his Congregatioun, aught, according to our bonden deuitie, to stryve in our Maisteris caus, evin unto the death, being certane of the victorie in him." [15]

In 1560 Parliament voted to establish the Scottish Confession of Faith. Papal jurisdiction was abolished in Scotland, and the *de facto* establishment of Protestantism was secured.[16] The strong prophetic emphasis is seen in the Second Scotch Confession, or the National Covenant of 1580, subscribed to "by the

---

[14] *A Compendious Book of Godly and Spiritual Songs, Commonly Known as "The Gude and Godlie Ballatis"* (ed. Mitchell), p. 204; see Kidd, *Documents*, p. 695.
[15] John Knox, *The History of the Reformation in Scotland,* in *Works,* vol. 1, p. 273.
[16] McCrie, *op. cit.,* pp. 205, 206; Robert Sangster Rait, "Scotland: History," *Encyclopaedia Britannica,* vol. 20, p. 153.
      Article 18, of the first Confession of Faith of Scotland, adopted in August, 1560, vigorously repudiated the papal church as the synagogue of Satan: "Because that *Sathan* from the beginning hes laboured to deck his pestilent Synagoge with the title of the Kirk of God, and hes inflamed the hertes of cruell murtherers to persecute, trouble, and molest the trewe Kirk and members thereof, as *Cain* did *Abell, Ismael Isaac, Esau Jacob,* and the haill Priesthead of the *Jewes Christ Jesus* himselfe, and his Apostles after him. It is ane thing maist requisite, that the true Kirk be decerned fra the filthie Synagogues, be cleare and perfite notes, least we being deceived, receive and imbrace, to our awin condemnatioun, the ane for the uther. The notes, signs, and assured tokens whereby the immaculate Spouse of *Christ Jesus* is knawen fra the horrible harlot, the Kirk malignant, we affirme, are nouther Antiquitie, Title usurpit, lineal Descence, Place appointed, nor multitude of men approving ane error." (The Scotch Confession of Faith, A.D. 1560, in Philip Schaff, *Creeds,* vol. 3, pp. 460, 461.)

King, the Council and Court, at Holyrood House," in which this strong declaration appears:

"And theirfoir we abhorre and detest all contrare Religion and Doctrine; but chiefly all kynde of *Papistrie* in generall and particular headis, even as they ar now damned and confuted by the word of God and kirk of *Scotland*. But in special, we detest and refuse the usurped authoritie of that *Romane* Antichrist upon the Scriptures of God." [17]

Mary, Queen of Scots, returned to Scotland in 1561. It was soon obvious that the return of the queen was a menace to the Protestant cause in Scotland. Not only had Mary refused to ratify the Acts of 1560, by which Parliament had abolished the papal jurisdiction, but after her return she still withheld her ratification.[18] Mary was asked to join a league of Catholic powers planned by Pius IV, the cardinal of Lorraine, the emperor, and Philip of Spain, for suppressing Protestantism, and it was generally thought that she secretly joined it.[19] But in 1567 the queen was forced to abdicate in favor of her son, and the Acts of 1560 establishing the new religion were confirmed.[20]

3. ASSEMBLY NAMES PAPACY THE PROPHESIED ANTICHRIST. —Those were stormy times, and there were frequent dramatic conflicts between Queen Mary and Knox, who was minister at St. Giles. But he was mainly occupied with the establishment of the Reformed Church in Scotland. The affairs of the country were now in Protestant hands, with Knox as a powerful force, his public statements virtually having the weight of public manifestos. Grindal, bishop of London, reporting by letter to Bullinger at Zurich concerning "affairs of Scotland" in 1567, cited the Acts passed in the general assembly by which the "true religion of Christ is established, and the impious superstition of the papists abolished." The prophetic element was again in the forefront, the first and part of the second of the fifteen items being:

---

[17] Philip Schaff, *Creeds*, vol. 3, p. 481.
[18] Wylie, *op. cit.*, vol. 3, p. 509; McCrie, *op. cit.*, pp. 219, 251-256, 281.
[19] T. G. Law, "Mary Stewart," chap. 8 in *The Cambridge Modern History*, vol. 3, p. 271; McCrie, *op. cit.*, p. 288.
[20] Brown, *op. cit.*, vol. 2, pp. 244-246.

15

"1. First, then, not only are all the impious traditions and ceremonies of the papists taken away, but also that tyranny which the pope himself has for so many ages exercised over the church, is altogether abolished; and it is provided that all persons shall in the future acknowledge him to be the very antichrist, and son of perdition, of whom Paul speaks.

"2. The mass is abolished, as being an accursed abomination and a diabolical profanation of the Lord's supper; and it is forbidden to all persons in the whole kingdom of Scotland either to celebrate or hear it." [21]

Knox continued to lecture on Daniel's prophecies concerning the great apostasy, and still thundered against the decisions of the Council of Trent, and the slaughter of the Huguenots in France. Such was the testimony of this fearless witness. A man of courage and sagacity, and of earnestness blended with inflexible austerity, Froude called him "perhaps in that extraordinary age its most extraordinary man." [22] At his funeral Morton, newly elected regent of Scotland, declared, "There lies he, who never feared the face of man." [23]

III. Knox's First Sermon a Comprehensive Prophetic Exposition

1. SCOTTISH REFORMATION IS FROM THE "KYRK OF ANTICHRIST."—John Knox sounded out his prophetic testimony as with a trumpet. [24] In the very title of his *Hystory of the Reformatioun of Religioun Within the Realme of Scotland,* he states that it Contains "The Maner and by what Persons the Light of Christis Evangell Hath Bene Manifested unto This Realme, After That Horrible and universall Defectioun from the Trewth, which hes Cume by the Meanes of that Romane Antichryst." [25]

At the outset of his history Knox gives a list of thirty-four articles of faith attributed to the Lollards of Kyle, taken from the Register of Glasgow back in 1494, when they were summoned before the tribunal on the charge of heresy. Of these

[21] *The Zurich Letters* [1st series], 1558-1579, p. 199.
[22] James Anthony Froude, *History of England,* vol. 4, p. 63.
[23] McCrie, *op. cit.,* p. 340.
[24] When the Scotch Protestants first organized to advance the Reformation, aware that their conduct would be misinterpreted, they appointed certain ones among them to commit their proceedings to writing. Later they resolved that a narrative of their proceedings should be written from these records. Knox was chosen to make this compilation. From a letter written by Knox in 1568, it appears that he had decided to withhold the history from publication during his life. (*Ibid.,* pp. 495, 496.)
[25] Knox, *The History of the Reformation,* in *Works,* vol. 1, p. 1.

the seventeenth reads, "That the Pape exaltis him self against God, and abuf God." And the thirty-second declares, "That the Pape is the head of the Kyrk of Antichrist." [26] Then, after the martyrdom of Patrick Hamilton—whose dying words were, "Lord Jesus, receive my spirit! How long wilt Thou suffer the tyranny of men?"—and of George Wishart, Knox tells how, in 1547, he was led to undertake the public work of preaching the truth about the Papacy.[27]

2. KNOX OFFERS TO PROVE DEGENERACY OF THE PAPACY.— In 1547 Knox, wearied of moving from place to place by reason of persecution for his faith, purposed to leave Scotland to visit the schools of Germany. But the fathers of his pupils urged him to go to St. Andrews, that he might benefit the group at the castle, as well as help their own children. This Knox did, and began not only to teach the usual subjects of "humane Learning," but to read to them from a catechism, and also from the Gospel of John. The castle leaders were much impressed, especially the Protestant preacher John Rough, and began to urge that Knox take the "Function of Preacher" upon him. But Knox refused, saying he would not run where God had not clearly called him. The leaders decided they would issue a public call through John Rough, who in public meeting, preached on the election of ministers and charged Knox not to refuse the call, which those present supported. Bursting into tears, Knox withdrew to his chamber, greatly troubled, and was sober and silent for many days.[28]

Then a crisis arose that drew Knox into the pulpit. A Catholic controversialist, Dean John Annan, had long troubled John Rough in his preaching. "By his Pen," Knox had fortified Rough with doctrinal arguments against Annan, and had driven him from Biblical grounds and compelled him to take shelter in the authority of the church. But Knox contended that the "Church" must first be defined. The "Immaculate Spouse of Iesus Christ"

---

[26] *Ibid.*, pp. 6-12.
[27] *Ibid.*, pp. 74-76, 188-192.
[28] *Ibid.*, pp. 74, 185-188.

must be distinguished from "Spirituall Babilon," "the mother of Confusion," lest they embrace a "Harlot, instead of the chaste Spouse," and submit themselves to Satan, thinking him to be Jesus Christ. Then follows this remarkable public declaration and challenge by Knox before the open audience:

> "As for your Romane Church, as it is now corrupted, and the Authority thereof, wherein stands the hope of your Victory, I no more doubt but that it is the Synagogue of Sathan; and the Head thereof, called the Pope, to be that man of Sin of whom the Apostle speaketh, then that I doubt that JESUS CHRIST suffered by the procurement of the visible Church of Jerusalem. Yea, I offer my self by word or writing, to prove the Romane Church this day farther to degenerate from the purity which was in the dayes of the Apostles, then was the Church of the Jewes from the Ordinance given by Moses, when they consented to the innocent death of JESUS CHRIST. These words were spoken in the open audience of the Parish Church of Saint Andrewes, after the said Dean John had spoken what it pleased him, and had refused to dispute." [29]

Then the people urged him to lay his proofs before them in a public address, declaring:

> "We cannot all reade your writings, but we can all hear your Preaching: Therefore we require you in the Name of God, That ye let us heare the approbation of that which ye have affirmed: For if it be true, we have beene miserably deceived." [30]

3. PROOF BASED ON BEASTS AND LITTLE HORN OF DANIEL 7. —Knox consented, and the next Sunday was accordingly appointed for Knox to "expresse his minde in the publike Preaching place." On that memorable day Knox—

"took the Text written in Daniel, the seventh Chapter, beginning thus: And another King shall rise after them, and he shall be unlike unto the first, and he shall subdue three Kings, and shall speak words against the most High, and shall consume the Saints of the most High, and thinke that he can change Times and Lawes: And they shall be given unto his hands untill a time, and times, and dividing of times, &c. In the beginning of his Sermon, he shewed the great love of God towards his Church, whom he pleased to forewarne of dangers to come, so many yeers before they come to passe. He briefly treated of the state of the Israelites, who then were in bondage in Babylon, for the most part, and made a short discourse of the four Empires, The Babylonian, The Persian, That of the Greekes, And the

---

[29] Knox, *The Historie of the Reformatioun of Religioun Within the Realm of Scotland,* book 1, pp. 75, 76.
[30] *Ibid.*, p. 76.

fourth of the *Romanes;* in the destruction whereof, rose up that last Beast, which he affirmed to be the Romane Church; for to none other power that ever hath yet beene, do all the notes that God hath shewed to the Prophet appertain, except to it alone; And unto it they do so properly appertaine, that such as are not more then blinde, may cleerly see them." [31]

4. LITTLE HORN SAME AS MAN OF SIN AND BABYLON.—But that was not all. Knox next showed that Daniel's "little horn" was identical with Paul's "man of sin" and John's "Whore of Babylon"—three paralleling descriptions of one single Antichrist.

"He shewed that the Spirit of God in the new Testament gave to this King other new names; to wit, *The man of sin,* The *Antichrist,* The *Whore of Babilon.* He shewed, That this *man of sin,* or *Antichrist,* was not to be restrained to the person of any one man onely, no more then by the fourth Beast, was to be understood the person of any one *Emperour.* But by such names the Spirit of God would forewarne his chosen of a body and a multitude, having a wicked head, which should not onely be sinfull himself, but also should be occasion of sin, to all that should be subject unto him (as Christ Jesus is the cause of Justice to all the Members of his Body) and is called the *Antichrist.*" [32]

5. THE MERCHANDISE OF BABYLON.—Then, after showing that the pope's laws were opposed to God's laws, and his system of works was contrary to God's provision of justification by faith, and commenting on papal laws commanding to abstain from meats and from marriage, which Paul denominates the "doctrines of devils," Knox discussed the "notes of that Beast," as given in Daniel 7:25—the speaking of great words and blasphemies—and cited the pope's claims as fulfillment. Then he said:

"If these (said he) and many other, easie to be showne in his own *Cannon-Law,* be not great and blasphemous words, and such as never mortall men spake before, let the world judge. And yet (said he) is there one most evident of all, to wit, *John* in his Revelation sayes, That the Merchandise of that Babylonian Harlot, *among other things, shall be the bodies and souls of men.* Now let very Papists themselves judge, If any before them, took upon them power to relax the pains of them that were in Purgatory, as they affirme to the people that daily they do, by the merits of their Masse, and of their other trifles." [33]

---

[31] *Ibid.*
[32] *Ibid.*
[33] *Ibid.*, p. 77.

Then Knox invited any or all to examine his authorities, and stated that he was prepared to sustain his positions.

"If any here (and there were present Master *Iohn Maire,* the University, the Sub-Prior, and many Cannons, with some Friers of both the Orders) that will say, That I have alleadged Scripture, Doctor, or History, otherwise then it is written, let them come unto me with sufficient witnesse, and by Conference I shall let them see, not onely the Originall where my Testimonies are written, but I shall prove, That the Writers meant as I have spoken." [34]

6. STROKE AT ROOT OF TREE OF EVIL.—The boldness and the clarity of this sermon, which was the "first that ever John Knox made in publike," astonished all. Some said, "He not only hews the branches, but strikes at the root." Others said, "If the Doctors, and *Magistri nostri,* defend not now the Pope and his Authority, which in their own presence is so manifestly impugned, *the devill may have my part of him, and of his Lawes both.*" And yet others said that Wishart was burned for much milder language. Would not Knox suffer the same? A report of this sermon having come to the ears of the bishop, a "convention of gray-Friers, and black-Fiends" was appointed. Nine heretical articles were extracted from the utterances of Rough and Knox, and the preachers were successively summoned to appear before the convention to justify or vindicate themselves, the second article being "2. The Pope is an Antichrist, and so is no member of Christs mysticall body." [35]

The Papacy lost ground by this dispute, as the papal disputants were worsted. But all in the castle, and many in the town, openly professed the Reformed doctrine as a result, and testified the same by partaking of the Lord's supper in the same manner as it is now administered in the churches of Scotland— the first time the emblems were celebrated in this way in that country. [36]

7. LATER CONCEPTS UNCHANGED CONCERNING ANTI-CHRIST.—A letter sent from the Continent in 1554, while Knox

---

[34] *Ibid.*
[35] *Ibid.,* pp. 77, 78.
[36] *Ibid.,* p. vii.

was in exile, contains two excerpts that show his unchanged burden and concept concerning Antichrist:

"And greatter iniquitie was never frome the beginning, than is containit in worshipping of an abominabill ydoll; for it is the seill of the league whilk the Devill hes maid with the pestilent sons of the Antichryst, and is the verie cheif cause why the blude of Godis Sanctis hes bene sched neir the space of ane thousand yeirs." [37]

"We knaw that he sall, and that with expeditioun, when Sathan and his adherentis, idolateris, and worschipperis of that blasphemous beast, filthie personis, and feirfull schrinkeris frome the treuth of God, sal be casten in the stank burning with fire, whilk never sal be quencheit." [38]

Knox's strong convictions on the non-apostolic character of Rome were vigorously phrased, as will be observed:

"As far as I am concerned I am absolutely convinced, that whatever is done in the Roman church is contradictory to Christ's blessed rule, and is nothing else than a lethal poison; and whosoever drinks of it drinks death and damnation to himself. . . .

"The malice of your bishops is only too evident, their impure lives contaminate the very air; the innocent blood they shed cries to God for vengeance; the idolatry and abominations they with impunity commit perverts and defiles the whole country. And none amongst you has the courage to do away with these villainies. Will not God consider you guilty? Do not deceive yourselves, dear brethren. Do not sleep in your sins, for vengeance is near to all the disobedient. Flee from Babel, if you do not want to partake in her destruction." [39]

Thus spoke Knox, one of the great figures of the Reformation. Fearless as a leader, weighty in counsel, and champion of right, he was in constant battle with what he deemed the powers of darkness. Like John the Baptist, his strong voice cried out in the wilderness of apostasy, warning men to flee from the wrath to come. And from first to last prophecy was his guiding light.

IV. Lord Napier—First Scottish Expositor of the Revelation

JOHN NAPIER (Neper) (1550-1617), lord of Merchiston, distinguished Scottish mathematician and devoted adherent of the Protestant cause, was born near Edinburgh. Son of the mas-

---

[37] Knox, *A Godly Letter . . . to the Faithful in London, Newcastle, and Berwick*, in *Works*, vol. 3, p. 212.
[38] *Ibid.*, p. 213.
[39] Translated from Brandes, *op. cit.*, p. 494.

DISTINGUISHED EXPOSITORS IN THREE GENERATIONS

Sir John Oldcastle (Left), Wyclifite Knight, Martyred for Maintaining That the Pope Is Antichrist; Lord John Napier (Center), Scottish Mathematician, Writer of First Important Scottish Work on Prophecy; Johann Bengel (Right), Professor at Denkendorf, Witnessed as Living Protest Against Surrender to Rationalistic Preterism

ter of the mint (Sir Archibald), he entered the University of St. Andrews in 1563. From St. Andrews he apparently went to the University of Paris, to prosecute his studies. Later he traveled in France, Italy, and Germany.

Napier is celebrated as the inventor of logarithms. His famous work, *Mirifici Logarithmorum Canonis Descriptio* (Description of the Wonderful Canon of Logarithms), was published in 1614. He also devised certain formulas in trigonometry, and introduced the present use of the decimal point. Napier was one of the first English writers to make any valuable contribution to mathematics, his discoveries marking an epoch. He also invented a mechanical device known as "Napier's bones," for the performance of multiplications and divisions and the extraction of square and cube roots.[40]

In 1588 Napier was one of the Edinburgh commissioners to the General Assembly, and in 1593 was made a member of the committee appointed to ensure the safety of the church.

---

[40] Buchan and Minto, *op. cit.;* Mark Napier, *Memoirs of John Napier of Merchiston,* pp. 27-30.

After five years of study, in 1593, Napier completed his *Plaine Discovery of the Whole Revelation of Saint Iohn*,[41] which he dedicated to King James VI. He prayed the king to deal justly with his godly Protestant subjects. The *Encyclopaedia Britannica* says, "This book . . . is the first important Scottish work on the interpretation of scripture." [42] Napier calculated that the day of judgment would probably come not later than 1700. Commending his piety and erudition, Adam Clarke says:

> "So very plausible were the reasonings and calculations of Lord Napier, that there was scarcely a Protestant in Europe, who read his work, that was not of the same opinion." [43]

1. EVERY PROPHETIC DAY TO BE TAKEN FOR YEAR.—Napier's work on the Revelation is in the form of a series of propositions, with elucidations, the first of which reads: "In propheticall dates of daies, weekes, monethes, and yeares, everie common propheticall day is taken for a yeare." [44]

Contending that a prophetic week is a "weeke of yeares," and a Jewish or Greek common year is a year of "360 daies" (as was commonly supposed at that time by many expositors, disregarding the Jewish luni-solar year), he quotes Numbers 14:34 and Ezekiel 4:5, 6 for the year-day principle,[45] and cites the seventy weeks as evidence of fulfillment, in these quaint words and the odd spelling of the day:

> "In the seventie weekes of Daniel, a day to be taken for a yeare, extending in the whole to 490 yeares; otherwise, that prophecie of the Messias comming, would not fal upon the just time of Christs comming, as necessarilie it ought to doe. So then, a propheticall day is a yeare, the week seven yeres, the moneth thirtie yeares (because the Hebrew and Grecian moneth hath thirtie daies) and consequentlie the prophetical yeare is 360 years." [46]

2. FIFTH AND SIXTH TRUMPETS MOHAMMEDANS AND TURKS. —Propositions 3 and 4, on the fifth and sixth trumpets, are

---

41 Translated into French by G. Thomson (3d ed. in 1607, at La Rochelle), and into German by De Dromna (published in 1612 at Gera); and published in 1615 at Frankfurt am Main.
42 *Encyclopaedia Britannica*, vol. 16, p. 75, art. "Napier, John."
43 Adam Clarke, General Preface, in his *Commentary*, vol. 1, p. 21.
44 John Napier, *A Plaine Discovery of the Whole Revelation of Saint Iohn*, p. 1; see also introductory Table of Conclusions, opposite p. 1.
45 *Ibid.*, pp. 1, 2.
46 *Ibid.*, p. 2.

applied to the Mohammedans and the Ottoman Turks, with Mohammed as the fallen star. Napier suggests the 150 years involved may possibly be from Zadok, in 1051, to "Changius Chan," in 1201, and touches hazily upon the year 1296.[47]

3. NAPIER LOOKS FOR JUDGMENT ABOUT A.D. 1700.—Napier looked for the day of judgment about the year 1700, and believed the latter day "beginneth to approch." This view he based on the six-thousand-year premise, and on the fact that God had given the time prophecies of Daniel and of Revelation by which the approach of the judgment might be known. Citing the 1290 and 1335 year-days, and remarking on the short space between their endings, Napier thought the 1335-year period might begin with the taking away of the Jewish ceremonies in A.D. 365, under Julian, and therefore extend to 1700.[48]

4. 1260 DAYS, 42 MONTHS, AND 3½ TIMES IDENTICAL.— Proposition 15 applies the three great time periods—of the Little Horn, the Witnesses, and the Beast—to one and the same period.

"The 42. moneths, a thousand two hundred and threescore propheticall daies, three greate daies and a halfe, and a time, times, and a halfe a time mentioned in Daniel, and in the Revelation, are all one date." [49]

Expounding the woman of Revelation 12, Napier makes her "signifie the Church of Christ fled into the wildernes" for 1260 days. But as verse 14 says this is three and a half times ("a time, and times, and half a time"), the periods must be identical. And the same as "the raigne of the Antichrist, is blaspheming of God, and oppression of Gods Sainctes, the treading of spirituall *Jerusalem* under feet." [50] This period, he thought, began about A.D. 300 or 316, according to Proposition 36.[51]

5. PROPHETIC DAYS FULFILLED IN JULIAN CALENDAR TIME. —In Proposition 16 Napier asserts that the 1260 prophetical

---

[47] *Ibid.*, pp. 3-5.
[48] *Ibid.*, pp. 16-22; see also introductory Table of Conclusions.
[49] *Ibid.*, p. 22.
[50] *Ibid.*, pp. 22-25.
[51] *Ibid.*, pp. 64, 65.

days, the 42 months, or the three and a half times signify "everie one of them, 1260 Iuliane yeares," that is, solar years, approximately. He says that they cannot be natural or common days, and gives his reasons therefor. He does not, however, include the 2300 evening-mornings of Daniel 8:14 in this category, but regards them as literal days.[52]

6. TWO WITNESSES ARE THE TWO TESTAMENTS.—Proposition 21 declares, "The two witnesses mentioned (Reve. 11) are the two Testaments," and remarks, "In that language of Latine, wherein they have bene used most, these 1200. years & more, they are called *Testamenta* from the word *Testis,* which is to say a *Witnesse*."[53]

7. WOMAN OF REVELATION 12 REPRESENTS TRUE CHURCH. —Proposition 22 states, *"The Woman clad with the Sunne (chap. 12.) is the true Church of God."* Expanding, Napier adds, "Spirituall Hierusalem, which is Christes Church by diverse Scriptures, is also called Christes Spouse in the Revelation." And referring to the symbol of marriage, he remarks, "Idolatrie being called spiritual whordome, necessarily the true worshipping of God is represented by perfect Spousage."[54]

8. CALLS ROME THE MYSTICAL BABYLON.—Proposition 23 declares that *"the whoore, who in the Revelation is stiled spirituall Babylon, is not reallie Babylon, but the verie present Citie of Rome."* Napier then develops these contrasts:

"In the former proposition was described the holie Spouse of Christ, here is to bee described the filthie Whoore of Sathan, there that Ladie, who is adorned with the Sunne, Starres, and heavenlie vertues: here that Adultresse, who glories in golde, silver, precious stones, and worldlie pleasures: there shee, who is persecuted by the Dragon, here she unto whome the Dragon doeth give authoritie: There she, who is chaced into the wildernes, and hath no lodge to hide her in; here she who impireth above all people, and is the Metropolitane citie of the world. And finallie, seeing in al things this Whoore, or whoorish *Babylon,* is contrarious to Christes holie Spouse, lette us, and all Christians trie her out, as our detestable and

---

[52] *Ibid.*, pp. 24, 25; introductory table.
[53] *Ibid.*, p. 32.
[54] *Ibid.*, pp. 33, 34.

deadlie enemie, and see what *Babylon* she is. We say then, that this *Babylon,* is not that reall *Babylon* of *Chaldee,* but *Rome,* for these reasons. First, for that this *Babylon* is called *mysterium Babylon,* that is to say, mysticall or figurative *Babylon:* Therefore, it is not *Babylon* it self in *Chaldee.*" [55]

9. SEVEN HILLS: SEVEN FORMS OF ROMAN GOVERNMENT.—

In support of seven-hilled Rome as Babylon, Napier cites Virgil, Propertius, Tertullian, Jerome, Eutropius, and others. And he concludes, "And so for assured certenty, this whorish & mystical *Babylon,* is verilie *Rome.*" [56] The seven hills are interpreted as "seven sorts of royal governments; . . . *Kinges, Consulles, Dictators, Trium-vires, Tribuns, Emperours, and Popes.*" The popes were "not come to government" until after the reign of the emperors.[57]

10. TEN-HORNED BEAST IS LATIN EMPIRE.—

Proposition 24 asserts, *"The great ten-horned beast, is the whole bodie of the Latine Empire, whereof the Antichrist is a part,"* [58] and Napier sets forth the following as proof:

"For firste (saieth the Text) the Woman that sate upon this Beast, is the great Citie, that sitteth over the Kinges of the earth: So the chiefe seate and citie of the *Latine* or *Romane* Empire, is that great citie *Rome,* that had Empire over all the kingdomes of the earth. Secondly, saith *Daniel, there shal foure cheif kingdomes arise upon earth, under the figure of foure beastes:* Whereof (by plaine interpretation hee saith) the fourth beast that had these ten horns, is the fourth kingdome of the earth: And so it is, that the firste greate kingdome or Monarchie being of the *Babylonians:* The seconde, of the *Medes* and *Persians:* The thirde, of the *Graecians.* The fourth and laste, is certainlie the Monarchie of the *Latines* or *Romanes:* and therefore, that fourth beaste which both there in *Daniel,* & here in *Iohns Revelation,* hath ten hornes, must necessarilie be the *Romane* or *Latine* Empire." [59]

The ten kingdoms were *"Spaine, France, Lombardie, England, Scotland, Denmarke, Sweden,* The kingdome of the *Gothes* in *Italie,* and of the *Hunnes* in *Pannonia* or *Hungary,* and the *Exarchat* of *Ravenna.*" [60]

---

[55] *Ibid.,* p. 34. This first reason was supported by a series of supplemental arguments.
[56] *Ibid.,* pp. 35, 36.
[57] *Ibid.,* p. 37; see also pp. 157, 166.
[58] *Ibid.,* p. 36.
[59] *Ibid.,* pp. 36, 37; and introductory table.
[60] *Ibid.,* p. 157.

11. Two-horned Beast Likewise Antichrist.—Proposition 25 reads, *"The two horned Beast, is the Antichrist and his kingdome, it alone."* Citing Paul, in 2 Thessalonians 2, where the Man of Sin seeks to be as God and assumes temporal power, Napier believes the horns signify spiritual and temporal power. Commenting further, he says:

"So in Paule, he came with power, and signes, and lying wonders, and in all deceaveablenesse of unrighteousnesse. Whereby (doubtlesse) that man of sinne, and sonne of perdition, even the verie Antichriste, whome *Paule* there described, is this very same two-horned beast, mentioned here by *Iohn.* And for confirmation hereof, the properties of this two-horned beast (cap. 13) are the selfe same properties of the false Antichristian Prophete (cap. 19.)." [61]

12. The Pope, Not a Turk or a Jew, Is Antichrist.— Proposition 26 declares, *"The Pope is that only Antichrist, prophecied of, in particular."* He must operate "under the name of a Christian," and "must sit, saith *Paul,* in the Church of God." Denying he can be a Turk or a Jew, Napier says:

"There is one particular Apostatik kingdome, who is the chief and principall of al Antichrists, and is that great Antichrist, whom *Paul* calles the *man of sinne, and sonne of perdition, adversary to God, and an extoller of himselfe above all that is called God,* with divers other epithets conteined 2. *The.* 2. Leaving therefore al other smaller Antichrists, this great Antichrist and chiefe heade of all Antichrists, is he whome here we have to trie out, whom (for remooving of all doubts) wee say cannot be the *Mahomet,* neither any *Turk, Iewe,* or *Ethnick."* [62]

13. 666 Is Number of Name, Not Years.—Proposition 29 states, *"The name of the beast expressed by the number of 666 (cap. 13) is the name λατεινος onely."* This is confirmed by Irenaeus. Napier insists that this is the number of the name of the first or ten-horned beast, and not the number of years, as some interpret it. [63]

14. Mark of Beast Is Profession of Obedience.—In Proposition 30 Napier defines the mark of the Beast thus:

"The marke of the Romane beast, is that invisible profession of servi-

---

[61] *Ibid.*, p. 40, and introductory table.
[62] *Ibid.*, p. 41.
[63] *Ibid.*, pp. 52, 53.

*tude and obedience, that his subiects hath professed to his Empire, since
the first beginning therof, noted afterward by the Pope, with divers visible
markes."* [64]

15. STILL HOLDS AUGUSTINIAN THEORY OF MILLENNIUM.
—On the thousand years of Revelation 20, however, Napier,
still held to the Augustinian theory, in modified form, thus:
*"The thousand yeares that Sathan was bound (Revel. 20.) began
in Anno Christi 300. or thereabout,"* that is, from the time of
Sylvester I. Napier's reason for choosing A.D. 300, or its approximate, follows:

> "For proofe hereof, it is evident by histories, that after the continual
> and successive tyrannie of Ethnick Emperours, and last of *Diocletian,* (who
> in one moneth made seventeene thousand Martyrs) there arose about this
> 300. year of Christ, *Constantine* the greate, a Christian and baptized Em-
> perour, who, and whose successors (except a few of short raign) maintained
> Christianisme and true religion, to the abolishing of *Sathans* publique
> kingdome: and therefore, say wee, this yeare *Sathan* is bound." [65]

As to the loosing, Napier refers to the armies of Gog and
Magog under the sixth trumpet as "loosed about the yeare of
God 1296, . . . or rather (as histories priseselie report) about
the yeare of God 1300." [66] For the space of the thousand years
"the Devil and his raging tyrantes of this world, were restrayned
from that high degree of universall tyrannie, that they both
before and after used." [67] And, conformable to Augustinianism,
the first resurrection is understood as spiritual—which is the
resurrection from antichristian errors,[68] and the second, the general or bodily resurrection.

V. Prophetic Interpretation Established on Sound Principles

The mariner freshly freed from dense fog which has shut
out sea and sky from view, looks to the stars for his course, in the
early dawn before the night is wholly past, in order to learn his
exact position on the sea. Thus it was with the church of the

---

[64] *Ibid.,* p. 53.
[65] *Ibid.,* p. 62; see also pp. 232, 233.
[66] *Ibid.,* p. 62.
[67] *Ibid.,* p. 233.
[68] *Ibid.,* p. 234.

Reformation. Having escaped the shrouds of papal mist and darkness which had so long enveloped her, she turned her eyes to the heavenly lights of God's Word to find her spiritual bearings and to the study of prophecy to ascertain her position on God's chart of prophetic fulfillment.

In restudying the prophetic statements of Daniel, Jesus, Paul, and John, the Reformers discovered the striking resemblance between the features of the gross apostasy portrayed in these picturesque symbols and the Roman church portrayed in history. Therefore they pointed to the pope and his system as the falling away, the Man of Sin, the Antichrist, the persecuting Little Horn, the corrupt woman of Babylon.

The development and dominance of the Antichrist had covered many centuries. Thus the fulfillment was found in history rather than in any short period of time. Further, the long-accepted interpretations of Daniel 2 and 7—the four kingdoms followed by the breakup of Rome—and the seventy weeks, lent weight to the long view of historical fulfillment and the year-day principle.

Accepting these basic considerations, the other time periods given in the Scripture were now likewise treated, and opened new vistas of understanding. God's guiding hand in history became discernible. History did not remain any longer a confusing mass of incomprehensible events, but became intelligible as the outworking of a divine plan with definite laws and a definite purpose.

This discovery of the historical basis of prophetic interpretation is one feature of the inspiring work of the Reformers, which, regrettably, our generation has practically forgotten. Their firm conviction of having a definite place in God's great unfolding plan of history gave them that strength and that courage which led them to brave all difficulties, dangers, and death itself. Only if we reorientate ourselves to these same guiding lights of prophecy shall we find strength, courage, and surety in the bewildering aspect of our time.

CHAPTER TWENTY-ONE

Rome's Counterattacks

on Protestant Interpretation

I. Reformation Followed by Catholic Counter Reformation

The Papacy suffered a major setback through the Reformation. The help of the monastic orders was sought, but they were so decadent that they had lost the respect of the people. The Dominicans and Franciscans, peddling relics and indulgences, had become the butt of ridicule and mockery. At this crisis Loyola and his companions offered their services, to go wherever the pope should designate, as preachers, missionaries, teachers, counselors, reformers. A new order was created, authorized in 1540, which infused a new spirit and spread rapidly over Europe. Like a wounded giant, Romanism arose in desperation to recover her lost prestige and enlarge shrunken territory.

From 1540, then, the Counter Reformation may be dated. Within fifty years the Jesuits had planted stations in Peru, Africa, the islands of the East Indies, Hindustan, Japan, and China, and before long in the Canadian forests and the American colonies. Their members secured important chairs in universities. They became counselors and confessors to monarchs, and were the most able of all Catholic preachers. By 1615 they had a membership of thirteen thousand. Thus through the Jesuits the Counter Reformation, next to the Protestant Reformation itself, became the most memorable movement in the history of modern times.[1]

---

[1] Albert Henry Newman, *op. cit.*, vol. 2, pp. 365 ff; Joseph Hergenröther, *Handbuch der allgemeinen Kirchengeschichte*, vol. 3, pp. 289 ff.

1. Protestant Tide Met by Counterwave of Resistance.
—The sixteenth and seventeenth centuries therefore present
a dual religious aspect—a Protestant and a Papal side. Reformatory action is soon matched by decisive reaction. Through the revival of learning and the invention of printing, the Scriptures
were translated, multiplied, and circulated as never before.
Prophetic exposition was revived, and made great advances.
Interpreters had arisen in groups, like constellations of stars.
But the Protestant Reformation was countered by a sharp papal
reaction, or Counter Reformation, and the rising tide of spiritual
life and liberty was met by a counterwave of Catholic resistance.

Against the Confession of Augsburg, Rome erected her
Council of Trent, formulating her canons and decrees, and
rigorously imposing the Creed of Pius IV. Luther and his followers were matched by Loyola and his Jesuits, and sound prophetic interpretation was attacked through specious counterinterpretations. When the Reformation broke out simultaneously in different countries of the Old World, the Papacy did not
at first seem to sense the full significance of what was taking
place. Time was required for this to be grasped. And this lull
before the gathering storm gave the Reformation opportunity
to establish itself before a serious attempt was made to stop it.
Then the sixteenth-century Reformation was succeeded by the
great papal reaction in the latter half of the sixteenth and the
first half of the seventeenth centuries.

2. Fivefold Aspect of Counter Reformation.—This far-
flung movement was fivefold. It included: (1) The formal recognition of the order of Jesuits, (2) the actions and decrees of the
Council of Trent, (3) the Catholic countersystems of prophetic
interpretation, (4) the establishment of the Index, and (5) the
widespread revival of persecution. In these the Papacy was revealed in the role of the persecuting Antichrist through actions
so glaring as to invite general recognition.[2] Our discussion will
center on these five basic factors.

---

[2] Guinness, *History Unveiling Prophecy,* pp. 131, 132; see also William Muir, *The Arrested Reformation,* pp. 147 ff.

II. Jesuitism Most Potent Assailant of the Reformation

Among all the instruments and forces with which the church assailed the Reformation—the Jesuits, the Council of Trent, the Index, the counterinterpretations, and the Inquisition—none was more potent than the Jesuits, whose work was inwrought into all the others. In Jesuitism the consummation of error and in the Inquisition the maximum of force were arrayed against Protestantism.[3] This militant Company of Jesus, constituted by the bull, *Regimini Militantis Ecclesiae,* of Paul III in 1540, directed that those who enrolled in this army were to bear "the standard of the Cross, to wield the arms of God, to serve the only Lord, and the Roman Pontiff, His Vicar on earth."[4] Declared Hagenbach:

"The Jesuit Order . . . is the genuine double of the Reformation. From the very outset of the Reformation, the Jesuit Order hung upon its heels as closely as a shadow."[5]

Thus at the very time the so-called Protestant "poison" of heresy sprang up in Germany, the papal "antidote" to the poison sprang up in Spain. Whereas Luther did not foresee the extent of the Protestant involvement that would grow out of his revolt, neither did Loyola envision the extent of the Jesuit movement that he had initiated in founding his order. The contrast is personified in the men themselves. Luther was led to the fountain of truth through the Scriptures, and rested in the mercy of God through Christ. Loyola hung upon Mary as the dispenser of mercy, and sought closeness to Christ through the mysterious host of the altar sacrament. Luther, on the one hand, was led to separate from the church, but Loyola, on the other, became the most effective tool the church had produced.[6]

III. Loyola's Holy Militia for Defense of the Faith

IGNATIUS OF LOYOLA, or Don Inigo Lopez de Loyola (1491-1556), subtle and capable founder of the Society of Jesus, was

[3] Wylie, *op. cit.*, vol. 2, p. 426.   [4] *Ibid.*, p. 386.
[5] Hagenbach, *op. cit.*, vol. 2, p. 404.   [6] *Ibid.*, pp. 404, 405.

born at the castle of Loyola in the province of Guipuzcoa, Spain, eight years subsequent to Luther, and eighteen years before the birth of Calvin. Descended from a family of knights, and serving in the royal court of Ferdinand and Isabella, he was charmed by the glitter of arms, fame, and gallant deeds. In 1521, at twenty-nine, he was in command of a garrison at Pomplona, Navarre. Ordered to withstand the combined forces of the invading French troops and the revolting Spaniards, he was seriously wounded by the shattering of his leg, which became a useless log. This unfitted him for a soldier's career and caused him to limp throughout life.

During this long period of painful confinement *The Life of Christ,* by Ludolphus of Saxony, and the popular *Flowers of the Saints* came to his hands. They made the deepest impression upon him, particularly the lives of Francis of Assisi and Dominic. He determined to follow in their steps, abandon the world, and become a soldier of Christ. He resolved to make a pilgrimage to Jerusalem, which he accomplished in 1523. But the provincial of the Franciscan Order in the Holy Land ordered him to return home and to study diligently before going to the Mohammedans, whom he wished to convert.

Distributing his goods among the poor, and donning a hermit's garb, Loyola subjected himself to the discipline of the school of Barcelona. Grammar and language did not appeal to him, but he became absorbed in the writings of the mystics and ascetics, such as Thomas à Kempis. After studying further at Alcalá de Henares and Salamanca, Loyola repaired to Paris in 1528, entering Montaigu College, from which he received his M.A. in 1534, and later lived in Saint Barbara College.

1. SPIRITUAL ARMY PLANNED, WITH DRILLS FOR SOUL.—Here in Paris, with six others of like mind, such as Peter Faber (Pierre Lefèvre) and Francis Xavier, he drew up plans for a new order of traveling missionaries. This was the age of military companies in Italy, and theirs was to be a "Company of Jesus." As its name indicated, it was to be a spiritual army, a fighting order, a holy militia for the prosecution of the faith

and the education of the young. Ignatius always had before him the concept of military drill—to discipline the soul as the drill sergeant molds the body. To this end he developed his *Exercitia Spiritualia* (The Spiritual Exercises), first written in Spanish—a strict method to enable the individual by means of the theory of discernment to ascertain the will of God, and then by means of special exercises to fit himself to carry out that will.[7]

In 1534 these seven men took the vow of poverty and chastity, and pledged themselves to go to the Holy Land as missionaries or for the purpose of tending the sick. If this plan should prove impracticable they resolved to go to Rome and place themselves at the disposal of the pope for any purpose. After they had obtained their ordination in 1537, Ignatius drew up a *Formula Instituti,* which the pope, Paul III, reluctantly approved. Loyola, Lefèvre, and Xavier sought audience with Paul III, and explained their project, which was destined to have such far-reaching influence. The aim was to win to God all kingdoms of the world. That meant to bring them all into the fold of the mother church, and to establish the pope's absolute supremacy over all earthly potentates. In the interim the pope engaged Loyola's two assistants as teachers of theology in the Roman University.

2. Authorized in 1540, Yearly Grows More Powerful. —Paul III confirmed the order in 1540. The authorizing bull *(Regimini Militantis Ecclesiae)* was published, and the Company of Jesus formally recognized—a holy militia pledged to fight perpetually for the Papacy against all assailants everywhere, at all costs. The bull had limited the society to a membership of sixty, but this limit was removed by a second bull, *Injunctum nobis,* in 1543. Ignatius was unanimously chosen as its first general in 1541. The intent of the new order was the preservation and dissemination of the faith. In addition to vows of poverty and chastity, the members were obliged to promise unconditional obedience to the Roman see. Whatever they were

---

[7] Hulme, *op. cit.,* pp. 416, 417.

asked to perform they were to do without objection or delay, and to go unquestioningly wherever sent. Then their ambitious goal was to become the universal and principal order of the Roman church. Though they took the name of Society of Jesus (Jesuits), the Protestants termed them *Jesuwider* (against Jesus).[8]

Their influence was felt immediately. They grew more powerful and comprehensive year by year, employing science, art, culture, politics, foreign missions, trades, and industry. They began to preach, as Protestants were accustomed to do, in the streets and marts, coming to be among the most eloquent preachers of the age. The churches were too small for the multitudes that flocked to hear them. They gained access to houses and hospitals, and sought influence over students and youth. At Rome they were scattered out through the various churches. Then they began to spread throughout Italy, Portugal, Germany, and especially in Austria and Bavaria. They hemmed in the Protestant movement on all sides. Some cities, such as Ingolstadt and Cologne, opened their doors; others opposed them.

Their doctrinal system was based mainly upon Thomas of Aquinas, and they became the zealous defenders of it, especially in those points such as the papal infallibility, the pope's universal episcopate, and his absolute supremacy over every earthly potentate. They further brought into practice four principles: (1) the idea of "Probabilism," which teaches that in a case where the conscience is undecided as to what should be done, one is not necessarily bound to the more certain and probable meaning, but may even take a less certain view, if this were supported by weighty reasons; (2) the doctrine of "Intentionalism," which means that an action is to be judged according to the intention with which it was performed, even if in itself sinful; (3) the distinction between philosophical and theological sin; and (4) the permissibility of a secret mental reservation *(reservatio mentalis).*[9]

---

[8] Hagenbach, *op. cit.*, vol. 2, p. 408; Hulme, *op. cit.*, p. 419.
[9] Kurtz, *op. cit.*, vol. 2, p. 431.

3. INFLUENCES TRENT AND BECOMES FORMIDABLE FORCE.—
In 1540 two Jesuits left Portugal for the East, and in 1542 a
Jesuit college was dedicated at Goa, capital of the important
Portuguese port of Western India. The discovery of the new continents in the west, which had slightly preceded the Reformation
age, and the serious losses sustained in Europe stimulated Jesuit
interest in foreign missions—the East Indies, China, Africa,
Japan, and America.[10] By 1545 papal permission was given the
Jesuits to preach in all churches and public squares, and to
absolve. By the time of Loyola's death the order boasted one
thousand members and one hundred colleges.[11] Thus Protestant
aggression was matched by Catholic zeal.

In 1558 LAINEZ was elected second general of the order. At
the Council of Trent he successfully exerted his power and skill
in behalf of papal supremacy. His vision of the society extended
far beyond that of Loyola, its founder. The alliance with the
Papacy now became more intimate, and close connection with
the cabinets of the various countries was established. The
Jesuits became entrenched in the universities. They were among
the best teachers in the land, and held public disputations. Even
Protestants began to send their children to them because of
the scholastic progress they could make. Thus the great Reformation began to be outflanked in its own fastnesses, and its
conquests were checked.[12]

It was under the generalship of CLAUDIO ACQUAVIVA (1581-
1615), however, that the order entered upon a career of universal
significance as an army for the defense of the Papacy.[13] New
developments occurred that made it the most formidable force
in the ecclesiastical affairs of the time, the society boasting 13,112
members at Acquaviva's death, and operating in thirty-two
provinces.[14] Thus the Jesuit order was led increasingly to combat
Protestantism, to seek out the weak places in the Protestant
positions, to regain the lost ground, and to promote the world-
wide dominion of the Papacy.

[10] Hulme, *op. cit.*, pp. 425, 426.
[11] Hagenbach, *op. cit.*, vol. 2, p. 408.
[12] Hulme, *op. cit.*, pp. 448, 449.
[13] Kurtz, *op. cit.*, vol. 2, p. 427.
[14] Hulme, *op. cit.*, p. 452.

IV. Two Irreconcilable Systems Clash at Trent

The conflict between Romanism and Protestantism was basic and irreconcilable. The Romanist believed in the authority of the church; the Protestant, in that of the Bible. The one yielded his conscience to the priest; the other, to God alone. The Romanist believed in the pope as the visible representative of Christ on earth; the Protestant looked, instead, upon the pope as Antichrist. The one regarded the church—meaning the hierarchy—as the depositary of all spiritual truth; the other looked upon the clergy as ministers of the church, not as the church itself. The Romanist, satisfied with the teaching of the church, was content to leave the Bible to the learned; the Protestant, on the other hand, held that it was to be diligently and reverently studied by all, as the Word of God. The one dreaded its spread as tending to heresy; the other multiplied translations as the assurance of soundness, and sought to introduce them to every household.[15]

The rising tide of Protestantism forced the issue. The Romanist held that the merits of Christ could be made ours only through the sacraments, and these could be administered only by a duly ordained priest. The Protestant received the sacraments merely as aids to faith. The one looked up to heaven through a host of mediatory priests and saints and the Holy Virgin; the other contended that there is only one mediator between God and man—Christ Jesus our Lord. Thus the two systems stood forth in absolute and irreconcilable opposition at the Council of Trent, where the council expressly condemned what the Reformation taught.

1. REFORMATION TRUTHS STIGMATIZED AS HERESY.—The Council of Trent—beginning in 1545 under Paul III and ending in 1563 under Pius IV—crystallized its actions into decrees that became the permanent law of the Catholic Church.[16] The recovered Reformation truths were there rejected and stigma-

---

[15] Geikie, *op. cit.*, pp. 484, 485.
[16] Philip Schaff (revised by David S. Schaff), "Trent, Council of," *The New Schaff-Herzog*, vol. 12, pp. 1, 2.

PAINTING BY TITIAN

COUNCIL OF TRENT—ROME'S ANSWER TO THE REFORMATION

The Council of Trent Rejected the Protestant Positions, and Crystallized Many of the Accretions of the Centuries, Making Them the Permanent Law of the Catholic Church. Thus Trent Was Rome's Answer to Protestantism, Seeking to Block Its Progress, to Reform Abuses in the Roman

tized as pestilential heresy. In one sense Trent became the culmination of the Counter-Reformation. It was Rome's definitive answer to the Reformation. Here a threefold movement got under way—the blocking of the progress of the Protestant Reformation, a reformation in discipline or administration, and the reconquest of territories and peoples lost to the church.[17]

2. LUTHER APPEALS IN VAIN FOR FREE COUNCIL.—Back in November, 1518, Luther had appealed for a free Christian council, to be held on German soil. But the papal bull of June 15, 1520, condemned forty-one of his propositions as heretical, scandalous, and false. It ordered all Luther's books burned. He and his followers were enjoined to renounce their errors, and were threatened with severest censure and punishment in case of obstinacy. In return, on December 10, 1520, Luther burned the pope's bull, together with a copy of the papal decretals. This aroused the wrath of Rome, and in January, 1521, the pope launched a bull of excommunication against the Reformer. But between the time of Luther's appeal to a general council, in 1518, and the convening of the Council of Trent in 1545, Bibles in German, Danish, Swedish, Icelandic, and English (Tyndale's New Testament and Coverdale's complete Bible) had been published, and the Reformation established in Germany, Switzerland, Sweden, Denmark, and England.

V. Historical Background, Call, and Scope of Council

From the very beginning of the Reformation many, both Catholics and Protestants, had wanted a general council representing all Christians, in which the disputed doctrines could be discussed and the abuses of Rome corrected. After the development of the Protestant positions the Catholic prelates felt a council to be imperative, in order that the fundamental positions of the Catholic Church relative to the controverted points could be restated. This frustrated all hope of reconciliation with the Protestants. The council convened in 1545, at Trent, a

---

[17] Hurst, *op. cit.*, vol. 2, pp. 532-534.

town in the Austrian Tyrol. The large majority of those in attendance were Italians.[18] The council was controlled from Rome.

The Reformation had taken the most ardent advocates of reform out of the Catholic Church, leaving the conservatives and reactionaries in the ascendant. The conflict consequently lay between the Protestants and the church, and the Protestants were told that their deadly opponent must act as judge. Everyone knew how the church would interpret the questions at issue.[19] Both German and British Reformers, therefore, rejected the conditions and the procedure.

Tedious negotiations sprang up between the emperor and the pope in an endeavor to effect a compromise. On the Protestant side a formula was drawn up whereby the Protestants were willing to accommodate themselves to certain points of the established Catholic doctrine, but they held fast to the basic Protestant principles. This was known as the Augsburg and Leipzig Interims of 1548. There was much opposition, especially among the free cities such as Magdeburg—but division marked the Protestant reaction.

1. DISCUSSIONS FOCUSED ON LUTHER'S POSITIONS.—Luther's basic positions were: (1) that Holy Scripture contains all things necessary to salvation, and that it is sacrilege to place tradition on a level with the Scripture; (2) that certain books, accepted as canonical in the Latin Vulgate, are apocryphal and not canonical; (3) that the meaning of Scripture is plain, and can be understood without churchly commentary, by aid of the Holy Spirit. The early discussions of the council cover these very questions, as can be seen from the decrees of the fourth session.[20]

2. PROTESTANT POSITIONS CONDEMNED BY TRENT.—Luther's propositions were condemned by the council. Tradition and Scripture were ostensibly placed on a par, though by implica-

---

18 Hulme, *op. cit.*, pp. 430-433.
19 Wylie, *op. cit.*, vol. 2, p. 113.
20 Landon, *op. cit.*, vol. 2, pp. 184, 185.

tion Scripture is made subservient to tradition through insistence that it be understood only in the light of the tradition of the church, specifically, the "unanimous teaching of the Fathers." [21] The Latin Vulgate was declared the one authentic version, with the intermingled apocryphal books as canonical. The Scriptures were declared not capable of being understood in and of themselves.[22] Justification by faith, as it was proclaimed by Luther, was condemned;[23] and no books of religion were to be printed without examination and approval by the church.[24] Such, in brief, were the council's decisions on these points.

The molding Jesuit influence, it should be added, was attested by the fact that the two noted Jesuits, Salmeron and Lainez, who served as the pope's theologians, and who had been enjoined by Loyola to resist all innovation in doctrine, were invited to preach during the council. They soon ingratiated themselves into the good will of the delegates. And by their unusual knowledge of the fathers, the conclusions of scholastic philosophy, and of Catholic doctrine, they came to wield a preponderant influence in the council.[25]

VI. Decisions Crystallized Into Catechism and Creed

The council stressed medieval Catholicism as the sole custodian of truth and compacted it with iron bands into a rigid system of doctrine, incapable of any alteration or essential reform. The decrees of the council were confirmed, January 26, 1564, by a bull of Pius IV. In December of the same year the Creed of Pius IV—a brief summary of the doctrinal positions of the council in the form of a creed—was immediately received throughout the Catholic Church as an accurate, explicit, and official summary of the Catholic faith.[26] The publication

---

[21] *Canons and Decrees of the Council of Trent* (trans. by Schroeder), session 4, April 8, 1546, pp. 17-19. The decision of the fourth session of the Council of Trent for the equal authority of Scripture and tradition, ruling out the Protestant standard of Scripture only, controlled the rest of the council's dogmatic decisions, and its results were ultimately seen in the Creed of Pius IV. (Kidd, *Documents*, p. 355.)

[22] *Canons and Decrees of the Council of Trent*, session 4, April 8, 1546, pp. 18, 19; Theodore Alois Buckley, *A History of the Council of Trent*, pp. 117, 118.

[23] *Canons and Decrees of the Council of Trent*, session 6, Jan. 13, 1547, pp. 33-35.

[24] *Ibid.*, session 4, April 8, 1546, pp. 18, 19.

[25] Hulme, *op. cit.*, p. 435.

[26] Buckley, *op. cit.*, p. 519; Philip Schaff, *Creeds*, vol. 1, pp. 96-99.

of the Latin *A Catechism of the Council of Trent,* authorized
by the council, followed in 1566. It was a manual of instruction
chiefly for priests. These two documents set the standard of
Catholic faith and practice to the present day. Only two cardinal
Roman Catholic tenets have since been added—the Immaculate
Conception (of Mary), in 1854, and the infallibility of the pope
and the universality of his episcopate, in 1870.[27]

The Creed of Pius IV utterly denies salvation to those who
differ from Rome; requires unreserved adherence to the published canons and decrees of preceding councils, as well as of
Trent.[28]

VII. Articles Added to Nicene Creed by Creed of Pius IV

This Creed of Pius IV is the authoritative epitome of the
canons and decrees of the Council of Trent, which every Catholic
priest is sworn to receive, profess, and maintain.[29] It commences
with the Nicene Creed, but a series of new articles is added,
which summarize the specific Roman doctrines as determined
by the Council of Trent and reject the doctrines of Scripture
recovered by the Reformation. The new articles in essence
are tradition equal with, or actually superior to, the Scriptures
as a rule of faith; interpretation of Scripture by unanimous
consent of Fathers; seven sacraments (baptism, confirmation,
the eucharist, penance, extreme unction, orders, and matrimony) and the ceremonies of the Catholic Church; definitions
and declarations of the Council of Trent concerning original
sin and justification; the mass and transubstantiation; communion in one kind; purgatory and invocation of saints; veneration
of images and use of indulgences; obedience to the bishop of
Rome; acceptance of the canons and councils, particularly the
Council of Trent; and no salvation outside of the true Catholic
faith.[30]

---

[27] A convenient chronological summary of council proceedings, in English, appears in
Landon, *op. cit.,* vol. 2, pp. 180-241.
[28] Joseph Faà di Bruno, *Catholic Belief,* pp. 250-254.
[29] James F. Loughlin, "Pius IV," *The Catholic Encyclopedia,* vol. 12, p. 129.
[30] Faà di Bruno, *op. cit.,* pp. 250-254; Philip Schaff, *Creeds,* vol. 1, pp. 98, 99, especially
footnote 1, p. 99.

These constitute Rome's deliberate and final rejection and anathema of the Reformation teachings of the Word—a decision to which she must unalterably adhere, and thus confess herself irreformable.

VIII. Speech of Archbishop of Reggio, January 18, 1562

The Reformers had appealed to the inspired Scriptures as the sole rule of faith and practice. Trent answered the claim by asserting the presence of continual inspiration residing in the Catholic Church, and making tradition the outgrowth of this continual, churchly inspiration. It appealed to the long-established change of the Sabbath into Sunday as standing proof of the inspired authority of the church, declaring that the change had not been made by the command of Christ but on the authority of the Catholic Church, which change Protestants accept. Ever since Trent the change of Sabbath into Sunday has been pointed to by Roman Catholics as the mark, or sign, of the church's power to be able to change even the fourth commandment of the Decalogue.[31]

1. SABBATH CHANGED BY AUTHORITY OF CATHOLIC CHURCH. —In the first session of the closing period of the council the tradition of the church was boldly set above Scripture, and the fact that the church had changed the Sabbath into Sunday, not by command of Christ, but by its own authority, was offered as proof. These remarkable statements occur in a speech made in the seventeenth session, on January 18, 1562, by Caspar del Fosso (or Gaspare Ricciulli), archbishop of Reggio di Calabria:

"Since the Scripture received its authority not from human will, but from God Himself, for that reason there was never any sane man who would have presumed to contradict it or oppose to it anything false, inconsistent, or idle. Likewise the church acquired from the Lord no less authority, so that whoever has heard or rejected her may be said to have heard or rejected God Himself. To her it has been given to distinguish between the canonical and apocryphal, the catholic and the heretical, to interpret the scriptures

---

[31] See vernacular *Catechisms*, such as those by Keenan, Geiermann, and Tuberville.

faithfully, to reject foreign and harmful things, and to embrace useful things. Therefore not amiss did Augustine say that he would not believe the Gospel if the authority of the church had not admonished him to . . . .

"Such is the condition of the heretics of this age that upon nothing do they rely more than that, under the pretense of the word of God, they overthrow the authority of the church, as if the church, His body, could be opposed to the word of Christ, or the head to the body. Nay, rather, the authority of the church, then, is most emphatically illustrated by the Scriptures; for while on the one hand she recommends them, declares them to be divine, presents them to us to be read, in doubtful matters explains them faithfully, and condemns whatever is contrary to them; on the other hand, the legal precepts taught by the Lord in the Scriptures have by the same authority become invalid. The sabbath day, the most distinguished day under the law, has passed over into the Lord's day; circumcision enjoined upon Abraham and his seed under such threatening that he who had not been circumcised should be destroyed from among his people has been so set aside that the apostle asserted, *If ye be circumcised, ye have fallen from grace, and Christ profits you nothing.* These and precepts similar to these have not become invalid by a declaration of Christ (for he says that he came to fulfil the law, not to abolish it), but they have been changed by the authority of the church. For should this authority be overthrown (since heresy is bound to exist), who would make known the truth, and confound the obstinacy of the heretics? All things will be confused, and heresies which have been condemned by the authority of the church will soon return." [32]

2. CLOSING ACCLAMATIONS AT CONCLUSION OF SESSION.—At the close of the last session, after the decrees of the council had been read, the motion to end the council and to seek confirmation of all decrees and definitions from Pope Pius IV was assented to. Then the cardinal of Lorraine led in the acclamations of the fathers, which reached a climax in the pledge to confess the faith of the Council of Trent and observe its decrees.

"The Cardinal: We all believe thus; we all think the same, agreeing and embracing them, we all subscribe. This is the faith of blessed Peter and of the Apostles; this is the faith of the Fathers; this is the faith of the orthodox.

"Reply: Thus we believe; thus we think; thus we subscribe." [33]

---

[32] Translated from Mansi, *op. cit.*, vol. 33, cols. 529, 530; Latin original also in *Concilium Tridentinum Diariorum, Actorum, Epistularum, Tractatuum Nova Collectio* (A New Collection of the Journals, the Acts, the Epistles, the Sermons of the Council of Trent), vol. 8, pp. 294, 297; see also Fra Paolo Sarpi, *Histoire du concile de Trente*, vol. 2, pp. 260, 261. For English translation of this extract see *Source Book for Bible Students* (1940 ed.), p. 604. For data on Del Fosso, see Heinrich Julius Holtzmann, *Kanon und Tradition. Ein Beitrag zur neueren Dogmengeschichte und Symbolik* (Canon and Tradition. A Contribution to the More Recent History of Dogma and Symbols), p. 263; see also *Source Book*, pp. 603, 604.
[33] *Canons and Decrees of the Council of Trent*, session 25, Dec. 3, 4, 1563, pp. 256-258.

In closing, the cardinal exclaimed, "Anathema to all heretics," to which the delegates answered, "Anathema, anathema." The council closed with this statement and response, after which the 265 delegates were commanded to sign the edicts of the council before leaving the city. Trent had ended.

IX. Power of Persecution Employed Anew

Under Pius IV (1559-1565), Catholicism reached a low ebb. Everywhere it was on the defensive, as one stronghold after another had passed into the hands of a victorious Protestantism. Pius V (1566-1572) became the first fighting pope of the new Roman Catholicism. Behind him was the reorganization effected by the Council of Trent; the revived Inquisition [34] and the Congregation of the Index; and, above all, the Company of Jesus. Catholicism once more boldly assumed the offensive. [35]

The Papacy now put forth strenuous efforts to restrict the Reformation to the narrowest limits, and, as far as possible, to recover her lost ground. This was carried out not only by polemics and attack and by missions to the heathen but by the persecution and suppression of Protestantism. Three of the weapons of reaction Rome drew from Spain, which still retained the spirit of the Crusades—the Jesuits, their counterinterpretation of prophecy, and the Inquisition, which was revived in 1542, as the tribunal for the whole church. [36]

1. VAST SCOPE OF REPRESSIVE MEASURES.—The great papal reaction of the sixteenth and seventeenth centuries included, according to Guinness, the founding of the Order of the Jesuits; the Marian persecutions in England; the wars in France against the Huguenots; the burning of heretics by the Inquisition in Spain; the decrees and anathemas of the Council of Trent; the attempt of the Duke of Alva to exterminate the Protestants in the Netherlands, with the slaughter of 18,000 in six years; the

---

[34] The Roman Inquisition was founded by Paul III, in 1542, through his bull *Licet ab initio*. (Kidd, *Documents*, p. 346.)
[35] Thomas M. Lindsay, *A History of the Reformation*, vol. 2, p. 606.
[36] Kidd, *The Counter-Reformation*, chap. 3, see also chap. 2, p. 23; Alfred Baudrillart, *The Catholic Church, the Renaissance and Protestantism*, pp. 156, 157.

PAPAL MEDAL COMMEMORATES ST. BARTHOLOMEW'S MASSACRE

Pope Gregory XIII Memorialized the Dread St. Bartholomew's Massacre of 1572, with a Representation, on the Reverse Side of the Medal, of the "Slaughter of the Huguenots" (*Ugonottorum Strages*) (Reproduced in Insert), to Commemorate the Slaying of 50,000 of These French Protestants

fearful Massacre of St. Bartholomew in 1572; and the invasion of the Spanish Armada in 1588. Religious fanaticism, flamed to white heat by these controversies, can probably be traced as a motive for the Jesuit attempts on the life of Queen Elizabeth, the Gunpowder Plot in 1605, the outrages of the Thirty Years' War (1618-1648), the massacre of 20,000 Protestants in Magdeburg in 1631, and the barbarities of Count Tilly in Saxony, as well as the massacre of 40,000 Protestants in Ireland in 1641 and the wholesale slaughter of the Waldenses in 1655.[37]

By these acts the Papacy stood revealed again as the persecuting Antichrist. The ecclesiastical woman was riding hard upon the civil beast, with its claws and iron teeth in action, and strong horns, and its ferocity mounting.

2. RELENTLESSNESS OF THE INQUISITION.—The Inquisition was the punishment of spiritual or ecclesiastical offenses by

---

[37] Guinness, *History Unveiling Prophecy*, p. 131.

physical pains or penalties. The principle had existed since Con-stantine's day. In medieval times it was employed by individual bishops, the church pointing out the heretics and the state pun-ishing them. In 1203 Innocent III censured the indifference of the bishops and appointed the Abbot of Citeaux his delegate in matters of heresy, giving him power both to judge and to punish heresy. This was the beginning of the Inquisition as a separate institution, and as managed by the Dominican and Franciscan orders.[38]

The Spanish Inquisition arose in the closing decades of the fifteenth century. It was a peculiar kind of Inquisition—under royal control, with the sovereigns appointing the Inquisitors, and the fines and confiscations flowing into the royal treasury. The first burning under its provisions took place in 1481, under the relentless inquisitor-general Torquemada. This was car-ried out under the terms of thirteenth-century decretals, which made the state subservient to the Holy Office and rendered any suspect or heretic incapable of public office.[39]

Its close relation to civil authority, its terrible secrecy, and its relentlessness made it a dreadful curse to unhappy Spain. In a century and a third 3,000,000 are said to have perished in that land. Llorente has calculated that during the eighteen years of Torquemada's presidency 114,000 persons were accused, of whom 10,220 were burned alive, and 97,000 were condemned to perpetual imprisonment or public penitence. This was the instrument used to bring the Spanish people into conformity with the Spanish Counter Reformation, and to crush the grow-ing Protestantism of the Low Countries, Corsica, and Sardinia.[40]

X. Prohibited Books Condemned by Roman Index

The leaders of the Counter Reformation in Italy were de-termined on more than the dispersion of Protestant communi-

---

[38] Thomas M. Lindsay, *op. cit.*, vol. 2, pp. 597, 598.
[39] *Ibid.*, vol. 2, p. 599; see Rafael Sabatini, *Torquemada and the Spanish Inquisition*, pp. 114-117.
[40] Thomas M. Lindsay, *op. cit.*, vol. 2, p. 600.

16

ties or the martyrdom or banishment of missionaries of evangelical thought. They resolved to destroy the "seed and seed-bed"—the cultivation of independent thought and scholarship—and so to "extirpate" all traces of the Reformation. The Inquisition in Italy and Spain attacked the schools of learning and the libraries in which the learning of the past was stored.[41]

Torquemada, already mentioned as Inquisitor-General of Spain, had served as an example, burning six thousand volumes at Salamanca in 1490 on the pretext that they taught sorcery. The burning of heretical writings had been in vogue throughout the Middle Ages. The bishops, universities, and, of course, the Inquisition had long endeavored to discover and destroy writings deemed dangerous to the dogmas of the church. But after printing was invented the task was more difficult. The edict of the archbishop of Mainz (1486), prompted by the number of Bibles printed in the vernacular, sought to establish a censorship of books.[42]

In 1547 Sixtus IV ordered the University of Köln to see that no books were printed without previous license, with penalties for infraction. By a constitution of Leo X, approved by the Fifth Lateran Council,[43] no book could be printed in Rome which had not been expressly sanctioned by the papal vicar and master of the palace, and in other places by the bishops and Inquisitor of the district. And that was confirmed by the Council of Trent.[44]

Some uniformity was necessary for the condemnation of books, and this led to lists of prohibited works (Louvain, 1546 and 1550; Köln, 1549; Sorbonne, 1544 and 1551, et cetera). Paul IV drafted the first papal Index in 1559. It listed sixty-one printers and prohibited the reading of any books printed by them. It also gave a long catalog of authors, all of whose writings were forbidden. The Council of Trent appointed a commission which drafted a set of rules governing a new papal index of

[41] *Ibid.*, p. 602; see also Putnam, *op. cit.*, vol. 1, chaps. 4-6.
[42] Thomas M. Lindsay, *op. cit.*, vol. 2, p. 602.
[43] Schroeder, *op. cit.*, p. 504.
[44] *Canons and Decrees of the Council of Trent*, session 25, Dec. 3, 4, 1563, p. 276.

prohibited books. This new Index was published by Pius IV in 1564. The Congregation of the Index (a special commission of cardinals to deal with the question of prohibited books) was instituted by Pius V in 1571. Although it was distinct from the Inquisition, it worked along with it.[45]

In the ten rules drawn up by the Trent commission, all writings of the most noted Reformers were absolutely prohibited and all religious writings of any other heretic. The Vulgate was declared the only authorized version, and the vernacular versions were to be allowed only to certain authorized persons, under restrictions. Books dealing with controversies between Catholics and heretics were placed under the same restrictions as vernacular Bibles. Books in the nature of lexicons, concordances, and the like, reproducing the work of heretics, had to pass the strictest censorship and expurgation before publication.[46] The Index, however, had little effect north of the Alps, in the lands of the Reformation. Even in France, papal Germany, and northern Italy a succession of daring colporteurs carried prohibited tracts, Bibles, and religious literature throughout the lands.[47]

The Index of 1564 remained the standard index, regarding both rules of censorship and inclusiveness of its lists, until the revision in 1897 by Leo XIII,[48] with other books added from time to time. The Congregation of the Index, which had become a permanent institution, undertook to pass a final opinion upon all publications—a task beyond accomplishment. But it was a powerful weapon in the arsenal of militant Catholicism.

Such was the essence of the Counter Reformation.

---

[45] Thomas M. Lindsay, *op. cit.*, vol. 2, pp. 603, 604; Putnam, *op. cit.*, vol. 1, chaps. 7, 8.
[46] *Canons and Decrees of the Council of Trent*, session 25, Dec. 3, 4, 1563, pp. 273-275; Thomas M. Lindsay, *op. cit.*, vol. 2, pp. 603, 604; Putnam, *op. cit.*, vol. 1, chaps. 7, 8.
[47] Thomas M. Lindsay, *op. cit.*, vol. 2, pp. 604, 605; Putnam, *op. cit.*, vol. 1, chap. 9.
[48] Hulme, *op. cit.*, pp. 453, 454.

CHAPTER TWENTY-TWO

Jesuits Introduce

Futurist Counterinterpretation

I. Counterinterpretations Divert Protestant Applications

For some time following the launching of the Reformation, Roman Catholic leadership carefully avoided exposition of the prophecies of Daniel and the Apocalypse. They seemed unable to parry the force of the incriminating Protestant applications of the prophecies concerning Antichrist, which were undermining the very foundations of the Catholic position. Upon the first outbreak of Luther's antipapal protest two Catholic doctors, Prierias and Eck, in the true spirit of the recently concluded Fifth Lateran Council (1512-1517), had boldly reasserted the Lateran theory and declared the papal dominion to be Daniel's fifth monarchy, or reign of the saints, and identified the existing Roman church with the New Jerusalem.

But what of the various prophecies of the Antichrist that was to do its exploits between the time of Rome's iron empire and the saints' reign? In Germany, Switzerland, France, Denmark, Sweden, England, and Scotland there had been simultaneous and impressive declarations by voice and pen that the Papacy was the specified Antichrist of prophecy. The symbols of Daniel, Paul, and John were applied with tremendous effect. Hundreds of books and tracts impressed their contention upon the consciousness of Europe. Indeed, it gained so great a hold upon the minds of men that Rome, in alarm, saw that she must successfully counteract this identification of Antichrist with the Papacy, or lose the battle.

She felt the tremendous force of the arguments used against her. And she discovered, to her dismay, that she could no longer hold her members by mere ritual, dogma, or force. There must be reasoned evidence and plausible exposition of Scripture prophecy to counter the largely unbroken harmony of the reformed positions. Catholicism must have preachers who would match the dynamic Reformation eloquence and scholarship. The Jesuits were summoned to aid in the extremity, and cleverly provided the very method needed both for defense and for attack.

From the ranks of the Jesuits two stalwarts arose, determined to lift the stigma from the Papacy by locating Antichrist at some point where he could not be applied to the Roman church. Whereas Luther and some of his associates had, in the early part of the Reformation, doubted the canonicity of the Apocalypse, Catholicism could now pose as the actual defender of the New Testament canon, as against the inconsistency of the Reformers, who had boasted that they rested their case solely on Holy Writ.

1. CONDEMNED REFORMATION ON POINT OF AGREEMENT.— The Reformers in all lands had been unanimous in applying most of the prophecies of Antichrist to the Papacy, though some applied one or two symbols to Mohammedanism, as a paralleling Eastern Antichrist. In fact, it was this united Protestant stand on the Papacy that became the spring of their reformatory action. It was this clear understanding of the prophetic symbols that led them to protest against Rome with such extraordinary courage and effectiveness, nerving them to break with her, and to resist her claims, even unto death. These positions were, moreover, shared by hundreds of thousands, and were adopted by both rulers and people. Under their influence, whole nations abjured allegiance to the bishop of Rome. It was clearly a crisis of major proportions. Of this wholesale Protestant testimony *The Catholic Encyclopedia* charges:

"To the 'reformers' particularly the Apocalypse was an inexhaustible quarry where to dig for invectives that they might hurl them against the Roman hierarchy. The seven hills of Rome, the scarlet robes of the cardinals, and the unfortunate abuses of the papal court made the application easy and tempting." [1]

In the reaction that followed, Catholicism loosed all its reserves upon the adherents of the Reformation. But the Counter Reformation did not merely condemn the Reformation in general; it attacked the prophetic positions on which all Protestants were agreed. It repudiated the interpretation which they embodied in their solemn confessions and sealed with their blood. It thus attacked and condemned Protestantism's prophetic spring of action.

2. APPLICATION TO PAPACY MUST BE DIVERTED.—Rome had felt the cumulative force of these prophecies. She must somehow offset them. There was no way but to deny their applicability to the Papacy, as their integral existence in the Scripture could not be denied. The Catholic citadel must be defended on prophetic grounds. The persistent Protestant application to the Papacy of Antichrist, under the various symbols, must be countered and turned if the Protestant prophetic fortress was to be overwhelmed. The incriminating finger of prophecy— pointed by Daniel, Paul, and John—must be diverted. The symbols must be pushed out of the entire field of medieval and contemporary history.

II. Two Conflicting Alternatives Brought Forth

Rome's answer to the Protestant Reformation was twofold, though actually conflicting and contradictory. Through the Jesuits RIBERA, of Salamanca, Spain, and BELLARMINE, of Rome, the Papacy put forth her Futurist interpretation. And through Alcazar, Spanish Jesuit of Seville, she advanced almost simultaneously the conflicting Preterist interpretation. These were designed to meet and overwhelm the Historical interpretation

---

[1] C. van den Biesen, "Apocalypse," *The Catholic Encyclopedia*, vol. 1, p. 598.

of the Protestants. Though mutually exclusive, either Jesuit alternative suited the great objective equally well, as both thrust aside the application of the prophecies from the existing Church of Rome. The one accomplished it by making prophecy stop altogether short of papal Rome's career. The other achieved it by making it overleap the immense era of papal dominance, crowding Antichrist into a small fragment of time in the still distant future, just before the great consummation. It is consequently often called the gap theory.

According to the Protestants, the vision of Babylon and the supporting Beast is divinely interpreted in chapter 17 of the Apocalypse. It was on this that the Reformers commonly rested their case—the apostate woman, the Roman church; the city, seven-hilled Rome; the many waters, the many peoples; the Beast, the fourth, or Roman, beast of Daniel; the sixth head, the Caesars; and the seventh, the popes. Concerning the two alternatives, presented by Ribera and Alcazar, consigning Antichrist either to the remote past or future, Joseph Tanner, the Protestant writer, gives this record:

"Accordingly, towards the close of the century of the Reformation, two of her most learned doctors set themselves to the task, each endeavouring by different means to accomplish the same end, namely, that of diverting men's minds from perceiving the fulfilment of the prophecies of the Antichrist in the Papal system. The Jesuit Alcasar devoted himself to bring into prominence the *Preterist* method of interpretation, which we have already briefly noticed, and thus endeavoured to show that the prophecies of Antichrist were fulfilled before the Popes ever ruled at Rome, and therefore could not apply to the Papacy. On the other hand the Jesuit Ribera tried to set aside the application of these prophecies to the Papal Power by bringing out the *Futurist* system, which asserts that these prophecies refer properly not to the career of the Papacy, but to that of some future supernatural individual, who is yet to appear, and to continue in power for three and a half years. Thus, as Alford says, the Jesuit Ribera, about A.D. 1580, may be regarded as the Founder of the Futurist system in modern times."[2]

Roman Catholics as well as Protestants agree as to the origin of these interpretations. Thus the Roman Catholic writer G. S. Hitchcock says:

---

[2] Joseph Tanner, *Daniel and the Revelation*, pp. 16, 17.

"The Futuristic School, founded by the Jesuit Ribera in 1591, looks for Antichrist, Babylon, and a rebuilt temple in Jerusalem, at the end of the Christian Dispensation.

"The Praeterist School, founded by the Jesuit Alcasar in 1614, explains the Revelation by the Fall of Jerusalem, or by the fall of Pagan Rome in 410 A.D." [3]

Similarly, Dean Henry Alford (Protestant), in the "Prolegomena" to his *Greek Testament,* declares:

"The founder of this system [Futurist] in modern times . . . appears to have been the Jesuit Ribera, about A. D. 1580." [4]

"The Praeterist view found no favour, and was hardly so much as thought of, in the times of primitive Christianity. . . . The view is said to have been first promulgated in any thing like completeness by the Jesuit Alcasar . . . in 1614." [5]

E. B. Elliott states precisely the same fact, only assigning slightly different dates;[6] and many others, such as Dr. Candish, of Edinburgh, support the charges. Thus the fact is established.

Catholics dared not admit that the dynasty of the popes had fulfilled the prophecies of the Man of Sin, or that Babylon the Great was the Roman Catholic Church. Yet it was clear that no other power or system existing during the early and the later Middle Ages really answered the description. Hence, some declared that Babylon meant *pagan* Rome. Others, of the Futurist School, which won general acceptance among the Catholics, declared that these prophecies regarding Antichrist were still largely unfulfilled, and insisted on a literal interpretation, especially of the prophetic time feature.

Futurism contended insistently for an individual Antichrist, not a system or dynasty; for a diminutive three and a half literal years, not twelve and a half centuries; for an individual Jew of the tribe of Dan, a clever infidel, to set himself up in the Jewish temple at Jerusalem, not a succession of bishops in the Catholic Church. Thus the prophecies allegedly had only to do with the first few centuries after Christ, and then three and a half years

---

[3] G. S. Hitchcock, *The Beasts and the Little Horn,* p. 7.

[4] Henry Alford, *The New Testament for English Readers,* vol. 2, part 2, p. 351 (bottom numbering).

[5] *Ibid.,* pp. 348, 349 (bottom numbering).

[6] Elliott, *op. cit.,* vol. 4, pp. 480-485.

sometime in the future. Between the two was the great gap of the spreading centuries with which prophecy had nought to do. Antichrist obviously had not come—because the time of the end had not come.

III. Ribera Initiates Futurist Counterinterpretation

FRANCISCO RIBERA (1537-1591), of Salamanca, Jesuit scholar, writer, and critic, was born in Villacastin, Spain. Educated at the University of Salamanca, he later specialized in the Scriptures, as well as in Latin, Greek, and Hebrew, in which he became a recognized expert, receiving a doctorate in theology. Joining the Jesuit order in 1570, at the age of thirty-three, he was soon called by Alvarez to teach and write on the Scriptures at the University of Salamanca. Serving as confessor and biographer of the famous Carmelite nun and mystic, St. Theresa, he began the composition of his famed commentaries in 1575. This writing was interspersed with preaching for a period of sixteen years.[7] It was under these circumstances that he began his controversy with Protestant Historical School interpretation.

About 1590 Ribera published a 500-page commentary on the Apocalypse, denying the Protestant application of Antichrist to the Church of Rome. Ribera's death at fifty-four halted the preparation of further commentaries. Those that were printed passed through several revised editions—at Salamanca about 1590, Lyons and Antwerp in 1593, Douay in 1612, and Antwerp in 1603 and 1623.

1. GIST OF RIBERA'S PROPHETIC EXPOSITION.—Ribera assigned the first few chapters of the Apocalypse to ancient Rome, in John's own time; the rest he restricted to a literal three and a half years' reign of an infidel Antichrist, who would bitterly oppose and blaspheme the saints just before the second advent. He taught that Antichrist would be a single individual, who would rebuild the temple in Jerusalem, abolish the Christian religion, deny Christ, be received by the Jews, pretend to be

---

[7] *Enciclopedia Universal Ilustrada*, vol. 51, pp. 330, 331.

God, and conquer the world—and all in this brief space of three
and one-half literal years!

Ribera made Revelation 12 refer to the persecution of the
church when she would be compelled to flee into the wilderness
during this very last three and a half years of time, which period
coincides with Antichrist's reign. Ribera also believed that at
that time Christian Rome would be overthrown because of her
sins. He placed the one thousand years, which he regarded as
an indefinite period, between the cross and the coming of Antichrist just before the second advent, but repudiated Augustine's
view of the temporal rule of the saints on this earth; instead, he
placed the ruling saints with Christ in heaven during the thousand years.

2. PLACES ANTICHRIST'S COMING AT CLOSE OF SEALS.—
Ribera expounded the Apocalypse much as if it were a commentary on the prophecy of Matthew 24, making it begin with
the early period of the church.[8] Under the first seal the white
horse and rider signify the gospel triumph of the apostolic era;
under the second seal the red horse, ridden by the devil denotes
the early persecutions; the third seal's black horse, heresies; the
fourth seal, the violent persecutions of the church by Trajan;
and the phenomena of the sixth as the signs preceding Christ's
second coming, spoken of in Matthew 24 and Luke 21.[9] But the
sealing vision under the sixth seal and all that follows in the
Apocalypse, he applied to the brief time of Antichrist at the
end of the age.[10]

3. PLACES TRUMPETS UNDER SEVENTH SEAL.—Under the
seventh seal the punishment of those who were not sealed by the
angel of Revelation 7 (under the sixth seal) is depicted by the
seven trumpets. The first six trumpets come before the death of
Antichrist; the seventh, after.[11] The seven trumpets are the

---

[8] For a convenient summary in English of Ribera's commentary on the Apocalypse, see
Elliott, *op. cit.*, vol. 4, pp. 481-483.
[9] Francisco Ribera, *Sacram Beati Ioannis . . . Apocalypsin Commentarij*, chaps. 6, 7, pp.
135 ff.
[10] *Ibid.*, chap. 8, pp. 173, 174; chap. 10, pp. 210, 211.
[11] *Ibid.*, chap. 8, pp. 173, 174; chap. 11, p. 211.

preachers of truth, and the judgments are to lead men to repentance. The locusts of the fifth trumpet are cruel and barbarous invading armies proceeding against those without the seal of God. The evil angels of the sixth trumpet are those loosed to impede the salvation of men.[12]

4. DEATH OF WITNESSES IS LITERAL TIME.—In Revelation 11 the temple and the Holy City prefigure the church, the treading underfoot being by Antichrist's followers. And the period of the death of the Two Witnesses is likewise a symbol of the three and a half literal years, under the tyranny of Antichrist.[13]

5. ANTICHRIST'S PERSECUTIONS BUT THREE AND A HALF YEARS.—In Revelation 12 Ribera's Futurism comes more sharply into view. In Revelation 1-11 he has dealt with signs of the future, up to the time of Antichrist; but in chapters 12-22 he describes the outcome of the seven seals, the rule of Antichrist, the persecutions of those times, the final judgment, and the blessedness of the saints.[14] The woman travailing in the last time is the church just before the three and a half "times," or literal years, of Antichrist. Ribera interprets the dragon as Satan, and identifies it with the fourth beast of Daniel 7.[15] After the three horns are disposed of, the seven unite with Antichrist, or the Little Horn, who now has everything his own way.[16] Citing Irenaeus, Ribera makes 666 the number of the name of Antichrist, which name cannot be known until he comes.[17]

6. JUDGMENTS UPON ROME FOR ULTIMATE APOSTASY.—In Revelation 17 Ribera admits the woman to be not only pagan Rome but also Rome Christian after a future falling away from the pope.[18] He admits, further, that before the consummation the ten kings, prefigured by the ten horns, will overthrow Rome just prior to the coming of Antichrist.[19] Therefore in Revelation

---

[12] *Ibid.*, chap. 8, p. 175, chap. 11 [i.e. 9], p. 188; chap. 9, p. 196.
[13] *Ibid.*, chap. 11, pp. 211 ff, 118 [i.e. 218]. Denying the year-day principle, Ribera nevertheless makes the 3½ days of the death of the witnesses a sign to the faithful of the three and one-half years of the last persecution under Antichrist. (*Ibid.*, p. 223.)
[14] *Ibid.*, chap. 10, pp. 209, 210.   [15] *Ibid.*, chap. 12, p. 231.
[16] *Ibid.*, chaps. 12, 13, pp. 232-234.   [17] *Ibid.*, chap. 13, pp. 263-265.
[18] *Ibid.*, chap. 14, pp. 282, 283.   [19] *Ibid.*, chap. 22, p. 445.

18 Rome's burning is in judgment for the sins both of pagan Rome and of Rome apostatized from the pope.[20]

7. REPUDIATES AUGUSTINIAN EARTHLY MILLENNIUM.— The thousand years of Revelation 20 are declared by Ribera to be the whole time, from the binding of Satan by the death of Christ until the coming of Antichrist.[21] He agrees with Augustine in placing the millennium during the Christian Era, but repudiates the Augustinian view of the millennial period as the reign of the church in this world; rather he regards the saints as reigning in heaven.[22] He believes he has discovered the right view— that the number 1,000 may be elastic, or figurative, or at least indefinite.[23]

8. ANTICHRIST'S REIGN COUNTED BY LITERAL DAYS.—Ribera makes the other prophetic time periods literal time, as seen in his prophetic exposition of the 1260 days of the Two Witnesses of Revelation 11, though even this is elastic:

"*And they shall prophesy 1260 days.* It signifies a time of three years, and a half not complete. . . . Gloss: *Note that these days do not completely make up three years and a half, just as Christ did not complete a half year of preaching.* And since it is probable that they will begin to prophesy at the same time in which the tyranny of Antichrist will begin, seeing that, as it were, they had been given as his antidote, they are killed by the same Antichrist on the 20th day before the end, and before his death.

"But it is not to be passed by without the question why he numbers the time of their prophecy by days, when he numbers the time of Antichrist by months? Simple and plain is the answer that the time of Antichrist was not numbered by years, because it was shorter, and easier, since they were not whole years, but by months, since 42 whole months were given for the persecution of Antichrist. So therefore, the time of prophesying of the two prophets is not counted by years, nor by months, since they were not to be whole years or months, and therefore it remained that it should be computed by days." [24]

Of Antichrist's three and a half literal years Ribera repeatedly speaks.

"As there are granted to Antichrist three years and a half for the probation of the good and the blinding of the wicked. . . . So to Antiochus was

---

[20] See Elliott, *op. cit.*, vol. 4, p. 483.
[21] Ribera, *op. cit.*, chap. 20, pp. 374, 375, 386, 387.
[22] *Ibid.*, pp. 375, 384.   [23] *Ibid.*, pp. 387, 388.
[24] *Ibid.*, chap. 11, verse 3, p. 118 [i.e. 218].

given a period of 2300 days against the daily sacrifice. Dan. 8 & 9; seventy weeks were cut off upon the people Israel and upon Jerusalem. For of these numbers, to which there are many similar in the Scriptures, no other plan than that recited, either ought to be sought, or can be, except rarely, set forth." [25]

"*And they shall tread underfoot the holy city.* Now no one of the expositors doubts that here is to be understood the holy ecclesiastical state, which was signified by Jerusalem, which was called the holy city, where were the temple, priests, and sacrifices. Hence he has reference to the universal church, which *before* he indicated by the two parts of the temple, *now* by the holy city Jerusalem, which for *forty-two months,* that is three years and a half, he says is to be trodden down by Antichrist and his followers, that is, to be vexed, oppressed, and occupied." [26]

9. BABYLON IS ROME PAST AND FUTURE, NOT PRESENT.—The power and learning of the Jesuits, says Maitland, enabled them to hold out the menace to Rome that she would someday fall away from the faith and, despite her boast of perpetual purity, become the mother of harlots and abominations of the earth—though here they tread carefully. But Ribera does not allow that to be the Rome of his day, which is the "mother of piety, the pillar of the Catholic faith, the mistress of sanctity"; the reference, he contends, is to Rome "as she once was under the pagan emperors, and as she will be in the end of the world, after she has fallen away from the pope." [27]

Thus in Ribera's commentary was laid the foundation for that great structure of Futurism, built upon and enlarged by those who followed, until it became the common Catholic position. And then, wonder of wonders, in the nineteenth century this Jesuit scheme of interpretation came to be adopted by a growing number of Protestants, until today Futurism, amplified and adorned with the rapture theory, has become the generally accepted belief of the Fundamentalist wing of popular Protestantism. Although Ribera launched the Futurist system of interpretation, it was popularized and made to register by the astute Cardinal Bellarmine, with his effective phrasings and polemical power, as will be noted next.

---

[25] *Ibid.,* chap. 9, p. 192.
[26] *Ibid.,* chap. 11, p. 214.
[27] *Ibid.,* chap. 14, pp. 282, 283; see also Charles Maitland, *op. cit.,* pp. 377-379.

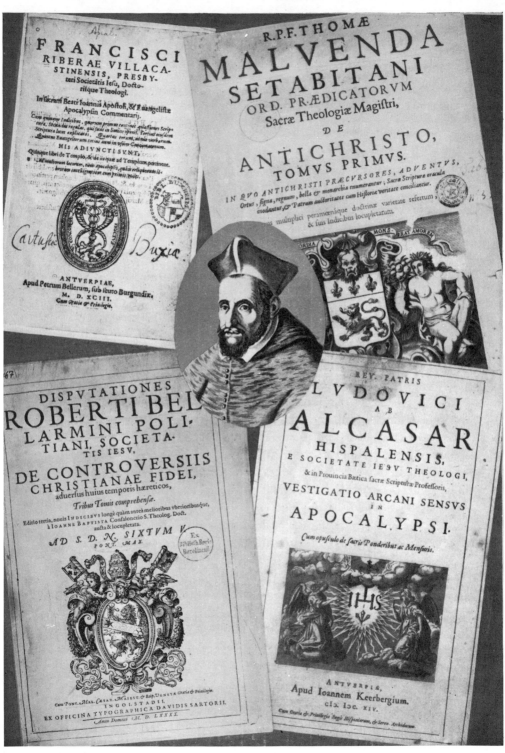

JESUIT COUNTERINTERPRETATIONS PARRY REFORMATION EXPOSITION

Ribera's Treatise Introduced Futurist Antichrist Theory, Followed by Malvenda (Upper, Left and Right); Cardinal Bellarmine (Oval) Launches Attack on Year-Day Principle (Lower Left); Alcazar Projects Entirely Opposite Preterist Theory Regarding Prophecy (Lower Right). See Pages 506-509

IV. Bellarmine Centers Attack on Year-Day Principle

ROBERT BELLARMINE (1542-1621), Italian cardinal and ablest and most renowned of all Jesuit controversialists, was born in Tuscany, his mother being the sister of Pope Marcellus II. In 1560, when he was eighteen, he entered the novitiate of the Jesuit order, and spent three years studying philosophy at the Collegium Romanum, going from thence to Florence as a teacher of the classics. Here, at twenty-two, he was authorized to preach on Sundays and holy days. By 1564 he was studying and teaching at the college of Mondovi, in Piedmont, not yet having begun the study of theology.

In 1567 he was called to Padua, and two years later to Louvain, where he completed his studies, was ordained, and began to teach theology. In 1576 Bellarmine returned to Rome, under appointment by Gregory XIII, to teach controversial theology to young clerics going forth as missionaries. In 1592 he became rector of the Roman College, and was made a cardinal in 1599, by Clement VIII, who said, " 'The Church of God had not his equal in learning.' " [28] He was made archbishop of Capua in 1601, but in 1605, when appointed chief adviser of the Holy See in the theological department, he resigned his see.

Between 1576 and 1589, in addition to his teaching, Bellarmine lectured to large audiences. He insisted that the prophecies concerning Antichrist, in Daniel, Paul, and John, had no application to the papal power. This formed the third part of his *Disputationes de Controversiis Christianae Fidei Adversus Huius Temporis Haereticos* (Polemic Lectures Concerning the Disputed Points of the Christian Belief Against the Heretics of This Time), published between 1581 and 1593. This was the most detailed apology of the Catholic faith ever produced, and became the arsenal for all future defenders and expositors. [29] It called forth a host of counterwritings from Protestant leaders, who considered him their greatest adversary. About this time the

---

[28] Sydney F. Smith, "Bellarmine," *The Catholic Encyclopedia*, vol. 2, p. 412.
[29] Kidd, *The Counter-Reformation*, pp. 185, 186.

Ecclesiastical Annals of Baronius appeared as the counterpart to the *Magdeburg Centuries*.[30] Both Bellarmine and Baronius were created cardinals for productions that filled the armory of Rome with effective weapons. Because of the importance of the man and the weight of his works, we shall carefully examine Bellarmine's position. He greatly augmented the case for Futurism over the work of Ribera.

1. CAPITALIZES ON LUTHER'S HESITATION OVER APOCALYPSE. —Bellarmine's method was astute. As a Catholic, he held the canon of Scripture as dependent upon tradition. But Luther and certain other Reformers had at first questioned the canonicity of the Apocalypse. So Bellarmine now posed as a defender of the New Testament canon against the leader of the Reformation, who had avowedly rested his case on the Bible. Thus Luther's best weapon was adroitly turned back upon him.[31]

2. MAIN ASSAULT CENTERED ON YEAR-DAY APPLICATION.— Bellarmine's assault on the Protestant interpretations of prophecy was centered upon the year-day principle, which, since Joachim, had risen to general notice and wide acceptance among both Catholics and Protestants. He went out of his way to do this, perhaps, says Maitland, tempted by hope of an easy victory.[32] In citing Ezekiel 4, Bellarmine contended that it could not apply, because Ezekiel did not lie on his side 390 years; and, further, that the "angelic" days of Illyricus and Chytraeus were nowhere to be found.[33]

Determined to nullify the year-day principle, used by Protestants as the basis of the 1260-year period of Antichrist's tyranny,

---

[30] CAESAR BARONIUS (1538-1607), father of Catholic Church history, was born in Sora (Campania). He studied law and theology in Veroli and Naples, and then went to Rome in 1557. He was asked to write an effective Catholic Church history to counter the influence of Protestant *Magdeburg Centuries*, which had made heavy inroads on the Roman church. Clement VIII selected him as his confessor, and appointed him cardinal in 1596, and librarian of the Vatican in 1597. The success of Baronius' learned and laborious *Annales Ecclesiastici* (12 vols., 1588-1607) soon attracted widespread attention. Written in a rather grandiose style, his *Annales* attempt to show the continuity of Catholicism. (Herzog, *Real-Encyklopädie*, art. "Baronius.") It was Baronius' belief that history simply discloses the God-willed world position of the Roman church.

[31] Robert Bellarmine, "De Verbo Dei," book 1, chap. 19, in *Disputationes Roberti Bellarmini . . . De Controversiis Christianae Fidei, Adversus Huius Temporis Haereticos*, tome 1, vol. 1, pp. 17, 18.

[32] Charles Maitland, *op. cit.*, pp. 373, 374.

[33] Bellarmine, "De Summo Pontifici," book 3, chap. 8, in *Disputationes*, tome 1, vol. 1, pp. 190, 191. On Matthias Flacius Illyricus and Chytraeus see chapters 14 and 17 in this volume.

he sought to deprive this symbol of its Scriptural support through making Scripture dependent upon tradition. It should not be forgotten that his first argument against it is "the common opinion of the ancients," who believed in a literal three-and-a-half-year reign of Antichrist. In this endeavor he searched not only the fathers and the Scriptures minutely, but apparently the whole field of Protestant exposition as well, citing them facilely, and telling effectively wherein they differed; he did this to neutralize their influence.[34]

3. ASSIGNS SYMBOLS TO PAST AND FUTURE.—Bellarmine assigned the apocalyptic symbols to the distant past and the distant future, thereby eliminating application to the long papal ascendancy of the Middle Ages. Antichrist had not yet come, for he was to abolish the daily (continual) sacrifice *(iuge sacrificium)* of the mass, according to Daniel 12:11.[35] The seventy weeks, he held, were weeks of years only because of the specific Hebrew word. He could not contravene this. But a prophetic "time," he contended, simply denoted a unit—such as a day, a year, or a millennium.

"For by 'time' ought to be signified, without a doubt, some one number; as one day, one week, one month, one year, means one lustrum, one jubilee, one century, one millennium; but if we should accept one millennium, then antichrist will reign 3500 years, which the adversaries do not admit. If we accept one century, the time of antichrist will be 350 years, which they also do not admit, and the same is plain concerning one jubilee." [36]

4. EXPLOITS VARIATIONS ON TIME OF ANTICHRIST.—If the Antichrist had been reigning in the church for centuries, there should be a recognized, exact, and uniform date of beginning. But, as Bellarmine pointed out, on this Protestants differed widely. Some had dated the 666 or the 1260 years from the beginning of the fall of Rome, about A.D. 400, and others from Gregory, about 600, others from Phocas, 606 [37]—the dates ranging from 200 to 773, 1,000, or even 1,200. So he chided them for being asleep, instead of on the watch, because they could not

---

[34] *Ibid.*, p. 190.
[36] *Ibid.*, chap. 8. Translated from the Latin.
[35] *Ibid.*, chap. 7.
[37] *Ibid.*, chap. 3, pp. 186, 187.

agree on the definite time of Antichrist.[38] This vulnerable position Bellarmine attacked as also being contrary to prophetic specification.

Furthermore, the spiritual supremacy of the Papacy had lasted more than 1260 years, and the secular domination more than 666.[39] In addition, Luther's own name yielded 666.[40] The Protestants had said that Rome was the seat of the Beast; but Bellarmine countered with Jerusalem, "where also their Lord was crucified." Whereas the Papacy had preserved Rome, the Antichrist is to destroy Rome.[41] Rome means Babylon, he admitted, but only in its pagan empire, and possibly again in the future, at the end of the world.[42]

In book 5 Bellarmine put limits to the temporal jurisdiction of the pope, claiming that he had not immediate temporal power but only spiritual power. For this reason Bellarmine's work on the Controversies was put on the Index by Sixtus V.[43] Possibly it was also in disfavor because it quoted so many arguments of opponents, such as the evidences, sometimes from Catholic sources, offered to prove that the pope is the predicted Antichrist. However, the pope died before the book was printed, and when the Index was issued, Bellarmine's book was not mentioned.

V. The Twofold Issue—Antichrist's Nature and Duration

It should ever be remembered that the heart of Bellarmine's thesis—which was both clever and plausible, though deceptive—was simply this: (1) Antichrist is an individual Jew, and not an apostate Christian system. (2) *Therefore the length of his exploits must harmonize with the life period of one man—three and a half literal years, and not 1260 years.* This he premised upon the teachings of the early fathers, whose views were constricted and who were then without the later perspective of the year-day principle for the longer time prophecies. In doing this,

[38] *Ibid.*, chap. 7, p. 190.   [39] *Ibid.*, chap. 8, p. 190; chap. 3, p. 186.
[40] *Ibid.*, chap. 10, pp. 191, 192.   [41] *Ibid.*, chap. 13, pp. 194, 195.
[42] *Ibid.*, book 4, chap. 4, pp. 211, 212; see also Charles Maitland, *op. cit.*, p. 376.
[43] Kidd, *The Counter-Reformation*, pp. 185, 186.

Bellarmine denied or ignored the clearer testimony of many reverent Catholics who had asserted, from Joachim's time onward for four centuries, that historical developments had identified Antichrist as a system, or organization, or falling away in the church—involving centuries of time, and therefore bringing to light the year-day principle as the only consistent interpretation harmonizing with the prophetic symbols.[44]

Bellarmine discussed in detail—his works fill nine ponderous folio tomes—the standard prophecies pertaining to Antichrist, and others besides.

It is interesting to observe that he sometimes flung back against the Protestants certain prophetic interpretations which they had used against the Papacy. Thus, to Chytraeus the "fallen star" of Revelation 9 symbolized the Papacy, and the "locusts" were its army of clergy and monks; but to Bellarmine the same symbols represented Luther and his followers.[45] And to the opposers of the Protestant movement this interpretation had convincing appeal.

1. CONTENDS FOR AN INDIVIDUAL, NOT A SYSTEM.—Pressing the twofold issue of the *nature* and *length* of the operation of Antichrist, Bellarmine places against the Protestant portrayal of Antichrist as an apostate system (a ruinous, ruling hierarchy in the church) the opposing picture of Antichrist as a single man, a Jew, in whom will dwell all the power of the devil, the same as all the power of God dwelt in Christ.[46]

2. MAKES DANIEL'S LITTLE HORN A SINGLE KING.—As to the prophecies, Bellarmine finds in the Little Horn of Daniel 7, as well as in chapters 11 and 12, a single king—Antiochus—who would take away three kings and subdue seven others to himself, and yet admittedly was a figure, or symbol, of Antichrist, and who, he contends, would therefore be one man only, and not a kingdom.[47]

---

[44] Treated fully in Volume I of *Prophetic Faith;* see also No. 10, under Brute, in this volume, p. 82.
[45] Bellarmine, "De Summo Pontifici," book 3, chap. 23, in *Disputationes,* tome 1, vol. 1, pp. 203, 206.
[46] *Ibid.,* chap. 2, pp. 184, 185; chap. 12, pp. 193, 194.
[47] *Ibid.,* chap. 2, p. 185.

3 Only "Forerunners" of Antichrist Depicted by Paul.

—Bellarmine excludes 2 Thessalonians 2 from application because it involves a long apostasy under many rulers—the forerunners of Antichrist—and therefore could not refer to Antichrist himself.[48] On this argument Bellarmine places Protestant and Catholic teaching in opposition, quoting first from the Protestant *Magdeburg Centuries* concerning the apostate system operating in the Church of Rome:

"The apostles teach that Antichrist will not be one person only, but a whole kingdom through false teachers presiding over the temple of God, that is in the Church of God, in the great city, that is in the city of Rome." [49]

Bellarmine stresses, in contrast, the Catholic "single man or single throne" concept:

"For all Catholics think thus that Antichrist will be one certain man; but all heretics teach as cited above that Antichrist is expressly declared to be not a single person, but an individual throne or absolute kingdom, and apostate seat of those who rule over the church." [50]

4. Arguments in Behalf of Literal Time.

—Revelation 13 and 17, Bellarmine argues, both mention ten kings who will be ruling over the earth when Antichrist comes, and assumes that both chapters limit his reign to a literal three and a half years. Hence, both Daniel and John speak of but one single king,[51] and that individual has not yet come.[52]

In supporting this contention, Bellarmine insists that the "1260 days" of Daniel and John are but a literal three and a half years—a period that a single man could compass; and as there is a difference of thirty days between the 1260 and the 1290 days, Bellarmine contends that Enoch and Elias, the two witnesses, will be slain "one month ["30 days"] before Antichrist is destroyed." [53] Moreover, the difference between the 1290 and the 1335 days in Daniel 12 is seized upon as forty-five literal days before the actual end of the world, when Antichrist will be slain. Thus Bellarmine's long and tortuous arguments on Antichrist

---

[48] *Ibid.*
[50] *Ibid.*
[52] *Ibid.*, chaps. 3, 4, pp. 186-188.

[49] *Ibid.*, p. 184.
[51] *Ibid.*, p. 185.
[53] *Ibid.*, chap. 8, pp. 190, 191.

all center on these two interdependent points—Antichrist's nature and duration.

5. ASSERTS ROME NOT YET DIVIDED.—In the heading of chapter 2, "De Summo Pontifice," Bellarmine expressly states that Antichrist is yet "to come," and chapter 3 is devoted to showing that "Antichrist has not yet come." [54] Chapter 5 declares that the Roman Empire is not divided according to the demands of prophecy—that is, the nations ruled by Roman kings—and until this happens, Antichrist cannot have come. The complete desolation of the Roman Empire must come, Bellarmine avers, before the advent of Antichrist, and this has not yet taken place. The Roman legs of iron are "very long," he adds, and are in two parts, East and West; furthermore, no toe is a leg. [55] The Protestants had contended that the "letting" power of the Roman Empire had been removed, and that the Papacy had followed upon the fall of Rome. On the contrary, Bellarmine contends that the succession of the Roman emperors had continued so that the statue of Daniel 2 always had one leg to stand on. Here are his words, literally translated:

"That this has not ever been thus far fulfilled is clear since, up to this time, the succession and name of the Roman emperors remains, and by the marvelous providence of God, when the western Empire fell, which was one of the legs of the statue of Daniel, there remained the whole empire in the east, which was the other leg. But since the eastern Empire had to be destroyed by the Turks, as now we see done; again God raised up in the west the former leg, that is, the western Empire, through Charlemagne, which empire endures up to now." [56]

6. POPE NOT ANTICHRIST BECAUSE OF LONG DURATION.— Chapter 8 deals with the duration of Antichrist. On this he cites Irenaeus, Hippolytus, Cyril, Theodoret, Jerome, Augustine, Primasius, Gregory, Bede, Anselm, Haymo, Arethas, Richardus, and Rupertus—all of whom wrote before the recognition of the year-day principle relating to the longer periods. Bellarmine's argument is explicit.

---

[54] *Ibid.*, chaps. 2, 3, pp. 184, 186.   [55] *Ibid.*, chap. 5, p. 188.
[56] *Ibid.*

"The fifth argument is taken from the duration of Antichrist. Antichrist will not reign except for three years and a half. But the Pope has now reigned spiritually in the church more than 1500 years; nor can anyone be pointed out who has been accepted for Antichrist, who has ruled exactly three and one-half years; therefore the Pope is not Antichrist. Then Antichrist has not yet come." [57]

7. CAPITALIZES UPON PROTESTANT DIFFERENCES OVER 666. —Chapter 10 is devoted to an extended discussion of the number 666, whether a name or the number of years, and the variance of Protestant interpreters is emphasized, citing Bullinger, the *Magdeburg Centuries,* and Chytraeus.[58] Chapter 13 concerns the seat of Antichrist, which the Protestants placed in the city of Rome, proving the same from Revelation 17 and 2 Thessalonians 2. This, Bellarmine says, is fallacious, because as long as the pope has his throne in Rome the seat of Antichrist is not Rome but Jerusalem. This is his final statement on the seat of Antichrist:

"The Pope is not antichrist since indeed his throne is not in Jerusalem, nor in the temple of Solomon; surely it is credible that from the year 600, no Roman pontiff has ever been in Jerusalem." [59]

Such are the leading counterarguments and positions of the astute Bellarmine.

VI. Viegas Supports Futuristic Scheme

BLASIUS VIEGAS (1554-1599), Portuguese Jesuit scholar, was born at Evora, and united with the Jesuit Society in 1569. He taught theology for twelve years at Coimbra and Evora, and wrote a scholarly and lengthy commentary on the book of Revelation. Viegas claimed the Jesuits to be the spiritual order anticipated by Joachim, and, like Ribera and Bellarmine, centered everything in a future three and a half years of time. He interpreted "taking away of the daily" (Dan. 8:13; 12:11) as the abrogation of the mass, but thought the 1335 were possibly year-days, extending to the judgment. However, he disapproved of Ribera's exposition of the ten kingdoms and the thousand years,

---

[57] *Ibid.,* chap. 8, p. 190.   [58] *Ibid.,* chap. 10, p. 191.   [59] *Ibid.,* chap. 13, p. 195.

and made Revelation 20 refer to the endless reign of the saints.[60]

As to Babylon, Viegas declared:

"From these words it appears that, by the Babylon of the Apocalypse, Jerome understood Rome. But the name of Babylon is to be applied, not to that Rome which, under the Popes, now professes the name of Christ, but to that Rome which, before she received Christianity, worshipped idols, and to that which will exist in the time of Antichrist, which John, in this and the next chapter, describes as about to fall away from the Pope, and therefore from the faith. I think, therefore, with Tertullian and Jerome, that throughout the Apocalypse, and especially in this chapter and the next, the name of Babylon and the Harlot do describe the city of Rome under that twofold state, and that this passage foretells the future calamity and destruction of the city about the time of Antichrist. . . .

"Now, as the angel here declares to John that the *ten* Kings will hate the Harlot, and will entirely desolate and burn her, it may be gathered plainly that, a little before Antichrist's coming, or at least in the beginning of his reign, the city of Rome will be overthrown and burnt by those ten Kings: for, when Antichrist rules, there will be, not ten Kings, but seven." [61]

In making these concessions to the requirements of prophecy, remarks Maitland, the Jesuits received no check from their superiors. Rome's spokesmen may therefore be considered as acknowledging both past and future identity with Babylon.[62]

VII. Lapide Supports Ribera and Censures Alcazar

CORNELIUS OF LAPIDE (1567-1637), Belgian Jesuit, professor of Biblical exegesis at Louvain and later at Rome, famous for his Bible commentaries,[63] followed Ribera and Viegas in his explanation of the Apocalypse. At the same time he censured Alcazar, the Preterist, for making assertions without proof, and for his employment of allegorical interpretation. Lapide contended that the seals, trumpets, and vials belonged to the future and asserted that the first beast of Revelation 13 was Antichrist, and the second his precursor and assistant.[64] Notwithstanding Alcazar's exposition of the Apocalypse, and despite its own defects and the criticisms of other famous Jesuits, the Lapide com-

[60] *Enciclopedia Universal Ilustrada,* vol. 68, p. 982.
[61] Blasius Viegas, *Commentarii Exegetici in Apocalypsim Ioannis Apostoli* (1599), chap. 17, sec. 3, pp. 798, 799; this translation is taken from Charles Maitland, *op. cit.,* p. 380.
[62] Charles Maitland, *op. cit.,* pp. 380, 381.
[63] *Enciclopedia Universal Ilustrada,* vol. 15, p. 720.
[64] Cornelius Cornelii a Lapide, *Commentarius in Apocalypsin S. Iohannis,* pp. 9, 10.

mentary established itself, because it defended the church and its primate against the Protestant application of the term *Antichrist*. Said Lapide:

" 'Ch. xvii. I say that Babylon, both in this chapter and the following, is Rome; not Christian, as she now is, but unbelieving and Pagan, as she was in St. John's time, and as she will be again in the time of Antichrist. This may be proved; first, because Pagan Rome is that great city which had dominion over the kings of the earth; and in the last verse St. John says that the woman Babylon is that city. She has, moreover, seven hills, as it is said in verse 9, which agrees with no other city than Rome. Secondly, St. John declares that the name of Babylon is not to be taken here literally, but mystically, for he says,—A mystery; Babylon the great.' " [65]

On the great controversy over 2 Thessalonians 2, Lapide declared:

" 'Who opposeth and exalteth himself above all that is called God. The Apostle here explains the name of Antichrist; namely, that he is one who will oppose himself to Christ, and to God, and to all divinity. Ridiculously, therefore, does Wolfgang Musculus [Protestant] say:—Antichrist means Vicar of Christ, which the Pope pretends to be, therefore he is Antichrist. . . .

" 'Moreover, if Antichrist means Vicar of Christ, then Peter and Paul, and all the Apostles, were Antichrists, for they acted as vicars of Christ. "We are ambassadors for Christ, as though God did beseech you by us; we pray you in Christ's stead." Now an ambassador performs his embassy in the stead of a king, and is a king's vicar.' " [66]

VIII. Malvenda—Antichrist Only Appears Before End

THOMAS MALVENDA (1566-1628), Spanish Dominican exegete, Hebrew scholar, and historical critic, was born in Valencia, Spain. Entering the Dominican order in his youth, he was already teaching philosophy and theology at thirty-five. Malvenda's criticism of Baronius' *Annales* led the latter to call him to Rome as a critical adviser, and to aid in annotating the Index Expurgatorius. Malvenda's own *De Antichristo* (Concerning the Antichrist) was published at Rome in 1604.[67] In 1608 he returned to Spain, where he undertook the translation of a new

————
[65] *Ibid.*, chap. 17, verse 6, translated in Charles Maitland, *op. cit.*, p. 384.
[66] Lapide, *Commentaria in II Epist. ad Thessalonicenses*, chap. 2, verse 4, p. 671, translated in Charles Maitland, *op. cit.*, p. 385.
[67] E. Macpherson, "Malvenda," *The Catholic Encyclopedia*, vol. 9, p. 577.

version of the Old Testament in Latin, with comments. It was completed only to Ezekiel when he died.

In this work Malvenda cites the views of Ephraim of Syria, Jerome, Chrysostom, Cyril, Augustine, Theodoret, Prosper, Gregory, Bede, and others, to show that leaders of the early church expected a Jewish Antichrist just before the end of the world; this he considers a most thoroughly established matter, and declares that "Antichrist will not come unless near the end of the age." [68] Thus he rests on the fathers, ignoring the swelling chorus of more recent Catholic witness.

In chapter 32 Malvenda emphasizes that no one can know "the exact and predetermined time when antichrist will come and the world be brought to an end." Two chapter headings reveal Malvenda's strong support of Ribera's futurism—"Antichrist Not To Come Unless Near the End of the Age" (chap. 31), and "Exact Time of the Coming of Antichrist and of the End of the Age to Be Wholly Unknown to Man" (chap. 32).

---

[68] Thomas Malvenda, *De Antichristo* (1647 ed.), vol. 1, book 2, chaps. 31, 32, p. 122.

CHAPTER TWENTY-THREE

Seventeenth Century

Begins With Battle

Protestantism and Catholicism now stand face to face in opposition over the prophecies, each with its weapons of argument drawn. The issues having been clearly enunciated, the battle is begun between the distinctively Protestant and papal interpretations, the two positions being irreconcilable. Stalwarts in the Protestant ranks arose to defend and perfect the Historical School of interpretation, though some compromisers adopted the Catholic countertheories—particularly the Preterist scheme, which will soon be considered.

This chapter will be devoted to the continuation of this conflict, touching on the Jesuit Alcazar, projector of the Preterist counterinterpretation; Brightman, the English Presbyterian who answered Bellarmine's challenges, as well as Pareus the German Calvinist. Notice will then be taken of Grotius of Holland, the first Protestant recruit to Preterism, and Hammond, its first convert in England.

I. Alcazar Projects Conflicting Preterist Interpretation

Not satisfied with Futurism's deflection of Protestant interpretation, and in a further but differing attempt to absolve the Papacy from the stigma of Antichrist, the Jesuit Alcazar was moved to proffer the Preterist theory of counterinterpretation. This scheme contended that the prophecies of Revelation were descriptive of the victory of the early church, as fulfilled in the downfall of the Jewish nation and the overthrow of pagan Rome, and in this way limited their range to the first six centuries of the Christian Era, and making Nero the Antichrist.

1. LIMITED TO EARLY OVERTHROW OF JEWS AND PAGANISM. —LUIS DE ALCAZAR, or Alcasar (1554-1613), Spanish Jesuit of Seville, in order to meet Protestant positions, devoted himself, from 1569 onward, first to the study of philosophy and then to the study of Scripture. Despite his incessant activities his 900-page commentary, *Vestigatio Arcani Sensus in Apocalypsi* (Investigation of the Hidden Sense of the Apocalypse)—the result of forty years' study—was published posthumously, in 1614.[1] In this work dedicated to the Catholic Church, he made a new attempt to interpret the Apocalypse by this Preterist scheme of exposition, that is, by the thesis that the prophecies were fulfilled in the past.

Applying the New Jerusalem to the Catholic Church, Alcazar contended that the Apocalypse describes the twofold war of the church in the early centuries—one with the Jewish synagogue, and the other with paganism—resulting in victory over both adversaries. Revelation 1 to 11 he applied to the rejection of the Jews and the desolation of Jerusalem by the Romans. Revelation 12 to 19 Alcazar allotted to the overthrow of Roman paganism and the conversion of the empire to the church, the judgment of the great Harlot being effected by the downfall of pagan idolatry; Revelation 20 he applied to the final persecution by Antichrist, and the day of judgment; and chapters 21 and 22, referring to the New Jerusalem, he made descriptive of the glorious and endless triumphant state of the Roman church.[2]

2. SUMMARIZING VIEW OF ALCAZAR'S POSITIONS.—In greater detail Alcazar made the seals the early expansion of apostolic Christianity, its vicissitudes, poverty, and persecution; then God's longsuffering, warnings, and punishments allotted to the Jews;[3] the trumpets, the judgments on fallen Judaism;[4] the Two

[1] *Dictionnaire d'histoire et de géographie ecclésiastiques*, vol. 2, cols. 13, 14, art. "Alcazar"; Elliott, *op. cit.*, vol. 4, p. 484.
[2] Luis de Alcazar, *Vestigatio Arcani Sensus in Apocalypsi*, pp. 35-370.
[3] *Ibid.*, pp. 110, 113, 115.   [4] *Ibid.*, pp. 115, 118, 119, 124.

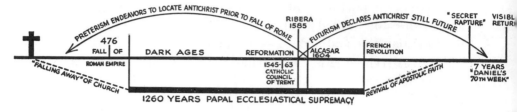

ANTICHRIST SHIFTED EITHER FORWARD OR BACKWARD

Ribera Thrust Antichrist Into the Future, Confined to Three and One-half Literal Years; Alcazar Pushed Antichrist Back Into the Early Centuries—Both of Them Outside the Middle Ages and the Reformation Period, Designated by All Protestants for Antichrist's Reign of 1260 Literal Years

Witnesses, the doctrine and holy lives of the Christians; and after the persecutions Christianity arising with new glory and converting many Jews.[5] Revelation 12 was the apostolic church bringing forth the Roman church; the first beast of Revelation 13 was declared to be the persecuting arrogance of pagan Rome, and the second beast, its carnal wisdom;[6] Revelation 17, the mystical meaning of idolatrous ancient Rome; and Revelation 18, its conversion to the Catholic faith.[7]

Revelation 20 presented the era of the peaceful and public exercise of the Catholic religion, with the thousand years as a mystical number—the fullness of time until the coming of Antichrist—and Revelation 21, the Roman church or New Jerusalem.[8] Thus all except those in the latter part of chapter 20—that is, the events at the end of the millennium—were believed fulfilled in the early ages of Christianity, or by the fifth and sixth centuries. The forty-two months, or 1260 days, of the Witnesses' preaching in sackcloth Alcazar applied to the early Jewish persecution of the Christians, paralleling the former persecution of the Jews by Antiochus for three and one-half years. In this explanation Alcazar omitted any specific application of the three and one-half days' interval of the Witnesses' death;[9] and he interpreted similar time periods rather vaguely.[10]

---

[5] *Ibid.*, p. 124.
[7] *Ibid.*, pp. 143, 148.
[9] *Ibid.*, pp. 123, 124, 572, 573.

[6] *Ibid.*, pp. 126, 130.
[8] *Ibid.*, pp. 155, 156, 880, 881.
[10] *Ibid.*, pp. 572, 573, 598, 643, 689.

Alcazar was the first to apply Preterism to the Apocalypse with anything like completeness, though it had previously been applied somewhat to Daniel. It thus pioneered the way for acceptance first by Hugo Grotius of the Netherlands, and later by the German Rationalists, as will be noted.

3. CONFLICT BETWEEN OPPOSING INTERPRETATIONS.— Though the Jesuits had laid much stress on minor differences among Protestant expositors as evidence of the unsoundness of their positions, yet these same Jesuits differed and warred even more violently among themselves.

Alcazar was fully aware that he contradicted certain of the fathers, differed from the Futurists Ribera and Viegas, and was in conflict with Malvenda. While approving of the concept of the spiritual resurrection held by Augustine, he contended against his view of the binding of Satan, as well as that of Ribera and of Viegas.[11] And he strongly disagreed with Malvenda on the interpretation of the Babylon of Revelation 17 as all the multitude of the wicked, declaring it to be pagan Rome; he also disagreed with Ribera and Viegas over the admission that Babylon might be Rome in the last days, becoming heathen again, and persecuting Christians.[12] Alcazar made the church's millennium of rest to date from the downfall of old pagan Rome—his apocalyptical Babylon—with the destruction of Roman idolatry in the spiritual fires of the Catholic religion.[13] Such, in brief, was Alcazar's Preterism.

II. Compromising Protestants Adopt Preteristic Scheme

This battle of the Protestants with Rome on the prophecies was not, however, without some advantages. It forced an intensified study of the prophecies by the later Reformers, in defense of their positions. Two results followed. With some, it strengthened the true prophetic positions of the past, revealing certain inconsistencies and correcting mistakes. The clearest of all expositions were brought forth thereafter. But with others there

---

[11] *Ibid.*, pp. 877, 879, 882.   [12] *Ibid.*, pp. 801, 802.   [13] *Ibid.*, pp. 881, 143.

was bewilderment, capitulation, and acceptance of the Roman Catholic counterinterpretations and positions. Despite many protests Alcazar's Preterist scheme gained a strong foothold among certain Protestants, especially among rationalistic scholars. The Preterist view was soon adopted and taught, with various modifications, by the Protestant Hugo Grotius of Holland in his *Annotationes* (1644), and by Hammond of England in his commentary (1653), whom Le Clerc, his Latin interpreter, followed. Then came the noted Catholic bishop of Meaux, Bossuet, the great antagonist of Protestantism, who capitalized on minor Protestant divisions.

BRIEF PREVIEW OF LATER DEVELOPMENTS ESSENTIAL.—Only in the light of future developments can the real significance of these first counterinterpretations of Rome be sensed and appraised. We therefore again digress briefly to sketch the leading later developments, so that the spreading conflicts, and ultimately the virtual overthrow of the historic Protestant positions, may be watched in the making. The fuller story will unfold in later chapters, in historical sequence.

First, as to Preterism's penetrations into Protestantism, we may note that in 1791 J. G. Eichhorn (1752-1827), the noted German rationalist, revived and republished Alcazar's Preterist interpretation. Soon he was joined by other rationalist scholars, such as G. H. A. Ewald (1803-1875), G. C. F. Lücke (1791-1855), W. M. L. De Wette (1780-1849), Franz Delitzsch (1813-1890), and Julius Wellhausen (1844-1918). And since 1830 numerous British and American scholars have followed Eichhorn. In 1830 Prof. Samuel Lee of Cambridge, likewise injected Bossuet's Preterist interpretation into the discussion. Prof. Moses Stuart, of Andover (1780-1852), introduced Preterism into the United States about 1842, and Dr. Samuel Davidson reiterated it in England in 1844. These, and many others, all contended with the Papacy that nothing beyond the destruction of pagan Rome and Judaism was intended by the prophecies concerning Antichrist in the Apocalypse.[14]

---

[14] See Volume III of *Prophetic Faith*.

As to Futurism, for some three centuries this view was virtually confined to Romanists, and was refuted by several masterly Protestant works. But early in the nineteenth century it sprang forth afresh, this time among Protestants—Samuel R. Maitland, William Burgh, J. H. Todd, and more recently it has been adopted by most Fundamentalists. In 1826 Maitland revived Ribera's Futurist interpretation in England. The Plymouth Brethren, organized in 1830 by John Nelson Darby, at Dublin and Plymouth, also laid hold of Maitland's interpretation. And when the High-Church Oxford Movement (1833-1845) gained ascendancy in Britain, it rejected the Protestant Historical School of interpretation and generally adopted Futurism, though some among them swung to Preterism. Bursting into full flame in 1833, it seized upon Maitland's interpretation as an argument in favor of reunion with Rome.[15] German rationalism, on the other hand, increasingly flouted prophecy and prediction. Thus the Jesuit schemes of counterinterpretation were more successful than their authors had ever dared anticipate.

The tragedy of modern Protestantism thus playing into the hands of Romanism is expressed by Tanner:

"It is a matter for deep regret that those who hold and advocate the Futurist system at the present day, Protestants as they are for the most part, are thus really playing into the hands of Rome, and helping to screen the Papacy from detection as the Antichrist. It has been well said that 'Futurism tends to obliterate the brand put by the Holy Spirit upon Popery.' More especially is this to be deplored at a time when the Papal Antichrist seems to be making an expiring effort to regain his former hold on men's minds." [16]

We may rightly conclude that, in the slight division which existed among the Reformation groups regarding the application of the Little Horn of Daniel 7—though all were agreed that the Papacy was Antichrist—lay the foundation of that later hesitancy, confusion, and retrenchment concerning Antichrist and the year-day principle that followed the impact of the Counter

---

[15] The introduction of Futurism among English prophetic writers is more fully discussed in Volume III of *Prophetic Faith*, chapters 28 and 34.

[16] Tanner, *op. cit.*, p. 17.

Reformation systems of interpretation, which were devised to divide, confuse, and defeat the Reformation. Had there been a clear and united concept and conviction on this point, the whole story of the aftermath of the Reformation might have been different. But through this division the Protestants were out-maneuvered and divided, their power curtailed, and their witness enfeebled and broken. This will again come up for discussion in Volumes III and IV of this work.

III. Brightman Confutes Futurism and Stresses Year-Day

THOMAS BRIGHTMAN (1562-1607), Puritan scholar, and one of the fathers of English Presbyterianism, was born in Nottingham. Educated at Cambridge, from which he received his B.A., M.A., and B.D. degrees, he became rector of Hawnes in 1592. A constant student, he always carried his Greek Testament with him, which he read through every two weeks—even perusing it while riding, so as to lose no time. His disaffection with the established church became increasingly apparent, and he became one of the founders of the Presbyterian Church in England.[17]

1. BATTLES POSITIONS OF BELLARMINE AND RIBERA.—Deeply stirred by Bellarmine's promulgation of the Futurist theory of interpretation, Brightman wrote *Apocalypsis Apocalypseos* (Revelation of the Revelation), dedicated to the Reformed churches of Brittany, Germany, and France, which up to 1644 had run through four editions, with later reprints.[18] This commentary was popular with the Protestant churches of the time because of its vigor of thought and language and its able answer to Cardinal Bellarmine. It sought to set a "clear torch-light" before them. A sixteen-chapter section entitled "The Confuting That Counterfeit Antichrist: Whom Bellarmine describeth, and

---

[17] *Dictionary of National Biography*, vol. 2, p. 1247.
[18] *Apocalypsis Apocalypseos . . . et Refutatio Rob. Bellarmini de Antichristo Libro Tertio de Romano Pontifice* (A Revelation of the Revelation . . . and Refutation of Robert Bellarmine Concerning Antichrist in Book Three Concerning the Roman Pontiff). Originally written about 1600, before Queen Elizabeth's death, it was first printed at Frankfurt (1609), then Heidelberg (1612), with English editions at Amsterdam (1615) and Leyden (1616). It was issued in his collected *Workes* at London (1644).

laboureth to prove by arguments with all his might" [19] was incorporated into his commentary, following Revelation 17, in which Brightman reviewed thoroughly and effectively the objections urged by Bellarmine. The avowed object of this refutation was likewise to prove that the pope is that Antichrist whose reign is limited to 1260 years, and is foredoomed by God to utter destruction.

When Brightman saw, for the first time, a copy of the Jesuit Ribera's original Futurist exposition, he was aroused to indignation. Of it he says:

"For when as I had by chance light upon *Ribera,* who had made a Commentary upon this same holy Revelation; *Is it even so* (said I) *doe the Papists take heart again, so as that book which of a long time* before they would scarce suffer any man to touch, they dare now take in hand to *intreat fully upon it?* What? was it but a vain image or bug, at the sight whereof they were wont to tremble a few years since, even in the dim light, that now they dare be bold to look wishly upon this glasse in this clear sun-shine, and dare proclaime to the world, that any other thing rather is poynted at in it than their Pope of *Rome?* O we sluggish and lazy creatures, if we suffer that! I thought it fit therefore that the croking of these fellowes should be somewhat repressed, thinking it worth my labour to make the Iesuites see, how wickedly they rage, how foolishly they trifle, how they understand nothing of the mysteries, how it cannot be possible that they should have any wit or reach at all in this matter." [20]

Brightman takes Ribera to task for his clever effort to shift the pope out of the field of prophecy.

"Indeed *Francis of Ribera* the Iesuit, thrust his whole Prophecy almost into these straits, wisely indeed to save his Popes head, but as touching the truth, exceedingly perversly. For why, were men that lived by the space of these 1500. yeeres which are now past, since the writing of the Apocalypse, altogether devoyd of this felicity." [21]

Brightman's other discussion of prophecy—*A Most Comfortable Exposition of . . . the Prophecie of Daniel* (from 11:36 through 12)—was included in his *Scholia,* and was issued at Basel (1614), Leyden (1616), and again in London in 1644.[22] Its

---

[19] Inserted with the running title "Against Bellarmine," between chapters 17 and 18 of *A Revelation of the Apocalyps,* in his *Workes* (1644 ed.), pp. 612-746.
[20] Brightman, *A Revelation of the Apocalyps,* Preface, in *Workes,* sig. B₁r.
[21] *Ibid.,* chap. 1, p. 8.
[22] Brightman, *A Most Comfortable Exposition of the Last and Most Difficult Part of the Prophecie of Daniel,* in *Workes,* pp. 891-970; see pp. 891, 894.

avowed purpose was to prove the conversion and restoration of the Jews after the destruction of their last three enemies—the Roman Empire, the Saracens (king of the south), and the Turks (king of the north).

2. SEVEN CHURCHES: SEVEN PERIODS, WITH THYATIRA AS ROME.—In his commentary on Revelation, Brightman interprets the seven churches as so many periods, applying the Thyatira church to the Roman Jezebel, Sardis to the Reformed churches of Switzerland, France, Holland, et cetera, and Laodicea to the Church of England [23]—with which he is not in sympathy.

3. FIFTH TRUMPET—150-YEAR PERIOD OF SARACENIC WOE. —Brightman places the fulfillment of the seven seals all prior to Constantine, the silence in heaven being the peace procured by Constantine.[24] But the early trumpets he expounds as the great heresies which befell the church, and the barbarian woes on the Western Roman Empire, the fourth being the Vandals. The fifth trumpet, darkening a third part of the sun (the church in Africa), he assigns to religious persons in the West and to the Saracens in the East, and the sixth trumpet to the Turks [25]— which oppressed by their tyranny not only the false church but also the true church—the latter, Brightman significantly adds, "began to come forth abroad at the year 1300." [26]

Brightman's prophetic time periods are all determined on the year-day principle. The five months, or 150 days of the locust woe, he allots to the Saracen ravages of Syria, Mesopotamia, Armenia, and Persia, beginning about A.D. 630, to their overthrow by the Emperor Leo Copronymus, about 780—a view later adopted by Daubuz.

"We define this first over-running of the *earth* by the *Saracens* in an *hundred and fifty yeers*, not because at the end of these yeeres they were straightwayes cast out of those Countries, which they had conquered, but because they had ill success afterwards in their battels against the *Romans*,

[23] Brightman, *A Revelation of the Apocalyps*, chaps. 2, 3 in *Workes*, pp. 75 ff., 91 ff., 125.
[24] *Ibid*., sig. B₁v.
[25] *Ibid*.
[26] *Ibid*., chap. 20, p. 816.

being often conquered, put to flight and slain, hardly *holding* that which they had gotten, much less getting any more." [27]

4. SIXTH TRUMPET: TURKISH WOE FROM A.D. 1300.—The "hour, day, month, and year" of the Euphratian woe, Brightman regards as a period of 396 years (365 + 30 + 1), measuring the duration of the Turkish power, dated by their revival under Othman, about A.D. 1300—and thus leading to about 1696. [28]

5. 1260 YEARS OF WITNESSES FROM CONSTANTINE.—Brightman expounds Revelation 10 as the revival of study of the Bible and the prophecies in the West at the time of the rise of the Turks under the period of the sixth trumpet—perhaps a reference to the Waldenses. He makes the 1260 year-days of the Witnesses date from the time of Constantine until about 1558—the warring against the true church and the Scriptures beginning afresh at the Council of Trent. In Revelation 12 the church was persecuted by the dragon (the barbarians). Constantine the Great, the man child, superseding the heathen emperors, threw the dragon down from heaven, and the pure church fled into the wilderness. [29]

6. BOTH BEASTS OF REVELATION 13 ARE PAPAL.—The casting down of Pagan Rome in Revelation 12 is followed by its restoration in new form in Revelation 13. In Revelation 13 Brightman makes both of the two beasts the popes and their empire, only at successive times—the first beginning with Constantine, wounded by the Goths but healed by Justinian and Phocas; the second from Pepin onward. It should also be noted that Brightman was about the first to mention Justinian's decree as a determining epoch in papal greatness. [30] He says further:

"This beast hath a double place, whence he ariseth, one out *of the Sea,* and another *out of the earth;* he hath a double power, also, *Civill* and *spirituall. . . .* Which double tyrannie is most clearly to be seen in the *Pope of Rome alone;* so that we cannot doubt, but that he is both the *beasts.*" [31]

[27] *Ibid.,* chap. 9, p. 300.

[28] *Ibid.,* p. 324. Brightman takes the 365 days of the natural year, instead of the 360 days of the "prophetic year," which would have given a total of 391 years (360 + 30 + 1), which was followed by certain others.

[29] *Ibid.,* sig. B₂v.

[30] *Ibid.,* sig. B₂r; chap. 13, p. 433.

[31] *Ibid.,* p. 420; see also chap. 17, pp. 605, 609.

7. SEVEN VIALS ARE JUDGMENTS UPON PAPACY.—The seven vials of chapter 16 are the judgments, or retributions, upon the Papacy, begun by the Reformation.[32] And the Jews are the kings of the East after they embrace the faith of the gospel, against whom the Turk will war. Under the seventh seal the Turkish as well as the popish powers will be destroyed.[33]

8. SEVEN-HILLED ROME SEAT OF ANTICHRIST.—Brightman then refers to Revelation 17, which "maketh mention but of one of them only; comprehending both under one." [34] As to the city and seat of Antichrist, he declares emphatically:

"*Rome* is the City where the heads of *Antichrist* remain fixed, therefore *Rome* is the seat of *Antichrist*. You can never escape the dint of this Argument (O ye Papists!) while you live. It must needs be as fixed, strong, and durable, as the Mountains themselves of your Rome. . . .

"*The seat of the seven Kings is the seat of Antichrist, Rome the City with seven Hils, is the seat of the seven Kings: For the heads are both the Mountains, and the Kings; Therefore Rome is the seat of Antichrist.*" [35]

The seven heads Brightman expounds as "seven forms of government"—kings, consuls, dictators, decemvirs, tribunes —with emperors as the sixth form, and the popes as the seventh. Thus, "the seventh King must govern in the same place, where the seven Hils are." [36]

9. PAPAL PERIOD 1260 YEARS: NEITHER 3½ NOR 3,500.— Proving the pope to be Antichrist, and challenging Bellarmine's suggestion of three and a half times possibly totaling 3,500 years, Brightman says:

"I will whisper as low as I can, and will tell you in your eare, that the *time of dayes* is not one day, but three hundred and threescore dayes, *times* twice so much; namely, seven hundred and twenty; *half a time,* an hundred and fourescore: So likewise *the time of yeers is three hundred and three-score yeers; times, seven hundred and twenty, half a time an hundred and four-score. So the time of moneths* is twelve moneths, *times* four and twenty, *half a time* six; I pray you think of these things when you are awake, and in the mean time sleep sweetly and soundly all those three thousand

[32] *Ibid.,* sig. B₃r, v.
[33] *Ibid.,* sig. B₈v. In his *Exposition . . . of Daniel,* Brightman defines the king of the north thus: "It is not then to be doubted, but that the King of the North is the Empire of the Turkes." (*Workes,* p. 921).
[34] Brightman, *A Revelation of the Apocalyps,* chap. 13, in *Workes,* p. 446.
[35] *Ibid.,* chap. 17, p. 586.
[36] *Ibid.,* pp. 586-589.

five hundred yeers, which you have inforced your adversaries to make by your calculation." [37]

Pressing hard on the year-day principle, from Numbers 14:34 and Ezekiel 4:6, Brightman gives the pope, as Antichrist, not three and a half years, but 1260 years.[38] And as evidence that Rome is mystical Babylon, Brightman cites many early writers, such as Jerome and Augustine.[39]

10. ANTICHRIST APPEARED UPON ROME'S BREAKUP.—Summoning the earlier witnesses, and ringing the changes on the general historical understanding of Antichrist's appearing upon the breakup of the Roman Empire, Brightman makes a convincing argument for papal Rome as succeeding pagan Rome, and thus fulfilling 2 Thessalonians 2. Then he adduces the historical testimony of later centuries as contemporary witnesses testifying to Antichrist's historical appearance in fulfillment of the prophecies.[40] In Daniel 7, Brightman asserts, the Little Horn sprang up together with the ten horns, or kingdoms, into which Rome was divided.[41]

11. HOLDS MODIFIED AUGUSTINIAN VIEW OF MILLENNIUM.— On the millennium, however, Brightman still clings to a modified, or Protestant, version of Augustinianism, beginning the thousand years with Constantine, in the fourth century, and running on to Wyclif, in the fourteenth, who, with his contemporary preachers against Antichrist, Brightman says, constituted the first angel of Revelation 14, preaching the gospel again. The second angel threatening the fall of Rome represented those ministers who followed Wyclif, chief among them, John Huss and Jerome of Prague, whereas the third angel was Luther.[42]

Brightman's view of the resurrections is also singular. He clings to the spiritual resurrection idea of Augustine, the first being in the fourth century after Constantine's triumph, as "many from al places in the west, with all theire indeavour seek-

[37] Brightman, "The Confuting That Counterfeit Antichrist," chap. 8, in *A Revelation of the Apocalyps,* in *Workes,* p. 686.
[38] *Ibid.,* p. 687.   [39] *Ibid.,* chap. 1, pp. 612 ff.
[40] *Ibid.,* chap. 2, p. 636.   [41] *Ibid.,* p. 626.
[42] Brightman, *A Revelation of the Apocalyps,* sig. B₂r, pp. 475-480.

inge to attayne to the sincere Religion." Then, "the second
resurrection is brought to passe by the second and full callinge
of the Jewes." But in Revelation 21 and 22 Brightman is back
on sound ground, for he teaches that this refers to the happiness
of the church in the earth renewed, with the New Jerusalem
descending out of heaven.[43]

IV. Pareus Exposes Futurism and Establishes Historical System

DAVID PAREUS (1548-1622), Calvinist professor at Heidelberg, was born in Silesia and educated at Hirschberg and Heidelberg. He entered the ministry in 1571, taking up pastoral duties
in the diocese of Worms, but lost his post because he was a Calvinist. In 1584 he was made professor of Old Testament at Heidelberg, and became one of the great lights of the university. His
fame spread far and wide, drawing students even from Hungary
and Poland. In 1587 he issued a German Bible with notes, the
so-called Neustadter Bibel, and held disputations over the Augsburg Confession. He received a D.D. degree in 1593, and in
1602 was made professor of New Testament, still at Heidelberg,
which position he held for twenty years, or until his death.[44]

Between 1604 and 1617 Pareus issued several treatises
against Bellarmine, summoning all Protestants to meet the
Jesuit danger. At the first centenary anniversary, or Evangelical
Jubilee, of the Reformation, in 1617, he set forth the proposition
that everyone, in order to be saved, must flee the Roman Papacy.
This drew upon him the resentment of the Jesuits.

In thirty theses he demonstrated that the Papacy bore all
the marks of Antichrist that Daniel, Christ, Paul, and John had
given. He published the results of his thirty years' study and lectures at the university in a Latin work, *In Divinam Apocalypsin
... Commentarius*. This commentary followed soon after that of
Brightman, and was first published in 1618, with reprints in
1622 and 1642. An English translation by Elias Arnold, *A Commentary Upon the Divine Revelation,* appeared in 1644.

---

[43] *Ibid.*, sig. B₂v.
[44] Julius Ney, "Pareus," *The New Schaff-Herzog*, vol. 8, p. 353.

Pareus excoriates the contradictory positions and subterfuges of the Futurists Ribera and Bellarmine, as well as the Preterist Alcazar.[45] "What thinkest thou," he demands of the pope, "dost not thou at least think that in some part it [the Revelation] belongs to thee? . . . Hath not Paul sufficiently noted that thou art he that sitteth in the temple of God as god? . . . the whorish woman sitting upon the mountains: nor oughtest thou not to suspect all these things?"[46] Then Pareus calls upon all kings to make Rome desolate, according to prophecy, and not to be Antichrist's vassals.

Pareus paints a comprehensive picture of the baleful teachings of both Futurism and Preterism. He asserts that only a madman could assign the task outlined in Daniel to the feigned Antichrist to be accomplished during the Futurist's three and a half years; namely, be acknowledged by all Jews as the Messiah, sit in the Hebrew temple, kill three kings and subdue seven others, repair the ruins of Rome burned by those ten kings, chase out the pope from thence, sit there as monarch, blot out the Christian religion, and subdue the whole world.[47] The logic of his strictures was impressive.

1. VIEWS ON SEALS, TRUMPETS, AND ANTICHRIST.—Pareus regards the seals as covering the whole Christian dispensation— the first four signifying by the four horsemen the successive periods of the apostles, of pagan persecutions, of heresies, of the rise of Antichrist;[48] the sixth, the judgment and wrath of the Lamb. The trumpets cover the same time as the seals, the fifth and sixth referring to the conquests of Mohammedanism, and the seventh to the consummation. The five months of the locusts are based upon the common length of the ravages of the locusts. Pareus refers to the Western and Eastern Antichrists—the Papacy and Mohammedanism. The 1260 years he extends from 606 to 1866—beginning with Phocas' recognition of the Roman

---

[45] David Pareus, *A Commentary Upon the Divine Revelation* (1644 translation), Preface, p. 2; also pp. 304, 346, 347.
[46] *Ibid.*, Preface.
[47] Pareus, *In Divinam Apocalypsin . . . Commentarius*, col. 460.
[48] *Ibid.*, chap. 6, cols. 239, 240, 249.

pope, and ending in 1866, though for the elect's sake the Lord will shorten it.[49]

2. HOLDS THE BEAST TO BE ANTICHRIST.—The first beast of Revelation 13 is the papal Antichrist, surviving the ten kings of Rome's division, and is to be destroyed by Christ's second advent. Pareus applies this first beast to the Papacy's imperial power, and the second beast to the spiritual power of pope and priesthood. He applies the number of the beast to *Lateinos,* and to the word *Romanus* in Hebrew letters.[50] The first angel of Revelation 14 he assumes to be Wyclif and others, like Huss and Jerome; the second, Luther and the other Reformers; the third, all the evangelical preachers since Luther.[51] The seven vials are the judgments on the Catholic Church.

The beast of Revelation 17 is Antichrist clothed with the skin of the Roman Empire. Like Napier and Brightman, Pareus makes the seven mountains seven forms of Roman government: kings, consuls, dictators, decemvirs, tribunes, pagan emperors, and Christian emperors, and the eighth the popes. The ten horns include Hungary, Spain, France, England, Denmark, Russia, Croatia, Dalmatia, Aragon, Sardinia, Portugal, Bohemia, Sweden, and Norway—not actually ten, but all the kingdoms of the Christian world.[52]

3. CONFUSED ON THE MILLENNIAL PERIOD.—On Revelation 20 Pareus admitted confusion, frankly confessing, "The more I think upon it, the less I find how to untie the knot that troubled so many." [53] He attempted to explain it nearly on the Augustinian principle—Satan bound and having no power over the nations after the destruction of Jerusalem, the rejection of the Jews, and the acceptance of the Gentiles, with the loosing, at the time, of Gregory VII, about 1073.[54]

Antichrist and the enemies of Christ are not destroyed till

---

[49] *Ibid.,* chaps. 6-9; see also Elliott, *op. cit.,* vol. 4, pp. 474-479.
[50] Pareus, *A Commentary Upon the Divine Revelation* (1644), pp. 305, 306, 317, 318.
[51] *Ibid.,* pp. 338, 343, 350.
[52] Pareus, *In Divinam Apocalypsin,* cols. 905, 906, 916.
[53] *Ibid.,* col. 1075.
[54] *Ibid.,* col. 1079.

the advent. Such is the interpretation given by Pareus at the close of the era and century of the Reformation.

V. Grotius—First Protestant to Adopt Alcazar's Preterism

HUGO GROTIUS, or van Groot (1583-1645), Dutch jurist, statesman, historian, and theologian, was born at Delft, and attended the University of Leyden. He accompanied Johann Oldenbarneveldt to France, to the court of Henry IV. In 1603 he was appointed to be states-historiographer and later advocate-general of the fisc for the provinces of Holland and Zeeland. Grotius maintained that the ocean is free to all nations, the famous doctrine of *mare liberum*.

In 1613, at the age of thirty, he was made pensioner of the city of Rotterdam. Being one of the leaders of the Remonstrant party, or Arminians, he was condemned to life imprisonment in 1618. But after a few years, escaping from prison in a book chest, he went to Paris, where he was gladly received by the king, and where he wrote (1625) his famous *De jure belli et pacis* (Concerning the Law of War and Peace), which made him the Father of International Law.[55] During that period he also wrote his *De veritate religionis Christianae* (On the Truth of the Christian Religion), which was translated into many languages, including Arabic and Urdu. In his *Annotations to the New Testament* he applied the historical-philological method. He had nothing to do with dogmatism, and tried to bridge over the differences between the warring factions. In 1631 he entered the Swedish service, under Gustavus Adolphus and became Swedish ambassador to the French court.[56]

Extremely liberal in his religious views, he was a friend of the Jesuit Petavius. Grotius held the Reformation to be an unwarranted schism, and moved as closely as possible to Rome. His avowed aim was to bring peace out of the horrible conflict between the Catholics and Protestants which was devastating

---

[55] Buchberger, *Lexikon;* H. C. Rogge, "Grotius," *The New Schaff-Herzog*, vol. 5, pp. 85, 86.

[56] Hyma, *op. cit.*, pp. 189, 190.

Europe (it was the time of the Thirty Years' War), and he used his diplomacy to that end while serving as Swedish ambassador to Paris. His anonymous anti-Protestant *Commentatio ad Loca Quaedam N[ovi] Testamenti Quae de Antichristo Agunt* (1640) (Commentary on Certain Texts Which Deal With Antichrist) sought to remove the great prophetic stumbling block to re-union. To this end he followed the Jesuit Alcazar's Preterist interpretation. In fact, he believed the Jesuits so fully that he believed the pope was not mentioned in any of the prophecies.[57] For example, he applied the three and a half years to Domitian, and the number 666 to Trajan.

When Grotius' authorship of the book was detected, it turned all orthodox theologians against him. His misinterpretations so stirred Cocceius, of Bremen, that he wrote a commentary on all the prophecies relating to Antichrist, the excellence of which won him a theological professorship in 1643. Maresius (Desmarets), a Belgian theologian, in his review of Grotius' *Commentatio,* declared that not only did the united Belgic Church believe the pope to be Antichrist but all the Reformed in all the world as well.[58] Grotius labored in favor of the union of all Christian bodies. In his mediatory work he drew nearer and nearer to the Catholic Church, so that finally he came to the point where he counseled all Protestants to return to the Catholic faith.

This fatal change on the part of Grotius, in 1640, marked a fork in the Protestant road, as others, following the lead of Grotius, began to take the divergent path veering away from the Protestant highway of sound interpretation. His lead unquestionably had greater influence upon Protestants than did the works of the Jesuit Preterists who originated the system. Here follow the Preterist expositions of Grotius.

1. APOCALYPSE RESTRICTED TO JEWS AND ROMANS.—He holds that Revelation 1 to 11 constitutes a history of the Jews

---

[57] Hugo Grotius, *Commentatio,* pp. 38, 46. Published anonymously; author identified in the British Museum Catalogue.
[58] Samuel Maresius, *Dissertatio de Antichristo,* p. 4.

and their overthrow in the early centuries, and that chapters 12 to 20 are limited to the Christian victory over pagan Rome, with the destruction of idolatry.[59]

2. SEALS AND TRUMPETS: JEWISH-ROMAN CONFLICTS.— The seals Grotius applies to the period from Christ to the Jewish-Roman wars,[60] and the trumpets to the events leading up to the historic fall of Jerusalem.[61]

3. FORTY-TWO MONTHS LIMITED TO TEMPLE OF JUPITER.— The forty-two months of Revelation 11 are assigned from the time of the building of the pagan temple of Jupiter in Jerusalem until the revolt of Barcochba, whom he designates as the beast from the bottomless pit.[62]

4. BEAST: ROME WITH PERSECUTIONS UNDER DOMITIAN.— Grotius holds the first beast of Revelation 13 to be Roman paganism, the deadly wound the destruction of Rome, the three and a half times as three and a half years of persecution under Domitian, and the two-horned beast from the earth the cult of magic. The number 666 he applies to Trajan (53-117), based upon his first name (Ulpius). In Revelation 17 the beast's seven heads are Roman emperors, and the ten horns, or kings, who rule with the beast one hour are the Ostrogoths, Visigoths, Vandals, Gepidae, Lombards, Heruli, Burgundians, Huns, Franks, Anglo-Saxons.[63] The seven last plagues were the tribulations that came upon the Roman Empire.[64]

5. WOMAN OF BABYLON: PAGAN ROME.—Revelation 17, the seven hills, the woman, and Babylon are all made to refer to pagan Rome.[65]

6. 1,000 YEARS: FROM CONSTANTINE TO TURKS.—Grotius begins the thousand years of Revelation 20 with Constantine's edict of 311, and ends it with the rise of the Turkish Empire, a thousand years later, in 1311—and makes the Holy City repre-

---

[59] Grotius, *Annotationes in Novum Testamentum* (Annotations on the New Testament), p. 1197.   [60] *Ibid.*, pp. 1164-1169, 1175.   [61] *Ibid.*, pp. 1175-1183, 1195.
[62] *Ibid.*, pp. 1190, 1192.
[63] Grotius, *Commentatio*, pp. 33-47; *Annotationes*, pp. 1205-1211, 1215, 1223.
[64] Grotius, *Annotationes*, pp. 1234-1238.
[65] *Ibid.*, pp. 1252, 1261; *Commentatio*, pp. 49-56.

COMMENTATIO	A
ad Loca quædam	PARAPHRASE,
N. TESTAMENTI	AND
quæ	ANNOTATIONS
DE ANTICHRISTO	Upon all the Books of the
agunt, aut agere putantur,	New Teſtament:
EXPENDENDA ERVDITIS.	Briefly explaining all the difficult places thereof.

COMMENTATIO
ad Loca quædam
N. TESTAMENTI
quæ
DE ANTICHRISTO
agunt, aut agere putantur,
EXPENDENDA ERVDITIS.

KÖNIGLICHE
BIBLIOTHEK
BERLIN

AMSTELODAMI,
Apud IOH. & CORNELIVM BLAEV,
cIↃ IↃ c XL.

A
PARAPHRASE,
AND
ANNOTATIONS
Upon all the Books of the
New Teſtament:
Briefly explaining all the difficult places thereof.

By H. HAMMOND, D.D.

LONDON.
Printed by J. Fleſher for Richard Royſton at the Angel in Ivie-lane.
M DC L III.

FIRST PROTESTANT WORKS TO ADOPT PRETERIST COUNTERINTERPRETATION

Grotius of Holland (Left) and Hammond of England (Right) Introduce Alcazar's Counterview Among Protestants, Confining Prophecy of Revelation to the Overthrow of Judaism and Pagan Rome in the Early Centuries

sent Constantinople, taken by the Turks in 1453.[66] Such was the curious Preterist interpretation of the first Protestant who went over to the camp of the Jesuit Alcazar.

VI. Hammond—First English Proponent of Preterism

HENRY HAMMOND (1605-1660), called the "Father of English Biblical Criticism," was born in Chertsey and educated at Eton and Magdalen College, Oxford. Ordained in 1629, he was given a living at Penshurst, Kent, and was a frequent preacher at Paul's Cross. In 1643 he was made archdeacon of Chichester and member of the Westminster Assembly, but never

---

[66] Grotius, *Annotationes*, pp. 1268, 1270, 1271.

524

sat with them. And in 1645 he was made canon of Christ Church and was one of the royal chaplains.

Hammond was author of fifty-eight works,[67] his *Paraphrase and Annotations* (1653) being the best known. In this he followed Grotius closely in his Preterist views, though without naming him. Le Clerc, who translated Hammond's *Paraphrase* into Latin in 1698, indicated that the name was omitted that it might have a more ready hearing. He was apparently the first English cleric to abandon the Protestant Historical School for the Jesuit counterview. Employing the Preterist key in explaining the Apocalypse, he stressed the expression, "Things which must shortly come to pass."

A brief fivefold summary will suffice to cover Hammond's main positions. (1) The first beast of Revelation is, by him, restricted to pagan Rome, the seven heads to seven Roman emperors—and the ten horns are ten kings as well.[68] (2) The two-horned beast, of the same chapter, is applied to the heathen priests, and the persecution as resulting from the edicts against the early Christians.[69] (3) Revelation 17 is likewise limited to the vile iniquities and cruel persecutions of imperial Rome, and by the seven heads, or kings, are specified Claudius, Nero, Galba, Otho, Vitellius, Vespasian (then reigning), and Titus (then yet to come).[70] (4) Revelation 18, similarly considered, is a portrayal of the desolation of heathen Rome by the barbarians, under Alaric and others.[71] (5) Revelation 20 is expounded by Hammond as portraying the thousand years of tranquillity and freedom from persecution, after the conversion of Constantine, with the resurrection as the flourishing condition of the church under the Messias. The loosing of Satan is set forth as the time of the Mohammedan incursions, Mohammedanism being also called Gog and Magog, and the compassing of the city is the siege of Constantinople, in 1453.[72] Such are the astonishing declarations of Hammond, the first English Protestant Preterist.

---

[67] *Dictionary of National Biography*, vol. 8, pp. 1126-1130.
[68] H. Hammond, *A Paraphrase, and Annotations Upon All the Books of the New Testament*, p. 967.
[69] *Ibid.*, pp. 967, 968.
[70] *Ibid.*, pp. 984, 985.
[71] *Ibid.*, p. 990.
[72] *Ibid.*, p. 996.

VII. Counter Reformation Regains Lost Ground for Church

By the middle of the sixteenth century the Protestant Reformation had taken firm root in all countries north of the Alps, with the exception of France and the Netherlands. Thus Europe, for the most part, seemed lost to the Holy See.[73] But the Catholic Counter Reformation began, with a program of reform in the Roman church, along with the formation of new religious orders. The church set about recovering the lands from which it had been driven. Its two chief instruments were the Jesuits and the Inquisition, and a third was the Council of Trent.[74]

1. PROTESTANTISM DIVIDED INTO OPPOSING GROUPS.—The dissensions among the Reformers, between 1555 and 1580, led to the crystallization of three groups—Protestants, Reformed, and anti-Trinitarians; or Lutherans, Calvinists, and Socinians.[75] So, while the forces of the Catholic Revival, or Counter Reformation, were gathering strength, Protestantism was losing vitality through its internal dissensions. The primary principle of Protestantism is the right of every Christian not only to have direct access to the Scriptures, but to interpret them for himself. This inevitably invited variance. The extravagances of radicals led the leaders to fall back on the right of sovereigns to direct the religion of their own territories.

The theologians did their part by producing authoritative statements of belief, as the Confession of Augsburg, in behalf of the Lutherans at the Diet of Augsburg in 1530, the *Fidei Ratio* of Zwingli, and the *Confessio Tetrapolitana* of the mediating cities. Meant at first as apologies, these documents became symbolical formularies. Each state decided upon its own religion, and each set of opinions became fixed.[76] Each of the three divisions of Protestantism had its own habitation, name, and following. All had some degree of organization and crystallized into three systems, incompatible with one another. Lutherans and Calvinists began to persecute each other. Thus the Jesuits

---

[73] Kidd, *The Counter-Reformation*, pp. 9, 10.
[74] *Ibid.*, p. 10. See chaps. 3 and 5 on the Roman Inquisition and on the Jesuits, and chap. 4 on the Council of Trent.
[75] *Ibid.*, p. 189.   [76] *Ibid.*, pp. 189 ff.

were able to win back Poland.[77] Religious wars developed in the Netherlands and France, and a concerted Catholic reaction followed.[78]

2. HALF OF EUROPE REGAINED FOR PAPACY.—Thus the reaction spread, with varying results, over Britain, the Baltic lands, Switzerland, and Savoy.[79] The Catholic Church held her own and resisted all opposition in Italy, Spain, and Portugal. In France the Wars of Religion ended in a compromise, with France largely Catholic. In the Netherlands the success of the reaction was but partial. In England it failed. Scotland remained Calvinist, and Ireland overwhelmingly Catholic. In Sweden the reaction failed. The Catholic revival penetrated Germany, and this cradle of the Reformation lost more to the reaction than any other nation.[80] The emperor was head of the state, and in theory, the successor of the Roman emperors and of Charlemagne, was lay head of Western Christendom and patron and protector of the Roman church. But the imperial dignity was only in name. Actually he was only a king and overlord. The great vassal dukes were virtually independent.

In this way the marked early advances of the Reformation were checked. In Belgium, Catholicism won, as well as in various parts of the Lower Rhine. Bavaria became thoroughly Catholic, and in Austria, Hungary, and Bohemia, Protestantism became virtually extinct. The Protestant doctrines were repressed with an energy equal to that with which they had first been advanced. And the chief factor in it all was the Jesuits.[81] Thus half of Europe was secured for the Roman Catholic Church, and Protestantism split into two groups, Protestant and Reformed.[82] The gains were largely on the side of the Roman Catholic Church, which had been effectually renovated and reorganized for battle at the Council of Trent.[83]

---

[77] *Ibid.*, pp. 195, 196.
[78] *Ibid.*, chap. 10.
[79] *Ibid.*, chap. 11.
[80] *Ibid.*, pp. 233, 234.
[81] *Ibid.*, pp. 241-259.
[82] The terms *Protestant* and *Reformed* are here used in their historical sense: *Protestant* to mean "Lutheran," and *Reformed* to mean "Calvinist."
[83] *Ibid.*, p. 262.

No.	Name	Date	Page	1 John 2:18 Antichrist	Matt. 24:15 Abom. of Des.	4 Metals	Dan. 2 Clay-Iron	Stone	4 Beasts	10 Horns	Dan 7 Little Horn	3½ Times	Judgm
1	Martin Luther	1522	266	Papacy	Papacy	B-P-G-R	Mod. Kgdms.	Christ's Kgdm.	B-P-G-R	Listed	Papacy, Turk	Phocas-	After
2	Philipp Melanchthon	1543	285	Papacy, Moham.		B-P-G-R	Mod. Kgdms.	Messian. Kgdm.	B-P-G-R	Listed	Mohammedism	(Hazy)	P.-Ove
3	Andreas Osiander	1545	295	Papacy	Papal Trad.				(B-P-G)-R		Papacy	412-1672	
4	Nicolaus von Amsdorf	1554	303	Papacy	Papal Trad.				(B-P-G)-R				
5	Johann Funck	1558	308	Papacy		B-P-G-R			(B-P-G)-R		Papacy		
6	Virgil Solis	1560	313	Papacy					B-P-G-R		Papacy		
7	Nikolaus Selnecker	1579	323	Pope, Turk			B-P-G-R		B-P-G-R	Listed	Turk		
8	Georg Nigrinus	1570	325	Papacy					B-P-G-R	Listed	Pope-Turk	1260 Years	
9	David Chytraeus	1572	329						(B-P-G)-R		Papacy	412-1672	
10	Johann Oecolampadius	1530	336	Papacy (Man of Sin)		B-P-G-R		Kgdm. of God	(B-P-G)-R	Listed	Papacy		
11	Heinrich Bullinger	1557	339	Papacy	Papacy (Man of Sin & Beast)	(B-P-G)-R	Divisions	Everlasting	B-P-G-R	Listed	Papacy	1260 Years	
12	George Joye	1545	361	Papacy (Man of Sin & Beast)					B-P-G-R		Papacy		
13	Nicholas Ridley	1554	364	Papacy	Papacy	B-P-G-R	Divisions		B-P-G-R	Divis.			
14	Hugh Latimer	1553	368	Papacy					(B-P-G)-R				
15	Thomas Cranmer	1582	387	Papacy							Papacy		
16	John Bale	1550	395	Papacy	Papacy				(B-P-G)-R		Papacy		
17	John Jewel	1562	405	Papacy	Papacy				(B-P-G)-R		Papacy		Justinian-
18	Anglican Formulas	c. 1563	423	Papacy (Also Harlot)				Future Kgdm.					
19	John Knox	1547	445	Ch. of Rome (Also Man of Sin, Babylon, Harlot)					B-P-G-R	Fall of R.	Papacy		
20	John Napier	1593	455	Pope					B-P-G-R	Listed		1260 Years	
21	Francisco Ribera *	1590	489	Future Infidel					4th, Satan		Fut. Antichr.	Literal	
22	Robert Bellarmine *	1593	495	Future Jew	(Rome Not Yet Divided; Antichr. Not Yet Come) (To Reign in Jerusalem)						Single King	Literal Lit., Fut.	
23	Blasius Viegas *	1601	502	Future									
24	Thos. Malvenda *	1604	505	Future Jew (Time of Coming Antichr. Unknown—At End of Age)									
25	Thomas Brightman	1614	512	Pope		(B-P-G)-R			(Ṣ-P-G)-R	Divis.	Papacy	Years	
26	David Pareus	1618	518	Pope & Turk									

* Futurists

VIII. Consensus of Reformation Writer Conviction

COVERAGE OF TABULAR CHARTS.—A summarizing view of the leading positions of the principal Reformation writers on prophecy is presented here. Beginning with Luther in the sixteenth century, it is extended to include the first Catholic Futurist and Preterist counterinterpreters and their earliest Protestant followers. The same general plan of tabulation is here followed as was pursued with the pre-Reformation interpreters (pages 156, 157), only now an increasing number of areas are included in the widening scope of study. (The post-Reformation expositors appear in similar form in a concluding summary at the close of the volume.)

Two tabular charts are now needed, one to cover the book of Daniel and the other the book of Revelation. The leading features found in Daniel 2, 7, 8, 9, 11, and 12, including their respective time periods, are listed in sequence. Similarly, the principal teachings of these expositors are given on the seven churches of Revelation 2 and 3, then the seven seals (Revelation 6, 7), the seven trumpets (Revelation 8, 9), the Two Witnesses (Revelation 11), the woman and the dragon (Revelation 12), the two beasts and the number (Revelation 13), the angels and the mark (Revelation 14), the seven vials (Revelation 16), the scarlet woman, Babylon, and the beast (Revelation 17), the thousand years of the millennium

| m-Goat | Dan. 8 | | | Dan. 9 | | | Dan. 11 | | Dan. 12 | | 6000 Yrs. |
	Ex. Horn	Daily	2300 Days	70 Weeks	1 Week	Cross	Willful Kg.	Kg. of North	1290 Days	1335 Days	
P-G P-G	Papacy Papacy		Literal	Yrs. (2d Darius) Yrs. (2d Artax.)	34-41	Begin. Midst	Papacy Papacy	Papacy Papacy, Turk	37-1372 37-c. 1372 Yrs.-Combined—to End		Near End Near End Near End
		Gospel Worship		457 BC-AD 34	-34	End			261-1550	261-1595	
P-G				Yrs. (2d Artax.) 456 BC-AD 34		End		Papacy	Years	Years	
P-G	Papacy			Years 457 B.C.-A.D. 34 Cyrus, Yrs.	Long Period -34	End		Antichrist Papacy Papacy	Yrs. to End		
							Papacy				Near End
							Papacy	Papacy			
		Lit. Days Literal		490 Years 490 Years					Years	365-1700	End c. 1700
		Mass Mass		Wks. of Years			Antiochus		Lit., Fut.	Lit., Fut. Yrs. to Judgm.	
								Turks			

(Revelation 20), and the New Jerusalem of Revelation 21 and 22. Their strikingly similar teaching on Antichrist, the Abomination of Desolation, and the Man of Sin, set forth by Christ, Paul, and John, also appear in separate columns.

The expositors serially listed on the two charts are not always identical, as some interpret Daniel but not the Revelation, or vice versa. Lesser lights, who merely reiterate, are omitted because of space limitations. They only serve to intensify the predominant positions. The broadened scope of interest and interpretation in this era is apparent. Reading *horizontally,* we obtain a comprehensive summary of the teachings of these principal writers; but reading down *vertically,* we get at a glance the collective convictions of the Reformation and Counter-Reformation writers on these major points. This method is indispensable to reaching sound and fair conclusions. The main teachings of the era may thus be deduced.

SUMMARY OF CONCLUSIONS.—The most marked characteristic of the Reformation period is the virtually unanimous belief that the Papacy is assuredly the predicted Antichrist, variantly called the Little Horn of Daniel 8, the Abomination of Desolation, the Man of Sin, the Beast, Babylon, and the Harlot of Old and New Testament prophecy. The four empires of prophecy, followed by the division of the Roman fourth, are taken as axiomatic. It is similarly the majority view that the Little Horn of Daniel 7 and the willful king of Daniel 11 also indicate the

529

				2 Thess. 2		Rev. 2, 3	Rev. 6, 7		Rev. 8, 9				Hr.-Dy.-Mo.-Yr.	Rev. 11	
No.	Name	Date	Page	Man of Sin	Hinderer	7 Churches	4 Horses	6th Seal	4 Trumpets	5th Trumpet	5 Months	6th Trumpet		2 Witnesses	42 Month
1	Martin Luther	1522	266	Papacy	Imp. Rome	Literal	Distress	Afflictions				Mohammedans			
2	Philipp Melanchthon	1543	285	Papacy	Imp. Rome										
3	Andreas Osiander	1545	295	Papacy	Imp. Rome										
4	Nicholaus von Amsdorf	1554	303												
5	Virgil Solis	1560	313												
6	Matthias Flacius	1556	315	Papacy (Also Antichrist, With Turks)										O.T., N.T.	
7	Alfonsus Conradus	1560	318	Papacy (Also Antichrist, Little Horn)					Calamities on the Church						
8	Georg Nigrinus	1570	325	Papacy	Pagan R.										
9	David Chytraeus	1572	329	Papacy								Mohammedans			
10	Heinrich Bullinger	1557	339	Papacy	Pagan R.	Chr. Era			Calamities	Saracens		Turks		Martyrs	
11	Johann Funck	1558	308	Papacy										O.T., N.T.	
12	William Tyndale	1550	354	Papacy (Also Antichrist, Little Horn)											
13	Nicholas Ridley	1554	364												
14	John Hooper	1550	380	(Antichrist & Abom. of Desolation)			4th, Papal								
15	Thomas Cranmer	1582	387	Papacy			Papal Aptcy.								
16	John Bale	1550	395	Papacy		Chr. Era	Aptcy. in Ch.	Judgments	7 Ages to Judgment Day						
17	John Jewel	1562	405	Papacy	Pagan R.										
18	John Foxe	1587	412	Bp. of Rome (Also Antichrist)								Turks			
19	John Napier	1593	455	Papacy										O.T., N.T.	
20	Francisco Ribera*	1590	489	Not Yet Come	Rome		Early Tribul.	Antichrist	Punishments	Mohammed. Armies	1051-1201	Turks, c. 1300		Ch. Under Antichr. Enoch & Elias	Literal
21	Robert Bellarmine*	1593	495												
22	Blasius Viegas*	1601	502	(Antichrist Still Future)			All Seals Are Future		All Trumpets Are Future						Literal
23	Cornelius a Lapide*	1620	503	Future			All Seals Are Future		All Trumpets Are Future						Literal
24	Luis de Alcazar†	1614	507	(Rev. 1-11: Rjctn. of Jews; Dstrctn. of Jer.)			Early Spread of Ch.		Judgments on Judaism (Rev. 12-19: Overthrow of Pagan R.)					Christians	Literal
25	Thomas Brightman	1614	512	Papacy	Pagan R.	7 Periods	All Prior to Constantine Cover Whole Chr. Era		Barbarians	Saracens	630-780	Turks	1300-1696	Christians	
26	David Pareus	1618	518	Papacy						Parallel Seals		Mohammedan Conquests			
27	Hugo Grotius†	1640	521	(Rev. 1-11: Overthr. of Jews)	(P. Not in Proph.)		Early Jew.-Rom. Wars		Prior to Fall of Jerusalem (Rev. 12-20: Chr. Victory Over Pagan R.)						
28	Henry Hammond†	1653	524												Paganism

* Futurists
† Preterists

Papacy. There are some variations on these two symbols as referring to the Papacy, but never on the Papacy as the pre-eminent Antichrist. Every Reformer holds that steadfastly.

Until the Jesuit Counter-Reformation writers made their appearance, at the close of the period, the Historical School view of prophetic interpretation prevailed. There were virtually no exceptions. Then the Jesuits, coming to the aid of the Papacy, adroitly introduced the diverting, though conflicting, Futurist and Preterist schemes.

The same Protestant unanimity is true of the application of the year-day principle for most prophetic time periods, which principle forms an inseparable part of the Historical School thesis. Not until the appearance of these same Jesuit counter-interpreters do we find any serious challenge to this uniform principle among Protestants, and even Catholics, though the precise timing of the periods was a matter of slow perception and gradual correction over a period of centuries. The 2300 days, it will be observed, were the least understood of all, and the last to be placed and to be included under the year-day principle.

These features may well be compared and contrasted with the pre-Reformation writers (pages 156, 157) and the post-Reformation expositors (pages 784-787). Likewise with the Jewish expositors, on page 194. A technical table of leading writers on the seventy weeks appears on page 430. Similar tables for the

EXPOSITORS ON REVELATION (For Daniel, See Preceding Opening)

| Rev. 12 | | | Rev. 13 | | | | | Rev. 14 | Rev. 16 | Rev. 17 | | | | | Rev. 20 | Rev. 21, 22 |
Woman	Dragon	1260 Days 42 Months	1st Beast	42 Months	2d Beast	666	Mark	3 Angels	7 Vials	Harlot	Babylon	Beast	10 Horns	7th Head	1,000 Yrs.	New Jerusalem
Pure Ch.		Years	Imp. Rome / Papacy	Yrs. (Phocas) / Papacy	Papacy / Teachers	Yrs. (Greg.) Romith Romith	Subservience		5th, Papacy	Papacy / Papacy	Papacy -Papacy / Papacy	Nations / Rome	Listed	Pope	August.	
Church	Years	Years	Papacy / Papacy / Papacy	Yrs. 606-		Yrs. Lateinos		Worship	5th, Papacy	Papacy / Papacy	Papacy / Papacy	Rom. Emp.		Popes		
True Ch.		Years 441-1701	Papacy / Pagan R. / Rom. Emp.	1260 Yrs. / 1260 Yrs.	Papal R. / Papacy	Name / Latin Ch. / Lateinos				Papacy	Papacy	Nations / Rome			Pre-mill. / August.	
	Devil	261-1521	Pagan R. / Papacy / Papacy		Papal R. / Papacy	97-763 / Years		Gosp. Prch.	5th, Rome	Rom. Ch / Papacy / Papacy	Papacy / Papacy				August.	
			Papacy / Papacy				Allegiance			Papacy / Papacy / Papacy	Papacy / Papacy / Papacy	Papacy / Rome				
True Ch.	Years	Years	Papacy / Papacy / Pagan R.		Prelates / Bp. of R.	Name / Romanus		Preaching		Papacy / Papacy	Papacy / Papacy	Papacy / Rome	Nations	Popery	August.	
True Ch. Church	Satan	Yrs. 316- Lit., Fut.	Lat. Emp.	1260 Yrs. / Literal / Literal	Papacy	Lateinos / Name of Antichr. / Luther		Obedience		Papacy / Pgn. R. & Fut. Aptsy.	Papacy / Pgn. R. & Fut. Aptsy. / Pagan R.	Lat. Emp.	10 Kings / 10 Kings	Popes	August. / Cross-Antichr.	
Apstlc. Ch.			Fut. Antichr. / Fut. Antichr. / Pagan R.		Precursor / Carnal Wisdom				Future	Pgn. R. & Fut. Aptsy. / Pgn. R. & Fut. Aptsy. / Pagan R.	Pagan R. / Pagan R.	Pgn. R. & Fut. Aptsy.	10 Kings		Saints' Rgn. / Cath. Rgn.	Cath. Ch.
Pure Ch.	Pagan R.	Years 606-1866	Early Pap. / Papacy	Years	Later Pap. / Sp. Power	Lateinos		Preachers / Preachers	Retributions / Judgments	Papacy / Papacy	Papacy / Papacy	Papacy	Kgdms.	Popes / Popes	August. / August.	New Earth
	Domitian	Domitian	Pagan R. / Pagan R.	Domitian	Magic Cult / Pgn. Priests	Trajan			Tribulations	Pagan R. / Pagan R.	Pagan R. / Pagan R.	Pagan R.	Kings / Kgdms.	Titus	311-1311 / August.	Constantinople / Constantinople

earlier centuries occur periodically in Volume I, and for subsequent centuries in Volumes III and IV.

We repeat, for emphasis, that the primary principle established in the minds of the Reformation writers was that the Roman Papacy was in verity the predicted Antichrist, disclosed under an impressive series of symbolic names, so as to make the identification full, rounded, and inescapable. Antichrist was at first held back from early development by the dominant Roman Empire, the breakup of Rome opening the way for its development. Furthermore, it was declared to be an ecclesiastical system, not an individual. Its seat was in seven-hilled Rome, not in Jerusalem. It was primarily the apostasy within the Christian church, not simply the antagonism of Mohammedanism outside of and against the church. The Mohammedan Turks were clearly sensed in the sixth trumpet and the sixth vial. Further, the 1260 prophetic days were years, the same as the forty-two prophetic months, and the three and a half prophetic times, or years. These refer to different aspects of the same common power and its various manifestations. And the Reformers sensed that they were well along in that designated period.

The prophecies covering the Christian Era were looked upon as picturing the conflict between Christ and Antichrist, though involving the nations in which the battle was to be staged. The end of the warfare was drawing near, they were persuaded, and the judgments of God upon the impenitent would erelong be poured out, at the approaching end of the age, when both the Papacy and the Turk would come to their destined end. These expositors knew approximately where they were in the grand outline. Practically all the way through the Reformation period, however, the Augustinian view of the thousand years, or millennium of Revelation 20 still held Christendom in its grip, though in modified Protestant form. Only as we come to the close of the Reformation and enter upon the seventeenth century expositors, is this great misconception rectified.

CHAPTER TWENTY-FOUR

King James I

Turns Prophetic Expositor

I. Preview of the Post-Reformation Characteristics

During the Post-Reformation period of the seventeenth and eighteenth centuries literally hundreds of Protestant commentaries, large and small, appeared in Britain, the European continent, and for the first time in the New World. Notwithstanding varying degrees of clarity and perception, there was, nevertheless, remarkable unity on the essentials. These expositors did vastly more than answer the specious countersystems of the Jesuits. They built an increasingly solid and symmetrical system, which was progressively developed and perfected by investigation and experience—a system sealed and demonstrated by an ever-growing correspondence with the continuing course of events.

With the exception of relatively few, like Grotius and Hammond, who adopted Catholic Preterism, all held the Historical School of interpretation, as to general outline. And several notable advances marked the century. There was now, for example, almost complete agreement that the fifth and sixth trumpets represented the Saracens and Turks. Other advances will be noted as we progress.

From the fifth century onward the binding of Satan, as introducing the millennium, was regarded by the Catholics as a past event. Earlier Protestants retained a similar interpretation, with the outbreak of persecution at the close of the Middle Ages considered as the loosing of Satan for a little season, prior to the great judgment day. The church of the Middle Ages had believed herself living in the millennial period. But by the middle of the seventeenth century the period had so lengthened that this idea was hard to uphold. A basic change in the thinking of Protestantism took place, as the futurity of the thousand years of Satan's binding, introduced by a literal resurrection of the saints at the advent, again became a fundamental of sound interpretation. And so the last of the determining factors of sound interpretation [1] was reinstated.

Before the world was aware, the backbone of the Lateran theory was broken. The millennial thousand years, again established as future, were bounded by the two literal resurrections. Thus the medieval Augustinian position was at last flanked and turned, and the pretended kingdom of Christ on earth was seen to be but the "Babylonian Empire of Antichrist." Various creedal symbols and Confessions of Faith appeared based solely on the Bible.

There was also a gradual recognition of the vital place occupied by the 2300 year-days, and for the first time the 70 weeks were connected with the 2300 days. The coming destruction of the earth by fire was once more stressed. Unhappily, extremism and fanaticism likewise came in again to blight—in England among the Fifth Monarchy men. And the religious wars had a definite bearing on the state of interpretation.

Because of the number of expositors and commentators, only the leading writers who make a definite contribution can be presented in detail, minor contributions simply being noted. We begin with a survey of the British expositors, then follow with the German, French, Dutch, and Swiss, reserving the seventeenth-century American writers largely for Volume III, as the background of the great American advent and prophetic awakening of the nineteenth century. The English writers were, happily, rather insulated from the constant bickerings of the Lutheran and Reformed churches.

---

[1] See Volume I of *Prophetic Faith*.

II. Downham Expounds Stone, Daily, Turkish and Papal Periods

GEORGE DOWNHAM, or Downame (d. 1634), English theologian, whose *A Treatise Concerning Antichrist,* the second book of which was a refutation of Bellarmine, leads the vanguard of English Protestant works on prophecy over in the seventeenth-century line, was born in Chester. He was professor of logic at Cambridge. James I appointed him one of his chaplains and nominated him bishop of Derry in 1616. Written to prove that "the Pope Is Antichrist," and "against all the objections of Robert Bellarmine," this treatise by Downham denies the Catholic position that "the stone that smote the Image be Christ at his first coming, and his Kingdom immediately following unto the end." On the contrary, in it he contends that the kingdom is "to be set up at the fall of Antichrist, it appeareth by these Arguments." [2]

1. POPE TAKES AWAY DAILY TILL PROPHETIC PERIOD ENDS. —Downham gives the standard interpretation of Daniel 2, with the following listing of the divisions of Rome—"Britons, Saxons, Franks, Burgundions, Wisigothes, Sueves and Alans, Vandals, Alemans, Ostrogothes, Greeks," and cites a number of reasons why the Little Horn of Daniel 7 is "Antichrist, or the Pope of *Rome.*" [3] This power in Daniel 8 Downham presents as the exceeding great horn that takes away the "daily," which he defines as the "true Doctrine and Worship of God according to his Word," and which point is repeated and emphasized as the other characteristics of the Papacy are outlined; this interference with the "daily," he contends, would last to the end of the 2300 evening-mornings, or 1150 "compleat days," and these "days are years" [4] (reaching to the Protestant Reformation).

2. ALSO IDENTIFIED AS KING OF NORTH.—Also depicting the Papacy as the "King of the North" in Daniel 11, Downham has

---

[2] George Downham, *A Treatise Concerning Antichrist,* pp. 3, 4.
[3] *Ibid.,* pp. 6, 15.
[4] *Ibid.,* pp. 45, 49, 133.

him coming to his end.[5] And over in Revelation 13 Antichrist follows the imperial Roman emperors, or sixth head.[6]

3. YEAR-DAY PRINCIPLE IN TIME PROPHECIES.—In explaining the 1260 year-days, or forty-two months, or three and a half times of Revelation 11, 12, and 13, as well as those of Daniel 7 and 12, Downham contends that a time is a year, "which in propheticall use containeth 360 dayes."[7] Seeking to find the starting point of the 1260-, 1290-, 1335-, and 391-day periods— all of which are recognized as based on the prophetic year-day principle—Downham suggests several possible dates. The 391 years (360 + 30 + 1) "do appertain unto the solution [loosing] of the Turks," and this Downham puts from about 1169, or from about 1300. The 1335 years will, he believes, end in the "glorious state of New Jerusalem."[8]

4. DOWNHAM DATES 1260 YEARS FROM JUSTINIAN AND PHOCAS.—The "time, two times and half" of the "Beast or little horn, that is, the Pope," are placed by Downham after his "rise into his Kingdom after the ten horns." The time of Justinian is suggested, when there came the "open manifestation of his Kingdom." This would be from about A.D. 600, "according to the round number," when Phocas recognized the pope as universal bishop, and when Gregory began to "deform the Church with rites and superstitions." On the thousand years, however, Downham still holds the Augustinian view, dating them from Constantine, in the fourth century.[9]

III. James I—Royal Expositor Cites Prophecies to Fellow Kings

Queen Elizabeth had been in frequent perplexity over the conflict between her Catholic and Protestant subjects, the latter looking upon the hierarchy and liturgy of the Roman church as remnants of Antichrist, from which the country needed to be purged. The Second Scotch Confession of Faith, for example, declared:

---

[5] Ibid., pp. 122-124. [6] Ibid., pp. 138, 140. [7] Ibid., pp. 125, 132.
[8] Ibid., pp. 133, 138, 139, 142, 143. [9] Ibid., pp. 139-143.

"In special, we detest and refuse the usurped authoritie of that *Romane Antichrist* upon the scriptures of God, upon the Kirk, the civill Magistrate, and consciences of men." [10]

In this atmosphere and persuasion the Scotch reared and trained their young KING JAMES (VI of Scotland, and later James I of England) (1566-1625), only child of Mary Queen of Scots and Henry Stewart Lord Darnley. Upon the abdication of his mother, in 1567, he was proclaimed king of Scotland—of course under regents until he became of age. His marriage to Anne of Denmark brought him into still closer relation with the Protestants. His rule in Scotland was disturbed by continued political and religious strife, particularly between the Presbyterians and Catholics, until in 1586 he entered into a treaty with England which turned out favorably for Protestantism. In 1603, when Queen Elizabeth died, he became king of England. The notable Gunpowder Plot occurred in 1605, the results of which were disastrous to the Catholics. The production of the Authorized Version, or King James Bible (published in 1611), was proposed by James in 1604. The rules governing the translation were drawn up by James himself. [11]

1. PAPAL BEAST SPRINGS FROM RUINS OF ROME.—When only twenty years of age, [12] King James wrote his remarkable *A Paraphrase Upon the Revelation of the Apostle S. Iohn,* as an "Epistle to the Whole Church Militant." With others, he held the view that the locusts were the different orders of monks, and their king the pope. [13] "The Pope is the plague for breaking of the first Table and the Turke for breaking of the second," [14] he

---

[10] Philip Schaff, *Creeds,* vol. 3, p. 481.
[11] On James I, consult Samuel R. Gardiner, *History of England;* William Sanderson, *A Compleat History of James I;* Arthur Wilson, *The History of Great Britain, Being the Life and Reign of King James the First.*
[12] The sequence of seventeenth-century British rulers, and their religious views, will help in understanding trends among interpreters:
James I (1603-1625). Protestant; commentator on prophecy.
Charles I (1625-1649). Married a French Catholic.
Cromwell (1648-1658). Independent; at first a sympathizer with Fifth Monarchy movement.
Charles II (1660-1685). Restored Episcopacy; inclined toward Roman Catholicism.
James II (1685-1688). Openly a Catholic.
William and Mary (1689-1694) } Religious tolerance provided.
William III (1694-1702)
[13] James I, *A Paraphrase Upon the Revelation,* in *Workes,* pp. 26-31; *A Premonition to All Most Mightie Monarchs, Kings, Free Princes, and States of Christendome,* in *Workes,* pp. 320, 321.
[14] James I, *Paraphrase,* chap. 9, "Argument," in *Workes,* p. 26.

THE WORKES OF THE MOST HIGH AND MIGHTIE PRINCE IAMES

BY THE GRACE OF GOD, KING OF GREAT BRITAINE, FRANCE AND IRELAND, DEFENDER of the FAITH, &c.

PVBLISHED BY IAMES, BISHOP of Winton, and Deane of his MAIESTIES CHAPPEL ROYALL.

1. REG. 3. VERS. 11.

Lee, I haue giuen thee a Wiſe and an vnderſtanding heart.

LONDON
PRINTED BY ROBERT BARKER AND IOHN BILL, PRINTERS TO THE KINGS moſt Excellent MAIESTIE.
ANNO 1616.
Cum Privilegio.

ſwallowed and dried vp that flood ſuddenly. " The Dragon therefore or the diuel, became more wrathfull and enraged then before againſt the woman, or the Church, and went about by ſome other way, to make warre againſt the reſt of the womans ſeed, who kept the Commandements of GOD, and had the teſtimonies of CHRIST to GOD the Father, that they were choſen and called, for theſe are onely the true poſteritie of the Church, *to wit*, the ſucceſſours in grace, faith and trewth. " And I ſtood vpon the Sea ſhore, I meane, it ſeemed to me that I ſtood vpon the Sea ſhore, becauſe I did wait to ſee come out of it, which repreſented all peoples and nations, ſuch powers, as Satan would imploy to fight againſt the Church; for the declaring whereof this Viſion was ſhewn vnto me, and whereof theſe two laſt great wonders were but the introduction, that by theſe things paſt, as the roote, I might the better vnderſtand the branches, which are to bud forth thereof as followeth.

CHAP. XIII.

ARGVMENT.

The Popes ariſing : His deſcription : His riſing cauſed by the ruine of the fourth Monarchie the Roman Empire : The riſing of the falſe and Papiſticall Church, her deſcription, her conformitie with her Monarch the Pope : The great reuerence borne to the Pope by many nations, and not onely to him, but to his Legates. A generall defection ſo great, as there ſhall not be an other viſible Church, but the Popedome : Of the firſt Pope who did take to himſelfe all their blaſphemous and arrogant ſtyle.

N then I ſaw a beaſt riſing out of the Sea, *to wit*, from among the number of Nations and peoples; I ſaw a Monarchie choſen and erected vp by this Dragon the deuil, and it had ſeuen heads and tenne hornes, and tenne diadems vpon the tenne hornes : the ſignification of theſe heads and hornes, was declared vnto me by an Angel, as ye ſhall heare in the place conuenient hereafter, and vpon theſe heads was the name of blaſphemie : for they by the perſecution of the Saints, and adorning falſe gods, ſhall both by word and deed blaſpheme the name of the Eternall God. ' This beaſt or Monarchie, is the fourth King or Monarchie whereof *Daniel* prophecied, *to wit*, euen that Monarchie which preſently reignes, and hath the power of the other three remained in it, for it is farre greater then they : And therefore as that Monarchie of the Leopard, gat that name becauſe of the ſwiftnes of the conqueſt : and that of the Lion, becauſe of the mightines and cruelty therof : and that of the Beare, becauſe of the ſtrength and long ſtanding thereof ; ſo this is called like the Leopard, *to wit*, in ſhape, whereof commeth her agilitie : headed like a Lion, becauſe his ſtrength is in the head, as ye heard already : and legged like a beare, becauſe

in

D 2

KING JAMES I, OF BRITAIN, EXPOUNDS THE PROPHECIES

Title Page of Works of James I (Left); Portrait of Monarch by Vaniomer (Center); and Page From the King's Exposition of the Beast of Revelation 13 Written When But Twenty, With the Power, Following Upon the Breakup of Rome, as the Fourth Prophetic Empire (Right) declared. Revelation 13 King James explained pointedly as "the Popes arising: His description: His rising caused by the ruine of the fourth Monarchie the Romane Empire: The rising of the false and Papisticall Church; her description; her conformitie with her Monarch the Pope." [15] The propriety of this venture was defended by James, bishop of Winton, the king's court chaplain, in these words:

"I may safely say; That *Kings* have a kinde of interest in that Booke [the Revelation] beyond any other: for as the execution of the most part of the *Prophecies* of that Booke is committed unto them; So it may be, that the Interpretation of it, may more happily be made by them: And since they are the principall Instruments, that GOD hath described in that Booke to destroy the *Kingdome* of *Antichrist,* to consume his State and Citie; I see not, but it may stand with the Wisedome of GOD, to inspire their hearts to expound it." [16]

2. PAPACY CALLED PROPHESIED BABYLON AND ANTICHRIST.— The "Argument" for chapter 15 declares, "The faithfull praiseth God for the Popes destruction, and their deliverance," and for "the plagues which are to light on him and his followers." Chapter 18 says, "The Pope by his Pardons makes merchandise of the soules of men: Heaven and the Saints reioyce at his destruction, albeit the earth and the worldlings lament for the same"—the Papacy being constantly denominated Babylon.[17]

On Revelation 20 James asserts that Satan, "having been restrained for a long space, by the preaching of the Gospel, at last . . . is loosed out of hell by the raising up of many new errors . . . , especially the Antichrist and his Clergie," citing 2 Thessalonians 2 [18]—still the Augustinian position. This papal Antichrist is signified "by the pale horse, in the fourth seale, by the king of the Locusts in the fifth trumpet, by *Babylon,* in the 11. and 18. Chapter, by the second Beast rising out of the sea, in the 13. Chapter, and by the woman clad with scarlet in the 17. chapter." [19] Then King James charges that the pope, calling himself

15 *Ibid.*, chap. 13, "Argument," p. 39.
16 James, bishop of Winton, "Preface to the Reader," in James I, *Workes,* sig. D₄r; also cited in William Harris, *An Historical and Critical Account of the Life and Writings of James the First,* p. 36.
17 James I, *Paraphrase,* in *Workes,* pp. 47, 57.
18 James I, *A Fruitfull Meditation,* in *Workes,* p. 75.   19 *Ibid.,* p. 77.

universal bishop, ruling through the centuries, and usurping Christ's office, has lately sent out his Jesuits to stir up the princes of the earth, and to league them "together for his defence" and to root out all who "professe Christ truely." This he contends, is all being done "for the revealing of this Prophecie." [20] It is little wonder that the king's book on the prophecies was placed on the Roman Index. [21]

3. APPEALS TO KINGS TO STUDY APOCALYPSE.—As king of Great Britain, James favored the Anglican Church, suppressing the Puritans and disappointing the Catholics. Some of the latter, instigated by the Jesuits, conspired to blow up the king and Parliament (1605). This Gunpowder Plot, frustrated at the last moment, implanted a deep antipathy toward Rome in the hearts of the English. Parliament enacted drastic measures against Catholics, accompanied by a new oath of allegiance. Cardinal Bellarmine injected himself into the controversy, but James sent forth an appeal *(Premonition),* in 1609, to all the rulers of Christendom, in which he identified the Papacy as the "mysterie of iniquitie," urging them to action concerning the encroachments of the Papacy upon church and state, as well as to the defense of the authority and privilege of kings. [22] As might have been expected, there was a rather indifferent reception abroad. It was burned in Florence, forbidden to be translated or printed in France, and refused in Spain. [23]

James insists, in his appeal, that the identity and time of Antichrist were the chief questions upon which they differed, and concerning which they must soon search the Scriptures (especially Revelation 13, 17, 18). The king contends that Rome is the "Seat" of that Antichrist, and has become a second Babylon, Sodom, and Jerusalem in its persecution. Twenty folio pages are devoted to the subject of Antichrist. [24]

4. 42 MONTHS—PERIOD OF ANTICHRIST'S REIGN.—James

---

[20] *Ibid.,* p. 78.
[21] Harris, *op. cit.,* p. 112.
[22] James I, *Premonition,* in *Workes,* pp. 287-292; Harris, *op. cit.,* pp. 105-109.
[23] Harris, *op. cit.,* pp. 111-113.
[24] James I, *Premonition,* in *Workes,* pp. 308-310.

holds that the time of the worship of the beast (the forty-two months) is the period of the reign of Antichrist. This he locates between the first and second advents.[25] The seven forms of the Roman government of Revelation 17, he asserts, are kings, consuls, dictators, decemvirs, military tribunes, emperors, and then popes. The reign of Antichrist immediately followed the government of the emperors, he stated. This Antichrist, he adds, is plainly described four times in Revelation, chapters 6, 9, 13, 17, and the ten horns of Revelation 17 and Daniel 7 are the kings of divided Europe.

5. TIME TO TURN FROM WORSHIP TO DESOLATION OF BEAST. Concerning the responsibility of the monarchs of Christendom toward Antichrist, James wrote this remarkable passage, closed with a strong appeal:

"Therefore I take these ten *Kings* [in Daniel 7 and Revelation 17] to signifie, all the Christian *Kings,* and free *Princes* and *States* in generall, even you whom to I consecrate these my Labours, and that of us all he prophesieth, that although our first becomming absolute and free Princes, should be in one houre with the Beast; . . . and at the very time of the beginning of the planting of the *Antichrist* there; and that we should for a long time continue to worship the *Beast,* having *one . . . minde* in obeying her, . . . and kissing her feete, drinking with her in her cup of Idolatrie, and *fighting with the Lambe,* in the persecution of his Saints, at her command that governeth so many Nations and people: yet notwithstanding all this, wee shall in the time appointed by GOD, . . . converted by His Word; . . . *hate the Whore, and make her desolate, and make her naked,* by discovering her hypocrisie and false pretence of zeale; and shall *eate her flesh, and burne her with fire.* . . .

"*To flee from Babylon, lest they bee partakers of her sinnes, and consequently of her punishment Which warning I pray God that yee all,* my *Beloved Brethren and Cousins, would take heed unto in time, humbly beseeching him to open your eyes for this purpose.*" [26]

6. APOCALYPSE BECOMES EFFECTIVE WEAPON.—Attacks like that of the Jesuit Suárez (1613), and of the Cardinal of Peronne (1615), resulted. But James defended his thesis. On the other hand, numerous exhortations were dedicated to the royal commentator—by Napier of Scotland, Groser of Switzerland

---

[25] *Ibid.*, pp. 309-311.   [26] *Ibid.*, pp. 325-327.

(1605), Cottière of France (1615), Bishop W. Cowper (1623), and Aventrotus of Spain (1616)—all of whom took similar positions. Thus the Apocalypse, though at first depreciated by some of the Reformers, became one of their most effective weapons, even in the hands of a powerful king, while the Jesuits in their counterinterpretations sought to wrest it in favor of the Roman church. James' example proved a powerful stimulus to others. That this could and did happen is tremendously impressive.

IV. Mede Confirms Historical Interpretation and Year-Day Principle

JOSEPH MEDE, or Mead (1586-1638), professor of Greek at Cambridge, was born at Berden, Essex, and educated at Christ's College, Cambridge, from which he received M.A. (1610) and B.D. (1618) degrees. His accomplishments in philosophy, history, mathematics, physics, and antiquity were conspicuous. He twice refused the provostship of Trinity College, Dublin. With the Puritans, he held the pope to be Antichrist, but took no part in the theological controversy between Calvinists and Lutherans. He was widely informed, and maintained an extensive foreign correspondence.

Mede declined official position, preferring to teach. With deep insight into the divine Word, he made prophecy his special study, and materially advanced the science of interpretation. His expository fame rests chiefly on his *Clavis Apocalyptica* (The Key of the Revelation),[27] which sets forth the structural outline of the Apocalypse. This, he maintained, was prerequisite to its sound interpretation.

Mede's *The Apostasy of the Latter Times*, also devoted to prophecy, was issued in 1641 and 1644, and reprinted, significantly enough, in 1836 and 1845. His *Daniel's Weekes* was published in 1643, 1648, and 1677. His *Works* were first collected in 1648, followed by an enlarged edition in 1663-4, and reprinted

---

[27] Published in 1627, and in 1632 and 1642. Translated into English by Richard More in 1643.

in 1677. Such was the popularity and the permanence of his writings.

1. SYNCHRONISM OF FOUR PROPHECIES OF 1260 YEARS.—Mede did what interpreters had previously failed to do. In his *Key of the Revelation* (Part 1) he laid down the basic principle that, for the correct understanding of the Apocalypse, it is first necessary to fix the order and mutual relationships of its principal visions from internal evidence, apart from the question of their interpretation. He sought out, accordingly, the synchronism and succession of the visions, or the order of the prophecies found in the Apocalypse. Their mutual relationship provided a valuable clue to their significance. Then in part 2 (the Commentary based on this method) he gave the historical illustrations in harmony with the proper synchronisms. He is said to have been the first to attempt a tabular scheme to illustrate a commentary.[28]

The first synchronism Mede established was that of what he termed "a noble quaternion of prophecies," remarkable for the equality of their times: (1) The three and a half times, or 1260 days, of the woman in the wilderness; (2) the forty-two months of the domination of the beast; (3) the forty-two months of the treading under foot of the outer court of the temple; and (4) the 1260 days of the witnesses prophesying in sackcloth. Mede contended that not only are these times equal in length, but they begin at the same time and end together, and must therefore synchronize throughout their course. They reach from the era of the rise of the Papacy, and extend on to the era of the overthrow.

2. ALL VISIONS FIND RELATIONSHIP TO 1260 YEARS.—He also contended that the revived Roman head of the first beast of Revelation 13 parallels the second, or lamblike, beast, which acts for the revived head, and that these are necessarily synchronous. He then traced the remaining visions of the Apocalypse as they are related to these central visions, seeking to establish the con-

---

[28] Joseph Mede, *The Key of the Revelation . . . With a Comment Thereupon*, pp. 1, 27-29; Guinness, *Romanism*, p. 272; Elliott, *op. cit.*, vol. 4, pp. 487-489.

nection of the entire series of visions—apart from the question of interpretation.

Mede's revival of interpretation of the millennium as still future was epochal in its repudiation of the Augustinian theory, which computed the thousand years' binding of Satan as from Christ's first advent, or from Constantine's time. Mede placed it from the second advent onward, believing it would be introduced by the literal resurrection of the saints and the destruction of Antichrist.[29]

3. MEDE'S COMMENTARY AUTHORIZED BY BRITISH PARLIAMENT.—It is noteworthy that Mede's *The Key of the Revelation* —with Preface and comprehensive summary by Dr. William Twiss, prolocutor of the Westminster Assembly, and translated from the Latin into English by Richard More, one of the burgesses in the English Parliament—was authorized for publication by none other than the British House of Commons in 1642.[30] Thus the censorship of this Puritan Parliament accepted as orthodox this exposition of the Historical School of prophetic interpretation, called by some the "continuistic view." And at the time Mede's work was approved by the Parliamentary Committee Concerning Printing, the large Westminster Assembly of 121 divines, headed by Dr. Twiss, drew up the Confession of Faith, which was subsequently adopted by the Presbyterian Church. This confession endorses the Historical School of prophetic interpretation regarding the Papacy as declared in chapter 25, sec. 6:

"There is no other head of the Church but the Lord Jesus Christ: nor can the Pope of Rome, in any sense be head thereof; but is that Antichrist, that man of sin and son of perdition, that exalteth himself in the Church against Christ, and all that is called God. [Footnote refs: "2 Thess. ii, 3,4, 8,9; Rev. xiii, 6."]"[31]

---

[29] According to Dr. Worthington, in a sketch prefixed to Mede's *Works* (1663-64 ed.), Mede was led by the law of synchronisms to again place the millennium in the future, contrary even to his own inclinations. The deceptions of Mohammedanism that came in the Augustinian period, Antichristian idolatry, and persecution of the servants of Christ—indications that the devil was not chained—were all determining factors.

[30] The authorization by the committee of Parliament, dated February 21, 1641, and April 18, 1642, appears opposite the title page (1650 ed.).

[31] Philip Schaff, *Creeds*, vol. 3, pp. 658, 659.

Thus premillennialism rose again to real eminence in the seventeenth century, and high on the list of its exponents stands the illustrious Mede. He also made a valiant stroke against Futurism, and its literal three and a half years. So the year-day principle was again sustained.

V. Comprehensive View of Mede's Prophetic Positions

1. DANIEL 2 AND 7: FOUR KINGDOMS ARE ABC OF PROPHECY.—Declaring the "four kingdoms in Daniel" to be "The A. B. C. of prophecy," Mede asserts that these four kingdoms are a *"Propheticall Chronology* of times measured by the succession of foure principall Kingdomes," and that all the kingdoms of this world should ultimately become the everlasting kingdom. Elsewhere Mede calls this outline the "SACRED KALENDAR and GREAT ALMANACK of PROPHESIE." [32]

"THE FOUR KINGDOMS in *Daniel* are twice revealed: First, to *Nebuchadnezzar,* in a glorious *Image* of Four sundry Mettals; secondly, to *Daniel* himself, in a *Vision* of Four diverse Beasts arising out of the Sea. The intent of both is by that succession of Kingdoms to point out the time of the *Kingdom of Christ,* which no other Kingdom should succeed or destroy. . . .

"The same Kingdoms of the *Gentiles* are typified here which were in the former of *Nebuchadnezzar's Image;* namely, the *Babylonian, Persian, Greek,* and *Roman.* . . .

"This *Universal Kingdom* of the *Son* of man revealed in the clouds of Heaven, which *Daniel* here saw, and which the Angel expounds to be the *Kingdom of the Saints of the most High,* is the same with that voiced in the *Apocalypse,* upon the sound of the seventh Trumpet, *All the Kingdoms of the World are become the Kingdoms of our Lord and of his Christ.*" [33]

2. LITTLE HORN THE GREAT PAPAL APOSTASY.—Mede asserts the Little Horn to be "an Apostasie from the Christian faith," or the "Antichristian state" of Rome, which was to continue 1260 years, and which the enemies of true exposition seek to fasten upon Antiochus Epiphanes, for but three and a half literal years. [34]

---

[32] Mede, *The Apostasy of the Latter Times,* p. 69.
[33] Mede, *Mr. Mede's Answer to Mr. Hayn's Second Letter,* in *Works* (1677 ed.), book 4, pp. 743, 744.
[34] Mede, *The Apostasy,* pp. 71, 73, 75.

3. 1260 YEAR-DAYS SYNCHRONIZE WITH SIMILAR PERIODS.—
Mede declares that the 1260 year-days of the "wicked Horn" are
the same as the periods in Daniel 12, the forty-two months of the
Witnesses, the treading down of Jerusalem, the profanation of
the Temple and City of God, and the Beast's blasphemous and
persecuting reign. As to Futurism's claims, he says:

"Our adversaries would have them literally understood for *three single
years and a halfe,* as though it were an *History,* and not a *Prophesie:* but
besides the use of the prophesie to reckon dayes for yeers, I think it would
trouble any man to conceive how so many things as should be performed
in this time, should be done in three single yeeres and a halfe. 1 Ten
Kingdomes founded at the same time with the Beast. 2 Peoples, and multitudes of nations and tongues to serve and obey him. 3 To make warre with
the Saints and overcome them. 4 To cause all that dwell upon the earth to
worship him. 5 *Babylon* to ride the Beast so long, that all nations shall
drinke of the wine of her fornication, the Kings of the earth commit fornication with her, yea the Merchants and all those that had ships in the Sea,
to grow rich by trading with her. Mee thinkes all this should aske much
more than three yeares works, or foure either. . . . Therefore 3. years & a
half historically taken, cannot be the time of the Churches Apostasie, and
the Antichristian sovereignty of *Rome:* and if it cannot be taken historically,
it must be taken *prophetically,* every day for a yeare; & so 1260 dayes
counted so many yeares shewes the extent of those . . . [latter times] to be
1260 years." [35]

4. ROME'S TEN DIVISIONS ENUMERATED.—Mede's list of
the ten divisions of Rome in 456 is: " (1) Britans, (2) Saxons,
(3) Franks, (4) Burgundians, (5) Wisigothes, (6) Swevians and
Alanes, (7) Vandals, (8) Almaines, (9) Ostrogothes, . . .
(10) Greeks." [36]

5. SEVENTY WEEKS "CUT OFF" FOR JEWS.—Recognizing
four possible decrees from which to date the seventy weeks,
Mede held that they were cut off from a longer term for the
Jews:

"The word נחתך here translated *determined* or *allotted,* signifies properly *to be cut,* or *cut out,* and so may seem to imply such a sence, as if
the Angel had said to *Daniel,* Howsoever your bondage and Captivity under
the Gentiles shall not altogether cease, untill that succession of Kingdoms,
which I before shewed thee, be quite finished: yet shall God for the accom-

---

[35] *Ibid.,* pp. 72, 73.   [36] *Ibid.,* p. 82.

plishing his promise concerning the *Messiah,* as it were, *cut out* of that long term a certain limited Time, during which, the Captivity of Judah and Jerusalem being interrupted, the Holy City and Common-wealth in some measure shall again be restored, and so continue till Lxx. Weeks of years be finished." [37]

Mede, like Scaliger before him and Wood and Hales after him, pivots the seventy weeks on the destruction of Jerusalem in A.D. 70 rather than on the almost universally preferred crucifixion. He suggests starting from the second year of Darius Nothus: Nabonassar Era 327-817, or Olympic years 355-845 (421 B.C.-A.D. 70); but he prefers beginning from the sixth year of Darius Nothus: N.E. 331-821, or Olympic years 359-849 (417 B.C.-A.D. 74), placing the end of the temple sacrifices in the midst of the seventieth week. He bases a separate sixty-two weeks on the A.D. 33 crucifixion date as the midst of the sixty-second week, with the starting point in the seventh year of Artaxerxes Mnemon, not Longimanus: Olympic years 379-813 (397 B.C.-A.D. 37). [38]

6. Confused Relation of Seals and Trumpets.—On some points Mede was behind some of his predecessors. For example, he retrogressed on the first six seals, which he limited to pagan Rome; and regarded the trumpets as the unfolding of the seventh seal. So the seals were made to extend only to the time of Diocletian and Constantine, and the overthrow of paganism. [39]

7. Trumpets: Barbarian Incursions, and Saracens and Turks.—According to Mede, the first four trumpets were successively tied to Alaric, Genseric, Odoacer, and Totila. The fifth trumpet was fulfilled in the Saracens; and the sixth, by the Turks from the Euphrates. This, he adds, is in harmony with the best expositors. The fifth and sixth trumpets are explained, moreover, on the year-day principle, which is to be particularly noted, especially for the sixth—the 150 year-days of the "locusts" are given as the beclouding years of Saracenic ravages on the

[37] Mede, *Daniels Weeks,* p. 140 in *Works* (1648 ed.).
[38] *Ibid.,* pp. 141-146; 154-159.
[39] Mede, *The Key of the Revelation,* "Comment," part 1, pp. 30-123.

Italian coast, from A.D. 830 to 980.[40] The Euphratean horsemen's hour, day, month, and year, Mede takes as 396 years (365 + 30 + 1) from the taking of Baghdad, about A.D. 1057, to the taking of Constantinople in 1453.[41] The seventh trumpet is yet to come.

8. BEASTS OF REVELATION 13 SYMBOLIZE ROME.—In Revelation 12 the woman and the dragon are carried by Mede back to Constantine's war with, and overthrow of, paganism. And in Revelation 13 the first beast of that chapter is the papal secular empire, and the second the bishop of Rome and his clergy— with the pope as the "seventh and last head of the Romane Common-wealth, in the Citie standing upon seven hils." The Beast's name is *Lateinos*.[42]

9. VIALS ARE WOUNDS INFLICTED UPON PAPACY.—In Revelation 16 he suggests the vials are the wounds inflicted by the Waldenses, Albigenses, Wyclifites, and Hussites, Luther's labor, and that of other Reformers, and Elizabeth's reign—with some vials still future. The seat of the Beast is Rome, and the drying up of the Euphratean flood is the coming exhaustion of the Turkish Empire.[43] The Babylon of chapter 17 is the apostasy at Rome that Paul denominates the Mystery of Iniquity.[44]

10. SECOND ADVENT INAUGURATES MILLENNIUM.—The brightness of Christ's coming will destroy Antichrist and inaugurate the millennial period.[45] On this, Mede was clear as crystal, and was immovable.

11. 1,000 YEARS BOUNDED BY TWO RESURRECTIONS.—

"*The seventh* Trumpet, *with the whole space of* 1000 *years thereto appertaining, signifying the great Day of Judgement, circumscribed within two resurrections, beginning at the judgement of* Antichrist, *as the morning of that day, and continuing during the space of* 1000 *years granted to* new Ierusalem, (*the Spouse* of Christ) *upon this* Earth, *till the universall resurrection and judgement of all the dead, when the wicked shall be cast into*

---

[40] *Ibid.*, pp. 84-110. Like Brightman, Mede employs the natural, or solar year, not the "prophetic year" of 360 days.
[41] *Ibid.*, "Compendium," on chap. 9:3, 13, 14, and "Comment," part 1, pp. 110-112.
[42] *Ibid.*, "Comment," part 2, pp. 38-48, 65, 75, 76.
[43] *Ibid.*, "Comment," part 2, pp. 114-118.
[44] Mede, *Apostasy*, pp. 46-53.
[45] Mede, *The Key of the Revelation*, "Comment," part 2, pp. 121-125.

Hell *to be tormented for ever, and the* Saints *translated into* Heaven, *to live with* Christ *for ever."* [46]

12. NEW JERUSALEM IN THE MIDST OF EARTH.—The New Jerusalem is to become the capital of the new earth, "placed in the midst of our world." [47]

To get the full picture, let us note paralleling Roman Catholic activities in the field of prophetic exposition.

VI. Battle Over Douay-Rheims Catholic Bible Notes

The Protestant versions of the Bible, and the argument that Rome was keeping the Word of God from the people, drove the English Catholics to make their own translation. Sir Edwin Sandys said that the Protestant cry that the "Lord of Rome was no other than that imperious bewitching Lady of Babylon," together with the dissatisfaction of their own members, led to the Catholic translation. [48] The Roman Catholic English College of the University of Douay, France, put out its English version of the New Testament at Rheims in 1582, and the complete Bible in two volumes at Douay in 1609 and 1610. The full significance of the marginal notes, which started a battle royal, may be profitably noted, and briefly compared. There is essential agreement with the Protestant interpretation of the four world powers of Daniel 7. The basic difference comes over the interpretation of the Little Horn. The general note at the beginning of the chapter reads, "Prophetical visions of Christ and of Antichrist," and note *c* states that the "foure beastes do signifie the foure Monarchies of the Chaldees, Medes and Persians, the Grecians, and the Romanes." [49] Notes *d, e, f, g* give additional detail concerning the four kingdoms named, while *h* says:

"The litle horne becoming so great and strong, as to overcome al the

---

[46] *Ibid.*, "Compendium," on chap. 20.

[47] *Ibid.*, "Coniecture," sig. T₁v.

[48] SIR EDWIN SANDYS (1561-1629), son of Archbishop Edwin Sandys, was a member of Parliament, and one of the leaders of the Virginia Company. In 1599 he wrote *Europae Speculum. Or, A Survey of the State of Religion in the Westerne Parts of the World*, from which (1638 edition, p. 164) this statement is taken. The authorship of this anonymous treatise is identified in the British Museum Catalogue.

[49] *Holie Bible Faithfully Translated in English Out of the Authentical Latin* (Douay, 1609, 1610), Daniel 7, margin, vol. 2, pp. 790, 791.

other, signifieth Antichrist; whose outragious furie shal continue but a shorte time." [50]

The ram and "buckgoote" of chapter eight symbolize the Persians and Grecians.[51]

There was sharp discussion and criticism of the Catholic notes, as seen from George Wither's *A View of the Marginal Notes of the Popish Testament* (1588). Wither follows a three-fold progression, giving the text, Catholic note in italics, and then the Protestant answer in bold type. Thus he quoted the Douay note to Apocalypse 12:14 which denies the year-day principle citing two Protestants in rebuttal:

"This often insinuation that Antichrists reigne shall be but three yeeres and an halfe, Dan. 7.25. Apocalipse 11.2.3. and in this chapter v.6.c.13.5. prooveth that the heretikes be exceedingly blinded with malice, that hold the pope to be Antichrist, who hath ruled so many ages." [52]

William Fulke published in 1589 a parallel New Testament with a Protestant translation from the original Greek (the "Bishops' Bible") paralleling the Rheims translation from the Latin, and with accompanying notes. The issues are exemplified in the contrasting notes on Matthew 24:29:

"RHEM.8. 29. Immediatly. *If the latter day shal immediatly follow the persecution of Antichrist, which is to endure but three yeres and a halfe, as is aforesayd: then is it meere blasphemy to say, Gods Vicar is Antichrist, and that (by their owne limitation) these thousand yeeres almost.*

"FULKE.8. You have sayd, that the persecution of Antichrist, should endure but three yeeres and a halfe, but you are never able to prove it of vsuall yeeres, therefore it is no blasphemy to say, the Pope is Antichrist, though his tyrannie hath continued almost a thousand yeeres. But rather it is blasphemy, to say the Pope is Gods Vicar: for that importeth God and Christ to be absent from his Church. Otherwise the holy Ghost supplieth the want of his bodily presence, untill he come againe to iudgement." [53]

Considerable space is devoted to Paul's Antichrist [54] and also to the prophecies of the Apocalypse. It is well to keep the modern Catholic interpretation in mind, as attested in the Challoner

---

[50] *Ibid.*, p. 792.
[51] *Ibid.*, p. 793.
[52] George Wither, *A View of the Marginal Notes of the Popish Testament, Translated into English by the English Fugitive Papists resiant at Rhemes in France*, p. 296.
[53] William Fulke, annotation on Matt. 24:29 in *The Text of the New Testament of Iesus Christ*, p. 88.
[54] *Ibid.*, on 2 Thessalonians 2, also Revelation 13, 17, 18, 20, 21, pp. 658 ff., 882 ff.

revised editions of the Douay Version. For example, the interpretation of the everlasting kingdom of Daniel 2: *"A kingdom.
Viz., the kingdom of Christ in the Catholic Church, which cannot be destroyed."* [55]

The 2300 days of Daniel 8:14 are considered but literal, and
are confined to Antiochus. Thus:

"Unto evening and morning two thousand three hundred days. That is,
six years and almost four months: which was the whole time from the beginning of the persecution of Antiochus till his death." [56]

The seventy weeks of Daniel 9, however, are properly recognized as "of years." [57]

On 2 Thessalonians the Catholic comment is ingenious:

"Ver. 3. *A revolt.* This *revolt,* or *falling off,* is generally understood,
by the ancient fathers, of a *revolt* from the Roman empire, which was first
to be destroyed, before the coming of Antichrist. It may, perhaps, be understood also of a *revolt* of many nations from the Catholic Church; which has,
in part, happened already, by the means of Mahomet, Luther, and c., and it
may be supposed, will be more general in the days of Antichrist.—Ibid.
The man of sin. Here must be meant some particular man, as is evident
from the frequent repetition of the Greek aritcle ὁ, *the* man of sin, *the* son
of perdition, *the* adversary or opposer, ὁ ἀντικείμενος. It agrees to the wicked
and great Antichrist, who will come before the end of the world.
"Ver. 4. *In the temple.* Either that of Jerusalem, which some think he
will rebuild; or in some Christian church, which he will pervert to his own
worship: as Mahomet has done by the churches of the east." [58]

The Babylon of Revelation 17 is expounded in alternatives,
with bias toward pagan Rome:

"Babylon. Either the city of the devil in general; or, if this place be
to be understood of any particular city, *pagan Rome,* which then and for
three hundred years persecuted the church; and was the principal seat both
of empire and idolatry." [59]

On Satan's binding and the two resurrections in Revelation
20 this is the Douay teaching:

"The power of Satan has been very much limited by the passion of
Christ: for a *thousand years;* that is, for the whole time of the New Testament: but especially from the time of the destruction of *Babylon* or pagan

---

[55] Douay Bible, note on Dan. 2:44.   [56] *Ibid.,* Dan. 8:14.
[57] *Ibid.,* on Dan. 9:24, 25.   [58] *Ibid.,* on 2 Thess. 2:3, 4.   [59] *Ibid.,* on Apoc. 17:5.

Rome, till the new efforts of *Gog* and *Magog* against the church, towards the end of the world. During which time the souls of the martyrs and saints live and reign with Christ in heaven, in the *first resurrection,* which is that of the soul to the life of glory; as the *second resurrection* will be that of the body, at the day of the general judgment." [60]

The divided front of doctors of the Roman church is clearly admitted and the conflicting schools of Futurism and Preterism recognized:

"As to the time when the chief predictions should come to pass, we have no certainty, as appears by the different opinions, both of the ancient fathers and late interpreters. Many think that most things set down from the 4th chapter to the end, will not be fulfilled till a little time before the end of the world. Others are of opinion, that a great part of them, and particularly the fall of the wicked Babylon, happened at the destruction of paganism, by the destruction of heathen Rome, and its persecuting heathen emperors. Of these interpretations, see Alcazar, in his long commentary; see the learned Bossuet, bishop of Meaux, in his treatise on this Book." [61]

VII. Historical Interpretation Sustained by Various Groups

James I, who wished to remain head of the church and maintain the bishops, had not gotten along well with the Puritans, who wanted a more democratic church government than the Anglican Church provided. He was vexed with the Puritans, who were unwilling to use the Anglican Prayer Book. Then his son Charles I married a French Catholic, and made life so unbearable for the Puritans and nonconformists that twenty thousand came to America between 1629 and 1640. [62] First landing at Boston, in 1630, they founded Massachusetts Bay Colony.

Under Charles the English Government became more oppressive, and faced the solid opposition of the English Puritans and Scotch Covenanters. In 1642 the Long Parliament took the reins into its own hands and abolished Episcopacy. In 1643 the Westminster Assembly, a council created by Parliament, met to advise Parliament as to the new form of church government throughout Britain. [63]

---

[60] *Ibid.,* on Apoc. 20:2.
[61] *Ibid.,* on Apoc. 22:10. (It is to be remembered that both Alcazar and Bossuet were Preterists.)
[62] Hyma, *op. cit.,* p. 255.
[63] *Ibid.,* pp. 255-259.

VIII. Uncompromising Declaration of Westminster Standard

It is noteworthy that, though the Church of England in her strongly antipapal Thirty-nine Articles refrained from identifying the Pope as the "man of sin," the Westminster Confession of Faith (1647), ratified and established by Act of Parliament in 1646, did so identify him. Thirty-five times is 2 Thessalonians appealed to, and the Apocalypse fifty-seven times. Many of the most prominent Westminster divines were united upon two main points—premillennialism and the first resurrection. They publicly confessed and preached them. Apart from ten or eleven Independents, seven Scottish commissioners, and two or three French divines, most of the ministers were graduates of Oxford and Cambridge, in Episcopal orders, voting in favor of Presbyterian government, Puritan discipline, and high Calvinism.[64]

The Confession of Faith formulated by this Assembly of Divines stayed in with the doctrinal standards of the Continental, English, and Irish Reformers. It was in agreement with Article 80 of the Irish Articles of Religion of 1615, which had earlier declared:

"The Bishop of *Rome* is so far from being the supreme head of the universal Church of Christ, that his works and doctrines do plainly discover him to be *that man of sin,* foretold in the holy Scriptures, *whom the Lord shall consume with the spirit of His mouth, and abolish with the brightness of His coming."* [65]

Woven into the *Westminster Confession of Faith,* which may be regarded as the strongest premillennialist symbol of Protestantism, are the Historical interpretation of the Antichrist, in which is implicit the year-day principle, and the premillennial expectation of the advent:

"There is no other head of the Church but the Lord Jesus Christ: nor can the Pope of Rome, in any sense be head thereof; but is that Antichrist, that man of sin and son of perdition, that exalteth himself in the Church against Christ, and all that is called God."

---

[64] Nathaniel West, "History of the Pre-Millennial Doctrine," in *Second Coming of Christ. Premillennial Essays,* pp. 369-372.
[65] Philip Schaff, *Creeds,* vol. 3, p. 540. (Presumably composed by Archbishop James Ussher.)

"As Christ would have us to be certainly persuaded that there shall be a day of judgment, both to deter all men from sin, and for the greater consolation of the godly in their adversity: so will he have that day unknown to men, that they may shake off all carnal security, and be always watchful, because they know not at what hour the Lord will come; and may be ever prepared to say, Come, Lord Jesus, come quickly. Amen." [66]

The turbulence of the Fifth Monarchy men was unable to divert the Assembly from the Protestant interpretation of the prophetic symbols or commit it, in reaction, to a rationalistic Preterism. Light is not opposed to darkness more than is the Westminster symbol to the rationalistic Preterism, which had tortured the Apocalypse into a mere epic upon the destruction of Judaism and paganism, or the Temple and the Pantheon.

With these solemn affirmations of the Protestant churches of the seventeenth century, the voices of the leading expositors of all Protestant persuasions of the age agree, as their writings testify.

And now for a few other Protestant expositors to fill out the picture and to indicate continuing emphasis on Antichrist.

IX. Whetenhall and Willet Press Antichrist Identity

Passing with only a word Thomas Whetenhall, whose *A Discourse of the Abuses Now in Question in the Churches of Christ, of Their Creeping in, Growing Up, and Flowrishing in the Babilonish Church of Rome* (1606) describes "this great Antichrist Papa" as "sitting as God in the Temple of God," we note ANDREW WILLET (1562-1621), professor of divinity. Born at Ely, and prebendary there in 1587, Willet wrote *Synopsis Papismi* (Synopsis of Popery), which was considered one of the ablest discussions of its kind. And in his *Hexapla in Danielem* (Sixfold Commentary on Daniel) the power of Daniel 11:36 ff. is identified as the "antichrist of Rome." He seems to have been one of those who regarded Antiochus as a mere forerunner of Antichrist, but the pope himself as the real fulfillment. After expanding upon his self-exaltation, Willet identifies him as

---

[66] *Ibid.*, vol. 3, pp. 658, 659, chap. 25, sec. 6, and pp. 672, 673, chap. 33, sec. 3.

also the Antichrist of Paul, in 2 Thessalonians 2, sitting in the "Church of God." He bases this conclusion on an elaborate historical survey of the steps in its rise to power. This is followed by an extensive answer to Bellarmine's attempt to "wipe away this marke." [67]

X. Forbes—Clear on Antichrist and Year-Day; Confused on Millennium

PATRICK FORBES (1564-1635), titled Scottish divine (Lord of Corse and Baron of O'Neil), was born in Aberdeenshire, and became bishop of Aberdeen in 1618. In his *An Learned Commentarie Upon the Revelation* he identifies the Beast of Revelation 13 as the Roman Antichrist, as "all sound Interpreters agree," the time of whose raging is 1260 year-days.[68] The hour, day, month, and year of the sixth trumpet was identified as the period of the Mohammedans.[69]

The Beast of Revelation 17 is likewise the Papacy. The eighth head (after the seventh is gone), coming out of the fourth, or Roman, beast of Daniel 7, is similarly the "man of sinne." [70] Forbes attacks the arguments of the Futurist Jesuits Bellarmine and Ribera, and the "Rhemish doctors." [71] But he, too, adheres to the papal scheme of the one thousand years from the time of Constantine.[72]

XI. Ramsay—"Out of Babylon" the Authority for Leaving Rome

ANDREW RAMSAY (1574-1659), Scottish clergyman and Latin poet, was probably educated at the University of St. Andrews. He studied theology in France, where he was later given a professorship in the University of Saumur. Returning to Scotland in 1606, he was admitted minister of Arbuthnot. In 1620 he became professor of divinity in the college of Edin-

---

[67] Andrew Willet, *Hexapla in Danielem*, pp. 450, 455.
[68] Patrick Forbes, *An Learned Commentarie Upon the Revelation*, pp. 91, 108. (Likewise the forty-two months and "a time, times, and half a time," p. 221.)
[69] *Ibid.*, pp. 93, 221.
[70] *Ibid.*, pp. 116-118.
[71] *Ibid.*, p. 183.
[72] *Ibid.*, p. 221; unpaged "Summe of the Booke."

MEDALS MEMORIALIZE PAPAL CLAIMS AND ASSUMPTIONS

Paul II Likens Slaughter of Bohemian Heretics to Hunting Wild Boars (First Pair, Left); Julius III Consigns England to Ruin Under Edward VI (First Pair, Right); Leo X Appropriates Title "Lion of the Tribe of Judah" (Second Pair, Left); Fallen England Is Revived by Pope Julius Under "Bloody Mary" (Second Right); Calixtus III Asserts "All Kings Are Obedient to It"—the Triple Crown (Third Pair, Left); Gregory XV Decrees "Heavenly Honors" to Five (Third Pair, Right); Louis XIV Asserts "Heresy Extinguished," Through Revocation of Edict of Nantes, in 1685 (Fourth Pair, Left); Alexander VII Borne Aloft as He Elevates the Host (Fourth Pair, Right)

burgh, and also rector. In 1629 he was made subdean of the Chapel Royal at Holyrood, and in 1646 was again appointed rector of Edinburg University—from which he was later separated because of his protests against the innovations coming into the church.

He preached a sermon, *A Warning to Come Out of Babylon,* upon receiving the former Jesuit Thomas Abernathie into the Reformed Church of Scotland, and gave as answer to the challenge of Rome for authority to depart and secede from Rome the divine command of the Apocalypse to come out of mystic Babylon, which he proves from Scripture to be the Antichrist church of Rome.[73]

XII. Paralleling Witness of Coins and Medals

Apart from published writings on prophetic exposition in book, tractate, or broadside form, there is a paralleling line of testimony wrought out by artisans and cast in metal at the behest of pontiffs and potentates. These are the authoritative telltale medals, coins, and medallions of the time. Here, for instance, the essence of papal assumption through the centuries is disclosed in this unusual form. Many notable examples are preserved in the numismatic divisions of the British Museum, Bibliothèque nationale, Vatican Library, and similar institutions. Here the attitude of the Papacy toward heretics, the proud assumption of earthly and heavenly powers and titles, and alleged papal supremacy over the state, are skillfully wrought into enduring metal. (The papal medal commemorating the slaughter of the Huguenots in the St. Bartholomew's Massacre of 1572, appears on page 480; a large plaque noting the burning of Savonarola, on page 148.)

Similar witness is borne by the coins of civil rulers—the world powers of prophecy are in sequence, climaxing with Rome; the several nations into which Rome was divided, including those soon "plucked up"; the transmission of the title *Ponti-*

---

[73] Andrew Ramsay, *A Warning to Come Out of Babylon,* pp. 3-13.

fex Maximus from pagan to Christian Roman emperors, and thence to its assumption by papal pontiffs, are matters of metallic record. Moreover, the very symbolism of prophecy appears in these coins and medals, as the ram for Persia, and the he-goat for Greece, with Rome as the woman sitting on the seven mountains (reproduced in Volume I of *Prophetic Faith*). Later, a modern papal medal of a woman as the church, holding a golden cup in her hand, appears in Volume IV. Some of the medals paralleling the field of Volume II are reproduced on page 556.

CHAPTER TWENTY-FIVE

Similar Expositions

in Various Protestant Groups

The Reformers had had little time to devote to the study of the millennium, so fully were they occupied in their warfare against Rome's apostasy and externalism, and in the restatement and defense of the great doctrines of grace, the reorganization of the church, and the repulsion of the papal claims. Most of them had remained hampered, however, with the Augustinian view and reckoning of the millennium. They deemed the end of the world nearing, and looked for the speedy advent of Christ to destroy the papal Antichrist, and introduce the state of eternal glory. But they thought the thousand years were past, and that Satan had been loosed for a little season.

Now that Mede had led the way back to premillennialism, others took up this and other corrections and improvements, as well as establishing the Historical view against the attacks of the Futurists and Preterists. Often there were battles royal between the three groups. The beliefs of several lesser and greater lights in the Protestant ranks will be scanned, and then the Fifth Monarchy expositors will be dealt with.

I. Geree—Mysteries of Prophecy Clarified by Fulfillment

JOHN GEREE (1601?-1649), English Puritan, pastor of Tewkesbury, and prebendary at St. Albans, Hertfordshire, in his *The Down-Fall of Anti-Christ*, based on 2 Thessalonians 2:8, contends at the outset that "Prophesies cease to be Mysteries, when by accomplishment they became Histories," and proceeds to show how the identity of Antichrist, which was as yet unknown to the early church, became clear when fulfilled by the "succession of the Popes of Rome." [1]

II. Trapp—Reformation Wound of Beast Healed by Jesuits

JOHN TRAPP (1601-1669), vicar of Weston-on-Avon, in his commentary on the epistles and the Revelation of John, gives as one interpretation of the wounding of the papal "Beast" of Revelation 13 "the falling away of Protestants from the Popedome, from the daies of *Wicliffe, John Husse,* the *Waldenses, Luther,* to this present." But the healing, he notes, is under way by the Sorbonists, Jesuits, and the "Trent-fathers." [2] The two-horned beast is the Roman clergy, and the call out of papal Babylon has resulted in multiplied thousands coming out of Catholicism. [3] But, like all early Reformation predecessors, Trapp still holds that Satan was bound by the chain of a "succession of Christian Emperours" for a thousand years, from Constantine to Boniface VIII, when persecution began to wane, with the "first resurrection" as the awakening from "Romish superstitions." [4]

III. Clear Note Sounded in Anonymous Exposition

An anonymous work, *Rome's Downfal,* dealing with the angelic message of Revelation 14, applies it thus:

"In the 6th and 7th [verses] is shewed, that the Gospel in the latter days shall be preached with great success, for he saw an *Angel flying in the midst of Heaven, having the everlasting Gospel to preach unto them that dwell on the Earth.* Here is in the following verse made mention of more *Angels, i.e.* Evangelical Ministers, preaching the Gospel against the Beast and Beast Worshippers." [5]

[1] John Geree, *The Down-Fall of Anti-Christ: or, The Power of Preaching, to Pull Down Popery,* sig. A4r,v.
[2] John Trapp, *A Commentary or Exposition Upon All the Epistles and the Revelation of John the Divine,* p. 543.
[3] *Ibid.,* p. 569.
[4] *Ibid.,* pp. 583-585.
[5] *Rome's Downfal; Wherein Is Shewed That the Beginnings Thereof Call for Praise and Thanksgiving,* p. 4.

"No power of man shall be able to stop" these messages. Only God is to be feared, honored, and worshiped, and not Antichrist. The result will be "the downfal of the Romish Power." Babylon is here declared to be the same as Paul's Antichrist of 2 Thessalonians 2—"a succession of Popes"—with "every particular exactly verified in him." [6]

IV. Bernard—Catholic Witnesses Substantiate Protestant Claims

NICHOLAS BERNARD (d. 1661) was born about the beginning of the seventeenth century, and was educated at Cambridge. Having migrated to Ireland, he was ordained by Archbishop Ussher in 1626. He became the archbishop's chaplain and librarian, and then was made dean of Kilmore. He received an M.A. from Oxford in 1628, and in 1637 became dean of Ardagh. Probably about 1649 he returned to England, and was appointed preacher of Gray's Inn, London, as well as chaplain to Oliver Cromwell. Shortly before his death Bernard published *Certain Discourses*—a painstakingly documented tracing of the "consent of the Fathers" of the first four centuries, which testifies to the fact that the "successor to the Emperour in Rome" is the "man of sinne." [7]

Bernard says that an endless number of authors have given their testimony that *"after* the Emperour was *put out* of *Rome,"* the "Bishop of *Rome* had succeeded him, *viz.* after the 600 years after Christ." Then he parades the testimony of Catholic leaders from A.D. 1100 onward to show how, prior to the Reformation, the prophecies on Antichrist had been applied to the apostate See of Rome—by the bishop of Florence, Archbishop Eberhard of Salzburg, Honorius of Autun, Bernard of Cluny, Joachim of Floris, John of Salisbury, Robert Grosthead, Occam, Petrarch, the Waldenses, Wyclif, Purvey, Huss, and Savonarola. [8]

Next the witness of English bishops is summoned—like

---

[6] *Ibid.,* pp. 5-7.
[7] Nicholas Bernard, *Certain Discourses, Viz. Of Babylon (Rev. 18.4.) Being the Present See of Rome,* p. 117.
[8] *Ibid.,* pp. 118-125.

Jewel, Abbot, Whitgift, and Andrewes—to testify of papal Rome as Babylon, Antichrist, and the Man of Sin.[9] And this is all stressed to show that Antichrist is a successive dynasty, and not an individual pope—Bernard basing his argument on the prophecy of Daniel 7, with its four empires, and on Revelation 17, with its seventh head as the successive government of the pope reigning as head of the church.[10]

V. Guild—Antichrist Not an Individual but a Succession

WILLIAM GUILD (1586-1657), Scottish divine, was born at Aberdeen and became a minister there. A Doctor of Divinity, he was made principal of King's College in 1640, though displaced in 1651 for his devotion to the royalist cause. He was author of several works on prophecy, one being entitled *Anti-Christ Pointed and Painted Out in His True Colours, or The Pope of Rome, Proven to Bee That Man of Sinne, and Sonne of Perdition, Fore-prophesied in Scripture*. In this he brought to bear the supporting witness of Roman Catholics who died in the communion of that faith. Contending that Antichrist is *"not one individual person, but a continued succession of manie,"* [11] he devoted eighteen chapters to the prophecies of Paul (2 Thessalonians 2) and John (Rev. 12, 13, 17, etc.) concerning the claims, chronology, and characteristics of Antichrist, closing with his final ruin and destruction.

Another volume by Guild, *The Sealed Book Opened,* was similarly designed to prove the identity of "that *Roman* Antichrist," and the increasingly insistent note that "her final destruction is surely at hand." He connected the symbols of Daniel 7 and Revelation 13, citing the archbishop of Salizburg (Eberhard II) in 1240 as evidence.[12] He contended that the reign of the saints will not be on the earth but in heaven.[13]

---

[9] *Ibid.*, p. 126 ff.
[10] *Ibid.*, pp. 168, 169.
[11] William Guild, *Anti-Christ Pointed and Painted Out,* p. 6.
[12] Guild, *The Sealed Book Opened. Or, A Cleer Explication of the Prophecies of the Revelation,* pp. 149, 173.
[13] *Ibid.*, p. 309.

VI. Heylyn Expresses General Longing for Antichrist's End

PETER HEYLYN, or Heylin (1600-1662), theologian and historian, author of some fifty works, was born at Burford, Oxfordshire, and educated at Oxford. About 1631 he became chaplain to Charles I, but was ejected by the Republicans because of his High Church partisanship. In a sermon preached in 1661, on the ten virgins, he stressed the nearness of the end, from Daniel 7.[14] To this he added these signs: *"The Nations are shaking: the Devil is roaring: the Turks are falling: envy is boiling: the Papists are raging: the Elect are crying.* To which we may add: *The Virgins* ["Protestants"] *are sleeping"*—and all this before the approaching "Downfal of *Babylon."* Therefore he urged preparation for the coming storm and tribulation.

VII. More Sustains Historical School Against Innovation

HENRY MORE (1614-1687), nonconformist educator and philosopher, was born at Grantham, of Calvinist parents, and from childhood took a deep interest in questions of theology. Having studied Greek and Latin at Eton, and having completed his education at Christ's College, Cambridge, in 1639, with an M.A., he thenceforth lived almost entirely within the walls of Christ's College. A man of profound learning, he was a distinguished religious leader.

More refused all preferments, including the mastership of Christ's College, the deanery of Christ's Church, the provostship of Trinity College, Dublin, the deanery of St. Patrick's, and two bishoprics. He believed he could do God greater service in private than in public station. He loved music, shrank from theological disputes, and was author of numerous works, chief among which were: *A Modest Enquiry Into the Mystery of Iniquity* (1664); *An Exposition of the Seven Epistles to the Seven Churches* (1672); *Apocalypsis Apocalypseos, or the Revelation of St. John the Divine Unveiled* (1680); and *A Plain and Con-*

---

[14] Peter Heylyn, *A Sermon Preached in the Collegiate Church of St. Peter in Westminster,* pp. 8, 9.

*tinued Exposition of the Several Prophecies or Divine Visions
of the Prophet Daniel* (1681). Between 1672 and 1675 he translated his English works into Latin.

1. DENIES PROPHETIC "ABSURDITIES" PERMEATING PROTES-
TANTISM.—More refuted the "follies" and "absurdities" of both
Ribera's Futurist and Grotius' Preterist interpretations, and sustained Mede and the Historical system with its papal Antichrist
and year-day principle on the prophetic periods, a millennium
yet future, and a literal resurrection.[15] Denying that the Little
Horn of Daniel 7 is Antiochus, and insisting that it symbolized
the Papacy, More said:

> "These things are so plain that nothing can be plainer. Wherefore
> the *little Horn* in the Seventh Chapter is a part of the *Roman* Empire,
> a Power there whose Reign cannot be circumscribed within the Compass
> of *Three Years and a half,* but these Years must be resolved into 1260
> Days, and these 1260 Days into so many Years, or no Sense can be made
> of the Prophesie." [16]

2. CLEAR ON PAPAL ANTICHRIST AND YEAR-DAY.—In his
exposition of Daniel he gives the standard historical interpretation of Daniel 2 and 7, with Rome the fourth kingdom divided
into ten kingdoms. The Little Horn is the Papacy, with blasphemous claims, which is similarly portrayed in Revelation 13
and 17.[17] The 490 years of Daniel 9 were *"cut out"* for the Jews.[18]
And the power of Daniel 11:37, 38 is the same Antichrist that
Paul describes in 2 Thessalonians 2, with the Turk indicated
in the last few verses as the king of the north coming to his end.[19]

VIII. Broughton Rebuked for Reviving Porphyry Theory

Notice should be taken of HUGH BROUGHTON (1549-1612),
who in the first part of the seventeenth century revived the early
Porphyry theory of confining the third kingdom to Alexander
in person, and reserving the fourth for the Legidae and Seleu-

[15] Henry More, *A Modest Enquiry Into the Mystery of Iniquity,* book 2, chaps. 1-3, 7-10;
An Antidote Against Idolatry, book 5, chaps. 15, 16; book 6, chap. 1, in *The Theological Works
of Henry More.*
[16] *Ibid.,* book 5, chap. 15, p. 120.
[17] More, *A Plain and Continued Exposition of . . . the Prophet Daniel,* pp. 4-54.
[18] *Ibid.,* p. 105.
[19] *Ibid.,* pp. 203-215.

cidae—from among which he chose eleven kings, the last of whom was Antiochus Epiphanes as the Little Horn. Acceptance of this view, in Porphyry's time, was confined to a few writers in the East—Jacob of Nisibis, Ephraim the Syrian, and Polychronius. This concept lay largely dormant until, in 1590, Broughton discovered it in the long-lost work of Polychronius (c. 430), and soon blended his own extravagances with this Porphyrian scheme of the kingdoms and the horns.[20]

Both in his *Daniel With a Brief Explication* and in his *A Revelation of the Holy Apocalyps* (1610) Broughton had expounded the fourth beast as divided Macedon. Thus:

"The Beare had but one head: the Lyon one: & the fourth beast: the parted Macedonians but one: that beast is not named, because it was the same nation with the former but is distinguished from the former by ten hornes or kings, five Ptolemies and five Seleucj or Antiochi, that vexed Iudah." [21]

Broughton declared that it was Antiochus, as the Little Horn, who spoke the "great things" and "raged against the temple properly three yeares and an half," and brought in the Papacy as the two-horned beast of Revelation 13. But, like others, he began the thousand years back in the early centuries.[22]

Broughton's commentaries, in turn, fell into the poetic hands of Ben Jonson,[23] the dramatist, who satirized the conflict over the fourth beast in one of his leading plays, and fastened responsibility for reviving the Seleucid theory of the fourth empire squarely upon Broughton. The general familiarity of contemporary playgoers with the specifications of Daniel 2 and 7 is evident by the dialogue between Dol and Mammon in *The Alchemist* (1610), where, citing Broughton's position, Jonson has his characters use sketchy expressions like "after Alexander's death," "the two that stood, Seleuc', and Ptolemy," "made up the two legs, and the fourth beast," "Gog-iron-leg and South-iron-leg," "then Gog-horned," "then Egypt-clay-leg and Gog-

---

[20] Charles Maitland, *op. cit.*, pp. 428, 429. See Volume I of *Prophetic Faith* for a fuller discussion of Polychronius.
[21] Hugh Broughton, *A Revelation of the Holy Apocalyps*, p. 26.
[22] *Ibid.*, pp. 26, 27, 34, 35.
[23] BEN JONSON (1573-1637), friend of Shakespeare and writer of many plays, is buried in Westminster Abbey.

clay-leg," "last link of the fourth chain." [24] Then Face enters, and discussion centers on how the rabbis differ from Broughton concerning the fourth beast—that it is Rome and not divided Greece—and Dol says:

> "And the force
> Of King Abaddon, and the beast of Cittim:
> Which Rabbi David Kimchi, Onkelos,
> And Aben Ezra do interpret Rome."

Then comes this telltale colloquy:

> "*Face.* How did you put her [Rome] into 't?
> "*Mam.* Alas! I talked
> Of a fifth monarchy I would erect.
> With the philosopher's stone, by chance, and she
> Falls on the other four straight.
> "*Face.* Out of Broughton!
> I told you so. Slid, stop her mouth." [25]

The significance of such general familiarity with the prophecies as to allow or warrant such terms and expressions, and any understanding of the controversy stirred up by Broughton, should not be overlooked. These were days of universal interest in, and familiarity with, the prophecies.

IX. Positions of Fifth Monarchy Expositors

The Reformation had to resist a differing but false chiliasm such as came in to afflict the early church—"a secular kingdom of the saints, set up by fire or sword, and before the resurrection." [26] Such were the wild notions of Thomas Münzer and some of the Anabaptists, the Prophets of Zwickau, the French Prophets of Dauphiny, and later, the Fifth Monarchy men who arose in the time of Cromwell and the Puritan revolt in England—all unjustifiably claiming support from the Apocalypse.

These Fifth Monarchy men were strongly represented in Cromwell's army, and looked for the establishment of his power as the commencement of a new reign of Christ on earth, in succession to the four great monarchies of prophecy. Their wild

---

[24] Ben Jonson, *The Alchemist*, Act IV, Scene 3, in his *Plays and Poems*, p. 74.
[25] *Ibid.*, p. 75.
[26] West, *op. cit.*, pp. 362, 363.

destructiveness quickly brought them into conflict with Cromwell's government, which in 1657 flung their leaders into prison, and later, in 1661, put a definite end to their insurrections. However, despite their fallacious notions as to the part they were to play in the events to occur, it might be worth while to study the prophetic interpretation of these Fifth Monarchy men. Their expositions of the prophetic symbols and the chronology of their time periods were strikingly similar to the great students of prophecy who had no connection with them—save in the Fifth Monarchy aspect and the time-setting emphasis.

They stood with Mede on the firm Scripture platform of a *future* millennium, soon to be introduced in connection with Christ's Fifth Monarchy, and in repudiation of the *past* millennium of Augustine, which had warped the thinking of mankind for thirteen centuries. Morever, the discussion of relationships between the 2300 years as inclusive of the 70 weeks, as well as of other time periods, advanced by Tillinghast and others was a distinct advance step in a progressive development, the significance of which will be increasingly apparent as we come to the beginning of the nineteenth century.

1. To Establish Kingdom by Forcible Overthrow.—The extremists among the Fifth Monarchy men believed that civil and military power were to be in the hands of the saints, and with these powers the saints were to overturn the thrones of kings and cause their kingdoms to hate the Papacy, the woman of Revelation 17, and make her desolate, and in this way would be brought about the fulfillment of Revelation 17:16.

2. Archer Affords a Sample of Exposition.—Henry Archer, preacher of All-Hallows, in London, taught that Christ and the saints would visibly possess a monarchical state and kingdom in this world. He traced the four world powers of Daniel 2, insisting that the divisions of the fourth beast could not be reunited, and made the stone kingdom the Fifth Monarchy, to be set up by Christ at His second advent in glory. Tracing the same from Daniel 7, Archer applied the Little Horn to the

"Papacie," whose 1260 year-days were drawing to a close.[27] Adding the 1260 years to A.D. 406, he arrived at 1666; then, he declared, would come the ruin of Antichrist, with the reign of Christ following, about 1700.[28] A tractate, *The Glory of Christ, and the Ruine of Antichrist Unvailed* (1647), by "T. C." (Thomas Collier, a traveling Baptist preacher from the west of England), set forth a similar position.

X. Cromwell's Clash With Fifth Monarchy Extremists

OLIVER CROMWELL (1599-1658), greatest of the Independents, formed his original army of "Ironsides" from one thousand pious, resolute men who longed to see the age of Christ's kingdom ushered in. His favorite doctrine was the second coming of Christ and the reign of His saints.[29] By 1648 the leaders and most of the officers of the army were Independents. This resulted in a definite split and controversy with the Presbyterians. In the crisis of 1649 the Rump Parliament put Charles I to death, and Cromwell took over the reins of government as lord protector of England—and in turn persecuted the Catholics and Anglicans.

A petition was once presented to the council of officers " 'by many Christian people dispersed abroad throughout the county of Norfolk, and City of Norwich,' " asking for the establishment of the Fifth Monarchy, that is, the reign of Christ and His saints, which, according to Daniel 7:27, was to supersede the four monarchies of the ancient world.[30] In 1653 Cromwell dissolved the Rump Parliament and created a new one from the Independents, who considered themselves the saints called of God to establish His kingdom. The speeches of the new Parliament were enriched with Scripture, often resembling sermons. At the opening of Parliament, Cromwell reminded the members:

"Why should we be afraid to say or think, That *this* may be the door to usher-in the Things that God has promised; which have been prophe-

---

[27] Henry Archer, *The Personall Reign of Christ Upon Earth*, pp. 7-53.
[28] *Ibid.*, pp. 47, 54.
[29] John Lord, *Beacon Lights of History*, vol. 4, p. 99.
[30] Samuel Rawson Gardiner, *History of the Commonwealth*, vol. 1, p. 29.

sied of; which He has set the hearts of His People to wait for and expect? . . . We are at the threshold. . . . And we have thought, some of us, That it is our duties to *endeavour* this way; not merely to *look* at that Prophecy in Daniel, 'And the Kingdom shall not be delivered to another people.' " [31]

In 1653 a majority of the Little Parliament set themselves, under the leadership of General Harrison, to carry out reforms, preparatory to the divine reign. These included dissolving universities, confiscating church tithes, and superseding all other laws by the laws of Moses. But this was interrupted by the resignation of Parliament. Certain preachers, however, kept teaching that Christ was setting up the Fifth Monarchy. They believed that the Spirit of prophecy had been vouchsafed to them, enabling them to see future events, and that it was Christ's design to destroy all antichristian forms.[32]

Cromwell reprimanded the monarchy men for planning to overthrow the government, particularly while the Jesuits were trying to regain favor for the pope. But they called him a usurper, whose usurpation of the government was the only hindrance to the reign of Christ. Cromwell sought to instill religious tolerance. At his right hand in this effort was the renowned Baptist poet, John Milton. The renewal of censorship by Parliament in 1643, requiring that no book, pamphlet, or paper should be henceforth printed, unless first approved and licensed by such as should be thereto appointed, occasioned Milton's great address to Parliament for freedom of the press, which reviewed the history of censorship.[33]

Cromwell also tacitly permitted the return of the Jews to England, from which they had been officially excluded for three hundred years.[34] He and his followers were responsible for a marked increase in personal piety, as well as for constitutional reforms. He is also to be given credit for bringing the cessation of the terrible Waldensian persecution of 1655.[35]

---

[31] *Oliver Cromwell's Letters and Speeches*, part 7, speech 1, p. 356 (2d pagination).
[32] John Stoughton, *Ecclesiastical History of England*, vol. 2, pp. 63-72.
[33] John Milton, *Areopagitica: A Speech for the Liberty of Unlicens'd Printing, to the Parliament of England*, in *The Works of John Milton*, vol. 4, pp. 293-354. The Westminster Assembly attempted to persuade Parliament to enforce the licensing ordinance against John Goodwin, Roger Williams, Milton, and others (*Ibid.*, notes, pp. 366, 367).
[34] See chapter eleven under Manasseh ben Israel.
[35] Discussed in Volume I of *Prophetic Faith*.

We now note leading Fifth Monarchy expositors.

XI. Tillinghast Makes 70 Weeks Part of 2300 Years

JOHN TILLINGHAST (1604-1655) was born in Sussex and educated at Cambridge, from which he received his B.A. in 1624-25. By 1636 he was serving as rector of Tarring Neville. Then he was inducted as rector of Streat (1637), and about 1643 was a frequent preacher in London. In 1650 he became an Independent and joined the newly formed church in Suffolk, being rebaptized in 1651, when he was called to work in the Yarmouth church. Several Independent churches then extended calls to him to serve as pastor, and he responded to Trunch. Tillinghast came to share the millenarian views of the Fifth Monarchy. In 1655 he went to London to remonstrate with Cromwell and to visit those of like faith who filled the prisons at that time. He died while he was in London, early in June, 1655, probably of overexcitement.

Tillinghast's millenarianism was of the spiritual rather than the militantly fanatical type. Except for his Fifth Monarchy view of the immediate coming and kingdom of Christ, he was in line with the Protestant orthodoxy of his day. Although the basis of his chronology was rather unclear, his contribution to the understanding of the prophetic periods was the principle that the 2300 years, as the longest time prophecy, included the 70 weeks, and the other year-day prophetic periods—the 1260, 1290, and 1335 years.

1. THE FOUR MONARCHIES AND THE FIFTH.—In the visions of Daniel 2 and 7 Tillinghast sees the kingdoms of Babylon, Persia, Greece, and Rome, the last of which as the Little Horn includes the mixed civil-religious empire of the contemporary kingdoms of Christendom under the long domination of the papal Beast or Antichrist.[36] He expects the imminent end of the dominion of this power at the close of the 42 months of treading the Holy City underfoot, of the 1260 days of the woman hiding

---

[36] John Tillinghast, *Knowledge of the Times*, pp. 315-322, 64, 65.

in the wilderness, the time, times, and a half of the Beast, and the wearing of sackcloth by the Two Witnesses [37] (Christ's true "Magisterial and Ministerial" power); [38] and before long the Stone—the Fifth Monarchy, the visible kingdom of Christ and the saints—is to destroy the Antichristian kingdoms and fill the whole earth. [39] But there is to be an interval between this and the final destruction of the Beast and the scarlet woman (Antichrist's ecclesiastical and civil power). [40]

The prophecies concerning Antichrist, he contends, cannot be applied to the Turk, but to the Papacy. But he says that when the Jews again become God's people, after the 1290 days, the term Antichrist may be equally applied to the Turks, for the Jews, restored to Palestine, become the king of the south (Daniel 11:40 ff.), and "push at the *Turk* and Pope both," who combine as king of the north, and are destroyed, as they besiege Jerusalem, by the coming of Christ. [41]

2. THE 1260 AND 1290 YEARS.—Tillinghast says that the days and months are not natural, but "Prophetical," and that the 42 months are the 1260 days, "making up but one and the same number of years." [42] The 1260 days (also the three and a half times and the 42 months) he runs from A.D. 396, when *"the Civil power of the* Roman *Empire began to go to decay,"* to 1656. [43] He begins the 1290 days in A.D. 366 (which he assigns to the emperor Julian) and ends them at the same time as the 1260, with the beginning of the Jews' deliverance, "at the end of Antichrist's Reign," in 1656, [44] differing thus from Mede, Alsted. and Archer.

3. 1335 YEARS END WITH 2300.—He begins the 1335 years, like the 1290, at A.D. 366, which he identifies as the date of "the taking away of the daily sacrifice, and setting up of the abomination"; and he ends the 1335 with the 2300 at 1701—the end of the age and the beginning of Christ's personal reign on earth for a thousand years. [45]

---

[37] *Ibid.*, pp. 16-19.   [38] *Ibid.*, sig. A₄r.   [39] *Ibid.*, A₅r-A₈r.
[40] *Ibid.*, pp. 15, 16, 20.   [41] *Ibid.*, pp. 69, 70, 74, 76.
[42] *Ibid.*, pp. 23, 27.   [43] *Ibid.*, pp. 56, 97.
[44] *Ibid.*, pp. 22, 97, 129, 130.   [45] *Ibid.*, pp. 129, 130, 306.

4. THE SEVENTY WEEKS INEXACT.—He ends the 70 weeks at the cross, but makes the period only 486 years, disregarding the latter part of the seventieth week.[46] Having decided, on exegetical grounds, that the going forth of the commandment was in the twentieth year of Artaxerxes Mnemon, he contends that there must be 486 years between that year and A.D. 34, although this *"account will superabound the account of all Historians,"* because he is "bound to account as many years betwixt time and time as *Daniel* doth, though Human Writers will not allow it." [47] He frequently contends with Mede, but he does not seem to be familiar with his contemporary, Ussher, and seems to disregard the more exact chronology available in his day.

5. 2300 YEARS INCLUDE 70 WEEKS.—The 2300 days cannot be literal days applied to Antiochus, but signify 2300 "years compleat," he asserts, from *"the beginning of the Persian Monarchy, viz.* in that year the Scripture calls the first of *Cyrus."* [48] He extends them to 1701, ushering in Christ's personal coming, the Jews' redemption, the final overthrow of the Beast and the Turk, the binding up of the Dragon, the destruction of the Fourth Monarchy, the thousand-year reign of the saints on earth.[49]

Tillinghast proffers a new principle for the understanding of Daniel 8 and 9; namely, that the 2300 years of Daniel 8:14 are a larger period embracing the 70 weeks of years as a lesser period.

"This seventy weeks is a lesser Epock comprehended within the greater of two thousand and three hundred years, consisting of four hundred and ninety dayes; for seventy weeks being reduced into dayes, amount to the aforesaid number, which according to the Prophetical way of speaking is so many years, *viz.* four hundred and ninety years." [50]

Tillinghast thus reasserts the application of the year-day principle to the 2300 years, advanced by Nicholas of Cusa [51] two centuries earlier, but largely neglected since; and his inclusive

---

[46] *Ibid.*, pp. 217, 306. [47] *Ibid.*, pp. 278-281.
[48] *Ibid.*, pp. 127, 132-134. [49] *Ibid.*, pp. 305-307.
[50] Tillinghast, *Knowledge of the Times*, pp. 152, 153. (Reproduced in facsimile on p. 310.)
[51] See chapter 5 of this volume.

principle marks another step toward the later interpretation of the 2300 years as beginning synchronously with the 70 weeks, a principle which plays a vital part nearly two centuries later in the renewed investigation of the prophecies in the early nineteenth century. At that time it formed an axiomatic part of the exposition on three continents.[52]

XII. Goodwin—Turkish and Papal Periods and Future Millennium

THOMAS GOODWIN (1600-1680), celebrated Nonconformist, was born at Norfolk and educated at Cambridge. In 1625 he was preacher at the university, and in 1632 he became vicar of Trinity Church, Cambridge. Resigning his preferments when he did not conform to all his bishop's ideas, he withdrew from the university and went to Holland in 1639. Returning to London shortly afterward, he became minister of an Independent congregation, and in 1643 was elected to the Westminster Assembly.

One of the most distinguished leaders of the Congregational party, and author of numerous theological works, he became head of Magdalen College, Oxford, in 1650, and was vice-chancelor of the university. He was one of Cromwell's most intimate advisers, attending him on his deathbed. When he was commissioner for the inventory of the Westminster Assembly, he and John Owen drew up the Amended Westminster Confession of 1658.

1. 1335 YEARS END AT RESURRECTION AND MILLENNIUM.— Goodwin taught that the 1335 years would reach to the end, which would be introduced by the resurrection, with the thousand-year reign of Christ following. He called the Apocalypse the story of Christ's kingdom, and believed the Lord would reign with His saints in a world especially prepared, called "the world to come."

2. TURKISH WOE DATED FROM 1453 TO 1849.—Goodwin followed Mede in his general scheme of the Apocalypse, and ex-

---

[52] See *Prophetic Faith*, Volumes III and IV.

pounded the fallen star of the fifth trumpet as Mohammed, with the locusts as the Saracens. The period of the sixth trumpet he held to be that of the Turk, dated from 1453, and "being one year, one month, one day, and one hour (prophetically three hundred and ninety-six years), would not thus be fulfilled according to the latter date, until 1849." [53]

3. PROTESTANTS MAKING IMAGE TO PAPACY.—The dragon of Revelation 12 he expounded as pagan Rome, and the Beast of Revelation 13, as the description of "the Pope and his Antichristian church," [54] whereas certain Protestants tend to set up an "image of old Popery in a Protestant reformed way." [55] The 1260 year-days, he said, may end "about A.D. 1866." [56] For a time Goodwin believed not only that the Fifth Monarchy would be that of Christ and His saints, but that it would come "after the Fourth Monarchy is destroy'd by the Sword of the Saints, the followers of the Lamb." [57] Goodwin also felt that France was the predicted "tenth part" of papal Christendom, or the ten kingdoms comprising the city of Babylon that would fall away from support of the Papacy as is noted on page 724. This appeared in one of his printed sermons, not in his regular works.

XIII. Homes and Overton Base Millennium on Resurrection

NATHANIEL HOMES, OR HOLMES (1599-1678), Puritan divine, was born in Wiltshire and educated at Magdalen College, Oxford, and Exeter College, from which he received the degrees of B.A., M.A., B.D., and D.D., between 1620 and 1637. He was said to have been highly skilled in Hebrew. He was made rector of St. Mary Staining as a Calvinist, but he changed his views, becoming a millenarian and having some of the beliefs of the Fifth Monarchy. He then served several Independent congregations, but upon enforcement of the Act of Conformity (1662), Homes gave up his cure.

---

[53] Thomas Goodwin, *Expositions . . . on the Book of Revelation*, p. 596. (The 396 is calculated as 365 + 30 + 1.)
[54] *Ibid.*, pp. 596, 597.
[55] *Ibid.*, p. 602.
[56] *Ibid.*, p. 603.
[57] Goodwin, *A Sermon of the Fifth Monarchy*, title page.

His sermon on 2 Peter 3:13, *The New World; or, The New Reformed Church* (1641), expresses his clear premillennial views. His most noted work is *The Resurrection Revealed: or the Dawning of the Day-Star.* This stresses the millennium as still in the future, and is based on the literal resurrection of the dead saints and the change of the living, the coming destruction of the world by fire, with Antichrist as the archenemy of the truth of the coming glorious estate. Peter Sterry [58] makes this introduction:

"Like a peece of rich coine, it hath been long buried in the earth, but of late dayes digged up againe; it begins to grow bright with handling, and to passe current with great numbers of Saints, and learned men of great Authority. As the same Star at several seasons is the Evening-star, setting immediately after the Sunne, and the Morning-star shining immediately before it; So was this Truth the Evening-star to the first coming of Christ, and giving of the Spirit, setting together with the glory of that Day, in a night of Antichristianisme: Now it appears againe in our Times, as a Morning star, to that blessed Day of the second effusion of the Spirit, and the second appearance of our Saviour in the glory of the Father." [59]

OVERTON CONTENDS RESURRECTION BEGINNING OF IMMORTALITY.—The literal resurrection concept is increasingly stressed in the treatise by Richard Overton (fl. 1646) titled *Man Wholly Mortal.* The full explanation of the title page will suffice to give its scope:

"A Treatise wherein 'T is proved, both Theologically and Philosophically, That as *whole man sinned,* so *whole man died;* contrary to that common distinction of *Soul and Body:* And that the *present* going of the Soul into *heaven* or *hell,* is a meer *Fiction:* And that at the *Resurrection* is the beginning of our *immortality;* and then actual *Condemnation* and *Salvation,* and not before.

"With Doubts and Objections answered and resolved, both by *Scripture* and *Reason;* discovering the multitude of *Blasphemies* and *Absurdities* that arise from the Fancie of the *Soul.*

"Also, divers other Mysteries; as, of Heaven, Hell, the extent of the Resurrection, the New Creation, *etc.* opened, and presented to the tryal of better Judgments." [60]

---

[58] PETER STERRY (d. 1672), Cromwell's chaplain, was a decided premillennialist. Educated at Cambridge, and one of the Westminster divines, he became preacher to the Council of State in 1649. He preached weekly to Cromwell and frequently before the House of Lords and House of Commons. He also had responsibility for certifying the fitness of ministers.

[59] Peter Sterry, Introduction, in Nathaniel Homes, *The Resurrection Revealed.*

[60] Richard Overton, *Man Wholly Mortal,* title page. Signed "R.O.," but identified in the British Museum Catalogue.

XIV. Sherwin Focuses Attention on 2300-Year Terminus at Millennium

WILLIAM SHERWIN (1607-1687?), receiving appointment to a "sequestered living" at Wallington, in Hertfordshire in 1645, was also a lecturer on the prophecies at Baldock, but was believed to have been ejected in 1662. Most of Sherwin's works were published anonymously, and sometimes were reprinted with different titles. From 1671 onward Sherwin's attention was often focused on the 2300 days as prophecy's longest and most decisive period. Sherwin stressed the 2300 days as years reaching to the "blessed time," which period he calculated would end in 1700, synchronizing with the terminus of the 1335 years.[61] In his heavy style he emphasized two personal comings of Christ in convergence with the millennium—one at the beginning and the other after a little space at its close. Sherwin quotes frequently from Mede and other expositors.

1. PROPHETIC PERIODS OF TURK AND PAPACY.—Sherwin holds the first four trumpets to be the incursion of the barbarians upon Rome, with the fifth and sixth woe trumpets as the Saracens and the Turks, in the seventh and thirteenth centuries respectively—the Saracens rising about A.D. 600, and the "Turks day, hour, moneth and year, *viz.* 396. years [365 + 30 + 1], Rev. 9. 11. being the sixth Trumpet, or second Woe beginning about *An. Dom.* 1300." [62] The 1260 days of the Witnesses are likewise years, the same as the Beast's "contemporary" three and a half times of persecution of the church, which period, Sherwin believes, reaches to 1666 years after the ascension of Christ.[63]

2. SEVENTH TRUMP BEGINS MILLENNIAL PERIOD.—Like Mede, Sherwin begins the thousand years with the seventh trumpet and the New Jerusalem state, "for which time Satan is

---

[61] William Sherwin, *The Scheme of God's Eternal Great Design* (large sheet), recto (following the title page *The True News*), and *A Brief but Weighty Appendix to the Scheme,* pp. 8-10, in his *The Saints First Revealed and Covenanted Mercies;* Sherwin, *The Times of Restitution,* p. 57.
[62] Sherwin, *A Scheme of the Whole Book of the Revelation of Jesus Christ,* pp. 2, 8, in *The Saints First Revealed;* Sherwin, *A Brief but Weighty Appendix,* p. 10.
[63] Sherwin, *A Brief but Weighty Appendix,* p. 10; Sherwin, *An Additional Supplement to the Irenicon,* p. 19, in *The Saints First Revealed;* Sherwin, *The Times of Restitution,* pp. 58, 59, 76, 77.

bound, and Christ reigneth personally with his Saints," and the New Jerusalem being the "mother citie of Christ's said Kingdom." Then, at the close of the thousand years Satan will be loosed for "his last most provoking and desperate attempt." Then will come the resurrection of the wicked and the general judgment.[64]

3. CHRIST'S KINGDOM TO SUPERSEDE EARTHLY KINGDOMS.— Concerning the prophecies of Daniel, Sherwin believes that the fourth, or Roman, monarchy of Daniel 2, and its divisions, will be followed by "Christ's Kingdome on earth." [65] He holds, however, that the "stone" of Daniel 2 began first to be set up at the first advent, which was some sixteen hundred years past, in the time of the last, or Roman, empire. (This, he believes, will be superseded by the thousand-year reign of Christ with the saints.) In the paralleling prophecy of Daniel 7, with the Little Horn as the pope's reign for "1260 days of years," the saints are at last to possess the everlasting kingdom.[66] In Daniel 8 the 2300 days are years, and in chapter 9 the 70 weeks are 490 years,[67] with the latter part of Daniel 11 paralleling the sixth, or Turkish woe, trumpet,[68] which Turkish power shall come to his end without help at the same time as the Papacy.

4. ENDS 1290 IN A.D. 1656; 1335 IN 1700.—The "1290 dayes of years" of Daniel 12 Sherwin dates from Julian the Apostate, ending them in 1656, while the 1335 years, from the taking away of the daily, extend forty-five years longer to the "standing up of Michael" in 1700—in which period would come a "gathering" of the pope with his armies for the last great conflict.[69] This, he states, is the same as the pope's rise for one hour with the ten crowned horns.[70] The 2300 years he here dates "from the Captivity of *Babylon* to Christs appearance, leading to the end of 1700 years since Christs birth." [71]

---

[64] Sherwin, *A Scheme of the Whole Book of the Revelation*, p. 3.
[65] Sherwin, *An Additional Supplement*, p. 2.
[66] *Ibid.*, pp. 3, 4.   [67] *Ibid.*, pp. 4, 5.
[68] *Ibid.*, pp. 19, 37.
[69] *Ibid.*, pp. 21, 40; Sherwin, *A Brief but Weighty Appendix*, p. 8; Sherwin, *The Times of Restitution*, p. 57.
[70] Sherwin, *An Additional Supplement*, p. 40.
[71] Sherwin, *The Times of Restitution*, p. 74.

5. TURKISH PERIOD AS YET NOT EXPIRED.—In *The Prodo-mus,* Sherwin speaks of the "2300 years of the four Gentil Monarchies," [72] and states that the first of the trumpets "took away the very seat and mansion of the Dragon, that he that till that time Letted might be taken out of the way, that Antichrist might come in his room, as the Apostle Paul foretold, 2 Thess. 2.7." [73] Of the relationship between the papal 1260 years and the Mohammedan fifth and sixth trumpets, we read:

"But from the time Antichrists forty two months begun, to the end of the sixth Trumpet, or the second Woe, we have the fourth Trumpet proceeding in the ruine of the Empire in the West, and the fifth Trumpet is the beginning of the ruine of it in the East, *ch.* 10. by the Mahumitan Saracens, those Locusts out of the bottumless pit, hurting all but the green fruits sealed to be preserved from that first Woe Trumpet, as was foreshewed, *ch.* 7. who destroyed one half of the Eastern Empire; and after the other Mahumitan Locusts under the sixth Trumpet, namely the Turks took away the other part of the Eastern Empire, whose 396 years are not yet expired, till the end of the sixth Trumpet, and the second Woe, as is said, *Rev.* 11.14. which is to be at the rising again, and the ascension of the Witnesses." [74]

6. NATIONS TO TURN UPON AND DESTROY PAPACY.—Revelation 13, Sherwin says, describes the "false Apostolical Church, (from about *Anno.* 406)," the first beast being its political capacity and the second its "Ecclesiastical capacity," this dual capacity "making up one body with his Clergy." [75] His reign is the period of the Two Witnesses in sackcloth when the "Pastours" fed the woman "in her Wilderness-condition 1260 days of years." [76] This apostasy is the same as the "false Antichristian Apostatical Church of spiritual *Babylon,*" bewildering the nations, with the plagues poured upon her and the kings hating and desolating her—at last to be overthrown by Christ in the Armageddon battle. [77] Then the binding of Satan and the reign of Christ and His saints are "Synchronals," and all the seals, trumpets, and vials end in the thousand years.

7. RESURRECTION AT ADVENT INTRODUCES MILLENNIUM.—Sherwin asserts that "the great Personal appearance of the Com-

---

[72] Sherwin, *The Prodromus* (1674), "To the Reader," in *The Saints First Revealed.*
[73] Sherwin, *The Irenicon, or Peaceable Consideration of Christ's Peaceful Kingdom,* p. 17, in *The Saints First Revealed.*
[74] *Ibid.*
[76] *Ibid.*
[75] *Ibid.,* p. 18.
[77] *Ibid.,* pp. 18, 19.

ing of Christ, now shortly approaches." [78] This, he declares, will be visible and glorious, in the clouds of heaven, with the trump of God to raise the righteous dead and to catch up the righteous living, who will pass through a momentous change. The introductory statement reads:

"*A plain and evident Discovery of the two Personal Comings of CHRIST, one at the beginning of his Thousand years Reign, REV. 20.4, with his holy and blessed raised Saints in the New Jerusalem, come down from God out of Heaven, REV. 21. the other after the little space when the Thousand years are ended.*" [79]

---

[78] Sherwin, *The Everlasting Gospel* (second part, *A Plain and Evident Discovery*), p. 1, in *The Saints First Revealed.*
[79] *Ibid.*

CHAPTER TWENTY-SIX

Approaching End
of Papal Period Predated

The English had grown weary of the power exercised first by the Puritans and Presbyterians (1640-1648), and then by the Independents under Cromwell (1648-1658). So the English Revolution of 1688 took place. This marked the cessation of papal power in England. James II, last Catholic king of England, abandoned his throne and fled, and the victories of William of Orange in Ireland and on the Continent followed, terminated in the Treaty of Ryswick, in 1697. Encouraged by the English Revolution, the Vaudois refugees in Switzerland began their "glorious return" in 1689, under the leadership of Henry Arnaud, cutting their way through opposition back to their native Piedmontese valleys.[1]

Among expositors the approaching end of the papal period was stressed increasingly. HANSERD KNOLLYS, in his *An Exposition of the Eleventh Chapter of the Revelation* (1679), insisting on the year-day principle for all portrayals of the 1260 days, remarks that there is variation among expositors as to their beginning and ending, but says time and fulfillment will demonstrate the certainty of their ending.[2] Then will come the advent. And the clear note of the second advent as the hope of the church rings through these various writings, as witness the touchingly significant signature "By a *Lover* of the *Second*

[1] Guinness, *History Unveiling Prophecy*, pp. 153, 154.
[2] Hanserd Knollys, *An Exposition of the Eleventh Chapter of the Revelation*, pp. 12, 13.

Coming of our Lord *JESUS,* and of the *Blessed Myllenium"* to the work, *A Modest Inquiry Into the Meaning of the Revelations, in a Letter to All Such as Wait for the Kingdom of Christ.*

I. Beverley Extends 2300 From Persia to Advent

During the reign of William III (1688-1703) toleration was granted all Protestant dissenters in Great Britain, which resulted in liberty and tranquillity. Between 1687 and 1701 THOMAS BEVERLEY (fl. 1670-1701)—concerning whom we know little except that he was an Independent minister—published more than a score of short treatises, many with curious titles, emphasizing the approaching end of time.[3] Note their scope. In a tract, *Command of God to His People to Come Out of Babylon, Revel. 18.4. Demonstrated to Mean the Coming Out of the Present Papal Rome* (1688), the ending of the 1260 years is anticipated about 1697—within "Nine or Ten Years." Another, his *Pattern of the Divine Temple,* argued further that the temple in heaven, or New Jerusalem, would be seen opened "at the end of the 1260 *Days* of the *Apostasie,* 1697. That there may be a Daily Preparation in Conformity to it, until It *comes down from Heaven* at the end of the 2300 *Evens. Morns.* Dan. 8:14 and of the 1335 *Days,* Dan. 12.12 at 1772." [4]

A survey of Beverley's writings discloses that his *Kingdom of Jesus Christ Entering Its Succession at 1697 According to a Calendar of Time* (1689) was based on "the Four Monarchies, and by the Time, Times, Half Time Allowed to the Papacy, and the Ten Kingdoms; as the Last State of the Roman, or Fourth Monarchy Then Ending; Given in *Daniel* and Expounded by the *Revelation,* in Consent With All History." [5] His *Prophetical History of the Reformation; or the Reformation to be Reformd; in . . . 1697* (1689) dealt with "the 1260 Years Allowed to the *Beastian Kingdom,* as to the *Roman Apostasie:*

[3] Forty separate entries in British Museum Catalogue.
[4] Thomas Beverley, *The Pattern of the Divine Temple,* title page.
[5] Beverley, *The Kingdom of Jesus Christ,* title page.

(Which Because It Is to End in 1697. Must Therefore Have Begun 437.)" [6]

Beverley's *An Appeal Most Humble, Yet Most Earnestly, by the Coming of Our Lord Jesus Christ, and Our Gathering Together Unto Him,* treats on "the Thousand Years State of the Saints; the Dead Raised First, and of the Living; the Remaining Chang'd in It, and of the Wicked-Dead-Raised." [7] His *The Universal Christian Doctrine of the Day of Judgment: Applied to the Doctrine of the Thousand Years Kingdom of Christ* (1691) attempts to show that Christ's "Judging the *Quick* and the *Dead;* and His Appearing, and His Kingdom, Which, Seeing It Must Have Some Duration, the Scripture 1000 Years, Is on Great Proof Preferr'd." [8]

Becoming a prisoner in Fleet in 1691 through some miscarriage of justice, Beverley protested, in his Petition to the High Court, that he was no fanatic, but simply that God had summoned his mind to "contemplate that great prophesied frame and scheme of the grand futurities." Set free, Beverley dedicated his *Catechism of the Kingdom of Our Lord Jesus Christ in the Thousand Years* (1690) to all Christians and bishops. In this he asserts that the resurrected saints will "sit on thrones and judge angels and the world with Christ; and reign with Him a thousand years, not *upon* earth, but *over* the earth." [9] Beverley's preaching and writing had a telling effect upon inquiring minds. When Konrad Brüssken, court-chaplain at Offenbach, Germany, on a visit to England, had heard Beverley preach, he was impressed, after a personal interview, to translate and publish a portion of his *Scripture-Line of Time,*[10] which he did.

1. 2300 YEARS FROM PERSIA TO CHRIST'S KINGDOM.—The consideration of the none-too-well-understood 2300 year-days, initiated by Cusa in the fifteenth century, and now carried forward in the seventeenth by Tillinghast, Nigrinus, and Sherwin,

---

[6] Beverley, *The Prophetical History of the Reformation,* title page.
[7] Beverley, *An Appeal Most Humble,* title page.
[8] Beverley, *The Universal Christian Doctrine of the Day of Judgment,* title page.
[9] Beverley, *Catechism of the Kingdom of Our Lord Jesus Christ,* p. 2.
[10] *Herrn Thomas Beverley's . . . Zeit-Register,* translated by Konrad Brüssken.

is again taken up by Beverley. He believed the period to extend from Cyrus, the typical restorer of Jerusalem, on to Christ, with the New Jerusalem as the great antitype. This concept he developed in *A Scripture-Line of Time* (1684). Beverley's basic "Proposition" is significantly this:

"That the 2300 *Days* are a definitive *Line of Time,* from the beginning of the *Persian Monarchy,* to the very End of the *Monarchies,* and till the Supream Monarchy of Christ." [11]

Repeating, like the strain of a song, but with different words in the several stanzas, Beverley declares that the 2300 years extend from Persia to the literal New Jerusalem, from Persia to the breaking of Antichrist without hand, from Persia to the stone cut out of the mountain without hand, from Persia to the kingdom of Christ, from Persia to the fall of Mystical Babylon, from Persia to the night of earth's monarchies and the morning of Christ's kingdom, from Persia to the cleansing of the sanctuary.[12] Two citations must suffice:

"The *Vision* of the 2300 *Evenings* and *Mornings,* dates most exactly, and precisely the Time from the very Beginning of the *Persian Monarchy* or the *First of Cyrus* to the *cleansing of the Sanctuary,* at the *new Jerusalem,* and the *breaking of Antichrist without hand,* or by the *stone cut out of the Mountains without hand,* at the Kingdom of Christ, *Dan.* 8. 14. 25." [13]

"Those 2300 are not the *Gauge of the daily Sacrifice taken away,* but of the whole *Vision,* from the *Persian* through the *Grecian,* to the end of the *Roman, Antichristian Monarchy,* and the *Kingdom of Christ.*" [14]

This was a sharper, clearer concept than any had had before his day.

2. YEAR-DAY IS PROPHETICAL "CYPHER OF TIME."—Ten times the 2300 years is called "the vision," [15] though the year-day prophetical "Cypher of Time" is applied to all time periods, on the basis of Ezekiel 4:6.[16] And "the vision" is declared to embrace in its 2300-year span the whole Antichristian apostasy until the end, and to constitute the longest time period, while the eve-

[11] Beverley, *A Scripture-Line of Time* (part 1), "An Explication of Daniel's Grand Line of Time, or of His 2300 Evenings and Mornings," p. 6.
[12] *Ibid.,* pp. 1-18.
[13] *Ibid.,* p. 1.   [14] *Ibid.,* p. 14.
[15] *Ibid.,* p. 15.   [16] *Ibid.,* p. 1.

ning-mornings are interpreted as signifying full prophetic days, and thus complete years in fulfillment.[17]

3. RELATES 70 WEEKS, 1335, AND 2300.—Beverley insists that the "Daily" or "continual" is not to be limited to the Jewish sacrifices, as the word is "applicable either to sacrifice, or service and worship in general," and to "tyrannous *taking away the daily Worship of the Saints.*" [18] He applies the expression to the latter.

Beverley gives a graph which includes the 70 weeks, but without much explanation. Though he fails to integrate the 70 weeks with the 2300 days, Beverley makes this important statement, which in reality dates them with the 70 weeks. The intent seems obvious:

"Every *Vision of Daniel's* except the following *Vision* of the seventy Weeks, which has the high and noble Subject of the *Death* and *Resurrection* of our Lord *Jesus Christ* . . . runs expressly to the *last* End and *Kingdom of Christ.*" [19]

"The 70 Weeks are dated from the *going forth of the Word;* the 1335, from the *taking away of the daily:* And in the *Apocalyptick Prophecy* we shall find some certain Epoch of each numeral Line: but there being no *Epoch* to these 2300 *Ev. Mor.* but the general *Epoch* of the *Vision* one and the same, as we shall find, with the *seventy Weeks,* That must be the *Epoch.*" [20]

4. TERMINATES 1260 YEARS IN 1697.—In the second part of his *Scripture-Line of Time,* Beverley holds that the forty-two months, or 1260 days, *"measur'd by the exactest Rules* of Prophecy, *and found . . . to begin at the Cessation of the* Christian Western Empire," will end in 1697.[21] The papal Man of Sin is sitting in the temple, and the 1260 days are the same as the three and a half times of the woman, and of the Witnesses. Of this period, which had not yet ended, Beverley declares:

"The 1260 *Days of Mourning,* and of the *Church in the Wilderness* are not yet run out, the *Beast* is yet in Power; the *Tenthliness* [tenth part] *of the City is not yet fallen, the Kingdom of Christ is not yet proclaimed.*" [22]

---

[17] *Ibid.,* pp. 14, 15.   [18] *Ibid.,* pp. 15-17.
[19] *Ibid.,* p. 12.   [20] *Ibid.,* p. 16.
[21] *Ibid.* (part 2), "Of the Great Line of Prophetical Time . . . The 1260 Days of the Witnesses," p. 90.
[22] *Ibid.,* p. 29.

This "tenth part of the City" will be referred to with increasing frequency by other writers.

5. RELATIONSHIP OF FOUR MAJOR PERIODS.—Of the relationship of the 1260, 1290, 1335, and 2300 years, Beverley leaves this thought-provoking but not too clear record:

"The 1260 Days immediately following in Account, as concurrent with the 42 Months, shew, They are taken out of the 2300 *Morn.* and confirm this to be the Time of the Daily taken away, because the *Daily taken away* is the Character of the first Point of Time to the *Twelve hundred ninety;* of which Twelve hundred, sixty must needs be part, seeing they go on to 1335 at the end of all; and so many cannot be found in the 2300, which is the Date of the whole *Vision of the daily taken away,* or in so great a Number, but in these 1290, joyn'd with 1335." [23]

6. SARACEN LOCUSTS AND TURKISH WOE PERIOD.—In section 10, on the woe trumpets, Beverley states that the "Mahometan Saracens are the Locusts" of the fifth trumpet, with their five months.[24] And the sixth trumpet includes the Turks and the taking of Constantinople in connection with the hour, day, month, and year period, and involving the year 1453.[25]

7. LIVING IN LAST PORTION OF DANIEL 2.—Beverley holds the standard view of the four monarchies, as the stream of time, on to the end of time, with the kingdom of Christ now near at hand:

"It is true, The *Four,* as *Universal Monarchies,* are together the great *Canale* of Time, till the *glorious Kingdom of Christ,* whatever great States or Kingdoms were coexistent with them or any of them at any Time, or have arisen since, do not mingle with this stream, which runs strait on to this end. . . . And because of this real substantial *calendar* of Time in these *Monarchies,* the first Act of *Christ's Kingdom* is recorded by the *Apostle Paul* to be the *putting down all Rule, Authority,* and *Power,* referring especially to these *four Monarchies,* the great Emblem of such Rule and Power; viz. when the *Kingdoms of this World become the Kingdoms of the Lord* and of his *Christ,* Rev. 11.15. Then all this *Calendar* of *Rule* and *Power* is at an *end.*" [26]

8. SEVEN CHURCHES COVER CHRISTIAN ERA.—The seven churches of Revelation cover the Christian Era, "*contemporizing with whole* Apocalyptick Time."

[23] *Ibid.,* p. 46.   [24] *Ibid.,* pp. 21, 124 ff.   [25] *Ibid.,* pp. 21, 22, 149 ff.
[26] Beverley, *A Scripture-Line of Time* (part 1), "2300 Evenings and Mornings," p. 10.

"It is certain, There hath been a *Christian Church* in all Ages from the *Resurrection of* Christ, to this Day, and shall be to the *New Jerusalem,* and to the *End of the World."* [27]

As to the "true church in the wilderness" of the Dark Ages, Beverley observes:

"But now the Church was indeed out of view, by the *Apostasie,* introduc'd by the *Gentiles* the *Beasts people* under the other *Beast;* so that the *False Church* hid the *True,* as in a *wilderness:* The *Gentiles* crowded the *True worshippers* into a *clos'd Temple, The Daily was taken away; The witnesses* were in *Sackcloth,* where then could the True Church be seen? All was scatter'd, no Body of a Church appear'd, but the Antichristian; to this state things grew more and more under the Regnancy of the Beast till the Woman was fled from the *Serpent* himself." [28]

The Turkish horseman is set forth as the king of the north, soon coming to his end, with the Jews as the kings of the east.[29] At that very time the Mohammedan king of the south, symbolized by the Saracens, or locusts, and the king of the north, the Turkish horsemen, according to the military language of Daniel's time, will go into action.

II. Burnet—Earth Renovated by Fire at Millennium's Close

THOMAS BURNET (1635-1715), English divine and author, was born in Yorkshire and educated at Christ's College, Cambridge, becoming master of Charter House in 1685. He resisted the attempt of James II to make a Roman Catholic pensioner of Charter House, and after the Revolution of 1688 became chaplain to William III. In 1680 he wrote *Telluris Theoria Sacra* (Sacred Theory of the Earth), with an English version enlarged and modified in 1684. Six editions were printed by 1726. Burnet maintained that the earth, like a giant egg, had its internal shell crushed at the deluge, and that the entombed waters burst out, the fragments of the shell forming the mountains, and at the same catastrophe the equator was diverted from its original coincidence with the ecliptic.[30]

---

[27] *Ibid.,* pp. 62, 63.
[28] Beverley, *A Scripture-Line of Time* (part 2), "The 1260 Days of the Witnesses," p. 79.
[29] Beverley, *A Scripture-Line of Time* (part 1), "2300 Evenings and Mornings," pp. 43-45.
[30] *Dictionary of National Biography,* vol. 3, pp. 408, 409.

Burnet contended that the earth must undergo a thorough change by fire before the great consummation, when the saints are to dwell upon it. Paradise will be restored on the renewed earth, after it had run its predicted course—creation week being the type. Placing the millennium on earth before the great renovation, had brought discredit upon it. In vain had men dated it from the days of Christ or Constantine. Moreover, only those changed by the literal first resurrection will have part in it. That great day is near, he urged, as the sun of time is near its setting.

1. New Earth Out of Deluge of Fire.—Burnet stated that the "Sex-millennial" duration of the world (the 6,000-year theory) was very much insisted upon by the Christian fathers, and he added: "Which yet I believe is not so much for the bare Authority of the tradition, as because they thought it was founded in the History of the *Six days Creation* and the *Sabbath* succeeding." [31] He cited nearly a score of early fathers in its behalf. Burnet firmly believed in a coming deluge of fire that will overflow this earth like the deluge of old, not destroying it, but only its form and fashion. Burnet contended that the millennium was the soul of the Apocalypse, the key that unlocked it. After this great conflagration the earth will be renewed, and in that new earth the saints will dwell forever. [32]

2. All Prophecies Terminated by Millennium.—Passing to the Bible prophecy phase, and alluding to the fifth kingdom in Daniel's prophecies, Burnet declares that the seven seals, seven trumpets, and seven vials all reach to the millennium and first resurrection, and "all terminate upon that great period." [33] But of the time periods—the forty-two months of the treading of the Holy City, the 1260 days of the witnesses, the woman in the wilderness for 1260 days, the forty-two months' war by the beast—he says, "They do not reach to the end of the world." [34]

---

[31] Thomas Burnet, *The Theory of the Earth*, vol. 2, pp. 34, 35.
[32] *Ibid.*, pp. 35, 36. Burnet takes due notice of the mistaken expectation of some around A.D. 500, but explains that this was based on the Septuagint Chronology, which is about 1500 years longer than the Hebrew.
[33] *Ibid.*, pp. 37, 154.   [34] *Ibid.*, p. 37.

Burnet then attacks the evasions, inconsistencies, and absurdities of the spiritual or allegorical resurrection,[35] advocated by the Preterist Hammond and others—contending that if the first resurrection is spiritual, the second must be also.[36]

3. Renovation of Earth Dropped Under Apostasy.— Burnet next shows, by documentation, that the doctrine of the premillennial second advent was commonly held by the primitive church up to Nicea,[37] and that in the first and second centuries the literal resurrection of the flesh was understood. Jerome, in the fifth century, was an open enemy,[38] and in the Christianization of the empire after Constantine, and with the Augustinian theory of the then-present millennium, the doctrine of the renovation of the earth was dropped. The doctrine has always been displeasing to Rome. And how could it be otherwise when she contends that Christ is already reigning through His vicar the pope.[39] On this he adds:

"The *Apocalypse* of St. John does suppose the true Church under the hardship and persecution, more or less for the greatest part of the Christian Ages. . . . But the Church of Rome hath been in prosperity and greatness, and the commanding Church in Christendom, for so long or longer, and hath rul'd the Nations with a Rod of Iron. . . . And the *Millennium* being properly a reward and triumph for those that come out of Persecution, such as have liv'd always in pomp and prosperity can pretend to no share in it or benefit by it." [40]

4. Various Signs of Approaching End.—Because of the coming storm, with all the volcanoes of earth ready to burst forth, there will be precursors to herald its tragic fate. Christ plainly foretold these—celestial signs in sun, moon, and stars, and terrestrial omens on earth and sea.[41] Earthquakes will increase, the sun and moon will be darkened, and there will be a giant meteoric shower—the last celestial sign.

III. Cressener—Antichrist's 1260 Years From Justinian to *c.* 1800

Drue Cressener (*c.* 1638-1718), native of Suffolk, was educated at Christ's College and Pembroke Hall, Cambridge, re-

---

[35] *Ibid.*, pp. 152-154. [36] *Ibid.*, p. 154. [37] *Ibid.*, vol. 2, pp. 173-176.
[38] *Ibid.*, p. 180. [39] *Ibid.*, p. 182. [40] *Ibid.*
[41] *Ibid.*, vol. 2, pp. 91 ff.

ceiving the degrees of B.A., M.A., B.D., D.D., between 1661 and 1708. Church of England vicar successively of Framlingham, Suffolk, and Wearisly (1677), and Junior Proctor of the University of Cambridge (1678), in 1700 he was given the vicarage of Soham, and was prebend of the cathedral church of Ely.

During the reigns of Charles II and James II a mighty change had come over the clergy in the Church of England. The religion of Rome not only had become fashionable at court but was the religion, secretly or openly, of the reigning kings. In addition, the sufferings of the episcopal clergy during the fifteen-year ascendancy of Cromwell and the Puritans had tended to make them look upon the Puritans as their chief enemy. As a result, they came to look upon Catholicism with less disfavor, and even with a desire for fellowship and union.

This could not but have a modifying effect upon men like Hammond, and upon the exposition of prophecy that concerned the Church of Rome. Cressener wrote strongly against this change, saying that in the time of James I one doctrine of the church was the explicit charge that the Roman church is Babylon and Antichrist. In fact, it was such a cardinal article of faith that even the king wrote upon it,[42] as is noted elsewhere.

1. URGES REVIVAL OF REFORMATION POSITIONS.—In 1689, the year of the coronation of William of Orange as William III, Cressener published his *The Judgments of God upon the Roman Catholick Church,* dedicated to the king, urging the speedy revival of the Reformation. In 1690 he put forth *A Demonstration of the First Principles of the Protestant Applications of the Apocalypse,* dedicated to Queen Mary. In this Cressener stresses the fact that the *Homilies,* approved by the Articles of Faith, charge that the Church of Rome is Babylon.[43] He well answers the contentions of Alcazar and of Bellarmine, showing that Babylon is neither Rome pagan, as it existed under the old

---

[42] Elliott, *op. cit.,* vol. 4, pp. 499, 500; Guinness, *History Unveiling Prophecy,* pp. 179, 180.

[43] He cites the third part of *Homily Against Idolatry,* and the sixth part of the *Homily Against Rebellion;* he also cites Jewell, Abbot, Whitgift, Andrewes, Bilson, Morton, and Hooker. For the *Homilies,* see pp. 424, 425.

A

DEMONSTRATION

OF THE

FIRST PRINCIPLES

OF THE

Proteſtant Applications

OF THE

APOCALYPSE.

Together with the Conſent of the Ancients
Concerning the Fourth Beaſt in the 7th of *Daniel*,
and The Beaſt in the *Revelations*.

By *DRUE CRESSENER*, D.D.

LONDON:
Printed for *Thomas Cockerill*, at the *Three Legs* in the
Poultrey over-againſt *Stocks-Market*. MDCXC.

THE

JUDGMENTS of GOD

UPON THE

Roman-Catholick Church,

FROM

Its firſt Rigid Laws for Univerſal Conformity
to it, unto its laſt End.

WITH

A Proſpect of theſe near approaching Revolutions,

244
PART I.

Conſeq. 3.

The Judgments of God
This would very much confirm that which is elſe-
where endeavoured to be demonſtrated, That,

The time of the Beaſt muſt be at an end about the
year 1800.

For the three laſt Vials according to the Example of
thoſe before them, are to continue each of them about
fourty years, and they are yet to come. But the laſt
of them may be ſuppoſed to finiſh its buſineſs in a ſhorter
time, and then the end of the Beaſt muſt be ſome year
that time.

By *DRUE CRESSENER*, D.D.

LONDON,
Printed for *Richard Chiſwell*, at the *Roſe* and *Crown*
in St. *Paul's Church-Yard*, MDCLXXXIX.

APPENDIX.

THE

CONSENT

OF THE

ANCIENTS

Concerning the

Fourth Beaſt

In the VIIth Chapter of *Daniel*;

AND

THE BEAST

In the *REVELATIONS*.

LONDON:
Printed for *Thomas Cockerill*, at the *Three Legs* in the
Poultrey over-againſt *Stocks-Market*. MDCXC.

APPENDIX.

" ſhall be divided, *declaring what were thoſe Ten Horns that were*
" *ſeen by Daniel.* —— And again, —— *Daniel* did diligently fore-
" ſignifie the dividing and ſharing of the fourth Kingdom at
" the end of it, by the *Ten Toes* of the Image. —— And ſpeaking
" of the Number of the Beaſt, which he had before made to be
" a time of the fourth Beaſt in *Daniel*, cap. 24. he pitches upon
" *Latinos,* —— Becauſe *his Kingdom*, ſays he, *hath that Name*;
which we know muſt be the *Roman* Monarchy. —— And *Irenæus's*
Teſtimony may paſs for the Senſe of the moſt judicious of the
Fathers at that time; for he appears to have been the moſt di-
ligent Searcher into the Book of *Daniel*, and the *Revelations*, of
any of the firſt Ages. See lib. 5. contra Hæreſ. cap. 24. H: had
enquired of thoſe that had ſeen St. *John* face to face, and of thoſe that
had given the cleareſt Reaſons for their Expoſitions of the Revelations,
and had examined all the ancient and approved Copies of it.   Lib. 3.

CENTURY III.

Tertullian, preſently after *Irenæus*, in his Book againſt the
Jews, after having quoted *Daniel* cap. 2. about the Second Coming of Chriſt, adds: —— *Of which Second Coming, the ſame*
Daniel alſo ſays, And behold one like the Son of Man, coming in the
Clouds of Heaven; which is in the 7th chapter of *Daniel*, and
muſt therefore by him be expected to come at the end of the
Fourth Beaſt there, of which he ſays, in his Apology to the Emperour, —— *The Diviſion of the* Roman *Empire into Ten Kings, brings*
on Antichriſt. —— According to the deſcription of the riſing up of the
11th Horn of the 4th Beaſt after the Ten. And again ſays, That *that*
time of Antichriſt was at hand; which therefore muſt be in the
time of the *Roman* Kingdom, and ſo muſt the Fourth Beaſt, to
which that Horn did belong, be the ſame Kingdom.
Hippolytus Martyr. de conſummatione Mundi.] —— " I bring, ſays
" *he,* the teſtimony of a Witneſs worthy to be believed, the
" Prophet *Daniel*, cap. 2, & cap. 7. *where he ſays*, That the firſt
" *Beaſt ſignifies the* Babylonian *Kingdom, and the fourth ſignifies the*
" *Romans.* And then, about the Ten Horns, —— Who are theſe,
" but the Empire of the *Romans*, and the Little Horn, Antichriſt?
" —— *And a little before,* —— " This Prophecy will perſuade all
" that have any judgment in them, That the four Kingdoms in
" the 2d and 7th chapter, are the ſame.
St. Cyprian

CRESSENER FORECASTS BLOW TO STRIKE PAPACY ABOUT 1800
A Full Century Before the French Revolution Drue Cressener Defended Protestantism Against
Catholic Charges of Novelty and Modern Invention (Upper Left and Lower Two); At the Same
Time He Began the 1260 Years With Justinian, and Anticipated Their End About 1800 (Upper
Right, With Insert)

pagan emperors, nor Rome paganized at the end of the world, as Ribera and Malvenda would have it. But it is Rome papal, as existent from the sixth century onward to their own time. He argues that it is Rome, idolatrous and antichristian, under its seventh, or papal, head, which receives the deadly wound but is revived, and which exists all through the time of the Witnesses, from the breakup of the old empire into ten kingdoms, until Christ's second coming to take the kingdom.[44]

2. First to Date 1260 From Justinian Era.—Cressener's book lives up to its title, incontrovertibly establishing the papal identity of Babylon in a series of connected propositions. Moreover, Cressener sets forth Justinian's era as the beginning point of the 1260 years—with their ending as about A.D. 1800. This is apparently the first clear declaration of its kind. Truly, Cressener's book was a major contribution. His heavily documented and monumental *Demonstration,* written to prove "that the church of Rome" is the "Great Enemy of God's Church," submits this challenge at the very outset:

> "*Where-ever was there an Empire since the writing of the Prophecy, but that of the* Roman *Church, that was so* Universal *for 1260 years together, as to have all that dwell upon Earth, Peoples, and Multitudes, and Nations, and Tongues, to worship it? What Ruling Power, but that, so* Ancient, *as to have the* Blood of Prophets, and Saints, and of all that were slain upon Earth, *of that kind for that space of time, to* be found in it? What Rule but that, had ever so long a duration in the World, as to continue set upon an Hill, much less upon seven Hills, for so great a space of time, or so as to answer the whole length of the time of the* Saracen, and Turkish *Empires in the Two first Woes?"* [45]

3. Seated in Temple as Head of Church.—Though Cressener disposes of the quibbles and arguments of the Futurists Ribera, Malvenda, and Bellarmine, and the Preterist contentions of Alcazar, Grotius, and Hammond, his chief effort is positive and constructive. Thus in book 4, chapter 7, Cressener shows in detail how Justinian laid the firm foundation of a gen-

---

[44] Elliott, *op. cit.,* vol. 4, p. 500.
[45] Drue Cressener, *A Demonstration of the First Principles of the Protestant Applications of the Apocalypse,* Preface, pp. viii, ix.

eral uniformity in religion—detailing the episode of Justinian's imperial edict concerning the faith, challenged by some, with appeal for submission to Pope John, as "Head of all churches." And this, Cressener establishes, was inserted in the Civil Code, with penalties for infraction, and constitutes the beginning.[46] Thus was the pope legally seated in the temple of God. All this is fully documented from the sources.[47]

4. Unanimous Consent for Rome as Fourth Empire.— Coupled to this work is an Appendix—"The Consent of the Ancients Concerning the Fourth Beast in the VIIth Chapter of Daniel; and the Beast in the Revelations." This impressive aggregation of outstanding witnesses from each of the early centuries, in chronological order, shows the virtually unanimous consent of the fathers, which was the requirement of the Council of Trent, session 4, that the fourth empire was that of the Romans.[48] For the Jews the general statement of Abravanel is cited, that "it appears to have been the *common* Tradition of the learned *Jews*"; [49] and for the fathers Jerome is quoted, thus:

> "*Let us therefore affirm that which* ALL ECCLESIASTICAL WRIT-ERS *have delivered to us, That about the end of the World, when the Kingdom of the* Romans *is to be destroyed, there shall be Ten Kings, who shall divide the* Roman *Empire amongst themselves; and there shall arise after them an eleventh small King.*" [50]

5. Protestants Not Innovators but Restorers.—The second point of early agreement, as presented by Cressener, was that the Antichrist would emerge after, and out of, these ten divisions of Rome.[51] Century by century Cressener traverses the years, summoning the testimony of Justin Martyr, on through Tertullian, Hippolytus, Cyprian, Methodius, Victorinus, Chrysostom, Sulpicius, Jerome, Theodoret, and lesser lights up to Gregory I—with the full reference for each.[52] Thus wavering Protestants and determined Catholics were confronted with evi-

---

[46] *Ibid.*, pp. 306, 307.   [47] *Ibid.*, pp. 313-317.
[48] Cressener, *A Demonstration of the First Principles*, Appendix, p. 4.
[49] *Ibid.*, p. 5.   [50] *Ibid.*   [51] *Ibid.*, p. 6.
[52] These witnesses are all considered in *Prophetic Faith*, Volume I.

dence that the Protestant Historical School of interpretation was truly the interpretation of the early church, and that instead of being innovators, true Protestants had simply revived and carried forward the primitive positions, whereas the Catholic counterinterpreters and those who follow them had departed from the early faith. This was stressed effectively.

6. PROPOSITIONS COMPASS PROPHETIC PICTURE OF ROME.— This remarkable book is unique in its structure, its chapters being based on a series of twenty-five propositions, with their rules and corollaries, as well as certain observations and queries.[53] Thus Proposition 1 reads: "Babylon, *Revelat. 17, is the City of* Rome *in an Antichristian and Idolatrous Domination,*" with the corollary to Proposition 3 reading, "Babylon *cannot* be Rome-Pagan." Proposition 6 contends that "the Beast all over the 17th Chapter, is *the Beast in the time of its last Ruling Head.*" Proposition 8 says, "*The Term of the Beast all over the 13th chapter does signify the First Beast, shown V. 1,* with the second beast as the false prophet, meaning the hierarchy in Proposition 9, Corollary 1, and Proposition 25, Corollary 2. Proposition 10 asserts, "*The Seven Heads, the Ten Horns in the 13th and 17th Chapters, are the same thing*"—the beasts are one and the same. Proposition 11 avers, "*The Judgment of the Dead,* Rev. 11.18, *is the General Judgment at Christ's Second Coming,*" and the Beast that killed the Witnesses the same as the Beast in the other chapters.

7. TIME OF LITTLE HORN NOT YET EXPIRED.—Proposition 14 declares that "*the Kingdom of the Son of Man,* Dan. 7, *is the Second Coming of Christ in glory.*" Then Proposition 15 and its corollaries add that the fourth kingdom of Daniel 7 is the same as the Beast of Revelation, and the last head of the Beast of Revelation is the same as the Little Horn of the fourth beast of Daniel 7—with the time not beginning until after the division of the Roman Empire into ten kingdoms, and its time not yet ended.

---

[53] Cressener, *A Demonstration of the First Principles*, "A Table of Propositions."

8. SEVEN HEADS AND TEN HORNS DISCUSSED.—Proposition 17 states that the Beast of Revelation, with seven heads, comprehends the rule of the Romans in the *"Successive Changes of the Government of that Nation; The Ten Horns, the division' of the Empire into so many several Sovereignties."* And note these: Proposition 19 says that the sixth king is the imperial government of Rome in the time of St. John. And Proposition 22, brings the sixth head, or western empire, to an end by "the Heruli and Gothish *Kings of* Italy." Proposition 23 and Corollaries 1-3, contend that the forty-two months of the Beast are the same as the 1260 days of the Two Witnesses in sackcloth—which period represents the *"True Church of Christ during all the time of the Reign of the Beast."* In Propositions 24 and 25 Cressener asserts that the Beast is the secular power of the Roman church in idolatrous union, and in Corollary 1 to the last proposition he avers that the second beast is *"a succession of Ecclesiastical Persons, having Supream Power in Ecclesiastical Affairs."*

9. FIFTH AND SIXTH TRUMPETS: SARACENS AND TURKS.— In his first book, *The Judgments of God Upon the Roman Catholick Church,* Cressener submits a series of cumulative theorems [54] built around the seven trumpets, seals, and vials. Theorem 1 reads, *"The Woe of the seventh Trumpet destroys the power of the Beast."* Theorem 5 says, *"The whole time of the Beast is within the time of the Trumpets,"* and under "Consequences," that *"the Kingdom of the Beast is an Object of the Trumpets."* And Theorem 19, Consequence 1 adds, *"The Saracens and Turks are the Woes of the fifth and sixth Trumpet."*

10. TENTH PART OF CITY ONE OF TEN KINGDOMS.—The significant series of statements that follows is built upon by other eighteenth-century writers who followed Cressener. Theorem 21: *"The Streets of the great City* [Rev. 11] *are the Dominions of* Babylon." Consequence 1: *"The tenth part of the City is the*

---

[54] Cressener, *The Judgments of God Upon the Roman Catholick Church,* "Suppositions and Theorems," unpaged, following preface.

tenth part of the Dominions of Babylon." Consequence 2: *"The tenth part of the City is one of the ten Kingdoms, that were given to the Beast."* Theorem 25: *"The killing the Witnesses is the fiercest Persecution of the Church, and about the end of the Beast."* Theorem 27: *"The three days and an half,* ver. 9, *are at least three years and a half."* Theorem 28: *"The Dead Bodies of the Witnesses,* ver. 9, *cannot signifie literally";* therefore (Consequence 2), *"the killing of the Witnesses cannot be a general Massacre of the Protestants,"* but must be (Theorem 29) the *"Suppression of the True Religion, in* all *parts of the Jurisdiction of the Beast."* Theorem 32: *"The Resurrection of the Witnesses is the reviving of the true Religion in* some *of the Dominions of the Roman Church where it has been suppressed"*—and this resurrection "is not yet past."

11. HOUR OF JUDGMENT FOLLOWS REFORMATION.—Theorems 34 and 35 inform us that the preaching of the everlasting gospel to every nation is the preaching of a general reformation of the Roman church in the time of the Beast, and the hour of God's judgment is "about the same time with the preaching of the everlasting Gospel." Theorems 36 and 37 add that the hour of God's judgment is the beginning of the final ruin of the Roman church, and cannot come before the Reformation. Theorem 44 continues, "The seven Vials are an orderly succession of Judgments upon the Beast to bring him to his ruine." Theorem 47: "The Hour of God's Judgments is the beginning of the time of the seven Vials"—though Cressener thought the vials were in the process of being poured out. Then, after Theorem 51, is Cressener's Consequence 4: "The time of the Beast does end about the Year 1800." And Theorems 53 to 60 connect the events of the last vials with the third woe or seventh trumpet.

12. 1260 YEARS FROM JUSTINIAN TO 1800.—After discussing the evidences for fixing the beginning date for "the 1260 years of the Reign of the Beast," Cressener draws the really epochal conclusion (written in 1689, be it remembered):

"The first appearance of the Beast was at *Justinians* recovery of the *Western* Empire, from which time to about the year 1800 will be about 1260 years." [55]

Cressener rejects the earlier dates for the beginning because they came before the breakup of Rome, and thus would not fit the prophetic specification that the divisions arise first, and then the Little Horn appear among them.[56] Pressing the point that the city of Rome must be wrested from Gothic control by Justinian in order to date the period, he then follows with this second remarkable statement, even more precise:

"For if the first time of the Beast was at *Justinians* recovery of the City of *Rome,* then must not it end till a little before the year 1800." [57]

13. SIXTH TRUMPET WOE PERIOD ENDS C. 1800.—Tying this terminus of the 1260 years to the fast-expiring series of woe trumpets, Cressener incidentally alludes to the "period" of the sixth trumpet (the day, month, and year) in these words:

"For the third Woe ends not before the last end of the Beast; It is that, which ruines him; And by its character of coming quickly after the second Woe, and by the known end of the period of the second Woe (from the day, month, and year assigned for the continuance of it) the third Woe must necessarily begin within a very few years; Wherefore the continuance of the execution of that Woe upon the Beast must be about an 100 years, that is, from a few years hence to about the year 1800." [58]

That was the really remarkable forecast of Cressener.

IV. 1335 Years End Simultaneously With 2300

A remarkable pamphlet called *The Mysteries of God Finished: or an Essay toward the Opening of the Mystery of the Mystical Numbers* deals with Daniel's 2300 Days, 1290, and 1335, with the time of the witnesses prophecy of 1260 days, and the Beasts reign of 42 months. It, too, is based on the clear premise of "A Day for a year, as is usual in Scripture." [59] Of the 2300, the author states:

"I conceive this Number of 2300 was headed, or doth take its beginning from the Year God translated the *Babylonian Monarchy* to the *Medes*

---

[55] *Ibid.,* p. 309.   [56] *Ibid.,* p. 310.
[57] *Ibid.,* p. 312.   [58] *Ibid.,* p. 313.
[59] *The Mysteries of God Finished,* p. 6.

and *Persians,* which was the third and last of *Belshazzar's* Reign, who was also the last of the *Babylonian Kings."* [60]

Several reasons are set forth for fixing upon the year the vision was given as the initial year. The 2300 years are therefore dated, by the writer, from the first year of Medo-Persia on to the "Churches Deliverance." [61] Moreover, the relationship of the 1335 years is described thus: "Whenever these 1335 Years begin, they end with the 2300 Years also." [62] Of the 1260 and 1290 year-days, this unknown writer likewise says, "Though they may end together, yet they cannot begin together." [63] This would imply that he meant to begin the 1290 years in 395 with the terminus in 1685, for he reckons the 1260 years of the papal Antichrist as beginning in 425 and ending in 1685. [64]

The 2300 years nearly cover the time of Daniel's four monarchies— perhaps from 601 B.C.—which would lead possibly to 1699, when the reign of Antichrist would be accomplished. [65] Thus, he adds, the 1260, 1290, and 1335 all fall within the sweep of the 2300 years. Thus the 2300 years are increasingly a subject of earnest study.

---

[60] *Ibid.*
[61] *Ibid.,* p. 7.
[62] *Ibid.,* p. 30.
[63] *Ibid.*
[64] *Ibid.,* p. 31.
[65] *Ibid.,* p. 33.

CHAPTER TWENTY SEVEN

German Expositors
Parallel British Positions

I. Few Advances Among Post-Reformation German Expositors

In Germany the force of the Reformation seemed to have spent itself. With some notable exceptions there were few expositors of importance in the first half of the seventeenth century,[1] and virtually no advance in prophetic exposition. In fact, in various cases there was less clarity than in the platform of the Reformation founders, and even retrenchment. Because these expositors clung to the idea that the writings of Luther and his immediate associates were almost canonical, their commentaries more and more lost the vigor of new light and life.

The Reformation had lost itself, regrettably, in a maze of theological contentions. Every important center had its own formula, built about its party creed. Thus the Post-Reformation period became conspicuously an age of creeds, symbols, confessions, and rigid theological systems. Note them: The Articles of Marburg (1529); the Confession of Augsburg (1530); the Wittenberg Concord (1536); the Articles of Schmalkald (1537); the Second Helvetian Confession (1566); the Lutheran Formula Concordiae (1580); the Thirty-Nine Articles (1562); the canons of the Synod of Dort (Reformed) (1619); and the Westminster Confession (1647). As a consequence of this bondage to formulas, it was also the age of huge books of theology, which were

---

[1] Farrar, *op. cit.*, p. 380, note 3.

issued in astonishing numbers—their dogmatic inflexibility leading to sharp contention. Papal infallibility had been set aside, but in their perplexity of opinion men yearned for some arbitrary authority.

1. WAR OF PENS SUPPLANTED BY WAR OF SWORD.—In Germany the war of pens over the prophecies concerning Antichrist had given way to one of the most destructive religious wars the world had ever witnessed—the Thirty Years' War, from 1618 to 1648. It changed Germany into a desert and was interspersed by decimating pestilences. In this armed conflict between the Evangelical Union and the Catholic League, the former succumbed. Finally, in October, 1648, the Peace of Westphalia was signed, despite the fulminations of the papal nuncio. The pope denounced it in a bull, and declared it null and void. But in it Catholic, Calvinistic, and Lutheran princes agreed to tolerate each other—within carefully defined limits. Suppressed evangelical truth had at last emerged from papal dominance.

2. FUTURE MILLENNIUM SUPPLANTS PAST MILLENNIUM.—In the Lutheran and Reformed groups the question of the future millennium, rather than a millennium already in the past, was a delicate and divisive issue. The abbot Joachim of the twelfth century, returning to the view of the early fathers, had given the cue. The Anabaptists and later Protestants followed him. CELLARIUS (Borrhaus) of Basel (1551) had emphasized that the faithful martyrs were chiliasts, and COLLADON of Lausanne (1581) had interpreted Revelation 20 in the same way. In the seventeenth century this position became slowly but increasingly general, though not without opposition, among the Protestants of Continental Europe. It was the last of the abandoned factors emphasized in the early church to be restored.

As in England, the proximity of the end became a matter of common belief and expression. The nearer the ominous year A.D. 1666 approached, or other similar years of expectation—when some were looking for the ruin of Rome—the more did calendars and prognostications affirm that the great catastrophe impended. But regardless of the differences in time the destruction of Antichrist at the advent was clear and sure.[2]

II. Minor German Expositors Parallel English Positions

1. NICOLAI INTERPRETS 1260 YEARS.—PHILIPP NICOLAI (1556-1608) was the son of a pastor and received a good education, partly in Wittenberg. In 1590 he wrote his doctor's thesis, *De duobus antichristis primaris Mahumete et Romano pontifice.* He was a talented poet, and has given many hymns and songs to the Protestant church in Germany. Some of them have found their way into the English-speaking world, as, "O Morning Star! How Fair and Bright," and "Wake, Oh, Awake! for Night Is Flying."

When the Spaniards approached Unna, his parish, he had to flee, because he had not minced words to make clear his convictions about papal Rome. In 1601 he became the chief pastor of St. Catharine in Hamburg.[3]

In his *History of the Kingdom of God,* although not setting a definite year for the coming of the end, he held that all prophetic time comes to an end in 1670—the 1260 years, the 1335 days or years, the time period given in Revelation 9, the time mentioned in Ezekiel 38 and 39, as well as the 1600 furlongs of Revelation 14. The conjectures which led him to this year (1670) are rather difficult to follow. Nevertheless, his book, which appeared in Latin in 1597 and was translated and printed in German in 1626, found a widespread circulation and evoked a number of commentaries. His antipathy against the Calvinists was so strong that he considered them to be the locusts coming out of the smoke of the pit. (Revelation 9.)[4]

---

[2] Annotated Bibles in Swedish (1622) and Danish appear in the seventeenth century, with illustrative cuts on Daniel and the Apocalypse from Luther's Bible appearing—in this way essentially the same witness was carried in Scandinavia relative to the prophecies common in Central Europe. Annotations parallel the leading Continental Lutheran positions.

[3] *Allgemeine Deutsche Biographie,* art. "Ph. Nicolai."

[4] Daniel Springinsguten, *Kurtzer Begriff und Theologische Prüffung der . . . Zeit-Rechnung des . . . Herrn D. Philippi Nicolai,* pp. 11 ff; Caspar Heunisch, *Wolgegründtes Bedencken über dem . . . 1670. Jahr. Ob in demselben der Jüngste Tag zu hoffen oder zu vermuthen sey?* sig. A₂r.

2. PISCATOR BOUNDS MILLENNIUM WITH RESURRECTION.—

JOHANNES PISCATOR (1546-1625), Calvinist Heidelberg professor, was born in Strassburg, where he received his education and finally became professor at the university. Later, in 1574, he was appointed professor of philosophy at Heidelberg; but, being inclined toward Calvinism, which was anathema in Heidelberg, he was compelled to relinquish his chair (1577). After several years of wandering he was called to be the head of the department of theology in the newly founded school of higher learning in Herborn. Here the most fruitful period of his life began. The commentaries on practically all the books of the Bible which he edited were of the best in his time and are esteemed even in our day.[5] Great numbers of students came to him from all the Reformed countries. During the long conflict of pen and sword prominent evangelical theologians faced the charge of heresy for discussing a still future millennium as a source of hope for that dark hour. Piscator refers Revelation 20 to the future triumphant church, when wars would cease during the thousand years, the martyrs being resurrected at the beginning and reigning in heaven during the millennium. This period is followed by the deliverance of the saints from the final persecution, the destruction of the wicked, and the great executive judgment after the general resurrection at its close.[6]

3. PROLAEUS WOULD HAVE KINGS EXPEL BABYLON.—On

July 10, 1631, ANDREAS PROLAEUS, or Proel, pastor of Stolp, Pomerania, dedicated his thirty lectures on Babylon, Revelation 17, 18, and 19, to Gustav Adolph, king of the Swedes, Goths, and Wends. He tells in his preface how the Swedish Evangelical Church had the seal of the Lord on her forehead and had withstood the swarm of locusts from the abyss, which flew over the sea to damage and to devour the flourishing and blossoming Swedish church. But the church stood firm and confessed her faith in the Word of God and the Lamb. Therefore God delivered her from the detestable vermin.

---

[5] *Allgemeine Deutsche Biographie,* art. "Johannes Piscator."
[6] Johannes Piscator, *Commentarii in Omnes Libros Novi Testamenti,* p. 568.

"And your majesty being descended from such a noble, pope-hating house and being given by the Lord such a kind-hearted disposition, you do not only hate the whore, but even much more love the lamb Jesus Christ and keep his commandments. And in these two things combined really lies perfection. . . . There are many who are full of hatred against the whore but they are also void of love to the Lamb and that, of course, is of no avail." [7]

4. HOFMANN ENDS FIFTH SEAL IN 1747.—In 1667 MAT-THAEUS HOFMANN (b. Schweidnitz, Silesia), in his *Chronotaxis Apocalyptica* (Chronology of the Apocalypse), asserted that no vision extends beyond the seventh trumpet, which reaches to the end of the world—the seven churches, seals, and trumpets paralleling each other. He looked for the fifth era to end in 1747.[8]

III. Gerhard—Noted Lutheran Theologian

JOHANNES GERHARD (1582-1637) is considered an example and a master of Lutheran orthodoxy, the most important and most influential teacher of his time. He had the rare gift of combining a polemic scholarship with a serene piety and devotion. His spiritual father was Johann Arndt, the author of *Das wahre Christentum* (True Christianity). After receiving his doctor's degree in Jena (1605), he was called by the duke of Coburg to be superintendent of Heldburg. The duke tried to keep him in his domains by all means, but in 1616 he left for Jena, to become a university teacher, and later became the rector of the university. With admirable skill he steered the university through the tribulations of the Thirty Years' War and kept up its standard and fame in spite of all difficulties.

His most renowned works are his *Loci Theologici* (Jena, 1610-32) and his *Confessio Catholica,* in which the evangelical and catholic doctrines are presented in a masterly way. Both were reprinted again and again. He helped in editing a popular exegesis of the Bible, and he himself prepared the books of Genesis, Daniel, and Revelation. In his *Adnotationes in Apoca-*

---

[7] Andreas Prölaeus, *Babylon. Das ist: Theologischer Schrifftmässiger Erklärung des sechsten General-Gesichtes der . . . Offenbahrung S. Johannis 17.18. 19. Capitels,* sig. A₂r-A₃v.
[8] Matthaeus Hofmann, *Chronotaxis Apocalyptica,* pp. 70, 76, 213.

lypsin he holds to the historical view of interpretation.[9] Some of his interpretations are worthy of special mention.

1. APOCALYPSE COVERS CHRISTIAN ERA.—For example, Gerhard holds that the Apocalypse deals with the church from the time of John the apostle on to the end of the world.[10] The four horsemen are expounded as Christ Himself, riding the white horse in power and victory, and carrying His bow of the gospel, whose arrows pierce the heart (signifying the preaching of the gospel by the Apostolic church); the red horse, ridden by the devil, represents wars, persecutions, and bloodshed; the black horse is famine; and the pale horse is pestilence. However, Gerhard adds a further interpretation: The horse of the church goes forth, white at first, then red under persecutions, afterward blackened by heresies, and finally pale with the hypocrisy of the bishops, until it becomes sick unto death.[11] The woman of Revelation 12, the pure church, flees into the desert and disappears. Then the Roman beast arises from the sea, on whom rides an impure woman—the Antichristian church of Revelation 17.[12]

2. SYMBOLS APPLIED TO PAPAL ROME.—The seven trumpets are applied by Gerhard to heretics of various sorts, used by the evil angels, whom God permits to be the instruments for stirring up the church. His view of the fifth trumpet is as follows: He interprets the star fallen from heaven as the Roman pope, who holds the key to the bottomless pit (the power of freeing souls from purgatory through indulgences); the smoke as the false doctrine which darkens the rays of the Sun of Righteousness; the locusts as the various orders of monks who propagate papal errors.[13] The forty-two months "contain 1260 days, that is, years," but "we cannot know exactly whence the beginning of the computation is to be started." [14] The time, times, and a half are three and a half years. If they are turned into months,

9 *Allgemeine Deutsche Biographie*, art. "Johannes Gerhard."
10 Johannes Gerhard, *Adnotationes in Apocalypsin*, Prolegomena, p. 2.
11 *Ibid.*, pp. 43-45. 12 *Ibid.*, p. 49.
13 *Ibid.*, pp. 56, 57, 63-65. 14 *Ibid.*, p. 72.

they make forty-two months; if those months are turned into days, they make 1260 days, by numbering thirty days to a month.[15] All those periods refer to the duration of the Antichristian tyranny.[16]

Gerhard understands the two beasts of Revelation to be, first, the pagan Roman Empire with its ten horns, representing ten provinces of the empire; and second, the papal kingdom with its two horns of ecclesiastical and civil power.[17] He is positive that the number of the beast is the number of the Roman pope, but offers various interpretations of the number 666, without coming to a definite conclusion. He cites its possible derivation from *Romith, Ecclesia Italika,* and *Lateinos;* also Luther's application of it to the years of duration of the pope's worldly kingdom.[18] Gerhard applies the first angel of Revelation 14 to Luther, and the second angel's message to the warning against Babylon, the kingdom of Antichrist, whose capital is Rome.[19]

3. VIEWS ON BABYLON AND THE TEN KINGS.—The woman Babylon, of Revelation 17, is also the Roman Antichristian church, scarlet with the blood of saints, riding upon the Beast of the Roman Empire, which she has subjugated.[20]

The seven mountains are the seven hills of the city of Rome. The seven kings are the successive forms of government of the empire, with the pope as the seventh, or eighth, head.[21] The ten horn-kingdoms are those which were subject to the ancient Roman Empire, namely: "1. Syria. 2. Aegyptus. 3. Asia [Minor]. 4. Graecia. 5. Africa. 6. Hispania. 7. Gallia. 8. Italia. 9. Germania. 10. Polonia," and the neighboring kingdoms. Others give a slightly different list.

4. AUGUSTINIAN MILLENNIUM.—Gerhard still follows the Augustinian theory of the millennium, placing it from about 300 to about 1300, when superstition began to increase in the

15 *Ibid.,* p. 94.
17 *Ibid.,* pp. 96, 97, 102.
19 *Ibid.,* p. 110.
21 *Ibid.,* pp. 129, 131.
16 *Ibid.,* p. 99.
18 *Ibid.,* p. 106.
20 *Ibid.,* p. 126.

world, and the orders of monks began to increase, and the Turks began to overrun the Eastern Empire.[22] He sees western and eastern Antichrists in the Papacy and Mohammedanism.[23]

IV. Helwig Finds 666 in Vicarius Filii Dei

It is always well to note the pioneer expositor on any given point. It is desirable to observe his qualifications, the soundness or weakness of his positions, and the setting and contributing factors leading to that initial conclusion. We now come to apparently the first attempt to compute the numerical values of the component Latin letters from the title *Vicarius Filii Dei* (Vicar of the Son of God), which yield the number 666, and which came increasingly to be cited, with similar 666-yielding titles, around the time of the French Revolution.

That Master Helwig, writing under the pseudonym of "Irenechoreaus," [24] was seemingly the first to compute from this particular name, is attested not only by our own researches but by the testimony of E. B. Elliott, who doubtless made the most exhaustive investigation from the sources of any of the writers on the Apocalypse of which we have knowledge. On this point he is of particular interest to us, although part of his writings are spotted with strange and peculiar notions, which led him to rather farfetched conclusions.[25]

To Elliott may be added the similar witness of Züllig in 1840,[26] and it will be desirable to find in what setting this attempt occurs, and on what basis the number is computed. Note first the one who introduces this calculation.

MASTER ANDREAS HELWIG, or Helwich (*c.* 1572-1643), of Friedland, was a teacher of the classics for twenty-seven years, and author of an Etymological Greek Dictionary and a volume on Greek Vowels and Synonymns (1602). He was rector in Berlin (1611-1614) when he wrote on the Antichrist, and was

---

[22] *Ibid.*, pp. 144-146.
[23] *Ibid.*, p. 147.
[24] Given as Helwig's pseudonym in *Preussische Staatsbibliothek*, Berlin, official catalog.
[25] Elliott, *op. cit.*, vol. 3, p. 255, note.
[26] Züllig, F. J., *Die Offenbarung Johannis*, II Theil, p. 237.

professor of poetry at the University of Rostock (1614-1616).[27]
He was invited to teach in the gymnasium [28] of the Grey Convent
in Berlin, but declined, accepting a call instead to the Gym-
nasium at Stralsund, where he continued as teacher for several
years. His specialty in language and his conspicuous ability in
Greek and Latin won him the standing of royal crown poet.[29]
In 1612, at the close of his rectorship in Berlin, he wrote his
Antichristus Romanus (Roman Antichrist).

1. COMPUTES FIFTEEN TITLES IN THREE LANGUAGES.—Helwig's *Antichristus Romanus,* with the opening heading "demonstration of the name of Antichrist, to which indeed that mystical number in Apocalypse 13, last verse, answers," cites certain
Hebrew names, such as *Romith,* which yield 666, applied by
writers to the pope. He also cites five Greek names, some reaching back to the third century, such as *Lateinos,* each similarly
yielding 666. He then cites certain Latin names, used by, or
applied by others to, the pope. These are *(a) Vicarius Filii Dei,*
(b) Ordinarius Ovilis Christi Pastor, (c) Dux Cleri, and *(d) Dic
Lux*—each likewise yielding 666.

2. COMPUTES NAME FROM EXPANDED EQUIVALENT.—A difficult problem of the church, Helwig says, concerns Antichrist.
"Has he come or not? And if he has already come, what is his
true and genuine name, prefigured by Saint John in the Apocalypse, in which is mentioned that number of triple six each,
666?" [30] Contending that Antichrist has come, and is found in
the Papacy, of which the pope is head, Helwig declares:

"Consequently, when we shall have brought forth the name of this
Antichrist by prescribed laws, everyone will at once know that as the name
of Antichrist has not been thus far disregarded, so the number in reference
to it has been too little taken note of. Without doubt, by God's help, I will
show that this is Vicarius Filii Dei." [31]

---

[27] C. G. Jöcher, *Allgemeines Gelehrten-Lexicon,* part 2, col. 1477.
[28] A liberal arts junior or preparatory college where Latin, Greek, and Hebrew were basic, in contrast to commercial or other schools.
[29] Johannes Zehlicke, *Schulschriften aus d. Provinz Pommern Commentarii de Gimnasio Grypisvaldico,* p. 46.
[30] Andreas Helwig, *Antichristus Romanus, in Proprio Suo Nomine, Numerum Illum Apoc-alypticum (DCLXVI) Continente Proditus,* sig. A₃v.
[31] *Ibid.,* sig. B₁r.

Helwig shows that the mystic name (1) must yield the required number; (2) must agree with the papal order; (3) must not be a vile name applied by enemies, but acceptable to Antichrist himself; and (4) must be one of which he can boast. Helwig takes *Vicarius Filii Dei* as an expansion or equivalent of the officially used shorter papal title *Vicarius Christi,* and shows that it conforms to these four requirements, citing Sleidanus in his *Commentariis Suis Historicis,* lib. 2, for the decretal of Aeneas Sylvias, which employs the title *Vicarius Christi* only.

3. EXPLAINS CHOICE OF VICARIUS FILII DEI.—Explaining his emphasis of *Vicarius Filii Dei,* Helwig checks it by his four rules:

"But behold this present [name] (Vicarius Filii Dei) in every way is such as is required. For first, it is a Latin name, and most exactly renders with significant letters that Apocalyptic number; then it harmonizes wholly and always with the papal order in itself (even though by hypothesis [ex hypothesi]), as no pontiff denies; then it is not offensive or vile as imposed upon him by adversaries, but is especially honorable to this very one, venerable, and formidable to others: which all the pontiffs have now already ascribed to themselves for more than 600 years (as is apparent), and do ascribe today, and wish to be ascribed: on which account they vehemently glory and boast with an execrable voice that they hold, shared as it were with the omnipotent God, the rule throughout the earth in human affairs. This [is] what, among other things (for who may investigate all the swelling words of papal bulls?), that decretal of Pope Aeneas Sylvius (who wished later to be called Pius) makes clearly evident—[that decretal] published in the year 1459 at Mantua which John Sleidan notes in his historical commentaries, vol. 2—in which he [the pope] took care that nobody should appeal from the pope to a Council because he said that, in the nature of things, nothing greater could be found above the Vicar of Christ." [32]

4. SELECTED DESPITE BELLARMINE'S OMISSION.—Helwig tells why he computes the number from *Vicarius Filii Dei,* when it is a lengthened equivalent of his official title *Vicarius Christi.*

"Wherefore, since that extended name [productum—lengthened, drawn out], *Vicarius Filii Dei,* is best adapted to the Roman Antichrist, in which truly are all the conditions [met] which Bellarmine has thus far demanded for the name of his pope. Hence that this is the true and peculiar name of the very Antichrist, as clearly is it evident from those things which we have brought out into the open, so must it surely be established." [33]

---

[32] *Ibid.,* sig. C₂r,v.   [33] *Ibid.,* sig. D₄v.

5. Asserts Pontiff Is Prophesied Antichrist.—

"If Antichrist is not the very Pontiff of Rome, it follows among other things that the citation of the blessed Paul, 1 Tim. 4:3, must not be taken of Antichrist, although almost all the fathers and theologians so accept it." [34]

Helwig says that the pope makes himself vicar of the Lord Jesus, though Christ does not need any vicar; desires to be called father of the whole church, though no one is to be called father; is called highest priest and pontiff of Christians, though One is our high priest; assumes himself to be head of the church, though only Christ is head, and foundation of the church, though Christ is the only Foundation. [35]

In summary, there are four points to be remembered concerning Helwig: (1) As to his competency in this ancient language research problem, he was a professional teacher of Latin, Greek, and Hebrew for twenty-seven years, and had already written two or three well-known works on classical philology when he made his calculation of the 666. (2) He listed and computed many different names in three different languages, all yielding 666, but preferred *Vicarius Filii Dei* of the Latin. (3) Helwig's computation, based on *Vicarius Filii Dei,* was expressly stated to be an expansion of the actual historical title of the Pope, *Vicarius Christi*—and therefore upon an equivalent, and not the actual title. (4) This computation lay largely dormant until the time of the French Revolution, when computations based upon this and other titles of the pope became increasingly common.

V. Cramer—One of the First German Premillennialists

Daniel Cramer (1568-1637), stanch Lutheran pastor and professor, at the gymnasium in Stettin, wrote a book on the Apocalypse which is largely a treatise against the empire of Antichrist in the Orient and the Occident. [36] In this exposition the characteristics of the seven churches are found in the different religious movements and churches of his day, including the

---

[34] *Ibid.*, sig. C₄v.   [35] *Ibid.*, sig. E₃r,v.
[36] Daniel Cramer, *Apocalypsis oder Offenbarung S. Johannis.*

Waldenses and Hussites. According to Cramer, many of the Reformation churches have now a name to live, but are dead—especially the Zwinglians and Calvinists.[37] The Laodiceans are neutral and lukewarm, halting between two opinions. The seals and trumpets indicate persecutions and tribulations, with the fifth trumpet applied to the pope and his retinue, and the sixth to Mohammed and his hordes. Antichristianism comes to its climax in the Roman popes, with the forty-two prophetic months as the time of his power.[38]

Cramer holds that the woman of Revelation 12 is the true church, and that the dragon is Satan, whereas the first beast of chapter 13 is pagan Rome—the same as the fourth beast in Daniel 7.[39] Cramer repeatedly calls seven-hilled Rome the seat of Antichrist, and makes the second beast papal Rome, and the forty-two months the time of the popes, who seek to wield both kingly and priestly swords.[40] On the 666 he gives both versions. He reckons it as years, and also considers it possible that it could be applied to a person, for instance Lateinos, or PAULO V. VICE DEO.[41]

The plagues are punishments upon papal Christianity spread back over the centuries.[42] The woman of Revelation 17 is the Papacy, borne up by the kings of the earth—Germany, Bohemia, Hungary, Poland, Sweden, Denmark, Norway, Scotland, England and France—the bird being "known by its feathers."[43] The thousand years are neither the old earthly chiliastic view of Cerinthus, nor the first millennium of the Christian Era, nor a thousand years beginning with Constantine, but are introduced, and the reign of grace begins, with the preaching of Luther. Cramer was thus one of the first German premillennialists. We are living, God be praised, in this evangelical kingdom. Therefore the reign of the gospel will continue for one thousand years as the real *Regnum gratiae*. As nobody lives for a thousand years, therefore the end cannot

---

[37] *Ibid.*, fols. 2, 11-17.
[39] *Ibid.*, fols. 47-51.
[41] *Ibid.*, fols. 50, 55.
[43] *Ibid.*, fols. 68, 69.

[38] *Ibid.*, fols. 26-46.
[40] *Ibid.*, fol. 53.
[42] *Ibid.*, fols. 63, 64.

20

be seen till the last day. But the closer we come to the end, the more we shall find that the devil will take hold of his old helpers, the pope and the Turk, until their abominable teachings will be accepted practically by everybody, and when Christ comes, faith will hardly be found on earth, according to an old prophecy.[44]

VI. Alsted Ends the 1335 Year-Days in A.D. 1694

JOHANN HEINRICH ALSTED (1588-1638), noted teacher and prolific writer, was born and educated at Herborn. He became professor of philosophy there in 1615, and professor of theology in 1619. He represented the Reformed Church at the Synod of Dort (1618-1619), and in 1629, as a result of the unrest of the war in Germany, went to the newly founded University of Weissenburg, in Transylvania. His *Tractatus de Mille Annis* (Treatise on the Thousand Years) (1618) was followed by his *Theologia Prophetica* (Prophetic Theology), and then his *Triumphus* (1675), which appeared in English as *Beloved City, or the Saints Reign on Earth a Thousand Years*. He contended that before it is fulfilled, every prophecy is a riddle. But when fulfilled, it is plain and understandable.

The Little Horn of Daniel 7 was applied literally to Antiochus Epiphanes, and in type to the "Roman Antichrist," which powers Alsted similarly saw in Daniel 11.[45] The seven seals in the Apocalypse represent the history of the church. Under the first four seals the four horses indicate the following: the white horse, the apostolic church; the red horse, the church under pagan tyrants; the black horse, the time of the heresies; the pale horse, the sick condition of the church under the rise of Antichrist in the time of Boniface III (606); the fifth seal, the time of the martyrs; the sixth seal, the reign of Antichrist from 606 onward for a thousand years.[46] The seven trumpets, according to Alsted, are included in the seventh seal, symbolizing

---

[44] *Ibid.*, fols. 81 ff.
[45] Johann Heinrich Alsted, *Theologica Prophetica*, p. 558.
[46] *Ibid.*, pp. 848, 849.

the apostasy of the church, beginning with the time of Boniface III, progressing through the corruption of gospel doctrines, the time of growing papal power, the pollution of the sweet waters of the Scripture by the papal decretals, the darkness of Antichristian error. Under the fifth trumpet comes the fall of the Roman Antichrist from the heavenly church, the locusts representing the clergy. Under the sixth trumpet comes the full revelation of Antichrist, and the mighty angel, Christ, with the open Book, sounding the call for the Reformation; and under the seventh, the completion of the Reformation and the conversion of the Jews, followed by the kingdom of Christ.[47]

The treading underfoot of the city for the period of forty-two months is 1260 years from the time of Sylvester, when the falling away of the church began as Constantine removed from Rome to Constantinople, which apostasy reached its climax in the time of Phocas and Boniface.[48]

The two beasts of Revelation 13, Alsted envisions as the two stages of Roman Antichrist—the ten-horned beast from the sea, imperial Rome; and the two-horned beast, papal Rome. The term *Lateinos* is linked with the mystic number 666.[49]

This same dual form of Rome is likewise seen in the Beast of Revelation 17, with the seven heads as the seven forms of government of imperial Rome leading up to papal Rome. The ten horns, in turn, are tabulated as standing for "Hispania, Hungaria, Anglia, Dania, Polonia, Dalmatia, Croatia, Portugallia, Bohemia, and Svevia." [50]

Revelation 18 and 19, in Alsted's mind portray the downfall and destruction of the papal rule.[51]

VII. Hoë—Redeemed Saints Spend Millennium in Heaven

MATTHIAS HOË VON HOENEGG (1580-1645) of Saxony was born in Vienna and educated at the University of Wittenberg. At twenty-one he became a licentiate in theology and lecturer

[47] *Ibid.*, pp. 850-853.
[49] *Ibid.*, p. 856.
[51] *Ibid.*, p. 860.

[48] *Ibid.*, pp. 852, 853.
[50] *Ibid.*, pp. 859, 860.

in the university, and later a Doctor of Theology. In 1602 he
was called to the court of Dresden as third chaplain. Because
of his manners and ability he soon rose in favor with the elector,
and after fulfilling a number of commissions in the provinces
he became in 1613 the chief court chaplain in Dresden. To comprehend the situation correctly, we have to understand that at
that period the intellectual as well as the spiritual life in Germany was centered in the courts of the different princes, and lay
in the hands of those persons who knew how to influence the
princes. These persons were the confessors, the court chaplains,
and favorites. Therefore some historians are not far amiss when
they contend that the history during that period lay in the
hands of two priests: Hoë, court chaplain of John-George of
Saxony; and Lämmermann, priest-confessor of Ferdinand I.

Hoë, a stanch Lutheran and violently anticalvinistic, preferred rather to unite with the emperor, which meant with
Rome, than with the Calvinistic princes of Germany. His works,
Triumphus Calvinisticus (1614) and *Prodromus* (1618), reveal
his spirit. In these works flares up the deep-seated hatred and
enmity which separated the two Protestant confessions and
illuminated with sinister glow the centennial celebrations and
jubilee of a Protestant Germany. A few months later the great
drama of the Thirty Years' War began. Hoë, inducing the elector to side with the emperor, became therewith instrumental in
bringing about the almost complete annihilation of the Moravian Church and other evangelical bodies in Bohemia and
Silesia. In his 99 theses against the Calvinists he is so violent
that even the bishop of Cologne (1622) congratulated Saxony
on her return to the bosom of the mother church. But in reality
that was not the case, because at the same time, for nearly thirty
years, Hoë worked on his *Commentarius in Apocalypsin*,[52]
wherein his theological position toward the Catholic Church is
made perfectly clear. Therefore in him we have the strange and
sorrowful spectacle that he, although theoretically sound in his

---

[52] Matthias Hoë von Hoenegg, *Commentarius in . . . Apocalypsin* (1671 ed.), title page.

views about the Papacy, yet by his violent hatred against his coreligionists helped not only to weaken the Protestant cause but even to wreck it in certain parts of the German Empire and to strengthen the power of Rome.[53]

His general positions of interpretation are as follows:

Under the first four seals he sets forth the horsemen as the gospel church, persecution, hunger, and death;[54] the first four trumpets as heretics; the fifth, the Roman Pope (Antichrist); the sixth, the Turks (the Eastern Antichrist); and the seventh, the overthrow of both Antichrists in the last judgment.[55] He also suggests that the "kings of the east," of the sixth plague, are probably Japan, Persia, and other Asiatic countries who, drunk with the wine of Babylon, will embrace the Papacy, or the "Lamb-Dragon religion," and receive the three evil spirits from the mouth of the dragon, beast, and false prophet. How this will come about is illustrated by the activities of the Jesuits of the present century.[56] The seventh plague, the day of judgment, he avers, will end the Papacy.[57]

The two beasts of Revelation 13, Hoë states, are "the old Roman Empire" and the papal "Roman Antichrist." [58] After discussing many opinions concerning the 1260 days and 42 months, he concludes that the times are indefinite, and known only to God.[59] The woman Babylon is Antichristian Rome, the papal see.[60] Hoë declares the Alcazar view on the 1,000 years to be "silly," and interprets this period as beginning with the end of the persecutions at the time of Constantine's rise to imperial power, and ending about 1300 with the rule of the Papacy on the one hand and of the Turks on the other.[61]

VIII. Cocceius Denies Grotius' Fallacy; Reaffirms Historical View

JOHANNES COCCEIUS, or Koch (1603-1669), was born at Bremen and educated in Bremen and Holland, specializing in

---

[53] *Allgemeine Deutsche Biographie*, art. "Hoë von Hoenegg."
[54] Hoë von Hoenegg, *Commentarius in . . . Apocalypsin* (1671 ed.), vol. 1, pp. 213, 217, 223, 226.
[55] *Ibid.*, pp. 268, 272, 273, 275, 290, 325, 401.
[56] *Ibid.*, vol. 2, p. 36.
[58] *Ibid.*, vol. 1, pp. 443, 475.
[60] *Ibid.*, p. 503; vol. 2, p. 87.
[57] *Ibid.*, p. 38.
[59] *Ibid.*, p. 360.
[61] *Ibid.*, vol. 2, pp. 270, 275.

ancient Biblical languages. In 1629 he became professor of
Biblical philology at Bremen, then professor of theology at
Franecker in 1636 and at Leyden in 1650. He composed a famous Hebrew dictionary, and definitely affected the religious
tendencies of his day. He helped lead men back to the Bible,
but carried the system of figurative interpretation to extremes.

He certainly led out in a new way of approach to theological
problems. He based his exegesis first on the original text of the
Bible, and stood for the principle that the passages should be
explained according to their real meaning in their original
connections and in agreement with each other, and not according to church dogma. By him the Reformed Church in the
Netherlands was deeply influenced. Unfortunately he had a
tendency to allegorize, and therewith his own exegesis was somewhat discredited.[62]

Cocceius' conception of the historical phases of the proph-
ecy led him to write a work on Daniel which refuted Bellarmine's theses and proved the pope to be Antichrist. In this work
he interprets the kingdoms of Daniel 2 as Babylon, Persia,
Greece, Rome, followed by the divided kingdoms rising from
the Roman Empire; yet in the four beasts of Daniel 7 he sees
Constantine and the succeeding Catholic emperors; the Arian
Goths, Vandals, and Lombards (who devour the three ribs of
Italy, Gaul, and Spain); the Mohammedans; and the empire of
Charlemagne (the ten horns being the various ruling houses of
the Holy Roman Empire through the centuries, and the Little
Horn the Roman pope).[63] It was an odd sequence.

He makes the "time, times, and a half," as well as the
forty-two months, the 1260 days, and even the three and a half
days (as "years of years"), all refer to 1260 years, within which
also is embraced the 1,000 years, but regards the "2300 evening-
mornings" as literal days in the time of Antiochus and the
Maccabees.[64] As for the seventy weeks, Cocceius remarks that

---

[62] Max Göbel, *Geschichte des Christlichen Lebens in der rheinisch-westphälischen Evangelischen Kirche*, vol. 2, pp. 147-160.
[63] Johannes Cocceius, *Observationes ad Danielem*, in *Opera*, vol. 3, pp. 323-325; 335-337.
[64] *Ibid.*, pp. 338, 343, 344.

our faith should not hang on chronology, yet we do not throw away the argument derived from time, by which to prove that Christ came. He regards the period as being "not less than 70 weeks, that is 490 years," but inexact, for he extends it "between the decree of Cyrus and the ascension of Christ and the overthrow of the city." Like Mede, he makes the sixty-two weeks a separate period, which he reckons from the time of Darius (Nothus) to the thirty-third year of Christ.[65]

The 1290 days, which "no one doubts" are years, he reckons as ending with the restoration of the mass in certain parts of Germany, and therefore beginning in 332 or 333, in which he locates, for some unknown reason, the Council of Nicaea, where the false prophets erected an image to the Beast.[66]

In 1643 Grotius' interpretations stirred Cocceius to write a commentary on all the prophecies relating to the Antichrist, in which the preface bemoans the loss of clear understanding by recent commentators in glossing over the prophecies.[67] He shows how the popes fulfill the specifications of Antichrist, and how Rome is the seat of the Antichrist, handed over to the woman riding the Beast at the fall of the pagan empire.[68] He points out that the beasts of Daniel 7 are combined in the first beast of Revelation 13, and applies the symbols to the Papacy, with the Little Horn as the Roman pope.[69] The seven heads are the same as those noted in Revelation 12:3, the divisions of the Roman Empire (Italy, Greece, Asia Minor, Palestine, Africa, Spain, Gaul); and the ten horns, those mentioned in Revelation 17:12, the kings of the Christian world (Italy, Spain, France, England, Scotland, Denmark and Norway, Switzerland, Poland, Hungary).[70] The second beast from the earth is the rule of ecclesiastics, with the two horns denoting legitimate office and hypocrisy, and the image the papal Antichrist.[71]

---

[65] *Ibid.*, pp. 350, 351.
[66] *Ibid.*, p. 366.
[67] Cocceius, *Illustrium Locorum de Antichristo Agentium Repetitio* ("A Repetition of the Notable Places Dealing With Antichrist"), in *Opera*, vol. 9, p. 103.
[68] *Ibid.*, pp. 107, 109.
[69] *Ibid.*, pp. 122, 123; cf. pp. 131, 132.
[70] *Ibid.*, pp. 122, 118, 130.
[71] *Ibid.*, pp. 124-126.

The number 666 is found in *Lateinos, Romith, Paulo V., Vice Deo*, etc., but various other interpretations are given which are not entirely clear.[72] The woman of Babylon is papal Rome.[73]

IX. Calovius Combats Grotius' Adoption of Catholic Interpretation

ABRAHAM CALOVIUS, or Kalau (1612-1686), was born in East Prussia and educated at the University of Königsberg. He became rector of the Gymnasium at Danzig in 1643 and professor of theology in the University of Wittenberg in 1650. He represented the most exclusive form of Lutheranism, and being purely a polemical writer, his life consisted of a continuous chain of bitter controversies with the Romanists and Calvinists. To his *Biblia Novi Testamenti Illustrata* (The Books of the New Testament Explained) he added Grotius' annotations, which he refuted wherever he disagreed,[74] with the purpose of combating the Preterist views of Grotius. In his notes on Matthew 24 Calovius denied Grotius' theory of Antiochus, in connection with the abomination of desolation, and disagreed with his sidestepping of Catholicism as Antichrist and Babylon.[75] "Grotius perverts everything," he complained.[76] Calovius enumerated many Greek and Latin authors in support of the Historical view of prophecy.

X. Lucius and Comenius on the 1260 Years

JOHANN ANDREAS LUCIUS (1625-1686), Spener's predecessor at Dresden, devoted many years to prophetic research, citing many able commentators. He prepared 231 sermons and issued them in a ponderous work *On the Apocalyps*. Contending the 1260 days to be prophetic days, or years, he began them with Boniface III, in 606.[77] He interpreted the fourth beast of Daniel 7 as well as that of Revelation 13 as the Roman Antichrist, or the kingdom of the pope and his sovereignty, with the mark of the

---

[72] *Ibid.*, pp. 126, 127.
[73] *Ibid.*, pp. 130, 131.
[74] Abraham Calovius, *Biblia Novi Testamenti Illustrata*, vol. 1, title page.
[75] *Ibid.*, vol. 1, pp. 413, 414; vol. 2, p. 1866.
[76] *Ibid.*, vol. 2, p. 1841.
[77] Johann Lucius, *Die Offenbahrung . . . Johannis*, pp. 630, 631.

Beast the confession of the Roman religion.[78] But he likewise held to the Augustinian view of the resurrection, and the millennium as beginning with the days of Constantine.

JOHANN AMOS COMENIUS (1592-1670), well-known Slavic minister, philologist, and educational reformer, as well as bishop of the Moravian Brethren, issued anonymously in 1664 *Die geöffnete Offenbarung* (The Opened Revelation), in which he placed the 1260 years from 395 to 1655, and ended the prophetic periods there. In 1655 he published *Licht in Finsternis* (Light in Darkness) at Amsterdam.

XI. Pietism Stresses Vital Christianity Instead of Dogmatics

For centuries the Papacy had opposed efforts at reform from sincere men within her own ranks. Luther, Zwingli, Calvin, and Knox were raised up to bring about the needed reformation, and to reinstate Christ as the only Founder and Head of the church, with His Word as the only rule of faith and practice. In some matters these noble pioneers fell short in the application of correct principles and sound fundamentals. Then the masses of their followers, instead of correcting these inaccuracies, began to emphasize the divine call of their leaders and the virtual inerrancy of the Reformation symbols.

Great things had been promised by the Reformation. Gifted men had testified fearlessly, and martyrs had sealed their faith resolutely with their blood. Though the Lutherans, Reformed, Baptists, and Brethren disagreed on many things, they were solidly united on the identity of Antichrist and the necessity of gathering out a people from Rome's communion. But, like all previous spiritual advances, the first love grew cold, and the Sardis condition became general.

1. HOLINESS BURIED UNDER STERILE DOGMATISM.—The stagnation and unregenerate life of the evangelical state churches needed the powerful remedies proffered by the Pietists,

---

[78] *Ibid.*, pp. 754, 755, 828.

the Moravians, and later the Wesleyans. Such men as Spener, Zinzendorf, Ziegenbalg—and then Wesley and Whitefield—heralded the breaking of the day.

A breath of fresh life came from the Pietists, this movement arising in Germany in the latter part of the seventeenth century. Johann Arndt (1555-1621) and Johannes Cocceius (1603-1669) might be called its forerunners. But its full development is to be ascribed to Philipp Spener (1635-1705) and his associates. Spener saw living holiness buried under formalism and sterile theology.[79] Pietism was passionate for the holiness about which orthodoxy was indifferent, and was indifferent about the formulas for which orthodoxy was passionate.

2. SPENER'S POSITIONS CENSURED BY THE WITTENBERG FACULTY.—Spener's views were adopted by Francke, Anton, Schade, and others. These held Bible meetings at Leipzig, trying to do what Wesley later attempted at Oxford. They were violently denounced—Spener being compelled to leave Dresden and Francke being driven from Leipzig. But Pietism found a home at Halle.[80] Controversy arose, however, between the Pietists on the Halle faculty and the orthodox on the faculty of Wittenberg; the latter censured as heretical 283 propositions found in Spener's writings.[81] But the influence of Pietism was perpetuated in the Moravian Brethren, Count Zinzendorf being a disciple of Francke.

XII. Spener—Pietist Founder Holds Same Prophetic Positions

PHILIPP JAKOB SPENER (1635-1705), learned father of Pietism, was born in Alsace and educated in Strassburg by Lutheran teachers, in strict orthodoxy, but the food for his soul he found largely in books of pious writers, like Arndt's *True Christianity* and Baile's *Praxis pietatis*. Upon completion of his courses of study, he traveled in Switzerland, where he saw the life and institutions of the Reformed Church. He also came to

---

[79] Farrar, F. W., *History of Interpretation*, pp. 380, 381.
[80] *Ibid.*, p. 382.
[81] Herzog, *Real-Encyklopädie*, art. "Spener."

Geneva, where he lived in the home of Leger, the pastor of the Waldenses. He served as pastor at Frankfurt am Main from 1666 to 1686, where his preaching was intensely practical and spiritual. He requested a thorough preparation before partaking in the Lord's supper, especially the first time. Upon request, he instituted special devotional meetings for religious instruction and prayer, called Collegia Pietates.[82]

Here in Frankfurt he wrote, in 1675, the little work *Pia Desideria: Oder Hertzliches Verlangen* (Pia Desideria, or Deep Longing), urging that the reformation be completed, and insisting on regeneration. This book made a profound impression on all Christian circles, influencing many toward leading a better Christian life, but causing also storms of protest from the orthodox camp. Devotional circles and prayer groups were introduced in many churches. This book made Spener the father of Pietism.

In 1686 he was called to Dresden to become the first chaplain of the court, which was practically the highest position the Lutheran Church had to offer at that time. But inasmuch as Spener insisted on a Christian life even at the court and at the universities, his career became rather stormy, and when the elector Frederick III of Brandenburg and Prussia invited him to come to Berlin to be provost of the Nicolaikirche, he accepted. The Prussian monarch, opposed to all religious fanaticism, tried to establish peace between the warring factions of Protestantism, and he saw in Spener a useful instrument to that purpose. Spener had therefore the opportunity to exercise a tremendous influence on all ecclesiastical matters in Brandenburg and Prussia.[83]

Spener was one of the finest characters the German Lutheran Church has produced. He is considered to be the Reformer of the Reformation, standing foursquare on the basis of Luther, accepting all his basic positions, including his definite stand

[82] Paul Grünberg, *Philipp Jakob Spener*, p. 519; Herzog, *Real-Encyklopädie*, art. "Spener"; see also Carl Mirbt, "Pietism," *The New Schaff-Herzog*, pp. 53-67.
[83] Herzog, *op. cit.*, art. "Spener"; see also Mirbt, "Pietism" in *The New Schaff-Herzog*, pp. 53-67.

against the Roman church as it is revealed in the Scriptures. He drew all his strength from these essential principles, and his chief burden was to bring to pass a real reformation of the heart in every church member.

He laments bitterly in his *Pia Desideria* that even though some Catholics understand and believe that the pope and his see are the Antichrist, and would like to join the real church, yet they do not see any change in our lives, no divine power manifested; therefore they conclude that no real church exists any more on earth but all are in Babylonian confusion.[84] And on the following page he proclaims:

"We cannot be thankful enough for the great blessings which God has bestowed upon us through the work of the Reformation, in having opened Himself the doors of the Roman-Babylonian captivity and led us out into the glorious freedom. However, as the Jews should not have been satisfied with leaving Babel, but were commanded to build the house of the Lord and to establish His services, in like manner we should never be contented with having left Babel, but should carefully correct all still existing shortcomings."[85]

1. CHOSE PROPHETIC THEME FOR DOCTORAL DISSERTATION. —Spener's interest in the prophecies found expression already early in his life in his choice of Revelation 9:13 and onward as the topic for his doctoral thesis (1664). In preparation he read sixty commentaries, tabulating their contents.[86] He saw paganism glossed over in the Papacy, Rome as the prophesied Babylon, with the pope and his clergy as the predicted Antichrist. Constantine's recognition of the Catholic state church had caused the apostasy and had resulted in the Dark Ages. Spener deeply lamented the fact that the Reformation had not simply come to a halt but had retrogressed. Not everything was completed with the Reformation; many things had to be done still. The reformation of the doctrine is only the first step; the reformation of the life has to follow.[87]

---

[84] Philipp Jakob Spener, *Pia Desideria* (2d ed., n.d.), pp. 46, 47.
[85] *Ibid.*, p. 48.
[86] Grünberg, *op. cit.*, vol. 1, p. 153.
[87] *Ibid.*, pp. 516 ff.

2. His Clear Conceptions About Papal Rome.—Spener's fundamental position toward the Papacy and his zeal for the pure doctrine, which he expressed in many sermons and written statements, were later collected and compiled by Georg Pritius and appeared under the title *D. Philipp Jakob Speners Gerechter Eifer wider das Antichristische Pabstthum* (D. Philipp Jakob Spener's Righteous Zeal Against the Antichristian Papacy). Among these statements are the following:

"In order that the Antichrist might rise, the power of the pagan authorities and of imperial Rome must be broken; only then the ecclesiastical profession could acquire the position which was adequate to its arrogance." [88]

"This beast has the appearance of a lamb. It has shaped itself outwardly in the similitude of our Saviour, Jesus Christ, the lamb; that means, that the form of true Christianity and of the power of Christ is found within it, but it speaks like the dragon and carries inwardly the characteristics of Satan in its disposition to lie and to kill. This beast is the Antichrist and is called also the false prophet. Rev. 19:20. . . . These beasts do not represent individual kings or men but entire kingdoms." [89]

"Therefore the judgments of God shall fall upon the Roman Papacy and especially upon that profession [ecclesiastical] which is utterly corrupted. We might well say (if we mean by it the papacy itself and not the hidden remnant of the children of God in it), it is real paganism brushed over with Christian paint. And as in olden times God laboured in vain with the Jews to lead them to repentance, in like manner he worked with the papacy but without avail. He roused again and again witnesses of truth to correct and to chastise it. He employed different means to let the light of truth shine into the eyes of the Papacy, so that, if it had willed, it could have accepted the light. Some 100 years ago complete new groups protested and separated—the Waldenses and the Hussites—and then the blessed reformation of Luther took place. And today we visualize how the Papacy fills its cup of iniquity by the persecution of the true believers and forced reformation. It uses all the violence foretold in Rev. 13:15; 14:12, 13; 17:6; 18:24. And that will be the last which will draw God's vengeance upon it, since it has become drunken with the blood of the saints and true believers." [90]

In Revelation 14:8 the angel proclaims that Babylon is fallen.

"The downfall of the Papacy is evident, yet it will become worse. Up till now it is not a complete decline, because we see, that after this procla-

---

[88] Jo. Georg Pritius, D. *Philipp Jakob Speners Gerechter Eifer wider das Antichristische Pabstthum*, p. 13.
[89] *Ibid.*, p. 16.
[90] *Ibid.*, pp. 146, 147.

mation a number are left, who worship the beast and its image and receive its mark. Rev. 14:9, 10. It has still great power, because it is a time in which the patience of the saints is needed (v. 12), and many even have to expect death for the sake of Jesus (v. 13). Whereas Rev. 18:4 commands, even after the voice had proclaimed that Babylon is fallen, 'Come out of her, my people, that ye be not partakers of her sins, and that ye receive not of her plagues.' Therefore a remnant of the people of God is still left, after that first fall of Babylon who should come out, and then Babel has to expect more plagues." [91]

3. HELD THOUSAND YEARS STILL IN THE FUTURE.—When some in the pietistic circles began to develop eccentric ideas about the thousand years, and a storm was raised by the orthodox, Spener tried to tone the matter down, declaring that no vital portion of the faith was involved, but that he personally maintained that these thousand years of the Apocalypse had not yet begun, nor had they ended.[92]

In summation, it is significant that, irrespective of nationality or denominational affiliation, virtually all—except the few who yielded to Rome's expositorial sophistries—held the Papacy to be the Antichrist of prophecy.

---

[91] *Ibid.*, p. 184.
[92] Spener, *Theologisches Bedencken,* unpaged, 1692.

CHAPTER TWENTY-EIGHT

French Huguenots
Hold Prophetic Banner High

From the 1572 Massacre of St. Bartholomew onward, the Huguenots, as the French Protestants were called, had a most precarious time. At last, at the close of the century, Henry IV extended religious toleration to the Huguenots, with the civil right to hold public office, by issuing the Edict of Nantes— sometimes called the "Charter of Protestant Liberties," dated 1598. Soon after, in their convocation at Gap, October 1, 1603, the Huguenots made this united declaration concerning Antichrist in their Statement of Faith:

"Not only so, but the same assembly formally resolved to append to the 31st article of the Confession of Faith a very explicit declaration to the same effect, wherein the church professed its conviction that the Roman Pontiff was the Son of Perdition, predicted in the word of God under the emblem of the Harlot clothed in scarlet, seated on the seven hills of the great city, and reigning over the kings of the earth, and uttered its confident expectation that the Lord would consume him with the Spirit of His mouth and finally destroy him with the brightness of His coming." [1]

Before taking up the seventeenth-century expositors, we pause briefly to note one of their writers just before the close of the previous century, whose life gives us a glimpse of the rigors of the time.

I. Du Jon Holds Prophetic Day Stands for Literal Year

FRANCOIS DU JON (c. 1545-1602), Huguenot leader, better

[1] Henry M. Baird, *The Huguenots and Henry of Navarre*, vol. 2, p. 453.

known under his Latin name Junius, was tender and timid by
nature, but equipped with excellent gifts. He studied law and
wanted to join an embassy to Constantinople, but missed the
party at Lyon. He began to read the New Testament, and resolved to study theology; therefore, he went to Geneva in 1562.
In 1565 he was called to Antwerp as preacher, and stood firm
at his post through all the vicissitudes of war and upheaval.
Not being of Flemish origin, he had to leave the country, and
was called to Heidelberg in 1568, where he became a collabo-
rator of Tremellius in translating the Bible into Latin. There
he published a work on the Apocalypse, *Apocalypsis Methodica
Analysi Notisque Illustrata* (The Apocalypse With a Methodical Analysis Elucidated With Notes) and, in 1593, a similar
work on Daniel.[2] He later was called back by Henry IV and
fulfilled a mission for the king. When he passed through Leyden, the university urged him to become one of its members,
which invitation he finally accepted.

The year-day principle for all prophetic time was expressly
declared by du Jon thus:

"*Daies* is commonly taken for yeares, that God in this sort might shew
the time to be short, and that the space of time is definitely set downe by
Him in His counsaile." [3]

"The daies must be reckoned for so many yeares, after the example of
the Prophets Ezechiel and Daniel." [4]

He considers the best time to start the 1260-year period
with the death of Jesus in 34, which brings him to 1294, the
time of Boniface VIII.[5] In this he differed from all others.

II. Revocation of Edict of Nantes the Prelude to Persecution

Picture the setting of the seventeenth century. Midway
through we find Louis XIV (1643-1715) sitting on the throne of
France, after the death of Cardinal Mazarin, taking the reins in

---

[2] Eugène and Emile Haag, *La France Protestante* (1st ed.), vol. 4, pp. 381-389.
[3] François du Ion, [Jon], *The Apocalyps, or Revelation of S. Iohn* (English translation,
1596), p. 30.
[4] *Ibid.*, p. 124.
[5] *Ibid.*, p. 125.

his own hands in 1661. With his mistress, Madame de Maintenon, by his side, and the Jesuit confessor Père de la Chaise
behind her, the king is guided politically by the opportunist
maxims of Cardinal Richelieu. Attempting to suppress the Jansenists and quartering his dragoons on the Huguenots, he
deprived both of all rights. In the Piedmontese Alps the sur-
vivors of the dreadful Waldensian massacre still clung to their
ancient mountain fastnesses. In England, James II was
struggling to restore papal domination, and to enslave the children of the Puritans. Then, in France, came the Revocation
of the Edict of Nantes—the crowning perfidy of king and court
—with the wail of thousands of Protestants robbed of their
children.[6] This was but the prelude to the last papal persecution of the Huguenots, which was later to be followed by the
French Revolution with its retributive element.

1. LAW OF 1681 AUTHORIZED FORCIBLE CONVERSION.—Back
in June, 1681, a terrible law authorizing the wholesale conversion of all Huguenot children, from seven years of age upward,
had struck terror to the hearts of parents. It was a deadly blow
at the existence of the Protestant family. Priests and monks
could ensnare the children into confession of the Roman faith
and tear them away from the parental home. The noted Huguenot Jurieu uttered his flaming protest against this outrage in
his *Derniers efforts de l'innocence affligée* (Last Efforts of
Afflicted Innocence), and had to flee to Rotterdam. Then, as
the parents and older children still clung to their faith, the
dragoons were commissioned to convert them.[7]

2. ATTEMPT TO EXTIRPATE FOLLOWED BY GREAT EXODUS.—
But the statute still remained. So the Edict of Nantes was
revoked in 1685, and all gatherings of Protestants forbidden
on pain of death. Their ministers were ordered to leave within
fifteen days. If the lay people attempted to leave the country,

---

[6] While the king is responsible before history, it is generally recognized that behind Louis
was Louvois Le Tellier, the war minister, his "evil genius," technician and spokesman of the
church.
[7] Baird, *The Huguenots and the Revocation of the Edict of Nantes*, vol. 1, pp. 494, 495.

the men would be sent to the galleys, the women imprisoned, and their goods confiscated. Marriages were declared null and void. All the children born thereafter must be baptized by Roman priests. And all Protestant churches must be torn down.[8]

Louis XIV decreed these stringent measures for the specific extirpation of the Huguenots.[9] And for this he was adorned with a medal struck at Rome—reading on one side *Sacr. Romana Restituta* (The Roman Rites Restored)[10]—and lauded as a second Constantine who had severed the head of the dragon of heresy.[11]

Then came the great exodus. Nothing could stay it. About 184,000 Protestants left the province of Normandy, and a very moderate calculation suggests that 400,000 left France and found refuge in England, Holland, Switzerland, Germany, and America. France lost by this exodus the most learned and industrious of her citizens.[12] Many other thousands, whose flight was frustrated by the government, died by the gallows, or in dungeons and galleys. In 1686 Louis XIV even sent 14,000 men under Marshal de Catinat to join the Piedmontese army in enforcing submission of the Vaudois.[13]

3. CALLED THEMSELVES "CHURCH IN THE WILDERNESS."— For a whole century the French Government and the Papacy joined hands in an attempt to crush the Huguenots, who, like the Waldenses before them, called themselves the *Eglise du désert* (Church of the wilderness), for they had to meet in caves, forests, and desolate places.[14] Even their baptismal and marriage certificates were dated from "The Wilderness." Their meeting places and the whereabouts of their pastors had to be kept carefully secret. These pastors had to wander about, separated from their families, ever watching for spies, and

8 The Edict had been partially abrogated by Richelieu in 1628, by the Edict of Alais, or Ales.
9 Baird, *The Huguenots and the Revocation of the Edict of Nantes*, vol. 2, pp. 28 ff.
10 *Ibid.*, p. 66.
11 It was hailed particularly by Bossuet, bishop of Meaux, Count Bussy Rabutin, and Madame de Sévigné (*Ibid.*, pp. 53, 54), but deplored by Vauban, minister of fortifications.
12 *Ibid.*, pp. 99-107.
13 Guinness, *History Unveiling Prophecy*, p. 152.
14 There are wonderful vestiges in the little French village of Mas Soubeyran north of Nimes, which was the headquarters of the Camisards for a certain period.

constantly changing their location.[15] Though Louis XIV declared, in 1715, that the Reformed Church was extinct, nevertheless the courageous preachers of the church in the wilderness preached on in the place prepared of God, though countless numbers were imprisoned and perished.

III. Pacard Opens Century With Standard Protestant Positions

GEORGE PACARD (d. 1610) was pastor of the church of La Rochefoucould in southwestern France. After having studied theology, probably in Geneva, he became pastor of the aforementioned church. At the time of the Bartholomew massacre he fled to Geneva, but soon re-entered France, where we find him as pastor of Châtellerault in 1574. In 1578 he was a deputy to the synod of Sainte Foy, and in 1594 he was a member of the commission charged to defend the Protestant faith against the Catholic ecclesiastics. In 1579 he wrote a book called *Théologie naturelle ou Recueil contenant plusieurs argumens contre les Epicuriens et Athéistes de notre temps* (Natural Theology or a Collection Containing Several Arguments Against the Epicureans and the Atheists of Our Time).[16] This contained also *le traité de l'Ante-Christ* (The Treatise on the Antichrist) which was separately reprinted in 1604 under the title *Description de l'Antechrist, et de son royaume* (Description of the Antichrist and of His Kingdom). It was "gathered from the Prophecies of the Holy Scriptures, from the Writings of the Fathers, and from History," according to the title page. Contending that "nothing has come by chance," Pacard cites the fate of the Jewish church, city, and temple, and then refers to Antichrist's usurpation of the church—sitting in the temple of God, surrounded by the kings and princes of the world, made drunk by the wine of her fornication, and soon to be discomfited at the second advent.[17]

---

[15] CLAUDE BROUSSON (1647-1698), French Protestant lawyer, manifested great zeal in behalf of his persecuted brethren. Obliged to flee to Switzerland for refuge in 1683, he practiced law at Lausanne. Returning to France, he passed through the horrors of persecution, doing much to organize "worship in the Wilderness" and preaching day or night in the caverns and in the woods. A heavy price was set on his head. After another visit to Switzerland and Holland, he returned to his French churches, was arrested, imprisoned, and hanged before being racked. (*La grande encyclopédie*, art. "Brousson, Claude.")

[16] Haag, *op. cit.* (1st ed.), vol. 8, pp. 62, 63.

[17] George Pacard, *Description de l'Antechrist, et de son royaume*, Preface, pp. vii, viii.

1. A System Springing From Rome's Division.—It will be well to take a survey of the expositions of this initial writer. Chapter 3 discusses the conflicting assertions of the doctors of Rome as to Antichrist, and in contrast contends that he will not be a single man but a system or succession, citing ancient writers in contrast to the "sophistries of Bellarmine." Pacard shows Antichrist was to constitute a general apostasy in the church, be erected on the ruins of the Roman Empire, and will last until the second advent.[18] The pope is Antichrist, not Mohammed.[19] Discussing the prophetic side, Pacard affirms that history plainly states that Rome was divided into ten parts, and that three were cut down, then asserting, "Daniel's prediction has been fulfilled."[20]

2. Rules 1260 Years From Seven-hilled Rome.—In chapter 6 Pacard shows that Antichrist, even according to many Roman doctors, will sit on a throne in the Christian church, and not in the city of Jerusalem.[21] In chapter 8 he proceeds to show that the place of his seat of residence is seven-hilled Rome.[22] Dealing next with the terrible persecution inflicted upon dissenters,[23] Pacard longs for the approaching end of the 1260 year-days:

"We are therefore waiting patiently for the end of the 1260 days ordained for the great beast, after which God will deliver his people, and this beast will feel the fierce wrath of the Lord."[24]

3. Marshals Thirty Historic Witnesses on Antichrist.— Coming to the historical side, Pacard cites some thirty select witnesses—the famous speech of Arnulf, at the Council of Rheims (991), and the witness of Berenger, Bernard, John of Salisbury, Joachim, and a dozen others—as well as the Waldenses, Beghards, Eberhard of Salzburg, and Wyclif—citing their statements in brief.[25]

4. Daniel's Little Horn, Paul's Man of Sin, John's Beast.—Chapter 12 deals with the Biblical side, making the

---

[18] *Ibid.*, pp. 21, 27.
[21] *Ibid.*, p. 69.
[24] *Ibid.*, p. 157.
[19] *Ibid.*, pp. 38 ff.
[22] *Ibid.*, pp. 106, 115.
[25] *Ibid.*, pp. 164-177.
[20] *Ibid.*, p. 64.
[23] *Ibid.*, pp. 152-157.

argument from Daniel's Little Horn, Paul's Man of Sin, and John's two-horned beast.[26] The pope's power to change the law of God at will is the subject of chapter 14, and the omission of the second commandment and the division of the tenth is noted.[27] Pacard charges the Papacy was corrupting the faith by (1) false interpretation, (2) audacious additions, and (3) sacrilegious eliminations.[28]

5. THREE AND A HALF TIMES = 42 MONTHS = 1260 DAYS. —Having demonstrated that Antichrist is not a single man but a continuing system, Pacard deals with his duration determined by God, as featured in Daniel 7:25 and 12:5, as well as Revelation 13:5 and 12:4. The three and a half times are the same as the 42 months, or 1260 days—years according to the inspired prophetic reckoning.[29]

IV. Cottiere—Two Witnesses Are Two Testaments Prophesying 1260 Years

MATTHIEU COTTIERE (Cotterius) (fl. 1625) was a student in Geneva in 1604, then preacher at Pringé and Tours. He was deputy to the National Synod of Alais in 1620, rebuilt the church of Tours, which was demolished in 1621, and was again deputy to the Synod of Charenton in 1631. He wrote several books, his earliest being *Explicatio Apocalypseos* (Explication of the Apocalypse).[30] In his *Manuel ou briève description de l'Eglise Romaine* (Manual or Brief Description of the Church of Rome), Cottière expounds the Two Witnesses as "the Old and New Testaments." [31] These Witnesses extend over the 1260 years.[32] This is the same 1260 years when the woman was nourished in the wilderness, and also the three and a half times—which "means so many years." [33] Cottière takes due note of "that famous deserter from the holy ministry and from his religion," Ferrier, and speaks of the time of Phocas when the see of Rome received a notable increase.[34]

[26] *Ibid.*, pp. 182-185.   [27] *Ibid.*, p. 230.   [28] *Ibid.*, p. 233.
[29] *Ibid.*, pp. 314-317.   [30] Haag, *op. cit.* (2d ed.), vol. 4, col. 753.
[31] Matthieu Cottière, *Manuel ou briève description de l'Eglise Romaine*, p. 88.
[32] *Ibid.*, p. 89.   [33] *Ibid.*, p. 80.   [34] *Ibid.*, pp. 96, 97.

V. Cappel Begins Seventy Weeks With Seventh of Artaxerxes
(457 B.C.)

JACQUES CAPPEL (1570-1624), Lord of le Tilloy and eminent Protestant theologian, was born at Rennes. His father, a judge, had to flee because of his religious convictions. But Jacques was left in Sedan to study theology. His father died in exile soon after, and the mother, with the younger children, reduced to dire poverty, renounced the faith in order to receive a subsistence for the children. Stricken by grief and remorse, she soon followed the father into the grave. The girls and the little brother were sent to a convent. In 1593, after having completed his studies, the first thing Jacques did was to secure the release of his brother and sisters from the convent. He also recovered his paternal possessions, the estate of Tilloy. In 1596 he was called to Sedan by the duke of Bouillon to be pastor as well as professor of Hebrew in the seminary. Here he completed his lifework.[35]

Cappel was distinguished as an exegete, philologist, historian, and antiquarian, and during extensive travels in Italy and Germany formed the acquaintance of many noted Protestants. He was the author of many theological works, most of them written between 1611 and 1622. Among them we find *In Apocalypsin D. Johannis* Συνοψις, printed in 1605.

In 1616, taking up the cudgels against Ferrier, the apostate Protestant minister, Cappel wrote *Les livrées de Babel, ou l'histoire du siège romain* (The Flunkeys [Footmen] of Babel or the History of the Roman See), dealing with the issue of Antichrist. Dedicated to the prince of Sedan, now marshal of France, who was his former pupil, the book stresses the consent of scholars in many nations that the pope is Antichrist. Many chapters deal with the exposition of Revelation and Daniel; and one chapter, with the three advents of Christ. There are two striking characteristics of his prophetic interpretation. The first is his consecutive arrangement of the prophecies—those of

---

[35] Haag, *op. cit.* (2d ed.), vol. 3, cols. 720-726.

the Revelation following those of Daniel and earlier, which he ends at the cross. Thus he completely separates Daniel's prophetic periods from those of the Revelation, so that, for example, the 1260 days of John are not the same as Daniel's "time and times and the dividing of time." The second distinctive interpretation is his assigning fixed time values to some of the outline prophecies—for example, fifty years each to the seals and 150 years each to the trumpets. (Title page appears on page 648.)

1. PROPHECIES COMPASS CHRISTIAN ERA.—The Apocalypse cannot extend from John's time to the end, he insists, unless the "1260 days make up as many years, and unless every seal and every trumpet embraces a certain length of time." Placing the seven churches in John's lifetime, he counts the seals, beginning with the death of John, from A.D. 100 to A.D. 400, with fifty years for each seal.[36] The trumpets, following the sixth seal (presumably, therefore, included in the seventh), are each given five months, like the fifth trumpet, that is, 150 years—the first (400-550) being the barbarian invasions of Europe, the second (550-700), the Lombards, Persians, and Mohammedans, and so on.[37]

2. HOLDS HISTORIC POSITION ON OUTLINE PROPHECIES.— Cappel makes the first beast of Revelation 13 the old Roman state up to the year 500, and the two-horned beast from the earth the Papacy—the two horns being the claim of spiritual and temporal power.[38] The paralleling prophecies of Daniel 2 and 7 are declared to compass Babylonia, Medo-Persia, Greece, and Rome, in connection with which several supporting Jewish expositors are also cited.[39]

3. BEGINS 490 YEARS IN 457 B.C.—Although rejecting the reckoning of Cardinals Damian, Bellarmine, Alcazar, and others who make the 1260 days literal, Cappel treats the 1290 and 1335 days as only literal days applied to Antiochus,[40] and the

---

[36] Jacques Cappel, *Les livrées de Babel, ou l'histoire du siège romain*, pp. 863, 864.
[37] *Ibid.*, p. 865.   [38] *Ibid.*, pp. 902, 903.
[39] *Ibid.*, pp. 998, 999.   [40] *Ibid.*, p. 1013.

2300 days similarly;[41] yet he makes the 70 weeks "a period of 490 years," starting from the seventh year of Artaxerxes, at 457 B.C., and sealing and fulfilling all the prophecies of Daniel and of earlier times with the death of Christ. Note the clarity of his reasoning:

"The weeks are to begin with the publishing of the edict of Artaxerxes Longimanus, an edict obtained by Ezra in the seventh year of his reign. . . . Therefore, from that edict to the baptism of our Lord, who by the voice of the Father was declared the Christ and the Prince of our salvation, there are sixty-nine entire weeks. . . . And during the seven weeks the places and the ditches shall be rebuilt in a time of anguish. These seven weeks enclose Ezra's and Nehemiah's government from the seventh year of Artaxerxes Longimanus to the sixteenth year of Darius the Bastard, from the year 457 down to the year 408." [42]

VI. De Launay—True Jerusalem Is Persecuted by Beast

PIERRE DE LAUNAY (1573-1661), Lord of de la Motte and of de Vaufarlan, was born at Blois in 1573 and died at Paris in 1661. He had all the qualities inherent which predestined him to the highest position in the state. But when his elder brother died, to whom he was deeply attached, he renounced all the positions he held and resolved to devote his time entirely to studies. At the age of forty he learned Hebrew and became one of the outstanding expositors of the Bible in his time. He wrote numerous works, of which two are of particular interest to our study: *Paraphrase sur le prophète Daniel* (Paraphrase of the Prophet Daniel) and *Paraphrase et exposition sur l'Apocalypse tirée des Sainctes Ecritures et de l'histoire* (Paraphrase and Exposition of the Apocalypse, From the Scriptures and History). The latter he published under the pseudonym of Jonas le Buy.[43] In this work he recites the ravages of the Visigoths, Ostrogoths, Vandals, and other barbarian nations who broke up the Roman Empire, which empire, in turn, became the seat of the papal Antichrist.[44] De Launay likewise applies the Two Witnesses to

41 *Ibid.*, p. 1004.   42 *Ibid.*, p. 1005.
43 Haag, *op. cit.* (1st ed.), vol. 6, pp. 427-429.
44 Pierre de Launay, *Paraphrase et exposition sur l'Apocalypse, par Ionas le Buy*, pp. 121 [i.e. 221] ff.

the Old and the New Testament, their message trodden down, and lying ignominiously wounded in the schools and universities of the "Antichristian Church of Rome." [45]

Discussing the fallacies of the Jesuit Ribera, De Launay insists that the treading of the Holy City is the violence and oppression visited by the Beast against the church. (Revelation 13 and Daniel 7.) "Thus have the Roman Antichrist and its supporters ravaged the church and persecuted." [46] This time of oppression, he adds, is 1260 year-days: "It also goes without discussion that the 1260 days, according to prophetic style, mean 1260 years, each day corresponding to a year." [47]

VII. Amyraut Puts Millennium After Judgment of Little Horn

Moise Amyraut (1596-1664) was one of the most distinguished and influential theologians of the seventeenth century. He was born at Bourgueil. First studying law at Poitiers, he was led to enter the ministry by reading Calvin's *Institutes*. Studying theology at Saumur, under Cameron, he served as pastor at Saumur and Charenton, and became one of the leading professors at Saumur, and finally rector of the school in 1639. He was a deputy to the Synod of Charenton in 1631 for the province of Anjou and was also held in high esteem by the Catholics. He secured from Louis XIII cancellation of the obligation of Protestant deputies to speak to the king only upon their knees.[48]

He was a prolific writer, and published many sermons—among them one upon the Apocalypse. He was a poet, and we have from him 150 Christian sonnets. In his *Du règne de mille ans, ou de la prospérité de l'Eglise* (On the Thousand Years Reign, or the Prosperity of the Church) Amyraut takes issue with the dominant Augustinian concept of the kingdom of the saints in Daniel 2, and opposes De Launay in the latter's chiliastic interpretations. He maintains that the kingdom of the saints comes only after the ruin of the iron and clay, and in the prophecy of Daniel 7 is received only after the judgment of the Little

[45] *Ibid.*, p. 299.   [46] *Ibid.*, p. 307.   [47] *Ibid.*
[48] Haag, *op. cit.* (2d ed.), vol. 1, cols. 186-206; *La grande encyclopédie*, art. "Amyraut."

Horn. Then will come the triumphant state of the church in its celestial abode.[49]

VIII. De Mornay Says Papacy Is Prophesied Antichrist

PHILIPPE DE MORNAY (1549-1623), illustrious Protestant, Lord of Plessis Morly, was born at Buhy. Influenced by his mother, who had secretly embraced the new Protestant doctrine, he openly espoused Calvinism. Finishing his education in Paris, he traveled in Switzerland, Germany, and Italy. For a number of years he was engaged in the service of the king of Navarre, as king's counselor, governor of Saumur, superintendent of the house and crown, and later becoming minister of state, and the grand diplomat of the Huguenot party, the most truly representative Protestant of France and the most steadfast and trustworthy advocate of peace.[50] In 1598 his book *Traité de l'institution de l'Eucharistie* (Treatise on the Institution of the Eucharist) brought upon him the disapproval of the court.[51] He wrote numerous other works including *Le mystère d'iniquité: c'est à dire, l'histoire de la Papauté* (The Mystery of Iniquity: That Is, the Story of the Papacy). (Title page reproduced on page 648.)

1. PRESENT POPE PART OF SYSTEM OF INIQUITY.—In 1611 he wrote *Le mystère d'iniquité,* under his full name and titles. The Latin edition was dedicated to King James I of England and the French edition to Louis XIII.[52] De Mornay declares that the present pope, Paul V, corresponds fully to the description of the great antichristian system of iniquity given by John and Paul, and shows how this power has usurped the throne which belongs to the eternal Son of God, the sole ruler of His church.[53] Yet this great apostasy had to come, for it was predicted in the Scriptures, even as well as the fact that the kings of the earth

---

[49] Moyse Amyraut, *Du règne de mille ans,* pp. 124, 125.
[50] Baird, *The Huguenots and the Revocation of the Edict of Nantes,* vol. 1, pp. 16 ff.
[51] *La grande encyclopédie,* art. "Mornay (Philippe de)."
[52] Baird, *The Huguenots and the Revocation of the Edict of Nantes,* vol. 1, pp. 60, 61.
[53] Philippe de Mornay, *Le mystère d' iniquité,* Preface, p. xii.

would unite in their counsels to surrender their power to the Beast.[54] On this he was very explicit.

2. APPLIES ALL PROPHETIC EPITHETS TO ROME.—Re strained by pagan Rome at first, the Papacy now makes all the nations drink from her cup. De Mornay castigates her for her simony and similar iniquities, and her benefits which are sold for a price.[55] John called her the Harlot, Paul the Man of Sin, the predicted Antichrist. But more than all the arguments and historical statements in the body of the work, the two illustrations given in the book rankled in the hearts of the Roman Catholics. The one represented symbolically the approaching downfall of the papal see, under the guise of a strong tower, like the tower of Babel, resting on perishable wooden supports to which the flame is already applied; and the other represented Pope Paul V, with the most blasphemous of certain inscriptions placed on an arch of triumph erected in Italy to his honor, as PAULO V. VICE DEO CHRISTIANAE REPUBLICAE, by which they had unwittingly affixed to him the exact number of the Beast.[56]

IX. Bourignon—Court of Rome Is Harlot of Apocalypse

ANTOINETTE BOURIGNON (1616-1680), visionary, was born at Lille. Claiming to be inspired to re-establish the spirit of the primitive gospel, she gave up the liturgy of Rome, emphasizing the spiritual worship of God. Expelled from France, she fled to Belgium, Holland, and northern Germany. She wrote numerous volumes, and among her principal works are: *Témoignage de la vérité* (Testimony of the Truth), *Traité du nouveau ciel et du règne de l'antéchrist* (Treatise About the New Heaven and the Rule of Antichrist), *Le renouvellement de l'ésprit évangélique* (The Renewal of the Evangelical Spirit), *L'Antéchrist découvert* (Antichrist Unveiled).[57] She comments thus on Antichrist:

---

[54] *Ibid.*, p. 597.
[55] *Ibid.*, p. 603.
[56] *Ibid.*, frontispiece and second illustration; Baird, *The Huguenots and the Revocation of the Edict of Nantes*, vol. 1, p. 61.
[57] *La grande encylopédie*, art. "Bourignon (Antoinette)."

"People think that Antichrist will not reign on the earth until we see him bodily. This is a great error, for he has long been reigning through his doctrine and his spirit of error, though he is not discerned. He occupies the throne of God, and rules over all christendom under a false appearance of holiness and piety, thus winning the whole world. He has spread such thick darkness on the whole world, that he is discovered by none, and people would think to be committing sin if they were suspecting the court of Rome of being the harlot of the Apocalypse, while she is that in truth." [58]

Such is the witness of a voice on the fringe of Protestantism.

X. Jurieu—France Considered Tenth Part of Papal City

PIERRE JURIEU (1637-1713), distinguished Huguenot leader and noted controversialist, was born at Mer, and schooled in philosophy at Saumur. He was the nephew of Pierre du Moulin.[59] A man of unusual scholastic attainments, he received his M.A. at nineteen. After travel and further study in Holland and England, and upon ordination, he succeeded to his father's pastorate at Mer, about 1671. In 1674 his reputation for learning won him the professorship of theology and Hebrew in the Huguenot Seminary at Sedan. Here for seven years he zealously guarded the Reformation against attacks particularly from Catholic Bishop Bossuet,[60] with whom he held controversies, as well as with the Jesuit Maimbourg—and championed vigorously the rights of his persecuted brethren in France. (Portrait on page 648.)

In 1681 the academy at Sedan was "desolated" when Louis XIV deprived Protestants of permission to give public instruc-

---

[58] Antoinette Bourignon, *L'appel de Dieu et le refus des hommes* (The Call of God and the Refusal of Men), p. 129.

[59] The caliber of some of these able French Protestant leaders and writers may be gauged by noting that Pierre du Moulin, or Molinoeus (1568-1658), noted controversialist, was author of some eighty different works. He escaped the Massacre of St. Bartholomew (1572). A tireless worker, he was professor of philosophy at Leyde, chaplain of Princess Catherine de Bourbon, who became the wife of Henry of Lorraine, and then pastor and professor at the Sedan Protestant Theological school. In 1615 he went to England, where he was called in counsel to King James I. In 1612 he wrote *Troisième livre de l'accomplissement des prophéties*.

[60] BISHOP JACQUES-BENIGNE BOSSUET (1627-1704), Catholic bishop of Meaux, king's counselor, highly educated in Jesuit schools, and accomplished orator and preceptor to the Dauphin, lauded the Revocation of the Edict of Nantes. Besides writing the *History of the Variations of the Protestant Church*, he also employed his skill in writing a commentary on the Apocalypse (*L'Apocalypse avec une explication*) based on the *Preterist*, not the *Futurist*, scheme. He sharply attacked Jurieu's positions, declaring pagan Rome and Judaism had long since fulfilled the predictions. On the other hand, he said the Catholic Church had already brought about the millennium—the period of the church's supremacy—and the Albigenses, Waldenses, numerous as Gog and Magog, had besieged the New Jerusalem, that is, the Catholic Church. The papal anathemas were the fire from heaven that would consume them. (*L'Apocalypse avec une explication*, p. 254; see also Elliott, *op. cit.*, vol. 4, pp. 501 ff. and 585 ff.)

tion. Upon the Revocation of the Edict of Nantes, in 1685, Jurieu went into exile at Rotterdam, where for twenty-seven years he was a resident—a pastorship and lectureship having been provided for him. Here his ardor drew him into controversy with Preterists Grotius and Hammond over the identity of the Antichrist and the time of his reign. A prolific writer, he was author of sixty works, one of which passed through twenty-two French and twenty-six English editions. Jurieu's *L'Accomplissement des prophéties ou la délivrance prochaine de l'église* (Exposition of the Apocalypse or the Coming Deliverance of the Church) was published just after the Revocation of the Edict of Nantes. In prophetic exposition he expressedly took Mede as his guide,[61] except in those portions involving later application.

1. REFUTES FUTURISTIC AND PRETERISTIC THESES.—Writing out of conviction, and in lucid style, Jurieu is very specific. But as he follows Mede so closely—such as in the enunciation of the seven seals, ten horns and seven heads [62]—these similarities will not be repeated and the analysis extended. Jurieu definitely refutes with force and in detail the papal Futurist and Preterist theses of Ribera, Bellarmine, et cetera.[63] He also bemoans the lapse of vigor that had come over Protestantism.[64]

2. MAKES FRANCE TENTH PART OF CITY.—Concerning the trumpets, Jurieu makes the first four the barbarian scourges of the Western Empire, to vex and destroy it, and the fifth and sixth the Saracens and Turks.[65] He believed the last persecutions had begun in 1655 with the Waldenses, spreading into other lands, and in 1685 by the Revocation of the Edict of Nantes. He therefore thought the three and a half year-days of the Witnesses lying dead in the street of the papal city, or empire—which he believed refers to France—might end in three and a half years. But he adds later:

"There are as yet in France more than *a hundred thousand persons* who either have not signed or have *repented* after their signing. If all these

---

[61] Pierre Jurieu, *The Accomplishment of the Scripture Prophecies* (English ed.), Introduction.
[62] *Ibid.*, part 1, pp. 54, 160.
[63] *Ibid.*, pp. 104 ff.
[64] *Ibid.*, Preface.
[65] *Ibid.*, part 1, pp. 55 ff.

must *fall off*, there is yet a long time to tarry. *Lastly* who knows, whether God will not begin to reckon the three *years* and a half untill other Princes have wholly extinguisht the *Reformation* in their dominions? 'Tis therefore rashness to affirm, *that deliverance must exactly come in such a year."* [66]

"And the spirit of life from God entered into them. These words teach us how the Reformation shall be reestablished in France." [67]

" 'Tis therefore evident that God does *here* testify, that sometime after these three years and a half of death, the Reformation shall be lifted up to a great glory, but not everywhere; 'tis only in that place, which is called the *street of the great City,* and is after called the *tenth* part of the city: for the whole destruction of the *Antichristian Kingdom* must not happen until some years afterward." [68]

He also judged that the tenth of the city destined to fall, as the Witnesses arose, would be France. [69] His thesis appears on the title page:

"Proving, that the Papacy is the *Antichristian Kingdom;* and that *that Kingdom* is not far from its Ruin. That the *present Persecution* may end in *Three years and half,* after which the Destruction of *Antichrist* shall *begin;* which shall be *Finisht* in the beginning of the *next Age:* and then the *Kingdom of Christ* shall come upon Earth." [70]

3. END OF 1260 YEARS BRINGS FALL OF POPEDOM.—Computing the 1260 years from A.D. 450 or 454, the death of Valentinian—on the year-day principle, and with 360 days to a year— would bring the fall of popedom about 1710 or 1714. [71] The Beasts of Revelation 13 are both the Antichristian Empire. [72] These ten kings, Jurieu held, are the continuation of the Roman Empire under the seven heads and ten horns, the seventh head being that of Antichrist, and the beast from the earth representing a new empire, called the Empire of the Church, or an Ecclesiastic Empire. The vials are interpreted as the means by which the papal empire would be brought to ruin, falling upon it since the tenth century. The second plague, for instance, is the crusades; the fifth, when Rome was forsaken and the popes resided at Avignon; the sixth involving the Turks. [73] Spreading

---

[66] *Ibid.*, part 2, p. 256.   [67] *Ibid.*, p. 258.
[68] *Ibid.*, p. 259.   [69] *Ibid.*, pp. 254 ff.
[70] *Ibid.*, title page of the whole work. See further quotations from this work in the chapter on predictions of the French Revolution, p. 726.
[71] *Ibid.*, part 2, pp. 54-57.
[72] *Ibid.*, part 1, pp. 98, 136 ff.
[73] *Ibid.*, part 2, p. 87.

back over centuries, these will soon reach their climax. Babylon is also the Antichristian Empire.[74]

4. ROME'S DIVISIONS PRECEDE CHRIST'S KINGDOM.—There are frequent allusions to Daniel's four empires, the divisions of the fourth, and the fifth monarchy, as the kingdom of Christ, appearing *after* the ten divisions.[75] Daniel 7 repeats the grand outline, with only the Little Horn added as Antichrist.[76] Besides these views he held strongly to the view that during the millennium the Jews will have the prominent share in governing the earth.[77]

---

[74] *Ibid.*, part 1, pp. 171-173.
[75] *Ibid.*, p. 290.
[76] *Ibid.*, p. 291.
[77] *Ibid.*, part 2, pp. 300-310.

CHAPTER TWENTY-NINE

Eighteenth Century
Marked by Contrasting Developments

I. Advances Countered by Serious Retrogressions

The eighteenth century—which completes the scope of Volume II—was a climactic period, witnessing the recognized close of one of the greatest of the prophetic time periods. It was a century of extreme contrasts. The seeds of the Jesuit Preterist counterinterpretation sprang up and began to bear their evil fruit of acceptance among German rationalists, and thence to similar groups in England and America. Furthermore, no sooner had premillennialists repudiated the false Augustinian theory of a past millennium, than postmillennialism, introduced among Protestants by a Protestant, swept like a scourge over a large percentage of the churches. And coupled to this was the tragedy of bitter reaction against all Christianity, false and true, as the insidious principles of infidelity and atheism reached their climax in the French Revolution.

On the other hand, the ending of the 1260 year-day period took place—anticipated for a full century by a line of expositors who believed France might be the instrument to accomplish it. Prophetic students on three continents watched for and recognized the fulfillment, which they duly attested. Prophetic interpretation in the hands of able men in Britain, France, and Germany—and now in America—continued to advance. Errors were corrected, and new principles were discerned. The great Lisbon earthquake-sign of the approaching end was clearly recognized. And just before the close of the century men in two different lands independently arrived at the identical conclusion that the 70 weeks of years are the *first part* of the 2300 year-days. Such were the prophetic high lights of this new century which we now enter.

1. PROFOUND EFFECT UPON PROPHETIC INTERPRETATION.— After the establishment of Protestantism by the English Revolution of 1688, came the expansion of Britain, the rise of America, the revival of religion, and the dawn of world-wide missions. Under the Peace of Ryswick (1697), between William of Orange and Emperor Leo I, there were various stipulations favorable to the standing of England. But in particular it marked the beginning of a new era of civil and religious liberty. Moreover, entry upon this new era had a profound effect upon prophetic interpretation. Fresh fulfillments of prophecy were recognized, and advanced study followed. Current progress in science, philosophy, and theology was reflected in prophetic exposition.

2. COMPLEXITIES SIMPLIFIED BY THREEFOLD GROUPING.— The tracing of prophetic interpretation from the eighteenth century onward becomes more complex. But by holding in mind the three basic schools of interpretation now operating, the analysis is still relatively simple: (1) The Historical School continues on strongly, strengthening and perfecting its interpretation; (2) the Jesuit Preterist School begins to be adopted seriously by an increasing group of Protestants; and (3) the Jesuit Futurist School, generally held among Catholics, becomes more aggressive, but is not adopted by any Protestant group until early in the nineteenth century.

3. DETAILS HARMONIZE WITH OVER-ALL PATTERNS.—If these three schemes are kept in mind, it will be easy to trace developments. Once an expositor is cataloged, it is a relatively simple matter to know what he believes on all major points, as those who hold to the respective schools run rather true to pattern. Thus the Historical School expositor will apply the year-day principle to all time periods, whereas this will be

21

denied by the other two schools. Likewise, the Historical School holds the Papacy to be the prophesied Antichrist, and such is denied by the other two schools. The discussion will begin with England.

II. Fleming Forecasts French Revolution as Prelude to Papal Overthrow

ROBERT FLEMING, JR. (c. 1660-1716), descended from a line of Scotch preachers. Born in Scotland, he early set his heart on the ministry. His father[1] took him to Holland in 1679, where he studied at Leyden and Utrecht. For a time he plodded through the whole round of scholastic literature, until it not only tired him but became "nauseating." "I resolved, therefore," he said, "to betake myself for the future to the study of the Sacred Volume alone," and to use other books only to help in the understanding of the same. Thus he continued to study and investigate.

Ordained at Rotterdam, in 1688, by Scotch divines who were refugees in Holland, he became pastor of the English church at Leyden, and in 1695 succeeded his father as pastor of the Scots church at Rotterdam. He was then invited to accept a call to the Presbyterian church in Lothbury, his acceptance being urged by William III. Distinguished for his learning and his piety, and author of nine volumes, he exerted great influence, William III frequently consulting him on the ecclesiastical affairs of Scotland. Fleming was proffered the principalship of the University of Glasgow, but he declined, preferring his humble charge as a Dissenter.

In 1701 he was lecturer at Salters' Hall—the very year in which he produced his small but remarkable discourse on the

---

[1] ROBERT FLEMING, SR. (1630-1694), educated at the universities of Edinburgh and St. Andrews, removed to Rotterdam in 1677 as pastor of the English church. Author of ten books, he was also an expositor of prophecy, writing *The Fulfilling of the Scripture* (1669), which went through several editions. Robert, Sr., held that the papal Antichrist had persecuted the Protestant witnesses in sackcloth, discussed "Antichrist's reigne," and looked for the fall of Babylon and the ruin and overthrow of Antichrist, which was approaching. He also stressed the destruction of Turkey under the sixth plague. He likewise wrote a book on earthquakes as premonitory signs (London: 1693). It was unquestionably from his father that Robert, Jr., inherited his strong taste for tracing "the divine hand in history."

rise and fall of the Papacy. The unsettled state of public affairs and the danger with which Protestantism was menaced particularly perturbed Fleming's later years. In the midst of such anxieties he published his work. (Title page of one of the editions and portrait of author appear on page 644.) At this time the power of France was at its height, William III maintaining an unsuccessful and hopeless struggle. Just at that time he wrote his improbable predictions.[2]

Nearly a century after Fleming's death the treatise became famous, being reprinted several times in England, Germany, America, and Scotland.[3] In 1793 and 1848 attention was drawn to the apparent historical verification of Fleming's prediction that the French monarchy would fall by 1794 at least, and that in 1848 the Papacy would receive a severe blow. In a "Postscript," Fleming takes note of the deflection of Grotius and Hammond from the "First Principles of the Apocalyptical Interpretations," thus: "My principal design in writing this postscript was to refute the hypothesis [Preterist] that Grotius and Hammond go upon."[4]

1. GETS CLUE TO JUSTINIAN BEGINNING FROM CRESSENER.— The title page announces it to be "Predictions respecting the Revolutions of France; the Fate of its Monarch, the Decline of Papal Power."[5] Writing concerning "the Great Antichrist, or Rome Papal," and his "era or epoch," in an endeavor to see when its fall would occur, Fleming offers a "Key" to "unriddle" it. Determining its beginning epoch from evidence offered by Joseph Mede, Henry More, and Drue Cressener, he holds (1) that Babylon is papal Rome, and the Papacy the seventh head of the Beast; and (2) that the 1260 days[6] are years, and all references to the 1260-year period are "synchronical and the same," citing the 70 weeks as proof, along with Ezekiel.[7] However,

---

[2] *Thomas Thomson*, "Life of the Rev. Robert Fleming," in Robert Fleming, *The Rise and Fall of Papacy* (1870 ed.), pp. vi-ix.
[3] Several editions were printed in London (1793, 1809, etc.), an American edition in 1794, one printed in Stettin, Germany, in 1800, and one in Edinburgh, Scotland, in 1870 (perhaps occasioned by the events of that time).
[4] Robert Fleming, *Apocalyptical Key* (1793 ed.), pp. 119, 136.
[5] In the 1701, 1793, and 1809 eds.
[6] Robert Fleming, *op. cit.* (1793 ed.), pp. 16, 17.   [7] *Ibid.*, pp. 17, 18.

PROPHETIC CONJECTURES

ON THE

FRENCH REVOLUTION,

AND OTHER RECENT

AND SHORTLY EXPECTED EVENTS:

EXTRACTED FROM

ARCHBP. BROWN,	1551	DR. H. MORE,	1663
REV. J. KNOX,	1572	REV. P. JURIEU,	1687
DR. T. GOODWIN,	1639	REV. R. FLEMING,	1701
REV. CHR. LOVE,	1651	REV. J.WILLISON,	1742
ARCHBP. USHER,	1655	DR. GILL,	1748

AND

A REMARKABLE ANONYMOUS PAMPHLET, 1747.

WITH AN

INTRODUCTION AND REMARKS.

SURELY THE LORD GOD WILL DO NOTHING, BUT HE
REVEALETH HIS SECRET UNTO HIS SERVANTS THE
PROPHETS. AMOS.

London:

PRINTED BY W. TAYLOR, SHOE MAKER ROW,
BLACK FRIARS,

FOR WILLIAM BUTTON, N° 24, PATERNOSTER ROW.

MDCCXCIII.

ILLUSTRATIONS

OF

P R O P H E C Y:

IN THE COURSE OF WHICH
ARE ELUCIDATED MANY PREDICTIONS, WHICH OCCUR

IN ISAIAH, OR DANIEL,

IN THE WRITINGS OF THE EVANGELISTS,

OR THE BOOK OF REVELATION;

And which are thought to foretell, among other Great Events,
A Revolution in France, favourable to the Interests of Mankind,
The Overthrow of the Papal Power, and of Ecclesiastical Tyranny,
The Downfal of Civil Despotism,
And the subsequent Melioration of the State of the World:

TOGETHER

WITH A LARGE COLLECTION OF

EXTRACTS,

INTERSPERSED THROUGH THE WORK, AND TAKEN FROM

NUMEROUS COMMENTATORS;

AND PARTICULARLY FROM

Joseph Mede, Vitringa, Dr. Thomas Goodwin, Dr. Henry More, Dr. John
Owen, Dr. Cressener, Peter Jurieu, Brenius, Bishop Chandler, Sir Isaac
Newton, Mr. William Lowth, Fleming, Bengelius, Daubuz, Whitby,
Lowman, Bishop Newton, and Bishop Hurd.

VOL. I.

LONDON.—M,DCC,XCVI.

A

DISCOURSE

ON THE

RISE AND FALL OF PAPACY;

WHEREIN

The REVOLUTION in FRANCE,

AND THE

ABJECT STATE OF THE FRENCH KING,

IS DISTINCTLY POINTED OUT.

DELIVERED AT LONDON, IN THE YEAR M,DCC,I.

BY ROBERT FLEMING, V.D.M.

LONDON: PRINTED, M,DCC,I.
EDINBURGH: RE-PRINTED, M,DCC,XCII;
AND
BOSTON: RE-PRINTED AND SOLD BY ADAMS AND LARKIN, COURT-
STREET, M,DCC,XCIV.

A

DISCOURSE

ON THE

RISE and FALL of PAPACY.

IF we may believe historians, says a learned man,
was, in seven years, the occasion
100,000 Christians. The mass
100,000 in three months.—
in the persecution of the
1,000,000 lost their
of the Jesuits till 1580,
900,000 perished,
of Alva, by the hang-
ergerius affirms, that
destroyed 150,000.
Rebellion, in which
the Lord Orery re-
reign of Charles
been destroyed in the
iedmont, in the Pa-
can full reckon
been in the gallies,
idolatrous harlot, so
ints, that a late author
sets up as a pattern

Dialogues, p. 161. See also his
ii. chap. 15, 16, &c.

Coming French Revolution Predicted Throughout Century Prior

Two Compilations Published During French Revolution as Proof of the Accuracy of Prophetic
Forecasts Naming France as Scene of the Coming Upheaval (Upper). Robert Fleming (Inset) in
1701 Wrote of the Approaching Blow to the Papacy, Which He Looked for About 1794.

the total destruction of Antichrist would not take place until the "appearance of Christ, upon the pouring out of the 7th Vial." [8]

2. LITTLE HORN SEATED LONG BEFORE 606.—Fleming bases his time calculation on the four world powers of Daniel 7 and the period of the Little Horn, which is the *"Papal Antichrist,"* supplanting the three kingdoms—"the *Exarchat,* the *Lombards,* and the *Authority of the Emperors in Italy."* [9] He states that "this great enemy was seated in his Regal Dignity long before the year 606."

3. TURKISH WOE DATED FROM CROSSING EUPHRATES.—The seven trumpets, Fleming holds, are the blows upon Western Rome by the barbarians in the first four trumpets. The star fallen from heaven in the fifth trumpet is the bishop of Rome; the dark pitchy smoke is the monks that swarmed about spreading error and idolatry. The locusts are the Saracens. The sixth trumpet brings the Turks from beyond the Euphrates, from which coming they date their rise. [10]

4. FIFTH VIAL TO VISIT BEAST BETWEEN 1794-1848.—Fleming begins the outpouring of the seven vials in the time of the Reformation, with the fifth upon the seat of the Beast.

"This judgment will probably begin about the year 1794, and expire about A.C. 1848; so that the duration of it upon this supposition, will be for the space of 54 years. For I do suppose, that seeing the *Pope* received the title of *Supreme Bishop* no sooner than An. 606, he cannot be supposed to have any Vial poured upon his seat immediately . . . until the year 1848." [11]

The basis for fixing upon the year 1794 follows:

"But as to the Expiration of this [4th] Vial, I do fear it will not be until the Year 1794. The Reason of which conjecture is this; that I find the Pope got a new Foundation of Exaltation, when *Justinian,* upon his Conquest of *Italy,* left it in a great measure to the *Pope's Management,* being willing to eclipse his own Authority, to advance that of this haughty *Prelate.*" [12]

---

[8] *Ibid.,* p. 19.
[9] *Ibid.,* (1701 ed.), p. xxxii (1793 ed., p. 26).
[10] *Ibid.* (1793 ed.), pp. 33-40.
[11] *Ibid.,* p. 59. "A.C." is "after Christ," or A.D.
[12] *Ibid.* (1701 ed.), p. lxix (1793 ed., p. 53).

5. 1848 TO BE EVIL YEAR FOR PAPACY.—Anticipating 1848 also to be an evil year for the Papacy, Fleming says:

"Therefore, 2, we may conclude that the *last head* of the Beast, which is the *Papal,* did arise either immediately upon the extirpation of the *Gothish* kingdom, or some time after. But it could not rise to its power immediately after, seeing *Justinian* did by the conquest of Italy revive the Imperial government again there, which by that means *was healed* after *the deadly wound* which the Heruli and the Goths had given it. Though I confess Justinian's conquests of Italy laid a foundation for the Pope's rise, and paved the way for his advancement: both by the *penal* and *sanguinary laws* which he made against all those that dissented from the Romish church, and by the confusions that followed upon *Narses* his bringing in the *Lombards.*" [13]

However, instead of extending the 1260 years from 606 to 1866, Fleming unjustifiably uses but 360 days to a year in fulfillment rather than a Julian year—casting away eighteen years in order to bring what he believes to be the exact measurement, which he sets forth as 1848.[14]

6. SECOND ADVENT DESTROYS PAPACY; BRINGS MILLENNIUM.—Fleming looks for the end of the Papal Kingdom and its destruction in the year 2000, at the coming of Christ, when the world enters upon that glorious *sabbatical millenary,* when *the saints shall reign on the earth, in a peaceable manner for a thousand years more.* After its expiration, Satan will be let loose to play a new game, and men will begin to apostatize from the truth almost universally. But when they have brought the saints to the last extremity, Christ Himself will appear in His glory and destroy His enemies with fire from heaven. (Rev. 20:9.) This denotes the great conflagration (2 Peter 3:10) after which come the resurrection and Christ's summoning of men before Him unto judgment. Perhaps the time of this judgment, Fleming thinks, would take up the greatest part, or the whole, or *another millenary* of years.[15]

7. FRENCH UPHEAVAL BRINGS REPRINTS OF FLEMING.—The trouble Fleming anticipated for France, he phrases thus:

---

[13] *Ibid.* (1793 ed.), pp. 24, 25.
[14] *Ibid.* (1701 ed.), pp. xxvi, xxvii (1793 ed., p. 22).
[15] *Ibid.* (1701 ed.), pp. xxxiv, xxxv (1793 ed., pp. 27, 28).

"I cannot but hope that some new Mortification of the *chief Supporters* of *Antichrist* will then happen; and perhaps the *French Monarchy* may begin to be considerably humbled about that time: that whereas the present *French King* takes the *Sun* for his *Emblem,* and this for his *Motto, Nec pluribus impar,* he may at length, or rather his Successors, and the Monarchy it self (at least before the Year 1794) be forced to acknowledg, that (in respect to neighbouring Potentates) he is even *singulis impar.*" [16]

In 1793, when the horrors of the French Revolution were at their worst, and Louis XVI was about to perish on the scaffold, Fleming's improbable prediction, written nearly a century before, was recalled. It was brought to public attention by extracts in newspapers and by reprints in England, Germany, and America. The impression produced was profound. In London, Terry simply republished, in 1793, the original 1701 edition as the best evidence, which none could gainsay. In the 1809 reprint this earnest appeal, based on the ending of the 1260 years, appears:

"How blind must they be, who see not the finger of God in all these changes, but still say, *Where is the promise of his coming?* Where is the fulfilment of the prophecies? *O fools, and slow of heart to believe what the prophets have spoken!*

"'Christians! Protestants! hasten from Babylon, the object of the Divine vengeance, *that ye partake not of her sins, nor receive of her plagues.* Beware of enlisting yourselves, directly, or indirectly, in defence of the *Man of Sin,* that hath so long tyrannized, and uttered his blasphemies, in the temple of God.'" [17]

8. 1848 Witnesses Another Crisis in Europe.—As to Fleming's second date, when the Papacy would be further weakened but not destroyed, 1848 brought another crisis. The Revolution of 1848 broke out in Paris on February 23, and by March 5 every country between the Atlantic and the Vistula had in greater or less degree felt the revolutionary fever. On March 15, a fortnight after the fall of Louis Philippe, a constitution was proclaimed at Rome, the Pope had fled to Gaeta, and an Italian Republic had been proclaimed. The eyes of Europe became giddy as they beheld the rapid whirl of events.

---

[16] *Ibid.* (1701 ed.), pp. lxviii, lxix (1793 ed., p. 53).
[17] *Ibid.* (1809 ed.), following title page.

FRENCH EXPOSITORS PARALLEL BRITISH AND OTHER CONTINENTALS

Cappel Identifies 457 B.C. as Beginning Year of the Seventy Weeks of Years (Upper Left and Center); Philipot's Answer to Jurieu on the Vials (Upper Right); With Jurieu's Portrait (Left Oval); De Mornay's Discussion of the Papal Mystery of Iniquity, With Graphic Illustration of Its Precarious Position (Lower Center); and Author's Portrait (Right Oval)

The year 1848 was an important one in this era. And Fleming's point was that the stroke upon the Papacy would probably begin about the year 1794 and expire about the year 1848,[18] a period which involves the pouring out of the fifth vial upon the seat of the Beast.

9. FLEMING NEVER EMPLOYED VICARIUS FILII DEI.—Be it particularly noted that, despite wide quotation to the effect that Fleming himself computed the number of the Beast upon the name *Vicarius Filii Dei,* it is only a supplemental statement by the reprinter, first appearing in an *appended* section of the 1793 reprint. It is introduced by the explicit words: "In addition to what Mr. Fleming has said, the Editor begs leave to subjoin the following." [19] There follows an "Explanation of the Mark of the Name of the Beast" (in the 1809 edition it is called "Frontlet of the Beast"), giving 666 as the numerical significance of the name *Vicarius Filii Dei,* which, the editor says, the popes "have assumed to themselves," and "caused to be inscribed over the door of the Vatican" [20]—though without any documentation. Nowhere in the 1701 edition and nowhere in the body of the original reprints of 1793 and onward does *Vicarius Filii Dei* appear—only the Greek title *Lateinos,* mentioned by Irenaeus, and a Hebrew title or two.[21]

We now turn to a completely different exposition—an innovation in the matter of the millennium.

III. Whitby Projects His New Postmillennial Scheme

The eighteenth century in England was distinguished by the rise of a new millennial theory—that of Whitbyanism. It was an elaborate effort to set aside the chiliastic view, and was asserted to be a new hypothesis, or new discovery—the world's conversion under an increased potency of grace. It was a spiritual millennium, consisting of the universal triumph of the gospel and the conversion of all nations in the thousand years *before* the coming of Christ.

---

[18] *Ibid.* (1793 ed.), p. 59.
[20] *Ibid.* (1809 ed.), pp. 105, 107.

[19] *Ibid.* (1809 ed.), p. 104 (1793 ed., p. 138).
[21] *Ibid.* (1793 ed.), p. 26.

A
PARAPHRASE
AND
COMMENTARY
ON
The New Testament.

VOLUME II.

Containing a Plain
EPISTLES,
WITH
A Discourse on the Millennium.

To which is added,
A CHRONOLOGY of the New Testament, a Map, and Alphabetical Table of all the Places mentioned in the Gospel, Acts, or the Epistles.

With Tables
Of the Matters contained, and of the Words and Phrases explained throughout the whole Work.

By DANIEL WHITBY, D.D.
And CHANTOR of the Church of SARUM.

The Second Edition.

LONDON:
Printed by J. Barber, for Awnsham and John Churchill, at the Black Swan in Pater-Noster-Row, 1706.

A
TREATISE
OF THE
True Millennium:

Shewing that it is not a
REIGN of PERSONS,
Raised from the Dead,

but of the
CHURCH

Flourishing Gloriously for a
THOUSAND YEARS

AFTER THE
Conversion of the Jews,

AND THE
Flowing in of all Nations to them thus Converted
TO THE
CHRISTIAN FAITH.

DANIEL WHITBY LAUNCHES HIS POST-MILLENNIAL THEORY

Title Page of Whitby's Commentary (Left) Containing His Revolutionary Treatise on the Millennium; Portrait of Whitby (Center); and Initial Page of Whitby's Post-Millennial Treatise (Right) Attacking the Premillennial Position of the Protestants and the Augustinian Theory of the Millennium Held by the Catholics

DANIEL WHITBY (1638-1726), originator of the postmillennial theory, was born in Northamptonshire. Educated at Trinity College, Oxford, from which he received the B.A., M.A., B.D., and D.D. degrees, he was made chaplain to the bishop of Salisbury in 1668, and prebend of Yatesbury in the Cathedral church. Finally he became rector of St. Edmund's in Salisbury. Fairly popular as a preacher, he is better known for his voluminous writings, about thirty-nine works in all. A persistent student, of unquestioned erudition and ability, he was primarily a controversialist. His *Protestant Reconcilor* (1683) encountered violent opposition and was ordered publicly burned at Oxford.

Whitby's most noted work was his two-volume *Paraphrase and Commentary on the New Testament* (1703), which had reached its seventh printing by 1760. In the latter part of this work he set forth an elaborate 26-page "new hypothesis" on the thousand years. The postmillennial scheme, of which he was the avowed originator, appeared in chart form as a substitute for a commentary section on the Apocalypse, which he declined to attempt.[22] Whitby passed through a number of opinions before coming to his ultimate positions; and his theory, based on unproved assumptions and without support of Scripture, clearly contravened the faith of the church for sixteen centuries.

This theory asserted that the conversion of the world, under large outpourings of the Holy Spirit, would be at the time of the national establishment of the Jews,[23] along with the overthrow of the pope and the Turk. This he denominated the "first resurrection." A universal reign of paradisiacal righteousness, peace, and victory was scheduled to come next, before the second advent. Postmillennialism thus places the advent at the *end,* instead of the beginning, of the thousand years.[24] The theory was built upon the interpolated text of Justin, misap-

---

[22] West, *op. cit.*, in *Premillennial Essays*, pp. 378, 379.
[23] Daniel Whitby, *A Paraphrase and Commentary*, p. 688.
[24] See diagram on p. 652.

| PRESENT AGE | GRADUAL WORLD BETTERMENT | ETERNITY |

SPIRITUAL
RESURRECTION
(CONVERSION
OF JEWS)

SOULS IN HEAVEN

CHRIST
COMES AT
CLOSE

WHITBY PLACES MILLENNIUM PRIOR TO SECOND ADVENT

Whitby's Post-Millennial Theory, as Its Name Implies, Shifts the Second Advent
to the Close of the Thousand Years, Instead of Introducing the Period, as in the
Premillennial View of the Early Church, Which View Had Been Restored by
Joseph Mede and Most Expositors for a Century After His Time

plied passages of Irenaeus, misrepresentations of Christian chiliasm by Origen, Dionysius, and Eusebius, and by twisted quotations from the fathers, apocryphal writings, and Sibylline
oracles.[25]

Whitbyanism asserted that the thousand years were still
future, and that under the preaching of the gospel all opposing
forces would give way, and there would be restraint of Satan's
power. Thus the kingdom of Christ would come upon the
earth under the seventh trumpet—with Islam gone, the Papacy
gone, Brahmanism, Buddhism, and all heathenism gone, atheism, infidelity, secularism, false science, and philosophy gone,
and Satan shut up for one thousand years, the heathen nations
all converted, the whole world reformed, the times of restitution completed, and those of refreshing present—and all before
Christ personally and visibly appears.[26]

Eminent divines began to embrace it, and wrote upon it
—Vitringa (d. 1722), then Edwards and Hopkins in North
America, and Bellamy, Scott, Faber, Brown, and Fairbairn in
Britain. But the very century that gave the Whitbyan theory
to the world provided a vigorous protest against it. Astronomers,
philosophers, nobles, and poets, as well as divines, stood forth
in strong protest. Bengel helped turn the tide in Germany. Then
came a host of stalwarts—Zinzendorf, Roos, Jung-Stilling, and
others in Continental Europe. Sacred poetry in the hands of

---

[25] L. S. Chafer, "An Introduction to the Study of Prophecy," *Bibliotheca Sacra*, January-
March, 1943 (vol. 100, no. 397), p. 128.
[26] West, *op. cit.*, in *Premillennial Essays*, pp. 379, 380; Whitby, *op. cit.*, p. 696.

Watts, Wesley, Cowper, Montgomery, and Heber re-emphasized the premillennial story in impressive phrases.[27]

I. THE RESURRECTION APPLIED TO THE CHURCH.—Whitby's position is stated simply in the title of his treatise, which is both comprehensive and explicit. The resurrection is the glorious renewal of the church. It reads:

"A Treatise of the True Millennium: shewing that it is not a reign of persons raised from the dead, but of the church flourishing gloriously for a thousand years after the conversion of the Jews, and the flowing-in of all nations to them thus converted to the Christian Faith." [28]

2. FIRST AND SECOND RESURRECTIONS DENIED.—This is expressly stated in a chapter summary.

"*Arguments against the literal Resurrection, and the Reign of Martyrs upon Earth a thousand years.* First, *From the Inconsistency of it with the happy State of Souls departed,* ¶ I. Secondly, *From the accurate Description of the Resurrection in the Holy Scripture, without any mention of a first and second Resurrection, and with such Descriptions of the Qualities of the Bodies raised, the efficient Cause, of the Time, Circumstances, and Consequents of it, which suit not with the Doctrine of the Millennium.*" [29]

3. ANTICHRIST'S FALL MUST PRECEDE MILLENNIUM.— Whitby declares:

"The true *Millennium* will not begin till the fall of *Antichrist;* nor will the *Jews* be converted till that Time, the *Idolatry* of the *Roman Church* being one great Obstacle of their Conversion." [30]

"These instruments of Satan being thus slain and overcome by *Christ,* Satan is bound *a thousand Years.*" [31]

4. SECOND ADVENT A SPIRITUAL EFFUSION.—Whitby's definition of the second advent is explicit.

"There shall be then a *full Effusion of the Holy Ghost* . . . somewhat resembling that which was vouchsafed to the first Ages of *Christianity.*" [32]

This indicates a spiritual second advent in the form of a Pentecostal outpouring of the Spirit.

5. SAINTS SEPARATED FROM CHRIST DURING MILLENNIUM.—

---

[27] West, *op. cit.*, in *Premillennial Essays,* pp. 384, 385.
[28] Whitby, *op. cit.*, p. 687.   [29] *Ibid.*, p. 708.   [30] *Ibid.*, p. 696.
[31] *Ibid.*, p. 703.   [32] *Ibid.*, p. 700.

Christ is in heaven, and the saints are on earth during Whitby's millennium. Then He comes to earth.

"Since *Christ* is to continue in Heaven till the Completion, or Consummation of all Things, spoken by the Holy *Prophets,* if the *Millennium* were any of them, *Christ* must continue in Heaven till the Consummation of that also, and therefore is not to come down from Heaven to reign on Earth till the *Millennium be* ended." [33]

"I believe then, That after the Fall of *Antichrist,* there shall be such a glorious State of the *Church,* by the Conversion of the *Jews* to the *Christian* Faith, as shall be to it *Life from the Dead;* that it shall then flourish in Peace and Plenty, in Righteousness and Holiness, and in a pious *Off-spring;* that then shall begin a glorious and undisturbed Reign of *Christ* over both *Jew* and *Gentile,* to continue a thousand Years, during the Time of *Satan's binding;* and that, as *John the Baptist* was *Elias,* because he came *in the Spirit and Power of Elias;* so shall this be the *Church of Martyrs,* and of those who had not received the *Mark of the Beast* because of their entire Freedom from all the Doctrines and Practices of the *Antichristian Church,* and because the Spirit and Purity of the Times of the *Primitive Martyrs* shall return." [34]

6. EFFECT UPON PROTESTANT CHURCHES WAS PROFOUND.— So Whitby begins his millennium with the living saints on earth, and Christ and the dead of ages past in heaven. He ends the period with the Lord's personal literal descent, accompanied by the spirits of just men made perfect. This postmillennial advent brings the day of judgment and the destruction of sinners, and the day of eternal salvation for the saints.

The effect upon the Protestant church was profound. As men came to contemplate an intervening millennium of peace and safety, they ceased to be eager and alert for the second advent. The principle of accommodation became ascendant. Men came to substitute the expectancy of death for Christ's coming. With such, Whitbyanism muffled the warning note, "Behold, I come quickly." Gill was impelled to cry in alarm: The churches have a name to live but are dead; both ministers and churches are asleep. And Bengel declared, in distress: This slumbering age needs an awakener. The day star of the advent hope was lost sight of by thousands, as they dreamed of a

---

[33] *Ibid.,* pp. 707, 708.   [34] *Ibid.,* p. 696.

golden age without Christ. Further note of Whitbyanism will be taken later. The repercussions increase with the passage of time.

IV. Daubuz Holds Firmly to Historical School Interpretation

CHARLES DAUBUZ (1673-1717), exiled Huguenot, was born in Guienne, France, his father being a Protestant pastor. Upon the Revocation of the Edict of Nantes (1685), the family left France, but his father died upon reaching England. Finally they settled in Yorkshire, England. He was educated at Christ Church, Oxford, and in Queens College, Cambridge. After receiving his B.A. and M.A., he became librarian of the college. He was tall, swarthy, and possessed of a powerful voice. In 1696 he accepted the mastership of a grammar school in Sheffield. However, he soon received orders in the Anglican Church, and was made vicar of Brotherton, in Yorkshire, where he wrote his *Perpetual Commentary on the Revelation of St. John,* which was published by his widow.

One of its features is a Symbolical Dictionary, in which the general significance of the prophetic symbols, especially those of the Apocalypse, is laid down. There, under "Babylon," Rome is signified, because the power of Babylon passed successively to Persia, Macedonia, and then Rome, first pagan and then papal.[35]

1. PLACES SARACENIC WOE FROM 612-762.—Believing that the seven churches are the church universal till the end of time, Daubuz explains the trumpets largely as Mede and Jurieu explain them, the fifth and sixth being the Saracens and Turks. Holding to the year-day principle, he places the five months, or 150 years, of the fifth trumpet, from Mohammed's opening of his mission to the Saracen caliph's removal to Baghdad, 612-762. Daubuz is not clear on the sixth trumpet. But the seventh is the signal for the resurrection of the just, after which is to come the time of the millennium.[36]

---

[35] Charles Daubuz, *A Perpetual Commentary on the Revelation of St. John* (1730 ed.), pp. 24, 25.
[36] Elliott, *op. cit.,* vol. 4, pp. 514-516.

2. Two Beasts Are Civil and Ecclesiastical Rome.—

The beasts of Revelation 13 Daubuz expounds as representing Rome, first civil and then ecclesiastical.[37] The seven heads are successive forms of government, and the ten horns are the original divisions, with their modern counterparts, which are: Italy and Germany, France, Spain, England with Ireland, Scotland, Hungary, Poland with Lithuania, Denmark with Sweden and Norway, Portugal, and Greece.[38] Note is also taken of other lists as given by Whiston and Allix.

3. Eberhard's Tabulation Noted; 1260 Years (476-1736).

—The early Latin tabulation of Eberhard, bishop of Salzburg at the Diet of Ratisbone, in 1240, is quoted.[39] The forty-two months are placed as from A.D. 476 to 1736.[40] The seven vials are made to spread over the centuries, the sixth drying up the Turkish power.

4. Two-horned Beast and Babylon Declared Papal.—

The two-horned beast is taken to represent the whole body of the corrupted clergy, as the former beast was that of the laity.[41] The Babylonish woman of Revelation 17 is the Papacy.

5. Resurrection Literal and Millennium Future.—

Daubuz' clear position on the future millennium and the literal resurrection, with the New Jerusalem being the habitation of the church—a touch of Whitbyanism—is best cited by the following extract:

"They who will right or wrong explain this *Life* or *Resurrection,* to signify the Resurrection of the Church in general, will find it hard to shew, why those, who are said to be *dead* still, and to *live again* during this first Resurrection, must not be said to be *dead,* and not to *live again,* in the same sense as they are so said in v. 12. to be *dead,* who are there to *stand,* that is to be *raised again* to stand before God, in order to be tried and judged. . . . But if this second Resurrection be of the Bodies, why must not the other? Are not both expressed in the like Terms. If this consequence be denied, then I challenge any Man to prove, that there is ever to be any bodily Resurrection of the Dead. For at this bold rate we may easily evade

---

[37] Daubuz, *op. cit.,* chap. 13 (1720 ed.), p. 576 (1730 ed., pp. 412 ff.).
[38] *Ibid.* (1720 ed.), pp. 556, 557.
[39] *Ibid.*
[40] Elliott, *op. cit.,* vol. 4, p. 517.
[41] Daubuz, *op. cit.* (1720 ed.), p. 576 (1730 ed., pp. 502, 503).

the force of all the Texts in Holy Writ, which mention the Resurrection of the Dead, and thus fall into that folly of those, who in the times of the Apostles, did, as some still do." [42]

V. Unknown Writer Revives Eastern-Western Antichrist Theory

In 1719 the anonymous writer of *An Exposition of the Revelations* places Antichrist's kingdom principally in the East, though duly recognizing the woman of Revelation 17 as the apostate Papacy. The two legs of Nebuchadnezzar's image are taken as the basis of East and West—the western being broken by the northern invasions, and the eastern by the Saracens and Turks, under the second and third woes; the ten toes are the resultant divisions, at the end of which Christ's kingdom will succeed. [43]

1. LITTLE HORN THE TURK; LOCUSTS THE SARACENS.— In harmony with this now largely discarded view, the writer makes Rome the fourth beast of Daniel 7, the ten horns the ten divisions, and the Little Horn the Turk—and similarly brings Turkey into the latter part of Daniel 11. [44] In chapter 8 the details of the invasion of Western Rome are set forth from the first four trumpets. [45] Chapter 9 then presents Mohammed as the fallen star, and the Saracens as the locusts with the power of scorpions to torment and oppress. "The five months makes 150 years," [46] for which several possible dates are suggested, but the period is not definitely delimited.

2. TURKISH TRUMPET PERIOD CLIMAXES IN 1471.—The sixth trumpet is taken to symbolize the Turks, who were "to slay the third part of men in a Day, a Month, and Year, in which time (396 years) the *Turkish* Empire came to its height, 1471." [47]

3. THEORY PROJECTED INTO TWO BEASTS OF REVELATION 13.—This East and West theory is pursued further under the two beasts of Revelation 13. The first, with the ten horns, sprang up in the West—and the ten horns are France, Spain, England,

[42] *Ibid.* (1720 ed.), p. 933.
[44] *Ibid.*, p. 15.
[46] *Ibid.*, pp. 28, 29.

[43] *An Exposition of the Revelations*, pp. 14, 15.
[45] *Ibid.*, p. 23.
[47] *Ibid.*, p. 29.

Portugal, Poland, Denmark, Sweden, Prussia, Sicily, and Hungary; the two-horned second beast is the Ottoman Empire.[48]
The woman on the scarlet beast is the "tyranny of the Popedom" over the western emperor and the kings.[49]

VI. Isaac Newton Employs Scientific Approach to Prophecy

SIR ISAAC NEWTON (1642-1727), mathematician, philosopher, and outstanding genius of his age in the realm of scientific research, was born in Lincolnshire, and grew up in a
religious atmosphere. Attending grammar school at Grantham,
he was conspicuous for his mechanical ingenuity with windmills,
water clocks, and sundials. In 1665 and 1668 respectively, he
received a B.A. and an M.A. from Trinity College, Cambridge.
His early interests centered in mathematics.

In 1665 Newton discovered differential calculus, and after
the alleged episode of the falling apple in 1666, began to specu-
late on the laws of universal gravitation—that the attraction
which one particle has for every other is proportional to its
respective mass plus the square of the distance. He thereby explained how the planets are kept in their courses. Newton then
began to study the nature of light and the colors of the prismatic
spectrum, and in 1668 experimented with small reflecting tele-
scopes. Einstein pays extraordinary tribute to him thus:

"The two-hundredth anniversary of the death of Newton falls at this
time. One's thoughts cannot but turn to this shining spirit, who pointed
out, as none before or after him did, the path of Western thought and research and practical construction. He was not only an inventor of genius
in respect of particular guiding methods; he also showed a unique mastery
of the empirical material known in his time, and he was marvellously in-
ventive in special mathematical and physical demonstrations. For all these
reasons he deserves our deep veneration. He is, however, a yet more significant figure than his own mastery makes him, since he was placed by fate
at a turning-point in the world's intellectual development."[50]

Newton began to lecture at Cambridge in 1669 and wrote
several vital scientific books, the greatest being his *Principia*

[48] *Ibid.*, p. 45.
[49] *Ibid.*, p. 61.
[50] Albert Einstein, "Isaac Newton," *The Observatory*, May, 1927 (vol. 50, no. 636), p.
146.

(1685-1687). He became a member of the Royal Society in 1671, and represented Cambridge in the Convention Parliament of 1689-1690, when his interest in prophecy began. In 1692-1693 he was studying the formation of sun and planets, maintaining that they could not be produced by natural causes alone, but only by an intelligent Agent and divine Power. In 1694 he was working on the lunar theory, and in 1696 was appointed warden of the mint, being advanced to master of the mint in 1699, at a salary of £1500 annually. In 1703 he became president of the Royal Society, which position he held by annual re-election till his death. In 1705 he was knighted by Queen Anne. His sepulcher is in Westminster Abbey. He never married.

Newton's skillful enunciation of celestial law and motion, his accuracy of statement, and his clearness of demonstration has never been surpassed. His aim was to find a simple rule by which the motion of the heavenly bodies of our planetary system could be calculated.[51] The breadth of his mind led him to take the expansive views of things natural and divine. He studied nature as a whole, history as a whole, chronology as a whole— and in connection with these, prophecy as a whole, in both Daniel and the Apocalypse. And in tracing prophecy through history and chronology, Newton utilized in the latter his unrivaled astronomical skill.[52] His *Observations Upon the Prophecies of Daniel, and the Apocalypse of St. John* (1733), which was not published until six years after his death, was the outcome of forty-two years of study. (Facsimile of title page, with portrait, on page 664.) From 1690 onward he had correspondence with the philosopher John Locke (d. 1704), over questions relating to the interpretation of prophecy.[53]

1. NEWTONIAN METHOD REVEALED IN MANUSCRIPT.—In writing on prophecy Newton employed the same exactness in finding the facts and applied the same strictly logical method

---

[51] Einstein, *op. cit.*, p. 147.
[52] Guinness, *Romanism*, p. 276.
[53] *Dictionary of National Biography*, vol. 14, p. 391.

of deduction that he used in the fields of mathematics and physics. For instance, on the second advent he tried to gather all available material, and we find in an auction catalog under several items:

"243 PROPHECIES. 'PROPHESIES CONCERNING CHRIST'S 2D COMING,' . . . *about* 15,000 *words,* . . . AUTOGRAPH. . . .

"245 PROPHECIES. OBSERVATIONS UPON THE PROPHECIES OF DANIEL AND THE APOCALYPSE OF ST. JOHN, A VAST COLLECTION OF DRAFTS OF VARIOUS CHAPTERS AND SECTIONS, . . . *about* 300,000 *words,* AUTOGRAPH. . . .

"247 PROPHECIES. A FAIR COPY, WITH CORRECTIONS, OF A WORK ON INTERPRETATION OF THE PROPHECIES, (*no title*) . . . *about* 40,000 *words,* . . . HOLOGRAPH." [54]

The systematic method employed by Newton in reaching his general conclusions concerning the prophecies on the advent is illustrated in one of these manuscripts, *Prophecies Concerning Christ's 2d Coming.* In this 15,000-word, forty-page study are listed prophecies pertaining to the second advent.[55] Item 235, a miscellaneous group not considered suitable for publication, contained *De Antichristo* (1727). These manuscripts are in addition to 231 published works. Such is the amazing record of this busy teacher and reverent scientist.[56]

2. KEY TO ALL PROPHECY FOUND IN DANIEL.—Part 1 of Newton's *Observations Upon the Prophecies,* comprising 231 pages, pertains to the prophecy of Daniel. He begins with a remarkably keen and clear definition of prophetic terms and symbols.[57] He maintains that Daniel is the key to all other prophecy, and insists that "to reject his Prophecies is to reject the Christian religion"; as to its unity he says, "The prophecies of *Daniel* are all of them related to one another, as if they were but several parts of one general prophecy." [58] The first prophecy —of Daniel 2, where the foundation is laid—is the easiest to understand, yet each succeeding vision adds something to the

---

[54] Item 5, 243, 245, 247, *Catalogue of the Newton Papers, which will be sold by auction by Messrs. Sotheby and Co.* (1936), p. 69.
[55] This original autograph manuscript of forty pages, small quarto ($8\frac{1}{2}$ x $6\frac{1}{2}$ in.), is now in the Advent Source Collection.
[56] "That the greatest philosopher of which any age can boast, was a sincere and humble believer in the leading doctrines of our religion and lived conformably to its precepts, has been justly regarded as a proud triumph of the Christian faith." (Joseph Thomas, *Universal Pronouncing Dictionary of Biography and Mythology,* p. 1814.)
[57] Newton, *Observations,* pp. 16 ff.
[58] *Ibid.,* pp. 24, 25.

former. The standard Historical School interpretation of the prophetic symbols is maintained—Babylon, Persia, Grecia, and Rome.[59]

3. LITTLE HORN MUST BE WEST OF GREECE.—Daniel 7 introduces "several new additions"—the lion's two wings, the three ribs in the mouth of the bear, the leopard's four heads, the fourth beast's eleven horns, and the Son of man coming to the Ancient of Days, sitting in judgment.[60] The identity of the same four kingdoms—Babylon, Persia, Grecia, and Rome— is stressed, together with the fact that the ten kingdoms arising out of Rome are to be sought in the Western Roman Empire —in the nations to the west of Greece.[61]

4. LITTLE HORN IS SEER, PROPHET, AND KING.—The ten kingdoms are listed by Newton as follows: (1) Vandals and Alans, (2) Suevians, (3) Visigoths, (4) Alans in Gallia, (5) Burgundians, (6) Franks, (7) Britains, (8) Huns, (9) Lombards, (10) Ravenna.[62] The eleventh horn, as a horn in the Latin empire contemporaneous with the division of Western Rome, occupies chapter 7. Its unique characteristic is portrayed thus:

"But it was a kingdom of a different kind from the other ten kingdoms, having a life or soul peculiar to itself, with eyes and a mouth. By its eyes it was a Seer; and by its mouth speaking great things and changing times and laws, it was a Prophet as well as a King. And such a Seer, a Prophet and a King, is the Church of *Rome*.

"A Seer . . . is a Bishop in the literal sense of the word; and this Church claims the universal Bishoprick.

"With his mouth he gives laws to kings and nations as an Oracle; and pretends to Infallibility, and that his dictates are binding to the whole world; which is to be a Prophet in the highest degree." [63]

5. CHARACTERISTICS AND CHRONOLOGY OF LITTLE HORN.— The Papacy's attempt to change times and laws is the burden of chapter 8, together with the plucking up of the three horns (Ravenna, the Lombards, and the principality of Rome),[64] the embracing of the Roman religion by the remaining kingdoms, and the achieving of temporal dominion.[65] The three and a half

---

[59] *Ibid.*   [60] *Ibid.*, p. 28.   [61] *Ibid.*, p. 73.
[62] *Ibid.*, p. 47; for detailed data and evidence, see pp. 47-73.   [63] *Ibid.*, p. 75.
[64] *Ibid.*, pp. 76-84.   [65] *Ibid.*, pp. 90-113.

times are declared to be "1260 solar years" in fulfillment, on the basis of a prophetic year of 360 days.[66]

6. Cleansing of Sanctuary Is Still Future.—The Persian ram and the Grecian goat are treated in chapter 9, with the notable horn of the goat meaning the first kingdom, which was founded by Alexander. The great horn, being from the body of the goat, must be found in the goat's original dominions. And such a little horn was the kingdom of *Macedonia*, from the time that it became subject to the *Romans*. This kingdom, because of the victory of the Romans over Perseus, king of Macedonia, ceased to be one of the four horns of the goat and became a dominion of a new sort, a horn which grew mighty but not by its own power, a horn which rose up and grew potent under a foreign power, the power of the Romans.[67] On Daniel 8:13 Newton demonstrates that the prophecy was fulfilled not in Antiochus but in the Antichrist. "Daniel's days are years," but no clear point from which to date the period is given.[68] Newton concludes:

"The Sanctuary and Host were trampled under foot 2300 days; and in *Daniel's* Prophecies days are put for years: but the profanation of the Temple in the reign of *Antiochus* did not last so many natural days. These were to last till the time of the end, till the last end of the indignation against the *Jews;* and this indignation is not yet at an end. They were to last till the Sanctuary which had been cast down should be cleansed, and the Sanctuary is not yet cleansed." [69]

7. Seventy Weeks Dated From 457 b.c.—Newton reasons that the seventy weeks of Daniel 9 are from j.p. 4257, or 457 b.c., as follows:

"*Seventy weeks are cut out upon thy people, and upon thy holy city, to finish transgression,* &c. Here, by putting a week for seven years, are reckoned 490 years from the time that the dispersed *Jews* should be re-incorporated into a people and a holy city, until the death and resurrection of Christ." [70]

"Now the dispersed *Jews* became a people and city when they first returned into a polity or body politick; and this was in the seventh year of *Artaxerxes Longimanus,* when *Ezra* returned with a body of *Jews* from cap-

66 *Ibid.*, p. 114. 67 *Ibid.*, pp. 115-120. 68 *Ibid.*, p. 122.
69 *Ibid.*, pp. 123, 124. 70 *Ibid.*, p. 130.

tivity, and revived the *Jewish* worship; and by the King's commission created Magistrates in all the land, to judge and govern the people according to the laws of God and the King, *Ezra* vii.25. There were but two returns from captivity, *Zerubbabel's* and *Ezra's;* in *Zerubbabel's* they had only commission to build the Temple, in *Ezra's* they first became a polity or city by a government of their own. Now the years of this *Artaxerxes* began about two or three months after the summer solstice, and his seventh year fell in with the third year of the eightieth *Olympiad;* and the latter part thereof, wherein *Ezra* went up to *Jerusalem,* was in the year of the *Julian Period* 4257." [71]

Ptolemy's canon was cited by Newton for his chronology, which he based on three of the eclipses recorded by Ptolemy— in the seventh year of Cambyses, and in the twentieth and thirty-first years of Darius I.[72] In determining when Artaxerxes' regnal years began, Newton did not follow the common practice of reckoning them from December, according to the canon (Egyptian) years, for he knew that Ptolemy had adjusted them to the Egyptian calendar; neither did he reckon them as Persian lunar years, from the spring, for such a regnal method, derived from archaeology, was unknown in Newton's day; rather he counted them as beginning with the date of accession. Newton assumed Artaxerxes' accession to have been delayed seven months after his father's death, until his actual exercise of kingly authority upon the ending of Artabanus' control of the government. Thus he arrived at a starting point some months later than the canon would indicate:

"Now he [Xerxes] reigned almost twenty one years, by the consent of all writers. Add the 7 months of *Artabanus,* and the sum will be 21 years and about four or five months, which end between midsummer and autumn *An. J. P.* 4250 [B.C. 464]. At this time therefore began the reign of his successor *Artaxerxes.* . . .

"His 7th year therefore began after midsummer *An. J.P.* 4256 [458 B.C.]; and the Journey of *Ezra* to *Jerusalem* in the spring following fell on the beginning of *An. J.P.* 4257 [457 B.C.]." [73]

---

[71] *Ibid.,* pp. 130, 131.

[72] *Ibid.,* p. 141. The eclipse of the seventh year of Cambyses is now known also to modern archaeologists from an ancient clay tablet recording its occurrence in the Babylonian lunar calendar—the 14th of Tammuz in the seventh year of Cambyses—agreeing not only with Ptolemy's date for it in the Egyptian calendar but also with the placing of that eclipse in "—522," or 523 B.C., by modern astronomical calculation. (Franz X. Kugler, *Sternkunde und Sterndienst in Babel,* vol. 1, pp. 61, 70, 71.) This is the only recorded eclipse in the sixth and fifth centuries B.C. that ties a regnal date to a Babylonian lunar year, Ptolemy's canon year, and a B.C. year.

[73] Newton, *Observations,* pp. 142, 143.

UNIVERSITY PROFESSORS CONSPICUOUS EXPOSITORS OF PROPHECY

Joseph Mede, Brilliant Cambridge Professor, Writes Remarkable *Key to the Revelation*, Marking Real Exposition Advance (Left); Sir Isaac Newton (Oval), Genius of His Age in Scientific Research, Likewise an Expositor, Whose *Observations on the Prophecies* Set a New High in Interpretation (Right)

8. SEVENTY SABBATIC YEAR-WEEKS TO A.D. 34.—Newton reckons the seventy weeks to the year of the crucifixion, which he puts in A.D. 34 (in the 490th year of the period), by assuming five Passovers in the period of Christ's public ministry.[74] He counts the seventy weeks by Jewish years, beginning in the fall—those of the Sabbatic-year and Jubilee-year series, which began on the tenth day of the seventh Jewish month, the Day of Atonement.[75]

"If you count in *Judaic* years commencing in autumn, and date the reckoning from the first autumn after *Ezra's* coming to *Jerusalem,* when he put the King's decree in execution; the death of *Christ* will fall on the year of the *Julian Period* 4747, *Anno Domini* 34; and the weeks will be *Judaic* weeks, ending with sabbatical years; and this I take to be the truth: but if you had rather place the death of *Christ* in the year before, as is commonly done, you may take the year of *Ezra's* journey into the reckoning."[76]

Newton outdoes Mede in separating, not only the 62 weeks, but also the 7 weeks, one week, and even the half (midst) of the week—numbers which have been almost universally re-

---

[74] *Ibid.,* pp. 131, 156, 157.   [75] Leviticus 25:9.
[76] Newton, *Observations,* pp. 131, 132.

garded as component parts of the seventy. Newton's 7 weeks
are a period of 49 years immediately preceding the second advent, in which the literal Jews restore Jerusalem; he runs the
62 weeks from the 28th year of Artaxerxes to the birth of Christ,
J.P. 4278-4712 (or 436-43, 2 B.C.); the one week, from the cross
to the seventh year thereafter, until the calling of the Gentiles;
the half week, A.D. 67-70, ending with the taking of Jerusalem
by Titus.[77] This odd view was not shared by others.

9. TIME FOR INCREASE OF KNOWLEDGE HAS COME.—In
Part 2 (pp. 235-323), dealing with the Apocalypse, Newton reverts to Daniel 12:4, and remarks how prophetic knowledge
will be on the increase, for "in the very end, the prophecy
should be so far interpreted as to convince many." An angel
must fly through the midst of heaven with the everlasting gospel
to preach to all nations before Babylon falls, and before the
great tribulation and end of the world. He then concludes,
"If the general preaching of the Gospel be approaching, it is
to us and our posterity that those words [Dan. 12:4] mainly
belong." [78]

10. PRE-ADVENT RECOVERY OF LONG-LOST TRUTH.—Newton then makes this impressive declaration: "The many and
clear Prophecies concerning the things to be done at *Christ's*
second coming, are not only for predicting but also for effecting
a recovery and re-establishment of the long-lost truth, and setting up a kingdom wherein dwells righteousness." [79] And this
will be in the days of the voice of the seventh angel when he
shall begin to sound.

11. CALLED TO INTERPRET, NOT TO PROPHESY.—In this
connection Newton enunciates the sound principle, *Let Time
Be the Interpreter,* thus:

"The folly of Interpreters has been, to foretel times and things by this
Prophecy, as if God designed to make them Prophets. By this rashness they
have not only exposed themselves, but brought the Prophecy also into
contempt. The design of God was much otherwise. He gave this and the

---

[77] *Ibid.,* pp. 132-136.   [78] *Ibid.,* pp. 250, 251.   [79] *Ibid.,* p. 252.

Prophecies of the Old Testament, not to gratify men's curiosities by enabling them to foreknow things, but that after they were fulfilled they might
be interpreted by the event, and his own Providence, not the Interpreters,
be then manifested thereby to the world." [80]

Many interpreters in recent times, Newton states, have
made helpful discoveries in prophetic exposition. He therefore
gathers that "God is about opening these mysteries." It was
this thought that stirred him to study, and he states that if he
should contribute anything useful, he would have achieved his
"design." [81]

12. 150- AND 391-YEAR WOE PERIODS DATED.—Newton
agrees in general with Mede on the seals and the first six trumpets, but takes him to task for not making the vials "synchronal
to" the trumpets; he gives the first four trumpets—the barbarian
tribes falling upon the Eastern Empire under the first, and upon
Western Rome under the second, third, and fourth—in detail. [82]
The fifth trumpet, or first woe, is the Saracenic locusts, whose
150 years he doubles—five months and five months—from 637
to 936 inclusive. [83] The sixth trumpet, or second woe, sounds to
the wars of the king of the north, or the Turks, led by Alp-
Arslan. The four kingdoms of the Turks, seated upon the
Euphrates, began to erect their empire in 1063, and in 1453 they
took Constantinople and extinguished the Byzantine Empire,
or Eastern Rome. For this period Newton takes 391 years inclusive (360 + 30 + 1), not 396 (365 + 30 + 1), as does Mede,
and remarks: "The interval is called an hour and a day, and a
month, and a year, or 391 prophetic days, which are years." [84]

13. THE WOMAN AND THE TWO BEASTS.—Newton has an
unusual interpretation of Revelation 12, 13, and 17. The woman
is the church—originally pure, but degenerating until she becomes the impure woman of Revelation 17, sitting on the seven
hills. After the pains of Diocletian's persecution the church is
delivered of a man child (the Christian Roman Empire, begin-

---

[80] *Ibid.*, p. 251.					[81] *Ibid.*, p. 253.					[82] *Ibid.*, pp. 295-303.
[83] *Ibid.*, pp. 303-307.					[84] *Ibid.*, p. 307.

ning with Constantine), who is caught up to the throne. The woman flees to mystical Babylon, or the "spiritually barren Empire of the Latins." When the dragon (Satan, personified in the pagan Roman Empire) sees that he is dethroned in favor of the man child, he persecutes the woman in the reign of Julian the Apostate. The earth (the Greek, or Byzantine, Empire) helps the woman by giving the Beast (the Western Roman Empire) a deadly wound; but the dragon goes to the Eastern Empire to make war with the faithful remnant of her seed, whom she has left in the East. Thus the western Beast is revived and given the seat and power of the pagan dragon; and the ten horns, or kingdoms, receive power "the same hour with the Beast." The woman, having "fled" from her former pure state, reigns *spiritually* over the Beast and the ten kings, and *temporally* as the eleventh horn of the Beast (the same as the Little Horn of Daniel's fourth beast). Nourished in this spiritual wilderness for 1260 years by the merchants of the earth, she becomes drunken with the blood of saints. The second beast, from the earth, is the church of the Greek Empire, which meanwhile makes an image to the western Beast, whose name is *Lateinos,* and whose number is 666.

After the killing of those religious bodies which will not worship the western Beast and his eastern image, a new temple is built for them, into the inner court of which retire the 144,000 saints, or the Two Witnesses—not new churches but descendants of the primitive church, represented by Smyrna and Philadelphia, the two faultless but persecuted, witnessing churches, which alone of the original seven were worthy of having their candlesticks placed in this new temple. But the outer court, or outward form of the church, is trodden underfoot for 1260 years by the Gentiles, who worship the Beast and his image.[85]

14. PASSOVER AND ATONEMENT TYPES OF TWO ADVENTS.— Tremendously impressive are Newton's declarations concerning the relationship between the visions of the Apocalypse, the

---

[85] *Ibid.,* pp. 279-286.

temple service, the dressing of the candlesticks, and the Day of Atonement, carried out through the seven seals.

"The Temple is the scene of the visions, and the visions in the Temple relate to the feast of the seventh month: for the feasts of the *Jews* were typical of things to come. The Passover related to the first coming of *Christ,* and the feasts of the seventh month to his second coming: his first coming being therefore over before this Prophecy was given, the feasts of the seventh month are here only alluded unto." [86]

15. SEALS IN SETTING OF PRIESTLY MINISTRY.— In the first vision John sees Christ, our High Priest, in the midst of the golden candlesticks, "dressing the lamps," this dressing being the sending of the seven epistles to the seven churches of Asia. The first four visions of the seals relate only to the civil affairs of the heathen *Roman* Empire, and under the fifth, the perversions and persecutions of the Man of Sin are revealed.[87] Then, after the lamps were dressed, the door of the temple was opened, and John saw the throne and the ark of the testament in the most holy, and the attendant scene.[88] Newton then remarks on how for seven days before the Day of Atonement, the high priest was constantly in the temple studying the book of the law.[89]

16. SEALING WORK TIED TO DAY OF EXPIATION.—Then the seventh seal was opened on the "Day of Expiation." And there was silence in heaven as the High Priest entered the most holy place and carried the smoking incense before the ark, and the solemnity of the Day of Expiation consummated.[90] With this, the sealing was connected.

17. EITHER SEAL OF GOD OR MARK OF BEAST.—Newton then describes how certain features of the Day of Atonement are reflected on the final day of judgment. According to the Jews, three books were opened in judgment: (1) the book of life, in which are written the names of the perfectly just, (2) the book of death, in which are the names of the very wicked, and (3) a book of those whose judgment is suspended till the Day of Expiation. In those first ten days of penitence the Jews

pray and fast, that on the tenth day their sins may be remitted and their names be written in the book of life.[91] Then, on the tenth day, returning home from the temple—

"they say to one another, *God the creator seal you to a good year*. For they conceive that the books are now sealed up, and that the sentence of God remains unchanged henceforward to the end of the year. The same thing is signified by the two Goats, upon whose foreheads the High-Priest yearly, on the day of expiation, lays the two lots inscribed, *For God* and *For* Azazel; God's lot signifying the people who are sealed with the name of God in their foreheads; and the lot *Azazel*, which was sent into the wilderness, representing those who receive the mark and name of the Beast, and go into the wilderness with the great Whore.

"The servants of God being therefore sealed in the day of expiation, we may conceive that this sealing is synchronal to the visions which appear upon opening the seventh seal." [92]

18. INFIDELITY TO PUT STOP TO PAPAL DOMINANCE.— Whiston, Newton's successor in the chair of mathematics at Cambridge University, tells how Newton maintained significantly that before primitive Christianity could be restored the power of infidelity in a "main revolution" would be used to put a stop to or block the popedom that had so long corrupted the church.[93]

---

[91] *Ibid.*, pp. 266, 267.
[92] *Ibid.*, p. 267. In a supplemental chapter (pp. 309-323), in observations "differently drawn up by the author in another copy of his Work" (p. 309), an even more detailed account of the same is given of events of the seventh month.
[93] Whiston, *Essay on the Revelation of St. John* (2d ed.), p. 321; Elliott, *op. cit.*, vol. 4, p. 521; Guinness, *History Unveiling Prophecy*, p. 190.

CHAPTER THIRTY

Advances in Exposition; Lisbon Earthquake Noted

I. Lowth—The 2300 Years Extend to Antichrist's End

WILLIAM LOWTH (1660-1732), son of an apothecary, was born in London and educated at St. Johns, Oxford, from which he obtained the B.A., M.A., and B.D. degrees (1679-1688). His first work was *A Vindication of the Divine Authority of the Old and New Testaments* (1692), against Le Clerc. In 1696 he became chaplain to the bishop of Winchester, and about 1700 rector of Buriton. Lowth wrote several highly esteemed works, the most noted being *A Commentary Upon the Larger and Lesser Prophets.*[1]

1. DATES PAPAL HORN PERIOD FROM BONIFACE (606).— Lowth's *Commentary Upon the Larger and Lesser Prophets* interprets the Little Horn of Daniel 7 as the Papacy, exercising ecclesiastical as well as temporal power, the three kingdoms subdued being the Exarchate of Ravenna, the Greeks in Italy, and the Franks. Daniel 7 is paralleled by Revelation 13 and 2 Thessalonians 2. The papal attempt to abrogate divine as well as human law is stressed, and the three and a half times, or forty-two months, is 1260 year-days from Boniface III, in 606.[2] The papal rule will be destroyed, Lowth contends, when the destruction of the present state of affairs ends at our Lord's coming.

---

[1] Issued in separate parts, 1714-1725: afterward assembled various editions—3d ed., 1730; 6th ed., 1765.

[2] William Lowth, *A Commentary Upon the Larger and Lesser Prophets* (3d ed., 1730), p. 382.

2. 2300 YEARS EXTEND TO END OF ANTICHRIST.—Lowth mentions the literal application of the 2300 days to the invasion of Antiochus, as about six years and four months, reckoning 360 days to a year; however, he regards Antiochus as merely a type of the Antichrist, and concurs with Lloyd and Newton in the opinion that—

"These *two thousand three Hundred Days* are a Line of Time that is to be extended to the End of the Times of *Antichrist:* taking each *Day* for a *Year,* according to the Genius of the Prophetical Writings." [3]

This year-day principle, he adds, is used in the periods of Daniel 7 and 9, and the 1290 and 1335 year-days which, like the 2300, lead to the cleansing of the sanctuary. The "wilful king" of Daniel 11:36, 37 is explained as the papal Antichrist.[4]

II. Whiston Applies Year-Day Principle to Prophetic Periods

WILLIAM WHISTON (1667-1752), Baptist theologian and mathematician, and Newton's successor as professor of mathematics at Cambridge, was born in Leicestershire. His employment when a boy as his father's amanuensis—his father being a Presbyterian minister—gave shape to his entire life. Educated at Cambridge in mathematics and philosophy, he received his B.A. and M.A. degrees. He was ordained a deacon by Bishop Lloyd in 1693, and became acquainted with Newton. While chaplain to the bishop of Norwich, he wrote his first book, *A New Theory of the Earth* (1696), to confirm the Genesis record on Newtonian grounds. In 1698 he was vicar in Suffolk.

A hard worker, he conducted an early service in the chapel daily, preached twice a day in his church, and gave catechetical lectures. In 1701 he was nominated by Newton to Cambridge for the chair of mathematics, succeeding Newton in 1703, and giving up his vicarage. Whiston was one of the first to give lectures with experiments, and was the first to popularize the Newtonian theories. In 1715 he started a Society for Promoting

---

[3] *Ibid.*, p. 385.
[4] *Ibid.*, pp. 385, 402.

Christian Knowledge, and was attacked by Anthony Collins for his prophetic interpretations.

Whiston had a stormy time with some of his theological views. His learning was indisputable, but he was charged with heresy. He believed that infidelity might be the only means of stopping the papal enslavement before true Christianity could be restored. In 1726 Whiston made models of the tabernacle of Moses and the Temple at Jerusalem, lecturing upon them in London, Bristol, and Bath. He also lectured on earthquakes as a fulfillment of prophecy. In 1737 he made a successful translation of Josephus that has remained the most popular standard version. In 1747 he left the Church of England and joined the Baptists. He was the author of fifty volumes.[5]

1. HOLDS BASIC PRINCIPLE OF DAY FOR YEAR.—Whiston's major work, *An Essay on the Revelation of Saint John* (1706), begins with the basic proposition of "a Day for a Year," meaning sometimes a year of 360 days, sometimes the Julian year of $365\frac{1}{4}$ days.[6] Maintaining the standard historical exposition of Daniel 7, he denies that the fourth kingdom could be the Seleucidae, or the Little Horn Antiochus.[7] In this he cites Mede, More, Cressener, and others, in copious, heavily documented footnotes.

---

[5] His works in the British Museum Catalogue occupy 15 columns.

[6] William Whiston, *An Essay on the Revelation of St. John* (2d ed., 1744), pp. 2, 3.

Whiston explains his method of turning prophetic days into literal years—to reckon by the type of year which would naturally be used at the time of the writing, or the beginning of any given prophetic period. For example, he uses the 365¼-day year for John's prophecies, because the Julian calendar was in use in the Roman world in John's time and onward. But he reckons the 2300 days and the 70 weeks of Daniel as 360-day years, because they date from the time of the Persian Empire. Whiston thought that the "Chaldean" year, employed by the Persians, had 360 days. Actually, as proved from contemporary documents discovered by modern archaeology, the Babylonians and Persians—as did the Jews also—used a year of 12 lunar months, about 11 days shorter than the true solar year, which they corrected by inserting an extra month periodically. (See Sidney Smith, "Calendar: Babylonian and Assyrian," *Encyclopaedia Britannica*, vol. 4, p. 576.)

The supposed *calendar* year of 360 days, used by Whiston and a very few other prophetic writers, is not to be confused with the 360-day "*prophetic year*" used by later expositors, derived from the equivalence of the prophetic periods of the three and a half times and the 1260 days. With the Biblical interpretation of a "time" as a "year," it can be reckoned that three and a half years (which are also 42 months) are equal to 1260 days, if the months are 30 days each. From the Jewish writer's point of view, this was reasonable enough, for although he had calendar months of 29 or 30 days, he called the 29-day month "hollow," or deficient, and the 30-day month "full." An ideal or theoretical year of "full" months would be 360 days long. (Even today we often use a theoretical month of 30 days in computing interest.) But it must be remembered that such a 360-day year was symbolic, not literal, even to the writer of the prophecy. The Jewish, Babylonian, and Persian luni-solar year would, over a long period, always be equivalent to the same number of true solar years. Those prophetic interpreters who use this 360-day "prophetic year," derived from the periods denoting 1260 days, regard it as a symbolic year composed of symbolic days which are equated, according to the year-day principle, with literal, natural years, and therefore they count the fulfillment in true solar years.

[7] *Ibid.*, pp. 22-26.

2. DATING THE 1260 YEARS OF PAPAL ANTICHRIST.—Whiston makes the second beast of Revelation 13 the same as Daniel's Little Horn and Paul's Man of Sin, and declares Babylon is the Papacy seated in seven-hilled Rome.[8] Recognizing the possibility of the fulfillment of the 1260 years between 476 and 1736 as the dominion of the ten "Antichristian Kingdoms," he considers the period of 606 to 1866 as the period of the Papal Little Horn.[9] Whiston cites Allix, Mede, Howell, and others on the ten kingdoms, and he discusses the uprooted three as the Ostrogoths, Lombards, and Heruli.[10] In arguing for the continuity of the kingdoms with Rome, he also cites Howell for the revival of Justinian's Code (which gave sanction to the Papacy) as still "the general Law of Christendom, one kingdom excepted." [11]

3. DATING THE 2300, 1290, 1335, AND 396 YEARS.—In his first edition Whiston cites at length Cusa's statement, made "full 250. years ago relating to this matter," in introducing the 2300-year period, "which determines the Period of the Church's Pollution to 2300 days from the time it was seen." He counts 2300 years of but 360 days each, totaling a fraction less than 2267 Julian years, from J.P. 4162 (B.C. 552) to J.P. 6429 (A.D. 1716).[12] In determining the 70 weeks, Whiston likewise uses weeks of years of 360 days each, beginning at Artaxerxes' twentieth year, 445 B.C. The sixty-ninth week he ends in A.D. 32 followed by the crucifixion, but no reference is given to the end of the seventieth week.[13] The 1290- and 1335-day periods are Julian years, for they are applied to the Christian Era, perhaps A.D. 70 + 1290 = 1360, the very time of Wyclif's famous opposition to Antichrist, and A.D. 70 + 1335 = 1405.[14] The Ottoman Turkish-Woe period of 396 years ($365\frac{1}{4}$ + 30 + 1 + 15 days) Whiston places from 1301

---

[8] *Ibid.*, pp. 70, 111-113.   [9] *Ibid.*, pp. 275, 281, 282.
[10] *Ibid.*, pp. 283-288.   [11] *Ibid.*, pp. 251, 252.
[12] *Ibid.* (1st ed., 1706), pp. 10, 236, 237. See also (pp. 270, 271) the 1260 days and other periods which Whiston ended in 1716 in his first edition. These interpretations were perforce revised, some of them to 1736, in his 1744 edition. In 1724 his *The Literal Accomplishment of Scripture Prophecies* (p. 86) placed the end of the 2300 days "still future, at A.D. 1731, or 1749, or perhaps at 1754," but by 1744 he had given up this idea, for he cited Josephus for 2200 "evenings and mornings," or a period of 1100 literal days in the time of Antiochus. (*Essay on the Apocalypse* [2d ed.], pp. 10, 11.)
[13] Whiston, *A Short View of the Chronology of the Old Testament, and of the Harmony of the Four Evangelists*, pp. 199, 200.
[14] Whiston, *Essay on the Revelation* (1744 ed.), pp. 268-271.

LISBON EARTHQUAKE (1755) RECOGNIZED AS HARBINGER

On Both Sides of the Atlantic, the Lisbon, Portugal, Earthquake of February 6, 1755, Was Declared a Herald of the Approaching End of All Things

to 1697, following Brightman, Cressener, and Lloyd.[15] The ending point he identified as Prince Eugene's great victory over the Turks, followed by the Peace of Carlowitz in 1699, as the Ottomans ceased to be the terror of Christendom. Whiston inclines toward *Lateinos* as the name yielding 666.[16] And he makes the Turk the last power of Daniel 11:44.[17]

III. Lisbon Earthquake Recognized as Sign of Approaching Advent

As previously noted, contemporary recognition of prophesied epochs or events, as rapidly as they have been fulfilled, has characterized the centuries. Both the middle and the close of the eighteenth century record such an attesting witness. The first was the Lisbon, Portugal, earthquake, of 1755, and the second was the French Revolution, which resulted in the ending of the papal 1260 years through the stroke of the arms of France. We here note the first.

---

[15] *Ibid.*, pp. 203, 318, 319.   [16] *Ibid.*, pp. 293-295.   [17] *Ibid.*, p. 319.

1. Called Herald of Approaching End.—The Lisbon earthquake was definitely recognized at the time of its occurrence as a harbinger of the approaching advent. "A.B.," for example, in *The Gentleman's Magazine* (London), February, 1756, declares that this "tremendous judgment and dreadful catastrophe" corresponds to Luke 21:25, 26, and is set forth as a herald of the "glorious kingdom of the millennium." [18] Asserting that it cannot fail to "awaken the world to serious and devout contemplations," and to "compare it with the prophecies relating to, and now fulfilling in this its last days," [19] he denominates it "one of the infallible omens," a "signal from the King of heaven." Calling attention to the fact that Lisbon is inhabited by perhaps the most bigoted zealots of the Roman faith, and that it was where "the most dreadful tribunal of the inquisition emitted the infernal flames with the greatest fury and hottest violence," A.B. makes this remark:

"For my own part, I do really suppose, from the present condition of *Europe* compared with *Luke* xxi.25,26, that this is surely nothing less than *the outstretched arm of God prepared to break the earth in pieces with a rod of iron, and to cleanse and purify it from all pollutions and filthiness both of flesh and spirit,* to make way for the glorious kingdom of the millennium; like *the voice of the first angel* (chap. xiv.v.6,7.) *to call all nations every where to repent while it is day,* and make all pious men *now look up, for their redemption draweth nigh; when he shall appear again with healing in his wings."* [20]

2. Day of Fasting Celebrated on Anniversary.—Asserting it was "seemingly supernatural, as if it came to pass by the direction of a *particular* providence, to confound the wisdom, and silence the audacious infidels of the age; such as show plainly, *that the Lord was in the earthquake, and that it was his angel that troubled the waters,"* [21] A.B. makes reference to the appropriateness of a fast day, with appropriate prayers on the part of Protestants. And that such a day of fasting was appointed and carried out in the Anglican Church is attested by a remark-

---

[18] "A.B." in *The Gentleman's Magazine* (London), February, 1756, p. 69.
[19] *Ibid.*, p. 68.
[20] *Ibid.*, p. 69.
[21] *Ibid.*

able packet of pamphlets and sermons bound together, and lodged in the British Museum. They were prefaced by a hand-written index listing the twenty-one sermons comprising this special volume of sermons preached in connection with this fast day of February 6, 1756.

The names on this roster are impressive—a bishop, seven M.A.'s, five D.D.'s, two LL.B.'s, and a chaplain to the king, making up fifteen of the twenty-one. *A Discourse Preparatory to the Religious Observance of the Day of Publick Fasting and Humiliation, Appointed by Authority, to Be Kept on Friday the Sixth of February 1756, on the Occasion of the Late Earthquakes Abroad, and Particularly at Lisbon* (1756) was prepared by Henry Stebbing, D.D., chaplain in ordinary to His Majesty.

Thomas Alcock, preaching at Plymouth, stated:

"The affrighted Inhabitants of *Lisbon,* and of many other Places, thought the *Lord was come to smite the Earth with a Curse*—thought the *great and terrible Day* of Judgment was at Hand, *in the which the Heavens shall pass away with a great Noise, and the Elements shall melt with fervent Heat: The Earth also and all the Works that are therein shall be burnt up.*" [22]

3. FULFILLMENT OF OUR LORD'S PROPHECY.—Then follows this observation on the meaning of the catastrophe:

"Nor was it without Reason, that they entertained these Apprehensions: As there were Signs almost sufficient to make them expect that Catastrophe. For our Saviour has foretold; *that there shall be Wars and Rumors of Wars, Nation shall rise against Nation, and great Earthquakes shall be in divers Places, and Famines, and Pestilences, and fearful Sights, the Sea and the Waves roaring; Mens Hearts failing them for fear, and for looking after those Things which are coming on the Earth: For the Powers of Heaven shall be shaken:* That these shall be the *Beginnings of Sorrows,* and some of the previous Signs of his Coming. And though the *Lord* still *delayeth his Coming, yet seeing all these Things most certainly shall be dissolved,* we know not how soon, *what Manner of Persons ought we to be in all holy Conversation and Godliness! Looking for, and hasting unto the coming of the day of God!*" [23]

4. HUMBLE HEARTS WHILE AWAITING FULFILLMENTS.—

---

[22] Thomas Alcock, *A Sermon on the Late Earthquakes, More Particularly That at Lisbon,* p. 40.
[23] *Ibid.*

Bishop Lavington of Exeter preached a sermon on the general fast day, which was published at the request of the mayor and chamber. Declaring "this Event is the greatest Call in its Kind which has been known in the Memory of any Person living, or (I think) recorded in History," the bishop appealed for a humbling of heart and a true spirit of contrition.[24] After referring to Luke 21 and the signs of the second advent, including great earthquakes, the bishop said:

"I do not think that we have Light enough in these Matters to pin down this Prophecy to these Events; nor to determine how near or how far off Christ's second Coming may be. There seem to be other Prophecies not yet accomplished, which must be accomplished before this comes to pass. But, as the *Resemblance* between what we now see, and what shall be seen, when the last Catastrophe comes, naturally connects them together in our Thoughts; so it will always be our Wisdom, when we see such Signs as these, *so far to be apprehensive that the End of all Things is at Hand,* as to *be sober and watch unto Prayer.*" [25]

Then he called for the gathering of the people (Joel 2:16) to plead with God to spare the people, and to put away disaffection, and apathy, and compromise with the "Great Apostasy." He concluded by declaring none can put "any stop to the Forerunner of the Lord's Coming," [26] though the precise day and hour is known to no man.

IV. Vitringa Compromises on Year-Day and Postmillennium

CAMPEGIUS VITRINGA (1659-1722), learned Dutch theologian, was born at Leeuwarden, on the Zuider Zee, and educated at the University of Franeker. In 1681 he was made professor of Oriental languages, and two years later professor of theology and afterward of sacred history in the same institution. In his *Anacrisis Apocalypsios Johannis Apostoli* ("Examination of the Apocalypse of John the Apostle"), Vitringa interprets the two beasts of Revelation as papal Rome and the false teachers of

---

[24] George Lavington, *A Sermon Preached in the Cathedral-Church of Exeter, on the General Fast-Day, February 6, 1756,* p. 19.
[25] *Ibid.,* pp. 20, 21.
[26] *Ibid.,* p. 26.

Antichrist, such as the Dominicans and Franciscans;[27] the image as the Inquisition, and the mark as the profession of faith of the corrupt Roman church.[28]

The successive states and fortunes of the Christian church from John's time to the great consummation, including the desolations of the Saracens and Turks, are deemed represented by the seven churches [29] and seven seals.[30] The seven trumpets, illuminating the seventh seal, cover the whole period again, showing the judgments of God upon the persecutors of the church—the first five covering pagan Rome and its successors, the sixth and seventh, papal Rome—and the seven vials are to be referred to the seventh trumpet, designating the last judgments upon corrupt Christian Rome.[31] Favoring Scaliger's concept of a year for a century, Vitringa suggests the interpretation of three and a half times as three and a half centuries—from Waldo to the Reformation, but he also follows the more usual year-day principle in the forty-two months or 1260 days, which he says refer to the period of the corrupt church of Antichrist, or Babylon, and whose terminus will be recognized when it comes. He sees in this an allusion also to certain literal periods of three and a half years such as the drought of Ahab's time and the persecution under Antiochus.[32]

On the millennium Vitringa adopts the view just previously set forth by Whitby, to whom he refers—a view which considered it as a spiritual reign brought about by the complete victory of the reformed church, with the world completely evangelized, and answering to the description of the New Jerusalem.[33]

V. French Work Continues Prophetic Interpretation

THEODORE CRINSOZ DE BIONENS (1690-c. 1750), Swiss Protestant theologian and renowned Orientalist, founded a school at Lausanne. He was definitely an individualist, refusing to sign

---

[27] Campegius Vitringa, *Anacrisis Apocalypsios*, pp. 585, 612, 613.
[28] *Ibid.*, pp. 621, 623.   [29] *Ibid.*, pp. 74, 82, 96, 112, 126, 146, 161.
[30] *Ibid.*, pp. 249, 255, 261, 267, 275-278, 319.
[31] *Ibid.*, pp. 328, 329.   [32] *Ibid.*, pp. 462-464.
[33] *Ibid.*, pp. 849, 857 ff.; see also Elliott, *op. cit.*, vol. 4, p. 513.

the Consensus with the clergy at Geneva, and as a result he was not allowed to publish his translation of the Bible.[34] No new or unusual contribution appears in his work on Daniel and the Apocalypse. A brief summary discloses its similarity to other expositions of the time.

The seven churches span the Christian Era from early days on through pagan persecution, then popularity, next the tyranny under the popes during the Thyatira period, next the Reformation, and on to the judgment.[35] The seals are thought to apply to the empire out for conquest, but only up until Julian the apostate.[36] The trumpets are clearly punishments upon the corrupted church, first by the early barbarians. Then the fifth trumpet symbolizes the Saracens, with the five months as 150 years; the sixth indicates the Turks, who were to afflict for some 400 years.[37]

The tenth part of the city of Christendom is believed by Crinsoz to be one of the kingdoms into which Rome was divided, which severs connection with the Papacy.[38] Revelation 12 discloses the final triumph of Christianity over paganism during the time of Constantine, the dragon representing pagan Rome, under its various forms of government.[39] The first beast of Revelation 13 is obviously the Western Roman Empire, and the 1260 years are suggested as beginning in 445, which would end them in 1715, when Louis XIV died.[40] The two-horned beast indicates the popes, who have authority in matters of faith as well as in discipline; and the image of the Beast, he fancied, pictures the German Empire beginning with Charlemagne. The 666 could be deduced from *Lateinos*.[41] And the plagues are clearly judgments on the Roman Catholic Church.[42] Babylon is, of course, the Papacy.[43]

On Daniel 8 the author maintains that the 2300 evening-mornings are "prophetic days," and that church and state are to

---

[34] *Nouvelle biographie générale*, vol. 12, col. 473.
[35] Théodore Crinsoz de Bionens, *Essai sur l'Apocalypse, avec des éclaircissemens sur les prophéties de Daniel qui regardent les derniers tem[p]s* (Essay on the Apocalypse, With Elucidations on the Prophecies of Daniel Which Concern the Latter Times), p. 7.
[36] *Ibid.*, pp. 80-115.   [37] *Ibid.*, pp. 120-176.   [38] *Ibid.*, pp. 210, 211.
[39] *Ibid.*, pp. 215-233.   [40] *Ibid.*, pp. 240, 241.   [41] *Ibid.*, pp. 251-256.
[42] *Ibid.*, pp. 285-306.   [43] *Ibid.*, pp. 310-322.

be trodden for 2300 years, which period, he says, cannot begin
with the 1260 years, as that would be too late.[44] He contends:

> "Nothing is more natural than to place its beginning [the 2300 days]
> at the very date of this prophecy. Daniel was honored of this second vision
> on the third year of Belshazzar, which was, as we stated, the year 555 B.C.,
> to which 1745 must be added to make up the two thousand three hundred
> years, so that we have good reason to hope that, after the year 45 of the
> century in which we live, the church will be cleansed." [45]

The 1290 years are dated from A.D. 455 to 1745, and the
1335 are terminated in 1790, when the time of blessedness would
be at hand.[46] So much for Crinsoz.

VI. Pyle Condemns Grotius' Attempt to Compromise Protestantism

THOMAS PYLE (1674-1756), son of a rector, was educated at
Cambridge, from which he received the B.A. and M.A. degrees.
In 1697 he was ordained by the bishop of Norwich. Whiston,
chaplain to the bishop, notes that Pyle was one of the two best
scholars he ever examined. He served as minister at St. Nicholas
Chapel, Lynn, and then as rector of Outwell and Watlington. An
impetuous but eloquent preacher, he gained some popularity,
and wrote *The Scripture Preservative Against Popery* (1735).

1. EXACT DATING OF 1260 YEARS STILL SECRET.—Discussing
the Antichrist, symbolized by the Little Horn of Daniel 7 and
Revelation 13, and the problem of the exact placement of the
1260 years, Pyle declares it to be—

"of the highest Concern to Christians to attend to, whether they can precisely fix the *Beginning* and *End* of this remarkable *Period,* or not. Idolatry,
Saint Worship, Image Worship, Persecution, Monkery, and forged Miracles,
are *Marks* clear enough to warn us against the Danger of being seduced into
the *Apostacy,* tho' the *Date* of its *Rise* and *Continuance* remain yet a
Secret." [47]

Condemning Grotius' attempt to effect a compromise between Protestant and Catholic interpretation, he says:

"That great Scholar racked all his Inventions and Ingenuity in order

---

[44] *Ibid.,* pp. 391, 392.
[45] *Ibid.,* p. 392.
[46] *Ibid.,* p. 431.
[47] Thomas Pyle, *A Paraphrase With Notes on the Revelation of St. John,* Preface, p. xiii.

to explain those odious Characters not of *Rome Christian,* but of *Heathen Rome.*" [48]

In support he cites Mede, More, Jurieu, and Vitringa.[49]

2. FOLLOWS STANDARD PATTERN FOR TRUMPETS AND BEASTS. —On the trumpets Pyle follows the now standard pattern—the first four upon Western Rome (Goths, Vandals, Visigoths, Huns, Heruli),[50] and the fifth and sixth the Saracens and Turks. The Beast of Revelation 13 and 17 he maintains to be the same as the fourth power of Daniel 7.

VII. Rudd Confutes Whitby's Postmillennial Theory

SAYER RUDD, M.D. (d. 1757), was in 1716 assistant in a Baptist church in London, and was ordained in 1725, securing a living at Turner's Hall, London. In 1733 he traveled in Europe, visiting Paris, and then obtained his M.D. at Leyden. The Baptist Board accused him of heresy. Though he defended himself in a series of tracts (1734-1736), he was disowned by the board. In 1738 he conformed to the Established Church, and received a living at Walmer. Rudd wrote a number of works, the best known of which is *An Essay Towards a New Explication of the Doctrines of the Resurrection, Millennium, and Judgment* (1734)— the substance of several discourses on Revelation 20. Rudd confutes the theory of Whitby with the searching question, Where are Christ and the raised saints to reside during the thousand years?

1. DAILY: REMOVAL OF TRUE WORSHIP BY PAPACY.—In his Introduction Dr. Rudd goes to considerable pains to explain his view of the *daily sacrifice.* Here are his precise words:

"*And from the time that the daily sacrifice shall be taken away, and the abomination that maketh desolate set up, there shall be a thousand two hundred and ninety days.* By the *daily sacrifice* here (as it alludes to the Jewish state) I understand, the pure worship of God under the gospel; and by its being *taken away,* the suppression or corruption of that worship, by the antichristian tyranny taking place on the rise of the papal apostasy.

---

[48] *Ibid.,* p. xvi.
[49] *Ibid.,* p. xvii.
[50] *Ibid.,* pp. 58-61.

This, I suppose, may be intended in the next words, which seem to me in a great measure explanatory of the last, *and the abomination that maketh desolate set up. Abomination* in scripture frequently signifies idols, and so here aptly represents the idolatry of the *Romish* church, by which a desolation is made in the pure doctrine and discipline of the gospel." [51]

2. BOTH RESURRECTIONS AND SATAN'S BINDING STILL FUTURE.—On the millennium Rudd concludes, after an extensive discussion, that "Satan *has not yet been bound,* and consequently that *the Millennium* is not commenced." Answering the question, "When do they [the thousand years] begin?" he gives a twofold reply: (1) after the destruction of the Turk and the Pope; and (2) upon the second coming of Christ.[52] This involves the first resurrection, Dr. Whitby to the contrary notwithstanding. Here are Rudd's words on that:

"And having likewise endeavoured to remove all that Dr. *Whitby* has advanced against this doctrine in his celebrated treatise of *the Millennium;* I hope, none of my readers will think much, if I lay claim to his own words, with a very small alteration, and conclude the argument with saying: THUS WILL TRUTH PREVAIL AT LAST, BUT TO THE RUIN OF THIS FIGURATIVE RESURRECTION." [53]

VIII. Gill—Stalwart Defender of Historic Positions

JOHN GILL (1697-1771), eminent Baptist expositor and Orientalist, was born in Northamptonshire. Ordained in 1718, and well trained and thoroughly versed in Hebrew and Latin, he settled as pastor at Horsleydown, where he preached for fifty years. A Wednesday evening lectureship was formed for him in 1729, which he held till 1756. In 1748 he was granted the D.D. degree at Aberdeen. Author of numerous works, especially expositions on prophecy—and on Hebrew vowel points and accents—Gill held the outpouring of the seven vials to be still future in his day. He maintained the usual teaching on the trumpets. He also held that the kingdom of God would be established only after His enemies—including Antichrist—are

[51] Sayer Rudd, *An Essay Towards a New Explication of the Doctrines of the Resurrection, Millennium, and Judgment,* p. 14.
[52] *Ibid.,* pp. 196, 197.
[53] *Ibid.,* p. 273.

destroyed, and Satan bound. The millennium will be bounded by the two literal, corporeal resurrections, and the eternal kingdom is to be on earth, not in heaven.[54]

The swirl of current controversy over conflicting schools of interpretation, Christian and Jewish, can be felt in these clear and powerful writings. The pages are heavily and accurately documented with reliable sources. For example, the Little Horn of Daniel 7 is "not *Titus Vespasian,* as *Jarchi;* nor the *Turkish* empire, as *Saadiah;* nor *Antiochus Epiphanes,* as many Christian interpreters; for not a single person or king is meant by a horn, but a kingdom or state, and a succession of governors." [55] Thus he concludes:

"And since no other has appeared in the *Roman* empire, to whom the characters of this horn agree, but antichrist, or the pope of *Rome,* he may well be thought to be intended." [56]

1. INCLINES TO 1260 YEARS FROM 606-1866.—Under 2 Thessalonians pagan Rome's restraint is dwelt upon, retarding the manifestation of Antichrist's usurpation of the seven hills until the empire's breakup.[57] And in his *Revelation* the identity of the Beast of Revelation 13 with the Man of Sin and the Little Horn is impressively portrayed—the seat (Rome) given by the removal of the capital to Constantinople. The blasphemous claims and titles of the "Romish antichrist" are recited, and the period of his power is discussed. Catholic defenses are duly noted.[58] Concerning the 1260 year-days, we note his impressive statement:

"Hence it appears, that 1260 prophetic days, that is, years, contain the whole period of antichrist's reign and continuance; so that could we tell where they began, it might be exactly known when his reign will end;

---

[54] John Gill, *An Exposition of the Revelation,* pp. 232 ff.
[55] John Gill, *An Exposition of the Prophets,* on Daniel 7:8, vol. 6, p. 306.
[56] *Ibid.*
[57] *Ibid.,* on 2 Thess. 2:5, vol. 9, pp. 242, 243.
[58] Bishop Walmesley, writing under the fictitious name of "Signor Pastorini," launched his *General History of the Christian Church From Her Birth to Her Final Triumphant State in Heaven* (1771), soon translated into Latin, German, and French. He divided the New Testament era into seven ages, answering to the seven seals, trumpets, and vials—with the fourth age, from 620-1520, marked by the rise of Mohammedanism, and the Greek Schism, with the fall of Constantinople as a judgment upon the latter; and the fifth age beginning with the "apostasy" of Luther and the Protestant locusts to last five prophetic months, or 150 years (p. 154 in 1834 ed.), and with sixth and seventh ages still future.

but for want of knowing the former, the best of calculators have failed in the latter: but seeing the time when he was made universal bishop by *Phocas,* bids fair for the time of his open appearance, and the beginning of his reign, and of his blasphemy, which was in the year 606, to which, if we add 1260, the expiration of his reign will fall in the year 1866; so that he may have upwards of an hundred and twenty years yet to continue; but of this we can't be certain; however, the conjecture is not improbable." [59]

2. 2300 YEARS REACH TO CLOSE OF SIXTH MILLENARY.—Gill's view of the 2300 days is equally succinct:

"These 2300 days may be considered as so many years, which will bring it down to the end of the sixth millennium, or thereabout; when it may be hoped there will be a new face of things upon the sanctuary and church of God, and a cleansing of it from all corruption in doctrine, discipline, worship and conversation." [60]

IX. Thomas Newton—Representative of Protestant Historical Positions

THOMAS NEWTON (1704-1782), bishop of Bristol, was born at Litchfield and educated at Christ's Church, with A.B. and A.M. degrees. Ordained in 1730, he became curate to Dr. Treback at St. George, whose daughter he later married. He rose through a series of preferments from morning preacher in Spring Garden Chapel (1738) to lecturer at St. Georges (1747), chaplain to the princess of Wales (1751), then prebend in Westminster Abbey (1757), and precentor of York (1759), until finally he was made bishop of Bristol (1761), and dean of St. Paul's (1768).

In 1754 Newton lost both his father and his wife. He distracted his mind from his grief by composing his *Dissertations on the Prophecies,* which ran through eighteen editions, and was translated into German and Danish. This deservedly popular work compares the prophecies with the historical events fulfilling them. It contends that nothing is more self-evident than that the prophecy of the millennium and first resurrection is not yet fulfilled, and that Satan was not bound in the Middle Ages.

---

[59] John Gill, *Exposition of the Prophets,* on Revelation 13:5.
[60] *Ibid.,* on Daniel 8:14, vol. 6, p. 319.

1. FOURTH EMPIRE IS ROME, NOT SELEUCIDAE.—Dissertation 13 is a comprehensive exposition of the four empires of Daniel 2, with the fourth as Rome and not the Seleucidae, then the divisions, and the coming kingdom. The witnesses of the early centuries are summoned and the attacks of Porphyry duly noted. Dissertation 14 treats of Daniel 7 in a similarly thorough way. It gives various lists of the ten-horn divisions, including Eberhard's (1240) exposition and other early and later writers, contends that the Little Horn is Western Rome, and denies the Antiochus Epiphanes distortion by Porphyry.[61]

2. END OF 1260 YEARS WILL REVEAL BEGINNING.—Newton notes both Justinian's decree of 533 and Phocas' decree of 606, from which some date the 1260-year period.[62] Concerning this and related periods, he says:

"Here are then those different periods assigned, 1260 years, 1290 years and 1335 years: and what is the precise time of their beginning and consequently of their ending, as well as what are the great and signal events, which will take place at the end of each period, we can only conjecture, time alone can with certainty discover." [63]

3. END OF 2300 YEARS LIKEWISE FUTURE.—Dissertation 15 compasses the Persian ram, the Grecian goat, and the Roman horn. Of the 2300 days, Newton declares:

"These two thousand and three hundred days denote the whole time from the beginning of the vision to the cleansing of the sanctuary. The sanctuary is not yet cleansed, and consequently these years are not yet expired. When these years shall be expired, then their end will clearly show from whence their beginning is to be dated, whether from the vision of the ram, or of the he-goat, or of the little horn. It is difficult to fix the precise time, when the prophetic dates begin, and when they end, till the prophecies are fulfilled, and the event declares the certainty of them." [64]

Dissertations 16 and 17 deal with Daniel 11—between the seas being the Holy Land—and are made the climax, with the Turkish power going forth with fury to fight the Russians.[65] Dis-

[61] Thomas Newton, *Dissertations on the Prophecies* (1796 ed.), pp. 157-195.
[62] *Ibid.*, p. 276.
[63] *Ibid.*, p. 277.
[64] *Ibid.*, p. 218.
[65] *Ibid.*, pp. 273, 274.

sertations 22 and 23 present Paul's Man of Sin as the Roman
Papacy.

4. 150- AND 391-YEAR TIME PERIODS OF TRUMPETS.—Passing to the Apocalypse, Dissertation 24 deals with the seven
churches, seven seals, and seven trumpets. The first four trumpets depict the barbarian scourges on Western Rome, and the
fifth and sixth describe the Saracens and Turks and the downfall of Eastern Rome. Mohammed is the fallen star, and the
five months, or 150 years, extend from 612 to 762.[66] The four
angels of the sixth trumpet are the "four sultans" of the Turks.
On the time period of this second woe Newton makes this impressive statement in 1754:

"If it be taken mystically, and the *hour,* and *day,* and *month,* and
year be a prophetic *hour,* and *day,* and *month,* and *year,* then a *year* (according to St. John's, who follows herein Daniel's, computation) consisting
of 360 days is 360 years, and a *month* consisting of 30 days is 30 years, and
a *day* is a year, and an *hour* in the same proportion is 15 days; so that the
whole period of the Othmans *slaying the third part of men,* or subduing
the Christian states in the Greek or Roman empire, amounts to 391 years
and 15 days. Now it is wonderfully remarkable, that the first conquest
mentioned in history, of the Othmans over the Christians, was in the year
of the Hegira 680 and the year of Christ 1281. For Ortogrul 'in that year
(according to the accurate historian Saadi,) crowned his victories with the
conquests of the famous city of Kutahi upon the Greeks.' Compute 391
years from that time, and they will terminate in the year 1672: and in that
year, as it was hinted before, Mohammed the Fourth took Cameniec from
the Poles, 'and forty-eight towns and villages in the territory of Cameniec were delivered up' to the sultan upon the treaty of peace. Whereupon
Prince Cantemir hath made this memorable reflection, 'This was the last
victory by which any advantage accrued to the Othman state, or any city or
province was annexed to the ancient bounds of the empire.' " [67]

"Here then the prophecy and the event agree exactly in the period of
391 years; and if more accurate and authentic histories of the Othmans
were brought to light, and we knew the very day wherein Kutahi was taken,
as certainly as we know that wherein Cameniec was taken, the like exactness
might also be found in the 15 days." [68]

5. SEVEN VIALS AND MILLENNIUM YET FUTURE.—Dissertation 25 discusses the pagan Roman dragon, the papal Beast of

<hr>

[66] *Ibid.,* p. 427.
[67] *Ibid.,* p. 431.
[68] *Ibid.*

Revelation 13, with the two-horned beast as the Roman clergy.[69] The seven vials are held as still future.[70] Spiritual Babylon of Revelation 17 is the Papacy. And the millennium and resurrection are literal and yet future, at the close of which will come the general resurrection and the loosing of Satan—followed by the earth made new.[71]

X. De la Flechere—2300 Years Expiring; French Revolution Impending

JEAN GUILLAUME DE LA FLECHERE, or John William Fletcher (1729-1785), associate of Wesley, was born in Nyon on Lake Geneva, Switzerland, removing to England while he was still young. Soundly converted, he joined the Methodists, and became vicar at Madeley, where he labored in close association with Wesley. He was author of several works.[72] Of La Fléchère, Southey says, "No church ever possessed a more apostolic minister."[73] In one of his remarkable letters, with all probability addressed to Wesley in 1755, concerning the "impending Revolutions," appears this serious declaration: "We are come to the last times, the grand catastrophe of God's drama draws near apace."[74]

1. IRON DIVISIONS; MINGLED WITH PAPAL CLAY.—As the basis for such a conclusion, La Fléchère cites the four empires of Daniel 2, and the division of the fourth—the Roman Empire "divided into ten kingdoms, these were still *united together by the Clay,* i.e. the Pope's erroneous religion and idolatrous worship." The next event, then, is the coming of the stone kingdom. Next, from Daniel 7, he presents the same four kingdoms, the division of the fourth, and the divisions' names—with the Little

[69] *Ibid.*, A masterly presentation of Middle Ages' witnesses—Gerbert, Berengar, Fluentius, Joachim, Peter de Bruis, Arnold of Brescia, the Waldenses—appears in the 1796 ed., pages 449-452.

[70] *Ibid.*, pp. 499, 500.

[71] *Ibid.*, pp. 521, 522.

[72] His works were gathered into nine volumes in 1803. There are four columns of items in the British Museum Catalogue.

[73] Thomas, *op. cit.*, p. 1002.

[74] *Posthumous Pieces of the Late Rev. John William de la Flétchère . . . to Which Is Added a Letter Upon the Prophecies, Never Before Published* (3d ed.), pp. 368, 369.

Horn as the obtruding Papacy, uprooting Lombardy, Burgundy, and the Vandals. His persecution and his allotted period, soon to expire, ends with his destruction.[75]

2. Cleansing of Sanctuary to End Disfigured Worship. —Third, La Fléchère presents Daniel 8, with its Persian, Macedonian, and Roman powers—the bishop of Rome waxing exceeding great, casting down kings and emperors, and taking away the daily sacrifice, that is he "abolished or quite disfigured the true worship of God and Jesus, and cut down the truth to the ground, with his army." To the question, *"How long* the church should be thus corrupted and desolate?" the answer was, "Till the end of the 2300 days, and then the sanctuary should be cleansed." [76]

3. 2300 Years End in Present or Next Generation.— Stressing the importance of this number that fixes the beginnings of things to come on the earth, La Fléchère insists that the 2300 are prophetic days, signifying whole years. He then states that they must start with the time of the vision, about 550 B.C.—giving considerable data in behalf of this year—and so leading to A.D. 1750, when the cleansing of God's church should take place; then he expatiates on the pollution of the sanctuary by the Papacy's doctrine of justification by works and outward performances.[77] And, noting the variation in chronologies, he adds and puts down 1770, with this impressive word:

"Chronologists may mistake in a few years, but cannot err upon the whole; and as God is true and faithful, so it is manifest, that the prophecy of 2300, must be fully accomplished in our days, or those of the next generation." [78]

4. Year-Day Principle Applied to All Time Periods.— Denying that this cleansing had anything to do with the time of Judas Maccabaeus or Antiochus Epiphanes, or even the time of Luther, he applies it to the time of the "end"—"the word end signifies plainly, the catastrophe of God's drama, the last act

[75] *Ibid.*, pp. 370, 371.
[77] *Ibid.*, pp. 373, 374.
[76] *Ibid.*, p. 372.
[78] *Ibid.*, p. 375.

of the wicked tragedy men have been acting for near 6000 years." [79] He then argues that the "latter days" of Daniel 10 and the "end" of chapter 8 mean the same; the 2300 days form a "compleat proof." But he surveys the 1260 years, under the three and a half times, forty-two months, and 1260 days—putting 360 days to the "prophetic year," and touches the 1290 and 1335, and the time of their reckoning.[80]

5. LUKEWARMNESS PARALYZES CHURCH OF LAST DAYS.— La Fléchère then comes to the lukewarmness that is to paralyze the church in the last days.

" 'As the love of many will be cold,' and there will be, comparatively, no faith upon the earth, the apostacy foretold by all the prophets will soon take place; begin, in all probability, by the Lutherans in Germany, and follow in all the Protestant countries. Here cruelties unheard of since the beginning of the world, will be the refining fire of our decayed Faith; part of the reformed Christians will be destroyed by the sword, or by famine; part will be carried into captivity, part will remain to serve their cruel conquerors, who (notwithstanding their falling away from the pure, outward worship) will treat them in a most terrible manner." [81]

6. FORSAKING OF PAPACY FOLLOWED BY CLIMAX OF AGES.— With this he couples the death and resurrection of the Two Witnesses, the fall of the tenth part of the city, and the call out of Babylon; Rome will be destroyed amid revolutions, and the grand climax will be the second glorious advent of Christ.[82] The ten kings will rebel and forsake the whore, as pictured in Revelation 18 and 19. The climax comes when the thousand years end, and Satan is again loosed to—

"seduce two powerful nations *Gog and Magog;* but this second almost Universal Rebellion will be quenched, as prosperously as that of Antichrist. How long the world shall last after this, no one knows, not even the Angels of God; but it is certain that all those things must come to pass before the Conflagration of this Globe, spoken of by St. Peter, as well as before the Second Resurrection and Judgment." [83]

7. FRENCH PROTESTANTS AWAIT FRENCH REVOLUTION.— La Fléchère brings this remarkable letter to Wesley on prophecy

---

[79] *Ibid.*
[81] *Ibid.*, p. 379.
[83] *Ibid.*, pp. 383, 384.

[80] *Ibid.*, pp. 377, 378.
[82] *Ibid.*, pp. 380, 381.

WESLEY AMONG THE PROPHETIC EXPOUNDERS OF HIS DAY

John Wesley, Distinguished Founder of Methodism (Inset); His Well-known London City Road Church, Where He Included Prophetic Exposition in His Preaching (Left) ; and Prayer Room, in His Home Next Door, the Secret of His Spiritual Power (Right)

to a close with the general expectation of the Protestants of France for the predicted Revolution:

"I know, that a good part of an hundred thousand Protestants, scattered in France, expect some great revolution, that will turn at last to their good, and re-unite them to the children of above 200,000 of their brethren, that were either expelled the kingdom, or forced to leave it, because they 'would not take the mark of the beast in their hands or on their foreheads.' " [84]

XI. R. M. Places 2300 Years Between B.C. 558 and 1742

In 1787 an anonymous writer whose initials were R.M. published, in two editions during the same year, *Observations of Certain Prophecies in the Book of Daniel and the Revelation of St. John Which Relate to the Second Appearing of Our Lord, Shewing That It Is Highly Probable That the Tremendous Day in which It Shall Be Revealed Will Shortly Come.*

1. 2300 YEARS FROM VISION TO 1742.—Contending that, previous to the end, there shall be more than an ordinary preaching of the gospel, this writer refers to it as the coming jubilee. Here is his conclusion:

"This jubilee or cleansing of the sanctuary must begin within 2300 years from the time of Daniel's vision of the Ram and He-Goat, mentioned in chap. viii.; for in verse 14 of that chapter, it is said that the vision shall be until 2300 days. These days are to be understood as years: in the prophecies of Ezekiel, we read that God appointed that each day should denote a year; and by so interpreting Daniel's 70 weeks, relating to the first coming of Christ, the time exactly corresponds with the event; so we have a sure confirmation that Daniel's days are to be understood as years.

"Now the vision was in the third year of Belshazzar, king of the Chaldeans, 558 years before the Christian aera, and therefore the 2300 years ended A.D. 1742, at which time the sanctuary and the host were no longer to be trodden under foot, but to be cleansed." [85]

2. PAPAL ABOMINATION TAKES AWAY TRUE WORSHIP.— Commenting on the daily, R.M. says:

"The taking away of the daily sacrifice, and the setting up of abomination, is the taking away of the true christian worship, as instituted by

---

[84] *Ibid.*, p. 388.
[85] R. M., *Observations of Certain Prophecies*, pp. 6-8.

Christ and his Apostles, and the setting up of the doctrines and commandments of men, superstition, and idolatry, &c. in lieu thereof, which is mentioned by St. John under the appellation of the woman's flying into the wilderness. The daily sacrifice is a Mosaic term for the true worship of God, suited to' the time in which Daniel lived; but even the Apostles sometimes spoke in like manner, giving Christians the name of Jews." [86]

The 1260 year-days, however, he places from 405 to 1666, with the 1290 ending in 1696, and the 1335 in 1741.[87]

XII. Wesley, Following Bengel, Sets Consummation for 1836

JOHN WESLEY (1703-1791), distinguished founder of Methodism, was born in Lincolnshire. Educated at Charterhouse school, London, and Christ Church, Oxford, he was distinguished for his attainments, especially in logic. His father advised him to make religion the business of his life, and his mother, who understood Greek and Latin, approved of the plan. He was profoundly impressed by reading the works of writers who inculcated "the religion of the heart." He was ordained a deacon in 1725. After receiving his M.A. in 1726, he became his father's curate in 1727, and lived and officiated mainly at Wroot. In 1728 he was ordained a priest of the Established Church.

Returning to Oxford, he found his brother Charles, and they, together with two undergraduates, associated themselves in a society for "religious improvement." They were nicknamed "methodists," and sometimes "Bible Moths," "the holy club," and "Bible Bigots." Later Hervey, Whitefield, and others became members of the society. In 1735 the Wesleys accepted an invitation to Georgia to preach to the Indians and the colonists, and sailed in October. On the voyage to America John Wesley met twenty-six German Moravians whose simplicity and piety made a favorable impression upon him ere they arrived in Savannah early in 1736. Returning to England in 1738, Wesley wrote, "I, who went to America to convert others, was never myself converted to God." [88]

---

[86] *Ibid.*, pp. 8, 9.　　　　　　　　　　[87] *Ibid.*, pp. 12-14.
[88] Thomas, *op. cit.*, p. 2453.

In 1738 Wesley met, and was greatly influenced and really converted by, the Moravian Peter Böhler. He decided to visit Herrnhut because of his connection with and liking for the Moravians, and so traveled to north Germany. It was on this trip that he became acquainted at Marienborn with Count Zinzendorf. Upon his return to England he followed the example of Whitefield, and preached in the open fields at Bristol and elsewhere, as well as in churches and chapels everywhere. Though sometimes interrupted by mobs, and in several instances barely escaping death, he carried on his preaching, and persecution only confirmed his convictions. He traveled much on horseback, and preached several sermons daily. In fact, in fifty years he scarcely missed a day.[89] As his work grew, both in America and Europe, he was known as a great preacher in both hemispheres.

Wesley believed in the main doctrines of the Church of England, but departed later somewhat from her ritual and discipline. He separated from the Moravians in 1740, and soon afterward broke with Whitefield over "free grace" and predestination. His prose writings fill thirty-two volumes. Few religious leaders through the centuries have been instrumental in effecting more good. Thus began the great Methodist movement that has since grown to such gigantic proportions.

1. FOLLOWS BENGEL IN LOOKING TO 1836.—In his *Explanatory Notes Upon the New Testament,* Wesley holds that the book of Revelation extends from the Old Jerusalem to the New Jerusalem, and the seven trumpets to the end of the world—the sixth being Mohammedanism. Soon after he began to write, he became acquainted with the great work of Bengel, and believed that the translation and use of many of his notes would be more effective than his own.[90] He even followed Bengel's curious and complicated chronology. Thus on Revelation 10:6, he says, *"The Non-chronos* [not a whole "time"] here mentioned" seems to reach from 800 to 1936; the "Turkish Flood" (Revelation

---

[89] *Ibid.,* p. 2454, citing Coke and More, biographers of Wesley.
[90] John Wesley, *Explanatory Notes Upon the New Testament,* p. 219. For Bengel, see p. 709.

12:12, 16), which runs "higher and higher," "reaches the Woman *in her place;* and will, till near the End of the half time [1836], itself be swallowed up, perhaps by means of *Russia,* which is risen in the room of the Eastern Empire." [91]

2. PAPAL BEAST TO BE OVERTHROWN IN 1836.—The first beast of Revelation 13 is the "Romish papacy," [92] connected with the city of Rome. The second beast (verse 11) is to come out of the earth—out of Asia. "But he is not yet come: tho' he cannot be far off. For he is to appear at the End of the forty-two Months of the first Beast." [93] The woman Babylon is the papal city, likewise "Antichrist, the man of sin." [94] This brief exaltation will end in 1836, with the Beast "finally overthrown." [95]

3. A PREMILLENNIALIST AT FIRST.—Throughout the early part of his career Wesley was a premillennialist, in the sense that he looked upon the new earth state as the millennium. In fact it is called such in the hymns for which he took joint theological responsibility with his brother Charles. [96] For example, in a 1748 edition of their hymnal called *Hymns for Our Lord's Resurrection,* hymn 22 contains the following lines:

"Then the whole earth again shall rest,
    And see its paradise restored.

.   .   .   .   .

"O wouldst Thou bring the final scene,
    Accomplish the redeeming plan,
    Thy great millennial reign begin."

Wesley's notes on the book of Revelation constituted a milestone in his thinking in regard to the time of the millennium. In the introductory comments he said that he had never really understood this book until he read the works of Bengel, and that his own commentary followed Bengel's closely. (A comparison of the two works will show this in respect to the millennium.) Wesley thenceforth advocated Bengel's double millennium, and expected the first, on this earth, to begin in 1836.

---

[91] *Ibid.*, pp. 274, 287, 289, vs. 12, 6, and 16.   [92] *Ibid.*, pp. 290-296, v. 1-5.
[93] *Ibid.*, p. 299, v. 11.   [94] *Ibid.*, p. 313, v. 3; p. 316, v. 11.   [95] *Ibid.*, p. 303, v. 8.
[96] Thanks are due to Mrs. Kathleen B. McMurphy, who is preparing a doctrinal dissertation on eschatological poetry of the eighteenth century, for supplying this information.

4. Two Millenniums Follow Times of Beast.—These periods, he says, "do not precede, or parallel, but wholly follow the Times of the Beast." Moreover, the first of

"these thousand Years bring a new, full, and lasting Immunity from all outward and inward Evils (the Authors of which are now removed) and an Affluence of all Blessings. But such a Time . . . is still to come." [97]

However, the reign of these souls with Christ during the second thousand years is not on earth but in heaven.

XIII. Purves Anticipates 2300 Years Will End in 1766

James Purves (1734-1795), Scotch sectary, was born in Blackadder, Berwickshire. Selected by a "fellowship society" in Berwickshire for their pastor, he was sent to Glasgow college to study, mostly Latin, Greek, and Hebrew. In 1776 he moved to Edinburgh, taught school, and was elected pastor of the society there. He wrote a number of works. In his *Observations* (1777) Purves begins the 2300 days "with the Empire of the Medes and Persians." [98] The "vision being said to be for many days" indicates the cleansing or "making just the sanctuary, was a very distant event; the *season* or *time* in which it was to be effected, being 2300 *prophetic days* [years] distant from the beginning of the *Empire* of the medes and persians." [99]

Then Purves adds, "Having fixed the beginning of the 2300 *days*, the end of them is next to be enquired into." [100] Beginning with 534 B.C., Purves ends the 2300 years in 1766, [101] when the justification would take place. Others, such as Imrie [102] and Taylor, [103] had been making similar inquiry.

---

[97] *Ibid.*, p. 327, v. 2.
[98] James Purves, *Obesrvations on Prophetic Time and Similitudes*, p. 1.
[99] *Ibid.*, pp. 4, 5.   [100] *Ibid.*, p. 5.   [101] *Ibid.*, p. 6.
[102] David Imrie, minister at St. Mungo in Annandale, wrote *A Letter . . . Predicting the Speedy Accomplishment of the Great, Awful and Glorious Events Which the Scriptures Say Are to Be Brought to Pass in the Latter Times.* (Published at Edinburgh in 1755; reprinted at Boston, 1756). This looked for the speedy fall of Antichrist—the three and a half times of the Beast—about 1794. (Pages 10-12.) Coupled with this, he extended the 2300 years from 538 B.C., the first year of Medo-Persia, until the cleansing or justification of the sanctuary. (Page 12.) Imrie cites Fleming, Newton, and Mede.
[103] Laughlan Taylor, minister of Larbert, in *An Essay on the Revelation of the Apostle John* (1763), says that the 2300 days of Daniel 8:14 "signify years," calculating the beginning from the time of the vision—perhaps 532 B.C. They end "according to this calculation, about the year 1761" (p. 141), when the sanctuary should be cleansed.

CHAPTER THIRTY-ONE

Pietism's Advances

Counterbalanced by Rationalism's Inroads

I. Growth and Extension of Pietism's Influence

It is essential to have a bird's-eye view of the eighteenth-century efforts toward a revival of godliness. In Germany they centered around Spener, in Berlin, and Francke, professor of divinity in the University of Halle. There followed the solicitation of contributions for the purchase of books for the religious instruction of the poor, the erection of schools, and the building of a great orphan home. The spirit of piety affected the city and extended to other parts of Germany and beyond.

1. PIETISM SPREAD AND ADVANCED BY FRANCKE.—AUGUST HERMANN FRANCKE (1663-1727) was brilliant as a lad and deeply religious. By 1685 he had received his M.A. from the University of Leipzig, with Hebrew as his major. He went to Lüneburg, where he studied the Bible under Superintendent Sandhagen. These studies made the deepest impression upon him and caused him to surrender his life to Christ. He visited Spener in Dresden, and was a welcome guest in his home. In 1689 he returned to Leipzig and lectured on the epistles of Paul. He followed Spener's example, and instituted clubs for Bible study and devotion. Although some of the professors of the University of Leipzig were at first associated with him and many students and citizens attended, differences and discussions arose, and the participants were nicknamed "Pietists."

In 1690 his lectures were forbidden, and he left Leipzig for

Erfurt. But soon opposition arose there, and he had to leave the town. His friend Spener, by now in an influential position in Berlin, secured for him a pastorate and professorship at Halle. In fact, the chairs of theology in this newly founded University of Halle were filled by the disciples of Spener. Francke's deep desire to help the suffering made him accept some orphans into his home, out of which grew the big orphanage, the normal seminary, the divinity school, and the Royal Pedagogium. The latter was reserved for the sons of noblemen. Count Zinzendorf received a part of his education there. By the time of Francke's death more than 2,200 children had been instructed in his institutions. Francke's Bible studies attracted large audiences and deeply affected the life of the community. His supreme emphasis was upon the Bible and practical Christianity rather than upon dogma and scholastic subtleties.

Among those who opposed him were some who declared the church to be so pure and holy as to be above the possibility of reform. To others, the Lutheran creed was absolute truth. Some even declared the decision of the clergy was equally authoritative with the Scriptures.[1] While at Halle, Francke wrote his *Introductio ad Lectionem Prophetarum* (1724).

2. ZINZENDORF ESTABLISHES COLONIES EVERYWHERE.—NICOLAUS LUDWIG, COUNT OF ZINZENDORF (1700-1760) was born in Dresden, Saxony. He became the founder of the "Brüdergemeinde," the Brethren's Church—a church within the church. Because of his receiving persecuted families of the old Moravian Church into his estate, the connection is established with the old "Unitas Fratrum" of the Bohemian and Moravian Brethren. He traveled extensively in Europe and America, consolidating the Moravian colony at Bethlehem, Pennsylvania. In Zinzendorf and his Moravian brotherhood, the undying force of practical Christianity reappeared, and the spirit of missions was really born within this brotherhood. They founded missions in Green-

---

[1] Albert Henry Newman, *op. cit.*, vol. 2, pp. 528 ff.; see also T. Förster, "Francke," *The New Schaff-Herzog*, vol 4, pp. 367, 368.

land and the West Indies, among the Hottentots and the Papuas.[2]

In 1710 Zinzendorf had gone to the Seminary of Halle, where as a pupil of Francke he experienced the quickenings of spiritual life. He founded a society called the "Order of the Grain of Mustard Seed." After studying law at Wittenberg, and traveling in Holland and France, Zinzendorf entered into the civil service of the crown of Saxony, but not many years thereafter went to live on his estates near the border of Bohemia. A few members of the Moravian church driven from home by persecution, sought refuge with him. The settlement was called Herrnhut (under the Lord's guard, Hutberg). Under Zinzendorf's fostering care it grew until it became the Church of the United Brethren, established in 1727—including direct descendants of the Hussites of Bohemia, who had been crushed by cruel and prolonged persecution.

II. Horch—2300 Extending to Kingdom, Includes Lesser Periods

HEINRICH HORCH (or Horche) (1652-1729), Reformed theologian, was born in Eschwege, and studied theology and medicine in Marburg. There he was deeply influenced by the Spener Pietistic Movement. In 1683 he became a minister at Heidelberg, and two years later court preacher at Kreuznach, returning to Heidelberg in 1687, there to receive the Doctor of Theology degree. He was also pastor of the Church of the Holy Spirit, and became involved in controversies with the Jesuits over questions in the Heidelberg Catechism.

In 1690 Horch became court chaplain and professor at Herborn, holding unorthodox views, especially concerning the millennium. He associated with Separatists, sponsoring their movement. This led to his suspension in 1698, following which he traveled extensively, preaching in the market squares, cemeteries, and wherever he found an opportunity. He was arrested several times. He was erratic and intractable, and for a period

---

[2] Farrar, *op. cit.*, p. 390; see also Herzog, *Real-Encyklopädie*, art. "Zinzendorf."

suffered from a mental illness, from which he later recovered. His last years were spent in Kirchhain, near Marburg, where his time was occupied largely in writing books. To the end he held that the church had become corrupt and needed reforming. He was a man of unusual gifts, sincere and zealous, but stubborn. He wrote a great number of treatises in German and Latin.

1. INTEREST IN PROPHECY AROUSED BY BEVERLEY.—One of Horch's first works on prophecy was prompted by reading Beverley, as translated by Brüsske. It was called *Das A und das O oder Zeitrechnung der gantzen H. Schrifft* (The Alpha and Omega or Time Reckoning of the Holy Scriptures). He considers the 2300 years the "guide to the entire succeeding chronological order of the Scriptures up to the glorious kingdom of Christ." [3]

2. 2300 YEARS FROM CYRUS TO CHRIST'S KINGDOM.— Horch declares they began with Cyrus and will last till the destruction of Antichrist and the establishment of Christ's kingdom—past the four kingdoms of Babylonia, Persia, Grecia, and Rome.[4] His detailed statement on the 2300 years follows:

"What period spans the 2300 evenings and mornings? From the Persian monarchy to the end of the Roman, by the destruction of Antichrist. . . . What kind of days are the evening-mornings? Those are prophetic days—or so many years. Had these prophetic days already begun in those days? Yes. Ezekiel had to bear the iniquity of Israel for 390 days and the iniquity of Judah for 40 days, and each day stood for a year. Ezek. 4:5, 6. . . . As Moses says: And the evening and the morning were the first, second, third, etc., day, till the Sabbath, the last day of the week; in this manner time shall continue till the glorious kingdom of Christ as the right day of rest of the saints at the end of the world. Heb. 4:9, Acts 3:20, Rev. 20:6." [5]

3. TRUE SANCTUARY WORSHIP INTERRUPTED BY PAPACY.— Horch holds that the sanctuary, which had been built, had the true daily sacrifice or worship, but this daily would be interrupted for a time—the Little Horn to stand up against the Prince

---

[3] Heinrich Horch, *Das A und das O oder Zeitrechnung der gantzen H. Schrifft* (1697), p. 169.
[4] *Ibid.*, p. 163.
[5] *Ibid.*, pp. 164-167.

of princes during a long part of the period [6]—while the 2300
years would stretch across the centuries.

4. 2300 Years Embrace All Periods.—This 2300 years embraces the seventy weeks, the 1260 years, the 1290, and 1335,[7]
which reach to the kingdom of God.[8] Horch was evidently the
first German expositor to recognize the 70 weeks as a subordinate
part of the 2300 years. He does not, however, begin the two
periods together, but starts the 2300 years with the year in which
Cyrus gave the permission to rebuild Jerusalem. As this order
was not carried out for seventy-five years, Horch calls this interim
the period of obstacles or resistance, but includes it in the 2300-
year period.[9] After the passing of this interval the 70 weeks or
490 years began, and extended three and one-half years beyond
the death of Christ.[10]

5. Dead Works of Sardis Must Be Shaken Off.—Horch,
in the Revelation, applies Sardis to the post-Reformation church,
to which some of the dead works had clung, to be shaken off in
the Philadelphia period.[11]

6. Periods of Saracenic and Turkish Trumpets.—The
trumpets are judgments against the Roman Empire—the reign
of the Saracen locusts to last 150 years, the time of their great
spread,[12] beginning in 622, and the Turkish sixth trumpet of 396
years (a year, a month, and a day, or 365 + 30 + 1) to extend
from 1057 to 1453.[13] The saints will not reign with Christ until
the beast and the false prophet are cast into the lake of fire.[14]

7. Angelic Messages Against Papacy Yet Future.—In
later books the Little Horn as Antichrist is iterated and reiterated,[15] and the three angelic messages of Revelation 14, are considered still future.[16] Such were the leading positions on prophecy advocated by Horch.

[6] *Ibid.*, pp. 168, 169.   [7] *Ibid.*, pp. 170, 171.   [8] *Ibid.*, p. 163.
[9] *Ibid.*, p. 172.   [10] *Ibid.*, p. 176.   [11] *Ibid.*, pp. 188, 189.
[12] *Ibid.*, pp. 206, 225.   [13] *Ibid.*, p. 207.   [14] *Ibid.*, p. 240.
[15] Horch, *Mystische und Profetische Bibel* (The Mystical and Prophetic Bible), chaps.
7, 8.
[16] Horch, *Die Filadelfische Versuchungsstunde* (The Philadelphic Hour of Trial), pp. 2, 3.

III. Wide Study and Concern Over 2300 Years

1. JEWS AND PIETISTS AGITATED OVER APPROACHING TERMI-
NUS.—In an anonymous treatise in 1702, titled *Aufrichtiges
Bedencken* (Sincere Doubts), by a Pietist, the writings of GEORG
HERMANN GIBLEHR, pastor at Aspach, are cited and discussed.
The propriety of studying prophetic time periods and dates is
stressed, and mention made of a belief among certain Polish
Jews who, around 1700, looked for the judgment day on the
basis of Daniel 8:14. Hildebert of Nürnberg is quoted concerning 120 Jews who had left Poland for Palestine, believing the
day of their salvation was drawing nigh. The writer then emphasizes the universal study of the last days among Pietists, as
well as other scholars in Germany, Italy, Spain, France, England,
and America. Expositors such as Jurieu, Beverley, and Giblehr,
all look for the ending of the great prophetic period around
1715, 1740, 1772, or 1785—thus differing only a few years in
their expectancy.[17]

Emphasis is given to the belief that "we today" (the people
at that time) live in the "Philadelphia Age" of the seven
churches, and the belief of Pietists, such as Spener and Petersen,
is set forth, that the 2300 days are literal years.[18] The first and
second resurrections are also stressed, as bounding the millennium.[19]

2. GIBLEHR ANTICIPATES JUDGMENT AT 2300 YEAR'S END.—
In a religious periodical called *Unschuldige Nachrichten von
Alten-und Neuen Theologischen Sachen* (Unbiased Reports of
Old and New Theological Matters), issued in 1708 by "Servants
of the Divine Word," Giblehr's tractate on the time of the last
judgment, issued in 1702, is reviewed. The tract was reprinted
several times within the year.[20] Giblehr is cited as stating, on page
36, that the cleansing, or justifying, of the sanctuary and the end
of the 2300 literal years mean the last judgment, and that he

---

[17] *Aufrichtiges Bedencken*, pp. 12-14.
[18] *Ibid.*, pp. 15, 21.
[19] *Ibid.*, pp. 24, 39, 40.
[20] "Georg Hermann Giblehrs Unvorgreiffliche Gedancken von dem erfundenen Termino
des jüngsten Gerichts. 1702," *Unschuldige Nachrichten von Alten-und Neuen Theologischen
Sachen*, 1708, p. 764.

looked to 1760 as the supreme year.[21] Giblehr is then quoted concerning the 1260 days of Daniel 7:25 and 12:2, and Revelation
11:2; 12:14; and 13:6; with the statement that they all refer to
the 1260 literal years of the oriental and occidental Antichrist,
with the 1335 years beginning in A.D. 425, when Pope Anaceleto
(Celestine I) started the reign of Antichrist, which will *continue
till* the last judgment.[22]

IV. Berlenburg Bible—2300 Years Reach to Christ's Kingdom

The eighteenth century was marked by a quest for truth
and further enlightenment. Many, not satisfied with the dogmatism of the established churches, searched diligently the prophetic word, which yielded increasing treasures to the reverent
student. The result was a spiritual awakening that found its
expression under different forms, as the Pietism of Spener and
Francke, the Moravian Brethren under Zinzendorf, Quakerism
in England, and Jansenism among the Catholics in France.
Movements with a more mystical or even theosophical bent also
sprang into existence. Among the most noteworthy are the Philadelphian groups, in England and Germany. In the latter country
their chief sponsor was Count Casimir of Seyn-Wittgenstein and
Berleburg, under whose protection a most remarkable work was
completed, the so-called *Berlenburger Bibel*. It is an eight-vol-
ume work, edited by theologians like Haug, Scheffer, Seebach,
and Edelmann, who produced the German version and added
numerous highly helpful notes, which indicate a good insight
into the prophetic elements of the Bible. This Bible encountered
much opposition from orthodox circles, but on the other hand it
was cherished among many, even outside the Philadelphian
groups. It is interesting to note how its influence reached to
America.

A German, Christopher Saur, imported many Bibles from
Germany, among them numerous copies of the Berlenburg
Bible, which were much preferred by the Ephrata Mystics, the

---

[21] *Ibid.*, pp. 765, 766.   [22] *Ibid.*, pp. 766-768.

Dunkers, and the Mennonites. He began to print the Scriptures, using the Berlenburg Bible as the principal pattern. It went to press in 1743, in Pennsylvania. So before an English Bible was printed in the New World, the Berlenburg Bible was reprinted in Germantown.[23]

1. 2300 YEARS END AT KINGDOM'S ESTABLISHMENT.—In the notes on Daniel, on the exceeding great horn of Daniel 8:9, Antichrist is recognized, which exalted itself above God and cast down truth to the ground. The notes indicate that there is more than one reason to believe that the 2300 year-day period refers not only to Antiochus but to the whole time of the great conflict between the powers of darkness and the people of God from the time of Daniel to the end of the world.[24] God's people will be suppressed, persecuted, and tormented during the new dispensation, first "by the rule of the pagan dragon, and then by the ten-horned beast, and finally most cruelly, spiritually and physically, by Antichrist and his followers." But when the 2300 years expire, "then shall the sanctuary of God come to its own, which will become a reality in the glorious kingdom of Christ." If the 2300 years begin with the time of Daniel's vision, the grand terminus will come in 1748.[25]

2. 70 WEEKS CONNECTED WITH THE 2300 YEARS.—Tied into "the great line of time"—the 2300 years—are the "seventy year-weeks reaching to the death of the Messiah." In the discussion of Daniel 9 these statements occur, which recognize fulfillment in natural years:

"Without doubt Daniel is shown here the beginning of the great time-period of the 2300 years of which the 70 weeks would carry us to the death of the Messiah. . . .

"In reckoning these 70 weeks as year weeks we get the sum of 490 years. There is no reason to presume a different kind of years than those of 365 days as it is generally understood by the Scriptures." [26]

3. CROSS IN FOURTH YEAR OF 70TH WEEK.—Asserting that the 70 weeks "came to an end in the fourth year after Christ's

[23] P. Marion Simms, *The Bible in America*, pp. 120 ff.
[24] Berlenburg Bible, Notes on Dan. 8:11-14, Old Testament, pp. 645-647.
[25] *Ibid.*, p. 647.　　　　　　　　[26] *Ibid.*, p. 655. Translated from the German.

violent death," to make reconciliation and to establish righteousness, the Berlenburg note says:

"They [70 weeks] are exactly measured off, that nothing could be added or subtracted nor that the measure given could be any longer or shorter according to the Divine decision.

"[are determined] upon thy people and thy city from which you came and who are so dear to your heart. It is generally understood that this is the period which God had set apart for the Jews during which they should remain a people and Jerusalem be rebuilt. Within this period, more precisely at the end of it some one should appear to resist transgression, to check and consume it. . . . At that time Christus should appear to destroy the works of the Devil. 1. Joh. 3.8." [27]

4. Seventy Weeks Dated From Artaxerxes Longimanus. —The decree beginning the period is limited to Artaxerxes Longimanus, thus:

"It cannot be the command of Cyrus; there should be more weeks or else they would end too early . . . for the same reason it cannot be the command of Darius Hystaspis, because from the time of his decree to the death of Christ are 50 to 60 years more than the 70 weeks or 490 years comprise. The latter would end before the birth of Christ.

"Therefore, it is understood by a more thorough investigation, which certainly comes closer to the purpose, that it is either the order of Artaxerxes Longimanus which Ezra received in the 7th year of Artaxerxes' reign and which bestowed many privileges upon the Jews as can be seen in Ezra 7:7, 8, 11 or that of the 20th year of Artaxerxes given to Nehemiah, (Neh. 2:1-5) permitting to build walls around the city and therewith making it again a city. Sir. 49:15. And even if the reign of Artaxerxes should have started nine years earlier, so that he should have reigned in the lifetime of his father or that the latter should have died earlier, from his 20th year to the 30th year of Christ would be 483 years and only one week of seven years is left for the suffering, death, and resurrection." [28]

5. Christ's Ministry First Half of 70th Week.—The seventieth week is delineated in this way:

"This week began when Jesus was baptized in His 30th year and began His ministry. Luke 3:23. This ministry He continued for three and a half years until His death. After His death the disciples continued the work for another three and a half years, while He had already ascended to His Father and sat down at His right hand." [29]

---

[27] Ibid.
[28] Ibid., p. 656. The reference to the possibility of Artaxerxes' reign beginning nine years earlier, is an allusion to the interpretation of Petavius and Ussher. See page 428.
[29] Ibid., p. 658.

6. Lesser Periods Begin a.d. 412; 1335 Ends 1748.—The commentators in the Berlenburg Bible began the 1260, 1290, and 1335 year-days about a.d. 410. Therefore the last period, the 1335, would end synchronously with the 2300 years, in 1748.[30] They are clear and strong on the literal resurrection at the advent, and stress the glorious appearing of Christ at the end of the world, when the resurrection of the just will take place. This great Bible exerted a potent influence.

V. Swedenborg—Spiritual Advent and Carnal Jerusalem Theories

Emanuel Swedenborg (1688-1772), Swedish scientist and Spiritist, must not be overlooked. Son of a Swedish clergyman, he was born in Stockholm, and took a precocious interest in religious matters. In 1734 he published *Prodromus Philosophiae Ratiocinantis de Infinito et Causa Finali Creationis* (A Philosophical Argument on the Infinite and the Final Cause of Creation), which also tried to establish a *nexus* between body and soul. From this time he applied himself to discovering the nature of soul and spirit by means of anatomical studies, and published a number of books. Later in life he professed to obtain a new and free access to the supernatural, claiming ability to communicate with inhabitants of the spirit world. Believing himself to be the recipient of celestial revelations, he published his experiences in *Arcana Coelestia* (Heavenly Secrets), during 1749-1756. In this he stresses a fanciful correspondence between the natural and spiritual that led to grave extremes.

Swedenborg also wrote *The True Christian Religion*. He claimed that the old church of Christianity passed away and all things became new in the founding of the New Jerusalem church —the judgment enacted in the world of spirits in 1757.[31] He not only interpreted the Bible in an allegorical way but saw in its verses enshrined an inner spiritual sense, or rather a series of spiritual meanings. He treated the book of Revelation in the

---

[30] *Ibid.*, p. 677.
[31] J. F. Blunt, *Dictionary of Sects*, pp. 579-583.

23

same manner. Books which did not yield to a spiritual interpretation were set aside. On angels he remarked:

"There is not a single angel in the universal heaven who was originally created such, nor any devil in hell who was created an angel of light and afterwards cast down thither; but all, both in heaven and in hell, are from the human race." [32]

The year 1757, he insisted, marked the transition into a new age of the world, by the coming of the Lord to spirits and to men in the opening of his Word in its spiritual sense. The good were to recognize the Lord Jesus Christ in His glorified humanity, and follow Him in a life of faith and charity, and so compose the new Christian heaven. [33] Such was his strange interpretation of the Revelation.

VI. German Rationalists Adopt the Preterist School

Deep shadows intermingle with the golden sunshine of the century. Along with the growth and spread of Pietism in Germany, Rationalism began to take root and expand disturbingly. The nearer we approach the time of the French Revolution, the more the generation of rationalistic and higher critical expositors grows in influence, having adopted the Preterist School of interpretation. Their writings were characterized by much research and philological learning, blended with a startling frankness in religious skepticism. It also broke out in other countries. In Bengel's day FIRMIN ABAUZIT (1679-1767), of Geneva, [34] published a work, in 1730, titled *Discours historique sur l'Apocalypse* (Historic Discourse on the Apocalypse), which was the first, in this period, to attack the canonical authority of the Apocalypse. [35]

Soon after the middle of the century the skeptical spirit broke forth sharply in Germany. In 1765 SEMLER [36] published a

[32] George Trobridge, *Swedenborg, Life and Teaching*, p. 179.
[33] Frank Sewall, "Swedenborg," *The New Schaff-Herzog*, vol. 11, p. 186.
[34] Born in Uzes in Languedoc, he was, after the Revocation of the Edict of Nantes, placed in a Roman Catholic Seminary, from which his mother recovered him, and succeeded in bringing him to Geneva. There he received his education and spent his long life. He was considered to be one of the most learned men of his time, and was a friend of Newton, Rousseau, and Voltaire.
[35] Elliott, *op. cit.*, vol. 4, p. 524.
[36] JOHANN SALOMO SEMLER (1725-1791), called the father of German rationalism, was born at Saalfeld. Educated at the University of Halle, he became professor of theology there. In 1757

work by Oeder, entitled *Christliche freye Untersuchung über die so genannte Offenbarung Johannis* (A Free Investigation Into the So-called Revelation by John), denying both its apostolicity and its literary beauty, and charging it with extravagances. This launched the Semlerian controversy, which lasted until 1785. Semler was answered by Reuss of Tübingen (1767), Knittel of Wolfenbüttel (1773), and Schmidt of Wittenberg (1775). The genuineness of the book of Daniel was also impugned by English Deism, French Skepticism, and German Rationalism.[37]

In 1786 HERNNSCHNEIDER published his commentary on the Apocalypse, explaining it as a poem limited to (1) the overturning of Judaism, (2) the overthrow of heathenism, and (3) the final universal triumph of the Christian church. This became the model of the celebrated work of JOHANN GOTTFRIED EICHHORN (1752-1827), in 1791.[38] The scheme is simple, as described by Johann Leonard Hug (1765-1846).[39]

There are three cities in the Apocalypse: *Sodom* (or Egypt), *Babylon*, and the *New Jerusalem*. The seven trumpets refer to Sodom, or Old Jerusalem, and its destruction, where Christ was crucified. The seven vials pertain to the destruction of Babylon, or pagan Rome, of the seven hills on the Tiber. Consequently, Jerusalem and Rome are the two cities, or religions, that were to be destroyed. Thus the New Jerusalem, continues this smooth contention, can only stand for Christianity and its triumph, taking the place of the former two religions. Therefore the book of Revelation is devoted to the description of the dissolution of Judaism, the abolition of heathenism, and the dominion of the world by the doctrines of Jesus.

This subtle, modified Preterism, traceable back through

---

he succeeded to the directorship of the seminary. Semler did not adhere to the then-prevalent idea of verbal inspiration and attacked especially the Apocalypse, attributing it to a fanatical group of Jews in Alexandria, who wished to propagate the concept of the nearness of the end of the world. He points to the fourth book of Ezra and the book of Enoch as its sources. He asserts that the theory of the world's lasting 6,000 years is purely apocryphal and the number 666 a childish play with figures and an insult to attribute such a fantasy to the apostle John. He propounds these ideas in his *Neue Untersuchungen über Apocalypsin* (New Investigation of the Apocalypse), pages 28, 29, 34, 35, 76.

[37] Carl August Auberlen, *The Prophecies of Daniel and the Revelations of St. John* (trans. by Saphir), pp. 9, 10.

[38] Elliott, *op. cit.*, vol. 4, pp. 525, 565.   [39] *Ibid.*, pp. 526-529.

Bossuet, Grotius, and Hammond, to Alcazar, came to be rather generally accepted. Later JOHANN GOTTFRIED HERDER (1744-1803) came to emphasize the Jewish catastrophe, whereas GEORG HEINRICH AUGUST EWALD (1803-1875), FRIEDERICH BLEEK (1793-1859), and WILHELM MARTIN DE WETTE (1780-1849) stressed that of the heathen Rome—but included both catastrophes.[40] And the names of Corrodi, Bertholdt, von Lengerke, Schleiermacher, Knobel, and Lücke also belong in the later list,[41] as well as Moses Stuart (1780-1852) in America,[42] and Samuel Davidson (1807-1898) of England,[43] as will be noted in Volume III.

Then, ERNST WILHELM HENGSTENBERG (1802-1869),[44] typical of others before him, softened toward the Papacy because of his concern over German infidelity and Rationalism, while holding to much of the Historical School of interpretation. He joined with the Rationalists and Catholics in their efforts to subvert the Protestant application of the Apocalyptic symbols, and contended that if a definite era were to be fixed for the beginning of the thousand years scarcely any other would be so suitable as the first Christmas Eve of the year 800, the day of the inauguration of the Western Christian, or Holy Roman, Empire.[45] Hengstenberg, commenting on Bengel, admitted that Chiliasm is the necessary consequence of the Protestant view, for the thousand years' reign, according to the Apocalypse, begins only with the destruction of the Beast.[46] Serious inroads were made by these Rationalist teachings. We must not forget what Hengstenberg has done to defend the revelations of Christ in

[40] *Ibid.*, pp. 565, 566.

[41] Auberlen, *op. cit.*, pp. 9, 10.

[42] In the early nineteenth century STUART inoculated the American ministry with anti-Protestant Preterism, using this to combat the prophetic interpretations of William Miller and his associates—denying that Revelation 13 applies to the Papacy, and denying that the thousand years are still future.

[43] Similarly in England, DAVIDSON, in the interest of the same Preterist theory, assailed the Reformation view. He said, "Little do we believe that the Papacy is to be found in the Little Horn of Daniel's Beast, in the Man of sin predicted by Paul, or the Antichrist of John." (*Introduction to the New Testament*, vol. 3, p. 623.)

[44] This conspicuous Lutheran leader was born in Fröndenberg, Prussia, studied in Bonn, and in 1824 went to Berlin, and became a lecturer on theology at the university. By 1827 he became editor of the *Evangelische Kirchenzeitung*. He was author of several commentaries, notably *Christologie des Alten Testaments* (Christology of the Old Testament) (1829-1835).

[45] Ernst W. Hengstenberg, *The Revelation of St. John*, vol. 2, p. 334; Auberlen, *op. cit.*, p. 12.

[46] Hengstenberg, *op. cit.*, vol. 2, p. 351.

the Old Testament against Rationalism. His commentaries on the Gospels, as well as on the Apocalypse, will always be of the greatest benefit for all practical theologians.

Bengel likewise resisted this radical diversion of the twentieth chapter from its relation to the nineteenth. No one was able effectually to oppose him, though few Preterists had the courage to abandon the false view of the Papacy which had obtained increasing sanction. Let us note Bengel.

VII. Bengel Projects Strange Modification of Year-Day Principle

JOHANN ALBRECHT BENGEL (1687-1752), stalwart German defender of the Historical School of interpretation in the midst of compromises and surrender, was born in Württemberg. Studying first at the gymnasium at Stuttgart, he pursued his theological studies at Tübingen, specializing in the Sacred Text and in philosophy. His bent toward Pietism is disclosed by the fact that his favorite authors were Arndt, Spener, and Francke.

In 1713 Bengel was made professor at Denkendorf for the training of candidates for the ministry. And for twenty-eight years he also served there as pastor. He early became convinced that the pope was the predicted Antichrist and that the millennium was yet future. In 1734 Bengel, as Germany's first reverent textual critic, issued an edition of the Greek New Testament, together with an *Apparatus Criticus*, which became a standard work. In 1740 appeared his *Erklärte Offenbarung Johannis* (Explanation of the Revelation of John), and his *Gnomon oder Zeiger des Neuen Testaments* (Gnomon or Hand of Time in the New Testament) in 1742, each passing through numerous editions. His books were soon translated into most European languages.

In the year 1741 Bengel was made prelate of Herbrechtingen, and in 1749 he became councilor and prelate of Alpirsbach. Conspicuous for his conscientious piety, his thorough education, his sane and rational opinions, he was one of the foremost men of his time. His critics could not accuse him of visionary fanaticism.[47] Believing that the world was approaching the termination of a great prophetic period of 666 years, Bengel urged the importance of individual preparation for the millennial reign of Christ on earth, which he expected to begin in 1836.

Twenty years a close student of prophecy, he confirmed the general Protestant Historicist view of the Apocalypse, and stood forth in exegesis as the Continental champion of the future millennium.[48] Rejecting the Augustinian theory, and regarding the Apocalypse as chronological like Daniel's prophecies, he turned the eyes of a multitude of followers to the kingdom of God as a future blessed hope, culminating in the second advent, when man shall be redeemed from dust to immortality. His school of exposition was followed by Prelate Oetinger, Rieger of Ludwigsburg, Prelate Roos, and many others, including Wesley.

1. FORMULATES ARBITRARY TIME UNIT FOR PERIODS.— Bengel's millennial view was singular in that it was "double"— a thousand years on earth followed by a thousand years in heaven.[49] In his chronological works he endeavored to fix and blend the number of the Beast with the date of the beginning of the millennium, which he placed in 1836. Bengel's most characteristic principle of expounding prophetic time—that of a month for approximately fifteen years—was wholly arbitrary and groundless. To deduce his principle, he conjectured that the Beast's number signified 666 years, and that this must

---

[47] Christoph Hoffmann, *Mein Weg nach Jerusalem* (My Way to Jerusalem), part 1, p. 26. Bengel's great contribution to evangelical Christianity does not lie so much in his chronological writings or in his computations for measuring prophetic time, but in his introduction of the idea that the Bible should be considered as the revelation of God's plan, in which Christ is the supreme, all-overshadowing Center. He did not consider the Bible as merely a textbook for dogmatics, but as a progressive unfolding of the divine plan of redemption, with the second coming of Christ as its glorious culmination. "Because the ultimate goal of all time-periods mentioned in the Bible is the coming of Christ in glory."—Jakob August Dorner, *Geschichte der protestantischen Theologie besonders in Deutschland* (History of Protestant Theology, Particularly in Germany), pp. 654, 655. He thus gave evangelical thinking a new impetus and guided it into completely new channels. This was also the motive of his writings on the Apocalypse—*Erklärte Offenbarung Johannis* (1740) and *Sechzig erbauliche Reden über die Offenbarung* (Sixty Edifying Addresses on the Apocalypse) (1747). And although we cannot rely upon his computations, as they have been superseded by subsequent events, his fundamental contribution—of viewing the Bible as a whole, and explaining the Bible by the Bible—should never be forgotten.

[48] Auberlen, *op. cit.*, p. 365.

[49] Johann Christian Friedrich Burk, *A Memoir of the Life and Writings of John Albert Bengel* (trans. by Walker), p. 294.

equal the Beast's numeral period of forty-two months. Thus one prophetic month $= 666$ divided by $42 = 15\ 6/7$ years.[50] Through such fantastic fractional arithmetic he came to infer that 1836 would begin the first of the two millenniums. Even in this he was followed by Wesley and many others. It was in 1724 that Bengel became convinced that the Beast's number of 666 is "a period of time," the same as the forty-two months of the Beast's blasphemy.[51] And in 1727 he abandoned the strict year-day reckoning and attempted to correct the time periods by this modified scheme.[52]

2. BEAST IS PAPACY, WITH SHORTENED TIME PERIOD.—The woman of Revelation 12 symbolizes the church, bringing forth Christ, the male child, and the "1260 prophetic days are 657 ordinary years in full. And if you reckon these from 864 to 1521, you will certainly not be far from the truth." [53] The Beast of Revelation 13 is the "ecclesiastico-political power opposed to the kingdom of Christ," connected with Rome and existing at the present time—the Roman Papacy founded by Hildebrand, or Gregory VII, and to be cast into the lake of fire.[54] The Beast considered as to his seven heads is the papal power transmitted through a long succession of popes; but when "the last head," and especially the Beast himself as "the eighth," shall rage, he is become a personal individual. The "horns" are ten kings existing in this same last period; the Beast out of the earth is probably Jesuitism, or possibly Freemasonry; the angel messengers of Revelation 14 he presumes to be Arndt and Spener, with the third yet to come.[55]

The three and a half times, comprehending within its scope the forty-two months and the Beast's number, 666, is set at 1058 to 1836. This latter year is anticipated as the time of the destruction of the Beast and of the binding of Satan.[56]

---

[50] *Ibid.*, p. 288.
[51] *Ibid.*, p. 283.
[52] Oskar Wächter, *Bengel und Oetinger, Leben und Aussprüche* (Bengel and Oetinger, Life and Sayings), p. 22.
[53] Johann Albrecht Bengel, *Gnomon of the New Testament* (Edinburgh, translation), vol. 5, pp. 258, 259; see also his *Erklärte Offenbarung*, p. 415.
[54] Bengel, *Gnomon*, vol. 5, pp. 269-289; vol. 2, pp. 749, 750.
[55] Burk, *op. cit.*, pp. 301-303. [56] Bengel, *Gnomon*, vol. 5, p. 373.

3. Calculates Thousand Years to Begin in 1836.—The woman sitting on the Beast in Revelation 17 is Rome.[57] The seven plagues are still future, with the last raging of Antichrist from 1831 to 1836.[58] The thousand years' binding of Satan is concluded by the first resurrection, which introduces the second thousand years. Bengel says:

"XIII. Babylon will become desolate followed by the downfall of the Beast.

"XIV. At the downfall of the Beast the 1000 years of the captivity of Satan begin. Revelation 19, 20.

"XV. After those 1000 years then Satan will be freed for a little time. Rev. 20:3.

"XVI. At the beginning of that little time, the souls of those who were killed will come to life and from this time till the resurrection of the remaining dead will be one thousand years." [59]

On the idea of a first millennium on earth and a second in heaven, which was Bengel's basic contribution, he says:

"4. The 1000 years of captivity of Satan are still in the future. Babylon is still existing. The beast has not yet perished. As long as the beast continues its activity, Satan is also active. He has been excluded from heaven, but on earth he sustains the third Woe. Only after this he will be thrown into the pit and finally into the lake of fire. . . . 5. The saints will reign with Christ 1000 years in heaven. The thousand years in which Satan is bound and the thousand years in which the saints rule are differentiated." [60]

4. Cross in Midst of Seventieth Week.—On the seventy weeks, Bengel earlier followed Clauswitz in part, who held these to be year-weeks—490 years, a complete number—commencing with the rebuilding of Jerusalem under Persia, dating from the seventh year of Artaxerxes, with the crucifixion of Christ in the midst of the seventieth week.[61] Later, however, Bengel abandoned reckoning by whole years, and by applying his curious arithmetical formula, he lengthened the 490 years to 555 years and a fraction, making them reach from the second year of Darius Hystaspes to seven years after the death of Christ.[62]

57 Bengel, Sechzig erbauliche Reden, pp. 483, 487.
58 Burk, op. cit., p. 293.
59 Ibid., p. 294; Bengel, Erklärte Offenbarung Johannis, pp. 74, 75.
60 Bengel, Schrifftmäszige Zeit-Rechnung (Computation of Time According to the Scripture), p. 265.
61 Bengel, Das Neue Testament, pp. 974, 975; Schrifftmäszige Zeit-Rechnung, p. 187.
62 Bengel, Das Neue Testament, pp. 974, 975, 986.

5. 2300 DAYS ARE LITERAL YEARS—UNDATED.—The 2300 days of Daniel are 2300 literal years.[63] Vainly do some try to tie this to Antiochus Epiphanes, he adds, but he offers no terminal date. Such is the strange admixture of ideas disclosed by Bengel.

6. COLONIES IN SOUTHERN RUSSIA AND TRANSCAUCASIA.— Many of the common people in Germany were greatly moved by the Pietism of Spener and Francke and the teaching of Bengel. Around the end of the century many left their homes in Württemberg and settled in southern Russia under the leadership of Christoph. Hoffmann,[64] some in anticipation of Bengel's indications about Russia and his great date, 1836. Others went to Transcaucasia, and again others settled in Hungary and Rumania.[65]

VIII. Petri First to Begin 70 Weeks Synchronously With 2300

JOHANN PHILIPP PETRI (1718-1792), apparently the first expositor to begin the 70 weeks synchronously with the 2300 days, was born the son of a carpenter, near Hanau, Germany. He attended the gymnasium of Hanau, and finished his theological studies at the universities of Halle and Marburg. Later he became pastor of the Reformed Church in Seckbach, a suburb of Frankfurt am Main, where he served from 1746 to 1792. Energetic and studious, he was particularly interested in the prophecies.[66] He was author of eleven treatises on the prophecies, ranging from 24 to 212 pages.[67] It is interesting to note that the spread of the disorders of the Seven Years' War over Germany, together with the serious state of the church, inspired him to study the numbers of Daniel and the Apocalypse till he felt he had a clear understanding of them.

---

[63] Bengel, *Schrifftmäszige Zeit-Rechnung*, p. 182.
[64] Jakob Prinz, *Die Kolonien der Brüdergemeinde* (The Colonies of the Moravian Brethren), pp. 11 ff.
[65] Paul Hoffmann, *Die Deutschen Kolonien in Transkaukasien* (The German Colonies of Transcaucasia), p. 18.
[66] *Festschrift zum 200 Jährigen Jubiläum der Einweihung der evangelischen Marienkirche zu Frankfurt am Main-Seckbach* (Special Publication for 200-Year Jubilee of the Dedication of the Protestant Church of Mary at Seckbach, Frankfort on the Main), p. 41.
[67] F. W. Strieder, *Grundlage zu einer Hessichen Gelehrten und Schriftsteller-Geschichte* (Survey of the History of the Scientists and Writers of Hesse), vol. 10, pp. 319-322.

Aufſchluß

der

Zahlen Daniels

und der

Offenbahrung Johannis

allein mit Grund göttliches Worts ohne
Beyhülf menſchlicher Zeit-Rechnung.

J. P. P.

P. zu.

1768.

Shortly Before the French
Revolution These Two Ex-
positors Proffered a Key for
Unlocking the Difficulty in
Dating the 2300 Years, Which
Became Burnished Through
Use During the Nineteenth
Century

PETRI AND WOOD BEGIN 2300 YEARS WITH 70 WEEKS

Petri of Germany Announced in 1768 That the 2300 Years Began Synchronously With the 70
Weeks (Left); Church of Which He Was Pastor at Seckbach (Bottom); Hans Wood of Ireland, in
1787, Took Essentially the Same Position (Upper Right). Discussed on Pages 719-722

1. PETRI'S TWELVE PROPHETIC NUMBERS.—Petri's first published treatise, in 1768, was a 24-page *Aufschlusz der Zahlen
Daniels und der Offenbahrung Johannis* (Explanation of the
Numbers of Daniel and the Revelation) "based upon the divine
Word." Twelve prophetic time numbers, six from Daniel and
the same number from Revelation, are treated: (1) the 2300
days—the largest number and including all others—applied
typically to days, literal days in the time of Antiochus, but principally as prophetic days, or literal years, with the key to their
chronological beginning found in the 70 weeks;[68] (2) the 70
weeks with their subdivisions—Christ baptized in the 483d
year—with both periods beginning simultaneously in 453 before
Christ's birth, and the 2300 years ending in 1847, the end of the
abomination;[69] (3) the 1290 year-days, which Petri likewise ends
in 1847, and therefore begins in A.D. 557, as the beginning of
abomination in the church of Christ;[70] (4) the 1335 years, which
extend forty-five years beyond the 1290, or to 1892—preparatory
years for the eternal rest;[71] (5) the three and a half times of the
Little Horn of Daniel 7:25, which Petri interprets as the Mohammedan Turks;[72] (6) the same period of Daniel 12:7; (7-10)
the 1260 years and their paralleling numbers of the Revelation,
likewise ending in 1847 [73] (thus beginning about 587-590, with
Gregory I); and (11, 12) the two beasts of Revelation 13, both
symbolizing the same blasphemous religio-political empire, to
whom the same time is applied.[74]

2. MILLENNIAL VICTORY FOLLOWS CHRIST-SATAN CONTRO-
VERSY.—In 1769 Petri published *Aufschlusz der drey Gesichter
Daniels* (Unfolding of the Three Visions of Daniel). J. D.
Michaelis, reviewing both pamphlets, demanded clear informa-

---

[68] Johann Philipp Petri, *Aufschlusz der Zahlen Daniels und der Offenbahrung Johannis*
(signed J. P. P., identified by other of his works), pp. 5, 6.
[69] *Ibid.*, pp. 9, 10.   [70] *Ibid.*, pp. 10, 11.   [71] *Ibid.*, pp. 11, 12.
[72] *Ibid.*, pp. 12, 13. Petri recognized two Antichrists, however, the Western Antichrist
being the Papacy. See his *Das nahe Tausendjährige Reich Christi* (The Imminent Thousand-
Year Kingdom of Christ), Preface, unpaged; see also his *Die Stunde der Versuchung bey vorhandener Eröfnung des Sechsten Siegels*, pp. 27, 28.
[73] Petri, *Aufschlusz der Zahlen Daniels*, pp. 15-22.
[74] Petri, *Gründlicher Beweis zur Auflösung der Gesichter und Zahlen Daniels und Offenbahrung Johannis* (Well-grounded Evidence for the Solution of the Visions and Numbers of
Daniel and the Revelation of John), pp. 52, 53.

tion on the thousand years. Petri responded with *Das nahe Tausendjährige Reich Christi und darauf folgende Reich des Vatters* (The Imminent Thousand-Year Kingdom of Christ and the Succeeding Reign of the Father), declaring that the main portion of the Revelation is devoted to the controversy between Christ and Satan, while Revelation 20-22 gives a description of the victory of Christ. This controversy has its appointed time in these various time periods, but the victory is in the thousand years.

3. MILLENNIAL REIGN BEGINS AT ADVENT IN 1847.—In 1774 Petri wrote *Die Offenbahrung Jesu Christi durch Johannem* (The Revelation of Jesus Christ by John), declaring that the seven churches, seals, trumpets, and vials all run parallel—the seventh beginning in 1847, and the thousand years beginning at that time.[75] Petri's explanation is explicit:

"According to my explanation of the visions of Daniel, it is to be easily seen that the seventy weeks and the 2300 evenings and mornings of Dan. 8. begin together in the same year. Therefore at the time of the birth of Christ, 453 years of both these periods had passed; what remains and has to be done is the cleansing of the abominations and the consecration of the sanctuary at the coming of Christ, 1847, . . . whose kingdom and victory begins therewith and lasts during that glorious Sabbath year, Hebr. 4, Rev. 20, for 1000 years.

"4) At the end of the 1000 years follows a little time in which Satan will be released and attack the camp of the saints." [76]

In other writings Petri strikes at the concept of a golden age before the advent.

4. SEVENTY WEEKS PROVIDE KEY TO UNLOCK 2300 DAYS.— Petri's first treatise, although not claiming to calculate the time of the advent, undertakes to explain the numbers in Daniel, the first and most important being the 2300 days, and the 70 weeks, which give the clue to its beginning. The 490 years are located, he says, by three landmarks: the end of the 7 weeks, which he places in Nehemiah 2; the end of the 62 weeks in the 30th year of Christ, at His baptism; and the crucifixion three and a half

---

[75] Petri, *Die Offenbahrung Jesu Christi durch Johannem,* p. 14.
[76] *Ibid.,* p. 112. Translated from the German.

years later in the midst of the week. Here is Petri's statement:

"The angel showed the thirtieth year of Christ or the 483d year of the 70 weeks and therefore the 453d year as the birth of Christ, so that was the correct explanation of the sealed vision of the 2300 days. 453 years of the 2300 had passed at the birth of Christ and the remainder of this number continues from that date to A.D. 1847, as 1847 plus 453 makes 2300." [77]

He ignores secular chronology, and indicates no event for the starting point; his key date is the 30th year of Christ's life. He does not designate 453 B.C., but 453 years *before Christ's birth*. It has generally been assumed that he had 453 B.C. in mind, but he merely subtracts, and observes that the date of Christ's birth is in dispute, with a possible discrepancy of several years in historical dates. [78]

In the following year he uses more exact time statements, and makes the point that his 1847 is not necessarily the accepted A.D. 1847.

"By this Nehemiah could know who received such a command (in the second chapter) in the month of Nisan in the 20th year of Arthasasta [Artaxerxes], as well as all of Israel that now seven weeks or forty-nine years of the seventy weeks (as well as 49 years of the 2300) had passed. . . . Seven weeks and 62 weeks make 483 years, which in the 30th year of our Lord had been completed of the 70 weeks, and at the same time of the 2300 years. . . . In the middle of the 70th week, three and one-half years later, therefore, in the year 486 and one-half, at the time of the Easter festival in the month of Nisan, at 3 o'clock in the afternoon, when Christ died on the cross, 486½ years of the 2300 had also been completed. Now the dark vision was clear to Daniel and the people of God had received an unmistakable pivotal point of time, by which it was possible to recognize exactly the beginning of the 2300 before as well as after Christ. . . .

"Since 453 years of the 2300 have elapsed at the time of Christ's birth, so the remaining will bring us to the year 1847 when the sanctuary will be dedicated. As far as the calendar is correct, so far will the end of the 2300 be correct. The proof here rests not upon shaky Persian or Greek dates, but upon the Word of God." [79]

He states the principle that unlocks the 2300 years, in relation to the judgment-hour cleansing of the sanctuary, in these impressive words:

---

[77] Petri, *Aufschlusz der Zahlen Daniels*, p. 9.   [78] *Ibid.*, p. 24.
[79] Petri, *Aufschlusz der drey Gesichter Daniels*, p. 30.

"And therefore, I find that the commentators up to now could not possibly understand the vision, because they separated the second vision Dan. 8 and 9 [the seventy weeks from the 2300 days]. It is impossible to cut off one piece of this vision and then to understand the whole of it without its [proper] connections. Therefore such commentators neither could find the beginning nor the end of the seventy weeks." [80]

"The foundation for the complete understanding was laid in His first coming through the suffering and the death; but the fight and the destruction will continue to go on in His church among the people of Christ until the time of the cleansing of the sanctuary which is the day of judgment, when the Ancient of days will give the Son of man and His holy people the kingdom, power, and might under the whole heaven as was shown Daniel in the first vision in chapter 7, vs. 14, 27." [81]

5. THE SIGNIFICANCE OF THE PETRI CONTRIBUTION.—The significance of the Petri contribution looms before us in its true proportions in the light of the following retrospect: The year-day principle, as applied to the 70 weeks by the Jews centuries before Christ, was generally accepted by Christians; next was added the application of the principle to the 1260 days by Joachim, about A.D. 1190. This, in turn, was extended to the 2300 days by Villanova about 1297 and Cusa in 1440—dating its beginning from the time of the vision. During the Reformation men like Funck (1564) were perfecting the chronology of the 70 weeks, which was generally connected with the death of Christ, but as yet unconnected with the 2300 years. Then post-Reformation writers, like Tillinghast (1644), and later Beverley, concluded that the 2300 days embraced the 70 weeks. Sherwin and Beverley anticipated the terminus of the 2300 years about 1700, and Horch looked toward 1790; others fixed upon dates but a few years different.

And now Petri, in 1768, evidently was the first to begin these related greater and lesser periods together; he began both periods 453 years before Christ's birth, with the cross in the midst of the seventieth week, and ended the longer period in the year 1847 after Christ's birth. After him came others who did practically the same thing; in the nineteenth century the majority of expositors calculated backward from the time of

---

[80] Petri, *Gründlicher Beweis*, p. 15.   [81] *Ibid.*, p. 22.

Christ to a starting point in B.C. 457, or 453, to begin the 2300 years with the 70 weeks.

To recapitulate: The 70 weeks as years, long accepted, had become firmly established in prophetic interpretation, located by a majority with reference to the death of Christ. The growing conviction of the soundness of the year-day principle for the 2300 days also, especially as keyed to the 70 weeks by Petri, set the stage for the next expected test of that principle, namely, the anticipated ending of the 1260 years in the last decade of the nineteenth century. The recognition, in turn, of the fulfillment of this expectancy, under the events of the French Revolution period, laid the foundation for the great emphasis upon the approaching terminus of the 2300 year-days in the early decades of the nineteenth century, as will be seen in Volumes III and IV of *Prophetic Faith*.

IX. Wood Begins the Periods Simultaneously

HANS WOOD (died *c.* 1803), pious layman of Rossmead, Ireland, like Petri of Germany, used the 70 weeks as the solution to the beginning of the 2300 years about the same time. He likewise averred that Daniel 9 is the key to Daniel 8, as the 70 weeks were cut off for the Jews. In 1787 he wrote anonymously on the Revelation, which he "considered as alluding to certain services of the Jewish Temple; according to which the visions are stated, as well in respect to the objects represented, as to the order in which they appeared." [82]

1. SEVENTY WEEKS ARE FIRST PART OF 2300 DAYS.—The 2300 years included the 70 weeks, says Wood.

"He comprehended the two parts under one great sum of years, two thousand three hundred; then, at the end of these years, *the sanctuary shall be cleansed,* which implied the acceptance of all the tribes of Israel; the Sanctuary considered as the Church of God in that season when, according to the Apostle, 'Israel shall be saved.' " [83]

But Daniel did not as yet understand how to calculate them.

---

[82] Hans Wood, *The Revelation of St. John*, title page.
[83] *Ibid.*, *"Appendix on Daniel,"* p. 382.

Coming to chapter 9, Wood tells how the angel came to clarify the chronology of the 2300 years. Next the relation of the 70 weeks to the 2300 days is set forth:

"The Visions of the seventh and eighth Chapters were explained at the time; the latter by this Angel Gabriel, except in the declaration of the two thousand three hundred days: he is now come to instruct the Prophet in them also. The discourse which follows can be well apprehended only in the reference to the long line of years, which was the *matter* Daniel was now to be made to understand, and the *Vision* he was to conceive. The date from which the years became current is here set down; the portion of them allotted for the residence of the Jews in their land is assigned; the remainder is attributed to the desolation." [84]

Wood begins the 2300 years synchronously with the 70 weeks of years, but he places the "one week" within the 70 weeks—not at the end, but after the sixty-fourth week.[85] He ends the seventieth week with the capture of Jerusalem by the Romans; he begins the 70 weeks at 420 B.C. Then, beginning the 2300 at the same time, he arrives at the end of the longer period by calculating: $2300 - 420 = 1880$. He holds that the kingdom of righteousness will be established when the full period expires.[86]

William Hales, the English chronologer, bases his conclusions on Wood, whom he cites in 1799.[87] Later, in the Anglican *Orthodox Churchman's Magazine* for December, 1803, Hales, writing in this journal under his well-known pseudonym, "The Inspector," after referring once more to the anonymous author of a commentary on the Revelation, and giving full title-page data, attributes it to the "most sagacious and original expositor, perhaps, since the days of Mede," on the relationship of the 70 weeks and the 2300 days. He then adds:

"I am now at liberty to divulge the name of this truly pious, learned, and respectable Layman, which his obstinate modesty forbad, during his lifetime, the late *Hans Wood*, Esq., of Rossmead, in the county of Westmeath, Ireland; who *is gone to his reward!*" [88]

---

[84] *Ibid.*, p. 388.
[85] William Hales, *A New Analysis of Chronology*, vol. 2, p. 518.
[86] Wood, *op. cit.*, pp. 382, 386 ff, 477.
[87] Hales, *The Inspector*, pp. 205, 206. For a fuller discussion of Hales, see Volume III of the present work.
[88] *Orthodox Churchman's Magazine*, December, 1803 (vol. 5), p. 342.

2. Fifth and Sixth Trumpets Begin in 630 and 1030.—

Wood applies the fifth and sixth trumpets to the Saracens and Turks—the 150 years of the Saracen locusts extending from the invasion of Syria in 630 to the defeat in Cilicia, in 780, and the Turkish period beginning in 1030.[89]

3. Papal Antichrist Follows Imperial Rome.—The four

empires of Babylonia, Medo-Persia, Grecia, and Rome are set forth as the foundation for the papal phase of Rome under the first beast of Revelation 13.[90] The second beast signifies Constantinople, the seat of Roman dominion after the empire in the West had fallen.[91] The papal Antichrist is coupled to the "Antichristian woman" of Revelation 17. The seven heads are forms of Roman government, one of them being the imperial; and the eighth head is the "Universal Bishop." [92] In Revelation 20 the millennium follows the "resurrection of the just." [93]

4. Little Horn Papacy; Turk in Daniel 11.—In chrono-

logical sequence the four beasts of Daniel 7 are portrayed in detail and identified, according to the Historical School, with the eleventh horn—coeval with the ten—as the Papacy, having the character of Seer, and dominating for three and a half prophetic years; the Ottoman power is described in Daniel 11:44, 45.[94]

5. Daily Taken Away by Innovations in Worship.—

Wood declares the 1290 years are to be dated from the taking away of the daily sacrifice, which he defines as the substituted innovations in "divine worship" brought forward by the eleventh horn, and resulting in the "profanation of the temple." And the activity of the image of the beast and the expulsion of the woman to the wilderness is just at the end of these prophetic periods.[95]

6. Reckons Subordinate Periods Back From 1880.—Pre-

suming there can be no "reasonable doubt" that the 70 weeks ended in the capture of Jerusalem by the Romans,[96] Wood dis-

---

[89] Wood, *op. cit.*, pp. 108, 109.   [90] *Ibid.*, pp. 176, 177.   [91] *Ibid.*, p. 191.
[92] *Ibid.*, pp. 178, 179, 230.   [93] *Ibid.*, p. 324.
[94] *Ibid.*, pp. 364 ff., 470, 471.   [95] *Ibid.*, pp. 476, 477.   [96] *Ibid.*

closes how he brings the terminus of the 2300 years to A.D. 1880.

"From the great term 2300, deduct 420; the remainder 1880, is the year of Our Lord, according to our stating, with which the great term may be presumed to end. Again, from the year of Our Lord 1880, deduct 1290; the remainder will shew the year in which the 'daily sacrifice was taken away, and the abomination that astonisheth,' set up, viz. the year of Our Lord 590, the year in which Gregory the Great ascended the Papal Chair, whose ordinances in the Church, which we have specified where the occasion required to speak of this Prelate, closely correspond with Paul's notices to Timothy concerning the *latter times*. From the same 1880, deduct the Woman's abode in the wilderness, viz. 1260 years; the remainder will give the year of expulsion, 620, the year we concluded on, from historical circumstances, when the cruelty and treason of the Jews of Palestine, in the reign of Heraclius, were related." [97]

7. LAST MESSAGE, ARMAGEDDON, AND ETERNAL KINGDOM.—Wood opined that the death of the Witnesses is between 1847 and 1850, and the angel with the everlasting gospel was then to go out among the nations with his special message. Next would come the gathering of the Western powers to Armageddon, to overthrow the great city; then with the sanctuary cleansed, the kingdoms of the world would become the kingdoms of our Lord. [98]

In New England, as in old England, the same prophetic faith was preached. Many of the earlier ministers of the New World were clear exponents of the Historical School of interpretation, including the year-day principle. The full account of the colonial American and early national expositors of prophecy appears in *Prophetic Faith,* Volume III.

---

[97] *Ibid.,* pp. 477, 478.
[98] *Ibid.,* pp. 478, 479.

CHAPTER THIRTY-TWO

Predictions of French Revolution

and Papal Overthrow

The papal reaction of the seventeenth century was followed by the French Revolution of the eighteenth. For more than a century before the Revolution developed, a line of expositors of the Protestant Historical School not only had predicted from the prophecies of Daniel and the Apocalypse the approaching end of the 1260 years of the ecclesiastic supremacy of the Papacy, but had set forth France as the probable instrument, and infidelity as the possible means of the coming overthrow. When, therefore, the French Revolution broke forth in 1789, not only did new writers solemnly discourse on contemporary fulfilling prophecy, but various compilations of past statements were assembled and printed. Let us note them.

I. Towers Reprints Imposing List of Predictions

JOSEPH LOMAS TOWERS (1767?-1831)[1] furnishes an example, with his *Illustrations of Prophecy,* based on predictions in Daniel and Revelation of "A Revolution in France," and "The Overthrow of the Papal Power, and of Ecclesiastical Tyranny." (Title page reproduced on page 644). In this unusual treatise there is allusion to and citation of expositors in this imposing list, spreading back over a hundred and fifty years: Brightman (1644), Durham (1660), Mede (1663), More (1680), Goodwin

---

[1] Towers was educated at St. Paul's School and New College, Hackney, and preached as a Unitarian minister. In 1792 he was made librarian of Dr. Williams' library, resigning in 1804.

(1683), Jurieu (1687), Cradock (1696), Fleming (1701), Whiston (1706), Waple (1715), Vitringa (1719), Daubuz (1720), Robertson (1730), Pyle (1735), Lowman (1745), Bishop Newton (1748), and Johnson (1794).[2] We note but one—Thomas Newton's (1704-1782) widely quoted observation on France, which was this:

"Rome therefore will finally be destroyed by some of the princes, who are reformed, or shall be reformed from popery: and as the kings of France have contributed greatly to her advancement, it is not impossible, nor improbable, that some time or other they may also be the principal authors of her destruction. France hath already shown some tendency towards a reformation, and therefore may appear more likely to effect such a revolution." [3]

II. Goodwin—France Should Deliver Stroke Against Rome

Many single works, or portions, were also reprinted, as that of THOMAS GOODWIN (1600-1680), under the title *The French Revolution Foreseen, in 1639. Extracts From an Exposition of the Revelation, by an Eminent Divine of Both Universities, in the Beginning of the Last Century.* Citing Goodwin's remarks on Revelation 11:13, this reprint repeats these words of 140 years before:

" 'By the tenth part of the city, I understand (as Mr. Brightman before me) some one tenth part of Europe, which, as it all once belonged to the jurisdiction of Rome, (and is in this book called Ten kingdoms) so now again upon the Gentiles, or idolatrous Papists, their recovering the outward courts, shall now, at last, more or less, come under the jurisdiction of that city, but especially, or at least this tenth part of it here intended.' " [4]

1. UPHEAVAL TO COME IN ONE OF TEN KINGDOMS.—After referring to the Witnesses, "triumphed over and slain during these three years and a half," but resurrected again to the accompaniment of an earthquake, Goodwin gives this further definition of the "city": "City being put here, (as it often is in this book) for the extents of the jurisdiction of the city of Rome,

---

[2] The dates in this series refer to time of publication of the various writers' works.
[3] Cited from Thomas Newton, *Dissertations on the Prophecies* (2d. ed.), vol. 3, p. 308.
[4] Thomas Goodwin, *The French Revolution Foreseen*, pp. 6, 7; see also pages 13 and 14, where the reference is made to Goodwin.

which had those ten European kingdoms allotted to it, Chap. xvii." [5] The earthquake is then explained: A "mighty commotion, with an alteration of the face of things (either civil or ecclesiastic) shall fall out in a tenth part of the city, and shall accompany or usher in this rising of the witnesses." [6] Further, "By and through this earthquake's falling thus out in a tenth part of the city, this tenth part of it is so shaken, that it falls; that is, it ceases to be a part of the city, or to belong unto its jurisdiction any longer";—the earthquake arising "from within that kingdom itself." [7]

2. France Should Be Honored With Stroke.—Discussing the churches and saints within the "Kingdom of France," who have been greatly persecuted by the Papacy, and conjecturing which of the ten kingdoms, or of the ten states in Europe, and what tenth part thereof, shall first have this great privilege, Goodwin adds:

"'It may be hoped, and looked for, that their Kings, in the end, should be of the number of those Kings, who, as you have it Chap. xvii. are to be brought on to *hate the whore,* and *to burn her with fire.* And so that this voice here, which calls these Witnesses (who there have ever prophesied in sackcloth) up to Heaven, may proceed from one of these Kings. And so as that kingdom [France] had the first great stroke, so now it should have the honour to have the last great stroke in the ruining of Rome.' " [8]

3. Cites Supporting Opinion of Jurieu.—Then in a footnote the anonymous British reprinter adds:

"In order to shew that Dr. T. Goodwin was not singular in his interpretation of this passage of Scripture, I subjoin the sentiments of two others, the one a French, the other a Scotch Divine. The first is Peter Jurieu, a French Protestant Minister at Rotterdam, who in 1689 published a Treatise, entitled, 'The Accomplishment of the Prophecies of Scripture.' " [9]

Citing Jurieu's exposition, which "coincides entirely with the doctor in opinion," he quotes concerning the tenth part of Antichrist's kingdom, which shall be taken away from it: "What

---

[5] *Ibid.,* p. 7.
[8] *Ibid.,* p. 13.
[6] *Ibid.,* p. 8.
[9] *Ibid.,* pp. 13, 14.
[7] *Ibid.,* pp. 8, 9.

is this part of the city that shall fall? In my opinion we cannot doubt that it is France." [10] His fuller statements are quoted hereafter.

III. Jurieu—France Will Start the Breakdown

In 1686 Jurieu, previously noted, writing a full century before the French upheaval, on *The Accomplishment of the Scripture Prophecies, or the Approaching Deliverance of the Church,* dealing in chapter 13 with the resurrection of the Two Witnesses, says:

"Now, what is this *tenth part of this City,* which shall fall? In my opinion, we cannot doubt that 'tis *France.* This *Kingdom* is the most considerable *part,* or piece of the *ten horns,* or *States,* which once made up the great *Babylonian City:* it fell; this does not signify that the *French Monarchy* shall be riun'd; it may be humbled." [11]

"But who must begin this last revolt? 'Tis most probable, that *France* shall. Not Spain, which as yet is plunged in *superstition,* and is as much under the *tyranny* of the *Clergy* as ever. Not the *Emperor,* who in *Temporals* is subject to the *Pope,* and permits that in his *States* the *Archbishop of Strigonia* should teach, that the *Pope* can *take* away the *Imperial Crown* from him. It cannot be any Countrey but France, which a long time ago hath begun to *shake off the yoke of Rome.*" [12]

"Seeing the *tenth part* of the *City* which must fall, is *France,* this gives me some hopes that the death of the *two witnesses* hath a particular relation to *this Kingdom.*" [13]

IV. Philipot—France to Contribute to Papal Ruin

JACQUES PHILIPOT's *Eclaircissements sur l'Apocalypse de S. Jean* (Elucidations on the Apocalypse of St. John) devoted a number of pages to the part he felt France would play in the coming overthrow:

"As the king of France did his utmost to enhance the glory of Popery, it will be the king of France who shall mostly contribute to her ruin." [14]

This was written, be it remembered, a full century before the French Revolution. Philipot finished his manuscript in

---

[10] *Ibid.,* p. 14.
[11] Jurieu, *op. cit.,* part 2, chap. 13, p. 265.
[12] *Ibid.,* p. 266.
[13] *Ibid.,* p. 267.
[14] Jacques Philipot, *Eclaircissements sur l'apocalypse de S. Jean.*

August, 1685, just two days before the arrival of the dragoons, who destroyed his home, and only the manuscript was saved from the wreckage. Having reached a port of safety, he compared it with the writings of the distinguished Jurieu, and was delighted to find virtual agreement.

1. 1260 YEARS DATED FROM A.D. 445 TO 1705.—Like Mede, he commences the seven trumpets under the seventh seal, and the seven vials under the seventh trumpet, when will come the deliverance of the church.[15] Discussing Revelation 17, he holds that the seven kinds of rulers were kings, consuls, decemvirs, military tribunes, dictators, emperors, and popes; the ten horns were kingdoms and sovereignties—this being deduced 'from the two horns of the Persian king of Daniel 8.[16] He identifies the pope as the seventh head of the beast with the ten horns, and as the two-horned beast. He is the eighth king and therefore the false prophet and consequently the Antichrist,[17] the same as Paul's son of perdition, of 2 Thessalonians 2, with his fantastic claims of power and honor.[18] The 150 years of the fifth trumpet are applied to the Jesuits from 1540 to 1690. The 1260 years are begun with Leo I in 445, which would lead to 1705 as possibly the terminal year of "the reign of the beast." [19]

2. SURPRISING CHANGE TO COME IN FRANCE.—Stating that the "earthquake" was symbolic, not literal, he says, "It is a sure thing that earthquakes in the Scriptures mean great changes occuring in the nations," and adds, "There will be a surprising change in France"—a change of which "the whole world will be glad, except the clergy, the monks and the Jesuits." [20] Then Philipot gives his reasons succinctly why he believes France is the "tenth part of the city."

"It may be asked what reasons I have in believing that it is France, rather than any other kingdom, which is referred to by this tenth part of the city, which is to fall by the earthquake. My reasons are these. I take it for granted, first, that the city here mentioned is Babylon, that is the Papal empire, the church of Rome, the empire of Antichrist. This

15 *Ibid.*, preface.   16 *Ibid.*, pp. 6, 7.   17 *Ibid.*, pp. 34, 35.
18 *Ibid.*, pp. 170, 171.   19 *Ibid.*, p. 246.   20 *Ibid.*, pp. 208, 209.

has been proved. I take it for granted, secondly, that France is one of the ten horns of the Beast, one of the ten kingdoms which should be formed, according to Daniel, out of the debris of the Roman empire, and that, according to St. John, she should rise at the same time with the Beast, that is, with the Papal empire. This is evident from history. The French monarchy, like all the neighboring states, was established upon the ruins of the Roman empire, and grew at the same time as the bishop of Rome. I take it for granted, thirdly, that France is a place and a part of the *city,* that is of the Papal Empire." [21]

3. DEATH OF TWO WITNESSES IN FRANCE.—The fourth point pertains to the beauty and power of France, with her king as the "most Christian King," and "Eldest Son of the Church." This leads Philipot to conclude that the expression refers "to France rather than any other kingdom, or fief of the Papal empire"; thus he concludes:

"Since the death of the Two Witnesses takes place in France, and in such a surprising manner, why should there be any hesitation in concluding that this tenth part of the city which shall fall is France?" [22]

V. Willison Looks to France as Tenth Part

Another widely circulated reprint was titled *A Prophecy of the French Revolution, and the Downfall of Antichrist; Being Two Sermons Preached Many Years Ago, by the late Rev. Mr. John Willison, Minister of the Gospel at Dundee. And Now Reprinted From the Original, Which May Be Seen at the Publishers* (1793). JOHN WILLISON (1680-1750), Scotch divine, author of the original of this reprint, was born in Stirling, and educated at the University of Glasgow. Licensed by the Presbytery in 1701, he was ordained in 1703, encountering some opposition. In 1705 the former minister took possession of his pulpit, the magistrates refusing help. In 1716 he moved to Dundee, his ministry being marked by controversy. He published an apology for the Church of Scotland in 1719, and in 1733 one of his sermons was published under the title *The Church's Danger.* Willison went to Cambuslang to study the revival associated with Whitefield, and returned to his own parish to start a similar

---

[21] *Ibid.,* p. 209.   [22] *Ibid.,* p. 210.

movement. In 1745 he published *Popery Another Gospel.* He was the author of nine principal works.

1. HISTORIC BACKGROUND OF ROMAN ANTICHRIST.—Inasmuch as we have not previously noted this expositor, a brief panorama of his prophetic views is here given. Beginning with the apostolic age, Willison tells how "every Sermon made new Conquests and Additions to the Church, till every City and Corner of the vast *Roman* Empire was stored with Christians"; [23] then he turns to the "Kingdom of the *latter Days,* or towards the End of the World, of which *Daniel* speaks in his Prophecy, Dan. ii. 28,44 and Dan. vii.27." The stone is the eternal "Kingdom of Christ," to be established only after "the Days" of the kings which would divide the Fourth Monarchy, or Roman Empire, among them. "This empire was to be divided into ten Kingdoms, called in the *Revelation* ten Horns, as represented in Dan. ii.41 by the ten Toes of the Feet of the Image." [24]

2. THE FORERUNNERS OF ANTICHRIST'S FALL.—The last days would be characterized by the overthrow of Babylon or Antichrist, the destruction of the Turkish Empire, the ingathering of the Jews, and the fullness of the Gentiles. Coming directly to the time and circumstance of the "Destruction of Antichrist, or the Papal Power," promised for the latter days, he observes that "Scripture is more particular, about the Time of its being fulfilled, than any other." [25] He then proceeds to enumerate the forerunners of Antichrist's fall and to tell of Christ's coming to deliver His people from this tyranny.

First, there will be a great defection among the churches, an increase of formality, sleepiness of the virgins, and ministers corrupting the glorious doctrines of the gospel. False teachers, infidelity, scoffers, will deride the promise of Christ's coming to destroy Antichrist. This is caused in part by the mistakes of those who have "prefixed Times for it, that there will remain but little Faith in any about his glorious Appearance for his Church,

---

[23] John Willison, *A Prophecy of the French Revolution,* p. 16.
[24] *Ibid.,* pp. 16, 17.   [25] *Ibid.,* p. 20.

when behold he is just at the Door." Thus "Adversaries of the Truth have been much hardened in their Infidelity." [26]

3. SIGNS OF CHRIST'S SECOND ADVENT.—Second, there will be unprecedented world trouble, fear, and distress, as certified by Daniel 12:1. And before Christ's coming strange sights will appear in the heavens, and on the earth, earthquakes, wars, upheavals, and universal distress, before the deliverance.[27] Third, when Christ appears, the church's enemies will be most confident and secure, "particularly when the *Romish Harlot* is lifted up with pride by her Success," saying, *"I sit a Queen and shall see no Sorrow."* [28]

4. MANY BELIEVE FRANCE WILL EFFECT FALL.—Fourth, the climax of his argument (stated, be it remembered, half a century previous to the reprint of 1793):

"Before Anti-christ's Fall, one of the ten Kingdoms which supported the Beast shall undergo a marvellous Revolution, *Rev.* xi. 13. *The same Hour there was a great Earthquake, and the tenth Part of the City fell.* By which *tenth Part,* is to be understood one of the ten Kingdoms into which the great City *Romish Babylon* was divided: This many take to be the Kingdom of *France,* it being the tenth and last of the Kingdoms as to the Time of its Rise, and that which gave *Rome* Denomination of the Beast with ten Horns, and also it being the only one of the ten that was never conquered since its Rise. However unlikely this and other prophesied Events may appear at the Time, yet the Almighty Hand of the only wise God can soon bring them about when least expected. Though the Church should be wrapt about with the blackest Clouds and thickest Darkness for a Time, that will be no Stop to God's great Designs." [29]

Then the compiler and reprinter in the early days of the Revolution concludes, "France was to be cut off from the dominion of Rome. How wonderfully this has been brought about, we have seen." [30]

---

[26] *Ibid.*, pp. 20-22.
[27] *Ibid.*, p. 22.
[28] *Ibid.*, pp. 22, 23.
[29] *Ibid.*, pp. 23, 24.
[30] *Ibid.*, p. 29.

CHAPTER THIRTY-THREE

French Revolution

Leads to Papal Wound

I. Constitutes Turning Point in Modern History

Having attained the peak of its power under Innocent III, the Papacy began gradually to decline. This decline was sharply accentuated by the Protestant Reformation, though the Papacy partially recovered itself in the Counter Reformation. But in the latter half of the eighteenth century deep hostility toward the Roman court developed on the part of numerous Catholic governments. There seemed to be no way of reconciliation. The sovereigns were making rapid progress toward "depriving the Roman See of all its secular prerogatives." [1] Lord Chesterfield, in 1753, had sensed the beginning of a great revolution in France.[2] Even on the Iberian Peninsula, where Catholicism ruled supreme, movements were under way to shake off the yoke of its most energetic servants, the Jesuits. In Portugal they were implicated in the judicial investigations resulting from an attempt on the life of the king, and finally were driven out of the kingdom in 1759. Later they were expelled from France, Spain, and Naples. The pope himself abolished and annulled the Society of Jesus on July 21, 1773.[3]

Hostile elements gathered under the surface in France against the papal tyranny. A new danger menaced the city of

---

[1] Leopold Ranke, *The History of the Popes,* vol. 2, p. 433.
[2] Thomas Carlyle, *The French Revolution,* vol. 1, p. 17; Guinness, *History Unveiling Prophecy,* p. 206.
[3] Ranke, *op. cit.,* vol. 2, pp. 441 ff.; Hergenröther, *op. cit.,* vol. 3, pp. 456, 457.

the seven hills. Infidelity seemed bent on confederating together in an anti-Christian league to consume the Papacy. The new constitution of France, declaring the universal rights of man, soon swept away all special privileges enjoyed by the Catholic Church. In vain did the pope's bull denounce it, and prohibit its acceptance by the clergy. The Jansenists watched with satisfaction as the Roman church received this blow, and the clergy that had so cruelly persecuted them were overthrown—some 40,000 priests who had refused the oath being expelled.

Pius VI tried futilely to arrest the progress of the reforming spirit and to stay the advancing tide of revolution. But his anathemas were unheeded. General war broke out that uprooted dynasties, and changed the face of Europe. France poured her legions into Belgium, Holland, the Rhenish provinces, and Austria. And in 1798 she made herself master of Italy—the deluge sweeping over the patrimony of Peter. This we shall note with some detail.

As the time of Justinian, in the sixth century, when the bishop of Rome achieved legally recognized headship of the churches, was a turning point between the ancient and medieval worlds, so the time of the eighteenth-century French Revolution, when the 1260 years of the papal era were closing, was similarly a turning point in the history of the modern world. It brought forth forces that made a permanent change in the thoughts and actions of mankind.[4] It was indeed the complementary epoch. The infidelic and atheistic became the initial keynote of the time.[5] It was an era of daring unbelief, presumption, and defiance of God. It was the beginning of modern world wars, with peace gone from the world, seemingly forever.

More than that, it was also the beginning of modern missions, of Bible societies, of expansion of political, religious, and intellectual freedom, of liberty of speech and press, of popular education for the masses, of mighty religious revivals, of reformatory movements, of the development of rapid communication

---

[4] Sir Archibald Alison, *History of Europe* (1789-1815), vol. 1, pp. 47-49.
[5] George Stanley Faber, *The Sacred Calendar of Prophecy*, vol. 1, p. 74; vol. 3, p. 363.

and transportation. Truly, it was a turning point in modern history.

II. Far-reaching Implications of the Upheaval

The French Revolution was one of the momentous events in the history, not only of France, but of Europe and even the whole world. It introduced a new mode of political thinking, and released forces which are not yet spent. The ideas and conceptions underlying the French Revolution were of such a nature that they would of necessity lead to violent clashes with the established order. Vehement convulsions had to precede the establishment of such a social order, if ever it should be realized.

In the epochal Declaration of Human Rights it is stated that all men are born free and have equal rights. Those rights are: liberty, the right to hold property, and security against all oppression. The government that recognized these rights should be the only legitimate sovereignty. All are equal before the law; the poor no less than the rich are to be protected by it. None should be molested for their opinions and religious convictions. Every citizen should have the right to speak, write, and print what he wishes. War should never be waged except in self-defense. All men are brethren. Such were the background concepts.

To sense the full impact of these principles, one must visualize them as proclaimed at a time and in a country where absolutism still ruled supreme; where the Catholic Church had long enjoyed complete sway over the whole populace; where by ruthless persecution she had succeeded in crushing all dissenting movements; where the majority of the people, although nominally free, were poverty stricken beyond belief, and held in ignorance and superstition by a relentless grip.

Little wonder that these ideas were like sparks falling into dry timber, kindling a conflagration far beyond the intentions of their originators—a conflagration in which the throne, the church, the nobility, the whole old social order and all for which it stood, were burned like chaff. Alas, out of its violence, terror, and streams of blood emerged a completely different form of life than anticipated, not so much caused by its own choice as by external pressure and the momentum of circumstances—the dictatorship of Napoleon, and with it the birth of nationalism.

Democracy and nationalism are two forces which are the legacy of the French Revolution—two mighty impulses in the life of man, which, however, man has not been able to master even to this day. Some of the portentous events of the French Revolution will now be given in greater detail in connection with the impression they caused on serious Bible students of the time, and in relationship to prophetic interpretation.[6]

III. The First Revolutionary Acts in 1789

One of the first signs of the gathering storm that would soon sweep over France was the fact that the king found himself obliged to convoke "les Etats generaux" (Estates-General) in 1788—which body was almost forgotten, and had not met in more than a century. It was made up of three estates—the clergy, or first; the nobility, or second; and the commons, or third. Delegates were elected in 1788, and in May, 1789. Twelve hundred assembled—some 300 of the first estate, 300 of the second estate, and 600 of the third.

At the very beginning a difficulty arose over the question of votes—should they be counted by head or by estate? As this question was not resolved in a manner satisfactory to the third estate, the latter, on June 17, proclaimed itself the "National Assembly." This was the first revolutionary act. The king annulled this decision, whereupon Mirabeau declared that the Assembly would not disperse, and on July 9, 1789 it declared itself to be the "Constituent Assembly."[7] On July 14, 1789, the proletarians of Paris seized and destroyed the huge royal fortress of the Bastille, the grim, visible emblem of absolutism. In August the National Assembly heatedly debated the question of the

---

[6] See Adolphe Thiers, *Histoire de la révolution Française;* Alphonse de Lamartine, *History of the Girondists;* Carlyle, *The French Revolution; The Cambridge Modern History,* vol. 8, ("The French Revolution"); A. Aulard, *The French Revolution, A Political History, 1789-1804;* Guinness, *History Unveiling Prophecy.*
[7] J. Isaac, *Histoire révolution-empire première moitié du XIXe siècle,* pp. 8-12.

tithes, or taxes, for the clergy. In the same month the Assembly adopted its "Declaration of the Rights of Man and of the Citizen." And in October a mob marched to Versailles and urged the king to come to Paris to recognize the tricolor of the revolution.[8]

IV. The Break With the Catholic Church

In November the Protestants were raised to political equality, with full religious freedom. On the other hand, the Catholic Church was deprived of all of its property, though the clergy was assured of receiving a reasonable remuneration. The higher clergy protested vehemently, and excited the king against the Assembly. Then followed, in July, 1790, the Decree of the Civil Constitution of the Clergy, by the National Assembly. Its outstanding points are in Title I, Article IV:

"No church or parish of France nor any French citizen may acknowledge upon any occasion or upon any pretext whatsoever, the authority of an ordinary bishop or of an archbishop whose see shall be under the supremacy of a foreign power, nor that of their representatives residing in France or elsewhere; without prejudice, however, to the unity of the faith and the intercourse which shall be maintained with the Visible Head of the Universal Church, as hereafter provided." [9]

And Title II, Article I reads:

"Beginning with the day of publication of the present decree there shall be but one mode of choosing bishops and parish priests, namely that of election." [10]

That meant a clear break with Rome and its hierarchial and political influence, and a return to the principles of original Christianity.[11] Many bishops and clergymen refused to accept this new relationship. And the pope, after a period of hesitation, condemned the Civil Constitution of the Clergy. From thenceforward the bitter struggle between the Revolutionists and the

---

[8] *Ibid.*, pp. 13, 14; see also Edmond de Pressensé, *The Church and the French Revolution*, pp. xxi, xxii.
[9] *Translations and Reprints From the Original Sources of European History*, vol. 1, no. 5, "The French Revolution," p. 26.
[10] *Ibid.*, p. 28.
[11] See 1 Timothy 3.

THE BURSTING STORM OF THE FRENCH REVOLUTION

Victims Headed for the Guillotine as the Knitting Women Counted the Rolling Heads. The Reign of Terror Was an Explosion of Infidelity, Immorality, and Massacre Without a Previous Parallel. Voltaire (Inset), by His Acrimonious Infidelity, Prepared the Way for the Outburst, Followed by Others Determined to Form an Antichristian League to Consume the Papacy

church began, which ended not only in the elimination of the church in France but in the overthrow of the Christian religion and the proclamation of the Goddess of Reason in the Cathedral of Notre Dame, now converted into the Temple of Reason.

V. The Break With Royalty in 1791

Louis XVI, a pious Catholic, decided to break with the Assembly after the condemnatory bull of the pope, and established secret relations with foreign countries. He tried to flee from France on June 20, 1791. Discovered, he was brought back to Paris, and now for the first time a republican movement came to the forefront, which in time gained overwhelming power and became more and more radical, although for the time being the Assembly did not take action against the king.

The general European situation became more menacing month by month, and war was imminent. Finally, on April 20, 1792, war was declared. Under the stress of circumstances the Assembly had to enforce the sternest measures to assure the defense of France and rally the people, which led to an upsurge of political fanaticism and a purge of all so-called untrustworthy elements. Fanaticism, once loosed, is like a fury—not satisfied until it is choked with blood. All these different elements finally led to the Reign of Terror, when human life meant nothing, and the heads of royalty and nobility, of high and low, rolled into the gutter.

Robespierre, the idealist and theorist of the revolution, having reached the summit of his power, ruthlessly brushed away even his former co-workers, and the frenzy of terror reached undreamed-of heights. At the same time he, as the high priest of reason, directed a most eloquent address to that "supreme Being" whose cult he had instituted.

VI. The Climax of Revolutionary Frenzy in 1793

In the latter part of 1793 the revolutionists abolished the old calendar of the week and introduced a new one, dating it from September 21, 1793, with new names for the months, and ten-

24

day periods for weeks—and with each tenth day devoted to the
new worship. Pastors who continued to observe the weekly
day of the past were to be imprisoned.[12]

Liberty now became the new god. Trees of Liberty were
planted in streets and squares, around which rich and poor
danced. The tricolor of France, the rights of man, the national
holidays, and the Constitution became the new ritual. Now, the
great of the present having been massacred and the illustrious of
former ages having been insulted, there remained nothing but
heaven itself for them to direct their fury against. Paché, Hébert,
and Chaumette, leaders of the municipality, expressed their determination to "dethrone the King of Heaven, as well as the
monarchs of earth," and prevailed upon Gobel, apostate constitutional bishop of Paris, to abjure the Christian faith (November 7, 1793).[13] Shortly after, Hébert and his group appeared at
the bar, on November 10, and declared that "God did not exist,
and that the worship of Reason was to be substituted in His
stead." [14]

In November, 1793, atheism reached its zenith, with its
mockery of the rites of the church. On the tenth of November
the commissioners of the Convention dressed up an ass in sacerdotal habit, loaded it with the symbols of Christianity, and tied
the Old and the New Testament to its tail. It was then led in
mock procession through the town by two *sansculottes* bearing
a sacred cup, out of which they gave the animal sacramental wine
to drink.[15] Arriving at their destination, the crowd piled books
of devotion into heaps, and burned them to ashes amid blasphemous shouts. A prostitute was enthroned as "Goddess of
Reason," and received adoration by the National Convention
and the mobs of Paris, the populace donning red caps to show
their loyalty to the new regime.[16] It is to be remembered, however, that this was a revolt against the Roman Catholic departure

---

[12] De Pressensé, *op. cit.*, pp. xxi, xxii.
[13] Alison, *op. cit.*, vol. 2, p. 88.
[14] *Ibid.*, pp. 88, 89.
[15] Joseph Galloway, *Brief Commentaries Upon Such Parts of the Revelation and Other Prophecies as Immediately Refer to the Present Times*, vol. 1, p. 113.
[16] Alison, *op. cit.*, vol. 2, pp. 89, 90.

from the true faith, for the Papacy was the only religion they knew. This revolt was therefore against the caricature rather than against the genuine.

After incarnate reason was set up, war against fanaticism was demanded, and worship of the true God punished as a crime. "Liberty, Equality, Fraternity," were the catchwords with which revolutionaries sought to allure the French nation.

"Thus on the 3rd of Frimaire of the Year II (Nov. 24, 1793) upon the application of Chaumette, the Commune of Paris passed the following resolution:

" 'Whereas the People of Paris has declared that it will recognise no other religion than that of Truth and Reason, the Council General of the Commune orders:

" '1. That all churches and temples of whatever religion or sect has existed in Paris shall immediately be closed.

" '2. That all priests and ministers of whatever religion shall be held personally and individually responsible for all disturbances of which the cause shall proceed from religious opinions.

" '3. That whosoever shall demand that either church or temple shall be opened shall be arrested as a suspect.' " [17]

It was the first time in the annals of mankind that a great nation had thrown off all religious principles and openly defied the power of heaven itself.[18] In May, 1794, Robespierre induced the Convention to renounce its belief in a Supreme Being, and then at a festival in June he acted as the high priest of Reason and marched at the head of a procession, with the symbols of atheism and vice. Coupled to these, there were wholesale massacres in Paris and throughout France. According to some, more than two million perished—mock trials were held, with the people dispatching the condemned.

It was the era of the holy guillotine, with the dreadful instrument of decapitation in daily use. Not only nobles and ecclesiastics, but every class suffered. At last the revolutionary fever exhausted itself, and reaction stayed the effusion of blood.

Although war was declared against fanaticism, the revolutionists tried to enforce their ideas with precisely the same fanati-

[17] Aulard, *op. cit.*, vol. 3, p. 161; see also William Holden Hutton, *The Age of Revolution*, p. 256.
[18] Galloway, *op. cit.*, vol. 2, pp. 64-66.

cism. Perhaps it would be interesting to note a statistical account wherein Alison gives the number of victims who fell to their mad rage.

Guillotined by sentence of the revolutionary
  tribunal _____ 18,603
Women and children killed in La Vendée _____ 37,000
Men slain _____ 900,000
Victims at Nantes _____ 32,000
Victims at Lyons _____ 31,000 [19]

VII. Reign of Guillotine Followed by Wars of Napoleon

Following the overthrow of the monarchy and the abolition of religion in France, accompanied by their fearful massacres, came the enormous destruction of life through the wars of Napoleon. Revolutionary France had had to face armed resistance on the part of Austria and Prussia. In 1792 the first war broke out. In 1793 England and the Dutch Republic entered the conflict. Later, during the war against Austria and Sardinia, Napoleon assumed control of the French Army. In 1796 he crossed the Alps, defeated the Sardinian forces, and entered the Po Valley. He also defeated the Austrians, and they sued for peace at Campo Formio in 1797. Thus the reign of the guillotine was followed by the reign of the sword.

With the rise of Napoleon a new era began, and France became the scourge of Europe. The armies of France were now led on an unparalleled career of conquest. Arrogant, unscrupulous, selfish, remorseless, ambitious, and tireless, Napoleon's military genius and administrative ability was blended with utter disregard of moral considerations. Napoleon sacrificed the lives of millions, overturned the thrones of Europe, and thought to revive the empire of Charlemagne as he strove to obtain the mastery of the Old World.

Napoleon's career as ruler and conqueror divides into two periods; first, his seizure of the reins of power as first consul in

---

[19] Alison, *op. cit.*, vol. 2, pp. 399, 400

1799. This was followed by a victorious campaign against Austria and the treaty of Luneville in 1801. In the same year Napoleon signed a concordat with Pope Pius VII, in which it was stated that the first consul nominate the bishops, and the bishops the priests. All have to swear the oath of allegiance and receive a salary from the state. The pope has to recognize the sale of the estates of the church. But, on the other hand, the Catholic clergy is recognized as an official and privileged body in the state.

In the second period a third coalition was formed against France, consisting of England, Russia, and Austria, but with Napoleon's brilliant victory at Austerlitz (1805), Austria had to submit to his terms. In 1806 Prussia was crushed, and in the battle of Friedland (1807) the Russians were defeated. Not the same success, however, followed his forces in Spain. Yet in 1810 he was at the height of his power. Then followed his disastrous invasion of Russia, the rise of Prussia, and his defeat at Leipzig —and finally Waterloo, which closed his career forever.

By many voices in different lands and through various vehicles the end of the papal period was perceived as due and under way. The sudden shock of the French Revolution sent the Protestant church back to the Scriptures for the meaning. Thus in the Edinburgh *Missionary Magazine* for 1796 the fact was publicized that the reign of Antichrist was hastening toward its end. Note it:

"By the general consent of prophecy, the reign of Antichrist, is now hastening to an end. The aspect of providence, for some time past, has quickened our expectation of his fall. This will pave the way for the overthrow of every system by which the empire of iniquity and error has been maintained; and this again will be succeeded by the age of righteousness and truth." [20]

VIII. Bell—France Accomplishing the Fall of Antichrist

In the London *Evangelical Magazine* of 1796 appear two illuminating articles by GEORGE BELL, on the "Downfal of Anti-

---

[20] *Missionary Magazine* (Edinburgh), vol. 1, p. 185.

christ," written July 24, 1795. He contends first that though man may not presumptuously inquire into God's secrets, it is our duty to seek knowledge of those things He has revealed. Then he asserts that God often overrules the actions of men to bring to pass entirely different objectives. He then comes directly to the time of the rise and fall of Antichrist, based on the internal evidence of the prophecy. First, its rise would not be until after Western Rome's division, and we are therefore "not to look for his appearance before the year 407." [21]

1. BELIEVES ANTICHRIST AROSE ABOUT 537.—Again, he would not appear until after the "subversion of the imperial government of Rome," and "this obstacle was taken out of the way in the year 476." It would appear soon thereafter, but "not instantly." [22] Bell's third point is based on the seven heads or governments, the sixth being the emperors—that form falling in 476 under Augustulus. Then the Gothic kings chose Ravenna as their seat of government, but held Italy from 476 to 553—but "lost the government of Rome in the year 537." [23] So the papal was to follow the imperial. He concludes:

"If this be a right application of events to the prophecy, then Antichrist arose about the year 537, or at farthest about the year 553. He continues 42 months, or 1260 prophetical days, that is, 1260 years, Rev. xiii.5.; consequently we may expect his fall about the year 1797, or 1813." [24]

2. DATING THE 1260, 1290, AND 1335 PERIODS.—Turning next to the evidence from Daniel, Bell alludes to the oft-repeated 1260 years, or forty-two months, or three and a half times, during which Antichrist will "scatter the power of the holy people." [25] The 1290 years "takes its date from a time of remarkable apostasy." Of this period Bell says:

"The holy city is to be trodden under foot by the Gentiles, or Papists, who, though they are Christians in name, are Gentiles in worship and practice; worshiping angels, saints, and images, and persecuting the followers of Christ. These Gentiles take away the daily sacrifice, and set up the abomination that maketh the visible church of Christ desolate for the space of 1260 years. But this is a longer period by 30 years." [26]

[21] *The Evangelical Magazine,* 1796 (London), vol. 4, p. 54.   [22] *Ibid.*
[23] *Ibid.*, p. 55.   [24] *Ibid.*, p. 56.   [25] *Ibid.*   [26] *Ibid.*, p. 57.

Then the 1335 years extend forty-five years beyond the 1290 years and seventy-five years beyond the reign of Antichrist.[27]

3. 1260 YEARS FROM JUSTINIAN TO REVOLUTION.—The second article concentrates on the Justinian date when, after the Ostrogothic withdrawal to Ravenna, the army of Belisarius approached Rome, which opened its gates to the Roman general in December, 537; tracing the transfer of the Roman emperor to Constantinople, and then the shift of the Goths to Ravenna, Bell says the pope is left, *"as it were, the governor and principal at Rome."* [28] Then, logically coming to the predicted earthquake, which "signifies a revolution," and France as the tenth part of the Babylonian City—when "One of the ten kingdoms under the dominion of Rome would fall off, or revolt from her jurisdiction"—he declares, "Have we not seen, in one of the ten kingdoms, a most astonishing revolution? Have we not also seen that kingdom fall off of the papal jurisdiction?" Bell then concludes, saying, "Have we not good ground to hope that the accomplishment of the prophecies, respecting the rising of the witnesses and the fall of antichrist, is near at hand?" [29]

IX. American Clergyman—Anticipates Papal Overthrow in 1798

Yet another magazine declaration, in the London *Baptist Annual Register,* this time by an American clergyman, apprehends the overthrow of the papal government at Rome before his letter could reach Britain. Since it was written March 31, before the captivity of the pope could have become known in America, the significance becomes apparent.

"Letter on Prophecy, with A Particular Reference to The Fall of Rome into the Hands of the French. From the Rev. Dr. **** of America Dated—March 31, 1798.

"We are not able so accurately to fix the meaning of those prophecies, that are now about to be accomplished, as we shall easily do a few years hence. However, I cannot help thinking, that Rome will soon fall into the hands of the French, and that the Pope will be deprived of all his

---

[27] *Ibid.*   [28] *Ibid.*, pp. 98, 99.   [29] *Ibid.*, p. 104.

temporal dominions; that is, that he will soon cease to be a beast . . . which I apprehend is nigh at hand, and, *perhaps, will be accomplished before this letter can reach Great Britain.* The Pope, being deprived of his temporalities, will be nothing but a false prophet, and then the seventh trumpet will sound." [30]

The editorial comment on the foregoing prediction reads:

"Dr. . . .'s conjectures respecting the speedy fall of the civil papacy has been remarkably accomplished—was so indeed a few days before he wrote, though he could not possibly know it. Many with Dr. . . . plainly foresee what the present commotions of Europe are designed to produce, and will produce, viz., the ruin of the pope and turk, and all the antichristian governments that support them." [31]

INSENSIBILITY OF CHURCH GIVES ALARM.—Still another contributor, in the same issue, asserts his belief that the tenth part of a city signifies "one of the tenfold divisions of the great Babylonish city. . . the principal street or kingdom of Europe," or France, as plainly stated, and concludes his remarks thus: "O that men were wise to see what God is about!—The general insensibility of the church of Christ alarms me more than all besides." [32]

X. Priestley—French Revolution Is Earthquake in Action

JOSEPH PRIESTLEY, L.L.D., F.R.S. (1733-1804), English clergyman, philosopher, and scientist, was born in Yorkshire. The friend of James Watt and Franklin, he had his preliminary education at the Dissenters' Academy at Daventry, and through his investigation of gases, and the discovery of oxygen in 1774, he pioneered in lifting chemistry to a science. He ministered to a small congregation at Needham Market, Suffolk, and was ordained in 1762 at Warrington. In 1761 he was tutor at the Academy of Warrington, and in 1767 went to Leeds, where he became a Socinian and where he began to occupy a central position in the first period of the Unitarian Movement. In 1774 Priestley spent three months abroad with his patron, the Earl of

---

[30] *Baptist Annual Register,* January, 1799, p. 144. (Italics in the original.)
[31] *Ibid.,* p. 146.
[32] *Ibid.,* p. 147.

Shelbourne, but a few years thereafter he retired from Shelbourne's service, and in 1780 moved to Birmingham.

Priestley opposed the government's attitude toward the American colonies, a fact which led to his being mobbed in 1791, his house being burned, and his manuscripts and instruments being destroyed. Facile in French, German, and Italian, as well as in Hebrew, Syriac, and Aramaic, he was author of some eighty items, including *The History and Present State of Electricity* (1767), and *History of the Corruption of Christianity* (1782). He wrote against Paine and Volney, and upheld the Biblical faith. In 1793 he contemplated removal to America for the sake of his three sons. So he resigned his charge on February 21, 1794, and preached his farewell sermon March 30. The "Fast Sermon" of February 28, hereafter cited, was therefore preached just before leaving for America, where he resided at Northumberland, Pennsylvania, for the remainder of his life.[33]

1. CALAMITOUS TIMES TO AFFLICT PAPAL NATIONS.—His famous sermon, titled *The Present State of Europe Compared with Ancient Prophecies*, preached at the Gravel Pit Meeting in Hackney, was based on Matthew 3:2, "Repent ye, for the kingdom of heaven is at hand." Priestley contended that "great calamities such as the world has never yet experienced," were to precede the coming of the kingdom of Christ. In this sermon, preached during the height of the French Revolution, he stated further:

"These calamities will chiefly affect those nations which have been the seat of the great antichristian power; or, as all Protestants, and I believe justly, suppose, have been subject to the see of Rome. And it appears to me highly probable, as I hinted in my last discourse on this occasion, that the present disturbances in Europe are the beginning of those very calamitous times." [34]

2. PAPAL LITTLE HORN TO BE DESTROYED BY ADVENT.— Bidding his hearers to "look back to the antient prophecies and

[33] *Dictionary of National Biography*, vol. 16, pp. 357-376.
[34] Joseph Priestley, *The Present State of Europe Compared With the Ancient Prophecies*, p. 2.

compare them with the present state of things," he showed that the Little Horn of Daniel 7 was "the Papal power," to be destroyed when the judgment shall sit. After mentioning the awful period of trouble of Daniel 12:1, Priestley averred that the New Testament prophecies on the fall of Antichrist, such as 2 Thessalonians 1:7, corresponded with those of the Old Testament, and were to be accomplished suddenly by the second coming of Christ and not before.[35]

3. REVOLUTION IN FRANCE THE PREDICTED EARTHQUAKE.— Citing Sir Isaac Newton, Whiston, and Clarke, on the part the "prevalence of infidelity" was to play in putting a stop to the papal tyranny, Priestley said:

"This great event of the late revolution in France appears to me, and many others, to be not improbably the accomplishment of the following part of the Revelation, chap. xi.3. 'And the same hour there was a great earthquake, and the tenth part of the city fell, and in the earthquake were slain of men (or literally, *names of men*) seven thousand, and the remnant were affrighted, and gave glory to God.'

"An earthquake, as I have observed, may signify a great convulsion, and revolution, in states; and as the Papal dominions were divided into ten parts, one of which, and one of the principal of them, was France, it is properly called *a tenth part of the city,* or of the mystical *Babylon.*" [36]

4. KINGDOMS ELEVATING PAPACY TO OVERTHROW HER.—"It is farther remarkable, that the kings of France were those who gave the Popes their temporalities, and the rank they now hold among the princes of the world. And it is foretold, Rev. xvii.16, that 'those kings who gave their power and strength unto the beast, these shall hate the whore, and shall make her desolate and naked, and shall eat her flesh, and burn her with fire. For God has put it in their hearts to fulfil his will, and to agree to give their kingdoms unto the beast, until the words of God shall be fulfilled.'

"May we not hence conclude it to be highly probable, that what has taken place in France will be done in other countries?" [37]

The certainty, suddenness, and unexpectedness of the approaching expectancy rested as a burden on Priestley's heart.

XI. Bicheno—1260 Years From Justinian to Present Revolution

JAMES BICHENO (d. 1831), dissenting minister and school man, of Newberry in Berkshire and of London, was author of

---

[35] *Ibid.,* pp. 2, 8, 9.   [36] *Ibid.,* pp. 25, 26.   [37] *Ibid.,* pp. 26, 27.

numerous works. His *The Signs of the Times; or the Overthrow of the Papal Tyranny in France, the Prelude of Destruction to Popery and Despotism; but of Peace to Mankind* was first published in 1793. With an American reprint in 1794, it had passed through its sixth edition by 1808. This was followed by his *Restoration of the Jews* (1800), and his *Destiny of the German Empire* (1801).

From the very first, Bicheno considered the awful judgments inflicted by the French Revolutionists as retribution upon the Papacy for her agelong bloody persecution of the saints. Falling on the royalty, nobility, and clergy, the affliction was thus visited upon the chief abettors. So strongly did he feel this that he protested the antirevolutionary writings of others. So Bicheno discussed the papal tyranny of the past, and the judgments on popery then taking place before the eyes of men rather than attempt a systematic exposition of the Apocalypse.

1. INFIDELIC FRANCE IS TWO-HORNED BEAST.—Bicheno held the standard view of the four kingdoms of Daniel 2 and 7— Babylonia, Medo-Persia, Grecia, and Rome—followed by the division of Rome. The three and a half times were 1260 years, and the Little Horn was the spiritual tyranny of the Roman Empire.[38] In Revelation 12 the tyranny of the dragon was that of pagan Rome and civil tyranny, and the ten-horned beast from the sea represented ecclesiastical or spiritual tyranny of the Papacy.[39] He held, further, that the two-horned beast from the earth was Louis XIV, or at least of that tyranny which the family of the Capets have exercised to the great oppression of the Christian church.[40] In harmony with this interpretation Bicheno sought to place the number 666 upon France, and suggested the name of Ludovicus (XIV).[41]

2. PROPHETIC PERIODS DATED FROM A.D. 529.—In the prophetic time periods Bicheno extends the 2300 years from 481 B.C. to A.D. 1819, when some great event or events will take place. The 1260-, 1290-, and 1335-year periods he begins together

---

[38] James Bicheno, *The Signs of the Times* (1799 ed.), pp. 10-13.
[39] *Ibid.*, p. 14.   [40] *Ibid.*, p. 17.   [41] *Ibid.*, p. 24.

in 529, when Justinian's Code was first published, and consequently ends them in 1789, 1819, and 1864 respectively—the
final year being the blessed one.[42]

3. STANDARD POSITIONS ON TRUMPETS AND VIALS.—The first
four trumpets are the barbarian scourges of the Western Empire, the fifth is the Saracens for 150 literal years, and the sixth
is the Turk for 396 years (365 + 30 + 1), dated from about 1300
to 1697.[43] France is the tenth part of the city Babylon, and the
earthquake is the French Revolution; the Apocalyptical city is
not Rome as some understand it, but the anti-Christian states of
Europe.[44] The Turk is the king of the north in Daniel 11, and
the seven vials are the great judgments of God against the Papacy.[45]

4. CONSUMMATION TO FOLLOW GOSPEL PREACHING.—Bi-
cheno endorses in his conclusion the views of Dr. Hartley.[46] He
applies the climax of our Lord's prophecy of Matthew 24 to the
terrible commotions of the revolutionary times, and predicts
that there would speedily come the preaching of the gospel
throughout the world to heathen and to Jew, that would gather
God's elect—maintaining that the great consummation is nigh
at hand. He is completely absorbed in those portions of prophecy relating to events of the present, as they were unfolding before the eyes of mankind.

---

[42] *Ibid.*, pp. 54-56.
[43] *Ibid.*, pp. 131, 138-152.
[44] *Ibid.*, pp. 127, 187, 188.
[45] *Ibid.*, pp. 165-187.
[46] *Ibid.*, pp. 114-116.

CHAPTER THIRTY-FOUR

The Deadly Wound

Ends the 1260 Years

I. Papal Government Supplanted and Pontiff Banished

The immediate problem is to trace the overthrow of the Papacy in Italy in 1798. One of the most interesting accounts, as well as a very trustworthy one, of the overthrow of the papal government is by Richard Duppa,[1] in *A Brief Account of the Subversion of the Papal Government, 1798.*[2] Of this work Duppa says, "It was written with the strictest attention to truth; the facts were recorded by one who was witness to the events." And he adds, "After a lapse of nine years, no part has been invalidated." [3]

1. NAPOLEON'S GOAL WAS FREEING OF ROME.—In 1796 Napoleon Bonaparte, on his way to overthrow the pope, incited his soldiers with one of his fiery speeches to the effect that they still had one offense to avenge. The hour of vengeance had struck. To restore the Capitol, to awaken the people of Rome, blunted from centuries of slavery, were to be the fruits of their victories; they would mark an epoch in history. Hearing of this, Pius VI (1775-1798)—born in 1717 as Giovanni Angelico Braschi, and died in 1799—attempted to fortify his position and

---

[1] RICHARD DUPPA (1770-1831), English lawyer, writer, and artist, studied art in Rome as a youth. Educated at Trinity College, Oxford, and Middle Temple, he received an L.L.B. from Trinity Hall, Cambridge. He was also an F.S.A. Duppa published a dozen works, besides classical schoolbooks, travels in Europe, and biographies of Michaelangelo, Raphael, and others.

[2] Third edition enlarged and more heavily documented and illustrated. London: Murray, 1807. (2d ed., 1799).

[3] R. Duppa, *A Brief Account of the Subversion of the Papal Government, 1798*, Preface.

neglected nothing that might prevent the great catastrophe. Meantime he sent an emissary to Napoleon at Milan and proposed an armistice, offering heavy reparations and the surrender of Ancona, Bologna, and Ferrara—the northern portion of the papal territory.[4]

The French Directory demanded that the Papacy revoke, retract, and disannul all bulls, briefs, rescripts, and decrees affecting ecclesiastical affairs in France issued since the beginning of the Revolution in 1787. This Pius VI refused, declaring he would oppose it with force, and broke off the parley. Napoleon took Imola, the Romagna, the duchy of Urbino, routed the papal army, and made new overtures to the pope.

2. TOLENTINO FOLLOWED BY KILLING OF DUPHOT.—The Directory wished Napoleon to destroy the Papacy,[5] and directed that no successor to Pius VI be elected to the papal chair. It hoped as a consequence, to deliver Europe from the papal supremacy.[6] But Bonaparte negotiated the Treaty of Tolentino, on February 19, 1797, by which the Pope was to abandon Avignon, Venaissin, Bologna, Ferrara, and Romagna (Peter's patrimony), in addition to heavy indemnities.[7] The papal treasury was unable to meet the monetary demand, and the populace of Rome was showing increasing hostility to the papal government. The pope could scarcely appear in public without being hissed.[8] Revolution was in the air. Incendiary placards were posted on the one hand, and on the other the French were exposed to increasing insults. A crisis approached.

Joseph Bonaparte was sent to Rome as French ambassador, and sought to quiet the situation. But on December 27, 1797, a riot threatened, and the papal government ordered the mutineers to disperse. Duppa records that some in the mob, "proceeded to make public harangues, and pretended to shew clearly,

[4] I. Bertrand, *Le Pontificat de Pie VI et l'athéisme revolutionnaire*, vol. 2, pp. 340 ff. The population of the Ecclesiastical State was given as 2,200,000.
[5] George Trevor, *Rome: From the Fall of the Western Empire*, p. 439; Duppa, *op. cit.*, p. 14.
[6] Alison, *op. cit.*, vol. 3, p. 551n.
[7] Duppa, *op. cit.*, p. 5.
[8] Pius VI, *Historical and Philosophical Memoirs of Pius the Sixth and of His Pontificate* (translated from the French), vol. 2, pp. 314 ff.

by several texts of scripture, that the time was at hand to over-throw the existing government."[9] The papal troops advanced, and the revolutionists sought refuge at the French embassy. The pontifical soldiers followed and opened fire. Then the French general Duphot sought to quiet the melee, but was shot, and dispatched with papal bayonets.[10]

3. BERTHIER'S TROOPS ENTER ROME BY INVITATION.—The killing of General Duphot brought on the crisis. The ambassador left Rome in indignation. Reparations were refused, and the Directory, on January 1, 1798, ordered General Berthier,[11] then in Milan, to march upon Rome and conquer it, and to establish a Roman republic.[12]

General Berthier advanced, but stopped outside of Rome, awaiting an invitation to enter. Patriots invited him to do so. Thus the French troops entered Rome on February 10, 1798. Berthier immediately pledged by proclamation that the Catholic "cult" should remain untouched.[13]

4. PROCESSIONAL LAUNCHED TO STAY EVIL DAY.—As a last resort the church had had recourse to a vast religious processional through the streets of Rome, with venerated relics, in the hope of staving off the evil day. An elaborate proclamation was issued January 15, 1798, in the form of a printed poster[14] signed by the papal secretary. The three special relics paraded were a portrait of the Saviour supposed to have been painted by supernatural agency, a miraculous picture of the Virgin Mary and the child, and the supposed chains by which St. Peter was fettered.[15] These

---

[9] Duppa, op. cit., p. 9.

[10] Historical and Philosophical Memoirs, vol. 2, p. 328; The London Packet, Jan. 19-22, 1798, p. 2.

[11] LOUIS ALEXANDRE BERTHIER (1753-1815), prince of Wagram and confidant and associate of Napoleon, was born at Versailles. He served under Lafayette in the United States from 1778 to 1782, and at the outbreak of the French Revolution was appointed major general of the national guard at Versailles. By 1795 he had risen to chief of staff of the Army of Italy, and as Napoleon's representative, proclaimed the Republic of Rome and effected the captivity of the pope in 1798. Berthier accompanied Napoleon into Egypt as chief of staff, and aided in victory over the Directory in 1799, becoming minister of war (1799-1808). Made marshall of France in 1804, he was constantly at Napoleon's side until 1814. In 1809 he became chief of the general staff of the grand armée, and was created prince of Wagram in the same year.

[12] The London Packet, Jan. 19-22, 1798, p. 2.

[13] Duppa, op. cit., pp. 34, 35, 91.

[14] Invito Sagro e Notificazione (Sacred Invitation and Proclamation); see also English translation in Duppa, op. cit., pp. 17-24.

[15] Pictured in Duppa, op. cit., p. 18.

were then placed on exhibition on the high altar of St. Peter's, and visited by the people of Rome and the surrounding country. Prayer, fasting, and penitence were urged, and liberal indulgences promised. But the French Army came on.[16] Priests went throughout the city preaching the end of the world and, as customary, calling on miracles to sustain their prophecies. They little dreamed that they were so near the close of their power.

5. Roman Republic Is Re-established.—Berthier called upon the commander of St. Angelo to open the fort. He asked two days for decision, but Berthier gave only four hours. So the fort was evacuated, three thousand French troops taking possession, and taking over the city, with certain cardinals, princes, and prelates as hostages to ensure quiet. From that moment onward Pius VI confined himself to the Vatican. Heavy reparations were exacted for the assassination of General Duphot. Then a petition, drawn up and signed by the French partisans in Rome, demanding a change of government and regime of liberty, was followed by an imposing public demonstration. The Tree of Liberty was planted on the capitol hill,[17] and the new government was established on Pluviose 27 (February 15), when the sovereignty of the people was proclaimed and the re-establishment of the Roman Republic was effected.[18]

6. Papal Arms and Insignia Removed.—Berthier came to the capitol escorted by a military band, received the acclaim of the great concourse, and gave formal recognition to the Roman Republic and its provisional government.[19] He then ordered the papal arms and insignia everywhere removed. Thus the change was effected without bloodshed. Later when the Sacred Congregation of Propaganda was suppressed, their College at

---

[16] *Historical and Philosophical Memoirs*, vol. 2, p. 326.
[17] Duppa, *op. cit.*, pp. 34, 35.
[18] *Ibid.*, pp. 37-39; *The Times* [London], no. 4141, March 12, 1798, p. 3; *The London Packet*, March 5-7, 1798, p. 2; *The London Chronicle*, March 10-13, 1798 (vol. 83, no. 6089); Duppa, *op. cit.*, pp. 185-188. The 75-page *Constitution of the Roman Republic, Translated From the Authentic Italian Edition* (1798) is a "Declaration of the Rights and Duties of Man and of Citizens," with a tabulated series of Articles of (1) Rights and (2) Duties, followed by the text of the Roman Constitution. (Original title: *Costituzione della Repubblica Italiana, adottata per acclamazione nei comizj nazionali in Lione*. Anno I., 26 Gennajo 1802.)
[19] Duppa, *op. cit.*, pp. 36, 37, 40.

Rome was closed and the building used as a warehouse for confiscated property, and their printing presses and type were sent
to France.[20] Vatican Palace was stripped of its valuables, and
the sacerdotal vestments of the pontifical chapels were burned
for the gold and silver of the embroidery.[21]

7. Pius VI Dethroned on Anniversary in Sistine Chapel.
—Meantime, on this very same day—February 15—on the
anniversary of his elevation to the pontificate, Pius VI repaired
to the Sistine Chapel, and was receiving the felicitations of the
Sacred College of cardinals, when, in the midst of the ceremony,
shouts penetrated the conclave, intermingled with the strokes
of axes on the doors. Soon General Haller, a Swiss Calvinist, with
a band of his soldiers, broke into the chapel, and declared that
the pope's reign was at an end.[22] (Painting appears on page 754.)
His Swiss guards were dismissed, and republican soldiers substituted. Ferrara, Bologna, and Romagna (Peter's patrimony) were
taken over, and the cardinals were stripped of authority and
possessions. Eight were arrested and sent to the Civita Castel-
lana.[23] The glory, honor, and power had vanished. Soldiers were
quartered in the papal palace. Such was the stroke of the sword
at Rome. It was the end of an epoch in papal history long before
predicted in the prophecies of Holy Writ. Trevor goes so far as
to say:

"The territorial possessions of the clergy and monks were declared
national property, and their former owners cast into prison. The papacy
was extinct: not a vestige of its existence remained; and among all the
Roman Catholic powers not a finger was stirred in its defence. The Eternal
City had no longer prince or pontiff; its bishop was a dying captive in
foreign lands; and the decree was already announced that no successor
would be allowed in his place."[24]

8. Treasures Demanded and Banishment Decreed.—The
pope's banishment from Rome was then decreed, and Haller was
again chosen to inform him. Appearing on the afternoon of

---

[20] *Ibid.*, p. 92.
[21] *Ibid.*, pp. 59, 60; Alison, *op. cit.*, vol. 3, p. 558; *Historical and Philosophical Memoirs,*
vol. 2, p. 343.
[22] Duppa, *op. cit.*, pp. 43-47; *The European Magazine,* July, 1798, vol. 34, p. 7.
[23] Alison, *op. cit.*, vol. 3, p. 559.
[24] Trevor, *op. cit.*, p. 440.

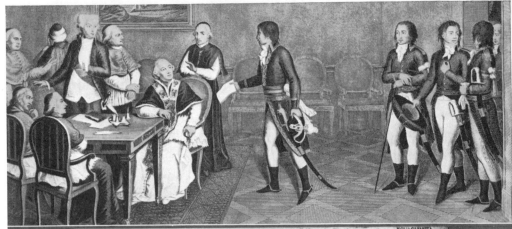

LIBERTÉ   EGALITÉ

ARMÉE D'ITALIE

Au Quartier général devant Rome le 27. Pluviôse VI année
de la République Française une et indivisible.

Le Citoyen Alexandre Berthier Général en Chef.

LE Peuple Romain est rentré dans les droits de la Souveraineté en proclamant
son indépendence, en se donnant le Gouvernement de l'ancienne Rome,
en se constituant République Romaine.

Le Général en Chef de l'Armée Française en Italie déclare au nom de la
République Française qu'il reconnoit la République Romaine indépendente,
et qu'elle est sous la protection spéciale de l'Armée Française.

Le Général en Chef de l'Armée reconnoit au nom de la République
Française le Gouvernement Provisoire qui lui est proposé par le Peuple Souverain.

En conséquence toute autre autorité Temporelle émanée de l'ancien Gouvernement
du Pape est supprimé et n'exercera plus aucune fonction.

Le Général en Chef fera toutes les Dispositions necessaires pour assurer
au Peuple Romain son indépendance. Pour que son Gouvernement soit bien Organisé,
pour que les nouvelles Loix soient basées sur la liberté & l'egalité,
il prendra toutes les mesures necessaires pour assurer le bonheur du Peuple
Romain.

Le Général Français Cervoni est chargé de pourvoir à la police, et à la
sureté de la Ville de Rome, ainsi que d'installer le nouveau Gouvernement.

La République Romaine reconnue par la République Française comprend
tout le pays qui était resté sous l'autorité temporelle du Pape après
le traité de Campo-Formio.

Alexandre Berthier.

LIBERTA'   EGUAGLIANZA.

RISPOSTA PRONUNZIATA DAL GENERAL BERTHIER
SUL CAMPIDOGLIO

ARMATA D'ITALIA

Nel Quartier Generale avanti Roma i 27. Piovoso (15. Febbraro)
anno VI. della Repubblica Francese una e indivisibile.

Il Cittadino Alessandro Berthier Generale in Capo.

IL Popolo Romano è rientrato ne' diritti della Sua Sovranità proclamando
la sua indipendenza, attribuendosi il Governo dell'antica Roma, e
continuandosi Repubblica Romana.

Il Generale in Capo dell'Armata Francese in Italia dichiara in nome
della Repubblica Francese che riconosce la Repubblica Romana indipendente,
e ch'essa è sotto la protezione speciale dell'Armata Francese.

Il Generale in Capo dell'Armata riconosce in nome della Repubblica
Francese il Governo Provvisorio che gli è proposto dal Popolo Sovrano.

In conseguenza ogni altra autorità Temporale emanata dall'antico Governo
del Papa è soppressa e non eserciterà più funzione alcuna.

Il Generale in Capo farà tutte le Disposizioni necessarie per assicurare
al Popolo Romano la sua indipendenza. Perchè il Governo sia bene
organizzato, perchè le nuove Leggi siano basate sulla Libertà, e l'Eguaglianza,
egli prenderà tutte le misure necessarie per assicurare la felicità del
Popolo Romano.

Il Generale Francese Cervoni è incaricato di provvedere alla Polizia
ed alla sicurezza della Città di Roma, e d'installare il nuovo
Governo.

La Repubblica Romana riconosciuta dalla Repubblica Francese, comprende
de tutto il paese ch'era restato sotto l'autorità temporale del Papa dopo il
trattato di Campo-Formio.

Alessandro Berthier.

Roma 15. Febbrajo 1798, primo di della Libertà proclamata nel Foro Boario, e ratificata sul Campidoglio
col Libero voto emesso in voce, ed in scritto da innumerabili Cittadini.

FRENCH ULTIMATUM RESTRICTS PAPAL AUTHORITY IN 1798

General Haller Presenting Berthier's Ultimatum to Pope Pius VI, in the Sistine Chapel at the
Vatican, on February 15, 1798 (Upper); The Declaration of the End of Former Papal Authority,
With French Original at Left and Italian Translation at Right (Center), and Inset of Berthier,
Who Signed the Declaration; and Pius VI, Sent From Rome to France, Where He Died (Lower)

February 18, he demanded the pope's treasures. When the pope protested that the Tolentino Treaty had left him nothing, Haller demanded and took the two rings on his fingers, including the Fisherman's ring—though only by threat. (This was returned the following day.) Haller told the prelate to be ready to leave the next morning at six. He protested his age—of eighty-one— and illness, Haller nevertheless insisted, and threatened force. Given forty-eight hours to settle the affairs of the church, he was to leave before daybreak.[25] (Painting of departure appears on page 754.)

It was still night, February 20, 1798, and stormy with lightning and thunder, when the carriage crossed the city, preceded by two men with torches—the guards pointing out the dome of St. Peter's. Both hisses and prayers came from the crowd that had assembled. Within ten days Pius VI had been dethroned, imprisoned, exiled, his private library confiscated, his state given up to plunder, and his subjects to military control. Reaching Sienna, Pius and his party stopped at an Augustinian convent. But while they were there, an earthquake destroyed several buildings. The Pontiff was therefore housed outside the city in a country home called Hell, a fact that elicited the sarcasm of the unbelieving.[26]

9. DIES AT VALENCE, FRANCE, IN 1799.—But the pope was still in the heart of Italy. So Pius VI was transferred to Florence, constantly under guard of French dragoons. Next his transfer to Parma was decided upon, the departure to take place at 2 A.M. As the pope was suffering from partial paralysis, his guards had great difficulty in effecting the transfer. From here he was taken to Turin, and finally to the French fortress at Valence, in Dauphiny,[27] arriving there July 14, 1799, broken with fatigue and sorrow. He died there on the 28th.[28]

---

[25] *The European Magazine*, July, 1798, vol. 34, pp. 7, 8.
[26] Bertrand, *op. cit.*
[27] Pennington, *op. cit.*, pp. 449, 450.
[28] In the Gallery Room of Pius VI, in the Vatican Museum, his life is portrayed in a series of sixteen pictures, the last in the series showing his expulsion, the coach by which he was escorted to France, his arrival at the destination, and his demise.

II. Official Handbills Reveal Facts of Overthrow

About fifty official handbills and circulars, many in parallel-ing French and Italian columns, were printed and posted in Rome during the papal overthrow and the establishment of the republic under Berthier in 1798. These constitute about the highest source evidence obtainable, and are not commonly ac-cessible. They are therefore summarized here, the more impor-tant being quoted from.[29] Nos. 1 and 2 assure respect for public worship and its ministers and for ambassadors, and warn French officers of violation.[30] No. 5, dated Year 1, Pluviose 27 (Feb. 15, 1798), announces that Berthier has appointed civil authorities in the six territories of the republic. No. 7 gives a pompous speech of Berthier in which he says that at the capitol, bearing an olive branch, free Frenchmen have re-established the altars of liberty, erected by the first Brutus.[31]

1. PAPAL GOVERNMENT SUPPRESSED, REVERTING TO PEOPLE. —The famous Bill No. 8, in parallel French and Italian, dated Pluviose 27 (February 15), is a formal declaration by "Citizen Alexander Berthier, General in Chief." In this he makes the announcement:

"The Roman people are now again entered into the rights of sover-eignty, declaring their independence, possessing the government of ancient Rome, constituting a Roman Republic.

"The General-in-chief of the French army in Italy declares, in the name of the French Republic, that he acknowledges the Roman Republic inde-pendent, and that the same is under the special protection of the French army.

"The General-in-chief of the army acknowledges, in the name of the French Republic, the provisional government which has been proposed by the sovereign people.

"In consequence, every other temporal authority emanating from the old government of the Pope, is suppressed, and it shall no more exer-cise any function. . . .

"The Roman Republic, acknowledged by the French Republic, com-prehends all the country that remained under the temporal authority of the Pope, after the treaty of Campo-Formio.

"ALEXANDRE BERTHIER."

---

[29] Based on complete sets in the Paris Bibliothèque nationale and the British Museum.
[30] Duppa, *op. cit.*, pp. 35, 180, 181.   [31] *Ibid.*, p. 37.

"Rome, the 15th of February, 1798; first year
of Liberty, proclaimed in the Roman Forum,
and ratified on the Capitol, with free voice,
and subscribed to by innumerable Citizens." [82]

2. ROMAN POPULACE CASTS OFF PAPAL YOKE.—Bill No. 9,
likewise of the same date (February 15), titled "Acte du Pepule
[peuple] Souverain" (An Act of the Sovereign People)—certified
and signed by three notaries, and confirmed by General Berthier
—makes this clear-cut declaration:

"The people of Rome, long tired of the monstrous despotism under
which they groaned have on various occasions tried to shake off this yoke.
The magic of public opinion and political interests combined into a mighty
force have not allowed their efforts to succeed. And a despotism of that nature becomes the more insulting the more its weakness and arrogance corresponds to its misery. But at last, the people, fearing to be exposed to an
hideous anarchy and in despair to fall under even a worse tyranny have
mustered all their courage in order to evade these sinister consequences and
to reclaim the primitive rights of their sovereignty.

"Assembled in the presence of the Eternal and the whole universe, they
solemnly and unanimously declare to have had no part whatever in the
crimes and assassinations committed by the government against the French
Republic and her nation. They disapprove of these crimes and detest their
originators and invoke upon them (vow them) eternal shame.

"They further have suppressed, abolished and crushed the political,
economic, and civil authorities of the former Roman government and have
constituted themselves a free and independent sovereignty in taking up all
executive and legislative powers which its legitimate representatives shall
exercise according to the immortal rights of man based on the principles of
truth, justice, liberty, and equality.

"They have declared that their desire is that no attack against religion
or the spiritual authority of the pope should be made and that they reserve
to themselves the right by their representatives to provide for the comfortable sustenance [of the Pope] and to ensure the safety of his person by a
national guard.

"These representatives shall present themselves in the name of the
Roman people. The government has also asked the following citizens
[names follow] to approach the citizen Alexander Berthier, general-in-chief
of the French army in Italy, imploring the powerful protection and the
friendship of the generous French nation, whose gallant examples serve
them as a lesson in the task of their own regeneration.

---

[82] Proclamation of the Establishment of the Roman Republic in the name of the French
"Army of Italy" (See facsimile on p. 754), in the collection of Official Bills and Circulars
Printed and Posted in Rome . . . 1798; in Bibliothèque nationale, Paris; Duppa, *op. cit.*, pp.
37-39; see also *The European Magazine*, vol. 33, March, 1798, p. 208.

"The present act has been signed by several thousand persons who, with many others, have read, approved and confirmed it by their acclamations on the Capitol. On the 27. Pluviose in the 6. year of the Republic."

3. COLOSSUS OF IMPOSTURE DESTROYED.—Bill No. 17, dated February 21 (Ventose 3)—the day following the pope's departure from Rome—is a violent charge against the old government, and is signed by five consuls, the secretary general of the consulate, General Berthier, and the minister of war. It reads:

"The provisional consuls of the Roman Republic to the soldiers of the former government: 'Soldiers: The despotism which was afflicting humanity and which was weighing so heavily upon the descendants of the illustrious Romans; this colossus of imposture and immorality which was governing this beautiful land has just been destroyed by a sublime movement of the Roman people. Soldiers, you will wish to have a part in this grand event.'"

4. UNION OF SACRED AND PROFANE DISSOLVED.—Bill No. 28 gives an extract from a speech by Citizen Gagliuffi on February 23. He says:

"Already has proud and penurious hypocrisy fallen to the ground. Already is this grotesque union of the sacred and the profane being dissolved. At last, are the sweet maxims of gospel morality allowing us to seek and propagate righteousness and truth. The ministers of the sanctuary may henceforth—according to the duties of their sublime institution—bring peace and consolation into homes and hearts. The representatives of the Republic will ever keep the trust which the people of Rome have committed to us with such piety and universal joy.—Thanks be therefore rendered unto thee, O supreme and immortal Being, on whom the destiny of all creatures depends. Touched, at last, by the woes which pressed upon us so heavily: Monopoly, Favoritism, Privilege, and alas! perhaps Religion itself, a Religion honored by the lips only and denied by the hearts,—do graciously sanctify our Liberty, bless our Equality, and preserve our Republic!"

5. RELIGIOUS INTERESTS SEPARATE FROM POLITICS.—Bill No. 34, addressed to the Roman people and clergy, signed by the president of the republic and five consuls, and dated February 26, stating that the government is "based on the gospel," and declaring, "God has established a gospel of peace and pardon," commends good priests and warns the evil, and admonishes:

"In the pulpit, at the altar, at the confessional, give the people of both sexes to understand that religious interests are separate from politics. O thou, benignant and generous people of Rome, be no longer led astray by infernal wolves disguised as heavenly lambs. Shun and denounce the fanatic who betrays both religion and the Republic, and who, therefore, is the implacable enemy of thy present and future felicity. Hail with open arms the righteous man, the brother or magistrate who would thee enlighten, protect and save."

6. France Formally Notified of Change.—A fourteen-page tract, bound in with the bills, published in French and Italian, includes a letter from the minister of foreign affairs in Rome to Talleyrand, minister of foreign affairs in Paris, dated February 28 (Ventose 10), giving notice that the Roman people have chosen a new government comprising all the territory formerly under the temporal power of the pope after the treaty of Campo-Formio. It is signed "Corona." Talleyrand's answer follows, expressing the great satisfaction of the French Directory, and is dated Ventose 25.

III. Code of Justinian and the Code of Napoleon

There is yet another factor which was brought about by the French Revolution. The Revolution had given a totally new concept to man of his dignity, his rights, his relationship to his fellow men. There must follow, of necessity, a new concept of law.

The French had long felt the need of a new and more unified law; therefore, the revolutionists promised, among other things, a new code for the people. However, it needed the strong will and leadership of Napoleon to complete the codification of civil laws. In 1804 this task was finished and the code was accepted. This became the first great codification of law since the time of Justinian. Under the auspices of Justinian, Roman law was codified by 529, and in an imperial rescript in 533 the Roman bishop was recognized as the head of all the churches, and given full authority as such. This recognition, as well as that of the canons of the first four ecumenical councils, was incorporated into the Justinian Code. Thus the Catholic faith was recognized as the only orthodox religion of the empire, and the two mighty forces of state and religion were legally united.

Now, in the first general codification of law after so many centuries, a complete break between these two forces was achieved. The French Civil Code contains nothing which savors of an allegiance of the spiritual power of the pope and the state, and is far from giving the pope any authority whatsoever. It is purely a secular code.

IV. Retributive Character of Deadly Wound

The retributive character of the French Revolution should not be forgotten. In its sheer destructive effects it was considered to constitute a judgment doubtless without a parallel in human history.[33] It was directed primarily against Catholicism, not Protestantism, and was a reaction against her excesses. Terrible as was the destruction of Jerusalem by the Romans under Titus, says Guinness, it sinks to secondary place when compared with the wholesale slaughter by massacre and war that first affected France, then Italy, and other nations of Europe. "If it inflicted enormous evil, it presupposed and overthrew enormous evil." [34]

1. Visited With Plague of Infidelity and Immorality. —The France of St. Bartholomew—of the Wars of the Huguenots, of the Revocation of the Edict of Nantes, and of the suppression of the Jansenists—was visited with a retributive plague of infidelity and immorality that was fearful. The monarchy that had banished the Huguenots was overthrown and abolished in a national convulsion of revolutionary excess and crime wherein the restraints of law and order gave way. The monarchy was brought to an end on the scaffold, the aristocracy abolished, estates were confiscated, prisons crowded, rivers choked with victims, churches desecrated, priests slaughtered, religion suppressed, and the worship of a harlot as the Goddess of Reason was substituted for the worship of the host on the altars of the Roman church.[35]

---

[33] Guinness, *History Unveiling Prophecy*, pp. 226-229.
[34] Thomas H. Gill, *The Papal Drama*, p. 342.
[35] The summary given by Guinness is here followed closely.

2. Holy Roman Empire and Church Crash Together.—
France, a prey to infidelity, anarchy, and the guillotine, then communicated revolution and antiecclesiasticism to surrounding nations. Democratic revolution was succeeded by military despotism. Italy, Austria, Germany, Poland, Spain, Portugal, and Russia were invaded by the armies of France. Many Catholic nations which had ruled for centuries were crushed by Napoleon. The Holy Catholic Church and the remnant of the Holy Roman Empire were alike prostrated—the empire and the papal crown going down in the common ruin. They had stood side by side for a thousand years. The Holy Roman Empire had risen with Charlemagne, who attempted to revive the imperial power of the Caesars. He had combined Germany, Italy, and France into a single empire, which had warred against and crushed the Hussites, and had stood against Luther in the days of the Reformation, inflicting on Germany the horrors of the Thirty Years War in the time of Gustavus Adolphus. Now, stripped of Italian territory, driven back from the plains of Lombardy, the Holy Roman Empire came to be totally suppressed.

3. Piedmont and Spain Reap Bloodshed and Misery.—
Piedmont, which had suppressed and all but exterminated the Waldenses, turning their valleys into slaughterhouses, was in turn overrun by merciless invaders. Spain, which had crushed the Reformation within her borders and in other lands, by the horrors of the Inquisition and the auto-da-fé, was now delivered over to dreadful bloodshed and misery, and during the seven years of the Peninsular War the Inquisition was suppressed.

4. Climax of Reversal Reached in Rome.—In Italy the reign of the pope of Rome was ended by a Swiss Calvinist leading the French military. Stripped of his possessions, and his temporal government abolished, the pope was carried away captive to the camp of the infidels, to die in a foreign land, where his priests had been slain and his name and office made a mockery, with Rome given up to plunder and desecration. Even as the pope was being hurried away from the scene of his dethrone-

ment—the Sistine Chapel—he was taken, ironically enough, through a hall covered with a fresco representing the bloody massacre of St. Bartholomew's day.[36]

The downfall of the papal government excited little sympathy. The oppressions and the tyranny of Rome over Christendom were remarked upon with bitterness. Many rejoiced in the overthrow of a church which they considered idolatrous, even though the overthrow was attended with the immediate triumph of infidelity. When news of the papal defeat at Rome reached Paris, Director Merlin declared that for fourteen centuries there had been cumulative demand for the destruction of this power opposed to society. And in the Court of the Ancients, Bordas actually held "a funeral oration of the Papacy," on March 14, 1798.

5. BIBLE AND MISSIONARY SOCIETIES HAVE BIRTH.—Papal hostility had been exerted in two ways: (1) By the suppression of the Scriptures, and (2) by the torture and death of its preachers and converts, which were effected by means of the Inquisition. The French Revolution ended both—French arms abolishing the Inquisition in France in 1798, and temporarily in Spain in 1808. Moreover, the extraordinary circulation of the Scriptures began during the French Revolution. Never should it be forgotten that both missionary and Bible societies had their birth at this very time, the British and Foreign in 1804, and the American in 1816.

6. TEMPEST OF WAR GAVE IT WINGS.—Begun in France, the spoliation of the fallen church and its head had spread quickly to other countries of Europe, until the stroke of the sword struck at Rome. The tempest of war gave it wings, sweeping into Belgium and the Rhenish provinces of Germany, where ecclesiastical changes similar to those in France took place.

In 1796-1797 French dominion, established by Bonaparte's victories in northern Italy, was similarly accompanied by French Democratism and infidelity and antipapalism. Then Rome itself

---

[36] Pennington, op. cit., p. 450.

became the goal, as the French armies urged marching forward on the papal capital.

7. Looked as If Papacy Were Dead.—In Rome all the cardinals were involved in the indiscriminate proscription. Eight were imprisoned, and several renounced the Roman purple and sought asylum away from Rome. It looked as if the Papacy were dead. In fact, half of Europe thought "the Papacy was dead." [37]

The blood of the saints was avenged. France had for years yielded the neck to the papal yoke, and helped to bind other nations. Now she had abolished papal tithes, suppressed her monasteries, confiscated her church lands, and despoiled her priests. [38] Pennington says, "The same God who visits the iniquities of the fathers upon the children unto the third and fourth generation had made him [the pontifical head of the church] the victim of His retributive justice." [39]

V. Papal Establishment and Overthrow Are Counterparts

The evidence is incontestable that the eighteenth-century overthrow of the Papacy, stemming from the French Revolution, was the clear counterpart of the sixth-century papal establishment. Justinian first recognized by law the pope's absolute ecclesiastical supremacy, and virtually gave the saints into his hand, placing the civil sword at his ultimate disposal. And now, 1260 years later, springing from the French Revolution, the land that for centuries had been the mainstay of the Papacy, abolished the pope's age-old supremacy, declared the clergy totally independent of the See of Rome, vested the election of bishops in departmental authorities, made a national profession of atheism, and then actually overthrew the papal government.

In 533 was given the notable decree of Justinian, the pope's powerful sixth-century supporter, recognizing his ecclesiastical supremacy. And by a decisive stroke of the Roman sword at

---

[37] Joseph Rickaby, *The Modern Papacy*, p. 1, in *Lectures on the History of Religions,* vol. 3 [lecture 24].
[38] Alexander Keith, *The Signs of the Times*, vol. 2, p. 470.
[39] Pennington, *op. cit.*, p. 450.

Rome, in the spring of 538, the way was opened for a new order of popes and the beginning of a new epoch. And now in 1793, just 1260 years after Justinian's 533 imperial fiat, came the notable decree of the Papacy's once powerful supporter, France —eldest son of the church—aimed at the abolition of church and religion, and their unholy union with the state, followed by the decisive stroke of the sword at Rome in overthrow of the Papacy in 1798—an act marking the end of the epoch begun 1260 years before.

The two are clearly counterparts. In the first the supreme civil power of the time was employed for the aggrandizement of the pope, framing laws with that special objective in view, and subjecting all spiritual authority to him. And now, in the reaction, the supreme civil power of the hour was bent on the pope's overthrow, and on the recovery of all the usurped political authority which he had assumed. One was the beginning, and the other the termination, of an epoch foreknown of God, and determined—perhaps unwittingly—by men.

Amid the chaos of falling kingdoms and decaying pagan religions of the early centuries, the massive plans of the Papacy occupied the central place. They formed the point of integration, and constituted the principle around which the ancient world could wrap its wracked form. Constantine realized that in the vast, unorganized Christianity within his realm lay the essential principle of unity needed by his empire, and which later became the dominating concept in the Middle Ages. Rome is thus seen to be the meeting point of all history, the papal succession filling the space from Caesar, and Constantine, and Justinian, and binding all ages into one.[40] And similarly the final events of prophecy cluster decisively around her.

---

[40] William Barry, *The Papal Monarchy*, p. 428.

CHAPTER THIRTY-FIVE

End of Period

Recognized and Proclaimed

When the stroke had fallen, and the pope had been taken captive, a chorus of voices in England, Continental Europe, and America witnessed to the ending of the 1260-year era of the Papacy. In rapid succession some of the typical and impressive testimony uttered at the time will be noted.

I. King Recognizes and Proclaims End of 1260 Years (1798)

EDWARD KING, F.R.S., F.S.A. (1735-1807), was educated at Cambridge, and in 1763 admitted to the bar. He wrote extensively from 1767 onward. A wealthy uncle made him financially independent. He contributed several papers to the "Archaeologia," and became a fellow of the Antiquarian Society. Tenacious in his views on prophecy, he wrote *Morsels of Criticism* in 1788 and *Remarks on the Signs of the Times* in 1798.

1. CLEAREST RECOGNITION OF TERMINUS OF PAPAL PERIOD. —King is perhaps the most explicit of all expositors of prophecy in recognition of the momentous ending of the 1260 years, which he declares had just terminated. This appears in his *Remarks on the Signs of the Times*,[1] published shortly after the captivity of the pope and the overthrow of the papal government in February, 1798. The author's first attempt in the field of exposition, his *Morsels of Criticism,* made little impression. He there alludes

---

[1] Edward King, *Remarks on the Signs of the Times* (Philadelphia ed., 1800), p. 19.

765

to the "1260 years," [2] and later discusses the 2300 years, noting the divergent Septuagint rendering of 2400. [3]

2. 2300 DAYS ARE YEARS FROM PERSIA.—To King the number 2300 "seems to afford us an uncommon degree of light and information." Allowing these days to be *"prophetical days,* and to denote *years,* consistently with the interpretation of so many other parts of prophecy," King computes them from "the time of the full establishment of the power of the Ram, (i.e. of the Medo-Persian Empire, by the conquest of Babylon in the year 538 A.C.)." He believes they reach to 1762, or possibly from 525 A.C. to A.D. 1775, with the diminution of the Mohammedan power, that "for so many ages has been the cause of the *desolation,* and of the long subversion of truth." [4]

3. PROPHECIES COVER INTERVAL BETWEEN ADVENTS.—In the preface of his *Remarks on the Signs of the Times,* King begins with the statement that for many years he had made the Holy Scriptures his "constant study," and that he has reached the full conviction of the truth of divine prophecy. Being "fully persuaded that we were rapidly advancing to one of the most interesting periods of the world," he seeks to "awaken the attention of mankind, to the approaching scene of things." He endeavors to show that apocalyptic prophecy is "an account, in *chronological order* of the great overruleing events" that lie between the first and second advents. [5] He stresses the Saracenic and Turkish woes upon the Eastern Church. [6] In common with many others, he believes that the seven vials are in process of fulfillment. He exclaims, "With what awful astonishment must we behold the Events of the present day!" [7]

4. 1260 DAYS HAVE ENDED "THIS YEAR," 1798.—Contending that *"Great Babylon,* undoubtedly meant *Rome;* the Proud *City on seven hills; so long deemed Mistress of the world,"* King refers to the wrath and vengeance being visited upon her, how

[2] King, *Morsels of Criticism* (2d ed., 1800), vol. 2, pp. 194, 195.
[3] *Ibid.,* pp. 231, 232, 240, note. On Septuagint rendering of Daniel 8:15 see *Prophetic Faith,* Volume III, pp. 377-380.
[4] King, *Morsels,* vol. 2, pp. 232, 233.   [5] King, *Remarks,* p. [3].
[6] *Ibid.,* p. 4.   [7] *Ibid.,* p. 16.

she is scourged, torn to pieces, and consumed with fire, violence, and anger, and then makes this impressive declaration of the currently accomplished ending of the 1260 years:

"Is not the *Papal power,* at Rome, which was once so terrible, and so domineering, at an end?

"But let us pause a little. Was not *this* End, in other parts of the Holy Prophecies, foretold to be, *at the* END *of* 1260 *years?*—and was it not foretold by Daniel, to be at the END of *a time, times, and half a time?* which computation amounts to the same period. And now let us see;—hear; —and understand. THIS IS THE YEAR 1798.—And just 1260 years ago, in the very beginning of the year 538, *Belisarius* put an end to the Empire, and Dominion of the Goths, at Rome.

"He had entered the City on the 10th of the preceding December, in triumph, in the name of *Justinian,* Emperor of the East: and had soon after made it tributary to him: leaving *thenceforward* from A.D. 538, No POWER *in Rome,* that could be said *to rule over the earth,*—excepting the EC-CLESIASTICAL PONTIFICAL POWER."[8] (Facsimile reproduction on page 768.)

5. TEMPORARY LOSSES DO NOT AFFECT PROPHECY.—Due cognizance is taken of Rome's later brief recapture, after 538, as without bearing on the prophecy, in these words:

"It is true; that after this entry of Belisarius, Rome was twice re-taken by *Totila,* and the *Goths.* But instead of setting up any Empire there, he, the first time, carried away *all* the Senate, and drove out all the in-habitants; and, the second time, he was himself soon defeated, and killed; and Rome was recovered for *Justinian* by *Narses.*

"Still, however, no Dominion, No *Power ruling over the World,* ever had *any seat* there, any more, except the *Papal."*[9]

6. ENDING OF 1260 YEARS ESTABLISHES BEGINNING.—Then comes King's impressive conclusion, and reasoning, on the his-torical terminus of the 1260 years, in relation to coming events.

"We have reason to apprehend then, that *the* 1260 *years are now com-pleted.*—And that we may venture to date *the commencement* of that period, not, as most Commentators have hitherto done, either from *Pepin's* giving the Pope *Ravenna;* or from *Charlemagne's* determining, and ad-judging the Pope to *be God's Vicar on earth;* but from *the End* of the *Gothic Power at Rome.* Because both those other circumstances were only (like subsequent gifts, or acquisitions of territory, and revenue,) mere aug-mentations of splendour, and confirmations of that state of *Ecclesiastical*

---

[8] *Ibid.,* pp. 18, 19.   [9] *Ibid.,* p. 20.

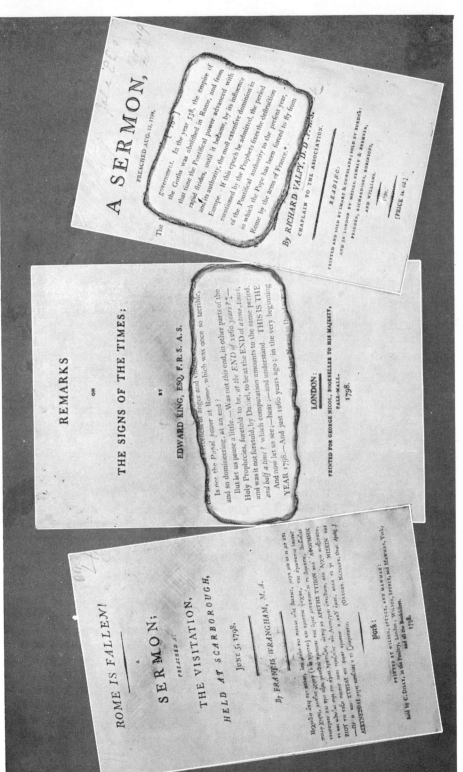

END OF 1260 YEARS IN 1798 ATTESTED BY MANY

Sample of Contemporary British Heralding of Ending of Prophetic Papal Period (Left); Edward King Designates Dethroning of Pope as Marking End of Prophetical 1260-Years Epoch (Center); Richard Valpy Recognizes 538 and 1798 as Constituting the End Years of the Prophetic Period. The Same Recognition Was Noted in Germany and America

Supremacy, in which the Papal Power had been left, at Rome by *Belisarius,* on his driving out the Goths, and ruining their kingdom.

"And if these things are so;—then truly that Great City *Babylon is fallen,—is fallen;—is thrown down; and shall be found no more at all.* And nothing remains, but for us to wait, with awful apprehensions, for the End. Even for the completion of the further *closing events,* which are, in the emblematical language, of Holy Prophecy, described as being at hand." [10]

7. TIME OF TROUBLE PRECEDES CRUSHING OF IRON AND CLAY.—So impressive were these words that four decades later the Millerite *Signs of the Times* quoted two full columns, urging its readers to "weigh every word." [11] Connecting the "tremendous events of the times" with preparation for the second advent, the establishment of the everlasting kingdom, and the imminent smiting of the emblematic feet of iron and clay by the stone, King adds:

"And we are expressly told, that this was an intimation; that the Great Empires of the World, the remains of the Roman Empire, should be broken in pieces, by certain *Instruments of God's Wrath.* Whilst it is moreover added, that, in the latter days, *there should be a Time of Trouble, such as never was since there was a nation, even to that time.*" [12]

8. WRITES UNDER SENSE OF SOBERING RESPONSIBILITY.— But one more excerpt will be noted:

"We approach unto the latter days!—I tremble whilst I write! God forbid I should mislead any.—But if I do apprehend aright; I must—I ought to speak, and write with circumspection, that which I apprehend.

"I am no rash enthusiast.—I desire to be exceedingly guarded against error; and I have not the least presumptuous idea of intending to prophecy. —The word of Prophecy is sealed for ever.

"I desire only to apprehend what is written." [13]

9. 1260-YEAR ENDING NOT NULLIFIED BY NEW POPE'S ELECTION.—In footnotes to the 1800 edition of *Morsels of Criticism,* King takes particular note of the re-election of a pope in 1800, with these words:

"Another *Pope* has indeed been elected at *Venice* in this year 1800;— but without any possession of *Rome;* or of its territories;—without the

---

[10] *Ibid.,* pp. 20, 21.
[11] "'The 1260 Years of Papal Triumph," *The Signs of the Times, and Expositor of Prophecy,* Feb. 22, 1843 (vol. 4, no. 23), p. 177.
[12] King, *Remarks,* p. 22.   [13] *Ibid.,* p. 28.

Ecclesiastical Revenue;—without Dominion;—without Power;—a Shadow, and not a Substance;—and with regard to any continuance of *Papal Dominion at Rome,*—a flighter, and more feeble continuance of the appearance of *Roman Papal Power,* than even *Augustulus* was of the continuance of the Power of the *Western Roman Emperours.*

"Unless therefore the *Pope* be restored to his Territorial Possessions, and Dominion, and Residence *in Rome;* there is an end of *Roman Pontifical Greatness;* and the 1260 years are ended, which were named, in Holy Prophecy, for the continuance of the usurped *Ecclesiastical Empire* of the *City on seven hills,* and of the *little horn* of the furious emblematical Monster." [14]

II. Valpy Proclaims 1798 in Sermon to Reading Association

RICHARD VALPY, D.D., F.S.A., MRSL (1754-1836), noted schoolmaster, was rector of Stradishall in Suffolk and chaplain of the Reading Association. Trained at Pembroke College, Oxford, from which he received the B.A., M.A., B.D., and D.D. degrees between 1776 and 1792, he was also a fellow of the Society of Antiquaries. He became headmaster of Reading School in 1781, retaining connection with it for fifty years, and bringing it to enviable scholastic heights. In 1787 Valpy was collated with the rectory at Stradishall. He published both a Greek and a Latin grammar in 1809. Twice refusing a bishopric, he retired from active schoolwork in 1830.

In a *Sermon* based on Matthew 24:44 ("Be ye also ready"), preached August 13, 1798, before the Reading and Henley Associations, the Woodley Cavalry, and the Reading Volunteers, at the consecration of the colors,[15] Valpy expounded the momentous events of the spring at Rome as fulfillment of the close of the prophetic period of the 1260 years. The sermon was "printed at the request of the Corps, before which it was preached."

1. END OF 1260 YEARS FIXED FOR 1798.—Declaring that "God has never left Himself without witness," and that "history is indeed but a record of the completion of prophecy," Valpy comments on the "present awful events" that involve the world,

---

[14] King, *Morsels,* vol. 3, p. 353, note.
[15] Richard Valpy, *Sermons Preached on Public Occasions,* vol. 1, pp. 143 ff.

and the "disastrous revolution, which have plunged Europe into blood." He declares, "The hand of God is filling up, by instruments of the most fearful execution, the great outline, which he had traced before by his Prophets and his Apostles." [16] Then comes this luminous declaration:

"Among the Prophecies, which must have excited your attention, are those, which relate to the present state of Rome. If with all Protestant Commentators, we understand the Roman Pontiff to be represented under the figurative emblems of Daniel, and the Author of the Revelations, and by the still clearer description of St. Paul, we must be struck with the completion of the prophecy. Daniel and St. John mention the period of 1260 years from the establishment to the extinction of that government. In the year 538, the empire of the Goths was abolished in Rome, and from that time the Pontifical power advanced with rapid strides, until it became, by its influence and its authority, the most extensive dominion in Europe. If this epoch be admitted, the period mentioned by Prophets fixes the destruction of the Pontifical authority to the present year, in which the Pope has been forced to fly from Rome by the arms of France." [17] (Facsimile on page 768.)

2. BEGAN WITH GOTHIC EXPULSION AND PAPAL ELEVATION.
—In added notes, in the published sermon, Valpy adds:

"In the year 538, the Goths were driven from Rome, and at that time the aspiring Vigilius, by his secret intrigues with the artful Theodora, was promoted to the Pontifical dignity, which he purchased with 200 pounds of gold: an unequivocal proof of the character of a *man of sin*.

"During the Pontificate of Vigilius, the pretensions of the successors of St. Peter to a general superiority began to be openly asserted; and shortly after, their supremacy was publicly acknowledged. It was at this time that the Pope assumed the title of Vicegerent of Jesus Christ. . . . Now too celibacy was more generally enjoined. The use of Holy Water was first publicly recommended by Vigilius in 538." [18]

3. EXPULSION OF POPE DRAWS ATTENTION TO PROPHECY.—
Valpy then traces the growth of papal power and the growing acquisition of "strength and of territory." He discounts the temporary exiles occasionally suffered by the pontiffs, and mentions Bishop Newton's observation that we must see the conclusion before we can precisely ascertain the beginning of this notable period. Then he adds, "If we have now witnessed the fall of the

---

[16] *Ibid.*, pp. 144-146.   [17] *Ibid.*, pp. 146, 147.   [18] *Ibid.*, p. 258.

Pope's temporal dominion, it cannot be an unprofitable task to endeavor to trace its origin." [19] Valpy then remarks significantly that "on the expulsion of the Pope from Rome, the attention of many contemplative persons was turned to the prophecies relating to that power." [20]

4. INCREASE OF KNOWLEDGE IS OF PROPHECIES.—In the same notes "On the Prophecies Relating to the Fall of Rome," he says:

"It is not therefore a subject of wonder that *many should run to and fro* in tracing these events to the designs of the Almighty declared in Prophecy; for thus *knowledge shall be increased;* and thus we may *prepare to meet our God.*" [21]

Valpy quotes from leading expositors, such as Newton, Faber, Woodhouse, and Kett, who had shed light on prophecy. He especially mentions King—"of extensive erudition and ingenuity, and of accurate Biblical knowledge"—who, he notes, likewise begins the 1260 years in 538,[22] and so ends them in 1798.

5. PROPHETIC EXPOSITION INTERWOVEN IN "POETICAL CHRONOLOGY."—Valpy's large library of about three thousand volumes, sold at auction in 1832, contained many works on prophecy. His rather unique *Poetical Chronology* of history touches upon calendars, such as the construction of the Jewish calendar —and in his introductory remarks on years he says, "Whenever a complete year, or a series of years, is mentioned, a solar year is always understood." [23] In it he traces Babylon, Medo-Persia, Grecia, and Rome. Under each leading year noted Valpy gives the significance in verse, interweaving the prophetic aspect. For example:

"330 Three hundred thirty, Persia's empire ends:
Great Alexander Cyrus' throne ascends.
Short was his reign: the eighth returning spring
Stopt in mid triumph the victorious king.
One horn cut off, lo! four new horns arise;
Three hundred one divides the mighty prize." [24]

[19] *Ibid.,* pp. 260, 261.   [20] *Ibid.,* p. 262.
[21] *Ibid.,* p. 254.   [22] *Ibid.,* pp. 253-269.
[23] Valpy, *Poetical Chronology of Ancient and English History,* p ix
[24] *Ibid.,* p. 17, with footnote reference to Daniel 8:8.

III. Wrangham—Prophetic Demand Is Now Fulfilled

FRANCIS WRANGHAM, M.A. (1769-1842), classical scholar, was educated at Magdalene College, Cambridge, winning the Sir William Browne medal for the best Greek and Latin epigrams. He secured his B.A. and M.A. degrees in 1790 and 1793. Ordained in 1793, he became a member of the Trinity College staff, four times winning the Seaton prize for academic achievement. While serving as curate and rector for different congregations, he was examining chaplain to Vernon Harcourt, the Archbishop of York. In 1825 he was prebend at Chester Cathedral, and in 1828, archdeacon of East Riding. He wrote frequently on emancipation from Catholicism.

1. EARTHQUAKE ACCOMPLISHED FACT; BABYLON FALLEN.— In an impressive sermon *Rome Is Fallen!* (see page 768) from Revelation 14:8, preached at Scarborough, June 5, 1798, Wrangham uses these words:

"*It is done—There* has been *a great earthquake, such as was not since men were upon the earth, so mighty an earthquake and so great—and the cities of the nations* have fallen: *and great* BABYLON *has come in remembrance before God, to give unto her the cup of the wine of the fierceness of his wrath.*" [25]

2. REJOICES OVER PROPHETIC ACCOMPLISHMENT.—Back in 1795 he had written thus on "The Destruction of Babylon";

"Hear then, proud ROME, and tremble at thy fate!
The hour will come, nor *distant is its date*
(If right was caught the Prophet's mystic strain,
Which awe-struck Patmos echoed o'er the main)
The hour, which holy arts in vain would stay,
That prone on earth thy gorgeous spires shall lay." [26]

And now, in 1798, he declares:

"What Protestant does not rejoice—to hear that those thunders at length are silent, which issued during so long a period from the gloomy recesses of the *Vatican* to convulse EUROPE; shaking the allegiance of subjects, and 'hurling princes from their thrones!' What lover of peace does not exult—to learn that those lightnings, which so often blasted

---

[25] Francis Wrangham, *Rome Is Fallen!* p. 19.   [26] *Ibid.*, p. 9.

the olive of CHRISTENDOM, are quenched for ever! Ought we, who should anxiously wish the Prophecies fulfilled, to weep over their accomplishment?" [27]

3. INFLUENCED BY KING'S CLEAR APPLICATION.—Wrangham speaks highly of Edward King, whose clear application evidently influenced his own conclusions, and of the still earlier David Hartley,[28] and his *Observations on Man,* who expatiates on the image of Daniel 2, the beasts of Daniel 7, and the setting up of Christ's kingdom.

Hartley had declared, "How near the dissolution of the present governments, generally or particularly, may be, would be great rashness to affirm. CHRIST will come in this sense also *as a thief in the night.*" [29] He refers to the critical circumstances into which the world was entering.

IV. Daubeny—France Pulling Down Usurping Antichrist

CHARLES DAUBENY, LL.B., D.C.L. (1745-1827), in a discourse (1798), on *The Fall of Papal Rome,* emphasizes the approaching second advent, presenting the past fulfillment of prophecy as assurance of the accomplishment of the remaining unfulfilled portions. He declares that before the Christian faith shall gain that universal prevalence in the world, the great antichristian power that had exalted itself in the temple of God, "is to be brought down and destroyed"—Antichrist being identified as the "Papal Church of Rome." [30] Then occur these passages:

"The Papal power has long been upon the decline. It received an irrecoverable wound at the period of the Protestant Reformation; since which time it has been gradually sinking into an insignificance preparatory to its final extinction. That event has now taken place; an event in which all nations are more or less concerned. For in the accomplishment of an important prophecy, which respects the progress of Christ's kingdom upon earth, what nation can be uninterested?" [31]

"We have seen that nation, whose former sovereigns contributed much to the elevation of the Papal throne, now employed as the more immediate

---

[27] *Ibid.,* p. 12.   [28] *Ibid.,* p. 1.
[29] David Hartley, *Observations on Man, His Frame, His Duty, and His Expectations,* vol. 2, p. 380.
[30] Charles Daubeny, *The Fall of Papal Rome,* p. 25.   [31] *Ibid.,* pp. 26, 27.

instrument in God's hand, to pull down the idol that has been set up in the Temple." [32]

V. Simpson—1260 Years Accomplished Before Our Eyes

DAVID SIMPSON (1745-1799), theologian and religious writer, was born in Yorkshire and educated at St. Johns College, Cambridge, from which he received an M.A. He was successively curate of Ramsden in Essex, Buckingham, and Old Church in Macclesfield. In all three charges his alleged Methodism gave offense, and in the last place he was silenced by the Bishop of Chester. However, friends erected Christ Church for him at Macclesfield, where he officiated until his death. His numerous writings included *Key to the Prophecies* (1795—with a third edition in 1812), and *A Plea for Religion and the Sacred Writings* (first published in 1797 with numerous later editions). On the title page it appears that this latter volume was "Addressed to the Disciples of Thomas Paine, and Wavering Christians of Every Persuasion."

1. COMPREHENSIVE SKETCH OF LITTLE HORN.—Simpson sketches Daniel 7—the ten divisions of the Roman Empire, the arising of the Little Horn among the ten, subduing three of the ten and usurping their dominion, and increasing in power until it had obtained a peculiar kind of power and jurisdiction over all the seven other horns.[33] This dominion was to continue three and a half times (a time being a year of 360 days) or a total of 1260 years, at the end of which it would be destroyed. Then he traces the accomplishment—the Roman Empire was dismembered, the bishop of Rome arose, and three of the ten states ("the *senate* of *Rome*, the *kingdom* of *Lombardy*, and the *exarchate* of *Ravenna;* three governments all in *Italy*") were subdued, the pope assuming a triple crown.[34]

2. 538 BEGINNING ACCORDS WITH 1798 ENDING.—Simpson next discusses the dates fixed by some for beginning the 1260

---

[32] *Ibid.*, p. 30.
[33] David Simpson, *A Plea for Religion*, p. 134.
[34] *Ibid.*, pp. 134, 135.

years—606 (from Phocas), 666 (the apocalyptic number), and 756 (when the pope became a temporal prince). The time of Gregory I is also mentioned. But he adds this footnote:

"There is some reason, from the present appearances of things, to suppose, that the 1260 prophetical years must be calculated from a period somewhat earlier than the commencement of the seventh century. The year of our Lord 538 accords with the downfall of the Pope's temporal dominion A.D. 1798." [35]

3. FULFILLING THIS DAY BEFORE OUR EYES.—Referring then to the signs of the approaching end, Simpson asks pointedly:

"Are not abundance of these *predictions* fulfilling at this day before our eyes? . . .

"Does it not seem that those 1260 years are upon the point of expiring?" [36]

4. BEAST'S CLAWS CUT AND TEETH DRAWN.—Expatiating on the prophesied changes that had taken place, and on how the nations that "for so many ages had given their power unto the *Beast,*" were to "turn against that *Beast,* and use means for its destruction," Simpson then asks:

"Is not this part of the prophecy also, in a good degree, fulfilled at the present moment? Have not all the CATHOLIC powers forsaken his HOLINESS of *Rome* in the time of his greatest need? And is not He, who, a few ages ago, made all *Europe* tremble at the thunder of his voice, now become weak like other men? Are not the claws of the *Beast* cut, and his teeth drawn, so that he can no longer either scratch or bite? Is he not already, in our *own day,* and before our *own eyes,* stripped of his temporal dominion?" [37]

5. PRESENT FULFILLMENT POWERFULLY CONFIRMS TRUTH. —Now comes this climactic declaration:

"Is it not extremely remarkable, and a powerful confirmation of the truth of *Scripture prophecy,* that just 1260 years ago from the present 1798, in the very beginning of the year 538, Belisarius put an end to the empire of the *Goths* at *Rome,* leaving no power therein but the *Bishop* of that *Metropolis?*

"Read these things in the *prophetic Scriptures;* compare them coolly with the present state of Europe, and then, I say again, deny the truth

[35] *Ibid.,* p. 138.
[36] *Ibid.,* pp. 164, 165.
[37] *Ibid.,* p. 165. (There is frequent footnote reference to such expositors as Hartley, Tillotson, Newton, Hurd, Hallifax, Clayton, Lowman.)

of *Divine Revelation,* if you can. Open your eyes, and behold these things accomplishing in the face of the whole world. *This thing is not done in a corner.*" [38]

VI. Thube Asserts Papal Wound of 1798 to Be Healed

CHRISTIAN GOTTLOB THUBE was pastor at Baumgarten, Mecklenburg-Schwerin, in Germany. In 1789 Thube looked forward to a great day of vengeance for the papacy in 1836— influenced by Bengel's curious mode of calculation. [39] In 1796, in *Ueber die nächstkommenden vierzig Jahre* (Something About the Next Forty Years), Thube recorded a sermon preached by request before the duke of Mecklenburg in 1775, in which he predicted that a great revolution would break out within fifteen years, [40] and which actually began in France in 1789.

1. PAPACY IDENTIFIED AS BEAST AND BABYLON.—Thube held the Papacy to be the prophesied Beast and Babylon—citing Revelation 13, 2 Thessalonians 2, Daniel 7 and 11:36-45— "whom I consider to be all one and the same person, whom I call the Antichrist." [41]

2. USUAL VIEWS ON LEADING PROPHECIES.—In his book on Daniel, Thube offers a new translation of Daniel from the original. The standard view of the four kingdoms of Daniel 2 and 7 is held. [42] However, concerning the Little Horn of Daniel 7, Thube develops an unusual theory. He anticipates its appearance in the immediate future, and sees in the French Revolution a forecast of its disastrous powers. Like Bengel, he believes that world events would reach their climax in 1836. The judgment sitting in heaven takes place while this tyrant rules upon earth. [43] The ending of the seventieth week he places in A.D. 37, with the crucifixion in A.D. 30, [44] and 1836 as the great year of crisis. [45]

3. WOUNDING OCCURRING BEFORE OUR EYES.—Thube then

---

[38] *Ibid.,* p. 166.
[39] Christian Gottlob Thube, *Handbuch der Gottsgelahrtheit* (Handbook of Divinity), p. 300.
[40] Thube, *Ueber die nächstkommenden vierzig Jahre,* pp. 4, 5. See also Thube, *Das Buch des Propheten Daniels . . . 1797* (The Book of the Prophet Daniel), Appendix I, pp. 180, 181.
[41] Thube, *Ueber die nächstkommenden vierzig Jahre,* p. 22.
[42] Thube, *Das Buch des Propheten Daniels,* pp. 50-54, 92-95.
[43] *Ibid.,* pp. 96-100.   [44] *Ibid.,* pp. 125, 130.   [45] *Ibid.,* pp. 30, 100.

deals with the French Revolution, and all the infidelic and atheistic excesses attendant, closing with these words:

"The most remarkable thing is that the French compelled the pope to make peace under the most oppressive conditions. The prophecy concerning the wounding of the beast, which we find in Revelation 13:14, is being fulfilled before our eyes. This wound, however, shall sooner or later be healed again. Then will come to pass what has been written in Revelation 13:11-17." [46]

4. TIME PERIODS ON BENGEL'S YEAR-DAY BASIS.—In 1799 Thube published a work on the book of Revelation, which discusses in detail the prophetic time periods of the Apocalypse.[47] These are all reckoned on the prophetic-day principle in which he follows Bengel's fractional modifications.[48] The pure woman is the true church in the wilderness and the Babylonian woman is the false church; the Papacy is also the beast from the sea.[49]

He also thought, like some writers before him, that the Papacy received a preliminary wound when Pope Gregory VII died in misery away from Rome and later counter-popes were battling each other. He likewise believed that under Urban II, the originator and promulgator of the Crusades, the early wound was healed.[50]

5. WOUND BY THE SWORD TO BE HEALED.—The French Revolution stroke against the Papacy is stressed as only a wound that would be healed, not as the extinction of the Papacy, as some anticipated. Thus:

"The beast has received a deadly wound, Rev. 13:12. It received the wound by the sword, verse 14.

"This was fulfilled by the French who with sword in hand banished the pope and his cardinals from Rome, dissolving the Papal States and erecting a so-called Roman Republic.

"The present condition of the Papacy is the following: it received a wound by the sword and yet it is alive. How long this condition will continue and under which form this still continuing life will exist, is not yet to be decided with certainty. The deadly wound will be healed, but whether it will take a short or long time we do not know; nor do we understand now in which manner and by which process it will come to pass." [51]

---

[46] *Ibid.*, p. 189.
[47] Thube, *Anleitung zum richtigen Verstande der Offenbarung Johannis* (Guidance to the Right Understanding of the Revelation of John), pp. 37, 38.   [48] *Ibid.*, p. 48.
[49] *Ibid.*, pp. 94, 103.   [50] *Ibid.*, pp. 105, 106.   [51] *Ibid.*, pp. 123, 124.

VII. Galloway—Two Testament Witnesses Dead From 1792-1796

JOSEPH GALLOWAY (*c.* 1730-1803), American lawyer and Loyalist in Revolutionary times, was born in Maryland. He was one of Philadelphia's most popular and distinguished lawyers, and from 1756 to 1776 was a member of the Pennsylvania Assembly, serving as Speaker from 1766 to 1775. In 1774, he became a delegate to the Continental Congress, in which he took a prominent part. He discouraged radical action and proposed a union between Great Britain and the colonies. In 1776 Galloway joined the British Army. On the capture of Philadelphia he was made police magistrate, and superintendent of the port. He soon removed to England, however, his remaining years being devoted to the study of prophecy, resulting in several published works in this field. One of his most important works was, *Brief Commentaries Upon Such Parts of the Revelation and Other Prophecies, as Immediately Refer to the Present Times.*

1. BEAST FROM ABYSS THE CENTRAL FIGURE.—Galloway had an abhorrence of the revolutionary and infidelic principles of Republican France. Being interested mainly in the fulfillment of prophecy during his time, he devoted a long chapter to the two faithful Witnesses and their slaying by the Beast from the bottomless pit.[52] Following certain Protestant interpretations, reaching back to Mede, he held that the seven seals cover the history of the church of the early centuries, with the seven trumpets as the development of the sixth seal. These trumpets were God's judgments against the apostate church—the first four covering the Gothic invasions in the West, and the fifth and sixth the incursions of the Saracens and Turks in the East, which opened the pit of the abyss. The 1260 years might be dated from Phocas and Mohammed respectively.

2. DEATH OF WITNESSES FROM 1792 TO 1796.—Galloway gives a very detailed explanation, which led him to the conclusion that the Two Witnesses were slain in France. He maintains that the " 'beast that shall ascend out of the bottomless pit;' or,

---

[52] Joseph Galloway, *Brief Commentaries* (1809 ed.), vol. 1, pp. 50-144.

as it will presently appear, of *an infidel and atheistical power,* more hardened, more mischievous, and consummately wicked, than either of the two that rose before it." [53]

He, in contrast to many others, sees in the Two Witnesses neither Elias and Enoch nor yet Luther and Calvin, but the Old and New Testaments.[54] "These *two holy prophets and oracles of God,* alone, among all the *variety of things* upon the earth, can satisfy and fulfil the figurative description of the text." [55]

"Is it not by these two sacred and infallible records, . . . [which have] been preserved amidst the waste of all-devouring time, the ravages of wars, the wrecks of books, and even during the dark ages of Pagan sensuality, of Mohammedan ignorance, and Papal superstition. I ask, is it not by these two holy records *alone,* that God has been pleased to reveal and attest his righteous and immaculate will to mankind?" [56]

Concerning the Witnesses' prophesying in sackcloth, he writes:

"The evident interpretation of this trope is, that during the domination and persecutions of the Mohammedan and Papal hierarchies, the pure truths of God, attested by the 'two witnesses' shall lose a great part of their weight and influence in the world. They shall be misunderstood, misapplied, tortured, perverted, and corrupted by the two apostasies." [57]

They will be killed, he continues, by the beast ascending out of the bottomless pit. And who is this beast? It is "a power which should utterly efface from the minds of men, all the truths revealed to mankind by the two Testaments, and establish atheism in their stead: *atheism, the consummation of error, impiety, and sin!*" [58] It is the coming of an atheistic power that will conspire against and " 'kill the two witnesses of God;' or, as I have said before, extinguish in the minds of men all sense and influence of the sacred truths revealed in the Old and New Testaments." [59]

Where do we find such a power? There have always been individuals who have denied God.

"But if we search the annals of the world, we shall not find even a private society or sect, much less a civil community and state, which, before

[53] *Ibid.,* p. 54.   [54] *Ibid.,* p. 55.   [55] *Ibid.,* p. 56.
[56] *Ibid.,* p. 57.   [57] *Ibid.,* pp. 61, 62.   [58] *Ibid.,* pp. 75, 76.
[59] *Ibid.,* pp. 76, 77.

our day, has, in the most public manner proclaimed to all the nations around it, that THERE IS NO GOD! and made that position the basis of the constitution of its government. . . . It is obviously, that political and atheistical monster, the revolutionary power now ruling the French nation." [60]

Galloway thought (1) that the "little horn" is not a type of the pope, but of a different political power, to be explained hereafter; (2) that the pope in no part of the prophecies is referred to as a horn or temporal prince, but is only designated by the symbol of a beast, which signifies a cruel and wicked power, whether civil or ecclesiastical. (Verse 8.) And their dead bodies shall lie in the street of the *great city*. It is here not unworthy of remark that the prophet does not say that the *two witnesses* themselves be dead but only their " '*dead bodies* shall lie in the street of the great city.' " [61]

The great city at the time of the fulfillment of this prophecy cannot be Rome, as some commentators suppose, because it is a metropolis of a small territory, but it is Paris. It is compared to Sodom and Egypt, "remarkable among its contemporaries for the like depravity, and wilful ignorance of the true God. Papal Rome has been remarkable among its neighbours for neither." [62]

Verse 9. Their dead bodies will be seen three days and a half. That is "three *years* and an *half:* that is, *from the time of the final expulsion of the clergy* (when all practical religion ceased in France), *to the date of the decree for tolerating all religion.*" [63]

3. INFIDELIC FRANCE THE BEAST FROM EARTH.—Galloway likewise explained the seven-headed dragon, the Beast from the sea, and the Beast from the earth, in Revelation 12, 13, as pagan Rome, papal Rome, and infidelic France, respectively. The great confederacy of Babylon was still to be formed. The millennium is still future, and will be synchronous with the reign of Christ with His saints. Such was the teaching of the last expositor of the century we shall note.

---

[60] *Ibid.*, p. 78.
[61] *Ibid.*, p. 114.
[62] *Ibid.*, pp. 116, 117.
[63] *Ibid.*, p. 118.

VIII. Revolution Has Profound Effect on Interpretation

The effect of the French Revolution and the European upheaval upon prophetic interpretation was profound, and inaugurated a new era in the study of the Apocalypse. Many who lived to see with their own eyes the accomplishment of the stroke so long foretold had new hopes kindled within them respecting the nearness of the coming trump of judgment, and the promised kingdom of God.

In recording the deeds of the French Revolution, even historians called attention to the seeming fulfillment of inspired prophecy. History thus rose to its most exalted height as it became the interpreter of prophecy. And numerous religious writers of prominence recognized that the contemporary terrible judgments were an evident fulfillment of prophecy.[64] They declared that the 1260 years of papal ecclesiastical supremacy had indeed expired, and that the hour had come for the world-wide preaching of the gospel and the heralding of the impending hour of God's judgment. The prophecies concerning this hour are the field of study of Volumes III and IV.

---

[64] John Adolphus, *The History of France* (1790-1802), vol. 2, p. 379.

CHAPTER THIRTY-SIX

Summing Up the Evidence
of Volume II

I. Composite Picture of Post-Reformation Witness

In the comprehensive tabular charts which appear in the next two openings, the principal teachings of the leading post-Reformation expositors are assembled. Their expositions of the various chapters of Daniel and the Revelation appear in logical sequence for comparison and evaluation. These charts are based on the same general scheme followed for the pre-Reformation and Reformation interpreters on pages 156, 157, and 528-531, only having added details. This makes possible rather accurate and highly helpful comparisons.

The findings are most revealing. Nothing like a comprehensive pre-Reformation interpretation of the prophecies of Daniel and the Revelation appeared before those of Wyclif and Brute in Britain, late in the fourteenth century. Distinct light on isolated truths of prophecy had, of course, been seen and declared by various men in the twelfth, thirteenth, and early fourteenth centuries. The British expositors built, independently, upon these elemental foundations.

Two points stand out as common denominators among the group: first, the Papacy is the predicted Antichrist, under its various prophetic symbols; and second, prophetic time is to be understood on the recognized year-day principle. From the Renaissance onward prophetic exposition began steadily to unfold and expand. The Middle Ages, therefore, mark the gradual

No.	Name	Date	Page	1 John 2:18 Antichrist	Dan. 2 4 Metals	Stone	Dan. 7 4 Beasts	10 Horns	Lit. Horn	3½ Times
· 1	George Downham	1603	535	Papacy	(B-P-G)-R	Kgdm of Chr.	(B-P-G-R)	Listed	Papacy	1260 Yrs (600-)
2	James I of England	1600	536	Papacy			(B-P-G)-R	Divis.	Papacy	1260 Yrs to End
3	Joseph Mede	1631	542	Papacy	B-P-G-R	Kgdm of Chr.	B-P-G-R	Listed	Papacy	1260 Yrs
4	Henry More	1664	563	Papacy	(B-P-G)-R		(B-P-G)-R	Divis.	Papacy	1260 Yrs
5	Hugh Broughton	1607	564		B-P-G-Alexander's Successors			Kings	Antiochus	(Literal)
6	John Tillinghast	1655	570	Papacy	B-P-G-R	Kgdm of Chr.	B-P-G-R		Papacy	396-1656
7	William Sherwin	1670	576	Papacy	(B-P-G)-R	Kgdm of Chr.	(B-P-G)-R	Divis.	Papacy	1260 Yrs
8	Thomas Beverley	1684	581	Papacy	(B-P-G-R)	Kgdm of Chr.	(B-P-G-R)	Kgdms	Papacy	437-1697
9	Drue Cressener	1689	588	Papacy			(B-P-G)-R	Kgdms	Papacy	Just.-c1800
10	"Mysteries . . . Finished"	1699	596	Papacy			(B-P-G-R)			425-1685
11	George Pacard	1604	627	Papacy			(B-P-G)-R	Divis.	Papacy	1260 Yrs
12	Pierre Jurieu	1687	636	Papacy	B-P-G-R	Kgdm of Chr.	B-P-G-R	Kgdms	Papacy	454-1714
13	Johannes Cocceius	1701	613	Papacy	B-P-G-R		B-P-G-R	Listed	Papacy	1260 Yrs
14	Robert Fleming, Jr.	1701	642	Papacy			B-P-G-R		Papacy	Just.-1794
15	Sir Isaac Newton	1727	658	(Papacy)	B-P-G-R	Kgdm of Chr.	B-P-G-R	Listed	Papacy	1260 Yrs
16	William Lowth	1700	670	Papacy (Beast, Man of Sin)			(B-P-G-R)		Papacy	606-1866
17	William Whiston	1706	671	Papacy			B-P-G-R	Kgdms	Papacy	606-1866
18	Th. Crinsoz de Bionens	1729	678	Papacy						
19	Thomas Newton	1754	684	(Papacy)	B-P-G-R	Kgdm of Chr.	B-P-G-R	Kgdms	W. Rome	533 or 606
20	Jean G. de la Flechere	1800	687	(Papacy)	B-P-G-R		B-P-G-R	Listed	Papacy	1260 Yrs
21	R. M.	1787	691	(Papacy)						
22	James Purves	1777	694							
23	Heinrich Horch	1712	698	Papacy	B-P-G-R	Kgdm of Chr.	B-P-G-R		Papacy	(Years)
24	Georg Her. Giblehr	1702	701	Papacy			(B-P-G-R)		Papacy	1260 Yrs
25	Berlenberg Bible	1743	702	Papacy						c410-
26	Johann Al. Bengel	1740	709	(Papacy)						1058-1836
27	Johann Ph. Petri	1768	713	(Papacy)			(B-P-G-R)		Turks	587-1847
28	Hans Wood	1787	719	Papacy	(B-P-G-R)	Kgdm of Chr.	B-P-G-R		Papacy	620-1880
29	John Willison	1745	728	Papacy	(B-P-G-R)	Kgdm of Chr.	(B-P-G-R)	Divis.	Papacy	
30	George Bell	1795	741	Papacy (Also Babylon)			(B-P-G-R)	Divis.	Papacy	537-1797
31	James Bicheno	1793	746	Papacy	B-P-G-R		B-P-G-R	Divis.	Papacy	529-1789
32	Edward King	1798	765	Papacy	(B-P-G-R)		(B-P-G-R)		Papacy	538-1798
33	Richard Valpy	1798	770	Papacy			B-P-G-R		Papacy	538-1798
34	David Simpson	1797	775	Papacy (Also Beast)			(B-P-G)-R	Divis.	Papacy	538-1798
35	Christian G. Thube	1789	777	Papacy	B-P-G-R	Kgdm of Chr.	B-P-G-R	Divis.	Papacy	

recovery of the lost prophetic truths of the church of the early centuries, together with certain advanced positions. This all followed the fifth-century collapse of exposition, and its virtual extinction for five hundred or six hundred years. Now the former lights were burning again, and new lights were being added.

In the second era traversed—that of the Reformation—marked advances were made in rapid succession by the great Reformation leaders in various lands and languages. There was steady clarification. Point after point became established. The earlier confusion over the kingdom of God, as the dominant Catholic church on earth, was expressly repudiated. Instead, its establishment at, and through, the second advent of Christ was constantly emphasized. The fact of the 70 weeks, as 490 years extending to Christ's first advent, had never been lost, but its precise timing now became increasingly clear and accurate. The

Ram-Goat	Grt. Horn (Dan. 8)	Daily	2300 Days	70 Weeks (Dan. 9)	Cross	Kg of Nor. (Dan. 11)	1290 Days (Dan. 12)	1335 Days
	Papacy	Worship	1150 Yrs			Papacy	Years	Yrs to N. Jer.
				417-74	(33)			
Beast; Babylon; Man of Sin) (Papacy=2-Horned Beast of Rev. 13)				490 Yrs		Turks		
		Worship	Cyrus-1701	Ends 34	34	Turk & Pope	366-1656	366-1701
(2300 Yrs to Sanct.)		Worship Worship Worship	-1700 Per. to End	490 Yrs Yrs to Cr.		Turks Turks	-1656 Years Yrs fr. Daily	-1700 Yrs to End Yrs to End
			601-1699				395-1685	-1699
P-G	Rome		Literal 2300 Yrs	490 Yrs 490 Yrs 457-34	(33) 34			
			Years (552-1716) 555-1745	Years 445-32+	33	Turks	Years 70-1360 455-1745	Years 70-1405 455-1790
P-G P-G P-G	Rome Rome Pap.	Worship Worship	Yrs-Not Exp. 550-1750 558-1742	Yrs to 1st Adv.		Turks	Years Years	Years Years
P-G P-G		Worship	534-1766 Cyrus-End 540-1760	490 Yrs	Midst		Years Years	Years 425-Jdgmt
	Papacy		Visi.-1748 Years 453-1847	Yrs to Chr. Yrs to Chr. 453-37	Midst Midst Midst		c410- 557-1847	410-1748 557-1892
France 10th Part of City) France 10th Part of City)		Worship	420-1880	420-70		Turks	590-1880 537-1827	537-1872
P-G P-G			481-1819 538-1762			Turks	529-1819	529-1864
				-37	30	Papacy		

prophetic time periods of Daniel were practically all held to be on the year-day principle, though the 2300 years—which extended the farthest in time—was the haziest, and the last to be included and allocated.

The millennium had a particularly hard struggle. First, the Augustinian theory, in revised form—placing the thousand years from the fourth to the fourteenth centuries—still held Christendom in a viselike grip, and along with it went a spiritualized resurrection. Not until the Reformation was far advanced was the millennium wrested from its false medieval position and again placed in the future, introduced by the second advent and the literal resurrection of the righteous. This was re-established by Joseph Mede, and the great majority soon followed his exegesis.

The paralleling character of the seven churches, seven seals, and seven trumpets as covering the Christian Era, grew in

785

No.	Name	Date	Page	2 Thess. 2 Man of Sin	Rev. 2, 3 7 Churches	Rev. 6, 7 / 7 Seals 4 Horses	4 Trumpets	5th Trumpet	Rev. 8, 9 / 7 Trumpets 5 Months	6th Trumpet	Hr-Dy-Mo.-Yr
1	George Downham	1603	535	(Papacy)						Turks	391 Yrs (1350-
2	James I of England	1600	536	Papacy		4th=Papacy		Monks			
3	Joseph Mede	1631	542	Papacy	7th=Seals	7th=Trumps	Barbarians	Saracens	830-980	Turks	396 Yrs (-1453)
4	John Tillinghast	1655	570		(2300 Yrs Includes 70 Weeks, 1260, 1290, 1335 Yrs)						
5	Thomas Goodwin	1654	573	(Papacy)	(Follows Mede)	(7th Seal=Trumpets)		Saracens		Turks	1453-1849
6	William Sherwin	1670	576	Papacy	(Follows Mede)		Barbarians	Saracens	600-	Turks	1300-1696
7	Thomas Beverley	1684	581	Papacy	Chr. Era			Saracens		Turks (1453)	
8	Drue Cressener	1689	588	Papacy				Saracens		Turks	-1800
9	Johannes Gerhard	1643	602	Papacy		Tribulat.	Heresies	Monks			
10	Andreas Helwig	1612	605	Papacy (Also Antichrist)						Mohammed.	
11	Daniel Cramer	1618	608	Papacy	Chr. Era	Persecut.		Papal Retinue			
12	George Pacard	1604	627	Papacy							
13	Pierre Jurieu	1687	636	(Papacy)	(Follows Mede)		Barbarians	Saracens	Yr-Dys	Turks	(Yr-Dys)
14	Johann H. Alsted	1681	610	(Papacy Is Antichrist, Little Horn)		(Follows Mede)		Rom. Clergy		Antichrist	
15	Matthias Hoe	1618	611	(Papacy Is Antichrist)		Tribulat.	Heresies	Pope		Turks	
16	Johannes Cocceius	1701	613								
17	Robert Fleming, Jr.	1701	642	Papacy			Barbarians	Saracens.		Turks	(Years)
18	Daniel Whitby	1703	649	(Roman Ch. Is Antichrist) (Projector of Post-Millennialism; World Conversion, Spiritual Resurrection, New Jer. the Church)							
19	Charles Daubez	1720	655					Saracens	612-762	Turks	Yr-Dys
20	Sir Isaac Newton	1727	658	Papacy	Chr. Era	Pagan Rome	Barbarians	Saracens	637-936		1063-1453
21	William Whiston	1706	671	Papacy						Turks	1301-1697
22	Th. Crinsox de Bionens	1729	678		Chr. Era	Conquests	Barbarians	Saracens	150 Yrs	Turks	c400 Yrs
23	Thomas Pyle	1735	680	Papacy (Also Little Horn)			Barbarians	Saracens		Turks	
24	John Gill	1758	682	Papacy (Also Antichrist; Little Horn)			Barbarians	Saracens	Yr-Dys	Turks	(Yr Dys)
25	Thomas Newton	1754	684	Papacy			Barbarians	Saracens	612-762	Turks	1281-1672
26	John Wesley	1764	692	Papacy (Also Antichrist)			(Trumpets Cover Chr. Era)			Mohammed.	
27	Heinrich Horch	1712	698		Chr. Era (Sardis Post-Ref.)		Barbarians	Saracens	622-	Turks	1057-1453
28	Johann Al. Bengel	1742	709	(Papacy)							
29	Johann Ph. Petri	1768	713	(Papacy)	(Chr. Era)	(Chr. Era)	(Chr. Era)				
30	Hans Wood	1787	719	(Papacy)			(Barbarians)	Saracens	630-780	Turks	1030-
31	Jacques Phillipot	1685	726	Papacy (Also Antichrist)				Jesuits	1540-1690	(7th=Vials)	
32	Joseph Priestley	1794	744	Papacy (Also Little Horn)		(7th=Trumps)					
33	James Bicheno	1793	746				Barbarians	Saracens	150 Yrs	Turks	1300-1697
34	Edward King	1798	765	Papacy				Saracens	(Yr-Dys)	Turks	(Yr-Dys)
35	Richard Valpy	1798	770	Papacy							
36	Christian G. Thube	1796	777	Papacy							
37	Joseph Galloway	1798	779			Hist. of Ch.	Barbarians	Saracens	(Yr-Dys)	Turks	(Yr-Dys)

clarity. The five months of the Saracenic locusts of the fifth trumpet, and the 391 (or 396) years of the Mohammedan Turks of the sixth trumpet, became almost axiomatic, though their time placements differed.

The synchronous timing of all the 1260-year periods (whether 1260 days, forty-two months, or three and a half times) became increasingly clear. And improvement is to be noted in locating their chronology.

The disruption and confusion regarding the Antichrist and his length of dominance, introduced by the Jesuits at the close of the sixteenth century, simply drove vigorous Protestant expositors to a closer study and sounder exposition of prophecy— except for that small but growing number who were taken in by their plausible schemes. Then came the second attack on the millennium. Whitby placed it in the future, but *before* the second advent, and likewise spiritualized the resurrection. So now there were three millennial views struggling for position— the Catholic Augustinian teaching, the restored premillennial view, and finally the new popular Whitbyan postmillennial

EXPOSITORS ON REVELATION (For Daniel See Preceding Opening)

Rev. 11			Rev. 12			Rev. 13				Rev. 16	Rev. 17			Rev. 20
2 Witnesses	1260 Dys	10th of City	Woman	Dragon	1260 Dys 3½ Times	1st Beast	42 Months	2d Beast	666	7 Vials	Harlot	Babylon	7th Head	1000 Yrs
Years / Years			Church	Pagan R.	Years / Years	Papacy / Papacy / Civil R.	Yr-Dys / Yr-Dys / Yr-Dys	Papacy / Papacy	Lateinos	Falling	Papacy / Papacy	Papacy / Papacy	Popes / Pope	August. / August. / Pre-Mill.
Church	396-1656 / Cross-1666	France	Church / Church	Pagan R. / Pagan R. / Pagan R.	396-1656	Papacy / Papacy / Papacy	396-1656 / -1866 / 1260 Yrs	Prot. Im.		Papacy / (1335 Yrs to End) / End at M.	Papacy			Pre-Mill. / Pre-Mill. / Pre-Mill.
Tr. Worship / Protestants	437-1697 / Just.-c1800 / Years	1 of 10 Kgdms / 1 of 10 Kgdms	True Ch. / True Ch.		437-1697 / Just.-c1800 / Years	Papacy / Papacy / Civil R.	437-1697 / Just.-c1800 / 1260 Yrs	Hierarchy / Papal R.	Romith	Judgments	Papacy	Papacy / Papacy / Papacy	Popes / Pope	Pre-Mill. / (Pre-Mill.) / August.
Papal Era			True Ch.	Pagan R.	Years	Papacy / Pagan R. / Rome	1260 Yrs / 1260 Yrs	Papal R. / Papacy		Vicarius Filii Dei / Lateinos Judgments	Papacy	Papacy / Papacy	Popes	August. / Pre-Mill. / Pre-Mill.
Living / Sylv.-(Yrs)		France	True Ch.	Pagan R.	454-1714	Papacy / Imp. R. / Imp. R.	454-1714 / Papal R. / 1260 Yrs	Eccl. Emp. / Papal R. / Papal R.	Lateinos	Falling / 7th Jdgmt	Papacy	Papacy / Papacy	Papacy / Papacy	Pre-Mill. / Pre-Mill. / August.
Years		France			Years	Papacy / Papacy	Hierarchy / Just.-1794	Lateinos / Lateinos		Falling / 6—Turk	Papacy / Papacy	Papacy / Papacy	Papacy	Pre-Mill. / Pre-Mill. / Post-Mill.
True Church			Church	Pagan R.		Civil R. / W. Rome	476-1736 / 606-1866	Eccl. R. / Greek Emp.	Lateinos / Lateinos	Falling	Papacy / Papacy	Papacy / Lat. Kgdm / Papacy		Pre-Mill. / (Pre-Mill.) / (Pre-Mill.)
Years / 606-1866		1 of 10 Kgdms / (2300 Yrs to End)		Pagan R.	Years	R. Emp. / Papacy / Papacy	445-1715 / Years / 606-1866	Popes	Lateinos	Judgments / Future		Papacy / Papacy		(Pre-Mill.) / (Pre-Mill.) / (Pre-Mill.)
Years / Years		France	Church	Pagan R.	Years / -1836 / Years	Papacy / Papacy / Papacy	533 or 606 / -1836	R. Clergy / East. Emp.		Future	Pap. R.	Papacy / Papacy / Papacy		Pre-Mill. / Pre-Mill. / Pre-Mill.
587-1847			Church / Church		864-1521 / 587-1847 / 620-1880	Papacy / Papacy / Papacy	1058-1830 / 587-1847	Jesuitism / Papacy / East. Emp.	Years	Future	Papacy	Papacy / (Papacy)		Post-Mill. / Pre-Mill. / Pre-Mill.
In France / 445-1705		France / France / France		Pagan R.	445-1705 / 529-1789	Papacy / (Papacy) / Papacy	Papacy / 529-1789	Louis XIV	Ludovicus	Judgments	Papacy / Papacy / Papacy	Papacy / Papacy / Papacy	Papacy	(Pre-Mill.) / Pre-Mill. / (Pre-Mill.)
538-1798					538-1798 / 538-1798	Papacy / Papacy	538-1798 / 538-1798			Falling	Papacy / Papacy	Papacy / Papacy		(Pre-Mill.) / (Pre-Mill.)
O.T., N.T. / 606-			True Ch.	Pagan R.	—	Papacy / Papacy	606-	France			Papacy / Papacy	Papacy / Papacy		(Pre-Mill.) / Pre-Mill.

innovation, which was adopted by a growing section of Protestantism.

Two special time features should be closely noted:

1. The gradual clarification of the problem of the 2300 evening-mornings. From the time of Arnold of Villanova (1297) onward, but particularly from Nicolas Krebs of Cusa (1440), the year-day character of the period was gradually established, in harmony with all other time prophecy. At first no better clue to its timing was had than from the time of the vision, at the very beginning of Persian dominance. Meantime, clarification came on the exact timing of the 70 weeks from the seventh of Artaxerxes, in 457 B.C. This position was advanced in various lands.

Finally Tillinghast, in 1654, saw that there was a definite connection between the 70 weeks and the 2300 days. Beverley and others sensed that the larger period dated from Persia. But Petri of Germany (1762) was the first to declare that they begin together, which concept was to mean so much to expositors of the nineteenth century, as will be seen in Volumes III and IV.

2. Throughout the century prior to the French Revolution,

France's key place as the "tenth part" of the great papal "city," Babylon, to fall away from the support of Rome and end the papal dominance, became an increasingly common conviction. And the last decade of the eighteenth century was the time for which men watched, and awaited the events forecast. The climax came when the captivity of the pope, in 1798, was recognized as fulfilling the prophetic specifications of the deadly wound by the sword, but which was destined to be fully healed.

The majestic outline of Daniel 7—the four world powers of Babylonia, Medo-Persia, Grecia, and Rome, the ten divisions of the fourth, or Roman, empire, the upspringing of the Papacy among the permanent divisions of Rome, with its persecution of the saints, its attempts upon the appointed times and laws of God, and its blasphemous assumption of titles and prerogatives of God—was now all seen in sharp perspective. Daniel 7 was almost entirely fulfilled. Only the final judgment scenes remained, which were destined soon to become the new focal point of interest and concern—and in definite connection with the specifications of Daniel 8:14, and its cleansing of the sanctuary, whatever that might mean.

To this survey should be added the American evidence, appearing in Volume III, pages 252, 253. Then the entire expositional picture for the seventeenth and eighteenth centuries, Old World and New, will be before us. The comparisons and contrasts are interesting. But the fundamental emphasis is identical —the historical sequence of empire, the Antichrist Little Horn, and the year-day nature of all time periods. The same progressive unfolding and the same correction of minor inaccuracies obtain—the same earnest effort to place the 1260-, 1290-, 1335-, and 2300-year periods for Daniel, and the attempt to find the relationship between the 70 weeks and the 2300 years, and between the 1335 and the 2300. The correspondence over the trumpets is impressive in the Revelation, with Pre-Millennialism—and all that it implies and involves—as another common denominator.

II. Conclusions Deducible From Volume II

In evaluating the evidence assembled in Volume II we may therefore logically conclude that the two major points of emphasis in prophetic interpretation, which stand out predominantly in the period covered, are (1) the well-nigh universal identification of the Papacy as Antichrist, and (2) the allotted time, chronology, and recognized close of its special prophetic period—and all in relation to the divine plan of the ages.

The church of the early centuries looked simply for an individual Antichrist, to whose exploits a literal three and a half years was then most naturally and logically assigned. To these early Christians all future time was foreshortened, because they expected the end of the age to come soon. Although their view reached beyond the actual breakup of Rome, it was circumscribed by the fact that Antichrist had not yet developed historically, and so could not possibly be identified in advance with certainty.

In later centuries the conviction developed that the Antichrist of prophecy was an extended system of organized apostasy, already long established within the church. As the centuries passed and the corruptions in the dominant church became more and more evident, the cry was increasingly raised that the various prophetic symbols of Antichrist—the Little Horn, Beast, Babylon, Harlot, Man of Sin, Mystery of Iniquity, and so forth —fitted Romanism just as a custom-made shoe fits the foot.

The sequence, the timing, and the character of the papal Little Horn seemed inescapable. First, Rome *had* come as the fourth prophetic empire; next, Rome's breakup *had* followed; and then, after Rome's partitioning, the Antichrist, or Little Horn, *had* appeared, pushing its way up through these permanent divisions of Roman territory and meeting all the specifications predicted. The logic of the reasoning seemed invulnerable. So it came to be commonly recognized that the concurrent "1260 days," assigned for Antichrist's special exploits, were obviously in *prophetic or symbolic time,* as verily as the other specifications of the Antichrist were symbolic. Understood in this way, the time feature became clear and consistent, and the conclusion inescapable.

It is likewise to be noted that all the great time periods of prophecy have been progressively discerned. They have always been recognized during the process of contemporary fulfillment. Thus, as noted in Volume I, the 70 weeks were seen by the Jews, writing in the third century before Christ, to be weeks of years. And it is known that there was widespread expectancy of the Messiah about the time of Jesus. In fact, Jesus Himself came saying, "The time is fulfilled," with the acknowledged fulfillment appearing in His own life and death.

In the early centuries of the Christian Era the 1260 days were believed to center on the still future Antichrist. But until its actual appearance, and the long extent of its duration came to be recognized, the year-day principle was not extended to include this period. From Joachim (1190) onward, however, the 1260 prophetic days, as symbolizing years, were increasingly recognized by Jew as well as Christian, and by Catholic and non-Catholic alike. And beginning with Arnold of Villanova (1297), Walter Brute (1393), and Nicolas Krebs of Cusa (1440), the 1290, 1335, and 2300 days of Daniel were similarly seen to represent years.

With the Reformation came the full chorus of Protestant voices, hundreds strong, declaring the contemporary fulfillment of prophetic symbolism in the Papacy. Although some made supplemental application of one or two of the prophecies to the Turks, and there was a variety of timing in the attempt to locate the 1260 years, the unanimity of conviction concerning this rapidly expiring segment in the career of the Papacy was most significant.

During the Reformation and post-Reformation periods, the predominant Historical School system of prophetic interpretation took on impressive proportions, based on the accepted fulfillment of the anticipations of earlier times—the historical interpretation of the symbolic prophecies, and the year-day time periods—with the Papacy fitting inescapably into the continuous sequence of unfolding history. That sequence was not only historical but logical and inexorable—the four empires *without a break between them;* the disintegration of the Roman fourth empire, *likewise without a gap* following Rome; and then the appearance, among the still shifting fragments, of the Little Horn Antichrist in the early Middle Ages, *similarly without a parenthesis,* or blank space, intervening after Rome's breakup.

It was the Jesuit countersystems of Futurism and Preterism that deliberately injected the scheme of a great gap of centuries, for the obvious purpose of shielding the Papacy from uncomfortable scrutiny and censure, by shifting the application to the remote future or the distant past. The obvious inconsistencies of these two systems have been duly noted. Protestants did not at first accept these Catholic counterinterpretations. Nevertheless, the device succeeded to an unanticipated degree, and confusion ensued.

Meanwhile, the focal point of prophetic emphasis shifted to the closing date of the 1260-year period. Many had searched back to earlier times, seeking to assign the beginning of the era of the Little Horn to some point in the fifth, sixth, or seventh centuries. Now many began to look forward, endeavoring to compute the approaching end of the 1260 years. The story has been unfolded of how a sizeable number proclaimed the ending of the time in the aftermath of the French Revolution, and declared the capture of the pope in 1798 the exact counterpart of the prophetic demand. Clearly another epoch had been fulfilled in the sweep of prophecy, and was contemporarily recognized and declared.

III. Main Features Established, Not Variant Details

Emphasis upon the obvious soundness of the main positions of the Historical School of interpretation should not be construed as commendation of the many conflicting and often incongruous details of various expositions. Rather, endorsement is confined to those basic features only—those clear, major aspects upon which there was unity. These positions have been established by the cumulative testimony of the reverent scholarship of the centuries. Not only were they clearly recognized during the course of fulfillment, but they have since been confirmed by the passage of time and the clarifying perspective of the years.

These various mountain peaks of unified exposition, which stand out in overtowering prominence, and are generally recognized as established, bear the attesting stamp of demonstrated soundness. Mark it: These conclusions were reached progressively—first in anticipation, then in contemporary recognition, and finally in the retrospective conviction that the historical counterpart had clearly matched the inspired prediction. Subordinate details were realigned and corrected. Earlier inaccuracies on lesser features were superseded by sounder positions.

Moreover, the chronological placement of the great time periods was clarified and certified by obvious fulfillment. When the beginning and the close of a prophetic period are seen in historical perspective, and are found to be in perfect correspondence and in harmony with the facts, then the soundness of the application may be regarded as checked and certified. Thus with the 70 weeks of years, the close of which involved the death of Christ in the seventieth week of years. The same is true with the special 1260-year era assigned by the Almighty to the course of the papal Little Horn, obviously stretching from Justinian on to the deadly wound that followed as the aftermath of the French Revolution. The consensus of competent, reverent scholarship may then be well conceded as having established the soundness of the exposition. Such essentials form the heart and essence of prophetic interpretation.

IV. Epilogue

With this section we bring this volume to a close. The two towering mountain peaks of supreme historical interest and concern that we have passed in our journey from the Renaissance onward, across the centuries, are: first, that mighty religious awakening, or revolt, known as the Protestant Reformation of the sixteenth century; and second, that epochal turning point in modern history, the French Revolution at the close of the eighteenth century. The great historical importance of these two intriguing events is universally recognized. But they are of even greater significance and concern to the student of prophecy. From the wealth of source materials treated in this volume —which might at times seem bewildering—two vital facts have emerged, which are of greatest importance to our quest.

1. THE REFORMATION POSITION ON ANTICHRIST.—We have seen the remarkable unanimity of belief of Reformation leaders in every land that the Antichrist of prophecy is not to be a single individual—some sort of superman—who will wrack and wellnigh wreck the world just before the second advent of Christ. Instead, they found that it was a vast system of apostasy, or rather, an imposing counterfeit of truth which had developed within the jurisdiction of that divinely appointed custodian of truth, the Christian church. Although ostensibly proclaiming the principles of Christianity, it denied the very essence of Christian faith—the apostolic spirit of truth, freedom, tolerance, and love—and perverted the very doctrine of Christ. Of this they were profoundly persuaded. This Antichristian system, which had developed within the inner precincts of the church, the Protestants declared to be the Papacy of history, in fulfillment of prophecy. Such was the unanimous witness of the Reformation. That was the basic emphasis of the Reformation century.

The corollary was inseparably attached thereto: Protestantism recognized with ever-increasing clarity the paralleling fact that a definite time period had been marked out in the counsels of the Almighty for the career of this great antichristian system of prophecy, during which it would develop, reach the climax of its power, and do certain exploits, as well as come to its greatest humiliation. This prophesied period was depicted as three and a half prophetic "times," or forty-two prophetic "months," or 1260 prophetic "days," which are repeatedly portrayed in both Daniel and the Apocalypse, but which are actual years in fulfillment according to the clear year-day principle. These are accepted as established through the universally acknowledged interpretation of the 70 weeks of years, and applied to most of the other time prophecies. This 1260-year period of the apostate power became increasingly the object of inquiry, to ascertain when it began and therefore when it would end.

This system of interpretation was vigorously challenged at its height by two Catholic attempts to parry the application of the symbols to the Papacy. The Jesuits Ribera and Bellarmine sought to substitute for the Protestant Historical School of interpretation the countering Futurist School of speculative literalism, which leads to extravagant supposition and fanciful conjecture. But prophecy that is written in symbolic language must be symbolically explained. And it follows with inescapable logic that time features thrust in among such symbols must similarly have symbolic time values.

The Jesuit Alcazar's Preterist School of interpretation—the other defensive system—was likewise found to be wholly unsatisfactory, because its interpretation of virtually all these symbolic events as already fulfilled in the early history of the church cannot be upheld except by straining beyond measure either the events or the text. Therefore the Historical School explanation, with its long-range view and consistency in both outline and time prophecy, is obviously the most reasonable, sound, and satisfactory. This was the second high point which came to light in the study of the prophetic faith of our Protestant forefathers. Practically all stood on the sound platform of Historical interpretation.

2. French Revolution a Turning Point.—True, the Protestant Historicists differed considerably as to when to begin and when to end the 1260-day period of Antichrist, but they were all united in the conviction that a period of 1260 years had been allotted to him, and that it was drawing toward its

close. The precise location of the period could scarcely be determined with accuracy until the closing event took place. This is one of the clear characteristics of prophecy—that history is the true and final interpreter of prophecy. The farther we proceed across the stretching years, the greater the number of voices we hear expecting extraordinary events to happen in connection with the close of the eighteenth century, or the beginning of the nineteenth, and which would profoundly affect the Papacy. When the thundering storm of the French Revolution actually broke, it was commonly recognized, and clearly pointed out by many in different lands, that this was the long-expected finale of that epoch. It was solemnly declared that the great time period of 1260 year-days was ending; that the Papacy had received a wound which was obviously grave, though not necessarily fatal.

But this very French Revolution upheaval, which gave the predicted stroke by the sword to the Papacy, impressively brought to light a new conception of man. It cut mankind loose from the bondage of ecclesiastical authority, clothed in the awe-inspiring mantle of allegedly divine sanctions. It snapped the fetters of superstition that had held men in constant fear, and which were only too readily forged by the clergy of a system whose aim was to dominate rather than to enlighten and to serve. And if the papal system received a heavy blow in the theological and prophetic fields through the Reformation, it received an even greater stroke in some ways, through the emancipation of reason by the French Revolution. The shackles of superstition were stricken from the wrists and ankles of humanity, and mankind was seemingly delivered out of Catholicism's hand.

Not only was this period remarkable for these emancipating events, but it can be considered a fundamental turning point in modern history in a much broader sense. This may easily be seen from the following facts: Shortly before, during, and after this time, the greatest advances in man's history were made, advances upon which our modern civilization is built—for example, the harnessing of the power of steam (1788-1807), and the first experiments with electric light and power, which have produced the Industrial Revolution that has caused profound changes in all spheres of human thought and activity.

The world had been locked into national and racial compartments, isolated by long-standing hostilities, and sharp limitations in communication and transportation. Now came the great expansion of political, religious, and intellectual freedom which lay at the foundation of all advances. Along with freedom of speech and press came religious revivals and the world-wide missionary enterprise, as great organizations were formed to foster them. These, in turn, were followed by Bible and tract societies. Great reformatory movements and developments followed in educational and in health and temperance lines. That is its larger aspect. The close of the 1260 years was verily the end of the old and the beginning of a new epoch. It changed the trend of history, as will be seen in Volume IV.

So at this turn of the century may be found the beginning of all those far-reaching influences that molded the succeeding century, and which are continuing to operate. But the implications reach not only forward into the future but back into the past. Another discovery was made in that era—the finding of the Rosetta stone in Egypt in 1799, the deciphering of which became the magic key that unlocked the secrets of Biblical archaeology. This not only cleared away many of the mists that had hung like a pall over the early ages of history, but gave us a greater and richer understanding of the Bible and its prophecies. And this, in turn, has provided an antidote for the virus of rationalism projected by the French Revolution.

Such a focusing of vital events, and the bringing forth of new wonders, all having their common beginning around the end of the eighteenth century, indicate beyond peradventure that an old epoch had come to its end and a new era had begun, just as prophecy had predicted. The further specifications of the prophecies, and their contemporary recognition, will be followed through in Volumes III and IV.

ACKNOWLEDGMENTS

IN CARRYING through to completion an enterprise as extensive as this volume in the *Prophetic Faith* set, the competent aid of experts has been imperative at various stages of the project. This has involved collaboration in the investigating, gathering, and translating of the sources, criticism of the completed manuscripts by experts, technical checking of all citations and data, critical copy editing, proofreading, and indexing, and effective illustration and mechanical production. Indebtedness is here expressed to all in these categories who have made possible the completion of Volume II, and specifically to the following:

To F. A. Dörner, of Berlin, Germany, for collaboration in the long quest for the sources in the great Preussische Staatsbibliothek in Berlin, where he joined me, both in 1935 and in 1938, as well as at the Nationalbibliothek of Vienna, in the search for evidence, which was continued in the interim, and up to the outbreak of World War II; to Jean Vuilleumier and Johann Weidner for similar co-operation in the Bibliothèque nationale and Bibliothèque de la société de l'histoire du protestantisme français, in Paris; to Alfred Vaucher for effective aid in the various libraries of Rome, Florence, and Torre Pellice, Italy, and at the Bibliothèque publique et universitaire at Geneva, Switzerland, in which latter institution we were joined by Daniel Walther; and to W. E. Read, R. A. Anderson, and L. W. Normington at the British Museum in London.

Acknowledgment for essential translation help is here made to the late William W. Prescott and Grace Amadon for the Latin, to John F. Huenergardt for German, to Jean Vuilleumier for French, to Erich W. Bethmann for both German and French, and to Theodore De Luca and Edgar Brooks for Spanish.

Gratitude is similarly expressed for valuable criticisms and suggestions from the readers of Volume II, several of whom have lived, studied, and taught in Europe, and whose familiarity with European languages, history, and religion made their critiques of unusual value. These were:

R. A. Anderson, instructor, S.D.A. Theological Seminary.

H. M. Blunden, chairman, International Radio Commission.

L. L. Caviness, professor of Biblical languages, Pacific Union College.

M. L. Neff, book editor, Pacific Press Publishing Association.

F. D. Nichol, editor of *Review and Herald*, Washington, D.C.

R. L. Odom, editor of *Our Times*, Nashville, Tennessee.

George McCready Price, scientist; author, teacher, Loma Linda, California.

H. M. S. Richards, international radio commentator, Los Angeles, California.

W. E. Read, administrator and research investigator, London, England.

D. E. Rebok, president of the S.D.A. Theological Seminary, Washington, D.C.

H. L. Rudy, formerly educational secretary, Northern Europe.

A. W. Spalding, director, social education, Madison College, Tennessee.

W. H. Teesdale, president, Home Study Institute, Washington, D.C.

Daniel Walther, professor of church history, S.D.A. Theological Seminary.

Similar indebtedness is expressed to special readers of major sections of the manuscript, whose expert knowledge in given fields has been a safeguard both to author and reader. These include:

Abraham Shinedling, editorial staff of *International Jewish Encyclopedia*—Jewish writers.

Frank H. Yost, professor of church history, S.D.A. Theological Seminary—pre-Reformation period.

Otto Schuberth, professor of Reformation history and education in Central Europe—Reformation period.

Richard Ruhling, administrator and author from Central Europe—Bohemian expositors.

Jean Vuilleumier, former editor Paris *Les Signes de Temps*—French interpreters.

Special mention is to be made of kind personal interest and help from Raymund Klibansky, formerly professor of medieval philosophy at Heidelberg University, and now of Oriel College, Oxford, on Nicolas Krebs of Cusa; A. I. Ellis, superintendent of the British Museum Library; William W. Rockwell, former librarian of Union Theological Seminary; George Henderson, chief of reading room and stacks in the New York Public Library; Louis Ginzberg, Talmudist, Jewish Theological Seminary of America; Joshua Bloch, head of Jewish Division, New York Public Library; and M. R. Thurber, book editor of the Review and Herald Publishing Association, and his excellent research staff—Julia Neuffer, Edna Howard, and Eunice Rowe.

Gratitude is here expressed to my faithful secretary, Thelma Wellman, for preparing the comprehensive index.

Due acknowledgment is here recorded for vital aid from the great state, national, church, and university libraries, and historical society archives of the Old World and the New, which institutions not only afforded unusual research privileges, but made possible extensive photostat and microfilm copying of materials which form the factual basis of this volume. The uniform courtesies and co-operation extended, together with special opportunities afforded, made the quest both pleasant and fruitful, and expedited the search. An Advent Source Collection of over seven thousand documents was thus made possible for permanent reference and verification. There were numerous other institutions from which individual items were secured, but the libraries most heavily drafted upon for the sources were the following:

Andover Newton Theological Seminary Library, Cambridge, Massachusetts.

R. Biblioteca angelica, Rome, Italy.

Biblioteca apostolica vaticana, Vatican City, Rome, Italy.

Biblioteca nazionale Vittorio Emanuele, Rome, Italy.

R. Biblioteca casanatense, Rome, Italy.

R. Biblioteca nazionale centrale, Florence, Italy.

Bibliothèque de la société de l'histoire du protestantisme, français, Paris, France.

Bibliothèque nationale, Paris, France.

Bibliothèque publique et universitaire, Geneva, Switzerland.

British Museum Library, London, England.

Harvard University Library, Cambridge, Massachusetts.

Bodleian Library, Oxford University, Oxford, England.

Cambridge University Library, Cambridge, England.

Nationalbibliothek, Vienna, Austria.

Preussische Staatsbibliothek, Berlin, Germany.

New York Public Library, New York, N.Y.

Library of Congress, Washington, D.C.

> Rare Books Division.
>
> Union Catalogue Division.
>
> Inter-Library Loan Section (through which single volumes were borrowed for photostats or microfilms from libraries all over the United States).

Union Theological Seminary Library, New York, N.Y.

Bibliothek des Evangelischen Predigerseminars, Wittenberg, Germany.

Trinity College Library, University of Dublin, Dublin, Ireland.

Trinity College Library, University of Glasgow, Glasgow, Scotland.

S.D.A. Theological Seminary Library, Washington, D.C.

Review and Herald Library, Washington, D.C.

Columbia University Library, New York, N.Y.

Wisconsin State Historical Society, Madison, Wisconsin.

University of Nebraska Library, Lincoln, Nebraska.

Henry E. Huntington Library, San Marino, California.

University of Chicago Library, Chicago, Illinois.

John Carter Brown Library, Providence, Rhode Island.

Appendices

APPENDIX "A"

Fundamental Fallacies of Futurist System

Because of the far-reaching implications and later effects of Futurism, we here list the fundamental weaknesses of this Jesuit counterinterpretation.

1. DESIGNED TO RELIEVE PRESSURE ON ROME.—Ribera's and Bellarmine's Futurism was deliberately designed to *counter* the interpretation not only of virtually all Protestants but likewise of that large group of pious Spirituals within Catholicism's own ranks whose application of the prophetic symbols concerning Antichrist pressed uncomfortably upon the papal hierarchy. Futurism was an expedient designed to relieve that pressure and to divert the application of Antichrist from the papal system. Protestant writers had pressed fulfillment in the Papacy with unbearable logic. So recourse was had by the Jesuits to ridicule, play upon words, and clever turning of phrases in an attempt to confuse the issue and win the case. That is a questionable basis of exposition.

2. VIOLATES PRINCIPLE OF CONSISTENT PROPHETIC SYMBOLISM.—Futurism breaks the law of harmonious prophetic symbolism—that all factors in symbolic prophecy must be consistently applied. Thus a symbolic "woman," denominated "mystery" and seated on a seven-headed beast, clearly stands for something different from what the actual words describe. It is true that not all Apocalyptic prophecies are symbolic. There is no reason, for example, to consider the recital in Daniel 11 as symbolic prophecy, for here the prophet speaks of kings, battles, and leagues, or of taking cities and conquering countries, not of figurative beasts, horns, and tempests; neither is there any indication that Revelation 20, which speaks of Satan, the saints, the dead, the resurrection, and the nations, means anything but Satan, the saints, the dead, the resurrection, and the nations.

As a rule, there is no difficulty in distinguishing literal from figurative language. Winged lions, composite beasts, multiple heads and horns, winds, waters, and Babylon on her seven hills are all obviously symbols. And even if the prophecy did not in many cases supply the interpretation of the symbols, no one could possibly mistake the figurative nature of the language. But Futurism is based largely on literalism, and literalism, paradoxically enough, leads to grotesque conclusions if applied to symbols. Therefore the impossibility of maintaining a consistent literalism leads to confusion.

If the Futurist admits that a scarlet woman seated on a seven-headed beast is not a woman on a beast, but is a false religious system enthroned

in a seven-hilled city, and supported by the civil power, how can he insist
that the Two Witnesses (identified by the prophecy itself as the two symbolic olive trees) must be literal persons preaching in sackcloth, and lying
unburied in the streets of literal Jerusalem for three and a half literal days,
and demand an extremely unlikely series of varied exploits performed in
a very short time by a future superman Antichrist?

3. MAKES PROPHETIC TIME MEANINGLESS.—As a consequence of confusing the figurative and the literal, Futurism mixes prophetic and literal time.
The three and a half days of the Two Witnesses are admitted by Ribera as
also prefiguring, on the year-day principle, three and a half actual years;
but the prophetic three and a half times, or years, applied to the woman
and the Little Horn (both obviously symbolic figures), he considers simply
literal years. Such confusion is utterly inconsistent and illogical. Anyone
would expect to find literal time in a literal prophecy, but symbolic time
obviously belongs with symbolic prophecy. And whereas Ribera holds to
three and a half years, Bellarmine, whose main assault is upon the year-day
principle, destroys all dependability of prophetic time by making it mean
anything—either days or months, years or millenniums. Confusion is worse
confounded when Ribera makes the Little Horn, with its three and a half
years, refer to a yet future Antichrist, and Bellarmine applies it to Antiochus
Epiphanes, for three and a half years way back in the time of the Maccabees,
thus resurrecting the contention of Porphyry the sophist.

4. REMOVES APPLICATION FROM HISTORICAL VERIFICATION.—Futurism
removes the application from the tangible check of historical fulfillment
where it can be tested, and gets it into the future where necessarily imagina-
tive treatment of predicted but as yet unfulfilled events cannot be checked
against anything solid or historical as a guide. It is therefore without limit
as to speculative possibilities that can scarcely be gainsaid. If literalism
leads to absurdities, futurity of application leads to fantasy.

5. ARBITRARY GAP AN UNJUSTIFIABLE DEVICE.—Futurism makes a great
gap between the events of the early centuries and the last, supposedly brief,
terrific struggle with a personal Antichrist at the end of the age. It violates
the principle of historical progression and unbroken sequence for the outline prophecies of Daniel and Revelation, recognized as established by most
Catholics as well as all Protestants of the time—the four consecutive world
powers, followed by the breakup of the fourth, and these in turn by Antichrist. The absence of any indication in the prophecies to account for such
a gap of centuries leaves as the only adequate reason for the theory the
necessity of parrying the application to the Papacy of the specifications set
by prophecy for that period following the breakup of Rome. So Futurism
deliberately overleaps the centuries of the Middle Ages and seeks to fasten
all eyes on a superman Antichrist at the end of the age.

(This did not convince the Protestants of the post-Reformation era,
for none accepted this device to relieve the pressure on Rome, produced by

inexorable Protestant application. Acceptance by Protestants had to wait until the nineteenth century.)

6. VIEW OF EARLY CHURCH BESIDE THE POINT.—Futurism ignores and repudiates the principle of progressive interpretation built up through fulfillment of prophecy. Futurism insists on clinging to the interpretations of the early church writers of things they expected shortly, but which were not yet fulfilled. In that time all the prophecies beyond the first advent of Christ, the rule of Rome, and its breakup were still in the future. They looked for a future Antichrist at the end of time, for to them the end was imminent. Paul found it necessary to explain to the Thessalonians that a falling away must come first, but he gave no hint as to whether that falling away would be of long or of short duration. John's prophecy, written many years later, probably extended their conception of the time until the consummation of all things; therefore it would never occur to them to interpret the 1260 days as years because, expecting their Lord soon, they could not possibly foresee the stretch of centuries ahead. But, because the early church saw certain prophetic fulfillments as future in their day, it does not therefore follow that more than a thousand or fifteen hundred years later they should still be future. The early church argument of the Futurists is therefore beside the point.

APPENDIX "B"

Inconsistencies and Inadequacies of Preterist System

As with Futurism, the far-reaching effects of Preterism upon the fortunes of Protestantism similarly call for a summarization of its basic weaknesses.

1. AN EXPEDIENT DESIGNED TO SHIELD ROME.—Preterist interpretation, like its Futurist companion, was conceived and brought forth to deflect application of the prophetic symbols concerning Antichrist away from papal Rome. This was attempted by arbitrarily ending the prophetic outline before the Papacy developed into the powerful system that became dominant during the Middle Ages. This is of itself questionable. No exposition deliberately designed to remove a stigma and to divert an uncomfortable application is without suspicion. Sound exegesis is a search for truth, not a deliberate attempt to counter an embarrassing exposition. The motive is wrong, and unavoidably raises question as to its sincerity and soundness.

2. PRETERISM AND FUTURISM CANNOT BOTH BE RIGHT.—Preterism and Futurism present conflicting concepts that are mutually destructive. Obviously, both cannot be right. If Antichrist be Nero, he cannot at the same time be a malign superman yet to come; if he be a pagan Roman emperor of the past, he cannot be a sinister Jew to appear at the end of the age. One contention neutralizes the other, and the one disproves and nullifies the other. The Jesuit apologists for Romanism went too far in projecting *two*

antagonistic solutions, and brought all exposition with which they had to do under grave suspicion.

3. VIOLATES PRINCIPLE OF CONSISTENT SYMBOLISM.—Preterism, like Futurism (already noted), violates the principle of consistent symbolism by denying its obviously symbolic character, and mixing it with literalism.

4. GLORIFIES PAPACY BY IGNORING ACTUALITIES.—Preterism gets rid of the prophetic indictments against papal Rome by applying them to early pagan Rome, then glorifying the church as the benevolent reign of the saints for a thousand years. It thus ignores her unhappy apostasies and corruptions, her arrogant assumptions, and her persecution of dissenters through the long centuries of her dominance. It glosses over the ugly facts by glamorizing the Roman church as the New Jerusalem, which will abide forever. But that theory is taken over bodily from fallacious Augustinian reasoning (treated in Volume I), with its spiritualization of the resurrection, its carnalization of the church, and its throwback of the millennium to the early centuries. It cannot be squared with the facts. The great gulf between the spiritual reign of the saints and the all too earthly rule of the medieval church is obvious.

5. DENIES ELEMENTAL PRINCIPLE OF BIBLE PROPHECY.—Preterism, in ending the seals and trumpets by the fifth or sixth century, neglects the greater period of the church and denies that prophecy is a revelation of the divine plan of all the ages. Yet the panorama of the great conflict between right and wrong, truth and error, Christ and Satan here on earth, carries through to the ultimate triumph of Christ and right, and the deliverance of the saints through the second coming of Christ and the destruction of sinners at the end of the age. It is impossible to eliminate from apocalyptic prophecy the final judgment and the second advent. Preterism substitutes an aborted story of redemption; it presents a stunted picture that ends before the tremendous conflicts of the church actually began.

The seals lead past the vicissitudes of the centuries to the triumph of the saints of God. (Rev. 7:15-17; 8:1.) Preterism leaves the church without a guide through the greater part of her history, and nullifies the very purpose and provisions of prophecy. The prophecies obviously extend past the judgments and calamities on pagan Rome to the finishing of the mystery of God, when the kingdoms of this world become the kingdoms of Christ the Lord—with the attendant resurrection, rewarding of the saints, and destruction of the sinners. (Rev. 11:15-18.) The dominant theme of Revelation is obviously the Christian church, not Judaism. Revelation 18 is clearly a picture of the destruction of spiritual Babylon, not the conversion of paganism.

6. LIKE FUTURISM IT LEAVES AN UNEXPLAINED GAP.—Preterism, then, like Futurism, has a fatal gap. It jumps from the events of the sixth century past the alleged thousand-year reign of the Catholic Church to the final persecution and day of judgment, thus violating the principle of the pro-

gressive sequence of prophecy, with an unexplained gap that leaves the church at large without any prophetic guide.

7. OFFERS NO ADEQUATE FULFILLMENTS.—Preterism places the Two Witnesses back in pagan Rome's day and makes the forty-two months literal time. But it presents no historical evidence of time, place, and events that adequately meets the specifications. It ignores the three and a half days of the Witnesses' death, after they had been slain and were then resurrected. Such vagueness is utterly inadequate. The specifications have to be trimmed, and history juggled to make them fit such a proposal. And if these specifications were fulfilled in early Roman history, then Futurism is wrong; and if Futurism's positions are right, then Preterism is wrong. One neutralizes the other, an indication that both are wrong.

Preterism was obviously an expedient, for it never commended itself to the Roman church as a whole. There have been relatively few Catholic Preterists. That is not the case, however, with Protestantism. Preterist principles have been adopted and adapted by those of rationalistic mind as the easiest way to compass the problem of prophecy, throwing it into the past, where it does not affect life today. It has had a sizable following among rationalists, of which Modernism is the modern counterpart.

This much, however, can be said of both Preterism and Futurism: Despite their defects and their inadequate and inconsistent teachings, they succeeded individually and jointly in their objective—that of splitting and confusing Protestant interpretation, and diverting the incriminating finger of prophecy either to the distant past or to the remote future, away from the uncomfortable facts of papal history throughout the Middle Ages and early modern history. That is the serious side.

APPENDIX "C"

Basic Errors of Whitbyan Postmillennialism

The bold premise of Whitby's revolutionary postmillennial theory discussed in chapter 29—that of the final victory of righteousness over sin through the gradual conversion of the world—was based on the philosophy that man, without any divine interposition, is inherently capable of infinite progress and increasing perfection in this present world. In time this appealing concept so captivated a large section of the Protestant church that we here analyze its fallacies and list its fundamental errors:

1. FLOUTS EXPRESS DECLARATION OF TWO RESURRECTIONS.—Whitbyanism boldly denies the explicit assertion of the Apocalypse that there are two resurrections. (Rev. 20:5, 6.) Nevertheless, it actually proceeds upon a spiritualized modification of the two. The fact of two resurrections, one for the righteous and one for the wicked, is borne out by various other declarations of Scripture—such as a resurrection unto "life" (the "better resurrection") for the saints, and a vastly different resurrection for the wicked, unto

"damnation." (John 5:28, 29.) The righteous, according to the Apocalypse, are raised at the beginning of the thousand years, the rest at its close.

2. ILLOGICALLY SPIRITUALIZES THE RESURRECTION.—Whitbyanism holds to the literality of the thousand-year period, or millennium, but arbitrarily and inconsistently spiritualizes the resurrection which introduces it and is therefore an integral part of it—declaring the resurrection to be that of souls dead in sin raised to spiritual life. But that violates consistent and harmonious interpretation—recognizing the over-all period as literal, but making an integral part only figurative. That creates conflict and confusion, and leads to false conclusions. The allegorization of literal prophecy is a wresting of Scripture.

3. HOLDS TO WORLD CONVERSION WITHOUT WARRANT.—Whitbyanism asserts the conversion of all humanity, Jew and Gentile, Christian and pagan, in direct contravention of the uniform testimony of Scripture that two classes will await Christ's coming at the end of the age—the righteous and wicked, wheat and tares, sheep and goats, saints and sinners—with the saints, dead and living, gathered unto Christ at His second advent, and the living wicked destroyed by the brightness of His coming. The theory of the universal triumph of righteousness is contrary to the uniform testimony of Scripture and to all human experience.

4. INTRODUCES MILLENNIUM WITHOUT SECOND ADVENT.—The elimination of the first resurrection of the just at the second coming of Christ (1 Thess. 4:16), introduces the millennium without an antecedent second advent. But the uniform testimony of Scripture and the general expectation of the early church were for a catastrophic end of the age and divine intervention through the second advent, which will be attended by the literal resurrection of the righteous, the destruction of the wicked, and the binding of Satan.

5. DISTORTS TIME AND NATURE OF ADVENT.—Whitbyanism distorts the second coming of Christ by shifting it to the close of the thousand years, instead of marking its beginning, and by denying its express characteristic —that Christ will come personally, visibly, literally, in power and glory, to reign triumphantly with His saints, first throughout the thousand years when Satan is bound, and then after the final destruction of the impenitent wicked at its close, to be with His saints forever.

6. WRONGLY BASED ON CONVERSION OF JEWS.—Whitbyanism builds its thesis around the conversion of the Jews, as part of a first spiritual resurrection, contrary to the express declaration of the Scripture that only spiritual Israel is to realize the promises, and to possess the *New* Jerusalem and the land of the *New* Earth forever. God rejected literal Israel when it rejected His only-begotten Son. So He turned to the Gentiles to constitute His peculiar. people.

Whitby's postmillennial theory of universal righteousness and peace is acknowledged to be but a hypothesis (a supposition, conjecture, assumption, opinion). It is a speculation that has not been borne out by subsequent historical developments. It is a theory without foundation in the Bible, in conflict with the teachings of the apostolic church, and contradictory to the faith of seventeen centuries. It denies all Reformation creeds—that Christ will come in judgment to a world in which both righteous and wicked will still be living.

It contravenes the test of time in the two centuries that have ensued—as witness the first and second world wars, which breakdowns of civilization have shaken the theory of progressive world conversion to its very foundation. By 1914 the majority of intellectuals had subscribed to the idea that the world was gradually progressing upward, as a result either of the force of evolution or of the mysterious workings of God's Spirit. But that concept crashed with World War I. And the final blow, for those who still hoped through, was delivered by World War II and the horrors of the atomic age.

The fundamental difference is between the concept of man getting worse, and God having to step in and end the world and create a new earth, and that of man getting better and better, and finally building his own new earth, and thus achieving perfection. The developments of today overthrow the second idea.

Bibliography

This list does not include works alluded to, and often named, but not cited in the text. It is virtually confined to those works for which specific credit appears in the footnotes. Because of the extraordinarily large number of sources and authorities listed in the Bibliography, book and periodical titles are not repeated in the Index. Page references to the works cited appear in bold type in the Bibliography in connection with each item. As sources predominate, the relatively few authorities have not been segregated—the publishing dates serving to distinguish them. Periodicals, manuscripts, and documents are listed separately.

BOOKS

Abravanel, Isaac. *Sefer Mayene Hayeshuah*. Stettin, 1860. **See pp. 227-231.**

Adam, Melchior. *Vitae Germanorum Theologorum*. Francofurti: Sumptibus Jonae Rosae Viduae, 1653. **See p. 154.**

Adolphus, John. *The History of France, From the Year 1790 to the Peace Concluded at Amiens in 1802*. London: George Kearsley, 1803. 2 vols. **See p. 782.**

Albiruni. *The Chronology of Ancient Nations*. Translated and edited by Dr. C. Edward Sachau. London: William H. Allen and Co., 1879. **See pp. 196, 197, 201.**

Alcazar, Luis de. *Rev. Patris Ludovici ab Alcasar . . . Vestigatio Arcani Sensus in Apocalypsi*. Antverpiae: Apud Ioannem Keerbergium, 1614. **See pp. 494, 507-509.**

Alcock, Thomas. *A Sermon on the Late Earthquakes, More Particularly That at Lisbon*. Oxford: Richard Clements, 1756. **See p. 676.**

Alford, Henry, editor. *The New Testament for English Readers*. See Bible, English. 1872.

Alison, Archibald. *History of Europe From the Commencement of the French Revolution in 1789 to the Restoration of the Bourbons in 1815*. Edinburgh: William Blackwood and Sons, 1835-42. 10 vols. **See pp. 732, 738, 740, 750, 753.**

Allgemeine Deutsche Biographie. Edited by R. V. Liliencron. Leipzig: Duncker & Humblot, 1875-1912. 56 vols. **See pp. 295, 296, 304, 326, 600, 601, 603, 613.**

Alsted, Johann Heinrich. *Theologia Prophetica*. Hanoviae: Sumptibus Conradi Eifridi, 1622. **See pp. 610, 611.**

Amsdorf, Nicolaus. *Fünff fürnemliche und gewisse Zeichen aus göttlicher heiliger Schrifft, so kurtz vor dem Jüngsten tag geschehen sollen*. Jena: Rödinger, 1554. **See pp. 305, 306.**

Amyraut, Moyse. *Du règne de mille ans, ou de la prospérité de l'Eglise*. Saumur: Isaac Desbordes, 1654. **See pp. 633, 634.**

Andrews, Charles M. *The Historical Development of Modern Europe, From the Congress of Vienna to the Present Time*. 2d ed. London and New York: G. P. Putnam's Sons, 1899, '98. 2 vols. **See p. 786.**

Archer, Henry, *The Personall Reign of Christ Upon Earth. In a Treatise Wherein Is Fully and Largely Laid Open and Proved, That Jesus Christ, Together With the Saints, Shall Visibly Possesse a Monarchicall State and Kingdome in This World.* London: Benjamen Allen, 1642. [Catalogued by the British Museum as John Archer.] **See p. 568.**

Aretius, Benedictus. *Commentarii in Apocalypsin.* Morgiis: Ioannes le Preux, 1581. **See p. 348.**

Auberlen, Carl August. *The Prophecies of Daniel and the Revelations of St. John.* Translated by Rev. Adolph Saphir. Edinburgh: T. & T. Clark, 1856. **See pp. 707, 708, 710.**

Aufrichtiges Bedencken über Herrn Georg Herman Giblehrs . . . erfundenen warhafftigen Terminum, oder eigentliche Zeit des letzten und Jüngsten Gerichts. Durch einen Liebhaber Schrifft-gemässer Philadelphischen Kern-Lehren. Erffurt: Joh. Christoph Stössel, 1702. **See p. 701.**

Aulard, [François Victor] A[lphonse]. *The French Revolution, a Political History (1789-1804).* Translated from the French of the 3d ed. . . . by Bernard Miall. New York: Charles Scribner's Sons, 1910. 4 vols. **See pp. 734, 739.**

Ault, Warren O. *Europe in the Middle Ages.* Rev. ed. Boston: D. C. Heath and Company, 1946. **See pp. 17, 21, 45, 46, 63, 66, 128.**

The Babylonian Talmud: Seder Nezikim, Sanhedrin, vol. 2 [Vol. 6], translated into English. Edited by I[sidore] Epstein. London: The Soncino Press, 1935. **See p. 191.**

Der babylonische Talmud. Vol. 7. Edited by Lazarus Goldschmidt. Berlin: S. Calvary & Co., 1903. **See p. 195.**

Bain, Robert Nisbet, and Roman Dyboski. "Poland: The Reformation to the Partitions," *Encyclopaedia Britannica,* vol. 18, pp. 132-137. **See p. 433.**

Baird, Henry M. *History of the Rise of the Huguenots of France.* New York: Charles Scribner's Sons, 1879. 2 vols. **See p. 623.**

————. *The Huguenots and Henry of Navarre.* New York: C. Scribner's Sons, 1886. 2 vols. **See p. 623.**

————. *The Huguenots and the Revocation of the Edict of Nantes.* New York: Charles Scribner's Sons, 1895. 2 vols. **See pp. 625, 626, 634, 635.**

Bale, John. *A Brefe Chronycle Concernyne the Examynacyon and Death of the Blessed Martyr of Christ Syr Johan Oldecastell the Lorde Cobham.* London: C. Davis, 1729. **See pp. 89, 90.**

————. *Select Works of John Bale, D. D., Bishop of Ossory. Containing the Examinations of Lord Cobham, William Thorpe, and Anne Askewe, and The Image of Both Churches.* Edited for the Parker Society by the Rev. Henry Christmas. Cambridge: The University Press, 1849. **See pp. 395-401.**

Barnes, [Robert]. *Workes of Doctour Barnes,* in *The Whole Workes of W. Tyndall, Iohn Frith and Doct. Barnes,* pp. 183 to 376 (second pagination). London: Ioan Daye, 1572 [i.e. 3]. **See pp. 360, 361.**

Baronius, Caesar. *Annales Ecclesiastici.* Coloniae Agrippinae: Sumptibus Ioannis Gymnici & Antonij Hierati, 1609-13. 12 vols. **See p. 504.**

Barry, William [Francis]. *The Papal Monarchy From St. Gregory the Great to Boniface VIII (590-1303).* New York: G. P. Putnam's Sons, 1902. **See p. 764.**

Bartolocci, Giulio. . . . *Bibliotheca Magna Rabbinica.* Romae: Ex Typographia Sacrae Congregationis de Propaganda Fide, 1675-93. 4 vols. See p. 195.

Baudrillart, Alfred. *The Catholic Church, the Renaissance and Protestantism.* Translated by Mrs. Philip Gibbs. London: Kegan Paul, Trench, Trübner & Co., Ltd., 1908. See p. 479.

—————, editor. *Dictionnaire d'histoire et de géographie ecclésiastiques.* Paris: Letouzey et Ané, 1912-. See p. 507.

Becon, Thomas. [*Works of Thomas Becon.* Vol. 1:] *The Early Works of Thomas Becon* [etc.]; [vol. 2:] *The Catechism of Thomas Becon . . . With Other Pieces;* [vol. 3:] *Prayers and Other Pieces of Thomas Becon.* Edited for the Parker Society by John Ayre. Cambridge: The University Press, 1843-44. See pp. 402, 403.

Bell, Arthur G. and Mrs. Arthur G. [Nancy]. *Nuremberg.* Painted by Arthur G. Bell; described by Mrs. Arthur G. Bell. London: Adam and Charles Black, 1905. See pp. 293, 295.

Bellarmine, Robert. *Disputationes Roberti Bellarmini . . . de Controversiis Christianae Fidei, Adversus Huius Temporis Haereticos.* Cologne: Anton & Arnold Hieratorus Brothers, 1628. 4 vols. in 2. See pp. 494-502.

Bengel, Johann Albrecht. *Dr. Johann Albrecht Bengels . . . Gnomon oder Zeiger des Neuen Testaments,* vol. 2. Edited by C. F. Werner. Ludwigsburg: Ferd. Riehm, 1860. See p. 709.

—————. *Erklärte Offenbarung Johannis oder vielmehr Jesu Christi.* Stuttgart: Fr. Brodhag, 1834. See pp. 441, 709-712.

—————. *Gnomon of the New Testament.* Translated, revised, and edited by Andrew R. Fausset and others. Edinburgh: T. & T. Clark, 1877. 4 vols. in 3. See p. 711.

—————. *Das Neue Testament.* See Bible, German. 1753.

—————. *Schrifftmäszige Zeit-Rechnung.* Tübingen: Johann Georg Cotta, 1747. See p. 712.

—————. *Sechzig erbauliche Reden über die Offenbarung Johannis oder vielmehr Jesu Christi.* New ed. Stuttgart: Evangelische Bücherstiftung, 1870. See pp. 710, 712.

Berlenburger Bibel. See Bible, German. 1726-39.

Bernard, Nicholas. *Certain Discourses, Viz. Of Babylon (Rev. 18.4.) Being the Present See of Rome.* London: John Crook, 1659. See pp. 561, 562.

Berthier, Alexandre. See France, Official Bills and Circulars, in section on Documents.

Bertrand, [l'Abbé] I[sidore]. *Le Pontificat de Pie VI et l'athéisme révolutionnaire.* Par l'abbé I. Bertrand avec la collaboration de M. le Chanoine Sauret, . . . et de M. l'abbé Clerc-Jacquier. Bar-le-Duc: Imp. de Bertrand, 1879. 2 vols. See pp. 750, 755.

B[everley], T[homas]. *An Appeal Most Humble, Yet Most Earnestly, by the Coming of Our Lord Jesus Christ, and Our Gathering Together Unto Him.* London: John Salusbury, 1691. [Author identified in Library of Congress catalogue.] See p. 582.

—————. *The Catechism of the Kingdom of Our Lord Jesus Christ in the Thousand Years,* [etc.]. London, 1690. See p. 582.

[————]. *The Command of God to His People to Come Out of Babylon, Revel. 18.4. Demonstrated to Mean the Coming Out of the Present Papal Rome.* 1688. [Author identified in the British Museum catalogue.] **See p. 581.**

————. *Herrn Thomas Beverley's . . . Zeit-Register.* Translated [from his *Scripture-Line of Time*] by Konrad Brüssken. Franckfurt und Leipzig: Georg Henrich Oehrling, 1695. **See p. 582.**

————. *The Kingdom of Jesus Christ Entering Its Succession at 1697. According to a Calendar of Time.* [n.p.: n.n.], 1689. **See p. 581.**

————. *The Pattern of the Divine Temple.* London: John Salusbury, [1689/90]. **See p. 581.**

————. *The Prophetical History of the Reformation; or the Reformation to Be Reformed; in That Great Re-Reformation: That Is to Be 1697.* [n.p.: n.n.], 1689. **See pp. 581, 582.**

————. *A Scripture-Line of Time, Drawn in Brief From the Lapsed Creation to the Restitution of All Things.* [n.p.: n.n.], 1684. **See pp. 582-586.**

————. *The Universal Christian Doctrine of the Day of Judgment: Applied to the Doctrine of the Thousand Years Kingdom of Christ.* London: [n.n.], 1691. **See p. 582.**

Bezold, Friedrich von. *Geschichte der deutschen Reformation.* Berlin: G. Grote'sche Verlags-Buchhandlung, 1890. (In Wilhelm Oncken, *Allgemeine Geschichte in Einzeldarstellungen.*) **See pp. 154-156.**

Bible, English.

1601. *The Text of the New Testament of Iesus Christ* [Rheims and Bishops' versions parallel, with refutation of the Rheims notes]. Edited by W[illiam] Fulke. London: Robert Barker, 1601. **See p. 550.**

1609-10. *The Holie Bible Faithfully Translated Into English, Out of the Authentical Latin.* [Douay-Rheims.] Doway: Lavrence Kellam, 1609-10. 2 vols. **See pp. 549, 550.**

1701. *The Holy Bible.* [Authorized Version.] London: Charles Bill, and the Executrix of Thomas Newcomb, 1701. **See p. 429.**

1841. *The English Hexapla, Exhibiting the Six Important English Translations of the New Testament Scriptures.* London: Samuel Bagster and Sons, 1841. **See pp. 52, 447.**

1872. *The New Testament for English Readers: Containing . . . a Critical and Explanatory Commentary,* by Henry Alford. Vol. 2, part 2. London: Rivingtons, 1872. **See p. 488.**

1914. *The Holy Bible Translated From the Latin Vulgate.* [Douay-Rheims.] Philadelphia: National Publishing Co. (Copyright, 1914, by John Murphy Company.) **See pp. 429, 551, 552.**

Bible, German.

(1534.) 1934-35. *Biblia, das ist, die gantze Heilige Schrifft, Deudsch.* Translated by Martin Luther. [Woodcuts by Hans Lufft.] Wittenberg: [n.n.], 1534. Facsimile reprint, Leipzig, 1934-35. **See pp. 265, 276.**

1726-39. *Die Heilige Schrifft Altes und Neues Testaments . . . Nebst Einiger Erklärung des buchstäblichen Sinnes.* [Berlenburg Bible.] 8 vols. folio. Berlenburg: [n.n.], 1726-39. **See pp. 703-705.**

1753. Bengel. *Das Neue Testament nach dem revidierten Grund text über-setzt und mit dienlichen Anmerkungen begleitet von Johann Albrecht Bengel.* Stutgart: Johann Benedict Metzler, 1753. **See p. 712.**

Bible, Greek.

1570. *Novum Testamentum Iesu Christi Filii Dei, ex versione Erasmi . . .* [with] *Glossa Compendiaria M. Matthiae Flacij Illyrici.* Basileae: Per Petrum Pernam et Theobaldum Dietrich, 1570. **See p. 318.**

Bible, Hebrew.

1724-27. *Sefer Kehilloth Mosheh.* Edited by Moses Frankfurt. Amsterdam, 1724-27. 4 vols. **See pp. 200, 201, 210, 212, 213, 218.**

1860-1902. *Mikraoth Gedoloth im Lamed Beth Perushim.* Warsaw, 1860-1902. 11 vols. **See pp. 192, 200, 201, 210-213.**

1899-1923. *Nebiim Ukethubim im Perush Rashi Uperush Mikrae Kodesh Cha-Rav Meir Loeb Malbim.* Wilna: Romm, 1899-1923. 12 vols. in 11. **See p. 210.**

Bibliander, Theodor. *Ad Omnium Ordinum Reip[ublicae] Christianae Principes Viros, Populumque Christianum, Relatio Fidelis.* Basileae: Ex Officina J. Oporini, 1545. **See pp. 338, 339.**

————. *Temporum a Condito Mundo Usque ad Ultimam Ipsius Aetatem Supputatio.* Basileae: Per Ioannem Oporinum, 1558. **See p. 339.**

Bicheno, James. *The Signs of the Times, in Three Parts. A New Edition With . . . an Appendix, Containing Thoughts on the Fall of the Papal Government; . . . With a Symbolical Vocabulary, for the Illustration of the Prophetic Style.* London: [n.n.], 1799. **See pp. 747, 748.**

Birnbaum, Philip, editor. *The Arabic Commentary of Yefet ben Ali the Karaite on the Book of Hosea.* Philadelphia: The Dropsie College for Hebrew and Cognate Learning, 1942. **See pp. 196, 206, 212.**

Blair, John. *The Chronology and History of the World.* London: [n.n.], 1768. **See p. 431.**

Blunt, John Henry, editor. *Dictionary of Sects, Heresies, Ecclessiastical Parties, and Schools of Religious Thought.* Philadelphia: J. B. Lippincott & Co., 1874. **See p. 705.**

Böhmer, Heinrich. *Luther in Light of Recent Research.* Translated by Carl F. Huth, Jr. New York: The Christian Herald, 1916. **See pp. 248, 261, 263, 278.**

Bossuet, Jacques-Bénigne. *L'Apocalypse avec une explication.* Paris: Sebastien Marbre-Cramoisy, 1690. **See p. 636.**

Bourignon, Antoinette. *L'Antéchrist découvert.* Amsterdam: Jean Rieuverts & Pierre Arents, 1681. **See p. 635.**

————. *L'appel de Dieu et le refus des hommes.* Amsterdam: Jean Riewerts & Pierre Arents, 1682. **See p. 636.**

Bradford, John. *The Writings of John Bradford.* [Vol. 1:] *Sermons, Meditations, Examinations;* [vol. 2:] *Letters, Treatises, and Remains.* Edited for the Parker Society by Aubrey Townsend. Cambridge: The University Press, 1848, 1853. 2 vols. **See pp. 376-380.**

Brandes, Friedrich. *John Knox, der Reformator Schottlands.* Elberfeld: R. L. Friderichs, 1862. **See pp. 447, 455.**

Bridget, Saint [of Sweden]. *Leben und Offenbarungen der heiligen Brigitta*. 2d ed. Revised, translated, and edited by Ludwig Clarus. Regensburg: G. T. Manz, 1888. 2 vols. in 1. (*Sammlung der vorzüglichsten Mystischen Schriften aller katholischen Völker*, vol. 10.) See p. 69.

Brightman, Thomas. *The Workes of That Famous, Reverend, and Learned Divine, Mr. Tho: Brightman*. London: Printed by John Field for Samuel Cartwright, 1644. See pp. 512-518.

Brigitta. See Bridget, Saint [of Sweden].

British and Foreign Bible Society. *Historical Catalogue of the Printed Editions of Holy Scripture*. London: The Bible House, 1903-11. 2 vols. in 4. See pp. 266, 429.

Brocard, James. *The Revelation of S. Iohn Reveled. Englished by Iames Sanford*. London: Thomas Marshe, 1582. See p. 348.

Broughton, Hugh. *Daniel With a Brief Explication*. Hanaw: Daniel Aubri, 1607. See p. 565.

————. *A Revelation of the Holy Apocalyps*. [London], 1610. See p. 565.

Brown, P. Hume. *John Knox, A Biography*. London: Adam and Charles Black, 1895. 2 vols. See pp. 445-447, 449.

Broydé, I. "Ben Meïr," *The Jewish Encyclopedia*, vol. 2, p. 677. See p. 199.

Brüssken, Konrad, translator. *Herrn Thomas Beverley's . . . Zeit-Register* [translated from *A Scripture-Line of Time*]. Franckfurt und Leipzig: Georg Henrich Oehrling, 1695. See p. 582.

Bruno, Joseph Faà di. See Faà di Bruno, Joseph.

Brute, Walter, and others. *Writings and Examinations of Brute, Thorpe, Cobham, Hilton, Pecock, Bilney, and Others; with The Lantern of Light, Written About A. D. 1400*. Philadelphia: Presbyterian Board of Publication, 1842. (*British Reformers* [vol. 1], Wicklif to Bilney.) See pp. 64, 65, 75.

Bryan, Michael. *Dictionary of Painters and Engravers, Biographical and Critical*. Rev. ed. Edited by Walter Armstrong and Edmund Graves. London: George Bell and Sons, 1886, 1889. 2 vols. See p. 313.

Buchan, David Stewart [Erskine], [11th] earl of, and Walter Minto. *An Account of the Life, Writings, and Inventions of John Napier, of Merchiston*. Perth: R. Morison and Son, 1787. See pp. 447, 456.

Buchberger, Michael. *Lexikon für Theologie und Kirche*. Freiburg im Breisgau: Herder & Co., 1930-38. 10 vols. See pp. 302, 308, 316, 521.

Buckley, Theodore Alois. *A History of the Council of Trent*. London: George Routledge and Co., 1852. See p. 475.

Bullinger, Heinrich. *Daniel Sapientissimus Dei Propheta*. Tiguri: C. Froschoverus, 1576. See pp. 344, 345.

————. *The Decades of Henry Bullinger, Minister of the Church of Zurich*. Translated by H. I. Edited for the Parker Society by the Rev. Thomas Harding. Cambridge: The University Press, 1849-52. 5 vols. in 4. See pp. 311, 339, 340, 342, 344.

————. *A Hundred Sermons Upon the Apocalips of Jesu Christe*. English ed. London: Iohn Day, 1561. See pp. 342-344.

Burk, Joh[an]n Christian Friedrich. *A Memoir of the Life and Writings of John Albert Bengel.* Translated by Robert Francis Walker. London: William Ball, 1837. **See pp. 710-712.**

Burnet, Thomas. *The Theory of the Earth.* London: R. Norton, for Walter Kettilby, 1684-90. 2 vols. **See pp. 586-588.**

Cahn, Zvi. *The Rise of the Karaite Sect.* New York: M. Tausner Publishing Co., 1937. **See p. 197.**

Calmet, Augustin. *Dictionarium . . . Sacrae Scripturae.* Translated by J. D. Mansi. Venetiis: Apud Sebastianum Coleti, 1757. **See p. 429.**

Calovius, Abraham. *Biblia Novi Testamenti Illustrata.* Hildburghausen: Balthesar Pensold, 1719. **See p. 616.**

Calvin, Jean. *Commentaries on the Book of the Prophet Daniel.* Translation and dissertations by Thomas Myers. Edinburgh: Printed for the Calvin Translation Society, 1852, 1853. 2 vols. **See pp. 436, 438, 439.**

————. *Commentaries on the Epistles of Paul the Apostle to the . . . Thessalonians.* Translated and edited from the original Latin, and collated with the French version, by the Rev. John Pringle. Edinburgh: Printed for the Calvin Translation Society, 1851. **See p. 438.**

————. *Institutes of the Christian Religion.* Translated from the Latin and collated with the author's last edition in French by John Allen. 7th American ed., rev. Philadelphia: Presbyterian Board of Christian Education, 1936. 2 vols. **See pp. 434, 436-438.**

————. *Tracts Relating to the Reformation.* Translated by H. Beveridge. Edinburgh: The Calvin Translation Society, 1844. 3 vols. **See p. 436.**

The Cambridge Modern History. Edited by A. W. Ward, G. W. Prothero, and Stanley Leathes. New York: The Macmillan Company, 1934. 13 vols. **See pp. 449, 734.**

Cappel, Jacques. *Les livrées de Babel, ou l'histoire du siège romain.* Sedan: Iean Iannon, 1616. **See pp. 631, 632, 648.**

Carlyle, Thomas. *The French Revolution: A History.* With an introduction by C. R. L. Fletcher. Oxford: University Press, 1928. (The World's Classics, vols. 125, 126). 2 vols. **See pp. 731, 734.**

Catalogue of the Newton Papers . . . Which Will Be Sold by Auction by Messrs. Sotheby & Co. [London]: Printed by H. Davy, [1936]. **See p. 660.**

Catechism of the Council of Trent. See Trent, Council of.

The Catholic Encyclopedia. Edited by Charles G. Herbermann and others. New York: Robert Appleton Company, 1907-14. 15 vols. and index. **See pp. 127, 129, 166, 476, 485, 486, 495.**

The Century Cyclopedia of Names. New York: The Century Co., 1906. (*The Century Dictionary and Cyclopedia,* vol. 9.) **See p. 401.**

Certain Sermons. See Church of England.

Chambers, George F. *A Handbook of Descriptive and Practical Astronomy,* vol. 2. Oxford: The Clarendon Press, 1890. **See p. 431.**

Church, R[ichard] W[illiam]. *Essays and Reviews.* London: J. and C. Mozley, 1854. **See p. 22.**

Church of England. *Certain Sermons or Homilies Appointed to Be Read in Churches in the Time of Queen Elizabeth of Famous Memory.* London: Society for Promoting Christian Knowledge, 1890. [Contains also the "Second Tome."] **See pp. 424, 425, 589.**

Chytraeus, David. *Auslegung der Offenbarung Johannis.* Rostock: Jacob Siebenbürger, 1572. **See pp. 330-332.**

Clarke, Adam. *The Holy Bible . . . With a Commentary and Critical Notes by Adam Clarke.* New York: Lane & Scott, 1850, 1851. 6 vols. **See p. 457.**

Cocceius, Johannes. *Johannis Cocceji . . . Opera Omnia Theologica, Exegetica, Didactica, Polemica, Philologica.* Amstelodami: Ex Typographia P. & J. Blaev, 1701. 10 vols. **See pp. 614-616.**

Coleman, Christopher B. *The Treatise of Lorenzo Valla on the Donation of Constantine.* New Haven: Yale University Press, 1922. **See p. 128.**

C[ollier], T[homas]. *The Glory of Christ, and the Ruine of Antichrist Unvailed, as They Are Held Forth in the Revelation, by the Seales, Trumpets, and Vialls.* London: [n.n.], 1647. [Author identified in the British Museum catalogue.] **See p. 568.**

Columbus, Christopher. *The Authentic Letters of Columbus.* Edited by William Eleroy Curtis. Chicago: Field Columbian Museum, 1895. **See pp. 167, 168.**

————. *Christopher Columbus, His Own Book of Privileges.* Edited and compiled by Benjamin Franklin Stevens. Introduction by Henry Harrisse. London: B. F. Stevens, 1893. **See p. 167.**

————. *First Letter of Christopher Columbus to the Noble Lord Raphael Sanchez Announcing the Discovery of America.* Facsimile from the Latin version of 1943, translated by Henry W. Haynes. Boston: Public Library, 1891. **See p. 175.**

————. *Libro de las Profecias,* in *Scritti di Cristoforo Colombo.* Edited by Cesare de Lollis, vol. 1, pp. 75-160. Roma: Ministero della Pubblica Istruzione, 1892-94. 2 vols. **See pp. 171, 173-175.**

————. *Select Letters of Christopher Columbus.* Edited by Richard Henry Major. London: The Hakluyt Society, 1847. **See pp. 162, 163, 165-168, 170, 174.**

————. *The Voyages of Christopher Columbus. Being the Journals of His First and Third, and the Letters Concerning His First and Last Voyages, to Which Is Added the account of His Second Voyage Written by Andres Bernaldez.* Translated and edited, with an introduction and notes, by Cecil Jane. London: The Argonaut Press, 1930. **See pp. 163, 166, 168, 175.**

Comenius, Joh[an]n Amos. *The Bequest of the Unity of the Brethren.* Translated and edited by Matthew Spinka. Chicago: The National Union of Czechoslovak Protestants in America, 1940. **See p. 107.**

A Compendious Book of Godly and Spiritual Songs, Commonly Known as 'The Gude and Godlie Ballatis.' Edited by A. F. Mitchell. Reprinted from the edition of 1567. Edinburgh: William Blackwood and Sons, 1897. **See p. 448.**

Conradus, Alfonsus. *In Apocalypsim D. Ioan. Apostoli Commentarius Alfonsi Conradi.* Basileae: Apud Petrum Pernam, 1560. **See pp. 319, 320.**

C[ottière], M[atthieu]. *Manuel ou brière description de l'Eglise Romaine.* Saumur: Iean Lesnier, 1653. **See p. 629.**

Coulton, G[eorge] G[ordon], translator and compiler. *From St. Francis to Dante. A Translation of All That Is of Primary Interest in the Chronicle of the Franciscan Salimbene (1221-1288). Together With Notes and Illustrations From Other Medieval Sources.* London: David Nutt, 1906. **See p. 25.**

————. "Reformation," *Encyclopaedia Britannica*, vol. 19, pp. 32-43. **See p. 433.**

Coverdale, Miles. [*Works of Bishop Coverdale.* Vol. 1:] *Writings and Translations of Myles Coverdale, Bishop of Exeter;* [vol. 2:] *Remains of Myles Coverdale, Bishop of Exeter.* Edited for the Parker Society by George Pearson. Cambridge: The University Press, 1844-46. 2 vols. **See p. 404.**

Cox, F[rancis] A. *The Life of Philip Melancthon.* Rev. ed. Boston: Gould, Kendall & Lincoln, 1835. **See pp. 286, 287.**

Cramer, Daniel. *Apocalypsis oder Offenbarung S. Johannis, sampt einer richtigen Erklerung.* Alten Stettin: Johann Christoff Landtrachtinger, 1618. **See pp. 608-610.**

Cranmer, Thomas. *The Works of Thomas Cranmer.* (Vol. 1:) *Writings and Disputations . . . Relative to the . . . Lord's Supper;* (vol. 2:) *Miscellaneous Writings and Letters.* Edited for the Parker Society by John Edmund Cox. Cambridge: The University Press, 1844-46. 2 vols. **See pp. 389-394.**

Creighton, M[andell]. *A History of the Papacy During the Period of the Reformation,* vol. 1. Boston: Houghton, Mifflin & Co., 1882. **See pp. 20, 110, 111, 115.**

Cressener, Drue. *A Demonstration of the First Principles of the Protestant Applications of the Apocalypse.* London: Printed for Thomas Cockerill, [1690]. [Date from the Library of Congress Union Catalogue.] **See pp. 590-593.**

————. *The Judgments of God Upon the Roman Catholick Church.* London: Printed for Richard Chiswell, 1689. **See pp. 590, 594, 596.**

[Crinsoz de Bionens, Théodore]. *Essai sur l'Apocalypse, avec des éclaircissemens sur les prophéties de Daniel qui regardent les derniers tem[p]s.* [*n.p.: n.n.*], 1729. [Author identified in Ant.-Alex. Barbier, *Dictionnaire des Ouvrages Anonymes,* vol. 2, p. 226.] **See pp. 679, 680.**

Cromwell, Oliver. *Oliver Cromwell's Letters and Speeches.* Edited by Thomas Carlyle. London: Chapman and Hall, 1849. **See p. 569.**

Cusa, Nicholas of. *D[octoris] Nicolai de Cusa Cardinalis . . . Opera.* Basileae: Ex officina Henric Petrina, [1565]. 3 vols. in 1. [Date from Union Catalogue in the Library of Congress.] **See pp. 126, 129-136.**

Czerwenka, Bernhard. *Geschichte der Evangelischen Kirche in Böhmen.* Vol. 1. Bielefeld and Leipzig: Velhagen and Klasing, 1869. **See pp. 32, 36-39, 121, 122.**

Daneau, Lambert. *Tractatus de Antichristo.* 2d ed. Genevae: Apud Eustathium Vignon, 1582. **See p. 349.**

Dante Alighieri. *The De Monarchia of Dante Alighieri.* Edited with translation and notes by Aurelia Henry. Boston and New York: Houghton, Mifflin and Company, 1904. **See pp. 23, 24.**

————. *The Divine Comedy of Dante Alighieri; Hell, Purgatory, Paradise.* Translated by Henry F. Cary. New York: P. F. Collier & Son, [1909]. (The Harvard Classics, vol. 20.) **See pp. 22-29.**

Daubeny, Charles. *The Fall of Papal Rome: Recommended to the Consideration of England: In a Discourse on Isaiah xlvi. 9, 10.* London: T. Cadell, Jun., and W. Davies, 1798. **See pp. 774, 775.**

D'Aubigné. See Merle d'Aubigné.

Daubuz, Charles. *A Perpetual Commentary on the Revelation of St. John. Wherein Is Contain'd* [etc.]. London: Benj. Tooke, 1720. See p. 656.

————. Same. Revised and abridged by Peter Lancaster. London: W. Innys, 1730. See pp. 655-657.

Davey, Richard. *The Nine Days' Queen—Lady Jane Grey and Her Times.* Edited, and with introduction, by Martin Hume. London: Methuen & Co., 1909. See p. 413.

Davidson, Samuel. *An Introduction to the New Testament.* London: Samuel Bagster and Sons, 1848-51. 3 vols. See p. 708.

Desmarets, Samuel. *Dissertatio de Antichristo.* Amstelrodami: Apud Ioannem Ianssonium, 1640. See p. 522.

Dibelius, F. W. "Selnecker, Nikolaus," *The New Schaff-Herzog Encyclopedia,* vol. 10, p. 346. See p. 323.

Dictionary of National Biography. Edited by Leslie Stephen and Sidney Lee. London: Smith, Elder, & Co., 1908-1909. 21 vols. See pp. 512, 525, 586, 659, 745.

Dictionnaire d'histoire et de géographie ecclésiastiques. See Baudrillart.

Döllinger, Joh[an]n J. Ign[atz] von. *Fables Respecting the Popes of the Middle Ages.* Translated by Alfred Plummer. London: Rivingtons, 1871. See p. 128.

[————]. *The Pope and the Council, by Janus.* 3d ed., rev. London: Rivingtons, 1870. See pp. 19, 105.

————. *Prophecies and the Prophetic Spirit in the Christian Era. An Historical Essay.* Translated by Alfred Plummer. London: Rivingtons, 1873. See pp. 22, 66, 68, 69, 71-73, 109, 127, 137, 143, 145, 147, 155, 156.

————. *Studies in European History; Being Academical Addresses* [etc.]. Translated by Margaret Warre. London: J. Murray, 1890. See pp. 23, 28, 203-205.

Dorner, Jakob August. *Geschichte der protestantischen Theologie besonders in Deutschland.* München: Cotta, 1867. See p. 710.

Douay Bible. See Bible, English. 1601, 1609-10, and 1914.

Downham, George. *A Treatise Concerning Antichrist.* London: Cuthbert Burbie, 1603. See pp. 535, 536.

Draper, John William. *History of the Intellectual Development of Europe.* Rev. ed. New York: Harper & Brothers, 1876. 2 vols. See pp. 160, 161, 163, 165, 168-170.

Du Jon, Fr[ançois]. *The Apocalyps, or Revelation of S. Iohn.* English translation. Cambridge: John Legat, Printer to the University of Cambridge, 1596. See p. 624.

Duppa, R[ichard]. *A Brief Account of the Subversion of the Papal Government. 1798.* 3d ed. London: John Murray, 1807. See pp. 749-753, 756, 757.

Egli, Emil. "Bibliander (Buchmann), Theodor," *The New Schaff-Herzog,* vol. 2, p. 169. See p. 338.

Eliezer, Rabbi. See *Pirkê de Rabbi Eliezer.*

Elliott, E. B. *Horae Apocalypticae; or, A Commentary on the Apocalypse.* 5th ed. London: Seeley, Jackson, and Halliday, 1862. 4 vols. **See pp. 67, 74, 177-181, 183, 195, 200, 216, 239, 307, 348, 414, 415, 488, 490, 492, 543, 589, 591, 605, 635, 655, 656, 678, 706-708.**

Enciclopedia Italiana. [Roma]: Instituto G. Treccani [etc.], 1929-39. 36 vols. **See p. 129.**

Enciclopedia Universal Ilustrada Europeo-Americana. Madrid: Espasa-Calpe, S.A. [imprint varies], [1907?-1930]. 70 vols, 10 vols. of appendices, and supplements to date. **See pp. 489, 503.**

Encyclopaedia Britannica. 1945 ed. (Published with the editorial advice of the faculties of the University of Chicago.) Chicago: Encyclopaedia Britannica, Inc., 1945. **See pp. 48, 62, 110, 111, 126, 128, 129, 385, 433, 447, 448, 457, 672.**

The Encyclopedia Americana. New York: Americana Corporation, 1942. 30 vols. **See p. 140.**

The English Hexapla. See Bible, English. 1841.

Erskine. See Buchan.

Evans, Austin Patterson. *An Episode in the Struggle for Religious Freedom. The Sectaries of Nuremberg 1524-1528.* New York: Columbia University Press, 1924. **See pp. 293, 294.**

Exeter, Bishop of. See [Lavington, George].

An Exposition of the Revelations, by Shewing the Agreement of the Prophetick Symbols With the History of the Roman, Saracen, and Ottoman Empires, and of the Popedom. London: Printed for M. Johnson, 1719. **See pp. 657, 658.**

Faà di Bruno, Joseph. *Catholic Belief: or, A Short and Simple Exposition of Catholic Doctrine.* Edited by Louis A. Lambert. New York: Benziger Brothers, 1884. **See p. 476.**

Faber, George Stanley. *The Sacred Calendar of Prophecy; or, A Dissertation on the Prophecies.* London: C. & J. Rivington, 1828. 3 vols. **See p. 732.**

Farrar, Frederic W. *History of Interpretation. Eight Lectures Preached Before the University of Oxford in the Year MDCCCLXXXV.* London: Macmillan and Co., 1886. **See pp. 67, 68, 185-190, 192, 195-197, 200, 209, 210, 212, 214, 226, 598, 618, 698.**

Ferguson, James. *An Astronomical Lecture, on Eclipses of the Sun and Moon, the True Year of Our Saviour's Crucifixion, the Supernatural Darkness at That Time, and the Prophet Daniel's Seventy Weeks.* Bristol: S. Farley, [1775]. **See p. 431.**

―――. *Astronomy Explained Upon Sir Isaac Newton's Principles.* London: The author, 1756. **See p. 431.**

―――. *Tables and Tracts, Relative to Several Arts and Sciences.* London: A. Millar and T. Cadell, 1767. **See p. 431.**

Festschrift zum 200 Jährigen Jubiläum der Einweihung der evangelischen Marienkirche zu Frankfurt am Main-Seckbach. Frankfurt am Main: Marienkirche, 1910. **See p. 713.**

[Flacius, Matthias]. *Catalogus Testium Veritatis.* Lugdun.: Ex typographia Antonij Candidi, 1597. 2 vols. [Author identified in British Museum catalogue.] **See pp. 316, 317, 349.**

Flacius, Matthias (and others). *Ecclesiastica Historia.* (Magdeburg Centuries.) Basle: [*n.n.*], 1560-1574. 8 vols. **See pp. 316, 317.**

Flacius, Matthias. *Etliche Hochwichtige Ursachen und Gründe Warumb das sich alle Christen vondem Antichrist und allem seinen Grewel der Verwüstung auffserst absondern sollen.* [*n.p.: n.n.*], 1570. **See p. 317.**

————. "Glossa Compendiaria," in his edition of the New Testament. See Bible, Greek. 1570.

Fleming, Robert. *Apocalyptical Key. An Extraordinary Discourse on the Rise and Fall of Papacy; or the Pouring Out of the Vials.* Printed from the original published [in his *Discourses on Several Subjects*] in the year 1701. London: G. Terry, [1793]. **See pp. 643, 645-647, 649.**

————. Same, with an appendix. London: W. Baynes, 1809. **See pp. 643, 647, 649.**

————. *Discourses on Several Subjects. The First Containing a New Account of the Rise and Fall of the Papacy.* . . . London: Printed for Andr. Bell, 1701. **See pp. 642, 643, 645-647.**

————. *The Rise and Fall of Papacy.* Edinburgh: Johnstone, Hunter, & Company, 1870. (Reprinted from 1701 ed.) **See p. 643.**

Fletchere, John William. See La Fléchère, Jean Guillaume.

Flick, Alexander Clarence. *The Decline of the Medieval Church.* New York: Alfred A. Knopf, 1930. 2 vols. **See pp. 19, 20, 22, 30, 37, 39, 40, 51, 59, 67, 69, 71, 106, 109-113, 121, 122, 139-141, 154, 155.**

Förster, T. "Francke, "*The New Schaff-Herzog,* vol. 4, pp. 367, 368. **See p. 697.**

Forbes, Patrick. *An Learned Commentarie Upon the Revelation of Saint Iohn.* Middelburg: Richard Schilders, 1614. **See p. 555.**

Foxe, John. *The Acts and Monuments of John Foxe: A New and Complete Edition; With a Preliminary Dissertation, by the Rev. George Townsend.* Vol. 1. Edited by the Rev. Stephen Reed Cattley. London: R. B. Seeley and W. Burnside, 1841. **See p. 363.**

————. *Acts and Monuments of Matters Most Special and Memorable, Happening in the Church.* 9th ed. London: Company of Stationers, 1684. 3 vols. **See pp. 20, 21, 61, 63, 64, 74-83, 85-94, 117, 119, 145, 149, 259, 358, 363, 365, 405, 415-417.**

————. *Conjectures on the Apocalypse.* See his *Eicasmi.*

————. *Eicasmi seu Meditationes, in Sacram Apocalypsin.* Londini: Impensis Geor. Byshop, 1587. **See pp. 414, 415.**

Froude, James Anthony. *History of England From the Fall of Wolsey to the Death of Elizabeth,* vol. 4. New York: Charles Scribner's Sons, 1890. **See p. 450.**

Fulke, W[illiam], editor. *The Text of the New Testament of Iesus Christ.* See Bible, English. 1601.

Fulke, William. [*Works.* Vol. 1:] *A Defence of the Sincere and True Translations of the Holy Scriptures Into the English Tongue, Against the Cavils of Gregory Martin,* edited for the Parker Society by Charles Henry Hartshorne; [vol. 2:] *Stapleton's Fortress Overthrown. A Rejoinder to Martiall's Reply. A Discovery of the Dangerous Rock of the Popish Church Commended by*

Sanders, edited for the Parker Society by Richard Gibbings. Cambridge: The University Press, 1843-47. **See pp. 421-424.**

F[unck], J[ohann], supposed author. *Anleitung zum verstandt im buch, das man nennet Apocalypsis.* With foreword by Melanchthon. Wittenberg: Zacharias Engelhaubt, 1559. **See p. 309.**

[————], supposed author. *Apocalypsis. Der Offenbarung, künfftiger geschicht Johannis . . . Auslegung.* Wittenberg: Zacharias Engelhaubt, 1558. (A second title of his *Anleitung.*) **See p. 309.**

————. *Ausslegung des anderntheils des Neundten Capitels Danielis.* Königsperg: Johann Daubman, 1564. **See pp. 309-312.**

————. *Chronologia: Hoc Est, Omnium Temporum et Annorum ab Initio Mundi . . . Computatio.* Wittebergae: Iohannes Schwertel, 1570. **See pp. 308, 312.**

Galloway, Joseph. *Brief Commentaries Upon Such Parts of the Revelation and Other Prophecies as Immediately Refer to the Present Times. With the Prophetic, or, Anticipated History of the Church of Rome. To Which Is Added, A Pill for the Infidel and Atheist.* London: Printed 1802: Trenton. reprinted by James Oram, for Daniel Fenton, 1809. 2 vols. **See pp. 738, 739, 779-781.**

Gardiner, Samuel R. *History of England From the Accession of James I to the Outbreak of the Civil War, 1603-1642.* London: Longmans, Green, and Co., 1883-84. 10 vols. **See p. 537.**

————. *History of the Commonwealth and Protectorate 1649-1656.* London: Longmans, Green, and Co., 1903. 4 vols. **See p. 568.**

Gardner, Edmund G[arratt]. *Saint Catherine of Siena.* London: J. M. Dent & Co., 1907. **See pp. 69, 71.**

————. *The Story of Florence.* London: J. M. Dent & Co., 1900. **See pp. 21, 145.**

Geffcken, [Friedrich] Heinrich. *Church and State. Their Relations Historically Developed.* Translated and edited with the assistance of the author by Edward Fairfax Taylor. London: Longmans, Green, and Co., 1877. 2 vols. **See p. 19.**

Geikie, John Cunningham. *The English Reformation; How It Came About and Why We Should Uphold It.* New York: D. Appleton and Company, 1879. **See pp. 31, 91, 352, 355, 360, 381, 385, 390, 391, 471.**

Geree, John. *The Down-Fall of Anti-Christ: or, The Power of Preaching, to Pull Down Popery.* London: Thomas Underhill, 1641. **See p. 560.**

Gerhard, Johannes. *Adnotationes in Apocalypsin.* Jenae: Sumtibus Christiani von Sahers, 1643. **See pp. 603-605.**

[Geveren, Sheltco a]. *Of the Ende of This World, and Second Comming of Christ, a Comfortable and Necessary Discourse, for These Miserable and Dangerous Dayes.* Translated by Thomas Rogers. [Author and translator identified in Halkett & Laing, *Dictionary of Anonymous and Pseudonymous English Literature,* vol. 4, p. 239.] London: Andrew Maunsell, 1577. **See pp. 404, 405.**

Giblehr. See "Georg Hermann Giblehrs Unvorgreiffliche Gedancken," under Periodicals.

Gieseler, Joh[an]n C[arl] L[udwig]. *A Textbook of Church History.* Vol. 3. Translated by John W. Hull; edited by Henry B. Smith. New York: Harper & Brothers, 1858. **See pp. 19, 35, 37, 67, 127, 154, 298, 308,**

Gill, John. *An Exposition of the Prophets.* Vols. 6, 9. London: [*n.n.*], 1758. **See pp. 683, 684.**

————. *An Exposition of the Revelation of S. John the Divine.* London: George Keith, 1776. **See p. 683.**

Gill, Thomas H. *The Papal Drama. A Historical Essay.* London: Longmans, Green, and Co., 1866. **See p. 760.**

Gillett, E[zra] H[all]. *The Life and Times of John Huss; or, the Bohemian Reformation of the Fifteenth Century.* Boston: Gould and Lincoln, 1863. 2 vols. **See pp. 35, 39-42, 106, 113.**

————. "Milicz," in M'Clintock and Strong, *Cyclopaedia of Biblical, Theological, and Ecclesiastical Literature,* vol. 6, p. 256. **See pp. 32, 33, 35.**

Ginzberg, Louis. "Akiba ben Joseph," *The Jewish Encyclopedia,* vol. 1, pp. 304-310. **See p. 195.**

Ginzel, F. K. *Handbuch der mathematischen und technischen Chronologie.* Leipzig: J. C. Hinrichs, 1906-14. 3 vols. **See p. 427.**

Göbel, Max. *Geschichte des Christlichen Lebens in der rheinisch-westphälischen Evangelischen Kirche.* Coblenz: K. Bädeker, 1849-60. 3 vols. **See p. 614.**

Goodwin, Thomas. *The Expositions of That Famous Divine Thomas Goodwin, D. D., on Part of the Epistle to the Ephesians, and on the Book of Revelation.* London: Simpkin, Marshall, and Co., 1842. **See p. 574.**

[————]. *The French Revolution Foreseen, in 1639. Extracts From an Exposition of the Revelation, by an Eminent Divine of Both Universities, in the Beginning of the Last Century.* London: J. Johnson, [1796?]. **See pp. 724-726.**

————. *A Sermon of the Fifth Monarchy.* London: Livewel Chapman, 1654. **See p. 574.**

Graetz, Heinrich Hirsch. *History of the Jews.* Reprint. Philadelphia: The Jewish Publication Society of America, 1940. 6 vols. **See pp. 196, 206, 223, 224.**

Grafton, Richard. *A Chronicle at Large and Meere History of the Affayres of England* [*etc.*]. London: Henry Denham, for R. Tottle and H. Toye, 1569. **See p. 313.**

La grande encyclopédie inventaire raisonné des sciences, des lettres et des arts. Paris: H. Lamirault et Cie. [etc.], [1886-1902]. 31 vols. **See pp. 627, 633-635.**

Grier, Richard. *An Epitome of the General Councils of the Church.* Dublin: William Curry, Jun., and Co., 1828. **See p. 175.**

[Grotius, Hugo]. *Commentatio ad Loca Quaedam N[ovi] Testamenti Quae de Antichristo Agunt, aut Agere Putantur.* Amstelodami: Apud Ioh. & Cornelium Blaev, 1640. [Author identified in British Museum catalogue.] **See pp. 522-524.**

————. *Hugonis Grotii Annotationes in Novum Testamentum.* Vol. 2, part 1. Erlangae in Ptochotrophio et Lipsiae apud Ioannem Carolum Tetzchnerum, 1756. **See pp. 510, 521, 523, 524.**

Grünberg, Paul. *Philipp Jakob Spener.* Vol. 1. Göttingen: Vandenhoeck & Ruprecht, 1893. **See pp. 619, 620.**

Guicciardini, Francesco. *The History of Italy.* Translated from the Italian by Austin Parke Goddard, 3d ed. London: Z. Stuart, 1763. 10 vols. **See p. 149.**

Guild, William. *Anti-Christ Pointed and Painted Out in His True Colours. Or, The Pope of Rome, Proven to Bee That Man of Sinne, and Sonne of Perdition, Fore-prophesied in Scripture*. Aberdene: Iames Brown, 1655. **See p. 562.**

————. *The Sealed Book Opened. Or, A Cleer Explication of the Prophecies of the Revelation*. London: Anthony Williamson, 1656. **See p. 562.**

Guinness, H. Grattan. *History Unveiling Prophecy or Time as an Interpreter*. New York: Fleming H. Revell Company, 1905. **See pp. 465, 480, 580, 589, 626, 731, 734, 760.**

————. *Romanism and the Reformation From the Standpoint of Prophecy*. New York: A. C. Armstrong & Son, 1887. **See pp. 336, 436, 543, 659.**

Guttmann, Michael. *Mafteah Hatalmud—Clavis Talmudis*. Breslau: D. Rotenberg, 1906-30. 3 vols. in 4. **See pp. 190, 191.**

Haag, Eugène and Emile. *La France protestante*. Paris, Genève: J. Cherbuliez, 1846-59. 10 vols. **See pp. 624, 627, 629, 630, 632, 633.**

Hagen, J. G. "Nicholas of Cusa," *The Catholic Encyclopedia*, vol. 11, pp. 60-62. **See pp. 127, 129.**

Hagenbach, Karl R. *History of the Reformation in Germany and Switzerland Chiefly*. Translated from the 4th revised ed. of the German by Evelina Moore. Edinburgh: T. & T. Clark, 1878-79. 2 vols. **See pp. 316, 466, 469, 470.**

[Hales, William.] *The Inspector; or Select Literary Intelligence for the Vulgar A.D. 1798, but Correct A.D. 1801*. London: J. White, 1799. [Author identified in his *New Analysis of Chronology*, vol. 2, p. 518.] **See p. 720.**

————. *A New Analysis of Chronology*. 2d ed. London: Printed for C. J. G. & F. Rivington, 1830. 4 vols. **See p. 720.**

Hammond, H[enry]. *A Paraphrase, and Annotations Upon All the Books of the New Testament*. London: Printed by J. Flesher for Richard Royston, 1653. **See pp. 524, 525.**

Harris, William. *An Historical and Critical Account of the Life and Writings of James the First*. London: James Waugh, 1753. **See pp. 539, 540.**

[Harrisse, Henry]. *Notes on Columbus*. New York, 1866. [Author identified in Library of Congress catalogue.] **See pp. 163, 166, 168, 171, 174.**

Hartley, David. *Observations on Man, His Frame, His Duty, and His Expectations*. 5th ed. London: Richard Cruttwell, 1810. 2 vols. **See p. 774.**

Hase, Karl (Charles). *A History of the Christian Church*. Translated from the 7th German ed. by Charles E. Blumenthal and Conway P. Wing. New York: D. Appleton & Company, 1855. **See p. 69.**

Hastings, James, editor. *Encyclopaedia of Religion and Ethics*. New York: Charles Scribner's Sons, 1928. 13 vols. in 7. **See p. 198.**

Headlam, Cecil. *The Story of Nuremberg*. London: J. M. Dent & Co., 1900. **See pp. 291, 293-295.**

Held, Friedrich, editor. *Dr. Martin Luthers Vorreden zur Heiligen Schrift*. Heilbronn: E. Salzer [1934]. **See p. 266.**

Helwig, Andreas. *Antichristus Romanus, in Proprio Suo Nomine, Numerum Illum Apocalypticum (DCLXVI) Continente Proditus*. Wittebergae: Typis Laurentij Seuberlichs, 1612. **See pp. 606-608.**

Hengstenberg, Ernst Wilhelm. *The Revelation of St. John Expounded for Those Who Search the Scriptures.* Translated by Patrick Fairbairn. New York: Robert Carter & Brothers, 1852. 2 vols. See p. 708.

Henry, Paul. *The Life and Times of John Calvin, the Great Reformer.* Translated by Henry Stebbing. New York: Robert Carter & Brothers, 1851. 2 vols. See p. 436.

Hergenröther, Joseph Adam Gustav. *Handbuch der allgemeinen Kirchengeschichte.* 3d rev. ed. Freiburg im Breisgau: Herder, 1884-86. 3 vols. See pp. 464, 731.

Herzog, Johann Jakob, editor. *Real-Encyklopädie für protestantische Theologie und Kirche.* Hamburg, Stuttgart, Gotha: Rudolf Besser, 1854-68. 22 vols. See pp. 295, 304, 316, 322, 323, 334, 496, 618, 619, 698.

Heunisch, Caspar. *Wolgegründtes Bedencken über dem antrettenden 1670. Jahr. Ob in demselben Der Jüngste Tag zu hoffen oder zu vermuthen sey?* Nürnberg: Johann Philipp Miltenberger, [n.d.]. See p. 600.

Heylyn, Peter. *A Sermon Preached in the Collegiate Church of St. Peter in Westminster on Wednesday May 29th, 1661.* London: Printed by E. C. for A. Seile, 1661. See p. 563.

Hills, Margaret T. *A Ready Reference History of the English Bible.* New York: American Bible Society, [1935]. See p. 52.

Historical and Philosophical Memoirs of Pius the Sixth and of His Pontificate Down to the Period of His Retirement Into Tuscany. Translated from the French. London: S. Hamilton, 1799. 2 vols. See pp. 750-753.

Hitchcock, George S. *The Beasts and the Little Horn.* In Catholic Truth Society (London) Publications, 1911. See p. 488.

Hoë von Hoenegg, Matthias. *Commentariorum in . . . Johannis Apocalypsin . . . Libri VIII.* Lipsiae & Francofurti: Impensis Haeredum Schürerianorum & Johannis Fritzschii, 1671. See pp. 612, 613.

Hoffmann, Christoph. *Mein Weg Nach Jerusalem.* Jerusalem: Christoph Hoffmann, 1881-84. 2 vols. See p. 710.

Hoffmann, Paul. *Die Deutschen Kolonien in Transkaukasien.* Berlin: Reimer, 1905. See p. 713.

Hofmann, Matthaeus. *Chronotaxis Apocalyptica Visionibus Apocalypticis Certas Temporum Periodos Assignans.* Jena: Johannes Bielckius, 1668. See p. 602.

Holtzmann, Heinrich Julius. *Kanon und Tradition. Ein Beitrag zur neueren Dogmen geschichte und Symbolik.* Ludwigsburg: Ferd. Riehm, 1859. See p. 478.

Homes, Nath[aniel]. *The New World; or, The New Reformed Church.* (A Sermon on 2 Pet. iii:13.) London: T. P. and M. S. for William Adderton, 1641. See p. 574.

————. *The Resurrection Revealed: or, The Dawning of the Day-Star.* London: Ibbitson, 1653. See p. 575.

Homilies. See Church of England.

Hooper, [John]. [*Works.* Vol. 1:] *Early Writings of John Hooper,* edited for the Parker Society by Samuel Carr; [vol. 2:] *Later Writings of Bishop Hooper,* edited for the Parker Society by Charles Nevinson. Cambridge: The University Press, 1843-52. See pp. 381-384.

Horch, He[i]nrich. *Das A und das O oder Zeitrechung der gantzen H. Schrifft.* Leipzig: Thomas Fritsch, 1697. **See pp. 699, 700.**

————. *Die Filadelfische Versuchungsstunde.* Marburg: Philip Casimir Müller, 1715. **See p. 700.**

————. *Mystische und Profetische Bibel.* Marburg: Joh. Kürssner, 1712. [Author identified by Staatsbibliothek, Berlin.] **See p. 700.**

Hulme, Edward Maslin. *The Renaissance, the Protestant Revolution, and the Catholic Reformation in Continental Europe.* Rev. ed. New York: D. Appleton-Century Company, Inc., 1915. **See pp. 175, 316, 468-470, 474, 475, 483.**

Humboldt, Alexander von. *Cosmos: A Sketch of a Physical Description of the Universe,* vol. 2. Translated from the German by E[lise] C. Otté. New York: Harper & Brothers, 1850. **See pp. 166, 169.**

Hurst, John Fletcher. *History of the Christian Church.* Vol. 2. New York: Eaton & Mains, 1900. **See pp. 127, 129, 473.**

Huss, Johann, and Jerome of Prague. *Ioannis Hus, et Hieronymi Pragensis Confessorum Christi Historia et Monumenta.* Noribergae: In Officina Ioannis Montani & Ulrici Neuberi, 1558. 2 vols. **See p. 116.**

Huss, John. *The Letters of John Hus.* Edited by Herbert B. Workman and R. Martin Pope. London: Hodder and Stoughton, 1904. **See pp. 117-119.**

Hutton, William Holden. *The Age of Revolution; Being an Outline of the History of the Church From 1648-1815.* London: Rivingtons, 1908. **See p. 739.**

Hyma, Albert. *Europe From the Renaissance to 1815.* New York: F. S. Crofts & Co., 1931. **See pp. 351, 384, 386, 387, 521, 552.**

Imrie, David. *A Letter From the Reverend Mr. David Imrie, Minister of the Gospel at St. Mungo, in Annandale. To a Gentleman in the City of Edinburgh. Predicting the Speedy Accomplishment of the Great, Awful and Glorious Events Which the Scriptures Say Are to Be Brought to Pass in the Latter Times.* Edinburgh: Printed in 1755. Boston: Reprinted by S. Kneeland, 1756. **See p. 695.**

Innes, Alexander Taylor. "Knox, John," *Encyclopaedia Britannica,* vol. 13, pp. 467-470. **See p. 447.**

Irving, Washington. *The Life and Voyages of Christopher Columbus.* London: Henry G. Bohn, 1850. **See pp. 163, 170.**

Isaac, J. *Histoire Révolution-Empire première moitié du XIXe siècle.* Paris: Libraire Hachette, 1932. **See pp. 734, 735.**

Isslcib, S. "Intcrim," *The New Schaff-Herzog,* vol. 6, pp. 21, 22. **See p. 316.**

Jacobs, Joseph. "Manasseh ben Israel," *The Jewish Encyclopedia,* vol. 8, pp. 282-284. **See p. 233.**

[James I, King of Great Britain]. *The Workes of the Most High and Mightie Prince, Iames, . . . King of Great Britaine.* Edited by Iames [Mountague], Bishop of Winton. London: Robert Barker and Iohn Bill. 1616. **See pp. 537-541.**

Jane, Cecil, editor. See Columbus, Christopher, *The Voyages of Christopher Columbus.* **See pp. 163, 166, 175.**

Janssen, Johannes, *Geschichte des deutschen Volkes seit dem Ausgang des Mittelalters.* Freiburg im Breisgau: Herder, 1883-86. 4 vols. **See p. 295.**

Jephet ibn Ali. *The Arabic Commentary of Yefet ben Ali the Karaite on the Book of Hosea.* Edited by Philip Birnbaum from eight manuscripts and provided with critical notes and an introduction. Philadelphia: The Dropsie College for Hebrew and Cognate Learning, 1942. **See pp. 196, 206, 212.**

————. *A Commentary on the Book of Daniel.* Edited and translated by D[avid] S[amuel] Margoliouth. Oxford: Clarendon Press, 1889. (*Anecdota Oxoniensia,* second series, vol. 1, part 3.) **See pp. 207-209.**

Jewel, John. *The Works of John Jewel, Bishop of Salisbury.* Edited for the Parker Society by John Ayre. Cambridge: The University Press, 1845-50. 4 vols. **See pp. 406-408.**

The Jewish Encyclopedia. New York and London: Funk and Wagnalls Company, 1901-06. 12 vols. **See pp. 195, 199, 202, 233.**

Jöcher Christian Gottlieb. *Allgemeines Gelehrten-Lexicon.* Leipzig: [*n.n.*], 1750-1819, 1897. 11 vols. **See p. 606.**

Jonson, Ben. *Plays and Poems.* 2d ed. With an Introduction by Henry Morley. London: George Routledge and Son, 1886. **See p. 566.**

Josephus, Flavius. *The Complete Works of Flavius Josephus.* Translated by William Whiston. Philadelphia: John E. Potter & Company, [188—?] **See p. 193.**

Joye, George. *The Exposycion of Daniel the Prophete, Gathered Out of Philip Melancthon, Johan Ecolāpadius, Chonrade Pellicane, & Out of Johan Draconite. &c.* [London: *n.n.,* 1550] **See pp. 361-363.**

————. Same. [*n.p.: n.n.*], 1545. **See pp. 361, 363.**

Juda, Leo. *Paraphrase Upon the Revelacion of S. John.* Translated from High Duche by Edmonde Alon, *Added to the Seconde Tome or Volume of the Paraphrase of Erasmus Upon the Newe Testament.* London: Edwarde Whitchurche, 1549. **See pp. 335, 336.**

Jurieu, Pierre. *The Accomplishment of the Scripture Prophecies, or the Approaching Deliverance of the Church.* Translated from the new French edition. London: [*n.n.*], 1687. **See pp. 637-639, 726.**

Kawerau, G. "Flacius," *The New Schaff-Herzog,* vol. 4, pp. 321-323. **See p. 316.**

————. "Magdeburg Centuries," *The New Schaff-Herzog,* vol. 7, pp. 123, 124. **See p. 316.**

————. "Musculus (Meusel), Andreas," *The New Schaff-Herzog,* vol. 8, pp. 59, 60. **See p. 322.**

————. "Stiefel (Styfel), Michael," *The New Schaff-Herzog,* vol. 11, p. 95. **See p. 320.**

Kehilloth Mosheh. See Bible, Hebrew. 1724-27.

Keith, Alexander. *The Signs of the Times, as Denoted by the Fulfilment of Historical Predictions, Traced Down From the Babylonish Captivity to the Present Time.* New York: Jonathan Leavitt, 1832. 2 vols. **See p. 763.**

Kidd, B. J. *The Counter-Reformation, 1550-1600.* London: Society for Promoting Christian Knowledge, 1937. **See pp. 479, 495, 498, 526, 527.**

————. *Documents Illustrative of the Continental Reformation.* Oxford: The Clarendon Press, 1911. **See pp. 251, 252, 258, 291, 448, 475, 479.**

[King, Edward]. *Morsels of Criticism, Tending to Illustrate Some Few Passages in the Holy Scriptures Upon Philosophical Principles.* 2d ed., with supplement. London: J. Davis, 1800. 3 vols. [Author identified in dedicatory letter.] **See pp. 765, 766, 769, 770.**

————. *Remarks on the Signs of the Times.* Philadelphia: reprinted by Jas. Humphreys from the London 1799 ed. 1800. **See pp. 765-769.**

Klibansky, Raymond. "Niccolò da Cusa," *Enciclopedia Italiana,* vol. 24, pp. 761-763. **See p. 129.**

Knollys, Hanserd. *An Exposition of the Eleventh Chapter of the Revelation.* [London?: n.n.], 1679. **See p. 580.**

Knox, John. *The Historie of the Reformatioun of Religioun Within the Realm of Scotland.* Edinburgh: Robert Fleming and Company, 1732. **See pp. 452-454.**

————. *The Works of John Knox;* collected and edited by David Laing. Edinburgh: The Wodrow Society, 1846-64. 6 vols. **See pp. 445, 448, 450, 451, 455.**

Krasinski, Valerian, Count. *Sketch of the Religious History of the Slavonic Nations.* Edinburgh: Johnstone and Hunter, 1851. **See p. 106.**

Kugler, Franz Xaver. *Sternkunde und Sterndienst in Babel.* Münster in Westfalen: Aschendorff, 1907-35. 2 vols. and 2 supplements. **See p. 663.**

Kurtz, [Johann Heinrich]. *Church History.* New York: Funk & Wagnalls, 1889, 1890. 3 vols. **See pp. 31, 48, 60, 111, 113, 469, 470.**

Labbe, Philippe. *Concordia Chronologica.* Parisiis: Typographia Regia, 1670. 5 vols. **See p. 429.**

Lactantius. *The Divine Institutes,* in *The Ante-Nicene Fathers,* vol. 7, pp. 9-223. New York: Charles Scribner's Sons, 1913. **See p. 281.**

La Fléchère, Jean Guillaume de. *Posthumous Pieces of the late Rev. John William de la Fléchère.* 3d ed. London: (Methodist) Conference Office, 1800. **See pp. 687-689, 691.**

[Lalande, Emmanuel]. *La vie et les oeuvres de maître Arnaud de Villeneuve.* Par Marc Haven [*pseud.*] Paris: Chez Chamuel, 1896. [Author identified from Library of Congress catalogue.] **See p. 72.**

Lambert, François, of Avignon. *Exegeseos in sanctum Divi Joannis Apocalypsim ... Libri VII.* Marburg: [n.n.], 1528. **See p. 303.**

Landman, Isaac. "Abravanel, Isaac," *The Universal Jewish Encyclopedia,* vol. 1, pp. 53, 54. **See p. 225.**

Landon, Edward H. *A Manual of Councils of the Holy Catholic Church.* Rev. ed. Edinburgh: John Grant, 1909. 2 vols. **See pp. 61, 104, 115, 180, 474, 476.**

The Lantern of Light, Written About A.D. 1400. See Brute, Walter, and others. **See pp. 64, 65.**

Lapide, Cornelius à. *Cornelii Cornelii a Lapide ... Commentarius in Apocalypsin S. Iohannis.* Antverpiae: Apud Henricum & Cornelium Verdussen, 1717. **See pp. 503, 504.**

Latimer, Hugh. [*Works,* vol. 1:] *Sermons by Hugh Latimer;* [vol. 2:] *Sermons and Remains of Hugh Latimer,* [etc.]. Edited for the Parker Society by George Elwes Corrie. Cambridge: The University Press, 1844-45. 2 vols. **See pp. 369-372.**

[Launay, Pierre de]. *Paraphrase et exposition sur l'Apocalypse* . . . par Ionas le Buy [pseud.]. a Genève: Chez Pierre Aubert, 1651. [Author identified from Library of Congress catalogue.] **See pp. 632, 633.**

[Lavington, George]. *A Sermon Preached in the Cathedral-Church of Exeter, on the General Fast-Day, February 6, 1756.* By the Lord Bishop of Exeter. Exon: Edward Score, [1756?]. [Author identified in British Museum catalogue.] **See p. 677.**

Law, T. G. "Mary Stewart," *The Cambridge Modern History,* vol. 3, pp. 260-293. **See p. 449.**

Lechler, [Gotthard]. *John Wycliffe and His English Precursors.* London: The Religious Tract Society, 1878. **See pp. 49, 51-54, 59-61, 74, 75, 94, 110, 111.**

Lee, Guy Carleton. *Source-Book of English History. Leading Documents Together With Illustrative Material From Contemporary Writers and a Bibliography of Sources.* New York: Henry Holt and Company, 1900. **See pp. 48, 60, 366, 381.**

Lee, William, "Knox, John," *The New Schaff-Herzog,* vol. 6, pp. 362-365. **See p. 446.**

Legge, Alfred Owen. *The Growth of the Temporal Power of the Papacy.* London: Macmillan and Co. 1870. *See p. 19.*

Lewis, John. *The History of the Life and Sufferings of the Reverend and Learned John Wicliffe, D.D.* London: Printed for Robert Knaplock, and Richard Wilkin, 1720. **See p. 51.**

Lindsay, James Ludovic. *Bibliotheca Lindesiana. Collations and Notes No. 7; Catalogue of a Collection of Fifteen Hundred Tracts by Martin Luther and His Contemporaries. 1511-1598.* Aberdeen: Privately printed, 1903. **See pp. 283, 285.**

Lindsay, Thomas M. *A History of the Reformation.* New York: Charles Scribner's Sons, 1917. 2 vols. **See pp. 479, 481-483.**

————. "Lollards," *Encyclopaedia Britannica,* vol. 14, pp. 340-342. **See p. 62.**

Lord, John. *Beacon Lights of History.* Vol. 4: *Warriors and Statesmen.* New York: Fords, Howard, and Hulbert, 1884. **See p. 568.**

Loserth, Johann. *Wiclif and Hus.* Translated from the German by M. J. Evans. London: Hodder and Stoughton, 1884. **See pp. 107, 110-116, 118, 121.**

Loughlin, James F. "Pius IV," *The Catholic Encyclopedia,* vol. 12, pp. 129, 130. **See p. 476.**

Lowth, William. *A Commentary Upon the Larger and Lesser Prophets: Being a Continuation of Bishop Patrick.* 3d ed. London: Printed for James and John Knapton, etc., 1730. **See pp. 670, 671.**

Lucas, Herbert, S. J. *Fra Girolamo Savonarola.* London: Sands & Company, 1899. **See pp. 143, 144, 150, 151.**

Lucius, Johann Andreas. *Die Offenbahrung* . . . *Johannis.* Dresden: Christian Bergens, 1670. **See pp. 616, 617.**

Luther, Martin. *D. Martin Luthers Werke.* Vol. 6. Edited by J. K. F. Knaake, G. Kawerau and others. Weimar: Hermann Böhlau, 1888. **See p. 267.**

————. *Dr. Martin Luthers Sämmtliche Schriften.* Edited by Joh[ann] Georg Walch. St. Louis: Concordia Publishing House, 1881-1910. 23 vols. in 25. **See pp. 181, 253-258, 261, 267-275, 278, 281, 282, 284.**

————. *Dr. Martin Luther's sämmtliche Werke.* Edited by Ernst Ludwig Enders and Johann Konrad Irmischer. Frankfurt am Main und Erlangen: C. Heyder, etc., 1828-70. 67 vols. **See pp. 277, 278, 281.**

————. *Dr. Martin Luthers Vorreden Zur Heiligen Schrift.* Edited by Friedrich Held. Heilbronn: E. Salzer, [1934]. **See pp. 265, 266.**

————. *The Familiar Discourses of Dr. Martin Luther.* Translated by Henry Bell. New ed., rev. & cor. by Joseph Kerby. London: Baldwin, Craddock, and Joy, 1818. **See p. 278.**

————. *First Principles of the Reformation; or, The Ninety-five Theses and the Three Primary Works of Dr. Martin Luther. Translated into English.* Edited by Henry Wace and C. A. Buchheim. Philadelphia: Lutheran Publication Society, 1885. **See pp. 255-258.**

————. *The Letters of Martin Luther.* Selected and translated by Margaret A. Currie. London: Macmillan and Co., 1908. **See p. 304.**

[————]. *Luther im Kreise der Seinen, Familienbriefe und Fabeln.* Leipzig: Insel Verlag, 1917. **See p. 281.**

————. *Passional Christi und Antichristi mit Bildern von Lucas Cranach dem Alteren.* Leipzig: Robert Hoffmann, [n.d.]. **See pp. 264, 276.**

————. Preface in *Commentarius in Apocalypsin Ante Centum Annos Editus* (attributed to John Purvey). VVittembergae: [n.n.], 1528. **See pp. 98, 284.**

————. *Quare Pape ac Discipulorum Eius Libri a Doctore Martino Luthero Combusti Sint.* Wittenberg: [n.n.], 1520. **See p. 259.**

————. *Schriften.* See Luther, Martin. *Dr. Martin Luthers Sämmtliche Schriften.*

————. *The Signs of Christ's Coming and of the Last Day.* London: [n.n.], 1661. (The substance of his *Ein tröstliche predigt von der zukunfft Christi . . .*) **See pp. 280, 281.**

————. *Supputatio Annorum Mundi Emendata.* Vuittembergae: Apud Georgium Rhau, 1545. **See p. 279.**

————. *The Table Talk of Martin Luther.* Translated and edited by William Hazlitt; to which is added the life of Martin Luther, by Alexander Chalmers, with additions from Michelet and Audin. London: H. G. Bohn, 1857. **See pp. 271, 272, 277, 278.**

————. *Ein tröstliche predigt von der zukunfft Christi und den vorgehenden zeichen des Jüngsten tags.* Wittemberg: [Hans Lufft], 1532. **See pp. 279, 280.**

————, translator. See Bible, German. (1534.)

Lützow, [Franz], Count. *The Life & Times of Master John Hus.* London: J. M. Dent & Co., 1909. **See pp. 115, 119, 122.**

M'Clintock, John, and James Strong. *Cyclopaedia of Biblical, Theological, and Ecclesiastical Literature.* New York: Harper & Brothers, 1867-1883. 10 vols. **See pp. 31, 32, 35, 94, 125-128, 321, 338, 354, 364.**

McCrie, Thomas. *Life of John Knox.* First complete American ed. (from the 5th Edinburgh ed. of 1831). Philadelphia: Presbyterian Board of Publication, [n.d.]. **See pp. 443, 445-450.**

Mackinnon, James. *Luther and the Reformation.* London: Longmans, Green, and Co., 1925-1930. 4 vols. **See p. 259.**

Macpherson, E. "Malvenda," *The Catholic Encyclopedia,* vol. 9, p. 577. See p. 504.

Magdeburg Centuries. See Flacius, Matthias.

Maitland, Charles (1815-1866). *The Apostles' School of Prophetic Interpretation: With Its History Down to the Present Time.* London: Longman, Brown, Green, and Longmans, 1849. See pp. 47, 67, 73, 74, 192, 307, 308, 493, 496, 498, 503, 504, 565.

Maitland, S. R. *The Dark Ages; A Series of Essays, Intended to Illustrate the State of Religion and Literature in the Ninth, Tenth, Eleventh, and Twelfth Centuries.* London: J. G. F. and J. Rivington, 1844. See p. 139.

Major, Richard Henry, editor and translator. *Select Letters of Christopher Columbus.* London: The Hakluyt Society, 1847. See pp. 162, 163, 165-167.

Malvenda, Thomas. *De Antichristo.* Lugduni: A Sumptibus Societatis Bibliopolarum, 1647. 2 vols. in 1. See pp. 494, 504, 505.

Manasseh ben Israel. *Menasseh ben Israel's Mission to Oliver Cromwell. Being a Reprint of the Pamphlets Published by Menasseh Ben Israel to Promote the Re-admission of the Jews to England, 1649-1656.* Edited, with introduction and notes, by Lucien Wolf. London: Macmillan & Co., Ltd., 1901. See pp. 220, 222, 223, 235, 236.

———. *Piedra Gloriosa o de la Estatua de Nebuchadnesar.* Amsterdam: an. 5415, [1655]. See pp. 235, 237, 238.

Mann, Jacob. *Texts and Studies in Jewish History and Literature.* Vol. 2. Philadelphia: Jewish Publication Society of America, 1935. See p. 197.

Mansi, Joannes Dominicus, editor. *Sacrorum conciliorum nova, et amplissima collectio.* Parisiis: Huberto Welter, 1901-27. 53 vols. See pp. 51, 59, 61, 91, 104, 114, 122, 141, 176-178, 180, 181, 183, 261, 307, 478.

Maresius. See Desmarets.

Marshall, Benjamin. *Chronological Tables.* With an appendix from Bishop Lloyd. Oxford: The Theater, 1713. See p. 429.

Matthew, F. D., editor. *The English Works of Wyclif Hitherto Unprinted.* London: Trübner & Co., 1880. See p. 53.

Mede, Joseph. *The Apostasy of the Latter Times.* London: Samuel Man, 1644. (Bound with his *Works,* 1648 ed.) See pp. 542, 545, 546, 548.

———. *Daniels Weeks.* London: Printed by M. F. for John Clark, 1643. (In *Works,* 1648 ed., pp. 137-176.) See p. 542.

———. *The Key of the Revelation, . . . With a Comment Thereupon.* London: Printed by F. L. for Phil. Stephens, 1650. (Bound with his *Works,* 1648 ed.) See pp. 542-544, 547-549.

———. *The Works of That Reverend, Iudicious, and Learned Divine, Mr. Ioseph Mede . . . Whereunto Are Added, Sundry Discourses on Other Texts . . . Together With Two Tables.* London: Printed by M. F. for John Clark, 1648. See pp. 542, 544, 547.

———. *The Works of the Pious and Profoundly-Learned Joseph Mede.* London: Roger Norton, 1677. See pp. 542, 543, 545.

Melanchthon, Philipp. *Philippi Melanthonis Opera Quae Supersunt Omnia.* Edited by C. G. Bretschneider. Halis Saxonum: Apud C. A. Schwetschke et Filium. 1834-60. 28 vols. (*Corpus Reformatorum,* edited by Henricus Ernestus Bindseil, vols. 1-28). See pp. 154, 288-291.

————. *Der Prophet Daniel ausgelegt durch D. Philipp. Melanth.* Translated from Latin by Justus Jonas. Wittemberg: [*n.n.*], 1546. See p. 289.

Menasseh. See Manasseh.

Merle d'Aubigné, J[ean] H[enri]. *History of the Reformation of the 16th Century.* New York: Worthington Co., [*n.d.*]. 5 vols. in 1. See pp. 248, 249, 288, 385.

Midrash Rabboth al Hatorah U Chammash Migloth. Berlin: Zusman, 1865-66. 3 vols. See p. 193.

Mikraoth Gedoloth. See Bible, Hebrew. 1860-1902.

Milman, Henry Hart. *The History of the Jews, From the Earliest Period Down to Modern Times.* New York: Hurd and Houghton; Boston: W. Veazie, 1864. 3 vols. See pp. 189, 214, 235.

Milner, Joseph. *The History of the Church of Christ.* With Additions and Corrections, by the late Rev. Isaac Milner. From the last London edition. Philadelphia: Hogan and Thompson, 1835. 2 vols. See pp. 37, 87, 88.

Milton, John. *Areopagitica: A Speech for the Liberty of Unlicens'd Printing, to the Parliament of England,* in *The Works of John Milton,* vol. 4, pp. 293-354. New York: Columbia University Press, 1931. See p. 569.

Mirbt, Carl. "Pietism," *The New Schaff-Herzog,* pp. 53-67. See p. 619.

————. *Quellen zur Geschichte des Papsttums und des römischen Katholizismus.* 5th ed. Tübingen: Verlag von J. C. B. Mohr (Paul Siebeck) , 1934. See p. 72.

A Modest Inquiry Into the Meaning of the Revelations. In a Letter to All Such as Wait for the Kingdom of Christ. By a Lover of the Second Coming of our Lord Jesus, and of the Blessed Myllenium. London: [*n.n.*], 1688. See pp. 580, 581.

Möller, W[ilhelm Ernst]. *Andreas Osiander. Leben und ausgewählte Schriften.* Elberfeld: R. L. Friderichs, 1870. See pp. 296, 298, 300, 301.

————. *History of the Christian Church in the Middle Ages.* Translated by Andrew Rutherfurd. London: Swan Sonnenschein & Co., 1893-1900. 3 vols. See p. 115.

More, H[enry]. *A Modest Enquiry Into the Mystery of Iniquity.* London: Printed by J. Flesher for W. Morden, 1664. See pp. 563, 564.

————. *A Plain and Continued Exposition of the Several Prophecies or Divine Visions of the Prophet Daniel.* London: Printed by M. F. for Walter Kettilby, 1681. See pp. 563, 564.

————. *The Theological Works of the Most Pious and Learned Henry More, D.D.* London: Joseph Downing, 1708. See p. 564.

Morison, Samuel Eliot. *Admiral of the Ocean Sea. A Life of Christopher Columbus.* Boston: Little, Brown and Company, 1942. 2 vols. See pp. 162, 163.

Morland, Samuel. *The History of the Evangelical Churches of the Valleys of Piemont.* London: Printed by Henry Hills for Adoniram Byfield, 1658. See p. 105.

Mornay, Philippes de. *Le mystère d'iniquité c'est à dire, l'histoire de la Papauté.* Saumur: Thomas Portau, 1611. See pp. 634, 635, 648.

Mosheim, Johann Lorenz von. *Institutes of Ecclesiastical History, Ancient and Modern.* Translated by James Murdock; edited by Henry Soames. London: Longman & Co. [etc.], 1841. 4 vols. **See pp. 126, 129, 360.**

Muir, William. *The Arrested Reformation.* London: Morgan and Scott, Ltd., 1912. **See p. 465.**

Musculus, And[reas]. *Vom jüngsten Tage.* [Erfurt: *n.n.*], 1559. **See p. 323.**

The Mysteries of God Finished: or an Essay Toward the Opening of the Mystery of the Mystical Numbers in the Scriptures, by the Scriptures, Without the Help of Human History. London: Printed for John Marshal, 1699. **See pp. 596, 597.**

Nanni, Giovanni. *Glosa Sive Expo[sitio] Super Apocalypsim Joa[n]nis Viterbiensis . . . de Statu Ecc[les]ie ab Anno Salutis M.cccc.lxxxi-Usque ad Finen mundi.* Genua: [*n.n.*], 1480. **See p. 308.**

Napier, John. *A Plain Discovery of the Whole Revelation of Saint John: Set Downe in Two Treatises.* Edinburgh: R. Walde-grave, 1593. **See pp. 457-462.**

Napier, Mark. *Memoirs of John Napier of Merchiston.* Edinburgh: William Blackwood, 1834. **See p. 456.**

Neander, Augustus. *General History of the Christian Religion and Church.* Translated by Joseph Torrey. Boston: Crocker & Brewster, 1850-56. 5 vols. **See pp. 32, 35-37, 40-43, 109, 111-113, 126.**

Nebiim Ukethubim. See Bible, Hebrew. 1899-1923.

The New International Encyclopaedia. 2d ed. New York: Dodd Mead and Company, 1930. 23 vols. (And supplements). **See p. 129.**

The New Schaff-Herzog Encyclopedia of Religious Knowledge. Edited by Samuel Macauley Jackson, and others. New York: Funk and Wagnalls Company, 1908-12. 12 vols. **See pp. 126, 127, 142, 145, 308, 316, 322, 323, 338, 446, 471, 518, 521, 697, 706.**

Newman, Albert Henry. *A Manual of Church History.* Philadelphia: The American Baptist Publication Society, 1933, 32. 2 vols. **See pp. 60, 122, 249, 385, 389, 447, 464, 697.**

Newman, Louis Israel. *Jewish Influence on Christian Reform Movements.* New York: Columbia University Press, 1925. (Columbia University Oriental Studies, vol. 23.) **See pp. 186, 209, 217.**

Newton, Sir Isaac. *Observations Upon the Prophecies of Daniel, and the Apocalypse of St. John.* London: J. Darby and T. Browne, 1733. **See pp. 659-669.**

————. Papers. *Catalogue of the Newton Papers . . . Which Will be Sold by Auction by Messrs. Sotheby & Co.* [London]: Printed by H. Davy, [1936]. **See p. 660.**

Newton, Thomas. *Dissertations on the Prophecies.* Northampton, Mass.: William Butler, 1796. **See pp. 685-687.**

Ney, Julius. "Pareus," *The New Schaff-Herzog,* vol. 8, p. 353. **See p. 518.**

Nigrinus, Georg. *Antichrists Gründtliche Offenbarung.* [*n.p.: n.n.*], 1586. **See pp. 327-329.**

————. *Apocalypsis, Die Offenbarunge Sanct Johannis . . . in Sechzig Predigten . . . ausgelegt.* Ursel: Nicolaus Henricus, 1573. **See pp. 325-327.**

————. *Ein wolgegründe Rechnung und Zeitregister von anfang der Welt.* Ursel: [*n.n.*], 1570. **See pp. 325-327, 329.**

Nolhac, Pierre de. *Petrarch and the Ancient World.* Boston, Mass.: D. B. Updike at The Merrymount Press, 1907. **See p. 29.**

Nouvelle biographie générale depuis les temps les plus reculés jusqu'à nos jours. Vol. 12. Paris: Firmin Didot Frères, Fils et Cie., Editeurs, 1856. **See p. 679.**

Ochser, Schulim. "Sahl ben Mazliah Ha-Kohen," *The Jewish Encyclopedia,* vol. 10, p. 636. **See p. 202.**

Oecolampadius, Johann. *Io. Oecolampadii . . . In Danielem Prophetam.* Genevae: E. Typographia Crispiniana, 1567. **See p. 337.**

Of the Ende of This World. See [Geveren, Sheltco a].

Ogg, Frederic Austin. *A Source Book of Mediaeval History.* New York: American Book Company, 1935. **See pp. 18, 23, 60.**

Osiander, Andreas. *Vermutung von den letzten Zeiten und dem Ende der welt, aus der heiligen Schrifftgezogen.* Nürnberg: J. Petreius, 1545. **See pp. 299-302.**

O[verton], R[ichard]. *Man Wholly Mortal. Or, A Treatise Wherein 'Tis proved, . . . That at the Resurrection Is the Beginning of Our Immortality [etc.].* London: [*n.n.*], 1655. [Author identified in the British Museum catalogue.] **See p. 575.**

Pacard, George. *Description de l'Antechrist, et de son royaume.* Niort: René Troismailles, 1604. **See pp. 627-629.**

Pareus, David. *A Commentary Upon the Divine Revelation of the Apostle and Evangelist Iohn.* Translated by Elias Arnold. Amsterdam: C. P., 1644. **See pp. 518-520.**

————. *In Divinam Apocalypsin. S. Apostoli et Evangelistae Johannis Commentarius.* Heidelbergae: Impensis Jonae Rosae, 1618. **See pp. 518-520.**

Paris, Matthew. *English History. From the Year 1235 to 1273.* Translated by the J. A. Giles. London: Henry G. Bohn, 1852-54. 3 vols. **See p. 47.**

Pastor, Ludwig. *The History of the Popes From the Close of the Middle Ages.* From the German of Dr. Ludwig Pastor. Edited by Frederick Ignatius Antrobus. London: Kegan Paul, Trench, Trübner, & Co., Ltd., 1898-99. 6 vols. **See pp. 71, 168, 169, 177, 178.**

Pattison, Mark. "Erasmus," *Encyclopaedia Britannica,* vol. 8, pp. 676-679. **See p. 385.**

Pennington, Arthur Robert. *Epochs of the Papacy From Its Rise to the Death of Pope Pius IX in 1878.* London: George Bell and Sons, 1881. **See pp. 47, 49, 52, 181, 259, 351, 755, 762, 763.**

Pestalozzi, Carl. *Heinrich Bullinger. Leben und ausgewählte Schriften.* Elberfeld: R. L. Friderichs, 1858. **See pp. 340, 342.**

Pétau, Denis. *Dionysii Petavii . . . De Doctrina Temporum.* Venetiis: Excudebat Bartholomaeus Baronchelli, 1757. 3 vols. **See p. 428.**

————. *Dionysii Petavii . . . Rationarium Temporum.* Venetiis: Apud Laurentium Basilium, 1733. 2 vols. **See p. 428.**

Petrarch, Francesco. *Epistolarum Sine Titulo Liber,* in his *Opera,* vol. 2, pp. 793-809. Basileae: Per Henrichum Petri, 1554. 4 vols. in 2. **See p. 31.**

————. *The Sonnets, Triumphs, and Other Poems of Petrarch.* Now First Completely Translated Into English Verse by Various Hands. With a Life of the Poet by Thomas Campbell. London: Henry G. Bohn, 1859. See p. 30.

Petri, Johann Philipp. *Aufschluss der drey Gesichter Daniels nebst dem Traum Nebucadnezars, nach dem Prophetischen Sinn.* Offenbach: Ulrich Weiss, 1769. See p. 717.

————. *Aufschlusz der Zahlen Daniels und der Offenbahrung Johannis.* [*n.p.: n.n.*], 1768. [Author identified by other of his works.] See pp. 714, 715, 717.

————. *Gründlicher Beweis zur Auflösung der Gesichter und Zahlen. Daniels und Offenbahrung Johannis.* Offenbach am Mayn: Ulrich Weiss, 1784. See pp. 715, 718.

————. *Das nahe Tausendjährige Reich Christi.* Offenbach: Ulrich Weiss, 1769. See p. 715.

————. *Die Offenbahrung Jesu Christi durch Johannem von Capitel I-XIX.* Frankfurt: Weisz, 1774. See p. 716.

————. *Die Stunde der Versuchung bey vorhandener Eröfung des Sechsten Siegels.* Offenbach am Mayn: Ulrich Weiss, 1778. See p. 715.

[Philipot, Jacques]. *Eclaircissements sur l'Apocalypse de S. Jean. Système Nouveau.* Amsterdam: Daniel du Fresne, 1687. [Identified in Ant.-Alex. Barbier, *Dictionnaire des Ouvrages Anonymes,* vol. 2, col. 10.] See pp. 726-728.

[————]. *A New Systeme of the Apocalypse, or Plain and Methodical Illustrations of All the Visions in the Revelation of St. John. . . . In Answer to Mr. Jurieu.* [Translation of *Eclaircissements sur l'Apocalypse de S. Jean. Système Nouveau*] London: [*n.n.*], 1688. See p. 648.

Philpot, John. *The Examinations and Writings of John Philpot.* Edited for The Parker Society by Robert Eden. Cambridge: The University Press, 1842. See pp. 374, 375.

Pirkê de Rabbi Eliezer. (The Chapters of Rabbi Eliezer the Great). Translated and Annotated by Gerald Friedlander. London: Kegan Paul, Trench, Trubner & Co., Ltd., 1916. See p. 199.

Piscator, Johan[nes]. *Johan Piscatoris Commentarii in Omnes Libros Novi Testamenti.* Herbornae Nassoviorum, 1613. See p. 601.

Pius VI, Pope. See *Historical and Philosophical Memoirs of Pius the Sixth.*

Poole, Reginald Lane. "Wycliffe, John," *Encyclopaedia Britannica,* vol. 23, pp. 821-824. See p. 48.

————. *Wycliffe and Movements for Reform.* New York: A. D. F. Randolph & Company, [1888]. See pp. 32, 48, 59-61, 109.

Poznanski, Samuel. "Calendar (Jewish)," in James Hastings, *Encyclopaedia of Religion and Ethics,* vol. 3, pp. 117-124. See p. 198.

————. *Miscellen über Saadja III. Die Berechnung des Erlösungsjahres bei Saadja.* Berlin: S. Calvary & Co., 1901. See pp. 200, 201.

The Prayer and Complaint of the Plowman, in Foxe, *Acts and Monuments,* book 5, vol. 1, pp. 453-463. London: Company of Stationers, 1684. See p. 63.

Prescott, William H. *History of the Conquest of Mexico.* Chicago: Belford, Clarke & Co., [1886]. 2 vols. See p. 170.

Pressensé, Edmond de. *The Church and the French Revolution.* Translated from the French by John Stroyan. London: Hodder and Stoughton, 1869. See pp. 735, 738.

Prestage, Edgar. "Portugal," *The Catholic Encyclopedia,* vol. 12, pp. 297-307. See p. 166.

Prideaux, Humphrey. *The Old and New Testament Connected in the History of the Jews and Neighbouring Nations, From the Declension of the Kingdoms of Israel and Judah to the Time of Christ.* Dublin: Printed by A. Rhames, for John Gill, etc., 1719. See p. 431.

Priestley, Joseph. *The Present State of Europe Compared With Ancient Prophecies; A Sermon, Preached February 28, 1794.* London: J. Johnson, 1794. See pp. 745, 746.

Prinz, J[akob]. *Die Kolonien der Brüdergemeinde.* Pjatigorsk, Moskba: Jakob Prinz, 1898. See p. 713.

Pritius, Jo. Georg. D. *Philipp Jacob Speners . . . Gerechter Eifer wider das Antichristische Pabstthum.* Franckfurth am Mayn: Anton Heinscheit, 1714. See pp. 621, 622.

Prölaeus, Andreas. *Babylon. Das ist: Theologischer Schrifftmässiger Erklärung des sechsten General-Gesichtes der heiligen geheimen Offenbahrung S. Johannis 17. 18. 19. Capitels.* Leipzig: Elia Rehefeld, 1632. See p. 602.

Purves, James. *Observations on Prophetic Time and Similitudes.* Part First. [n.p.: n.n.], 1777. See p. 695.

[Purvey, John, supposed author]. *Commentarius in Apocalypsin Ante Centum Annos Editus.* With preface by Martin Luther. VVittembergae: [n.n.], 1528. [Attributed to Purvey; see footnote to Luther's preface in Dr. *Martin Luthers Sämmtliche Schriften* (ed. G. Walch), vol. 14, col. 178, n.; Workman, *Dawn of the Reformation,* vol. 1, pp. 236, 305.] See pp. 98-100, 284.

Putnam, George Haven. *The Censorship of the Church of Rome and Its Influence Upon the Production and Distribution of Literature.* New York: G. P. Putnam's Sons, 1906, 1907. 2 vols. See pp. 141, 183, 482, 483.

Pyle, Thomas. *A Paraphrase With Notes on the Revelation of St. John.* London: Printed for Noon, 1735. See pp. 680, 681.

R. M. *Observations on Certain Prophecies in the Book of Daniel, and the Revelation of St. John, Which Relate to the Second Appearing of Our Lord; . . . To Which Are Added, Some Remarks Concerning the Last Antichrist and the Killing of the Witnesses.* [London?]: Printed for the Author, 1787. [The preface signed R.M.] See pp. 691, 692.

Rait, Robert Sangster. "Scotland: History," *Encyclopaedia Britannica,* vol. 20, pp. 146-162. See p. 448.

Ramsay, Andrew. *A Warning to Come Out of Babylon.* Edinburgh: in King James his College, by George Anderson. 1638. See p. 557.

Ranke, Leopold [von]. *The History of the Popes. Their Church and State.* Translated by E. Foster. London: H. G. Bohn, 1847-51. 3 vols. See p. 731.

Rapp, Georg, translator. See Savonarola, Girolamo, *Die erwecklichen Schriften.* See pp. 143-145, 153.

Registrum Johannis Trefnant, Episcopi Herefordensis, A.D. MCCCLXXXIX-MCCCCIV. Edited by William W. Capes. London: Canterbury and York Society, 1916. **See pp. 75-83, 85-87.**

Ribera, Francisco. *Francisci Riberae . . . In sacram Beati Ioannis Apostoli, & Evangelistae Apocalypsin Commentarij.* Lugduni: Ex Officina Iuntarum, 1593. **See pp. 490-494.**

Richard, James William. *Philip Melanchthon. The Protestant Preceptor of Germany. 1497-1560.* New York and London: G. P. Putnam's Sons, 1898. **See pp. 285-287.**

Rickaby, Joseph. *The Modern Papacy,* in *Lectures on the History of Religions,* vol. 3, [lecture 24]. London: Catholic Truth Society; St. Louis, Mo.: B. Herder, 1910-11. 5 vols. **See p. 763.**

Ridley, Nicholas. *The Works of Nicholas Ridley, D. D. Sometime Lord Bishop of London, Martyr, 1555.* Edited for The Parker Society, by the Rev. Henry Christmas. Cambridge: University Press, 1841. **See pp. 364-368.**

Rieger, Georg Cunrad. *Die Alte und Neue Böhmische Brüder,* vol. 1. Züllichau: Gottlob Benj. Frommann, 1734. **See pp. 32-34, 36, 107, 116.**

Robertson, James C. *History of the Christian Church From the Apostolic Age to the Reformation.* London: John Murray, 1874-75. [Imprint varies.] 8 vols. **See pp. 36, 37, 39, 40, 106, 111-113, 127, 128, 140, 141, 154, 170.**

Rogge, H. C. "Grotius," *The New Schaff-Herzog,* vol. 5, pp. 85, 86. **See p. 521.**

Rollin, Charles. *The Ancient History of the Egyptians, Carthaginians, Assyrians, Babylonians, Medes and Persians, Macedonians, and Grecians.* Translated from the French. New York: W. Borradaile, 1825. 4 vols. **See p. 429.**

[Rome, Republic of] *Constitution of the Roman Republic.* Translated from the Authentic Italian ed. [*n.p.: n.n.*], 1798. **See p. 752.**

Rome's Downfal; Wherein Is Shewed That the Beginnings Thereof Call for Praise and Thanksgiving. London: Printed for Tho. Parkhurst, 1689. **See pp. 560, 561.**

Roth, Cecil. *A History of the Marranos.* Philadelphia: The Jewish Publication Society of America, 1932. **See pp. 74, 220-223.**

————. *A Life of Menasseh ben Israel.* Philadelphia: The Jewish Publication Society of America, 1945. **See pp. 232, 233, 235.**

Rudd, Sayer. *An Essay Towards a New Explication of the Doctrines of the Resurrection, Millennium, and Judgment. . . . To Which Are Added Three Dissertations.* London: J. Blackwell, 1734. **See p. 682.**

Sabatini, Rafael. *Torquemada and the Spanish Inquisition.* London: Stanley Paul and Co., 1913. **See p. 481.**

Sanderson, William. *A Compleat History of the Lives and Reigns of Mary Queen of Scotland, and . . . James.* London: Humphrey Moseley, Richard Tomlins, and George Sawbridge, 1656. **See p. 537.**

Sandys, Edwin [Archbishop]. *The Sermons of Edwin Sandys, To Which Are Added Miscellaneous Pieces, by the Same Author.* Edited for The Parker Society by John Ayre. Cambridge: The University Press, 1842. **See pp. 418-420.**

[Sandys, Sir Edwin]. *Europae Speculum. or, A View or Survey of the State of Religion in the Westerne Parts of the World.* London: T. Cotes for Michael Sparke, 1638. [Author identified in the British Museum catalogue.] **See p. 549.**

Sarachek, Joseph. *The Doctrine of the Messiah in Medieval Jewish Literature.* New York: Jewish Theological Seminary of America, 1932. **See pp. 188, 190, 195, 197, 200, 201, 210-212, 214-217, 226, 231, 232.**

—————. *Don Isaac Abravanel.* New York: Bloch Publishing Company, 1938. **See pp. 223-225.**

Sarpi, Fra Paolo. *Histoire du concile de Trente.* Londres: De l'Imprimerie de Samuel Idle, 1736. 2 vols. **See p. 478.**

Sarton, George. *Introduction to the History of Science.* Baltimore: Williams & Wilkins Company, 1927-31. 2 vols. **See pp. 160, 161, 166.**

Savonarola, Girolamo. *Compendium Revelationum.* Extracts translated in Herbert Lucas, *Fra Girolamo Savonarola,* pp. 51-73. London: Sands and Company, 1899. **See pp. 150, 151.**

—————. *Die erwecklichen Schriften des Märtyrers Hieronymus Savonarola.* Translated by Georg Rapp. Stuttgart: Verlag von S. G. Liesching, 1839. **See pp. 143-145, 153.**

—————. *Auswahl aus seinen Schriften und Predigten.* Translated into German by Jos[eph] Schnitzer. Jena: Eugen Diederichs, 1928. *(Das Zeitalter der Renaissance; ausgewählte Quellen zur Geschichte der italienischen Kultur,* edited by Marie Herzfeld, series 2, vol. 10.) **See pp. 151, 152.**

Scaliger, Joseph. *Iosephi Scaligeri . . . Opus de Emendatione Temporum,* vol. 2. Genevae: Typis Roverianis, 1629. **See p. 427.**

Schaff, David S[chley]. *John Huss—His Life, Teachings and Death—After Five Hundred Years.* New York: Charles Scribner's Sons, 1915. **See pp. 33, 107, 114.**

—————. *The Middle Ages.* New York: Charles Scribner's Sons, 1907, 1910. 1 vol. in 2. (Philip Schaff, *History of the Christian Church,* vol. 5, parts 1 and 2.) **See pp. 29, 87, 88, 91, 106, 110-112, 114, 116, 121-123, 126-129, 136, 141, 143-146, 149, 150, 154, 155, 169, 170.**

Schaff, Philip. *The Creeds of Christendom, With a History and Critical Notes.* New York: Harper & Brothers, 1919. 3 vols. **See pp. 123, 287, 340, 448, 449, 476, 537, 544, 553, 554.**

—————. *History of the Christian Church.* (Vol. 5, parts 1 and 2 written by his son David S. Schaff.) New York: Charles Scribner's Sons, 1882-1910. **See pp. 29, 87, 88, 91, 106, 110-112, 114, 116, 121-123, 126-129, 136, 141, 143-146, 149, 150, 154, 155, 169, 248, 249, 251-254, 257-259, 262, 263, 297, 302, 316, 335, 337, 338, 340, 434, 435, 440, 441.**

—————. *Saint Augustin, Melanchthon, Neander.* Three Biographies. New York: Funk and Wagnalls, 1886. **See pp. 285-287.**

————— (revised by David S. Schaff). "Savonarola," *The New Schaff-Herzog,* vol. 10, pp. 214-218. **See pp. 142, 145.**

—————. "Trent, Council of," *The New Schaff-Herzog,* vol. 12, pp. 1-3. **See p. 471.**

Schaff-Herzog. See *The New Schaff-Herzog Encyclopedia of Religious Knowledge.*

Scharpff, Franz Anton [von]. *Der Cardinal und Bischof Nicolaus von Cusa als Reformator in Kirche, Reich & Philosophie des fünfzehnten Jahrhunderts.* Tübingen: H. Laupp, 1871. **See p. 137.**

Schmid, R. "Cusa," *The New Schaff-Herzog*, vol. 3, pp. 327, 328. **See pp. 126, 127.**

Schreckenbach, Paul, and Franz Neubert. *Martin Luther. Ein Bild seines Lebens und Wirkens.* 3d ed. Leipzig: J. J. Weber, 1921. **See p. 285.**

Schroeder, H[enry] J[oseph]. *Disciplinary Decrees of the General Councils.* Text, translation, and commentary. St. Louis: B. Herder Book Co., 1937. **See pp. 61, 104, 114, 115, 126, 141, 175, 176, 183, 261, 482.**

—————, compiler. See Trent, Council of.

Sefer, etc. See next word in title.

Selnecker, Nikolaus. *Die Propheten.* [*n.n.: n.p.*], 1579. **See pp. 323, 324.**

Semler, Johann Salomo. *D. Joh. Sal. Semlers neue Untersuchungen über Apocalypsin.* Halle: Carl Hermann Hemmerde, 1776. **See p. 707.**

Sewall, Frank. "Swedenborg," *The New Schaff-Herzog*, vol. 11, pp. 183-189. **See p. 706.**

Sherwin, W[illiam]. Ἐυαγγελιον . . . or *The Saints First Revealed and Covenanted Mercies Shortly Approaching.* London: [*n.n.*], 1676. [General title page for a work composed of tracts, some already published, with other material, in several paginations. See the "Account . . . July 27, 1672," p. 4. Bound with other separate works in a volume, listed under the binder's title *Pamphlets*, in the University of Illinois library. The British Museum, which seems to have an incomplete collection, catalogues each item separately.] **See pp. 576-579.**

—————. Χρονοὶ . . . or *The Times of Restitution of All Things.* London: [*n.n.*], 1675. Bound with *The Saints First Revealed and Covenanted Mercies* in *Pamphlets*. **See pp. 576, 577.**

A Short Catechisme, or Playne Instruction, Conteynynge the Summe of Christian Learninge, Sett Fourth by the Kings Maiesties Authoritie, for all Scholemaisters to Teache. London: John Day, 1553. **See p. 423.**

Silver, Abba Hillel. *A History of Messianic Speculation in Israel From the First Through the Seventeenth Centuries.* New York: The Macmillan Company, 1927. **See pp. 186-188, 191, 193, 195, 196, 199-202, 206-208, 210-219, 225-227, 231-233, 235.**

Simms, P[aris] Marion. *The Bible in America; Versions That Have Played Their Part in the Making of the Republic.* New York: Wilson-Erikson, Incorporated, 1936. **See p. 703.**

Simpson, David. *A Plea for Religion and the Sacred Writings: Addressed to the Disciples of Thomas Paine, and Wavering Christians of Every Persuasion.* With an appendix, etc. London: Printed for J. Mawman, 1802. **See pp. 775-777.**

Sismondi, J. C. L. Simonde de. *History of the Crusades Against the Albigenses, in the Thirteenth Century.* Translated from the French. London: Wightman & Cramp, 1826. **See p. 105.**

Smith, Preserved. *Luther's Table Talk; a Critical Study*. New York: The Columbia University Press, 1907. **See p. 278.**

Smith, Sidney, "Calendar: Babylonian and Assyrian," *Encyclopaedia Britannica*, vol. 4, pp. 576, 577. **See p. 672.**

Smith, Sydney F. "Bellarmine," *The Catholic Encyclopedia*, vol. 2, pp. 411-413. **See p. 495.**

Solis, Virgil. *Biblische Figuren des Alten und Newen Testaments*. Franckfurt am Main, [*n.n.*], 1560. **See pp. 313, 314, 346.**

Sotheby, S[amuel] Leigh. *Unpublished Documents, Marginal Notes and Memoranda, in the Autograph of Philip Melanchthon and of Martin Luther*. London: J. Davy, printer, 1840. **See pp. 287, 291.**

Source Book for Bible Students. Rev. ed. Washington, D.C.: Review and Herald Publishing Association, 1940. **See p. 478.**

Spener, Philipp Jakob. *Pia Desideria: Oder Hertzliches Verlangen*. Franckfurt au Mayn: Johann David Zunner, 1676. **See p. 619.**

————. Same. 2d ed. Leipzig: Koehler, [*n.d.*]. **See p. 620.**

————. Theologisches Bedencken. 2d ed. [*n.p.: n.n.*], 1692. **See p. 622.**

Springinsguten, Daniel. *Kurtzer Begriff und Theologische Prüffung der sinnreichen und mit grossem Fleiss auffgesetzten Zeit-Rechnung des Geistreichen Theologi Herrn D. Philippi Nicolai*. Rostock: Johann Richeln, 1666. **See p. 600.**

Stebbing, Henry. *A Discourse Preparatory to the Religious Observance of the Day of Publick Fasting and Humiliation, Appointed by Authority, to Be Kept on Friday the Sixth of February 1756, on the Occasion of the Late Earthquakes Abroad, and Particularly at Lisbon*. London: E. Owen, 1756. **See p. 676.**

[Stiefel, Michael]. *Ein sehr Wunderbarliche wortrechnung sampt einer mercklichen erklerung etlicher Zalen Danielis und der Offenbarung sanct Johannis*. [*n.p.: n.n.*], 1553. [Author identified in Staatsbibliothek, Berlin.] **See pp. 320-322, 346, 347.**

Stimmer, Tobias. *Neue Künstliche Figuren biblischer Historien grüntlich von Tobia Stimmer gerissen*. Basel: Thoma Gwarin, 1576. **See p. 346.**

Stimson, Dorothy. *The Gradual Acceptance of the Copernican Theory of the Universe*. New York: Baker & Taylor Co., 1917. **See p. 162.**

Stolberg, August. *Tobias Stimmer, Sein Leben und seine Werke*. Strassburg: J. H. E. Heitz, 1905. **See p. 347.**

Stoughton, John. *Ecclesiastical History of England, From the Opening of the Long Parliament to the Death of Oliver Cromwell*, vol. 2, *The Church of the Commonwealth*. London: Jackson, Walford, and Hodder, 1867. **See p. 569.**

Strayer, Joseph R., and Dana Carleton Munro. *The Middle Ages, 395-1500*. New York: D. Appleton-Century Company, Incorporated, 1942. **See pp. 17, 45, 46.**

Strieder, Friedrich Wilhelm. *Grundlage zu einer Hessischen Gelehrten und Schriftsteller Geschichte*. Vol. 10. Cassel: J. H. G. Griesbach, 1795. **See p. 713.**

Strype, John. *Memorials of the Most Reverend Father in God Thomas Cranmer*. A new edition, with additions. Oxford: The Clarendon Press, 1812. 2 vols. **See p. 391.**

Tanner, Joseph. *Daniel and the Revelation: The chart of prophecy and our place in it. A Study of the Historical and Futurist Interpretation.* London: Hodder and Stoughton, 1898. **See pp. 487, 511.**

Taylor, Henry Osborn. *The Mediaeval Mind: A History of the Development of Thought and Emotion in the Middle Ages.* 3d (American) ed. New York: Macmillan Company, 1919. 2 vols. **See p. 22.**

Taylor, Lauchlan. *An Essay on the Revelation of the Apostle John.* London: A. Millar, 1763. **See p. 695.**

Thacher, John Boyd. *Christopher Columbus, His Life, His Work, His Remains.* New York: G. P. Putnam's Sons, 1903. 3 vols. **See pp. 166, 167, 171, 173, 174.**

Thomas, Joseph. *Universal Pronouncing Dictionary of Biography and Mythology.* Philadelphia: J. B. Lippincott and Company, 1930. **See pp. 660, 687, 692, 693.**

Thomson, Thomas. "Life of the Rev. Robert Fleming," in Robert Fleming, *The Rise and Fall of Papacy.* Edinburgh: Johnstone, Hunter & Co., 1870. **See p. 643.**

Thube, Christian Gottlob. *Anleitung zum richtigen Verstande der Offenbarung Johannis.* Schwerin und Wismar: Bödner, 1799. **See p. 778.**

—————. *Das Buch des Propheten Daniels neu übersetzt und erklärt.* Schwerin und Wismar: Bödner, 1797. **See pp. 777, 778.**

—————. *Handbuch der Gottsgelahrtheit.* Minden: Martin Gottfried Franke, 1789. **See p. 777.**

—————. *Ueber die nächstkommenden vierzig Jahre.* Schwerin und Wismar: Bödner, 1796. **See p. 777.**

Tillinghast, John. *Knowledge of the Times, or, The resolution of the Question, How Long It Shall Be Unto the End of Wonders.* [To which is added] *An Appendix.* [Separate title page. Same imprint.] London: R. I. for L. Chapman, 1654. **See pp. 310, 570-572.**

[Towers, Joseph Lomas]. *Illustrations of Prophecy.* London: [n.n.], 1796. 2 vols. [Author identified in *Dictionary of National Biography.*] **See pp. 644, 723, 724.**

Translations and Reprints From the Original Sources of European History. Philadelphia: Published by the Department of History of the University of Pennsylvania, 1894-99. 6 vols. **See pp. 48, 735.**

Trapp, John. *A Commentary or Exposition Upon All the Epistles and the Revelation of John the Divine.* London: John Bellamy, 1647. **See p. 560.**

Trefnant, Johannes. See *Registrum.*

Trench, Richard Chenevix. *Lectures on Medieval Church History.* New York: Charles Scribner's Sons, 1877. **See pp. 22, 49, 52, 60, 67, 93, 106, 107, 110, 112, 115, 137, 176, 177.**

Trent, Council of. *Canons and Decrees of the Council of Trent.* Original text with English translation by H. J. Schroeder. St. Louis: B. Herder Book Co., 1941. **See pp. 475, 478, 482, 483.**

—————. *Concilium Tridentinum. Diariorum, Actorum, Epistolarum, Tractatuum Nova Collectio,* part 5 (vol. 8), Edidit Societas Goerresiana. Friburgi Brisgoviae: B. Herder, 1919. **See p. 478.**

Trevor, George. *Rome: From the Fall of the Western Empire*. London: The Religious Tract Society, 1868. See p. 750.

Trobridge, George. *Swedenborg, Life and Teaching*. New York: Swenborg Foundation, 1944. See p. 706.

Tschachert, Paul. "Funck," *The New Schaff-Herzog*, vol. 4, pp. 410, 411. See p. 308.

Tyndale, William. [*Works*]. Vol. 1: *Doctrinal Treatises*, [etc.]; vol. 2: *Expositions and Notes*, [etc.]; vol. 3: *An Answer to Sir Thomas More's Dialogue*, [etc.]. Edited for the Parker Society by Henry Walter. Cambridge: The University Press, 1848-50. See pp. 354-358.

Tyndale, Frith, and Barnes. See Barnes.

Ubisch, Eduard Edgar von. *Virgil Solis und Seine Biblischen Illustrationen*. Leipzig: Ramm & Seemann, 1889. See p. 314.

Ullman, Karl. *Reformers Before the Reformation, Principally in Germany and the Netherlands*. Translated by Robert Menzies. Edinburgh: T. & T. Clark, 1855. 2 vols. See pp. 127, 154.

The Universal Jewish Encyclopedia. . . . An Authoritative and Popular Presentation of Jews and Judaism Since the Earliest Times. Edited by Isaac Landman. New York: The Universal Jewish Encyclopedia, Inc., 1939-1943. 10 vols. See pp. 199, 218, 225.

Ussher, James. *Annales Veteris Testamenti, a Prima Mundi Origine Deducti*. London: Ex Officina J. Flesher, 1650. See p. 428.

—————. *The Annals of the World*. Translated from his *Annales*. London: E. Tyler, 1658. See p. 428.

V[alpy] R[ichard]. *Poetical Chronology of Ancient and English History; With Historical and Explanatory Notes*. 4th ed. Reading: Smart and Cowslade, 1804. [Author identified in British Museum catalogue.] See p. 772.

—————. *A Sermon Preached August 13, 1798*. Reading: Smart and Cowslade, 1798. See pp. 768, 770.

—————. *Sermons Preached on Public Occasions. With Notes, and an Appendix*. 2 vols. London: Sold by Longman, etc., 1811. See pp. 770-772.

Van den Biesen, C. "Apocalypse," *The Catholic Encyclopedia*, vol. 1, pp. 594-599. See p. 486.

Vaughan, Robert. *John de Wycliffe, D.D., A Monograph*. London: Seeleys, 1853. See p. 53.

—————. *The Life and Opinions of John de Wycliffe, D.D., Illustrated Principally From His Unpublished Manuscripts*. 2d rev. ed. London: Holdsworth and Ball, 1831. 2 vols. See pp. 48, 49.

Viegas, Blasius. *Commentarii Exegetici in Apocalypsim Ioannis Apostoli*. Eborae: Apud Emmanuelem de Lyra, 1601. See p. 503.

Villanova, Arnold of. *Tractatus de Tempore Adventus Antichristi*. Printed in part in Heinrich Finke, *Aus den Tagen Bonifaz VIII*, pp. 129-159. Münster i. W.: Druck und Verlag der Aschendorffschen Buchhandlung, 1902. See p. 72.

Villari, Pasquale. *Life and Times of Girolamo Savonarola*. Translated by Linda Villari. London: T. Fisher Unwin, 1899. See pp. 143-147, 149, 150, 152, 153.

Vitringa, Campegius. *Anacrisis Apocalypsios Johannis Apostoli*. Armstelodami: Ex officina Henrici Strickii, 1719. See pp. 677, 678.

Wace, Henry, and C. A. Buchheim. See Luther, Martin, *First Principles of the Reformation*.

Wächter, Oskar. *Bengel und Oetinger. Leben & Aussprüche*. Gütersloh: Bertelsmann, 1886. See p. 711.

Waddington, George. *A History of the Church From the Earliest Ages to the Reformation*. London: Baldwin and Cradock, 1833. See pp. 88, 144.

————. *A History of the Reformation on the Continent*. London: Duncan and Malcolm, 1841. 3 vols. See pp. 248, 252-254.

Walch, Johann Georg, editor. See Luther, Martin. *Luthers Sämmtliche Schriften*.

[Walmesley, Charles, Bishop]. *The General History of the Christian Church, From Her Birth to Her Final Triumphant State in Heaven*. By Sig. Pastorini [pseud.] 2d American ed. New York: John Doyle, 1834. [Author identified in Library of Congress catalogue.] See p. 683.

Wesley, John. *Explanatory Notes Upon the New Testament*. Vol. 3. 1st American ed. Philadelphia: Pritchard and Hall, 1791. See pp. 693, 694.

West, Nathaniel. "History of the Pre-Millennial Doctrine," *Second Coming of Christ. Premillennial Essays of the Prophetic Conference, Held in the Church of the Holy Trinity, New York City. With an Appendix of Critical Testimonies*, pp. 313-404. Edited by Nathaniel West. Chicago: F. H. Revell, 1879. See pp. 553, 566, 651, 652.

Whetenhall, Thomas. *A Discourse of the Abuses Now in Question in the Churches of Christ, of Their Creeping in, Growing Up, and Flowrishing in the Babilonish Church of Rome*. Imprinted 1606. See p. 554.

Whiston, William. *An Essay on the Revelation of Saint John, So Far as Concerns the Past and Present Times*. Cambridge: University Press, 1706. See p. 672.

————. Same. 2d ed., greatly improv'd and corrected. London: Printed for the author; and sold by John Whiston, 1744. See pp. 669, 672-674.

————. *The Literal Accomplishment of Scripture Prophecies*. London: Printed for J. Senex, 1724. See p. 673.

————. *A Short View of the Chronology of the Old Testament, and of the Harmony of the Four Evangelists*. Cambridge: University Press, 1702. See p. 673.

Whitby, Daniel. *A Paraphrase and Commentary on the New Testament*. London: Printed by J. Barber, for Awnsham and John Churchill, 1706. 2 vols. See pp. 650-654.

Whitling, H. J. *Pictures of Nuremberg; and Rambles in the Hills and Valleys of Franconia*. London: Richard Bentley, 1850. 2 vols. See p. 293.

Willet, Andrew. *Hexapla in Danielem: That Is, A Six-fold Commentarie Upon the Most Divine Prophesie of Daniel*. Divided into two books. Book 1. University of Cambridge: Cantrell Legge, 1610. See pp. 554, 555.

————. *Synopsis Papismi, That Is, A Generall Viewe of Papistry*. London: T. Orwin, for T. Man, 1592. See p. 554.

Willison, John. *A Prophecy of the French Revolution, and the Downfall of Antichrist; Being Two Sermons Preached Many Years Ago.* Reprinted. London: J. Forbes, 1793. **See pp. 729, 730.**

Wilson, Arthur. *The History of Great Britain, Being the Life and Reign of King James the First.* London: Richard Lownds, 1653. **See p. 537.**

Winsor, Justin, editor. . . . *Narrative and Critical History of America.* Boston: Houghton, Mifflin and Company, 1884-89. 8 vols. **See p. 166.**

Winton, James, Bishop of. See James I, *Workes.*

Wither, George. *A View of the Marginal Notes of the Popish Testament, Translated into English by the English Fugitive Papists Resiant at Rhemes in France.* London: Printed by Edm. Bollifant for Thomas Woodcocke, [1588]. **See p. 550.**

Wolf, Lucien, editor. *Menasseh ben Israel's Mission to Oliver Cromwell.* London: Macmillan & Co., Limited, 1901. **See pp. 220, 222, 223.**

[Wood, Hans]. *The Revelation of St. John.* London: Printed for the Author and sold by T. Payne & Son, 1787. [Author identified by Halkett & Laing, *op. cit.*, vol. 5, p. 106.] **See pp. 714, 719-722.**

Wordsworth, Christopher. *Ecclesiastical Biography; or, Lives of Eminent Men, Connected With the History of Religion in England; From the Commencement of the Reformation to the Revolution; Selected and Illustrated With Notes.* 4th ed. London: Francis & John Rivington. 1853. 4 vols. **See pp. 354, 364, 365, 380, 381, 405, 406.**

Wordsworth, John. *The National Church of Sweden.* (The Hale Lectures, 1910.) London: A. R. Mowbray & Co. Ltd., 1911. **See p. 69.**

Wordsworth, William. "Wicliffe," *Ecclesiastical Sonnets,* Part II, Sonnet XVII, in *The Poetical Works of William Wordsworth,* [vol. 3], pp. 369, 370. Edited by E. de Selincourt. Oxford: At the Clarendon Press, 1946. **See p. 62.**

Workman, Herbert B[rook]. *The Dawn of the Reformation.* London: Charles H. Kelly, 1901-02. 2 vols. **See pp. 22, 23, 34, 36, 40, 51, 53, 74, 91, 93, 109, 110, 114-116.**

―――. *John Wyclif, A Study of the English Medieval Church.* Oxford: At the Clarendon Press, 1926. 2 vols. **See pp. 60, 62, 91.**

Workman and Pope. See Huss, John, *Letters.*

Wrangham, Francis. *Rome Is Fallen! A Sermon . . . 1798.* York: Wilson, Spence, and Mawman, 1798. **See pp. 768, 773, 774.**

Wyclif, [John]. *The English Works of Wyclif Hitherto Unprinted.* Edited by F. D. Matthew. London: Published for the Early English Text Society, by Trübner & Co., 1880. **See p. 53.**

―――. *John Wyclif's De Veritate Sacrae Scripturae.* Edited by Rudolf Buddensieg. [*n.p.*]: Published for the Wyclif Society by Trübner & Co., 1905-07. 3 vols. **See pp. 55, 57, 58.**

―――. *The Last Age of the Chirche.* Edited with notes by James H. Todd. Dublin: University Press, 1840. ["Now first printed from a manuscript in the University Library, Dublin (the collection of Archbp. Ussher).'] **See p. 59.**

————. *Select English Works of John Wyclif,* edited from original mss. by Thomas Arnold. Oxford: Clarendon Press, 1869-71. 3 vols. **See pp. 53, 60.**

————. *Tracts and Treatises of John de Wycliffe, D.D.* Edited by Robert Vaughan. London: The Wycliffe Society, 1845. **See pp. 53, 54, 58.**

————. *Writings of the Reverend and Learned John Wickliff, D.D.* London: Religious Tract Society, 1831. (*British Reformers,* vol. 1, Wickliff to Bilney.) **See p. 54.**

————, translator. Bible version, in *The English Hexapla.* See Bible, English, 1841.

Wylie, J. A. *The History of Protestantism.* London: Cassell and Company, Limited, [no date]. 3 vols. **See pp. 51, 106, 291, 385, 424, 443, 445, 449, 466, 474.**

Züllig, Friedrich Jakob. *Die Offenbarung Johannis.* Stuttgart: E. Schweizerbarts Verlagshandlung, 1840. **See p. 605.**

The Zurich Letters. Edited for the Parker Society by H. Robinson. Cambridge: University Press, 1842-45. 2 vols. **See pp. 341, 450.**

Zwingli, Huldreich. *Zwingli Haupschriften,* vol. 7. Edited by Fritz Blanke, Ostar Farner, and Rudolf Pfister. Zürich: Zwingli Verlag, 1942. **See p. 335.**

DOCUMENTS

France. *Official Bills and Circulars Printed and Posted in Rome During the Establishment of the Republic Under General Berthier in 1798.* In Bibliothèque Nationale, Paris. **See pp. 754, 756-759.**

Invito Sagro e Notificazione. (Poster.) Issued by Guilo Maria, Cardinal della Somaglia. Roma: Nella Stamperia d[obliterated] Camera Apostolica, 1798. **See p. 751.**

PERIODICALS & NEWSPAPERS

Baptist Annual Register (London), 1794-97, 1798-1801. **See pp. 743, 744.**

Bell, George. "Downfal of Antichrist," *The Evangelical Magazine* (London), vol. 4, 1796, pp. 53 ff, 98 ff. **See pp. 741-743.**

Chafer, Lewis Sperry. "An Introduction to the Study of Prophecy," *Bibliotheca Sacra,* January-March, 1943 (vol. 100, no. 397), pp. 98-133. **See p. 652.**

Einstein, Albert. "Isaac Newton," *The Observatory,* May, 1927 (vol. 50, no. 636), pp. 146, 147. **See pp. 658, 659.**

The European Magazine, vols. 33, 34, 1798. **See pp. 753, 755, 757.**

The Gentleman's Magazine (London), February, 1756. **See p. 675.**

"Georg Hermann Giblehrs Unvorgreiffliche Gedancken von dem erfundenen Termino des jüngsten Gerichts. 1702. 4. von 7. Bogen," *Unschuldige Nachrichten von Alten-und Neuen Theologischen Sachen* (Leipzig), 1708, pp. 764-769. See pp. 701, 702.

[Hales, William]. Installment of a series signed "Inspector" in *The Orthodox Churchman's Magazine and Review* (London), December, 1803 (vol. 5), p. 342. [Author identified in his *A New Analysis of Chronology*, vol. 2, p. 518 n.] See p. 720.

[King, Edward]. "The 1260 Years of Papal Triumph" (excerpts from Edward King), *The Signs of the Times, and Expositor of Prophecy* (Boston), Feb. 22, 1843 (vol. 4, no. 23), p. 177. See p. 769.

The London Chronicle, March 10-13, 1798. See p. 752.

The London Packet, Jan. 17-22, March 5-7, 1798. See pp. 751, 752.

The [London] *Times,* March 12, 1798. See p. 752.

Missionary Magazine (Edinburgh), vol. 1, 1796. See p. 741.

Poznanski, Samuel. "The Anti-Karaite Writings of Saadiah Gaon," *The Jewish Quarterly Review,* January, 1898 (vol. 10, no. [2]), pp. 238-276. See p. 198.

"Rembrandt's Etchings for the 'Piedra Gloriosa,'" *The Jewish Chronicle* (London), July 13, 1906 (new series, vol. 3), pp. 39, 40. See p. 235.

MANUSCRIPTS

Cusa, Nicholas of. "Paulus Apostolus ad Galathas Scribens," Predigt 3, 1440. In Cusa's MS. library. See pp. 129, 135.

Klibansky, Raymond. Letter to L. E. Froom, dated October 17, 1938. See p. 136.

Newton, Sir Isaac. "Prophecies Concerning Christ's 2d Coming." 15,000 words, 40 pages, small quarto (8½ x 6½ in.). Original autograph manuscript in the Advent Source Collection, S.D.A. Theological Seminary, Washington, D.C. See p. 660.

Index

The classification in this Index is threefold. It includes the names of all expositors and other individuals cited, all prophetic terms employed, and topics discussed. The topics, however, are based upon key words rather than upon the subdivisions of the various subjects. The main discussions of the different commentators are indicated by the inclusive figures in italics, as pages *658-669* for Sir Isaac Newton. Comprehensive analyses of the principal Jewish, pre-Reformation, Reformation, and post-Reformation expositors appear respectively on pages 194, 156, 157, 528-531, and 784-787. Book, pamphlet, periodical, and manuscript titles are not repeated here, as they appear in the Bibliography, which begins on page 809, with page reference to all citations given in connection with each work.

Abauzit, Firmin, 706
Abomination of desolation, 33, 40, 58, 72, 77-80, 88, 91, 117-119, 210, 213, 272, 277, 280, 305, 306, 396, 411, 428, 529, 571, 616, 681, 682, 691, 715, 722, 742, 766
Abraham, 478
  bar Hiyya Hanasi, 211
Abravanel, Don Isaac, 187, 211, *223-232*, 237, 238, 240, 592
Absolutism, 48, 105
Acquaviva, Claudio, 470
Act of Six Articles, *see* Six Articles
Act of Uniformity (conformity), 386, 574
Adam, first, 135, 136, 174
  second, 135
Adiaphora, Adiaphoristic Controversy, 304, 315
Advent of Christ, first, 131, 134, 186, 238, 398, 404, 457, 535, 541, 544, 580, 630, 766, 784, 804
  second, 32, 43, 62, 72, 79, 92, 134, 161, 171, 186, 233, 235, 279, 281, 309, 321, 328, 330, 344, 383, 398, 401, 403, 489, 520, 521, 534, 535, 541, 544, 567, 578, 580, 588, 600, 627, 630, 646, 651, 653, 665, 689, 710, 730, 745, 766, 760, 774, 704-786, 793, 805, 807
  third after millennium, 630
Afendopolo, Caleb, 197
Africanus, 135
Ahab, 678
Akiba ben Joseph, Rabbi, 193, 195
Ailly, Pierre d', 45, 161, 162, 166, 174
Alaric, 415, 525
Alaric's sack of Rome, 348
Albano, Cardinal, 36, 37
Albert of Mainz, Archbishop, 140, 252, 482
Albigenses, 104, 398, 548
Albrecht of Prussia, 298, 311
Alcazar, Luis de, 214, 439, 486-488, 503, 506, *507-510*, 519, 522, 524, 552, 589, 591, 613, 631, 708, 794
Alexander, the Great, 199, 207, 212, 237, 267-269, 289, 312, 324, 362, 564, 565, 662
  divisions of his empire, 428
  V, 45, 46, 112
  VI, 141, 145-147, 169
Alexandrian School (Jewish), 185

Alfonso, V of Portugal, 224
  X of Castile, 173, 174, 221
Allegory, allegorism, 185, 107, 355
Allix, 656, 673
Alsted, Johann Heinrich, 571, *610, 611*
Alva, duke of, 479
Ambrose, 317, 339
America, 18, 552, 640, 641, 647, 692, 693, 697, 701, 745, 765
  Advent and Prophetic Awakening in, 12, 534
American Bible Society, 762
Amoraim, 188
Amsdorf, Nicholas, 243, 255, *303-306*
Amyraut, Moise, *633, 634*
Anabaptists, 386, 439, 566, 599
Anacleto, *see* Pope Celestine I
Anan, Dean John, 451, 452
Anan ben David, *197*, 206
Ananites, 197
Anathema, 49, 113, 732
Ancient of days, 661, 718
Angel of Revelation 14, first, 99, 517, 520, 604, 675, 700, 711
  second, 99, 517, 520, 604, 700, 711
  third, 99, 517, 520, 700, 711
  "Angelic Year," Osiander, 299, 300
Anglican Church, 386, 387, 540, 655, 675, 681, 692
Anglican Prayer Book, *see* Book of Common Prayer
Anglicans, 413, 428, 568
Anne, Queen (England), 659
Anne of Bohemia, 61, 109
Anselm, 501
Antichrist, a Jew of tribe of Dan, 76, 81, 116, 407, 461, 488, 489, 498, 505, 803, 804
  Catholic counterinterpretations, 484-532
  church of, 397, 398, 424, 450, 451
  Eastern, 322, 608, 657, 658
  empire of, 727
  Roman, 259, 295, 328, 330, 373-442, 449, 450, 484-489, 537, 554, 562, 610, 611, 613, 633, 729
  seat of, 502, 516, 540, 609, 615, 683
  synagogue of, 383
  Western, 322, 608, 657, 658
Antichrist's Tayle, 89, 90, 117

847

Anticlericalism, 46
Antigonus, 428
Antiochus Epiphanes, 214, 230, 231, 269, 270,
    277, 290, 324, 328, 337, 392, 437,
    492, 499, 508, 545, 551, 554, 564, 565,
    572, 610, 614, 631, 662, 671, 672, 678,
    683, 685, 688, 703, 713, 803
Antiquarian Society (England), 765, 770
Anti-Trinitarians, 526
Apocalypse, 13, 24, 28, 32, 34, 67, 75, 78, 119,
    121, 124, 142, 143, 150, 154, 170, 245,
    273, 277, 278, 284, 288, 298, 302, 307,
    309, 317, 319, 322, 326, 330, 335, 338,
    341-343, 347, 374, 382, 393, 397, 414,
    436, 442, 443, 447, 484-487, 489, 490,
    496, 502, 503, 507, 510, 513, 522, 525,
    540, 541-543, 550, 553, 557, 566, 573,
    587, 588, 603, 605, 608, 622, 624, 631-
    633, 636, 637, 651, 655, 659, 660, 665,
    667, 677, 679, 706-710, 713, 723, 747, 778,
    782, 794, 806, 807
Apocalyptical city, 748
Apostasy, Roman, 66, 336, 581
Apostolic, See, 177
    succession, 366
Appearing of Christ, 705
Aquinas, Thomas, 25, 204, 343, 469
Aramaic, 191
Archer, Henry, 567, 568, 571
Aretas, 343
Aretius, Benedictus, 348
Aristotelianism, see Aristotle
Aristotle, 18, 215, 226, 237, 299
Armageddon, 578, 722
Arminians, 521
Arndt, Johann, 602, 618, 709, 712
Arnold of Villanova, 71-73, 718, 787, 790
Arnulf of Orleans, 343, 411, 628
Artabanus, 663
Artaxerxes Longimanus, 192, 311, 312, 324,
    326, 345, 426, 428, 429, 431, 630, 632,
    662, 665, 704
    seventh year of, 309, 345, 787
Artaxerxes Mnemon, 547, 572
Articles of Marburg, 598
Articles of Religion, 446, 589
Arundel, Archbishop, 87, 89, 90, 93, 101
Asher, Bayya ben, 218
Ashkenazi ben Elijah Harofe, Eliezer, 219
Askew, Anne, 352
Atheism, 738
Atonement, Day of, 198, 222, 232, 664, 667,
    668
Augsburg, Confession, 287, 288, 465, 518, 526,
    598
    Diet, 253, 294, 441, 526
    Interim, 474
    Peace of, 350
Augustine, Augustinianism, 72, 80, 100, 160,
    173, 186, 237, 248, 320, 332, 339, 344,
    349, 358, 417, 436, 462, 478, 490, 492,
    501, 505, 509, 517, 520, 532, 534, 536, 544,
    567, 588, 604, 617, 633, 640, 710, 785, 805
Augustine friars, 369
Augustulus, 742, 769
Aurifaber, 308
Authoritarianism, 10
Auto-da-fé, 220, 221, 232, 761
Avignon, 17, 19, 20, 29-31, 34, 36, 46, 47, 68,
    70, 73, 176, 750

Babylon, 30, 31, 41, 73, 75, 79, 83, 86, 99,
    100, 102, 116, 121, 146, 152, 181, 183,
    190, 192, 197-200, 245, 257, 258, 274,
    277, 288, 290, 308, 314, 315, 317, 319,
    344, 356, 367, 368, 375, 378, 391, 396, 402,

    411, 412, 424, 437, 447, 452, 453, 455,
    459, 460, 487, 488, 493, 498, 503, 504,
    509, 517, 523, 528, 529, 546, 548, 549,
    551, 552, 557, 561-563, 577, 578, 581,
    583, 589, 591, 593, 595, 601, 604, 613,
    616, 620-622, 639, 643, 647, 655, 656,
    665, 667, 673, 678, 679, 687, 689, 707,
    712, 746, 748, 766, 769, 773, 781, 787, 789,
    802, 805
    fall of, 403, 769
    harlot, see Harlot
    Western, 31
    whore of, 20, 29, 79, 246, 356, 366, 368,
        383, 393, 404, 453, 519, 541, 602, 689
Babylonia, 185, 320
Babylonian, captivity, 11, 17, 19, 47, 68, 620
    city, 726, 743
    Empire of Antichrist, 534
    exile, 211
    Targum Onkelos, see Targum
    Targum Jonathan ben Uzziel, see Targum
    woman, 28, 67, 298, 305, 306, 315, 452, 453,
        778
Babylonians, 370
"Babylonical Beast," 366
"Babylonical Brood," 403
Babylonical synagogue, 375
Bacon, Roger, 47, 161, 166, 431
Bale, John, 356, 363, 395-401
Baptism, 86, 429
    infant, 441
Baptists, English, 386, 387, 672, 681, 682
Barcochba, 523
Barnes, Robert, 356, 358-361, 363, 369
Baronius, 495, 504
Basel, Council of, 122, 125, 126, 128, 176,
    180
Basil, 363
Basille, Theodore, see Becon
Bear, Persian, 190, 237, 264, 565, 661
Beast, 27, 75, 117, 193, 245, 246, 275, 293,
    301, 307, 308, 315, 319, 368, 382, 408,
    409, 442, 452, 458, 487, 528, 529, 537,
    541, 546, 554, 586, 594, 613, 615, 621,
    628, 633, 634, 645, 646, 656, 667, 679,
    681, 694, 700, 708, 710, 711, 712, 728,
    774, 776, 789, 802
    ascending from earth, 78, 85, 86, 415, 423,
        615, 638, 694, 747
    ascending from sea, 86, 136, 319, 331, 362,
        399, 415, 539, 611, 747, 778
    first of Revelation 13, 41, 78, 82, 99, 105,
        117, 136, 265, 274, 275, 307, 309, 318,
        320, 342, 356, 399, 415, 461, 503,
        508, 515, 520, 523, 525, 528, 543, 548,
        593, 604, 609, 611, 613, 615, 616, 631,
        638, 656, 657, 677, 679, 681, 683, 687,
        694, 715, 721
    from the abyss, 779
    image of, see Image of Beast
    mark of, see Mark of the Beast
    seat of, 265, 315, 342, 548, 645, 649, 667, 683
    second of Revelation 13, 77, 78, 85, 98,
        265, 274, 299, 300, 309, 320, 327, 330,
        335, 337, 342, 399, 415, 416, 461, 515,
        523, 525, 528, 543, 548, 560, 565, 593,
        604, 611, 613, 615, 629, 631, 638, 656-
        658, 667, 673, 679, 681, 687, 694, 711,
        715, 721, 727, 747
    with seven heads and ten horns, 28, 41, 76,
        85, 99, 265, 314, 319, 327, 331, 383, 399,
        415, 416, 460, 487, 593, 594, 703, 747
Beasts, see Beast
Becon, Thomas, 356, 401-403, 424
Bede, 58, 161, 501, 505
Beghard, 41, 43, 67, 628

Beguines, 67
Belisarius, 743, 767, 776
Bell, George, *741-743*
Bellarmine, Robert, 486, 493, *495-502*, 512, 513, 516, 518, 519, 535, 540, 555, 589, 591, 607, 614, 628, 631, 637, 794, 802, 803
Belshazzar, 135, 192, 597, 680, 691
Benedict XIII, 114
Bengel, Johann Albrecht, 652, 693, 706, 708, *709-714*, 777, 778
Benjamin ben Moses Nahawendi, 196, 206, 209, 240
Berenger, 628
Bernard, Nicholas, 561
of Clairvaux, 58, 343, 628
of Cluny, 349, 561
Berthier, Alexander, 751, 752, 756-758
Berthold, bishop of Chiemsee, 155
Beverley, Thomas, *581-586*, 699, 701, 718
Bible (*see also* Scripture), 18, 31, 35, 49, 62, 76, 90, 91, 93, 110, 138-142, 144, 145, 154, 158, 171, 206, 218, 244-248, 251, 263, 284, 294, 320, 334, 335, 339, 348, 352, 354, 361, 400, 413, 434, 435, 443, 471, 473, 482, 483, 485, 496, 515, 534, 549, 601, 614, 624, 632, 642, 657, 679, 697, 702, 709
Authorized version, 429, 537
Berlenburg, 702-705
Bishops', 418, 550
Bohemian, 140
Coverdale's, 355, 363, 389, 473
Dietenberger, 314
Douay, 549-551
Dutch, 140
English, Wyclif Bible, 51, 75, 92, 100
French, 140
German, 140, 263, 264, 266
Gutenberg, 140
Neustadter, Pareus, 518
Hebrew, 140, 223, 233
Latin Version (Osiander), 295
Picture, 313
Swiss, 313, 338, 447
Bible Bigots, *see* Wesley
Bible Moths, *see* Wesley
Bible prophecy, 116, 348
Bible societies, 732, 762
Bibliander, Theodor, 309, 332, *338, 339*, 343, 397, 426
Bibliothèque Nationale (Paris), 557
Bicheno, James, *746-750*
Bilney, Thomas, 368
Bionens, *see* Crinsoz
Bishop of Rome, primacy of, 378, 403
Bishops, 34, 35, 105, 115, 126, 132, 141, 203, 205, 221, 481, 540, 552, 763
Black plague, 204
Blair, John, 431
Bohemia, 31-33, 35, 36, 42, 45, 60, 105-107, 109-111, 118, 119, 121, 122, 126, 140, 180, 243, 271, 329, 336, 612
Pre-Reformation writers, 31-43, 105-123
Bohemian, Brethren, 123, 697
church, 31, 37, 39
Diet, 122
Reformation, 31, 105, 111
Bohler, Peter, 693
Bonaparte, Joseph, 750
Bonaparte, Napoleon, 734, 740, 741, 749, 750, 759, 761, 762
Code of, 759, 760
Boniface III, 331, 358, 398, 401, 422, 610, 611, 616, 670
Boniface VIII, 27, 28, 72, 74, 183, 344, 624
Book of Common Prayer, 386, 446, 552

Borgia, Roderigo, *see* Alexander VI
Borrhaus, 341
Bossuet, bishop of Meaux, 510, 552, 536, 708
Bottomless pit, 315, 331, 523, 578, 600, 603, 779, 780
Bourignon, Antoinette, *635, 636*
Bradford, John, 352, 353, 356, 370, *376-380*, 387, 402, 418
Braschi, Giovanni Angelica, *see* Pius VI
Brethren of the Common Life, 339, 433
Bride of Babylon, 323
Bride of Christ, 20, 130, 132, 143, 178, 451, 459, 548
Bridegroom of the church, 132, 134
Bridget of Sweden, 66, *68, 69*, 154, 155
Brightman, Thomas, 506, *512-518*, 520, 674, 723, 724
British and Foreign Bible Society, 762
British Museum, 557, 676
British Reformers, 246, 474
Brocardo, Jacobo, *348*
Brokes, James, bishop of Gloucester, 393
Broughton, Hugh, *564-566*
Brüssken, Konrad, 582
Brute, 52, *74-87*, 783, 790
Bucer, 439
Bull, 37, 48, 73, 104, 105, 112, 113, 121, 169, 179, 183, 232, 158, 259, 261, 284, 286, 294, 361, 398, 473, 598, 732, 750
Exsurge Domini, 258
Injunctum nobis, 468
Liquet by Julius II, 251
Pastor Eternus by Leo X, 183
Regimini Militantis Ecclesiae by Paul III, 466, 468
Unam Sanctam by Boniface VIII, 183
Bullinger, Heinrich, 338, *339-345*, 406, 427, 446, 449, 502
Bulls, *see* Bull
Burgh, William, 511
Burnet, Thomas, *586-588*
Buy, le Jonas, *see* Pierre de Launay
Byzantine Empire, *see* Greek Empire
Byzantines, 67, 307

Cabalism, Cabalistic, 67, 215, 216, 219, 226, 239, 320-322
Caesar, Claudius, 525
Julius, 85, 436
Caesars, 761, 764
Cajetan, Cardinal, 177, 294, 336
Calixtus III, 168
Calmet, 428
Calovius, Abraham, *616, 617*
Calvin, John, 309, 311, 340, 385, 397, 426, *432-441*, 446, 467, 633, 634
Calvinism, Calvinist, 297, 338, 385, 506, 518, 526, 527, 542, 553, 563, 599-601, 609, 616
Calvin's Confession of Faith, 435
Cambyses, 663
Campion, 421
Canon law, 255, 259, 299, 301, 305, 453, 454
Capito, 333, 439
Cappel, Jacques, 630
Captain of the Clergy, *see Dux Cleri*
Captivity of pope, 765
Cardinals, 20, 33, 34, 36, 37, 46, 69, 71, 116, 127, 135, 137, 146, 147, 149, 177, 256, 294, 336, 355, 398, 449, 478, 479, 486, 495, 496, 778
Carlstadt, 243, 259, 286
Carthusian, 74, 155, 171, 296
Cartright, Thomas, 420
Caspar del Fosso, *see* Archbishop of Reggio
Cassander, 428
Castellio of Savoy, *441*

Castle Church, 252
Catharinus, 266, 268
Catherine of Aragon, 387
Catherine of Sienna, 66, 68, *69-71*, 155
Catholic, 11, 13, 14, 32, 36, 41, 61, 66, 67, 73, 101, 104, 121, 122, 136, 143, 217, 244, 245, 314, 316, 320, 325, 336, 340, 354, 369, 385, 407, 413, 415, 416, 419, 426, 428, 432, 484, 486, 488, 493, 496, 498-500, 483, 484, 486, 488, 493, 496, 498-500, 521, 527, 530, 533, 535-537, 540, 551, 561, 568, 599, 627, 633, 641, `683, 702, 708, 761, 776, 790, 791, 794, 803
Catholic, Church, 9, 10, 13, 20, 22, 25, 26, 45, 49, 66, 93, 102, 114, 137, 139, 152, 155, 178, 181, 253, 254, 257, 261, 288, 316, 319, 325, 338, 356, 368, 371, 423, 432, 435, 440, 452, 453, 455, 463, 469, 471, 473, 475-477, 484, 485, 487, 488, 505, 507, 508, 520, 522, 526, 527, 536, 542, 551, 552, 589, 591, 594, 595, 612, 620, 653, 678, 699, 732, 733, 735, 760, 761, 784, 805
  Church as Christendom, 177
  clergy, 35, 60, 297, 560, 687
  League, 599
  resurgence, 351
Catholicism, 354, 364, 365, 373, 385, 389, 406, 419-421, 433, 477, 479, 483-487, 506, 510, 527, 549, 562, 589, 616, 635, 731, 738, 760, 773
Celestine I, 702
  V, 25
Celibacy of the clergy, 318, 334, 369, 389, 771
Cellarius, 243, 599
Censorship, 569
  papal, 183
Charenton, Synod of, 629, 633
Charlemagne, 106, 275, 358, 501, 527, 679, 740, 761, 767
Charles I (England), 552, 563
  II (England), 589
  IV (Bohemia), 31, 37, 204
  V, 262, 288, 294, 388, 432, 433, 436
  VI, 205
  VIII, 11, 145
  of Valois, 21
Charter of Protestant Liberties, *see* Edict of Nantes
Chaucer, 11
Chaumette, 738, 739
Chelcicky, 123
Chiliasm, chiliasts, 566, 599, 633, 649, 652, 708
Christ, 33, 36, 40-43, 57, 58, 60, 63-65, 68, 72, 73, 75, 78, 79, 81, 85, 88, 90, 95, 113, 114, 116-119, 122, 130-133, 135, 136, 174, 175, 193, 204, 217, 243, 245, 248, 249, 252, 254, 255, 261, 263, 264, 269, 270, 273-275, 277, 279, 281, 290, 296-300, 305, 314, 327, 336-338, 343, 357, 360, 361, 365, 367, 376, 378, 380, 384, 391-394, 398, 400, 402, 404, 406-408, 411, 418-420, 423, 424, 431, 437, 448, 449, 453, 466, 467, 471, 477, 478, 488, 489, 492, 499, 504, 518, 523, 529, 531, 535, 549-554, 567-569, 577, 578, 583, 587, 603, 608, 610, 611, 615, 621, 632, 646, 653, 668, 692, 694, 700, 704, 708, 711, 716, 718
  Advent of, *see* Advent
  ascension of, 80, 279
  death of, 345, 371, 417, 424, 439, 492, 632, 664, 718
  eternal High Priest, 334, 342

resurrection of, 134, 136, 279, 311, 345, 412, 662, 704
second coming of, 41, 42, 80, 121, 268, 278, 298, 306, 321, 323, 328, 356, 406, 419, 490, 548, 568, 571, 572, 579, 591, 593, 623, 646, 647, 649, 660, 665, 670, 677, 682, 691, 706, 716, 729, 730, 746
  signs of, 171, 279-281, 304, 305, 309, 322, 358, 419, 588, 730, 766, 772
Christendom, 10, 34, 75, 76, 102, 104, 113, 114, 126, 138, 144, 146, 147, 155, 163, 176, 179-181, 245, 252, 256, 278, 293, 298, 375, 379, 532, 540, 541, 570, 588, 636, 673, 762, 774, 785
  Western, 269, 527
Christian, Church, 23, 80, 83, 124, 186, 190, 231, 240, 246, 328, 374, 531, 551, 566, 586, 678, 707, 747
  dispensation, 488, 519
  Era, 12, 13, 158, 184-186, 193, 203, 221, 238, 240, 243, 348, 492, 507, 531, 585, 603, 609, 631, 673, 679, 691, 785, 790
  faith, 738, 774
  fathers, 336, 587
  writers, 426
Christiani, Pablo, 216, 217
Christianity, 10, 11, 31, 42, 73, 106, 169, 191, 203, 220, 221, 227, 228, 232, 243, 306, 313, 317, 333, 348, 488, 503, 508, 640, 669, 672, 679, 697, 705, 735, 738, 764
Christians, 14, 24, 31, 40, 102, 106, 113, 144, 151, 168, 171, 184, 186, 193, 203-205, 216, 220, 224, 226, 228, 230-233, 245, 248, 257, 267, 269, 273, 274, 279, 280, 305, 323, 329, 341, 462, 508, 525, 568, 582, 619, 647, 683, 689, 692, 775, 789, 790, 807
Christ's, church, 382, 397
  kingdom, *see* Stone Kingdom
Chrysostom, 160, 339, 438, 505, 592
Church, 10, 18, 32, 33, 36, 42, 43, 45, 48, 53, 59, 65, 66, 68, 69, 71, 75, 85, 89, 102, 114, 116, 127, 130, 132, 133, 143, 144, 152-154, 256, 271, 288, 315, 317, 318, 326, 334, 337, 342, 356, 368, 379, 380, 382, 407, 414-417, 436, 437, 450, 452, 456, 461, 466, 474, 475, 478, 481, 491, 497, 502, 504, 507, 513, 550, 552, 553, 560, 588, 594, 601, 603, 606, 620, 633, 634, 637, 652, 667, 669, 694, 730, 737, 744, 751, 755, 764, 784, 789, 793, 805
Church, and state, 123, 387, 440, 679, 764
  fathers, 160, 165, 169, 186, 233, 275, 373, 410, 445, 475, 478, 497, 498, 505, 561, 599, 627, 652
  militant, 436
  of England, 368, 385, 386, 389, 394, 406, 424, 514, 553, 589, 672
  of God, 144, 495, 500, 555, 719
  of Rome, 20, 22, 61, 89, 90, 94, 104, 151, 245, 253, 445, 447, 487, 489, 500, 557, 588, 589, 591, 629, 633, 661, 727
  of Satan, 392
  of Scotland, 449, 454, 728
  of the United Brethren, 698
  polity, 316
Chytraeus, David, 107, *329-332*, 348, 502
Citeaux, abbot of, 481
City, of God, 153, 437
  of Rome, 83, 331, 416
Clarke, Adam, 457
Clemangis of Paris, 72, 73,
Clement V, 72, 74, 204
  VI, 20, 29
  VII, 17, 49, 54, 68, 74

VIII, 495
Clergy, 39, 47, 48, 57, 66, 101, 111-113, 143, 149, 151, 155, 179, 316, 317, 392, 471, 499, 548, 578, 611, 620, 726, 727, 732, 735, 741, 747, 758
Cobham, *see* Oldcastle, Sir John
Cocceius, Johannes, *613-616*, 618
Coins and Medals, 556, 557
Collegia Pietates, 619
Collegium Romanum, *see* Roman College
Columbus, Christopher, 159, 161, *162-175*, 222-224, 241
Comenius, Johann Amos, 107, *617*, *618*
Communion, in both kinds, 38, 106, 121, 122, 149, 286, 294, 296, 360, 389
in one kind, 369, 389, 476
Company of Jesus, *see* Society of Jesus
Conciliar movement, or supremacy, 45, 46, 126
Concordat of Vienna, 126
Conditional immortality, 441
Conecte, Thomas, *154*
Confessio Tetrapolitana, 526
Confession, auricular, 51, 63, 77, 149, 337, 369, 389
Confessions of Faith, 353, 534, 553, 623
Forty-one Articles of Faith, 365
Helvetic confessions, 336, 340, 598
Thirty-nine Articles, 424, 553, 598
Westminster Confession of Faith, 544, 553, 573, 598
"Congregation of Satan," 448
Congregation of the Index, 479, 483
Congregationalists, 387, 573
Conrad of Waldhausen, 31, 36, 39, 107
Conradus, Alphonsus, *318-320*
Constance, Council of, 46, 61, 101, 114, 115, 118, 119, 121, 126, 176, 180
Constantine, 27, 28, 57, 92, 227, 228, 295, 296, 318, 348, 415, 417, 440, 462, 481, 514, 515, 517, 523, 525, 536, 544, 547, 548, 555, 587, 588, 609, 611, 613, 617, 620, 626, 667, 679, 764
Donation of, 28, 127, 128, 169, 299
Constantinople, 11, 126, 136, 219, 228, 231, 271, 272, 301, 358, 410, 524, 525, 548, 585, 611, 624, 683, 721, 743
bishop of, 275
Continental Congress, 779
Continual sacrifice, *see* Daily
Continuistic view, 544
Convent of St. Mark, 143
Convention parliament, 659
Cop, Nicolas, 434
Copernicus, 11, 18, 128, 160, 161, 297
Cornelius of Lapide, 503
Cossart, Gabriel, 429
Cottiere, Matthieu, 629
Counterinterpretation, 506, 510, 511, 525, 640
Counter-popes, 778
Counter Reformation, 12, 13, 25, 241, 464-532, 593, 731
Covenanters, Scotch, 552
Coverdale, 363, 403, 404
Cramer, Daniel, *608-610*
Cranach, Lucas, 263
Cranmer, 297, 351, 356, 364, 369, 370, 374, 376, 380, *387-394*, 402, 405, 424, 446
Cressener, Drue, *588-596*, 643, 672, 673
Crinsoz, Theodore, 678
Cromwell, Oliver, 222, 233, 235, 236, 561, 566, 567, *568*, *569*, 570, 573, 589
Cromwell, Thomas, 395
Cross, 34, 65, 145, 152, 240, 249, 263, 429, 431, 439, 572, 631, 703, 712, 717, 718

Crucifixion, 33, 100, 124, 181, 215, 279, 311, 345, 428, 431, 439, 498, 547, 664, 673, 707, 716, 777
Crusades, 46, 48, 77, 103-105, 113, 121, 176, 187, 204, 210, 301, 307, 638, 778
Crypto-Jews, crypto-Judaism, *see* Marranos
Cup of abomination, 41, 400
Curia, Roman, 30, 68, 113
Curio, Coelio Secundo, 375
Cusa, Nicholas Krebs of, 122, *124-141*, 161, 240, 298, 299, 317, 572, 582, 673, 718
Cusanus, Nicholas, *see* Cusa
Cyprian, 186, 592
Cyril, 501, 505
Cyrus, 135, 192, 199, 201, 206, 208, 230, 290, 311, 312, 363, 426, 439, 572, 582, 615, 699, 700

Daily, 58, 78, 79, 213, 230, 304, 306, 309, 493, 502, 535, 571, 577, 583, 585, 586, 681, 688, 691, 692, 721, 722, 742
Daneau, Lambert, 349
Daniel, 12, 13, 33, 39, 62, 64, 78, 79, 85, 89, 102, 104, 118, 119, 124, 134-136, 151, 154, 171, 187, 188, 192, 193, 202, 203, 212, 219, 225, 226, 239, 240, 261, 263, 266-269, 271-273, 284, 296, 298, 311, 314, 322, 324, 326, 327, 330, 341, 347, 353, 362, 363, 380, 392, 404, 406, 407, 410, 411, 419, 420, 423, 425, 437, 438, 440, 442, 450, 452, 458, 460, 484, 486, 495, 500, 518, 519, 529, 546, 563, 569, 572, 581, 597, 602, 614, 624, 628, 629, 631, 659, 660, 670, 673, 679, 686, 692, 703, 707, 710, 713, 715, 717-719, 723, 728, 767, 771, 783, 785, 790, 794, 803
Daniel 2, 322, 347, 362, 404, 423, 436, 438, 463, 501, 535, 545, 567, 570, 577, 585, 614, 631, 660, 687, 747, 774, 777
Daniel 7, 85, 201, 210, 212, 227, 229, 240, 268, 299, 305, 307, 309, 314, 319, 327, 330, 331, 337, 342, 343, 356, 379, 397, 403, 404, 410, 438, 440, 452, 467, 517, 529, 535, 536, 545, 549, 562, 564, 567, 570, 577, 592, 593, 609, 610, 615, 616, 631, 633, 645, 671, 672, 681, 683, 687, 746, 747, 774, 777
Daniel 11, 58, 208, 324, 337, 342, 363, 404, 409, 566, 610, 657, 671, 674, 685, 721, 748, 777, 802
Daniel ben Perahiah, 219
Dante, 9, 10, 18, 20, *21-29*, 30, 47, 53, 69, 411
Darby, John Nelson, 511
Darius, 192, 201, 231, 269, 270, 290, 339, 363, 426, 427, 439, 547, 615, 632, 663, 704, 712
Dark Ages, 160, 586, 620
Dato, Mordecai ben Judah, 219
Daubeny, Charles, *774*, *775*
Daubuz, Charles, 514, *655-657*
Davidson, Samuel, 510, 708
Day of the Lord, 64, 328
Days, shortening of, 89, 323, 401
Deadly wound, 523, 591, 731-764, 777, 778, 788, 792
Decalogue, 477
Declaration of Human Rights, 733
Deconsecration, 115
Decree of the Civil Constitution of the Clergy, 735
Decretals, 139, 259, 306, 361, 398, 611
De Cusa, von Cusa, *see* Cusa
Deism, English, 707
Delitzsch, 510

Deluge by fire, *see* Destruction of earth by fire
Democracy, 734
Destruction of earth by fire, 534, 575, 587
Devil, *see* Satan
De Wette, Wilhelm Martin, 510, 708
Dialecticism, *see* Scholasticism
Dic Lux, 606
Diets, 126, 293
  Augsburg, 297, 441
  Ratisbone, 656
  Spires, 294
  Worms, 262, 284, 294, 309
Diocletian's persecution, 77, 92, 462, 547
Dionysius, 652
Dispensation, 318
Dissenters, 432, 581, 628, 642
Döllinger, 22, 127
Dominic, St., 67, 467
Dominicans, 28, 47, 105, 142, 155, 251, 464, 481, 504, 678
Domitian persecution, 522, 523
Dort, Synod of, 598, 610
Downham, George, *535, 536*
Dragon of Revelation 12, 78, 81, 86, 264, 265, 309, 314, 459, 515, 528, 548, 572, 578, 609, 613, 626, 667, 679, 703, 747
  seat of, 667
Dragoons, 625, 727
Dürer, Albrecht, 293
Dunkers, 703
Duphot, General, 751, 752
Duppa, Richard, 749, 750
Duran, Simon ben Zemah, 218
Dutch Republic, *see* Low Countries
Dux Cleri, 77, 86, 606

Earth, destruction of, by fire, 534, 575, 587
Earthquakes and great earthquake of French Revolution, 59, 265, 672, 676, 677, 724, 725, 727, 730, 743, 746, 748, 773
Eastern Church or Eastern Christianity, 126, 269, 766
Eastern Roman Empire, 277, 501, 578, 605, 667, 686, 694
Eberhard II of Salzburg, 54, 55, 240, 325, 343, 363, 405, 561, 562, 628, 656
Ecclesia Italika, 604
Eck, Dr., 254, 258, 484
Ecumenical councils, first four, 759
Edict of Nantes, 623, 625
  revocation of, 351, 624, 625, 655, 760
Edom, 190, 191, 193, 199, 227, 230
Edward VI (England), 340, 351, 353, 364, 369, 373, 376, 380, 386, 389, 395, 396, 398, 402, 405, 417, 423, 424, 446
Egypt, 181, 197, 210, 319, 320, 368, 781
Eichorn, Johann Gottfried, 510, 707
Einstein, 658
Elhanan, Naphtali Herz ben Jacob, 219
Eleazar, Rabbi Tobia ben, 192, 193, 199, 213, 237, 240
Elias, Elijah, 42, 64, 131, 322, 323, 780
Elizabeth, Queen (England), 222, 350, 351, 386, 396, 402, 413, 418, 424, 480, 536, 548
Emperor, 35, 114, 296, 301
Empire, 10, 19, 23, 24, 54, 83, 207, 238, 262, 268, 269, 299, 317, 370, 374, 392, 409, 416, 462, 507, 588, 759
  of the church, 638
  of the Latins, *see* Latin Empire
Empires of the world, 769
End of, age, 91, 134, 136, 532, 571
  all things, 677
  world, 42, 43, 89, 171, 173-175, 195, 290,

291, 298, 299, 362, 404, 411, 412, 420, 421, 423, 498, 500, 505, 552, 583, 586, 587, 592, 599, 602, 610, 640, 665, 675, 693, 699, 703, 705, 729, 752, 776
England, 11, 18, 31, 44-46, 205, 220-223, 233, 235, 241, 245, 264, 268, 297, 340, 342, 350, 353, 356, 370, 377, 381, 384-386, 388, 389, 401, 410, 413, 418, 432, 443, 446, 473, 484, 512, 520, 527, 534, 537, 561, 566, 569, 582, 599, 625, 626, 634, 636, 640-643, 647, 655, 687, 697, 701, 708, 722, 740, 741, 765, 779
  Post-Reformation writers in, 533-597, 649-655, 658-695
  Pre-Reformation writers in, 44-101
  Reformation in, 350-425
English, church, 389
  crown, 433
  Deism, 707
  Revolution of 1688, 580
Enoch, 780
Ephraim of Syria, 505, 565
Ephrata Mystics, 702
Erasmus, 11, 223, 285, 333, 336, 339, 343, 354, 384
Erasmus' Greek New Testament, 318, 336, 354, 384
Established Church, *see* Anglican Church
Estates-General, 734
Euphrates, drying up of, 548
Europe, 10, 11, 15, 19, 30, 47, 59, 105-107, 109, 138, 139, 146, 204, 210, 216, 221, 241, 252, 283, 287, 291, 340, 382, 457, 464, 484, 522, 526, 527, 541, 599, 631, 647, 652, 675, 693, 732, 733, 740, 744, 745, 748, 750, 760, 762, 763, 765, 771, 773, 776
  Western, 18, 220, 221, 264
Eusebius, 160, 652
Eutropius, 460
Evangelical party (Germany), 294
Evangelical union, 599
Ewald, Georg, Heinrich August, 510, 708
Excommunication, 57, 60, 91, 112, 113, 146, 149, 183, 259, 261, 369, 390, 473
Exsurge Domini, 258
Ezekiel, 124, 135, 505
Ezra, 312, 632, 662-664, 704

Faber, Peter, 467, 468, 772
Falling stars, 322
False prophet, 67, 77, 78, 86, 301, 307, 613, 615, 621, 700, 727, 744
Famines and pestilences, 92
Farel, 435
Fast days, 315
"Father of English Biblical Criticism," *see* Hammond, Henry
Fathers of the church, 122, 406, 412, 423, 476
Ferdinand and Isabella, 164, 167, 169-171, 173, 220, 224, 467
Ferguson, James, 431
Ferrara, Council of, 126
Ferrara, Duchess Renate, 434
Ferrer, 74, 155, 205, 221
Ferrier, 629, 630
Feudalism, 10, 11
Feyerabend, 313, 314, 347
Fifth Monarchy men, 534, 554, 566-574
Fisherman's ring, 755
Flacianists, 316, 330
Flacius, Matthias, *315-318*
Fléchère, Jean Guillaume de la, *687-691*
Fleming, Robert, Jr., *642-649*, 724
Flood, 134-136, 151, 163
Florence, 21, 29, 71, 143-145, 147, 150

Florence, Council of, 126
Forbes, Patrick, 555
Forgiveness of sins, 113
Formula of Concord, 330
Formularies, 526
Fornication, 83, 119, 153, 368, 400, 412, 420, 546, 627
Forty-one Articles of Faith, 365
Four beasts, 84, 207, 218, 235, 237, 264, 314, 324, 347, 545, 549, 614, 721
Fourth beast, empire, or kingdom, 12, 54, 84, 240, 264, 307, 319, 343, 353, 392, 453, 460, 491, 529, 555, 565, 566, 572, 574, 581, 592, 593, 609, 616, 661, 685, 729, 789, 791
Four empires, kingdoms, monarchies, 54, 83, 187, 188, 190, 192, 193, 195, 199, 207, 210, 212, 218, 219, 226, 236, 238, 267, 289, 314, 323, 324, 330, 347, 362, 370, 379, 404, 419, 438, 452, 460, 463, 529, 545, 549, 562, 564, 566-568, 570, 581, 585, 597, 639, 645, 687, 721, 747, 791
Four horns—Alexander's generals, 201, 289
Four horsemen, see Seals, 1st four
Four winds, 347
Fox, Bishop, 360
Foxe, John, 20, 62, 76, 91, 149, 412-417
France, 11, 14, 19, 20, 27, 44, 46, 147, 153, 165, 221, 241, 245, 268, 302, 340, 342, 350, 351, 353, 356, 401, 410, 421, 432, 433, 439, 450, 456, 479, 483, 484, 512, 520, 526, 527, 540, 555, 624, 626, 634, 636-638, 640, 643, 646, 655, 674, 691, 701, 702, 723-728, 730-734, 737-741, 743, 746, 748, 759-763, 771, 777, 779, 781, 788
Post-Reformation, see Huguenots
Reformation writers in, 302, 303, 432-442
Francis I (France), 432, 434
Francis of Assisi, St., 67, 467
Franciscans, 35, 67, 147, 154, 161, 171, 302, 464, 467, 481, 678
spiritual, 20, 32
Francke, August Hermann, 696, 697, 702, 709, 713
Franklin, Benjamin, 744
Fraticelli, 67
Frederick II, 72, 85, 204
III, elector of Saxony, 249, 253, 286, 304, 619
Freedom of speech, 122
French, 11, 17, 19, 46, 71, 140, 447, 726, 745, 756, 759, 763, 778
civil code, see Code of Napoleon
Directory, 750, 759
Revolution, 12, 13, 605, 608, 625, 640-649, 674, 689, 691, 706, 719, 723-782, 787, 791-793, 795, 796
Frith, 363
Funck, Johann, 308-313, 426, 427, 718
Fundamentalists, 493, 511
Futurism, 486-506, 509, 511-513, 519, 528, 530, 545, 546, 552, 555, 564, 637, 641, 791, 794, 802-806

Gabriel, 720
Galileo, 18
Galipapa, Hayyim, 214
Galloway, 779-781
Gap theory, 487, 489
Gardiner, Stephen, bishop of Winchester, 373, 376, 402
Garret, 360
Gemara, 184, 188
Gematria, 187, 210, 216, 219, 231, 239
Genebrard, 307
Geneva, 435, 438, 440

Geneva Bible, see Bible, Swiss
Gengenbach, Pamphilus, 155
Gentiles, 80, 81, 203, 729, 742, 807
times of, 72
Gerhard, Johannes, 602
German (language), 32, 109, 139, 266, 406, 600, 609, 613, 744
Rationalists, Rationalism, 509-511, 640, 706-708
Reformed Churches, 287
Germany, 10, 11, 14, 18, 20, 46, 126, 127, 129, 154, 221, 241-332, 335, 340, 348, 350, 353, 356, 361, 410, 432, 451, 456, 469, 483, 484, 512, 598-600, 612, 630, 640, 643, 647, 689, 696, 701, 706, 710, 761, 762, 777
Post-Reformation writers in, 598-622, 696-722
Reformation in, 241-332
Gerson, John, 45
Gersonides, 218, 228
Giblehr, Georg Hermann, 701, 702
Gill, John, 682-684
Gillett, 34, 41, 113
Goat, 55, 362, 550, 558, 662, 685
Gobel, bishop of Paris in French Revolution, 738
Goddess of Reason, 737, 738, 760
Godhead, 344
Gog and Magog, 41, 100, 200, 201, 211, 274, 275, 462, 525, 551, 689
Goodman, Christopher, 447
Goodwin, Thomas, 573, 574, 723-726
Gospel of Jesus Christ, 41, 81, 82, 89, 94, 98, 114, 151, 170, 175, 257, 274, 305, 306, 331, 334, 335, 339, 419, 437, 445, 478, 490, 516, 539, 611, 613, 635, 681, 682, 729, 758
Gospel preached to world, 322, 329, 332, 595, 665, 722, 748
Gospels, 109, 171, 709
Goths, 331
Grace of Christ, 67, 251, 441
Great Schism, see Schism, Great
Great whore, see Babylon
Greek (language), 10, 11, 18, 106, 107, 136, 142, 233, 249, 259, 285-287, 340, 373, 406, 489, 550
Empire, 667
church, 31, 106, 107
philosophy, 184-186
Greeks, 370, 550
Gregory I, 275, 277, 331, 378, 379, 408, 421, 422, 499, 501, 505, 536, 592, 722, 776
VII, 106, 332, 344, 520, 711, 778
XI, 17, 36, 48
XII, 114
XIII, 128, 495
Grey, Lady Jane, 413
Grosseteste, Robert, 46, 47, 561
Grosthead, see Grosseteste
Grotius, Hugo, 506, 509, 510, 521-523, 525, 533, 591, 615, 616, 637, 643, 708
Grynaus, 315
Guild, William, 562
Guinness, 760
Gunpowder Plot, 480, 537, 540
Gustavus Adolphus, 521, 601, 761
Gutenberg Bible, 140

Hadrian, 77, 195, 337
Haggadah, 184, 189
Halachah, 184, 189, 190
Hales, William, 426, 432, 547, 720
Haller, General, 753
Hamilton, Patrick, 443

Hammond, Henry, 506, 510, *524, 525*, 533,
    588, 589, 591, 637, 643, 708
Harlot, 25, 27, 30, 40, 41, 72, 75, 79, 83,
    113, 117, 119, 152, 153, 246, 307, 335,
    392, 419, 420, 440, 452, 503, 507, 529,
    635, 636, 730, 760, 789
Hausmann, Nicolaus, 267
Hebdomads, seven, 217
  seventy, 363, *see also* Prophetic time periods,
    70 weeks
Hébert, 738
Hebraism, 185
He-goat, 54, 199, 201, 207, 237, 269, 289,
    691
Heidelberg Catechism, 698
Hell, 384, 549, 575
Helvetic Confessions, 336, 340, 598
Helwig, Andreas, *605-608*
Hengstenberg, Ernst Wilhelm, 708
Henry IV (England), 101
  IV (France), 521, 624
  V (England), 90, 101
  VIII (England), 351, 352, 363, 364, 368,
    369, 380, 385, 387-389, 396
Herder, Johann Gottfried, 708
Hernnschneider, 707
Heylyn, Peter, 563
Hierarchy (*see* Clergy), 39, 47, 48, 112,
    179, 471, 499
Hildebrand, *see* Gregory VII
Hildegarde, 296
Hillel I, 186, 189, 195
  II, 198
Hilten, Johannes, *154, 155*
Hipparchus of Nicea, 160, 161
Hippolytus, 397, 501, 592
Historical School of interpretation, 462, 463,
    486, 489, 506, 511-521, 525, 528-533,
    542-545, 552, 559, 563, 564, 593, 603,
    613-616, 641, 642, 655-657, 660, 708,
    709, 721-723, 790, 791, 794
Historicist view of the Apocalypse, 710
Hoe, Matthias von Hoenegg, *611-613*
Hofmann, Matthaeus, 602
Hoffmann, Christoph, 713
Holy, City, 80, 275, 315, 491, 493, 523, 547,
    570, 633, 662, 742
  Club, *see* Wesley
  Father, 254
  Ghost, *see* Holy Spirit
  Lateran Church, 179
  place, 118, 412
  Spirit, 135, 145, 173, 345, 399, 437, 474,
    511, 550, 651, 653
Homburg, Synod of, 302
Homes, Nathaniel, 574
Hooper, John, 340, 351, 356, 373, *380-384*
Horch, Heinrich, *698-700*, 718
Horn, conspicuous or notable, 54, 269, 362,
    535, 662, 703
  Little, 53, 55-57, 62, 207, 210, 213-215, 226-
    229, 231, 237-240, 261, 268, 269, 289, 290,
    305, 307-309, 324, 327, 330, 331, 336, 337,
    339, 344, 347, 362, 363, 410, 419, 436,
    452, 453, 458, 460, 463, 491, 499, 512,
    517, 529, 535, 545, 546, 549, 564, 565,
    567, 570, 593, 595, 610, 614, 615, 628,
    629, 633-645, 657, 661, 667, 670, 672,
    673, 683, 685, 687, 688, 699, 700, 715,
    721, 745-747, 770, 775, 777, 781, 788, 789,
    791, 793, 803
Horns, ten, 55, 88, 207, 210, 212, 228, 238,
    269, 298, 300, 301, 307, 324, 337, 344,
    347, 401, 438, 460, 517, 520, 523, 525,
    541, 577, 594, 604, 611, 615, 637-639,
    656, 657, 703, 726-728

Host, adoration of, 286
Howell, 673
Huguenots, 340, 450, 479, 557, 623-639, 655-
    657, 760
Humanism, 10, 11, 18, 155, 247, 433
Humanities, 10, 144
Hundred and forty-four thousand, 99, 667
Huss, 19, 32, 35, 37, 39, 46, 61, 106, *107-119*,
    121, 122, 176, 180, 271, 387, 413, 517,
    520, 560, 561
Hussites, 37, 121-123, 126, 179, 245, 336, 548,
    609, 621, 698, 761

Iberian Peninsula, *see* Spain
Ibn Bakhtawi, Joseph, 208
Ibn Ezra, Abraham, *211, 212*, 215
Ibn Yahya IV, Joseph ben David, 219, 240
Image of Beast, 78, 86, 99, 323, 622, 679,
    721
Images, 122, 294, 315, 389, 425, 678, 774
Immaculate conception, 476
Immortality, 215
Imrie, David, 695
Independents, 568, 570, 573, 574, 580
Index Expurgatorius, *see* Index of Prohibited
    Books
Index of Prohibited Books, 23, 140, 150, 465,
    482, 483, 498, 504, 540
Indulgences, Luther's Ninety-five Theses on,
    181, 251, 252, 283, 350
  plenary, 48, 51, 77, 112, 127, 149, 169, 251,
    252, 254, 263, 270, 334, 339, 464, 476,
    603, 752
Injunctum nobis, 468
Innocent III, 25, 94, 105, 204, 307, 344, 481,
    731
  VIII, 105
Inquisition, 11, 103, 105, 141, 148, 149, 165,
    176, 183, 187, 205, 209, 220-223, 232, 236,
    252, 293, 413, 432-434, 440, 466, 479-482,
    526, 678, 761
Inspector, *see* William Hales
Intentionalism, 469
Intercalation, 197, 198, 215, 222
Intercession of saints, 122, 334
Interdict, 112, 113
Interim compromise, 297
Irenaeus, 186, 332, 343, 397, 461, 491, 501,
    649, 652
Irenechoreaus, *see* Helwig
Irish Articles of Religion (1615), 553
Isaac ben Judah Halevi, 213
Ishmael, fourth power, 212, 230
Islam, 27, 187, 196, 207, 327, 652
Italian (language), 17, 19, 21, 29
Italy, 10, 11, 14, 18, 20, 21, 25, 29, 31, 44,
    68, 71, 136, 142, 146, 153, 178, 228, 256,
    333, 340, 342, 410, 456, 469, 481-483,
    527, 630, 646, 701, 732, 749, 755, 760, 761
  Pre-Reformation writers, 20-31
  Reformation writers, 441, 442

Jacob of Nisibis, 565
James, king of Aragon, 216
  I (England), 386, 457, 535, *536-542*, 552,
    589, 634
  II (England), 580, 586, 589, 623
Jansenists, Jansenism, 625, 702, 732, 760
Jarchi, 683
Jephet ibn Ali Halevi, 202, 206-209, 212
Jeroham, Solomon ben, 200, *201*
Jerome, 46, 109, 110, 112, 119, 121, 135,
    160, 186, 191, 343, 360, 387, 405, 460,
    501, 517, 520, 588, 592
Jerucham, Salmon ben, 208, 209
Jerusalem, 145, 152, 173, 174, 192, 195, 197,

201, 202, 206, 210, 214, 215, 228, 231, 263, 311, 312, 410, 467, 488, 489, 493, 498, 502, 531, 540, 551, 571, 628, 663, 665, 693, 700, 703, 707, 720, 721, 803
destruction of, 80, 81, 91, 190, 383, 426, 427, 488, 520, 523, 546, 547, 583, 665, 760
Dutch, 222
Pseudo-Jonathan Targum, *see* Targum
restoration of, 426, 489
spiritual, 459, 632
Jesuits, 220, 325, 327-329, 421, 428, 429, 432, 464-470, 475, 479, 480, 485-489, 493, 495, 502, 503, 507, 509, 513, 518, 521, 522, 524-527, 530, 533, 540, 541, 555, 557, 560, 613, 633, 640, 698, 711, 727, 731, 785, 791, 802, 804
Jesus Christ, 32, 40, 42, 58, 73, 78, 81, 82, 93, 177, 185, 187, 215, 217, 226-229, 239, 264, 268, 296, 327, 333, 334, 342, 353, 419, 452, 463, 601
Jewel, John, 340, 356, *405-412*, 424, 562
Jewish, calendar, 431, 772
church, 627
sacrifices, 584
synagogue, 507
wars, 337, 429
writers, 14, 158, 184-240, 530, 631, 683
Jewry, 184, 196, 197, 203
Jews, 11, 13, 14, 40, 73, 80, 81, 124, 128, 140, 184-240, 270, 272, 296, 298, 309, 311, 324, 328, 338, 378, 426, 489, 491, 507, 508, 516, 518-520, 522, 546, 569, 571, 586, 592, 611, 621, 639, 651, 652, 662, 668, 692, 701, 703, 718-720, 722, 729, 790, 807
conversion or restoration of, 72, 514, 572, 653, 807
return of, 280
synagogue of, 89
Jezebel, Roman, 514
Joachim of Floris, 21, 22, 24, 25, 33, 58, 68, 89, 91, 124, 142, 151, 154, 155, 171, 240, 296, 303, 307, 317, 343, 396, 397, 411, 496, 499, 561, 599, 628, 718, 790
Joachimite, 22, 33, 71
Johanan ben Zakkai, 190, 192, 193, 195, 199
John, 12, 24, 30, 62, 64, 78, 102, 104, 119, 136, 261, 273, 327, 353, 362, 367, 382, 393, 400, 401, 407, 440, 453, 463, 484, 486, 495, 500, 503, 518, 529, 560, 594, 628, 629, 634, 635, 668, 672, 678, 686, 692, 707, 716, 726, 728, 771, 804
II (Portugal), 163
VIII (Paleologus), 126
XXIII (pope), 112, 114, 118
of Constantinople, 422
of Salisbury, 46, 561, 628
of Stekno, 107
of Wesel, 154
the Baptist, 42, 58, 119, 131, 455
Jon François du, *623, 624*
Jonas, Justus, 243, 360
Jonson, Ben, 565
Josephus, 135, 184, 193, 237, 672
Joye, George, 356, *361-364*
Jubilee, jubilee period or years, 130-132, 134, 135, 299, 664, 691
Juda, Leo, 333, *335, 336*, 338, 340
Judah Hanasi, Rabbi, 195
Judaism, 191, 195, 200, 205, 214, 221, 233, 510, 707
Judgment, 64, 72, 86, 99, 117, 118, 132, 133, 151, 160, 181, 183, 227, 229, 268, 272, 275, 278, 281, 282, 289, 290, 305, 306, 321, 322, 330, 370, 371, 380, 383, 391, 399,

401, 411, 412, 414, 419, 440, 441, 491, 502, 516, 520, 531, 548, 552, 575, 577, 593-595, 601, 613, 633, 645, 646, 661, 675, 679, 689, 701, 717, 746, 782, 805, 807
day of, 419, 458, 507, 533, 548, 554, 582, 613, 668, 676, 701, 718, 805
Julian, Calendar, 128
period or year, 427, 428, 431, 458, 646, 663, 672, 673
the Apostate, 571, 577, 667, 679
Julius II, 175, 178, 179, 251
Jurieu, Pierre, 625, *636-639*, 655, 681, 701, 724-727
Justification, by faith, 38, 77, 127, 149, 297, 315, 419, 453, 475, 476
by works, 688
Justin Martyr, 343, 397, 592, 651
Justinian, 412, 515, 536, 591, 595, 596, 643, 645, 646, 685, 732, 743, 746, 759, 763, 764, 767, 793
Code, 203, 592, 673, 748, 759
Justinian's Decree, Edict, 515, 592, 685, 764

Karaite, Karaism, 196-202, 206-209, 211, 212, 215
Kempis, Thomas à, 467
King, Edward, *765-770*, 772, 774
of the north, 535, 571, 586, 748
of the north and south, 231
of the south, 571, 586
Kingdom, of Antichrist or Beast, 308, 539, 594
of Babylonians, 54, 55, 83, 135, 193, 200, 207, 210, 218, 225, 237, 267, 268, 289, 320, 324, 337, 347, 438, 452, 460, 545, 549, 570, 596, 614, 631, 655, 661, 699, 747, 766, 772
of Christ, (*see also* Stone Kingdom), 226, 227, 236-238, 362, 484, 534, 545, 551, 570, 573, 574, 577, 581-585, 587, 611, 639, 652, 657, 699, 703, 711, 716, 745, 769, 774
of God, 117, 337, 355, 682, 700, 782, 784
of Grecians, 54, 55, 83, 193, 199, 200, 208, 210, 218, 225, 230, 237, 267, 268, 289, 312, 320, 324, 337, 347, 438, 452, 460, 545, 549, 570, 614, 631, 655, 661, 699, 747, 772
of Medes and Persians, 54, 83, 124, 135, 192, 193, 199, 200, 208, 210, 218, 225, 230, 237, 267, 268, 289, 312, 320, 324, 337, 347, 438, 452, 460, 545, 549, 570, 572, 596, 597, 614, 631, 655, 661, 695, 699, 747, 766, 772
of Romans, 54, 55, 83, 191, 195, 199, 200, 207, 208, 210, 218, 225, 230, 237, 267, 268, 289, 320, 324, 337, 347, 438, 453, 460, 545, 549, 570, 592, 614, 631, 655, 661, 699, 747, 772
Kings, of Persia, 407
of the East, 516, 586
Kirk of Antichrist, *see* Church of Antichrist
Knollys, Hanserd, 580
Knox, John, 439, *445-455*
Kochba, Bar, 195

Labbe, Philippe, 429
Lactantius, 160, 186, 281, 405
Ladislaus, king of Naples, 112
Lainez, Society of Jesus, 470, 475
Lake of fire, 700, 712
Lamb, the, 85, 132, 416, 574, 601, 602, 621
Lambert, François, *302, 303*, 343, 443
Lang, Johannes, 256, 266
Last days, 158, 370
Last trumpet, 281

Lateinos, 291, 318, 332, 520, 548, 604, 609, 611, 616, 649, 667, 674, 679
Lateran Council, Third, 104
  Fourth, 25, 104, 307
  Fifth, 141, 175-183, 245, 482, 484
Lateran theory, 484, 534
Latimer, Hugh, 351, 356, 374, 376, 387, 390, 405, 424
Latin, 10, 18, 29, 32, 35, 109, 116, 233, 244, 249, 259, 283, 285, 335, 373, 385, 459, 475, 489, 505, 550, 563, 564, 600, 606, 608, 682, 694, 699
  Christendom, 258
  church, 318, 327
  empire, 460, 661, 667
Launay, Pierre de, 632, 633
Law of liberty, 89
Lee, Samuel, 510
Lefevre, Pierre, see Faber, Peter
Leger, Jean, 619
Leipzig interim, 315, 325, 474
Leo I (pope), 727
  X (pope), 141, 175, 178-180, 183, 251, 252, 257, 320, 482
  XIII (pope), 483
Leopard, Grecian, 190, 212, 237, 264, 289, 314, 661
Levi, Simeon ben, 237
Levi ben Gershon, see Gersonides
Liberty, Christian, 257
"Liberty, Equality, Fraternity," 739
Link, Wenceslaus, 253, 256
Lion, Babylonian, 264, 565, 661
Liquet, 251
Lisbon earthquake, 640, 674-677
Literalism, literalists, literality, 185, 196, 225, 239, 355
Little Horn, see Horn, Little
Lloyd, 429, 671, 674
Locke, John, 659
Locusts of Revelation, 41, 77, 331, 491, 499, 519, 537, 539, 547, 574, 578, 585, 586, 600, 601, 603, 611, 645, 657, 700, 721, 786
Lollards, Lollardy, 51, 52, 59, 60, 63, 66, 74, 78, 87, 90-92, 100, 101, 109, 179, 243, 360, 385
Long Parliament, 552
Lord Jesus, 40, 62, 119, 145, 174, 264, 323, 345, 391, 451, 478, 544, 553, 554, 584, 602, 706
Lord's day, 478
"Lords of the Congregation," 448
Lord's supper, 38, 75, 121, 286, 302, 321, 325, 409, 450, 454, 619
Lorraine, cardinal of, 449, 478
Lost tribes, ten, 235
Louis XIII, 633
  XIV, 624-627, 636, 679, 747
  XVI, 647, 737
Low Countries, 11, 18, 222, 353, 432, 433
Lowman, 724
Lowth, William, 670, 671
Loyola, Ignatius, 464-466, 469, 470, 475
Lucifer, 358, 394, 408
Lucius, Johann Andreas, 616
Lucke, G. C. F., 510
Lukas, Bishop, 123
Ludovicus XIV, 747
Lunar, and solar cycles, 427
  year, 57, 73, 311, 663
Luni-solar calendation, 198, 457
Luther, 35, 39, 77, 94, 106, 127, 142, 150, 175, 179, 181, 223, 241-280, 287, 288, 293-297, 302, 303, 309, 311, 316, 320-324, 326, 335-337, 339, 343, 350, 353-356, 358, 360, 385, 397, 426, 432, 433, 441-443,

465-467, 473-475, 484, 485, 496, 498, 499, 517, 520, 527, 548, 551, 560, 598, 604, 619, 621, 688, 761, 780
Lutheran, Lutheranism, 322, 323, 384-387, 526, 542, 599, 602, 608, 616, 618, 689
  Church, 287, 294, 304, 534, 619
  co-Reformers, 302
  creed, 697
  Formula Concordiae, 598
Luther's Bible, 356
Lyra, Nicholas de, 67, 307, 317

Maccabaeus, Judas, 688
Machiavelli, 155, 223
Magna Charta, 46
Maimonides, 67, 214, 215, 226, 228
Maintenon, Madame de, 625
Maire, John, 454
Maitland, Charles, 307
  Samuel R., 511
Malvenda, Thomas, 504, 505, 509, 591
Man of Sin, 20, 49, 53, 66, 75, 78, 245, 281, 288, 318, 319, 337, 356, 407, 411, 419, 420, 439, 452, 453, 461, 463, 488, 544, 551, 553, 555, 561, 562, 584, 628, 635, 647, 668, 673, 683, 686, 694
Manasseh ben Israel, 222, 223, 232-238
Manichaean sects, 176, 274
Manoel of Portugal, 205, 232
Marburg, Articles of, 598
  Conference, 297
Marcellus, Christopher, 177, 178
Marcellus II (pope), 495
Marcion, 274
Marco Polo, 162, 163, 166
Marguerite of Navarre, 434
Mariolatry, 337
Mark of the Beast, 77, 78, 85-87, 98, 100, 300, 305, 306, 342, 367, 447, 461, 528, 616, 617, 622, 649, 668, 678, 691
Marranos, Marranism, 73, 220-223, 232
Marsilius of Padua, 343
Martin V, 46, 61, 121, 169
Martyr, Peter, 405
Martyrs, see Persecution
Mary, Magdalene, 36
  Queen of Scots, 449, 537
  Tudor (England), 222, 351, 353, 370, 376, 381, 386, 389, 394, 396, 402, 413, 418, 446, 466
Mass, masses, 73, 103, 122, 286, 288, 294, 315, 382, 396, 408, 450, 453, 476, 502
Massachusetts Bay Colony, 552
Massacre of St. Bartholomew, 480, 557, 623, 760, 762
Matthew 24, 32, 40, 91, 151, 309, 329, 330, 344, 357, 404, 440, 490, 750, 770
Matthias of Janow, 31, 35, 37-43, 54, 107, 325
Maxentius, 417
Maximilian II (emperor), 330
Mazarin, Cardinal, 624
Mazzolini, Sylvester, 253, 484
Medals, see Coins
Mede, Joseph, 542-549, 564, 567, 571-573, 576, 637, 643, 655, 672, 673, 681, 720, 723, 779, 785
Medicis, 145
Meier, Sebastian, 343
Meir, Aaron ben, 198, 199
Melanchthon, Philip, 11, 154, 243, 259, 285-291, 295, 298, 304, 309, 316, 323, 325, 329, 335, 360, 361, 368, 426, 440
Menahem ben Aaron ben Zerah, 218
Menasseh, see Manasseh
Mennonites, 387, 703

Messiah (*see also* Christ), 124, 184-187, 195, 196, 199, 200, 202, 208-213, 215-219, 225, 226, 229, 231-233, 235-239, 288, 290, 311, 327, 457, 525, 546, 703
kingdom of, 212, 288
Methodists, Methodism, 687, 692, 693, 775
Methodius, 592
Michael, standing up, 577
of Cesena, 20
Middle Ages, 9, 10, 12, 17, 18, 22, 44, 47, 62, 67, 102, 103, 105, 109, 128, 139, 187, 190, 197, 203, 205, 217, 223, 423, 482, 486, 488, 497, 533, 684, 764, 783, 791, 803-806
Midrash, 184, 187, 190, 192, 193, 199, 206, 213, 237
Midst of week, 427
Milicz of Kremsier, *31-37*, 38-40, 54, 107, 110, 112
Militz, Karl von, 253, 254
Millenarian, 570, 574
Millenary, Sixth, 684
Sabbatical, 646
Millennium, 62, 67, 100, 186, 302, 332, 338, 440, 462, 492, 497, 508, 517, 528, 532-534, 548, 564, 567, 573, 578, 587, 588, 599, 601, 604, 617, 639, 640, 646, 649-655, 656, 675, 678, 682-684, 686, 687, 698, 701, 710, 712, 781, 785, 786, 805, 807
Milton, John, 569
Minorite friar, 20, 74, 315
Mirandola, Pico della, 343
Mishna, 184, 188, 195
Missionary societies, 762
Mohammed, Mohammedan, 57, 67, 72, 136, 163, 174, 196, 199, 204, 207, 214, 215, 217, 218, 221, 227, 235, 237, 238, 267-269, 274, 279, 289-291, 307, 308, 317, 318, 324, 327, 328, 331, 337, 338, 343, 344, 348, 378, 398, 407, 419, 457, 458, 461, 467, 485, 519, 525, 531, 551, 555, 574, 578, 586, 605, 609, 628, 655, 657, 686, 693, 715, 766, 779, 780
Monasticism, 286
Moravia, Moravian Church, 31, 36, 106, 107, 119, 612, 617, 618, 692, 693, 697, 698, 702
More, Henry, *563, 564*, 643, 671, 681, 723
Morland, Sir Samuel, 236
Mornay, Philippe de, *634-636*
Morning Star of the Reformation, *see* Wyclif
Moses, 124, 136, 185, 197, 215, 227, 699
Most holy place, 217
Mother of harlots, 493
Münzer, Thomas, 286, 566
Musculus, Andreas, *322, 323*, 504
Mystery of iniquity, 88, 116, 243, 356, 399, 419, 540, 548, 634, 789
Mystical Babylon, *see* Babylon
Mysticism, 66, 233

Nabonassar Era, 547
Nabuchadonozor, *see* Nebuchadnezzar
Nabugodonosor, *see* Nebuchadnezzar
Nahawendi, Benjamin ben Moses, *see* Benjamin
Nahmanides, Moses ben Nahman, 211, 215, 228
Nanni, Giovanni, of Viterbo, 307
Napier, Lord John, 447, *455-462*, 520, 541
Naples, 11, 21
Napoleon, *see* Bonaparte
Narses, 767
Nathan, Tanna Rabbi, 186
National Assembly (French), 734, 735, 737-739

Nationalism, 18, 19, 734
Neander, 34, 35
Nebuchadnezzar, 54, 63, 83, 84, 192, 199, 201, 235-238, 314, 347, 438, 545, 657
Nehemiah, 428, 429, 632, 704, 717
Nero, 92, 407, 507, 525
Netherlands, 14, 433, 526, 527
New earth, 315, 376, 587, 687, 807, 808
New England, 14, 722
New Jerusalem, 177, 181, 183, 484, 507, 508, 518, 529, 536, 548, 549, 576, 577, 579, 581, 583, 656, 678, 693, 705, 707, 805, 807
New Testament, 41, 60, 101, 109, 222, 263, 266, 309, 317, 318, 339-341, 354, 363, 375, 382, 394, 421, 435, 453, 459, 485, 496, 518, 529, 551, 616, 629, 633, 651, 709, 738, 746, 780
New World, 13, 168, 170, 222, 387, 533, 574, 703, 722, 788
Newton, Sir Isaac, *658-669*, 671, 746
Thomas, *684-687*, 724, 771, 772
Nicea, Council of, 440, 615,
Nicene Creed, 476
Nicolai, Philipp, 600
Nigrinus, Georg, *325-329*, 427, 582
Ninety-five Theses, 181, 252, 283, 284, 286, 294
Nisan, 717
Nonconformists, 386, 552, 563, 573
Nürnberg, 291, 294-297

Oecolampadius, Johann, *336, 337*, 338, 361, 397, 439
Old Testament, 40, 140, 174, 186, 191, 200, 212, 222, 233, 235, 309, 315, 318, 335, 338, 382, 394, 459, 505, 518, 529, 629, 633, 666, 709 738, 746, 780
Old World, 13, 465, 740
Oldcastle, Sir John, 52, 74, *87-91*, 101, 363, 387, 396
Olivetan, Robert, 433
Olivi, Pierre Jean, 59
Olympiads, 345, 427, 431
Olympic years, 547, 662
"Order of the Grain of Mustard Seed," 698
Ordinarius Ovilis Christi Pastor, 606
Origen, 186, 355, 652
Orthodoxy, 618
Osiander, Andreas, 270, 293, 294, *295-301*, 308, 362, 388
Othman, 515, 686
Ottoman Turks or Empire, 236, 458, 658, 674
Oxford, disputations, 405
Movement, 511

Pacard, George, *627-629*
Paché, 738
Paganism, 27, 507, 547, 620, 679, 805, 807
Paine, Thomas, 745, 775
Palestine, 199, 307, 468, 685, 701, 722
Papacy, 17, 19, 20, 23, 28, 39, 46-49, 52, 58, 62, 66, 69, 74, 95, 98, 102, 104, 106, 116, 126, 136, 137, 139, 140, 145-147, 154, 155, 159, 176, 181, 204, 226, 227, 231, 240, 243-245, 247, 252, 253, 255, 259, 261, 268, 271, 274, 275, 279, 280, 284, 295, 298-301, 305-309, 317, 319, 321, 322, 328, 331, 334-336, 339, 340, 344, 348, 353, 362, 363, 366, 367, 375, 381, 385, 390, 391, 396, 397, 399, 412, 414, 420, 421, 436, 437, 439-442, 445, 449, 451, 461, 465, 468, 470, 479, 480, 484-487, 499, 510, 511, 516, 518-520, 527, 529-532, 535, 539, 540, 543, 557, 564, 567, 568, 571, 577, 578, 581, 605, 609, 612, 620-622, 626, 629, 642, 643, 646, 649, 652, 656, 657, 661, 670,

673, 679, 681, 686-689, 694, 708, 709, 711,
721, 725, 730, 732, 739, 746-748, 750, 753,
762-765, 777, 778, 783, 788-791, 793-795,
802-805
Papal, empire, 727
  infallability, 469, 476, 599, 661
  primacy, 254, 358, 469
  Rome, 400, 581, 600, 603, 631, 667
  See, 281, 620
  wound of 1798, 777
Paradise, 25, 587
Paradiso, Jacobus de, *74*, 155
Pareus, David, 506, *518-521*
Paris, 31, 421, 433, 434, 737-739, 759, 762, 781
Parker Society, 341
Parkhurst, Bishop, 341
Parliament, English, 418, 540, 544, 568, 569
Passover, 198, 222, 232, 429, 431, 664, 667
Pastor Eternus, 183
Paul, 12, 32, 62, 64, 75, 78, 102, 171, 261,
  263, 277, 281, 288, 327, 330, 342, 353,
  356-358, 374, 375, 394, 407, 409-412, 417,
  419, 420, 423, 436, 637, 442, 461, 463,
  484, 486, 495, 500, 504, 518, 519, 529,
  550, 561, 562, 578, 585, 608, 629, 634,
  635, 673, 686, 727, 771, 804
  III (pope), 466, 468, 471
  IV (pope), 382, 390
  V (pope), 634, 635
Paulo V, 616
Paul's Cross, 402, 524
Peace, of Augsburg, 350
  of Ryswick, 641
  of Westphalia, 350, 599
Peasants' War, 284
Peninsular War, 761
Pentateuch, 140, 191, 192
Pepin, 358, 515, 767
Perahiah, Daniel ben, *see* Daniel ben Perah-
  iah
Pergamos, 343
Persecutions, 42, 58, 73, 98, 101-123, 131, 132,
  176, 203-206, 218, 220-223, 228, 275, 301,
  319, 323, 350-372, 387-394, 396, 413, 416,
  417, 443-446, 465, 479-481, 491, 507, 519,
  525, 533, 540, 569, 576, 595, 613, 625,
  628, 665, 698, 703, 733, 747
  Marian persecution, 413, 479
Persian lunar years, 663
Persians, 370, 550, 582, 766
Pestilences, 59, 91, 146
Petau, Denis, 428, 429, 431, 521
Petavius, Dionysius, *see* Petau
Peter, Apostle, 23, 24, 28, 69, 74, 77, 89, 90,
  113, 126, 132, 149, 169, 261, 327, 366, 372,
  378, 391, 394, 419, 424, 436, 478, 504,
  689, 732, 751
Peter's chair, St., 421
Petrarch, 411, 561
Petri, Johann Philipp, *713-719*, 787
Philadelphian groups, 702
Philip, of France, 21, 27
  II of Spain, 449
Philipot, Jacques, 648, *726-728*
Philippists, 316
Philo, 135, 185
Philpot, John, 351-353, 356, *373-375*
Phocas, Decree of, 277, 331, 344, 348, 358,
  379, 401, 415, 497, 515, 519, 536, 611,
  629, 684, 685, 776, 779
Picards, 41, 107
Piedmontese Alps, 625
Pietism, 617-622, 696-702, 706, 709, 713
Pilgrim Fathers, 386, 387
Pilgrimages, 48, 403
Pisa, Council of, 45, 46, 175, 176

Piscator, Johannes, 601
Pius IV, Creed of, 449, 465, 471, 475, 476,
  478, 479, 483
  VI, 732, 750, 752, 755
  VII, 741
Plagues, 613, 638
Plutarch, 311
Plymouth Brethren, 511
Poland, 36, 46
Polemics, polemical, 283, 284, 304, 421, 428,
  493
Pontifex Maximus, 557, 558
Pontiff, 755
Pontifical Authority, 771
Pope, 20, 22, 24, 25, 28, 33-35, 37, 41, 45,
  46, 49, 59, 67, 71, 74, 77, 82, 86, 88-90,
  94, 95, 100, 101, 110, 112, 116, 117,
  119, 125, 126, 128, 141, 147, 152, 155,
  161, 169, 177, 228, 229, 231, 238, 251,
  255, 256, 258, 262, 264, 267, 269-274,
  277, 280, 288, 296, 300, 305, 306, 309,
  317-319, 324, 327, 329, 333-335, 337, 343,
  344, 347, 349, 353, 356, 357, 361, 362,
  377, 385, 387, 388, 390, 392, 394, 397,
  415, 418, 437, 442, 448, 450, 452, 454,
  462, 463, 487, 491, 492, 498, 501-503, 513,
  516, 517, 519, 520, 522, 535, 537, 539,
  550, 554, 561, 571, 574, 577, 592, 598,
  604, 607, 608, 616, 620, 628, 630, 645,
  647, 651, 679, 687, 711, 726, 731, 735,
  741, 743, 744, 746, 749, 750, 755-760,
  763, 765, 769, 770, 772, 775, 781
  captivity of, 765
  of Rome, 41, 113, 226, 261, 323, 513, 515,
  535, 544, 553, 560, 683, 761
Popedom, 301, 335, 560, 638, 669
Popery, 299, 574, 726
Pope's supremacy, 149, 364, 443, 763, 772
Popes, Roman, 604, 609, 614, 615
Porphyry, 231, 564, 565, 685
Postmillennialism, 13, 14, 640, 649-655, 786,
  806, 807
Post-Reformation, *see* names of countries
Prague, 31, 32, 36, 37, 107, 112, 113, 121-123
  Four Articles of, 122
Predestination, 338, 435, 693
Prelates, 64, 88, 90, 98, 99, 143, 175, 314,
  317, 390
Premillennialism, 545, 553, 574, 609, 640, 710,
  786, 788
Pre-Reformation, 14, 87, 110, 158, 180, 336,
  527, 530, 783
Presbyterians, 537, 568, 580
Preterism, 244, 439, 486-488, 506-511, 519,
  522, 524, 525, 528, 530, 533, 552, 554,
  564, 616, 637, 640, 641, 643, 706-709, 791,
  794, 804-806
Prideaux, Humphrey, 429, 431
Prieras, *see* Mazzolini
Priestley, Joseph, *744-746*
Primasius, 343, 501
Printing, invention of, 11, 18, 137-140, 482
Probabilism, 469
Prolaeus, Andreas, *601, 602*
Propertius, 460
Prophecy, 75, 341, 353, 769, 770
  gift of, 145
Prophetic time periods:
  5 months—150 days—150 years, 77, 82, 173,
    458, 514, 519, 547, 585, 655, 657, 679,
    686, 700, 721, 727, 748
  7 weeks—49 years, 439, 632, 664, 665
  42 months, 76, 78-80, 82, 85, 301, 319, 328,
    343, 417, 436, 458, 492, 493, 508, 523,
    531, 536, 540, 541, 543, 546, 570, 571,
    578, 584, 585, 587, 594, 596, 603, 604,

609, 611, 613, 614, 629, 656, 670, 678, 689, 694, 711, 742, 787, 793, 806
62 weeks, 76, 82, 213, 547, 615, 664, 665, 716, 717
69 weeks, 673
70th week, 58, 76, 124, 213, 279, 290, 428, 429, 439, 457, 547, 673, 712, 718, 720, 777
70 Sabbatic year-weeks, 664
70 weeks or 490 years, 72, 82, 124, 151, 201, 208, 210-213, 216, 217, 230, 231, 239, 240, 270, 272, 290, 308, 309, 311-313, 324, 326, 337, 338, 345, 363, 426-432, 439, 457, 463, 493, 497, 530, 534, 546, 547, 551, 567, 572, 573, 584, 615, 630, 632, 641, 643, 662, 673, 691, 700, 703, 704, 712, 713, 715-720, 784, 787, 788, 790, 792, 794
  A.D. 33, 428, 429, 431, 547
  A.D. 34, 308, 309, 326, 624, 664
  457 B.C., 308, 309, 312, 431, 630-632, 662, 719, 787
396- or 391-year period, 536, 574, 576, 673, 686, 700, 748, 786
490 years, 309, 311, 312, 324, 345, 431, 457, 564, 572, 615, 631, 632, 662, 700, 703, 704, 712, 716, 784
666, 77, 86, 98, 99, 136, 275, 291, 300, 307, 309, 317-320, 327, 332, 342, 344, 399, 415, 461, 491, 498, 502, 522, 523, 604-606, 608, 609, 616, 666, 674, 679, 710, 711, 747, 776
1000 years—pause, 68, 100, 303, 332, 344, 349, 415, 417, 436, 441, 490, 492, 502, 508, 523, 525, 528, 532, 534, 548, 550, 551, 555, 564, 571-573, 576, 577, 579, 582, 601, 609, 610, 613, 614, 622, 633, 646, 651-653, 681, 682, 689, 694, 708, 710, 712, 716, 785, 807
1000 years' binding, 320, 417, 712, 807
1260 years or days, 13, 59, 76, 77, 79, 81, 91, 98, 124, 239, 240, 299, 300, 309, 316-319, 326, 327, 329, 331, 343, 348, 440, 458, 459, 492, 496, 498, 500, 508, 513, 515-517, 519, 531, 536, 543, 545, 546, 555, 564, 568, 570, 571, 576, 578, 580-597, 600, 603, 604, 611, 613, 614, 616, 624, 628, 629, 631, 633, 638, 640-649, 656, 662, 667, 670, 673, 674, 678-680, 683-685, 689, 692, 700, 702, 705, 711, 715, 718, 719, 723-782, 786, 788-792, 794, 796, 804
  end of, 580-597, 640-649, 723-782
1290 days, 67, 72, 76, 77, 79, 81, 82, 92, 100, 124, 200, 202, 208, 209, 211-213, 216-219, 231, 239, 272, 279, 290, 309, 329, 363, 436, 458, 500, 536, 570, 571, 577, 585, 596, 597, 631, 671, 673, 680, 681, 685, 689, 692, 700, 705, 715, 721, 722, 742, 743, 747, 788, 790
1335 years or days, 33, 59, 67, 72, 73, 76, 100, 124, 200, 206, 208-213, 216, 218, 219, 229, 231, 239, 272, 290, 309, 321, 329, 458, 500, 536, 570, 571, 573, 576, 577, 581, 584, 585, 596, 597, 600, 631, 671, 673, 680, 685, 689, 692, 700, 702, 705, 715, 742, 743, 747, 788, 790
2300 years, 125, 129, 133, 135, 136, 200, 202, 206-209, 211, 212, 216, 218, 219, 229-231, 239, 270, 290, 309, 313, 321, 427, 459, 493, 530, 534, 535, 551, 567, 570-573, 576-578, 581-585, 596, 597, 614, 632, 641, 662, 670, 671, 673, 679, 680, 684, 685, 688, 689, 691, 694, 695, 699-703, 705, 713, 715-719, 722, 747, 766, 785, 787, 788, 790
2400 years in Septuagint, 766
6000-year theory, 191, 211, 216, 279, 298, 299, 330, 338, 372, 458, 587

7000-year theory, 173, 174, 191, 215, 239, 299, 330
three and a half times, or years, 57, 76, 78, 79, 81, 82, 100, 207-210, 212, 229, 272, 277, 299, 301, 318, 319, 326, 328, 343, 407, 427, 436, 452, 458, 488, 490-493, 497, 498, 500, 502, 508, 516, 517, 519, 522, 523, 531, 536, 543, 545, 550, 564, 571, 576, 581, 584, 603, 614, 629, 631, 637, 638, 661, 670, 678, 689, 711, 715, 724, 742, 747, 767, 775, 786, 789, 793, 803
time and times and half a time, see three and a half times
Prophetic year (360 days), 646, 671-673
Protestant, church, 315, 350, 395, 441, 600, 741, 806
  Reformation, 9, 10, 13, 187, 240, 350, 464, 465, 473, 486, 526, 731, 774, 793
Protestantism, 350, 351, 356, 364, 365, 368, 373, 384, 385, 389, 418, 419, 434, 435, 447, 449, 470, 471, 479, 486, 493, 506, 510, 526, 527, 534, 537, 564, 637, 641, 643, 760, 787, 793, 804, 806
Protestants, 13, 14, 32, 58, 104, 110, 169, 170, 179, 229, 235, 240, 241, 245, 297, 302, 315, 316, 318, 325, 339, 352, 360, 373, 384, 385, 390, 401, 413, 417, 418, 426, 428, 432, 439, 441, 443, 449, 457, 465, 466, 469, 470, 473, 474, 479-481, 484, 486, 487, 493, 495-502, 504, 506, 507, 509-512, 517, 518, 521, 522, 524, 525, 527, 530, 532, 533, 536, 537, 550, 554, 560, 563, 570, 574, 593, 595, 599, 612, 625, 626, 634, 636, 640, 641, 675, 689, 691, 708, 735, 745, 771, 773, 779, 785, 790, 791, 793, 794, 802-804, 806
  of Judaism. 196
Ptolemy, Claudius, 11, 160-162, 166, 427, 428, 430, 431, 663
Purgatory, 122, 254, 288, 397, 453, 476, 603
Puritan Movement, 222, 381, 387, 406, 413, 420, 512, 542, 552, 553, 566, 580, 589, 625
Purves, James, 694, 695
Purvey, John, 52, 74, 92-100, 284, 561
Pyle, Thomas, 680, 681, 724

Quakers, Quakerism, 387, 702

R.M., 691, 692
Rabbinical calendation, calendar, 197, 198
Rabbinism, 195-198, 201, 206, 208
Ram, 54, 199, 201, 207, 269, 289, 362, 550, 558, 662, 685, 691, 766
Ramsay, Andrew, 555
Raphael, 150
Rashbaz, Simon ben Zemah Duran, see Duran
Rashi, Solomon ben Israel, 67, 209, 210, 228
Rationalism, 706-709
Reason, goddess of, 737, 738, 760
  temple of, 737
Recantation, 115, 116, 149, 381, 390
Reformation, 9, 11, 12, 14, 18, 20, 66, 87, 91, 100, 103, 106, 137, 138, 141, 142, 153, 155, 158, 175, 222, 223, 241-466, 470, 471, 473, 474, 476, 477, 479, 482-487, 496, 511, 512, 516, 518, 521, 527-529, 532, 561, 566, 581, 589, 595, 598, 611, 619, 620, 636, 638, 645, 678, 679, 710, 718, 761, 783-785, 790, 793, 795, 808
  churches, 609
  of the church, 71, 128, 144, 152, 158, 175
  writers, 405, 438, 527, 531
Reformed, Church of Scotland, 449, 557
  churches, 350, 512, 514, 526, 534, 599, 610, 618, 627, 678
  doctrine, 454

faith, 293, 378, 395, 443, 445, 522
movement, 100, 294
preachers, 402
Reformers, see Reformation, also names of countries
Reforms, 127, 445
Reggio, archbishop of, 477
Regimini Militantis Ecclesiae, 466, 468
Reign, of Antichrist, 541, 610, 727
of Terror, 737
of the Beast, see Reign of Antichrist
Reinhard, 154, 155
Remonstrant Party, see Arminians
Renaissance, 9-12, 17, 18, 29, 128, 136-138, 158, 433, 783, 792
Resurrection, first, 67, 332, 344, 440, 462, 517, 552, 553, 573, 587, 682-684, 687, 701, 712
literal, 62, 132, 281, 321, 322, 355, 412, 462, 517, 525, 534, 544, 548, 552, 564, 575, 578, 584, 587, 588, 595, 601, 617, 646, 652, 656, 785, 786, 802, 805, 807
of the church, 132, 134, 135, 656
second, 682, 683, 689, 701
Reuchlin, 11, 284-286
Revelation, 143, 273, 309, 314, 317, 327, 341, 342, 368, 383, 392, 411, 458, 460, 488, 502, 506, 513, 514, 519, 528, 529, 560, 581, 585, 602, 630, 631, 655, 672, 683, 693, 705-707, 715, 719, 720, 724, 729, 771, 777, 783, 785, 788, 803, 805
Revelation 13, 39, 77, 85, 99, 246, 264, 299, 307, 319, 327, 330, 331, 343, 356, 362, 375, 397, 440, 500, 502, 523, 536, 539, 554, 560, 562, 564, 565, 593, 606, 638, 670, 778
Revelation 14, 344, 399, 411, 440, 621
Revelation 17, 24, 25, 30, 39, 77, 79, 183, 299, 319, 327, 331, 335, 339, 342, 344, 356, 362, 393, 403, 407, 411, 440, 491, 500, 502, 508, 509, 513, 520, 523, 525, 539, 555, 562, 564, 601, 611, 687, 727
Revival of Learning, see Renaissance
Revolution, of 1688, 586, 641
of 1848, 647
Rheims, Council of, 336, 411, 628
Translation of the Bible, see Douay Bible
Ribera, Francisco, 486-488, 489-493, 496, 502, 503, 505, 509, 511-513, 519, 555, 564, 591, 633
Richard II (England), 109
Richelieu, Cardinal, 625
Ridley, Nicholas, 351, 356, 364-368, 370, 374, 376, 380, 387, 390, 405, 424
Rieger, 32, 34, 107
Robespierre, 737, 739
Rogers, John, 352, 373, 381
Thomas, 404
Rollin, 429
Roman, Beast, 85, 239, 314, 343, 603
bishops, 86, 126, 349, 378, 401, 759
College, 338, 495
court, 29, 255, 258
Empire, 10, 17, 23, 85, 86, 114, 116, 160, 186, 187, 196, 203, 227, 238, 261, 267, 268, 289, 305, 306, 317, 331, 342, 362, 363, 410, 416, 419, 421, 460, 486, 501, 514, 517, 520, 523, 527, 531, 539, 551, 564, 571, 577, 592, 604, 613-615, 628, 632, 638, 667, 668, 683, 686, 687, 700, 708, 728, 729, 743, 747, 761, 769, 770, 775
pontiff, 24, 72, 183, 288, 360, 438, 466, 502, 558, 608, 623, 771
Prince, 24
Republic, 752, 756, 758, 778
Senate, 29
Romanism, Romanists, 104, 235, 256, 297, 351,

373, 406, 412, 413, 418, 464, 471, 511, 616
Romans, 370, 428, 514, 522, 592, 721, 758, 760
Romanus, 415, 520
Rome, 10, 17-19, 22, 23, 27, 29, 30, 34, 35, 46, 49, 60, 64, 66, 68, 69, 73, 75, 77, 79, 83, 89, 99, 102-104, 110, 112, 141, 144-146, 150-152, 180, 181, 183, 187, 190, 192, 195, 201, 212, 219, 226-228, 237-239, 241, 244, 245, 253-256, 271, 272, 277, 281, 295, 296, 299, 300, 301, 312, 317, 319, 320, 327, 328, 331, 342, 350, 353, 358, 365, 378, 380, 382, 387, 388, 392, 393, 402, 405, 420, 431, 438, 455, 460, 473, 474, 476, 477, 482, 484-486, 491, 492, 496, 498, 500, 501, 503, 516, 517, 519, 521, 525, 531, 540, 545, 548, 549, 551, 557, 561, 564, 566, 588, 592, 593, 595, 599, 609, 612, 613, 615, 620, 622, 626, 635, 638, 647, 656, 661, 673, 683, 685, 694, 707, 712, 724, 725, 730, 743, 748, 750, 751, 753, 756-759, 761-764, 766, 767, 769, 770, 772, 776, 778, 781, 788, 789, 791, 803-805
Western, 657, 661, 681, 685, 686
bishop of, 77, 78, 82, 83, 85, 275, 331, 344, 358, 364, 378, 379, 381, 382, 393, 398, 403, 409, 412, 416, 417, 424, 476, 485, 548, 561, 645, 688, 728, 732, 775, 776
court of, 258
Imperial or Pagan, 12, 261, 295, 299, 488, 504, 508, 517, 523, 551, 574, 589, 591, 593, 611, 615, 621, 631, 678, 679, 681, 683, 707, 708, 721, 742, 747, 749, 781, 805, 806
divisions of, 12, 227, 261, 267, 268, 289, 328, 342, 343, 353, 362, 405, 410, 416, 517, 520, 531, 535, 546, 557, 567, 591, 592, 596, 614, 628, 639, 656, 657, 679, 683, 685, 687, 742, 747, 775, 788, 789, 791, 803, 804
Romith, 291, 300, 604, 606, 616
Rough, John, 445, 451, 454
Royal Society, 659
Rubens, 347
Rudd, Sayer, M.D., 681, 682
Rump Parliament, 568
Rupertus, 501
Rupescissa, Johannes de, 20
Russians, 685
Ryswick, Peace of, 580, 641

Saadia ben Joseph (al-Fayyumi), 200, 201, 206, 208, 212, 215
Saadia Gaon, 187, 198, 199, 212, 213, 683
Saba, Abraham, 219
Sabbath, 130, 131, 189, 221, 232, 238, 478, 699
change of, to Sunday, 477
Lord of, 130
millennial, 211, 216, 279
Sabbatical millenary, 646
Sachs, Hans, 293, 296
Sacraments, 40, 86, 152, 257, 294, 300, 357, 391, 471, 476
Sacred, College of Cardinals, 753
Congregation of Propaganda, 752
Volume, see Bible, Word of God
Sacrosancta Concilia, 429
St. Andrews Castle and Church, 445, 446, 451, 452
St. Giles Church (Scotland), 449
St. Paul's, 355, 371, 376
St. Peter's, 34, 35, 126, 178, 251, 752, 755
Saints of the Lord, 104, 300, 393, 405, 424
Salvation, 419
Sanctification, 38, 419

Sanctuary, 135, 210, 213, 216
    cleansing of, 583, 662, 671, 685, 688, 691,
        695, 701, 716-719, 722
Sandys, Archbishop Edwin, 356, 376, 417-420
    Sir Edwin, 549
Saracen, 40, 67, 274, 289, 304, 328, 343, 344,
        514, 533, 547, 574, 576, 585, 591, 594,
        637, 645, 655, 657, 678, 679, 686, 700,
        721, 750, 779
Saracenic woe, 514, 655, 766
Satan, 21, 40, 42, 59, 61, 67, 69, 71, 99, 256,
        264, 274, 281, 288, 299, 319, 322, 407,
        417, 421, 442, 448, 452, 454, 455, 462,
        463, 491, 539, 551, 576, 603, 609, 621,
        652, 667, 689, 706, 712, 716, 802, 805
    binding of, 320, 492, 509, 520, 533, 534, 544,
        551, 578, 682-684, 711, 807
    loosing of, 533
    seat of, 343, 368
    synagogue of, 61, 89, 99, 420, 452
    whore of, 459
Saur, Christopher, 702
Savonarola, Girolamo, 142-153, 223, 343, 397,
        557, 561
Scaliger, Joseph, 427, 428, 431, 547, 678
Scarlet woman, 246, 309, 335, 342, 528, 539,
        571, 802
Schaff, David S., 33, 129
Schism, Great, 11, 17, 19, 39, 48, 49, 61,
        114, 176, 272
Schisms, 176, 437, 521
Schleiermacher, 708
Smalkald Wars, see Schmalkalden Articles
Schmalkalden Articles, 297, 304, 322, 336,
        360, 598
Smalkaldic Wars, see Schmalkalden Articles
Scholasticism (Dialecticism), 10, 18, 29, 66,
        127, 189, 251, 286, 445
Scotland, 443, 451, 484, 527, 555
    Post-Reformation, writers in, 642-649
    Reformation in, 443-463
Scotch Convenanters, 552
Scottish, Confession of Faith (1560), 448, 449
    Second Scotch Confession of Faith (1580),
        448, 449, 536
Scriptarians, 196
Seal of God, 491, 668
Sealing work, 668
Seals, seven, 92, 98, 303, 319, 339, 398, 490,
        491, 503, 507, 514, 523, 528, 547, 578,
        587, 594, 602, 609, 610, 613, 631, 637,
        668, 678, 679, 686, 716, 779, 785, 805
    1st four, 92, 151, 278, 314, 384, 392, 397,
        490, 519, 539, 603, 610, 613
    5th, 92, 392, 397, 602, 610, 613, 668
    6th, 92, 274, 399, 490, 519, 610, 613, 631,
        779
    7th, 72, 92, 90, 303, 399, 490, 516, 519, 610,
        613, 631, 678, 727
Seat of Abomination, 382, 438
Second Thessalonians 2, 39, 41, 53, 64, 78,
        80, 117, 171, 261, 288, 299, 317, 318,
        327, 330, 339, 344, 357, 362, 374, 375, 403,
        406, 416, 417, 438, 440, 500, 502, 504,
        517, 539, 551, 553, 555, 561, 562, 564,
        578, 670, 683, 727, 746, 777
Secular arm, 91, 105, 115
See of Rome, 126, 168, 251, 258, 366, 382,
        383, 389, 392, 412, 421-423, 436, 468,
        495, 526, 561, 629, 630, 731, 745, 763
Seleucus, Seleucidae, 428, 685
Selnecker, Nikolaus, 323, 324
Semler, Semlarian Controversy, 706, 707
Separatists, Independents, 387, 698
Septemberbibel, 266
Septuagint Old Testament, 140

Servetus, Michael, 435, 439-441
Seven, candlesticks, 314
    churches, 273, 319, 342, 397, 514, 528, 585,
        602, 608, 631, 655, 678, 679, 686, 701, 716,
        785
    heads, 300, 319, 331, 410, 515, 523, 525, 611,
        615, 637, 638, 656, 711, 721, 742, 770, 802
    hills, 331, 343, 383, 409, 410, 416, 420, 422,
        460, 486, 487, 504, 516, 520, 523, 531, 558,
        591, 604, 609, 623, 628, 673, 683, 732, 766
    last plagues, 315, 523, 712
    seals, see Seals, seven
    trumpets, see Trumpets, seven
    vials, see Vials
Seven Years' War, 713
Seventy weeks, see under Prophetic time
    periods
Sforza, Cardinal, 147
Shammai, 189
Sherwin, William, 575-579, 582, 718
Sibylline Oracles, 652
Sigismund, king of Hungary, 114
    I of Poland, 433
Simony, 58, 63, 69, 99, 113, 119, 146, 152,
        318, 635
Simpson, David, 775
Sistine Chapel, 753, 762
Six Articles, 369, 380, 389
Six hundred and sixty-six, see Prophetic time
    periods
Sixtus IV (pope), 140, 154, 482
    V, 498
Smithfield, 101, 351, 352, 358, 360, 373, 374,
        377
    Martyrs Memorial Church, 352
Society, for Promoting Christian Knowledge,
        671, 672
    of Antiquaries, see Antiquarian Society
    of Jesus, 11, 467, 469, 479, 731
Socinians, 526, 744
Sodom, 181, 319, 368, 540, 707, 781
Sodomitry, 400
Solar year, 57, 73, 131, 311, 429, 459, 772
Solis, Virgil, 313
Son of perdition, 417, 450, 461, 544, 551, 553,
        623, 727
"Soul-Sleepers," see Conditional Immortality
Spain, 11, 14, 18, 44, 153, 161, 163, 165-167,
        171, 205, 220-225, 240, 401, 432, 479, 481,
        482, 520, 527, 540, 726, 731
Spalatin, 254, 255
Spanish, 11, 71, 223, 233
Spanish Armada, 480
Spener, Philipp, 616, 618-622, 696, 697, 701,
        702, 709, 712, 713
Spirit of God, 131, 410, 453, 808
Spiritual Babylon, see Babylon
Spirituals, 22, 30, 67, 243, 802
Spouse of Jesus Christ, see Bride of Christ
Stapulensis, 127
Staupitz, 244, 249, 256, 303
Stephen VI (pope), 204
Stiefel, Michael, 320-322
Stone, stone kingdom (see also Kingdom of
        Christ), 83, 199, 200, 206, 227, 235, 236,
        238, 289, 324, 336, 347, 403, 404, 423, 436,
        535, 567, 570, 577, 583, 687, 729, 760
Storch, 286
Strumpet, cursed, 94
    stinking, 400
Stuart, Moses, 510, 708
Stübner, 286
"Supreme Pastor of the West," 21
Swedenborg, Emanuel, 705, 706
Swinderby, 74
Swiss Guards, 753

Switzerland, 14, 426, 432-441, 484, 618
  Reformation in, 333-349
Sylvester (pope), 28, 169, 228, 440, 462, 611
Synagogue, 73, 143, 191
  papistical, 375

Tabor, 121
Taborites, 121-123, 243
Tallyrand, 759
Talmud, 184, 185, 188-191, 196, 197, 203, 204,
  206, 209, 214, 217, 218, 223, 298
  Babylonian, 188, 191
  Jerusalem, 188
Tanner, Joseph, 487
Targum, 184, 191, 192, 206, 237
Tartars, 187
Taylor, Lauchlan, 695
Temple, destruction of, 429
  of God, 41, 66, 78, 80, 85, 86, 263, 278, 295,
    301, 329, 356, 357, 375, 378, 392, 403, 405,
    408, 417, 423, 436, 437, 442, 491, 500, 519,
    554, 592, 627, 647, 774, 775
  of reason, 737
Ten, Commandments, 382
  horns, see Horns, ten
  kingdoms or kings, 419, 502, 517, 519, 520,
    541, 546, 564, 581, 591-595, 604, 661, 673,
    687, 689, 711, 724, 728-730, 743
  toes, 235, 268, 729
  virgins, 563
Tenth part of the city, 584, 585, 594, 595, 637,
  638, 679, 689, 726, 727, 744, 746, 750, 787
Tertullian, 186, 328, 343, 405, 460, 503, 592
Tetzel, 251, 252, 254
Theocracy, 145, 435
Theodicy, 23
Theodora, Empress, 771
Theodoret, 501, 505
Theodosius II, 203
Theresa, St., 489
Thirty Years' War, 233, 480, 522, 599, 602,
  612, 761
Thirty-Nine Articles, 424, 553, 598
Thomas de Vio, see Cajetan, Cardinal
Thomas of Stitny, 107
Thorpe, William, 52
Thube, Christian Gottlob, 777, 778
Thucydides, 311
Tiara, or triple crown, 19, 179, 345, 347, 361,
  391, 420, 448, 775
Ticonius, seven rules of, 67
Tillinghast, John, 567, 570-573, 582, 718
Time, and times and half a time, see Prophetic
  time periods
  of trouble, 89, 769
  or times of the end, 193, 230, 278, 372, 489,
    688
  shortened, 372, 520
Titus, 91, 208, 212, 525, 665, 683, 760
Todd, J. H., 511
Todi, Jacopone da, 74
Tolentino Treaty, 750, 755
Torquemada, Thomas de, 221, 223, 224, 481,
  482
Toscanelli, 163, 166
Totila, 767
Tower of London, 88, 90, 352, 360, 369, 376,
  389, 390, 402, 418, 421
Towers, Joseph Lomas, 723, 724
Tracy, 363
Tradition, 497
Trajan, 522, 523
Transubstantiation, 48, 49, 51, 58, 77, 122,
  337, 364, 369, 389, 476
Trapp, John, 560
Treaty of Ryswick, 580

Trent, Council of, 338, 406, 412, 450, 465,
  466, 470, 471-483, 515, 526, 527, 592
Trinity, 128, 168, 440
True church, 459, 514, 515
Trump, God's, 420, 579
Trumpets, seven, 67, 98, 314, 319, 338, 342
  399, 490, 503, 507, 519, 523, 528, 547,
  578, 587, 594, 602, 603, 609, 610, 631,
  645, 655, 678, 679, 681, 682, 686, 700,
  716, 727, 748, 779, 785, 788, 805
  1st, 98, 576, 578, 748
  2d, 274, 576, 748
  5th, 343, 457, 491, 514, 519, 533, 539, 547,
    574, 576, 578, 585, 594, 603, 609, 611,
    613, 637, 645, 655, 679, 681, 686, 721,
    727, 748, 779, 786
  6th, 98, 331, 343, 414, 457, 462, 490, 491,
    514, 519, 531, 533, 547, 554, 574, 576-
    578, 585, 594, 596, 609, 611, 613, 637,
    645, 655, 657, 679, 681, 686, 700, 721,
    748, 779, 786
  7th, 319, 399, 414, 490, 545, 548, 576, 595,
    602, 652, 678, 727, 744
Turkish woe, 515, 573, 576, 577, 645, 673, 766
Turks, 67, 105, 116, 136, 151, 154, 176, 231,
  237, 253, 258, 268, 269, 271, 272, 274, 289,
  290, 301, 303, 305, 307-309, 322, 324,
  329, 343, 344, 378, 414, 415, 457, 460,
  501, 514-516, 523, 524, 531-533, 537, 547,
  548, 564, 571, 572, 576, 578, 586, 591,
  594, 605, 613, 637, 638, 651, 655, 657, 674,
  678, 679, 682, 683, 685, 686, 700, 721,
  729, 744, 748, 779, 790
Two-horned Beast, see Beast, second of Revelation 13
Tyndale, William, 62, 354-358, 361
Tyndale's, Greek Testament, 354, 355, 473
  Illustrated Bible of 1550, 356, 363

Unam Sanctam, 183
Unitarian Movement, 744
Unitas Fratrum, see Bohemian Brethren
United Brethren, Church of, 698
Universal Church, 331
Universities, 11, 18, 44, 45, 140
  Basel, 333, 335
  Bologna, 21, 29, 44, 137, 142, 336, 750, 753
  Cambridge, 18, 44, 53, 60, 76, 137, 354,
    358, 361, 364, 365, 368, 376, 378, 387,
    395, 401, 417, 421, 512, 535, 542, 553,
    563, 570, 573, 586, 588, 589, 655, 658,
    659, 669, 671, 681, 765, 773, 775
  Cologne, 140
  Erfurt, 248
  Glasgow, 445, 728
  Halle, 697, 713
  Heidelberg, 44, 285
  Leipzig, 111, 618
  Louvain, 355, 364
  Marburg, 302
  Montpellier, 137
  Oxford, 18, 44, 48, 49, 59-61, 87, 107, 109,
    136, 139, 365, 354, 370, 373, 374, 380,
    390, 402, 406, 412, 524, 553, 561, 563,
    573, 574, 618, 651, 670, 692, 770
  Padua, 21, 125, 136
  Paris, 18, 29, 37, 44, 45, 71, 137, 456
  Prague, 18, 32, 44, 61, 106, 109, 111, 113,
    114, 121, 137
  St. Andrews, 456
  Salamanca, 137, 165, 489
  Tubingen, 285,
Urban II, 778
  V, 34, 35
  VI, 17, 48, 54, 59, 71, 74

Ussher, James, 428, 429, 461, 572
Utraquists, 122

Valentinian, 638
Valla, Lorenzo, 128, 343, 397
Valpy, Richard, *770-772*
Vandals, 514
Vatican, Vatican Library, 25, 316, 422, 557, 649, 752, 753, 773
Vaudois, 102, 580, 626
Vergerius, Petrus Paulus, *441, 442*
Vernal equinox, 198
Vespasian, 91, 213, 231, 525
Vestarian controversy, 420, 421
Vials, seven, 99, 503, 516, 520, 528, 548, 578, 587, 594, 595, 638, 656, 678, 682, 686, 687, 716, 727, 748, 766
   5th, 645, 649
   6th, 531, 656
   7th, 645
Vials of wrath, 67, 100, 265, 274
Vicar, Pretensed, 420
   of Christ, 19, 39, 41, 63, 71, 78, 82, 86, 88, 153, 154, 169, 177, 179, 300, 305, 377, 378, 382, 392, 398, 407, 424, 436, 466, 504, 550, 588, 607
   of Satan, 117, 358
   on Earth, God's, 767
Vicar-general, Christ's, 377
Vicarius Christi, 607, 608
Vicarius Filii Dei, 605-608, 649
Vice-Christ, 177
Vicegerent of Christ, 153, 179, 771
Viegas, Blasius, *502, 503*, 509
Vienna, Council of, 204
Vigilius (pope), 771
Villanova, Arnold of, *71-73*, 124, 718, 787, 790
Virgil, 460
Virgin Mary, 471, 751
Virgins, ten, 563
Vision, *see* Prophecy, gift of
Vitellius, Emperor, 525
Vitringa, Campegius, 652, *677, 678*, 681, 724
Vulgate, Latin Bible, 52, 140, 248, 249, 285, 474, 475, 483

Waldenses, 9, 32, 54, 102-107, 121, 123, 140, 176, 179, 236, 243, 245, 336, 340, 343, 398, 480, 515, 548, 560, 561, 569, 609, 619, 621, 625, 626, 637, 761
Waldo, Peter, 678
Wars of Religion, 527
Wartburg, 244, 262, 266, 286, 303
Watt, James, 744
Wellhausen, Julius, 510
Wenceslaus, King (Bohemia), 113
Werner, Hans, 158
Wesley, John, 618, 687, *692-694*, 710
Wesleyans, 618
Western Beast, *see* Papal Rome
Western church, 126
Western Empire, 10, 501, 514, 584, 594, 595, 661, 667, 748
Westminster, Abbey, 659
   Assembly, 544, 552, 573
Westphalia, Peace of, 350, 599
Whetenhall, Thomas, 554
Whiston, William, 656, 669, *671-674*, 724, 746
Whitby, Daniel, *651-655*, 678, 681, 682, 786, 806
Whitbyanism, *see* Postmillennialism
Whitefield, 618, 692, 693, 728
Whitgift, Archbishop, 340, 562

Whore, *see* Babylon
Wicked, destruction of, 601, 807
Willet, Andrew, *554, 555*
William of Orange, William III (England), 580, 581, 689, 641-643
Williams, Roger, 387
Willison, John, *728, 729*
Wimbledon, 74, *91-93*
Winchester, bishop of, 391
Wishart, George, 443, 445, 451, 454
Withers, George, 550
Witnesses, Two, 105, 274, 309, 314, 318, 342, 458, 459, 491, 492, 500, 507, 508, 515, 528, 546, 570, 578, 586, 591, 593-595, 629, 632, 637, 638, 689, 722, 724-726, 728, 743, 779-781, 803, 806
Wittenberg, 35, 249, 252, 258, 263, 266, 283, 286, 287, 302-304, 308, 315, 316, 320, 321, 323, 329, 330, 350, 600, 611, 616
   Concord, 598
Wolsey, Cardinal, 355
Woman, or church, in the wilderness, 79-81, 440, 458, 490, 515, 543, 570, 576, 584, 586, 603, 626, 627, 629, 692, 721, 722, 778
   of Babylon, 463, 616, 631
   of Revelation 12, 30, 76, 98, 246, 264, 274, 314, 315, 327, 415, 458, 459, 490, 508, 515, 528, 548, 578, 603, 609, 694, 711, 778
   on Beast of Revelation 17, 41, 53, 66, 77, 264, 315, 383, 400, 425, 460, 480, 558, 567, 603, 604, 609, 615, 656-658, 694, 712, 721
Wood, Hans, 547, *719-722*
Word of God (*see also* Bible), 39, 80, 81, 113, 115, 132, 143, 168, 208, 244, 259, 262, 277, 279, 297, 299, 300, 302, 317, 330, 334, 335, 338, 353, 361, 400, 403, 440, 443, 449, 463, 471, 477, 535, 541, 542, 549, 601, 623, 706, 717
Wrangham, Francis, *773, 774*
Wyclif, John, 11, 18, 19, 31, 37, 39, *44-65*, 74, 75, 87, 88, 92, 94, 100, 101, 109, 110-114, 116, 121, 122, 354, 363, 397, 413, 517, 520, 560, 561, 628, 673, 783
Wyclifites, 61, 107, 109, 110, 121, 179, 245, 336, 548
Wyttenbach, Thomas, 333, 335

Xavier, Francis, 467, 468
Xenophon, 311
Xerxes, 428, 663

Yahya IV, Joseph ben David ibn, *see* Ibn
Year-day principle, 33, 57, 67, 77, 80-82, 91, 124, 125, 129, 135, 136, 187, 195, 207, 208, 211-213, 216-219, 226, 231, 239, 240, 270, 317, 319, 329, 338, 415, 439, 457, 463, 495, 496, 498, 499, 501, 502, 517, 530, 536, 542, 545, 547, 564, 572, 580, 583, 596, 624, 638, 641, 646, 655, 662, 671, 672, 678, 688, 691, 718, 722, 778, 785, 787, 788, 790, 794, 803

Zakkai, Johanan ben, *see* Johanan
Zerubbabel, 663
Zbynek, Archbishop, 112
Zerah, Menahem ben Aaron ben, *see* Menahem
Zinzendorf, Count Nicolaus Ludwig, 618, 652, 693, *697, 698*, 702
Ziska, John, 121
Zurich Bible, *see* Bible, Swiss Bible
Zwingli, Huldreich, 302, *333-335*, 337-339, 340, 432, 526, 609